ISBN 978-1-331-69385-7
PIBN 10222448

1 MONTH OF
FREE
READING

at

www.ForgottenBooks.com

By purchasing this book you are eligible for one month membership to ForgottenBooks.com, giving you unlimited access to our entire collection of over 700,000 titles via our web site and mobile apps.

To claim your free month visit:
www.forgottenbooks.com/free222448

Similar Books Are Available from
www.forgottenbooks.com

EIFFEL TOWER
984 FEET 8 INS

STRASBURG
CATHEDRAL
465 FEET

COLOGNE
522
FEET

CATHEDRAL

GRAND PYRAMID
477 FEET

ST PETERS
ROME
429 FEET

ST PAULS LONDON
360 FEET.

NOTRE DAME 218 FEET

THE EIFFEL TOWER, PARIS.

THE

Sword and the Trowel;

A RECORD

OF

COMBAT WITH SIN AND OF LABOUR FOR THE LORD.

EDITED BY C. H. SPURGEON.

1889.

"They which builded on the wall, and they that bare burdens, with those that laded, every one with one of his hands wrought in the work, and with the other hand held a weapon. For the builders, every one had his sword girded by his side, and so builded. And he that sounded the trumpet was by me."—Nehemiah iv. 17, 18.

London:

PASSMORE & ALABASTER, PATERNOSTER BUILDINGS,

AND ALL BOOKSELLERS.

Index of Texts of Sermons, etc., by C. H. Spurgeon, in "The Sword and the Trowel," Vols. I.—XXV.

PREFACE.

We have now completed twenty-five years of our Magazine. The *Sword* has not lost its edge, nor has the *Trowel* grown rusty. Our dependence has been upon a strength which outrides the tide of time; and for this reason, and for this reason only, we have not been suffered to fail. This Magazine remains to bear witness for the Lord against abounding error, and at the same time to encourage and stimulate every holy endeavour to glorify the name of Jesus. Herein we rejoice, yea, and will rejoice, that while the present period is a sad victim to the energy of falsehood and worldliness, it is the object of Christian solicitude and endeavour to a very high degree. The weeds are shedding their seeds, but the wheat is ripening its corn. *Surely the harvest is drawing near!*

Next year, to begin another quarter of a century, we shall adopt a new wrapper for The Sword and the Trowel; but there will be no change in its doctrine, nor in its method of promoting it. Our colours are nailed to the mast.

Progress in the knowledge of truth does not imply the relinquishment of that God-given gospel which has throughout the centuries saved the souls of men. We ask our compeers whether the gospel of Paul, of Augustine, of Calvin, of Owen, and of McCheyne, did not assuredly bring salvation by Jesus Christ to those who knew nothing of "advanced theology," and they dare not question that it did. We ask them whether it does not still foster a true religious life, and they cannot deny it. We shall therefore keep to that which has been so long tried and proved; and all the more so, because we see nothing new in "the new theology" which is one half so likely to produce the same result. If he who doubts the Divinity of our Lord, and the plan of Substitution, is called a Christian by the advocates of novelties; even they have not gone so far as to deny the Christianity of those who firmly believe these glorious truths: therefore, on the very lowest ground, we resolve to take that road which is confessed to be safe, and in which a man may walk with the holiest. But more, we tremble at the disappointment which will surely come to those who lean on the bowing wall and tottering fence which the moderns set before them. A faith which knows not Christ as God, the divine Judge will not know at the last great day; and those who trample on the atoning blood will reap nothing but condemnation "in that day."

While we shall not bear the Sword in vain, but use it against error, our Magazine will fully represent the work of the Trowel, in upbuilding the cause of God. Throughout another year our friends have sustained *The College, The Orphanage, The Evangelists, The Colportage,* and *The Book Fund,* and we thank them with a full heart. To these is added *The College Mission,* which in Spain and North Africa has already done some little for foreign lands. This last will need to be greatly enlarged, and may safely be helped without injury to any other of the older missions. We are rivals to nobody, but hope to do our own work in quiet. We hope that, throughout the coming years, while we are spared to conduct these many enterprises, we may have the sympathy and the generous aid of the Lord's people, who judge us to be a fit agent in these matters. We need assistance; but we look for it to the Lord himself, and lift our heart in prayer to him, that he may direct his stewards to supply our needs.

Our child, in its new dress, still lives in its old house, and we entreat readers of the magazine and the weekly sermon, to think of the church in the Tabernacle in their prayers. Our congregations have never been more generally crowded than during the year 1889, and the number of conversions has never been more continuously cheering. The Spirit of the Lord is with us. But what if his gracious presence were withdrawn? Then might we call it *Ichabod*, for the glory is departed. We are filled with anguish at the very supposition of the good Lord's being grieved by the sin which he sees in us, so as to turn from us in anger. That were a grief we could not bear. Death would be desirable a thousand times beyond the least withdrawal of the sacred power. In vain the crowds, the societies, the ministry, if such a dire calamity should befall. Prayer must continually ascend that it be not so; for then the adversary would rejoice, and the gospel would be ridiculed as having proved a failure. Truly, it would not have failed, because our sins were thus sadly visited; but it would seem so among ungodly men, and "what would the Egyptians say?" May the Lord continue to bless his own work in our hand, *for his name's sake!*

Once more we offer our heartfelt gratitude to our readers and helpers; and we pray them to sustain us during the new period upon which we shall enter next month. Amid our perpetual engagements, the editing of this periodical is a heavy task; but we will press on while life and health shall last, and the Lord shall help us. Praying in the Holy Ghost, resting in the precious blood, trusting in God All-sufficient, and looking for the coming of our Lord, we set up our banner, and advance to a new year.

So writes,

The servant of the Lord's servants,

C. H. SPURGEON.

INDEX.

THE

SWORD AND THE TROWEL.

JANUARY, 1889.

The Eighth Wonder of the World.

BY C. H. SPURGEON.

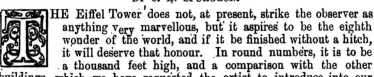

THE Eiffel Tower does not, at present, strike the observer as anything very marvellous, but it aspires to be the eighth wonder of the world, and if it be finished without a hitch, it will deserve that honour. In round numbers, it is to be a thousand feet high, and a comparison with the other buildings, which we have requested the artist to introduce into our engraving, will show how greatly it overtops any other erection of men. Who would wish to climb it? Happily for the ambitious, there will be lifts, which will bear the visitor to the summit in six or seven minutes; and then he can, at pleasure, look down upon Paris, which will lie low at his feet. The towers of Notre Dame scarcely reach to the first story of Mr. Eiffel's vast iron erection. No wonder that the workmen complain of the distance they have to climb before they can begin their day's work. Although only one-half is finished, it is no trifle to run up five hundred feet before you can commence your labour; to some of us it would be a good day's work to go up and down, even if the only labour required at the top would be refreshing the inner man.

The tower is said to have great strength to resist the wind. It could bear a strain of 3,284 tons of wind force, and this is nearly twice as much as has been experienced during the most violent tempest which has visited the city. So far, so well. As to the sustaining of the enormous weight by the foundations, this, we doubt not, has been attended to, for many of the most stupendous engineering works in iron have been produced by Mr. Eiffel, who ranks this as his masterpiece. Otherwise, one might well fear that so vast a mass of iron would press unduly upon the river banks, and upon the clay on which it rests, and would come to an untimely fall. We are told that it will be completed by the opening of the Exhibition, and that, when finished, it will be painted a light orange colour, which, it is said, will give it a dazzling golden appearance when the sun is shining upon it. Assuredly, it has the virtue of originality, if none beside.

Many have enquired as to the safety of the tower from lightning. It is affirmed that it will act as a huge lightning conductor for Paris, and, possibly, may be a safeguard to the whole city. Just so ; but what of the conductor itself, and those who may be venturing upon it ? Fears of this kind are answered by enthusiastic believers with a smile, and, for aught we know, the smile is the answer of wisdom ; but the following incident, recorded in *The Times* of Nov. 28, enables us to repeat our question without fear of being condemned as unreasonably nervous :—

"The Guion Line steamer *Alaska*, from New York, which arrived at Queenstown yesterday evening, brings intelligence of the ship *Edward*, from Havre, with a cargo of iron ore, whose captain reported that the vessel encountered a terrible electrical storm in the Atlantic, on the night of the 31st ult., when in lat. 41 42 N., long. 54 42 W., lasting for several hours. The vessel was continuously enveloped in lightning, which prostrated on the deck 11 seamen, and deprived them of sight for nearly half a day. The second officer and the boatswain were also dashed to the deck, and received serious injury, and the former was speechless for five hours. Three balls of fire exploded with a tremendous report over the main rigging, scattering flaming fragments over the ship, and driving the remaining members of the crew in terror into the forecastle. From 3 a.m. until 7 p.m. the captain and mate were the only persons on board capable of doing any work, and on them devolved the task of keeping the vessel before the easterly gale. The captain states that all on board the ship were trembling with fear during the time that the electrical storm lasted, which was the most terrible he ever witnessed ; and he adds that, no doubt, the iron ore with which the *Edward* was laden acted as a magnet to attract the lightning."

It is more to our point to believe that our reader will enquire— What is the use of this modern tower of Babel ? The enquirer knows as much as the writer. It is to be a feature in the great Exhibition, and to be talked of as the loftiest of 'buildings that man has yet piled upon the earth. There may be other recondite scientific uses; but this is probably the main object of the tower. To reach the greatest altitude, to overtop all other buildings : is not this an object worthy of this mass of metal, this expenditure of labour, this display of skill ? Perhaps. Certainly, in many other lines, this would seem to be consistent with the genius of the age. We go ahead, and everybody wants to lead the race. We must have everything bigger, noisier, more glaring, more amazing than any before us or with us. The old, silent toil for excellence, and the quiet realization of it, are out of date; we work by steam, and beat the drum to call the world's attention to every puff of the engine. The world is crowded with these Eiffel towers, and stunned, every now and then, with the crash of them. Men must be richer than millionaires, speakers must shout down all rival orators, writers must achieve a world-wide success, and even the maker of a pill must dose the universe and a world or two besides. "Excelsior!" Never mind how you build. It is needless to wait for iron; wood will be sooner put together, hay will be easier to carry up, and stubble, if you can only keep it together long enough, will be best of all. Let your manufactures deteriorate into rubbish, your finances run to bankruptcy, and your people pine into penury; it does not matter, so long as you are a great people, with great men at your head, able to boast great things.

This also would be little in the line of our business, if this spirit did not threaten the religious community as well as any other. It may come to pass that we also may desire to do some great thing, and may overlook the far greater importance of keeping close to the right and the true. If God gives to his servants a large sphere of usefulness, they must accept the responsibility with a grave gratitude; but if they have it not, they must not fret and fume, as though the proper object of life could be to fill a considerable space in the thoughts of men. The comfortable abodes which cluster around a cathedral are far more serviceable, and more to be desired, than a place among the clouds which hang over its lofty towers. If we will do our life-work well, we shall be nearer to happiness than if we neglect the commonplaces of duty to soar into the heavens of publicity. Usefulness is far more equally distributed than many think; for the results of insignificant actions are often greater than the consequences of brilliant deeds. The plants which come of life's sowings are not always in proportion to the size of the seeds. A nation's destiny may turn upon a word; while a torrent of eloquence may effect nothing. Let us serve our God; but as to our relative elevation among our fellow-mortals, let us fight against the self-idolatry, which would permit us to waste a moment's thought upon it.

Far be it from our churches to vie with each other, and go in to build their Babels. To be largest in number, to have the most intellectual persons in our ranks, to attempt the most ambitious missions—these are little enough as objects of ambition. Just now, the tendency is to seek to wield the most potent political influence in Parliaments, Councils, Boards, and Corporations. There may be reasons for this thirst for power; but we earnestly trust they will never even seem to have weight enough to decoy Christians from their legitimate calling; which is, not to win positions, but to win souls; not to canvass votes, but to convince consciences. The hunt after respectability is another form of this tower-building. So is the longing to have the finest building, the largest organ, the most learned doctor, the most eloquent preacher. What! In the worship of God is there to be competition? At our Maker's feet are we to try to outshine each other? Are sinners to contend who among them shall be the greatest, while they are crying, "Lord, have mercy upon us"? Are saints to rival saints as they together chant, "Not unto us! Not unto us! but unto thy name, O Lord, give glory"? Yet, we say it with great sadness, there is a tendency among all denominations to carry the competitions of trade and politics into the sanctuary of God. Zion and Bethel bid for hearers; the vicar and the pastor tout for customers; the choir, the organ, the stained-glass windows, are a part of the paraphernalia of the shop. This must be ended. At the very least, it must be avoided by all spiritual men, and whenever it is seen, it must be treated as unbearable.

Why should we say, "Go to, let us build a tower"? Do we not remember how the Lord stopped the work by confounding the language of the workers? Are not many of our confusions nowadays caused by our ambitions? May we not hope for the restoration of a pure language when we take more heed to the one foundation, and are content to build thereon those far smaller, but infinitely more precious, structures which can be fashioned from gold, silver, and precious stones?

Bad Reading, and those who Provide it.

BY G. H. PIKE.

OCCASIONALLY, when the public conscience receives a shock, some wholesome results follow; and we have recently seen this to be the case in regard to the circulation of bad reading. The truth is that, for some time past, the English law, as represented by Lord Campbell's Act, has been stronger than has been generally supposed; and the fine of one hundred pounds which a well-known London publisher had to pay in the Central Criminal Court, on the last day of October, was in itself conclusive proof, that, for years past, the law has been broken because no one took the trouble to put it in force. When the case came on before the Recorder, the Solicitor-General argued the case at considerable length, and so shocked the ears of the respectable jury by reading extracts from the works of the French author complained of, that the occupants of the box desired him to desist, having heard quite enough to ensure their verdict. The publisher had not only to pay the fine already named, he had to undertake that he would issue no more of the offending works; but then the old proverb about locking the stable-door after the steed was stolen was partially verified in this instance. Some tens of thonsands of volumes, the matter of which the prosecuting counsel described as *revolting*, have been let loose, and, being in as many homes, they will still poison the atmosphere for years to come. This is not the liberty for which Milton pleaded; it is a crime committed under a reign of too much license, which a proper police vigilance would not have allowed.

Commenting on this trial, a daily paper, which had previously frequently advertised the works in question, said that if anyone could read them "without an intolerable sense of nausea and disgust, he must have unusually strong nerves and unusually obtuse perceptions." Speaking of the author himself, the same paper says further : "He does not depict things vicious and brutal because there is an ethical or artistic lesson to be drawn from them, but simply and solely, as far as we can perceive, because he either delights in them, or because he supposes that they will delight the taste of depraved and degraded readers. . . . It was an outrage to write such books, it is an aggravation of the offence to translate them, and it makes the matter worst of all to issue them in a cheap and popular form." This is well, so far as it goes; but while advertisements of such books have been freely accepted by leading newspapers, some have sufficiently commended them to promote their sale. Now that the criticisms of the Solicitor-General have overridden all others, however; and now that the law has vindicated itself, we have reason for some satisfaction.

There can be no doubt that this trial, by the publicity it has given to the subject, and by the check the purveyors of printed garbage have received, has done good. The public begin to see, more than they have done before, the character of the deadly evil that is in their midst; and they are becoming impatient while unprincipled printers, in London alone, send forth hundreds of thousands of sheets weekly, which inflict untold evil on that susceptible class educated in our Board-schools. This represents quite a different department of the corrupt trade from that of French translations. Belonging to it are the weekly periodicals, some of which are far worse than others; the worst of all, perhaps, being the stories about adventures in crime, which appear in penny numbers, and which sometimes cost, by the time that they are complete, a considerable price for young people to give for a single book. Much of this garbage keeps within the letter of the law, and is therefore much more difficult to cope with than French importations, that, as a rule, may be supposed not to reach the hands of scholars in Board-schools. This is the reading that is chiefly doing harm among the young; and if, as some assure us, the circulation amounts to a quarter of a million sheets every working day, one may be able to form some notion of the moral havoc that is being effected.

The public are indebted to Mr. Samuel Smith, M.P., for calling the attention of Parliament to this evil; and for making other efforts, which have drawn forth a promise from the Government that they will do what the law enables them to do to check the circulation of impure reading. The writers who deal in this sort of thing make heroes of well-known criminal adventurers; and as such exploits readily appeal to the taste of the young and the ignorant, the numbers containing them soon command a large constituency. Some would tell us, that the children of the poor forget all that has been taught them in Board-schools soon after engaging in the serious business of life; and if this is so, it may also be true that it is owing to taking in so large a quantity of this corrupt reading, the natural tendency of which would be to wholly occupy the mind by excluding everything else. But human nature is the same, whether in low or high life, so that the humbler classes are not the only readers of what is vicious. Referring to the general tendency of the times, a daily paper lately said: "We can hardly wonder that publishers, more enterprising than scrupulous, when they see tales of vice and crime, of murder, forgery, and seduction, eagerly devoured by the educated classes, easily blind themselves to the wrong they are committing by supplying similar stories to a different class of palates. A vitiated taste in fiction, and, to some extent, in poetry, too, has been visible in English society for many years past, and novel writers of great ability and power of imagination have not hesitated to minister to it. The evil has spread downwards, and we are now confronted with the gigantic growth to which Mr. S. Smith has called attention." This shows us where we are, and the dangers to which we are exposed by the plague that has come upon us. The demon that carries on this conspiracy, is, as it were, a hydra-headed monster, and his operations are carried on in many directions at the same time. What with the importation of novels and pictures from France, the production of costly indecent books, which can only be obtained by the initiated, the circulation of penny dreadfuls and more expensive horrors, we are in a bad way indeed. Though one would not say that the present is the most corrupt time that has been known during the Christian centuries, we have, undoubtedly, a greater supply of impure reading than was ever known before.

In the old times of two or three generations ago, when the majority of people could not read, the mental pabulum that found its market in provincial towns and secluded villages alike was represented by the production of the Catnach Press, in St. Giles's, broadsides relating to startling current events, and songs which those who were ignorant of the alphabet could learn from hearing others repeat them. From the curious collection which Mr. John Ashton has just made of the songs* more particularly of other days, we find that so far from having advanced, we have actually gone back; for when compared with some of the things we have mentioned, the songs for which authors in St. Giles's attics received the honorarium of half-a-crown each were quite harmless productions. The subject of popular songs is one in which Macaulay and other students of our social customs have shown themselves to be greatly interested, and the times were when writers of songs exercised great influence over the popular mind. Mr. Ashton's book will be valuable for purposes of reference, showing what ideas ruled among the common people, before music-halls and faster ways ministered to more vicious tastes. Of course we do not refer to the old ballads to commend them, but rather to show that we have, as a nation, not much amended our literary ways since patterers and flying stationers sold their wares to wondering rustics. "Rough though some of these street ballads may be, very few of them were coarse," says Mr. Ashton; and we may add that the old ballads did not generally instil criminal sentiments as is now done by the tales which have highwaymen and burglars for their heroes.

The results of evil reading are continually becoming manifest. The result may actually be nothing less than murder, the murderers being mere children. A tragedy at Maidstone, in which two boys were the chief actors, is proof of this; and if the traffic in blood-and-thunder papers continues, more things of this kind will surely happen; indeed, at the time of writing, a boy of eleven is charged with a capital crime, which suggests that these papers have been his tutors. Again and again, the cases in police-courts have shown how readily children advance from reading to action. They will run away from honest work in some instances, and actually arm themselves, and "take to the road." They have done this in England; and a story which lately came from Chicago shows that the effects are the same in the United States.

There were two boys, who having gone through a course of reading about burglars and "gentlemen of the road," quite naturally made arrangements for themselves adopting the same profession. Accordingly, they ran away from home, dug for themselves a cave on a vacant piece

* "Modern Street Ballads." By John Ashton. Author of "Social Life in the Reign of Queen Anne." With Fifty-six Illustrations, Chatto & Windus, 1888. Price 7s. 6d.

of ground, and set up as thoroughly equipped bandits. Hen-roosts and clothes-lines were preyed upon, and even houses were broken into ; for of course carpets, rugs, and chairs were needed for their cave. While living in this manner, they even indulged in the freak of capturing two little girls, on the road between school and their home, and these were confined as captive queens ! They were finally arrested for stealing game chickens ; but being of such a tender age, they were to be pitied as much as blamed, because they had merely acted out in real life what their more guilty instructors had taught them.

Notwithstanding all, however, it is a very encouraging feature of these times that the supply of what is good is as large as it is, and that it is of such high quality from a literary point of view. Were the Scriptures ever before so extensively circulated ? Was there ever such a Bible House seen in the world before as that which is now a chief architectural ornament of Queen Victoria Street ? We suppose that in round numbers the issues of the Religious Tract Society reach over half a million a day. Great advances have been made in the quality of the periodicals and tracts. When we look at the rich banquet provided in the volumes of *The Leisure Hour*, and *The Sunday at Home*, for 1888, we realize that the best that money can procure is provided for the subscribers. *The Boy's Own Paper*, and *The Girl's Own Paper*, stand at the head of their class; and those who started them, under our enterprising and lamented friend, Dr. Samuel Manning, little thought that their efforts would be so instantly and widely appreciated. When our brother, Mr. Charles Bullock, a quarter of a century ago, began to provide reading that the Evangelical clergy could circulate in their parishes, he little thought of the vast proportions his work would assume, or that an Archbishop of Canterbury would confer on him the distinction of B.D., in recognition of his distinguished services in editing *The Fireside, Home Words, The Day of Days*, and *The Fireside News.* In the case of the Manchester carpenter, John Cassell, how could he foresee what gigantic proportions the tree he planted would assume ? *The Quiver*, which he started three or four years before his death, still retains all the charms of youth and freshness, as an examination of the volume for 1888 will pleasantly show.

We might extend the list through several pages ; but the above are typical publications, and they show how good and how abundant is the supply of elevating reading. We thus live in a favoured age ; and if the battle must go on between the pure and the impure, Christian people are only true to their cause when, by every means, they promote the circulation of what is good. Through the recommendation of its friends, why should not the circulation of *The Sword and the Trowel* be largely increased during the year 1889 ?

John Leland, the Apostle of Virginia, and American Baptists a Hundred Years ago.

BY ROBERT SHINDLER.

THE first British colony in North America was founded, in 1587, by Sir Walter Raleigh, in Virginia, which colony was so named after Elizabeth, the Virgin Queen of Great Britain. This settlement was not a success. The first abiding settlers in this new colony were chiefly cavaliers, from the upper classes of English society. They carried with them their notions of aristocratic government and religious formularies. They believed in the divine right of kings, and in the Church of England as the safeguard of the State, even as the king was Head of the Church, and "Defender of the Faith." In the Virginia charter of 10th April, 1606, the Church of England was made the religion of the State, and adherence to it a test of loyalty. This was long before the *May Flower* landed the Pilgrim Fathers at Plymouth Rock, and more than twenty years before Massachusetts Bay was colonized.

The first structure reared for the worship of God—the first, it would seem, in the whole of North America, and certainly the first in connection with British colonization—was set up at Jamestown. The patriarchal captain, John Smith, who figures so prominently and so favourably in the history of American colonization, gives a graphic description of it.

An awning, or old sail, was stretched to four trees, and walls were formed of rails of wood ; the seats were unhewn trees or cut planks, and the pulpit a bar of wood nailed to two trees. This was the first church. It was followed by a "homely thing like a barn, with crotchets,† covered with rafts, sedge, and earth ; so were also the walls, which could neither keep out wind nor rain." In this place prayer was offered morning and evening, and two sermons preached by "our minister, Mr. Hunt," until he died. Happy had it been for the State and the people if the same simplicity had characterized all ecclesiastical proceedings and laws. Far otherwise is the record of the historian.

The charter made non-attendance on Episcopal services a crime punishable with arrest and imprisonment, and, in some cases, with being sent, with all convenient speed, "into our realm of England, to receive condign punishment for his or her said offence."

Each governor promulgated his own code of laws in the spirit of the charter, directing his subordinates in all the details of administration. And so, as the governor was more or less a bigot, the laws were more or less severe. Every new-comer was required to give an account of his religious principles to the minister. If he refused, he was to be whipped : if he still refused, he was to be whipped twice, and to acknowledge his fault in church the following Sunday; and if he yet refused, he was to be whipped every day until he complied. The very severity of such laws

---

* History of the Baptists. By Dr. Armitage. Elliot Stock, London.
† Timbers forked or branching out, like *crotches* in a tree. The whims, fancies, and conceits of disordered and eccentric minds, commonly known—too much known, indeed —as *crotchets*, give no support to roof, walls, or anything, inside or out..

rendered them more or less inoperative ; but it placed a power in the hands of " unreasonable and wicked men " which they were not slow to use.

At that time the boundaries of Virginia were not very rigidly defined, excepting as by the coast and rivers. The present state is smaller than the old colony, but, even now, including Virginia West, which separated on the slavery question in 1861, it is larger than England and Wales by several thousand square miles. As the colony increased in inhabitants, the parochial system of the old country was acted on. Every parish was to have a church and a minister, and every householder was to pay his portion of taxes for their support. Tobacco was the staple product, and the minister's salary was changed from £80 to 16,000 lbs. of tobacco per annum, a pound of "the weed" being valued at twopence. Anyone who wilfully absented himself from church was to be fined fifty pounds of tobacco for each Sunday, and a Nonconformist was to pay £20 per month ; and if this continued for a year, he was to be apprehended, give security for his good behaviour, or remain in prison until he was willing to attend church. This was one way of understanding the injunction, " Compel them to come in."

This was the sweet and gentle spirit of the gospel of peace and love —that is, as they understood it, or, rather, mis-understood it. Whatever of bitterness, wrath, and uncharitableness, the Congregational Puritans of New England — Massachusetts especially — manifested towards the Quakers and Baptists of the Eastern States, the much-commended cavaliers, with their "gentle blood" and polished manners and ideas, were at least their match. The "brutal intolerance" of the English court under the infamous Stuarts was reproduced in the colony of the Virgin Queen.

It may very naturally be said, Could Baptist principles ever enter or take root under such oppressive and restrictive laws ? Yes, they did ; and they entered to stay ; and they have taken root downward, and borne fruit upward. Comparison of the population and the number of Baptist churches, ministers, and members in England and Wales and in Virginia, will show what amazing growth there has been, and prove that a mighty agency must have been in operation.

In England and Wales there are about twenty-six millions of inhabitants, and of these, 291,014 are members of Baptist churches, and 1,751 ministers, while churches number 2,642. In Virginia and West Virginia, there is a population of 1,667,177—rather more than one-fourteenth of that of England and Wales—while there are 1,608 Baptist churches, 868 ordained ministers, and a total membership of 230,266.

And yet there was no Baptist church formed in Virginia until 1714, and during the present century there has been a very large secession from the ranks of Regular Baptists to the body formed through the ministry of Alexander Campbell, who went to America, from the north of Ireland, in 1807, became pastor of a Presbyterian Church in Pennsylvania, but joined the Baptists in 1812.

Another Baptist triumph is that the Constitution of the United States has been formed very much on the model of Baptist Church polity ; not as a mere accident, but from actual study of the matter by the Revolutionary leaders, Patrick Henry, and Madison, both of whom were Presidents of the Republic in after days. Jefferson, a third leader, had an aunt, who was a member of a Baptist church in Goochland county. This aunt was a great favourite with him, and, when young, he frequently visited her, and attended Baptist meetings, and, it is said, in this way caught his first ideas of a democratic form of government.

During the Commonwealth, Virginia went in strongly for the king, and those of an opposite opinion were persecuted, some even to the death. Four men, who had been soldiers under Cromwell, were taken and hanged out of hand for their religious opinions, which were supposed to be treasonable. In 1661-2, an Act was passed amercing every one who refused to take his child to an authorized minister for baptism in the amount of two thousand pounds of tobacco. This was aimed at the Friends, for Baptists had no existence at that time in Virginia.

The improved state of things in England following the accession of William and Mary, did not alter the law in Virginia until twenty years after. There were a few scattered Baptists at that time in the state who resolved to assert their rights as British subjects. They appealed to their brethren in England for ministers, who, in 1714, sent them Robert Norden and Thomas White. The latter died upon the voyage. Thus, the first church was established in 1714. There were Baptists in other States, as in Pennsylvania and Delaware, and Maryland, and ministers from these colonies came into Virginia. Some Welch Baptists in Pennsylvania were also very active. A young man, of whom we shall have something to say in another paper, went with two ministers from New Jersey into Virginia. He felt prompted to preach, and obeyed the inward suggestions. His name was John Gano. The church of which he was a member called him to account for his disorderly conduct, but wisely requested him first to preach before them. He did so, and he was " called" and ordained.

The General Baptists soon became Particular, and turned from evangelical Arminianism to a healthy Calvinism, from which position, as a rule, their descendants have not receded.

" Down to the Revolution," says Dr. Armitage, " all the colonies, with the exception of Rhode Island, New Jersey, and Pennsylvania, had a church established either by law or custom, as the rightful controller of the spiritual interests of the people, and those of Massachusetts and Virginia were peculiarly intolerant. In these, the influence of the Baptists, as the champions of religious equality, was especially felt, as they resisted the legislative, judicial, and executive departments combined. They were emboldened in this resistance from the fact that they took and held a footing despite the combination against them, and by piecemeal wrenched from their foes the recognition of their rights." As time went on matters developed more rapidly. Men of equal power and energy and piety, and deep-souled earnestness of purpose, were raised up. Besides Dr. Isaac Backus, the historian, there were Drs. Stillman and Manning and John Leland, and others less distinguished. Drs. Stillman and Manning were both men of considerable culture, they were clerical in their dress and habits, and wielded a powerful influence with the more educated ranks of the denomination. John Leland was less cultured, but perhaps a greater preacher, and more popular than the others. "Every man in his own order." They worked on their lines; he worked on his: they in New England, and he in Virginia.

"Leland's convictions were as clear and deep as they well could be, but his tastes and habits, as well as his early training, all ran in other channels than those of his compeers. His powers were rare and natural: theirs were moulded by culture. They were polished, measured, graceful; he followed the instincts of mother wit, quick adaptation and eccentric eloquence. They reached the grave, the conservative, and thoughtful; he moved the athletic masses. They did more to begin the Baptist struggle under the Federalism of the East; he lived to finish the triumph in the radical democracy of the South." *

John Leland was born at Grafton, Massachusetts, in 1754, and was baptized at the age of twenty. He had gone through "most intense soul-agonies on account of his sins and exposure to the second death." His deliverance was clear, decisive, and thorough. He remembered the "hole of the pit," and knew who had raised him out of it. His testimony was therefore strong and clear, and unhesitating. His feet were on the rock, and his song was of redeeming love and sovereign grace. " By grace ye are saved " meant everything in his experience and his preaching.

A year after his baptism he started on his first preaching tour through New Jersey and Virginia. Whitefield had visited most of the colonies, both east and south, and his preaching had been blessed to tens of thousands. Many of the Congregational ministers, and some of the Presbyterians, had closed their pulpits against him, but they could not close the hearts of the people against the message he brought; for who can shut where God opens? Those of his followers who left the dry and cold teaching of a sleepy orthodoxy were known as "New Lights," and by degrees many of them became Baptists; and better even than that, they joyfully accepted such heart-stirring preaching as Leland's.

He settled for a time as pastor of the church at Mount Poney Culpepper County, and then removed to Orange County in the State of his adoption. But he could not confine himself to one narrow sphere: he went about in all directions preaching the gospel of the kingdom. In fifteen years he baptized seven hundred on their profession of faith. It has been said that he was the most popular preacher who ever resided in Virginia. He was a Calvinist, though he would not be bound either by Dr. Gill or Andrew Fuller. He tells us that one time when he was preaching his own soul got "into the *trade winds*," and when the Spirit of the Lord fell upon him he paid no attention either to Gill or Fuller, and five of his hearers confessed Christ. He did a noble work in Virginia, first as a minister of Christ's gospel, and then as an advocate of civil and religious liberty. When he entered, the state persecution had abated. "The dragon roared," he says, " with hideous peals, but was not scarlet-coloured."

A touching story is told in "English Hymns" (3rd edition, 1888) of John Leland's " Evening Hymn," which was copied from the *Century Magazine*, 1885. A lady records, in her diary of the siege of Vicksburg, under 5th June, 1863, that their house was struck by a shell. "The candles were useless in the dense smoke, and it was many minutes before we could see. Then we found the entire side of the room torn out.

* Dr. Armitage.

The soldiers who had rushed in said, " This is an eighty-pound Parrott."
It had entered through the front, burst on the pallet-bed, which was in
tatters ; the toilet service and everything else in the room being smashed.
The soldiers assisted H—— to board up the breach with planks to keep
out prowlers, and we went to bed in the cellar as usual.   This morning
the yard is partially ploughed by a couple that fell there in the night.
I think this house, so large and prominent from the river, is perhaps
taken for headquarters and specially shelled.   As we descend at night
to the lower regions, I think of the evening hymn that grandmother
taught me when a child :

> " Lord, keep us safe this night,
>   Secure from all our fears ;
> May angels guard us while we sleep,
>   Till morning light appears !

Surely, if there are heavenly guardians, we need them now."
    Leland began his ministry about a year before the war of Indepen-
dence.   "Scarcely was the first shot fired at Lexington," says Dr.
Armitage, " when every Baptist sprang to his feet and hailed its echo
as the pledge of deliverance, as well from domestic as foreign oppressors.
Leland was to the front."   The time had come to strike for freedom—
freedom to worship God according to conscience, and freedom from the
domination of a State Church, both Congregational and Episcopal.   The
Episcopal Church had lost, almost entirely, what it had ever possessed
of spiritual life, and many of its ministers were godless, carnal, and
scandalous in their lives.   The Baptists were now a considerable, though
not a numerous body.   They had some noble leaders, and they were
generally people with strong convictions, and men who knew " what
Israel ought to do ;" and they did it.   They were the first to suffer in the
war.   "Wherever the British standard was triumphant, their pastors were
obliged to flee from their flocks, their meeting-houses were destroyed,
and they were hated by all men."   Alongside of the battle for Independence, the battle of State-Churchism was fought, though in the latter
case without blood.   Men like Leland, with will and nerve and unflinching fidelity, were needed, and were not wanting.   Their resistance
to State-Churchism was well-organized, and their position gave them
such importance, that they could not be dispensed with by the asserters
of liberty.   Sixty churches met and addressed the State Convention of
Virginia.   They stated that "they were alarmed at the oppressions
which hung over America, and had determined that war should be made
with Great Britain, that many of their brethren had enlisted as soldiers,
and many more were ready to do so, and that they would encourage
their young ministers to serve as chaplains in the army which should
resist Great Britain.   Also, they declared the ' Toleration by the civil
government is not sufficient ; that no State religious establishment
ought to exist ; that all religious denominations ought to stand on the
same footing ; that, to all alike the protection of government should
be extended, securing to them the peaceable enjoyment of their own
religious principles and modes of worship.' "
    In the end their cause triumphed, as the world knows ; but it was not
until 1833, that Church and State were for ever separated, and all laws

sanctioning the connection removed from the statute books of all the states. John Leland lived to see the end of what he called the "felonious principle," dying in 1841, at the age of eighty-seven.

God has put honour upon the denomination in America, for no denomination has been more blessed and used by God in soul-winning. The churches have continued faithful to evangelical truth, moderate Calvinism being everywhere held and taught; and whatever of "down grade" there may be among Congregationalists in places, there is scarcely any among Baptists. Mr. Spurgeon's sermons are read all over the States; but his teaching finds no heartier echo anywhere than among the three million members of Baptist churches.

Launch out into the Deep.

LLOYDS' agents report, concerning a late gale, that "*The casualties are confined to coasters.*" This is often the case upon the sea of religious life. Those who hug the shores of the world, and never lose sight of its associations, are very liable to be blown on the rocks when the storms are out. They have to study men, circumstances, profits, and losses, and these are as rocks or quicksands to their integrity. Brave men have quitted the inviting but fatal coasts, and have sailed away to the deep seas of true trust in the living God, and these find sea-room in the gale, and ride out every storm. In the late tempests of heresy, it will be found, on reference to the wreck register, that great havoc has been made among the fleet of coasters, whose avocation has always been in the shallows. These know nothing of chart and compass, for they never go out of sight of the cliffs of society, and therefore are quite unable to keep clear of the dangers with which they have so long been flirting. If men only knew the more than earthly joy of being alone with God, and out of sight and sound of human reliance and influence, they would up with the anchor, and seek the glorious main, where apparent danger is real safety, and manifest solitude is the truest company. Farewell, ye sandy shores of human trust! Adieu, ye green hills of human admiration! At last, we lose sight of even you, ye highest peaks of trusted attachment! Now our soul waits only upon God, and our expectation is from him. Above, beneath, around, is the Godhead's fathomless sea! God the horizon, and the zenith, and the whole circle! Now we dare fly before the wind, and leap the billows with delight. There are no rocks or quicksands here! O coasters could ye but know this liberty and life, ye too would fly your present fancied safety.   *C. H. S.*

W. Evans Hurndall in East London.

THE horrible tragedies which have recently occurred at the East End have at least had the effect of directing public attention to that vast and crowded area about which respectable people know too little. We have had descriptions true to life, or coloured with sensational exaggerations; but now all alike are outdone by the details of the grim reality which has startled and shocked the public to a degree hardly ever

W. EVANS HURNDALL, M.A.

before paralleled. Some of us have long known that the streets of London at night represent the very saddest phase of sin in our fallen world; but because the subject was not one to be talked about, or written about, the truth has not been understood because it has been so little known. Now, however, whether respectability will have it so or not, the hideous thing has stalked forth out of the darkness to proclaim its true character in the broad daylight of our every-day life. We are not pessimists, for we know too much of the work that Christians are carrying on to allow of our taking despairing views of the situation. But while we do not anticipate a repetition in London of the French Revolution, and while we regard the Whitechapel murderer as a ghoulish phenomenon which will not repeat itself once in a century, *the victims* of the nocturnal adventurer are representatives of a class the existence of which ought to alarm us on account of its numbers. To write as some do, as if the entire East-End were given over to evil, or as if the mysterious murderer were a fair sample of its population, is absurd. At the same time, it were folly to shut our eyes to the fact, that there is in our midst an evil power which will undermine the very foundations of society, unless it be overcome.

Having recently given some articles on the far-reaching work of the most popular Baptist pastor at the East-End of London, we would now direct attention to the invaluable services of Mr. Brown's near

EMIGRANTS SENT TO CANADA BY MR. HURNDALL.

neighbour, W. Evans Hurndall, M.A., who belongs to the Congregational denomination. Like Mr. Brown, Mr. Hurndall is the director of a great and comprehensive Mission, as well as the pastor of a church. The preaching of the Sabbath is followed up by earnest labour among the people during the six days of the week. He did not build for himself a Tabernacle. After serving for a time elsewhere, he lighted upon the spacious old chapel in Harley Street, Bow Road, whose first pastor, in the days of William IV., was the eloquent brother of James Parsons, of York. When Mr. Hurndall first appeared on the scene, twelve years ago, the outlook was of that melancholy kind which is peculiarly characteristic of chapels which have "had their day." If the building had ever been crowded at all, it must have been with cobwebs and empty seats. To build up a church, and attract a congregation, was an achievement which grandly testifies to the power of the gospel simply and earnestly preached.

2

Mr. Hurndall was born at Berkeley, in Gloucestershire, in 1845. At the age of twenty-one he succeeded his father as partner in an extensive manufacturing business at Bristol; and in this sphere he gained much experience concerning men and manners, which he has been enabled to turn to good account in the ministry. In the Western Metropolis Mr. Hurndall became associated with the church at Castlegreen, where he taught the young men's Bible-class, the attendance of which he saw increased from thirteen to about one hundred and fifty members. Soon after this he settled in London, to advance the interests of his firm ; and while thus engaged during the week, he devoted his services on the Sabbath to a congregation at Putney, where the building soon filled. Being so far successful, Mr. Hurndall decided to give up business, and devote himself wholly to pastoral work. Pressing invitations from several

A CHRISTMAS DINNER IN A POOR HOME.

quarters would have made an early settlement easy; but the young preacher preferred to enter St. John's College, Cambridge. At Cambridge he was throughout very successful ; he won the essay prize given by his college, and also an exhibition ; and in 1879 he took the degree of M.A., three years after he had accepted the pastorate at Harley Street, Bow Road.

Great success at once attended Mr. Hurndall's ministry, and his efforts to organize a working church in his densely-populated district. The renovation of the old chapel, at a cost of £2,000, was undertaken, and since that date an additional £4,600 has been expended in necessary enlargement, and in providing new rooms. The ordinary congregations were exceedingly crowded, while the membership of the church became as numerous as the seats in the chapel. This success was the more gratifying because it was in East London, where, in an ordinary way, so small a proportion of the people are amenable to Christian influences. Since then, Mr. Hurndall has more thoroughly organized his forces, and correspondingly extended his operations. Apart from his tract-visitors, who now number nearly one hundred, and who call upon some thousands of families every week, he has nine missionaries. One of these is an agent of the City Mission, whose salary is paid in part; the others, with one exception, devote the whole of their time to the work, and four, being women, are able to render special service. In his last account, the support of these missionaries amounted altogether to only £518 18s., the total amount received in the year for mission purposes being nearly £2,000.

The church's field of enterprise is the world; the field in which the Harley Street church expends its energies is East London, which becomes more and more unfashionable year by year. Had Mr. Hurndall studied his own advancement and ministerial prestige, he certainly would not have chosen such a sphere, though he could not have found one of greater usefulness. He must have been willing, at the outset, to make great self-sacrifice; but perhaps at first, as a younger man and less experienced veteran, he could not see quite all that his action involved. Even in a dozen years the outlook has altered in a degree that could not have been anticipated when the start was made; and, in a sense, the change that is ever going on is not for the better. Think of the different state of things which now obtains from the days when Harley Street could show its row of carriages on Sunday, waiting to carry home the wealthy persons who attended on the ministry of Edward Parsons! People were then content to reside in the district where they carried on their business, and made their money; nowadays they are not content unless they can at least sleep in a more congenial region. Our friend complains that people take their departure "just as soon as they can grow wings big enough." He then adds, with caustic wit, that "a gentility is prevalent which cannot endure the letter E at the end of its postal address. S.E. or N.E. may be tolerated, but bare, unadorned E. is shunned by many with far more eagerness than Satan himself." This habit which people have contracted of hastening away to quarters which are better chiefly because there is no E. in the postal address, is condemned, because "there is less excuse for leaving than many apprehend. East London is not unhealthy. Many parts will compare favourably with the most aristocratic metropolitan regions." If possible, Mr. Hurndall would retain those whom the poor cannot part with without incurring additional suffering, he even pleads for "the immigration of those who are sufficiently human to realize that there are other people in the world beside themselves." He actually makes the "startling suggestion" that the Sovereign herself should pass part of her time in Bow or Whitechapel, in a palace reared by the unemployed on a selected healthy site. He thinks that such a concession would be a graceful *finale* of the Jubilee, since it would touch the most sensitive spot in the heart of the people. "Victoria would go down among kings and queens as Queen Pre-eminent, with a strange halo encircling her name; because, in an age of self-indulgence she was content to dwell among her poorer subjects."

Meanwhile, while people who are anxious about their social standing are migrating to more congenial regions represented by the other three letters of the compass, the hungry crowd of those who have to be satisfied with E. on their postal address, daily increases in volume. Taken in its social aspect, the saddest characteristics of the East End become more intensified in proportion as the population increases. Thither, in a never-ceasing stream, gravitate all kinds of people who have lost their footing in the world; some being examples of misfortune, while others are victims of their own folly or sin. At the best of times, the great area shows an unnatural amount of poverty and suffering; but in times of exceptional distress it is a world of despair.

Is it, then, a world without any light on its horizon, and are its myriads to be abandoned to their fate without pity? So far from there being no encouraging signs, Mr. Hurndall assured us, that on the whole the people are getting better. The chief cause of their extreme poverty and consequent suffering is early and improvident marriages. Drink is the next cause of misery. In reference to the hardships caused by the over-crowded state of the labour-market, it is thought that the Government should give more attention to the condition of the unemployed—an opinion in which all heavily-burdened ratepayers should heartily concur. When Britons can go round the world on their own possessions; and when the richest colonies for all practical purposes are limitless, unemployed persons who are intensely anxious to obtain work should have direction and help granted them in accordance with the truest principles of political economy. At all events, the distressing scenes which take place every morning outside the Docks are discreditable to the nation; for if men who can work in the Docks, but who daily ask piteously for work in vain, can work in the Colonies, why are they not taken there in larger numbers? Mr. Hurndall believes that emigration will be one of the most profitable departments of his enterprise. While he is no alarmist, he fears that there may be trouble ahead unless this great question of want of employment is generously dealt with. The acute misery of the people had much to do with the first explosion of the French Revolution; and if any similar storm-cloud ever gathers in this great city, what human power could stop its disastrous progress? If nothing short of drastic measures will bring relief, the pastor is not even afraid to try such a prescription. He says, "It is childish folly to brand proposals as 'Socialistic,' and therefore to denounce them." "All proposals should be treated upon their own merits, and examined without foregone conclusions." While uttering such common-sense sentiments, Mr. Hurndall recognizes the truth, that there is still work to be done which can only be done by Christianity and its messengers. He says, "the root-matter is this, after all, that the people themselves need to be changed, and nothing in the universe can effect this but Christianity. Carry Christianity to the people, and its many fruits with it."

Let us now look at a few of the cases which came under the notice of Mr. Hurndall and his missionaries.

In one room there is a young man who is still under twenty-five years of age, who has been compelled to lie in bed during four years under peculiarly painful circumstances. At the too early age of twenty he was married; and about a fortnight after the wedding-day he met with an accident that permanently injured the spine, thus making it necessary for him to lie on his back. Instead of yielding to despair, as he might have been excused for doing, this brave young fellow still sets a striking example of patience and industry. While still obliged to remain in one position, he learned to make wool-work on frames, and at this he is constantly employed. A market for what he makes is found by Mr. Hurndall, so that a small but regular income is secured. The young wife, who appears to be a fitting companion for such a man, does her part with uncomplaining cheerfulness; a testimony to her character in this respect being seen in the clean and tidy room. Such an example of industry as this shows that none need really despair if they will but persevere.

A more commonplace, but still deserving case is that of a family of eight—man, wife, and six children—who were found all living in one room. The man being laid up by sickness, the duty of looking after him, and also of earning a livelihood for the family, devolved upon the woman, whose only resource consisted in making match-boxes at $2\frac{1}{4}$d. a gross. Even at such employment she contrived to keep herself and children out of the workhouse, which was her main ambition. We may moralize as we will about the folly of such persons taking upon themselves family responsibilities without any suitable provision; but when a woman is found devotedly toiling to get bread for her sick husband and six children, by making boxes at less than a farthing a dozen, Christian instinct prompts the giving of some assistance. These are the people that Mr. Hurndall assists in their laudable endeavours to keep out of the ranks of pauperdom.

In a general way, Mr. Hurndall is not in favour of free teas; but occasionally it may not be amiss to invite a number of the poor to such an entertainment. A short time ago, we were present at such a gathering, when an opportunity was afforded of seeing representatives of the classes who are fighting life's hard battle at the East End; those honest and struggling poor, whom to assist is the truest charity.

The first who enters is a woman, who has arrived at that age which is accounted the best part of life; but she is very poor, and has no change of clothes in which to appear on this festive occasion. Her unhappy lot is to do what she calls shirt-work at eightpence a dozen; she works at home with a machine which cost £7 10s., and on account of which she pays 1s. 6d. a week. As it requires four good hours to turn out a dozen, it is almost impossible to do double that quantity, because the same hands have to do the house-work as well. The result is that the earnings are about a shilling a day, twenty-five per cent of which must go towards the gradual paying off of the great debt on the machine. This reckoning only applies to times when trade is brisk. In dull seasons, shirts, even at eightpence a dozen, are by no means plentiful, and may even have to be waited for during many weary weeks.

The next subject is a married woman, whose sick husband and five children depend upon her for support; a mangle, for which she has been helped to pay £4 10s., being her only means of earning money. It is hardly possible to get a shilling a day at such an occupation; for when we learn that there are seven other mangles in the same street, it becomes plain that the artisans who construct these useful machines have a better time of it than the women who depend upon them for a livelihood.. The multiplication of mangles stimulates competition, thus bringing the price down from three-halfpence to a penny a dozen ; and how genuine a grievance this is, we should speedily realize if we had ourselves to provide for a household of seven by such an occupation. Of course, this sad-looking woman receives some assistance from Mr. Hurndall, and those who supply the funds will be glad to hear that she does so. These cases are merely representative of many others.

Through being subject to fits, the next subject does nothing but attend to her children ; and as eight out of eleven have survived to need attention, she does not lack employment. Her husband is a steady man, who has been a teetotaler for five years : but, notwithstanding, things have seemed to go against him ; for, after filling a situation in a mat factory for twelve years, the growing hardness of the times at last took away his employment. His only resource is now to go through the terrible ordeal of seeking work at the Docks, and those who know what kind of a scene is to be witnessed outside of the gates in the early morning, and again at noon, when some are taken on for half a day, will feel for him. Here, then, at all events, is a family which has not been brought down by drink ; and there are many others of the same kind, people who do their utmost to keep themselves above the low-water mark of pauperism, and who count it a privilege to attend religious meetings.

Another subject, whose work is that of a trousers finisher, at two-pence-halfpenny a pair, is lower down, if possible, than the others, her wages being equivalent to about a halfpenny an hour. It will be observed, however, that wages cut down to the lowest point do not represent the chief affliction of these women ; for two of the number have husbands disabled by sickness, and one has a son doubly ruptured.

Their testimony in regard to drunkenness is that drinking is nothing like so bad as it used to be ; but that still the drink is a main cause of poverty and suffering. The fact comes out that in wet or wintry weather bad shoes hinder people from attending the meetings. Many of these people, who have reached middle life, are unable to read, and deeply do they regret their ignorance. Mr. Hurndall finds that some who come forward to join the church have not yet mastered the alphabet.

Such are the kind of people who are reached and benefited by the church at Harley Street ; and the work is done by those who hold very uncompromising notions respecting the inspiration of the Bible and the doctrines of grace. In regard to Modern Thought, the pastor holds very clearly-defined opinions, maintaining that its fundamental idea is a mistaken one, that it tends to lessen the authority of Holy Scripture ; that it exalts man; that it lays little emphasis upon prayer ; and that it lessens the sense of the sinfulness of sin. If the objection is raised that he is "putting back the clock," his reply is, that "Christianity which goes according to a clock is likely to be a very queer faith. Theological clocks are among the most cranky pieces of mechanism that the world has ever been cursed with. No faith worth a farthing can travel by a clock; it must move with the sun. Now, here comes the question : Is there a sun to go by ? Modern-thought people seem to doubt or deny. We contend that there is, and that it is found in the faith which was once for all delivered to the saints, this being wholly of Christ the great Sun of Righteousness. If my clock does not agree with the Sun, I had better alter it until it does." For "abreast of the times" he substitutes "abreast of the apostles."

There is thus no uncertain ring about the preaching at Harley Street Chapel. It is a gospel that shows its divine character by its effect upon the poor. By living close by, at 16, Cottage Grove, Bow, Mr. Hurndall shows his preference for dwelling among his own people. In another paper we hope to show what is being done by means of emigration, as well as in other ways, and meanwhile, we commend the pastor and his work to all who have at heart the cause of the poor. Now that winter has settled down upon the East End, those who are devoting time and energy to work such as Christ himself would have commended, should receive the most generous encouragement.

G. H. P.

Self-Searching.

THE newspapers the other day told us that "*the Searches Bill was advanced a stage.*" We are glad to hear that anything has been advanced in a Parliament which is degraded by obstructionists: but what the Bill may be this deponent sayeth not. Yet this is sure, that we have each need, not only to pass such a Bill, but to carry it out. May be, because *we* are slow in so doing we are brought into more trials. *God* hath undertaken this work in answer to our prayer, "Search me, O God!" Did we know what we asked for? Those pains, those depressions, those losses and crosses. Were these black horses sent to bring with them, as in chariots of iron, "deep searchings of heart"? It is highly probable, and it would be our wisdom, and our relief, if we more voluntarily set about heart-searchings, and as the practical result, put away every evil thing.

C. H. S.

This End of the Streets of Glory.

AN old writer says, "*The streets of glory have their beginnings on earth.*" This witness is true. What is heaven but eternal life; and this is life eternal, that we know the only true God, and Jesus Christ whom he hath sent. This we already know, and have believed. Heaven is rest, and in taking Christ's yoke upon us and bearing his yoke we have already found rest unto our souls. Heaven is communion with saints, and with their Lord, and this we also have the privilege of enjoying in a delightful measure. Heaven is holiness, and the Spirit hath wrought in us the beginnings and elements of perfection. Heaven is victory, and in him that hath loved us we are more than conquerors even now. Heaven is hallowed service, and this day "he hath made us unto our God kings and priests." Heaven is glory, and when we suffer for righteousness' sake "the Spirit of glory doth rest upon us."

Truly the old preacher spake as an oracle, and the light of prophecy gleamed from his eye when he said, "The streets of glory have their beginnings on earth." Let us walk as far down those streets as we may.

C. H. S.

Strange Notions of Religion.

BY C. H. SPURGEON.

WITH how little God is satisfied, according to the notions of men ! That Thrice Holy One, who, in the Scriptures, is described as requiring truth in the inward parts, and the love of all the heart and soul, and strength, is dreamed of by worldlings as a Deity who, by a sort of witchcraft, is propitiated by pious words, or clerical persons, or pecuniary gifts. While considering the vain hopes of worldlings, frailer than spiders' webs, and more illusive than the mirage, we have given the words of Watts a fresh sense, and cried—

> "Great God, on what a feeble thread
> Hang everlasting things!"

One would think that the gate to eternal life was by no means strait, and that to enter it required no striving. Men have strange notions as to what they must do to be saved. These ideas take forms which are absurd in essence, and sometimes ridiculous in appearance. We remember the true story of the gentleman who was thrown from his horse in the hunting-field, and was carried into a house, and found to be fatally injured. A sporting friend, finding that he must die, offered to hasten off and bring a clergyman, evidently supposing that something might be lacking which the ordained person could supply. The dying man declined the aid of the rector or vicar, for, said he, "*I attended my own parish church last Sunday.*" He evidently felt that he had taken in his full supply of religion for the week, and that it covered all the emergencies of the period.

No doubt, religion is viewed by many as a blackmail paid to avert misery, or a decent homage rendered to a superior power, or a kind of exemption-money in lieu of personal service to a mysterious Lord. It is, to such, not a part of life, much less the essence and soul of character; but a thing to be done and done with, as we observe a matter of etiquette or propriety, and then take our pleasure. What a mistake lies at the bottom of all this! True religion means the love of God, and a delight in his ways. It is not the saying nor the doing of this or that, but the being reconciled to God and his commands and ways, and the exercise and enjoyment of friendship towards him, and intercourse with him. Such a thing as unpleasant religion is impossible. How can there be such a thing as forced love, or unwilling friendship? If these things are true, they are voluntary and pleasurable. What a different affair is this from going to church, having prayers in the house, taking the sacrament at intervals, and giving a guinea to the poor-fund! These things are done by genuine Christians; but they are scarcely mentioned, and never over-valued. They are such a matter of course to the hearty believer that the idea of trusting in them never occurs to him. His trust is in another and a higher than himself, and in gifts, and deeds, and prayers, which are of more than mortal origin.

The story has often been told of the sporting lord who made no pretence to religion, nor even to morality; but, on the contrary, rather gloried in his free-thinking and his free living. His time came to enter eternity, and he was laid low by a sickness which was the forerunner of death. One of his wild companions, calling upon·him, was greatly surprised to see the parson coming out of the bedroom, and mentioned the fact to the sick man. The explanation was soon given in sporting language : " Yes," said the departing libertine, " I am trying to hedge." He feared that his speculation in free opinions and ungodliness might turn out to be a loss, and so he was speculating a little in the other direction, to save himself in some degree. He was carrying out for spiritual things what he had often tried in betting on the turf. The story did literally occur. The conduct which it sets forth has struck bolder and more honest sinners as rather a mean piece of business, and they have been heard to say that, having been in the service of the devil all their lives, they were not prepared to desert.him at the last. Such a consideration has small weight with those selfish beings whose one thought is to enjoy themselves at as little risk as possible; or, if at great risk, then to discover some secret method of insurance by which the pleasure of the sin could be enjoyed, and the punishment of the sin could be escaped.

There are among us,'self-contained and self-satisfied persons, who can dispense even with the minimum of religion which others concede, because they are so good without it, that it would seem superfluous to care about it. If they pay respect to its outward forms it is from deference to society, but not from any personal need for the performance. Very wonderful are these superior persons. They assert that they are quite as good as religious people, and, in some points, a great deal better. They themselves assure us that this is the case, and they ought to know. They are so excellent. that to contemplate their own virtues is, to them, far more exhilarating than the worship of God. Such worthies remind us of the eccentric nobleman, who talked to himself in his travelling carriage all the way from Brighton to London, and ended by inviting himself to dinner, as the most pleasant companion he had ever travelled with. Surely to them there can be no higher heaven than eternally to enjoy their own society ! Alas ! when they wake up from their present delusion, and see themselves as God sees them, this supposed paradise will darken down into the worst of hells; for of all society, the most degraded will be that of one who dared insult his Saviour by the proud pretence that his own righteousness rendered faith in the cross needless, and indeed made the redeeming death a superfluity. It would be difficult to make a table of degrees of sins; but assuredly, though self-righteousness may seem a small evil towards man, its Godward character is of the blackest. It refuses mercy, it denies truth, it depreciates grace, it dishonours the Saviour; it is, in fact, a rebel in the robes of a courtier, or, as Thomas Adams would have said, "a white devil."

From the religion which is without righteousness, and from the righteousness which is without religion, may the Lord deliver us !

A Rescue in the Gulf of Finland.

I SHALL not soon forget a scene which I witnessed recently in the Gulf of Finland. I was on board the steamship *Golden Horn*, bound for St. Petersburg. One day, shortly before noon, the steward pushed into the cabin to tell me that there was a raft with two men on it, and that they were raising a signal of distress. I immediately went on deck, and could see in the distance something floating on the water, with two persons on it. Our good captain (Captain Leisk) at once had the steamer put in the direction of them. On coming nearer, we found that there were a man and a woman on the keel of a boat which had been capsized. The man was standing up, and the woman kneeling with one hand clutching the boat, while with the other she was beckoning to us in the most excited way. One of our boats was lowered, and soon returned with the two shipwrecked people. They were poor Finns from an adjacent island, and could not speak a word of English. They had been away to another island, and were returning home with a cargo of wood, hay, and—I was about to add *stubble*, for to the eyes of an Englishman it looked very worthless stuff. Their boat was a rough affair, with two rude sails, and in a sudden squall it had been overturned. After we got them on board, the captain had their boat righted and baled out. While this was being done the poor creatures were partaking of something to eat and drink. They seemed very grateful for the kindness they received. The woman was weeping incessantly. The captain found her a few dry articles of clothing, and I gave her my travelling rug. We took them as near to the island to which they belonged as we well could, and then put them into their own boat, and soon they were rowing away towards their home, which no doubt they reached in safety. But what excitement prevailed during the scene which I have thus poorly described! From the captain to the humblest sailor, all seemed intensely interested. The steward, cook, and nearly everybody, were rendering assistance. Sailors are amongst the bravest and kindest of men, and I was glad to have an opportunity of being in their company at a time when their better qualities were in exercise.

Now for the thoughts suggested by the foregoing incident. One thing was uppermost in my mind, and it was a desire that Christians might only be as much in earnest in rescuing people from eternal death as the captain and crew of the *Golden Horn* were in saving those poor Finlanders from a watery grave. Everything was forgotten at the time but the one purpose of delivering two fellow-creatures from danger. O brethren, let us arouse ourselves to save poor sinners who are perishing all around us. Shame upon us for our sloth in a matter of life and death! Let us

"Rescue the perishing, care for the dying,
  Snatch them in pity from death and the grave."

The efforts made to rescue those people were *prompt*. When it was once discovered in what imminent peril they were placed, no time was lost in going to their aid. Every moment is of value at such a time. Delay is dangerous, for procrastination may mean the loss of lives. In spiritual matters we need to act with more promptitude. While we are talking about reaching the masses the masses are sinking into the black waters of eternal death. How foolish and even sinful it is to be squabbling about little matters of procedure in Christian service while thousands are dying! If our captain and officers had retired to the cabin to hold a committee-meeting about what should be done, in all probability those two people would have been in eternity long ere their talk was done. But they were not so foolish. They set to work with all eagerness. The captain stood giving orders with the utmost readiness and the greatest urgency, and was not satisfied till he saw our boat speeding over the waters to the assistance of those in distress. This is what we need as Christian workers. We must be up and doing at once. By all means we must save some. Whatsoever our hands find to do, we must do with our might.

In saving men *there should be no respect of persons.* Those two people belonged to another country; but they were human beings, who stood in need of help, and that help was not withheld because they were strangers and foreigners. Our one business is to seek the salvation of all mankind, of whatever tribe and tongue. We are bidden to go into all the world, and preach the gospel to every creature. We are debtors both to the Greeks and to the barbarians; both to the wise and to the unwise. There is no difference, for the same Lord over all is rich unto all that call upon him. Those Finlanders were very *poor.* They looked wretched objects; they could not in any way repay those who rescued them; but they had lives to lose, and that was sufficient to awaken sympathy. We also must seek the salvation of the poorest. All have souls to be saved or lost. Let us be as anxious to save a peasant as a prince. "My brethren, have not the faith of our Lord Jesus Christ, the Lord of glory, with respect of persons." Oh, that we had less desire for the presence of the fashionable and wealthy in our congregations, and thought more of that immortal soul which belongs as much to the meanest as to the noblest!

Again: we must not merely rescue people, but endeavour to restore the loss which sin has caused the sinner. It would have been only half a kindness to save those Finlanders, and leave their boat to drift away; for their livelihood depended upon it. But when their boat was recovered, and they were placed within it, they were in a position to help themselves. Now, of course, in a spiritual sense, we cannot undo what has been done by sin; but we can help to alleviate its temporal consequences. We can assist the discharged prisoner to obtain honest employment, or help the poor drunkard to gather about him once more the comforts of a home. This is of the utmost importance, and is, perhaps, too much overlooked by the churches. May we all arise to the holy and blessed work of saving men, and carry out that work in a Christ-like way. On the great ocean of life moral and spiritual wrecks are all around us. On every hand there are signals of distress, if we had but eyes to see them. Let us strive to imitate him who came to seek and to save that which was lost.

C. W. TOWNSEND.

The Christian who was trusted.

A CHRISTIAN Santal was once going through several villages to
make an extensive purchase of rice. In the first of the villages he
got part of what he required, in the second also he got some baskets, and
so forth, all for cash payments. But when he brought out his money at
the last village, he found that he was twelve shillings short of the sum
necessary to pay for what he had bought; and as the Santals never give
credit, the man had no alternative but to ask the seller to take back
twelve shillings' worth of the rice. Meanwhile, the seller had perceived
that he had to do with a Christian; and as this impression was confirmed
on his directly putting the question, he declared, without more to do,
that he would be content in the meantime with the partial payment,
and would trust to the buyer that he would soon bring him the balance.
Herein was a great marvel for that part of the earth.

Unfortunately, the tax-collector came next day to the village to collect
the dues. The man who had parted with his rice on credit was not
able to pay his dues fully at once, and told, by way of excuse, what
had befallen him, and how he had hope of being paid before long. The
tax-gatherer deemed it incredible that a Santal should part with his goods
without getting the money for them. His suspicion was very greatly
confirmed by the fact that the man could give neither the name nor the
residence of his debtor, and only took his stand upon this, that he was
a Christian, and would certainly pay the twelve shillings ere long. Even
the other villagers did not believe the story, and the collector sentenced
the supposed liar to a suitable measure of stripes. A few days after,
the Christian returned and paid his debt. His creditor had scarcely
recovered from his undeserved ill-treatment; but he forgot his pains
in the joy of being able to vindicate himself and his honourable
debtor before his neighbours and acquaintances. He called them all
together, and said triumphantly: "You laughed at me lately because I
trusted to the word of a Christian. There he is. Look well at him.
I have not dunned him for his debt. I knew neither his name nor
where he lives, and yet he has come to pay me the twelve shillings!"—
From "Modern Missions and Culture."

Lost Jewels.

THEY are searching in the Adriatic, near to Trieste, for a valuable
case of jewels, which was lost in September, 1812, when a French
corvette was sunk by an explosion. It is seventy-seven years ago, and
yet they search for the jewels; the original owner must long ago have
died, yet others set great store by the gems. The case is at the bottom
of the sea, which can only be searched at great expense, yet the rocks
will be ransacked, or the mud upturned. Have any of us lost our jewels
of fellowship with God, power in prayer, joy in the Holy Ghost, and
delight in the Lord? Let us not rest until we find them. If we go to
the bottom of the sea of humiliation, and seek amid the depth and
darkness, yet let the labour be continued till once again we wear upon
our neck and arm the priceless love-tokens of our heavenly Bridegroom.

C. H. S.

The Gospel in New Guinea.*

THE conquests of the gospel in the South Seas have all along been wonderful, many of the smaller islands being transformed into gardens of the Lord ; and now the greatest achievement of all in those sunny regions—the reclamation of New Guinea from idolatry and cannibalism—is making rapid progress.   In the future, the names of such veterans as Chalmers, Macfarlane, and Lawes, will be intimately associated with the honourable service.   People who love to read about adventure on the virgin soil of unexplored countries will find plenty of instruction and entertainment in Mr. Chalmers' pages.   The author warns his readers that he has made no effort to produce "a finished book," the bulk being made up of what was written while on his travels. This will not detract from the value of a book which describes the progress which Christianity is making in the great island continent, which is about 1,400 miles long and nearly 500 miles wide at its broadest part. What there may be in the interior beyond vast stretches of grand scenery, great mountain ranges, and broad rivers, no traveller has yet been able to tell.   There are remains of an older civilization, from which the people have fallen.   All savage races show that so far as they themselves are concerned, they have miserably fallen ; and in no single case have they ever been found to be rising in the social scale until reached by the gospel.   Mr. Chalmers says, "The influence of the gospel of peace is already so marked, that it is working rapid changes in the thoughts and habits of the natives. Succeeding missionaries and observers can never see these people in the same stage of savagery as when we acquired their friendship."

But while the prospect of success is fair to the Christian missionary, there are clouds on the political horizon.   Our author says : " If New Guinea is handed over to Queensland—and this seems to be by no means improbable—there will be a repetition of one of the saddest and cruellest stories in Australian history ; the weaker race will go to the wall, and might will be substituted for right.   The young colony will not readily admit that the savage has any rights, and it is altogether too fond of the doctrine that the day of the savage is gone, and it is time that he made way for the robuster, so-called civilized race."

In giving a few extracts, which will convey to the reader a clear notion of the country and its people, we will begin with

A LOCAL DISEASE.

Elephantiasis seems very prevalent ; there are many swollen legs. I have found on all my travels that elephantiasis prevails on the banks of the rivers ; yet I believe that the most healthy localities to be found in New Guinea will be the banks of the rivers at the mouths.   Twice in the twenty-four hours there is a general cleaning up by the tide, a constant supply of fresh, good water, and no unpleasant smells, and the villages are all built on the sandy spits where no water can rest.

---

* Pioneering in New Guinea. By James Chalmers. With a Map and Illustrations engraved by Edward Whymper from Photographs taken by Lindt of Melbourne.   The Religious Tract Society.   Price 16s.

A NATIVE MAN OF FASHION.

Here comes a swell in the most fashionable dress. His woolly hair is tied well back, and round it is a circle of bright red hibiscus flowers, backed by a coronet of beautiful feathers, and enlivened in front with a chain of white shells. On his forehead is a frontlet of shells ; between the eyebrows a round shell, with a finely cut piece of tortoise-shell something like a large watch-wheel, and on each temple the same. In his nose is a large piece of round shell, and hanging from his ears are various fancy pieces of tortoise-shell. His face is one mass of red ochre, and round his neck is a large necklace made of small shells, and hanging underneath are a crescent-shaped pearl shell and a large boar's tusk. On his arms are arm-shells, and wrought armlets and new bowstring guards, and round his waist a large carved belt made from the bark of a tree and coloured red and white; his trousers consist of a narrow strip of native cloth of various colours, and ends hanging down in front, and under his knees and ankles are very nicely knitted garters and anklets. He feels himself handsome, and knows that he is now being admired.

PRAYING AND TEACHING.

Sunday, October 14th (among the cannibals of the Gulf in 1883). Last night in the dark we had evening prayers. The deacon gave a short address, I, through him, another; then he engaged in prayer. It was a strange, weird meeting. There were about a dozen present, and we taught them to pray, "O Lord Jesus, give us light, save us." Nothing more ; it was quite enough. And will he not answer them ? Long the deacon spoke to them and told them of God's love

Last night in the dark an old fellow got up and spoke : "Tamate (i.e. teacher), we are glad you have come again, that we all might see you, as we heard so much of you : we thought you must be a spirit, now we see you are a man like ourselves, only white." We have just had service, a hymn, a few verses of St. Matthew, and prayer by the deacon in the Elema dialect. The deacon also gave an address on God's love to man, and his desire that all might be saved . . .

October 16th. Slept outside on the platform, and had a splendid night. Arnako fulfilled his promise, given at Orokolo, and for long held forth on Adam and Eve, Noah and the Flood ; and both he and Arnadaera spoke about Jesus our Lord and his love . . . They listened well, asked questions, and expatiated freely. Soon after sunset it commenced, and when I sought sleep it was still going on. Although not a prepossessing people, yet they seem kind, and would, I believe, listen to the gospel, and receive it as good news from God to man. When I awoke, the sun, I found, had preceded me, and they were then, perhaps still, talking and listening. I went into the dubu, and looking my friend Arnako, who was now quite hoarse, in the face, I said, " Arna, have you been at it all night ?" He replied, "Yes, and when I lay down they kept asking questions, and I had to get up, go on, and explain. But enough, I am now at Jesus Christ, and must tell them all about him." Yes, my friend had reached him to whom we all must come for light, and help, and peace. When Arna had finished, there was but one response from all their lips : " No more fighting, Tamate;

no more man-eating ; we have heard good news, and we shall strive for peace."

NATIVE GARDENS.

Near. all their dwelling-houses they have small flower-gardens. A platform is made about ten feet high, surrounded with a fence, and inside, earth brought from far inland and the coast, is placed, to the thickness of about two feet, various kinds of plants are grown, but in the majority tobacco prevails. I think these gardens furnish further evidence that there is a kind of civilization amongst these people ; and this taste for the beautiful can surely be worked upon with much good result.

NEW GUINEA AS A MISSIONARY FIELD.

This is indeed a splendid field for missionary labour. Will the church of Christ in the South Seas give the men, and the church in Britain and the Colonies the money, with a few more missionaries? How niggardly we act in everything for Christ. We speak too much of. sacrifices for the gospel's sake, or for Christ. I do hope we shall for. ever wipe the word sacrifice, as concerning what we do, from the missionary speech of New Guinea. May there never be a missionary or his wife in this mission who will speak of their " sacrifices," or of what they have suffered !

THE PHYSIQUE OF MISSIONARIES.

They (the Motumotuans) were anxious to know if their teachers were big men, and when I told them they were, they were greatly delighted. Not only do savages look for physique in these teachers, but more civilized nations like appearance also. It is a grand mistake to send out men of small stature to these savages.

BAPTISM OF CONVERTS.

On Sunday afternoon we returned to Maiva, when we met five people anxious for baptism—one, a good old friend, who begged earnestly to be received into the church of Christ. On the Monday there was one of those soul-stirring gatherings that are met with in these heathen lands, composed of a crowd of natives who have come to see the first native converts baptized, into the church of Christ, the converts themselves, and the mission-party. Only after a long period of preparation as catechumens, and receiving instruction, and after a thorough public profession of faith in Christ, do we baptize them. . . . The enlightening goes on, and one after another is led from the dense darkness, through the glimmering light, on to the full light of glorious freedom in Christ and his cross—set free from their superstitions by his truth. But not in the present or following generation will the superstitions of these people be entirely overcome. There are nearly two thousand people being taught on New Guinea connected with our branch of the mission ; and it may safely be hoped the young will know little of the past, and they will be free from much their parents believed.

Easily Tested.

TO such as, in the midst of the darkness that doubt has created, are seeking a place of true rest for the soul, the following may be useful:

A few weeks ago, at the close of our Sunday-evening service, a young lady sought an interview with the writer, in his vestry. She was in a troubled state of mind, owing to the inner battle between the Holy Spirit's light and her own native darkness. God had made known his love to her, and the good Spirit was leading her; but at that time there was no settled peace. Surrounded in society with practical atheists, and herself reading some of the most poisonous religious literature of the day—the poison, however, being cleverly and fiendishly concealed under the coating of pious expressions—it was scarcely to be wondered at that her great difficulty was in believing "the record that God hath given of his Son."

In short, her difficulty was this: Could she absolutely rely upon the (to her, at that stage, so-called) Word of God as a worthy agent in her salvation? Supposing the Bible to be human, and not divine, or only partially divine; and the distinction between the divine and the human portions not defined distinctly, or left to clever wits to discover; how, in such a case, could she be *sure* that her confidence was not misplaced, and her hope a complete delusion? This was her "stone of stumbling"—a "stone," by the way, placed in her path by religious impostors, who traduce the gospel to which they are indebted for their daily maintenance. After she had opened her heart to me, I quietly said, "You desire rest of soul, and an assurance of acceptance with God: let us see if this Bible meets your case." We then turned together to several Scriptures, as follows:—

"Come unto me, all ye that labour and are heavy laden, and I will give you rest." "I am the Bread of life: he that cometh to me shall never hunger: and he that believeth on me shall never thirst." "I am the light of the world: he that followeth me shall not walk in darkness, but shall have the light of life."

When we had read these, and many others, I said, "Now, in each Scripture that we have read, there is *a distinct promise in the present tense.* If words mean anything at all, these mean that Jesus Christ promises specific blessings on specific conditions. You are not asked to work at some knotty problem, the true solution of which you will never know this side eternity; but most distinctly you are invited to participate in a *present blessing.* In your case, the validity of the Scriptures must be settled, not by argument, or appeal to ancient documents (which, however, constitute proofs beyond the shadow of a doubt), *but by your personal experience.* You may easily test the truth, or otherwise, of our Lord's promises. And now I ask you, in his name, will you venture upon his bare word, and take the consequences?"

All was not clear yet: there came another objection, and I proceeded— "Let me use an illustration. Suppose that you were in deep poverty, and hopelessly in debt. In your extremity, a gentleman—whose reputation for benevolence is not wholly unknown to you—hands you a cheque, the amount of which will cover your present liabilities, and provide for your near future. Under such circumstances, would you argue thus: 'Well, this gentleman has given me a cheque, and, if it is genuine, it will meet my need; but then, I am not sure of its genuineness; it may be a cruel trick to awaken my hopes, and then dash them to pieces again, leaving me worse than before. Now, considering the fact that such roguery exists, I will lay this cheque by until proof is forthcoming of its honesty'?"

Here my enquirer laughed, and I saw that the arrow had hit the mark; so I continued: "I see that you recognize the absurdity of the position supposed. Now, tell me, what would be your readiest method of ascertaining the genuineness of the cheque; for, remember, *as a cheque* it is worthless?"

My enquirer replied immediately, "Why, present it at the bank for payment." "Exactly so; and now do you see my point? This is precisely what I want you to do with my Lord's promises—*his cheques*, we may say."

Then there came a pause, and the tearful eyes were an index to the work within. In a few minutes she rose up, and said, "I see it all now; HE bids me come and rest—I WILL. I take him now and here to be ALL to me." And so it was settled. Subsequent events have proved the reality of her trust.

Reader, put JESUS to the test: that is just what he likes—"Prove me now herewith." All difficulties vanish when HE is received into the heart. St. Bernard sang sweetly and correctly :—

> "When once thou visitest the heart,
>   Then truth begins to shine:
> Then earthly vanities depart,
>   Then kindles love divine."

You will never get any good through criticizing or merely admiring God's promises. They must be received, and personally tested, before their power and sweetness can be known; and, once known, there remains no room for doubt.

> "If our love were but more simple,
>   We should take him at his word;
> And our lives would be all sunshine
>   In the sweetness of our Lord."

Cardiff.   F. C. SPURR.

Medical Mission Work in Travancore.

BY E. SARGOOD FRY, MEDICAL MISSIONARY, NEYOOR.

IN *The Sword and the Trowel,* of September, 1888, there are two articles bearing on Mission Work in India, the one narrating the short but noble life of Dr. T. S. Thomson, the other drawing attention to the work recently commenced among the lepers of India. As a kind of supplement to these two articles, it may be of interest to glance once more at the field of labour once filled so well by Dr. Thomson, which is now the corner of the great harvest field apportioned to the writer of the present paper.

The band of young men, who were trained in medicine and surgery by Dr. Thomson and his predecessor, Dr. Lowe, still do good service in the eight branch dispensaries connected with the Mission, and month by month they meet the medical missionary with reports of the work that has been done, of the seed that has been sown in hearts softened by affliction, and of one and another who, by divine grace, are turned from "darkness to light," and "from the power of Satan to serve the living God." A young man who has for some months been under treatment at the central hospital at Neyoor, and on whom a successful operation for the removal of dead bone has been performed, has given evidence of a simple faith in the Lord Jesus Christ, and is about to be baptized in the hospital with his family.

This being the jubilee year of the establishment of the Medical Mission in Travancore, a new and more commodious hospital is now being erected, the funds for which are almost all in hand; indeed, as Hudson Taylor has remarked, "All is in God's hand, and to be put into our hands when the proper time comes." Last, but not least, a separate "Leper Ward" in connection with the "Mission to the Lepers of India" has been begun, and medical help, kindness, and the glorious gospel, are being brought to bear upon these afflicted ones, for whom also Christ died.

May the Holy Spirit breathe through these various agencies, so that dead souls may be made alive! We are in need of a Pentecostal shower of blessing; for amongst our forty-five thousand professing Protestant Christians of South Travancore, we have to deplore much coldness of spiritual life. The visit of Messrs. Mateer and Parker last year did much good. Will all readers join in prayer that Travancore may be a " garden of the Lord"?

Notices of Books.

Metropolitan Tabernacle Pulpit for the Year 1888. Passmore and Alabaster.

WITH thankful heart we issue the thirty-fourth annual volume of sermons. Despite frequent illnesses, no week has been without its discourse, though on one occasion, at least, we were within measurable distance of a failure, through sheer inability to hold the pen. In their separate form the sermons have gone forth in their thousands, and now in their compacter shape we hope they will secure a lodgment in many a library. We trust our friends will continue to sustain the sale for the truth's sake.

The Interpreter; or, Scripture for Family Worship. By C. H. SPURGEON. Passmore and Alabaster.

WE are greatly rejoiced that our publishers see their way to the reissue of *The Interpreter* in parts, for thus it will come within the reach of the many. There will be twenty parts at sixpence each; or the whole can be had bound for twelve shillings and sixpence. We took great pains to make this book suitable for reading at family prayer, and from the testimony of many who have used the volume we believe we succeeded. A large edition of the work was cleared out, but as it was printed on fine paper it was somewhat costly, and it is with much pleasure that we see a cheaper edition prepared for the press. In the best form it will still be obtainable, but in these sixpenny parts we trust it will reach many more homes. May the Lord restore the spirit of pure devotion which delights in family prayer; for we fear that this holy institution is dying out in many quarters.

Our Own Picture Book. By EMMA MARSHALL. Nisbet and Co.

EXACTLY what it professes to be. A very varied assortment of engravings;

these are used as texts for short chats with the little ones. This is a splendid Christmas-box for those who are beginning to read. What must the sensation be of reading a page of letterpress for the first time in one's life? Assuredly, a good engraving must be a great help to the struggling scholar.

How the Home was Won Back. A Story for Mothers. By Mrs. G. S. REANEY. Nisbet and Co.

For years in the East of London Mrs. Reaney's ministry was "a blessing to mothers." Manchester mothers, among the humbler classes, will, by this time, have learned to love her for her work's sake. This little book is intended for those higher in the social scale. It is full of practical wisdom for both daughters and their mothers. *But*—reviewers always keep a large store of "buts"—what a poor compliment the writer pays to her husband's Nonconformist brethren! In their ranks she could not find or imagine a helpmeet worthy of her model daughter, without going to the Novelists' "Stores" for "a nice curate, if you please." "The priest, all shaven and shorn, that married the maiden all forlorn," appears to be as absolute a necessity to the bride's new home as to "The House that Jack built."

Left Behind. By JENNIE CHAPPELL. Shaw.

SCHOOL-BOYS will like the story. As it is all about one of themselves it is not likely to be "left behind."

Adeline Mayling. By DAVID NEWTON. Primitive Methodist Book Depôt.

A GOOD Methodist story. The fidelity of a loving sister is the silver thread which runs through the entire narrative. It is full of interest, and well illustrates the Scripture:—"He that trusteth in the Lord, mercy shall compass him about."

Raphael Tuck and Sons, of London and New York, take a leading place in producing works of art for the season. Some of their productions will be more acceptable to High Churchmen than to those of less florid taste, and of simpler creed; yet such works as " *the Infant St. John with Lamb* " will be acceptable to all. In books and booklets, this firm is as successful as usual. " *Harbour Lights*" strikes us as a specimen of how poetry and the pencil, working together, make scenes visible to the eye, and almost audible to the ear. In a special line of high art, the name of Raphael Tuck is to the front. The works of the firm are so well known, that we need only mention that they are supplying the market, as usual, with a great variety of beautiful things for the season. Cards, books, and copies of great pictures, are proffered, so that both the juvenile with his pence, and the nabob with his guineas, can find opportunity for expenditure.

Mr. H. J. Drane, Lovell's Court, Paternoster Row, sent us specimens of Gift-books for the season, but they were too late for the December number. They are as attractive a set of things as we have yet seen, and in some respects, we set them above all we have hitherto reviewed.

In a box at six shillings, we have *Songs of Love and Joy. Poems by Dr. H. Bonar.* This is simply perfect, and we may safely call it *the* gift-book of the season. Four books in boxes, at 2s., entitled, " *The Talking with Jesus series*," are each so good, both spiritually and artistically, that we know not which to choose, but are glad to have lingered over all four. Any one of these would be just what you are looking for to give Jane a present which may not only please, but profit. Following these are charming books at one shilling, and others at ninepence. We advise our friends to write for a catalogue, for when we reach so low down as 6d. and 4d., and still find beauty and art, we give up the task of making a list. *On the Sea-shore*, in the shape of a scallop, is finely poetical throughout, and is only 1s. Booklets fashioned as thistles, shamrocks, and rose-leaves, are striking, and will

please many—they only cost sixpence. Autograph Albums, also at 1s., will suit the juveniles. Altogether, it is our duty, as well as our pleasure, to commend Mr. Drane's issues to the special attention of the Christian public.

Year by year we use *the calendars of Bemrose and Son*, tearing off the number day by day. The figures are sufficiently bold to be conspicuous even in a large room. There are three sorts, each costing a shilling.

The Day of Days. Home Words. The Fireside. Hand and Heart. Volumes for 1888. 7, Paternoster Square, E.C.

THESE four serials, edited by our honoured friend, Mr. Bullock, are as good as ever, and we do not see how they can be better. The "Home Words Office" is the seat of a great Religious Tract Society, which supports itself by its own sales. "Success to it," say we.

Favourite Bible Stories for the Young. Illustrated. Nelson and Sons.

ILLUSTRATED indeed. We have seen nothing better this season. For taste and beauty these publishers are always to the front. A cheap and handsome present for a child. We prefer it to most of the books of the season.

Pictures and Stories of Animal Life. By JAMES WESTON. Partridge.

A DAINTY shilling's-worth. In the most entertaining manner children are introduced to many of those forms of animal life which stupid people do not admire. This is a rare book for a New Year's gift.

The Children's Treasury of Pictures and Stories for 1889. Nelson.

So good that we don't see how it could be better. Cheap too.

Nursery Land. By FREDERIC E. WEATHERLY. Illustrated by HELENA J. MAGUIRE. Hildesheimer & Faulkner.

A GEM of gems. Nothing can be more artistic, or better adapted to fill all Nursery-land with an uproar of jubilation. Cannot some good spirit make us all trotties again?

The Sermon Bible. 1 Kings to Psalm LXXVI. Hodder and Stoughton.

ANOTHER volume of a condensed compilation, which will be of the utmost service to poor, hard-pressed preachers. It is all stolen material, but the sources are honestly given. We cannot vouch for the quality of every particular stone in this mosaic; but, as a whole, it will be a great work. Get this second volume at 7s. 6d., and secure the one before it, and you will have no need of spoil, for you will have enough and to spare.

The Happiest Half-hour. Sunday Talks with Children. By FREDERICK LANGBRIDGE, M.A. Religious Tract Society.

VERY good reading. We are not carried away by it; but still it will be useful to friends who want something to read to the youngsters on Sunday.

The Biblical Treasury of Expositions and Illustrations. Old Testament Series. Vol. IX., Jonah to Malachi. New Edition. Sunday-school Union.

EVERY teacher, without a single exception, should possess a full set of the Biblical Treasury, and in so doing he will have by him a great store of Scriptural illustrations. This is one of the very best things which the Sunday-school Union has ever done; and in its present form, issued in volumes according to the order of the books of the Bible, it is simply invaluable to the rank and file of the great army of Sunday-school teachers.

Bible-class Notes on the First Seven Chapters of the Gospel of St. Luke. By OLD CHRISTOPHER. Second Edition. Jarrold and Sons.

FAR beyond the average of such notes as to depth and spirituality. Old Christopher is true to the gospel of the grace of God, with which we believe, from his *Notes,* he has a truly personal acquaintance through the inward teaching of the Spirit of God. This is a handsome book externally, and within, it has the beauty of truth and grace. We do not observe much that is astonishing; but, what is better, we find abundance of gracious, edifying teaching. We hope Old Christopher will be encouraged to bring out all the rest of the Gospel which he has so well begun.

The Antichrist, Babylon, and the Coming of the Lord. By G. H. PEMBER, M.A. Hodder and Stoughton.

THE triple title of this little book points to three distinct essays. In this, as in his previous works—"Earth's Earliest Ages," and "The Great Prophecies"—the author adheres to the primitive literal school of interpretation. In fact, like De Burgh, B. W. Newton, and Mr. Govett, of Norwich, he is a "*Futurist*"; while Elliot, of the "Horæ Apocalypticæ"; Cumming, and our good friends Mr. and Mrs. Guinness, have preferred the more modern system, generally known as the "*Historico-Prophetic.*" This causes a divergence of views which, happily, does not imperil collision, for they travel on totally different lines of interpretation; but they are alike evangelical and pre-millennial. They concur where they are never likely to collide, in looking for the coming of our Lord. Some of our friends may be curious enough to ask by which train (of expectation?) we prefer to book. Well, in our little wisdom, we will give them an answer as opaque as a Delphian oracle. The sentence is borrowed from Seneca. "*Veritatis simplex oratio est.*" We observe that Mr. Pember holds his Bible in his hand, and asks no other help, as by the aid of exegesis he aims to unfold the sacred text. The scenery through which his train travels is Scriptural. By the historic route you have saloon-carriages, furnished with libraries of secular history, heraldry, astronomy, and the inductive sciences, in profusion enough to prove that the Apocalypse could have been of little use to our poor progenitors. If you strain the language of metaphor with a lively suggestion, and put a little colour into your pictorial narrative, extraordinary coincidences will crop up, and our fear is that some of the historic coincidences of the historico-prophetic school are simply coincidences, and nothing more. Mr. Pember's favourite text is 1 Cor. x. 32: "*Give none offence, neither to the Jews, nor to the Gentiles, nor to the church of God.*" You see here in these three classes the triple thread of his meditations. We commend them to your evening hours.

Musings in Green Pastures; or, Food for the Lambs of Christ's Fold. By EDWARD CARR, Minister of Ebenezer Chapel, Leicester. Gadsby, Bouverie Street.

RICH dainties for Zion's pilgrims. There are still left among us a few who love the good old ways, and have a sweet tooth for covenant truth; and such will enjoy the gracious teachings of Mr. Edward Carr. To us it has been a relief to turn from reviewing modern theology, rotten at the core, to the sound, spiritual, devout musings of this man of God. The book costs 1s. 9d. Only simple-hearted believers will think it worth reading. The worldly-wise will sneer at its experimental testimony; but that will not matter, so long as the God of saints blesses it, and the saints of God are blessed by it.

John Hazelton : a Memoir. By W. J. STYLES. Robert Banks and Son. Price 3s.

MR. STYLES has written with the ardour of a friend, and with the skill of a practised hand; and hence he has produced a memoir which must be eminently satisfactory to all associated with Mr. Hazelton, either in his family or in his church. To us this biography has furnished special enjoyment, for Mr. Hazelton came from our own town of Colchester, and became a member of that same Baptist church with which we often worshipped. Many of the names mentioned awaken happy memories in our heart. Mr. Hazelton was led to embrace what we should have called *hyper-Calvinism*, if we had not seen from these pages that the word is distasteful. We only mean by that designation a doctrine which goes beyond Calvinism: suppose we call it *stronger Calvinism*. Mr. Hazelton faithfully adhered to those views which were advocated by Dr. Gill; but he held them with courtesy and peacefulness. How he went from Mount Bures to Bungay, from Bungay to Guyhirn, from Guyhirn to Clerkenwell; and how he fulfilled in Clerkenwell a faithful and useful ministry of thirty-six years, we have here written with an able pen.

Those who love the doctrines of sovereign grace will be refreshed by the allusions here made to the good men, now departed, who stood firm in their day. Many of these we knew, and esteemed. Those religionists who will not see the special beauty of the Strict Particular Baptist, might do themselves a service and a pleasure if they were to read this memoir, to see the nature of " the sect which is everywhere spoken against." No concealment is used, and no apologies are offered : the author is convinced that he is in the right, and hence he writes out of his heart in all naturalness, and lets you see both himself and his friend in a clear light. This is as it should be.

The points of difference between us and friends like brethren Hazelton and Styles are not unimportant; but we have far more points in common. We wish prosperity to the churches holding strong doctrine : may they be multiplied. It is a pleasure nowadays to meet with a man who believes anything; but a far greater joy to meet with one to whom the Scriptures are really inspired, and to whom the doctrines of grace are marrow and fatness.

John Hazelton's place will not easily be filled. He was a good man and true. Clerkenwell misses him. May the Lord raise up a faithful successor, and may the good man himself, through this memoir, though dead yet speak.

The Waldensian Church in the Valleys of Piedmont, from the Earliest Period to the Present Time. By the late JANE LOUISA WILLYAMS. Religious Tract Society.

THIS is a very desirable book. Those who have no work upon the Vaudois church should get it at once. We need not give it a full review, for this is the second edition, and we are sure that the work will make its own way, for the subject is of perennial interest to all who love the gospel of our Lord Jesus Christ.

Sunday Afternoons at Rose Cottage. By E. M. WATERWORTH. Religious Tract Society.

TEN capital chats with the children. Printed in good type, and written in simple language. We know some little ones that are very delighted with the book, and never seem weary of hearing it read. This is the best recommendation.

Heroes of Every-day Life. By LAURA
M. LANE. Cassell and Co.

CAPITAL. We have here no heroes of
ten centuries ágo, or of lands ten
thousand miles off; but we have men
and women of our own time and town,
of our own common-place order. This
is just the sort of book to spread
abroad. It will do good in a thousand
ways. Old England is not lost yet
while among her sons and daughters
such brave spirits are reared.

Mothers of the Bible. By Rev. CHAS.
LEACH, F.G.S. Nisbet and Co.

VERY good. Nothing to set the
Thames on fire, but something to feed
the flame which burns so happily on
the domestic hearth.

Louisa of Prussia, and other Sketches.
By Rev. JOHN KELLY. Religious
Tract Society.

THESE princesses and queens seem to
have been very good ladies, and indeed,
for their station in life, quite remarkable for piety; hence it is well to
record their doings. And yet we have
met with many a life among the poor,
infinitely richer in all that can edify
and elevate. When we get a little
from a queen, we are justified in
thinking much of it; and yet, as a
rule, it is no more than the hyssop on
the wall, while in every-day life we
see grace comparable to the cedar in
Lebanon. To many, this story of
royalties will have unusual charms,
and they will read, we trust, to profit.

*Robert Morrison, the Pioneer of Chinese
Missions.* By WILLIAM JOHN
TOWNSEND. Partridge and Co.

A BIOGRAPHY of the first class. As
cheap as it is good. So richly illustrated, and so much of it for eighteen-
pence! Get it for the Sunday-school
library at once.

The Makers of British India. By W. H.
DAVENPORT ADAMS. With a Map
and twelve Illustrations. John
Hogg.

MR. DAVENPORT ADAMS is great in
the use of the pen, and in this case he
has a thrilling subject to descant upon.
Young Englanders ought to know how
their fathers subdued a great nation:
thus may they learn courage and perseverance. Our sons ought also to know

what follies and mistakes British conquerors are prone to exhibit : thus may
they learn to treat a vanquished race
with the consideration which may con-
done past oppression. This is fine
reading, and such as we like to commend in preference to this all-pre-
vailing fiction—which is mere wind.
In the last great day men will be
startled to discover how much the
crime, the hollowness, the heartless-
ness of this generation is due to the
surfeit of novels to which it is treating
itself. We make our lives fictitious by
feeding upon fiction.

*Martyr Scenes of the Sixteenth and
Seventeenth Centuries.* Designed and
drawn by EDWARD BACKHOUSE and
WILLIAM BELL SCOTT. Etched by
W. B. SCOTT. Hamilton, Adams,
and Co.

THOSE who keep alive the memory of
heroic saints by such works as these,
are doing good service to their generation. Our Quaker friend, E. Backhouse, who has now gone among the
shining ones, had, by the aid of his
friend, William Bell Scott, prepared a
dozen telling martyr-pictures to illustrate some of his writings: they are
given here with short explanations.
The scenes are a little out of the common way of such things, and are therefore all the more to be prized. Foxe
kept to a beaten track of anti-Romanist
sufferers; but here we have Congregationalists, Quakers, and Gospellers
of all sorts. The power to discern
truth, and to follow it at all costs,
is a privilege of the elect, which,
whatever of trial it may cost them, is
in itself more precious than hid treasure. "Few there be that find it."

*Heart and Thought Memories of Eastern
Travel.* By T. HOLMES, Bolton :
J. W. Gledsdale, Deansgate.

MR. HOLMES has a special correspondent's eye. Travelling over lands
which have been observed and written
upon without stint, he yet spies out
new objects of a striking kind, and
these he paints in graphic language.
We had sooner read these unpretentious and perfectly natural pages than
all the learned observations with which
the profound Dr. Von Drone has favoured the present and future ages.

The Mother's Friend. Volume for 1888. Hodder and Stoughton.

VERY good and taking. Will make its own way. The volume is tastefully got up, and is cheap.

Our Boys and Girls. Volume for 1888. Wesleyan Methodist Sunday School Union.

SEVERAL other annual volumes give twice the amount for a shilling which we find here. The magazine is very fair at a halfpenny, and we wish it success.

Horner's Stories for the People. First and Second Series. Horner & Son, 27, Paternoster Square.

WE commend these penny stories, only wishing that they would kill the penny dreadfuls. There is a fulness of gospel truth in most of these stories which makes us desire to see them widely scattered among the tale-lovers of the period. Bound together, the stories make attractive volumes.

Sunbeams. By F. E. WEATHERLY. Illustrated by E. K. JOHNSON and E. WILSON. Hildesheimer & Faulkner.

THIS is wonderfully fine, and æsthetic —in fact, a little "too too." Little folks who have such play-books ought to grow up artists. We wonder if they will.

Sunshine for 1888. G. Stoneman, 67, Paternoster Row.

DR. WHITTEMORE must have needed all his wit, and more, to find sunshine in all the months of 1888. In this volume he presents us with the Sunshine of the year for eighteen-pence. Well, there was not much of it. Surely this is good money's worth. You can hardly buy sunshine too dear in this foggy little island. Dr. Whittemore is never more at home than in conducting a juvenile magazine.

The Leisure Hour. Volume for 1888. Religious Tract Society.

THIS is a gorgeous volume. For range of reading, freshness of style, wealth of illustration, and sterling instruction, what can beat it? It is excellent as a serial, and equally good as a bound volume: for the material is not for the month only, but for all time.

Anecdotes on Bible Texts. Ephesians to II. Timothy; Titus to Revelation. By J. L. NYE. Sunday School Union.

THESE collections of anecdotes are well arranged, and must be of great service to teachers and preachers. Good value for a shilling.

Sunny Faces. Bible Pictures and Stories Partridge.

THESE are two shilling books for the children. Full of pictures. Just the thing for Christmas.

Early Days. 66, Paternoster Row.

A LIVELY magazine done up in a neat coloured cover for 1s. 6d. Contents very excellent.

Onward. Volume XXIII. 1888. Partridge.

CANON WILBERFORCE makes a striking frontispiece. The year's issue forms a handsome volume. We do not think it a miracle of cheapness at three shillings, but certainly it is very handsomely bound, and the contents are wide-awake.

The Onward Reciter. Vol. XVII. Edited by THOMAS E. HALLSWORTH. Partridge and Co.

IF there is little strikingly new in this seventeenth volume, who can wonder? There must be an end to telling extracts at some time or other. To us it is wonderful that this serial has held out so long, and kept up its character for interest. The complete set of this work would set a Temperance man up for life.

Fancy Fair Religion; or, The World Converting Itself. By Rev. J. PRIESTLEY FOSTER, M.A. Swan Sonnenschein and Co.

THIS is not a jot more severe than true. The Christian heart is bowed in sad prostration before the Lord at the recital of the shameful things which are being done to raise money for the thrice-holy Lord. This shilling pamphlet should be universally read, and then, perhaps, there might come an end to tomfoolery in the name of Jesus. All who are getting up a bazaar should read the wholesome words of Mr. Foster, and it is possible that the form of the business will be greatly altered.

Voices of the Spirit. By GEORGE MATHESON, D.D., Minister of St. Bernard's, Edinburgh. Nisbet.

To our mind, a very valuable work. It costs only 3s. 6d., but it gives no less than ninety-five meditations or sermonettes upon different phases of the Holy Spirit's offices and operations within the soul. We feel sure that it must be exceedingly helpful to students of the Word, and to preachers of the same. At the same time, it will aid the devout emotions of those who do not aspire to instruct, but only long for vigorous spiritual life in their own souls.

Not Cunningly devised Fables. By the late Rev. ALEXANDER EWING. With Memorial Sketch by Mrs. Ewing. Hodder and Stoughton.

THE title is taken from one of the sermons : a vicious method, which ought not to be followed, for it misleads. The book is made up of sermons which deserve to live, for they bear witness to living truth. The brief memoir excites our tender sympathies for the widowed lady, who therein treasures up the relics of her husband's life, and makes us wish that such a career could have been lengthened. The discourses are full and deep, and always distinctly upon the right side. The preacher felt no difficulties as to the need and the justice of substitution. The gospel is not hidden away in these pages, nor even dimmed by qualifications and apologies. Would that all modern sermons were of this clear evangelical type !

The Pulpit Commentary. II. Samuel. Kegan Paul and Co.

DIGGING the knife here and there into this great mass of commenting, we seem always happy in getting a slice of satisfactory material. This is a garden full of flowers and fruits, and he must be singularly sleepy who cannot gather a handful worth carrying away. This Second of Samuel is a good book for preachers, and it has been but little used : we shall expect to hear something which will strike and stick when preachers are familiar with this huge tome, which is a mountain of exposition.

Notes.

THE CHRISTIAN WORLD, in its review of the nondescript Conference on "Evangelical" Preaching, which was held in the month of November, very accurately says of it: "It started from nothing, and it ends nowhere." This may serve as a very fair description of much of the less pronounced theology of the period. We view matters from a point of view which is precisely the opposite of *The Christian World;* but we come to the same conclusion as it has done, namely, that what is sought to be palmed off upon the public by many as Evangelicalism, "on its intellectual side, lies neither here nor there, but is consistent with the most widespread differences of belief." You may believe anything, everything, or nothing, and yet be enrolled in the "Evangelical" army— *so they say.* Will there arise no honest, out-spoken evangelicals among Dissenters to expose and repudiate this latitudinarianism? Are all the watchmen asleep? Are all the churches indifferent? We quote, however, from our antagonistic cotemporary that we may reproduce its testimony to our correctness of judgment. It cannot be supposed to be a witness biased in our favour, but it says, " *It is now established* by abundant signs that Mr. Spurgeon is well within the mark in asserting that among Nonconformist preachers there is a very marked defection from the doctrinal standard maintained by their fathers, and still upheld by him ; and every day that defection is becoming more visible." We do not now need this testimony, for ministers who at first denied our impeachment have passed far beyond that stage, and admitting the truth of what we objected to, are glorying in the defection as a happy advance, a laudable piece of progress, a matter not needing defence, but deserving to be carried still further. Is it not so? If it be so, upon whose heads will rest the guilt of this evil hour ? The "Evangelical" leaders of the day, who are dallying with the grossest heresies must answer for it in the day of the Lord's appearing.

As John Bunyan has, by a thousand-horse power engine, been dragged into the Down-Grade controversy, as though he was, or would have been, opposed to our protest, we thought we would look into his works, to see if he had ever been opposed to a creed; and, as our readers will have guessed, we soon found that he had one of his own, exceedingly full and clear. It seems like a joke, that the most reckless of our opponents should attempt to put Honest John on the wrong side; and, in no spirit of jest, but in downright earnest, we suggest to any who are inclined to repeat the clumsy experiment, that they should first study Bunyan's own Confession of Faith. As we are half afraid that they will decline the task, we make them a present of his belief upon the Doctrine of Election. If *they* should not take delight in reading it, there may be others who will. At any rate, the Scriptural teaching which he sets forth in his homely way deserves consideration. Thus wrote the author of "The Pilgrim's Progress":—

OF ELECTION.

"1. I believe that election is free and permanent, being founded in grace and the unchangeable will of God. 'Even so then at this present time also there is a remnant according to the election of grace. And if by grace, then is it no more of works: otherwise grace is no more grace. But if it be of works, then is it no more grace; otherwise work is no more work' (Rom. xi. 5, 6). 'Nevertheless the foundation of God standeth sure, having this seal, The Lord knoweth them that are his' (2 Tim. ii. 19). 'In whom also we have obtained an inheritance, being predestinated according to the purpose of him who worketh all things after the counsel of his own will' (Eph. i. 11).

"2. I believe that this decree, choice, or election, was before the foundation of the world; and so before the elect themselves: had being in themselves; for, 'God, who quickeneth the dead, and calleth those things which be not as though they were' (Rom. iv. 17), stays not for the being of things to determine his eternal purpose by; but having all things present to him, in his wisdom, he made his choice before the world was. Eph. i. 4; 2 Tim. i. 9.

"3. I believe that the decree of election is so far off from making works in us foreseen, the ground or cause of the choice, that it containeth in the bowels of it, not only the persons but the graces that accompany their salvation. And hence it is, that it is said, we are predestinated 'to be conformed to the image of his Son' (Rom. viii. 29), not because we are, but 'that we SHOULD BE holy and without blame before him in love' (Eph. i. 4). 'For we are his workmanship, created in Christ Jesus unto good works, which God hath before ordained that we should walk in them' (Eph. ii. 10). He blessed us according as he chose us in Christ. And hence it is again that the salvation and calling of which we are now made partakers, is no other than what was given us in Christ Jesus before the world began; according to his eternal purpose, which he purposed in Christ Jesus our Lord. Eph. iii. 8—11; 2 Tim. i. 9; Rom. viii. 29.

"4. I believe that Christ Jesus is he in whom the elect are always considered, and that without him there is neither election, grace, nor salvation. 'Having predestinated us unto the adoption of children by Jesus Christ to himself, according to the good pleasure of his will, to the praise of the glory of his grace, wherein he hath made us accepted in the beloved. In whom we have redemption through his blood, the forgiveness of sins, according to the riches of his grace . . . . that in the dispensation of the fulness of times he might gather together in one all things in Christ, both which are in heaven, and which are on earth; even in him' (Eph. i. 5—7, 10). 'Neither is there salvation in any other: for there is none other name under heaven given among men, whereby we must be saved' (Acts iv. 12).

"5. I believe that there is not any impediment attending the election of God that can hinder their conversion and eternal salvation. 'Moreover, whom he did predestinate, them he also called: and whom he called, them he also justified: and whom he justified, them he also glorified. What shall we then say to these things? If God be for us, who can be against us?' . . . Who shall lay anything to the charge of God's elect? It is God that justifieth. Who is he that condemneth?' &c. (Rom. viii. 30, 31; 33—35). 'What then? Israel hath not obtained that which he seeketh for; but the election hath obtained it, and the rest were blinded' (Rom. xi. 7). 'For Israel hath not been forsaken, nor Judah of his God, of the Lord of hosts; though their land was filled with sin against the Holy One of Israel' (Jer. li. 5). When Ananias made intercession against Paul, saying, 'Lord, I have heard by many of this man, how much evil he hath done to thy saints at Jerusalem: and here he hath authority from the chief priests to bind all that call on thy name,' what said God unto him? 'Go thy way: for he is a chosen vessel unto me, to bear my name before the Gentiles, and kings, and the children of Israel' (Acts ix. 13—15).

"6. I believe that no man can know his election, but by his calling. The vessels of mercy, which God afore prepared unto glory, do thus claim a share therein: 'Even us (say they), whom he hath called, not of the Jews only, but also of the Gentiles. As he saith also in Osee [Hosea ii. 23], I will call them my people, which were not my people; and her beloved, which was not beloved' (Rom. ix. 24, 25).

"7. I believe, therefore, that election doth not forestall or prevent the means which are of God appointed to bring us to Christ, to grace and glory; but rather putteth a necessity upon the use and effect thereof; because they are chosen to be brought to heaven that way; that is, by the faith of Jesus Christ, which is the end of effectual calling. 'Wherefore the rather, brethren, give diligence to make your calling and election sure.' 2 Pet. i. 10; 2 Thess. ii. 13; 1 Pet. i. 12."

As loving friends pressingly wish to know

of the Editor's whereabouts and welfare, I venture to give them what else I should never think of writing—namely, a little account of matters personal.

When I left home it was with great difficulty I tottered up the stairs of Herne Hill station, and I felt quite spent while waiting for the train by which I reached Dover; therefore I stopped by the sea for the night. Our friend, Miss Dawson, cheered me by a call. How much the Orphanage is indebted to her for taking our sick children into her hospitable home, I cannot express in words. She has by her own bounty supplied us with a Convalescent Home for our Girls—and with something better than any institution can ever be.

On Tuesday morning I crossed the Channel with exceeding comfort, and reached Paris, whither Mr. and Mrs. Passmore had preceded me, to make all arrangements. I was very weak, but felt better than when I left home. At Paris our party remained till Thursday evening, our kind deacon, Mr. Higgs, and his wife, helping to cheer us. Thursday night saw me on my way to Marseilles. The night journey was a trial, but it proved a light one, for sleep made the long miles slip away unobserved, and Mr. Allison, a third deacon, and Mr. Ladds, secretary, kindly ministered to me. The day was clear and bright at Marseilles. The Mediterranean soon drives away colds; and when Marseilles is without wind, its weather is genial. A ride round the Prado and the port helped to bring on a restful night, and on Saturday I was on the road to Menton, enjoying the warm sun, the balmy air, and the continuous succession of lovely views. The Lord that healeth us was tenderly doing his gracious work by his great minister, the sun.

Rooms were ready at Menton, and Christian friends had sent in bouquets of flowers to express their welcome. The host and hostess at Hôtel Beau Rivage are of the kindest sort, and never fail to make our party feel quite at home at once. The first Sabbath was literally, as well as spiritually, a day of rest, and I found myself free from pain, but weak to an extreme. Since then the days have usually been more sunny than our midsummer, and though by no means scorching, yet delightfully warm and balmy; so that each day I have been out in the air, and have rapidly improved, and at the time of writing I am well until I reach my knees. The feet continue to swell in a very disagreeable manner night by night; but as they get right by the morning, the doctors assure me that it is only weakness. Soon may that weakness disappear, that I may be able to climb the Alpine staircases of the Tabernacle, and may be able to stand during a whole service, which at present I could not do. This once accomplished, the pleasurable duties of my ministry will have more charm for me than all the ease and health which this sheltered and sunny paradise can afford me. It is a daily sorrow that my dearest

companion cannot be with me, and that she continues to suffer at home; but we see the hand of God in our afflictions, and in the needful separation which they involve, and we drink together from a secret well which flows both in Norwood and in Menton, and fills our hearts with peace.

I have to thank friends, who have *not* written me during the time of my retreat, for the thoughtfulness of their abstinence; but I am also grateful to several who could not withhold glad tidings of souls saved through reading the sermons. I could not blame anyone who aroused me in the middle of the night with news of sinners brought to Jesus, backsliders restored, and saints sustained in their dying hours. I never yet felt too weary or too ill to listen to the bells of heaven as they rang out over "one sinner that repented."

The best news from home flies to me as on dove's wings, and brings me peace of heart. God has blessed the work of brethren Fullerton and Smith far beyond all previous experience. Hundreds declare that they have found the Saviour, and many more have been awakened. The officers of the church, and all the workers, are bent upon making up for my absence; and I trust they will succeed in doing far more than that. A spirit of prayer is poured out, and zeal is aroused, and from this, under the divine blessing, welcome results must follow. The special blessing of Mr. William Olney's ability to be once more at all meetings calls for devout gratitude; for the Lord uses him greatly as a leader in stirring up the hearts of others by his own ardour in every holy work. It is a severe loss to the work that my beloved brother should be for a time laid aside; but even this only calls out double diligence from my good brethren, and thus in weakness the church finds its strength renewed. How can I do otherwise than praise the Lord for his goodness, and take heart?

The various preachers who have supplied the pulpit have been graciously assisted, and the people have been edified. Mr. McNeil set the vast audiences on fire. He will be a great gain to London.

Friends at home and here press me to remain a longer time than usual, that I may the longer continue in vigour when I return; but I must see what progress I make. When I feel well and strong I cannot stay out of the pulpit; but I have not reached that point at this present. I will not be away a day more than is necessary.

It is no doubt true that those who address great audiences and superintend important enterprises must rest after a period of unusual strain, or else they will break down very seriously. If ever a human being has had a supremely severe pressure of mind to endure, I think I am at least his equal in endurance. Hence it may not be an unmixed evil that my bodily pain rendered me incapable of mental effort, and that at this present I have no choice in the matter, but must cease from preaching.

One would like to keep on for ever telling the great message; but the next best thing is to be gathering strength to begin again, while for a season silence is compulsory. Of course, by the time this reaches the reader, a great change may have occurred, for, in preparing a magazine a thousand miles from home, one has to take time by the forelock, and commence early in the month, and all the more so when one is quite uncertain as to how long health may permit writing of any sort.

Friends must not imagine, as some of them evidently do, that the *Book Fund* has ceased its gracious work on account of the more pressing illness of Mrs. Spurgeon. She was compelled to suspend the issue of books for a season, but she soon began again. The packing, &c., have been largely left in other hands, but the management and book-keeping are still with her, and preachers of all denominations are still obtaining parcels of books. There is no improvement in the condition of the vast number of poor ministers; but, owing to agricultural depression, their incomes grow less and less. How can they buy books when they can scarcely buy bread? Many thousands have now been helped from Mrs. Spurgeon's Book Fund, and we trust that the supply will never cease to be forthcoming and forthgoing. The heart of the lone and languishing worker is cheered by help to her holy enterprise. We hope to be able next month to give our readers some account of the *Auxiliary Book Fund* which, under the charge of Mr. Bagster, has been for about a year supplementing Mrs. Spurgeon's work by supplying books to Christian workers who are beyond the range of her efforts.

The hopes that we expressed last month respecting MESSRS. FULLERTON AND SMITH'S SERVICES AT THE TABERNACLE were more than realized before the mission closed. The numbers in attendance increased nightly, until, at the closing service, not only was the Tabernacle densely packed, but overflow meetings were held in three rooms in the College, and some thousands of persons were unable to gain admission. All who had professed to find the Saviour were asked to meet the workers in the lecture-hall, at the close of the public services, and very soon the hall was quite full. Those who were present will not soon forget the scene when, in response to Mr. Fullerton's request, some hundreds of hands were held up in token of blessing received during the mission.

In order to deepen the impressions that had been made, and to strengthen the new life that had been implanted, a meeting was held on *Wednesday evening*, *November* 28. Nearly five hundred invitations were sent out to those whose names had been taken by the workers, and the greater part of them met for tea, while afterwards, notwithstanding an almost tropical downpour of rain, the lecture-hall was well filled with workers, converts, and enquirers. Messrs. Fullerton and Smith came over from Bloomsbury for the first half-hour, and gave wise and weighty counsels to those who had been brought to decision. When they left, Mr. William Olney took the chair, and delivered a soul-searching and spirit-stirring address upon the evidences of the work of regeneration; Mr. Harrald expounded and applied Acts xi. 26—28 to the various classes present; Mr. Chamberlain sang and spoke, and then asked any who had been brought to decision during the mission just to rise, and declare that fact. In less than half-an-hour, no less than fifty-one persons bore oral testimony to what the Lord had done for them at the special services, and many more would have spoken if there had been time. The converts were of all ages, and of both sexes; there were "young men and maidens, old men and children," praising the name of the Lord for the great things he had done for them. The whole proceedings of the evening were of such an interesting and profitable character, that it was decided that a similar meeting should be held every Tuesday evening, for the present, for further instruction and confirmation of the converts, and for the guidance of those who are not yet fully decided. The success of the mission has been a great joy to the officers and members of the church, the students of the College, and other workers who helped in the sowing and the reaping; and they join in prayer that the work of revival may continue to spread until thousands more are won for the Saviour.

An effort was made to get Messrs. Fullerton and Smith to hold a few more special services at the beginning of the year, but their engagement at Exeter Hall prevented them from taking more than the Watch-night service, on *Monday*, *December* 31. Let us all pray for a great outpouring of the Holy Spirit on those who will be gathered at the Tabernacle at that meeting.

On *Monday evening*, *December* 10, the Tabernacle prayer-meeting partook of the character of a farewell to the four students of the Pastors' College who are shortly leaving for the foreign mission field—viz., Messrs. Clark, Roger, Patrick, and Huntley. Mr. William Olney presided; prayer was presented by Mr. Huntley; Mr. Minifie (secretary of the Students' Missionary Association); and Mr. F. Thompson (one of the Tabernacle missionary collectors); and addresses were delivered by Mr. Scrivener, a missionary from the Congo, and Messrs. Clark and Roger, who are going to that region. Mr. Harrald explained that Mr. Patrick, who was leaving for Tangier, North Africa, would be supported by Mr. Spurgeon, who hoped to send out many more missionary students as the doors were opened, and his funds permitted. Mr. Patrick briefly spoke. Mr. William Olney and Mr. Dunn gave the departing brethren a few words of loving counsel and encouragement, and then quite a large number of students and other brethren commended them to the Lord in prayer. There was a dense fog outside, and some of it penetrated the lecture-hall, where the meeting was held, but there has seldom been a happier or more enjoyable gathering.

Farewell meetings for the missionary students have also been held at Beulah Chapel, Thornton Heath; Devonshire Square Chapel, Stoke Newington; the Y.M.C.A. Aldersgate Street; and several other places; resulting in increased interest being taken both in the College and in the work of missions to the heathen.

COLLEGE.—Several students are leaving us for the foreign mission field. Mr. J. A. Clark, and Mr. J. L. Roger, who have been accepted by the Baptist Missionary Society for work on the Congo, will be sailing about the time that this magazine is issued. Mr. N. H. Patrick is leaving this month for Tangier, North Africa. We have undertaken to support him, and we hope to be able to send out other brethren to labour amongst the twenty millions of Mahometans in that region. Mr. G. A. J. Huntley has been accepted by the China Inland Mission, but the date of his departure is not definitely fixed. We ask our readers to pray very specially for these beloved brethren, that their lives may be spared, and that they may be the means of winning many souls for the Saviour. There are several other students who desire to go as missionaries to the heathen when the Lord opens the door for them.

Mr. A. A. Witham has sailed for America. He hopes to be able to raise a Baptist church in Washington Territory. Mr. R. Hughes, who went to the United States a few months ago, has settled at Londonville, Ohio. Mr. F. Dann's health broke down under the great extremes of climate in Minnesota, so he has returned to England with the hope of engaging in pastoral work here. His address is 35, Broad Street, Reading.

Mr. A. W. Curwood goes next month to settle at West Hartlepool, where there appears to be a wide sphere of work, though not without many difficulties.

The following brethren have removed:—Mr. W. H. Smith, from Minchinhampton, to Haddenham, Thame; Mr. J. O. Stalberg, from Faringdon, to Stanwell Road, Penarth, South Wales; Mr. J. B. Warren, from Shouldham Street, to Irthlingborough, Northamptonshire; Mr. C. Welton, from Driffield, to Morley, Yorkshire; and Mr. W. Coller, from Mitcham, Adelaide, to Broken Hill, South Australia. Mr. C. W. Townsend his left Plumstead, and is preaching in connection with the Evangelization Society.

During the President's absence the students have been greatly interested and instructed by the Friday afternoon lectures delivered by the Revs. David Davies, J. Jackson Wray, and Dr. Sinclair Paterson.

On *Friday afternoon and evening*, November 23, the twenty-fourth anniversary of the Students' Total Abstinence Society was held, under the presidency of Professor Cheshire, when it was reported that every student in the College was an abstainer. On the following Friday evening, the annual *soirée* of the Students' Total Abstinence Union was held at Hackney College. Out of the two hundred and fifty-three students in the six colleges in the Union, two hundred and thirty-six are abstainers, a larger proportion than in any previous year.

EVANGELISTS. — *Messrs. Fullerton and Smith* have had a very successful mission at Bloomsbury Chapel, of which we shall give fuller particulars next month, when we shall also be able to present a report of the services at Peckham Park Road, which are being held while these "Notes" are in course of preparation. The Evangelists are to be at Exeter Hall from January 4 to 27; and in February they go to the Shoreditch Tabernacle and Dalston Junction Chapel.

Mr. Burnham has been obliged to rest during the past month, but he reports himself as better, and hopes to be able to resume work this month at Puddletown, Bere Regis, and Shefford. In each of these places he has already conducted two missions.

Messrs. Harmer and Parker have completed their series of services in connection with the Conference of General Baptist Churches in the Bradford district. Mr. A. White, the secretary of the Conference, writes:—"A week was spent at Queensbury (the mother church of the district), a week at Sandy Lane, a fortnight at Denholme, another at Allerton, and the mission closed with a week's services at Clayton. The meetings have been well attended, especially considering the stormy weather; and large numbers have manifested their desire after the better life by coming into the enquiry-rooms at the various churches. Mr. Harmer's simple, earnest, and effective gospel addresses have been warmly appreciated, and Mr. Parker's solos and efficient leadership of the service of praise have proved very useful in attracting people to the services, and in helping them to decision. The services will be ever remembered by many in this neighbourhood who have found blessing through them."

After leaving Bradford, Mr. Harmer joined *Mr. Chamberlain*, for a week's mission at Redditch. Concerning this, Pastor E. W. Berry writes:—"This is Mr. Harmer's third visit to us, and the services have been more largely attended than on any former occasion. Many have professed conversion, and the members of the church have been wonderfully quickened." Mr. Harmer has since been to Orpington, and he is now at Crewkerne, with Mr. Parker.

' Pastor D. Macmillan writes as follows, with regard to *Mr. Carter's* visit to King's Langley, Hunton Bridge, and Leavesden :— " In each place souls have been won for Christ, and the people of God encouraged and helped. A very pleasing feature has been the work done among the elder scholars of our Sunday-schools, many being led to decision." Mr. Carter is now at Farnworth, by Bolton.

Pastor W. Pettman writes thus about *Mr. Harrison's* services, at Bath :—" Our brother's visit has been the occasion of much blessing, and the earnest prayers of the church have been graciously answered. Large congregations were attracted each evening, and many were led to come out as enquirers, a considerable number of whom give good evidence of true conversion. Brother Harrison's clear and earnest preaching of the truth was deeply impressive. In the preparation for these services, and the actual engaging in them, the church has been much revived." This month Mr. Harrison goes to Bristol and Sittingbourne.

ORPHANAGE.—The magazine has to be issued before the Christmas festivities are over, so we must postpone our account of them until our next number. We need not, and we will not, postpone our thanks to the generous friends who evidently intend the children at Stockwell to enjoy themselves as thoroughly as on former occasions. We are also very grateful to all who have again helped to ensure the success of the Orphan-

age choir visits to Portsmouth, Gosport, Cowes, Southampton, and Winchester.

COLPORTAGE.—During the past month the colporteurs have been busier than usual, on account of the increased demand for books, Christmas cards, &c., for presents. The total value of sales was . £733 5s. 8d. This widespread distribution of the Scriptures, with Christian and sound, healthy literature, cannot fail to produce salutary and saving effects throughout the country in the districts occupied. But there are hundreds of localities equally needy, in which the same valuable work might be done, if only a church or association would guarantee the £10 a year required by this association. All denominations can combine to do this, as the work is carried out on unsectarian lines, while the subscription required is very small, considering that it secures the entire services of the agent for the locality. We hope to receive numerous applications for the extension of the work during the new year.

The secretary has visited Salisbury during the month, and addressed a meeting in Brown-street Chapel, explaining the work, and advocating its claims. Rev. G. Short, B.A., presided.

Any information or co-operation will be gladly given on application to the Secretary, W. Corden Jones, Colportage Association, Metropolitan Tabernacle, Newington Butts.

Baptisms at Metropolitan Tabernacle :— November 29, two.

Pastors' College, Metropolitan Tabernacle.

Statement of Receipts from November 15th to December 14th, 1888.

	£	s.	d.		£	s.	d.
Mr. William Buchan	1	0	0	Collected at Drummond-road Chapel, per Pastor B. Briggs ...	4	11	0
From a friend	50	0	0	Collected at Bell-street Chapel, Romsey, per Pastor J. Smith	1	0	0
A Presbyterian, Edinburgh ...	5	0	0	*Monthly Subscription:*			
From Victoria Chapel, Wandsworth-road, per Pastor E. Henderson ...	4	0	0	Mr. R. J. Beecliff	0	2	6
Nameless	1	0	0	Weekly Offerings at Met. Tab. :			
D. E. G., Wilts.	0	5	0	Nov. 18 ... ... 25 3 3			
Mr. D. J. Pillai (for missions) ...	10	0	0	„ 25 19 10 0			
Mr. Armstrong, Warrambeen ...	10	0	0	Dec. 2 18 2 6			
Lambda	5	0	0	„ 9 4 0 0			
A friend	5	0	0		66	15	9
Mrs. Pole	1	1	0				
Mrs. Russell...	2	0	0		£169	17	3
Mr. A. Robertson	2	2	0				
Mrs. Arnold	1	0	0				

Stockwell Orphanage.

Statement of Receipts from November 15th to December 14th, 1888.

	£	s.	d.		£	s.	d.
The South West London Band of Hope Union, per Miss Carr	2	2	0	Collected by Miss Keay	0	7	0
Mrs. E. Wild	0	10	0	Messrs. Fannett and Neden	2	2	0
Mercies received by A. U.	0	1	0	His steward	1	1	0
Miss M. Anderson... ...	0	5	0	Jack, South Lambeth	0	3	0
Mr. James Scott	2	0	0	Collected by Mrs. Willmot	0	14	6
				Collected by Miss L. Wilson	0	5	0

£ s. d.

	£	s.	d.
Collected by Miss Bodle ...	0	4	0½
Collected by Mr. and Mrs. Mason	0	7	6¾
Collected by Mr. Binstead	1	4	0
The Misses Hyyet and Delves	0	4	6
Mr. Lockwood	0	4	10¾

	£	s.	d.
	2	5	0
Mr. James Slater	1	1	0
Miss E. Weymouth	0	5	0
Sale of ring	0	5	0
Balance left from the late Miss Chicken's estate, per Mr. A. J. Vining	0	7	6
Mr. J. Dodwell	0	2	6
The Young Women's Bible-class at the Orphanage, per Mrs. James Stiff ...	0	13	0
Collected by Miss E. Betts ...	0	6	0
Miss S. Chidlaw ...	5	0	0
Mr. G. Smith	0	10	0
Collected by No. 2 girls, per Mrs. Clark	0	6	7
From Lewes, 6d. per week ...	1	6	0
Collected by Mr. Platt	0	4	1
Mr. S. Slodden	0	2	6
Collected by Miss Potts	1	0	0
Mrs. Shaw	2	2	0
Mr. John Barnes	0	10	0
G. C., Tain, Ross	0	10	0
Three Arniston miners	1	0	0
A friend, Edinburgh	1	0	0
From a friend	50	0	0
Captain J. Williamson	10	0	0
Carlisle Baptist Sunday-school, per Pastor A. A. Saville	0	7	6
Mr. G. C. Howe	1	0	0
Mrs. Smith, in memoriam ...	1	0	0
Mr. John Best, J.P.	1	0	0
Mrs. William Hicks	1	1	0
Part proceeds of lecture at Cranswick, by Pastor C. Welton	0	7	6
Farley Green Mission-room	0	11	7
"Rookery" children's box	0	5	0
Mrs. Robert Davies	2	0	0
Mr. James Gilmour	1	0	0
Mr. W. McEwing	2	0	0
Miss A. Leeder	0	10	0
Mr. J. H. Mills	0	5	0
Mrs. Lewis	1	1	0
Mr. T. Underhill, per Mrs. Whittard	2	2	0

Per Mrs. Nelson :—

	£	s.	d.
Collected	1	1	0
Mr. J. W. Nelson (ann.)...	1	0	0

	£	s.	d.
	2	1	0
Mr. S. Ager	1	0	0
Young Women's Bible-class, Westbourne Grove Chapel	0	5	0
Mr. Lawrence Shepherd	0	0	0
Mr. J. Newling	0	10	0
Mr. D. H. Lloyd	5	0	0
Dr. Berdoe	1	0	0
Mrs. Hooper, per Pastor H. J. Preece	0	10	0
From the haven of peace	5	0	0
Miss M. Bassham	0	5	0
Mr. W. R. Deacon	5	0	0
Mrs. M. Fryer	0	10	0
Mr. R. Sherringham	0	5	0
Mr. James Spence...	0	3	0
Nameless	0	10	0
Miss Green	1	1	0
Miss F. Cook	0	3	0
Mr. and Mrs. W. Diaper... ...	0	10	0
P. W. A.	4	4	0
A widow's mite, Dundee... ...	0	5	0
Miss A. Shelly	0	10	0
M. C. S. F.	1	0	0
Miss M. Trevenen	0	10	0
Miss M. Smith	1	0	0

Collected by Mrs. James Withers :—

	£	s.	d.
Mrs. J. Davis	0	2	6
Mr. James Boorne ...	1	0	0
Mrs. Hammond .	0	10	0
	1	12	6

£ s. d.

	£	s.	d.
Mrs. Walker	2	2	0
Mr. George Anderson	0	10	0
Miss Hawkes	0	5	0
Mr. T. Steer...	1	10	7
Mr. William Paine	2	2	0
D. E. G., Wilts.	0	7	0
Mr. E. McDonald, per Mrs. Armstrong	2	0	0
Collected by Miss Armstrong, and her nurse, and Miss Maggie McNeil	16	0	0
Mrs. J. C. Higham	5	0	0
J. J., Harrogate	2	0	0
Mrs. Williamson	0	15	0
Mr. J. Ball	0	5	0
Mrs. Swift	1	0	0
Miss Toward, per Mrs. J. A. Spurgeon	1	1	0
Executors of the late Mr. E. Boustead (second instalment of legacy) ...2037	7	8
A friend, per Pastor H. Jones ...	1	0	0
Mr. C. Fowle	1	1	0
Mr. T. Vickery	1	1	0
Mr. W. Kelley	0	0	0
Captain W. J. Robertson	1	1	0
Mrs. Best, per Mr. G. C. Heard ...	0	0	0
Collected by Miss Retford	0	1	9
Mrs. Job, per Pastor J. S. Paige ...	0	0	0
Mattie Seaton	0	10	6
Orphan girl's collecting card, M. Watson	1	1	0
Collected by Miss M. Thomas	1	3	0
Mrs. Wainwright, jun.	1	1	0
Mr. J. Handy	1	0	0
Collected by Miss E. L. Rawlins ...	0	10	3
Mrs. Mannington	1	1	0
Mrs. Brown	0	10	0
Mrs. Hall	0	10	0
Miss L. C. Greenlees	0	5	0
Mrs. Ferguson	0	2	6
Collected by Mrs. Nelson ...	0	2	6
A friend	5	0	0
Miss A. V. Wicks	0	2	6
Mrs. Pole	1	1	0
Mrs. Lowe and daughters ...	2	0	0
Miss Pester	0	5	0
One of the dear Lord's little ones ...	0	5	0
Miss S. Thomas	0	1	6
Mrs. Seivwright	0	2	0
Mr. Edward Adam	1	0	0
Mrs. Russell	1	0	0
Mrs. E. Barrat	1	1	0
Mr. George Turner	0	5	0
Mrs. R. A. Snell	1	0	0
W. W., Carluke	1	0	0
Mr. R. R. Nelson	3	0	0
Mrs. Wilkinson	5	0	0
Mrs. Leask	0	10	0
Mrs. Belcher	0	10	0
Miss England	0	3	0
Scissors, A. T., per Miss Anna Thatcher	0	2	6
Additional proceeds of harvest thanksgiving service, per Pastor J. Stanley	0	1	6
E. P., Brixton	0	3	0
E. Y. B. C.	1	0	0
B. P.	1	0	0
L. K. D.	0	17	6
J. B. C.	1	10	0
Miss E. Bates	0	10	0
Mr. W. T. Chesterman	1	0	7
Mrs. Arnold...	3	0	0
Mr. H. R. Parker	1	1	0
Miss Janet Burdon, per Mrs. Spencer	1	0	0
Miss E. A. Fysh	0	1	0
Miss M. D. Macleay	2	0	0
Miss E. Swabey	0	5	0
Mr. W. Woolidge	0	10	0
Mrs. Benham	5	0	0

Collected by Miss Jesson :—

	£	s.	d.
Mr. W. Stanyon			0
The Misses Bennett			0
Miss Eames			0
Miss Paynes...	0	5	6
	0	17	6

	£	s.	d.
Mrs. Dunlop	1	0	0
A mite	0	10	0
Mr. H. Munday	1	5	0
D. A.	0	5	0
Mr. G. Nowell	5	0	0
Mrs. W. Colthup, per Mr. J. Wood	0	10	0
Captain Allenby, per Mr. S. J. Dobson	0	5	0
Mr. G. Gibbs	1	1	0
Stamps from Sunderland	0	1	0
Mr. John Farkinson	1	0	0
Mr. Smith Nutter	1	1	0
Miss R. Smith	2	0	0
Mr. MacDowell	0	2	6
Mr. G. Russell	2	0	0
Mr. and Mrs. Gregory	2	10	0
Mr. J. Harridence	1	0	0
Messrs. J. D. Williams and Son	1	1	0
Mr. William Mingins	1	0	0
Mr. William Mathewson	70	0	0
Miss Buckle	1	0	0
For Jesus' lambs	0	5	0
Mr. H. Humphry	0	5	0
Miss E. Ellis	0	6	0
Messrs. Hine Brothers	1	1	0
The Misses Bashall	5	0	0
Mrs. Hall	0	1	0
Dr. Mackintosh	1	0	0
Mrs. McKenzie	0	10	0
A. J. F.	0	1	0
Mr. W. Driver	0	2	0
Mr. John Malcolm	1	0	0
Mrs. Reed	1	0	0
Mrs. Mathewson	1	0	0
Mr. J. Wilson	1	0	0
Mrs. Reid	0	5	0
Miss M. A. Downs	5	0	0
Miss H. Fells	0	10	0
Mr. H. Davie	0	5	0
Mr. H. Greenwood Brown	2	2	0
Miss E. Brotherton	0	10	0
Mrs. Dodwell	0	10	6
Mrs. Spindler	5	0	0
The Countess of Seafield	10	0	0
Mr. Henry Tribe	10	0	0
E. Janem	10	0	0
Mrs. Irwin	0	5	0
Master B. Dennish	0	5	0
Mrs. Shurmer	0	7	0
A friend, per Mrs. Shurmer	0	10	0
Mr. C. Wadland	1	0	0

Meetings by Mr. Charlesworth and the Orphanage Choir:—

	£	s.	d.
Cross Street, Canonbury	7	7	0
Brecon	16	12	11
Cardiff	163	15	0
Clifton Chapel, Peckham	10	0	0
Hammersmith	14	6	0
Gunnersbury, towards expenses	1	14	6
Surbiton Baptist Chapel	9	9	6

Annual Subscriptions:—

	£	s.	d.
Mrs. Appleton	1	1	0
Mrs. Bagster	1	1	0
Captain James Ewing	1	1	0

Monthly Subscriptions:—

	£	s.	d.
Mr. E. K. Stace	0	10	0
Mr. S. H. Dauncey	0	2	6
Sandwich, per bankers	2	2	0
F. G. B., Chelmsford	0	2	6

Christmas Festivities:—

	£	s.	d.
Mrs. Shearman	2	2	0
Mr. and Mrs. Frame	1	0	0
Mr. and Mrs. H. Proctor	1	0	0
Mrs. Joslin	0	10	0
Mr. J. E. Saunders, for new shillings for 250 girls	12	10	0
Adelphi	1	0	0
Eskdale Shepherd	0	10	0
Miss Cousin	2	0	0
A member of the Church of England, Sheffield	0	2	6
Mrs. Virtue	1	0	0
Miss B. Fox	0	5	0
Miss Clover	0	5	0
Mr. Spencer R. Turner	3	0	0
Miss R. Daniell	0	5	0
Miss J. Matthews	0	5	0

Collected by Miss Anna Thatcher:—

	£	s.	d.		£	s.	d.
Mrs. Dobbs	1	0	0				
Mrs. W. Mannington (Isfield)	0	5	0				
Mr. J. Mannington	0	5	0				
Mrs. J. Mannington	0	5	0				
Mr. and Mrs. Caffyn	0	5	0				
Miss Caffyn	0	2	6				
Mrs. Faulconer	0	3	0				
Mrs. and the Misses Hamshar	0	4	0				
Mrs. Charles Mannington	0	2	6				
Miss Mannington	0	2	0				
Mrs. Oyler	0	2	0				
Mrs. Guy	0	2	0				
Mrs. Porter	0	2	6				
Anna Thatcher	0	3	0		3	3	6

	£	s.	d.
Emma	0	5	0
E. S. D.	0	5	0
Mrs. Warmington	1	0	0
Mr. S. Cornborough	4	0	0
Mr. J. Wood	0	0	0
Mr. W. Colthup, per Mr. J. Wood	0	0	0
Miss R. Smith	0	10	0
Miss C. E. Smither	1	0	0
K. M.	0	5	0
Miss M. A. Mundy	0	5	0
Mr. J. Wilson	0	5	0
H. E. S.	2	2	0
Mr. E. Goodman	0	10	0
Mrs. McGregor	0	10	0
Mr. James Jackson	1	1	0
Mr. W. Hillier	0	5	0
Mr. E. Upward	1	0	0
	£2,694	11	5

List of Presents, per Mr. Charlesworth, from November 15th to December 14th, 1888.—PROVISIONS :—20 lbs. Currants; 20 lbs. Raisins, Mrs. C. Reynolds; 1 New Zealand Sheep, Mr. A. Seale Haslam; 1 Cake, 1 parcel Sweets, Miss Dawson; 1 sack Potatoes, Mr. J. Walton; 28 lbs. Oatmeal, Anon.; 8 Geese, Mr. W. Paxman; 1 dozen Stilton Cheeses, Mr. J. T. Crosher; 6 bushels Onions, Mr. D. Parkins; 1 bag Potatoes and 1 bag Turnips, Mr. J. Walker; 2½ boxes Valencias, Mr. T. Wray; 3 boxes Valencias, 56 lbs. Currants, 7 lbs. Orange Peel, 7 lbs. Lemon Peel, 42 lbs. Sugar, 1 lb. Spice, Mr. J. T. Daintree; 1 sack Flour, Mr. J. Lawman.

BOYS' CLOTHING.—6 pairs Knitted Socks, Miss Hicks; 10 pairs Knitted Socks and 2 pairs Knitted Stockings, Mrs. Lenton; a quantity of Neck Ties and 1 pair of Boots, Anon.; 18 pairs Boys' Slippers, Mr. G. H. Kerridge; 12 pairs Socks, Miss Jones; 12 Flannel Shirts, The Misses Dransfield; 12 Bows and 1 Shirt, Miss Harper; 5 Suits and 1 Waistcoat, S. H. W.; 4 pairs Socks and 6 pairs Stockings, Mrs. Gregory; 12 pairs Socks, Mrs. Dexter; 12 Bows, Mrs. S. E. Knight.

GIRLS' CLOTHING.—12 Flannel Petticoats, Miss Burton; 8 Dolls, Miss Salter's Bible-class; 13 Articles, The Misses S. and C. Sharlow; 6 Articles, Mrs. Penstone; 59 Articles, The Ladies' Working Meeting at Tabernacle, per Miss Higgs; 6 Articles, Miss F. Leeder; 6 Knitted Petticoats, S. N. A.; 3 Aprons, 6 Dolls, Mrs. S. E. Knight; 1 box of Clothing, &c., M. E.; 6 Flannel Petticoats, Two Friends, per Mrs. Penstone; 21 Garments, The Chatham Ladies' Working Meeting; 64 Articles, Miss Harper; 3 pairs Stockings, 4 Petticoats, M. B. C.; 34 Articles, Mrs. E. M. Lott; 20 Articles, Mrs. J. Harding;

2 Flannel Petticoats, Mrs. Peel; 12 pairs Knitted Socks, Mrs. Kine; 4 Woollen Articles and 12 Hand-kerchiefs, Mrs. H. Verrall; 15 Articles, Mrs. Mannington; 56 Articles, Mrs. Kemp; a quantity of Articles, Mrs. Spooner.

GENERAL.—1 Scrap Book and 4 Small Books, Miss Dawson; 1 Jet Chain, 1 pair Earrings, a Well-wisher, E. H.; 1 box Fancy Articles, Messrs. Axtens Brothers; 1 Scrap Book, Mrs. S. E. Knight; 1 piece White Calico and 1 piece Unbleached Calico, Mrs. Wainwright, sen.; 9 Scrap Books, 4 Work Bags, Miss Harper; 4 pairs Fancy Slippers, Mr. J. A. Maitland; 50 copies of "Illustrations," Mr. F. G. Heath; a quantity of Cards, Miss Bagster; 1 small box of Artificial Flowers, Messrs. Morley and Lanceley; 1 box of Useful Articles, Mrs. Ling; 1 box Fancy Articles, Mr. T. Barrett; 2 boxes Arti-ficial Flowers, The Bon Marché.

Colportage Association.

Statement of Receipts from November 15th to December 14th, 1888.

Subscriptions and Donations for Districts:—

	£	s.	d.
Mr. R. Scott, for Colchester District ...	10	0	0
Sellindge, per Mr. Thomas R—— ...	10	0	0
Worcester Colportage Association ...	30	0	0
Mr. Thomas R——, for Bower Chalk ...	6	0	0
Southern Baptist Association ...	50	0	0
Repton and Burton-on-Trent, per E. S.	20	0	0
Bower Chalk Baptist Church	5	0	0
Maidenhead, per Miss Lassells	10	0	0
Metropolitan Tabernacle Sunday-school, for Tring	10	0	0
Rendham District, per Rev. J. Hollier	5	0	0
Mr. J. J. Tustin, for Burstow and Horley	10	0	0
M. A. H., for Orpington... ...	5	0	0
£171		**0**	

Subscriptions and Donations to the General Fund:—

	£	s.	d.
M. C. S. F.	0	10	0
Mr. A. Todd	0	5	0
D. E. G., Wilts.	0	5	0
Mrs. Williamson	0	15	0
L. K. D.	0	10	0
S. W., per Mr. S. R. Pearce ...	1	0	0
£3		**5**	**0**

Society of Evangelists.

Statement of Receipts from November 15th to December 14th, 1888.

	£	s.	d.
Mrs. Raybould	1	0	0
Mr. William Grant	2	0	0
D. E. G., Wilts.	0	3	0
Mrs. Everest	0	10	0
Thankoffering for Messrs. Harmer and Parker's services at Allerton...	8	11	3
Mr. Armstrong, Warrambeen ...	10	0	0
Thankoffering for Messrs. Harmer and Chamberlain's services at Hull ...	2	2	0
Thankoffering for Messrs. Harmer and Chamberlain's services at Redditch...	3	5	0
The Misses Kirtley	5	0	0

	£	s.	d.
Thankoffering for Messrs. Harmer and Parker's services at Clayton	6	10	0
Thankoffering for Messrs. Harmer and Parker's services at Sandy Lane ...	2	2	0
Thankoffering for Mr. Boyall's services at Grantham	0	14	0
Thankoffering for Messrs. Fullerton and Smith's services at Metropolitan Tabernacle	30	0	0
£71		**17**	**3**

for General Use in the Lord's Work.

Statement of Receipts from November 15th to December 14th, 1888.

	£	s.	d.
Miss Wood	1	0	0
E. H., Cheltenham, per Pastor C. Spurgeon	5	0	0
£6		**0**	**0**

Friends sending presents to the Orphanage are earnestly requested to let their names or initials accompany the same, or we cannot properly acknowledge them; and also to write to Mr. Spurgeon if no acknowledgment is sent within a week. All parcels should be addressed to Mr. Charlesworth, Stockwell Orphanage, Clapham Road, London.

Subscriptions will be thankfully received by C. H. Spurgeon, "Westwood," Beulah Hill, Upper Norwood. Should any sums sent before the 13th of last month be unacknowledged in this list, friends are requested to write at once to Mr. Spurgeon. Post Office and Postal Orders should be made payable at the Chief Office, London, to C. H. Spurgeon; and Cheques and Orders should all be crossed.

THE

SWORD AND THE TROWEL.

FEBRUARY, 1889.

Whose God is Jehovah?

A SHORT SERMON, BY C. H. SPURGEON.

"I am the God of Abraham, the God of Isaac, and the God of Jacob."—Exodus iii. 6.

IT was great condescension on the part of the glorious Jehovah to give himself this title. There is such a difference between God and the greatest and the best of men, that it is a wonderful stretch of mercy that he should call himself "the God of Abraham, Isaac, and Jacob." It is still more marvellous that God should give to a creature property in himself, the Creator. That God is God is a glorious fact, but that he is *our* God has about it an infinite glory of tenderness, and love, and condescension. When I can say, "This God is mine," have I not said the greatest thing that man can say, and too great a thing for man to say if God himself had not first declared it? The patriarchs could call Jehovah their God, because, first of all, God himself said, "I am the God of Abraham, the God of Isaac, and the God of Jacob." The title-deeds to this possession must be drawn up by God himself. What right have I to God's love? None; but I must have far less right to God's self. Let us praise and bless Jehovah our God, as we read our text, and say together, "This God is our God."

When informed that God has called some men his own we naturally wish to know what sort of men they were. Who were these favourites of heaven? Is it possible that we can ever be numbered among such choice spirits?

Here are eight particulars, and upon each one I shall be very brief.

I. Abraham, and Isaac, and Jacob, THESE THREE, WERE CHOSEN MEN.

It would have seemed a most unlikely thing that Abraham should call Jehovah his God. He lived on the other side of the Euphrates with his fathers, who served other gods, and the Lord appeared unto Abram, and called him, and said to him, "Get thee out from thy country, and from thy father's house"; and Abram obeyed the voice of

4

God. But why was Abraham chosen? There were many other decent men in Charan. There were multitudes of other men on that side of the flood who were serving other gods. Why came the word to Abraham ? "Even so, Father, for so it seemed good in thy sight." I know no other answer to the question. Abraham was called of God according to the eternal purpose of divine grace, and, therefore, he came forth to sojourn with the Lord in Canaan.

As to Isaac, he was the son of Abraham. Do you think that he had claims to divine favour because of natural descent? It was not so, for there was one born unto Abraham before him, even Ishmael, whom his father loved, and for whom he prayed, " Oh, that Ishmael might live before thee! " But the purpose of God must stand ; and Isaac was chosen to the covenant heritage, and Ishmael received his portion in this life, and went his way to be the father of earthly princes and nations. "In Isaac shall thy seed be called," was the divine purpose ; and so it must be.

The third of the chosen is Jacob. He is the son of a saint, and the grandson of a saint ; but grace runs not in the blood ; for you remember that he had an elder brother born at the same birth, a twin with him, and yet it is written, " Jacob have I loved, and Esau have I hated." In the particular matter of the covenant inheritance, Jacob was called into the service of Jehovah, and Esau was left by his own choice to follow out his own worldly purposes. It was in a sovereignty for which the Lord vouchsafes no reason that Jacob was chosen ; so Paul tells us, and so it was.

Abraham, Isaac, Jacob, these three are the Lord's because he chose them for himself. A line of electing love threads these three names together as pearls are threaded on a string of silk. Whatever of mystery there may be about it, it is according to the word of God ; and so must it be.

II. If this should seem obscure and difficult to you, believe it, and leave it ; for the next remark is, that THESE THREE WERE BELIEVING MEN.

By the grace of God Abraham believed. When the call came to him he believed God, and he went forth not knowing whither he went. God promised to give him a land for an inheritance which he had never seen, and when he came to it the Canaanite was still there in full possession. Firmly he believed God, and dwelt as a stranger in a strange land, and yet found himself at home with God. When God promised him that he should have a son, though it was contrary to nature, he believed, and in due time the promise was fulfilled to him ; for no man ever believed God in vain. Abraham was so truly a believing man as to be the very father of believers. His sacrifice of Isaac showed that his faith would go to the very uttermost. This is the man whom the Lord calls his own ; Jehovah is the God of all who trust him with childlike confidence. To the last, his life was one of true, simple-hearted, and yet princely faith in God.

Isaac was equally a believer, and his quiet, patient life proved it. Read his life-story. He dwelt at home, and he addicted himself to the arts of peace ; but he believed, and therefore never quitted the pilgrim life, nor even, when blind, doubted the word of the Lord his

WHOSE GOD IS JEHOVAH ?

God. Such men, whether great as Abraham, or peaceful as Isaac, are the Lord's, and the Lord is theirs; for faith is the mark of their high privilege.

Jacob was a man of many and manifest infirmities, but he was a great believer. Let us never so think of the faults of Jacob as to forget that he was a man of surpassing excellence in the matter of faith in God. If there were nothing else to prove it, that midnight wrestling at the brook of Jabbok, when he dared to say even to God himself, "I will, not let thee go, except thou bless me," proved the depth of this patriarch's faith. Here was the evidence that Jehovah was his God. Not doubting, but believing, is the hall-mark of heaven's true silver.

Neither Abraham, nor Isaac, nor Jacob yielded to the worship of idols. They reverenced no symbols, nor kissed their hand to the queen of heaven, nor adored the Great Invisible through any sign or emblem. Jehovah abhors such worship, for he has said, "Thou shalt not make unto thee any graven image nor any likeness of anything that is in heaven above, nor in the earth beneath, nor in the water under the earth. Thou shalt not bow down to them, nor worship them." The one·Invisible Jehovah, the living God that made heaven and earth, was the sole object of the worship of these gracious men. They believed in God, and adored the Lord believingly. Spiritual faith is the great mark of distinction between the man of God and the man of the world. To many there is no God, or if there be any God, they are sorry that there is one. The man that loves God rejoices in God, delights in God: atheism to him would be·absolute misery. All the heaven that we want or expect is to be with God, and to be like him ; and those who can say this may know that the Lord is theirs, since they trust in him.

III. Advance another step : THESE THREE WERE ORDINARY MEN. Abraham, Isaac, Jacob—who were these ? We pronounce their names with great reverence ; but, in themselves, there is no more about these three names than if I said "Brown, Jones, and Robinson." I bless God that it is not written, "He is the God of Nimrod the mighty, or of Methuselah the aged, or of Solomon the wise, or of Samson the strong," but· "the God of Abraham, Isaac, and Jacob," who were, of themselves, only common Bedaween of the plains. These were not kings, but little sheikhs, presiding over their own families and servants. Though Abraham was wealthy, yet, as compared with the riches of a London merchant, he was a poor shepherd. No foot of land he called his own; his house was a tent ; his possessions were sheep, and goats, and cattle, and his life was that of a gipsy. There were thousands of men, richer, mightier, more renowned than Abraham, Isaac, and Jacob ; yet it is not written that God was the God of the kings of the East, or of the men of renown of that age, but he was the God of Abraham, of Isaac, and of Jacob. Turn hither, ye three angels; if there be a place where ye may rest, it is not where the Babylonian monarch walks in all his pride, but beneath the oak of Mamre, where a keeper of sheep shall bring forth water and wash your feet. Jehovah loves to visit the lowly ; he dwells with humble minds. To this day he is seldom the God of the worldly great, or the worldly wise, but his grace seems to say, " I am the God of that farmer, that blacksmith, that tailor, that shoemaker.   I am the God of that poor woman whose eyes ache as she stitches so many hours to earn her scanty living; the God of that widow woman, who has trusted me, and I have fed her; the God of that young lad from the country, whose one desire is that he may serve his mother's God."

" When the Eternal bows the skies
   To visit earthly things,
With scorn divine he turns his eyes
   From towers of haughty kings.

" He bids his awful chariot roll
   Far downward from the skies,
To visit every humble soul,
   With pleasure in his eyes."

The homes of the poor, the laborious, and the forgotten, are visited by the God of grace, and thus the word is fulfilled, "I am the God of Abraham, and of Isaac, and of Jacob"—the God of common people, who are little esteemed among men.

IV.   Fourthly: THESE MEN WERE IMPERFECT MEN; yet the Lord avows himself their God.   There were moments when even Abraham's faith failed him, and when, like other orientals, he condescended to equivocations.   His character is grand : he is worthy to be called the father of the faithful, but still he was imperfect.   To a higher degree Isaac was imperfect too.   We cannot help feeling that the good old man was rather weak in that day, when he must needs bless Esau because Esau made savoury meat for him.   We should have thought that one able to bestow so great a blessing would have been absorbed in higher things.   The facts recorded in Scripture about good men are not to be looked upon as solitary incidents, but as representative events, and hence we see the weak stuff of which Isaac was composed. It is not for us to find fault with Isaac, but it is for us to thank God that he was the God of Isaac, who was not perfect; for hence we gather hope that he may be our God also.

As to Jacob, he had many faults, largely taken from the mother's side—from that crafty family over which Laban presided.   Jacob was wonderfully human, and like ourselves.   Yet, brethren, God was his God.   He runs away from home, as well he may, for he has done his brother wrong; but when he dreams, God appears in the dream.   He gets to Laban, and there it was " diamond cut diamond," one trying to get, and the other to keep; but even then he looked to the God of his fathers, and the Lord brought him through.   He comes back, and when he fears Esau, he cries to God as naturally as a child cries to its father; and right along till he went down into Egypt, you can see that his trust is in the God of Abraham and Isaac, who was his own God.   Yet he was imperfect; and I stand here to thank God that the Bible does not conceal the failings of believing men.   If they had been absolutely perfect, I should have said, " There is no hope for me"; but as I see that even the saints were not altogether saintly, I thank God that he has not made them all white as marble, and then set them up in niches, saying to us poor mortals, "You stand down there, and look up at them, but you can never be one of them." No, the Lord has put the saints among us, that we may imitate their faith, and have God for our God, as they had.

, V. Here let me say, in the fifth place, that THESE THREE WERE ALL DIFFERING MEN : they are very much unlike each other. Abraham stands alone, gigantic as a mount ; Isaac is like a valley after a hill ; Jacob is beaten about as the seashore. You cannot put the three in one class as to their conformation of mind, or their mode of action. They exceedingly differ. Learn from this that we must not pick out one good man, and read his life, and say, "I·have to be like that man." When you find that your experience is not like that of another believer, you must not hence conclude that you are no child of God. No, no. Jehovah is the God of Abraham ; but do not judge yourself by Abraham, because he is a greater man than you are : for God is also the God of Isaac. Sit down in quiet with Isaac. Do you reply, "Alas! I do not feel quite so calm as Isaac : I am often tossed to and fro, and troubled in my family"? Then, go to Jacob, and see how the Lord heard even him.

I do not want you, Abraham, to be like Jacob ; I should be sorry that you should come down so low ! You, Isaac—I am not going to urge you to be like Jacob ; you are better as Isaac. And you, Jacob, you cannot be Isaac, and yet God is your God. Let each man of God be God's man, according to his own manhood. Was not God the God of Luther ? Who dare deny it ? But was he not the God of Calvin ? Will anybody question that the seer of Geneva walked with God ? But was Calvin Luther ? or Luther Calvin ? And there is Zwingle, over there in Zurich. He is not at all like Calvin, nor in the least like Luther ; but I see God in Zwingle as well as in Luther : and why not ? Surely God, who is to be seen in wrens as well as in eagles, in the tiniest fish as well as in the great whales ; who is to be seen in the sparkling dewdrop as well as in the raging of the tempestuous sea, is to be seen in all kinds of characters where his grace is found. Read right joyfully these words : "I am the God of Abraham, the God of Isaac, and the God of Jacob."

VI. But I pass on, for I have scarcely time to observe, in the sixth place, that THESE THREE WERE ALL PRAYING MEN. There is that about them all. One is not like the other till you get him on his knees ; but when he is on his knees Abraham prays likes Isaac, and Isaac prays like Abraham, and Jacob prays like Abraham, and Isaac. There is no difference between them when they come to draw near to God. They are alike, dust and ashes, yet they alike prevail with God. Mind this: prayer is the essential mark of grace. The Lord is not your God unless in prayer you plead "Our Father." A prayerless soul is a godless soul. Oh, if you want this God to be your God, you must be men of prayer, and only as you love the mercy-seat can you read your title to the possession of divine grace. Like Abraham, get up early to your secret place and plead with God ; like Isaac, walk in the fields and meditate ; like Jacob, wrestle and prevail ; so shall the Lord be your God.

VII. And the consequence was, in the seventh place, that THESE THREE MEN WERE PRESERVED BY THE POWER OF GOD. Their fight was different, but their victory was the same.

As to Abraham, I should like to be exactly like him, if I might. He seems to me to move with calm dignity and grave joyfulness. You never see him fluttered. He is undisturbed because of the greatness and solidity of his faith. He deserved to be called "His Serene Highness." He was always equal to emergencies; indeed, nothing appeared to be an emergency to him. The great father of the faithful could even turn soldier and pursue the kings who had carried away Lot. Whatever he does, he does it thoroughly well, because he believes in the Lord always. Oh, it is a grand thing to have Abraham's faith, and so to conquer from day to day without defeat!

Isaac—a milder, gentler, softer character—yet wins the day, and makes his life to be a success. He digs wells. The Philistines fill them up, and he digs more. What a victory of patience! When they filled these, he still digged more till they ceased to molest him. Oh, the triumph of calm long-suffering! There is nothing braver, after all, than giving way and yielding your rights, because you feel that the Lord will take care of you, and you are in no need to quarrel with petty Philistines. Isaac was no warrior, but no one could harm him. Jacob had a severe battle in life : he might expect to have a fourfold measure of troubles, as he had four wives. He had stepped aside from the right path, and made his way difficult. And then that bargaining with Laban—that haggling—trouble must come of it. Many of the troubles of God's people come from not walking by faith, and from trying to match the men of the world in their tricks and moves. Policy is of no use to believers in God, "for the children of this world are wiser in their generation than the children of light," and we shall be beaten if we try conclusions with them on their own lines. If we walk by faith, doing the right thing, and trusting in God, we shall baffle all adversaries, for the Lord will be on our side.

However, as in Jacob's life there was a line of true faith in God, and a resolve to do the right, he came out safely from all his afflictions. The Lord had said of his chosen, "Touch not mine anointed, and do my prophets no harm," and therefore these men of God were safe. Neither Philistine, nor Canaanite, nor Egyptian, could touch them. When God is our God, his angels are our guard, his providence is our protection, himself is our shield and our exceeding great reward. Come under the wing of Jehovah, and you shall find a most secure abode. Jacob became Israel, the prevailing prince, not by what he did as he touched that crafty forehead, but by what he did when his sinew shrank, and as he fell he clutched the covenant angel with "I will not let thee go, except thou bless me." Prayer did for Jacob what craft could never have done. Try the power of prayer, and leave the power of craft to those who like it.

VIII. And now my eighth particular is—THESE THREE MEN ARE ALL LIVING MEN. This we might never have thought of except the Saviour himself had said, "God is not the God of the dead, but of the living." These three men still live as Abraham, Isaac, and Jacob. Their bodies were laid in Machpelah to pass away in rottenness, and there is no relic of them left; but the Lord knows where they are. He is well aware as to the abode of their soul and their spirit. The body shall rise again; for the Saviour was arguing upon this point when he used this expression—

."God is not the God of the dead, but of the living": the soul still lives, for God is still the God of the whole man. Beloved, is God your God? Then you shall never die. Is God your God? Then you shall live for ever, for he is not the God of the dead, but of the living. You shall pass out of this world by what is called "death," but the reality of death can never pass upon the believer. Jesus says, "He that believeth in me, though he were dead, yet shall he live. He that liveth and believeth in me shall never die." It is not death to pass out of this world unto the Father. The real death in which the soul is separated from God for ever—for that is the second death—that shall never pass upon the man who is joined unto God in Christ by a love from which there is no separation. Wherefore let us joyfully set up our banners. We are numbered with the immortals. We shall take our place in eternal youth hard by the throne of him who says, "I am that I am," and we shall see the ages glide away, while we,

"Far from a world of grief and sin,
With God eternally shut in,"

shall live with the God of Abraham, the God of Isaac, and the God of Jacob, world without end.

How my Bible-class Grew.

BY MRS. H. L. GIBSON.

I HAVE often been asked the question, "How did you manage to get such a large Bible-class?" My answer has been, "I did not get the class, it grew." I little dreamt, when I began twelve years ago, that it would ever be so large; but, like the "little seed," it has grown from a very small beginning to a "great tree."

I live in a town where there are a great many mills and factories, and consequently many young women. I often wished to do something for the spiritual good of this interesting class of the community, but did not know very well how to begin. One or two girls, who had got good at a small Sabbath-school class which I taught for some time, but which I was prevented from continuing, came and begged me, if I could not teach them on Sabbath, to take them during the week. I consented to do so, provided they could get two more to come with them. The following week four presented themselves; and this was the beginning of my young women's Bible-class.

At first I intended that it should be only for Christians, as I thought something of this kind was needed to supply a felt want, viz., a class to instruct young believers more fully in the ways of the Lord. A week had not passed away, however, when one of the four asked me if she might bring a companion with her. "Is she converted?" I asked. "No; but she is very anxious to come." "Bring her, then, she may perhaps get a blessing," I replied. Another and another desired to come; and this I took as an indication from the Lord that I should receive all who would come, and make it a regular Bible-class.

From the beginning it has been quite unsectarian. Not one of the four belonged to the congregation with which I was connected. One was Established; one, Free Church; one, United Presbyterian; and one, Congregational. This has continued all through, the members of the class comprising representatives of all denominations. I would never waste my time in merely seeking to gather members to any particular Church, much as I love my own. My aim has ever been higher, even to win souls to Christ—work that will last throughout eternity.

Each week new members were added to the class, not by any special effort of mine, but by the girls themselves bringing their friends and companions. Thus it became known in the different factories and mills. Three weeks after its formation, one of the young women was awakened, and soon after was brought to decision for Christ. Another and another followed in quick succession; and each one who trusted him was eager to bring others to hear the glad news which, by the Spirit's power, had led her to the feet of Jesus.

At the close of the first session of nine months, there were fifty-six on the roll; next year, seventy-seven. Then the kitchen of my house, in which we had always met, became too strait for us, so much so that I had to forbid them bringing any more. One girl came to me at this time, saying that, if I would allow her to bring a careless companion to the class she herself would stay away to make room for her; "Although," she added, "I will be sorry to do so; but having got blessing myself, I would like my friend to come, for maybe she will get the blessing too." She was, of course, allowed to bring her friend and to come herself also. This, however, made me decide to look out for another place of meeting. Accordingly, we in a short time removed to the hall of the church which I attended. Every week brought fresh members. The hall was soon as crowded as the kitchen had been, until the numbers on the roll reached two hundred or more each year. About this time, the Lord was graciously pleased to pour out his Spirit upon us; and many were brought out of darkness into his marvellous light.

There is nothing of an outward kind to attract. Many fall into the mistake of supposing that the interest of such a large class can be kept up only by the aid of music, story reading, and such like. My experience has been very different. I have used nothing but the Word of God; and I believe this to be the secret of the success of my class. The more we honour God's Word, the more he will honour our work; for he has said, "Them that honour me, I will honour." I consider it of great importance that the young women should be brought into personal contact with the Word. Each one has her Bible in hand, and during the lesson turns up the passages to which I may refer; and these are marked by many of them. In this way they obtain a knowledge of their Bibles, which they would not otherwise have.

I prepare very carefully, spending over each lesson seven or eight hours every week. As soon would I think of having no class at all, as of going to it unprepared. But while I seek to give instruction, my chief aim is conversion: and never once would I teach without appealing to, and pressing upon, my class the acceptance of Christ as their Saviour and Substitute. I also give an opportunity, at the close of each meeting, to any who may wish to converse with me, besides setting apart an evening each week, on which any of the young women may come to my house to get counsel and direction on the all-important matter of their salvation. Many have taken advantage of these opportunities; and not a few have in this way been united to Christ.

I look upon personal dealing as a most important part of a teacher's work, and I never lose an opportunity of speaking to the members of my class about their spiritual state when I meet them *alone*, either in the house, or by the way. I also try to know them all by name, and to take an interest in all that concerns them.

Another thing that has helped me very much is a little Prayer-meeting we have for twenty minutes, before the class gathers, at which two or three of the young women plead for the presence of the Spirit on the lesson that is to be taught. This has been a great source of strength to me, and often, when in fear and trembling, the simple earnest prayers of these godly young women have filled me with a power not my own. I believe in the power of prayer; for our God is a great God, and he has said, "According to your faith be it unto you." None are admitted to this meeting, unless they take part in it. Some have said to me, "We wish that we could do a similar work amongst young women; but, you see, God has given you the talent, and we have no talent!" Now this is a great mistake; God has given to every one of us talents for which we are accountable to him: but it is not so much great ability, as earnestness of purpose, perseverance, and tact that are needed for such a work.

Many look upon our mill and factory workers as a sort of *lower species*. It is a great mistake; for, while there are so many who are rough and uncouth, there are also many of the finest specimens of womanhood amongst them, ay! and many noble Christians too. The way to raise them is to teach them God's truth, and anxiously to seek to bring them under its power; nothing else will do. It is not amusement they need, but something that will satisfy them, not only in time but throughout eternity. They require earnest and faithful dealing and warning; for their temptations are many and great. Even careless girls know when they are *faithfully* dealt with, and despise in their hearts those who are only "half-and-half" in their dealing with them. During these twelve years, one thousand young women have passed through the class. Many of these are now in different parts of the earth; not a few have gone into the eternal world. Some of these, by their lives as well as by their bright and happy deathbeds, have left a clear testimony behind them that they have gone to be with Jesus; over the end of others we will draw the veil.

I have had many precious testimonies as to how helpful the class has been, not only in leading to decision for Christ, but in preventing many from being led in the wrong way. As one lately said, "But for the class, where would I have been?" The results are with God. This is our sowing time, and he can make it also our harvest season; at all events, the reaping time is coming, when sowers and reapers will rejoice together.

One word to fellow-teachers. Teach with a single eye to the glory of God, and aim at the conversion of each soul under your care; anything short of this will not stand when God begins to reckon with us concerning our work. If we would have the "Well done!" at last, we must be faithful in the discharge of our duties now. And let our practice be consistent with our teaching, otherwise we shall have no influence for good over those under our care.

W. Evans Hurndall in East London.

(SECOND ARTICLE.)

THE visiting missionaries continually meet with numbers of interesting cases; but although they may be admirably adapted for their work, they are not often able to give descriptions of what they see; and in their own way they can talk of their adventures better than they can write about them. Let us refer to a few more cases selected from that great world of the East End, which, in some respects, is one of the greatest mission-fields in the whole world.

We naturally become very indignant against working men who ill-use their wives; but infamous as many of the charges under this head undoubtedly are, there are sometimes extenuating circumstances. Can we put ourselves in the place of some of these men, who may have grievances of which we, happily, know nothing? There are men who would be very different from what they are if they were not dragged down into the mire of home surroundings.

Take the case of Mrs. Slut—her representative, not her real name—whose besetting sin prompted her to spend hard-earned money at the gin-palace, when she ought to have laid it out with the baker and grocer. She is prevailed upon to attend a meeting; but as meetings alone, however good in themselves, are not a cure for dram-drinking, she falls back into her old habit, proving that she would need a model of patience, indeed, to bear with her. On a certain day, when the man hastens home to a meal, instead of finding the table ready, all things are in a state of dirt and confusion, because, having received some money to which she was entitled, Mrs. Slut had forthwith taken it to the gin-palace. Of course, under such conditions, there will be much noise, and many threatenings; and something more than ordinarily serious would happen if the missionary were not on the spot to act as peacemaker. Such subjects as these, however, are sometimes reformed, and live ever after as glorious trophies of mission work.

Mr. Hurndall gives one of the largest Christmas dinners in London: and some saddening sights are witnessed in connection with the filling-up of the forms. The friend who supplies the information about the representative Mrs. Slut, tells us, that on a day when a number of these forms were filled up, he saw a crowd gathered at one of the stations, composed of the most wretchedly haggard faces he had ever looked upon. We are sorry, too, to find, that he thinks that the general outlook of this winter is quite as bad as it was a year ago. How can we expect it to be otherwise, until the labour market is relieved on a greater scale, by those being sent to the colonies who are willing to go?

Having devoted special attention to barbers and coffee-house keepers, this same observer tells some curious facts, especially about the former. According to the testimony of one of their own number, hairdressers are the most drunken of any class in London, while they are also much addicted to gambling, many of the lower kind of coffee-houses being little better than gambling-hells. Among both of these classes, Sunday labour is generally the rule, only one barber's shop in fifteen, and about one coffee-house in seven, in this locality, being closed on the Sabbath.   In all of these places, evangelical papers are circulated, and are read by customers, as well as by the poor seven-days-a-week servants, and the masters and mistresses.   The papers thus circulated are sure to have some good results ; but they are outdone in this respect by the special services which are held every Sunday evening, at the, Bow and Bromley Institute, after the ordinary service at Harley-street chapel, and bring together quite another congregation.

Thus, the missionary who has found so many friends among barbers and coffee-house keepers, says, "Grand things have been done for my district by our special mission-services ; twelve men, eighteen women, four boys, and four girls, have professed conversion.   Some will make good workers for Christ."   There are not many pastors who preach to two such congregations as Mr. Hurndall draws together on Sunday nights during the winter.   His own chapel is crowded ; and, leaving that, he finds another expectant and crowded congregation at the Institute already named.   The people who attend are the more interesting on account of their East End characteristics.   They are " the working classes," without doubt.   Here, too, are men who seem to have such a shrinking from attending a meeting at all, that they will not come without their wives ; and here are women who cannot conveniently leave home to appear at public worship until after eight in the evening, when their children are in bed.

The privation through which some of these people pass is terrible indeed.   Another of Mr. Hurndall's visitors tells of a man, his wife, and three children, to whom a succession of privations happened which were quite enough to unhinge the mind.   The man, after twelve years of service, was obliged, through ill-health, to leave his situation.   Then a child, five years old, was lost on the road between home and school for some days, and fright ended in the little one's death.   Next came scarlet fever ; and the father, who was very ill himself, then lost his reason. The excessive grief of the wife made her ill also, so that she had to be removed to an infirmary, with her baby.   Who would comfort such poor people if it were not for the mission visitors ?

The female missionary, who gives the above facts, can also tell of many striking cases of good received at the late Sunday-night service at the Bow and Bromley Institute.   In one instance, a woman who had not been in a place of worship for three years, was converted, with two of her companions.   Another case was that of a man, who, perhaps, through being so severely tried by want of work, became cross-grained in temper, until he was more of a terror than anything else to his household.   The family would, at times, be without food for days together ; but the grace of God touched his heart at the Bow and Bromley Institute ; and, despite all, he became such a changed character, that the children were quick to notice the difference.   Then comes a case of sorrow, which might well shame many of us who too soon complain when affliction comes, and who, perhaps, are too ready to make privation an excuse for shirking duty.   A mother has had a daughter ill for five years, and more than half that time the young woman has been in bed.   The elder woman is a feather maker ; but although they are often short of things necessary, the sick daughter's room is always clean and well kept.   More than that, the invalid has found her Saviour during the time she has been laid aside. What a commentary is this on the words, "It is good for me that I have been afflicted"! It is in the poor rooms of the East End, in company with such friends as Mr. Hurndall's visitors, that we best see the other words of the Psalmist verified, "He forgetteth not the afflicted"; "He heareth the cry of the afflicted"; "For thou wilt save the afflicted people."

But let us proceed, and take notice of one or two of those cases which show us what is really meant by hard times for those who have no capital but their labour.

Monotonously alike as these suburban East End streets may seem to be to casual visitors, it is surprising what variety there is in the life-stories that are to be heard in the rooms, some being as touching as others are tragic.

In one house, for example, there is a man whose father was of good social standing, and a town councillor. He served his apprenticeship in the regular way to a mechanical trade, and the referees who acknowledge him show the poor fellow to have been well connected. Eventually, however, he had to take a situation in a sugar refinery ; but when that trade declined, in consequence of the French, and others, thinking well to send us sugar under cost price, the firm became insolvent, and all their employés were cast adrift upon the world. Since that date, the man, who has a wife and four children, has not been able to obtain any regular work ; and, like others in such sad circumstances, he has parted with everything that is worth a shilling. Mr. Hurndall gave him a few shillings, as trading capital, and with this he bought a quantity of fish, to sell again, by which means he hoped to ward off actual starvation until he could return to his own trade.

Men like the above do not belong to that class of noisy impostors who parade the streets to make capital of their sham poverty. In the majority of instances, if they were not sought out, the public would know nothing of their sufferings. The most touching cases of all are those of bread-winners whose health and strength become undermined through want of the food which cannot be obtained, but without which work cannot be properly done.

The next example is a man who has also a wife and four children depending upon him, but whose health has suffered through want of proper food and clothing, until the seeds of consumption have been sown in his constitution, and he has been obliged to enter the infirmary. Think of all this coming upon a man at the age of thirty-two ! Can we wonder that he lay uneasily on his sick bed, and partook sadly of the comforts unstintingly provided for him in the hospital ; or, at last, that he became sufficiently imprudent to disobey the surgeon's order, and turn out, because he knew that his wife and children were wanting the barest necessaries of life ? He has nothing better to depend upon than work at the docks ; but though in an advanced state of consumption, he says he will drop at his work rather than let his dependants starve, if he can help it. When called upon by Mr. Hurndall's agent, the wife was nursing a sick baby ; but, notwithstanding, she was trying to make match-boxes, the price for which is under threepence a gross. A little help was given, such as flannel-shirts for the husband, and grocery for the family, accompanied with words of cheer and Christian sympathy. There is no danger of pauperizing in assisting such subjects; and if, instead of giving to got-up impostors in the streets, people allowed such almoners as these Christian visitors to dispense their bounty, the money would reach the right objects, instead of being worse than wasted.

The next case is that of a man and wife without children, and whose only resources are what the woman can earn at finishing trousers at twopence farthing a pair, the man having lost the sight of one eye, and being otherwise afflicted. Under such conditions, it is hardly so much living, as an actual fight for existence. The case of another woman in a bare room, with one child, almost naked, and unable to help herself through expecting another, is not a whit less deplorable. It was the monotonous old story of the husband being out of work. He was about as intensely anxious as a man could well be to provide what was necessary, and at last obtained a situation which might, probably, very barely supply the needs of the family. Even such an observer as the late Samuel Morley favoured the notion that the main part of the want and misery in London was the direst of wasteful drinking; but although a proportion may be traced to that cause, we go wide of the mark if we make out drink to be the chief cause of trouble. The great thing to remedy is the terribly overcrowded state of the labour market, mainly brought about by too early and improvident marriages.

A family, which another visitor describes as "very steady people," consists of a carpenter, who has been out of work for six weeks, and can only get anything to do now and then. As a rule, the winter means to them severely hard times at the best, being obliged to live from hand to mouth in a truly distressing manner. If we ask, How do such people live at all? the very suggestive incident of a little girl being sent out to sell enough rags to procure a pound of bread to give a meal to nine persons, helps to give an answer. There is no drinking, nor do they crave relief so much as work. The wife does a little with her needle, but with a husband out of work and seven hungry youngsters around her, it is hardly the mother's fault if some of these latter occasionally go breakfastless to school.

Apart from this, however, what shall be said about an afflicted woman of seventy-six years trying hard to support herself amid the fierce labour competition of the East End? When in tolerable health she can do a little with her needle; but that failing, she is partly dependent on what a relative is able to give her, and on what she receives from Mr. Hurndall's fund. Still, being in full possession of the Christian's hope, the old lady presents a rare picture of content; and when she talks of how good the Lord is to her, she is not dealing in mere unmeaning words. To see Christian patience of the most genuine sort, we need to look in upon some of the poorest homes of the East End.

In hundreds of other homes comes the same testimony to the difficulty of getting work, and of the impossibility of living without it. In one front room are man, wife, and two children, who, through the former having nothing to do, would at times have nothing to eat but for what they receive from Mr. Hurndall. Then you come upon a woman in an underground room, who, while depending on a mangle, has sometimes only fifteen-pence with which to find her board for a week. In another room there is a family of six, the children sleeping in one corner ; and, after paying five shillings a week rent, the parents do not know which way to turn to get a few pence to buy food.   A jacket finisher at three farthings each, and a husband out of work, is another characteristic case.   A similar case of devotion is seen in the case of the wife and daughter of a cabinet-maker, who make match-boxes at twopence farthing a gross, while the husband and father is too ill to work.   Thus, there are many aged widows struggling for a livelihood on the one hand, and, on the other hand, many wives and children who are suffering the greatest privation on account of men being either out of work, or too ill to do any if work could be got.   It should also be well borne in mind that this illness, with its disablement, is often occasioned by sheer want of the bare necessaries of life.

It is a pleasant thing to turn from all this to that *El Dorado* of working people, our great Dominion of Canada.   Here, at all events, is a country where people can settle without fear of being in one another's way, and where, at least for those who are willing and able to work, there will sure to be good lodgings and an abundance of food.   It may be true that at times we hear murmurs of complaint from those who have gone out ; but when such is the case, we commonly suspect that some mistake has been made which might have been avoided if a little ordinary precaution had been observed.   If intending emigrants will accept the social representations of interested railway shareholders instead of ascertaining what the officially appointed agents in London have to say, it is not surprising if they are misinformed and disappointed.   We are happy to say that this is not usually the case with those who go out from the East End.   "Discouraging statements as to the condition of the labour market in Canada have appeared in some English newspapers," remarks Mr. Hurndall ; "but the intelligence which has reached us suggests strongly that the Press is assuredly not infallible.   All the letters that have come are of a hopeful character."   There is a class of loafers who will even go out to the colonies by way of adventure ; and when they land they are no more prepared to work in the New World than they were in the Old.   They are loafers still, and such will they remain wherever they may be.

All we have to do in the present instance as impartial witnesses is to quote the testimony of those who have actually gone out and accepted such work as there is to be done.   This is evidence that no one can gainsay.

One boy went from Mr. Hurndall's district, who, on landing and presenting his letter of introduction, was invited to sit down to a dinner consisting of "roast beef, apple pudding, cheese, two kinds of cakes, green peas and potatoes"; the board thus furnished being in point of fact typical of the superabundance of that land of plenty.   The young emigrant adds:—"I got a situation after I came from dinner on the day I landed—eight dollars a month, board and lodging—with a cattle-dealer that has a small farm.   They are very nice people, and it is just like home.   I have every comfort there, and it is a very nice place, ten miles from Ottawa. . . . I could have lots of places—one at Montreal, the instant I came ashore.   There is work for thousands out here."   A second lad obtained a similar situation, while a man got work at three dollars a day, which enabled him to set up what, to him, was quite a large establishment. Then a working man, who for years lived a life of great privation in East London, sends a letter from Ottawa which shows how great and rapid the progress of the country has been, and how unlimited are the openings for hard-working people of the right kind. He says :—"There are still standing at Ottawa some of the old log-huts that were put up in the time of the first settlement. Now there are the stately Parliament buildings, Government offices, General Post Office, churches of all denominations, immense hotels, streets of beautiful stores (Spark-street being the principal), and in suburban parts of the city, beautiful villas of very handsome design, all fitted up with the very latest domestic comforts. The beautiful verandahs and porches give quite a splendid appearance to the houses, and they are very pleasant to sit in in the evening; and the gardens that surround the villas are fine. Altogether the scene is lovely and enchanting. I am at work on one of these villas. I believe the value is six thousand dollars. . . . The Canadians are very early people. They are out to their business very early in the morning. They are all work. It is no use whatever for anyone to come out here who is not useful and willing to work ; but for a man who is so, there is a living for him ; and as a friend of our landlord, who is rich now, and started a poor man, said, ' If a man cannot live in this country, he cannot live in any.' The city is lit up with the electric light, and also the major part of the stores."

Another young man writes :—"Glad to say all our party is going on very comfortable. H. has got a steady job until Christmas at thirty-and-a-half cents (one and threepence farthing) per hour. D. is pick and shovel man, one dollar and seventy-five cents per day, which is seven shillings. Each of us works ten hours per day. The principal men wanted out here [Ontario] are bricklayers, thirty-six cents per hour; labourers nineteen cents; plasterers, thirty-and-a-half cents. Farm labourers twenty dollars per month and all found, to good men. It is no use anybody coming out here without they make up their mind to work."

Of course we do not mean to say that all prosper alike; some do not do all they hoped to accomplish. "One or two, not successful at first, by energy and pluck have secured employment," remarks Mr. Hurndall, who adds that "Canada is a land where grit is needed. People who want to lean against a wall and think, had better remain in England, and gravitate to the workhouse."

To give a few more testimonies about the country :—a married man, sent out by Mr. Hurndall, says: "I get nineteen dollars a fortnight, and do not work near so hard as I did in England." We will close these extracts with one which came from a married man, who had suffered terribly in London through want of work :—"You will be pleased to hear that I got work the morning after we landed at Ottawa, with a firm of builders here, who have a great deal of work, and therefore I have every reason to suppose that it will be constant work, both summer and winter. We are all well and happy. We put our whole trust in God to guide us, and he does so in his great mercies to us. I put my whole trust in him before I left Euston, and I never felt the least fear or anxiety. You must accept our sincere thanks for your kindness, and your kind attention, and also your missionaries—and your seeing us off at Euston."

Thus the over-crowded labour market is relieved on a small scale; and we often wonder why, in the case of so great a country as ours, possessing colonies practically without limit, more is not done in the way of sending destitute but able-bodied people to the lands which will not only afford them plenty, but will themselves be richer for their labour. Meanwhile there is no truer charity than that of helping these poor people to help themselves. When we think of what the pressure really means in the case of those who feel it most severely, we shall the more thoroughly sympathize with those women whose husbands commit suicide because the anguish they bore could be borne no longer.

We may here mention that, on Christmas Eve, Harley-street Chapel presented an example of "Keeping Christmas" on a scale such as is not often seen, even in London. As we were not there, we shall chiefly borrow a description of the scene from our fashionable contemporary, *The Morning Post*:—

" A distribution of Christmas dinners, on a large scale, took place at the Harley-street Chapel; provision being made for some 12,000 of the poor of East London, representing in all 2,345 families. The Lord Mayor and Lady Mayoress attended early in the evening, and were warmly greeted by the recipients, who had already gathered in the building. Mr. Hurndall briefly opened the proceedings, after which the Lord Mayor said that it had been suggested that he should establish a fund for the purpose of dealing with the distress that existed in the East-end; but while in some cases such funds might do good, and might be so administered as to be a benefit to the poor, he was, nevertheless, constrained to say that, judging from the experience of what he had seen three years ago, he should not feel disposed to open any fund at the Mansion House unless there were proper and better centres for its distribution than had existed on the last occasion. Provision for the distribution should, of course, be adequate; but, above all, they should be discriminating; and he was inclined to think that the real poor did not, on the occasion to which he referred, receive all the benefit from the fund that they were entitled to. Many who did not deserve assistance were then the recipients of it. He was not going to commit the same mistake, but would rather take a centre such as that in which they were assembled, with a man at the head of it with the character of Mr. Hurndall, and do all he could to assist him. Referring to the wider question of the removal of the causes of distress, he expressed the belief that something might be done by means of emigration if properly organized under the Government, though he thought the Government had to a great extent cut the ground from under their feet by not maintaining Crown Colonies more than they had done. He felt, too, that some bar should be placed upon the admission of pauper foreigners into London, and hoped that some scheme might be devised by which land which was not now cultivated, but was capable of being so used, might be brought into cultivation. After further urging that the drink traffic should be more vigorously dealt with, he concluded by wishing a merry Christmas to all those present. The dinners which were given away during the evening consisted of joints of beef and materials for

Christmas puddings. The distribution was carried out under the direction of a committee; the total cost, which was raised by subscription, amounting to £550."

We may add that the weight of the food distributed on this occasion was 12 tons, 12 cwt., 52 lbs., divided as follows: 9,582 lbs. of beef, 11,326 lbs. of materials for puddings, 7,368 lbs. of bread.

At his residence, 16, Cottage Grove, Bow, Mr. Hurndall gives up three rooms for this mission work, one for an office, one for storing provisions, and one for clothing (which Mrs. Hurndall superintends). Parcels of clothing are always welcome. The Editor of *The Sword and the Trowel* would like to see such brethren as Archibald Brown and Evans Hurndall overdone with money and goods, and wishes that he may live to see them in such happy difficulties.

But while Mr. Hurndall renders all the help he can to needy and deserving people, the mission he superintends has for its first object the carrying of the gospel to the poor. Apart from this Home Mission work, the burden of his pastorate year by year grows heavier. None save those who have to do it know what it is to have to preach with freshness to crowded congregations week by week. Nor is his pen idle. For some years he has very successfully edited *The Shield and Spear*, a penny monthly magazine published by Mr. E. Stock. The little volume, *Thoughts by the Way*, published when he was a Bible-class leader at Clifton in 1870, deserves to be reprinted as a treasury of bright and useful things. He has also by request supplied sermon sketches and homilies for 1st and 2nd Corinthians in *The Pulpit Commentary*. Thus the operations carried on represent a many-sided work, which confers immense benefit on the very poorest of people at the East End. G. H. P.

Eyes Right.

"LET *thine eyes look right on*"—Proverbs iv. 25—like one ploughing, who must not look back. Look straight before thee. Had Eve done so, she would have looked on the command of her God, not on the forbidden tree. Had Lot's wife looked straight before instead of behind her, she would, like her husband, have been a monument of mercy. Achan was ruined by neglecting this rule of wisdom. David's example calls the holiest of us to godly jealousy: he looked when he should not, and fell into sin. In asking the way to Zion, be sure that your "faces are thitherward;" for the pleasures of sin, and the seductions of a tempting world, do not lie *in* the road. They would not therefore meet the eye looking right on—straight before us. They belong to the bye-path on the right hand and on the left, or to some backward track. It is only, therefore, when the Christian lingers, turns aside, or turns back, that they come in sight. Take the racer's motto—"This one thing I do." Eye the mark, and press to it. Onwards, upwards, heavenwards.

CHARLES BRIDGES.

A Plea for Calvin.

BY DR. WILLIAM GRAHAM.

BUT why plead in any wise for Calvin or Calvinism? Their works praise them in the gate, and speak for both. Never since the beginning of Christianity has any man or system produced such immense, heavenly, and heroic fruits. That great mountain has sheltered many a valley, shaped by its rise, and lying at its foot. That deep digging and ploughing has made fruitful many a barren waste. That fountain of divine grace has parted into a four-fold river, and made paradise on every side. Nearly all the heroisms, most of the liberties, much of the highest wisdom and character of these three hundred years, trace themselves back straight to that lonely man. The children of his home died and left him solitary; the children of his spirit grew a great and mighty nation. The last and best biographer of Calvin, Kampschulte, points out that his Reformation is the only one that steps beyond the limits of his birthplace. Huss was more a political and Bohemian Reformer. Luther's Reformation, while deeply Christian, having its roots nourished by relations to his "dear German nation," has never struck kindly in any other soil. Calvin, living in Geneva, a free city, put off the Frenchman as he put off the Romanist, and came forth in his system a man and a Christian. From his hands the Reformation became a movement independent of nationality, and produced a truly Christian and Catholic church. Hence the breadth of his influence has touched all orders of mind. The highest in genius and culture rise in their mien of soul and measure of praise as they look up to him; and many a peasant, with God's grace stirring mightily within, amidst a poor lot and dreary toils, has felt the bracing air of his stern doctrine and noble aims. Pass out from Geneva. See how he moved through and joined together the Swiss Reformed Churches, and had all but gained over into union the German Reformation too! See how, though he never revisited his old France, yet his soul marched on at the head of the Huguenots, and but for black St. Bartholomew, had made France the central Christian power in Europe! See how, in France also, a hundred years after, it was his truth, indirectly felt, that roused the grand and saintly spirits of Port Royal! These two men, Calvin and Pascal, have lifted up the French mind out of its usual chasm into an unwonted sublimity. In Holland, Calvin gave a body to the meditations which had been cherished by Thomas à Kempis, in the serene air of his monastery, and created its noble army of thirty-six thousand martyrs. Calvin's voice in his letters was a word from an emperor; when about to die they saluted him. Ten years of added life to Edward VI., and Calvin, in his Reformation, would have shaped English Christianity, and saved us from a conflict which is again deepening around us at this hour. As it was, he was the teacher and inspirer of the Puritans; and men like Oliver Cromwell and John Milton, John Bunyan and John Howe, John Owen and, though differing in opinion, yet like in spirit, Richard Hooker, can answer well for the nobleness and beauty of souls that surrender themselves to divine grace. Shall we forget to call Scotland to bear testimony? John Knox was, as Guizot says, no disciple of Calvin, but an equal; yet he learned much from him, and

Scotland, to this hour, owes much of its Reformation to the sovereign intellect and example of Calvin. And was not the whole Covenanting struggle one for divine grace, spiritual independence, and human liberty? Our own old Secession and Relief Churches called no man master but Christ, yet they look up to Calvin as one of his best scholars; and in later years, under Chalmers, and in a revived Christianity, and the Free Church, the old truth has given new tokens of its undying power. In Germany also, the only system that has broken up Rationalism is that of Schleiermacher, which asserts, though with many defects, the person of Christ and the power of grace. But time would fail to tell of all the victories of the truth. It is the great spiritual force at this moment in America; for the Pilgrim Fathers carried Calvin with them; and it still lives in strength amid thousands of churches, and has been embodied afresh, and with marvellous skill and learning, in the great book of Charles Hodge, the patriarch of Presbyterianism. And away in far-off islands of the seas, and in continents to east and west, these principles rescue multitudes at this hour from heathenism, and bear fruit in homes of piety and churches of God. I venture, then, to claim for Calvinism, or rather the Christianity which it in good measure represents, a power no future age can exhaust. Its difficulties, after all, lie in its high thoughts and holy living; and these, while they awe, and sometimes repel, at last attract and win men. The future of the church and the world is contended for by these three—Romanism, Rationalism, and pure Christianity. I have no fear for the issue. There may be swayings to and fro over the wide battle-field of contest; but I am sure that the army that has deep convictions of sin, and lofty views of God and his grace, has elements of intellectual truth, moral power, and divine reinforcement that shall gain the day. These elements shall emerge after every failure, and at last stand fast and for ever. These are truest to God and to man, for God's praise and for man's good; and these meet in him who has redeemed man from his lowest sin, by that death on the cross in which he has revealed God in his highest glory.

Anecdotes of Early American Baptists.[*]

DR. ISAAC BACKUS, the historian of the American Baptists of former days, lived from 1724 to 1806, and so saw all the stages of the Revolution, and his brethren, as well as his country, free. He had had no small hand in the transactions which led up to this happy result. His mother, Elizabeth (Tracy) Backus, was a strong as well as a devout Christian. She was in her "first love" when her son Isaac was born, and she brought him up in the fear and love of God. With many others, she became a dissenter from Congregational State Churchism, refusing to pay the tax. In the fall of 1752, when ill, and seated before the fire, wrapped in thick clothing to induce perspiration, the officers came and took her off to prison. It was a dark and rainy night, about nine o'clock. The officer thought that being sick of a fever she would rather pay her rates than be cast into gaol—and gaols were gaols then. But he did not reckon her aright. With a heroism worthy of a David, and with the spirit of Christ-like love to her persecutors, we find her saying:—

"Oh, the condescension of heaven! Though I was bound when cast into this furnace, yet I was loosed, and found Jesus in the midst of the furnace with me. Oh, then I could give up my name, estate, family, life, and health freely to God. Now the prison looked like a palace to me. I could bless God for all the laughs and scoffs made at me. Oh, the love that flowed out to all mankind! Then I could forgive, as I would desire to be forgiven, and love my neighbour as myself."

Great is the grace and strong the faith when weak women become "mighty through God." Such women are to be found now, no doubt ; but where shall we look for them ? The pleasure-loving "ladies" of the present day are not made of this stern stuff. Hearts of oak will not be found among them.

In Massachusetts and Connecticut the adherents of George Whitefield and Jonathan Edwards, who insisted on the Scriptural principle of churches being formed of converted people, were called New Lights and Separatists. They greatly swelled the ranks of the Baptists, who stood well-nigh alone in the maintenance of this important principle. The colleges were under the control of the State Church party, and the President of Yale showed what manner of spirit he was of when he expelled two students and their tutors for attending a private meeting for divine worship conducted by a layman. The young men pleaded that it was where their godly father attended ; but no matter, they were expelled.

In 1758 the General Assembly of Georgia passed a law making the Church of England the. church of the province. It established two parishes—Christ Church, Savannah, and St. Paul's, Augusta. Under this law Daniel Marshall was arrested one Sabbath "for preaching in the parish of St. Paul," contrary to the "rites and ceremonies of the Church of England." The congregation was assembled in "a beautiful grove under the blue sky, and he was on his knees making the opening prayer," when a hand was laid on his shoulder, and a voice heard, saying, "You are my prisoner"! He was a white-headed old man of sixty-five. The venerable man of God rose, and gave security to appear the next day at Augusta, and the constable—one Samuel Cartledge— released him, the preacher offering no word of remonstrance or rebuke. But the matter did not end there. Marshall's wife was present, and she was a woman of spirit, and courage, and faith, and zeal withal, and eloquent in speech. She remonstrated stoutly with the constable, and with equal authority, and solemnity, and earnestness, bid the man flee from the wrath to come, and seek the pardon of his sins and the salvation of his soul. Her words told. The man did repent and seek salvation. Mr. Marshall afterwards baptized him ; he became a deacon, and subsequently a pastor, dying so lately as 1843, ninety-three years of age. Verily "two are better than one," and it is better for a man to have a good wife than to be alone. All honour to you, Mrs. Martha Marshall! and God be praised for the grace given you !

There was an Edward Batsford, who emigrated from England in 1771. He was converted at Charleston, and was sent by the church there as a missionary into Georgia. The above D. Marshall had removed into Georgia, where Colonel Barnard introduced Batsford to him. Batsford was simply a licentiate, and Marshall was a veteran pastor. The latter said to the young recruit—

" Well, sir ; you are to preach for us ? "

" Yes, sir, by your leave. But I am at a loss for a text."

" Look to the Lord for one," was Marshall's answer.

He preached with great freedom from the words, " Come and hear, all ye that fear God, and I will declare what he has done for my soul." The old pastor found a blessing under the sermon ; and, taking the young man by the hand, said: " I can take thee by the hand, and call thee brother, for somehow I never heard *convarsion* better explained in my life." He took the young man home to his house, and to his heart, and they were David and Jonathan together until Marshall was called home.

Norwich, Connecticut, has been a large centre of Baptist power. Dr. Lord was the pastor of the State Church there when Whitefield was labouring there with his well-known success. At first Dr. Lord, who was a good man, was inclined to work with Whitefield, but his prejudices were allowed to get the better of his piety, and he began to persecute and oppress. There was a large secession from his church to form a Separatist congregation, and out of this movement the Baptist church was evolved. The Doctor came poorly off, for many refused to pay the tax, and he was reduced to the necessity of collecting the tax himself. One day he called upon a barber named Collier:—

"Mr. Collier," said he, "I have a small bill against you."

"A bill against me, Dr. Lord? For what ? "

"Why, your rate for my preaching."

"For your preaching? Why I have never heard you ; I don't recollect that I ever entered your meeting-house."

"That's not my fault, Mr. Collier; the meeting-house was open."

"Very well," said the barber, " But, look here, I have a small bill against you, Dr. Lord."

" A bill against me ? For what ? "

" Why, for barbering."

" For barbering ? I never before entered your shop."

" That's not my fault, Dr. Lord, my shop was open!"

This keen argument of the barber *cut* the conversation, and Dr. Lord followed suit.

Mr. Whitefield's preaching was greatly blessed in Connecticut and New York States, and he often found more sympathy among the Baptists than among either Presbyterians or Congregationalists, though some of the latter consorted with him. A remarkable sermon was given by the great preacher at the parsonage house, Centre Groton. The upper windows of the house were removed, and a platform raised in front, facing a large yard full of forest trees. When Whitefield passed through the window to this stand, he saw a number of young men who, like Zacchæus at Jericho, were perched on the limbs of the trees. At that time it was no unusual thing, under his preaching, for a secret irresistible influence to descend on the congregation. The multitude would surge to and fro, a cry of agony would arise; many would fall to the earth in a state of unconsciousness, and then as suddenly awake full of ecstatic joy. The kind-hearted preacher asked them to come down, saying :—"Sometimes the .power of God falls on these occasions, and takes away the might of strong men. I wish to benefit your souls, and not have your bodies fall out of those trees." They came down, and several were prostrated under the sermon. Great numbers were converted on this occasion, and more than one of the young men became preachers of the gospel.

The first Baptist Church, New York city, met in the house of Nicholas Eyers. He was a brewer, and a noble-minded, discreet and godly man. He was baptized in 1714. There were eleven other candidates. For fear of the rabble the baptism was to take place at night. The company went to the river, and five females were immersed, when Mr. Eyers was seized with the conviction that they were not acting faithfully in shunning publicity. He remembered the word addressed to the Master, "No man doeth anything in secret, when he himself seeketh to be known openly." He therefore consulted the other candidates, and they agreed to postpone their baptism until the morning. Mr. E. then waited on the governor with a request for protection, which he not only gave, but went with many respectable citizens and witnessed the ordinance, remarking, "This was the ancient manner of baptizing, and is, in my opinion, much preferable to the practice of modern times." Mr. Eyers afterwards got his house licensed for worship, and he was chosen the first pastor of the church.

John Gano has been named in a previous article. His grandfather Francis Gano was a French Huguenot, and had to fly from Guernsey, in consequence of the revocation of the Edict of Nantes. He settled in New York state. John's father resided at Hopewell, New Jersey, where John was born in 1727. After his ordination, he was sent by the Philadelphia Association on a mission to the South. While in the back settlements of Virginia, he overheard the family with whom he lodged saying, "This man talks like one of the Joneses." On inquiry he found the "Joneses" lived about twenty miles off, their peculiarity being that "they did nothing but pray and talk about Jesus." He determined to see *his own likeness*, as he said. So, the next day he rode over. He found a large family—Welsh, we might gather, from the name—some of whom had been recently converted. They were engaged in worship. The sick father was lying before the fire, groaning with pain, and Gano accosted him by saying : —

"How are you ?"

"Oh! I am in great pain," said the sick man.

"I am glad of it," said Gano.

"What do you mean?" said the old man, somewhat excited.

"I mean," said he, "that whom the Lord loveth he chasteneth." The old man at once fell in love with him.

Gano reached North Carolina in company with another young man. Arriving at a plantation, they were invited to stay all night.

"Are you a trader ?" the planter asked of the young preacher.

"Yes," was his reply.

"And how do you succeed ?"

"Not so well as I could wish."

" Perhaps your goods do not suit?" said the planter.

"No one has complained of them," Gano replied.

"Probably you set your price too high ?"

"No," said Gano, "these are my terms : If gold tried in the fire—yea, that which is better than fine gold, wine and milk, durable riches and righteousness—if these will suit you, you may have them without money and without price."

"Oh!" said the planter, "I believe you are a minister."

Gano gave him proof of this by declaring unto him the freeness and fulness of the grace of Christ.

When Gano reached Charleston, he had to preach for a Mr. Hart. There was a large congregation, and a "brilliant audience," among whom were twelve ministers, one of them being Mr. Whitefield. A momentary fear of man came upon him, and then he thought, "I have none to fear and obey, but God," and he was strengthened. On his return to North Carolina during the French war he was informed that he was to be seized as a spy. When he reached the place where he was told he would be arrested, he stopped at the inn, and asked if the people could come to hear a sermon on a week-day. The landlord told him there was to be a general muster for the county. Gano, instead of stealing off, sent to the Colonel who was to arrest him, to ask if it would be agreeable to him to have a short sermon addressed to the regiment before military duty. The Colonel accepted the proposal, and the men gave profound attention, excepting one man, whom Gano censured for his conduct. The Colonel thanked the preacher, rebuked the man, and Gano went on his way.

On·reaching the Blue Ridge, a storm overtook him, and he entered a house for shelter. The owner asked him if he was a "press-master," he said he was. The man was alarmed and asked if he took *married ones*. Gano assured him he did, that his Master's service was good, with high wages,,and he wanted him to enlist, and his wife and children also. He then exhorted him to volunteer to serve the Lord Jesus.

After various changes, Gano settled at New York city, where he remained twenty-five years, and saw many trials, but great blessing on his ministry.

When the War of Independence was over, and Washington proclaimed peace, there were great rejoicings. After the proclamation was made, followed by three huzzas, John Gano gave thanks to Almighty God for his mercy, and an anthem was rendered by voices and instruments. Gano died in 1804.

A remarkable incident in connection with the War of Independence is told in relation to Colonel Joab Houghton. While proceeding to the Baptist meeting-house at Hopewell, New Jersey, he met a messenger with the news of the defeat at Lexington. He kept silence until the service was ended, and then, in the open lot, told the story of the cowardly proceedings of the royal troops, the retreat of Percy, and the gathering of the pilgrims around the hills of Boston. Then, pausing, and looking over the silent crowd, he said slowly : "Men of New Jersey, the red coats are murdering our brethren in New England. Who follows me to Boston ?" Every man in the audience stepped out into line, and cried, "I !"

Colonel Houghton fought through the war. He was every way a valiant man. A band of marauding Hessians had entered a house at More's Hill, New Jersey, for plunder, stacking their arms at the door. The colonel seized their arms, and made the leader and a dozen men prisoners, almost in sight of the British army.

The Colonel was a member of the Hopewell Baptist church, and died in 1793.

Dr. Shepherd, of Stathens, a young physician, visiting a patient, got hold of Norcott's book on Baptism. He read it, and became a Baptist, and subsequently a pastor, presiding over a church at Brentwood, New Hampshire, which had twelve branch meeting-houses and four hundred and forty-three members.

The church at Newport, New Hampshire, worshipped in a barn beside a river. Thomas Baldwin the Good, as he was called, once preached there, when such a divine power was realized that the meeting continued till quite late at night. Mr. Baldwin had to ride all night to meet an engagement in the morning. Mounting his horse, and picking his way through the forest, he mused over the hallowed meeting in the barn. The fire burned, and he began to sing. The words were the well known American hymn, which then sprang, as it were, to his lips :—

> " From whence doth this union arise,
> That hatred is conquered by love ? "

We have not exhausted our list of anecdotes ; but our paper will only admit of two more, which may be taken as points of contrast.

Morgan Edwards went from Wales to New York in 1761. Landing one morning, he thought he would try and find a Baptist. He wandered up and down, and looked here and there, but could discern no trace of one. At length he saw an old man sitting in his doorway, with a red cap. He thought, " This is an old inhabitant, I will ask him." " Can you tell me, sir, where any Baptists live in this city ? " " Baptists ! Baptists ! " said the old man, musingly. " Baptists, I really don't know as I ever heard of anybody of that occupation in these parts." Times have changed since then.

There was a great revival in Georgia in the years 1812-13, 1820, and 1827. Between fifteen thousand and twenty thousand were added to the church. This was promoted greatly by the labours of Dr. Adiel Sherwood, who preached with power from on high. One Lord's-day he preached before an association at Antioch, Morgan county. The power of the Lord came down. At the close of the sermon he asked all who wished for the prayers of the assembly to present themselves. A young gentleman of high standing and culture was the first. He was afterwards known as Dr. John E. Dawson, a brilliant, pathetic, and useful preacher. It is estimated that four thousand people that day sought the prayers of the church, and that sixteen thousand persons, directly or indirectly, were gathered in in two years as the result of that sermon. Oh, for seasons like the past ! Lord, send them !

R. SHINDLER.

The Auxiliary Book Fund.

THE history of the rise and progress of "Mrs. Spurgeon's Book Fund and its Work" must be familiar to most of the readers of *The Sword and the Trowel.* If there are any who are still unacquainted with the narrative, we should advise them to procure the charming volume in which the Founder of the Fund herself tells the story of its commencement, and of its loving and beneficent ministry during the first ten years of its existence.*

In the last Annual Report of her work, Mrs. Spurgeon wrote:—

"It has always been a grief to me that I have to limit my grants to one class of men—poor *pastors of churches.* I dare not extend the work beyond them, or my strength would utterly fail. But the *need* of books is felt by workers of all conditions, and in scores of cases a gift of suitable volumes to a devoted lay-preacher would bring in a splendid interest of glory to God, and gracious influence over poor sinners. There are the 'Local Preachers,' for instance; a grand body of men, doing noble service for the Lord, worthy of all sympathy and help; yet I have to refuse their applications, because my work is already so heavy and pressing that, to open the Fund to any but poor pastors, must practically result in the closing of it to everybody.

"Listen to the pleading of one of these good men, and then join me in asking the Lord to raise up a friend, who will do for them what God has enabled me to accomplish during the past twelve years for those who have the care of the churches:—'I write you,' he says, 'on behalf of poor "locals," who, I understand, are outside the pale of your Fund. Would it were not so; for I feel we are, of all workers, the most forgotten! Many of us are poor in purse, and short of time, and in need of teaching; yet we do our best to quit us like men. We walk many miles, preach often, and endeavour to glorify the Master in the salvation of souls. Oh, that we could have a share in this blessed book-distribution! If it is so great a boon to our brethren in the recognized ministry, how much greater a benefit would it confer on us, who have to labour with our hands for the bread which perisheth, and, in consequence, have so little spare time to study and ponder God's Word!'

"This is a real cry for help; will it touch the heart of any who can respond to it?"

The cry for help *did* touch the heart of one who *could* respond to it, as will be seen from the following extracts from a letter signed by Mr. Sydney S. Bagster, of the Conference Hall, Mildmay Park ·—

"Dear Mrs. Spurgeon,
    "Have you received a response to pages 9 and 10 of 'The Book Fund and its Work, 1887'? If not, I should like to offer to take up the work you there suggest should be done by some one.

"I will note a few points:—

"1. My own work as a (so-called) layman, engaged in preaching and teaching, with my affection for the contents of my own bookshelves, leads me to a lively sense of the needs of those so engaged, but not so provided as I am; while my eager welcome to any addition to my treasures leads me to realize somewhat the joy of those poorer than myself at the sight of a helpful book.

"2. My hearty sympathy with *old-fashioned* theology would lead me to

---

* "Ten Years of my Life in the Service of the Book Fund: being a Grateful Record of my Experience of the Lord's Ways, and Work, and Wages." By Mrs. C. H. Spurgeon. Third Edition. Sixth Thousand. Price 3s. 6d. In superior binding, gilt edges, with new Portrait and Autograph. Price 5s. Passmore and Alabaster.

follow closely the lines of ' The Book Fund,' save that *The Treasury of David* would be beyond the loftiest aspirations of a 'local'; or, at least, only in special circumstances could one be thus enriched.

" 3. I need hardly say that, while myself a Baptist, no distinction whatever would be made as to the applicant's denomination.

" 4. The question of funds I do not feel would be a difficulty, as one would only use what was given, assured that the Giver would not fail to give as much as he thought enough.

   *   *   *   *   *

" 7. Will you let me know whether my offer meets with the approval of the Founder of ' The Book Fund,' and whether she would assent to the formation of an ' Auxiliary Book Fund,' to make grants to preachers (other than pastors) whose means are too small to permit of their purchasing ? "

To this communication Mrs. Spurgeon replied :—

" Dear Sir,—Your letter gladdens my heart exceedingly, and I thank the Lord for inclining your mind to this important and much-needed work. I note with joy your purpose to keep to the ' old-fashioned ' truths, and to make your work unsectarian, and I wish you ' God speed ' with all the hope inspired by the fulfilment of a long-cherished desire. Yes, you are quite right, the *Lord* will send you the *means* to carry out the work he gives you to do, and a perfect trust in him will bring all needful help. I shall be delighted to render you any assistance in my power ; and if you will tell me *when* and *how* you propose to commence work, I will turn my promise into a performance.

   *   *   *   *   *

" No one else has ' offered himself willingly' for this work—I bless the Lord that *you* have done so. May his sweet and gracious dealings with me be repeated in your happy experience ! I feel almost too glad and thankful to be able to express myself as I would—I am overwhelmed with the goodness of the Lord in thus granting me the desire of my heart.

" Yours very sincerely,

" (Mrs. C. H.) SUSIE SPURGEON."

Notices of the proposed work were sent to *The Christian, Word and Work*, and *Service for the King ;* and as the result of the publicity thus given, applications came, and the distribution of books commenced. One of the earliest applicants was a provincial city missionary, who wrote :—

" I shall be most pleased and grateful for any books you may be kind enough to send me, having a rather long family (seven children), and one an invalid, not able to stand, also having to help my aged mother."

Another of the same noble army of Christian workers gave these reasons why he should have a grant from the Auxiliary Book Fund :—

" I have four meetings a week in my mission-room. I find I have to keep pegging away to get a little fresh food for the people. It is such a difficulty to buy a new book. . . . . I make and mend the boots for the family, and get up early in the morning ; even then I never hardly think of buying books. But, bless the Lord, I am happy in my work, I love it ! "

On receiving a parcel, the good man thus expressed his gratitude for the books :—

" I do appreciate them, and will try and profit by them. I have seen *The Treasury of David* several times ; I think it is lovely. If ever your fund gets rich and strong, and you are moved to send it to me, I should be so thankful."

A third provincial city missionary applied as follows :—

"At present I have to preach twice every Sunday, and, on an average, three times during the week, to the same people. Thus I find it rather difficult to present new matter at each service. In fact, I am feeling it to be a great mental and physical strain. Furthermore, I have charge of the ——— carriage-works, and every week have to address at least five hundred men."

A parcel was sent, and the recipient's thanks for the books were thus recorded :—

"I shall carefully and prayerfully read them, and do my best to personally appropriate all that is good within them ; and, by God's help, endeavour to communicate the good I receive to those among whom I labour."

*　　*　　*　　*　　*

The next two letters are from workers in connection with the Established Church :—

"I am very poor, of humble origin, and have had to fight my own battle in the world from the time that I was between fifteen and sixteen years of age. After having been brought to a knowledge of the truth as it is in Jesus, under the ministry of ———, I felt an intense desire to enter the ministry. [After mentioning the removal of difficulties, and his entering College, he says :—] I hope shortly to be ordained to the ministry in the Church of England ; but in going through this College course, all my little means have been entirely swallowed up. I have had to purchase many books which will be utterly useless in my ministry ; and, now, laying myself open to mission-work, I find great difficulty in preparing for it."

"I have charge of one mission-church near here, and preach there twice each week ; and on Saturday we open another mission-room, where I shall also have two sermons each week. I am also trying to get up a meeting for working-men one night a week."

In acknowledging the receipt of the parcel that was sent to him, this good brother writes :—

"I have had such a delicious revel amongst the sermons every spare moment since I received them ; and I felt very much fresher for Sunday. I am now saving my mites for a Commentary ; but with a sick wife and two children, I shall need a great amount of patience."

*　　*　　*　　*　　*

An evangelist, applying for a grant, and explaining his financial position, says :—

"When a station is not self-supporting, we receive a salary of 18s. per week. We have 4s. 2d. to pay for rent. I am married, and have two little girls, who cost 1s. a week for schooling. After paying rent and schooling, we have 12s. 10d. to live on and find clothes. This we have managed with, but I have been hindered very much by not being able to purchase books."

*　　*　　*　　*　　*

Many local preachers apply to Mrs. Spurgeon for books, although it has been frequently stated that her grants must be limited to pastors in actual charge of churches. These applications are now all forwarded to Mr. Bagster. The following letter from a warm-hearted Welshman was thus sent, and on receipt of the parcel from the Auxiliary he wrote to Mrs. Spurgeon the second note :—

"I am like Ishmael in the wilderness, unable to procure water, and dying of thirst, unable to procure that which is essential ; but, thanks be to God, that there is a Hagar who has found a well at 'Westwood,' which has quenched the parched tongues and thirsty souls of thousands of Ishmaels! My prayer is that the well will never run dry, but continue to pour out living water to thirsty souls, and that you will have health and strength to perform the heavy and arduous duties which have proved a blessing to many of God's servants."

"I am at a loss to find words to express my thanks to you for your kindness, and I may say that the meeting between your books and myself was of the same description as that of Jacob and Joseph; my heart was full, and no words can express that feeling. I have only 22s. per week, and a wife and four children, and I have had one of my little ones ill this four months, but I am pleased to say that the Lord has restored him."

    *   *   *   *   *

We can only spare the space for a few of the letters of thanks that have been received from those to whom grants have been made. The following will give a fair idea of the way in which the recipients express their gratitude :—

"I beg to acknowledge the receipt of the parcel of books to hand on Saturday, with very many thanks to you and the kind donor, Mrs. Spurgeon. They are beautiful, and will be very helpful. I prize them highly, and shall peruse them carefully As a lay preacher, I have conducted 2,298 Sabbath services, and travelled 13,995 miles in attending them. About 300 of the Sabbath services have been held in our own town, besides a large number of week-evening services."

"Mr. Spurgeon's *Sermon-Notes* I value very much; it is just the kind of thing I need. The books are all fresh to me, and are of a character fitted, undoubtedly, to help. I often take one of the services at ————, and I shall use Mr. Spurgeon's *Sermon-Notes* pretty freely; there is plenty of grip in them. The trajectories of Mr. Spurgeon's missiles are low,* and consequently hit pretty frequently."

"Parcel of books to hand, which I must say I am delighted with. By God's help, I trust they will not only make me wise to win souls, but to build them up in the knowledge of God. I do thank God there are such kind-hearted Christians as Mrs. Spurgeon and others, who are ever ready to help the needy. May God's richest blessings rest upon all who are supporting this good work! The books are more than one could expect, but it is the Lord's doings. They are a definite answer to prayer."

"My heart is filled with joy in receiving your very kind parcel of books, such a very nice Concordance, and all the other books. I do like to read and also to have, Mr. Spurgeon's books; they are always so fresh. Please to accept my heartfelt thanks, and may the Lord speed and bless you in this your work for him in cheering his servants ! "

"I most heartily thank you. I regard them as priceless treasures; even the sight of these books does me good. They are just the books that are likely to be a very great help to me. *My Sermon-Notes, Lectures to my Students,* and *Farm Sermons* are books that I have long coveted; but I had no idea that I should have the pleasure of saying that I have got the long-coveted prize in possession."

"I feel most thankful to you for the trouble you have taken in selecting such a good and profitable assortment; they are quite suitable to my situation." [This applicant, in a previous letter, explains that for upwards of forty years he has laboured for the Lord as a Sunday-school teacher and local preacher.] "My living," he says, "is rather precarious, it being obtained by buying, selling, and repairing second-hand boots and shoes."

---

* We hope the good brother does not talk like this when he is preaching. In the books sent to him he will probably see that short, simple, Saxon words will "hit" where long Latinized expressions "pretty frequently" miss the mark.

Friends will see from these letters that there is great need of books among local preachers, and that they are heartily grateful that an Auxiliary Book Fund has been started with the object of supplying their wants. No register of the denominations to which the applicants belong has been kept, but grants have been sent to Baptists, Bible Christians, Congregationalists, Episcopalians, "Joyful News" Evangelists, and Methodists of various sections. Some have been pastors in all but the name; others, city missionaries, evangelists, Scripture-readers, or students still in College. The distribution of books commenced on May 1st, 1888, and from that time until December 31st, 126 grants had been made, comprising 1,142 volumes:—

97 ".Lectures to my Students."
155 "My Sermon-Notes."
218 other books by Mr. Spurgeon.
672 books by other authors.

Mrs. Spurgeon has given £50 worth of books to the Auxiliary, and has also forwarded a large quantity of second-hand books given or offered to her by various friends. The cash account for the nine months, from April to December, is as follows:—

DR. RECEIPTS.	£ s. d.	EXPENDITURE.	CR. £ s. d.
To Two Donations ..	25 0 0	By Purchase of Books and Tracts ..	24 13 9
,, Sale of Old Books, and Stamps for Carriage	2 15 6	,, Postages, Stationery, and Carriage	2 18 11
		,, Balance carried to 1889 ..	0 2 10
	£27 15 6		£27 15 6

Mr. Bagster wishes us to say that all applications for grants are taken in rotation; and therefore, as he is a busy man, sometimes weeks may elapse before parcels are sent; but so long as the books and funds at his disposal will permit, he will attend to all duly-certified applicants who comply with the conditions laid down for the proper working of the Auxiliary.

The conditions attached to grants of books are:
1st. Only laymen who are regular and habitual preachers are eligible.
2nd. No person is eligible who can afford to purchase for himself.
3rd. In each case reference is required to some one—usually a minister—who will endorse the applicant's statement as to the 1st condition, and also state that, in his opinion, the applicant comes within the 2nd condition.
No names or addresses of those to whom grants are made will be published.
All communications needing a reply should contain a stamp.
The carriage of parcels by railway or carrier is *not* prepaid by the Fund.
Applications to be made by letter only, addressed:—
Mr. S. S. BAGSTER, 25, Newington Green, London, N.

It only remains for us to thank Mr. Bagster for having taken up this much-needed service for the Lord's poor preachers, and to wish for him as much success and blessing in his work as the beloved Manager of the Book Fund has found in hers during the past thirteen years.

𝕿𝖍𝖊 𝕳𝖔𝖑𝖞 𝕷𝖆𝖓𝖉 𝖆𝖓𝖉 𝖙𝖍𝖊 𝕭𝖎𝖇𝖑𝖊.*

DR. GEIKIE has become quite a worthy successor of John Kitto, who, in the earlier years of this century, won a well-deserved reputation as a writer who understood the art of making Bible subjects interesting to young persons and general readers. As regards the popular attractiveness of his style, Dr. Kitto had few equals in his own day; and, in his own department, Dr. Geikie has no superior in his. The books he has published are fine examples of good scholarship popularized; and next to his elaborate "Life of Christ," his last work will probably rank as the most useful that he has produced. In the most comprehensive sense, it is a book of illustrations gathered fresh in Palestine itself; so that while ordinary readers find plenty of entertainment, teachers and preachers have a rich treasure-house of material which they may explore with delight and use with good effect. "I visited Palestine," says the author, "with the intention of gathering illustrations of the sacred writings from its hills and valleys, its rivers and lakes, its plains and uplands, its plants and animals, its skies, its soil, and, above all, from the pictures of ancient times still presented on every side in the daily life of its people." No author ever more completely carried out his design ; and no reader is likely to be disappointed with the result. The readiest way of giving the reader an idea of the quality of the Doctor's work will be to make a few extracts. Here is a picture of the present condition under Turkish rule of

TANTURAH IN CÆSAREA.

It cannot be said that this neighbourhood is a very inviting one to the traveller, the natives being so savage and rude that their local feuds often give great trouble. Rock-hewn tombs are common, but the only use to which they are now put seems to be to hide away the bodies of men who have been robbed and killed. In one case, Captain Conder found in an old Jewish tomb six corpses, belonging apparently to strangers recently murdered. The number of skulls and bones in other tombs, he adds, astonished him, till he found that many of them were fractured, and was told that they had belonged to persons murdered by the villagers.

MELONS AT MUKHALID.

It is in the heart of the chief melon-growing district of Palestine, and must present a striking scene when the crop is being harvested. Hundreds of camels then wait their turn to be loaded with the huge fruit, or stalk away with a full burden of it. Peasants in their white turbans and skirts, the latter duly girt round them by a leather strap, assiduously gather the different kinds of melons, while the tents of the tax-collectors, pitched in the fields, show that these oppressors are on the look-out to lay a heavy hand on the produce, for the Government. How is it that great vegetable globes, like these melons, so full of water, thrive thus wondrously on so hot and sandy a soil? The camel-

---

* The Holy Land and the Bible. A Book of Scripture Illustrations gathered in Palestine. By Cunningham Geikie, D.D., Vicar of St. Martin's-at-Palace, Norwich. Cassell & Co., two vols., price 24s.

loads of them taken to the shore fill a thousand boats each summer. Indeed, if it were not for fear of the Bedouins, there need be no limit to the quantity grown.

EASTERN TOWNS.

No one who has not seen an oriental town can imagine its filthiness. The mud houses crumble into dust at a given rate daily, and all the garbage, offal, and foulness of daily life are thrown into the narrow lane, where the dust-hill is too far off. Rivulets of abomination soak out from a hole made for their escape at the side of each door. Nor is this the only kind of filth. There are no scavengers, and there is no decency.

THE MORTALITY OF CHILDREN.

More than a third of the children in Palestine, I was told, die in infancy, which is no wonder ; so ignorant are the people, and so dirty and unsanitary are their houses. Ophthalmia is epidemic, with blindness as its frequent result.

THE CURSE OF THE TURKISH RULE.

The hope of the peasant at Ascalon, that some of the Frank nations would soon come and take Palestine, is common to the whole population. Turkish government consists simply in collecting the taxes and quelling tumults, which often break out through oppression. The crops are assessed before the harvest, and are frequently left till over-ripe, the owner having to bribe the official with a larger share of them, to secure his coming in time to save what is left, before all the grain falls out of the dry ears. The taxes, moreover, are fixed without any regard to the amount of the crops, good years and bad having to pay alike, though nothing be left to the poor tiller of the ground. Bashi-Bazouks are sent out to gather the grain, or fruit claimed by Government, a fact that helps one to realize the extortion and villainy that follow. The Turk is the king of the locusts, his officials their desolating army. If the Kaimacan, or Governor, goes out with the soldiers, he and his followers must be fed and housed in the best style at the cost of the village. The soldiers also live at free quarters, and fleece the unhappy peasants at their will.

BEIT JIBRIN.

The town has an evil name, its population of well-grown, muscular men, who are thus very different from the peasants of other parts, being bold and insolent, though industrious, as a whole, and comparatively well-to-do. The father of the sheikh at whose side I sat had been a ruffian of the worst kind, the terror of the neighbourhood and of the townsmen. Tales of monstrous crimes committed by him were rife. It is said that if he heard of a man having married a handsome wife, he would invite the two to his house, and if he fancied the girl, would stab the husband on the spot, and make the widow marry him forthwith. Till his death no traveller dared visit Beit Jibrin, and the traders from Hebron would not venture to come near it with their goods. The Turks, however, have brought down the pride of the house since his death, for the family are now much reduced, as the ruinous condition of parts of the rough mansion showed.

THE MIRAGE.*

About noon, the most perfect deception that can be conceived exhilarated our spirits, and promised an early resting-place. We had observed a slight mirage two or three times before, but this day it surpassed all that I had ever fancied. Although aware that these appearances often led people astray, I could not bring myself to believe that this was unreal. The Arabs were doubtful, and said that as we had found water yesterday, it was not improbable we should find some to-day. The seeming lake was broken in several parts by little islands of sand, which gave strength to the delusion. The dromedaries of the sheikhs at length reached its borders, and appeared to us to have commenced to ford, as they advanced and became more surrounded by the vapour. I thought they had got into deep water, and moved with greater caution. In passing over the sand-banks their figures were reflected in the water. So convinced was Mr. Calmun of its reality, that he dismounted, and walked towards the deepest part of it, which was on their right hand. He followed the deceitful lake for a long time, and to our sight was strolling on its bank, his shadow stretching to a great length beyond. There was not a breath of wind ; it was a sultry day, and such a one as would have added dreadfully to the disappointment if we had been at any time without water.

A STREET IN JERUSALEM.

A few steps down David Street—the lane leading east and west from Joppa Gate to the Temple enclosure—brings you to Christian Street, which runs north; and close to this, on the under side, is the Church of the Holy Sepulchre. But what would any one think of the street called after the hero king of Israel, if suddenly set down at the end it ? It is a lane rather than a street, with houses, for the most part only two storeys high, on each side, the lower one being given up to shops—if you can call such dens by so respectable a name. Over the doors a continuous narrow verandah of wood, built at a slant into the houses, gives shade to the goods ; but when it was put up, or repaired in any way, is an insolvable historical problem. Its condition, therefore, may be easily fancied. The causeway of the street is equally astonishing ; for even a donkey, most sure-footed of animals, stops, puts its nose to the ground, and makes careful calculations as to the safe disposition of its feet, before it will trust them to an advance. No wonder there are no people in the streets after dark ; without a lantern they would infallibly sprain their ankles, or break a leg, each time they were rash enough to venture out. But during the day the stream of many-coloured life flows through this central artery of the holy city in a variety to be found, perhaps, nowhere else.

AN ANCIENT UNDERGROUND CITY.†

I visited old Edrei—the subterranean labyrinthine residence of King Og—on the east side of the Zamle hills. Two sons of the sheikh of the village—one fourteen, and the other sixteen years of age—

---

* Dr. Geikie quotes Major Skinner's description of this phenomenon.
† Dr. Geikie quotes Consul-General Wetstein's description of one of these wonderful relics of antiquity.

accompanied me. We took with us a box of matches and two candles. After we had gone down the slope for some time, we came to a dozen rooms, which, at present, are used as goat-stalls and store-rooms for straw. The passage became gradually smaller, until at last we were compelled to lie down flat, and creep along. This extremely difficult and uncomfortable process lasted for about eight minutes, when we were obliged to jump down a steep wall, several feet in height. Here I noticed that the younger of my two attendants had remained behind, being afraid to follow us ; but, probably, it was more from fear of the unknown European than of the dark and winding passages before us.

We now found ourselves in a broad street, which had dwellings on both sides of it, whose height and width left nothing to be desired. The temperature was mild, the air free from unpleasant odours, and I felt not the smallest difficulty in breathing. Further along, there were several cross streets, and my guide called my attention to a hole in the ceiling for air, like three others which I afterwards saw, (now) closed up from above. Soon after we came to a market-place ; where, for a long distance, on both sides of a pretty broad street, there were numerous shops in the walls, exactly in the style of the shops that were seen in Syrian cities. After a while we turned into a side street, where a great hall, whose roof was supported by four pillars, attracted my attention. The roof, or ceiling, was formed of a single slab of jasper, perfectly smooth and of immense size, in which I could not perceive the slightest crack. The rooms, for the most part, had no supports; the doors were often made of a single square stone; and here and there I also noticed fallen columns. After we had crossed several cross-alleys and streets, and before we had reached the middle of the subterranean city, my attendant's light went out. As he was lighting again by mine, it occurred to me that possibly both our lights might be put out, and I asked the boy if he had any matches. "No," he replied, " my brother has them." " Could you find your way back if the lights were put out ?" "Impossible," he replied. For a moment I began to be alarmed at this under-world, and urged an immediate return. Without much difficulty, we got back to the market-place, and from there the youngster knew the way well enough. Thus, after a sojourn of more than an hour and a half in this labyrinth, I greeted the light of day.

Hotel Beau Rivage, Mentone.

WE present our readers with the likeness of the homely, quiet hotel in which for several years it has been our great privilege to enjoy rest and Christian fellowship. Dr. Sewell, a courteous Canadian physician, residing in the hotel, was good enough to invite us, with Mr. Passmore, to stand upon his balcony while he took a view from below. The doctor was in the pursuit of photographs under difficulties in this case ; but he has succeeded, and we are grateful for the result. The nearness of the house to the road prevents its being made into an effective picture, especially as the road itself is narrow ; and then you have the sea, which is too skittish to furnish a foundation for a camera in which to take an instantaneous picture. Foreground on this and other grounds is out of the question. Our own apartments, on the first

6

floor on the right, are, so far as this picture is concerned, completely veiled by the palms; but that is not actually the case; we are not among the palms yet, but far more among the buffetings. A good deal, therefore, must be left to imagination before one arrives at the actual fact. "Things are not what they seem"; and the best photograph on earth can do no more than tell us "what they seem." In this instance things are better than they seem, and the hotel within surpasses the promise of its exterior. To us it seems as if the kindest and best people in all the world have been sojourning in this hostelry for the last three months, and that they have each one been more

thoughtful and sympathetic than every other. Until we came "down with a crash" our morning gathering for prayer at 9.30, and the reading through the Gospel of John, were bright beginnings of happy days. We were all there, and all there in time; and the Lord himself was with us indeed, and of a truth. Looking out upon the ever-changing sea, and ever feeling the joy of the unchanging God, this hotel has been to us none other than the house of God. It makes no pretensions to grandeur or vastness; but the host and hostess, Mr. and Mrs. Bernhard, devote themselves to the comfort of their guests, and those who have once come under their roof are very apt to return thither. The good people have no notion of our putting them into the magazine; but we hope they will forgive us for our kind intent.—C. H. S.

Notices of Books.

"Not Weary in Well-Doing;" or, the Life and Work of Mrs. Helen Lockhart Gibson. By her Husband. With Preface by Dr. A. A. Bonar. Simpkin, Marshall and Co.

THIS is a memoir which we recommend enthusiastically. Our subscribers must not be content with our brief note, but must *buy the book.* It is well written, but the value of it lies in what was written and done by this most exemplary woman herself. The gospel was her life, her food, her beauty, and her joy. She seemed to be good at everything: visiting, conversation, writing, giving addresses, and household management: she failed in nothing, for she did it with all her heart, resting in the Lord. There are no adventures in her life, no fine speculations, no great flourishes: she was a simple believer, living in her Lord and for him. It has been like waiting at the wells of Elim to read her biography, and we rise refreshed from it; therefore we feel that we can hardly put upon paper all that we feel. This holy woman shone as a lamp on earth, and she now shines as the stars for ever and ever.

We commend this life for its practical value. It will direct many godly women in their work, and suggest to them what to do; how to deal with special cases, and how to meet peculiar difficulties. It will breed quiet heroines, whose faith will be unabashed when ridiculed, and unabated when confronted by obstinacy. Even in the minor matter of dress she was a notable example, and took that happy middle course which avoids both the slatternly and the gaudy. In life and in death, by her calm repose on Jesus and his Word, she was a true mother in Israel. Happy is her husband that he had the companionship of so noble a helpmeet: may he be comforted in his immeasurable loss by the thought of her infinite reward. Greatly did we rejoice, when reading this charming book, to come across the following:—

"1888. The New Year opened brightly upon her, and thus she wrote:—'For more than a month I have had no breathlessness by night or by day. It is like a new world to me, and it is so nice to be able to run all over the house, and to do all my work, just as I used to do. I get out a great deal in summer, so I look forward to the bright days coming again.' It was the summer of glory, however, that was to burst upon her, before the bright days of another earthly summer should come. Meantime she was brightness itself in the domestic scene. 'As for me, I am never out; but I am as happy as I can be, praising him who has healed me, and done so much for me.' 'I am as happy as I can be'— yes, and with all the old winsome power of making others happy! The few Lord's-days she was now to spend on earth were radiant with spiritual joy. When I used to return home after service in the church, she would, with beaming countenance, say, 'How short the time looks since you left! I wondered when I heard your footstep at the door. I have had a service to myself; I sang, I prayed, I read the Bible, and I have had a sermon from Mr. Spurgeon.'"

It is worth working hard from day to day to prepare and revise sermons, to give to such an invalid a spiritual meal. There are doubtless thousands like her, "detained before the Lord"; and the thought that our penny sermon furnishes them with a preacher when they cannot get out to the public assembly, is more than a full reward for thirty-four years of continuous publication.

We have enriched the magazine with extracts from this lady's memoir: all intended to whet the appetites of our readers, and make them buy and read the work.

Professor William Graham, D.D. Essays: Historical and Biographical. Edited by his Brother. With Personal Reminiscences by Dr. W. M. TAYLOR, of New York. Nisbet.

THESE essays are exceedingly pleasant reading, and withal as profitable as pleasant. We have placed in our pages this month an extract from a lecture on Calvin and Calvinism, which will show the drift of Dr. Graham's theology. He has passed away from among us; and we are glad that Dr. W. M. Taylor was able to seize upon his mantle as he was taken up from among us, and now exhibits it to us in the form of an interesting memoir. Our readers will excuse the mournful pleasure with which we subjoin the closing paragraphs. Well do we remember our happy meeting at the table of our Lord ; but we little dreamed that it was the closing scene of such a life.

"But now these reminiscences must come to an end. The last time I saw my friend was in the month of July, 1887. I arrived in London on Saturday evening, the ninth of that month, intending to proceed early the next week to Homburg. Before I had been ten minutes in the hotel, Graham was in my room. He stayed with me till nearly ten o'clock; and arranged to meet me early next day and accompany me to morning service in the Metropolitan Tabernacle, that we might hear Mr. Spurgeon—which we did. The sermon of the great preacher that day was peculiarly tender. His text was Jacob's blessing of the sons of Joseph ; and as he had himself been, during the week, in the Essex pulpit that used tŏ be occupied by his venerable grandfather, his discourse was redolent of the experience through which there he had passed. It touched us both very deeply ; and at the close we went in to shake hands with the preacher. After a brief but cordial greeting, we went down with him to the communion service, at which Mr. Spurgeon seated us with the elders on the platform. He asked me to ' give thanks' over the bread, and Dr. Graham to 'give thanks' over the cup; and at the close of all offered a brief prayer himself. We had a delightful season ; and after it was over, Graham came with me to the hotel, dined, and spent an hour or two. Then I saw him take the omnibus to go to his friend Dr. Edmond, for whom, in the absence of his colleague, he was to preach that evening, and I went to worship in the Westbourne Church with my friend Dr. Morison. We hoped to see each other after my return from a three weeks' trip on the Continent ; but our plans were frustrated, and so *that* was our farewell. We had spoken our last word to each other—

' Ah! little thought we 'twas our last.'

But it *is* pleasant to think that the table of the Lord was almost the last place at which we were together on earth. May we meet at the table of celestial communion, to be for ever with the Lord !

"I cannot think of him as dead ; and in the highest sense he is not dead, for to quote from the first book he gave me—

' Saints that seem to die in earth's rude strife,
    Only win double life ;
  They have but left our weary ways
  To live in memory here, in heaven by love and praise ' "

" *Through Samaria*" to *Galilee and the Jordan.* By J. L. PORTER, D.D. Nelson and Sons.

THIS is a glorious volume: a royal feast for a Bible student. We speak from the experience of the couch of weariness, when we say that it is a rest and a refreshing to gaze upon the many scenes in the Holy Land so fairly depicted by the pencil, and then to read the fresh and life-like descriptions of Dr. Porter. However well acquainted the reader may be with Scripture cŏuntries, he will meet here with something which will be new to him, and as instructive as new. If you have money to spare, you will never grudge it upon such a book.

Jeremiah: his Life and Times. By Canon T. K. CHEYNE. Nisbet.

POOR Jeremiah is in the pit again, sinking in deep mire ; and, in addition, heavily chained. The Babylonians spared him ; but in this book he is in far worse hands than those of the Chaldeans.

The Temple of Solomon. By THOMAS NEWBERRY. James Nisbet and Co. Price one shilling.

NOTES of four addresses by the "Editor of the Englishman's Bible," to which work the lecturer refers us " for fuller and more complete information."

Seven, the Sacred Number. By RICHARD SAMUELL. Kegan Paul and Co.

IT is well known, and widely acknowledged, that "seven" is a number frequently used in a mystic sense throughout the Holy Scriptures. Hence the sanction and the sanctity it has acquired in legend and in lore outside the circle of divine inspiration. Who among our boys and girls has not heard of "the seven wonders of the world," "the seven wise men of Greece," "the seven champions of Christendom," "the seven sleepers of Ephesus," and sundry stories of similar order? Our author seems to imagine that he has wandered out of the beaten track, and turned up virgin soil; for he says, "Not finding in any English work such full information on the subject as he wished, he determined to seek it from the Scriptures themselves." Therefore he searches the Bible to find "sevens"; and they turn up, to his intense satisfaction, in endless variety. His finding is that "number pervades nature," and "seven predominates in Scripture." Were any particular friend of ours to ask for a private opinion, we might probably whisper in his ear that his discovery of "heptadic occurrences of words and phrases," taking his figures for granted, may and must, in many instances, imply much more of coincidence than design.

The main question with us, after all, is the moral of the whole work. You have to pick this up at odd points; but we are fairly posed at the main issue. One little sip from the stream of symbols may help such of our young friends as read our paragraphs out loud for mutual edification to a little liveliness. Here it is—"There is, occasionally, noticeable in Scripture a certain connection between the numbers *six* and *seven*. . . . Perhaps the most remarkable is in connection with the two genealogies of our Lord, given respectively by Matthew and Luke. . . . . It can be by no accident that our Lord is the sixty-sixth in descent from God, through Adam, in one line, and seventy-seventh in another. What, then, does it mean? Six is man's number, as seven is God's; and the two numbers being used here, doubt-

less point to the fact that our Lord was at once both Son of man and Son of God. So, in his very name, 'Ιησοῦς Χριστός, Jesus Christ, the human name, *Jesous*, contains six letters, and the official name, *Christos*, seven letters" (p. 456).

For dilettante students of divinity, this *farrago libelli*, a very medley of minute manuscript, may appear delightful. It is, certainly, too discursive to be dreary. "Sevens" our author has sought after, and "sevens" he has found. They are strewn about or strung together in countless multiples and combinations. All nature vibrates with the symphony, all science repeats the echo. "*Nunquam aliud natura, aliud sapientia dixit.*" In the study of sight or sound, you meet with it. Are there not seven colours in the sunlight, and are there not seven notes in music? (p. 385). In the Prayer-book, as well as in the Pentateuch, you discover the same arrangement. (Appendix G compared with chapter I.) Chronologies and genealogies, of course, run in corresponding order (p. 340). On the sincerity of the author we cast not a shadow of doubt. Is there anything worth a groat in his discovery? Well, we have carefully summed up the evidence, and we confidently leave the verdict to a competent jury of our subscribers.

Bible Studies: Studies in Mark and in Jewish History. The International Sunday-school Lessons for 1889. By GEORGE F. PENTECOST, D.D. Hodder and Stoughton.

THESE pages must be useful to teachers who wish to be prepared to meet their classes. They are gracious and edifying, though not very fresh or deep. The passage about our Lord's reception of little children and the baptism of such seems rather confused to be written by a Baptist, and we suppose that Dr. Pentecost still holds Baptist views. It would be hard to tell from that paragraph what he holds: we cannot say that we admire dubious voices upon such subjects.

Saved at Sea. By Mrs. O. F. WALTON. Religious Tract Society.

As brisk and bracing as a sea-breeze.

The Disciples' Prayer: being Notes of Sermons on our Lord's Prayer. By Rev. J. M. GIBBON. Elliot Stock.

GOOD things said in an original, and, sometimes, startling way. We have had to look at some sentences several times, for they looked awkward; but on further examination we have seen that the author must mean right. It must have been lively work to hear these sermons on what is commonly called "the Lord's Prayer," but which is far more accurately styled "The disciples' prayer." There is a rush and a dash about Mr. Gibbon's style, and withal a brave faithfulness, and a personal driving home of truth, which we greatly admire. We should not subscribe to every sentence here written, but we feel all the better for making the acquaintance of this living and struggling book.

The Sun of Righteousness, and the Dark River. By WILLIAM M. FERRAR. Elliot Stock.

A FAIRLY good book, if you will only take the trouble to find out its merits. But surely a volume of over three hundred and sixty pages ought to contain a syllabus, index, or key to its contents. We had to make our own survey before we discovered whether it was even broken up into chapters. At length we ascertained the titles of four fresh departures, which we pencilled on the fly-leaf for our own guidance. A brief preface tells us that the author, avoiding controversy, simply and sincerely upholds the Christian faith, in its broad acceptation, against scientific scepticism, modern thought, and open infidelity. This is an excellent design, and we welcome into the field any man who comes on this errand.

We became curious to know for whose benefit the work was compiled. Obviously not for believers, to certify them concerning truths of which they are fully assured! And, as obviously, not for adversaries, to smite them hip and thigh for invading our sacred territory. Well, we skimmed the surface till, at page 113, we got a solution of our riddle. The book is chiefly intended for labouring men, who, with little leisure for reading, seek intellectual treats of an evening by listening to free-thought lecturers. With many such we can well imagine the author has met in Tasmania, and he has longed to do them good. Nor can we think that he will be unsuccessful. Far be it from us to challenge his methods. If he opens his essays (notably chapters I. and IV.) with descriptions of the seasons, or of the scenery of nature, he certainly places his well-assorted library at the service of his friends by a supply of elegant and substantial extracts from pure literature. This should suggest a bright idea to amateur missioners of the gospel to rural towns and outlying hamlets. Intersperse bright passages from brilliant authors in your homely addresses. Jocular anecdotes are nearly played out: authentic history and genuine biography must take their place as we approach the twilight of a new century. The School Board will make it morally essential that teachers who, by lectures and other secular agencies, appeal to the common people of higher education, should do so in a nobler way than heretofore. The educated people must be regaled with wholesome food for the mind, and entertained with classic music rather than with nigger melodies. If this be so, there will be an end of much of the nonsense which degrades the present period, and men like our author will be welcomed with their solid teaching rather than mere jesters and story-tellers.

Beyond the Stars; or, Heaven, its Inhabitants, Occupations, and Life. By THOMAS HAMILTON, D.D. T. and T. Clark.

A GOOD book upon a grand subject. If there is nothing startling here, it is because Dr. Thomas Hamilton thinks more of the sobrieties of Scripture than of the marvels of speculation. His writing is solid: he dissipates dreams, but he establishes authorized hopes. He deals with the famous passage in Peter about "the spirits in prison," and has a blow at the dream of "the larger hope." Altogether, with its clear type, this is a book which a believer will enjoy all the more when he draws nearer to those blessed fields "beyond the stars."

When I was a Boy in China. By VAN PHON LEE, a Native of China, now resident in the United States. Blackie and Sons.

A CURIOSITY. Written by a Chinese youth. We already know most of the information, but it is curious to get it from a real Chinaman. The little book is written as one would suppose an Anglicized Chinese would write.

Life's Problems, Here and Hereafter. An Autobiography. By GEORGE TURESDELLE FLANDERS. Dickinson.

A MAN brought up in orthodox ways breaks loose from the Bible, and fashions a religion for himself. He is honest, but he is self-conceited; for he prefers the infallibility of his own mind to the infallibility of Scripture. He is convinced of the immortality of the soul, for *he sees a ghost—* a statement quite as easily doubted as any revelation of Scripture. He believes in God, and in providence, and he is specially strong in his belief in prayer—confirmed therein by a visit to Ashley Down, and the reading of Mr. Müller's Orphanage Reports. In fact, he arrives at right conclusions upon many points; but his religion lacks the heart which mourns for sin, and finds comfort in the Saviour's death. Lacking this, to our mind, it lacks the vital point. If this man is in the way, we fear that he tumbled over the wall, and came not in by the wicket gate. Yet, looking upon him with all his blunderings and maunderings about the future state, we love him as our Lord loved the young man in the gospel, and we pray that he may yet be led to the feet of Jesus. This book is an interesting study to one confirmed in the faith, as showing where mere reason may wander, and yet again, how the Bible may unconsciously sway those who think themselves most free from its influence. To those who are not strong on their feet the speculations of this free-lance might prove a snare, and, therefore, we recommend them to let them alone. In fact, we do not recommend the book to anybody; for, at its very best, it is but a fabric based upon the sand of human thought, and is not founded upon the rock of "Thus saith the Lord."

Anecdotes of Natural History. By Rev. F. O. MORRIS. Partridge.

JUST the sort of book to keep ever before the eyes of our young people. We are glad to look it over again, and renew our acquaintance with Harrison Weir and his large circle of animal friends. Two shillings buys this book.

Birds and Beasts. By Rev. J. G. WOOD. Shaw and Co.

WE have only to say that this is one of the Rev. J. G. Wood's Natural History books, and our readers know that something good is before us. Being profusely illustrated and handsomely bound, this is, no doubt, prepared for a Christmas-box. In our young days we had many a box which could not for a moment be compared with such a noble volume as this.

Crime, its Causes and Remedy. By L. GORDON RYLANDS, B.A. T. Fisher Unwin.

VERY sensible remarks upon crime and its punishment. All our parliament men should read it, and, indeed, all who regard themselves as philanthropists. Painful as the subject is, our author has managed to make his book extremely interesting.

Lewis's New Readings. Selections from the best Poets, Prose Writers, and Speakers. Lewis, Market Street, Manchester.

A WONDERFUL form of advertisement: a book worth a shilling is sold for a penny, and so the fame of *Lewis, of Manchester,* is kept ever green. The former selection of readings was cleverly made, and so is this.

Drake and the Dons. By Rev. RICHARD LOVETT, M.A. Religious Tract Society.

THE self-imposed task of the Editor to provide a really good boys' book in connection with the Tercentenary Celebration of the Defeat of the Spanish Armada has been admirably accomplished. The ancient chronicles have been allowed to speak for themselves, and there is much novelty in the old-fashioned style. The portraits, maps, and illustrations are as interesting as the text, and the whole combined makes up a capital book for boys.

Back Streets and London Slums. By FREDERICK HASTINGS. Religious Tract Society.

GRAPHIC writing, but truthful. It would do every godly man good to read and see what needs to be done, and must be done, before the church will have discharged her obligations to this city of millions. Altogether a remarkable little manual of the slums.

Curve Pictures of London. By ALEXANDER B. MACDOWALL. One shilling. Sampson Low and Co.

AN extraordinary series of diagrams, conveying a large amount of instruction as to the moral and social condition of London. Leaders of armies need good maps of the country they invade: these are social maps of the state of our vast city. The idea is novel and valuable. Lovers of statistics will value the painstaking which has compressed so much information into a small space, and set it before the eye in squares and lines. When we read of a Norwich of prostitutes, and a Huntingdon of known criminals, we have a more painful idea of our degradation than any figures could convey; and when we see the line of London's population overtopping that of Scotland, we are more appalled than when we only see the number written down in millions.

Tempted London : Young Men. Hodder and Stoughton.

WE have no doubt that these articles were written with the best intentions; but what may be the particular good to be compassed by their general reading we cannot tell. Our own impression is that young men are better if they know nothing about the vicious haunts of London than they ever will be if made fully aware of their ins-and-outs. Prurient literature, whose publication at the moment we thought absolutely imperative, has done more to defile our people than anything else attempted in modern times. We fear that the plan of reforming by giving publicity is of very doubtful efficacy: it advertises evil, and increases the temptation which it is supposed to expose. This may be an old-fashioned notion; but we dare not do other than express it, and thus our review will

not be favourable to the sale of this book, though it is well meant.

The Story of our Colonies. By H. R. FOX BOURNE. New and revised edition. With six maps. John Hogg.

A REALLY important compilation. We know not where else one could obtain all this information as to our colonies. We do not hesitate to say that a man who does not know the story of our various dependencies is not half educated, however fast he may jabber in French or in German. This should be read by all who think of going abroad, and by all who intend to stay at home. It is a fine volume for four-and-six.

Romance of the Mountains. By ASCOTT R. HOPE. John Hogg.

WHAT a book for boys! Not a religious work, but breezy and healthy, having, as a possible fault, the breeding of desires to climb Alpine summits and tempt the glacier's crevasses. These pages are sure to be read, for they are a web of stories, legends, adventures, scenes, and so forth, infinitely superior to fiction, and yet quite as romantic. Priced too low at 3s. 6d.

Short Biographies for the People. By VARIOUS WRITERS. Vol. V. Religious Tract Society.

THIS fifth portion makes up sixty short and useful biographies—or shall we say beautiful miniature portraits? Each volume costs eighteen-pence, and contains a world of charming instruction concerning the lives of the best of our race. Each life has a portrait in the forefront.

Upward and Onward: a Thought-Book for the Threshold of Active Life. By S. W. PARTRIDGE. Partridge & Co.

MR. PARTRIDGE is rather a philosopher than a poet; say rather, he is a little of each. His book has reached its thirteenth thousand, and has received genuine and well-earned tributes of praise. Sound sense is the life-blood of each line. There is no straining after the idiotic hypotheses of the period, and no decrying of the things on which the hopes of ages are reposing. His book will not astound, but it will instruct.

Notes.

SHOULD this month's magazine appear to fall short, the Editor begs to be forgiven. He had all manner of promising irons in the fire, and hopeful designs upon the anvil; but they have come to nought. A slip of the foot on this occasion has turned aside the cup from the lip. Three weeks, which would have been filled up with joyous intervals of writing alternating stretches of repose, have been dedicated to pains and patience. It is well, for so the Lord wills it; but it seems not well as, from the Editor's uneasy chair, we view our untidy work, and marvel that we have done it at all.

Well, if we must tell this poor little story —which in our small life bulges out into a striking incident—it happened thus:—It is our wont on the First Day of the week to break bread in memory of him who bade us "this do"; and this wont has been full of comfort and strength to the hearts of a little band of believers who have gathered in the Master's name, in the room of our hotel. On the last Sabbath of the year, our friend, Mr. Sommerville, and the friends at the Presbyterian Meeting-room, held their Communion Service, and according to our custom our own service was absorbed thereby, that we might in no way divide, but ever unite the family of our Lord. Having given a word from the heart to the hearts of those around the table, our work was done. This left the Sabbath afternoon quite free; and in order to enjoy as complete a rest as possible, four of us walked a short distance from the hotel to an empty villa, where we could sit, and sing, and read, and pray, and no one could visit us, because no one knew where we were. During that afternoon, sitting upon the covered balcony, we had the rolling sea below us, and the smiling hills around us, and enjoyed hearty Christian fellowship.

The rising of a cold and blustering wind rendered it expedient to retire within; and while the windows and doors were being secured on the upper story I quietly led the way downstairs. The stairs are amply carpeted in the middle; and had I walked on the carpet, and kept my hand on the balustrade, all might have gone well; but I trusted to my walking-stick; it slipped, as it was most natural that it should do, upon the smooth marble, and down went the massive form which was so little prepared for the consequent descent. The more those who were present reflect upon the incident of that one ill step, the more are they amazed that it led to nothing worse. With bowed head the sufferer from that fall adores the Lord, who hath said, "Underneath are the everlasting arms."

Our esteemed friend, Dr. J. R. Macduff, and others, have written to us of similar, and indeed almost identical experiences in connection with those luxurious man-traps—marble-stairways. There is room for a good racy article upon "the Falls of Men." In that production such questions might be discussed as "Is it better for a thin man or a stout man to fall? Is it better to fall backward or forward? In what figure is it best to close the performance?" To us there was matter enough for present meditation in lost teeth and trembling members. Our dear friends were in sad concern, and we rallied them with a cheery word about painless dentistry, sat down upon a chair, and joined with them in singing praise to God for so special an escape.

That Sabbath evening closed in with no great evil to deplore: a bruised knee seemed to be the only evil token. Soon the Scripture, which assures us that, if one member suffers, all the other members suffer with it, had a very emphatic illustration in our flesh, and bones, and tendons, and nerves; and in a day or two we also learned how intimate is the connection between flesh and spirit. To anguish of body followed shattering of mind, so that thought was confused. We now tell the story with a running pen, but a week ago we could not have written a line without blundering, or even forgetting what we had intended to have said.

It was at this time, when no one could tell whether the consequences would be merely to flesh and tendon, or to mind and thought, that I was called upon to telegraph to the beloved congregation at the Tabernacle, and I did so according to my best judgment, and the writing which was delivered to the clerk was in terms of clearest accuracy. I felt that, as I could be sure of nothing as to my own condition, I had better make no hasty statement. At the same time, I did not wish to raise a needless fear, and, therefore, I gave for a text Matthew vi. 34: "Take therefore no thought for the morrow: for the morrow shall take thought for the things of itself. Sufficient unto the day is the evil thereof." Alas! it pleased the movers of the wires to resort to the fifth instead of the sixth chapter, and consequently my brethren received the admonition, "Swear not at all"—a superfluity, to say no more.

Here, then, I find myself—lame through the fall, weak through its consequences, but in good hope that no evil will remain for permanent regret. I have risen out of utter prostration to fierce pain, and from that again to comparative ease; a fierce cough has left me with a feeble voice; and so one might go through a graduated list of miseries which have moderated into mercies; but what of it all? The good hand of the Lord is with us, and let his name be praised. Tribulation worketh patience, and patience experience, and the experience of one is for the profit of many, and the glory of God. I hope to be back as soon as I can walk, and to preach as soon as I can think out a sermon, and stand long enough to preach it.

The great kindness and true fidelity of the church at the Tabernacle have been proven beyond precedent by the present condition of its affairs. We cannot too greatly rejoice in God for sparing to us our beloved brother, Mr. William Olney, who, with other honoured helpers, has sustained the full burden of the service while our brother, J. A. Spurgeon, has been laid aside, and other church officers have also been disabled. Blessed be God for a people worth leading, and men of God in the church so fit to lead them!

The waters have met of late. Our venerable sire, John Spurgeon, paid a visit to his brother, Samuel Spurgeon, of Maldon, and, alas! during that visit his brother's wife died. This has been a great blow to our father, and he has been ill. C. H. S. was stricken down while seeking health, while his wife remained a special sufferer with increasing pain; then J. A. S. was again and again brought very low, and rendered unable for active service. Last of all, a trial for some little while expected came to its complete development, for our son Charles, of Greenwich, whose incessant labours have tried him with almost perpetual neuralgia of the head, has been compelled to follow the orders of the physician, and accept the loving suggestion of his church to take a voyage to New Zealand and back. He hopes to see his brother Thomas and return. God grant it may turn out to be a sure cure! It is a singular gathering of the floods of trial. But the Lord sitteth King for ever and ever.

According to promise, we give this month an account of the *Auxiliary Book Fund*, which we think will interest those of our readers who are helpers of Mrs. Spurgeon's work for poor ministers. Up to the present time Mrs. Spurgeon has been too ill to prepare any report of the operations of *her* Book Fund during the past year. If she is able to do so, she will write a brief record; but if her pain and weakness prevent her from doing this, she will send her subscribers the balance-sheet, list of contributions, and summary of gifts, that they may see that, although the worker has been laid aside for so much of the last twelve months, the work has gone on usefully, though more slowly than before, and that many poor pastors have had to rejoice over the parcels of books which have replenished their scanty stores.

Succeeding notes may contain repetitions, but it seemed good to tell the story from both sides.

Our readers will not fail to notice that our lists of contributions, together with the balance-sheets of the Pastors' College and Society of Evangelists, occupy eleven pages of the present number of the magazine. We have not reduced the quantity of general reading matter, but have inserted eight pages extra. Those who look down

the lists of donations can form only a very slight idea of the personal love for the Editor that is here represented, or of the sympathy which the donors express towards him in his protest against false doctrine and worldliness within the church. Out of the many hundreds of letters recently received from all parts of the kingdom, as well as from abroad, only *two* individuals have written in opposition to the course which the Editor has felt compelled to take.

On *Lord's-day evening, January* 6, after an impressive sermon by the Rev. Mark Guy Pearse, and before the communion service, the members of the church and congregation at the Tabernacle were invited to remain for a season of special prayer on behalf of the senior Pastor. The news of his accident had only become known to most of the members that day, although it happened a week previously. Scarcely a soul in the vast assembly moved; and as three of the elders and Brother Hewson led the supplications of the thousands present, it was a scene never to be forgotten, and, perhaps, unique in the history of the church of Christ. Earnest, sympathetic prayer was also offered for the recovery of Pastor J. A. Spurgeon, who was laid aside by illness, and unable to occupy his brother's place.

On *Monday evening, January* 7, the prayer-meeting at the Tabernacle was of a special character in connection with the "Week of United and Universal Prayer." In the absence of Pastor J. A. Spurgeon, Pastor J. Douglas, M.A., of Kenyon Chapel, presided, and gave an earnest, spiritual address, founded on Psalm ciii. 1—5. The following neighbouring ministers took part in the devotional service:—Pastors J. Creer, W. H. Edwards, W. Exton, W. Glanville, W. Mottram, B. Senior, and F. J. Smith. Mr. A. J. Arnold gave an interesting account of the principles and operations of the Evangelical Alliance, especially recounting marked instances of spiritual blessing and increase to churches in Asia Minor and other distant regions, through the meetings for united prayer promoted by the Alliance.

On *Lord's-day evening, January* 13, as the news from Mentone made it apparent that the Pastor's fall had injured him more seriously than had been at first supposed, the Rev. Newman Hall, who was preaching at the Tabernacle, somewhat shortened the service, and again almost the whole congregation remained to pray for the beloved sufferer in the distant land. Mr. Hall, Mr. William Olney, and three of the elders, pleaded in the name of the assembled multitude that pain might be abated, weakness removed, and health and strength restored; and *the prayers were heard*, for on the following evening, while a large number of the same people had met together to continue their prayers and supplications, a telegram from the Pastor arrived, announcing that he had that day been able to go out for a short ride. From this welcome news it was concluded that he was much better, and for this token of the divine faithfulness and lovingkindness grateful thanksgivings were expressed to the Lord.

POOR MINISTERS' CLOTHING SOCIETY.—
Mrs. Evans asks us to acknowledge, with thanks, the receipt of a parcel from B. H. R., Clapham. Contributions of money, materials for making up, or clothes, are always welcome.

A box of books was also received from C. B., East Dulwich, and at once forwarded to a country minister, who was very grateful for its contents.

COLLEGE.—Mr. J. L. Keys, jun., has completed his course with us, and settled at Tenbury, Worcestershire.

Mr. T. W. Medhurst, after serving the church at Lake Road, Landport, faithfully and well for nearly twenty years, is leaving Portsmouth, and going to Hope Chapel, Canton, Cardiff. We wish him great happiness and blessing in his new sphere.

Mr. T. D. Cameron, late of Willenhall, has gone to Millport, Cumbrae, N.B.; Mr. J. Davis, late of Millwall, has accepted the pastorate at Long Preston, near Leeds; Mr. J. Hart has removed from Potter's Bar, to Stotfold, Bedfordshire; and Mr. A. McDougall, from Oban, to Bunessan, Island of Mull, N.B.

We feel sure that many of our brethren will be interested in the following letters from their fellow-students in India and Australia. The sight of these signatures brings tears to our eyes, joy to our heart, and a prayer to our lips, as we remember each brother, and commend him to the Lord in grateful sympathy:—

"Calcutta, October 29, 1888.

"Beloved President,—We send you again our hearty greetings, and warmest love and sympathy. Many miles are between us, and the distance from you to us is far; but yet our love and esteem for you make us feel as if we were as near as we could be, and know no distance that is too far for us to reach. We are bound to you by ties that cannot be broken. We are one with you in sympathy, and prayer, and work; and one with you in the struggle for right, and the battle with wrong. We know no Lord or Master but him of the thorny crown and wounded side. We know no symbol but the cross, for by it we hold and are held. We know no book but the Bible in our conflict with evil. And so, by the sorrow of him who suffered unto death, of him who 'bore our sins in his own body on the tree', we struggle for 'the faith once delivered to the saints.'

"Your sorrows are ours, because we love you. Your burdens are ours, because we trust you. Your battles are ours, because we are 'bone of your bone, and flesh of

your flesh'; we are one in Christ in a union that unites us in all things.

"Our work is hard, and so is all work that is honestly done; but our hopes are great, and faith leaps forward to the time when we shall be 'complete in him'—our work, our desires, and hopes, and friendships all 'complete in him.' And so we stand with our hands stretched out to you, and to our brethren in Australia, and they to others in America, and they to others nearer home, till we fancy we see the whole world belted by men that love you, and pray for you, and will stand by you 'till death us do part.'

"Beloved President, believe us all to be, faithfully and lovingly, yours in the Lord Jesus Christ,

"G. H. HOOK, Lall Bazar, Calcutta.
"J. G. POTTER, Agra, N.W.P.
"JOHN STUBBS, Patna.
"GEO. J. DANN, Allahabad.
"ROBERT SPURGEON, Madaripore.
"W. S. MITCHELL, Dinapore.
"R. MAPLESDEN, Secunderabad.
"FRANK DURBIN, Colombo, Ceylon."

"Melbourne, Victoria,
"15th Nov., 1888.
"To the Rev. C. H. Spurgeon.

"Honoured and Beloved President,—We have been brought together from the different Colonies of Australia to celebrate the Jubilee of the Baptist Churches of Victoria. It naturally occurs to us to give expression in a letter at this time to the affection which glows in all our hearts towards you.

"We begin by assuring you of our continued love for the great foundation doctrines of the everlasting gospel, and of our determination, in the strength of God, to be loyal to the truth as it is in Jesus till we meet our Lord.

"We cannot cease to praise God for your personal influence over us, and for all the equipment for service and sustenance in labour we have received through you and the College.

"The main features of the Victorian Baptist Jubilee, which will make it gloriously memorable, are, the signal display of the hand of God in the origin and history of the Colonial churches, the raising of £50,000 for the Victorian Baptist Fund, and, notably, the presence with us of the honoured Dr. Alexander Maclaren. This servant of God has perceived our peculiar spiritual needs and dangers out here, and has counselled us how to meet them, and with an inspiration caught from God himself, his words have kindled in us an increasing love to Jesus, and a holier devotion to his service.

"We may not multiply words, but we cannot close our epistle without the old heart-grip with which we were wont of yore to part from one another.

"How can we avoid feeling how great a help to us, and to all the churches of Christ in Australasia, a visit from you would be? How can we refrain from again urging you to consider the desirability of such a visit, both for your own health's sake, as well as for our good? Do come and see us!

"May our fervent prayers gain for you fresh anointing for study, preaching, and endurance! We desire to stand around you, though so far away, as a body-guard of loving younger soldiers in the glorious service for the King. We cannot grasp your hand in a letter, but we know we may depend on the love which has never been withheld from your old students, who now subscribe themselves, in loyalty to King Jesus, and in love to you,

"WILLIAM CHRISTOPHER BUNNING, West Melbourne.
"ALFRED BIRD, Ballarat.
"EDWARD ISAAC, Brunswick.
"WILLIAM CLARK, St. Kilda.
"ROBERT WILLIAMSON, South Yarra.
"JAMES BLAIKIE.
"FREDERICK HIBBERD, Ashfield, New South Wales.
"W. WHALE, Brisbane.
"WILLIAM HIGLETT, Toowoomba, Queensland.
"JAS. R. COOPER, Portland, Victoria.
"A. J. CLARKE, Wooloomooloo, New South Wales.
"J. A. SOPER, Petersham, N.S.W.
"ROBERT McCULLOUGH, Tasmania.
"J. E. WALTON, Tasmania.
"JOHN DOWNING, Victoria.
"WILLIAM E. RICE, North Adelaide.
"THOMAS BREEWOOD.
"MATTHEW MORRIS, Kapunda, S.A.
"GEORGE D. COX, Geelong.
"F. G. BUCKINGHAM, South Melbourne.

EVANGELISTS.—The testimonies concerning the success of the work of our beloved brethren, *Messrs. Fullerton & Smith*, in Central and South London, are so numerous just now that we can only give extracts from the letters of thanks from the churches visited.

Pastor Williams (Upton Chapel) writes:—"The labours of these honoured servants of our Master were more appreciated than I can tell you, and the blessings enjoyed will, I am sure, be a source of permanent strength to our church, and an eternal joy to many hearts."

Pastor J. Baillie (Bloomsbury Chapel) says:—"We had been praying for great things, and expecting them, but we found the Lord able to exceed our petitions. Had you been present at the large enquirers' meeting which we held in the lecture-hall last night, your heart would have been rejoiced to hear the testimonies of God's power to save; and many steady, matured Christians added their witness to the fresh power and renewed consecration which they had experienced during the mission."

Pastor H. O. Mackey sends us a long and interesting report of the services at Peckham Park Road Chapel, from which we cull the following :—

"Mr. Smith's touching incidents, related with so much genuine pathos; his cheery songs and solos; and then Mr. Fullerton's solid expositions of Scripture, especially the foundation truths about sin, spiritual death, the need of a dying, atoning Saviour, and the infinite love of God as seen at Calvary, soon won the attention of the people, and the personal acceptance of the evangelists' messages. Seldom have we known a finer blending of the instructive with the earnestly exhorting to immediate . decision than was nightly listened to from Mr. Fullerton. On the Sunday afternoon, the meeting for men only was quite filled; and a grand sight it was to watch their faces as they listened to the racy, yet solemn appeals of both the brethren. The sound of their massive voices in the hymns was one to remember for many a day. Sunday evening saw the chapel packed long before the time for beginning the service, and hundreds went away disappointed, whilst a goodly number attended an overflow service in the schoolroom opposite. Best of all, great spiritual results have followed. No fewer than 150 persons went into the enquiry-room. Many of these have avowed their conversion to God, their newly-found faith in Jesus. Amongst these some are the children of the officers and members of the church, some are restored backsliders, and others are men and women who for many, many years have never gone inside a house of God. Although the mission only lasted nine days, it will not be merely a nine days' wonder; the neighbourhood has been touched, the church has been filled with joy, souls have been born again, and the Saviour has been greatly honoured."

Messrs. Fullerton and Smith conducted the Watch-night service at the Tabernacle. There was a good congregation considering the fact that New Year's Eve was one of the foggiest nights of the winter, and many who would have been present dared not venture out. Our brethren have been at Exeter Hall during the greater part of January, under the auspices of the Central Y.M.C.A. This month they go to Shoreditch Tabernacle and Dalston Junction Chapel.

Mr. Burnham has had to rest much longer than he anticipated, but he trusts that now he will be able to continue his work for some time. While resting at Malvern he has taken part in the united meetings for prayer. He has now gone to Dorset to fulfil engagements that had to be postponed through his illness, and afterwards he is to conduct a mission at Rotherhithe New Road. Pastor W. H. Broad kindly took Mr. Burnham's place at Ashdon and Radwinter. Brother Layzell writes: "Mr. Broad proved an excellent substitute. We have already seen the first-fruits from these services, and are prayerfully looking for the harvest."

Mr. Harmer's mission at Orpington, though held just before Christmas, was well attended, and productive of much blessing.

On New Year's Eve, in conjunction with *Mr. Parker*, he commenced a series of services at Crewkerne, which were so successful that they were continued until January 15th. Mr. Parker then went on to Falmouth, and Mr. Harmer, after a few days at home, went to March, Cambridgeshire. This month he is to be at Cheddar, Somerset; and Tuddenham, Ipswich.

Mr. Carter is much encouraged by the progress that is being made at Farnworth, Lancashire. He has recently put forth efforts to carry on evangelistic work · by means of two new literary productions— *The Pioneer Quarterly* and *Pioneer Papers*, published by Alexander and Shepheard. These are likely to be very useful, the *Pioneer Papers* especially. They are much better for giving away than ordinary tracts, for they contain nothing but the Word of God, judiciously arranged under special headings.

Pastor J. M. Steven gives this cheering report of *Mr. Harrison's* services at Romford:—"He has a most effective and impressive style of address, and by his clear and forcible exposition of the truth brings conviction home to the consciences of his hearers. Many have professed faith in Christ during his mission here."

ORPHANAGE.—*The Christmas Festival.*— By the kindness of many friends, everything calculated to make the children happy was supplied without stint, and the Christmas festivities of 1888 were in every respect equal to those of former years. The dining-hall was gaily decorated, and was worthy of the Knights of the Round Table; but, alas! the beloved President was a thousand miles away in quest of health and repose. On the tables, a box of figs, a cosaque, an orange, a Christmas card, and a new shilling were placed for every child; and when the merry party, numbering nearly half a thousand, trooped in, their eyes sparkled with gratitude, and the newcomers could not repress, at the same time, a look of sheer astonishment. A goodly number came to witness the sight, and the general verdict was, that it could not be surpassed at any Christmas gathering in the land. The trustees present were Messrs. W. P. Olney, W. C. Murrell, B. W. Carr, C. F. Allison, and H. Smith; and they each presided at a table, other friends making up the necessary number. Grace having been sung, and a few words spoken by the Head Master, Mr. Carr read the following letter from the President:—
"Dear Girls and Boys,—I wish you a Merry Christmas. Think of me as I shall think of you when you are eating the plum-pudding. Don't eat too much, but enjoy yourselves over head and ears.
"I hope you have each one deserved a thousand good marks during the year.

Mr. Ladds gives you good characters; but I do not think even he will dare to say that no boy is up to mischief, and that all the girls are quiet at all times. I think you are better than the average of laddies and lassies, and this makes me feel very happy about you. God bless you, and make you noble men and women in due time! I wonder which boys and girls will be missionaries; certainly not all, but all may be useful Christians. May the loving Jesus make you so!
"Give the Trustees three cheers, and do the same for the friends who give the shillings, the figs, and other things. I will be listening about two o'clock, and if I hear you cheering, I will cheer too; and if you hear my voice, you will hear me say, 'Another cheer for Mr. Charlesworth, the Matrons, and the Masters, &c.'
"Bless God when you go to bed for giving you a happy day, and ask him to make you his own children.
"Yours lovingly,
"C. H. SPURGEON."
Cheers for the absent President, with whom the children always associate Mrs. Spurgeon; cheers for the Vice-President and Mrs. James Spurgeon, and the Trustees; cheers for the Head Master, Secretary, and staff; and cheers for all donors; followed in succession: and if the echoes did not reach the President in his warm retreat, the fault could not be attributed to the youngsters, for contrary to the admonitions which others receive in the presence of company, they did their best to be heard as well as seen. When the Head Master called for "silent grace," every head was bowed, and in the deep and sudden hush, the eyes of many of the onlookers were moistened with tears; and as the children filed out to their play-rooms, many a heart breathed the prayer, "God bless the boys and girls of the Stockwell Orphanage!"
On *Wednesday, January* 2, the mothers and other friends of the children spent the afternoon and evening at the Orphanage, when they brought in the sum of £87 18s. 7d. as a practical expression of their gratitude that their fatherless boys and girls had found such a bright, happy, Christian home.

COLPORTAGE.—The New Year is beginning hopefully for the extension of the work of the Association, as arrangements are already made for the opening of two new districts, in connection with the Kent and Sussex Baptist Association, at St. Margaret's and Cowfold, respectively. It is hoped that other Associations will follow the lead, and share the good results so manifest from Colportage work in other districts.

Baptisms at Metropolitan Tabernacle.— January 3, seven.

Pastors' College, Metropolitan Tabernacle.

Statement of Receipts from December 15th, 1888, to January 14th, 1889.

	£	s.	d.		£	s.	d.
Part collection at New North Road Chapel, Huddersfield, per Pastor F. J. Benskin	3	7	0	Collected by Mrs. James Withers :—			
				Messrs. Heelas and Co. 1 1 0			
Mr. A. A. Lennard, per J. T. D.	0	5	0	Mr. P. Davies ... 0 10 0			
Mr. Thomas Scoular	2	0	0	Mr. G. Oakshott ... 0 10 0			
Miss M. M. Ferguson	1	0	0		2	1	0
Mr. and Mrs. W. Blott	5	0	0	A debtor to grace ...	2	0	0
Miss E. Hudson	0	7	0	Part valuation fee ...	5	0	0
Dr. and Mrs. Brougham	3	0	0	Mr. W. Casson ...	1	0	0
Mr. W. C. Greenop	1	1	0	Mr. A. Stewart ...	0	5	0
Mr. R. Greenwood	0	10	0	Dr. MacGill	1	1	0
Mr. J. Pentelow	1	0	0	Mr. and Miss Bloom	2	0	0
Mr. Elijah Bew	1	10	0	Mrs. Reed	100	0	0
Mr. R. Purser	0	10	0	*Annual Subscription :—*			
Mr. W. A. Macfie	1	0	0	Mr. Robert Morgan ...	1	1	0
Mr. J. Thornton	1	0	0	*Quarterly Subscriptions :—*			
A servant	0	5	0	Adelphi ...	1	10	0
Miss Brown	0	5	0	Mr. J. Wilson ...	1	11	9
Mr. J. Mortimer	0	5	0	Mrs. Elgee ...	0	10	6
Mr. C. W. Roberts	5	0	0	*Monthly Subscription.*			
Mr. W. H. Roberts	5	5	0	Mr. R. J. Beecliff	0	2	6
Mr. W. Parlane	10	0	0	Weekly Offerings at Met. Tab. :			
Mr. D. McKercher	1	0	0	Dec. 16 22 11 3			
Miss Ellen Cross	0	5	0	,, 23 24 10 0			
Mrs. Walker	0	5	0	,, 30 24 0 0			
Moiety of proceeds of Mr. Philip Phillips' lectures	5	0		Jan. 6 21 7 6			
Mr. R. Hunt, per J. T. D.	1	1	0	,, 13 15 10 0			
Mrs. Cracknell	0	3	0		107	18	9
Mr. H. Osmond	3	0					
Mr. and Mrs. Parker Gray	1	0			£280	5	6

Stockwell Orphanage.

Statement of Receipts from December 15th, 1888, to January 14th, 1889.

	£	s.	d.		£	s.	d.
Mansfield-street Sunday-school children, per Mr. E. Johnson	2	0	0	Stamps, Miss A. B. Leoder	0	0	9
Collected by Mr. Hinton ..	2	12	9	Sale of S. O. tracts	0	1	0
Mr. Thomas Howell	5	0	0	The executors of the late Mr. G. W. Petter	20	0	0
Shillings for 250 boys, Messrs. Alabaster and Passmore	12	10	0	Miss Coxeter's Bible-class	3	3	0
Miss E. E. Sharpington	0	10	0	Mr. S. Elson	2	10	0
Mrs. Sharpington	0	10	0	Mr. G. Askey ...	0	5	0
Collected by Mrs. Walker	5	7	0	Miss E. Mibroy ...	2	0	0
Miss Clarke ...	0	2	6	The Borough-road Sunday evening class, per Mr. G. Stanhope	0	10	6
Miss Farmer	0	2	6	Mrs. Monk ...	0	10	0
Miss McNab	0	10	0	Mr. W. Strain ...	0	5	0
Collected by Miss McArthur	0	17	6	Rev. W. Dovey ...	0	2	6
Mrs. C. Chapman	0	2	6	Postal order from Plymouth	0	2	6
Mr. F. W. Straker	5	0	0	Postal order from E. W. O.	0	1	0
Messrs. Lothian and Dougall	1	12	5	Miss Fort, per Mr. Henry Smith	1	1	0
Miss Turnbull	0	10	0	Mr. L. A. Spiller ...	0	2	0
Collected by Miss Pentelow	2	0	0	Collected by Mrs. Tullis	1	11	6
Stamps from Dalkeith	0	2	6	Mr. J. O'Gram ...	0	10	0
Mr. James Binstead	0	5	6	Collected by Miss J. Jones	0	7	6
Mr. James Lanchbury	0	5	0	Mr. H. Driver ...	0	10	0
Collected by Mrs. W. T. Clark	0	7	0	Mr. G. T. Jobbins ...	5	0	0
The scholars of Mauchline Free Church Sunday-school, per Mr. D. McKee	0	5	0	Mr. D. Rees ...	0	2	0
Mr. Williams	0	5	0	Mrs. Ferne. per Mrs. J. A. Spurgeon	1	0	0
Mr. D. Goodhall	0	1	0	Master A. B. McMaster	2	1	0
Mrs. Wiley	0	5	0	Mr. G. S. Miller ...	0	5	0
Postal order from Derby	0	7	6	Miss A. Blake ...	3	10	0
Miss E. M. Elford	0	12	0	Mrs. Fowler ...	0	2	6
Mr. E. J. Beaumont	0	4	6	Mr. H. Stevenson ...	0	10	6
Miss Sharp	0	10	0	John-street Baptist Sunday-school, Rodborough, per F. E. D.	0	10	0
Mrs. T. Frohock and friends	0	18	0	Mrs. Hassell	1	1	0
Mr. G. Saunders	1	0	0	Mr. W. E. Chamberlain ...	0	5	0
Mr. Robert D. Aldrick, per Bankers	0	10	0				

	£	s.	d.
Mr. J. Armstrong ...		3	0
Mr. T. J. Fowler ...	6	5	0
Mr. John Pugh ...	2	2	0
Mr. R. Walker ...	0	10	0
Miss E. H. Fielder...	0	2	6
Miss E. M. D. Mattick ...	0	5	0
Collected by Mrs. and Miss Boyd	0	14	0
Mrs. A. Rees ...	0	2	6
Mr. H. Trevanion ...	2	0	0
Mr. and Miss Taylor	0	10	0
Mrs. J. Houston ...	0	5	3
The Misses W. and E. Kay	0	2	6
Mrs. M. Penning ...	0	5	0
Mr. J. Thorn	0	5	0
Miss M. Muir	0	10	0
Mrs. M. Parsons	1	0	0
Mr. S. T. Hudson ...	0	7	0
Stamps from Glasgow	0	5	0
Mrs. Browne	0	2	11
Miss Derrick	0	5	0
Mrs. N. Sparrow	0	10	0
Mrs. Watts ...	0	2	0
Mrs. Cox, sen.	1	0	0
Miss McArthur	0	5	0
The teachers of Regent-street Sabbath-school, per Mr. T. Blayney	7	16	0
Mr. H. Robson, per Mr. B. W. Carr ...	25	0	0
Mr. R. A. James	5	5	0
Mrs. Jamieson	1	0	0
Mr. Thomas	0	4	0
Mr. W. A. Weightman	5	0	0
From Rad, per D. Watt	0	5	0
Mr. Taylor, per Pastor J. Small	0	6	0
Collection at breakfast table, on Christmas morning, by young friends at Hampstead	1		0
Fines in a business, per Mr. R. A. James	4	17	11
From a friend at Winchester	0	2	6
Collected by Miss L. J. Mumford	0	8	6
Mr. T. J. Hughes ...	0	5	0
Mr. Norkett	1	0	0
Sale of Goods	3	1	0
Mrs. F. Fakeley		7	0
Mrs. M. Rogers		10	0
A sermon-reader, Derby...		2	0
Mrs. Farmer...		10	0
Mrs. Fisher ...	0	5	0
Mr. C. Miller		10	0
Mrs. E. W. Price		6	6
Mr. W. Powell		2	6
The Young Women's Bible-class at the Orphanage, per Mrs. James Stiff	0	1	6
The Misses R. and L. Wigney ...	2	1	0
Mr. G. E. Elvin	0	1	6
Mrs. Bell	0		
Mr. W. J. Davidson	10	1	0
Mrs. E. Chambers	0		
Mrs. E. S. White	0	1	0
Mr. F. J. Aldridge...	1	2	0
Mr. H. C. Bridgman	0	6	6
Per Miss L. A. Blight:—			
Mr. Sharp ... 0 5 0			
Mr. E. S. Thoday ... 0 5 0			
Mrs. Thoday 0 5 0	0	15	0
Collected by Mrs. Carwithen	0	3	4
Collected by Miss N. Matthews			9
Mrs. K. Spender	0	14	3
Orphan boys' and girls' collecting-cards (first list)	87	18	7
Miss Edwards' Bible-class	0	7	0
Mrs. Eaton ...	0	5	0
Mrs. E. C. Tanner	0	2	0
Miss Wilmot	0	6	0
Mr. Robotham	1	0	0
Collected by Mr. G. Tolley	1	15	0
With best wishes from a friend, New Barnet	2	0	0
Mr. George Smith ...	0	10	0
A. J. F.	0	10	0

	£	s.	d.
Mr. L. W. Reed ...		5	9
Young Women's Bible-class, Lewin-road, Streatham, per Miss Davis	0	17	6
Mrs. Cracknell	0	3	0
Mrs. Atkinson	0	11	0
Collected by Mrs. Mott	0	18	0
W. B , per Miss Jones	0	2	0
Miss Jones ...	0	2	6
Per Pastor T. Greenwood :—			
Self ... 3 3			
Master T. Greenwood 0 2 0			
Master B. Greenwood 0 2 0	3	7	0
Postal order from Aberdeen	0	5	0
Mr. T. Scoular	2	0	0
Mr. B. E. Knight ...	10	0	0
Mr. H. J. Knight and brother ...	2	0	0
Mr. Thomas Bush ...	0	2	6
Mr. E. Vincent	0	5	0
Mrs. Ling ...	0	5	0
In memoriam, E. ...	1	0	0
Mr. A. M. Arthur ...	1	1	0
Miss Annie Pritchard	0	5	0
Mrs. Stewart and Miss Jane	0	10	0
Mrs. Younger	0	5	0
Mrs. Harrison	0	10	6
Mr. Henry Hill	1	1	0
Mr. H. L. Nunn ...	1	0	0
Miss Yockney ...	0	10	0
Mr. William Hill	1	1	0
A constant reader of Mr. Spurgeon's sermons	0	5	0
Allan and Percy White ...	0	10	0
Nemo ...	1	0	0
In memory of dear father and mother	1	5	0
Mr. J. Marshall	0	10	0
Mr. D. Thomas	1	0	0
Mr. M. Brown	0	2	6
Mr. Thomas P. Potts	0	10	0
Mr. J. Lock ..	1	0	0
Mr. W. Williams ...	0	2	6
Mrs. Cloat ...	0	2	6
Mrs. Alexander, per Mrs. Cloat	0	2	6
Mrs. Taylor ...	0	5	0
Mr. J. Hassall ...	1	0	0
Mr. W. Turnbull ...	5	0	0
Miss E. Skin	0	10	0
Miss J. Scott'	2	0	0
Mrs. Hutchison	1	0	0
Miss Pearce ...	1	1	0
Miss E. Pearce	1	1	0
A friend ...	0	1	6
Stamps from Wisbech	0	2	0
Mrs. Muntons ...	0	1	0
Two friends in Pitcairnfield	0	6	0
Scotch note from Aberdeen	1	0	0
Mr. J. Alabaster ...	20	0	0
Mrs. John Clarke ...	0	5	0
A friend ...	1	0	0
Mr. S. D. Lamb ...	0	5	0
Mr. James Martin ...	0	2	6
Mrs. Cuthbert ...	3	0	0
Miss J. Allan ...	0	2	6
Mr. T. T. Marks, C.E.	2	2	0
Mrs. Cockburn	1	0	0
A. J. R. ...	3	0	0
Rev. J. F. Linn ...	0	2	6
Mr. W. Anderson ...	0	10	0
Mr. W. L. Ferguson	1	0	0
An aged friend ...	0	5	0
Miss E. H. Nelson ...	0	2	0
Mr. George Jingey ...	1	0	0
Master J. E. Freeward ...	0	6	0
Rev. William Parry ...	0	5	0
Mr. James Lundie ...	0	5	0
Mrs. Lundie ...	0	2	0
Miss M. A. Mackay ...	1	0	0
Mr. H. Munro ...	1	0	0
Mrs. T. Poulter ...	1	1	0
Stamps from Arbroath ...	0	2	0
A widow ...	0	3	0

	£	s.	d.
Miss L. Belough	0	1	0
Miss M. M. Ferguson	0	10	0
Mr. James B. Falconer	1	0	0
Mr. and Mrs. W. Blott	5	0	0
Miss H. Jackson	0	14	0
Mr. John Smith	1	1	0
Mrs. J. Toller	0	10	0
W. H. D.	1	0	0
Mrs. Holcombe	1	0	0
Mr. William Church, jun.	0	5	0
Mr. A. Hobson	1	1	0
Mr. William Newton	0	5	0
G. A.	0	10	0
Rev. J. R. Macduff, D.D.	2	2	0
Mrs. C. Norton	0	5	0
Mr. P. T. Adams	1	0	0
Miss Louisa Bush	0	10	0
Pastor George Cobb	0	10	0
Miss Sprot	5	0	0
Mrs. Chapman	0	2	6
Miss E. Hudson	0	7	0
Mr. S. Ashton	0	10	0
Pastor W. G. Clow	0	5	0
Mr. J. B. Near	0	2	6
Mrs. Ellwood	2	0	0
Mr. G. Redman	1	0	0
Two friends	2	0	0
Dr. and Mrs. Brougham	3	10	0
Mr. A. A. Stephens	1	0	0
Miss Scarfe	0	1	0
A thankoffering	0	2	6
Mr. George W. Camps	0	2	6
Mr. William Dunn	1	5	0
Mrs. Ironside	1	0	0
Mr. and Mrs. Brown	0	5	0
Mrs. Chew	0	2	6
Mrs. J. G. Blake	0	5	0
Miss Murray	0	5	0
H. J. F. Meldrum	0	5	0
Mr. W. Turnell	0	10	0
Mrs. Puttock	0	2	6
Mr. A. Jungling	5	0	0
The Misses Cunnington	2	2	0
B. H.	0	10	0
Mrs. Keeley	0	10	6
Mr. William Mitchell	0	10	0
Mr. W. Pinkaman	0	10	6
Mr. and Mrs. Scruby	0	10	0
Mr. James Beere	0	10	0
Mr. Thomas Rose and family	0	10	0
Mr. W. C. Greenop	1	1	0
Mrs. R. B. Dall	0	5	0
Miss A. J. Mallett	1	0	0
Mr. W. O. Little	0	5	0
Mr. E. Davis	1	0	0
Mr. Whittaker	1	1	0
Mr. James Lunn	0	10	0
W. B.	0	10	0
Mr. C. Buchel	1	5	0
Mrs. Pepperdine and friend	0	5	0
Mrs. and Miss Hodges	0	6	0
Mr. F. H. Butler	0	10	0
Mrs. E. Campbell	0	3	0
Mr. G. D. Forbes	0	2	6
Mrs. Cave-B.-Cave	1	0	0
Collected by Miss Woodgate and her pupils	1	0	0
Mr. S J. Clements	1	1	0
Mr. H. Sprigg	5	0	0
A brother ploughman	0	10	0
A friend to the orphans	0	4	0
Postal order from Warrington	0	5	0
Mrs. Boyle	0	5	0
Mr. J. Patterson	0	10	0
Mrs. Briggs	0	5	0
Mr. James Fear	0	5	0
Mrs. Brodie	0	5	0
Mrs. Jackson	0	10	0
Miss Huckett	0	2	6
Mrs. Williams and friend	0	5	0
Mr. W. Oakley	0	2	0

	£	s.	d.		£	s.	d.
Mrs. Anderson	1	0	0				
Mrs. Mills	2	2	0				
Miss C. Field	0	2	6				
Mr. H. Thomas	1	1	0				
Miss M. Pitts	0	5	0				
Mrs. Speed	0	5	0				
Mrs. Salmon	0	5	0				
Mrs. Slade	0	10	0				
Miss Simpson	1	0	0				
Mr. W. Willis	0	12	6				
Mr. W. Longhurst	0	5	0				
Mr. and Mrs. Higgins	0	8	0				
Mrs. Bentall	0	10	0				
Mr. H. A. Matier	1	0	0				
Mr. R. Burgess	0	10	0				
Miss A. Mackenzie	1	1	0				
Mr. A. Ballard	1	0	0				
The Sittingbourne Baptist Sunday-school—boys	1	1	0				
The Sittingbourne Baptist Sunday-school—girls	1	5	0				
					2	6	0
M. B.	1	0	0				
C. G. C.	0	2	0				
W. and M. S., Glasgow	0	10	0				
G., Glasgow	0	2	0				
Mrs. Ferguson	2	0	0				
Mr. John How	1	0	0				
Mrs. Hepworth	0	10	6				
A. C. D.	0	10	0				
Mr. S. Armans	0	5	0				
Mr. W. Furse	1	1	0				
Mrs. Mitchell	0	5	0				
Mr. R. Dale	0	10	0				
Mr. T. Kirkpatrick	0	5	0				
Mr. J. Rugg	1	1	0				
Mr. E. Sparrow	1	0	0				
Mr. and Mrs. Underwood	0	6	0				
Mrs. Houlgate	0	5	0				
Miss Dunbar	0	10	0				
Mrs. Ewart	0	5	0				
Mr. W. Graham	1	0	0				
Rev. J. R. Wood	0	5	0				
Miss A. E. Seymour	0	2	0				
Mr. H. Lincoln, jun.	0	10	0				
G. R. M.	0	5	0				
Mr. C. J. Curtis	0	5	0				
Mr. Hartswell	0	2	0				
Per Mrs. Hickisson:—							
O. L.	0	2	6				
R. S.	0	2	6				
P. P.	0	2	6				
Mrs. Hickisson	0	5	0				
					0	12	6
Mrs. Thomson and friend	1	2	6				
Mrs. Dougall	1	0	0				
Miss E. Lander	0	1	0				
Bessie and Gerty Keylock	0	2	10				
Mrs. Jones	1	3	0				
M. A. D., Trowbridge	0	5	0				
Mr. S. Gallifant	0	4	0				
Widow's mite	0	2	0				
J. C., Paisley	0	5	0				
W. G., Berkhampstead	0	2	0				
Mr. Joseph Hill	10	0	0				
Pastor G. B. Richardson's Bible-class, Eynsford	0	9	0				
Mrs. F. Bridge	0	5	0				
Miss Camps	0	5	0				
Mr. C. H. Ruddick	0	3	0				
Mr. G. W. Irons	2	0	0				
Mr. R. Lewis	0	10	0				
Miss M. A. Moss	0	10	6				
Mr. Elijah Bew	1	10	0				
Workpeople at Southall Brothers and Barclay's, Birmingham, per Mr. J. B. Millard	2	3	0				
Mrs. Mitchell	2	0	0				
Mr. Peter Lamont	0	10	0				
Mrs. H. Kilborn	0	5	0				
Miss E. Kilborn	0	5	0				

	£	s.	d.
Miss H. Husk	0	5	0
Miss A. Barefoot	0	2	6
Mr. H. P. West	1	0	0
Mr. A. McCay	2	0	0
Collected at Sunday dinner-table, per Mr. W. Lewis	0	15	0
Dr. Habershon	10	10	0
Mr. J. B. Elgar	1	0	0
Mr. R. Purser	1	0	0
Mrs. E. Holdsworth	0	10	0
Miss Botsford	0	5	0
A few sermon-readers, per Mr. Thomas Weir	1	5	0
Mr. A. S. Hunter	4	1	3
Mrs. Moorhouse, per Mrs. Way	0	4	0
Friends in the country, per S. M.	0	12	0
Mr. W. A. Macfie	1	0	0
Collected by Miss A. H. Rust	0	6	0
J. and H. Letch	1	1	0
Mrs. Walsham	0	10	0
Mrs. Forbes	5	0	0
Mrs. Clarke	0	5	0
Mr. A. B. Todd	0	10	0
E. and M. H.	1	0	0
Mrs. Lane	0	5	0
Mrs. Frearson	5	0	0
Miss Frearson	0	5	0
A servant girl near Forres	0	2	0
Mr. J. Hooker	0	3	6
A friend in India, per Mrs. Newman	0	15	0
Pastor S. T. Williams	0	10	0
Collected by Miss Cutts	0	5	0
Collected at Llandrindod by Miss I. Harding	1	0	0
Widow Smith and two friends	0	3	0
Mr. Roger Bate	1	0	0
Miss E. L. Smith	0	10	0
Mr. T. Trotman	1	0	0
Miss Shaw	1	0	0
Mrs. Harris and friends	0	4	0
Mr. A. Barrett	1	1	0
Mr. R. Davies	0	5	0
Mrs. Owen Clover	0	15	0
Mr. J. Cook	2	0	0
Mr. J. Newcombe	0	2	6
Mr. A. Hobbs	3	0	0
Collected by Mr. W. Smith	0	10	0
Mr. R. Ellis	0	10	0
Mr. W. Green	0	5	0
Mr. J. Bazeley	0	10	6
Mr. D. Macpherson	0	5	0
"Sixty-eight"	1	0	0
L.	1	0	0
Mr. and Mrs. Drummond Grant	1	0	0
Mr. W. Dorward	1	0	0
Miss De Zoete	1	0	0
Mr. W. L. Maynard	1	0	0
A Burnham native	0	10	0
Mr. W. T. Martin	0	5	0
Mr. H. L. Heritage	0	10	0
A servant	0	5	0
Collected by Miss Hunter	3	11	6
A lover of Bible-truth, Torquay	1	0	0
Collection at Baptist Sunday-school, Niton, Isle of Wight	1	1	0
Mrs. Casburn	0	10	0
Mr. Frank Dodwell	0	5	0
Mr. W. Jones	1	0	0
Mr. Thomas Benton	0	5	0
Mr. N. Leeder	1	0	0
Janet Chalmers and friends	0	2	2
Mrs. Bell	1	5	0
Mr. J. Rossiter	2	2	0
Mr. J. Hole	0	5	0
Mrs. Joyner, sen.	0	10	0
"Rookery"	0	10	0
Mr. J. Aldington	0	8	0
Henley Tabernacle Bible-class	0	10	0
Mr. J. W. Barnaby	0	10	6
Mr. A. C. Barker	1	0	0
Miss J. Webb	0	5	0

	£	s.	d.
Mr. J. Reid	1	0	0
Mrs. Buik	1	0	0
Mr. J. Lewis	2	2	0
Mr. T. Farrow	1	0	0
Mrs. Johnstone	0	5	0
Mr. John McBeth	1	0	0
Willie and Edie Carter	1	0	0
E. A. and E. Dunstan	1	0	0
Mr. James London	0	2	6
Collected by Miss Evelyn Annie Sims	1	5	0
Stamps	0	2	0
Mr. W. Torrance	1	0	0
Mr. James Smith	1	0	0
Mr. and Mrs. David Lang	1	0	0
Mrs. Lees	0	5	0
Mr. T. Davies	0	10	0
Nellie	0	5	0
Mr. and Mrs. M. G. Hewat	2	0	0
J. Stormont and Alex. A. Bisset	0	8	0
Mr. Alex. Sutherland	1	10	0
Mr. Thomas Hoghton	0	10	6
Mr. and Mrs. Frank Watson	0	5	0
A thankoffering from three	0	5	0
Mrs. Struthers	5	0	0
T. P.	0	1	0
Mrs. Keddie	0	10	0
Pastor W. Fuller Gooch	1	1	0
Mr. and Mrs. W. Elliot	15	0	0
Mr. I. V. Ford	1	1	0
Mr. J. Mortimer	0	10	0
Mrs. Pearce	0	5	0
Mr. S. Ormrod	0	10	0
Mr. W. Manning	1	1	0
Mr. and Mrs James Perrett	2	2	0
Rev. S. K. Bland	0	10	6
Collected by Mrs. Plummer	0	13	0

Per Rev. J. R. Chrystal.

	£	s.	d.		£	s.	d.
Hamilton Sabbath-school	1	0	0				
A. M. W., G., Walter, R., J., and Willie Chrystal	0	2	9				
					1	2	9

	£	s.	d.
Miss M. J. Lewis	0	5	0
Mrs. Cook	0	5	0
Mrs. Parsons and friend	1	2	0
Mr. W. Phillips	1	0	0
Miss Cornell	0	2	6
A friend in Dingwall	1	0	0
A lover of Mr. Spurgeon's almanack	0	2	6
Postal order from Bearsden	0	10	0
Mr. John Carter	0	2	6
Miss I. Hood	0	5	0
Mrs. Perkins	1	0	0
Miss Janet Shaw	0	5	0
Mr. Ladbrook	1	0	0
P. and P.	0	5	0
Mrs. Callam	0	5	0
Mr. W. Glen	1	0	0
Mr. G. J. Guyer	0	10	0
Mrs. Oldfield	0	10	0
Mrs. Ferris	0	10	6
Miss Ferris	0	10	6
Mrs. Barnes	0	12	0
Donations at annual missionary meeting, U. P. Church, Stromness	1	1	0
Mr. and Mrs. J. H. Wicks	0	1	0
Miss E. Fisher	0	1	0
Children at Sunday morning school, Llangynidr		4	0

Colchester, per E. Spurrier:—

		£	s.	d.
Mrs. Arnold		2	5	
G. C.		2	0	
36, High Street		1	0	
E. Blaxill		0	10	0
Nellie and Eddie Spurrier		0	7	6
			6	

Collected by Mrs. Lang, Cheltenham :—

		£	s.	d.
Mr. J. Lance		0	5	0
Mr. J. Pillman, Plymouth		1	1	0
Rev. W. L. and Mrs. Lang		2	2	0
		3	8	0

	£	s.	d.
Madame Joubert	1	0	0
Mr. and Mrs. Robertson...	0	10	0
Mrs. Dalgleish	5	0	0
Mr. John Storey	1	10	0
Mr. John Hardy	0	5	0
Mrs. Haynes	0	2	6
Mr. W. Norton	0	10	0
Mr. and Mrs. J. H. Wale	2	0	0
Mrs. Batty	0	3	0
Mr. W. Badden	3	0	0
Mr. R. Mathieson	0	5	0
Mr. W. Chudley	1	1	0
Mr. G. S. Stowe	10	0	0
Mr. D. Imlach	1	0	0
A sermon-reader, B. B.	0	5	0
A truly sympathizing friend	0	3	0
Annie and Katie	0	5	0
Collected by Mrs. Barkwell ...	0	10	0
Mr. R. Ryman	10	0	0
Mr. C. W. Roberts	10	0	0
Mr. W. H. Roberts	5	5	0
Mr. W. Parlane	10	0	0
Mr. E. Frisby	2	2	0
Mr. S. H. Coles	0	10	0
Mrs. Bossingham	0	2	6
Devonshire Square Baptist Church, per Pastor E. H. Ellis	2	2	0
Mr. J. Wickham	1	0	0
Mr. W. Hawker	0	5	0
Mr. John C. Lance	0	5	0
Mrs. and Miss Goslin	0	4	0
Mrs. Pilgrim	1	0	0
J. W.	0	5	0
Mrs. Davies	0	5	0
Mrs. E. Dunnett	0	10	6
Otley Baptist Sunday-school, per Pastor P. B. Woodgate...	0	12	0
Mr. W. Rudd		10	0
In memoriam	1	1	0
First Free Church Sabbath-school, Blairgowrie	0	16	0
Mr. T. Fleetwood	1	0	0
Mary and Willie Thomas	1	0	0
Mr. R. F. Lewis	0	10	0
Mr. S. W. Powell (U.S.A.), per Mr. E. Powell	1	0	0
Mr. D. McKercher...	5	0	0
The Misses Murray	0	0	0
Miss E. Ramage	0	2	6
Mr. A. D. Taylor	1	0	0
Miss H. Jeggo	1	0	0
Mr. E. Martell	3	0	0
Mrs. F. Rowe	1	0	0
Mrs. Runcieman's Sunday-school class and a few well-wishers...	0	11	0
Mrs. S. L. Pakeman	1	1	0
Miss E. A. Pakeman	1	1	0
Master Stanley Jones	0	5	0
Miss May Jones	0	5	0
M. P.	0	5	0
Mr. James Cooper	0	2	6
Mr. Thomas Smith, jun.... ...	0	10	0
Mr. Henry Ward	0	5	0
Collected by Baptist Sunday-scholars, Niton, Isle of Wight	0	1	0
Mr. A. C. Johnston		2	6
Mr. Samuel Johnston		10	0
Miss Mann		10	6
Friends at Ludlow, per Mr. Sidney Cornock	0	7	6
Mr. J. E. Adams	1	0	0
Miss Jarman	0	10	0
Mrs. Bailey	1	1	0
Mrs. Haward	1	0	0
Miss Ellen Cross	0	5	0
Messrs. Henry Head and Co. ...	1	1	0
Mr. and Mrs. Butcher	0	10	0
Mr. T. Fleetwood	1	0	0
Mr. A. B. Todd	0	2	6
J. S. W. C.	0	2	0
Miss A. Sluce	0	10	0

	£	s.	d.		£	s.	d.
Collected by Mrs. C. Adlem :—							
P. L. E.		0	0				
P. M.		10	0				
S. B.		5	0				
G. H.	0	12	0				
G. W.		2	0				
Church of England		5	0				
A. Adlem and family	1	6	0				
					3	0	0
Louisa					0	2	0
Mrs. A. Alston ...					1	0	0
Mr. and Mrs. Potts					0	5	0
Birds from Paradise				...	2	0	0
A friend at Thurso				...	0	10	6
Mr. H. Osmond ...				...	2	0	0
Mrs. Pask ...				...	1	0	0
Mrs. M. A. Bucknell, per C. H. S.					2	0	0
M. B., Penpont ...				...	0	5	0
A sincere friend (less 2d. for postage)...					0	2	10
F. M. N. B. (less 4d. paid for postage and registration)					0	2	8
J. W. G.					0	10	0
Collected by Mrs. James Withers :—							
Mr. W. Moore	2	2	0				
Messrs. Hulas and Co. ...	1	1	0				
Mr. P. Davies ...	1	0	0				
Mr. E. P. Collier ...	1	0	0				
Mr. E. Harvey ...	0	0	6				
Mr. C. R. Stevens ..	0	0	6				
Mr. Robert Oakshott ...	0	0	0				
Mrs. Hampton ...	0	0	0				
Mrs. Ravenscroft ...	0	10	0				
Mrs. Collier	0	5	0				
Mrs. Paulton	0	5	0				
Mr. Wells	0	5	0				
Mrs. J. Davis	0	2	6				
					8	11	6
Miss M. E. Jenkins					0	2	6
Part proceeds of Christmas tree, per Pastor John Field, Ecton ...					6	10	0
Mrs. Gregory					0	10	0
Mr. R. Looker and friends ...					0	10	0
Mrs. Quilty					1	0	0
Mr. and Mrs. Morrison ...				...	1	0	0
Mrs. Milne ...				...	0	10	0
Mr. George Mitchell				...	1	0	0
Mrs. Bell ...				...	0	10	0
Pastor W. Sexton and friends ...					0	10	0
Mr. William Ronald ...					1	10	0
Mrs. Spear, sen.				...	0	5	0
Mr. T. C. McIntyre ...				...	10	10	0
Miss Florence Bousfield ...				...	15	0	0
M. N. W., Berbice				...	2	1	8
Mr. and Mrs. Parker Gray				...	3	0	0
Mrs. Bagster ...				...	2	2	0
Mr. H. Lodwick					0	10	0
A friend, Cumnock ...					0	5	0
Mr. D. D. Sinclair ...					0	10	0
Mrs. Martin					0	5	0
Mr. J. Minto					0	10	0
Rev. R. Colman					1	1	0
Collected by Mr. A. Bamford ...					1	0	0
Mr. T. Butcher					0	10	6
Mr. T. Bollard and friends ...					0	7	0
Part valuation fee					5	0	0
A country minister ...					0	3	0
Mr. W. King					0	2	0
Mrs. Bainbridge ...				...	2	2	0
Mr. John Broadley ...					5	0	0
Miss A. C. Foster					0	1	6
Collected by Mrs. Slater ...					0	3	0
Miss C. Hands					0	10	0
Mr. William Bates ...					5	0	0
Mr. E. O. Brown					1	0	0
Mr. W. Heywood ...					0	7	0
Miss R. Banister ...					0	10	0
The Misses M. and J. Gardner...					0	6	0
Mr. R. P. Froste					2	0	0
Miss E. Millar					0	3	6
Mr. William Casson ...					1	0	0
Mrs. Chiene					2	0	0

£ s. d.

Collected by Mrs. Clews:—
Mr. S. Lawrence — 5
Mr. Sloan .. — 5
Mrs. Kirkpatrick — 5
Mrs. Clews ... ... — 5
Mr. Dickie ... ... — 2 6
Mr. Scott 0 2 0
Mr. M'Garry — 0 2
Mr. W. Laurence — 1
Mr. Poynton ... — 1
— 1 8 6
Mr. W. Walker 1 1 0
J. C. 0 10 0
Mr. J. Johnson 0 5 0
Kent Street Sunday-school Bible-class 0 8 0
Mr. J. Crocker 5 0 0
Mr. T. N. Wade 1 0 0
Miss M. Pentelow 0 6 6
E. Webber 0 5 0
Baptist Sunday-school, Long Preston... 0 10 6
Mr. W. Murkin and friends ... 1 1 0
A reader of Mr. Spurgeon's sermons... 0 5 0
E. Morgan 0 5 0
Mrs. and the Misses Kemp 10 0 0
A friend 20 0 0
M. E. H. 0 5 0
Mrs. Bell 1 0 0
Mr. R. M. George 0 10 0
Mr. A. Welfare 0 1 0
Mr. W. Woolidge 0 10 0
B. C. Forder 0 15 0
Mr. J. Kerr 0 5 0
Mrs. Beare 0 7 6
Miss J. R. Moore 1 0 0
Miss E. Macnicoll 1 0 0
Mrs. Salt 0 3 0
Christmas offering from Baptist Chapel,
Garland Street, Bury St. Edmund's,
after services conducted by Mr.
Gordon 3 0 0
Dr. MacGill 2 2 0
Mr. and Miss Bloom 2 0 0
Donald 0 5 0
Collected by Mrs. Cockle... ... 5 12 0
Miss Budd 0 10 0
Rev. James Stephens, M.A. ... 1 0 0
Miss M. A. Chapman 1 0 0
H. F. and F. S. Gaylor 0 10 0
Mrs. Pollit 0 5 0
Miss G. M. Taylor... ... ... 2 2 0
E. A. V. 4 5 6
Mr. J. Grant... ... ... 0 3 0
Stamps from Insch... ... ... 0 5 0
Mr. C. Rogers 1 0 0
Miss H. F. Parker 0 5 0
Mr. A. Cowan 5 0 0
Mr. S. Foster 1 1 0
Mr. W. Kirkland 0 7 6
Mr. George Reid 10 0 0
Stamps 0 1 0
Mrs. Gregory 0 10 9
Postal order, Anon. 0 5 0
The Cowl Street Sunday-school,
Evesham 1 0 0
Mrs. E. M. T. Ambrose 0 8 0
A friend at Mentone 1 0 0
Mrs. M. Anderson 0 5 0
Mamma's mite for the little orphans .. 0 5 0
Mr. Thomas E. Sykes 3 16 0
Collected by Mrs. Way and Miss Payne 7 11 0
Teachers and Scholars of Eld Lane
Baptist Sunday-school, per Mr. H.
Letch 1 10 0
The children of the Baptist Sunday-
school, Lossiemouth, per Mr. William
Smith 0 10 0
Jack, South Lambeth 0 3 6
Mr. James Owers 0 10 0
Mr. John Courtnay 0 5 0
"H. C.," Torquay 5 0 0
Collected by Mr. H. Andrews 2 4 1

Mrs. Pickering 0 5 0
Mr. J. Hillier, Greytown, New Zealand 0 5 0
Communion collection at Boundary
Road Chapel, Walthamstow, per
Pastor A. Budgen 2 4 0
Miss Hagger 1 0 0
Mrs. Justican, per Mrs. James Spur-
geon 1 1 0
Young people's service, Immanuel
Church, West Brixton, per Mr. A.
Wilson ... ... · 5 0 0
Meetings by Mr. Charlesworth and the
Orphanage Choir:—
Southampton ... 15 3 6
Southsea 10 11 8
Winchester ... 13 2 0
Expenses at Barnsbury 3 0 0
Gordon Hall, per Dr. T. B. Stephenson 2 1 0
Brynmawr 46 14 0
Blackheath 6 7 0
Gosport 15 12 10
Portsmouth 51 0 5
Cross Keys, Mon. 40 0 0
Annual Subscriptions:—
Mr. W. Sewell 1 1 0
Mr. J. Baskervill (2 years' subs.) 0 10 0
Miss S. Thompson 0 12 6
Mr. Robert Morgan 2 2 0
Mr. Joshua Shaw 1 0 0
Mr. Alfred Smith 1 1 0
Mrs. Leechman 3 0 0
Mr. W. H. Pollard ... 0 10 6
Mr. and Mrs. C. E. Fox ... 50 0 0
Mrs. Gray 1 0 0
Mr. and Mrs. Edwin Smith 2 2 0
Miss H. A. Grose ... 0 10 6
Miss Grose 1 1 0
Mr. James Grose 2 2 0
Mr. M. Davies 5 0 0
Per F. R. T.:—
Mr. Probin 0
Mrs. Probin... ... 0
In memoriam, E. P. 0
Mrs. Adrian ... 0
Mr. R. Taylor 0
F. R. T. 0
In remembrance, J. R. T. 0
A. A. T. 1 1
The late Mrs. Baskerville 0 15 0
— 3 15
Mr. W. J. Norton 0 10 0
Mr. James Plumbridge 1 1 0
Half-yearly Subscription:—
Mrs. Hallett's children ... 0 12 0
Quarterly Subscriptions:—
The widow's mite 0 2
Mr. S. Bown 0 0
Mrs. Yates 0 0
Mrs. Elgee ... ...; 0 10 6
Monthly Subscriptions:—
Mr. E. K. Stace 0 10 0
Sandwich, per Bankers 2 2 0
F. G. B., Chelmsford ... 0 2 6
Mr. S. H. Dauncey ... 0 2 6
Christmas Festivities:—
Mrs. H. Rennard 1 0 0
G. D. C. 0 10 0
Mr. E. R. Daniells... ... ... 0 5 0
Mr. S. Pearce 1 0 0
Miss Lennard 0 5 0
Mrs. E. Freeman 0 3 0
The Misses R. and L. Wigney ... 1 0 0
Mr. E. Porter 0 5 0
M. G. 1 10 0
Miss M. Murray 0 10 0
Miss E. T. Beddome 0 2 6
Mrs. Keevil 1 0 0
Mrs. Taylor and friend . .. 0 6 0
Friends at Bures, per Miss E. A. Dupont 0 13 6
Miss A. Pratt 0 10 0

100   STOCKWELL ORPHANAGE.

	£	s.	d.
Endymion	0	10	0
Mrs. Elgee	0	5	0
Mrs. Lane	1	0	0
Mr. C. F. Alldis	0	5	0
Miss Horton	0	2	6
Miss P. M. Shaw	0	5	0
Miss A. Broom	0	2	6
Miss E. Newing	0	10	0
Mrs. Brake	1	0	0
Mr. Charles Norris	1	0	0
Mr. and Mrs. J. C. Smith ...	1	10	0
Mr. Edwin Davis...	0	10	0
Mrs. E. Johnson	1	0	0
Mrs. Sydenham	1	0	0
Friends at Risby	0	12	0
Mr. and Mrs. Baker	0	10	0
Mrs. B. Tice...	0	5	0
Mattie Tice	0	2	0
Lottie Tice	0	2	0
Bennie Tice	0	1	0
Maud and Grace Crathern ...	0	2	6
Collected by Miss Best, Helston:—			
Mrs. Cotton... ... ... 0 10 0			
Mr. Heynes 0 10 0			
Mr. Winkworth 0 1 0			
Miss Best 0 5 0			
	1	6	0
Collected by Miss Richards, Helston ...	1	6	2
Collected by Mrs. Cooper... ...	0	2	6
Mrs. Edwards	2	0	0
Grove Road, Gosport, Sabbath-school children and friends	0	10	0
Mr. and Mrs. Woodcock	0	5	0
A sermon-reader, Glasgow	1	0	
Mrs. Griffiths	1	1	
Mrs. Tebbutt	1	0	

	£	s	d.
Mrs. Wilshere	0	0	
Mrs. Barlow...	1	1	0
Mrs. Johnson	2	0	
Pastor R. E. Sears	0	0	
Mr. G. Lawrence and friends ...	12	1	0
Miss M. Hay	0	5	0
Mrs. W. Vinson	0	10	0
Mr. J. Beaumont	0	5	0
The Misses Rowland	0	5	0
A few friends at Bures, per Pastor G. Monk	0	16	6
Mr. C. Fleming	0	1	0
A servant	0	5	0
Mr. and Mrs. Chenery	0	1	0
Mrs. Stevenson	0	2	6
Pastor J. H. and Mrs. Barnard ...	1	0	0
Mrs. Rust	2	10	0
Mr. W. Jones	1	1	0
Miss E. Doerter	0	14	0
Miss A. Drayson	0	2	6
Mr. John Miles	0	3	0
Collected by Miss Reeve and Mr. W. B. Ashe	2	0	0
M. H....	1	0	0
Tom	0	2	6
Dora, Isabel, and Grace Walker ...	0	5	0
Mr. J. H. Padgett...	0.10		0
Mr. H. Hall	1	0	0
Mr. W. Johnson	0	2	0
Mrs. Macgregor	1	0	0
Mrs. Ely and friends	0	18	0
The Bible-class and friends at Hitcham, per Mr. C. P. Clover	0	10	0
	£1,315	2	9

Orphan Boys' Collecting Cards.—Abbott, H., 2s; Allison, S., 5s 2d; Barrett, F. B., 8s 3d; Bowen, W. G., 5s; Bull, L. O., 7s; Bates, W., 3s 3d; Burrows, G., 5s; Beadle, J. S., 2s 9d; Burnham, F., 16s 8d; Baker, J., £1 1s; Beer, A. J., 4s 6d; Burgoyne, W., 10s; Copsey, C., 9s; Carman, A. E., £1 2s; Cook, C., 4s 4d; Chamberlain, W., 4s 6d; Chandler, C., 4s; Cozens, H., 9s 3d; Cooper, C., 2s; Constable, F., 2s 6d; Clode, W., 10s 6d; Cartland, F., 2s; Deverall, G., 2s 7d; Drew, J., 5s; Earth-rowl, A., 8s 3d; Edwards, G., 10s 6d; Fitch, E., 8s; Greenhough, G., 5s; Green, A., 11s 1d; Goddard, C., 18s 6d; Golding, D., 15s; Gardiner, G., 2s; Gammon, A., £1 1s; Hodgson, W., 12s; Harris, W., 2s 9d; Heath, W., £1 1s; Horan, E., 3s 6d; Hatcher, J., 4s 1d; Hills, E., 2s 9d; Henderson, G., £1 1s; Ingram, W. A., £1 1s; Inward, W., 2s 3d; Jenning, R. W., 13s; Jansen, W., 6s 7d; Kent, J. W., 8s; Knap-pett, C. E., 6s 9d; King, A., 2s 6d; Lowne, J., 3s 6d; Lenderyou, A. V., 7s 3d; Long, H., 7s 6d; Med-calf, T., £1 1s; Morton, P., 2s 6d; Mead, H., 5s; Marks, A. T., 3s; Maclean, C., 3s; Manser, N. H., 5s; Newman, A. T., £1 2s 6d; Norton, R., 16s 8d; Ounsted, A., 4s 6d; Ponton, M., 3s 3d; Ponsford, H., 13s 7d; Payne, O., 4s; Peachey, A., 5s 6d; Pritchard, G., 13s 10d; Pegg, G. W., £1 1s; Pitney, F. G., 14s 2d; Rodwell, B., 15s; Rye, C., 5s 2d; Stoner, W., 5s 4d; Sargeant, E., £1 2s; Strike, A., 3s 3d; Surtees, J., £1 1s; Smith, R. A., 13s; Suttle, R., 10s 7d; Schofield, J. S., 5s; Tanner, J., 16s 6d; Trim, J. T., 8s 1d; Teasdale, H., 3s 2d; Unwin, E , 15s 6d; Vokes, E., 1s 6d; Warner, G., 5s; Walker, J., 6s; Westhrop, C., 6s; Wincott, J. S., 4s 3d; White, E. P., 2s 6d; Walker, C., 5s 6d; Winnen, J., 5s; Williams, A., 4s 6d; Williams, J., 4s 3d; Wilkins, J., 6s 3d; Ward, R., 5s; Wells, S. A., 10s; Bristow, J., 6s 6d; East, G., 7s 6d; Far, E., 2s; Fennall, A., 10s; Green, W. S., £1 1s; Mannell, W., £1 4s 6d; Moore, W., 4s; Mansell, E., 12s; Rathmell, W., 6s; Roberts, E. H., 13s; Rhodes, J. H., 5s; Rogers, W., 10s; Stringle, W., 1s 6d; Sanders, W. G., £1 1s; Uren, G., £1 1s 5d; Westbrook, H. J., 5s; Wallis, F. G., 2s 6d; Walker, A. J., 10s.—Total, £47 17s. 8d.

Orphan Girls' Collecting Cards.—Attfield, B., 13s 6d; Arnold, S., 13s; Attiken, E., 2s 6d; Aldrich, M., 5s; Arthur, P., 10s 6d; Allsopp, L., 1s; Bigglestone, M., 10s 6d; Bullock, L., 7s 2d; Broadhouse, N., 11s 9d; Bull, L., 6s; Bertwistle, E., 10s; Bird, A., 3s 6d; Bond, E., 3s; Burrows, F., 1s 10d; Beetham, A., 2s 7d; Boorman, V., 3s; Barlow, M., 7s; Brown, R., 7s; Cordwell, H., 9s 6d; Collis, H , 2s 6d; Cragg, A., 2s 1d; Cooper, K., 4s; Cousins, L., 5s 4d; Dickerson, E., 11s 6d; Doncaster, A., 1s; Donnelley, G., 9s 3d; Epps, F., 9s; Evans, A., 8s 6d; Guiver, K., 10s; Hall, F., 6s; Hoidge, A., £1; Hall, M., 4s 2d; Heath, K., 14s; Hobbs, M., 2s 6d; Hunter, F., 8s 1d; Howell, R., 4s 6d; Hallam, E., 11s 6d; Haydon, L., 3s 6d; Ingle, F., 9s 9d; Jacques, K., 2s 6d; Jackson, L., 7s 6d; Johnson, A., 1s 6d; Larkum, A., 6s 9d; Lailey, J., 6s; Lagdon, G., £1 1s 6d; Leitch, G., £1 1s 6d; McKinlay, F., 5s 6d; Mayhew, Z., 2s; Mockford, L., 8s 9d; Maynard, M., 4s 6d; Miles, M., 10s; Nutt, C., 4s 6d; Newton, K., 1s; Nash; M., 3s 1d; Orridge, A., 10s 7d; Palmer, B., 16s 6d; Pearce, A., 4s; Feepall, G., 4s 3d; Parker, A., 3s; Perry, R., 1s 7d; Page, L., £1 1s; Robottom, G., £1 1s; Richmond, B., 5s; Smith, A., £1 3s; Smith, K., 2s 6d; Soper, A., 10s; Seymour, J., 3s 6d; Smithers, L., 5s 2d; Stone, E., 2s; Smith, M., 5s 2d; Sawyer, V., 5s 6d; Shorter, E., 4s; Steel, M., 16s 6d; Skinner, E., 3s; Thorpe, E., 5s; Trepte, E., 10s; Valler, C., 4s; Veryard, R., 4s; Walker, K., £1 1s; Wright, K., 12s; Wil-liams, N., 2s 6d; Wale, E., 3s; Witham, P., 13s 1d; Woolfit, A., 4s 6d; Westwood, F., 10s; Youens, L., £1 1s; Bridgman, A., 5s 3d; Bennett, L., £1 1s; Bishopp, E., 12s 6d; Cable., F., 5s; Gray, E., 5s 4d; Hinchley, E., 3s; Holman, E., 11s 2d; Logan, K., 6s 2d; Moles, E., 2s 7d; Maycock, W., £1 1s; Page, M., 10s; Price, E., £1; Sharland, A., 1s; Warwick, L., 5s; Woodcock, J., 6s; Wilmore, E., 2s 6d.—Total, £40 0s. 11d.

List of Presents, per Mr. Charlesworth, from December 15th to January 14th, 1889.—PROVISIONS :— 1 Christmas Cake, and a few fancy packets of Sweets, Miss Morris; 3 dozen tins Beef, the Australian

Meat Company; 1 sack of Flour, Mrs. Collins; 1 case of Oranges, Mr. J. Gatward; 1 box of Oranges, Mr. E. Newman; 112 lbs. Corn Flour, Messrs. Brown and Polson; 1 case of Oranges, Mr. W. Taylor; 500 boxes of Figs, Mr. W. Harrison; 1 sack of Onions, Mr. F. Brown; 2 sacks of Potatoes, Mr. J. Edmead; 2 Bullocks' Heads, Mr. S. Rayner; 2 sacks of Potatoes, Mr. Watts; 1 sack of Flour, Mr. W. Medcalf; 1 hamper Aërated Bread, Mr. N. Read; 4 cwts. of Potatoes, Messrs. C. and A. Parker; 1 barrel of Apples, Mr. James Stiff; 224 lbs. Beef, Mr. Samuel Barrow; 6 bags of Sprouts, Mr. W. Vinson; an assortment of Grocery, &c., Miss Packeman; 36 lbs. of Beef, Mr. T. Round; 2 hampers of Grocery, The Misses J. and J. Wiseman; 4 cwts. Jam and 2 cwts. Fancy Sweets, Messrs. Chivers and Sons; 1 barrel of Apples, Mr. J. Cooper; 1 Hind of Beef, Mr. A. S. Haslam; 7 tins of Sweets, Mr. T. S. Price; 1 Shortbread, Mr. H. Mills; 1 large Loaf, Mr. J. Plant; 300 Fancy Cakes, Messrs. Peek, Frean, and Co.; 1 Leg of Salt Pork, Messrs. J. and J. Brough Nicholson and Co.; a quantity of Short Cakes, Mr. Dobson; 3 casks of Broken Biscuits, Messrs. Huntley and Palmer; 1 sack of Flour, Mr. Goddard; 28 lbs. of Baking Powder, Messrs. Freeman and Hillyard; 85 Pork Pies, Messrs. J. Tebbutt and Co.; 4 sacks of Potatoes, 5 dozen Savoys, Mr. Norkett; 1 sack of Cabbages, a Farmer; 224 lbs. of Rice, Mr. J. L. Potier; 2 dozen packets of Rizine, Mr. R. Speller; 7½ lbs. of Sweets, Rock Cakes, and Chestnuts, Mrs. Thompson; 6 lbs. Raisins, 6 lbs. Currants, Mrs. Hall; a quantity of Butter, Mr. E. J. Gorringe.

BOYS' CLOTHING.—11 Flannel Shirts, 6 Cotton Shirts, 4 Night Shirts, 7 pairs Socks, 4 Sheets, The Reading Young Ladies' Working Meeting, per Mrs. J. Withers; 13 Articles and 1 suit of Clothes, Mrs. Hunter; 3 Scarves, Mrs. White; 12 pairs Socks, The Misses M. and C. Sherwood; 12 pairs Socks and Stockings, Miss Morris; 1 Jacket and 3 Waistcoats, Mrs. E. A. Ventris; 10 Suits, 4 Coats, and 3 pairs Trousers, Mr. J. S. Smith; 20 Night Shirts, The Children's Sewing Circle, per Miss A. M. Davies; 10 Night Shirts and 24 Flannel Shirts, Mrs. G. Thompson; 12 pairs Cuffs, Miss L. Grove; 3 lengths Shirting, and 2 lengths Material, The Misses T. and B. Phillips; 3 pairs Gloves, Mrs. Wicks; 3 Jackets and Vests, Mrs. Read; 7 Scarves and 5 pairs Cuffs, E. C. M.; 6 Handkerchiefs, Mrs. Parsons; 2 Scarves and 2 pairs Stockings, Mr. J. Colver; 2 pairs Socks, Mrs. S. A. Whitehead; 17 pairs Socks, Mrs. Stockwell; 1 dozen Scarves, Miss Edwards; a quantity of Gloves, Scarves, Collars, Ties, &c., Messrs. S. and T. and E. Ellison; 8 Shirts, The Ladies' Working Society, Wynne Road, per Mrs. R. S. Pearce.

GIRLS' CLOTHING.—42 useful Articles, Miss Meares; 189 Articles, The Reading Young Ladies' Working Meeting, per Mrs. J. Withers; 22 Articles, Mrs. Hunter; 41 Jackets and Ulsters, Mr. T. Yorath; 8 Articles, Mrs. Brierley; 10 Articles, Mrs. E. Marshall; 6 Articles, Mrs. Dixon; 92 Articles, Mrs. E. Ventris; 9 Hats and 3 Ulsters, Mr. J. S. Smith; 5 Articles, Miss J. Shaw; 53 Articles, The Juvenile Working Society, Metropolitan Tabernacle, per Miss Woods; 109 Articles, Miss Chandler's Bible-class; 11 Articles, Miss E. A. Hargrave; 17 Articles. Miss J. Henry; 7 Pinafores, Mrs. Lindup and Miss Evans; 32 Articles, The Cheam Baptist Working Society, per Mrs. E. Cox; 66 Articles, Mrs. G. Thompson; 12 Handkerchiefs, Miss L. Grove; 9 Articles, Miss McKenzie; 6 Trimmed Hats, The Misses T. and B. Phillips; 6 pairs Stockings, Mrs. Casburn; 13 Articles, Miss Clarke; 52 Articles, The Ladies' Working Meeting at Tabernacle, per Miss Higgs; 50 Articles, The Fleet Baptist Chapel Working Society, per Mrs. Aylett; 21 Articles, The Chatham Ladies' Working Society, per Mrs. Harvey; 6 Articles, Miss Wood; 2 Articles, A. J. Holden; 1 Article, Miss Blinkhorn; 2 Articles, Mrs. Stockwell; 6 Articles, Mrs. Rolfe; 4 Articles, Mrs. Tye; 21 Articles, Miss Poole; 9 Articles, Miss Drake; 9 Articles, Miss Salter; 15 Articles, The Ladies' Working Society, Wynne Road, per Mrs. R. S. Pearce.

GENERAL.—A quantity of Toys, Miss Clarke; 6 Volumes, Rev. J. G. Van Rijn; 11 Volumes, Mr. E. A. Petherick; 2 boxes of Fancy Articles, Miss Descroix; 2 boxes of Artificial Flowers, Mr. H. Edwards; 2 Scrap Books, Mrs. E. A. Perkins; 1 Telescope, "In His Name"; 1 box of Artificial Flowers, Messrs. Quinn and Axten; a few Toys and Sundries, Mr. E. Newman; 1 Scrap Book, Miss Leaver; an assortment of Cards and Books, Religious Tract Society; a quantity of Cards, Mrs. Butting; 1 load of Firewood, Messrs. J. Keen and Son; 3 Articles, Anon.; a few Dolls, Mrs. Gunn; a few Cards, Anon.; 250 framed Christmas Cards, Pastor C. Spurgeon; 6 Scrap Books and 2 Neck Ties, Mrs. Hall; a few Books and Toys, Mrs. J. Robertson; 1 load of Firewood, Mr. Jonas Smith; 2 Scrap Books, Mrs. J. Withers; 1 dozen Books, A. J. Holden; a few Tracts and 6 Pin-cushions, Mrs. Dixon.

Colportage Association.

Statement of Receipts from December 15th, 1888, to January 14th, 1889.

Subscriptions and Donations for Districts:—

	£ s. d.		£ s. d.
Wilts. and East Somerset Association	25 0 0	Great Totham district ...	8 0 0
Ironbridge and Coalbrookdale...	7 10 0	Mr. R. W. S. Griffith, for Fritham	10 0 0
Castleton, Cardiff, and Penrhicewiber, per Mr. John Cory	20 0 0	Hadleigh district, per Mr. R. H. Cook ...	20 0 0
Pastor E. J. Farley, for St. Luke's	20 0 0	Ludlow district, per Mr. J. Evans	10 0 0
Wolverhampton district ...	10 0 0	Suffolk Congregational Union, for Thurlow ...	10 0 0
Cambs. Baptist Association	10 0 0	Ross district, per Mr. Thos. Blake	5 0 0
Tewkesbury district, per Mr. Thomas White ...	8 15 0	Wendover and neighbourhood	10 0 0
Norfolk Association, Neatishead district	10 0 0	Okehampton district ...	10 0 0
Yorkshire Association, Boroughbridge	10 0 0	Minchinhampton district ...	10 0 0
Mr. J. Dodson, for Littledale...	40 0 0		254 5
		Bethnal Green:—	
		Mr. C. E. Fox 5 0 0	
		Mr. W. R. Fox 5 0 0	
			10 0

	£	s.	d.
Essex Congregational Union, Pitsea ...			
	10	0	0
Oxfordshire Association :			
Stow and Aston 10 0 0			
Witney ... 20 0 0			
	30	0	0
Mrs. H. Keevil, for Melksham :	10	0	0
Great Totham district	2	0	0
Borstall	20	0	0
Newbury ...	10	0	0
Southern Baptist Association	50	0	0
Wolverhampton district ...	10	0	0
	152	0	0
	£406	5	0

Subscriptions and Donations to the General Fund :—

	£	s.	d.
Mr. H. Payne	0	2	6
Annual Subscriptions :			
Mr. F. Fishwick	2	2	0
Mr. F. Thompson ...	1	1	0
Mr. J. J. Cook ...	1	1	0

	£	s.	d.
Mr. J. Hall	1	1	0
Messrs. Cassell and Co.	2	2	0
Mr. E. Brayne	0	10	6
Mr. J. Passmore, jun. ...	1	1	0
Mr. R. Hellier ...	0	10	6
Mrs. R. Hellier	0	10	6
Mr. C. F. Allison ... ...·	5	0	0
	15	2	
Mr. W. A. Macfie ...	1	0	0
" Sixty-eight" ...	1	0	0
Rev. W. L. and Mrs. Lang	2	2	0
Mr. W. Parlane ...	10	0	0
Mr. A. Todd	0	5	0
Mr. H. Osmond	2	0	0
Part valuation fee	5	0	0
Mr. William Casson ...	0	10	0
Annual Subscriptions :—			
Mr. J. Stiff ...	1	1	0
Mr. W. Olney ...	1	1	0
Messrs. Hodder and Stoughton	2	2	0
	26	1	
	£41	3	0

Society of Evangelists.

Statement of Receipts from December 15th, 1888, to January 14th, 1889.

	£	s.	d.
Mr. John Barrie ...	1	0	0
Mr. James Baxter	1	0	0
Mr. and Mrs. W. Blott	5	0	0
Thankoffering for Messrs. Fullerton and Smith's services at Upton Chapel	20	0	0
Thankoffering for Messrs. Fullerton and Smith's services at Christ Church, Westminster Bridge Road ...	21	0	0
Thankoffering for Messrs. Fullerton and Smith's services at Bloomsbury Chapel	40	0	0
Miss H. Husk	0	5	0
Mr. W. A. Macfie	1	0	0
Miss Shillito... ...	1	1	0
Rev. W. L. and Mrs. Lang	1	1	0
Mr. R. Dawson	0	8	0
Thankoffering for Mr. Harmer's services at Orpington	4	0	0
Mr. E. E. Sawyer	25	0	0

	£	s.	d.
Mr. W. Parlane	10	0	0
Mr. D. McKercher	1	0	0
Thankoffering for Pastor W. H. Broad's services at Ashdon and Radwinter ...	0	10	0
Miss Ellen Cross	0	5	0
Mrs. Broadhurst ...	0	5	0
Readers of " The Christian Herald " ...	29	18	7
Part valuation fee	5	0	0
Mr. William Casson ...	0	10	0
Per Miss Susan Green :—			
Mrs. Mackenzie ... 0 10 0			
Mrs. Peter Fleming 0 10 0			
Mrs. and Miss Green 0 5 0			
Mrs. P. Cameron ... 0 1 0			
	1	6	
	£169	9	

For General Use in the Lord's Work.

Statement of Receipts from December 15th, 1888, to January 14th, 1889.

	£	s.	d.
J. W. Y.	1	0	0
Mr. C. Hunt...	1	0	0
Mr. G. Hacksley	0	5	0
Mr. Thomas Land... ...	0	7	6
Mr. S. Francis Smith, L.R.C.P.	4	0	0
Mr. James Wilson... ...	0	10	0
Mr. and Mrs. Way... ...	2	2	0
Mr. W. A. Macfie	1	0	0
Mr. T. L. Jones	1	0	0

	£	s.	d.
A sermon-reader, B. B.	0	5	0
Mr. W. Perry	0	10	0
Mr. William Moir ...	3	0	0
Part valuation fee	5	0	0
Miss Seivwright ...	0	1	6
S. P., Warrington...	0	10	0
	£20	11	0

Friends sending presents to the Orphanage are earnestly requested to let their names or initials accompany the same, or we cannot properly acknowledge them ; and also to write to Mr. Spurgeon if no acknowledgment is sent within a week. All parcels should be addressed to Mr. Charlesworth, Stockwell Orphanage, Clapham Road, London.

Subscriptions will be thankfully received by C. H. Spurgeon, " Westwood," Beulah Hill, Upper Norwood. Should any sums sent before the 13th of last month be unacknowledged in this list, friends are requested to write at once to Mr. Spurgeon. Post Office and Postal Orders should be made payable at the Chief Office, London, to C. H. Spurgeon : and Cheques and Orders should all be crossed.

PASTORS' COLLEGE.

Accoun for the Yea 1888.

RECEIPTS.		£	s.	d.
To ...y Offerings ...	...	1,176	5	3
Donations... ...	...	5,301	19	9
...hs by Students ...	...	419	13	8
...ost on Deposit Account ...	...	35	6	7
...nal Meeting ...	...	7	9	0
		7,007	14	3
Balance in hand 1st January, 1888	,,	1,385	15	10
		£8,393	10	1

PAYMENTS.		£	s.	d.
By Salaries	...	1,726	18	2
,, ...nd, ...ng, and ...al...	...	3,167	17	3
,, ...ng ...	...	87	16	7
,, Lighting, Cleaning, and Warming	...	173	11	5
,, Books, ...ng, Stationery, ...ng, Advertising, and ...ce ...es	...	292	17	8
,, Book-grants to ...ts on leaving	...	197	5	0
,, Preaching Stations—Home Missions and New Chapels	...	1,135	3	5
,, ...nal Conference—including Hire, Labour, and Decorations...		400	0	0
,, Furniture and Fittings ...	...	52	13	4
		7,234	2	10
,, Balance in ...nd, 31st ...er, 1888	...	1,159	7	3
		£8,393	10	1

Audited and ...co ...d, January 5th, 1889.

JAMES A. SPURGEON,
J. PASSMORE,
W. C. MURRELL,
J. BUSWELL,
   Finance Comm...

WILLIAM PAYNE, } *Auditors.*
H. ...H,

PASTORS' COLLEGE SOCIETY OF EVANGELISTS.

Account for the Year 1888.

RECEIPTS.

		£ s. d.	
To Donations	...	614 14 6	
„ Contributions by Sales ...	...	510 1 3	
		1,124 15 9	
„ Balance in hand, January, 1888	...	156 9 6	
		£1,281 5 3	

JAS. A. SPURGEON, } Finance Committee.
W. C. MURRELL,
JOS. PASSMORE,
J. BUSWELL.

PAYMENTS.

		£ s. d.	
By Salaries of and for Evangelists, and part of three others ... paid	...	909 5 1	
„ Travelling Expenses to and from places ...	...	141 5 2	
„ Printing	...	7 17 7	
		1,058 7 10	
„ Balance in hand 31st December, 1888	...	222 17 5	
		£1,281 5 3	

Audited and found correct, January 5th, 1889. { WILLIAM PAYNE, } Auditors.
{ H. SMITH, }

LOAN BUILDING AND RESERVE FUND.

Account for the Year 1888.

RECEIPTS.

		£ s. d.	
To Balance in hand, January 1st, 1888	...	408 3 7	
„ Repayment of Loans	...	1,233 13 5	
		1,641 17 0	

Loans outstanding, December 31, 1888 ... 4,543 3 4
„ Balance in hand ... 541 17 0
£5,085 0 4

THOS. H. OLNEY, Treasurer.

PAYMENTS.

		£ s. d.	
By Loans to Churches :—			
South London ... Sale	...	500 0 0	
Upwell ...	...	100 0 0	
Metropolitan Tabernacle.		500 0 0	
		1,100 0 0	
Balance in hand, December 31st, 1888		541 17 0	
		£1,641 17 0	

Audited and found correct, January 5th, 1889. { WILLIAM PAYNE, } Auditors.
{ H. SMITH, }

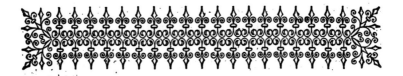

THE

SWORD AND THE TROWEL

MARCH, 1889.

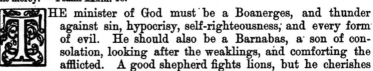

Special Pleading with the Specially Feeble.*

A SHORT SERMON BY C. H. SPURGEON.

"Behold, the eye of the Lord is upon them that fear him, upon them that hope in his mercy."—Psalm xxxiii. 18.

THE minister of God must be a Boanerges, and thunder against sin, hypocrisy, self-righteousness, and every form of evil. He should also be a Barnabas, a son of consolation, looking after the weaklings, and comforting the afflicted. A good shepherd fights lions, but he cherishes lambs. We have had of late to fight; but just now we will leave the wolves alone, and seek out the very feeblest of the flock, that lie faint and ready to die, and see if we may not be the means, in God's hand, of administering consolation to them.

Observe the curious blending in the text. "The eye of the Lord is upon them that *fear* him, upon them that *hope* in his mercy." These people both fear and hope; and yet fear and hope would seem to be contradictions. These opposites are sure to be found in every heart that is seeking the Lord, and they beautifully harmonize. That is a blessed state of mind in which fear keeps the door, and hope spreads the table. All is well when fear is the watchdog without, and hope is the lamp within. Those who have gone even a little way to heaven will begin to be familiar with paradoxes. The Christian life seems plain to those who know nothing about it; but those who possess it, find it to be a mystery. Within each believer's heart there is the company of two armies contending with one another. The life of God's people is made up of fearing the Lord, and hoping in his mercy.

* The Lord has lately thrown in my way many despairing ones; and, in my own sickness, I have prepared this sermon for them. May the Comforter use it! Will happy Christians put it in the trembler's way? Please see what you can do!

Those that hope in the Lord's mercy may be the very least of his people, but they are his true people, for his eye is upon them. They hope; and that is by no means so strong a grace as assurance. They hope only "in his mercy"; they have not gone far enough to look to his power or his immutability, though these are blessed grounds of hope. If you take hold upon the Lord anywhere, you have a hold of him: whether you touch the hem of his garment by hoping in his mercy, or lay hold upon his arm by grasping his power, you have him, and he is yours.

I speak now with those whose sole hope is hope in God's mercy.

I want you to notice, first, THAT THIS HOPE IS ONE, AND ONLY ONE. "Upon them that hope in his mercy." Have you any other hope? If so, it will fail you in the day of trial. The person I have in my mind's eye has no hope except in the mercy of God; but I will question him a little, just to see whether it is so.

Friend, *have you any hope in your own character?* I mark a kind of tearful smile as you hear the question. "Hope in my character, sir! Why, I am lost on that ground. I have done the things that I ought not to have done, and I have left undone the things that I ought to have done. My merit is demerit, and my desert is hell." I am glad to hear you say so, humbling as the admission is, because it is true of all, whether they think so or not. If any hope to be saved by their own righteousness, they are under a delusion. O self-truster, you are a living insult to the cross of Christ! If you can be saved through your own works, why did Jesus die? What need of an atoning sacrifice if man can win eternal life by his own merit?. Hope in God's mercy you may have; but hope in your own merit is a madman's dream.

But listen. *Have you no hope in external ordinances?* Have you not heard that we are born again in baptism? Don't you think that if you come regularly to holy communion a good hope will be yours? If you are a regular hearer of the gospel, and give a guinea or two to a charity, don't you think that this will lay the foundation of a good hope? Ah! I see my friend shake his head, as he answers, "Oh no, that will never do. I could not depend on rites and ceremonies—not even on those which are of God's ordaining. I must be a believer in Christ. I must have the pardon of my sins from Jesus; nothing else will ease my conscience." I am glad to hear you say so. It is a great relief to be delivered from all those foolish errors into which unthinking persons fall when they imagine that drops of water and priestly words, or the deep bath and Scriptural phrases, or consecrated bread and wine, or anything else, can avail in the least degree for the salvation of the soul. Nothing can help the man that is not saved by grace, renewed by the Spirit of God, and washed in the blood of the Lamb.

But, friend, *have you no trust in the priesthood?* Have you not heard that there are persons to whom God has given the keys of the kingdom of heaven, and that if you go to them in the proper way they can absolve you? When I come to this point, I do not know how to restrain my indignation. Beloved friends, trust in no man, whoever he may be. If he can trace his apostolical succession right up to Judas Iscariot, yet do not trust him: if he says that he has power on earth to forgive sins, do not believe him. Every minister of Christ has power to pronounce him absolved who believes in Jesus Christ; but beyond that declaratory power, there rests in no man power to forgive sin; and I am sure that if God has ever dealt with you by his Spirit, you will never be a victim of that delusion.

Some seem to fancy that there is *hope for sinners in scientific discoveries*. Nobody knows what will be found out next. Years ago, "everything was done by steam, and men were killed by powder"; but we have got long beyond that era, and are on our way to a glorious condition of things, if a great war does not blow us all to matches. They have discovered that our mother's Bible is not inspired, and that the glorious gospel of Jesus Christ is a worn-out fable. The new doctrine practically is—Let us eat and drink, for to-morrow we die; or if we do not die, it does not matter, for we shall all come right in the end. If the Lord has ever dealt with your soul, you will hate this infidelity, and the lying hope which grows out of it. God has spoken by his Word! Long lines of witnesses declare that Word to be true. Myriads have lived and died in the faith of it, and poured forth their blood for the defence of it. It must be true; and if there be no hope in the Word of God for an unpardoned sinner, then there is no hope for him anywhere. Yet the Lord Jesus has proclaimed no hope for a man who will not believe in him. If the Book declares that the unbeliever shall go away into everlasting punishment, then, depend upon it, he will do so, for the Book does not lie. Though men, pretending to be wise, would play the will-o'-the-wisp, and lead souls into marshes of doubt, where they sink into destruction, we will not be deluded by them. There is no hope in vain philosophy. You are shut up to the one hope of the text, "them that hope in his mercy."

Having thus talked of the folly of another hope, let us now consider the one commanded in the text. I have lately been greatly puzzled, saddened, and humiliated by having to deal with persons in despair. I have tried to rally them out of it, but not always with success. Let me try again while I show THAT THIS HOPE HAS GOOD FOUNDATIONS.

Dear friend, you are conscious that you have greatly sinned, and you are afraid that you cannot be saved. I rejoice in your sense of sin, but I lament your doubts of pardon. Let me give you hope, first, by a consideration of *the merciful character of God*. Everywhere in Scripture he is described as "the Lord God, merciful and gracious." He says of himself that "he delighteth in mercy"; and his saints were wont to sing of him, that "his mercy endureth for ever." His very name is love. He bids you forgive unto seventy times seven, and he will certainly do that himself which he bids you do. Come, then, indulge a hope of his mercy, and though you deserve nothing at his hands, believe that he will pass by your offences.

Let me encourage you to hope in his mercy, next, from the fact that *there is a gospel*. When the angels at first proclaimed the birth of Christ, they sang of good news for man. Every Sabbath-day the gospel is preached in ten thousand places, and everywhere it is good news. The essence of it is, "There is forgiveness for the greatest sin, for Jesus Christ has lived and died." Consider with joy that if there be a gospel it is not sent to mock you. Does not the very word "gospel" give you hope? If there is good news for men, may there not be good news for you?

Next, take hope from *the life and death of the Lord Jesus Christ.* You know how he lived among men. Did he ever reject a soul that came to him? When they brought to him her that was taken in the act of adultery, did he condemn her? When a woman, that was a sinner, washed his feet with tears, did he spurn her? He was so gentle, and so tender, that his life should make you feel that, if you would only trust him, he will receive you. But remember his death: the bloody sweat in the garden; the cruel scourging; the crown of thorns; the nailing to the cross; the groan of anguish. Why these? We are told, he died, "the Just for the unjust." If Jesus died for the guilty, despair is absurd. When the Son of God bows his head to die for men, mercy reigns without limit. Sin, brought into contact with the divine blood-shedding, vanishes at once.

I would ask the desponding to think of *the Holy Spirit.* Have you not heard that the Holy Spirit makes the bodies of men his temples, purifying them, sanctifying them? Why? To whom does he do this? To the guilty; to those who are weak, and feeble, and cannot rise out of sin. He helpeth them; but if they were good by nature, they would not want him. It is because they are hard that he comes to soften them: because they are dead, he comes to make them live. O trembler, the Holy Spirit would not have been provided unless God had intended to meet all your wants and difficulties.

And listen again. *We may pray.* Do you think that God would have bidden us pray, if he did not mean to hear us? You unbelievingly say, "He will never hear me." How dare you say that? If there be no pardon, why has he spared you to pray for it? Why does he let you live, and feel a desire to call upon his name, if he never intends to hear you? It would be a wicked hoax if a man invited poor people to his house to receive charity, and then, when they came there, denied them relief. God will not invite you to pray without intending to hear you. Take comfort from this.

If that does not cheer you, let me remind you of *the many who have come to Christ,* who tell you that they have been saved by him. I am one of them. I do not think that you are any worse than I was. I hope you are not. I do not think that you can be more careless than I was once; and, on the other hand, I do not think that you can be in greater despair than I was afterwards. I came to Jesus as I was, and I trusted him, and he did not cast me away. Dear heart, he cannot cast you away. I mean you who are reading these lines at this moment. Dare to hope in God's mercy, because so many others have hoped in it, and none of them have hoped in vain. If you met one of us who warned you, "Don't go to Jesus, he will refuse you," you might hesitate. But it is not so: we are unanimous in declaring that he will cast out none that come to him.

If you want any other word said to you, let me remind you of my text, "The eye of the Lord is upon them that fear him, upon them that hope in his mercy." It reminds me of a king sitting at a window. There is a splendid gathering in the square, and the king is looking down upon it. What can he be looking at? He passes over the helmets of the soldiery and the plumes of the ladies in their carriages. What is he looking at? The person for whom he searches is highly honoured. Transfer the picture to God, in the great heavens, looking down upon the whole mass of men. Whom is he looking for? He is looking for him who dares to hope in his mercy. Surely, this ought to encourage you to hope, since God has an eye for you, and looks for you beyond all others.

For a moment hearken to me while I try to exhort you to cast away doubts, THAT THIS HOPE MAY BE YOURS. Let me try to chase away objections.

Let me speak to those who despair. Is it, after all, true that your case is so peculiar? "Oh," say you, "*I have been guilty of the worst of sins!*" In the case of certain of you, I do not quite believe it. You have been, from early childood, amiable in temper, and excellent in moral character; and I do not like you to exaggerate, and make yourself out to be what you are not. You have enough to answer for without blackening yourself needlessly. "What are you driving at, sir? Do you want to prove that there is something good in me?" Oh, no! you are bad enough, and you are a deal worse than you think you are: I will warrant you that. But, still my drift is this—that worse sinners than you are have come to Christ, and have been saved. And why not you? If there is a door wide enough for a big sinner to go through, it is wide enough for you to go through too. A man had two dogs, and he liked them to go in and out of the house freely, and therefore he had two holes cut in the door. He was asked the meaning of this, and he answered, "That little hole is for the little dog." "But what is the big hole for?" Said he, "That is for the great dog." Then said one, "But the little dog might have gone through the same hole as the big dog, surely." "There!" said he, "I never thought of that." I want you to think of it: the little dog can pass where the big dog has entered. If the dying thief came to Christ, and was saved, why should not you? If Saul of Tarsus, blood-red with persecution, found room, there is room for you. Write yourself down as black as you like, but still remember that others as bad as yourself have been saved; and why not you?

I would like to put a question to you, but I must whisper it. Perhaps the other friends will not listen. Don't you think that when people have no hope, and are a long time despairing, there is a little sullenness in it? I do not want to say anything hard, but *may there not be just a spice of rebellion against God in your humility?* You want the Lord to deal with you in a marvellous manner; and as he does not choose to gratify you, you will not believe in him? You crave a remarkable dream; you long for a striking text to jump right out of the Bible and fix on you; and as you cannot get these special experiences, you will not believe in Jesus. I have put this very softly. Is there anything in it? If so, just shake yourself out of that sullen spirit. I pray you do so by God's grace. Don't put Christ away from you out of *a proud despair*. Accept his mercy as a common-place sinner. Don't want to be a great personage in the kingdom of Christ; but come as a common-place sinner, and accept such a Saviour as anybody else may accept. I am afraid there is just a tincture about you of wanting to be somebody—even though it be only to be worse than other people. I have known men take as much pride in blackening themselves with their sins as others have taken in their self-righteousness. You need not be so mighty proud of your rags: the very thought of them is detestable. Come just as you are, a common-place sinner, to take the common salvation which is provided in Jesus Christ.

Listen to me again. Do you not think that, when you despair and refuse to hope in God, *you are dishonouring him?* You say, "He will never forgive me." How can you say so? You do him much dishonour by that. "Oh, but he cannot!" Dare you use the word "cannot," in connection with omnipotent love? Unbelief gives God the lie. Despair is blasphemy against the infinite love and mercy of God. I am sure you would be ashamed to be guilty of that. Believe that the Lord is ready to forgive you. Come back to your Father's house with "I have sinned" upon your lip, and a full confession of your transgression written on the fleshy tablets of your heart. God grant that it may be so!

Let me try once more. So you think that God will never save you, but will leave you to perish? May I ask you *what good you think your death will do to him?* What profit is there in your blood? Suppose that you are lost, what gain is there to God in that? But suppose the Lord should save you. "Oh," say you, "He shall never hear the last of it!

> ' I will praise him in life, and praise him in death,
>   And praise him as long as he lendeth me breath.' "

He will be honoured then. You ought to hope that for his name's sake you may yet obtain mercy through Jesus Christ.

I will ask you another question. Suppose you should now discover that the Lord chose you from before the foundation of the world, that your name is written in his Book of Life, that he has bought you with his blood, and has espoused you to himself by an everlasting marriage, and means you to sit at his right hand, in his glory—suppose it is so, what will you say to yourself, in the happy days which are coming, for having thought so badly of the Well-beloved? If any of you has a dear friend at your side, or one nearer still than a friend, if there was ever a time when you used to think badly of the one you love so well, you cannot remember it without feeling a hot drop rising beneath the eyelid. It seems to me, that when I get to heaven and see my Lord, and am filled with his love, I shall marvel to think that I ever doubted him. Even now I want you to chide yourself for lack of trust in the dear Lord. Alas, that he loves you so, and yet you should not love *him!* Rock, Rock! Break! Break! The mighty rod of love hath smitten thee, pour forth thy streams of living love and deep repentance. Jesus loves thee. Oh, do not so live that afterwards thou shalt have to chide thyself for thinking so hardly of him. All the griefs that Christ bore do not so greatly vex his heart as that wicked thought of yours, that he is unwilling to forgive. By that thought you have stabbed him! By that hard suspicion you have nailed him to the cross! Oh, do not so; but, guilty as you are, believe that he forgives. Wretch as you are, believe that he saves. Trust yourself with him: this is all the gospel. "He that believeth, and is baptized, shall be saved," is the fuller form of it. "Believe on the Lord Jesus Christ, and thou shalt be saved," is the essence of it. Neglect it not.

Glow-worms.

BY THOMAS SPURGEON, OF AUCKLAND TABERNACLE, NEW ZEALAND.

"A GLOW-WORM, do you call it—that miserable, dull-coloured, half-inch, creeping thing, a glow-worm! There's precious little to go into ecstasies over, so far as I can see. A glow-worm, indeed! Well, it is a worm, right enough, and a poor enough specimen at that; but where the glow comes in beats me." The enthusiastic naturalist smiled in silence; but he thought the more. It was useless to expect admiration from such a critic. To him nature's choicest and most curious treasures were mean and miserable. The ignorant cannot judge. They are misled by appearances; and, alas, they often will not learn! The unenlightened one calls this little thing the most contemptible of worms; nor can he be persuaded that it is a gem most beautiful.

Suspend your judgment, courteous reader, on So-and-so. You do not know all. He may not be as mean a creature as he looks. Appearances deceive. Wait till you have learned what gifts and graces lurk within an uninviting exterior. The worm may be a glow-worm—crush it not. Uplift your heel, good sir. Bring it not down with violence, lest you stamp on a saint, and extinguish one of the lights of the world!

Special circumstances are necessary to reveal what is precious in certain characters. The dusk of evening and the shades of night are the special circumstances of the glow-worm. Then it is true to its name; a halo gleams about it; the grub is glorified. Then each tiny insect becomes a living flame, a fairy lamp, a mimic star.

Ah, yes! you should see the very ones you spurn and slight when their opportunity arrives. See them in the sick-chamber, or at the death-bed. See them when sudden accident or cunning treachery has turned the daylight into darkness. Then they rise to the occasion. Then their graces glisten: sorrow makes them shine. Perchance, dear reader, those whom you have once contemned have cheered you since, retaliating with sweet revenge by illuminating your darkest hour. Are you not glad you did not crush them?

There is a wonderful charm about the gleam of glow-worms, especially when they shine in myriads. The pale blue light of one or two may pass unnoticed, but of the shining host everybody says, "How beautiful!" Can I ever forget the glories of the Tikitapu bush? (Since then, alas, it has blazed with fiercer fires, belched forth from the flaming volcano of Tarawera!) There, in a cutting, was the glow-worms' rendezvous. The banks, on either side the road, were all a-twinkle. Ten thousand tiny stars sparkled from the grass and on the leaves. Every fern-frond was full of eyes. Bless the beaming beauties, beetles though they were! They sent us on our way rejoicing. I defy the most skilful pyrotechnist to produce anything half as lovely. The coloured fires, and prismatic fountains, and fairy lamps of the costliest *fête* are not within "coo-ee" of this exhibition. Modest little glow-worms, you have triumphed! Yours is the FIRST PRIZE FOR ILLUMINATIONS!

Learn, hence, a two-fold lesson. The brightest blaze is not always the most beautiful; and combination often makes amends for inefficiency and feebleness. Get together, you whose gifts are slender. Co-operate

and amalgamate, if your powers are few, and your purses poor. Do not
despise your own effort, but gleam in company.

"Shine like a glow-worm, if you cannot like a star."

Glow may be better than glory, after all. Light is preferable to lightning. I would rather be a glow-worm than a fire-fly, or a shooting-star,
for that matter. Would not you?

It is not every fraternity of glow-worms whose lot is cast in a public
thoroughfare; many are born to shine unseen. Do you think they
murmur? I came across an encampment of them once in some deep
caves, little frequented. There, from the rough roof, their pale radiance
streamed upon the else scarcely ever broken gloom. Yet these were as
bright and beautiful as those which tourists were admiring every day.
What cared they that so few saw them shine? God put them there,
and HE could see them always. What is your lot, and where your sphere,
good friend? Be content, though unobserved and unapplauded. You
may decorate a thorn-hedge with at least one diamond. You may glitter
in a cavern, and mitigate its gloom. Shine on. God in heaven sees
you, and will bless you.

Why are these worms luminous? "In order that they may seize their
prey," say some. Their victims are supposed to be attracted by their
beam, as sea-birds by a lighthouse, or moths by a candle. Poor silly
dupes, lured to their death by a pretty flame! This sort of thing is not
confined to insects and birds. A pair of bright eyes may decoy to
destruction. The glare of the theatre and dram-shop may entice to ruin.
The devil himself can pose as an angel of light.

Then, again, some hold that the glow-worm's light serves as a defence
against nocturnal enemies, as travellers kindle a watch-fire to keep the
beasts at bay. Riding at anchor, in the deep of darkness, these frail
barques hang up their lantern, lest some leviathan should run them
down. We shall do well to keep *our* beacons burning. A bold profession, a clear outshining, may save us from collision and disaster.

What if the Lord made these creatures lustrous merely that human
eyes might glitter with delight at sight of them? Let us be grateful
for glow-worms, for he who "made the stars also" made them too.

Perhaps they sparkle in the banks to teach us lessons. "We do our
little best," they say; "do you the same." "We get our light from
above; is not yours borrowed, too?" "We are never more pleased
than when, instead of praising us, onlookers say, 'How good and wise
is God to make such wondrous things!' for we desire to honour him.
Let *your* light so shine that men may glorify your heavenly Father."

It is a well-established fact, however, that the female glow-worm gives
the brighter light; the male can scarcely be said to glow at all. He
does his best, poor fellow; but he is not gifted with brilliance. His wife,
his sister, his fair cousin, and his aunt do the shining. (I ought to say,
in passing, that he can fly, while they are wingless. Nature always
compensates.) There is no help for it. We men must give the palm
for light and brightness to the gentler sex.

"A lamp is lit in woman's eye
That souls else lost on earth remember angels by."

I find that poets have so often compared women to "stars of the

night," and " gems of the morn," that they may not take it as a compliment to be compared to glow-worms. Yet, truth to tell, there can
scarcely be a better symbol; and if you would see sweet woman at her
best, behold her in the time of grief. Then her true beauty appears:
men are nowhere. Who, like her, can silently suffer and meekly bear?
Who, like her, can sympathize, and solace, and tend? Who more true
and faithful? Who so patient and long-suffering?

The glimmer of these lady glow-worms is thought by some to be the
flame of love. With these the amorous belles allure the sterner sex;
and wherefore not, if God has made them so? I am glad one poet names
it to their praise.

> "They call thee worm, thy love ungently name;
> Whilst thou, like Hero, lightest to thy nook
> Some bold Leander, with thy constant flame,
> Whose Hellespont may be this running brook
> Oh, let the wise man-worm his pride abjure,
> And his own love be half as bright and pure! "—*Blackwood.*

And who can tell but that some of those soft gleams denote the joy of
loving matrons welcoming their husbands home from business? (The
husbands have the wings, remember.) Next time I see a glow-worm,
I shall look out for her " worser half," and shall almost hope to hear
him say—

> " O Helen! O Helen! You're the light o' my dwellin'."

This is as it ought to be. Would that it were so in every home on
earth!

Farewell, bright little friends! Many thanks for the light you have
thrown on several subjects. We are worms, too; but we mean to be
glow-worms, and shine to the praise of our Redeemer, for

> " Poor helpless worms in him possess
> Grace, wisdom, power, and righteousness."

The True Apostolical Succession.

THE Church of Christ will never be denuded of faithful witnesses.
When one champion and honoured servant is removed, another is
found ready to take his place. "Moses my servant is dead." But, no
sooner is that announcement made, than Joshua is summoned from his
tent with the salutation and commission :—" Be strong, and of a good
courage." Elijah is carried up to heaven in a fiery chariot; but the
same hour Elisha stands before us, his worthy and accredited successor.
The thunder-tones of Luther are in course of time silenced; but the
voices of other faithful witnesses and sponsors are prepared in turn to
prolong the echoes. There is thus a blessed continuity in the Church
of Christ, a true Apostolic succession. No sooner is the mandate given,
" Remove the diadem, take off the crown," than some other is served
heir to it : some new shoulders ready for the burden :—some fresh hand
ready to seize the fallen banner and bear it onward. "The Lord gave
the word, and great was the company of those that published it."
(Ps. lxviii. 11.)—*Macduff's "Ripples in the Starlight."*

A Visit to Foreign Prisons.*

BY CHARLES COOK, OF HYDE PARK HALL, LONDON, W.

THE story goes that King Henry VIII., wandering one night in the streets of London in disguise, was met at the foot of one of the bridges by some of the watch; and, not giving a good account of himself, was carried off to the Poultry Compter, and shut up for the night without fire or candle. On his liberation he made a grant of thirty chaldrons of coals, and a quantity of bread, for the solace of night prisoners. A little personal insight and experience had awakened his compassion. There are prisons in other lands where the light of God's love never shines, and where the "Bread of Life" is never broken. May we, who are in happier case, sympathize with the inmates of such places, and feel it a privilege to carry to such the story of his love, who says, "I was in prison, and ye visited me!"

Having been to nearly all the prisons in Europe, as well as others in Africa and America, I here desire to give a short account of my endeavours to give the Word of God to those prisoners who were not provided with it, and to alleviate their sorrows.

EGYPT.

From seaboard to Soudan, from Alexandria to Philæ, did we travel, scattering the Word in villages and towns, on board the steamers, and in cells of prisons. In Cairo, the prisons were not so very bad; but in other places, and specially in Upper Egypt, the gaols were most unhealthy; it was no uncommon thing to find the water used for drinking purposes kept in the latrine, and a cesspool under the room where the prisoners slept. This was bad, indeed; but on enquiry of the authorities, I found over one thousand four hundred men in prison awaiting trial, and I was officially informed that many of them had thus been imprisoned for NEARLY SEVEN YEARS. This, and other instances of injustice, led me to lodge a strong protest at the Palace of the Khedive; and, writing to his Highness, I complained bitterly of the inhumanity of detaining prisoners so long before bringing them to trial. Whether through this letter or not, I was pleased to notice that three days afterwards *one hundred and fifty poor wretches were released*, and others were to follow. I "thanked God, and took courage"; and having been enabled to give copies of the Scriptures to all who could read in the prisons of Egypt, I left these miserable dungeons, with their chained and manacled inmates, and sailed for the classic shores of

GREECE.

Passing by the Island of Crete, in less than three days, from Alexandria, we reached the Piræus, and after a long and dusty drive, we enter Athens, to find one of our travelling companions stricken with ophthalmia, which he had contracted somewhere in Egypt.

---

* This is the second paper in which Mr. Charles Cook has called attention in our pages to his prison work. We deeply sympathize in his desire to bless these needy and suffering ones; and we think his lectures will enable friends to help him, if they invite him to their churches.

Visiting the prisons here, we were surprised to find them dirtier than those we had recently left, and quite as unhealthy ; for in one room we found ten men, in a room ten feet square; and in another, where thirteen men were confined—one being dangerously ill—the room measured twelve feet square, the only mode of ventilation we could see being the occasional opening of the door. No work was given the prisoners to do, and no books were provided for them to read; whilst the floors, stair-cases, and passages were simply thick with dirt. On our arrival, the chief prison in Athens was in a great uproar, as three men had escaped, and only one had just been recaptured. This man we visited, and gave him a copy of the gospels; but so dejected and miserable did the cap-tives all appear, that we first ordered them all to be supplied with coffee, and then left copies of the Scriptures in modern Greek for them all. Shame on the land of Homer and Demosthenes! and shame, indeed, on the authorities of Athens, to allow such dirt and misery to exist ! We wrote to the Minister, who has charge of the prisons, pointing out the need of reform, and complaining of the unsanitary condition of the place. We had to leave Athens before there was time to get an answer, but trust something was done to mend matters.

ITALY.

"It is no good going to Italy," said many friends, " you will never get the Scriptures into the prisons of that country." "Never venture, never win," replied I, " yet I will endeavour to do so." What is the result ? From Milan, in the north, to Naples, in the south; from Puzzuoli to Brindisi, in the old state dungeons of the Inquisition at Venice, to the convict prisons of Rome itself, have I had the joy and pleasure of distributing the Word of life. The people of Italy are struggling to be free from the thraldom of the priests; are far more loyal to King than to Pope ; and I was rather helped than hindered in my work by all the officials I came in contact with. Among the many interesting visits paid to the gaols of Italy, I select but one. We had run through Rome, visiting every prison it possesses, and leaving behind us our precious books without any opposition from the authorities, and reached Brindisi, where some six hundred convicts were imprisoned in the old castle. So eager were these men to possess the Scriptures, that they pressed round us so closely as to anger the governor, who was conducting us over the place. We were in one of the exercising yards—prisoners in chains all around us clamouring for our books ; the governor was about ordering the men into their cells, because of their noise, &c. Not a moment was to be lost; so, taking all the copies I had with me, and smiling the official into a good humour, I threw them into the middle of the yard. The noise of their chains clanking on the stones, and the scrambling of the convicts to obtain possession of those books, will ever live in my memory. In this country there are over five thousand men imprisoned for life, and these are known by their dress, which consists of red jacket, green cap, and dark trousers.

FRANCE.

" How long has this man to endure solitary confinement ? " I asked of the warder who was conducting me over the " Maison Centrale," of

Caen, in Normandy. " Ten years." "What is the effect of this on the prisoners ? " " It drives them mad," answered the officer. Descending into the lower part of the prison, I found a man in a " dark cell," and enquired the time he had been thus immured. " He has been in this cell twenty-five days, and has five more to stay," was the answer. The light of the lantern which I carried almost blinded the man. We gave away our books to the prisoners, and left the place.

No Roman Catholic Government supplies its prisoners with Bibles; but I am thankful to say that in many such countries I have travelled, visiting them with this object in view, and have been most gladly welcomed. The nine huge prisons of Paris alone occupied me nearly two years of what time I could spare from my own congregation in London. The prison discipline of France is extremely rigorous; but there is nothing about it which is calculated to reform a man, much less to convert him. The result is seen in the enormous number of men who are convicted again and again, and who, at last, have to be shipped as incorrigibles to New Caledonia.

AUSTRIA.

This was the most Papal country I had, as yet, seen. Several persons had been summoned for giving away tracts, and the wife of the chaplain to our own ambassador told me they were not allowed to hold a public prayer-meeting in their own house. We managed, however, to give away four hundred and fifty Testaments in four days in the streets of Vienna. By the aid of our credentials, we were soon in possession of the needful authority for visiting the prisons of Austria. It would not be wise, concerning this country, to speak in detail : enough to say that Protestants, Catholics, and Jews alike shared in the blessing of having the Word in their own language, we having received an official receipt for all the books which we gave away. Of course, I found that what could be done in Vienna it was possible to do in the provinces, and the receipt mentioned above was of great use to me.

HUNGARY.

Here we feel we are breathing another air. Though still under the rule of Austria, the Hungarians are a liberty-loving people ; and I had liberty given me to go where I liked, and do as I wished. In the capital—Buda-Pesth—in one day I supplied every prisoner with God's Word. Servians, Hungarians, Croatians, and others, all received the books with thankfulness. The ventilation of the prisons here was bad, the stench was horrible ; but the authorities thanked me for calling attention to it, and promised to remedy it. To God be all the praise.

I am trying to arrange with some of our ministering brethren at home to lecture on " The Prisons of the World," illustrating the journey by about thirty costumes, which I have brought from many lands. The lecture will deal with prisoners, and the costumes will illustrate the manners and customs of the ordinary people of the lands I have visited. Letters addressed to me, Hyde Park Hall, London, W., will find me.

Samuel Morley, the Merchant Philanthropist.*

SO far as the giving of his substance to the cause of God was concerned, Samuel Morley was the foremost benefactor of England during the present century. No one can read Mr. Hodder's interesting biography without seeing that this chief among merchant princes was what he was because he was a Christian. Mr. Hodder's hero bore a name that was familiar to everyone; but he differed in many essential particulars from the ordinary run of men who are supposed to deserve a biography after death. He was not a great scholar; in the conventional sense he was not a man of wide literary culture; in his views of gospel truth, and of moral duty, many, priding themselves on a more "advanced" liberality, would have called him narrow. He has left no copious diary, and few letters worthy of being printed; and his speeches, though marked by strong common-sense, were mainly exhausted by the occasions on which they were spoken. Many who knew the man as he was, and honoured him for what he did, at the same time wondered how the story of his life could be successfully told in a book. We are glad that Mr. Hodder's volume has justified the experiment. We see Mr. Morley as he lived and worked; and his story is worth the telling. It should stimulate young men to aim high, and to put Christ first in all the associations of life.

The Morleys are an old Nottinghamshire family, who, more than a century ago, possessed both wealth and influence. Samuel Morley, who died in middle-age, one hundred and twelve years ago, left three sons, and two of these, John and Richard, were the founders of the great firm in Wood Street. They were both of them shrewd men of business, as well as men of considerable capacity in other respects. Hitherto they had carried on the farm at Sneinton, and at the same time had been engaged in hosiery business at Nottingham. But with the changes that had come over their family life, there came changes also in their business relations. To meet the requirements of an increasing trade, it was mutually resolved that John should leave the old associations at Sneinton and Nottingham, and found a house in London, while Richard should carry on the farm, and at the same time extend the manufacturing business. The arrangement was, that while the London and Nottingham branches should be quite distinct as regarded the management, all accounts should be dealt with in London, and in both places the style and title of the firm should be "I. and R. Morley."

In 1798 John Morley married Sarah Poulton, of Maidenhead, and these were the parents of Samuel Morley. John came of Puritan stock; he was from the first an uncompromising Nonconformist, but he would, nevertheless, sometimes be seen in the family pew in Sneinton church.

"Content with small beginnings, he engaged part of a house in Milk Street, Cheapside, immediately opposite to the spot where, until quite recently, stood the City of London School. Instead of setting up a large domestic establishment in the suburbs, as many would

---

* "The Life of Samuel Morley." By Edwin Hodder. With etched portrait by Manesse. Hodder and Stoughton. Price 14s.

have done, he lived on the premises; and when, in course of time, business increased, he moved to larger and better quarters in Wood Street. . . . . When it was demonstrated to a moral certainty that success was ensured, and not till then, John Morley took a house in Homerton, where most of his children were born; and when, in the course of a few years, the continued prosperity of the business justified the step, he removed to a much larger house, in Well Street, Hackney, where he lived till the end of his long life."

Samuel Morley's days of childhood and youth were as happy as health, genial surroundings, and religion could make them. " His mother was a woman of character, of sweet and tender disposition, of intense affection, and of beautiful, unpretentious piety. His father was a man universally beloved, whose name stood well in the City, who was respected in a wide circle of religious and philanthropic workers ; in London, one of the best known Nonconformist laymen, and in his own home, always bright and genial."

As a schoolboy, young Samuel passed some time at Melbourne, in Cambridgeshire, and also at Southampton. Although he did well at school, he showed no uncommon piety in youth ; and at sixteen, in 1825, he commenced his career by entering the business house in Wood Street. What he was at this time is thus described by Mr. Hodder :—

" In many things the boy was father to the man. He was earnest in what he did. If he raced he raced as for his life ; and if he took his place in a tug of war, he pulled as if success or failure depended upon himself alone. His holidays were always spent at Hackney, except when an occasional visit was made, with his family, to the seaside. And happy holidays they were. There was the grand old garden, the large paddock with a pony to ride, and the companionship of brothers and sisters, and every encouragement from his parents to indulge in all healthy and manly recreations. Samuel loved his father and mother passionately, loved the home influences, and never associated the least notion of constraint with the family roof. It would be hard to say which exercised the greatest influence over him, his father or his mother. In after-life he used often to say, ' I am what my mother made me '; at the same time his father's influence was a most important factor in the formation of his character ; and no one who knew him can forget his constant reference to his father's opinions and sayings in such words as these, with which he would often commence or finish a sentence : ' As my dear father used to say.' "

He was content to commence in a humble way, by working for seven years in the counting-house as an ordinary clerk, walking to and fro between Hackney and the City, the hours of business being from soon after nine until seven in the evening. John Morley, senior, used to be seen, with his two sons, making the journey on foot before popular conveyances were available ; and during those morning and evening walks the father had many opportunities of teaching his children to become like himself—thorough-going Nonconformists as well as philanthropists, although he never unduly pressed his own views of religion and politics upon their acceptance. The rising merchant and his amiable wife became " celebrated for their hospitality; and among their visitors were all the prominent men of the day belonging to Nonconformist circles.

where Mr. Morley exercised, perhaps, a greater influence than any other layman of his time." Trained amid such associations, in a place which was then a centre of Nonconformity, it would have been singular indeed if the young Morleys had not done credit to their house. We have, of course, all along to bear in mind, that the days of Mr. Morley's youth and early business life were very different from our own, and there was then much self-denial in a man's openly avowing himself a Nonconformist.

Samuel Morley entered as heartily into his father's philanthropic enterprises as he did into the business; but, contrary to what might have been expected when all was so prosperous, he appears to have been in no hurry to marry; and, indeed, when he did come across the right lady, he did so by a sort of happy accident. Having occasion to call on Mr. Wilson, of Highbury, he was introduced to the Misses Hope, of Liverpool, and to one of these, Rebekah Maria, he was married in 1841. Mr. Morley found in his wife a thorough help, a woman who knew how to govern the home, and make it comfortable while he was engaged in the now rapidly-multiplying duties of life. He had already begun to develop into the philanthropist; and Richard Knill, later on, the friend of Mr. Spurgeon, was one of the first to receive a donation for his work at Wotton-under-Edge. Meanwhile there were many things in which such a man could not fail to be interested. Dissenters needed to be better represented in Parliament: the subject of primary education was being warmly debated; and the founding of *The Nonconformist*, by Edward Miall, proved that the denominations could use the Press with a power which their opponents could not excel. In all such matters Mr. Morley had a part. As time went on, and after the death of his father, in 1848, when, as it were, Samuel Morley stood more alone in the world, there were plenty of other enterprises which he was glad to stimulate. The Home Mission work of the Congregational Union he encouraged. The bettering of the condition of the working-classes in connection with theatre preaching, and the providing of better homes; parliamentary reform; the currency question; and the celebration of the bi-centenary of the two thousand confessors who left the Church of England in 1662, all won his aid. The Memorial Hall, on the site of the old Fleet Prison, in Farringdon Street, commemorates the latter celebration, and £6,000 was contributed to the building fund by Mr. Morley. His long term of parliamentary life, the Nottingham election riots, his return for Bristol, and the disappointments, hard labours, and successes which followed, may be regarded as distinct episodes in his busy life. It was contrary to the wishes of many far-seeing friends that he entered the House of Commons at all; and though he may have rendered useful service, he did so at an expenditure of strength which might have been given to what some considered his more legitimate calling.

The glimpses which are given of Mr. Morley's home-life, both at Stamford Hill and Tonbridge, are not only pleasing in themselves, but they reveal the sentiments he held in regard to many who are content to dwell on a sort of border-land between the church and the world. Thus, when his children were kept at a party, at a minister's house, where dancing, &c., was kept up until the small hours of the morning, Mr. Morley wrote to the pastor referred to :—

"There is a position, it appears to me, to be sustained between a rigid asceticism and moroseness on the one hand, and a laxity and negligence on the other; but, without going into details, I am sure that at the present time, and especially in the suburbs of London, the danger lies in the direction of the forgetfulness of this ruling principle of consecration, and, consequently, of undue approach to worldly maxims and ways. It was, therefore, with regret that I received a report of what transpired on the occasion to which your letter refers, because I thought the inevitable tendency of such proceedings would be to make it more difficult for some of us to keep back our children from ways and habits of life which, I am convinced, are injurious to their bodily and spiritual health. . . . It is not without reason, I think, that we look to you to check, rather than to stimulate, such tendencies in our circle."

From the above no sensible Christian person will infer that Mr. Morley was in any sense narrow in restricting the liberties of the Christian household.

"Mr. Morley was a kind and genial host. His attraction, however, was rather to his study than to the drawing-room, especially when his guest happened to be a man . . who could set before him, in a clear and practical fashion, some new scheme of public usefulness. He was not very social, in the ordinary sense of the word. He very often asked people to have a chop with him in Wood Street, at one o'clock; but in the days prior to his entry into Parliament, he rarely gave dinner-parties at home. The 'pleasures of the table' had no charms for him. He was simple in his tastes, never seemed to care for what is called 'good living,' and scrupulously avoided all habits of self-indulgence. He was, through life, exceedingly moderate in his food; and when he took wine he only took it in very small quantities, and for some years before the time of which we are now writing, he had abstained from it altogether. It is hardly necessary to say that, although not caring for these things himself, he did not force his opinions on others."

The picture we have of Mr. Morley as a business man is in all respects worthy of his Christian character. He never cut-down his workpeople's wages; but while seeking their interests, he was never satisfied with anything short of the best service. Knowing that one captain in a ship was enough, he did not like to give the word of command more than once; and he was not disposed to "make allowances for men who were dull and slow." If hasty words escaped him, he would be one of the first to make amends. There were thus, as was inevitable, flaws in his character, which no one lamented more than himself. "His best friends acknowledge that he carried imperiousness to a fault; and Mr. Morley himself averred that he had been all his life long trying to conquer his besetting sin of impatience." It has to be remembered, however, that the worries inseparable from managing so vast a concern were considerable. The house of Morley is the largest business of its kind in the Queen's dominions. When we find that two thousand letters would be delivered each day by the general post, followed by from sixty to a hundred by every succeeding post throughout the day, some idea of the magnitude of the concern may be formed.

The house in Wood Street was a school of training for many a youth or young man who was ambitious to make his mark in the world; and in many respects those who were engaged on the premises, found themselves encouraged to be steadfast in the Christian life. A Home Missionary Association was formed ; and at the station established in the neighbourhood of Golden Lane, a missionary was appointed at a salary of £120 per annum. The quarterly meetings of the employés were addressed by some of the leading ministers of the day.

Another interesting passage in Mr. Morley's life was that relating to his association with the newspaper press. "On June 8, 1868, the price of *The Daily News*, which had hitherto been threepence, was, mainly owing to the exertions of Mr. Morley, reduced to one penny." It would have been far more satisfactory if the Christian merchant, as one of the largest proprietors, could have exercised more influence over the editorial staff. One of the crying wants of London is a daily paper of a high moral tone—one not having two or three columns a day devoted to racing and betting. If it had occurred to Mr. Morley to render this great service, he could have carried it out as only few have the ability to do. It is still an anomaly that many provincial towns should be more favoured in regard to their daily papers than the capital.

Mr. Morley's philanthropy was local as well as general ; and thus, when, at sixty years of age, he removed from Stamford Hill to Leigh, near Tonbridge, the villagers of all ranks at once felt the benefit of having such a neighbour. Mr. Hodder says :—

"The drainage of the village was very imperfect : he had it put in a state of thorough efficiency, almost entirely at his own expense. The water was not good or abundant : he had a well dug, and machinery erected to pump and filter the water into a reservoir holding thirteen thousand gallons; he caused four fountains to be placed in the village, so that pure and good water could be within the reach of all, and a plentiful supply in a granite trough for dogs and horses. He found that there was no proper recreation-ground for the villagers : he caused one to be made and planted with trees, with a good road round it, and paths across it. The cottages needed radical improvement : he had some re-constructed, and new ones built of a model type. The villagers had no ground to cultivate as gardens: he set apart a plot of land for the purpose, cut it up into sections, and let them at a low rate. Cottage gardening was at a discount : he offered prizes for the best kept gardens and plants, and gave his gardener *carte blanche* to supply, free of charge, trees and shrubs to ornament the cottage gardens. In short, he found it a neglected village, and, as the gradual work of years, he transformed it into one of the neatest and prettiest in the country."

Christian work in the village was superintended by Miss Morley, for whose preachers her father erected an " undenominational chapel," the lady's views being "very nearly in accordance with those held by the religious community known as Plymouth Brethren." While he erected a baptistery, attended the services, and sometimes partook of the Communion in the school-room, and admired his daughter's devotion, Mr. Morley "totally disagreed with the opinions of many branches of the religious community with which she was connected." It was at Leigh, as a neighbour of Mr. Morley's, that Robert Moffat, the veteran missionary, spent his last days.

In the narrow limits at our disposal, it would, of course, be impossible
9

to give anything like a complete account of the many-sided philanthropic work of Samuel Morley; but those who are able to do so will do
well to look into the volume for themselves.. Who does not know of his
princely liberality? What part of Christian work has been unwatered
by his generosity? For steady continuous giving, he was not to be
outdone; and yet his wealth seemed ever to be increased thereby. In
this the Word of the Lord was fulfilled. The working-classes never
had a more honest and ardent friend; and among the enterprises which
he supported on their behalf, some fuller mention might well have been
made of the work at Lambeth Baths, superintended by the late G. M.
Murphy, a work to which Mr. Morley munificently contributed. Mr.
Morley's influence extended to all corners of the country; and his
departure has left a gap which will not be readily filled. His whole
heart went with the gospel of our Lord Jesus, and he often deplored
those departures from it which were cropping up in his own day, but
have become far more glaring since his departure. In the death of
Shaftesbury and Morley, the evangelical workers of Great Britain have
sustained a loss worthy of a mourning like that of "Hadad-rimmon
in the valley of Megiddo."

"By Dilution."

"WHAT is more unpleasant than to have to charge an opponent
with telling a lie? To use the term in its nude simplicity will
excite in an audience (on average occasions) the feeling of disgust
which, as Jeames Plush informed the master of the house, pervaded the
servants' hall in reference to a dinner of leg of mutton, suet pudding,
greens, potatoes, and beer: 'Substantial, sir, no doubt; but corse, sir,
very corse!' How can we remove the coarseness? By dilution. We
can say that our opponent reminds us of a conversation between a Friend
in Philadelphia, and one who had made some incredible statement:
'William, thee knows I never call names; but, William, if the Mayor
of this city were to come to me, and say, "Joshua, I want thee to find
me the biggest liar in all Philadelphia," I should come to thee, and say,
"William, the Mayor wants to see thee!"'..An English judge attained
the same end in this way: 'I should be sorry to say Brother Pearson is
the greatest liar of a lawyer I ever saw; but he is certainly more
economical of truth than any counsel on this circuit.'"

We copy the above from "*For Further Consideration.*" It has often
come before our thoughts while reading Down-Grade literature. Candour seems to have departed the earth. Words are now, in the case of
these gentlemen, often employed as instruments for concealing thoughts.
If the New Theology men would only say what they mean, and mean
what they say, we could deal with them; but, truly, the serpent is more
subtle than any beast of the field. If none enter heaven but those who
have the simplicity of little children, they are not likely to get there.
They would, if it were possible, deceive the very elect. We do not say
that they would be guilty of deliberate lying; but we do say that, if
they were to fall into that habit, we should expect them to do it in a
very natural and easy manner.

Central Africa and our Mission Stations.*

BY J. SALTER.

DR. -LIVINGSTONE lived and laboured to bring the sorrows and wrongs of the Dark Continent to the notice of Christendom. He travelled, he wrote, he died with Africa heavy on his heart. His powerful pen made Europe acquainted with the horrors of the slave trade. He had marched along the route of the slave caravan, and had seen the human skeletons that marked the line of march. He had passed the charred ruins of once flourishing villages, the inhabitants of which formed emaciated caravans for sale on the coast if they did not perish on the way thither. His sympathetic nature was consumed as a whole burnt sacrifice on the altar of inner Africa. Africa laid heavily on his heart, and in the heart of Africa he died.

The death of this great man has done more than his life, though the work that has been accomplished since his death could never have been achieved without the sacrificing of such a noble, self-denying life. He was the sun that shone on the dense darkness of the great Continent, though there were other contemporary luminaries of lesser magnitude that cast no small flood of light over the *terra incognita.* Mr. Saker, of the Baptist Missionary Society, lived and laboured long among the Cameroons. Some of his translations are before us while we write. Dr. Moffat, from the London Missionary Society, and his noble, heroic wife, spent their lives in South Central Africa, between the Molopo and the Zambesi, and many were the trophies they won for Jesus, among whom was Africana, the terrible freebooter. While there were pioneer missionaries in South Central Africa, there were others in the North-East of equal ability, endurance, and zeal. Among these, L Krapf, afterwards Doctor, and his able associate, J. Rebmann, both of the Church Missionary Society. The first of these was missionary among the Abyssinians, but that mission was abandoned in 1843, and the following year L. Krapf settled at Mombassa, and after two years he was joined by his indefatigable countryman, J. Rebmann. Krapf was the first to announce to Europe the existence of a snow-capped mountain at the equator, known as Kilimanjaro. The news at that time was received with a smile of incredulity on the part of those who were not quite so familiar with snow mountains as the discoverer ; for who would expect to find a mountain of snow under a tropical sun ? He also reported the existence of a lake in the centre, which subsequent visitors to the interior proved to be true. He was the first to discover the concord of affinities peculiar to all the languages of the Bantu family. This was first worked out in his grammar of the Swahili language, subsequently elaborated and remodelled by the late Bishop Steere. Krapf's dictionary of the Swahili language is the only one extant, and is a great work in itself. Rebmann made the first translation of any portion of the Scriptures in the Swahili language. His gospel of Luke was printed by the British and Foreign Bible Society.

* This paper, by our beloved brother, so long a missionary to the Asiatics, contains much that is deeply interesting to those who carry Africa upon their hearts. It strikes us as a very valuable paper.—C. H. S:

It is pleasant to linger among this noble band of veterans a while; for while their services are recorded in heaven, there is a chance of their being forgotten on earth. It is the divine order that one should sow and another reap. Reaping is a happy work, far more pleasant than sowing; and the age in which we live asks for reaping rather than sowing. Many will enter the harvest-field who do not care about ploughing and preparing the soil; and in the joy of harvest, the toil of the labourer in early spring is forgotten. But without the toiler of spring, there would be no precious sheaves to gather. Those early veterans in the mission-field had first to acquire an unknown tongue, discover its grammatical formation, formulate a dictionary, and even teach the natives the mysterious art of reading and writing. New-comers have all this to hand, and are often able to revise and reconstruct the productions of these pioneers, so that the veterans cease to be identified with the work they initiated with so much toil. Moffat, Saker, Livingstone, and a host of others, whose bones lie buried in the dark land, are now in the glory-land. "Yea, saith the Spirit, and their works do follow them"; and a glorious rest it must be to those weary toilers in the land of idols. In making these remarks, our mind is attracted to Krapf, Rebmann, and Carey. The last of these was the first in the field—not in Africa, but in India—whose early translation of the New Testament in Urdu is before us. I have no doubt but his heart rejoiced—and well might all the devoted brethren of Serampore rejoice with him—when such a work was completed; and it was a fit occasion to do so; but it is out of date now, having been revised, and the Dev Nagri character, in which it is printed, seldom used for that language. Indeed, a pioneer, though he lays the foundation on which others build, must not expect to produce a standard work. This, also, applies to the early missionaries—Krapf and Rebmann. Krapf was the first to reduce the singular language to order, to adapt it to Roman characters, and to produce the first grammar. But the aged Krapf has lived to see his noble work superseded by the laborious Bishop of Zanzibar. Bishop Steere has adopted a different literation from that used by Krapf, and has produced a grammar which will eclipse that of his forerunner in the work; but, then, the Bishop had the missionary's materials and tools to work with. Krapf's solid foundation is out of sight, and the bishop's noble and beautiful superstructure stands full in view.

Rebmann's translation will also cease to be a monument to his memory. It is in Krapf's literation. But the indefatigable Bishop lived to translate all the other parts of the New Testament, according to his own system, so that the Gospel of Luke, though forming part of the New Testament, is *not* in entire conformity with it. It is to the honour of the late Bishop that he felt a reluctance to obliterate the monument to the memory of the pioneer Rebmann; so, while he has altered the literation to bring it into fair conformity with his own great work, the translation remains as Rebmann's, and his work is thus bound up with that of the Bishop in the New Testament.

Bishop Steere's translation is in the Swahili of Zanzibar, Krapf and Rebmann in the Swahili of Mombassa, and, though only about one hundred and fifty miles apart, how soon changes in the language take place ! At Mombassa, a dislike is manifested to the " cb," and the " w," which are freely used at Zanzibar ; thus, *Inchi* (land) becomes *nti*, and *Bwana* (Lord) becomes *Bana :* among the Maiao and Makua, the r and the l are interchanged ; thus, God is *Muingu*, or *Mulungu*, or *Murungu ;* and yet this language belongs to a family of languages spoken from Zanzibar, in the Indian Ocean, to Old Calabar, on the Atlantic coast. In no other part of the world can a region be discovered where an unbroken system of intercommunication covers such a space of the globe. It is interesting to notice how soon, in some directions, the sound of a word becomes changed by an altered articulation ; and yet, in another direction, words may travel many hundreds of miles with little or no change. Stanley Pool is about two thousand miles from Zanzibar ; but mark the affinity in the following words :—

The chief's three dogs.

| Zanzibar. | Mbwa tatu wa Mfalme. |
| On the Congo. | Mbwa tatu a Mfumu. |

There is a strong element of intelligence and precision in this family group of tongues, inconsistent with a land always debased by slavery and cruel superstitious practices. Such intelligence and precision suggest a great past, which has been obliterated by Arab marauders, tribal wars, and heathen darkness. The history of this great continent is hidden, but we may predict a great future for both the language and the people.

Our missionaries have generally been the first to explore foreign lands, and bring to notice the rites and habits of the people ; but in Africa this work has been largely shared by adventurous travellers, such as Baker, Speke, Cameron, and especially by Livingstone and Stanley. In our youthful days we used to look at the mysterious map of Africa with its coast line of bays, lagoons, and rivers, coming from some imaginary source, and reaching the sea by a course equally imaginary, while the centre was filled up with lions, tigers, and elephants. In the map of to-day, these have all disappeared, and populous villages, towns, well-defined rivers and lakes appear where wild beasts were only supposed to roam. All this has been done at no small sacrifice of life and wealth. Native prejudices and customs have been no small impediments in the way of development. The extravagant presents expected by some chiefs, through whose territory the traveller wishes to pass, and the hostility of other chiefs against any European entering their country, have been serious obstacles in the way. The climate, too, has claimed a very serious death-rate. On the banks of the Niger and the Congo, an old, wide-spread belief still lives, that the white traveller steals away the spirits of the black men, and secretly conveys them, confined in some article of merchandise, to the coast, where they again put on their mortal tenements, and are made to work for the white man. We have met with Africans who attest the truth of this statement ; for they assert that they have heard a noise among the European merchandise, which was construed into the voice of such a captured spirit crying for liberty.

But the greatest enemies to the prosperity of the country are the Arab slave hunters, who have for so long a period held Africa from Whydah to Kiloa as a legitimate slave hunting-ground. At one time the Western coast was the great outlet of this inhuman traffic, but the occupation of Sierra Leone, and that portion of land that separates Ashanti from the sea, has closed the trade in that direction. This refuge for freed slaves has been maintained at a terrible cost, and has well earned the name of "the white man's grave." Slavers were captured in the Atlantic Ocean, and their human freight landed here under British protection. How far the slave trade influenced the interior of Africa from the West Coast, may be imagined from the Polyglotta Africana, compiled by Dr. Koelle, in 1854, in which he collected from freed slaves at Sierra Leone, specimens of language from more than 200 different tribes. Many of those liberated slaves were then rejoicing in their emancipation from a greater tyrant than the Arab hunter or the cruel master of the baracoon, for they were rejoicing in the liberty of the children of God. Our honoured S. Crowther, now Bishop of the Niger, rose from the ranks of the slave boys free at Sierra Leone.

But slavery checked in the West found a speedy outlet in the East. How long Zanzibar had been a slave market we cannot tell, but its name would suggest an early trade there. Its original name is Unguja, by which it is still known among the natives. It was a bold stroke to compel Syud Berghas to close the slave market of that island, for his interest was great in it. He levied a poll-tax on each man, woman, and child sold. In vain he was urged to repair his lost revenue by honourable trade, but he did not care to give up a certainty for an uncertainty. It needed an English man-of-war to appear off Shangani before the Sultan saw the wisdom of acceding to the English proposal. A church now stands on the grounds of the old slave market. Thus another great avenue for commerce in human sinew and bone was stopped in 1873. Still Africa continues a slave hunting ground, villages are still turned into blood and smoke, and the death track of the slave caravan is still noted, though we are willing and happy to think it has already felt the influence of civilization.

We have already referred to the great traveller and some of his contemporaries. We may now say how little has been accomplished that seems effectual to the removal of slavery from Africa. But Livingstone's death has done more than his life. His life laid open the land, his death has been a call to arise and occupy. It seemed to need the sacrifice of such a noble life to rouse the churches and nations of Europe to action. Well might the sons and daughters of the Covenanters take the lead in the noble work! Consecrated bands of Scotchmen went forth and occupied Blantyre, between the Zambesi and the Nyassa. These have gradually extended their influence along the shores of the lake. The Church Missionary Society occupied Uganda, at the northern end of the Victoria Nyanza, and planted intermediate stations along the long line of route; and the London Missionary Society has occupied Ujiji, on the Tanganyika, where Stanley discovered Livingstone, and they are extending their influence on the banks of this inland sea; while the Universities Mission, fixing their head-quarters at Zanzibar, have placed stations inland, among the Wakua and Waioo, till they reach the opposite shore of the Nyassa, about which are moving our brethren from Scotland. These are all scattered about the slave hunting ground between the East coast and the centre. Thus a noble work has been accomplished in comparatively few years, and predicts a glorious result.

So far, these preserves for hunting human game have been invaded; but this applies only to the Eastern and smaller half of the continent. Glancing from the Western coast to the centre, our expectation runs along the newly-discovered Congo ; the old Zaire and Lualaba united in one. We are indebted for what we know of this great river more to Stanley than to Livingstone. The knowledge of the importance of this water-way will exert an influence on Africa that cannot be overrated, for it is destined to become the highway to the centre. Along this line of route the missionaries from the Baptist Missionary Society, who do not appear on the East, are most prominent. Already they have planted stations on the upper river, and have more than twenty workers engaged at the gigantic task before them, and are calling on others to follow as they press forward to the lakes, and thus join hands with our brethren from the East coast. Comber, and other volunteers, have sacrificed their lives to the great task; others, baptized for the dead, have succeeded to their labours. Bentley has achieved a great work in the production of the grammar and dictionary that bear his name. This forms a grand stepping-stone between the West coast and the lakes, which missionaries and traders will highly value. The merchant has already passed on before, and an advanced station is now maintained at Stanley Pool; and here we are truly in Central Africa, being about equidistant from the Indian and Atlantic Oceans. This is a noble achievement, worthy the object in view. And yet Stanley Pool is five hundred miles distant from the most advanced station from the Eastern coast. A journey of five hundred miles of jungle land, with unknown swamps, no roads, and bridgeless rivers to cross, and where all burdens must be carried by the natives, is a very long way to travel. The water-way extends to Manynema, and perhaps further, so that possibly this distance may be shortened by two hundred and fifty miles by this water-way. Thus great things have been done. We say, "Praise the Lord ! Gird thy sword on thy thigh, O most mighty; and in thy majesty ride prosperously, because of truth and meekness and righteousness; and thy right hand shall teach thee terrible things."

We have thus far traced the triumphs of the churches in Central Africa, that we may the better understand the extent and nature of a change that is likely to discomfort most of these noble workers—a change which, though it may necessitate discomfort and re-organization, has, nevertheless, in it the death-knell of slavery, and the ultimate prosperity of the native churches of Central Africa.

Those mission-stations scattered about Central Africa cannot fail to excite the hostility of the prowling Arabs. They have ever, with much reason, regarded the European as unfavourable to their craft, and their influence at Uganda, and elsewhere, has been felt with baneful effect. Their hunting ground, to which time immemorial has given them an imaginary claim, is invaded. Still they have thousands of miles of native wold, left over which they can chase their human victims, secure from European gaze. But there is another and more important element now to the front. We live in an age when Europe is extending her protection to every part of the globe where it can be enforced. The broad plains of Africa could hardly escape the notice of our over-crowded nations seeking an extension of colonization and trade. The formation of the Congo Free States, of which Leopold, King of the Belgians, is nominal monarch, was grandly conceived and brought to a successful issue. Here a civilized government will ere long make its power felt, and mission-stations will not be exposed to the whims of vacillating chiefs, but secured by national protection; while a growing trade, aided by enforced law, will expel slavery in every form from the State. This is a happy forecast of a bright future.

The rest of Central Africa is already under European protection, in which Portugal, France, Germany, and England claim rights. How will this arrangement affect our mission-stations now under a foreign protectorate? Already our missionaries at Madagascar, Gaboon, and elsewhere have been discomforted by a foreign protection. Is there a similar discomfort looming in the future for our noble brethren of the Church Missionary Society, of the Universities' Mission, and our Scotch brethren on the Nyassa? Unfortunately all, or nearly all, the stations belonging to the Universities' Mission lie within the German Protectorate, and must more or less be affected by it. The same may be said of most of the stations belonging to the other societies. Indeed, the route to Uganda, with all the stations that mark that line of route, are now in German hands. Our Scotch brethren are removed from German influence, and will probably fall under British rule. Within the portion ceded to British rule, few mission stations exist; but, probably, the present circuitous route to Uganda will be abandoned for a direct route—the route that cost Bishop Hannington his life—now through the British Protectorate.

The slave hunters are aroused to desperation. They have made a combined attack on the station, at Stanley Falls, with too much success. They have come in collision with Germans, at Tanga, and left ten of their dead behind them. They have, also, measured their strength with our northern brethren on the lake. These are the dying struggles of a cruel giant. Christendom will rejoice when he is dead and buried.

French, English, and German companies are already formed, and these will cultivate trade over vast regions, and will, to a great extent, administer them. The British Protectorate includes Mombassa, the scene of J. Krapf's labours, where, indeed, he enjoyed the Sultan's authority "to convert the world"; it stretches from the coast to the Victoria Nyanza. This region has been reported unsafe for travellers, and even African cannibals have their reputed homestead there. Should the missions, under the German Protectorate, be too much under restraint, as they possibly may be, they must re-arrange and work under British protection. With slavery extinct, legitimate trade created, and European protection throughout the great Continent, the morning sun will dispel the darkness of the long night, civilization will extend, and, with this, we pray the gospel may run, have free course, and be glorified.

Who shall Keep the Keepers?

BY C. H. SPURGEON.

QUIS *custodiet ipsos custodes?* So say the Latins. Shepherds may keep the sheep ; but who shall pastorize the shepherds? A question of the weightiest import, both for the flocks and the pastors.

Politically, it is all very well to devise a form of government; but what if the governors themselves are ungovernable ? Look at poor France, whose first political necessity seems to be that her rulers should be ruled by a sense of justice, patriotism, and nobility. Given a Parliament where each man draws his pound a day, and secures his seat by promising to get subsidies for the district which returns him; he then sells his vote to those who will enable him to fulfil his promises, and a nation is dragged into needless expenses, which must end, sooner or later, in national bankruptcy. This happens in a republic, enjoying universal suffrage, which is, to some, the *beau-idéal* of perfect government. In our own land parliamentary institutions are becoming greatly degraded by the behaviour of certain representatives of the people. We may glory in our constitution ; but if God does not send us a race of true men to make up our House of Commons, where shall we be ?

Of vital importance is this enquiry religiously. What is to become of any body of Christians whose ministers are not loyal to their Lord and to his gospel ? When a church has over it a man of whom it can be justly said that he shows no sign of ever having been converted, what spirituality can be expected to survive ? When another preacher has one creed for the pulpit, and another for the private fraternal meeting, how can truth and honesty flourish in the community? When a third changes with the moon, and is not quite sure of anything, how can his hearers be established in the faith? We are not imagining cases ; there are too many who answer the description. Evil in the pulpit is poison in the fountain. In this case we find death in the great pot out of which all the guests are to be fed.

But who shall keep the keepers ? There is the great difficulty. This is a task beyond the power of the church and its most valiant champions. We might do well to watch the schools of the prophets, that more of deep devotion and fervent piety should be nurtured there. We might do no more than our duty if we were more jealously watchful over every election of ministers in which we take part, so that none were ordained but those sound in the faith, and filled with the Spirit. Even for these things, who is sufficient ? But if these were done to perfection, the plague might still break out among the teachers: their heads might be dazed with error, or their hearts grow chill with worldliness. We are thrown back upon him that keepeth Israel. It is well that it should be so. That which develops dependence upon God works for good.

All plans, however wise in themselves, and however effective they would be if we had to deal with honesty and truth, are baffled by the moral obliquity which is part of the evil. The men are not to be bound by creeds: they confess that such things are useless to them. Their moral sense is deadened by the error they have imbibed. They have become shepherds that they might poison the flock, and keepers of the vineyard that they might spoil the vines : if this was not their first motive, their course of action distinctly suggests it. There is no reaching them : they are bewitched and benumbed. Neither from within nor from without are healthy influences likely to operate upon them ; we must carry the case to the great Head of the church, and leave it in his hands. When' he ascended on high he received gifts for men ; and these gifts were men of differing offices, for the perfecting of his people. We have need that he should anew send us such men. May be we have forgotten to look to the ascended Lord. May be we have been gazing about us to find the men without looking first to HIM from whom they must come. Our Lord can speedily raise us up a new race of apo-stolic preachers from amid our youth, or he can convert those who are now the devourers of the churches. In the Reformation, many of the ablest leaders were called from among the priests and the monks; and to-day the Lord may breathe the life of faith into those who lie buried in sceptical philosophies. With him all things are possible. When we are at the end of our power and knowledge, we are on the confines of his omnipotence and omniscience. Let us bow our heads as we pass the frontier, and leave behind our own barren impotence to rejoice in his fruitful strength. Our confidence in the church of God lies not in her natural power, but in the fact that " God is in the midst of her; she shall not be moved."

Those who lament the declension of many among the present professed ministry should cry day and night unto the Lord to bless his people with pastors after his own heart. Let them also see to it that they walk wisely towards those they have. It behoves established believers to bear their testimony faithfully, but kindly, to young divines who are beginning to step aside ; for it may be that a gentle word may save them. In grosser cases, firmness may be needful as to the matter of quitting an unfaithful, Christless ministry ; or as to the removal of the false teacher.

In the happy instances in which the gospel is held and fully preached, the faithful should encourage, sustain, and help with all their hearts. Those who are faithful to the truth of God, should find us faithful to them. God will have his gifts valued, and his servants well treated. He has among his chosen ministers those who feel tears of gratitude welling up in their eyes when they think of the kindness of their churches; but there are other worthy men who are buffeted and battered, left without a decent maintenance, and never appreciated as they ought to be. For these the Lord himself will plead with his people, if there be not speedy improvement. Let not true shepherds be forgotten by the flocks to which they minister, nor by any of the faithful, lest their Master should be provoked to recall the gift which is not valued. Now, if never before, our eyes should be upon all the faithful of the land, to hold up their hands. No one must hold himself aloof lest that bitter curse should fall upon him which was of old pronounced on Meroz and the inhabitants thereof, because they came not to the help of the Lord against the mighty.

Little Mary the Martyr.

A 'MONTH'S mission in the Strand, London, has caused me to know that Fashion is not Beauty, but often the contrary in many respects. A lady asked me, the other day, what I thought of the "get-up" of the ladies we saw rushing into the theatres in their various costumes?

I said, "You have rightly named it 'get-up,' for it is indeed a 'get-up.' Many of them," I replied, "do not seem to have the least idea that Nature and Beauty are twin sisters." But it is so ; therefore, the more natural we are in our dress, life, and speech, the more useful and beautiful shall we become. No man or woman need be ashamed of being natural and simple in life and dress. We are all God's workmanship, and all that God has made is worthy of his divine power. But I have witnessed much of late, how Fashion, Sloth, and Vice can mar even God's workmanship. Some so-called ladies seem quite dissatisfied with the form with which God has endowed them. I heard one person remark that she must now prepare to "get herself up" in order to witness the "Cats" (some foolish play, I imagined), and the pit, I thought, was the right place for such a person to appear in. This lady thought she must try and assist Providence to improve her personal appearance; and what a fright she made herself look, to be sure ! She was only one among the many of both sexes I saw nightly rushing, in carriages, cabs, and hansoms, to these so-called places of amusement.

This same person asked me if I had been to see "The Babes in the Wood."

"No, madam," I replied; "life is too brief to waste in folly and foolery. I like pleasure that is lasting, and fun without sin ; but the main thing in this life is to bring glory to God, and to be made a blessing to others ; and all who neglect to do this, miss the real object of life. This life is not an accident, but part of a divine plan ; and I may miss my part altogether if I am careless, but I shall play a pleasant and profitable part during this life if I seek divine guidance. Therefore, the sooner a girl or boy seeks the Lord, the better it will be for them, as well as for those with whom they come in contact."

The person with whom I held this conversation, though she was a woman over seventy years of age, seemed to think there was nothing wrong in having dozens of young children employed on the stage, and trained for the pantomime. She could see no reason why mothers and fathers should not take their little girls and boys to witness such scenes. I told her my heart was pained, day after day, to see children being taken by hundreds to the theatres. I saw mothers rushing, with children in arms, fighting their way through the crowds into the pit. I said, "Madam, your conversation reminds me of a little girl I have heard about. It was an incident full of pathos. If you want interest, excitement, emotion, pathos, passion, and heroism, you need not go to the stage to get it. Listen, while I recite to you the story of this little heroic Christian girl."

"She lived in what is known in America as a frame-house, built with wood. All the houses round her were mostly of the same kind. One day there was a sad and sudden shout of 'Fire ! Fire ! Fire !' It was, alas ! too true. The fire-demon was abroad in fury, and the wind caused the flames to make great headway before much assistance could be given. In one house the husband rescued his fainting wife, who had become unconscious through the smoke. He then sprang from the window, and saved himself; and then, like a poor maniac, went rushing through the crowd, crying, and tearing his hair. And why ? Ah! that was the sad part of it. In his excitement he had saved his wife and himself; and then it dawned upon him that his three dear children were asleep upstairs, and there was no possible chance of reaching them. Poor man! he would have rushed into the burning house and perished with them but for strong friends who held him back by main force. But for them he would have destroyed his life in an utterly hopeless attempt.

"Soon the excitement became intense. Through the blinding smoke a weak voice was heard, and a dim form was seen at the top window. Little Mary was there, the heroine of my story. She was a sweet little Christian of twelve tender years. . She was hugging her little brother Bobbie, and a cry was raised from beneath :

"'Jump, we will catch you; jump, jump, quickly!' cried the crowd.

"She heard the shout from beneath, and instantly dropped her little brother into the outstretched hands, which, happily, caught the child in safety.

'Jump, jump, jump!' was again the continued shout.

But no voice was heard to reply. All thought she had succumbed; but soon her little figure was again discerned at the window.

"Jump, jump, jump!" said the people, with increased excitement; and so she did. It was her last leap in this life, but it was a grand one. She was safely caught by the crowd, and in her arms was a dear little baby, scarcely hurt. Alas! little Mary herself was terribly burned. She was soon taken into the house, and a doctor was tenderly examining her. He saw at once that she was doomed. She was unable to see : but still conscious. He did his best to alleviate her. sufferings, and found, on removing the burnt clothing from the child, that only one part of her body had escaped the fire, and that was a patch round her heart, where she had so tightly clasped her brother and the babe. Her sight was gone, her hair was burnt off, but around the chest and heart there was no mark of fire.

"'Her patience in death,' said my friend the doctor, who shed tears as he told me, 'was beautiful.'

"He said to her, 'Mary, do you know me?'

"'Yes, doctor,' was her reply.

"'I fear, my dear, I cannot do any more for you,' said he.

"'Never mind, never mind; thank you, doctor. I have saved Bobbie and baby, and Jesus has promised to save me, and he will, won't he. doctor?'

"'Yes, my dear, for he has done so already.' And he had scarcely said these words to encourage her, when Mary was no more.

"Do you tell me, madam, after this, that I need the stage or fiction to stir my imagination, or move my emotional powers? No, madam, I have no time to go and hear about the trials of those who never lived; nor to weep over events that never happened. But in the Bible, and in active service for Christ, I find full scope for all the faculties and emotions with which God has been pleased to endow me.

"I tell you, madam, I was moved, refreshed, and improved for having heard the touching story of little Mary, because it has four grand lessons running right through it. You here get truth with trial, and trust with triumph, all of which may be the portion of every believer."

The doctor who attended little Mary was the one who told this real, but romantic, story to a large congregation at the Metropolitan Tabernacle. I sat on the platform; beside me sat my dear friend, Mrs. Bartlett, who has since, like Mary, gone home to her reward. Our beloved President, C. H. Spurgeon, was chairman, and his big heart gave way during the telling of this incident by the American doctor. His manly face seemed none the less manly to me because a stream of tears came rolling down his face; on the contrary, I thought, "How like his Master! 'Jesus wept.'" They tell us this short verse, "*Jesus wept*," is the centre verse of the New Testament; if so, it is a fine pivot on which to swing the gospel of Christ's love.

Reader, ask yourself the question, "Are any tears ever shed over my life?" Does a mother, or sister, or wife, or pastor weep over you? If so, what is the cause of them? Remember, tears are caused by joy as well as sorrow. May God keep you and me from ever causing any tears of sorrow! May we create tears of joy!

Had I been asked to write an epitaph for Mary's tombstone, I think I should have written, "She saved others, herself she could not save."

J. Manton Smith.

Students of the Pastors' College and their Work.

MANY of the students now in the Pastors' College have the oversight of churches or missions in various parts of London or the country. We want our friends to know this, and to become better acquainted with our College work. Our aim is to send out good ministers of the gospel, and there is no better help in the education of such men than keeping them at work while studying. Many friends might help us to open up new places. We also need aid in subscriptions towards the work. In this laborious and anxious service we beg the aid of all lovers of the truth of God. The following is a brief summary of the work carried on by students now, or until recently, in the College :—

MR. A. CURTIS undertook the temporary pastorate of the Baptist church at *Hornchurch, Essex,* in November, 1886. The membership was then eighteen; it has since increased to thirty-eight, while several are waiting to be received. The Sunday-school has increased from ninety-five to one hundred and thirty-two scholars, and from ten to fourteen teachers. There is also a flourishing Band of Hope of over one hundred members. The Sunday congregations are extremely good, the chapel, which seats two hundred and twenty, being crowded in the evenings. In respect of finances, the people have done well, having, by means of two sales of work, and the kindness of several contributors, entirely cleared off the debt of £125 which was on the school, and they have also paid off £50 of the chapel debt. There is urgent need for enlarging the chapel, and this might easily be done, as it was built with a view to enlargement, and sufficient land was acquired for the purpose; but a debt of £125 still remains on the chapel, which must be cleared off before enlarging. This, however, our friends hope to do by next summer. The increased interest in every department of the work is exceedingly cheering. This cause, greatly aided by Mr. Abraham, of Hornchurch, is the child of the College.

MR. F. W. DUNSTER took up the work at Dell Road Baptist Chapel, *Grays, Essex,* eighteen months ago. At that time the church was not heartily united, but by God's blessing a better state of things now prevails. The membership has risen from twenty to fifty-three, while the congregations have been trebled, necessitating an extension, which furnished sittings for about seventy more people. The chapel now seats two hundred. The free-will offerings have been more than doubled, and a debt of £100 has been cleared off. A Temperance Society, Christian Band, prayer-meeting, cottage-meeting, and open-air services have been instituted, and resulted in much blessing.

MR. F. T. B. WESTLAKE has been labouring, since April, 1887, at *Parnell Road, Old Ford, E.* The results of the first twelve months' efforts are briefly as follow:—When Mr. Westlake went, there were twelve church-members; there are now fifty-three. In the Sunday-school there were three teachers and seventy scholars; the numbers at present are twenty and three hundred and sixty. Then there was but one service on Sunday, and no prayer-meeting; now there are two services, and three prayer-meetings. No tracts were distributed; now there are two thousand given away weekly. Bible-classes and other branches of work have also been established, the congregations have correspondingly increased, and the gospel has proved the power of God unto the salvation of many souls. When our brother went, he found what he modestly calls "a few slight difficulties." The chapel, which is an iron one, was sadly dilapidated, two hundred squares of glass were broken, the stoves had a habit of emitting all the smoke into the chapel during service, some of the seats (not being very strong) collapsed under pressure, while others, being badly painted, would hold fast the worshippers in one position, and refuse to let them go without paying, as penalty, a portion of their garments. These obstacles have been overcome, and the church is rejoicing in the manifest tokens of divine blessing.

MR. A. G. HASTE has been taking the oversight of the Baptist mission at *Bracknell, Berkshire,* since February, 1887. There are some twenty-five members on the books, the average Sunday morning attendance being thirty-six, and the evening seventy. The congregation meets in a most inconvenient room, and greatly needs a chapel, towards which the sum of £50 has been raised and handed over to Pastor C. H. Spurgeon, the treasurer of the building fund. There is a Sunday-school containing fifty-six scholars. This rising interest deserves aid from the Lord's stewards.

MR. T. ADAMSON has supplied the Baptist church, *Sunningdale, Berkshire,* for the past twelve months. The chapel has been recently enlarged, at a cost of £140, the whole of which has been paid off. The congregations are still increasing, and some believers have recently confessed Christ, and applied for baptism, while others are anxiously enquiring the way of salvation. The church has now a membership of forty-nine, and the Sabbath-school numbers fifty-three scholars.

MR. C. STANLEY founded a Baptist cause at *Silvertown, E.,* in September, 1887, and a church was formed in November of the same year, when seventeen persons were received into fellowship, nine of whom our brother had previously baptized, the rest being received by letter. The chapel, formerly known as the Drill Hall, was in a very dilapidated condition, and contained no furniture of any kind; but the friends who gathered round soon altered the condition of things, and made the place presentable. So well are the services attended, that it is difficult to find sufficient room to accommodate all who are present on Sunday evenings. The church now consists of forty-two members; and the Sunday-school, which commenced with ninety scholars and ten teachers, now numbers two hundred and twenty scholars and nineteen teachers. Much good work has been done by the Open-air Mission Band, which is conducted chiefly by young men and women who have been brought to the Saviour since Mr. Stanley commenced the work. A larger building being absolutely necessary to meet the existing needs of the work, a building fund has been started, and nearly £130 obtained. Mr. Spurgeon will be pleased to receive and acknowledge any contributions for this object.

, MR. G. H. JACKMAN commenced to preach at *Coggeshall, Essex,* in October, 1887. At that time the average attendance was twenty; at present it is about one hundred and twenty, and there is a membership of twenty-four. The chapel, on which there is a mortgage of £200, has been renovated during the year at a cost of about £45, which has been paid off. A Sunday-school was commenced the first Sunday in January, 1888, and there are now about forty children attending.

MR. N. H. PATRICK, who has just gone as a missionary to North Africa, preached, while in the College, at *St. Mary Cray, Kent,* where there is a chapel seating one hundred and twenty. The church numbers sixty-seven, and there is a Sunday-school, with eighty-two scholars and ten teachers. The congregations are almost entirely of the working-class, and the church has had heavy losses, especially through the emigration of the younger members. Nevertheless, there is encouragement in the work; the chapel is well filled, and two restored backsliders have lately been received into the church. Mr. A. W. L. BARKER has taken Mr. Patrick's place at St. Mary Cray.

MR. H. A. PHILLIPS entered upon work at *Mill End, Rickmansworth, Herts.,* in February last. The attendance has increased from forty to one hundred and sixty. Two backsliders have been re-admitted to membership, and four persons have been baptized, while several are under conviction of sin. Through visiting the people in their homes, a drunkard and his wife have been reclaimed. There is a Sunday-school of sixty scholars, and there is also a Bible-class. Our brother visits on Sunday afternoons, and though sin prevails on every hand, he hopes, "by prayer and plodding," to reach many who never attend the means of grace.

MR. H. CLARK went to labour at *Barking, Essex,* in August, 1887. At that time the Sunday evening congregation was about eighty; it has now doubled. The membership has increased from fifty to sixty-two. The school is very flourishing, numbering some two hundred and thirty scholars, with seventeen teachers. The blessing of God is resting on the work. The prayer-meetings are well-attended, and growing in interest and numbers.

MR. G. A. MILLER went to *Rochester, Kent,* two years ago, to start a Baptist cause there. No building being, at that time, obtainable in Rochester itself, the Workmen's Institute, at Strood, was hired. Much encouragement attended the work, and a church was formed last March, when twenty persons signed the covenant. The number of members now is thirty-eight. In April, the way was opened to hire a building in Rochester. This it was necessary to furnish. Seats, platform, harmonium, etc., were procured at a cost of £60, which amount has been entirely paid off. A Bible-class for men is held on Sunday afternoons, and a goodly company gathers together at the Monday evening prayer-meeting. Several have been baptized, and others are coming out to confess Christ. The shadow of the cathedral is no help to a Baptist cause, but the church is earnest and united, and hopes soon to have a home of its own, where it can better worship and work for the Master.

MR. A. W. CURWOOD has had charge of the little church at *Forest Row, Sussex,* for the past eighteen months. He has gone there himself once a month, and sent supplies the other three weeks, and this system has worked well. There were seven members when our brother went, and the number is now doubled. Besides these actual additions to the church, several conversions have taken place, but the friends have joined other churches. The chapel, which holds one hundred and fifty, is filled on Sunday evenings. It has lately been re-seated, and freed from debt.

MR. R. HUGHES, who lately went to the United States, for some time had the oversight of the church meeting at Zion Chapel, *Chesham, Bucks.* During his ministry, the church received an addition of forty-nine members, forty-two of whom our brother baptized. There are now about one hundred and twenty members. Since Mr. Hughes left, Mr. CURWOOD has been carrying on the work. The chapel, which seats three hundred, is filled every Sunday evening, and it has been decided to enlarge it, so as to accommodate two hundred more persons. A Sunday-school, Bible-class, prayer-meetings, and a Christian Band are all well-sustained, and a hearty spirit of love and unity dwells in the church. The friends have £40 or £50 in hand towards the proposed extension. As Mr. Curwood is leaving for West Hartlepool, other students will take up the work at Chesham and Forest Row.

MR. A. J. REID has, for some months, been conducting a mission' at *Theydon Bois, Essex,* a small village on the border of Epping Forest. Since the mission was started, four years ago, a steady work has gone on: many have been won to the Saviour by the preaching of the gospel, and ten have professed their faith by baptism. The average attendance on Sunday evenings is sixty. There is also a good work going on amongst the young people. The school numbers fifty scholars. During the past year, the mission-room, and site for proposed chapel, have been purchased, and presented to the President by F. L. Edwards, Esq., of Loughton.

MR. A. PRITER had the oversight of the church at *Cheam, Surrey,* till last August, when ill health compelled him to resign it. Since then MR. A. E. JOHNS has taken up the work. The chapel seats one hundred and eighty, there is an average attendance of about one hundred and thirty, the membership being seventy-three. There is also a Sunday-school, with one hundred children and fourteen teachers ; and there is an adult Bible-class, with about fifteen members. The cause has suffered somewhat lately through removals from the neighbourhood.

MR. J. L. ROGER laboured for a year at the village of *Shoreham, Kent.* During this time there were four who professed conversion, three of whom were baptized at Eynsford, and joined the Baptist church there. MR. D. H. HAY now carries on the work at Shoreham.

MR. ROGER, after leaving Shoreham, laboured at *Mitcham, Surrey,* for a few months, and the congregations in that time were nearly doubled. The membership is thirty, and the Sunday-school contains ninety scholars. Mr. Roger has been accepted by the Baptist Missionary Society for work on the Congo, and has already sailed for Africa, so another student will go to Mitcham.

MR. G. A. J. HUNTLEY, who is soon leaving for China, has been preaching for the past few months, on Sunday evenings, at *The Rock Mission, Camberwell.* The room seats about one hundred, and is full every Sunday. The Lord has greatly blessed the work, and conversions have taken place at nearly every service. A week's special mission was held recently, and was the means of much blessing. A Young Christians' Association has just been started, with a view to recognize and help young believers, and to foster and develop their Christian life and character, as well as to train them for service for the Master. This Association is heartily taken up and appreciated by the young converts.

Two brethren, MR. A. A. WITHAM (who has now gone to Washington Territory, North America), and MR. D. LOINAZ, have had charge of a mission at *John Street, Camberwell,* for the past few months. There are about forty members, and an average Sunday evening attendance of eighty persons. The congregations, though still small, have increased, and the outlook is hopeful. A prayer-meeting is held on Monday evenings; and an adults' Bible-class and a Tract Distribution Society are about to be started.

MR. W. E. WELLS has, for some time, laboured among the soldiers at *The Soldiers' Home, Buckingham Palace Road.* Our brother conducts a Bible-class there every Saturday evening. Much blessing has attended the work, especially latterly, in increased attendance, and in frequent manifestations of the divine favour. Mr. Wells has been privileged to baptize some who have been led to Christ through these classes, and he is in communication with many—some now far away from England—who at different times attended the meetings.

MR. W. C. MINIFIE, for some months past, has visited *The Throat Hospital, Golden Square,* every Sunday evening, and often during the week. The Sunday evening service, held in one of the wards, is made as attractive as possible, and has been attended with great blessing, many anxious souls having been led to the cross of Christ. Patients unable to rise from their beds are spoken to individually, and all are most willing to listen to what is said, and grateful for it. The President's sermons are gladly accepted by the patients, who come from various parts of England.

Two or three of the brethren preach from time to time for *The Evangelization Society.* Some go occasionally to help in *Miss Macpherson's Mission, Bethnal Green Road;* at *The Strangers' Rest, Ratcliff Highway;* and in other spheres where their assistance is sought.

There is also a *Home Visitation Society* in connection with the College, the object of which is to visit the people, leave the President's sermons, and try to get those who go to no place of worship to attend the Tabernacle services. A full report of this work was published in *The Sword and the Trowel* for June last.

The *Students' Missionary Association* is in a flourishing condition, and the brethren are glad to give missionary addresses wherever their services are sought. There is a museum belonging to the Association, containing curios, &c., from various parts of the mission field; and these greatly add to the interest of an address. Many missionary meetings have been held during the past year.

The *College Temperance Society* does a very useful work, and the students are in great demand to address Gospel Temperance meetings, Bands of Hope, &c. No fewer than one hundred and fifty meetings have been addressed by the students during the past year.

Our brethren are ready to work wherever a church of baptized believers can be gathered; and they ask for invitations from earnest friends in destitute places, who will back them up in missionary endeavours. Mr. Spurgeon encourages them in endeavouring, as far as possible, to form churches of which they may become the pastors when their College course is over.

We trust that this necessarily condensed account will interest our readers in the College. Many think of the orphans, but forget the students; yet surely both are equally worthy. The College appeals not only to our natural humanity, but to our spiritual nature. Help to train the men who are soon to be leaders in the churches of Christ.

10

A View in Old Mentone.

OUR friends must not imagine that Mentone is a dull, uninteresting place, made up of fine villas and great hotels. On the contrary, the old town is interesting, and full of old-fashioned bits. Here is an engraving of one of the streets leading down to the port —and a respectable street, too, perhaps a little out of repair through the earthquake. Did you say it was narrow? That is one of the beauties of it. Don't you see it? These good people are not like your proud citizens, who like to dwell alone, but they prefer to put their houses close together, that they may be near neighbours. This gives them shade in the hot summer days; and if you once felt the burning sun, you would think this a great matter. Moreover, you do not offend your friends by passing them without recognition because the road is broad and you are near-sighted. If you can shake hands across the street without going out of doors, is not this a convenience to friendship? Besides, if there happens to be a shop, you not only see but smell and touch the goods, as you pass close to them; and this saves the tradesman standing outside and crying "Buy, buy!" Seldom do carriages venture down the narrow streets; for you may have to wait long while another trap backs to a broader place, or you may have to back yourself, which is worse. This keeps the street quiet, and saves a lot of rattle; and who does not value this, after living in the roar of London? In the case before us there are steps, and so no traffic comes along, except that which is caused by one's own fellow-creatures, namely, foot passengers and donkeys. This allows the good women, and merry children, and men who have nothing to do, to sit out of doors, and get better air than there is likely to be within.

Truly, this little Jerusalem is "builded as a city that is compact together." Our visitors, as a rule, have a prejudice for broader thoroughfares; yet an excursion into the ancient streets is not without its charms to one who does not despise the narrow way, and wishes to see the people at home.—C. H. S.

Questions for "Down-Grade" Doubters.

DEAR MR. EDITOR,—At the recent meeting of the London Baptist Association, in endeavouring to show the inutility of the "seven statements" which it was proposed should be attached to Rule I. of the Constitution, I submitted the following seven questions. To these questions, which touch the very foundations of that mysterious theology in which so-called "Modern Thought" delights, no distinct answer is given by the seven statements. But, probably, they may be useful to others beside myself in the detection of error. I venture, therefore, to offer them to your readers for that purpose. The first question needs no explanation or comment.

I. Do you believe the Scriptures of the Old and New Testaments to be an *infallible* and *sufficient* guide in all matters of religious faith and practice?

II. Do you believe in the DEITY as well as *divinity* of our Lord Jesus Christ, *i.e.*, that he is himself God?
Note that a man may acknowledge Christ to be divine, as he might acknowledge the Bible to be divine, without admitting that he is God.

III. Do you believe that Christ, in his death, endured the *penalty* due to divine justice for human guilt?
Note—Many admit that he died for us, but exclude the idea of penalty from his death.

IV. Do you believe the Holy Spirit to be, not only a divine influence, but, in the true, real, and proper sense of the term, a divine person, and himself God?

V. Do you believe man to have become, by sin, a fallen creature, and to have lost, by his fall, his original peaceful, happy, and holy relations with his Maker?
Note—Schiller described the Fall as "a giant stride in the history of the human race."

VI. Do you believe that, by regeneration, man becomes possessed of a new and higher life, described as spiritual? that this life is only rendered possible by the mediatorial work of Christ? that it is only rendered actual by the work of the Holy Spirit in the soul? and that, apart from these means, it can never be enjoyed?

VII. Do you believe in the resurrection of the dead, as an event of the future, and not of continual recurrence?

I think, Mr. Editor, that these questions may be made of great service in determining the whereabouts of many a man, sermon, or book.

Yours faithfully,
JOHN TUCKWELL.

Bayswater.

[We agree with our correspondent that there is a ready way of dodging round the seven statements; but even such questions as those which he uggests will not bring slippery gentlemen to book. We feel ashamed to have to draw up statements, and put questions to those who should be brethren. Methods which the subtlety of error renders necessary are, nevertheless, greatly distasteful to simple, trustful hearts. We prefer to quit the company of those who plead that creeds have no binding power: they only too plainly avow their own characters. When one has to weigh words with a person, fellowship is out of the question. The phrases adopted by the L. B. A. look right enough, but it is clear that they can be every one of them evaded. Knowing what we do know of some who are called ministers of Christ, and in their heart of hearts do not believe the old gospel, we are saddened in soul, and wonder what next will come.—ED.]

Notices of Books.

A Concise History of the Church: from the Apostolic Era to the Establishment of the Reformation. By ALFRED E. KNIGHT. Partridge and Co.

CHURCH history is usually made wearisome, and is generally rather the history of a worldly organization than of the elect band by whom the truth of God was upheld. The present volume is of so popular a character that we could introduce it, not only to students, but to common readers, with the assurance that they would read the book quite through with much pleasure. The type is large and the lines are widely spaced, so that the reading is pleasant even to eyes which are losing their power. Mr. Knight seems to think that the seven churches of Asia were typical of stages of church life, and that we are nearing the end. His book is written in a devout spirit and from an evangelical outlook, and we trust it will make many of our plain church members well acquainted with the general run of religious history. This will be a refreshment to their faith, a stimulus to their zeal, and an excitement to their caution. The book is not very elegant in appearance, but we think its circulation will be greatly beneficial.

India's Needs: Material, Political, Social, Moral, and Religious. By JOHN MURDOCH, LL.D.

A PAMPHLET (octavo, 151 pp.) published at Madras, on sale at the offices of "The Christian Vernacular Education Society for India," No. 7, Adam Street, Strand. 1s. post free. Very interesting.

The Dawn of the Modern Mission. By W. FLEMING STEVENSON, D.D. Edinburgh: Macniven and Wallace.

To pious sympathy this small volume has a pathetic interest. It comprises a course of four lectures. The author had finished his course before its publication. Like a dream, it was alike the delight and distress of his deathbed. So enamoured of his theme! So embarrassed by his efforts to do it justice! His heart pined to revise the proofs; but his pulse failed. The task of revising them for the press fell on her to whom in life he was devoted.

His idea is a comprehensive survey of two centuries of Christian enterprise. The charm consists in lively photographs of light struggling with darkness among earth's tribes, where darkness has been slow to hail the daybreak. The lectures were delivered in connection with the Duff Missionary foundation.

Spiritual Decline of the Church of God. By ALFRED HILL. Elliot Stock.

A STIRRING address, delivered about twelve months ago, at the Clifton Church Institute, Brighton. Like a physician, our author feels the pulse of the Church, and mourns its feebleness.

The Devil's Mission of Amusement: a Protest. By ARCHIBALD G. BROWN. Morgan and Scott.

OUR brother Archibald Brown is one of the valiant in Israel, and he has here struck a mighty blow at a giant evil. Oh, that the blow may tell! It is all very fine to sneer, or to talk about exaggeration; but we know that our friend has written nothing but sober truth and surface truth. If he had gone into more private matters, he might have raised the blush upon the cheek of those who know how the amusements of the mission have, in sad instances, had their evil followings as surely as the amusements of the music-hall and of the theatre. We do not hesitate to assert that the characters of many hopeful young people have been shipwrecked, not by the avowed haunt of vice, but by the influence of the questionable entertainment in connection with their religious relationships. Pleasant lectures and wholesome singing were all very well when used for higher ends; but there has been a gradual coming down, till, in some cases, the schoolroom has endured what the theatre would have refused as too absurd.

This earnest warning ought to be poured like grapeshot upon the enemy, till the devil is driven to abandon the entrenchments of religious amusement. At present, in many cases, the prince of darkness feels himself as much at home in the church as in the world; and it is time that something was done to disturb his repose.

The Home of a Naturalist. By Rev. BIOT EDMONDSTON, and his sister, JESSIE M. E. SAXBY. Nisbet and Co.

THIS is a natural, unsophisticated book. In some respects, it reminds us of White's "Selborne," for it does for Shetland somewhat of the same kind of service that White did for the Hampshire parish : it make us feel as if we knew the place. The lover of natural history, and of stirring adventure in the wild waters of the north, will find himself held captive by the charms of these pages ; and we shall be surprised if he does not find his heart yearning after a sight of those primitive regions.

To our minds the book has more than its share of the records of folk-lore, and idle superstitions ; but, it may be, they were needed to complete the picture truthfully. Such a land must surely be "meet nurse" for elfin life, and uncanny fancy. It must have been a trying, but inspiring, life which fell to the lot of the Shetland doctor, who was often called to his patients from far over the sea, and had to encounter many a storm before he could reach the sick-bed which was wearying for him. His avocations made him well acquainted with the Shetlanders within doors, and his natural bent led him to become familiar with all forms of animal life outside. What he saw and heard is well written, and will please the reader.

Not for any special spiritual excellence ; but as a bright, refreshing bit of writing, such as may while away the weary hour, we commend this interesting work to our readers.

Thomas J. Comber, Missionary Pioneer to the Congo. By JOHN . BROWN MYERS. S. W. Partridge and Co.

YOUNG man, if you would have a place among the *immortals* of the armies of the Lord, follow the example set by this noble servant of Christ. Get this interesting book ; read it, and then act out its suggestions. Dear is the name of Comber to us. This friend Thomas studied most earnestly in our evening classes before he went to Regent's Park College ; and his brother, Dr. Comber, was one of our own College men. The family of Comber has given itself for Africa, and the name

will shine in the annals of the church of the Congo till time shall be no more. This life is superabundantly illustrated, and neatly produced. Let it be put in the school library. We believe the price is only 1s. 6d.

The Five Talents of Women. A Book for Girls and Women. By the Author of "How to be Happy, though Married." T. Fisher Unwin.

ALL who have read "How to be Happy, though Married," will expect a treat when they read this kindred production. Nor will they expect in vain. Good sense here expresses itself in wholesome proverb and quaint story. Our author can write *for* women, and *to* them. He is, therefore, you may be sure, no fool ; for women cannot endure fools to admonish them. He does not flatter, by any means, but he writes sense—such as sensible people will like to read. We believe we are doing real service to our friends when we say—Get this volume : it will make you laugh, at the very least, and that is good ; but it will leave behind a wise and happy impression, worth a hundred times the price of the work.

The Story of the Nations—Persia. By S. G. W. BENJAMIN. T. Fisher Unwin.

AGAIN and again have we commended to our readers the series of *The Story of the Nations*. Persia is the one which is now before us. Speak of fiction, it has no interest or charm when set side by side with the more than romance of such history as this ! Mr. Benjamin writes splendidly, and his theme is bright as the stars of heaven, with a glittering attractiveness · of many sparkling lights. You might read this "story" in separate chapters, and enjoy it : the book is so well put together that you may disjoint it without causing a fracture. From end to end the record of Persia is marvellous. That empire has been crushed many times, but has always been restored. We have by no means heard the last of it yet. Its vitality is a miracle among the nations. Taken for all in all, Persia in some respects excels each one of the other three great monarchies, and chiefly in this, that it lives on, while none of the others has more than a name to do so.

Turning Points in the Lives of Eminent Christians. By MARY E. BECK. Hodder and Stoughton.

THIS is likely to prove a very useful book. It would do well for reading at working-parties. The conversions described are those of men of eminence from every age and every quarter of the church, from Augustine to Bunyan, from Luther to Brownlow North. In the story of Richard Knill, the authoress has included the incident of that good man's talk with the little boy Spurgeon. She has a genius for condensation, and for setting out the notable bits. We cannot believe that these wonders of divine grace can be read without producing great searchings of heart. How we should like to hear of the real conversion of some who now figure in the outward church! The rampant error and riotous worldliness which are now saddening the godly, arise, to a large extent, out of the fact that we have in the ministry men who might be true preachers of the gospel if they were but converted. We want more personal turning-points to be visible, and we should see a grand turning-point in church-history.

These last words of ours must not, however, lead our reader to imagine that this is a controversial book. Our remarks are simply by-the-way: the volume itself is not responsible for them. We recommend its purchase. It costs 3s. 6d.

Christ and his People. By Nine Ministers of the Church of England. Hodder and Stoughton.

THIRTEEN discourses of the highest order of excellence. Clear as the sea of glass, but mingled with the fire of deep, believing earnestness. These sermons have appeared in *The Record*, and they well deserve to be put on more permanent record. Such preachers as Ryle, Richardson, Moule, Hoare, Everard, and others, need no commendation from us. They are not feebly evangelical, nor evangelically feeble; but they are masters in Israel. Here is a crown's worth of the old theology; and, whoever may gainsay it, no other form of teaching can compare with it for building up in holiness, or holding up in comfort. Whether such doctrine be taught within the Establishment, or out of it, we therein do rejoice, yea, and will rejoice.

Christianity in the Daily Conduct of Life. Hodder and Stoughton.

OUR unnamed author handles the subject of Christian character under a series of texts bearing upon the highest principles which govern our daily conduct according to the Word of God. We are glad to find that he adheres to the old-fashioned doctrines of Scripture. The secret piety of a true Christian life is well set forth in the chapters upon Humility, Forgiveness, Anger, and Purity; while the practical side is displayed by articles upon Honesty, Giving, Observance of the Sabbath, and the Conduct of Christ's Followers in Society. The careful and prayerful perusal of such chapters as these cannot fail to elevate the heart and cultivate the mind.

The Inner Mission. By T. B. PATON, M.A., D.D. Wm. Isbister.
Christian Solidarity. By HENRY STANLEY NEWMAN. S. W. Partridge and Co.

Two little books, which, though dissimilar in many respects, are yet alike in this, that they are each dedicated to the assertion of one and the same doctrine; forsooth, that Christianity is communistic, sympathetic, and socialistic. "The bearing of one another's burdens" becomes thus, not merely a duty, but a system that challenges diligent study how best it may be discharged. Dr. Paton's four addresses were delivered on divers occasions during the past fifteen years. They are dedicated to the memory of Samuel Morley. As they have pleased and edified privileged audiences before they were published, our praise is needless.

Mr. Newman is more sentimental; we do not say he is less sound. Charmed with a word, he chants "solidarity" in every chapter, on every page. His finding is that it means "fellowship." On the faith of divers dictionaries he gets assured of the fact; and he fancies that, like "solitaire," it is of French extraction. His ten stanzas are all on the one string of "Solidarity." Neither of these works has aroused our enthusiasm.

Angelic Apostasy, &c., &c. By P. GRANT, M.A. Edinburgh: Gemmell.

THE title-page of this work is voluminous. The excursions and discussions through which it conducts us are extraordinary. The author appears to observe a loyal allegiance to the absolute and unconditional authority of Holy Scripture; although he demurs to the human and traditional interpretation of much of the Divine record that passes current in our commentaries, and is endorsed by popular apprehension. He sets himself no easy task who aims to divert the current of theological literature. Some of his suggestions are sure to arouse the prejudice of those whom he is most anxious to propitiate, while they are not unlikely to foster the scepticism of those who sneer at an inspiration which (they will say) its own defenders claim a right to reconstruct at will. When he asks credit, in his preface, for honestly stating his ideas of things as he sees them in the light of his own judgment, availing himself of whatever assistance may lie within his reach, we cordially grant it, without consenting to follow his lead, and without compromising ourselves by accepting his conclusions. In a volume of such dimensions, comprising forty-six chapters and eight important appendices, there is room for a wide and frequent differing from the author; for we cannot see with the eyes of his understanding. His aim, we take it, is two-fold: first, to rectify a habit of reading as literal history certain records in the Bible, which were, according to ancient usage, purely symbolical; and, secondly, to show that in the antagonism of ingenious thinkers to certain explicit doctrines of the Bible, the obscurity is not in the teaching of the Holy Spirit, but the veil lieth on their own heart. The first fight is, of course, over the Book of Genesis, and its earliest chapters furnish the arena of the fiercest conflict. Of "the real meaning of the Genetic narrative," he writes thus:—"The two human creations mentioned in Genesis ii. 7 and 22 respectively are really different and distinct, both in their nature and purposes, from that of Genesis i. 27." He gives his reasons. They are so

satisfactory to himself that he says: "The distinction cannot reasonably be denied" (p. 33). In an appendix he tries to fortify his position. Here, however, he unfortunately gets into a fog. Referring to 2 Cor. xi. 3 (when he obviously means 1 Tim. ii. 13, 14), he observes that Paul "evidently read the history in the uncritically indiscriminating way in which ordinary readers still do. Such nice questions were not debated in his day. He was neither geologist nor antiquarian, but not the less fitted on that account to be a true preacher of the cross" (p. 210). Poor Paul! Truly was he "one born out of due time!" Our readers will not expect us to assent to this kind of reasoning. We have put a mark of interrogation against many another paragraph; but we have no space for further samples.

The Inspiration of Holy Scriptures. By DANIEL BAGOT, D.D., Dean. Hatchards, 1878.

THIS is a smart little essay, but it was not published yesterday. You can read it through at a sitting. As an evening's recreation it will amply repay you. The Dean has seized on a central point—the distinction between "inspiration" and "revelation"—from which to glance over a wide field of study. Granted that, in general, his panorama is well painted, yet there are colourings in places which we do not delight in. Our friends can easily find these out for themselves. "The occurrence in the Bible of objectionable sentiments" is a rough way of referring to the imprecatory psalms. His explanation of them we cannot possibly entertain. It is a pity that there should be even a speck in so sound a work on the canon.

Hooker. Book I. *Of the Laws of Ecclesiastical Polity.* Edited By R. W. CHURCH, M.A., Dean of St. Paul's. Oxford: Clarendon Press. London: Henry Frowde.

COMMENDATION is superfluous. One of the first and most famous of English classics, edited and annotated by Dean Church, and published by the Clarendon Press, carries its own testimonials on the title-page. Of course it is a school-book intended for students.

Pixie's Adventures from his own Point of View ; or, the Tale of a Terrier. By N. D'ANVERS. Shaw.

THE tale of this terrier is tied up with ribbons by the capital engravings, otherwise it would scarcely suffice to amuse even the smallest of a doggie's play-mates. The story is just a little too childish ; and we cannot see the value of a thousand marrow-bones in it, though the preface states that this was the joint reward of the two merry dogs whose names are set to this document.

The Cave by the Waterfall. By EDITH KENYON. Sunday School Union.

MOST wholesome lessons are woven into two interesting stories, suitable for young girls.

Vermont Hall. By M. A. PAULL. Hodder and Stoughton.

AN interesting story. Another shot at the demon Drink. Will the death-blow ever be given ?

The Lion of St. Mark : a Tale of Venice. By G. A. HENTY. Blackie and Son.

"UNDER twenty, charmed with Henty," may become a juvenile proverb ; for our author caters for boys, and knows their palate to a pinch of pepper. This is a soldierly-looking book, all scarlet and gold, and its outward appearance reminds us of a corpulent officer of a crack regiment. Within there is a mine of instructive history, intersected by a vein of rather strained adventure. A boy reviewer would call it "a jolly book." It costs six shillings.

Her Only Son. By the Author of "Jessica's First Prayer," "Nelly's Dark Days," &c. Houlston and Sons.

NOTHING more can be needed to commend this little book than the name of its author. It is as touching as any of her choice little stories. Its burden is "the Drink." It should be in every colporteur's pack, and it ought to be read by every big brewer in Britain.

With Steady Aim ; or, Herbert Ford's Life Work. By W. J. FORSTER. T. Woolmer.

A FAIRLY good story, to show how a good lad became a prosperous man through steadily pursuing an aim in life. Not very original or striking.

The Red Lion : a Temperance Tale. By JAMES CROMPTON. Sunday School Union.

VERY good. The Red Lion turns into the "White Lamb," and thus the plague of drink in the village is stayed. One of the best written of temperance stories. Put it in your library.

Two Enthusiasts. By EVELYN EVERETT GREEN. Religious Tract Society.

THE stories of Miss Everett Green are never dry, even to readers who have not the *entrée* of those baronial halls and quaint old moated mansions, in which, presumably, she is so much at home in the company of a wealthy heiress, a baron, or squire, or knight of the shire. These worthies are made to discourse on the responsibilities of wealth and position, the condition of the poor, the causes of want and crime, and various theories for the upraising of the sad and sinful. There is more of the sensational and improbable in this than in previous works of the same author which have come under our notice ; but we must add that there are not a few paragraphs of clear Christian teaching in the book.

Jack the Conqueror ; or, Difficulties Overcome. By Mrs. C. E. BOWEN. Partridge and Co.

A CHEAP shilling book, suitable for the village colporteur's pack. Mrs. Bowen says she wrote it "to show how great things even a child may effect by earnest resolve, if accompanied by energy and perseverance."

Will it Lift? the Story of a London Fog. Jack Horner the Second. "The Song of Sixpence:" for the Bairns. By J. JACKSON WRAY. James Nisbet.

WHAT a wonderful man this Jackson Wray must be ! We could not concoct a story for the life of us ; and he seems to reel them off by the mile at a time. Here are no less than three on our table now. Those who are more versed in tales, and such like, than we are, tell us that our friend is as good with the pen as with the tongue. *Then he must be good, indeed.* We best appreciate the vigorous, proverbial style of his writing. These are nuggets of gold upon the surface.

"Nothing to You"; or, The Home in Paradise Court. A Story for Maidens. By CHARLOTTE ELIZABETH TIDY. With Preface, by Rev. S. J. STONE, M.A. Partridge and Co.

JUST as, a short time since, "slumming" was the fashion, so East-end waifs and strays are just now the staple of story-tellers. In so far as they tend to evoke practical sympathy for the poor, we are glad to commend such tales to our readers' notice. But we do not care to travel too far into the dark continent of the utterly incredible. Nor can we advise "maidens" to read a book wherein, even in the delicate manner of our authoress, the arts of the seducer are referred to.

Climbing the Mountain Path. By B. SWAN. Glasgow: John J. Rae.

ONE of the "Snowdrop Series," and a really good story, setting in a lurid light the evils of the drinking customs of genteel society, and at the same time keeping the gospel well before the reader's mind. The "Snowdrops" are cheap at eighteen-pence, all things considered; but the sample before us abounds in printers' errors, and the chief illustration illustrates nothing but the carelessness of all concerned in its selection and location.

The Gate in Park Lane; or, Arnold Lane's Courtship. By the Hon. GERTRUDE BOSCAWEN. Nisbet.

COVER so pretty, and printing so good, that we should have liked to say a very good word for this simple country story; but really it has too little in it for us to do so.

Her Life's Work. By LADY DUNBOYNE. Nisbet and Co.

CHURCH organs will be loud in praise of this story, for it is admirably written from that point of view. The "life work" of the chief personage in the tale is, the building and endowment of a church and schools in a churchless village, where drunkenness and crime held sway. Much of the religion described is certainly not that of the Word of God, though it seems to accord with the Book of Common Prayer. Confirmation takes the place of regeneration, and works take the place

of grace. "Confirmation Vows"—title of chapter XI.—prepares the young people for "The First Ball"—title of chapter XII.; and of one of these newly-recruited "Christian soldiers" the record runs in a subsequent page: "He openly professes to disregard all religion, gambles recklessly, and drinks more than is prudent." Oh, that good church people would bring this wrong rite of Confirmation to the light of the Word!

Barbara's Brothers. By EVELYN EVERETT GREEN. Religious Tract Society.

THE author has a happy faculty for analyzing and vividly describing the inner life of young persons of the upper and upper-middle classes of society, and the temptations peculiar to their position. The vanity and vexation of spirit of those children of wealth whose lives are aimless and useless, and the happiness of those who devote themselves and their wealth to the service of the sad and suffering, are beautifully illustrated in this story, which is quite equal to any from the same pen.

Dinah's Son. By L. B. WALFORD. James Clarke and Co.

THE author is evidently anxious that his readers should "not mistake the purport of this little story," by supposing (as they probably would do) that he would damp the ardour of any youthful spirit inspired by the love of God and of the souls of the heathen, to go forth to mission-work in foreign lands. He tells us that the rather "he would have those who think they hear the divine call" see to it "that it is not the outcome of a restless nature, craving for excitement, or a novel field of action," to the neglect of evident service near at hand. The plot of the story is original, and gives scope for showing the worthlessness of worldly Christianity, and the soul-destroying poison of "the root of all evil." To lay the blame of the moral and financial ruin of his relatives to the charge of a godly youth, because his example was removed from the family circle, doesn't commend itself to our judgment.

Proverbs, Maxims, and Phrases of all Ages. Classified subjectively, and arranged alphabetically. In two volumes. Compiled by ROBERT CHRISTY. T. Fisher Unwin.

THESE are two splendid volumes. Students of proverbial lore will bless the laborious compiler. Chiefly is he to be praised for his system of arrangement, which is unique, and practically useful. We have many alphabetical lists of proverbs; but we have none in which the subjects are the basis of the arrangement, and the alphabetical commencement of the proverb is only followed as a secondary guide. We felt half sorry to see these volumes, because we are preparing a similar work, using for it the materials collected in our John Ploughman almanacks. We have almost completed our gathering of the proverbs, and are rapidly going on with the annotations thereon, and we were afraid that we were cut out of our market: but ours is a different thing altogether, and will suit, by its price, a class of persons who could not afford a guinea for these two volumes, which are, nevertheless, exceedingly well worth the money. We heartily recommend this publication, and wish it a large sale: it deserves it.

An Almanack for the Year of our Lord 1889. By JOSEPH WHITAKER, F.S.A. Whitaker.

WHITAKER'S Almanack again! We cannot pretend to review it: it is quite beyond praise. How any respectable person can get on without it we cannot tell; for it is your friend and informant at every turn. Complete, condensed, well arranged, varied, accurate: we could not suggest an improvement. It is a marvellous shilling's-worth.

Life and Times of Girolamo Savonarola. By PROFESSOR PASQUALE VILLARI. Translated by LINDA VILLARI. T. Fisher Unwin.

THIS is a standard life of the great Italian. The two volumes are worthy of their subject, and we cannot give higher praise. Our author is no partisan. We are happy to note that he does not *try to be impartial*, for whenever a writer is in that condition he becomes unjust; but he really is impartial, and both regards and reports facts with a well-balanced mind. Savonarola was sage and saint; but he was also a little off the square in his mind. When he fell to prophesying, and made one or two successful strokes, he deluded himself. Ever true, pure, brave, and we had almost added angelical, he was apt, at times, to believe in his reception of divine communications, when, in fact, he was in a dreamy or ecstatic state. This is very distinctly brought out by the biographer, without in the least diminishing our unbounded reverence for this Christian hero.

The labour of research involved in the production of these volumes impresses us. The theme is one of peculiar difficulty, and even with this new and revised edition, the writer does not seem quite content. Savonarola is too great for a biographer: he believed amid general doubt, he was pure amid universal licentiousness. God was in the man, and shone through him, and he was one of those born of the Spirit, of whom the Saviour said, "Thou canst not tell whence he cometh, or whither he goeth."

A Missionary Life: Stephen Grellet. By FRANCES ANNE BUDGE. James Nisbet and Co.

THOSE who are not acquainted with the life of Stephen Grellet, the French Quaker, should invest a shilling in the purchase of this little book. One called him St. Stephen Grellet, and the name was well deserved. He travelled everywhere, encountered every form of peril, and braved every kind of adversary. In him the Spirit of God had free course, and his life remains a proof that there are some among our race who can hear even the whispers of God; and who, hearing, are as ready to respond to the mind of God as is the hand of a man to obey the thoughts of his heart. Oh, that more of us were in such a condition! There are worlds of wonder open if we will but yield to the divine influences, and permit the Lord's own power to work us to his will.

Notes.

FRIENDS will not need me to say that I have recovered from the effects of my accident, if I am spared to preach the gospel in my own pulpit, as I hope to be doing before March magazine leaves the press. Writing in the middle of February, I feel myself to be, in many respects, in better health than before my painful descent, while the injured knee, after six weeks' gradual inprovement, is in such a state that I can walk a moderate distance. How great is the goodness of God in granting me this happy restoration, and the prospect of getting to work again! I thank heartily the very many friends who wrote letters of sympathy. If I have not answered them all, it is because I should have had no rest whatever if I had attempted the task, and I know they would not have wished me to find their affection the occasion of toil.

Will those members of the Christian public who are making up their minds to ask for a sermon, a lecture, a speech, a bazaar-opening, or something or other, be so very gracious to me as to note the following letter, which I have received from the Deacons of the Tabernacle? I think I must obey their thoughtful admonition, for what will become of all order and discipline if a minister does not pay due heed to his deacons? Moreover, I know, by very painful experience, the common-sense of the request. I have frequently gone a little beyond my tether, and have suffered a month's pain in consequence; and as soon as I have been half-well, somebody else has pleaded with me almost to tears to do the same thing again. I must this year be a little hard-hearted, and let the pleaders plead in vain. If I do my home-work, it is more than enough for one mortal man, and I must be happy to be able to keep on with it. I would, indeed, be grateful if friends could and would believe that I have not the strength of earlier years, and would excuse me when I cannot grant their requests. It is constantly the case that I have to write several letters before they will accept my answer in the negative; and this is one of the inflictions which I think I ought to be spared. It is painful to me to say "No" once; but it adds to the burden when another and another letter or deputation come with the same plea. I do not lack will, but power.

"Metropolitan Tabernacle,
"Newington, S.E., Feb. 8th, 1889.

"Dear Pastor,—At our meeting it was unanimously agreed to write you our strong and growing conviction, that you will be wise to husband your time and strength for home duties for the remainder of this year. We feel that you have, at times, overtaxed your immense powers by the attempt to compass work beyond any human endurance; and in the interest of the many 'works of faith and labours of love' in which you are the leader and main support, we must ask you to consider our fervent request to confine your engagements to those which, of necessity, arise, and to decline all invitations to go beyond these. Praying for you all help and blessing, and assuring you of our growing affection and esteem,

"We are,
"YOUR FELLOW-WORKERS AND DEACONS."

The German translation of *The Cheque Book* is having a very generous reception. The reviewers are puzzled by the title, but warmly commend the work; and the people are readily purchasing the parts as they appear. We hope by this means to speak with a multitude of Teutonic believers day by day.

We cannot do less than express our gratitude, deep and overflowing, to the men of God who have supplied the Tabernacle pulpit in our long absence. Specially do we desire for Mr. McNeill, on his coming to London, the best blessing of heaven. May he prove a standard-bearer of the truth, and a centre of holy influence in London! Every fresh voice for the old faith is a great gain in these days, when truth is fallen in our streets.

Many of our readers will rejoice when they learn that Mrs. Spurgeon *has* managed to write a brief Report of the work of her Book Fund during the past year, by taking advantage of the intervals between the paroxysms of pain which she continues to suffer. Friends who read this record may be inclined to think that it is like the water that David's mighty men drew out of the well of Bethlehem, when he longed for another draught of the cooling spring which had often refreshed him. They need not, however, refuse the cup that is filled for them, if they will praise the Lord for the blessing which has rested upon the work during 1888, and pray that, if it be his gracious will, a renewal of health and strength may this year be granted to the beloved Manager of the Fund. The Report will be sent to all subscribers as soon as it is ready, or it can be obtained for six-pence through any bookseller, or post-free for six stamps from Messrs. Passmore and Alabaster, 4, Paternoster Buildings, London.

Those who read "Son Tom's" bright article on "Glow-worms," in the present number of the Magazine, will be interested in hearing that a little "glow-worm," in the shape of a daughter, came to light up his Auckland home on Christmas-day, 1888. God bless both parents and child!

Son Charles left London on the 7th ult.,

in the steamship *Aorangi*, bound for New Zealand. We trust that he will return completely restored to health and strength, and that the Lord will graciously bless the work at Greenwich through the brethren who have kindly promised to serve the church at South Street during his absence.

A second box of books has been received from C. B., East Dulwich, and sent to a poor country minister, who was very grateful for the contents.

On *Tuesday evening, January 22*, the eleventh anniversary of MRS. ALLISON'S BIBLE-CLASS was celebrated by a tea in the Tabernacle school-room, and a public meeting in the lecture-hall. After prayer by Mr. W. Olney, Mrs. Allison made a brief statement with regard to her loved work, and her pleasure in meeting so many workers of the church that evening, and then recited "Ezekiel's Dream," and "Richter's Vision." The secretary reported that the class contributes to the part-support of a colporteur, the amount raised for this year being £20 4s. 8d.; also for Zenana Mission, £1 9s.; Rescue Society, 16s.; and a fund for poor non-members, £12 9s. 6½d. While the labours of Mrs. Allison are valued by the members, many of whom are Christian workers, they have also been owned of God in the conversion of sinners.

On *Tuesday evening, February 12*, the annual meeting of the TRAINING-CLASS in connection with the Tabernacle Evangelists' Association and Country Mission was held, under the presidency of Mr. James Stiff. After prayer by Mr. Guthrie, the secretary (Mr. C. Branscombe) stated that there are one hundred and ten members in the class; the attendance has been specially good lately, and much spiritual blessing has been experienced at the meetings. The chairman, on behalf of the class, presented to Mr. Elvin, the leader, four beautifully-modelled bronzes, and a written testimonial, expressing the members' appreciation of his services. Mr. Elvin gratefully acknowledged the gift, and addresses were delivered by several of the members.

COLLEGE.—Mr. W. Perrins, having completed his course with us, hopes to sail for the United States on the 2nd inst. We cordially commend him to the care of our brethren across the ocean. Letters may be sent to him to the care of Pastor R. Hughes, Londonville, Ohio.
Mr. F. G. Gathercole has removed from St. Neot's to Kimbolton, Huntingdonshire; and Mr. G. H. Trapp, from Towanda, to Covington and Sullivan, Pennsylvania, U.S.A. Mr. A. Hyde has accepted the pastorate of the new church at Formby, Tasmania; and Mr. H. G. Blackie has taken Mr. Hyde's place at Longford.
The London brethren will be called together as soon as possible after the Presi-

dent's return, to make arrangements for the next Conference of the Pastors' College Evangelical Association. In all probability, the meetings will be held *in the week commencing May 6*, that is, the week *after* the Baptist Union meetings.

EVANGELISTS.—*Messrs. Fullerton and Smith* spent nearly the whole of the month of January at Exeter Hall, in a mission under the auspices of the Central Young Men's Christian Association. The weather was very trying at the beginning, the dense fogs affected the attendances; but later on the hall was well filled, and large numbers professed to find the Saviour.
The evangelists have since been at Shoreditch Tabernacle, and are now at Dalston Junction Chapel. From there they go to Devonshire Square Chapel, Stoke Newington, then to Salters' Hall Chapel, Islington.

Mr. Burnham has conducted special services at Puddletown and Bere Regis during the past month. He had not long been at work before the unfavourable symptoms returned, making it clear that he must endeavour to carry out the doctor's recommendations, and take a sea-voyage, and reside for a year or two in a less trying climate than this. We hope soon to be able to announce that arrangements to this effect have been made. This month Mr. Burnham goes to St. John's Congregational Chapel, Ipswich; and also to Amersham.

Mr. Harmer's services at March were largely attended, and productive of great blessing. There were many remarkable answers to prayer during the meetings, and much cause for praise and thanksgiving. After a short rest, Mr. Harmer went to Cheddar, where several were brought to decision for Christ. He has since been at Ipswich, conducting missions at Tuddenham, Crown Street, and Washbrook; the latter part of this month he is going to Tewkesbury.

Mr. Harrison's mission at Stapleton Road, Bristol, is described as having been "remarkably successful in point of numbers, enthusiasm, and results." At Redditch, the services are reported as having been "rich in spiritual results." During the past month he has been at Sittingbourne and Bury St. Edmund's.

Mr. Parker reports successful services at Falmouth, Bourton, Ringstead, and Haddenham; and says that he is booked until the end of this month. He will be glad to hear from any brethren desiring his services. They can direct to the Tabernacle. Pastor C. T. Johnson tells of great blessing resting on Mr. Parker's work at Falmouth, and speaks of him as a very sound, earnest, and able evangelist.

ORPHANAGE.—We are very glad to hear that, during the past year, three hundred and thirty-three garments have been sent to the Orphanage by the Reading Young Ladies' Working Meeting. Will all the ladies accept our hearty thanks for their continued kindness to our fatherless family?

PERSONAL NOTES. — Among the many cheering letters received lately, is one telling us of the death of an earnest Christian worker, who was converted at one of our services at New Park-street Chapel, more than thirty years ago. Shortly before his departure, he told the minister who called to see him, that he went, one wet evening, to a meeting in an East End Mission Hall. As only eight people were present, an experience meeting was held, when it was found that five of them had been converted under our ministry. Bless the Lord!

A young man informs us of the following singular chain of circumstances leading to his conversion. In 1881, on a Lord's-day evening, when the Tabernacle was thrown open to all comers, he came, and heard a sermon upon the text, "Come unto me, all ye that labour and are heavy laden, and I will give you rest." Four years ago he went to Australia. On leaving that land, a few weeks since, a Christian lady gave him two of our sermons, and asked him to read them. He threw them into his trunk, and took no notice of them, till one day, on the voyage, having nothing to read, he suddenly remembered them. On taking them out, he found that one of the two was the very sermon he had heard in the Tabernacle more than seven years previously ("Christ's Word with You," No. 1,691). He read it, and re-read it, the Holy Spirit blessed the reading, and now he can sing—

"I came to Jesus as I was,
     Weary, and worn, and sad;
I found in him a resting-place,
     And he has made me glad."

The reading of the following letter gave us great joy during our recent season of suffering.

"Newark, N.J., U.S.A.

"Rev. C. H. Spurgeon,

"My dear Brother,—Four weeks ago, I began to use your book, *All of Grace*, in making plain to my people the way of salvation. Already God is blessing his Word, and your explanations and illustrations; and I want you to know that I join in your prayer that your work may be, 'by the power of God the Holy Ghost, used in the conversion of millions', some of whom shall come from my chapel.

"I know that he will, according to his promise in Matthew xviii. 19. I pray for you, and I ask that you will ask God to convert many in my chapel, to the glory of his name. For years I have wished to write you. God has made you a blessing to me ever since I heard you preach, twelve years ago. I will indulge in no words of praise, only to say I love you, I thank God for you, and pray him to bless you more and more in his service.

"For two years I was a missionary in Mexico; for five years I have laboured for the poor in this city. Pray for me, dear brother, that while health prevents my return to Mexico, God will abundantly bless my labours here.

"Very sincerely yours,
"J. H. POLHEMUS."

Baptisms at Metropolitan Tabernacle. January 31, sixteen.

Pastors' College, Metropolitan Tabernacle.

Statement of Receipts from January 15th to February 14th, 1889.

	£	s.	d.		£	s.	d.
Collection at Peckham Park-road, per Pastor H. O. Mackey	3	12	3	Christ Church, Aston, Birmingham, per Pastor G. Samuel	3	18	6
Do you love God? ...	50	0	0	Mr. John Cameron	1	0	0
What is your faith?	50	0	0	Collected at prayer-meetings at Mansion House Mission, Camberwell, per			
Keep thy mind stayed on him ...	50	0	0	Pastor G. W. Linnecar	0	10	0
Mrs. Raybould ...	1	0	0	A friend, per C. L.	0	2	6
Miss A. M. Morris... ...	0	2	6	From Scotland	25	0	0
Part collection at Upton Chapel, per				A sermon-reader's gratitude ...	0	10	0
Pastor W. Williams	6	5	1	Mrs. Griffiths	5	2	6
Pastor Thomas Whittle	0	5	0	Part collection at Lymington, per Pastor			
Pastor J. S. Poulton ...	0	5	0	John Collins	1	11	6
Mr. C. Allard ...	0	10	0	Rev. E. J. Farley	1	1	0
Rev. G. Hearson ...	2	2	0	*Monthly Subscription:—*			
Rev. E. J. Farley ...	1	1	0	Mr. R. J. Beecliff	0	2	6
Dear Grannie ...	1	0	0	Weekly Offerings at Met. Tab. :—			
First division of surplus income from				Jan. 20	14	7	6
estate of the late Rev. Thomas King,				„ 27	6	6	9
Semley	4	5	10	Feb. 3	11	12	6
Pastor C. Welton ...	0	10	0	„ 10	14	6	6
A mother's prayer answered, Edinburgh	1	1	0		—	—	—
An afflicted missionary in India	1	0	0		46	13	3
Miss Jephs	1	3	6				
Two sisters	1	5	0		£270	19	11
Mr. P. Mackinnon... ...	10	0	0				

Stockwell Orphanage.

Statement of Receipts from January 15th to February 14th, 1889.

	£	s.	d.
Mr. William Jones ...	0	6	
M. D., of Old Deer	5	0	
Captain C. M. Moller	10	0	
Collected by Mr. A. S. Barter	1	0	
Rev. J. F. Avery, per Rev. Dr. Booth...	0	6	0
In memory of Bertie ...	0	5	
Mr. T. Wells	0	5	
Mr. A. Stacey	0	4	
Westgate Sunday-school, per Mr. J. R. Birkinshaw	2	5	0
Miss J. Baigent	0	2	6
A. A. B.	0	5	0
Collected by Mr. J. Cooper	0	12	4
Clements and Newling's ticket-writers, per Mr. Hawkins	4	7	10
Collected by Mr. W. Armes ...	0	10	6
South Norwood Baptist Church, collection at communion-table, per Pastor J. Chadwick	1	10	
Rev. W. J. Guerrier, per Mrs. J. Spurgeon	2	2	0
A sincere friend	0	5	0
Mrs. M. Watson	1	2	6
Mr. H. Denby	2	0	0
Mr. T. Fordham	1	1	0
The Young Women's Bible-class at the Orphanage, per Mrs. James Stiff ...		5	7
Collected by Mrs. Dodwell ...	0	3	7
Collected by Mrs. Perry ...	0	0	0
Mr. G. Smith	10	0	
Miss M. A. Dobson	1	1	0
The Beauly Sabbath-school, per Mr. J. Paterson	1	0	0
Mr. William Swain	2	2	0
Mr. J. J. Pearce	1	0	0
Mrs. Fordham	3	0	0
Collected by Miss C. M. Stevenson ...	0	15	3
Mr. W. Snook	0	7	6
Bath	0	10	0
Orphan boys and girls' collecting cards (second list)	9	10	11
Collection at Townley Street Mission Hall, per Mr. R. H. Tomkins ...	0	11	6
Jack, South Lambeth	0	3	0
Mrs. Wakelin	1	1	0
Miss Farmer and Miss Gibbs	1	0	0
A friend in Canada...	0	12	0
Mrs. Hammerton	0	10	0
Mrs. T. Barrett	0	5	0
Mr. and Mrs. Frederick Sellar ...	2	2	0
Mr. C. Martin	0	7	6
Half contents of Helen, Sybil, Margie, Jean, Berta, and Willma's box, opened on New Year's day	0	9	
Dear Grannie	1	0	
Mrs. Ward	0	10	0
Mr. and Mrs. Norman	6	0	
Collected by Mr. James Miller	0	10	
First division of surplus income from estate of the late Rev. Thomas King, Semley	4	5	10
Lockerbie Mission Hall Sabbath-school	0	7	0
Executors of the late Mr. E. Boustead (additional interest on deposits) ...	34	17	2
Mrs. Elliott...	0	2	6
Miss A. E. Seymour	0	3	0
Mrs. Blyth	1	0	0
Mrs. Cooper and friends	0	5	0
Mrs. Garrett	0	3	6
Mr. John Harris	0	5	0
Pastor C. Welton	0	5	0
Mr. and Mrs. Froggatt	2	0	0
Mrs. Ferguson	0	10	0
Mrs. Chillingworth	0	10	0
Mr. William Howard	1	0	0

	£	s.	d.
Collected by Mrs. Coles	1	0	0
Mr. J. Spilman	0	10	0
Mr. F. J. Collier	2	2	0
Mrs. Vowles and friend	0	12	6
Mrs. McKessack	0	10	0
A Scotch reader	0	2	0
L. E. P., per Pastor Walter Brown ...	1	0	0
Mr. A. F. Rogers	1	1	0
Mr. W. Pickard	2	17	0
A Folkestone working-man ...	0	10	0
G. N., Edinburgh	1	0	0
Stamps from Bradford	0	2	5
Mr. John Thomson	0	2	6
Mrs. Raines	1	0	0
Miss Eyles	0	10	6
Proceeds of cottage tea-meeting at Great Barton, per Mr. R. M. Scott ...	0	11	0
Rev. Charles Miller ...	0	10	0
Mr. George Gibb and friends ...	0	9	0
Mrs. W. Warren, per Pastor E. Spurrier... ...	0	10	
Lynton Road Sunday-school ...	0	10	
Collected by Master Herries ...	0	7	
Collected by Mrs. R. C. Allen ...	0	12	
Mr. Charles Barker ...	1	0	
Mr. George Wight... ...	1	0	
Mrs. Harvey	2	0	
Mr. C. Ibberson	0	2	
Mrs. Bell	0	2	0
Miss A. Whatley	0	5	0
A constant sermon-reader, per Mr. Gilbert Finch	3	0	0
Mr. E. Joscelyne	2	2	0
Pastor W. Jenkins	0	4	0
Mr. George Sinclair	0	5	0
Mrs. John Froggatt	0	4	0
Mrs. Thompson	1	0	0
Mr. William Fyson	0	10	0
Baptist Sunday-school, Fraserburgh, per Pastor W. Richards	1	7	6
Collected at Watch-night service, at Penge Tabernacle, per Pastor J. Wesley Boud	5	0	0
Mr. D. Peck...	0	2	6
Mr. Sapsed, per Mr. Peck	0	4	0
Mr. S. Sargeant	1	0	0
Mrs. Doughty	0	10	0
The scholars of the Carrow Works Sunday-schools, Norwich	2	10	0
F. J. and friends	0	3	0
Ruthie and Jackie...	2	2	0
Miss Hall	0	12	6
Dr. Parry and friends, Bristol	5	0	0
H. H. K.	1	0	0
Collected by Master H. Kingsnorth ...	0	7	6
Mr. J. W. Green	1	0	0
Rev. Dr. Beith	1	0	0
Mr. A. McRae and friends ...	0	14	0
Dr. and Mrs. Fearn	5	0	0
Mr. W. Woolidge	0	10	0
A native of Norwood ...	1	0	0
Mr. T. D. Anderson	2	0	0
Mrs. and Miss Haywood	0	3	6
Mrs. Gifford...	0	5	0
Mr. P. Mackinnon	10	0	0
Mr. Joseph Wiles	1	1	0
Mrs. Talbot...	0	5	0
Mr. J. Culpin	1	0	0
A friend at Risby	0	2	0
An aged believer	0	6	0
Mr. Lawrence Shepherd	0	10	0
Mr. Thomas Thomson	3	0	0
Miss L. Fidkin	0	5	0
Collected by Mrs. Whittaker ...	0	10	0
Mr. L. Haigh	1	0	0

	£	s.	d.
A few friends at Irvine, per Miss Sarah Muir	2	0	0
Mr. W. E. Eastman	0	10	0
Per Mr. J. A. Abraham:			
Mr. W. R. Way ... 1 0 0			
Mr. H. S. Haynes ... 1 1			
Mr. J. A. Abraham ... 1 1 0			
Rev. A. M. Carter, B.A. ... 1 0			
Mr. H. Joslin, J.P. ... 1 1			
Miss Giles ... 1 1	6	4	0
Mr. James Woodward	0	5	0
Mr. E. E. Wright	2	10	0
Mr. R. Little	1	0	0
Mrs. Lauder's Bible-class	0	6	6
Mrs. Frost	0	10	0
Miss S. A. Whitehead	0	5	0
Per Miss E. L.	0	16	0
Miss E. L.'s Bible-class, St. Giles's Street, Edinburgh	0	5	0
C. L., and friend	0	7	6
Miss Westrope	0	10	0
Friends at Lionsgate Mission-room	1	15	0
Mr. John Horn	0	2	6
Mr. Evans	0	5	0
Collected by Mrs. E. Holiday	0	10	0
Sale of S. O. Tracts	0	1	0
Mr. E. Eno	0	3	0
Per Pastor W. Burnett:—			
Mrs. Burnett's box ... 0 12 0			
Mrs. Record's box ... 0 10 5			
Mr. Bolton's box ... 0 3 6			
William Burnett's box ... 0 16 6			
Mr. Perry's subscription ... 0 5 0			
Profits from various small books ... 0 4 0	2	11	5
Collected by Miss Riddle	0	4	0
Mr. C. Allard	0	10	0
Mr. H. C. Bridgman	0	1	6
Per Miss Bessie Dixon:—			
Miss Cutlack ... 0 3 4			
Miss Dean ... 0 2 8			
The Misses Dixon ... 0 7 6			
Mrs. Geale ... 0 1 6½			
Mrs. Harmer ... 0 1 3½			
Mrs. Jupp ... 0 5 0½			
Mrs. Peck and Mrs. Bullen ... 0 2 7½			
Mrs. Sear ... 0 5 2¾			
Mr. Swaffield ... 0 4 5			
Mr. Stuchfield ... 0 2 5½			
Miss Stichurst ... 0 1 8½			
E. J. Dixon's farthing fund ... 0 1 3½	1	19	1
Mrs. George	5	0	0
Executors of the late Mr. J. G. Paterson, Glasgow	1	0	0

	£	s.	d.
Per Mrs. James Withers:—			
Mrs. Haynes. Hoe Bridge ... 10 0			
Mr. Thomas Huntley ... 4 0			
Mr. J. O. Cooper ... 2 0			
Mr. D. Heelas ... 2 0			
Mr. Austin Woodeson ... 0 15			
Mr. Ernest Woodeson ... 0 12 0			
Mr. Henry Cooper ... 0 10			
Mr. G. W. Palmer ... 0 10			
Mrs. Whitfield ... 0 5	20	12	0
Donation from a friend	20	0	0
Mrs. Fraser	0	5	0
Mr. A. R. Coles	0	10	0
Mr. and Mrs. Jordan	1	1	0
Mrs. Crawley	1	0	0
Mr. G. Shrewsbury	1	1	0
Collected by Mrs. Griffiths from friends at Kingswood and Wotton-under-Edge ... 13 6 0			
Received for 12 dozen "John Ploughman's Almanacks" ... 1 4 0	14	1	
Mrs. Gray	0		0
B. G., Norwich	1		
A friend from Shepperton	0	1	0
Mrs. Brown	0	0	0
Part collection at Lymington, per Pastor John Collins	1	11	6
Mater	0	5	0
Meetings by Mr. Charlesworth and the Orphanage Choir:—			
The Soldiers' Institute, Portsmouth, per Miss S. Robinson ... 35 0 0			
Miss S. Robinson ... 5 0 0			
Miss Higgs (expenses of choir) ... 1 0 0			
Temperance Society, Barry Road Wesleyan Chapel, East Dulwich, per Mr. Jordan	2	10	0
Annual Subscriptions:—			
Mr. I. Vinall	1	1	0
Mr. E. R. Close	0	5	0
Per F. R. T.:—			
Mr. H. Keen ... 5 0			
Mr. S. Pewtress ... 5 0			
Mrs. George Dix ... 5 0			
Mrs. Henry Brown ... 0 10 0	1	5	0
Mr. E. H. Bramley	5	0	0
Monthly Subscriptions:—			
Mr. E. K. Stace	0	10	0
Sandwich, per bankers	2	2	0
F. G. B., Chelmsford	0	2	6
Mr. S. H. Dauncey	0	2	6
	£342	16	6

Orphan Boys' Collecting Cards (continued).—Barson, E. J., 2s; Gant, F. C., 5s 6d; Hill, G., 10s; Lewis, E. R., 3s; Langridge, J., 17s 6d; Moppett, F., 3s; Platt, A., 4s 6d; Virtue, C. F., 9s 2d—Total, £2 14s 8d.

Orphan Girls' Collecting Cards (continued).—Blake, C., 12s 4d; Donoghue, E., 13s 6d; Fenn, A., 5s 5d; Fitt, M., 3s; Freatby, E., 3s; Grimes, E., 10s; Haisell, J., 12s 5d; Hocking, L., £1 1s; Jackson, A., 5s; Lovell, E., 2s; Pennington, F., £1 1s; Sands, M., 17s 4d; Smith, P., 10s 3d—Total, £6 16s 3d.

List of Presents, per Mr. Charlesworth, from January 15th to February 14th, 1889.—PROVISIONS:—1 hamper Aërated Bread, Mr. N. Read; 18 Wild Rabbits, Mr. J. Cooper; 1 New Zealand Sheep, Mr. A. S. Haslam; 1 Cake, Miss Dawson; 18 Rabbits, Mr. S. Barrow; 1 Fowl, 1 bottle Jam, and a quantity of Honey and Butter, Y. M. A. G.; 6 Stilton Cheeses and 119 Pork Pies, Mr. J. T. Crosher.

BOYS' CLOTHING.—12 pairs Knitted Socks, Mrs. Barlow; 1 dozen Shirts, Mrs. Wilkinson; 3 articles, The Young Women's Bible-class at the Orphanage, per Mrs. J. Stiff; 12 pairs Knitted Socks, Mrs. Cunningham; 3 shirts, Mrs. Wilmshurst; 1 pair Socks, Anon.; 18 pairs Knitted Socks, The Misses Thompson.

GIRLS' CLOTHING.—14 articles, Mrs. Bartholomew; 39 articles, The Gosport Tabernacle Junior Dorcas Society, per Miss Hoare; 2 Pinafores, E. Fennall; 148 articles, The Young Women's Class at the Orphanage, per Mrs. J. Stiff; 1 Dress, Mrs. Wilmshurst; 2 Ulsters, 2 Hats, and 1 Pinafore, Miss Dawson; 1 Muffler and 3 Scarves, Mrs. Hicks; 17 articles, The Misses Thompson; 106 articles, and 35 Ribbon Bows, The Ladies' Working Meeting at Tabernacle, per Miss Higgs; 8 articles, Mrs. Muir; 49 articles, Miss Jones' Bible-class; 7 articles, The Misses Horton; 54 yards Dress Material, Mrs. Thompson; 57 articles, Mrs. J. Howard; 8 yards Red Flannel, 18 yards Unbleached Calico, The Misses Milner; 30 articles, The Juvenile Working Society, per Miss Woods.

GENERAL.—1 year's Magazines, Mr. J. B. Mead; 1 barge of Flints and Gravel, Messrs. Wills and Packham; 4 Dolls, Mrs Wilmshurst; a quantity of Almanacks and Date Cards, Mr. J. Tresidder; 2 volumes "Blue Lights," and 1 volume "Ready," Miss Robinson; 1 cask Blacking, Messrs. Carr and Sons; 6 fancy articles, Miss Jane Workman; a quantity of Magazines, Mr. J. W. Andrew; a quantity of Stationery, Mr. B. P. Bilbrough; 1 Doll, Mrs. Hall, per Mrs. J. A. Spurgeon.

Colportage Association.

Statement of Receipts from January 15th to February 14th, 1889.

Subscriptions and Donations for Districts:—	£	s.	d.
Mr. W. H. Roberts, for Ilkeston ...	10	0	0
Mr. Thomas Greenwood, for Brentford	20	0	0
Weston Turville Baptist Church ...	1	5	0
Greenwich, per Pastor C. Spurgeon ...	10	0	0
Stratford-on-Avon, per Mr. J. Smallwood	15	0	0
Kettering, per Mr. W. Meadows, sen...	10	0	0
Somers Town, per Miss Griffith ...	10	0	0
Bromley Congregational Church, Kent	10	0	0
Great Yarmouth Town Mission ...	7	10	0
Dorking District, per Mr. W. Drane ...	15	0	0
	£108	15	0

Subscriptions and Donations to the General Fund:—	£	s.	d.
Mrs. Raybould	1	0	0
Executors of the late Mr. Edward Boustead (additional interest on deposits)	20	18	4
Mr. W. Howard	1	0	0
Miss A. Whatley	0	2	0
Two sisters	0	10	0
Mr. P. Mackinnon...	10	0	0
Mr. A. Todd	0	5	0
Mr. A. Perren	8	0	0
Mr. D. Heelas, per Mrs. James Withers	1	0	0
Annual Subscriptions:—			
Mr. J. Buswell (for 1888)	1	1	0
Mr. Marshall, per Mr. Mears ...	1	1	0
Half-Yearly Subscription:			
Mr. H. B. Frearson	7	10	0
	£52	7	4

Society of Evangelists.

Statement of Receipts from January 15th to February 14th, 1889.

	£	s.	d.
Thankoffering for Mr. Parker's services at Ringstead	1	6	0
"Church of England," thankoffering for Mr. Spurgeon's sermons	10	0	0
Thankoffering for Messrs. Harmer and Parker's services at Crewkerne ...	6	7	3
Mr. and Mrs. Clarke	1	0	0
Mr. P. Mackinnon...	10	0	0
Mrs. B——, towards Mr. Burnham's support, 1889	50	0	0
Mrs. Hallows	0	5	0
Two sisters	0	10	0
Mr. G. W. Slater	0	10	0
Mr. R. P. Dayton	1	0	0

	£	s.	d.
Thankoffering for Mr. Burnham's services at Ulverston	0	10	0
J. M.	5	0	0
Mr. C. F. Whitridge	4	0	0
Thankoffering for Mr. Parker's services at Bourton	2	17	0
Thankoffering for Mr. Burnham's services at Bere Regis	1	3	0
Thankoffering for Mr. Burnham's services at Puddletown	1	18	6
	£96	6	9

For General Use in the Lord's Work.

Statement of Receipts from January 15th to February 14th, 1889.

	£	s.	d.
Mr. G. E. Medway	2	0	0
"Kemnay"	0	2	0
Mrs. Spencer	0	5	0
Mr. and Mrs. Haynes ...	0	16	0
Mr. H. Jones	0	5	0
"Reliance," per Mr. S. J. Dobson ...	5	0	0
	£8	8	0

Friends sending presents to the Orphanage are earnestly requested to let their names or initials accompany the same, or we cannot properly acknowledge them; and also to write to Mr. Spurgeon if no acknowledgment is sent within a week. All parcels should be addressed to Mr. Charlesworth, Stockwell Orphanage, Clapham Road, London.

Subscriptions will be thankfully received by C. H. Spurgeon, "Westwood," Beulah Hill, Upper Norwood. Should any sums sent before the 13th of last month be unacknowledged in this list, friends are requested to write at once to Mr. Spurgeon. Post Office and Postal Orders should be made payable at the Chief Office, London, to C. H. Spurgeon; and Cheques and Orders should all be crossed.

THE

SWORD AND THE TROWEL.

APRIL, 1889.

Growing on the Wall.

A DISCOURSE BY C. H. SPURGEON.

"He spake of trees, from the cedar tree that is in Lebanon even unto the hyssop that springeth out of the wall."—1 Kings iv. 33.

SOLOMON was a great botanist, and his range of knowledge was of the widest sort. In nature God has made an amazing variety—from the cedar to the hyssop. In the creation of his grace there is an equal variety. Certain saints for strength, and glory, and excellence, are as the cedars of Lebanon. Other believers, equally alive unto God, are small; their sphere is limited, and their position is difficult: they are like the "hyssop that springeth out of the wall." In order to complete a botanical system it is as necessary to mention the wall-flower as to mention the cedar. If any one of the plants that God has made be left out of the botanist's list, his knowledge is imperfect. So it is with the people of God: we must enumerate them from the least even unto the greatest, if we would comprehend the whole host. If we preach only to those who are strong, we shall be doing grievous wrong to those who are weak. If we mention only the captains of the Lord's host, we shall be despising the rank and file, who have to bear the burden and heat of the battle. To make full and complete proof of our ministry, it is quite as needful for us to think of the hyssop as to consider the cedar. The mercy is that, as Solomon did not forget the hyssop, so a greater than Solomon is here, and he does not overlook the very least of his people. In the records of his saints he puts down David, but he also notes the least of them, of whom our prayer is, that he may be as David, and David as the angel of the Lord.

11

There would have been no complete register of Jacob's children had Benjamin been left out; and of God's family the register shall be perfect, and no little Benjamin shall be omitted.

I want those of you who are conscious of being little in Israel to feel that the Lord knows you and remembers you. The Psalmist was happy because he could say—" I am poor and needy ; yet the Lord thinketh upon me." God has an eye to the least plant of his right-hand planting; and Jesus mentions, in his pleading, all his saints; those that be great, for they need his intercessions; and those that be little, for they cannot be forgotten of him.

Let us learn—from Solomon first, if you will, but chiefly from the greater than Solomon—this lesson, *never to despise the little ones in the church of God.* Never say, " Lord, what shall this man do ?" Never think of such a person—poor, obscure, destitute of gifts—and say, " Of what use is such a one in the church except to be a burden to it ? " Never imagine such evil in your hearts. Those members of the body that are uncomely are necessary; and of those who are little, Christ has said what he says not of the great ones : " Whoso shall offend one of these little ones which believe in me, it were better for him that a millstone were hanged about his neck, and that he were drowned in the depth of the sea." Be very tender of the feebler sort; and if you are tempted to be great, and to talk of your own attainments and perfections, mind what you are at, lest you offend the babes. Take heed, lest it happen to you, as it did to Israel of old in the days of the prophet, when the strong cattle pushed with horn and shoulder, and then God determined to be avenged on the strong because they regarded not the weak. Tread very tenderly when thou art among the tender. Injure no man by thy strength. If thy running be swift, run against no man; and if thou must smite any man, do it as gently as thy God smites thee; lest haply, being rough and untender, thou shouldst one day find God froward with the froward, and hard with the hard. If the wisdom of God creates hyssops, it is not for thee to despise them.

We are told, too, that Solomon " *spake* " of hyssops. I do not know what he had to say about them; but I am sure that his speech was wise. We, also, will speak of hyssops. " Who are they," say you—" these small plants ? " Well, I mean those people who have small abilities and powers. If they carry anything it must be ounces : if they do anything it must be done as with a child's hand. They never were, from their youth up, able to learn much ; and he that cannot learn is not likely to be able to teach. They still are, and probably always will be, men and women of one talent only. They are, for that reason, the hyssop on the wall ; but, moreover, they are placed in circumstances which are not very helpful to them. I know Christian persons who happen to be juniors in a family where all mock at them and persecute them for Christ's sake. They grow as upon a wall. Their foes are " they of their own household." Sometimes it is a wife who has the utmost difficulty to maintain a Christian profession at all in the teeth of a husband's hostility; and, perhaps, added to that, there is opposition from those who are the children of her own bosom. I have known young people placed as apprentices, or as domestics in the house, where every possible difficulty is thrown in their way if they serve God. When they kneel at their bed-side, they are assailed with, a roar of laughter. There is nobody to help them in the least, and everybody to hinder them. They are, like the hyssop that is to grow upon the wall, in very hard circumstances. With others much hindrance arises out of their extreme poverty. They cannot give anything to the cause of God, except it be the widow's two mites that make a farthing. Their noses are to the grindstone always. They have to do the rough work of the race, and consequently they cannot rise to large service of Christ. So they think, though I think otherwise.

Many are placed where their work and service in life allow them small gospel opportunities. Perhaps they do not get out more than once a fortnight to hear a sermon, and can scarcely ever come to the communion table. There are such occupations, and I believe there always will be as long as the world stands, wherein persons are obliged to forego the means of grace which others enjoy in such plenty. There are towns and villages in which the gospel is not preached. Nay, perhaps I may not say that it is not actually preached, but it is not preached with any fervour, or freshness, or power. I know some to whom the Sabbath, instead of being a day of refreshment, is a greater day of weariness than any other in the week, because the preaching they hear makes them sick at heart. The sheep look up, and are not fed; they are not led into green pastures of blessed gospel doctrine, but they are tantalized with philosophical essays. These, again, are like the hyssops that grow upon the wall.

These are the people that I desire to talk to and talk about. God give them comfort!:

I cannot forget the sunny skies beneath which I sat a little time ago. With all the clouds that have swept over my head, both natural and spiritual, I cannot forget that there are lands where "everlasting spring abides"; and if the flowers do wither, yet, at least, they bloom again so quickly that one scarce knows that they are gone. I thought of this text, and of what I am about to say, by noticing the walls of the garden, in which I sat, covered from top to bottom with flowers of all colours. Between the cracks of the stones that supported the terraces of earth, there were growing such flowers as we can only rear in our conservatories, and only dare plant out in summer. These abounded from the bottom of the wall to the top. Many plants take delight in walls; and though the place seems uncongenial, yet they bring forth sweet flowers, and shed a delicious perfume all around.

Well, then, I thought, first, *these flowers that grow on walls are suited for such places, and the places are suited for them.* That is what I want to say to you, dear friend. Have you been grumbling because you cannot do great service for God and come to the front? Do you complain of your situation? My dear friend, somebody must be in your position, and in all probability there is nobody so well fitted for it as you are. You say, "Oh, but I need so much patience." The mercy is that God is ready to bestow that great patience upon you. "It is a very hard place, sir," say you. Yes, but it would be as hard for somebody else as it is for you; and if somebody must fill it, are you not, in all probability, the best person to do so? How should God distribute his servants? Should it not be by putting each one where he is most fitted to be?

What would a commander do with his regiments in the day of battle? Would he not send each company where it could do the best service to the royal cause? So it is with the Lord. He has placed you where you are because you are the fittest flower to grow where he has planted you. Do you not know many others who would wither in your position? Oh, yes, I know you do. Mind that you do not wither yourself! But at the same time, I feel sure that, although you would not choose the place, yet there was infinite wisdom in his heart who chose you for the place. You are the right flower for the wall, and the wall is the right spot for you. We ought never to quarrel with our positions, for, after all, dear friends, if we fail, the fault is not in our tasks, or in our offices, but in ourselves. To be very quiet in the family, and to glide through it making everybody happy, and to be yourself unnoticed, may seem to be a very little thing, yet is it a difficult matter, and she that has accomplished it has done well. She is a flower that blooms on the wall. Some of you are just fitted for a quiet position, and such a position is just fitted for you. Do you say that you would have liked the high places of the field? Ah me! you do not know the trials which some of us endure in the front of the battle. If you cannot do well in a low estate, I am sure that you cannot do well in a high one. If your head swims on the level, what would it do if you had to stand on a high and beetling cliff in the teeth of the storm? Be in no hurry to change. I would not like to change my temptations. I know a little of the particular devil that worries me: I would rather not have another tempter. He might strike me in a fresh place, and I might not be so well able to guard myself. The old cross fits the shoulder best: a new cross might raise a second blister. Grow where you are. Transplanted flowers seldom come to much; but he that can abide in his calling, and be satisfied not to move unless God moves him, shall bring to God glory by his life.

A second thought: *hyssops and plants that are on the wall have their uses.* Not only the corn that grows in the field, and the fruits that hang on the trees, but the little hyssop and other wall-plants serve their ends. God's obscure people live not in vain. There is great usefulness in a sweet example; it yields far better preaching than eloquent tongues. The preaching of a pious servant, or a godly mother, or a holy tradesman is manifest to everybody. The humble saint may be no spokesman, may never put six sentences together, but yet he yields much for God by holy living. With a godly example will often go sweet influences of comfort. I know Christian people who, if they were gone home, would be terribly missed; not that a line they ever wrote would be remembered, or a word they ever said would be repeated, but they have been of use to everybody. Had you never an aunt of that kind, who was a mother and nurse to all the family? Had you not a brother who was the friend of you all? Did you never know a friend most lowly, yet most loving? The hyssop on the wall is the image of such unobtrusive usefulness.

And, let me whisper in your ear, you quiet people of God, you little ones, do you know what was chiefly done with the hyssop? It was only a little plant; but they gathered it, and when the blood was sprinkled on the lintel and on the two side-posts at the Passover, it is written,

"Thou shalt take a bunch of hyssop." So the hyssop was stirred round in the basin of blood, and all that it did was, that it conveyed the blood to the person, or to the door-post, that was to be sprinkled. Oh, if, in my humble talk, even though it be on a sick-bed, I can but convey the blood of sprinkling to a guilty heart! Oh, if by my telling out of the gospel of Jesus, though it may be with many tears and broken words, I may but make that blood drop on one seeking sinner to his soul's salvation, I shall not have lived in vain! Go on, then, you that cannot preach, or even teach in the Sunday-school! Go on; and, as often as you have opportunity, talk about that precious blood which cleanseth from all sin. You can speak, where, perhaps, I shall never be heard. There is a door-post accessible to you, and not to me ; a human heart over which you may have influence, though it be but the heart of your own little girl; and I may never have a chance to speak to her. Grow on, you hyssops on the wall; you have your uses.

A third point I noticed about plants that grow on walls, and it was this—*they make much of littles.* I saw a fuchsia, and a cactus, and all kinds of flowers, which I cannot mention now, all rooted between the cracks of the stones, and growing well, too. There was very little earth, but much beauty; very little space, but much fragrance. These plants went as deep as ever they could, sending their roots as far in between the cracks as possible, to get what little nourishment there was. So have I seen poor, humble-minded, lowly Christians, with very little ability, very little opportunity, and no worldly substance at all, but they have made a great deal out of very little : their lives have been so beautiful, their whole conduct has been so attractive, their words have been so full of Christ, that one wondered whence all their sweetness came. Though they had but little earth, they were deeply rooted. If they prayed, they *did* pray. If they heard a discourse, they *did* hear it, and were not half asleep. When they could commune with God's people, they did not waste time in idle chit-chat, but they talked earnestly of the things of God. To hear these poor Christians speak, was to perceive that they were intense; that what they believed, they *believed ;* that what they knew, they *knew ;* and that what they had received from God, they practised in their lives. I am afraid that we are, many of us, far too superficial; our roots go skimming over the surface. We have much earth to travel over, but we do not suck in as much nutriment as we might. God's hyssops have very little earth, but they get all they can out of it. Oh, it is grand to see a man who has no books but his Bible ; and what a scholar he is in that sacred lore ! He has no second book, except his hymn-book ; but see how pat he brings in the verses of the hymns! It would be a great blessing to many men if they had their books burned, so that they could not read anything but their Bible, although other books are very helpful to him that reads his Bible first and foremost. Unlettered Christians, by diligence and deep experience, may become so acquainted with the things of God as to be fathers in Israel; while others, with greater advantages, are feeble folk.

The fourth thing that I thought of as I sat and looked at my illuminated book on the garden wall was this: *they adorned the wall.* The wall looked far more beautiful than it would have looked without them. You have read, I suppose, "The Shepherd of Salisbury Plain."

From the day that book was written it became a most respectable thing to be a shepherd. You have read "The Dairyman's Daughter," too, I dare say. Well, every dairyman and every dairyman's daughter went up in the world as soon as that book became popular. These holy ones lived among sheep and cows; and the plain and the cowhouse were beautified by their presence. Yes, a servant makes her drudgery divine when she does it for the Lord. A man may glorify God by sweeping chimneys: he may bring honour to the Most High by being a coster-monger in the street. You may degrade a pulpit, and it is often done; but you may elevate the "scissor-to-grind" wheel of the streets by godliness. It matters not *what* we have to do, but *how* we do it. Put the most beautiful flower upon the wall, and it loses nothing by the wall; but it gives much to it. The flower that is growing in the garden-bed may be passed by unnoticed; but the flower on the wall is noticed because of the singularity of its position. I have seen pinks on the ruins of an old castle, which were not so fine as those I could grow in my own garden, and yet I valued them because they grew in that romantic spot. They seemed the fairer because, amid decay and ruin, they kept alive the freshness of beauty. O dear friend, do not be sorry that you are placed in a difficult situation, but adorn your position, and "adorn the doctrine of God your Saviour in all things."

I believe that sometimes, also, *these wall-plants help to hold the wall up.* Their roots twist themselves about the stones and hold them fast. In railway cuttings nothing keeps the earth up better than shrubs, or trees, or gorse. Life is a preservative always. Families are often kept together by almost unnoticed men and women. I am sure it is so in the Church. You that love your Lord, and live as he did—you that are true Christians, but unassuming, and unobserved—your secret prayers are known in heaven, though not on earth. Your communion is "with the Father, and with his Son Jesus Christ," and you bind the Church together better than any of us; and, perhaps, when the Lord shall mete out rewards to his people, I may have little, and you may have much. There is an old story, it is of Popish origin, yet it has no Popery in it, but rather the reverse. It is a story of a successful preacher who had converted many, and he thought that his reward would be great in heaven; but it was revealed to him that he would have none of the honour of the conversions. A poor old deaf man, who used to sit on the pulpit-stairs, and pray for him all the while he was preaching, would have the reward. So it may be. Blind, or deaf, or poor, and with little talent, you may, nevertheless, be the very backbone or right arm of a church. You may be keeping it together by that silent graciousness of yours; and, if so, will you not be content? Measure not your ministries by their glitter, or by the space they cover. Measure them by the grace that is in them, and by your obedience to God; so shall you weigh them in the balances of the sanctuary.

I merely throw out these things to be thought of: here is another hint: *hyssops on the wall sometimes get the full sun when others in better positions do not.* I have frequently noticed it. The sun comes gliding up in the East, and the garden under the wall is in the shade; but there is a plant on the top of the wall, in a queer and awkward place, but the sun kissed it or ever he was fully up; and all day long, when the sun has been spinning round the heavens, even to the last hour, when he dipped into the West, the lord of day seemed to toy with the floweret upon the wall. When half the garden lay in shade, the sun was smiling on its blossoms, and only when he set did he bid his favourite farewell. So have I seen the child of God, poor, afflicted, obscure, despised, living in the light of God's countenance always. The strong, the worker, the well-known giver, the man that stood forth in public life—I have seen him in the shade. I have heard him cry to God to manifest himself to him; and all this while the little one has had no need of such a cry, for he has basked in the light of Jehovah always. Ay, many of the Lord's sick ones can say, "In the night I am still with thee"; for though obliged to count the weary night-watches, they have not been dreary, for God has been there. If that is your portion, my dear brother or sister, I want to cheer you, and make you feel glad to be that little hyssop growing upon the wall.

Once more, *these plants that grow upon the wall have an opportunity of scattering their seeds in due time farther than others that grow in a more propitious place.* I had a plant that grew upon my wall. It was little at first, but it grew up, and up, and up, with its tall spike and yellow blooms, till I should think it had reached two or three feet in height. I liked to see it on the wall. I am not quite so certain that I want ever to see it again, for it has managed to multiply itself all over the garden till I regard its offspring as too much of a good thing. Its position on the wall gave it this opportunity. When the wind came it carried away the seeds, or, if the pods burst open, the seeds leaped forth to a wider area than if they had been growing on the ground. Certain men and women have more influence for good than others, because of their disadvantages, their difficulties, their trials, and their lack of talent. If I speak, and I am helped to speak well, many will notice the words I utter, but the spiritual sense will miss them; but if some lowly individual here shall say a half-dozen broken sentences earnestly, there will be nothing in the style to beguile the listener, and the matter itself will be carried home all the better. I wish that you would put this to the test.

"Oh, but I am so ill. I keep my bed." Beds are brave pulpits. Earnest words from sick beds go farther into hearts than fine orations from platforms. I am sure that it is so.

"Oh, but I am so very poor." Yes, and if men hear godly talks from the very poor, they think the more of them. Many a working man who hears my sermon, will go home and say nothing at all about it; but to-morrow morning, if one of you who work with him shall speak to him with tears in your eyes, he will say to his wife when he gets home, "Missus, do you know Will So-and-so?" "Yes, John." "Well, he has been talking to me about my soul. I heard Spurgeon on Sunday, and I forgot what he said; for, you see, he is a parson, and it's their usual way to talk of these things. But Will told me he had tried true religion, and that it was his comfort in his trouble. You know, Missus, he is a very poor man. He does not earn half the wages I do. He was telling me how happy he and his wife are together, and how their children have turned out a comfort to them. I think, Missus, that it would be a good thing if we were to turn over a new leaf." Do you not see that the man's position helps him in this talk ? This hyssop on the wall can throw its seeds farther because of the wall it stands on. Years ago, a man drew crowds to see him dance, because he had only one leg. It is odd, is it not? I should think a man with two might do it more daintily. And there are cases, no doubt, in which disadvantages are advantages. Remember this, and use your trials and infirmities for your Lord.

Having spoken to humbler saints, I finish by saying, that it is better to be the smallest believer than the greatest unbeliever; better to be the most obscure saint than the most applauded sinner. *It needs almighty power to make the smallest hyssop:* it needs divine grace to make the smallest Christian. He that makes great saints must make little saints, or they never will be made at all. So then, fearing, trembling, weak believer, God is seen in you and glorified in you. I wonder which reveals most of God—the telescope or the microscope. If I had here two men who were skilful in these instruments, it would be difficult even for them to decide. The man of the telescope would talk of the stars and of their wonders; but he of the microscope would glory that he had seen God's finger in a fly's eye and in a butterfly's wing. If they discussed the question, in which God's glory was best seen, they would never come to a clear conclusion. God is not less in the least than in the greatest; and so, dear child of God, the grace of God will be greatly seen in bringing you, a little saint, to heaven, and making you to sing the praises of God world without end. If I am ever so insignificant, this shall be my comfort: God made me a plant of his garden : God alone could have made me so ; and God is seen in me. As the broad heavens may be seen in a single drop of water, so God's omnipotence may be seen in the tiniest drop of grace.

And this is the last comfort. *Every blade of grass has its " ain drap o' dew."* Every hyssop on the wall has its own dew prepared for it. Say, O child of God, "Blessed Spirit, drop from above on me. Moisten my leaf, and bring my flower to perfection unto thy glory." May my God bless every one of you! You professed believers especially, may his blessing bind you fast together. Let us love each other heartily, and especially let us love those who are little in our Israel; and let us all try, like Solomon, to speak of the hyssop on the wall. God bless you, for Jesus' sake! Amen.

Copying the Crack.

IT often happens that a man made conspicuous among his fellows by dazzling deeds, is like Nebuchadnezzar's image in being compounded partly of precious metal and partly of miry clay. Every such man is certain to have a host of imitators, who succeed to admiration in reproducing the clay feet, but are not so successful with the golden head. A Chinaman had a cracked plate given him, with instructions to furnish a set like it. He did so : and every piece had a crack faithfully copied from the original. With many worshippers of faulty heroes, the crack is the one thing that is fairly well copied.—*From " For Further Consideration" : an admirable book. Published by Elliot Stock.*

Spiders.

BY THOMAS SPURGEON.

SCARCELY anyone has so much as half a good word for spiders. All the opprobrious epithets imaginable have been hurled at the poor insect. According to the ladies, it is "just horrid." According to housewives and domestics, it is a perfect plague; and even preachers of that gospel which calls nothing common and unclean refer to it only when they wish to illustrate some vice or other. Here are a few specimens. Bishop Hall saw a spider comfortably ensconced in his window, and straightway compared it to the "thieves by land and pirates by sea that live by spoil and blood." And is it not written in the commentaries of Manton:— "The spider spinneth a web out of her own bowels which is swept away as soon as the besom cometh; so do carnal men conceive a few rash and ungrounded hopes; but when death cometh, or a little trouble of conscience, these vain conceits are swept away"? Thomas Brooks is equally complimentary (?)—"There are some that would hammer out their own happiness, like the spider climbing up the thread of his own weaving."

Perhaps this unanimous antipathy is not to be wondered at. As to the ladies, it would be strange indeed if they admired a creature which, it must be confessed, "isn't a bit nice." Domestics may surely be forgiven for speaking ill of spiders, for do they not make more work than enough by their everlasting web-spinning, and do not a dozen come to the funeral when one is swept away? And I will say this for the preachers— they have Scripture to back them; for of all the times the insect or its web is mentioned, there is but one reference that is not connected with frailty or iniquity or hypocrisy.

Well, then, I suppose it must be admitted that spiders are not "nice." There is no disguising the fact. It is all very well to say that many of them are perfectly harmless; that they keep the flies down, and so on. We don't like them for all that: (it is surely an acquired taste with those who do). Into some minds they positively strike terror. And truly some of them are sufficiently hideous. Take the Australian Tarantula for instance—with its bloated body and long hairy legs. We are inclined to sympathize with the new-chum domestic who, lifting up her hands in horror, cried aloud, "Lor', mum, there's a triantelope!" and rushed shrieking from the room. Poor Bridget need not have been so scared, for their appearance is the worst of them. N.B. There are many things far less awful than they seem!

But is there nothing to say in the spiders' favour? Have they no good qualities? Can they teach us nothing? Let us see. Why, there is something even in their name. "SPIDER, a corruption of old English *spinder*—from *spin*, so named from spinning its web." So saith the Dictionary.

It is evidently true to its name. It is not itself a hypocrite, even if its web is an apt figure of a hypocrite's hopes. So that is one to the spider. Here endeth the *first* lesson.

A *spinner!* Not a bad occupation that! In a marriage register form, a lady of my acquaintance wrote herself down "spinster" in the column which should have recorded her occupation. That surely was a pardonable mistake, especially as in her case the description was virtually correct; for if she did not actually spin, she was a true worker. This stands to her credit. Who need be ashamed of honest toil?

> "When Adam delved and Eve span,
> Where was then the gentleman?"

So a spider is a spinster, *i.e.*, one who spins. Let idlers stand rebuked by the despised spider. This is the *second* lesson.

No. 3. is, *perseverance.* You all know the story of Robert Brúce and the indomitable spider. Go thou and do likewise.

If I could only remember them, I am sure there could be told plenty of stories, and true ones too, about spiders, that would make us think more highly of them than we are wont to do. Did not one of them once save the life of a persecuted saint? Fleeing from his foes, he crawled into one of· the caves of the earth that sheltered those of whom the world was not worthy, and as soon as he was safely in, a spider came and shut the door—yes, shut the door, by spinning a web over the opening. "He cannot be there," said his pursuers, "for see, there's a spider's web over the entrance"—and on they passed. The glory of such a deliverance must be the Lord's; but I feel inclined to call for three cheers for that spider.

And who would have thought a spider sensible to the charms of music? yet I read in D'Israeli's "Curiosities of Literature," of a certain officer confined in the Bastille who was greatly astonished when he played his flute (by special permission of the governor), "to see descending from their woven habitations crowds of spiders, who formed a circle about him while he continued breathing his soul-subduing instrument."

There is another equally authentic story of a spider in the same renowned prison-house, which always responded to the sound of the bagpipe. This love of music is a pleasing trait in the spider's character. Do you retort that one need not be particularly musical to appreciate the bagpipes? I confess it is not my favourite instrument. But some prefer it. Tastes differ. Perhaps this spider had a strain of Scotch blood in it. It may have been distantly related to Bruce's spider, for ought we know. Here again is the spider our teacher.

> "The man that hath no music in himself,
> Nor is not mov'd with concord of sweet sounds,
> Is fit for treasons, stratagems, and spoils;
> The motions of his spirit are dull as night,
> And his affections dark as Erebus:
> Let no such man be trusted."

There is one class of spider for which I own I have a certain sort of liking. He rejoices in the name of *Cteniza nidulans, alias* the Trap door Spider. Ever since I had an opportunity of seeing him in his haunts by the blue Mediterranean, I have taken a real interest in him. He is so cunning and clever. Having bored a long tube, or tunnel, in the side of a bank, he lines it with some macintosh material made on the premises; and at the opening of this strange home he constructs a door, fitted in a frame, and working on a hinge. It is so hung that it shuts of its own accord, and without slamming. (O spider, show our architects and builders how it is done!)

The outside of this door is for all the world like the surrounding bank, so that it is not readily discovered. Having found it, you try to open it, and are surprised to note that something keeps it back. The fact is, my lord spider, whose castle you have so unceremoniously besieged, is resisting. He has laced his fingers (Solomon knew what he was talking about when he spoke of the spider's *hands*) into the webbing of the door, and is doing his level best to keep the portal closed. More power to him, I say. Well would it be for us did we take as many precautions to live securely, and to keep out intruders. How often do we leave our communion and fellowship exposed, though Christ himself has bidden us "shut to the door"! We run too many risks. We do not challenge every thought. We should guard our homes and hearts more jealously. See to it, dear reader, that the door hinges all right, and swings to readily; and when unholy and mischievous interlopers come, take hold with your hands, and, at all costs, keep the intruder out.

Yet another spider has some of my respect. He is the water spider. He must be a thorough-going Baptist, for he spends most of his time in a state of immersion. The wonderful thing about him is, that he carries down with him a big bubble of air, and lets it escape into a dome-shaped cocoon, which he has previously constructed. Then he goes above for another; and so on, until he has sufficient air to last for a long time. In this diving-bell he lives, watches for his prey, eats his meals, and rears his family; returning to the surface only when his stock of atmosphere is running short.

Does it not occur to you that we have, in this curious specimen, a not inapt illustration of the Christian, who, compelled to live in an element which is not congenial to his new and better nature, can exist there only as he makes constant visits to the upper air, and secures fresh supplies of spiritual atmosphere? Fortified with this, he passes through conditions that else would destroy him, and, though in the world, is not of it. May we be ever thus!

Is my reader beginning to think better of spiders in general, and to see that there is something good, and worthy of imitation, in the humblest and ugliest? I am glad of that. The balance is inclined to drop, is it? Then let me add a few more facts that will surely kick the beam. Spiders are, without doubt, successful scavengers. Flies enough we have as it is, but the fourth of Pharaoh's plagues would be upon us if anything serious happened to the spiders. At God's command, they have set their traps and toils at every corner. I feel disposed (disinterestedly, of course) to wish them all success. Just now, at all events, I could wish that many more of the persistent little pests would accept the spider's kindly invite to walk into her parlour.

Nor is the web of the spider so absolutely useless as most folks think. So strong is it, that a single thread can bear six times the weight of its maker. Some articles of apparel have been manufactured from it, but sufficient quantities are not obtainable.

I will speak a word, too, in behalf of the much-abused cobwebs. Next time you cut your finger, try a cobweb. If it doesn't stop the bleeding almost immediately, it will be the first time I knew it fail. Really, I'm not joking. This is what the Americans call "a *true* fact."

But here is a greater wonder still. Some eyes will open wide, I dare say, when I assert that astronomers are not a little indebted to spiders! Celestial spheres and spiders are surely far removed. Yes, verily; but the astronomers are glad enough to get the fine threads the spiders spin to use as cross-wires for their telescopes. Fancy measuring the star-depths with spiders' webs! To what high uses may the meanest things be put! There is hope that our feeblest efforts for God may be of great service to him. "Base things of the world, and things which are despised, hath God chosen."

Thus have I taken the spider's part and sung his praises as best I could. Suppose we all resolve to speak a good word for the despised and downtrodden; to see the virtues which they surely have, rather than the vices, which too readily attract our eyes. Happy are we if we can see "good in everything"!

Let me conclude by quoting, in part, a fable I came across lately. "The Safest Place" is its title, and Joel Benton is its author.

"Disturbed outside, two spiders went
Into a church to pitch their tent;
Where each might spin her pretty nest,
With none to trouble, or molest.
When far within, one sought a pew,
And on its top her fabric drew.
But soon the sexton, prim and neat,
Brushed it aside beneath his feet.
The pulpit next she straightway took,
But when the preacher moved his book
One day, the web which she had spun
Was, in a moment, all undone.
At length, the spider walked around
Until her neighbour's home she found;
Then asked, "How is it you succeed,
While I am ever doomed to bleed?"
Then said her friend, "I took a spot
Certain to give a quiet lot;
To save myself from calls, or knocks,
I chose the *contribution box*."

"I shall look out for Jesus."

"MOTHER," said a dear little boy of eight or nine summers, as he quietly crept into his invalid foster-mother's bedroom one morning, "while I've been lying in bed, I've been looking up at the stars; and I thought they looked like angels. Then I said to myself, 'Suppose this was the Judgment-day, and these were the angels coming with the Lord, what should I do?' Then I thought, 'I'll look out for mother, and keep close to her'; but then I remembered how weak you are, and I said, 'No, mother couldn't help me, I'll look out for father; he's strong; and then I thought, 'No, I know father wouldn't be able to save me'; then I thought, 'I'll look out for Jesus, I know he can save me.'"

Let this little-child-language and this little-child-faith teach you, timid disciple. Look out for Jesus! He cannot fail you? You know he will not; for whilst you look out for Jesus, Jesus will look out for you.
F. E. B.

The Blood-marked Path.

AN Indian, addressing his brothers, said the Saviour had showed us the way to the Father, and, "lest we should miss it, he marked it with his blood."

Keep to the blood-marked path, brothers!
Keep to it all the way:
Follow the steps of the Saviour,
And nothing shall lead you astray.
Blood on the first step of pardon,
Blood on the next step of peace,
Blood-mark on gladness and sorrow,
Precious till sorrow shall cease.

Follow the blood-marked path, brothers!
Jesus has traced all the road:
Jesus has trod it before you,
Bearing a heavier load.
Go not where flowers are blooming;
Flowers must never decide:
Go not where many are pressing,
Only the blood be your guide.

Follow the blood-marked path, brothers!
Follow it in your thought,
Follow in practice and teaching,
Jewels to this are nought.
Follow it still in singing,
Praise it with every breath:
Follow it through the dark valley,
Follow it on to death.   WILLIAM LUFF.

"Are you Really?"

A YOUNG Christian stood in the midst of a workshop full of scoffers. Previous to his employment there, a professed and pronounced infidel had scattered his pernicious seed in every direction. On account of his aggressive and bullying manner, few, if any, of those who had respect for the truth of God's Word had dared to interfere. At length the new hand was taken on, and no sooner did he become aware of the awful company into which he had fallen, than, praying to God for strength, he resolutely confronted this servant of the devil. Day by day the battle waxed hard and furious; in the end, the sceptic was silenced if not convinced, of his error. At the close of almost the last discussion, one of the workmen who, previously to this, had remained a silent spectator, stepped up to the Christian, and said, "I'm on your side; I'm a Christian." "Are you really?" said he; "I should never have found it out, if you had not told me." The rebuke was keen, but it was well deserved, and came naturally to the lip of the earnest man.

We fear there are many cowards in the Christian church as well as out of it. If all renewed men would stand up for the honour of their Master whenever they heard his Word assailed, we should hear considerably less of the blatant scepticism now so prevalent in our midst. Many of Christ's followers have yet to learn that they are witnesses for him. Their lives are stunted and withered by their sinful cowardice. When Moses stood in the gate of the camp, he cried, "Who is on the Lord's side? let him come unto me"; and the Master cries after the same manner no less emphatically to-day. Oh, for a baptism of the Holy Ghost upon every individual believer in the Christian church! What a mighty witnessing for Christ there would then be! God send it, and send it at once!

Guernsey.   F. T. SNELL.

No Help : no Hope.

A PITEOUS advertisement, in one of the daily papers, ends with the words: "*No help : no hope.*" They sound like a funeral knell; or like the cry of some lone swimmer, whose strength has failed him, and the deep is closing over him. Thank God, it is not a cry which my reader needs to take upon his lips. For every child of God there is help in the great Father's heart and hand. What is more, for every creature there is help in the Creator, who forsaketh not the work of his own hands. What is best of all; for seeking ones, there is help for sinners; for, on their behalf, the Lord hath laid help upon one that is mighty, by raising up "a Saviour, and a great one." We may not despair, now that God, in human flesh, has come to the rescue of the guilty, and in that flesh has borne the condemnation which fell on man through sin. There is help, and therefore there is hope. It is a sort of constructive blasphemy to deny ourselves hope, since it involves the denial of honour to the divine Saviour. Is HE a failure? Is his work unfinished? Is his sacrifice insufficient?

Here is an advertisement which we insert gratis in *The Sword and the Trowel* :—

THERE IS HOPE, FOR THERE IS HELP.

Life up your head, despondent one, and look to HIM who now stands looking at you. From the window of love he gazes on your misery; look up to him from your low estate with the glance of hope. Do your eyes meet? His looks forbid you to be any longer the slave of fear! He shows you his wounds, and thereby heals your bleeding heart! He cries, "Look unto me, and be ye saved: for I am God, and there is none else."

                                                  C. H. S.

The Thirty Years' Peace.

HISTORY relates that Donald Cargill, the martyr, made from the scaffold the deeply interesting declaration, "I bless the Lord that these thirty years and more I have been at peace with God, and was never shaken loose of it; and now I am as sure of my interest in Christ and peace with God as all in this Bible and the Spirit of God can make me."

King Amaziah's Money-Difficulty.

BY DAVID JAMISON.

MONEY—most persons will, no doubt, agree at once to the statement— is a very good servant, but a very bad master. Perhaps, too, my readers will also allow that even as a servant much depends upon the way in which it is treated, whether, after all, it is a good servant or not. Good servants have a tendency and temptation, when their goodness is evidently appreciated, rather to presume upon the goodness, and to assume authority oftentimes in unasked advice and unauthorized action. And generally, when they do so, their goodness is very seriously dis-counted, not alone in the estimate of those with whose action they thus interfere, but often, too, in the effects which follow the interference, if it be permitted.

A servant, to be really good and to continue to be good, must, as servants go in general, be kept in his own place, and confined to his own province : and this is emphatically true of money. Valuable as it is, and useful as it is, and while it may need much effort and require much wisdom to make it, it needs more effort and requires more wisdom to manage it when it is made ; and so to manage it that there shall not be more of loss than of profit in its possession.

Many, very many persons, as we must all know, by allowing money to occupy too high a place in the ordering of their affairs and to interfere with matters, as if superior to them, in comparison with which it was really subordinate, have suffered a damage which it was utterly valueless and powerless to countervail.

One of the kings of Israel may be taken as furnishing an illustration, or rather as having come very near to doing so. For, fortunately for himself, a wise counsellor was at his hand, who prevented the illustration from being complete, and to whose wise counsel the king, in his turn, was wise enough to listen.

We have the story told us in the much-neglected Books of the Chronicles—in the Second Book, and at the twenty-fifth chapter—and its commencement should warn us against yielding to similar considerations nowadays, of fictitious rather than of real importance, by which we are more apt to be influenced than we should be; and its close will show us, that when, nevertheless, we give the preference to higher considerations, as we always should do, we shall never lose by doing it.

It is quite possible we may sometimes find ourselves in a similar per-plexity to that of Amaziah, the king referred to. And if, at such time or times, we act as he ultimately did, our policy may be condemned by some as Quixotic and unworldly. But we shall not find the apparent immediate loss a real loss, nor without, both at the time and afterward, its far more than counterbalancing compensation. There may rather, if it be best for us, result from it greater gain, even probably in hard cash, and certainly in higher and truer and much more lasting profit.

The story is as follows :—Amaziah, king of Judah, apparently soon after his coming to the throne, and after he had justly put to death those who had been concerned in the murder of his father, determined, for some unrecorded reason, on a war against the people of Edom. The war seems to have been a justifiable one enough, for no fault is intimated in Scripture, as being found with him on this account. But in order to be equipped for it, he not only musters and marshals his own available forces, enlisting all from the age of twenty years and upwards, but he also hires, at the same time, auxiliary forces to the number of one hundred thousand from the sister kingdom of Israel, at the cost of a hundred talents of silver—perhaps about £30,000. And here it was, in this last particular, that his fault comes in. Not only did this step manifest a want of confidence in God, who could equally have led the smaller as the larger army to victory; but the Israelites being at that time idolaters, it evidenced lack of jealousy for God's honour, as well as lack of faith in God's power.

A prophet is therefore commissioned to the king, who commands him to dismiss these troops, and warns him that should he disobey and lead them to the battle, their presence shall ensure, not his victory, but his defeat. The king in no way resents the prophet's interference, nor repudiates his interdict; but he is staggered at first, nevertheless, by a consideration of the money he must apparently lose if he obey.

He asks—"But what shall we do for the hundred talents which I have given to the army of Israel?" The prophet replies at once, "The Lord is able to give thee much more than this." And to his very great honour, it is recorded, that without any more ado, large as the sum was which he had lost, and much as he might look to suffer from the resentment of the Israelites so unceremoniously dismissed (that they did resent it, and that he did suffer, the chapter tells us), he nevertheless dismissed them at once, and leads his own troops alone to the fight.

He secures a complete victory also, even with the smaller army, and evidently, but that he did not continue to act with the same discretion afterwards, a bright page was then turned in the record of his life, which only his subsequent forgetfulness and folly brought abruptly and sadly to a close.

This is a story, a story (that part of it with which we have to do at present) in the main to the credit of king Amaziah. This question of his, however, "But what about the hundred talents?" what are we to say about it?

Well, it is easy enough to see, and easy enough to say, that it was wrong and unworthy in king Amaziah to allow this question—a question of mere money—to weigh with him for even a moment against his duty—the duty of instant compliance with the mandate of the man of God. And of course it was so. Nevertheless, before we blame him too much, let us just ask ourselves, how many of us could safely afford to throw a stone at him? If we ventured on censure of him should we not lay ourselves open to some such words as those of Paul, "Therefore thou art inexcusable, O man, whosoever thou art that judgest: for wherein thou judgest another, thou condemnest thyself; for thou that judgest doest the same things"?

If any ask, How so? can they challenge the reply, that only too many, not in the world only, but even in the church as well, allow this money-difficulty, all sordid and sorry though such an obstacle is, to come in between them and the interest of their souls in the one case; their full and loyal allegiance to God in the other?

. For, first, as to the world, what is so popular and powerful a competitor with the gospel for the attraction and attachment of men as, just, money? and what is it that so often, and so everywhere, and in so many cases, stands to the last between the soul and its salvation, perilling it and preventing it, as, just, "the love of money," which as the apostle says, "is the root of all evil"? Men of wisdom, men of sense, men who know that they have souls, and that these are immortal, men who are aware that there is a death and a judgment, and an eternity—a heaven or a hell before them—yet are so absorbed in money, that they forget all this, and live and labour and plan and propose all for earth, all for time, all for that which shall perish in the using—riches their only religion, gold their only god.

And they do this, thousands do it, heedless about all else, day by day, month by month, year by year, discovering, many of them, their folly only when it is too late, only when, in the midst of their selfish, their pelfish calculations, the cry breaks in, "Thou fool, this night thy soul shall be required of thee: then whose shall those things be, which thou hast provided?"

Amaziah shines in comparison with these; his was but a momentary hesitation; theirs is a lifelong mania; he chose God at length, at this time, at all events; they cleave to Mammon with purpose of heart.

Not only is it in the world, however, that this money-difficulty exerts so baneful an influence. In the church, too, its presence and its power are felt. Even among professing Christians, too many an ear is dulled to a "Thus saith the Lord," by the cropping up of such a question as this—"But what about the hundred talents?"

They, these professing Christians, are engaged perhaps in some trade or occupation which, however legitimate so far as human law is concerned, is one they yet can hardly carry on, such are its causes, concomitants, or consequences, with a clear conscience, or are able, therefore, without effrontery to ask God's blessing on it.

Or in a trade which is perfectly allowable in itself, they resort to expedients for making money which, though tolerated or even taught by the low, lame code of worldly morality, are yet incompatible with the letter and spirit of the gospel of Christ, and inconsistent with any proper profession of attachment or allegiance to him who "did no sin, neither was guile found in his mouth." And, as a consequence of engaging in this trade or adopting these expedients, when conscience twits them, or duty calls them, or some sermon or providence intimates their inconsistency to them, how often, even when they are on the point of doing what they know and acknowledge they ought to do, they are hindered and held back by such a question as this—"But what about the hundred talents?" What about the money I might make, or the money I might lose? And how often, too, not as in Amaziah's case, the colloquy and the conflict end in—"If I did it, the hopes of my gains would be gone; I could not—cannot do it!"

Too rarely indeed, as already intimated, is Amaziah's story paralleled in its finale here. Much to his credit he did not let the unworthy hindrance stand very long in the way of his duty. Large though the sum was he forfeited—some £30,000—he came very soon to ask, "What about it?" in a very different sense from that in which he asked it first.

And should not the worldling, should not the Christian of the present, put it and look at it in the differing sense as well? What about it? "What shall it profit a man, if he shall gain the whole world, and lose his own soul?"

It is true that money is valuable, money is necessary, and the possession of money is comfortable, and the loss or lack of money is awkward and annoying. But when money is brought into competition with the soul, with the light of God's countenance, with the hope of eternal life, with peace of conscience and joy in the Holy Spirit, oh, surely the wise, the rational man will say, "What about it?" and let it go at once, rather than prejudice, rather than peril, the far more important interest of his eternal well-being. Better, infinitely better, to be a Lazarus, if need be, here—that with Lazarus we may be hereafter—than to be a Dives on earth at the risk, and at the cost, of being a Dives in eternity.

Besides, there is no need that the Christian should be a Lazarus here. The prophet said to Amaziah in reply to his question, "The Lord is able to give thee much more than this."

And does not all the teaching of Scripture give a similar assurance to every Christian? Does it not say, for example, the Lord himself being the speaker, "Verily I say unto you, everyone that hath forsaken houses, or brethren, or sisters, or father, or mother, or wife, or children, or lands, for my name's sake, shall receive an hundredfold, and shall inherit everlasting life"? There is many a similar promise; and here, let me say—it really needs to be said—while there seems to be, with some, disinclination almost amounting, one would think, to disability to believe the promises of God in reference to money matters—though they may be believed in reference to everything else—there is no cause at all why this should be so. Giving does not impoverish God, nor does withholding make him richer. "The earth is the Lord's, and the fulness thereof." Surely such a thought about God is utterly unwarranted, utterly unworthy!

Look, then, at such matters aright. Be sure of this, that whosoever counts "all things but loss for the excellency of the knowledge of Christ Jesus," shall not only, no matter what he gives up for Jesus, receive a "much more than this" in the peace and the joy and the prospect of believers, but he shall also experience that "godliness is profitable unto all things, having promise of the life that now is." "The blessing of the Lord," let us never forget, "it maketh rich, and he"—and that cannot be said of riches gotten in any other way—"addeth no sorrow with it." If, then, any of us are like Amaziah in his first hesitancy, in similar circumstances, let us be like him also, and rather, in his ultimate decision, to trust in God and do the right. Whatever, we may be sure, we give up for God, God will "much more" make up to us. "THE LORD GOD OF RECOMPENCES SHALL SURELY REQUITE."—*From "Passim Papers."*

Covenanting Mountain Peaks.

BY W. Y. FULLERTON.

CIRCUMSTANCES recently led me to make a short sojourn in Ayr, where heroic memories of Wallace and Bruce linger, and poetic memories of Montgomery and Burns, both of whom were born here, abound. Indeed, the sentiment of the town may be said to be kept alight by Burns and the scenes of his poetry; while his birthplace and his monument annually attract thousands of visitors. In picturesqueness, the distant view of the almost alpine heights of the island of Arran, as seen from the sea-shore, is unsurpassed, especially when, in golden glory or in blushing glow, the sun sets behind the burnished peaks. It seems hard to understand how Burns should have seen this sight so often, and not have written a single line to show his appreciation of it: Arran and its charms are passed over in silence in his poems.

Those towering heights seen over the sea in many a changing aspect, seemed irresistibly to remind me of the noble Covenanters who, in their day, were like giants amongst their fellows, and who in the very district of which Ayr is the centre—it is "flowered with martyrs' graves"—wrought some of their noblest deeds. When not hidden by mist, those mountains were weird and sombre in their grandeur on cloudy days, and the days were few when the sun shone and caused all to stand out in clear and cloudless outline. Nor did we ever forget that round about the roots of the mountains was always the treacherous sea. Thus were those men of God who, in troublous times, stood firm amidst the change and turmoil : not wavering and driven with the wind and tossed, as so many were; yet, withal, sombre in their faith, though grand ; living not so much in the sunshine of Olivet as in the shadow of Sinai. Mistaken, doubtless, in some things, but heroes of God notwithstanding ; and when their sun set, the glory of their exalted character was revealed as clearly as the heights of Arran at the close of the day. Burns has not forgotten these brave men; and for that we are quite prepared to forgive his silence about the hills.

> "The Solemn League and Covenant
> Cost Scotland blood—cost Scotland tears ;
> But it sealed freedom's sacred cause—
> If thou'rt a slave, indulge thy sneers."

It is easy to criticize them while enjoying the fruit of their sacrifice. Yet, as Professor Wilson well says, "But for the single-hearted sufferings of these virtuous men, but for their resistance to tyranny—the proudest genius amongst us, perhaps even now, might have been clanking a chain, or adoring a wafer."

It is not our intention to enter into the history of this movement, or to speak in detail of its various events from the signing of the third Covenant in 1638 until the end of persecution in 1688, nor of the many martyrs who sealed their faith with their blood, especially during the second half of those fateful fifty years ; but as our attention was chiefly given to the summits of the Arran hills, there are seven sayings of these Covenanting saints which, like mountain tops, tower up from their record, and arrest our thought and heart. It is of these we write, and of so much history as is necessary to make them intelligible.

"YE HAVE GOT THE. THEORY; NOW FOR THE PRACTICE," was the utterance of the preacher Thomas · Douglas, at the Conventicle of Drumclog, when he was told Claverhouse was approaching with his dragoons; and, in a sentence, this gives us *the principle* of the Covenanters. On the Lord's-day, 1st June, 1679, a band of faithful men and women met together on Loudon Hill, and were quietly worshipping God after the fashion their consciences approved ; but the presence of fifty horsemen fully armed, and the watchmen dotted over the heights made it clear that danger attended the gathering. When the alarm was given, the preacher issued the striking order of the day we have quoted, and the armed men formed in line of battle. Two hundred and fifty of them, some with only pitchforks or scythes set on poles, waited the coming of the soldiers, singing the seventy-sixth psalm, to the tune Martyrs, the while. The morass which lay between the opponents frightened the dragoons, but the Covenanters, with their good theory, and a good conscience, plunged through it, and at last 'the dragoons fled, leaving forty dead and many wounded on what was afterwards always ·known as the only battlefield on which the Covenanters were successful—the field of Drumclog. Never did the word of the Lord Jesus, "They that take the sword shall perish by the sword," receive a more signal fulfilment than in the case of the Scotch heroes, and their very success in this first encounter raised in their ranks that fierce fanaticism which eventually proved their ruin on the battlefield. Let him that is without a single feeling of resentment towards his neighbour cast the first stone at them !

Many glimpses of deep tenderness are seen amidst the fierce struggle which show *the spirit* of these godly men. Richard Cameron, one of that band of preachers which includes such men as Matthew Mouatt, William Guthrie, Blackadder, and McKail, died in battle at Ayr's Moss. The battle of Bothwell' Brig had been fought and lost, and almost a year had passed, when Cameron and sixty friends were surprised by Bruce of Earshall, who came with a troop of horse. As at Drumclog the warriors united in praise before drawing their swords, here they joined in prayer, and one petition, enough to make one weep, Cameron repeated thrice : "LORD, SPARE THE GREEN, AND TAKE THE RIPE." In the fight which followed, Cameron, his brother, 'and seven others fell,' a few were taken prisoners, and the rest escaped over the moss where the soldiers could not follow. The head and arms of Cameron, being cut off, were taken to · Edinburgh where they were delivered with the words—" There are the head and the hands of a man who lived praying and preaching, and who died praying and fighting." That tender heart beating in that rough breast, showed indeed a spirit ripe for glory.

The records of those years have many incidents which show *the courage* of the Covenanted people. None is finer than the dying words of one of five men who were discovered in a cave in Glencairn, and instantly shot. He raised himself on his elbow, and cried with his dying breath, "THOUGH EVERY HAIR OF MY HEAD WERE A MAN, I WOULD DIE ALL THOSE DEATHS· FOR CHRIST AND HIS CAUSE." Truly, they counted not their lives dear unto them, and doubtless their martyr crowns shine bright !

One of the most thrilling incidents of the time of persecution was the death of John Brown at Priesthill. The answer of his wife to the taunt of his murderer after the cruel deed, is a sample of *the sacrifice* these true disciples gladly made for Christ. John Brown, overtaken by Claverhouse while digging moss in a field, was led up to his own door and, in his wife's presence, was asked to abjure the Covenants. He stoutly refused. He was then asked to swear he would never rise against the king, and again refused. Told that he must die, he begged time for prayer, and his prayer so touched the soldiers that none of them would shoot. Their commander himself fired the shot, and then turned to the wife with the angry question, "What think you of your goodman now?" to which the noble woman replied "I AY THOOHT MEIKLE O' HIM, AND I THINK MAIR O' HIM NOO THAN EVER." What grandeur of character such an answer displays! Well done, Isobel Brown!

But it is in the life of the saintly Peden that we see most of *the trust* these hunted people had in God. "He was a lonely man, and his loneliness was the result of his individuality." Men who walk near to God are always lonely, because there are so few of them. Enoch was, probably, the loneliest man of his generation, and Peden was another Enoch, who walked with his head in heaven and his feet on the earth. "O to be wi ye, Ritchie!" was the cry of his heart at the grave of Richard Cameron; but God spared Alexander Peden the martyr's suffering, and took him home in peace. "O sirs," he said, "will ye trust God, and give him credit? and he will help you in all your work. ... He will even, as it were, rock the cradle, if it were necessary for you. He will condescend as low as you desire him." We need not wonder that a man of such a spirit was powerful in prayer. Well do I remember how my heart was touched, as a boy, and how I received one of my earliest impulses towards prayer when I read of the deliverance God wrought on the hillside in answer to the cry of "Peden the Prophet." On the Carrick Hills, he and a small party were surrounded by soldiers, and unable to flee; he prayed that they might be delivered and their enemies scattered, and a sentence of his prayer is worthy of remembrance: "LORD, CAST THE LAP OF THY CLOAK OVER SANDY AND THESE POOR THINGS, and save us this one time, and we will keep it in remembrance, and tell it to the commendation of thy goodness, pity, and compassion." Immediately a mist came down and hid them so effectually that they escaped their pursuers. How beautiful the close intimacy with God, which can plead to be allowed to hide under the lap of his cloak! "He shall cover thee with his feathers, and under his wings shalt thou trust."

John Welch, of Irongray, is a famous name amongst this goodly company of confessors and martyrs. One incident in his life shows *the power* which rested on their testimony, as well as the boldness with which they spake. Engaged to preach at a gathering the next day, he took refuge from his pursuers in a house which he afterwards discovered belonged to an enemy of the Covenanters. In the course of conversation his host made no secret of his opposition, and mentioned the name of John Welch as being a specially obnoxious person, ignorant that the very man he hated was sitting at his table. The disguised preacher said, "I AM SENT TO APPREHEND REBELS. I know where he is to be found to-morrow, and will give him into your hands." His host was delighted, and early in the morning started, under his guest's guidance, in the hope of effecting a capture. His astonishment was very great when he saw his guide take his place at the head of the congregation, and greater still when he heard him, in the power of God's Spirit, pour forth his soul in an earnest exhortation to the people. The Word of God, quick and powerful—why have not we more faith in it?—reached his heart, and when the sermon was over, instead of apprehending the preacher, this man of influence went up to him, and warmly greeted him. "You said you were sent to apprehend rebels," said he, "and I, a rebellious sinner, have been apprehended this day." The men who can thus touch sinners' hearts have no need to be ashamed.

Only one more instance need be given ; but that one is, perhaps, the most touching in all the annals of martyrdom, and reveals *the separation* of these true disciples to their Lord. On the 11th of May, 1685, at Blednock, near Wigtown, Margaret Wilson and Margaret McLachlan were taken out to die for God and the Covenant—that Covenant which was Scotland's Magna Charta. It is said that remission had already arrived, but was kept secret by the cruel men in authority, Grierson and Legg. As neither of the two women would renounce their faith, the latter, who was older than her companion, was taken out to the sea edge, and, tied to a stake, almost at the ebb-mark, the incoming waves soon covered her. With that floating object before her, they again urged Margaret Wilson to recant ; and again she refused, saying that if she had not part with Christ's people she had no part with him. Her mother urged her to yield, but she loved not mother more than Christ. Then they tied her to a stake high up on the beach, and she had to wait long ere the laggard tide reached her feet. As it crept slowly upward, one, Major Windram, anxious to save her, rode out, and said, "Dear Margaret, say 'God save the king!' say 'God save the king!'" "God save him, if he will ; for it is his salvation I desire," was her answer. "She has said it! She has said it!" he shouted, anxious to give her the benefit of any doubt. And then they came to urge her to save her life by taking the oath of abjuration. But her strong faith prevailed, and she gave an answer that should be written in gold—an answer which might make a key-note for every separated life. "Take the oath!" they cried ; and firmly came the heroic reply, "I WILL NOT! I AM ONE OF CHRIST'S CHILDREN : LET ME GO"! They let her go ; they could not hold her back to forsake her Lord : serenely she raised a psalm amidst the sea—

> "'To thee, my God, I lift my soul!' she sang;
> And the tide flowed, and, rising to her throat
> She sang no more, but lifted up her face—
> And there was glory over all the sky;
> A flood of glory—and the lifted face
> Swam in it, till it bowed beneath the flood,
> And Scotland's Maiden Martyr went to God!"

Her holy heroism and Christian courage place this maiden in the front rank of those who have stood firmly for God in all ages. Turning our eyes, we see those with whom, in glory, she stands : and she is not a whit behind the chiefest. Look at these mountain summits :—

Margaret Wilson said : " I will not ! I am one of Christ's children .
let me go."

John Bunyan said : " I have determined, the Almighty God being

my Helper and Shield, yet to suffer, if frail life may continue so long,
even till the moss shall grow on mine eyebrows, rather than violate my
faith and principles ! "

Martin Luther said: " Here I stand : I can do no otherwise. God help me ! "

Peter said : " Whether it be right in the sight of God to hearken unto you more than unto God, judge ye : for we cannot but speak the things which we have seen and heard."

Nehemiah said : " I am doing a great work, so that I cannot come down. Should such a man as I flee ? I will not go in ! "

Joseph said: " How then can I do this great wickedness, and sin against God?"

The Covenanters were in this line of true nobility, and when we have half their fortitude it will be time enough to seek their faults.

Satan Satisfied.

" IF Satan could remodel the preaching of the day to suit himself, he would put the word *reformation* in the place of *regeneration;* he would insist that living is everything, believing is nothing; he would not object to having everybody belong to the church; he would have science and morality and sentiment abound in sermons ; he would represent religion as an outgrowth of human effort, improving as the world grows wiser; and he would endow a few chairs of " higher criticism " to prove that the Bible is not inspired, and was not written at the time, or by the men commonly supposed. He must be right well pleased with the way in which some men are preaching the gospel nowadays."

So far *The Central Baptist.* We suppose the paper refers to American preaching; and if so, it is sad to see how much it is like the English article. We have instances, sorrowfully abundant, of sermons which are as far removed from gospel as stones from bread. Just now, a preacher tells us that Jesus came very near to our humanity in that suffering and death *whose reason is not revealed to us;* another tells us that he holds the atonement, but does not believe that our Lord suffered the penalty of sin. Satan cannot but be pleased to have his work so cleverly done by professed ministers of Christ. He sets on foot no propaganda for infidelity, because the Down-graders are doing his work for him to his complete satisfaction.   C. H. S.

No Time for Doubts.

THE late Mr. William Munsie, of Glasgow, conspicuous, among other things, for his success during many years in imparting divine truth both to teachers and scholars, when asked if he had any doubts or fears, replied, " I have so much in Christ to think of, and so much to do for him, that I find little leisure for entertaining that question."

A True Incident.

"I *THOUGHT* it *was my mother's voice!*"
  The startled accents fell from one
Of Adam's fairest sons. The joy,
The hope, in bygone happy days,
Of parents passed into the skies.
A mother's love had checked the ill
That tried to spring up in his heart,
And nurtured with untiring zeal
The opening buds of promise there:
Goodness—truth—gentleness, and all
That stamped him one of God's chief works.
A mother's prayers had helped, and moved
The unseen hand to guide and guard
Her boy through childhood's way. But ere
One step was trodden in the path
Of *youthful* dangers, where the foe
Plies his temptations strongest, where
He finds the readiest victims; ere
This path was reached—that mother's voice,
Which in its last faint murmurs breathed
A prayer for *him*, was hushed in death.

    *   *   *   *

The boy grew on. The world's gay charms
Allured him from the path of life.
Pleasure, with siren voice, bade him
Partake the cup she held. He heard,
Tasted, and drank unto the dregs.
He now, spell-bound, was being led
Down to the gate of endless woe; but one
Who knew the worth of souls, and of
A word in season, spake that word
In earnest prayer, and gentleness and love.
        "Young man, beware!"
The loving tone—the gentle touch
Aroused the youth, who, starting, cried,
"I thought it was my mother's voice."
O blest awakening! The heart
Which sin had hardened, melted now
With deep contrition; and the voice
Of memory, which told of truths
Long since forgotten, now was heard
And heeded too. Then, after years
Spent in his Master's service, he
Has met again that mother blessed,
And her, whose words of warning seemed
The echo of a voice from heaven.

ANNIE TAYLOR
(Sister of the late Mr. G. M. Murphy).

"Our Enemies themselves being Judges."

A WORD MORE ON SUBSTITUTION.   BY JAMES L. STANLEY.

WHEN the Lord was preparing Gideon to go against the Midianites, he strengthened the confidence of his servant in the reality of the call by various manifestations and answers to prayer. It appeared as though enough had been done to satisfy the most exacting requirements; yet it pleased God to add to the previous signs another, and a most remarkable, confirmation. "Go thou with Phurah thy servant down to the host, and thou shalt hear what they say; and afterward shall thine hands be strengthened to go down unto the host." Gideon obeyed this direction; and in the stealthy visit which he paid to the camp of the enemy, heard from their own lips the words which expressed their doom. This is not the only occasion on which the enemies of God have borne witness against themselves. "Out of thine own mouth will I judge thee," expresses a principle which is often illustrated in God's dealings with men.

It is not only among the friends of truth that evidence in its favour is to be found: from the quiver of its enemies we may extract arrows that shall tell effectively against themselves. The opponents of evangelical doctrine have become increasingly persistent, subtle, and bitter in their attacks upon the truth, their destructive criticisms being chiefly levelled against that great foundation truth, the sacrificial character of the death of Christ.   Not having sufficient audacity flatly to deny what Scripture says, their ingenuity is devoted to the task of trying to make the Scriptures say what they were never intended to say. Knowing that they can never gain credence for their doctrines without some show of Scripture authority, they distort, and argue, and mystify, till they make it appear to their own satisfaction that the Word of God teaches exactly the opposite of what it really does teach.   They are not willing to be on the side of the Scripture: they want the Scripture to be on their side. They want the patronage of the Bible without the authority of the Bible.   To their mind, the simple believers in the Bible doctrine of the atonement are a biased and credulous people, the victims of an ancient superstition, who cling to childish traditions and exploded theories.

It may be well, therefore, to let some other witnesses speak, whose scholarly attainments will lift them above the charge of ignorance, and whose decidedly anti-evangelical sentiments will free them of all suspicion of favourable bias.

Dr. W. Lindsay Alexander, in his "System of Biblical Theology," Vol. II., in the course of an exceedingly able discussion on the mediatorial work of Christ, quotes the testimonies of four eminent Rationalistic writers in reference to the subject of Christ's expiatory work. First comes "Dr. Wegscheider, who may be regarded as the Coryphæus of the old Rationalist party in Germany, whose opposition to evangelical truth is well known. In stating what he calls the *Doctrina Biblica* on the subject of Christ's expiatory work, after referring to the Jewish notions of sacrificial atonement, and stating that the Jews do not seem to have connected these with the Messiah (a statement to which we, of course, demur) he proceeds thus: ' By the N. T. authors, however, this opinion was approved, and they transferred that famous prophecy in Isa. liii. to Jesus . . . . whence, by almost all the sacred writers, in order to remove the odium and ignominy of the punishment endured by Jesus Christ, it was so expounded, especially by Paul, that they showed the death of Jesus Christ as expiatory and also vicarious, as if the punishment incurred by the sins of all had been taken by him on himself, and that Jesus as a lamb, pure and immaculate, was destined by the Father himself to death as a piacular victim, who by his own blood washed away the sins of the world. They seem, therefore, to have attributed to the very obedience or virtue of Jesus a certain vicarious efficacy, whilst the author of the Epistle to the Hebrews asserts that whatever pertains to piacular sacrifices is accomplished by Christ in the heavenly temple. And clearly do all these writers assert that pardon of sins is granted to man by God, on the ground of no deed of theirs, or of any other cause, save the vicarious death of Christ alone, which they refer to God's supreme love to men.' "

The candour of this statement is admirable, and we can only lament that it was not accompanied by a simple faith. The writer does not regard the teachings of Scripture as of divine authority, and does not hesitate to dissent from what he finds there; but, it will be observed, that, on this point of doctrine, he is in no doubt as to what he *does* find there. There is no laboured and sophistical argument to make the Scriptures accord with his views: plainly and honestly he confesses that they do teach the sacrificial character of the death of Christ. Herein we have his testimony to a matter of fact: his opinion of that fact is quite another matter.

The next witness quoted is Dr. Von Ammon, another Rationalist divine. He says: " When the divine Teacher perceived that the end of his life was at hand, he compares his death, which elsewhere he teaches that he endured for the truth and the advantage of his followers, to a piacular sacrifice, by which was borne as a vicarious burden the punishment due to the sinner; and this comparison apostles and teachers, in lengthened line, have followed. For Paul teaches that Jesus was destined by the Father himself as a piacular victim; Peter calls him a lamb pure and immaculate; John declares that by his blood the sins of the world are washed away; the author of the Epistle to the Hebrews writes that all things that pertain to the sacrifices offered for sin are performed by Jesus in the heavenly temple." Here, again, we have a clear testimony as to what the Scriptures *do* teach, coming from one who, to quote Dr. Alexander's own comment, " goes on to apologize for such statements as accommodations to the weakness of those whom the apostles had to teach, and who required to be conducted to higher and purer notions of religion by means of images and allegories."

The third witness is Dr. Karl Hase, of Jena, another Rationalist, who gives this summary of the doctrine of the New Testament concerning the work of Christ: " In the N. T., Christ is set forth as sent by God to save the world ruined by sin. As the subjective condition of the salvation to be enjoyed through him, there must be repentance, conversion, and heart purity; as the condition of God's giving salvation or pardoning sin, the whole life of Christ on earth, in its separate moments, above all, his death as a ransom price for our sins, as a sin offering in our stead, in virtue of which we are redeemed from the bondage of sin, and obtain forgiveness of sins, eternal life, and peace with God."

The last witness is De Wette. He says: "The redemption which is through Christ consists in reconciliation with God, or in deliverance from the wrath of God and from condemnation; more specifically (1) in the forgiveness of sins, *i.e.*, the purification of the conscience from the feeling of guilt. (2) in deliverance from the feeling of sinfulness; hence (3) in trust in God; (4) deliverance from death, the punishment of sin, and the enjoyment of eternal life, and hope of eternal felicity"; again, "Christ has saved men principally by what he has done and suffered. . . . The death of Christ Jesus is the central, point of apostolic doctrine, and especially of that of Paul." "This death Jesus, the blameless and sinless, endured for the sins of men, accomplishing thereby, in the highest sense, what the sin-offerings of the O. T. were intended to accomplish, as a voluntary sin-offering, well pleasing to God, as the self-offering of the High Priest."

Such testimonies as these are valuable; not that the Christian believer really needs to be taught by Rationalists what the Bible contains, but it serves as a confirmation of his faith, and gives strength in opposition to scepticism, to find such frank avowal coming from pronounced antagonists to the gospel. It is no small comfort to reflect that the way is so plain that "the wayfaring man, though a fool, shall not err therein," and that where a perverse and learned ingenuity stumbles and falls, the childlike believer may walk in confidence and safety.

A few years ago, a Unitarian minister, giving an address before the Unitarian Club of Boston, U.S., said that fifty years' study of the Bible had brought him to the conclusion that "The vast majority of its readers, following its letter, its obvious sense, its natural meaning, and yielding to the impression which some of its emphatic texts make upon them, find in it orthodoxy. Only that kind of ingenious, special, discriminative, and—in candour I must say—forced treatment which it receives from us liberals, can make the Book teach anything but orthodoxy." "This witness is true"; and while we deplore the intellectual pride and perversity of heart which make men persist in a course of unbelief, in spite of such confessions, we think their position, bad as it is, preferable to that of the men who profess a certain reverence for the Scriptures, but by their dishonest subterfuge make them of none effect.

Secret Declension.

YOU will sometimes see a great landslip from the side of a mountain by which thousands of tons of stones and earth are precipitated into the plain; it is the work of a few minutes, but it had been prepared for months or years before by the water which, trickling down the mountain side, loosened the hold of the soil. And the great falls of professing Christians which now and again startle us, are not the work of a day, but the product of years of dubious faith and doubtful living.

Some Short Notes on Great Subjects

THE HITTITES.

IN his book about " The Hittites; the Story of a Forgotten Empire,"
Dr. A. H. Sayce conducts us into something more than "a by-path
of Bible knowledge." It was, of course, inevitable that, when the
ancient stones of the East spoke at all, they should confirm the truth
of Scripture. It was also to be expected that they would make clear
many references in the inspired historical books, which, to superficial
and self-confident critics, appeared to be wrong, because they were in
advance of their own knowledge. The expectation has not been disappointed. Until quite recent times, the Hittites were supposed to
have been nothing more than a small Canaanitish tribe; and, because
inferences from the Bible were opposed to such a supposition, the knowing ones were quick to note what they regarded as " the unhistorical
tone" of the Hebrew Scripture. Certain ancient stones at Hamath,
which Dr. William Wright did so much to recover seventeen years ago,
have given us a veritable romance of history. If one wishes to know
more of this almost forgotten nation, he can consult Canon T. K.
Cheyne's article on the Hittites in the new edition of the " Encyclopædia
Britannica." We are looking forward to an article worthy of the subject, and abreast of the latest discoveries, in the new edition, which we
believe has been long in preparation, of Dr. William Smith's " Dictionary
of the Bible."

If we ask Dr. Sayce who these Hittites really were, we see how the
supposed " unhistorical tone" of the passage, when the mere name of
the Hittites carries dismay to the besiegers of Samaria, really becomes
a confirmation of history:—"In the days of Rameses II., when the
children of Israel were groaning under the tasks allotted to them, the
enemies of their oppressors were already exercising a power and a
domination which rivalled that of Egypt. The Egyptian monarch soon
learned to his cost that the Hittite king was as 'great' a king as himself, and could summon to his aid the inhabitants of the unknown north.
Pharaoh's claim to sovereignty was disputed by adversaries as powerful
as the ruler of Egypt, if not indeed more powerful, and there was always
a refuge among them for those who were oppressed by the Egyptian
king."

DO NOT USE BIG WORDS.

The good brother who complimented Mr. Spurgeon by remarking that
the trajectories of his missiles were aimed low, would probably have
been more in his element a century ago, when an after-dinner walk,
translated into Johnsonese, was a " post-prandial perambulation," and
when the distinguished lexicographer himself, afflicted as he was with
some sort of xerophthalmia, practised, at certain seasons, that in-
judicious xerophagia which has since excited the curiosity of enquirers.
People formed very mistaken notions of Johnson's influence and merits
as a writer; but one thing that he did was to teach his disciples to
speak and write in that high-flown Latinized style which long survived,
and which lingers still. It is worthy of note, however, that men who
were head and shoulders above Johnson in point of genius, such as

Goldsmith and Cowper, did not copy his style at all, but wrote in a far plainer manner, and one which may still be read as an example of English at its best. In one place, Paxton Hood gives an illustration of the style of one of the Claytons—representative, we suppose, of all the others:—
"He never either could or would call a spade a spade; he would have spoken of it as 'that marvellous illustration of the inventive resources and manipulatory processes of the essential genius of the being we call man.'"

This failing is still so common that, even in this year's edition of "Sell's Dictionary of the World's Press," there occurs a passage giving advice to journalists, which preachers also may profitably take to heart. Here it is:—

"In promulgating your esoteric cogitations, or articulating your superficial sentimentalities, and amicable, philosophical, or psychological observations, beware of platitudinous ponderosity; let your conversational communications possess a clarified conciseness, a compacted comprehensibleness, coalescent consistency, and a concatenated cogency. Eschew all conglomerations of flatulent garrulity, jejune babblement, and asinine affectations; let your extemporaneous descantings and unpremeditated expatiations have intelligibility and veracious vivacity, without rhodomontade or thrasonical bombast; sedulously avoid all polysyllabic profundity, pompous prolixity, psittaceous vacuity, ventriloquial verbosity, and vaniloquent vapidity. In other words, talk plainly, briefly, naturally; keep from 'slang'; don't put on airs; say what you mean; mean what you say; *and don't use big words!*"

THE COUNCIL OF TRENT.

To understand Romanism in all its bearings it is so necessary to have a clear idea of what was discussed at this assembly, that the little volume, "The Council of Trent: a Study of Romish Tactics," by T. Rhys Evans, of Brighton, which the Religious Tract Society has just issued, deserves to be welcomed as a short cut to the knowledge of a difficult subject. It would need a very patient, persevering student to read what has been written by Protestants and Romanists on this matter; but Mr. Evans has made many rough places plain.

The city of Trent in the Tyrol, the Tridentum of ancient times, now belongs to Austria. It is a very picturesque old town, of about twenty thousand inhabitants. In the church where the council was held there is a famous picture, containing portraits of all the members.

The meeting of churchmen at Trent was reckoned as the Eighteenth General Council. The first meeting came off on December 13th, 1545; the last on the 4th of December, 1563.

Speaking of the early years of the Reformation, Mr. Evans says:—
"There arose from many quarters, and prompted by very diversified motives, a strong desire for a general council. Devout Catholics, shocked by church scandals, Lutherans, princes, and magistrates, angry at the ever-increasing ecclesiastical encroachments upon the civil domain, groaning peoples—all these were desirous for a council."

The decisions arrived at have for centuries been accepted as the standard creed of Romanism, so that in those decisions we are able to see the true character of popery. It was decreed, with the usual anathemas, that the canon of Scripture was to include the Apocrypha; and that, while traditions were to be of equal authority with the Bible, the church was to be the only interpreter. "The seven sacraments" were also confirmed. The effects of the council were chiefly disastrous to Italy. As Mr. Evans says, "'Italy against Europe' had been the watchword of Trent." He then quotes Edgar Quinet: "The holy chair throve at the expense of the political existence of Italy. The Papacy stifled in that country the breath of civil life; it absorbed the vital forces of Italy. . . . The grass grew upon the civil world as upon the Roman Campagna."

A GENERAL ON WAR.

The "Personal Memoirs of P. H. Sheridan," General in the United States Army, with portraits and maps, together make up two large volumes, which Messrs. Chatto and Windus have issued in this country. The work is really an autobiography, and the reader has more vivid descriptions of the civil conflict of a quarter of a century ago than he can hope to get in ordinary histories written by those who were not eye-witnesses. In one passage the late General shows that war implies a great deal more than mere actual fighting :—

"I do not hold war to mean simply that lines of men shall engage each other in battle, and material interest be ignored. This is but a duel, in which one combatant seeks the other's life ; war means much more, and is far worse than this. Those who rest at home in peace and plenty, see but little of the horrors attending such a duel, and even grow indifferent to them as the struggle goes on, contenting themselves with encouraging all who are able-bodied to enlist in the cause, to fill up the shattered ranks as death thins them. It is another matter, however, when deprivation and suffering are brought to their own doors. Then the case appears much graver, for the loss of property weighs heavy with the most of mankind; heavier, often, than the sacrifices made on the field of battle. Death is popularly considered the maximum of punishment in war, but it is not; reduction to poverty brings prayers for peace more surely and more quickly than the destruction of human life, as the selfishness of man has demonstrated in more than one great conflict."

MAKING HOME ATTRACTIVE.

Not before it was time, our outspoken friend, that true-hearted servant of the people, Archibald G. Brown, has raised his far-reaching voice in protest against the dangerous notion, that it is the mission of the church to provide congregations with amusements. Of course, those who profess to be abreast of the age, and to have cast away everything that is narrow and out of date, think that the pastor of the East London Tabernacle exaggerates, or goes too far; but others, who love to keep within the boundaries which Scripture prescribes, know well enough that Mr. Brown's position is impregnable.

It occurred to us, that, while this subject is engrossing the thoughts of many who take different views, we might just say, that home is the place where, at least, recreation should chiefly be found. Of course, we do not mean that young persons should never go out ; but we do insist that those who are so brought up that they find their principal pleasures at home, are highly favoured; their recreation is, indeed, in some degree, a safeguard; and when they grow older, they are not so disposed to exchange what has been tested and proved for the fatally vicious amusements, or indulgences, which tempt the unwary in the world.

In any middle-class home, even of the most modest kind, the appliances for recreation—which should always include self-improvement—ought not to be wanting; and home resources are much greater than anyone might suppose who has never given the subject attention. In looking through two such guide-books as "Indoor Games and Recreations" for boys, and "The Girl's Own Indoor Book," which the Religious Tract Society has just issued, we come upon a very remarkable variety of recreations, many of which improve while they entertain. The truth comes home to us very forcibly, that the recreation which can be found abroad is meagre, and of inferior quality, compared with what may be enjoyed at home. In the best sense, the Christian home should be the place of recreation for our young people.

The dangers attending the mixing up of religion and amusement in the church and congregation are very great. Any church, in which mere amusement is made a principal attraction, will inevitably degenerate until there is little or no religion left. If we are not mistaken, there is, at all events, one congregation in London which hears the date of "the annual ball" given out from the pulpit. Young persons reared under such conditions will be brought up for the world alone, and not for Christ. We hope that Mr. Brown will not recede an inch from the position he has taken up.

Can She Spin?

A YOUNG girl was presented to James I. as an English prodigy, because she was amazingly learned. The person who introduced her, boasted of her proficiency in ancient languages. "I can assure your Majesty," said he, "that she can both speak and write Latin, Greek, and Hebrew." "These are rare attainments for a damsel," said James; "but pray, tell me, *can she spin?*" For once this foolish Solomon was right; the high and mighty prince spoke common-sense.

Much the same test may be applied to Christian workers both in the pulpit and out of it. It is but a small matter that the worker can read three languages, and recite poetry, or can give birth to great thoughts, and utterance to fine language. *Does he win souls?* is the question which it is far more important to answer.

Had the fisherman a newly painted boat? Does he boast a pair of fine blue eyes? Can he sing a ballad of the sea? These are all idle enquiries in connection with the man's pursuit. *Has he caught any fish?* This is much more to the point, especially to the man's family at home, and all who depend upon his success. It is true, a first class fisher may often labour in vain ; but if his net always returns empty, how can he be called a fisher at all? A fisherman who never takes a fish, a preacher who never saves a soul from death! As well speak of a fire that never burns, a sun that never shines !

Notices of Books.

The Book Fund and its Work, for 1888. By Mrs. C. H. SPURGEON. Price 6d. Passmore and Alabaster.

THIS is to us as the water from the well of Bethlehem, which David felt to be all too precious, because it cost so much to those who brought it to him. Our dear wife has written in pain and weakness of an extreme kind. But what has been written will be prized by her dear helpers, and by others who care for poor ministers. There is to us an inexpressible sweetness in these pages. We wish every one of our readers would invest sixpence in the purchase of a copy: it would cheer the weary worker, and help the work itself.

Echoes from the Welsh Hills; or, Reminiscences of the Preachers and People of Wales. By Rev. DAVID DAVIES. Passmore and Alabaster.

THIS book we have seen before, and we then gave it our benediction. Here we have a cheap edition at 4s 6d., and it is to be had of our own publishers. "These Welsh people think a deal of their ministers!" And so would the English, if they could only understand the language, and were capable of that mystic, matchless fire which burns in a Welshman's heart. This is an attractive book.

The Expositor's Bible. The Pastoral Epistles. By Rev. ALFRED PLUMMER, D.D. Hodder and Stoughton.

THERE is much that is excellent in this exposition, but all this makes the more perilous the teaching which includes Baptismal Regeneration and Prayers for the Dead. This author is on some points a defender of the faith, but on others he is a very dangerous guide.

The Epistle to the Galatians. By Professor G. G. FINDLAY, Headingley College. Hodder and Stoughton.

THIS Exposition has a place of its own, and a very useful one. It keeps clear of the controversies which were once sure to arise out of comments upon this epistle, and it has little about it of the current phraseology of the schools. Largely practical, and keeping close to the text, it brings out the sacred teaching with much clearness and force. To a man who has other works upon the Galatians, it will be a welcome additional help. In this Commentary we have met with no trace of the modern spirit, but we have seen much to accept and enjoy. Having had to take exception to another of the volumes of *The Expositor's Bible,* we are glad to award, in this instance, our word of honest praise.

Cloudy Days: Short Meditations on some Texts of Scripture, for the Private Use of those in Trouble. By the Rev. FRANCIS BOURDILLON, M.A. Society for Promoting Christian Knowledge.

OUR esteemed friend, Mr. Bourdillon, here gives the world another of his quiet, gracious, and always suggestive meditations. Nothing of flash ever defiles his page with meretricious display: he is solid, deep, scriptural, and yet by no means dull and dreary. This is a honey-drop for a mouth which has been filled with wormwood.

Fugal Tunes, with their Associated Hymns. Edited by JOHN COURTNAY, Precentor. Sunday School Union.

HERE we have twenty-two of those grand old fugal tunes which have been so carefully expelled from modern psalmody. Never was there heartier singing than when these were used. What grand bursts of unanimous praise then rose from voices of all kinds! *Now* we go through the hymns at a gallop, and are glad to splash through the shallow stream of sound; but aforetime we bathed in the deeps of music, and swam in seas of harmony. Silly jests have been manufactured to throw the old tunes into disfavour; but equally silly ones could be made about the present hop, skip, and jump tunes; and, what is more to the point, facts can be stated which are not to their praise. We should be glad to see Hampshire, Refuge, America, Calcutta and the like, restored to the places they so richly deserve. A shilling will be well spent on these tunes.

13

A Manual of Introduction to the New Testament. By Dr. BERNHARD WEISS. Translated from the German by A. J. K. DAVIDSON. In 2 Vols. Hodder and Stoughton.

IN this work, of which only the first volume is before us, the author aims to compile a historico-scientific criticism of the origin of the New Testament Canon. His drift it would be difficult to explain in a few sentences to those who are not acquainted with "The foreign theological libraries." Even the word "Introduction" on the title page has a special significance, when it breaks on our ears with a German accent. The name of Dr. Bernhard Weiss must be familiar to many of our friends. Some years ago, Messrs. T. and T. Clark, of Edinburgh, published his "Biblical Theology of the New Testament" in three volumes. We called attention to it at the time. In the present treatise he aims to get behind that work; or, in other words, he sinks a shaft into deeper strata. Be his task pious or profane, we hold our breath for the moment as we watch his proceedings. According to a comparatively new principle, an attempt has been made to read and examine the writings of the New Testament from a human point of view. The *savans* called this a reaction against the fetters of tradition: their method was to challenge and combat, severally and separately, the authenticity and apostolic authority of each component part of these Scriptures. Their idea is to effect a complete disintegration, in order to a more scientific reconstruction. *We* call this "*an idea,*" because, as a positive fact, a century of labour has produced no result. *They* call it "*a science,*" although they are well aware that not one problem of theirs has ever been demonstrated with mathematical certainty from that "*human point of view*" which they like to talk about. Their scholars are all at issue with one another. The *vox populi* of Protestant Christianity has never proffered them a vote of thanks for their services. They have fostered scepticism, but they have never helped the struggling conscience of the *living* to a strong conviction which could become an anchor to their souls; nor have they fortified the *dying* even with so small a comfort as the rites of a church.

The "merit" of setting this precious ball in motion belongs to the Tübingen professor, Ferdinand Christian Baur (page 12). With the close of the year 1850, the elder representatives of the Tübingen school came virtually to an end (page 18). May they sleep in peace! Perhaps one of the most popular of these mole-eyed Germans, certainly one of the most ingenuous, is Edward Reuss, of Strasburg University. Well, he began by persistently defending the genuineness of the epistles; but in the fifth edition of his "Introduction" (1874), he entertained many doubts; and then, four years later, he adhered only to the second epistle to Timothy (page 419). Thus the deeper he delved, the darker he grew.

We turn back to the preface, which is obviously a postscript, and there we have Dr. Weiss's last utterance. He has been for thirty-four years a Professor of Theology at Berlin. His aim during that extended period has been to teach young ministers *to judge the Scriptures!* A questionable industry. Had he been a pastor instead of a professor, he might have tried to show his flock how the Scriptures judge *them.*

The apology that confronts the reader on the first page is almost pathetic. So fluctuating is the literary commodity in which the learned doctor speculates, that he regrets his inability to offer the most recent results of researches which were in progress while his manuscripts were in preparation for the press. Here is a perennial source of tears. They are for ever learning, but they never come to a knowledge of the truth. Their latest conclusions only last till the ink is dry with which they jotted them down.

Jonah. Old Lessons for the New Year. By CAPTAIN DAWSON. Shaw.

ALL Captain Dawson's writings are good and profitable. We don't think he quite catches the point of Jonah's character, and his reason for declining the great commission; but as far as they go, these lessons from Jonah are excellent. The little book is just the thing to give away.

The Way the Lord hath led Me; or, Incidents of Gospel Work. By C. S. London : G. Morrish.

LIKE all personal narratives written in the simplicity of a man's heart without the slightest concealment, or attempt at book writing, this is singularly interesting reading. Persons who do not agree with Charles Stanley will take pleasure in reading the narrative of his life and work. Those who have a spiritual life within them, akin to his own, will find a deeper interest arising from their sympathy with his obedience to inner guidance, and the calm practicalness of his faith in God. The story which we mean to quote has a Quaker-like flavour about it, and it is one of many of the same sort which he here records. Some others of his narratives remind us of William Huntington, but not of the coarseness and selfishness which mar many of the anecdotes in the Bank of Faith.

Mr. Stanley has right boldly declared the gospel of the grace of God, and has pursued a course which he believes to have been marked out for him by supreme authority ; so that he has not put his feet in another man's track, nor bound himself by the conventional bonds which have restrained the free Spirit in so many. We know little of his peculiarities, but, having simply perused "The Way by which the Lord hath led Me," we are deeply interested by the narrative. Whether an heir of heaven be a Plymouth Brother, or a Baptist, or an Episcopalian, is, with us, a far less matter than that he should possess the heavenly life, be true to his solemn convictions, reverent to the Word of the Lord, and zealous for the salvation of men. Here is the story, which, from among many others, we quote ; not as being the most remarkable, but as a fair specimen of many which lie imbedded in this personal story.

"It is important to look to the Lord every day for the guidance of the Holy Spirit, as we never know when and where he may use us in sovereign grace. I was crossing the country, one day from Bristol, where I had been preaching, to Tetbury. I had never been in that part of the

country before. On arriving at Wotton-under-Edge, I had some time to spare before going on. It was about five o'clock on a hot day in the midst of harvest. There was scarcely a person to be seen in the little town. I was very distinctly impressed from the Lord that I must preach the gospel there that afternoon, yet there appeared to be no people to preach to. Nearly all seemed to be out in the harvest field. Yet the conviction deepened that I must preach. I took a few tracts, and gave them where I could find anyone. I was standing in a little shop, speaking to a woman about her soul, when a man came running up the road, the perspiration streaming off his face. He turned into the shop, and said, 'Please, sir, are you a preacher of the gospel ?' 'Yes,' I said, 'I am, through the Lord's mercy, but why do you ask ?' He replied, 'I am the bell-man, and if you will preach to-day I will cry it.' 'Well,' I said, 'it was very much laid on my heart to preach the gospel here to-day, but I do not see any to preach to. Tell me, how is it you came in such haste, and asked me the question ?' He replied, 'I was working in the field, and a woman came past and told me some one was distributing tracts in Wotton, and it was just as if a voice had said to me, "You must run, and there must be preaching in Wotton to-day." That is why I left my work, and came immediately.' As he was the bellman, I involuntarily put my hand in my pocket to give him a shilling. 'Oh dear no, sir,' he said, 'I don't want the money, I want souls to be saved' ; and the earnestness and solemnity of the man confirmed his words. In half-an-hour he had washed himself, cried the preaching, and we were on the way to the Chipping preach."

Lessons on the (I.) *Works of our Lord* (II.) *Claims of our Lord.* By Flavel S. COOK, D.D., Chaplain of the Lock. Nisbet. One shilling.

THESE fifty-two Lessons form a year's course of instruction for Bible-classes and Sunday-schools. Concise, but comprehensive, they are admirably fitted to guide teachers in their preparations.

Passim Papers, in Prose and Verse.
By the Rev. DAVID JAMISON, B.A.
Belfast: Sabbath School Society for
Ireland, 12, May Street.

ON the old lines of the gospel, fresh
as spring flowers. These papers will
command a reading, and will benefit
all who give it to them. One and
sixpence is little for such good matter.
To promote the sale, we have inserted
one of the papers in this month's
magazine.

*Essays on Sacred Subjects for General
Readers.* By the Rev. WILLIAM
RUSSELL, M.A. Blackwood.

WE have been delighted with these
essays. Amid the surging torrents of
unbelief, these islets of strong and
confident testimony lift their rocky
forms, and we land upon them with
delight. Thoroughly learned, and in
every way masterly, these essays make
short work with Darwinism, and all
the other errors, which crowd the
temple of the nineteenth century's
monkey-god. The volume is a fine
one in every way. We fear that in its
present library form, at half-a-guinea,
it will have a small sale compared with
what it would have had in a smaller
and cheaper shape. Were we able to
do so, we should like to present a
copy to every minister in the Three
Kingdoms, in the hope that certain of
the better ones, who are slipping,
might find foothold by its means.
However, he that chooses to fall, cannot be held up; and such, we fear, is
a true description of many modern
teachers.

*Report of the Missionary Conference on
the Protestant Missions of the World,
held in Exeter Hall, London, 1888.*
Edited by the Rev. JAMES JOHN-
STON, F.S.S. Two volumes. Nisbet.

THESE volumes are of great value,
especially at this time, when missions
are somewhat roughly handled. The
Conference of last year was carried
out to perfection, and the papers and
addresses were wide in range, and of
a very high order. No one will ever
call these pages dull or dry: they are
rich with missionary information,
mostly supplied by the labourers themselves; and they reveal how far the

work has succeeded, and wherein it
has failed. We are on the eve of a
new departure in missions. Without
breathing a complaint against the old,
we shall welcome the new. The world
has to be evangelized, and he that can
show us how to do it, or even how *not*
to do it, is our friend.

As a compendium of missionary information from all parts of the church,
and all quarters of the globe, we consider these volumes to be altogether
priceless. The publisher marks them,
"Two volumes, 7s. 6d." Can he mean
that both are to be had for that
amount? If so, they are the greatest
bargain we have met with for many a
day.

*What are we to Believe? or, The Testi-
mony of Fulfilled Prophecy.* By
JOHN URQUHART. Second edition.
J. and A. Mack.

WE are right glad to see a second
edition of this precious treatise. We cannot too warmly comfend it. It is full
of the best defence of our holy faith.
We wish that every young man who
is beginning to doubt could be induced
to read these telling pages. Here he
will find such proof of the inspiration
of Scripture as none can overthrow.
History, which is the hand of God
acting, bears witness to revelation,
which is the hand of God writing.
Mr. Urquhart is entirely on the side
of faith, and his book is one which
ought to be scattered by tens of
thousands. No reader will find it
dull, but many will find it spiritually
establishing.

*Ruth: the Soul brought into Oneness
with Christ.* By GEORGE W. HILLS,
Vicar of Cambridge. Elliot Stock.

OUR author touches on a very delicate
theme, and does it with a careful hand.
These addresses, which spiritualize the
Book of Ruth, are of that good old-
fashioned order which the Puritans
would have enjoyed; but this evil
generation will take strong objection
to them. We are glad that there is a
vicar left who could venture upon such
a subject, and succeed so well in his
dealing with it. Still, the theme is
rather for the inner chamber of the
devout than for the promiscuous
assembly.

A Winter on the Nile, in Egypt, and in Nubia. By the Rev. CHARLES D. BELL, D.D. Hodder and Stoughton.

This is a delightful book. It will suit our readers when they desire to read something interesting and gracious. The good canon does not drag in pious reflections, but they come to him, or rather from him, as flowers from a watered garden. He is a traveller who does not overlay his notes with learned lumber, but writes very simply what he sees, and does it in the style of an educated gentleman talking with his friends who want to know what he has seen. Some of his notes upon evolution at the end of the book are so good that we cannot resist the temptation to give an extract:—

"On the theory of evolution, why should physical or mental development ever cease? That it has ceased, or not been uniformly progressive, is evident. Has man, in grandeur of conception or in powers of execution, surpassed the builders of these colossal pyramids, these awe-inspiring sphinxes, these splendid palaces and temples? Are these, the earliest monuments of the race, the work of the descendants of the ape and the baboon? Where is the development now? Are the modern Egyptians, in mental capacity or physical strength, in art or in science, superior to the men who reared the obelisk and hollowed out the tomb? Has not Egypt, the fountain of civilization, which drew an Herodotus, a Euclid, a Strabo, and a Plato to visit her universities, and to learn in her schools, become one of the lowest of the nations, needing the occupation of a foreign power to guard her frontier and to control her finance? If the theory of evolution had in it any truth—if man had to progress through an age of stone, and bronze, and iron, before he reached civilization, then the earliest nations should be the least developed, and be but little removed from the brute. But Egypt, the oldest historic nation, refutes this idea; and her majestic monuments, with their frescoes and sculptures, through which we read the daily life of the king, the priests, and the people, prove that in the times nearest to the creation of man she had attained to a higher condition of im-

portance and greatness than she has ever attained since. Hers is a development of degeneration. The descendants of this wonderful people, in outward appearance resembling the men we see in the sculptures and bas-reliefs on the monuments, can do nothing like them now, and cannot build or paint or write as their fathers builded and painted and wrote, cannot model the colossal statue or raise the magnificent pyramid. They have retrograded rather than advanced. They have lost the power of doing such works; their evolution is from higher to lower."

The Inspiration of the Scriptures. A Lecture. By PHILIP REYNOLDS, Pastor of Providence Baptist Chapel, Highbury. R. Banks and Son.

VERY good. The wilful sceptic will not be convinced, but the faithful will be established, by the line of argument here adopted. As a lecture, costing only threepence, this may go where a larger work could not enter; and, for certain, there cannot be too many voices raised in testimony to inspiration.

Light and Colour emblematic of Revealed Truth. By the late Major R. W. D. NICKLE. Edited by SARAH SHARP. Hodder and Stoughton.

WRITTEN in a devout spirit, and with the best intentions, but we do not care for pushing a figure into such nice points, and fine distinctions. That red, blue, yellow, and the other colours, may be, and are, admirable emblems of holy things we allow; but that we may regard their use in Scripture as dogmatic teaching we seriously doubt. This book is a religious curio, if nothing more.

By-Paths of Bible Knowledge. XII. *The Hittites.* The Story of a Forgotten Empire. By A. H. SAYCE, LL.D. Religious Tract Society.

THE pith of what is known of the empire of the Hittites. Those who are interested in that ancient, and yet newly-discovered, people, will not grudge half-a-crown for this book, which is one of the valuable series published by the Tract Society under the title of "By-Paths of Bible Knowledge."

Conversations at the Unity Club. Reported by a Member of the Club. Christian Commonwealth Publishing Company.

CLEVER pleadings for the peculiar views of the denomination which calls itself "*Christian.*" It is easy to write conversations in which you represent the views of others in your own way, and then set them right according ·to your own more accurate judgment; but it is quite another matter to turn into fact the pretty picture which you have drawn. On paper the thing is settled for ever, but in fact nobody is convinced, and nothing whatever is proved. We do not believe that Christian unity will come by the way which Mr. Moore here advocátes, though he argues with good temper and great skill. Churchmen and Methodists are a very long way off from his views, and Baptists, who may seem to be a little nearer, are by no means likely to accept baptismal salvation in any shape or form. We may all unite around the cross even now; but when the happy day of union shall come, and the whole church shall recognize "one Lord, one faith, and one baptism," the faith and the baptism will neither of them be quite the same as those accepted among our Campbellite brethren. We use the name, not by way of reproach, but by way of information. We do not know how we can better indicate the views which are advocated by *The Christian Commonwealth.* It seems to us that our friends, who claim for themselves the name of "Christians," just add one more to the many sects already existing, and this in the name of unity. O unity, what deeds have been done in thy name!

Church History. By Professor KURTZ. Translated by Rev. JOHN MACPHERSON, M.A. In three volumes. Vol. I. Foreign Biblical Library. Hodder and Stoughton.

THIS is obviously a colossal work. The first volume comprises 550 pages octavo of closely-printed matter. Such a theme is worthy of an author whose literary ability is of the highest order. We refrain for the present from attempting an adequate review, because we have before us only Vol. I., which is

a comparatively uninteresting sample. Some such introduction was requisite. Here it is. We are indulged with an exhibition of fossils picked up from the early centuries of Christianity. Here, too, are "doctrinal controversies that grew up independently on German soil"—("heresies," our author calls them). Nor does the writer forget "endeavours after reformation," which seemed, for the time being, to have proved futile.

Into the second and third volumes it has not been our privilege to peer; but judging from the part we have perused, we believe that our author provides a thoroughly reliable digest of the best information, and of the best sources of information, in every department, condensed into the smallest compass. If you want to give a series of lessons, or a course of lectures, this is a complete text-book. On the other hand, it is not a continuous tale skilfully woven together into chapters, like Macaulay's "History of England," or D'Aubigné's "History of the Reformation." What if it lacks all the qualities that lend enchantment to literature? That is no disparagement, for it was never designed to furnish circulating libraries with light reading. Enough that you are supplied with a comprehensive study, broken up into short sections, any one of which, if you are particularly interested in it, challenges further research.

Preacher, Pastor, Mechanic: Memoir of the late Mr. Samuel Deacon, nearly forty years Pastor of the General Baptist Church, Barton. *A Cabinet of Jewels.* (Vol. I. of Barton Memorials). By S. DEACON. Elliot Stock.

OUR venerable friend, Thomas Cook, must always be at work for the cause he loves so well. He is doing good service by issuing a memoir of a worthy of the General Baptist Connexion, and by re-issuing one of his simple books, which had a measure of popularity years ago. *The Cabinet of Jewels* is very homely, but as earnest as it is plain. The modern General Baptists will do well to return to the standing of the fathers. Mr. Cook is a genuine specimen of the solid, earnest believer of the old school.

Ephemerides. The Dayes of the Year. 1889. A London Almanack in the Olde Style. Unwin Brothers.

WE are sorry to mention so late in the year this quaint, curious, out-of-the-way sixpennyworth; but we counsel our friends still to secure it, if they like a racy bit. Six stamps sent to the publisher will buy it. It is not a religious almanack; but we note it as a literary rarity.

Faithful Words for Old and Young. Alfred Holness.

THIS magazine deserves support, because it is not written for amusement, but for practical salvation work. It keeps solidly to the gospel, and is truly what its name implies. The yearly volume deserves our praise.

St. Nicholas: an Illustrated Magazine for Young Folks. Volume XV. T. Fisher Unwin.

VERY wonderfully do our American brethren produce books for juveniles, and we do not wonder that they seek a market on this side of the water. St. Nicholas is not a *religious* magazine, and so is quite out of our line; but the illustrations which adorn it are marvellous.

The Century Illustrated Monthly Magazine. May, 1888, to October, 1888. T. Fisher Unwin, London.

IN the United States many processes of engraving seem to be in vogue, which, as yet, are not employed by English book-producers. For wealth of pictures, and for abundance of information, the volume of "The Century," for 1888, is second to none of all the secular serials. We have greatly enjoyed overhauling its contents. The chapters on Siberia are touchingly sad.

Jingles and Chimes, and Nursery Rhymes. With 75 Illustrations. By M. IRWIN. Shaw and Co.

YES, the real old nursery rhymes, and not a lot of new rubbish. Childish as the old jingles are, it would take a very clever man to make another of the sort. The new rigmaroles are not in the running at all; the little ones will not take to them.

The Sun. A Family Magazine for General Reading. Vol. I. Nisbet.

THIS weekly magazine has a blazing title, and it would be too much praise to say that it comes up to it in brilliancy; but the first volume is a good one, and deserves to the full its secondary emblem of the Sunflower. Its literary merit is high. It makes a fine book for six shillings. Who would not buy "The Sun" at that price in this murky island?

The Christian Worker's Magazine. An Advocate of Aggressive Christian and Philanthropic Effort. (Twopence monthly.) Marshall Brothers.

THIS first number is very good. This is a monthly record of work done under the lead of Mr. Edward Wright, far better known as Ned Wright.

The Tract Magazine, 1888. Religious Tract Society.

THIS is always a good, useful magazine, and may be circulated by those who wish to do good. The annual volume is neatly bound.

The Welcome: a Magazine for the Home Circle. Vol. XV. Partridge & Co.

MORE and more *welcome.* In every way first-rate.

The Methodist Family: an Illustrated Monthly Magazine. Vol. XIX. 61, Paternoster Row.

THOUGH we are not Methodists, we hold in high esteem "The Methodist Family." It is carefully edited, and contains much that tends to edification. Its tone is high.

China's Millions. Edited by J. HUDSON TAYLOR, M.R.C.S., F.R.G.S. Morgan and Scott.

OUR friend Mr. Hudson Taylor leads in a glorious work in China, and this record of the Inland Mission is always cheering. The volume deserves a place in every good man's library.

The Baptist Messenger, The Church, The Shield and Spear. These magazines, published by Elliot Stock, are each one excellent in its own way, and a really good pennyworth.

Mrs. Morse's Girls. A Tale of American Sunday-school Life and Work. By MINNIE E. KENNEY. Religious Tract Society.

WE should like to know something about the writer of this exceptionally good story, if story it is. We will hazard the guess that she is the "pastor's wife" of the narrative, who, by God-given tact and holy earnestness, won for Jesus a class of girls—gentle and simple—which had been the despair of the Sunday-school authorities. Here is every element of a soul-winning book. God speed it and its authoress!

Alma Ryan; or, Steadfast and True. By CHARLOTTE MASON. Shaw.

TELLS how an orphan girl—a young disciple—bore herself, and was "steadfast and true" to Christ when removed from her godly home, at the country vicarage, to the chilling atmosphere of a Belgravian mansion, where she suffered slow torture for conscience sake. Godly church people might make a worse choice than this of a book for a present to a young girl of the upper class.

Eagle and Dove. A Tale of the Franco-Prussian War, founded on Fact. By M. E. CLEMENTS. Nelson and Sons.

A CAPITAL story of the experiences of the inmates of a boarding-school for young ladies at Metz, during the whole period of the war, of which it furnishes a very cleverly-written epitome. The horrors of the beleaguered fortress are described with fidelity, and yet with the delicacy of a woman's pen. The writer says the story is intended especially for "the *girls* of this young generation": the boys will take good care to read it as soon as their sisters lay it down.

That Bother of a Boy. By GRACE STEBBING. Jarrold and Sons.

THIS example of unchecked mischief can do no good to anybody.

Uncle Steve's Locker. By BRENDA. John F. Shaw.

WE have thoroughly enjoyed reading this sweet story, and we think it takes rank with "Froggy's little brother," by the same author, for interest and beauty. Get it.

More than Conqueror. By HARRIETTE BURCH. Religious Tract Society.

THE temptations and trials of a young fellow in a house of business are here depicted, with the usual yielding on his part in the face of ridicule, and the ultimate victory gained through divine grace, over every temptation.

Gianetta: A Girl's Story of her Life. By ROSA MULHOLLAND. London: Blackie and Son.

A VERY well written story for girls. We could have wished the author had put a little more spiritual teaching into the mouth of the best character in the book (Aunt Eve) who carries out a good scheme of philanthropic work for the benefit of the poor Irish peasants. The chapters upon the evictions are very graphic. When the present unhappy agitations are over, we hope all will unite in a common effort for the good of Ireland. Oh, that the gospel would bring Ireland liberty and rest!

Little Lady Clare. By EVELYN EVERETT GREEN. Blackie and Son.

NOT at all a book for little ladies. Style somewhat stilted. Moral good.

Red Herring; or, Allie's Little Blue Shoes. By FRANCES ARMSTRONG. John Hogg.

SENSIBLE people will not expect to find the tale of a red herring very fresh, or fine, or large, nor that it would find a place in the *menu* of the fastidious; but boys and girls will relish the tale, and devour the entire herring, which is very well cooked.

From Squire to Squatter. By GORDON STABLES, R.N. John F. Shaw.

A DASHING story indeed: rather too much so for our liking, and yet one on which boys of pluck and spirit will feed, and these will grow into the men that Old England needs on flood and field, to keep up her greatness. Perhaps the one moral taught is the use of energy, physical stamina, and courage; and for some boys this is a necessary one. A spice of religion is thrown in; but in one instance a prayer seems rather too ghastly just before a fight with blacks.

IF any friends imagine that the growth of error in the Nonconformist churches has come to a pause, they are sadly mistaken. We have mournful evidence that the bad are growing worse, and some of whom we hoped better things are becoming unstable. The worst feature of the case is the want of moral honesty which allows persons to pass resolutions in which they do not believe, and to have one belief for the public, and another for private use. Years ago, the cry of Nonconformity was very loud against the Church of England, as a combination of men who vitally differed from each other: the inconsistencies of the Evangelical party were especially held up to reprobation, since they professed to accept a prayer-book which gives support to Ritualism. The protest was not without reason; but how can it now be maintained by the protesters, since the extent to which error is not only tolerated, but encouraged, in at least two of the Dissenting bodies, goes beyond the comprehensiveness of the Establishment? A man who occupies a chapel, and preaches contrary to the trust-deed, ought to hold his tongue in reference to elastic consciences. He who reads the creed of an Association in a non-natural sense should throw no stones at one who interprets the Church Catechism in an ingenious manner. We do not object to the Nonconformist protest; but when it comes from men who are themselves acting inconsistently, its force is gone.

The remarks made by Mr. Caine as to Mission operations are not to be set aside because of minor errors in his statistics and other matters. He will have done good service to the great cause if the managers of the societies will take to heart whatever is right in his somewhat severe strictures. There can be no need to pull down what is already built up; but there might be additions to the edifice. Missionaries, with their families, should not be stinted; but a body of young men might be sent out, pledged to remain for, say, five years, and then permitted honourably to return. These could be supported in plenty at about £100 a year each, and would be a great addition to the forces in the field. If the committees of the societies adopt all new suggestions which are prudent and promising, they will show themselves worthy of the occasion; but if not, the work will be done by those outside present organizations. To preach rather than to educate is the missionary's business; and what he preaches must be *the gospel*, or he might as well have remained at home. He who points out a flaw or failure in any good work should not be howled at as an enemy, but utilized to the utmost as an aid to wiser procedure. So far as any man is opposed to Missions, we are opposed to him; but so far as he can arouse us to deep regret that we have not

more success, and awaken us to make bolder attempts to gain it, we welcome him. The whole constituency of the Missionary Society should look into the questions submitted to the Christian public; and if this is done, a new interest will be aroused in the great enterprise of preaching Christ among the heathen.

Some eight years ago, our most worthy brother, Mr. Harry Brown, went out from our College to endeavour to win souls in India, and he has continued to do good service, as pastor of the church in Darjeeling during one part of the year, and as an agent of the Indian Evangelization Society during the other portion of it. In this way we furnished a worker for India who has been supported on the spot, and has been greatly blessed of God. We promised to supply his need, if need there should be; but he has managed to make his own way. We are, therefore, glad to make room for a request which he has sent to us.

"An appeal for a school in far-off Darjeeling may not at once commend itself to the readers of *The Sword and the Trowel*, but it may be that their attention has never been directed to the ever-growing European population, whose children need education, and whose circumstances compel that this education be given in India. Roman Catholics are alive to the fact, and have schools in all parts of the country, to which large numbers of Protestants send their children. The Jesuits are making Darjeeling one of their strongholds. The only other schools in the place are connected with the Church of England, and very sectarian; and it is much to be regretted that the tendency of that Church in India is decidedly away from Evangelicalism, towards either Ritualism on the one hand, or Indifferentism on the other. What need, then, is there for a school in Darjeeling, conducted, as George Müller puts it, upon Christian principles, *i.e.*, in which the teachers are believers, where the way of salvation is scripturally pointed out, and in which no instruction is given opposed to the principles of the gospel, and of a high-class character as to teachers and course of study!

"To meet this need, a circular has been issued, from which the following are extracts:—' It is proposed to start in Darjeeling a college for boys, and a college for girls, upon a purely undenominational basis, and yet with strict regard to the religious training of the pupils. With the view of making these institutions thoroughly successful, an efficient staff of first-class teachers will be engaged.'

"It is supposed that a sum of at least 50,000 rupees will be required to carry out the above scheme in a proper and satisfactory manner. Towards this sum one friend has offered to contribute 10,000 rupees, provided three others will come forward with a like sum of 10,000 rupees each, or provided any number of subscribers subscribe 40,000 rupees, so as to make up the sum of 50,000 rupees, required to start with. But no amount of money will suffice without God's blessing, and the prayers of his people are asked on this effort to meet a need, no less urgent, if not so universally recognized, as that for which missionaries plead. Any further communications may be addressed to D. Sutherland, Esq., Jessamine Villa, Darjeeling; or to H. Rylands Brown, The Manse, Darjeeling."

Our friends will have noticed with regret the terrible calamity which has fallen upon the Grimsby fishing-fleet. There are some seventy orphans left in that town through the fearful gale. We hope to take some few into the Stockwell Orphanage; but funds sent to the Relief Committee would be well applied. Our friend, Mr. Lauderdale, the Baptist pastor at Great Grimsby, would be glad to receive donations. The smack *C. H. Spurgeon* encountered a fearful storm. The disaster is thus described by our friend, Mr. Dobson:—

"From the lips of the skipper of the *C. H. Spurgeon*, this morning, I heard such a tale of hardship and suffering as I never have heard before from any of our men. As I have before mentioned, the *C. H. S.* is one of the best-built vessels in the port; that is, no doubt, the reason she has lived through all this rough handling. Last Saturday morning, about seven o'clock, the first sea struck the smack, taking, at one stroke, both the masts, every sail, and everything that was movable off the decks, including the boat, and half filled the ship with water. In this condition it was impossible to lie, so that the skipper and mate had to go to the head of the ship, and if possible get the anchor down to keep her head to the sea. In attempting to do this, another sea struck them, this time washing the mate overboard, and completely turning the ship round. This put the poor fellow out of the reach of any help, though the skipper said that he stood helplessly for some time, and watched him, until his heart grew sick, and then he turned away, so that he might not see him drown. When he turned to look again, the man lay upon the top of the water (his oil clothes keeping him up), but his spirit had gone. How the men on the smack lived through Saturday the skipper does not seem to know, as no less than seven of these huge seas rolled on board. During one of these the kettle, which was on the fire, was washed off, and the boiling water badly scalded the skipper. The mate was gone, as I have described. The third hand, in trying to do the mate's work, had his leg seriously injured; and by night the cook, who was a young man eighteen years of age, died through exposure and fright. At this time they were nearly two hundred miles from home. Sunday, the skipper said, was a long day; but towards night

another smack hove in sight, and seeing their distress, took them in tow, arriving in dock by last night's tide. The vessel presented a sad sight; you could never think it possible for the waves to have such power. This morning the skipper could neither open nor shut his hands, as they seem to have been half frozen to the pumps." The smack *C. H. S.* is not altogether an unsuitable type of its namesake: but those who desire to see either of the two vessels go down will have to wait a bit. They will both go to and fro, laden with fish, till their hour is come. Blessed be God, no sea can sink either smack or man till then!

Much aided in seeking the truth upon Believers' Baptism by our edition of Norcott's *Baptism Discovered*, Mr. H. N. Mitchell, minister of the Congregational church, Okehampton, Devon, after studying the Scriptures, has been baptized by Mr. Meyer, of Regent's Park Chapel. He is now without a charge, and seeks a Baptist pastorate. He has long been known to several of our brethren, and can be commended to any church needing a pastor. Churches needing gospel preachers can, at any time, apply to C. H. Spurgeon. We have men in the College ready, and there are, beside these, experienced brethren anxious to move, of whom we keep a list.

Mrs. Miller asks us to acknowledge, with thanks, the receipt of a parcel of clothing from S. E. Carter, Stockwell, for the Poor Ministers' Clothing Society. Such parcels are always acceptable.

On *Monday evening, February 25*, at the first prayer-meeting in the Tabernacle after the Pastor's return from Mentone, the area and first gallery were well filled, and a spirit of devout thankfulness and earnestness prevailed. About 200 of the Orphanage children were present, and their sweet young voices helped in the service of praise. Many brethren prayed, and the Pastor spoke at intervals, relating interesting incidents which had occurred during his absence. The more we attend prayer-meetings, the more are we confirmed in the belief that they are an admirable means of grace, and that they are a true gauge of the spiritual state of a church. Love of entertainment marks "zero," and love of prayer marks "summer-heat," in a church.

On *Monday evening, March 4*, a number of the Tabernacle subscribers to the Baptist Missionary Society met for tea, after which Mr. A. H. Baynes made a statement with regard to the work of the Society, especially in India, and replied to various questions. A denominational paper states that, "As a result of the gathering, an expression of unabated confidence in the management of the Society was given." This is not correct, as there was no expression either of confidence, or want of confidence. The friendly conference tended to awaken interest in mission-work in general, and to keep friends in touch with the actual working of the Society.

At the prayer-meeting in the Tabernacle, the singing and supplications were mostly of a missionary character; and addresses were delivered by Mr. A. H. Baynes; Mr. Percy Comber, of the Congo Mission; and the Pastor. Last year, the sum of £518 4s. 6d. was contributed from the Tabernacle to the Baptist Missionary Society, in addition to £170 for the Zenana Mission, and £200 raised by the Sunday-school for home and foreign missions. Beside this, we have our College Mission Fund, which is attempting work in North Africa, Mr. Patrick having gone thither.

On *Monday evening, March* 11, the annual meeting of the LADIES' BENEVOLENT SOCIETY was held in the Tabernacle lecture-hall. Addresses in advocacy of the work were given by Pastors C. H. and J. A. Spurgeon, and Messrs. W. Olney and J. W. Harrald. The receipts for the year covered the expenditure, which we would gladly see increased. The demands upon the Society continue as great as ever, if not greater; so the committee will be very thankful if other ladies of the church and congregation will help them by giving, working, or supplying materials that can be made up into garments for the poor. Mrs. Phillips, Metropolitan Tabernacle, will be happy to receive the names of fresh subscribers; and additional workers will be heartily welcomed on the Thursday after the first Sunday in each month. Our poor are more numerous than ever, and the notion that the church at the Tabernacle has "enormous revenues," and is composed of wealthy people, is pure fiction. The working-classes and the poor are with us: and we have no need to call them together, and ask them why they do not attend public worship. There they are, and we are glad to see them.

On *Tuesday evening, March* 12, the annual church-meeting was held at the Tabernacle. A large company met for tea, and other brethren and sisters came afterwards. It was a great family gathering, at which perfect harmony and Christian love prevailed. The statistics for the past year were as follow:—Additions, by baptism, 218; profession (persons previously baptized), 28; transfer, 61. Deductions, by dismission to other churches, 133; joining other churches without letters, 42; erasure for non-attendance, 91; emigration, 5; withdrawal, 1; exclusion, 5; deaths, 67. The number of members at the close of the year was 5,275. In connection with the Tabernacle church there are 26 mission-stations, with 4,110 sittings; and 28 Sunday and Ragged-schools, with 594 teachers and 7,811 scholars. The treasurer reported a balance in hand on every account except one, which exactly balanced. The Pastors cannot but express their gratitude to God that they and their

beloved fellow-workers have been enabled to steer the good ship for another year with its vast loading of precious souls. Who is sufficient for these things? We need in this great enterprise the prayers and sympathies of all the faithful.

The *Sunday services* at the Tabernacle were exceedingly well attended during the Pastor's absence, but since his return the building has been densely crowded. The multitudes are as eager as ever to hear "the old, old story"; and, blessed be the name of the Lord, to many of them "faith cometh by hearing"! Since his return, the Pastor has been very busy seeing candidates for church-fellowship. He was able to select, in three sittings, no less than 55, who have been proposed for membership. Day after day he returns wearied with the gladsome work of gathering in the sheaves. Owing to the wandering habits of Londoners, many leave us, and join other churches during the year; but even this has its good side, as it makes room for new-comers to hear the word, and live.

There is still room for more people at the *Thursday evening services*, although the congregations then are very large. Probably there are many who could not venture into the great crowds on Sundays, who would be glad to come on the week-evenings, if they knew that they could gain admission without tickets and without difficulty. Many of them would also enjoy the Pastor's prayer-meeting, in the lecture-hall, at six o'clock on Thursdays.

COLLEGE.—The following students have accepted pastorates during the past month. Mr. P. A. Hudgell, at Wrexham; Mr. H. Smith, at Faringdon; Mr. S. Jones, at Welshpool; and Mr. G. H. F. Jackman, at Coggeshall.

Mr. G. A. J. Huntley, who was accepted some months ago by the China Inland Mission, expects to sail for China on the 4th inst. Mr. R. Yeatman is leaving Widnes, Lancashire, and sailing this month for Canada. He hopes to find a suitable sphere of labour in Manitoba, or the North-West Provinces. We cordially commend him to our brethren in the Dominion, as a good man and true.

Mr. E. E. Fisk, late of Walthamstow, has gone to York; Mr. W. Gillard has removed from Croyde and Georgeham, to Uffculme and Prescott, Devonshire; Mr. W. J. Harris, late of Birmingham, has settled at Winchester; and Mr. Albert Smith has gone from Shefford to Shrewton, Tilshead, and Chitterne.

Mr. A. Bird has removed from Ballarat to Hawthorn, Victoria; Mr. A. F. Brown, from Woodstock, to Sussex, New Brunswick; Mr. G. H. Malins, from Plattsville, to Ridgetown, Ontario; Mr. J. E. Moyle, from Port Colborne, to Durham, Ontario; and Mr. G. C. Williams, from Mount Vernon, to Walnut Hills, Cincinnati, Ohio, U.S.A.

On *Friday evening, March* 8, the London brethren met at the College to make arrangements for the forthcoming Conference, and to spend a short season together in prayer and conversation upon the Lord's work. The meetings are to commence (D.V.) on *Monday, May* 6, at Dalston Junction Chapel. The great desire of the brethren who were at this meeting was that this year's Conference might be the most profitable spiritual gathering that has ever been held in connection with the College; and this result will be attained if all who are coming to the meetings, and all who take an interest in them, will "pray without ceasing" that the Holy Spirit's power may be realized more fully than ever before.

We shall be glad if friends in London will help us in lodging the country brethren. Beds for four nights in the week would be a great assistance to our hospitality committee.

On the night of the College Supper, *Wednesday, May* 8, we trust our helpers will be as liberal as they were last year, when we felt our eyes moisten as we saw their resolve to provide for our work, though some had turned away from us. *This year we shall need special help as much as ever.*

Special Notice. — Will all our London brethren kindly take note that the *tea and prayer-meeting for pastors, church-officers, and workers*, will be held on *Tuesday evening, May* 28, instead of May 21, as arranged ? Full particulars will be announced by circular as the time approaches.

EVANGELISTS.—Our Evangelists are diligently at work, and the Lord is with them in a remarkable way.

Our brethren *Fullerton and Smith* are still continuing their London campaign with much vigour and success. It is remarkable that, at the Shoreditch Tabernacle, and Dalston Junction Chapel, the services were held while the pastors were obliged to be absent through illness. Pastor W. Cuff writes:—"I heard from our deacons of the great and gracious blessing attending the services as they daily went on. We arranged for a meeting of the converts and enquirers immediately on my return. I met them on Saturday evening; that was a fortnight after the brethren had gone. Over two hundred came; amongst them were all classes and all ages. We had a most blessed time with them. . . . . . Already many have decided to join the church; some will join other churches. This is to me the glory of Fullerton and Smith's work—it blesses and helps the churches, all the churches round . . . . . I think this last visit of our two brave brothers has done our church and work more solid good than any previous mission."

During March our brethren have been at Devonshire Square and Salters' Hall Chapels ; and this month they go to Mildmay Park Conference Hall.

Mr. Burnham's services at Rotherhithe New Road were not without signs of blessing, although outsiders were not attracted in great numbers. His next mission was held at Harefield, near Uxbridge, where he had the welcome and efficient aid of Pastor W. H. Broad, and several were led to decision for Christ, while the believers were greatly strengthened in the faith.

Mr. Burnham has since been to Ipswich and Amersham; and this month he is to be at Hungerford Congregational Chapel.

Mr. Harmer's missions at Tuddenham; Crown Street, Ipswich; Washbrook, and Belstead appear to have been the means of blessing to many. During the latter part of March he has been at Tewkesbury; and this month he goes, with Mr. Chamberlain, to Lydgate, Todmorden.

Mr. Harrison had large congregations at Sittingbourne, and several persons professed conversion. During the past month he has had good services at Vernon Chapel, Pentonville, with Pastor J. T. Mateer, who was so successful as an evangelist before he succeeded our dear brother Sawday. This month Mr. Harrison is to be at Great Grimsby and Kidderminster.

Mr. Carter has been for some weeks at Farnworth, Lancashire, and the Lord has so blessed his labours, that he has promised to take charge of the work for a time, together with the church at Radcliffe; his hope being that, ultimately, the people will be able to support a pastor for the two places, if not one for each.

Mr. Parker continues to hold successful services. Pastor A. E. Johnson writes of much blessing experienced during his visit to Westbury, in connection with the local Sunday-school Committee; and Pastor D. Honour sends a cheering account of his mission at Deptford.

ORPHANAGE. — All our collectors are earnestly asked to note that the President hopes to meet them, at the Orphanage, on *Friday evening, April* 5. If any of them cannot be present, will they kindly send the amounts they have collected to the Secretary, Stockwell Orphanage, Clapham Road, London ? He will be happy to supply collecting-cards or boxes to any friends who are willing to have them.

COLPORTAGE.—This useful agency continues its unobtrusive, but plodding and vigorous work, with every token for good. Evidences of the continued necessity for pushing the sale of the Word of God, and literature of a sound moral and religious character, multiply. The results of reading pernicious serials are constantly printed in the newspaper reports of the criminal courts, while the necessity for checking the issue of the more outrageous publications has compelled the attention of Parliament to the subject. In the meantime, our seventy-eight men are scattered all over the land, diligently visiting, every month, thirty to forty towns and villages each, selling Bibles, books, and magazines, to the value of £728, besides regular house-to-house visitation, and simple preaching of the gospel in various ways.

The following is just to hand from a local superintendent of a new district, and calls for devout thankfulness that the Lord's seal is being put upon the effort at the start:—"B—— is getting known and liked. I give you one incident: In his calls with his books, he found a young farmer who was about to be married. He, with his intended, and their parents, being Christians, desired that the wedding-day might be marked by the conversion of some souls. They therefore offered to throw the house open on the Saturday evening for a meeting, if the colporteur would go and conduct it. We prayed for him at our Saturday evening prayer-meeting, while he conducted the little service as suggested. He told me yesterday that one was led to trust the Saviour that evening, and he is hopeful about two more, one of whom (a young man) promised to meet him last night."

Regular contributions to the General Fund are much needed, as from this source the Committee have to make up the deficiencies in the various districts, which in several instances are very heavy on account of special circumstances. The Secretary will be glad to correspond with friends wishing to open up new districts where £40 a year can be raised, or to acknowledge any contributions sent to him. Address—W. Corden Jones, Colportage Association, Metropolitan Tabernacle, Newington Butts, S.E.

In one district means to support a colporteur have been withdrawn on account of the "Down-Grade controversy"; but, happily, those who love the truth have rallied to the support of the work, and the attempt to stop it has been defeated. The Society, as such, has nothing to do with the controversy; and it is by no means a noble thing to assail Mr. Spurgeon through the colporteurs, whose only business is to scatter healthy literature, and preach the gospel.

PERSONAL NOTES.—A Primitive Methodist minister recently sent to Mrs. Spurgeon the following cheering note:—"I have been for some months calling to see an aged, retired London tradesman, who had attended various houses of prayer during his long career without apparent spiritual benefit. His home now is in a lonely part of the country, where he can get to no place of worship. I tried several times, but in vain, to point him to Christ. One afternoon, I found him sitting in his easy chair, as usual, because of his affliction, and I knelt in front of him, and was praying fervently that God would be pleased to reveal salvation to him, when the old man stopped me, crying out with great tears, 'I've got it! I've got it.' I enquired, 'How and when?' He replied, 'By reading this sermon of Spurgeon's.' I noticed that the text was 1 Timothy i. 15. 'This is a faithful saying, and worthy of all acceptation, that Christ Jesus came into the world to save sinners; of whom I am chief.' "Will you kindly tell your esteemed husband that God preaches down here in many a wayside cottage through his printed sermons?"

At the Tabernacle prayer-meeting, some weeks since, Mr. Warner, of the Irish Home Mission, related the following interesting incident:—A boy, who was in the employment of a friend of his, was sent by his master, month by month, to get *The Sword and the Trowel* for him. He thought, from the title of the magazine, that it contained stories about "battles and pirates"; and therefore, though he had not much money to spare, he bought a copy for himself as well as one for his master. He read it, it became the means of his conversion, and he is now a useful servant of Christ in the North of Ireland. *The Sword and the Trowel* lately has had a good deal to do with spiritual "battles and pirates." Oh, that the Lord would make it the means of the conversion of many more of its readers!

Baptisms at Metropolitan Tabernacle:—February 28, eighteen.

Pastors' College, Metropolitan Tabernacle.

Statement of Receipts from February 15th to March 14th, 1889.

	£	s.	d.
Mrs. Mulligan	0	10	0
Mr. Thomas S. Penny	2	2	0
Mrs. C. Norton	0	2	6
G. G., near John o' Groats	1	0	0
J. B. C.	1	0	0
Mr. Robert Gibson	10	0	0
Per Pastor J. W. Davies:			
Collection at Bromley Road Chapel	2 12 9		
Children's boxes	0 19 4		
	3	12	1

	£	s.	d.
Mr. A. Briscoe	12	10	0
Edward Ridgway, Sheffield	5	0	0
Collections at Beulah Chapel, Thornton Heath, per Pastor J. W. Harrald	4	4	0
Mr. F. W. N. Lloyd	5	0	0
Erin	1	0	0
A friend, Hackney	2	2	0
Mr. T. N. Wade	1	0	0
Mr. F. H. Cockrell	5	0	0
Miss C. M. Bidewell	0	5	0
Rev. E. P. Barrett	1	1	0

	£	s.	d.
Pastor R. Herries	1	0	0
Contribution from Baptist Church, Jersey, per Pastor C. A. Fellowes ...	1	0	0
Pastor R. Speed	0	15	6
The Misses Marlow	0	6	0
Mr. and Mrs J. C. Parry	1	0	0
Mr. H. R. Kelsey	2	0	0
Mrs. Jeanneret	1	1	0
Miss K. E. Cooper	0	5	0
Mr. John Brewer	5	5	0
Rev. G. D. Hooper	1	1	0
Collection at Victoria Place Chapel, Paisley, per Pastor John Crouch ...	5	0	
Mr. D. Norrie	1	0	
Miss M. E. Nicholson	3	0	
Big Lizzie	1	0	
Little Lizzie	0	1	0
Mrs. Walters	0	5	0

	£	s.	d.
Metropolitan Tabernacle Evangelists' Association and Country Mission Training Class	5	0	0
Mrs. Baldwin	2	0	0
Mrs. Allan	2	0	0
From M.	100	0	0
Friend	50	0	0
Mr. A. H. Huntley	5	0	0
Mr. W. Morgan	5	0	0
Weekly Offerings at Met. Tab. :—			
Feb. 17 ... ... 30 3 9			
,, 24 ... ... 40 15 6			
Mar. 3 ... ... 23 10 0			
,, 10 ... ... 28 0 9			
	122	10	0
	£371	12	1

𝔖𝔱𝔬𝔠𝔨𝔴𝔢𝔩𝔩 𝔒𝔯𝔭𝔥𝔞𝔫𝔞𝔤𝔢.

Statement of Receipts from February 15th to March 14th, 1889.

	£	s.	d.
Miss Stearman's class in St. Simon and St. Jude's Sunday-school, Norwich ..	1	2	0
Farness Sunday-school, per Mr. T. Middleton...	0	5	0
Collected by Miss J. Keay	1	8	1
St. Andrew's, Stockwell, Temperance Society, per Miss H. M. Bartlett ...	1	1	0
Mr. F. A. Perrons	0	5	0
Miss Wiley	0	2	0
Mr. F. Freeman	2	0	0
Mrs. S. Slodden	0	2	6
Mr. D. Smith	4	4	0
Executors of the late Miss Rachel Anthony	4	18	8
Miss Kavanagh, per C. H. S. ...	0	16	0
Collected by Miss M. A. Burman ...	0	7	6
The Leathersellers' Company	10	10	0
Mr. D. H. Lloyd	3	3	0
Collected by Miss Cowen... ...	2	7	0
Mr. J. E. Stephens (sale of old coin)...	1	0	0
Young Women's Bible-class at the Orphanage, per Mrs. J. Stiff ...	0	11	
Mrs. Strong...	0	10	
"A friend of yours and the orphans"	5	0	
Jack, South Lambeth	0	3	
Collected by Miss E. G. Comber ...	0	13	6
P. O., Weymouth, Jer. xlix. 2, Rev. ii. 10	1	0	
Mr. William Lewis	1	1	
Collected by Mr. Alex. Miller	6	0	0
Emily...	1	1	6
Per Mrs. J. A. Spurgeon :			
Mr. R. V. Barrow 2 2 0			
Mrs. R. V. Barrow... ... 1 1 0			
Sir Thomas Edridge ... 2 2			
Mr. J. Pelton 2 12 6			
	7	17	6
From a poor man, Ashdon	0	2	0
Mr. A. S. C. Amos... ...	0	5	0
Orphanage boxes at Tabernacle gates	4	1	2
Mr. Wadland	1	0	0
Mrs. Bedells...	0	2	6
Mrs. Dixon	1	0	0
Mrs. C. B. Hallett	0	5	0
Mr. John F. Wilkinson	0	2	0
Mr. Charles Walter	10	0	0
Mr. J. H. Matchett	0	2	0
Mr. J. Batten	0	10	0
Collection in Zion Chapel Sunday-school, Eastry	0	12	0
Messrs. G. M. Hammer and Co. ...	3	3	0
Mr. C. Ibberson	0	2	6
Mr. Thomas D. Adams	1	0	0
Mr. Thomas S. Penny	2	2	0

	£	s.	d.
Mr. H. Jackson	0	10	0
M. A.	0	2	0
Three little children, Blair Athole, N.B.	0	3	0
Mr. J. Cooper	1	0	0
Mr. J. H. Church	1	0	0
Mr. G. Becker	0	10	0
Per Pastor T. W. Medhurst .			
Miss Clara Martin 0 15 0			
Mr. Barham... ... ... 0 10 0			
Friends 0 5 6			
	1	10	6
A poor domestic	0	2	6
A thankoffering from Wilts. ..	0	5	0
Sydenham Chapel, Forest Hill ...	11	3	2
Mr. J. E. and Miss May Williams ...	0	3	0
Mr. John Martin ...· ...	1	10	0
Mrs. Thomas	3	0	0
Mrs. Young	0	6	0
J. B. C.	1	0	0
Mr. E. Williams	0	10	0
Mr. W. Rogers, per Mr. E. Williams...	0	10	0
Mr. P. Hooper	1	0	0
Mr. Robert Gibson... ...	10	0	0
Mr. James Clark, per Pastor W. Williams	31	10	
Mr. A. Briscoe	12	10	
Miss Bagshaw	0	5	0
Mr. J. Bickford	0	10	0
Per Pastor W. Jackson :—			
Tiptree congregation ... 1 0 0			
Mr. H. Birkin ... 0 5 0			
	1	5	0
Per Pastor J. W. Davies :—			
Collection at Bromley Road Chapel 2 10 6			
Collecting-box 0 11 2			
	3	1	8
Mr. J. Leeson	1	0	0
M. C. P., Gloucester	1	0	
Mrs. White	0	5	0
Mr. and Mrs. McIntyre and their children	0	15	0
Mrs. E. Workman	0	10	0
Collected by Miss E. Campkin ...	0	6	9
Collected by Mr. J. Gwyer ...	2	5	0
Collected by the employés of Messrs. Carter, Paterson, and Co., Penge ...	0	5	3
Miss Raitt	0	5	0
Mrs. Knott	0	5	0
Pastor R. E. Sears	0	5	0
In memory of Rev. E. Oldfield ...	1	1	0
Mr. P. Nicholson	1	0	0
Erin	1	0	0
Mrs. B. Joyce	1	10	0

	£	s.	d.
A friend, per J. R....	1	0	0
Mr. R. Beattie	0	10	0
M. P., Highbury	1	0	0
Mr. W. M. Grose	10	0	0
A friend of the orphans ...	0	10	0
Mrs. Wilson...	1	1	0
A thankoffering	0	10	0
St. Margaret's Hope, Orkney	5	0	0
Mr. George Reid	5	0	0
A friend, Hackney	4	4	0
Mr. J. Bovey	0	5	0
Miss E. Ellis	0	3	7
The Baptist Church, Crieff	1	0	0
S. and A. L....	0	5	0
Mr. and Mrs. Gowing	0	15	0
Collected by Master Herries	1	5	3
Edward Ridgway, Sheffield	5	0	0
Mrs. and Miss Stuart	0	7	6
Mrs. Smith	1	0	0
Mr. William Brown	0	2	6
A friend near Keighley	1	0	0
Mr. A. Storr...	1	1	0
Mr. G. Smith	0	10	0
Mrs. Waters	5	0	0
Mrs. Downing	2	0	0
Lochee Baptist Sunday-school	1	0	0
Collected by Miss A. Mackay	0	18	6
Mr. F. H. Cockrell	4	0	0
Mr. John T. Stevenson	5	0	0
Rev. E. J. Farley	10	0	0
Mrs. Milligan	2	0	0
W. S. ...	1	0	0
Mr. Philip Martin...	0	5	0
A lover of Jesus	0	10	0
Communion collection at Herne Hill, per Rev. F. C. Carter	1	3	3
Mr. A. Wilson	1	0	0
Mr. J. Gifford	0	7	6
Mr. F. Frank	2	2	0
Mrs. York	0	10	0
Mr. E. Webber	0	10	0
Messrs. G. Borwick and Sons	20	0	0
Collected by Mr. H. Lymberry	0	5	0
Sale of S. O. Tracts	0	3	0
The Girls' Bible-class, Baptist Chapel, Hatherleigh	0	2	0
Collected by Mrs. Gallyon	2	10	9
Dr. Shaw	2	2	0
Orphan boys' and girls' collecting cards (3rd list)	14	14	1
Mrs. Hewkley	1	1	0
Mr. and Mrs. J. C. Parry	2	0	0
Mr. H. R. Kelsey	5	0	0
Mr. George Gilbert, jun.	0	10	0
Mr. Samuel Cone	1	10	0
Mrs. Jeanneret	1	1	0

	£	s.	d.			
Postal orders from Belfast		1	5	0		
Mr. J. D. Lisset		0	5	0		
Mrs. Mutch, per Mr. Bisset		0	15	0		
Mr. J. Brown		1	0	0		
Given to Mr. Fullerton at Dalston Junction Chapel...		0	4	0		
Collected by M. M.		0	15	0		
Proceeds of entertainment by Mr. Kaye's boys		2	15	2		
Mrs. Worsdell		1	1	0		
E. B.		0	1	0		
Mrs. Orr		5	0	0		
R. W.		2	0	0		
Miss Hall		3	0	0		
W. Willis		0	1	0		
A sermon-reader for five years...		0	1	0		
Mary Anne Williams		0	0	0		
Big Lizzie		1	0	0		
Little Lizzie...		0	1	0		
Wick Baptist Sunday-school		2	0	0		
Miss E. Fyson		0	0	0		
Collected by Mrs. Johns		0	1	0		
Mr. John White		1	0	0		
Nemo		10	0	0		
Mr. James Morrison		1	4	0		
S. C., Bourton		0	0	0		
Collected by Miss Kate E. Buswell		5	0	0		
Mrs. Willson		0	0	0		
Mrs. Fowler		0	0	0		
Mr. W. Squbb		0	0	0		
Mr. J. Rice		0	0	0		
Collected by Mrs. James Withers:—						
Mr. William Moore	5	0	0			
Mr. M. H. Sutton	2	2	0			
Mrs. Collier	0	5	0			
Mrs. J. Davis	0	2	6			
				7	9	6
Mr. E. K. Stace		0	10	0		
Mr. S. H. Dauncey		0	2	6		
F. G. B., Chelmsford		0	2	6		
Sandwich, per Bankers		2	2	0		
Meetings by Mr. Charlesworth and the Orphanage Choir:—						
Hackney, Mare Street		7	13	6		
Hemel Hempstead...		10	7	6		
Twickenham		2	10	0		
Loughboro' Mutual Improvement Society		2	17	3		
Expenses, Great Hunter Street School		2	0	0		
Messrs. Higgs and Hill		2	2	0		
Boston		6	10	0		
Northcote Road, Wandsworth Common		12	9	7		
		£406	0	6		

Orphan Boys' Collecting Cards (third list).—Barter, A. S., £1; Bowles, E. C., 4s 7d; Borrows, L., 1s 8d; Cambridge, H., 2s 6d; Hawken, L., 10s 6d; Jarvis, H., 1s; Love, A., 4s; Morrell, H., 11s 3d; McArthur, K., 10s 4d; Peverall, W., 7s 7d; Sambell, F., 7s 2d; Tresidder, W. J., £1 1s; Taylor, G., 10s; Taylor, F., 5s; Worker, S., £1 1.—Total, £6 17s 7d.

Orphan Girls' Collecting Cards (third list).—Breakspear, A., 1s 6d; Boyles, L., 7s; Buddle, F., 3s; Castle, D., 3s 6d; Carr, A., 2s 6d; Ellis, A., £1; Haydon, E., 10s; Hollins, L., 1s 1d; Hoole, S., 6s 3d; Hewitt, H., 6s; Hocking, M., 10s; James, F., 1s 6d; Kemp, M., 14s 6d; Long, M., 2s; Martin, J., 7s 9d; Mash, L., 2s 6d; Neve, L., 5s; Paul, M., 2s 6d; Pope, A., 16s 3d; Richards, L., 7s; Rowsell, J., 3s; Scott, L., 8s 6d; Searing, S., 6d; Sayers, A., 2s 2d; Steele, E., 2s; Smith, J., 6d; Seymour, I., 1s; Tiley, R., 1s; Unwin, M., 2s 6d; Willmot, M., 3s; Ward, E., 2s 6d.—Total, £7 16s 6d.

List of Presents, per Mr. Charlesworth, from February 15th *to March* 14th.—PROVISIONS :—1 sack Potatoes, Mr. G. Batts; 224 lbs. Rice, Mr. J. L. Potier; 2 lbs. Tea, Miss S. Ellis; 1 New Zealand Sheep, Mr. A. S. Haslam; 3 jars of Butter, Mr. E. J. Gorringe.

BOYS' CLOTHING.—4 pairs Socks, Anon.; 13 Shirts, Mrs. Holcombe; 17 Shirts, The Ladies' Working Society, Wynne Road, per Mrs. R. S. Pearce; 48 Bows, Mrs. S. E. Knight.

GIRLS' CLOTHING.—4 pairs Socks, 2 pairs Cuffs, Mrs. S. Cound; 12 Articles, Mrs. Smith; 18 Articles, Mrs. Bartholomew; 10 Articles, Mr. J. Bickford; 38 Articles, The Ladies' Working Meeting at the Tabernacle, per Miss Higgs; 8 Articles, Miss Glazebrook and pupils; 12 Articles, Mrs. Kidner; 13 Articles, The Girls' Bible-class, Baptist Chapel, Hatherleigh; 6 Articles, Mrs. S. E. Knight, 57 Articles, the Juvenile Working Society, per Miss Woods; 7 Articles, Miss Marsh.

GENERAL.—1 volume "Ellen Montgomery's Bookshelf," Anon.; 100 copies "Sunday Text Search-ings," Miss Appleton; 1 Desk and 1 small Table, Mr. Dougharty; 11 Articles, Mrs. Mitchell; 6 Scrap Books, Mrs. Brooks; 1 dozen "The Words and Works of Jesus," Miss Tilly; 30 yards Hoggin, Messrs. Wills and Packham; 1 Quilt, Miss Marsh.

Colportage Association.

Statement of Receipts from February 15th to March 14th, 1889.

Subscriptions and Donations for Districts:

	£	s.	d.
Sellindge, per Mr. Thomas R—— ...	10	0	0
Mr. D. White, for Uxbridge ... ` ...	10	0	0
Cambridge Association	10	0	0
Mr. R. W. S. Griffith, for Fritham ...	10	0	0
Mr. John Cory, for Castletown, Cardiff, and Penrhicweiber	20	0	0
Repton and Burton-on-Trent, per E. S.	20	0	0
Home of Industry, Bethnal Green ...	10	0	0
Mr. R. Scott, for Colchester ...	10	0	0
Mr. R. Cory, for Cardiff & Penrhicweiber	20	0	0
Maidenhead, per Miss Lassells	10	0	0
Mr. J. J. Tustin, for Horley ...	10	0	0
M. A. H., for Orpington... ...	5	0	0
Mrs. Allison's Bible-class, for Orpington	11	5	4
Wilts. and East Somerset Association	25	0	0
Calne District	7	10	0
Tewkesbury District, per Mr. Thomas White	7	10	0
Wendover and neighbourhood	10	0	0

	£	s.	d.
Metropolitan Tabernacle Sunday-school, for Tring	10	0	0
	£216	**5**	**4**

Subscriptions and Donations to the General Fund:—

	£	s.	d.
Mr. G. Colyer	0	0	6
Mrs. C. Norton	0	2	6
Mr. Robert Gibson...	10	0	0
Erin	1	0	0
Mrs. Mackenzie	5	0	0
A friend, Hackney	2	2	0
Mr. A. Todd...	0	5	0
Mr. F. H. Cockrell	5	0	0
Mrs. York	0	10	0
Mr. and Mrs. J. C. Parry	0	10	0
	£24	**10**	**0**

Society of Evangelists.

Statement of Receipts from February 15th to March 14th, 1889.

	£	s.	d.
Thankoffering for Messrs. Fullerton and Smith's services at Exeter Hall ...	50	0	0
Thankoffering for Mr. Harmer's services at March ...	10	0	0
Thankoffering for Mr. Parker's services at Falmouth ...	8	13	6
Mrs. C. Norton	0	2	6
Mr. Robert Gibson	10	0	0
Thankoffering for Mr. Parker's services at Haddenham ...	6	11	9
Miss Clarkson	1	0	0
Thankoffering for Mr. Harmer's services at Cheddar	2	3	0

	£	s.	d.
Erin	1	0	0
Thankoffering for Mr. Harmer's services at Tuddenham	2	4	7
Thankoffering for Mr. Burnham's services at Rotherhithe New Road ...	0	15	0
Thankoffering for Messrs. Fullerton and Smith's servies at Peckham Park Road	10	10	5
Mr. and Mrs. J. C. Parry	0	10	0
Mrs. Allan	0	10	0
	£104	**0**	**9**

For General Use in the Lord's Work.

Statement of Receipts from February 15th to March 14th, 1889.

	£	s.	d.
Per Miss A. M. Morris ...	0	5	0
Mr. and Mrs. Gaunt ...	2	0	0
Mr. J. Pearmine	0	10	0
A friend, Barton-on-Humber	0	5	0
H. B. B.	0	2	6
	£3	**2**	**6**

"Nemo" will please note that we thought it best to place his £10 to the Orphanage account.

ERRATA.—£51 5s. 5d. for Orphanage, acknowledged in *The Sword and the Trowel* for February, from Portsmouth, ought to have been from Lake Road Chapel, Portsmouth, per Pastor T. W. Medhurst.

Mr. M. Davies, £5 for the Orphanage, in the same magazine, ought to have been Mrs. Davies, per Mrs. Mott.

Friends sending presents to the Orphanage are earnestly requested to let their names or initials accompany the same, or we cannot properly acknowledge them; and also to write to Mr. Spurgeon if no acknowledgment is sent within a week. All parcels should be addressed to Mr. Charlesworth, Stockwell Orphanage, Clapham Road, London.

Subscriptions will be thankfully received by C. H. Spurgeon, " Westwood," Beulah Hill, Upper Norwood. Should any sums sent before the 13th of last month be unacknowledged in this list, friends are requested to write at once to Mr. Spurgeon. Post Office and Postal Orders should be made payable at the Chief Office, London, to C. H. Spurgeon; and Cheques and Orders should all be crossed.

THE

SWORD AND THE TROWEL.

MAY, 1889.

A Word with the Obscure.

A SHORT SERMON BY C. H. SPURGEON.

"A woman named Damaris."—Acts xvii. 34.

E have all read the opening address of Paul to the philosophers on Mars Hill. We have not read the discourse itself, for *that* was never delivered. When he reached his subject, his congregation would listen no longer. They had gratified their curiosity, and when he made a bold declaration concerning Jesus and the resurrection of the dead, they would hear no more, and the meeting broke up.

Paul, no doubt, had high hopes as to the result of his reasoning with the men of Areopagus. It was like preaching in a duke's drawing-room to the leading spirits of society, and it was an opportunity none could despise. One would say to himself, "What a grand occasion! God grant that much may come of it!" He therefore prepared himself with care, and spoke in a learned style quite unusual to him. The results, however, were very small. Paul, out of councillors, philosophers, and judges, gathered fewer converts than he might have done out of the common people.

Three results followed his fragment of speech. Some mocked: these were the very learned ones, who had been pleased at his quoting one of their poets, and with his speaking of man as the offspring of God; but they had been irritated by what they thought the ridiculous idea of the resurrection of the dead. Plato had spoken of the immortality of the soul, and on that point there was room for profound thought; but the theory of the raising of the body was beyond endurance. When Paul spoke of a certain despised person as having risen from the dead, and

14

asserted that this man would judge mankind, they laughed at the idea as preposterous. We hear their sarcastic words, and see their contemptuous looks, and perceive that Paul has made no impression upon them. No audience under heaven is less likely to receive the Word than an assembly of philosophers. These receive not the wisdom of God, for they are wise in their own esteem.

A second sort did not laugh; they did not care enough about the matter one way or the other. As men of broad views, they were courteous, and replied to the preacher, " We will hear thee again of this." Probably the most of them were of the same spirit as flippant Felix, who said, " When I have a convenient season, I will call for thee." One of them had already lost an opportunity of hearing the news from the ship that was last in from Rome; and so he quickened his pace to get down to the shore. Another had missed a philosophical lecture, and felt annoyed. They declined to hear more for the present. Of this second class we have always more than of the first: they do not oppose us with mockery, but they repulse us by indifference.

Still a little handful remained to make up a third class. Paul must have greatly prized each one of that small company; and Luke, who wrote the account of the whole affair, was careful to make full report. He mentions Dionysius the Areopagite, one of those who had made up the council before whom Paul pleaded; and he does not overlook "a woman named Damaris." Who she was, where she came from, and what she was like, we do not know, nor can anybody inform us; but she came forward with the few who believed, and therefore her name is written in this honourable list: " a woman named Damaris." There were others; and although they were very few, a church was founded, which became a power in the city, so that Paul had not altogether laboured in vain. Thank God, we are not accountable for results: if our efforts are honest and faithful, the Lord accepts them. Paul, with a heavy heart, departed from among them; but the few cheered him, and, among the rest, " a woman named Damaris " threw in her portion of consolation. We, too, may derive benefit from her at this time.

I. My first remark is, that CONVERTS ARE VERY PRECIOUS IN EVIL TIMES. Luke notes them as particularly as if they were jewels: here is one, a man; yonder is another, a woman; and there are two or three others who are counted, though not named. In the day of mockery every convert was worth a Jew's eye; and this "woman named Damaris," who might not have been remembered had she been one among the thousands of Pentecost, is specially noted among the few of Athens. Converts who dare to believe in Christ when the great mass of people reject him are among the excellent of the earth.

Usually they are persons of a solid sort. My eyes twinkle as I read this verse. I will let you see what I mean. " Howbeit certain *men* clave unto him, and believed: among the which was Dionysius the Areopagite, and a woman named Damaris." What ? Is it really so ? " Certain men, among whom was a woman named Damaris." She acted upon the inspiring exhortation, "Quit yourselves like men. Be strong ! " She is, therefore, put down among men, even this " woman named Damaris." Those who will come out and follow Christ when the narrow way seems altogether without a traveller, are people of good metal. If they can go contrary to the stream when it is bearing away rank, fashion, and learning, they are worthy to be reckoned among true men-of-arms. Being strong of mind, clear in thought, and bold to do the right, they are choice spirits. Our converts, that come to us when there is a wide-spread religious movement, need to be watched with great care, lest they should be carried off when the stream flows in the opposite direction. We cannot highly value sons and daughters who join the church merely because their parents have done so; nor brothers and sisters who simply follow the family example in making a profession. Religion must be personal and individual. We are cautious when converts come in groups. I would have you come though your father and mother have come; but do not profess the faith because of the ties of relationship. Come on your own account, because of your own conversion. If you do this as the first in your family, and dare to say, "I will follow Christ if I go alone," then you are the kind of person for whom we have great need in these evil days. The principal want of the day is want of principle. This "woman named Damaris" was made of genuine stuff, for she was not ashamed of the apostle when the great ones around her made him the subject of their ridicule.

Persons who dare to confess Christ in evil times *are pretty sure to be genuine converts.* A certain class will always be mean enough to join a Christian church, if they fancy that something can be got by so doing. I have never tried to catch men with loaves and fishes, because such bait only attracts frogs, and not fish. Those who can be bought for church or chapel are not worth a farthing a dozen. These are not lovers of Christ's cross; but of Christ's money-bag. Their lot will be cast with Judas. The "woman named Damaris" had nothing to gain by siding with Paul; doubtless, she ran the risk of great persecution. She took the unpopular side when she stood out alone, following the man whom others rejected. This is the style of convert we covet.

Such persons are also very valuable, because *they will endure the test of persecution.* A woman who dared to confess her faith in Christ when so much was said against him by men of learning and repute, was sure to hold out against ordinary opposition. The preacher was called a fool and a babbler; but she clave to him none the less, and therefore she showed herself to be of that race which may be crushed, but cannot be conquered. We read of Jabez that he was more honourable than his brethren, because his mother bore him with sorrow; and I believe that the converts born to the church in days of persecution are more honourable and more reliable than others. They begin well. If plants live through the winter, they will not die in the spring and summer. If men and women can bear the sharp frosts of early ridicule and slander, they will easily put up with after-opposition, and will endure even to the end. It is very important that all additions to our church should be of the right kind; but they are not all such. I try to exercise, together with my elders, as great caution as is consistent with charity; but do what we may we are deceived by those who say that they are Christ's, and are not, but do lie. I feel, however, pretty sure of my men when they come to us in the teeth of opposition.

Such persons as this "woman named Damaris" are specially valuable, because they are generally *people of vigorous spiritual life.* Paul had only two or three converts at Athens, but he might have solaced himself with the old Greek fable of the fox and the lioness. The fox boasted 'of the number of her cubs, and taunted the lioness because she had but one. "Yes," said the lioness, "But that one a lion." Though Paul had but Dionysius the Areopagite, and this "woman named Damaris," the woman was of a noble breed. She believed unpopular doctrine, and confessed the Christ whom others despised. I venture to believe that the very fact that her name is here recorded implies that she was well known in those days. She was only "a woman named Damaris," but it was impossible to omit her name, she had written it too clearly upon the hearts of the saints. Certain I am that those who come to Christ when few are coming, and confess the faith in the midst of opposition, are the people who will leave deep footprints on the sands of time. These are no ciphers, but forcible personalities, whose influence will abide. Their courage proves that they are no triflers, but are bound to serve the Lord with diligence.

II. But, secondly, this little note which constitutes my text, shows me that CONVERTS ARE ALL VALUED by the Holy Spirit, and by the church of God. Observe that we have here the honourable name of "Dionysius the Areopagite." There are many legends about him, none of which I believe, and therefore I shall not repeat them ; but he was, evidently, a man of consequence, for he was one of the notable council of Areopagus. Well, well : but here is "a woman named Damaris," of whom the best Biblical dictionaries say, "Nothing whatever is known of this person." Her name is not left out. See, it is put down side-by-side with that of Dionysius. Grace creates true "liberty, equality, and fraternity." Dionysius? Yes, by all manner of means, put his name down. Damaris? Yes, by all manner of means inscribe her name also. The saints are each one chosen, beloved, and redeemed ; they are each one called by the Spirit of God, put into the family of love, and made joint-heirs with Jesus, and they shall all reign with him for ever and ever. Dionysius the Areopagite, and the woman named Damaris, are equally written in the Lamb's book of life.

Observe that *sex is no detriment.* How greatly God has blessed women in the midst of his church ! They have been highly favoured in their happy and holy experiences. If they were first in the transgression, they were last at the cross, and first at the sepulchre ; and no woman ever betrayed her Lord, or even denied him : that was left for men. I know of no wrong that is recorded of the female discipleship in the New Testament. There are sinners mentioned whom Christ made his disciples, but these loved much, and were the companions of those who ministered to him of their substance. Woman is raised to her right place by the tender hand of him who was "born of a woman."

Obscurity also does not diminish the value of the believer. What if we know nothing about "a woman named Damaris" : yet the Lord will have her name emblazoned in the roll of his chosen. She shall be his in the day when he makes up his jewels. Ah, my dear friend ! you may have very little talent, scant wealth, and no name; you may be quite hidden away among the masses ; but if you are a believer, you are on the roll of the armies of the Lord, and in that great day your name shall not be missed at the muster.

No sort of singularity shall make the believer of any less value. I do not know that there is much in it, but the woman's name, according to Cruden, means "little woman." Read for Damaris, "little dame." I have known, in the church of God, little men like Zacchæus, and little women, like Damaris, and yet they have been great in the kingdom of heaven. I have known persons physically deformed, who were spiritually beautiful. They were the life of the meetings for prayer; diligent as Dorcas, loving as Lydia, holy as Hannah, mothers in Israel like Deborah. The minister has often said, "I do not know what we should do without that little woman." So, too, many a brother who has been lame or blind has, despite his infirmity, been a man of great mind, and God has largely blessed him. Dr. Isaac Watts, the poet of the sanctuary, was a little man; and when he was spoken of in slighting terms, he said

> "Were I so tall to reach the pole,
> Or grasp the ocean with my span,
> I must be measured by my soul,
> The mind's the standard of the man."

This Damaris, whose name is little woman, is not the least among the thousands of Israel. Grace is the standard, and not the outward appearance. I want to say this, because unnoticed people are a little apt to be depressed on that account. If they join the church they cannot give any large contribution, nor shine as speakers, nor take up a leading position. Now, none of these things would cause the Lord to think any the more of you. Our Lord Jesus did not come into the world to save the talented, and the rich, and the famous: he came to save souls as souls, and he bought them for themselves, and not for their belongings and surroundings. When you give your heart to Jesus, do not imagine for a moment that he will despise you because you are not a great lady, or a person of consequence. Do not fret because the pastor scarcely knows you among so many. How can he know everybody? He would willingly be the shepherd of you all; but if he cannot be, remember that the Lord Jesus Christ, that great Shepherd of the sheep, will gladly fold you among his blood-bought flock. Your lot is obscure, your name is unspoken; you are little in presence, little in business, little in ability, little in every way; but the Lord despiseth not one of those little ones which believe in him.

Thus has "a woman named Damaris" taught us two truths. The most precious converts are those brought in in dark times, but none of them may at any time be lightly esteemed.

III. Now, thirdly, CONVERTS EXHIBIT MUCH THE SAME MARKS. No two converts are quite alike, and yet certain distinguishing marks are always upon them.

Note that it is written—"Howbeit certain men *clave unto him.*" That is an instructive expression: they "clave unto him." They clave to the despised preacher of Christ. The wise men had gone home laughing; but "a woman named Damaris" stood up for him, cast in her lot with him, and stuck to him. She could not be beaten off from avowing herself a convert to the doctrine which others derided, and a friend of the man whom they called "a babbler." In this way conversion frequently begins. There is a cleaving, first of all, to the preacher himself, because he boldly speaks the truth, and then a cleaving to the truth which he speaks. What he has said has come home to the hearer's heart, and so he resolves to hear more of it, and to keep to the services. The preacher is in earnest, and has done the man good, and so he cleaves to him when others slander him. This cleaving to the preacher, if it be of the right sort, is, at heart, a cleaving to the preacher's Lord. Bearing reproach with the servant is bearing reproach for the Master, where the heart is right. I am glad to see you become camp-followers, for I hope you will soon enlist as soldiers of the cross.

Better still, we find that *they believed.* It would have been of no use cleaving to Paul if they had not believed the gospel : but this they did. They trusted in the Son of God, who came from heaven to earth, and died, the Just for the unjust, to bring us to God. They trusted in him who rose from the dead. They left their idols and their good works, and placed their hope in the ascended Saviour, who is gone up into glory, and who will shortly come to judge the quick and dead. They believed : this was the great turning-point.

When they had believed, what did they do next ? Why, *they came forward and confessed their faith.* Did one say, "That is not in the text"? It is in the text. How could Luke have written down the name of "a woman named Damaris," if she had only believed in her heart, and not avowed her faith ? How could her name have come into the Acts of the Apostles if she had not given in her adhesion to the faith ? By cleaving to the shepherd she, in fact, joined the flock, and became a partaker of the sufferings of the followers of Jesus. She did not hide herself from the shame which dogs the footsteps of Christ's disciples. She owned herself a Christian, and took the consequences. This is the mark of true converts : they cannot hide their love, but openly confess it. The verse before us reads like an extract from the church book of Athens : "Certain men clave unto him, and believed : among the which was Dionysius the Areopagite, and a woman named Damaris, and others with them." Go, ye believers, and do likewise. Christ's people are compared to sheep, and sheep go together. Goats may wander one by one, but sheep are found in flocks. You do not meet a sheep all alone, unless it has gone astray. If you meet a Christian who has never joined a church you may call him a stray Christian. Converts went together in the olden time, as they do now.

IV. Fourthly, CONVERTS ARE HONOURED BY BEING JOINED TO CHRIST'S CAUSE.

Linked with the good cause and its advocate, they were honoured. This obscure and unknown little woman is united with Paul and his life-story, and with the work of the Lord in Athens. She is, in her measure, a founder of the church in Athens, and is honoured in the deed. She had taken no degree, she wore no star upon her breast; but still she was an honoured woman from the day in which she was willing to be put to shame for the sake of the apostle of Christ, and the cause he advocated.

Her name is inscribed in the sacred Book. It is no mean thing to have her name honourably written in Scripture. She clave to the apostle, and believed. What better thing could be said of her ? What more could she have done? "This is the work of God, that ye believe on him whom he hath sent." That godlike work she had performed.

Better still, *her name was inscribed in the Lamb's Book of Life.* "Notwithstanding, in this rejoice not," said Christ, "that the spirits are subject unto you; but rather rejoice, because your names are written in heaven." At the last great day, when the family register of heaven is read, "a woman named Damaris" will be there to answer to her name. If she were not there, he who redeemed her would stop the proceedings of the judgment, and ask, "Where is Damaris? On that day, at Athens, when the philosophers scoffed, she dared avow my name; and now I will confess her before my holy angels. Where is she? She cannot have perished by the way; for I give to my sheep eternal life, and they shall never perish. Where is she? Let the assize be suspended till my daughter is here." O dear soul, you have been a member of a church, perhaps, for years, and you feel quite overlooked; but you shall not be forgotten in that day. Jesus will remember you as he did the dying thief when he came into his kingdom. One would have thought that our Lord had enough to think of beside the thief; but when he entered into the glory of the Father, he would not be content to do so without the thief. He will remember the very least, and lowest, and poorest, and most despised of his dear blood-bought ones. If you have confessed him in the day of his humiliation, he will confess you in the day of his glory. I can imagine our Lord Jesus Christ, when he saw poor Damaris entering the golden gate, saying to the shining ones, "Make way for this daughter of the Lord; for she bravely owned my name when the proud councillors of Athens mocked. She shall reign with me; for she was willing to be rejected for my sake." This honour came to "a woman named Damaris," and it shall come to every child of God, however mean or obscure, that shall confess Christ in this evil and adulterous generation.

V. Last of all, learn that TRUE CONVERTS ARE MADE USEFUL. "That also is not in the text," cries one. It may not be in the words of the *text*, but this sermon is a proof of it. "A woman named Damaris," of whom we know so little, brings glory to God at this hour by what little we do know of her. She clave to Paul, she believed, and she confessed Christ in that dark day; and now, at this hour, she "being dead, yet speaketh." She speaks to us all the more because of her obscurity. This woman has spoken to me many a time for years. Often and often, when I have been reading the Scriptures to myself, a whisper has said, "Preach a sermon upon 'a woman named Damaris.'" I have said to myself, "I do not know anything about her." At last it came to my mind that this was the beauty of the case. Say that Jesus Christ saves people of whom nobody knows anything. Talk of her of whom nothing is known but that she clave to Paul, and believed in Jesus. Many who will hear or read the sermon will be like her, and God will bless the word to their comfort.

Damaris speaks to the encouragement of humble persons, lowly, and unknown. *You may come to Christ.* I dread lest any of you should think that you must be of importance before you can be saved. No; you must get rid of all notion of importance. We are all important to Christ because we have immortal souls; but our having money, or our displaying talent, or our wearing broadcloth or satin will not make us any more important in his eyes. Come to Christ, ye men in fustian, ye women in prints. If you swept a crossing and were clothed with rags you might believe and live. It is the soul that the Lord cares for, not the trappings. Come to Jesus, whoever you may be. Seek his face and trust him, because this humble woman named Damaris did so. Thus she is useful many long years after her death.

You that are saved, but remain unknown, *do not wish to be known.* How often have I longed that I could get where I should not be treated as a public exhibition ! You live under a glass case when once you are a public character. Everybody pries even into your domestic life; and falsehoods buzz about you like wasps. Do not court publicity, nor crave popularity : be quite satisfied to do your duty and serve your God, and never to be heard of; for the less you are heard of, and the less you are known, the more peaceful will your life be. You must accept as a cross that publicity which comes of being an example of faithfulness to your Lord ; but if nobody praises you, why do you want to be praised ? " A woman named Damaris " lost nothing by being unknown. Holy actions are spoiled if we wish them to be seen. I know a friend who wanted to give a present to another on her birthday, and the chosen article was bought secretly, but somehow it came to be seen by the person for whom it was intended, and the pleasure was spoiled. When you do anything for Jesus, do it by stealth. Hide your left hand behind you, and do not let it know what your right hand is doing. There is a certain bloom upon the fruit of grace which is the beauty of it : a single intrusive hand may rub it off. Like " a woman named Damaris," keep yourself unknown if you can serve Jesus the better in the rear rank. You shall be remembered, and your name shall be recorded, and you shall have your reward from the Lord alone. If you seek the applause of men, you have your reward, and a poor recompense it is ; but if you serve the Lord Christ, and wish only to be known of him who seeth in secret, then your reward shall be great.

I have done. What I have been aiming at all the while is that I may cheer you into the courage which will make you confess your Lord. You will increase the number of the Church by one, and that is something, yea, much, if done for Christ's sake. We seek not yours, but you. We want " a woman named Damaris," though she has no long purse, nor long tongue, nor long train. Jesus Christ wants her, though she is not wealthy, nor beautiful, nor forward. Oh, that she might be led to say, " That blessed Saviour who consorted with the poor and needy, and cast out none that came to him—he shall have my trust, and I will be his servant evermore. Write my name down along with ' a woman named Damaris ' ! "

Come, and welcome, ye hidden ones, for Jesus saith : " Him that cometh to me I will in no wise cast out."

Sleeping in Church.

BY THOMAS SPURGEON, OF AUCKLAND.

THE first case on record is that of Eutychus, who fell from a window while Paul was preaching. There were extenuating circumstances in his case. Those confirmed slumberers who so often quote him that one is led to suppose him their patron saint, should remember that circumstances alter cases. Theirs is malice aforethought. They sin (if I may be allowed the Irishism) with their eyes open. As if their pew were a couch, or a sleeping-car, they settle down quite cosily, as regularly as the Sabbath returns, and as punctually as the text is announced.

I speak not thus of all. Cases there are in which fatigue overpowers. One little knows what sorrows and sleeplessness have wearied some of the else most attentive hearers. It must be admitted, too, that if the preacher is dull as a beetle, the fault of the people is considerably minimized. But the inveterate sleeper we can neither spare nor pity. Henry Smith thus describes him :—"Another cometh to hear, but so soon as the preacher hath said his prayer he falls fast asleep, as though he had been brought in for a corpse, and the preacher should preach at his funeral." I feel inclined to say to such : "What! have ye not bedrooms to sleep and to snore in?" Under the most eloquent preachers I have seen them at it, and *heard* them too ; sleeping *soundly*, with shameful literalness. They would do well to imitate the Emperor Constantine and King Edward VI., of whom it is recorded that they would stand throughout the service, lest by any chance they might yield to drowsiness. I happened once on a good description of a sleepy congregation, away down at Drowsy Hollow, " where the congregations gather in the interests of sleep."

> " As they sit on Sabbath mornings in their softly-cushioned pews,
> They begin to make arrangements for their reg'lar weekly snooze.
> Through the prayer a dimness gathers over every mortal eye,
> Through the reading of the Scriptures they begin to droop and sigh ;
> In the hymn before the sermon, with its music grand and sweet,
> They put forth a mighty effort to be seen upon their feet.
> Then, amidst the sermon, throbbing with the gospel's sweetest sound,
> They sink down in deepest slumber, and are nodding all around."

Thus aptly does the poet describe them ; but, having discovered that these are the very sort of folk who, on their way home, say, "That was a stirring sermon we had this morning," I venture to add two home-made lines :—

> And yet, when they are going home, saith the sleeper to his wife,
> " I've never heard such stirring words in the course of all my life."
> And she, who had been sleeping too, thus made answer to her spouse,
> " 'Twas calculated, dear, to move, and will certainly arouse."

If the discourse is over long, there is some excuse. Moore gives this anecdote of Dr. Barnes: " Being sometimes inclined to sleep a little during the sermon, a friend who was with him in his pew one Sunday, having joked with him on his having nodded now and then, Barnes insisted that he had been awake all the time. 'Well, then,' said his friend, ' can you tell me what the sermon was about?' ' Yes, I can,' he answered, ' it was about half an hour too long.' " "Mamma," whispered a little fellow in church, " if you don't let me go to sleep, I shall holler ' Amen '; he's been talking long enough."

A prosy sermon is at least as good an excuse as a long one. "Some parsons put a lot of sleeping stuff into their sermons," says John Ploughman. Hugh Latimer tells of a sleepless woman, to whom drugs were useless. "Take me," she said, "to the parish church." He quaintly adds, " They had better come to church to sleep than not at all; for they may be caught napping."

That was a sad experience of a certain Scotch minister, who, being off duty, went to hear another, but had to record: "I laid my head down to get a good sleep; but never a wink could I get for the people about me, who were all snoring." Sydney Smith used to say, "Some preachers seem to think that sin is to be taken out of men as Eve was taken out of Adam—by first putting them to sleep." It was surely not a bad idea of his who once proposed to levy a tax on every dull good man who ventured to preach a sleepy sermon. There's a wrinkle for the Chancellor of the Exchequer!

Some amusing stories are extant of slumbering congregations, and the means taken to awaken them.

One day sleep had overtaken the audience of Dr. South, including its most illustrious member, King Charles I. Stopping, and changing his voice, the preacher called three times, "My Lord of Lauderdale!" when the earl woke up. "My lord," said he, "I am sorry to interrupt your repose, but I must beg you will not snore quite so loudly, lest you should waken his Majesty." He then went on with his sermon, but no one went on with his sleep.

The late Rev. Mr. More, of Selkirk, while preaching from these words of Moses, "I beseech thee, shew me thy glory," observing many of his hearers fast asleep, made a pause, on which they awoke. He then, in a very solemn manner, addressed them to the following effect: "Do you think, my friends, had Moses been asleep when the glory of the Lord passed by, that he would have seen it? The glory of the Lord in the dispensation of the gospel has just been passing by you, and yet you were all asleep." We may be sure his audience listened after that.

You remember how Rowland Hill managed it; somewhat eccentrically, of course. When preaching, one afternoon, he saw some sleeping; whereupon he paused, saying, "I have heard that the miller can sleep while the mill is going; but if it stops, he wakes. I'll try this method" —and so sat down, and soon saw an aroused audience.

Here let me quote an interesting historical fact:—"They had a strange, but effectual, mode of securing attention in the old American meeting-houses. A useful church-officer went about with a long wand, having a ball, or knob, on one end, with which to tap any man who would be overcome by sleep. From the other end of his wand there dangled a fox's tail, with which he politely brushed the faces of the women when he caught them dozing."

But what is to be done when the parson himself slumbers? That is worst of all. I remember to have read, in *The Cornhill Magazine*, an amusing account of a preacher who went fast asleep while he was preaching. He was always slow; but on this occasion he got slower and slower, until he stopped together. He passed from a sermon to a snore.

Another parson had gone to take service for a neighbour, a few miles off. He walked to the church, and, being in good time, went into the vicarage. "You seem tired," said a servant; "won't you have a glass of ale to refresh yourself after your walk?" Yes, he would; and he did. The afternoon was very hot, and the rustic congregation, who had been reaping and binding all the week, mostly fell asleep. There was a nasal murmuring among the people. The doors, too, were wide open, and the bumble bees sailed slowly down the aisle, adding to the hum. Thus, when the preacher went into the pulpit, he caught the sentiment of the congregation; and, putting his face reverently between his hands for a few seconds, remained in the same attitude, fast asleep.

And now, to pulpit and pew alike, let me say, "Let us not sleep, as do others." We are children of the day. The needs of our own souls, and the claims of others, call us to eternal vigilance. What a deal we may miss by dozing! Is it not written of the Transfiguration, "Now Peter and they that were with him were heavy with sleep: but when they were *fully awake,* they saw his glory" (R.V.)? Oh, to see all that there is to be seen of Christ, to view his glory, and to have its radiance streaming into our happy open eyes! "Wherefore he saith, Awake, thou that sleepest, and arise from the dead, and Christ shall shine upon thee."

A Suggestion.

SUGGESTIONS have played a remarkable *rôle* in their formative influence in the history of the world. Every achievement in the social life of our age has served as a suggestion or departing point for the next, the initial hint too often being held in contempt, instead of being, as would seem just, relegated to a place of honour in recognition of its useful service. Into the wisdom or otherwise of this method of action it is not our purpose to enter. But we are painfully aware that, while such a rule cannot be applied to the doctrines directly evolved from the Scriptures, yet there has grown up amongst us a company of teachers who, though too varied as to the opinions they hold to be described as a distinct *genus,* are united in this one point—they conceive that divine truth can be changed from year to year, or oftener, as it may please their whims. The leading feature of their creed (we must, we suppose, beg pardon for using such a word in this advanced age) consists in relegating to oblivion whatever was held sacred by their fathers, or even by themselves, but a short time since.

So it has always been—suggestions, which nowadays are made to be synonymous with doctrines, have played a sad part in the history of our humanity. Satan's approach to our Mother Eve was by way of suggestion; and perhaps no weapon of the evil one has been so effectively wielded for the undermining of the life of faith in believers, or in keeping others from the consideration of the things most surely to be believed.

But this line of thought would lead us aside from our purpose if we followed its tempting lure.

We fear that, while we are most laudably in earnest about the souls of Hindoos, Chinese, and Hottentots, our *very immediate neighbours* are sadly overlooked. Nearly every village in our land resounds with echoes of the old Macedonian cry for help, if we only had ears to hear them. This is especially true of the smaller of them, which were always excluded from Nonconformist help by reason of their very smallness, or remoteness from larger centres. Very many of these are now deprived of the little spiritual help by way of visitation that was once possible. These circumstances are not unknown, nor is much sympathy for the large mass of people so circumstanced wanting, as the discussions at our various gatherings fully attest. But what is needed is practical help, and that *at once*, in order to rescue the perishing. Whenever the question of help is mooted, the suggestions offered invariably take the form of a preaching-room or a preachers' plan. These are good wheresoever they are practicable, but *preaching* is not the most urgent spiritual instrumentality needed to-day in these rural districts. What is wanted is earnest pastoral work, which will be in touch with the daily life of our scattered agricultural population. In the family circle, at the bedside of the sick, or at the arm-chair of the aged pilgrim, how sweetly acceptable is the Christian teacher bringing "good tidings"! How gently, and yet how effectively, can a word of advice, or even of wisely-guided rebuke, be dropped! Though the latter might be often misconstrued, by reason of the ignorance of the recipient, yet it seldom misses its mark.

The long-continued depression in agriculture has caused an exodus of the younger and more able-bodied of the workers on the land, from under the village roof-tree into our colonies across the sea, or into our larger towns. But are the souls of the remaining—the very old, young, and poor—of no moment among us? Surely, in the æsthetic progress of our age, we have not yet reached the point at which the heathen axioms of Grecian social life have been equally accepted with her art? "Has the survival of the fittest" really become a rule of English life? We are glad to be able to bear record to what an extent the ambulatory visits of the colporteur have improved this sad state of things. But the very poverty of these village people, to which we have referred, acts as a stern limitation to the effect of such a blessed instrumentality.

This brings us to *the suggestion* which we would wish to present for consideration, prefaced by this crucial question: Are there not amongst us those who, though they may be deterred by various legitimate hindrances from going to earth's remotest bounds, in obedience to the Lord's command to every saved soul to bear his gospel, could nevertheless do very much at home—and are earnestly desirous of doing so? We are perfectly aware that thousands do find good work for the Master next their hand. But we opine that there are many who are freed from business, professional, or other ties to any particular locality, and who could, if they were so pleased, settle in any central locality in the country, and thus initiate a new sphere of Christian influence, without the slightest antagonism to present forms of work.

To make our *suggestion* clearer, we cite an actual case in point:—A friend, by the providential arrangements of God, removed to a large country town, the centre of a number of spiritually needy villages and hamlets. Among them was more than the usual proportion of deserted ones, so far as pastoral visitation by the episcopal incumbents was concerned. The religious agencies of the central town were most complete, but very little of this surplusage of energy flowed out to its clustering suburbs. The particular form of usefulness, to which our friend ultimately settled down, was altogether unknown. He accepted an invitation to see and converse with a poor villager who was tormented with doubts and fears to a terrible degree, who had for some time longed for converse with a Christian instructor. The vicar had been a non-resident for the greater part of the year, and no form of Nonconformist worship was held in the village. The moral condition of the parish was most saddening, as may readily be conceived. Others sought his aid, under like circumstances, and cottage-visitation soon revealed a depth of spiritual ignorance scarcely to be imagined by a dweller in the neighbouring respectable town. The issue of this investigation was, that our friend perceived a call to undertake a house-to-house visitation, in order to ascertain the places where his visits would be acceptable. Very soon his visits were looked forward to, and he became, to all who would receive him, a much-loved friend. This teaching from cottage to cottage soon bore fruit for the Lord. After this plan other villages were approached, until five of them furnished our evangelistic friend with as much work as he could well undertake, a tricycle affording him the means of loco-motion. On four mornings in each week he rode forth, armed with a supply of Spurgeon's sermons, Ryle's tracts, Oxenden's books, and such-like literature, which he changed from cottage to cottage as loan tracts, this method of operation furnishing him with abundant means for profitable conversation upon spiritual matters. These gospel missives were, in many cases, passed on by the first receivers to friends in out-lying farms, thereby refreshing unknown persons. Our friend often found himself, and that not always by accident, at the school-gate, at the mid-day dismissal hour, distributing among the children publications, such as *The British Workman, Band of Hope Review, Good Tidings*, &c., each containing a useful religious tract. By means of these little missionaries he was heralded, and the way prepared for an effectual entrance to the cottages of the parents. Families of children in houses by the wayside between the villages look upon him as their most welcome weekly visitor.

Of this much-needed form of work there is any amount ready to be taken up, the value of which is difficult to gauge. If the cracked and mended pot of the careful housewife of buried Pompeii has descended to us at this far-off date, as evidence of her care of such a humble utensil, what shall be the evidence of the existence of such a little-known helper in the Lord's vineyard, when the Lord of the harvest shall garner his fruits ?

Qadees, Qadayrât, Qasaymeh.

BY W. Y. FULLERTON.

TO pronounce these words take a Q, a K, and a G, mix them together, and dividing the result into three equal portions, use them for the initial letters of the words, giving voice accordingly. They are the Arabic names of three wells in the Wilderness of Zin, and it is a standing puzzle how to represent the Arabic sound in equivalent English. Indeed, we are almost inclined to take the advice of the elder Mr. Weller to his son, when, with reference to his surname, he advised him to "spell it with a ' we,' Samivel, spell it with a ' we.'"

To Bible students these wells are, perhaps, the most interesting places in the whole desert lying between Egypt and Palestine, between the Mediterranean and that part of the Red Sea known as the Gulf of Akabah ; yet, strange to say, they have only been visited by travellers on three occasions during historic times.

The great interest of Qadees is that, undoubtedly, it is the long-looked-for site of Kadesh-Barnea, from whence the spies went up to search out the Holy Land, and where from the smitten rock gushed forth the miraculous water. No satisfactory location for this Bible place could be found by any traveller until, in October, 1842, Mr. Rowlands, hearing of a spot called "Kadese," determined to find it. Unable at that time to pursue his purpose, he subsequently, on his journey home from Jerusalem, after some difficulty, came to the place. We cannot do better than give his own description of it from the appendix to Williams's "Holy City" :—

"Now, my dear friend, for *Kadesh*, my much-talked-of and long-sought-for Kadesh. You may conceive with what pleasure I tell you that I have, at length, found this important and interesting locality to my entire satisfaction. Our excitement (I can speak, at least, for mine while we stood before the rock smitten by Moses, and gazed upon the lovely stream which issues forth under the base of this rock) would be quite indescribable. I cannot say that we stood still—our excitement was so great that we could not stand still. We passed backward and forward ; examining the rock and the source of the stream ; looking at the pretty little cascades which it forms as it descends into the channel of a rain-torrent beneath ; sometimes chipping off some pieces of the rock, and at other times picking up some specimens and some flowers along a green slope beneath it. The rock is a large single mass, or a small hill of solid rock, a spur of the mountain to the north of it rising immediately above it. It is the only visible naked rock in the whole district. The stream, when it reaches the channel, turns westward, and, after running about three or four hundred yards, loses itself in the sand. I have not seen such a lovely sight anywhere else in the whole desert—such a copious and lovely stream."

When this description was published, persistent efforts were made by many other travellers to visit Qadees, but without success, as it is off the beaten track from Sinai to Hebron, and tribal difficulties among the Arabs prevented one tribe conducting pilgrims over the country of another. Grave doubts then began to be entertained as to the reality of Rowlands' discovery, and at length it came to be generally believed that no such place as Qadees really existed, and that the enthusiastic Rowlands had given a highly-coloured picture of some other place, perhaps Qasaymeh. Then it became a question whether there were three wells, two wells, or only one well, in the district—a well in the wilderness is a notable landmark—and some even said there was no well in the neighbourhood at all.

However, in May, 1878, Holland, one of the greatest of desert travellers, penetrated to this oasis ; but, unaware of the importance of the spot, left it for future investigation, and he died shortly afterwards.

It was left to Dr. H. Clay Trumbull, of America, to settle all doubts by his visit, on March 30th, 1881, to both Qadees which had been twice seen before, and Qadayrât, on which neither European nor American eyes had ever rested. In his large and learned book, " Kadesh-Barnea," he gives a most diverting account of his manœuvring with his Arab guides, and of the methods by which he at length induced the escort of the Teeyâyah tribe, at the risk of their baggage, and possibly their lives, to trespass on the Azâzimeh territory, where the well and camping-ground are situated. After a dreary march of eight hours over the wilderness, it almost looked as if, after all, the search would be baffled.

" But we kept up, and kept on ; and at 1.30, after nearly three hours of moving in the wady " (the dry bed of a winter water-course), " we suddenly turned sharply to the right, at a scarcely-noticed angle of the low limestone hill-range we had been approaching, and almost immediately the long-sought wells of Qadees were before our eyes.

" It was a marvellous sight ! Out of the barren and desolate stretch of the burning desert waste we had come with magical suddenness into an oasis of verdure and beauty unlooked for, and hardly conceivable in such a region. A carpet of grass covered the ground. Fig-trees laden with fruit, nearly ripe enough for eating, were along the shelter of the southern hill-side. Shrubs and flowers showed themselves in variety and profusion. Running water gurgled under the waving grass. We had seen nothing like it since leaving Wady Fayrân ; nor was it equalled in loveliness of scene by any single bit of landscape of like extent, even there.

" Standing out from the earth-covered limestone hills, at the northeastern sweep of this picturesque recess, was to be seen the ' large single mass, or small hill, of solid rock,' which Rowlands looked at as the cliff smitten by Moses, to cause it to ' give forth his water,' when its flowing stream had been exhausted. From underneath this rugged spur of the north-easterly mountain range issued the now abundant stream."

Then, after describing a number of pools round about, and the ground strewed with the camel and goat dung of centuries, and the water, which was remarkably pure and sweet, Dr. Trumbull continues:—

. " There was a New England look to this oasis, especially in the flowers, and grass, and weeds ; quite unlike anything we had seen in the peninsula of Sinai. Bees were humming there, and birds were flitting from tree to tree. Enormous ant-hills, made of green grass seed, instead of sand, were numerous. As we came into the wady we had started a rabbit, and had seen larks and quails. It was, in fact, hard to realize that we were in the desert, or even near it."

This, then, is the place which, being the third camping-ground from Sinai, became, after the discouraging report of the spies, the head-quarters of the pilgrim Israelites for thirty-seven or thirty-eight years ; the tribes, perhaps, wandering all over the peninsula, looked to this as their centre ; and, at the end of the exile, it was here they gathered to begin their victorious march into the promised land.

A clear conception of the features of this place will tend to solve many supposed Bible difficulties, and cause us to admire the wisdom and mercy of Jehovah, who did not, even amid abounding sin, allow his people, whom he brought out of Egypt, to perish in a dreary desert. With such a fertile plain, and with such a strategic stronghold as their rendezvous and rallying-point during their wilderness sojourn, the taunt of the sceptic as to the lack of pasturage for their cattle, or water for their flocks, loses all point. And there can be no doubt but that they camped here ; for both Hobab and Moses, who knew the desert thoroughly, would lead the people to such a pleasant place ; or even if they were unaware of it, which we can scarcely conceive, God knew of it, and the Guiding Pillar would surely bring them into these green pastures.

Thus, the place called at first Rithmah, probably on account of the broom growing round about, became Kadesh (" The Holy "), and from hence, in a few days, the Israelites might have easily invaded Palestine, and entered upon their rest. But unbelief stepped in, and failure, fol-lowed by swift judgment ; and hence the new name of En-mishpat was given to it. The people failed, in sending up the spies instead of believing the Lord's naked word ; the spies failed, in thinking more of the giants than of their God ; and again the people failed in attempting to invade the land after sentence of wandering had been passed upon them. Their unbelief was terrible—only paralleled by our own, which keeps us often from God's Canaan—yet it was well that none of these people (save two), who knew all Egyptian abominations, should enter into the land, else would the new country have been polluted. Thus, by over-ruling grace, the place of failure and judgment becomes the place of training and mercy. And it shall be even thus with thee, also, O child of God, though thine unbelief is none the less blameworthy, the grace of the Saviour shall be the more extolled ! The old man must die in the wilderness—only the new man can know God's rest.

When the tedious journeying around this central pivot was nearly over, again the tribes assembled their scattered camps at Kadesh, and again failure marked the spot. Excessive drought had dried up the wells, and the people murmured. Alas, they were little better than their fathers ! Worse than all, Moses and Aaron failed too, and in their impatience struck the rock instead of only speaking to it. " Must we bring you out water ? " For this they were condemned, like the rest, to die in the wilderness, and the Rock stands there to-day a symbol of the failure of even the best of men. Thus the fourth name, " Meribah," was given to this oasis ; but though the name changes, the teaching is still the same. What a marvellous spot is this ! Here, too, was Miriam buried, and, probably, here the earth opened to swallow Korah, Dathan, and Abiram. From yonder mountain, now called Jebel Madurah, then known as Mount Hor, Aaron looked down on the land and died ; and after further journeying, Moses, from Mount Nebo, saw the fair inheritance, but did not enter it.   Thus, God's judgments are true and righteous altogether.   But how great the mercy mingled with the judgment—the smiling plain, the fertile wady, and the gushing stream of Qadees plainly show!

Why always whisper? Why not speak out?

THE peculiar blessing of private prayer no soul can tell another.   Like heaven's best gift, it is unspeakable.   In secret, special nearness to our Immanuel is permitted; making plain to the soul's experience Peter's expression, "Whom having not seen, ye love ; in whom, though now ye see him not, yet believing, *ye rejoice with joy unspeakable and full of glory.*"   Indeed, in sweet, solemn, lonely prayer, sight, akin to that of Moses, is given, and we endure as " seeing him who is invisible."

At some such seasons, when the key is turned upon the world, and its din and sin are locked outside ; when he whose " visage was so marred more than any man" enters, and you " behold the King in his beauty," and the disciple is glad when he sees the Lord—then, at such times of gracious favour, why should we hold all the conversation with our best-Beloved in whispers?   We know that *he* can hear without the utterance of a syllable.   Jesus has more than a mother's insight.   She reads her child's thoughts before they are expressed, and knows the little heart's contents by the upturned face.   So is it with Jesus ; the heart's secrets are known unto him.   The mother is pleased for her child to *whisper* secrets ; but what pleasure would she lose if the voice was never raised above a whisper.   May it not be that, sometimes, your Lord and Master has reasons for saying, " Speak out!   We are alone " ?

One of the brightest and most consistent members of a village church was asked, " And how came you to be a Christian?" and this was her reply, "When I was in service, my godly master always had an hour each morning, after family worship, for private prayer, in his own room, upstairs.   I was curious to know how he spent his time ; so, one day, I listened at the door, and heard him talking to God just as though he was in the room with him ; just like I'm talking to you, sir.   And I said to myself, 'If that's how near God comes to him, and if that's how real his God is to him, master's God shall be my God'; and I began at once to seek him.   I hadn't long to seek before I found."

Let David's language be yours: "*My voice* shalt thou hear in the morning, O Lord; in the morning will I direct my prayer unto thee, and will look up."   Then, oftener will you be heard saying, "My soul doth magnify the Lord, and my spirit doth rejoice in God my Saviour."

F. E. B.

There is much sweetness at times in being able to use the voice in devotion.   It aids the mind, and gives vividness to the exercise.   We cannot, in many houses, gain so great an indulgence, for we should disturb others ; but when it is possible, and consistent with secrecy, it is certainly a high treat to pray aloud.   Our friend has also incidentally shown that the use of vocal language may be made a blessing to others. These simple facts are invaluable.   We wish more correspondents would favour us with the like.—C. H. S.   15

Elijah's Experience Re-told.

BY PASTOR F. E. MARSH, SUNDERLAND.

IN these days, when men are trying to do away with the supernatural, and robbing the Bible of all that they cannot tone down, or reasonably explain, it may be well to remind them that, however much it goes against human reason, the story of Elijah being fed by the ravens can be re-told in our own day. The following incident may help to strengthen one's faith, and it may also convince unbelieving believers of our gracious Father's care for his children shown in the smallest matters. In Elijah's days God used the ravens to supply his servant with food : here we have a dog being used for a like purpose.

There was a very poor saint, but a very bright one, in one of our northern towns, who, one day, had nothing to eat ; and, lifting up his heart to the Lord, on leaving the courtyard where he lived, in simple faith, said, " Lord, I am so hungry !" Meanwhile, a greyhound appeared, bounding down the street, and, making for the old man, dropped at his feet a large piece of meat which it carried in its mouth. The dog looked up in the old man's face, as if to say " It is for you," and made off as hard as it could go. To satisfy himself, the old man made enquiry at the butchers' shops in the neighbourhood, to see if the dog had stolen the meat ; but he could not find that it had. Thus God repeated his providence, as in the case of Elijah being fed by the ravens, and guided the dog to supply his child's need.

How full of meaning is that precious passage, " My God shall supply all your need according to his riches in glory by Christ Jesus" !

A gracious Provider—" God."
A glorious promise—" shall."
A good portion—" supply."
A gift that is perfect—" all."
A gain that is personal—" your."
A gladdened patient—" need."
A granary of plenty—" according to his riches in glory by Christ Jesus."

> " Why should I ever careful be
> When such a God is mine ?
> He watches o'er me night and day,
> And tells me, ' Mine is thine.' "

Artesian Eloquence.

THE only eloquence that has value is of the Artesian kind, springing up from deep and inexhaustible wells of conviction. If a speaker's mind is gripped by a sense of certainty, and his faith in the truth of his doctrines is held tight in the vice of absolute assurance, he has the immovable fulcrum for eloquence ; and if the truths, thus certainly believed are such as strongly stir his feelings, he has also the lever. If he has any power of speech whatever, any culture and equipment, it is strange if he be not eloquent. " Out of the fulness of the heart the mouth speaketh."—*From " For Further Consideration."*

Almost a Hundred.

THE memorial with which we occupy this page is sent us by one who knew this friend, and can testify to the truth of the record. It ought to strengthen the faith of many.

TO RECORD THE UNCHANGING FAITHFULNESS AND LOVE OF GOD
TOWARDS

MARY HAYMAN,

OF EXMOUTH.

SHE WAS BORN ON THE 3RD OF SEPTEMBER, 1788.

Shortly after her marriage to RICHARD HAYMAN, in September, 1808, she
experienced the converting power of the Holy Spirit,
and thenceforward, for fifty-three years, through much trial,
conflict, and sorrow, she prayed for the conversion of her Husband—
"Faint, yet pursuing."
Though it tarried long, the answer came at last;
then was her sorrow turned into joy, and her mouth was filled with praise.
Through their advancing years she proved that underneath
were the everlasting arms, for the Lord
wonderfully sustained and strengthened her to attend to all the
wants of her Husband, who became blind and helpless.
She cheered and comforted him to the end, and finally closed his eyes in
death, in March, 1878, in his ninety-first year, after a married
life of sixty-nine years and six months.
She then became the special care of her Heavenly Father, and he raised up
friends who gladly ministered to all her need, even as
she had ministered to others.
Her daily testimony to the close of her lengthened pilgrimage was that
the Faithful Promiser, continually gave
her to prove to the very utmost the truth of his own words
"As thy days, so shall thy strength be," and
"I will never leave thee, nor forsake thee."
All the days of her appointed time she waited until her change came,
and then, with undimmed faith, and in "the peace of God
which passeth all understanding," through "the precious blood of Christ,"

ON THE 8TH OF MAY, 1888,

Within four months of completing her one hundredth year,
she joyfully departed, to be for ever with the Saviour whom she had loved
and served for nearly fourscore years.
On the 13th of May she was laid in the same grave with her
Husband in the Cemetery at Withycombe,
"TILL HE COME."

"Like as a father pitieth his children, so the Lord pitieth them that
fear him."
"Bless the Lord, O my soul: and all that is within me,
BLESS HIS HOLY NAME!"

The Romance of Missions in the South Seas

AMONG many readers of to-day, fiction alone is supposed to possess
the charm of exciting interest and thrilling adventure. To such,
we would earnestly commend the reading of such biographies as the one
we purpose sketching briefly in the present paper. It has held us in
unbroken interest from its first page to its last, kindled anew our enthusiasm in mission work, and made us stronger in the confidence that
Christ's kingdom shall yet come in all the earth.

The story of the gospel's progress in the South Sea Islands, has been
endeared to God's people by the martyrdom of John Williams, at
Erromanga, nearly fifty years ago—November, 1839. The precious
blood then spilt devoted the islands to Christ, and the reward of that
martyrdom is seen everywhere.

John G. Paton was born May 24th, 1824, at Kirkmahoe, near Dumfries. His father was a working stocking-maker, living the humble,
holy life of a godly Scot, in the quiet recesses of his village and his
cottage. At five years of age, the home was changed from Kirkmahoe
to Tortherwald, then a busy, thriving, and populous village, but now
much deserted, the many small farms having been absorbed in one or
two large ones. A glimpse full of pathetic beauty is given of that abode
of piety. "Our home consisted of a 'but,' and a 'ben,' and a 'mid-
room,' or chamber, called the 'closet.' The one end was dining-room,
kitchen, and parlour; the other, my father's workshop. The 'closet' was
a very small apartment between the other two. This was the sanctuary
of that cottage home. Thither daily, and oftentimes a day—generally
after each meal—we saw our father retire and 'shut to the door,' and we
children got to understand, by a sort of spiritual instinct, that prayers
were being poured out there for us, as of old by the high priest within
the veil in the Most Holy place. Never in temple or cathedral, on
mountain or in glen, can I hope to feel that the Lord God is more near
than under that humble roof." It was no wonder that religion under
these influences stole into the child-heart, like a holy perfume.
Though four miles lay between them and the nearest kirk, such was
their love for God's house, that the whole family considered it a great
joy to attend every Sabbath, the father only thrice in forty years
being absent—"once, by snow so deep that he was baffled, and had
to return; once, by ice so dangerous, that he had to crawl back;
and once, by an outbreak of cholera in Dumfries." At home, religious
instruction was not neglected, mother and children going regularly
through the Shorter Catechism on the Sabbath evenings, the children
not regarding it as a task, but as a pleasure. For twelve years the
father was a missionary to the villages around, visiting the sick and
dying, praying and singing in their cottages, until, in 1868, three years
after his beloved wife's death, he went to his reward, to the sorrow
of all.

Before he was twelve years of age, little Johnnie Paton was set to

---

* John G. Paton, Missionary to the New Hebrides. An Autobiography. Edited by
his Brother. Hodder and Stoughton.

learn his father's trade at the stocking-frame, every spare moment being used in study, chiefly the rudiments of Latin and Greek. He had already trusted the Saviour, and longed to be a minister of the gospel or a missionary of the cross. A few years sped by, and, after a brief engagement in the Ordnance Survey, then occupied in making a map of the county of Dumfries, he became a district visitor in connection with a Presbyterian Church in Glasgow, entered for a short time as a student at the College, ultimately becoming a school teacher at Maryhill Free Church School. Later on, the Glasgow City Mission appointed him as agent in one of their districts—a very degraded one—filled with "avowed infidels, Romanists, and drunkards." Great opposition and fierce conflict were experienced in this labour, mainly from publicans and Papists, the young missionary on one occasion, being stoned and left in the street stunned and bleeding.

All this time the foreign mission work had been burning its way into Mr. Paton's heart, and clamouring for his practical devotion. Just at this time, the Reformed Presbyterian Church had advertised for a missionary to join the Rev. John Inglis, in his grand work in the New Hebrides. For two years they had appealed in vain, and in despair the Synod agreed to cast lots as to which minister of their number should leave home-work to go out as a missionary to the South Seas. The lot was arranged, and amid the strained silence of the assembly, the scrutineers announced the result as "so indecisive, that it was clear that God had not, in that way, provided a missionary." With tear-blinded eyes, young Paton watched the scene, longing to rise and offer himself as a missionary, yet held back by the fear that he might be mistaking his own desires for the will of God. After a few days continuous prayer, he called on Dr. Bates, who had helped him to his first appointment in Glasgow, and offered himself for the New Hebrides Mission, and returned to his lodging with a heart light with joy, feeling he had at last fallen in with God's great purposes concerning him.

Many of his friends opposed his resolve; not, however, his father or mother. But his determination once made was never repented; and, after a solemn ordination in Dr. Symington's church, Glasgow, in March, 1858, he sailed for the foreign mission field. The voyage out to Melbourne was a very pleasant one, the captain of the vessel being a godly Scotchman, who gladly availed himself of the missionaries' presence to have services regularly on board. At Melbourne they left the *Clutha*, and joined an American vessel going to Penang, the captain of it agreeing to land them at Aneityum, New Hebrides. The contrast between the two voyages was most striking ; in one vessel all was quiet and orderly, in the other all noise and profanity. When they reached Aneityum the captain refused to land them even in boats, fearing that if they once touched shore his men, who hated him, would never return. Leaving the vessel, the mission party entered boats sent from the shore ten miles distant ; but these being overloaded, became unmanageable, and a total wreck appeared imminent. After drifting in great terror for some hours, they were seen from the shore ; other boats were sent to their help, and, with great gratitude to God, they landed at Aneityum on the evening of August 30th, 1858.

The New Hebrides number in all some thirty islands, twenty being well inhabited, and eleven of them of considerable size, lying one thousand miles to the north of New Zealand.

After a little time spent in Aneityum, the largest island of the group, a meeting of the missionaries was called, to decide the place of settlement of Mr. and Mrs. Paton ; and, as a result, Port Resolution, in the island of Tanna, was named as their new sphere of service. A house was built by the paid labour of the natives, working under chiefs, who warily declined to promise protection to the mission families.

The first view of this savage people made Mr. Paton's heart to sink within him ; all the sentimental glamour of "innocent heathenism," indulged in by those who have never seen it, vanished before the stern reality of fact. He says—"The depths of Satan, outlined in the first chapter of the Romans, were uncovered there before our eyes, in the daily life of the people, without veil and without excuse." Cannibalism was rampant everywhere, the bodies of slain enemies frequently being eaten during the night of the battle. A few days after their settlement at Port Resolution, hearing a heart-piercing wail from the villages round, and enquiring its cause, they learned that a wounded man, just home from the battle, had died : and that *his widow had been strangled, that her spirit might accompany him to the other world !* No marvel that Mr. Paton should say, "Every new scene, every fresh incident, set more clearly before us their benighted condition and shocking cruelties, and made us long to speak to them of Jesus and of the love of God."

One of the first necessities was to learn their language, for they had no literature, and not even the rudiments of an alphabet. The way in which this was done was "to hire some of the more intelligent lads and men to sit and talk with us, and answer our questions about names and sounds." The religious sense possessed by the natives was mainly one of fear, its aim being "to propitiate this or that evil spirit, to prevent calamity or secure revenge. They worshipped the spirits of departed ancestors and heroes, through their material idols of wood and stone. Their whole worship was one of slavish fear; and, so far as I could ever learn, they had no idea of a God of mercy or of grace."

When, however, in the island of Aneityum the gospel began to master their hearts, they longed for a fuller knowledge of God through his Word ; they endured great hardships, and made great sacrifices to obtain it. The story of their efforts to obtain a Bible in their own tongue reads like a piece of romance. "For fifteen years, day and night, the missionaries kept toiling in translating the Book of God ; and all this time the willing hands and feet of the natives toiled in planting and preparing arrowroot to pay the £1,200, the cost of its printing and publishing. Year after year the arrowroot, too sacred to be used for their daily food, was set apart as the Lord's portion ; the missionaries sent it to Australia and Scotland, where it was sold by private friends, and the whole proceeds were consecrated to this purpose. On the completion of the great undertaking by the Bible Society, it was found that the natives had earned enough to pay every penny of the outlay ; and their first Bibles went out to them purchased with the consecrated toils of fifteen years."

In the island of Tanna Mr. Paton found the natives terribly superstitious. At one time a long drought was ascribed to the missionaries

and their God. Their lives were threatened, unless rain were speedily
sent; and when it did come, they credited the missionaries' prayers
with its bestowal.

Into this gloomy picture these pioneers had sent, for their encouragement, some gleams of light and brightness. One of the native teachers,
sickening and dying, left his message in these words: "I shall not
return again to Port Resolution, or see my dear Missi. (missionary),
but tell him that I die happy; for I love Jesus much, and am going to
Jesus."

Many were their dangers from the fickleness and treachery of the different chiefs, and miraculous the frequent deliverances from them. At one
time a man rushed furiously with his axe at Mr. Paton; but a kindly
chief, seizing a spade, averted the blow, and saved him from instant
death. The next day a wild chief followed him about for four hours
with his loaded musket, and though that weapon was often directed toward him, God restrained the murderer's hand. One evening he awoke
three times to hear a chief and his men trying to force the door of his
house; but they were made to retreat with their work undone.

During all this time the work of preaching the gospel was regularly
continued, and though few results were seen, it was manifestly not in
vain. Mr. Paton tells how that "several men, ashamed or afraid to
come by day, came to me constantly by night, for conversation and
instruction. Having seen the doors of the mission-house made fast, and
the windows blinded so that they could not be observed, they continued
with me for many hours, asking all sorts of strange questions about the
new religion and its laws."

Perhaps the saddest and most terrible difficulties were the revolting
wickedness and cruelties of the English traders who came to the island,
and by their atrocious excesses enraged the people against every white
face. They tried to stir up war in order to supply the ammunition at
fabulous prices; and when terrified by the natives' reprisals, pleaded in
abject terror for the missionaries to defend their lives. With a Satanic
malignity they landed four men infected with measles at different ports,
in order to spread the disease, destroy the natives, and supplant them
with their own harpies. "Most of them were horrible drunkards,
and their traffic of every kind among these islands was, generally
speaking, steeped in human blood." Later on, some of these traders
actually went the length of urging the natives to kill the missionaries,
as they felt them to be a powerful obstacle to their own wicked purposes. The heathen were more Christian than these civilized demons, and
the suggestion was rejected by them. Terrible trials were, however,
coming, and early in 1862, Mr. Paton was compelled to leave Tanna,
escaping only with his life; his house, printing-press, and mission-church
all being wrecked by the savage natives, goaded into treacherous
revenge by the cruelties of the white traders. The story of the book
ends here; but we know that since that time, the seed sown with so
many tears, and so much blood, has borne a marvellous harvest.

The Mission to Deep-Sea Fishermen.

THERE can be little doubt that, next to agriculture, fishing is one of the most ancient industries of Great Britain. It is said that Great Yarmouth has been a fishing station for something like one thousand four hundred years. It was inevitable that a considerable portion of the population of our sea-girt isles should choose this avocation, our coast-line being very extensive, and our tendencies as a race being towards adventures on the deep. Nor could it be otherwise that men would be tempted to go a fishing while fish could be found in such great variety, and of such tempting quality, as those which swarm in our seas. The rapid growth of this industry during the present reign is remarkable. In the days of our grandfathers, it was impossible to procure fish in a condition fit for food at long distances from the coast; and even at seaside places the supply was inconsiderable; for, as one authority on the subject tells us, "the fishing-boats were small, and there was little inducement to fish on a large scale, when the markets within reach were so few." Railways and steam-boats have extended the fishing business beyond what would, at one time, have been thought possible, by providing facilities for distributing the fish. The fishing fleet of the British Isles consists of something like seven thousand first-class boats, and between twenty and thirty thousand second and third class. Tens of thousands of men and boys are constantly engaged in this occupation. About a dozen large fleets are always out in the North Sea, each fleet being attended by steamers, which hurry off to one of the great ports as soon as they can be loaded up. Small boats ply between the fishing smacks and the steamers. Alas! from time to time many lives are lost on the stormy sea.

Much of the most important part of the work goes on in the dark hours, and when the fishing-ground is the North Sea, and the time mid-winter, it is impossible to realize what powers of endurance are needed by the men who watch or toil through the live-long night. What a luxury is fish! But at what a cost is it provided! There are twelve thousand fishermen always afloat in the North Sea alone; and these surely deserve a place in Christian sympathy. For the benefit of these men the Mission founded by Mr. E. J. Mather employs seven cruisers, each of which is said to be "a church, dispensary, temperance-hall, and lending library." On board of these adventurous Bethels, congregations assemble for public worship; and during the summer holidays the gospel is preached in their cabins by various pastors from England and Scotland.

The men and boys spend nearly the whole of their time upon the sea, except a week or so between each voyage of two months. In the old times they were little thought of; but about seven years ago the attention of Christian persons was drawn to the subject. It was during a cruise in 1881, that Mr. Mather took notice of a floating Dutch grog-shop, and he thought that something of a different kind ought to be provided. As was plainly seen, the proposed service could never be properly undertaken until a vessel was fitted out for the purpose; and a friend devoted £1,000 to the purchase of the "Ensign," the first mission-vessel. Since then, others have been added; and eventually, it is hoped that a vessel will be provided to accompany each fleet. "Happily, the nature of the work is such that the mission smacks do not interfere with the legitimate occupation of the trawlers. When a 'fishing breeze' is blowing, the nets are down, and the gospel ships fish like the rest, to maintain themselves; but when the sea is calm, and the men are unavoidably idle, the mission flags are hoisted, and the nets are spread to catch men."

By way of illustrating the power of the Bible on the sea, we will tell of something which occurred long before this Mission was founded.

Some years ago, a Sunday-school teacher in London found himself greatly encouraged in his work by a call from one of his old scholars, who had left the shore for the dangerous avocation of deep-sea fishing. Callers of this description, who have outgrown recognition, have a habit of making their identity certain by showing the copy of the Scriptures used while in the class; and this is what the sailor did. After this, he gave a chapter of his experience. He had been joined to a fishing company in Scotland; and on the boat, which was frequently away from shore for weeks at a time, he was the only hand who could read. Because time would otherwise have hung heavily on his hands when the hooks were baited, he who had once been a scholar on the Sabbath now read his Testament alone, till the men desired that he should read to them also. They had hitherto been a profane company; but a reformation was soon wrought among them. The master gave up the practice of swearing, and the others followed his example. After this, they resolved to keep the Sabbath. Prayer and reading of the Scriptures became regular things on board the little craft; and the men learned to read in their spare time. All became as thoroughly changed as though a miracle had been performed in their midst. Indeed, we may ask, is any miracle more wonderful than the transformation of the sin-hardened human heart?

Mr. E. J. Mather, founder and director of the Mission to Deep-Sea Fishermen, answers all enquiries at 181, Queen Victoria Street, E.C.

Tell your Minister.

A FRIEND of mine, a layman, was once in the company of a very eminent preacher, then in the decline of life. My friend happened to remark what a comfort it must be to him to think of all the good he had done by his gift of eloquence. The eyes of the old man filled with tears, and he said, "You little know! You little know! If I ever turned one heart from the ways of disobedience to the wisdom of the just, God has withheld the assurance from me. I have been admired, and flattered, and run after; but how gladly would I forget all that to be told of a single soul I have been instrumental in saving!" The eminent preacher entered into his rest. There was a great funeral. Many pressed around the grave who had oftentimes hung entranced upon his lips. My friend was there, and by his side was a stranger, who was so deeply moved, that when all was over, my friend said to him, "You knew him, I suppose?" "Knew him!" was the reply. "No; I never spoke to him, but I owe to him my soul!"—*From "Colloquies on Preaching" by Canon Twells.*

The Old Theology.

"The old theology dies hard."

OH, fatal folly; what avails
　The *new* theology in death—
When the huge thought of life-long sin,
　Shortens the palpitating breath?
No *Christ*, no *substitute*, no *blood*,
To plead before a holy God.

Whose is the old theology;
　And wherefore, *wherefore* should it die
Those dear, reviving types of old,
　Were they but solemn mockery?
Call they the sprinkled blood a sham?
And a mere farce, the Paschal Lamb?

How gloriously the *living* bird
　Soared singing to its native skies,
Dipt in its fellow's blood! and *here*
　The marrow of the gospel lies.
For very shame our face we hide,
Yet sing and soar; for Christ has died.

The old theology for power
　Eclipses every human plan;
And while the march of intellect
　Proclaims th' abilities of *man*,
We glory in a *shifted curse*,
And *Christ responsible for us*.

And shall God's old religion *die*,
　Since poor proud mortals love it not?
Because *they* keep their eyelids dry,
　Shall *weeping* sinners be forgot?
Never! Till misery shall cease,
The Christ of God shall be *their* peace.

I shudder as I see men dare
　To mutilate the Book Divine,
And steal, with ignorance of pride,
　The sweetness from this hope of mine;
But the whole earth—on sea—on shore
Holds but one Bible, and no more.

God's eye is on these mighty men,
　Of earthly fame and heavenly scorn;
Who boldly wield th' unholy pen,
　Of demon-like rebellion born:
Shall *he* his righteous wrath forego,
Because *they* will not credit woe?

Poor creatures : if the Holy Ghost
    Should overshadow them to-night,
And bring their hideous sins of heart
    Before their eyes in Heaven's light;
How keen would be their shame-faced plea,
" O Jesus, undertake for me ! "

How can it die, this blessed hope,
    This only refuge from despair ;
This scheme for glorifying Christ,
    Unfolded by the God we fear ;
This vital faith which flings its arms
About its God, in all alarms !

" He always wins who sides with God,"
    And so on Revelation's rock
I take my stand ; and though time's tide
    My faltering foothold seems to mock ;
Through time, through tide, my hope shall be,
CHRIST, and the OLD THEOLOGY.

M. A. CHAPLIN.

Galleywood, Chelmsford.

Can be had at 1s. per hundred of J. H. Clarke, 78, High Street, Chelmsford.

Learning to Sing.

THE following eight reasons why everyone should learn to sing are given by Byrd, in his " Psalms, Sonnets, and Songs," &c., published in 1588 :—
1st. " It is a knowledge easily taught and quickly learned, where there is a good master and an apt scholar."
2nd. " The exercise of singing is delightful to nature, and good to preserve the health of man."
3rd. " It doth strengthen all parts of the breast, and doth open the pipes."
4th. " It is a singularly good remedy for a stuttering and stammering in the speech."
5th. " It is the best means to procure a perfect pronunciation, and to make a good orator."
6th. " It is the only way to know where nature hath bestowed a good voice . . . and in many that excellent gift is lost because they want art to express nature."
7th. " There is not any music of instruments whatever comparable to that which is made of the voices of men ; where the voices are good, and the same well sorted and ordered."
8th. " The better the voice is, the meeter it is to honour and serve God therewith, and the voice of man is chiefly to be employed to that end."

" Since singing is so good a thing,
    I wish all men would learn to sing."

Post-mortem Salvation;

OR, CAN THOSE WHO DIE IMPENITENT BE AFTERWARDS SAVED?

THE words of the old Pilgrim Father, John Robinson, to the effect that probably fresh light would break forth from the Word of God, have been quoted to cover every kind of departure from "the good old way." Men stumbling on the dark mountains of error champion the cause of heresy by pretentions to greater light; thus falling into the old folly of calling darkness light; and proving the words of our Lord—"If therefore the light that is in thee be darkness, how great is that darkness!"

The truth is that we get more light concerning matters of divine revelation only as we get nearer to God, for "God is light;" and "in his light we shall see light." Light cannot by any possibility become darkness, neither can truth, in its pure and simple form, ever become error. Gold is gold; and, though it should be rolled into the thinnest leaf, drawn out into the finest wire, or reduced to an impalpable dust, every part of it would still be gold; by no process whatsoever could it be converted into brass or copper. And so, the more light we get upon the truth—or, in other words, the more the truth stands out in its own native beauty, the more will its excellence appear, and the more hideous will the distorted forms of error be seen to be. The oak is an oak, from the planting of the acorn until the majestic tree bows before the strokes of the feller: it cannot by any means become a briar or a thorn. But what is impossible in nature and science, what would be truly absurd in philosophy and history, may be, as some seem to think, quite possible in theology.

We go higher than theology, we go to revelation. Theology, as a system of man's compounding, though the elements be all Scriptural and true, may possibly be defective here or redundant there; but revelation never. It is God's voice, God's word, God's will, God's truth. We lay this down as a general principle, from which there can be no deviation; for "the words of the Lord are pure words, as silver tried in a furnace of earth purified seven times." All his words are true and right; and if anything therein seems hidden, it is not because *it* is obscure, but because *we* need more light. Speaking of God's Word, one has truly said:—

> "If aught there dark appear,
> Bewail thy want of sight;
> No imperfection can be there,
> For all God's words are right."

Seeing, then, God has in these last days spoken unto us by his Son, and left with his church the sacred truths he has once for all delivered to it, we are bound to "keep this commandment without spot, unrebukable, until the appearing of our Lord Jesus Christ." We must defend the truths of the gospel when they are assailed, and contend for them as a treasure, for the keeping of which we are responsible to God.

If our responsibility to God compels us to be faithful to our trust, so, also, should our compassion for man make us jealous of everything which would tend to remove from him healthy motives to care for his soul's eternal salvation. All that would tend to lessen his care for his own eternal well-being we ought to denounce.

Hence it is, that we contend earnestly against all those who make it a part of their teaching that there will come a time after death, when those who have died in the neglect of the great salvation shall have mercy offered to them once more, with a possibility of their being raised from the prison of despair to ultimate happiness and glory. This view is one among many relating to the future state of those who die in impenitence. The absolute annihilation of the wicked, at some period or other, is the extreme on one side, and the universal restoration of the sinful race of man to eternal happiness, is the extreme on the other.

Now, there could be no valid objection to either extreme, or to any of their various modifications, if they were not contrary to revealed truth.   If God *chose* in any such way to glorify himself, it must, of course, be in perfect consistency with himself, and with what he has made known of his holy will; for he can do nothing contrary to himself and his will.   *But has God revealed himself and his will to any such effect ?*   Is there anything in the Bible that looks that way ?   Has God anywhere said that, after the present state of probation has come to an end, there will be another ?   Has he said that after men have continued for years to disregard his just claims, refuse his entreaties, and reject his gospel, and after he has executed upon them the judgment of which they were forewarned, he will, by methods unexplained, extend to them again the offers of mercy, so that, after all, they may finally share the joys of his right hand with those who, through faith and patience, inherit the promises ?   If this is the will of God, he has somewhere stated it. It would be alike unjust and irreverent to suppose that, while stating with beautiful simplicity the terms of salvation offered in the gospel—that whoso-ever believeth in Jesus Christ shall never perish, but have eternal life, while urging his entreaties with all the arguments drawn from his mercy, from the personal dignity of the Redeemer, from the efficacy of his blood, and the imperativeness of his claims, and while holding over the head of the unbelieving the most terrible of threatenings, he should, nevertheless, in the midst of all, secretly determine that he would not act in strict accordance with his own declarations, but would act otherwise than he threatened. Surely, such a course would make it appear that he was either merely working upon men's fears, or that the awful doom denounced was the utterance of passion, and not the deliberate sentence of a truthful Judge. To suppose such a thing would be next to blasphemy, if not blasphemy itself.   Such proceeding on God's part is absolutely impossible.

We ask, therefore, for some positive statement from the lips of the Eternal, that he intends, at some future period, to open the gates of paradise to those who have been cast into hell for their sins.   An opinion, a theory, an inference will not suffice; nothing less than a positive statement will be sufficient.   We ask for this, but we ask in vain ; for the simple reason that no such passage can be found in either the Old or the New Testament. No, nor a single word sanctioning such an opinion.

To hold a sentiment so utterly without Scriptural foundation, cannot be harmless to anyone ; for such an error seldom comes alone.   For anyone to teach this baseless theory to others, must be mischievous in the extreme, and may end in the perdition of deceiver and deceived.

But if we have no positive testimony, nor even so much as a hint, in favour of post-mortem salvation, a great deal is said on the other side, plainly showing that the perdition of those who die impenitent is not only righteous, but endless ; that a gulf is placed between the saved and the lost which can never be passed over.

The condition of those who die impenitent may be considered under three terms, or heads.   It comprehends separation, privation, retribution.

Separation : separation from God and those beings who are in harmony with him.   The thought of this is unutterably painful and appalling to a gracious soul; for is not fellowship with God his greatest joy, even as union to him is his highest honour ?   But sin is a turning away from God, as if the Ever-Blessed were a repulsive Being ; and every act of sin is a further departing from God, making the distance greater.   Man does "not like to retain God in his thoughts"; and if we put his actions into words, they speak out the hostility of his heart :—"Depart from us ; for we desire not the knowledge of thy ways."   Sin is a "departing," a "going astray," a "turning of the back, and not the face," a *revolt* of the man from God ; and this is the course of all mankind, both where the gospel is preached, and where it is not preached ; and in this course man continues to the end, notwithstanding all warnings and entreaties, unless the hand of sovereign mercy interposes to pluck him as a brand from the burning.

Sometimes, even in this world, God seems to say of a man, "He is joined to idols; let him alone"; and when God thus, in this world, gives a man up, what hope or help is there for him? But might not God justly give up to his own ways any and every sinner, here in this life? There is nothing against it, except what God may find in himself, in his own love, and purpose, and grace. If he may justly give him up here, when he has hardened himself against God, he may justly do so in a fuller degree at death, and more terribly still at the resurrection. If he may justly give him up to his own ways, in life and death, and at the judgment, why not for ever? If when at first the stone started slowly rolling down the mountain-side there was no pause, but an accelerated downward progress, what is to reverse the nature of things, and roll back the stone to the sunny height of the mountain? In awarding to the impenitent sinner the awful doom of "everlasting destruction from the presence of the Lord, and from the glory of his power," God only gives to him the things he has chosen, the harvest of his own sowing. While God is God, and sin is sin, there can be no cancelling of the sentence, and no change in the portion of the sinner, excepting to deeper condemnation and despair. When once the tree has fallen *in the direction in which it leaned*, there it will lie for ever. God will, in effect, say to the hardened, impenitent one: "You have chosen to depart from me; take, therefore, that which is the result of your course. You have delighted in the things which I forbade and abhorred; take them, therefore, to the full, as your everlasting portion." But we mentioned also

Privation.—Privation, as here used, means the utter and eternal loss of all good. This must, of necessity, follow from being separated from God. He is essentially and eternally good. Separation from him must involve the loss of all good, for there is no good out of him. As sinners in this world, we have all forfeited all title and claim to God and goodness. Grace —the grace of God through Christ Jesus—makes its recovery possible, indeed, certain, to all who believe; yea, that which the believer gains by grace exceeds by far what he had lost by sin. "Where sin abounded, grace did much more abound." Everything in creation is laid under contribution to illustrate and set forth the good which God has provided for those who seek him—his best gifts in this world, and in the world to come. All that man needs and desires; all the grace, and holiness, and freedom, and happiness, that can be participated in here and hereafter, are summed up in this word "good" as belonging to God, and setting forth what he is. In view of his gracious provision for man's deep necessity, God says, in his gospel to the perishing children of men, "O taste and see that the Lord is good: blessed is the man that trusteth in him."

But the multitude—oh, how wickedly and wilfully, in many, many cases! —turn a deaf ear to all that God has said concerning salvation and eternal life; and as if no voice had spoken, and no call had been addressed to them, they still ask, "Who will show us any good?" "Lovers of pleasure, more than lovers of God," is the best that can be said of the world's votaries; while of many it must be added, "Whose god is their belly, and whose glory is in their shame, who mind earthly things"! The Lord leaves men to realize what they have sought as their chosen portion. The story of Dives is literally true of many. Earth's "good things," abused for selfish ends, are followed by their total loss and endless retribution.

When men have selfishly, wickedly, wilfully, and repeatedly chosen the sinner's portion, though entreated to choose differently, and have persevered to the end in their evil ways—is it not in the nature of things, having respect to the claims of justice and the honour of outraged mercy, that the righteous anger of the Omniscient Judge should burn unquenchably? that those who would have none of him should be eternally deprived of that which they refused? Is it in accordance with what God has revealed of himself, his law, his government of the universe, and of his salvation by Christ Jesus, that the gulf between the lost and the saved should be so bridged over in a future state that there may be a passage from the one state to the other?

Suppose, for a moment, that we allow the thing may be possible, allow it for argument's sake; how could the *moral* change be effected? Or, first, let us ask, seeing they had finally rejected Christ, and counted him and his sacrifice as worthless things, how can the sins of earth, countless in number, and the deeper, blacker, more horribly blasphemous crimes of hell, be removed and purged away? Can the fires of perdition cleanse them? Suffering in this world, unless sanctified by the grace of God, makes the sinner more rebellious; and can we hope that in the world beneath the effect will be different? The notion of suffering cleansing the soul from sin may have a place in the deceptive theology of Rome, but it has no place in the Scriptures of truth; and to them is our appeal.

Retribution was the other characteristic of the future of those who die impenitent; that is, they will be rewarded according to their works. All the descriptions given of the "Great Assize" present to our view a tribunal established in justice and righteousness; a deliberate proceeding of judicial investigation. The books will be opened and examined, and every one dealt with according to his deeds. There will be no passionate wreaking of vengeance upon irritating adversaries, unexamined and untried. The Omniscient Judge will calmly investigate every character, action, and plea, seeing to the bottom of everything; for "all things are naked and opened unto the eyes of him with whom we have to do."

It is a fact clearly stated in Holy Scripture, that the general resurrection will precede the general judgment; so that judgment will proceed "according to the deeds done in the body." The bodies of the wicked as well as of the justified will be raised; and as soul and body sinned in concert, so soul and body will suffer the just retribution of a holy God. "Depart, ye cursed, into everlasting fire, prepared for the devil and his angels," is the doom which Christ himself will then pronounce on the finally impenitent: and as if to strike the mind with a deeper awe, and give additional assurance of the certainty of the threatened doom, he adds: "These shall go away into everlasting punishment." It must be noted that he uses the same word to denote the duration of punishment as he uses to denote the duration of heavenly happiness, and the same word which is used elsewhere in Holy Scripture to denote the duration of the divine existence.

The retribution which God will deal out to the wicked at the general judgment is nowhere said to be corrective, but penal: not a chastisement in order to repentance and amendment, but a righteous retribution. "Woe unto the wicked! it shall be ill with him: for the reward of his hands shall be given him." He shall have his true desert. Having sowed to the flesh, he shall reap accordingly. The forbearance which endured so long will now be at an end. The wicked "goes away," is "driven away," and "cast into hell." All these terms imply his entire abandonment to his merited doom, and his final expulsion from all hope of mercy.

Such punishment must needs be *without remedy*. Let us quietly read together two verses of Holy Writ, and see if we can discern the least crack or cranny in the thick walls of the prison, through which the least ray of hope can penetrate. "The Lord Jesus shall be revealed from heaven with his mighty angels, in flaming fire taking vengeance on them that know not God, and that obey not the gospel of our Lord Jesus Christ: who shall be punished with everlasting destruction from the presence of the Lord, and from the glory of his power; when he shall come to be glorified in his saints, and to be admired in all them that believe (because our testimony among you was believed) in that day." And if the punishment will be *without remedy*, it will also be *without end*. Even in this world, we cannot conform to the will of God, and render even imperfect obedience, unless by the aid of divine grace. But in hell grace reigns not. The impenitent have already refused mercy's aid, and rejected her all-availing plea—the blood of Jesus Christ, the Lamb of God. Therefore there is neither hope nor help for them, and the doom of the disobedient must be theirs for ever.

Does nature shudder at the sentence? Does reason demur to its execution? Let us remember that God is able to fulfil his threatenings, and has already executed judgment in part on the devil and his angels. Let us also call to mind a transaction infinitely greater than the plunging of apostate angels into the dungeon of eternal despair—we refer to the offering up of his dear Son in all the agonies of Gethsemane and Calvary, when he was made a curse for us, that he might redeem us from the curse of the law.

Reader, beware of speculating upon salvation for the impenitent after death! It comes of that spawn of unbelief which suggested the first act of disobedience. The gospel is plain enough that, if we reject Christ, there remaineth no more a sacrifice for sin; and we cannot be saved without a sacrifice. Do not tamper with the delusion. Do not risk your soul, nor your soul's peace. "He that believeth on the Son of God is not condemned; but he that believeth not is condemned already." Oh, I beseech you, delay not a day, an hour, a moment to seek God's favour and grace! "Be ye reconciled to God." "Believe on the Lord Jesus Christ, and thou shalt be saved."

> "Turn to Christ your longing eyes,
> View his bleeding sacrifice:
> See through him repentance given,
> Pardon, holiness, and heaven:
> Glorify the King of kings,
> Take the peace the gospel brings."

Spiritual Cuckoos.

IT is a well known fact in natural history that, whether too lazy to rear a family, or from an entire dislike to parental responsibilities, or afraid to be late for its summer holiday, the cuckoo drops its eggs in the nests of other birds. Another fact concerning it is not so well known. One would think that a young cuckoo, on finding itself an interloper in the nest, would, out of sheer gratitude, endeavour to make things comfortable all round. But it is not so. Being generally a stronger bird, and broader in the back than those in whose nest it has found a home, it requires more room, and generally gets it by *turning the others out* of the nest. In spite of protest on the young ones' part, that they are the proper owners of the nest, and of the parent birds that they built it for their offspring, the disagreeable cuckoo claims more than the children's share, and thus abuses its position. How suggestive in these times is such a fact! Is it not in full swing in many quarters? Here is a church, happy and useful, holding the doctrines of the gospel with a good conscience, having a pastor who delights to preach the Word that has been the saving of his own soul, to the manifest joy and prosperity of the people. Into their midst comes one who, at first, seems just like the rest. He is received with warm and affectionate greeting, and made at home with them. But presently there is a disturbance in the hitherto warm and happy family nest.

What is it? There are uncomfortable suspicions of being crowded, and some one wants more room. The question is somehow started—hangs about in the air as a whisper—as to the old-fashioned and out-of-date views of the pastor and some of the deacons. They actually believe the Bible to be inspired, and quote its sayings as though God had spoken them. They believe in miracles, have a strange notion that they are saved by sovereign grace, and that God meant to save them from all eternity, and certainly would do so; and they even dare to hold that eternal punishment is the doom of the impenitent. It is whispered that no intelligent man believes these things now, and—well, it is evident that the old peace is gone. The centre of the commotion is found to be the recently received brother; and the church is fortunate if it does not lose its best members, and perhaps its minister, while the cuckoo holds possession of the nest, in which he has no right to be. In his case there is real guilt, for he knew, or ought to have ascertained before he joined, the things most assuredly believed among them.

Sometimes the spiritual cuckoo gets into the pulpit. An earnest, gospel-loving church, served by a true and faithful minister, is called upon to choose a successor. One such case we have in mind. It is thought that the candidate will preach the same gospel as his predecessor, although with, perhaps, more culture, and so attract the young. He is elected to the pulpit. He serves the church a few years, and such is his wondrous progress along the lines of advanced thought, that one Sunday he announces from the pulpit, that he could no more preach the sermons he preached when he first came amongst the people, than he could wear the knickerbockers of childhood. Then why not leave the pulpit? Get out of the nest! No, let others go, the people who invited and supported him in those early years. "Ah!" said an aged deacon, with the tears rolling down his cheeks as he related the incident, "would God he would now give us some of the knickerbocker sermons!" Such men may preach what they like—it is a free country—but let them, in all conscience, build their own churches, and not fancy they have a perfect right to the pulpits and the churches that were built by men who detest their doctrine, if such shadowy teaching as theirs can be called by that name. Mr. Cuckoo, build your own nest, and hatch your own eggs in it, and none will complain.

And, lastly. A number of ministers meet in holy fellowship, so much agreed in heart and faith, that there is no question of writing down or formulating a creed, as they agree to work in hearty and loving co-operation. Words are used to designate their position which have but one meaning. For years the association does good work, and brings much happiness to its associates. And then there come in those who are entirely opposed, in their faith, to the early founders. They introduce new meanings to old words, and for a long time assert that they hold the truth as held by the original associates. The story is well known. The evangelical nest is greatly disturbed; and, alas! it is not those who cause the disturbance who leave, they are most tenacious of their hold on the nest others have built, but the original founders are compelled to turn out. Where is the honesty, where the manliness of the thing? Surely, if a man finds himself entirely out of sympathy and belief with those whom he has joined, his course is clear: he should *himself* leave, and leave the rightful owners in possession.

Even the cuckoo may teach useful lessons. H. W. C.

Notices of Books.

The Stockwell Reciter: a Collection of Old and New Favourites for the Home, the School, and the Band of Hope. Edited by VERNON J. CHARLESWORTH, Head Master of the Stockwell Orphanage. Passmore , and Alabaster.

MR. CHARLESWORTH'S selection is well made. The pieces are worth re-citing, and worth hearing. For six pence we have here a wealth of good reading for those who do not recite; while for those who aspire to oratory, the book will be most valuable as a practising ground for voice and gesture. All our readers should get the sixpenny part of this useful work.

The Preachers of Scotland from the Sixth to the Nineteenth Century. By W. G. BLAIKIE, D.D. T. and T. Clark.

A VALUABLE volume. The lectures before us are an able tribute to those who in Scottish pulpits served, not Scotland only, but all our Lord's kingdom on earth. The ministry of Columba, the earliest apostle of Christianity to Scotland, though not strictly within the limits proposed by the author, is a welcome prelude to the stirring and pathetic voices of later witnesses. That was a remarkable balancing of favours, if, as is believed by some, Patrick was Scotland's gift to Ireland, as Columba was Ireland's messenger to Scotland.

The ten centuries between the introduction of Christianity and the Reformation tell a sad story of decay and ruin of the church which had been raised upon evangelical foundations. Let us note well the fact that decline in missionary zeal ran parallel with decline in spirituality within the church. The flame of devotion must be kept bright upon the home altar in order that Christ's servants may bear the lighted torch to dark lands.

In Scotland, as in Germany, there were Reformers before the Reformation. Hamilton and Wishart prepared the way for Knox, as Huss for Luther. The Scotch forerunners were both bold and powerful preachers, and both became martyrs. This chapter in the history of the Scotch pulpit reads like the Acts of the Apostles. A wicked hierarchy joined hands with the civil authority to silence the messengers of the Lord. Is it strange that the struggle was fierce? Romish rites and ceremonies had stripped the early church of every shred of its evangelical power, and robbed it almost of life itself. Knox looked upon the mass as an abomination and rank idolatry, as in very truth it is;· and the fire shut up in his bones burst forth in devouring flames. Royalty trembled before the prophet of the Lord God, and Israel saw deliverance. Strong, and sometimes rough, as the Reformers and Covenanters were, we must not think that their preaching was all granite and gall: the tender grace of the gospel was a characteristic feature of their pulpit; some of them were masters of pathos. James Lawson, the spiritual son and successor of Knox, was never heard but with tears, both of repentance and joy. John Welsh, of Ayr, the son-in-law of Knox, had a heart of such overflowing tenderness that his preaching was wonderfully moving. It was he who kept his plaid at hand, and often rose at night to pray, because, as he said, "I have three thousand souls to answer for, and I know not how it is with many of them."

Men who subscribed their names in their own blood to solemn covenants against popery and prelacy valued the pure gospel. There were chosen men for trying times. One was Alexander Henderson, a leader among the Westminster Assembly divines; another was David Dickson, an eminent preacher, but even more remarkable as an expositor of the deep things of God; a third was Samuel Rutherford, who was singularly successful in setting forth the love and loveliness of Christ, both in his sermons and letters.

Four hundred of the flower of the Scotch clergy were ejected from their livings in 1662. Then began "the killing time." The wolves were abroad, and neither pastors nor flocks had safety. Then was the preaching full of the very essence of the gospel.

It seems strange that a recoil from this fervently evangelical spirit should take place in the next century, and that many of the clergy should lose their grip upon fundamental truths. No wonder that the power of the pulpit declined when preachers courted the favour of fashionable society, sought literary distinction, and dropped saving truths to discourse upon bare morals. Infidelity became widespread, drunkenness became common among the clergy, and morality greatly declined among the people. Then came the evangelical revival of the eighteenth century, with sound and earnest men at the front again, and the power of the pulpit felt as in earlier days.

The history of the Scottish pulpit has many lessons for modern preachers. Professor Blaikie wisely points them out. Perhaps none is more clear than this: that the gospel of Jesus Christ best supplies the needs of every age. No other remedy for social wrongs and disorders is so effective. There need be no fear of failure in the pulpit so long as the gospel is faithfully preached; but ministers who think that they must ever be telling some new thing may here see that nothing is so attractive as the old, old story of Jesus and his love. Oh, that Scotland may learn as well as teach the lesson of fidelity to the truth! We fear that even in her faithful churches an unhallowed leaven has begun its work.

Flashes from the Welsh Pulpit. Edited by the Rev. GWNORO DAVIES. With an Introductory Paper by the Rev. T. C. EDWARDS, D.D. Hodder and Stoughton.

HEREIN are many precious things from the Welsh mountains, and some rather ordinary gatherings. We are afraid that the collector's preface indicates coming evil for the Principality; but we are grateful that at present the old truth has sway, and novelties are not so highly esteemed as in England. This collection of good things will be useful to the preacher, and interesting to the reader. We subjoin a passage which sets forth a glorious truth:

"SALVATION IS OF GRACE ALONE."

"The high priest goes into the middle court, clad in long flowing garments, the bells attached to his skirt ringing at every movement he makes. Now, you say, he is prepared to go into the holiest of all, and appear before God? No, not yet. He must lay aside his gorgeous robe and his bells, and enter the sanctuary with nothing but the clean linen garment upon his flesh. No bells must ring before God. Everything must be silent there, that the blood may speak. Ring the bells of your good works in your family circle, and in all your spheres of influence; but beware of ringing them before God. All must keep silence there. The blood alone must speak. At the same time, if the bells don't ring in the middle court, the people will take for granted that the priest within the veil is dead."

The Least of all Lands: Seven Chapters on the Topography of Palestine in Relation to its History. By WILLIAM MILLER, C.I.E., LL.D. Blackie.

THIS work contains most instructive remarks upon events of Old Testament history, derived from personal examination of the sites upon which they took place. As a corrector of mistakes, and a setter forth of the great battles of the old times in a vivid manner, Dr. Miller has done good service to Bible students. But we take grave exception to his remarks upon our Lord's life, so far as we understand them. We do not read without painful emotion that Jesus Christ "did not fashion the framework of his life on the pattern that he wished. The ideal that he realized was meaner than the one he aimed at." Such language shocks us, and makes us feel that all the pleasure we had in reading the earlier pages is curdled into indignation. Whatever else may be said to honour our Lord, these lines ought not to have been written by the Principal of a Christian College.

The Biblical Illustrator; or, Anecdotes, Similes, Emblems, Illustrations, &c., &c., gathered from a wide range of Home and Foreign Literature, on the Verses of the Bible. Galatians, 1 vol.; Ephesians, 1 vol. By Rev. JOSEPH S. EXELL, M.A. Nisbet and Co.

NEVER were books so crowded with matter, pressed down, and compressed as by an hydraulic ram. Taken from all quarters, the comments are of varied value, making up a solid mass of expository thought such as can be found nowhere else in such profusion. Given discretion in their use, the contents of these volumes must be of the utmost value to working ministers with little money to buy books, and less time to search them. Of course, we do not endorse every extract contained in this omnium gatherum, but at 7s. 6d. each there is an absolutely unrivalled quantity for money, to say the very least. If anything, there is too much; but instead of finding fault at a failure of keen discrimination in selection, we marvel at the comprehensiveness of the collection. What a worker Mr. Exell is!

What is Man? His Origin, Life-history, and Future Destiny, as revealed in the Word of God. By J. ANDERSON, M.D. London: J. Nisbet.

A BULKY volume, beautifully edited! While we refuse to endorse all his expositions of Scripture, we cannot refrain from congratulating the venerable author upon the sincere pleasure, honest pride, and heartfelt gratitude with which he dedicated it to his "dear wife" on his seventy-sixth birthday, last September. More than fifty years have rolled by since he first piloted the product of his pen through the press in a scientific work that befitted his medical profession, and bespoke his faith at the same time in the wisdom that cometh down from above. That disquisition on "The Nervous System" has been long out of print; but we gather from an "advertisement" that the substance of it is condensed in chapter II. of the present treatise.

Here, then, we ought to have the photograph of a mind gilded with the "Golden Alphabet." Like the Author of the long Psalm, he professes to have found the words of God sweeter than honey to his taste, while the Prophecies have exerted such a fascination over him that he has *seemed to himself* to have "more understanding than all his teachers."

As a Protestant he holds the right of private judgment, with the inevitable proviso that it involves the duty of personal research. The original text of both Old and New Testaments he has scanned daily and diligently. More than that, on many a critical passage he has marked the little variations which occur in the readings by such a comparison of codices and uncials as might only appear interesting to a microscopic criticism. A vein of conscientious industry pervades his studies, for which no prejudice of our own would prompt us to stint an eulogium. When we notice, however, that his Eschatology follows in the wake of those who teach "conditional immortality" and its concomitants, proclaiming "a larger hope" and a future probation for those who quit this life unsaved; and when we hear talk of probabilities as if they were predictions of the Bible, we hoist the cone all round the coast, and wait with tremulous anxiety for a report of wrecks.

Sunday Letters to a Schoolboy. By E. L. MONTAGU. Nisbet.

A FAIRLY good little book. Our lads would like it better if the style were livelier. It is possible to be pious without being prosy even on Sundays.

Notes for Boys. By an Old Boy. Elliot Stock.

THE author of these notes is fond of aphorisms. If his youthful learners have an equal taste for laconics, they may find here piquant counsels on "Morals, Mind, and Manners." His "own son" for whom these pages were prepared, must have been decidedly a smart young fellow if he could follow the "old boy" in all his Latin and French phrases without the aid of one or more lexicons. Likely enough the "old boy" thought this himself when he put a parenthesis on the title-page—*sic*, "Notes for boys (*and their fathers*)." If the boys cannot make out a passage, they are to ask their fathers. Very likely!

Ripples in the Starlight: Additional Fragments of Sunday Thought and Teaching. By J. R. MACDUFF, D.D. Nisbet.

DR. MACDUFF's stream of thought has rippled in the twilight and in the moonlight, and now in the starlight; we look for its rippling in the sunlight. Ripple when it may, it is a pure stream, and long may it continue to flow! Our friend, who elsewhere has given the Church great loaves, here brings forth cracknels, and dainty cakes.

God and Nature. By Rev. N. CURNOCK, F.R.M.S. Woolmer.

MR. CURNOCK is a thoughtful and poetical writer, and frequently strikes out new and valuable thoughts; but we do not think there is quite so much in his writing as there seems to be. He is deep, but not full. He will yet be clearer in style, and then he will be more powerful; for he has evidently large resources of mind, and the will to use them for the truth's sake. Our verdict on this little work is—*Too many flowers, sweet-smelling flowers though they be.*

Christianity according to Christ. A series of papers. By JOHN MONRO GIBSON, D.D. Nisbet.

THIS volume contains much excellent and deep thought; and we know, of a surety, that our friend is always true to the gospel of the blessed God. If it were not for this assurance, we should be inclined to pick a bone, here and there, with him. He seems to us to have, in his mind's eye, certain ultra brethren, who, from ignorance or wilfulness, mis-state orthodox truth; and in the process of correcting them, he seems to be taking the loose side. We do not believe that he does so in the least degree; but he may easily enough be thought to do so. We could not endorse all that he has to say; and yet we feel sure that he thought it needful to say it, to remove out of the way those mis-statements which are the weak points against which adversaries direct their attacks when they mean to assail the truth itself. Though bound to say as much as this, we are none the less glad to have read so many good things from his choice pen.

The Form of the Christian Temple; being a Treatise on the Constitution of the New Testament Church. By THOMAS WITHEROW, D.D., LL.D. T. and T. Clark, Edinburgh.

A THOROUGHLY learned book upon Church Government, arguing for presbytery in opposition to prelacy. In almost all his statements, we are at one with Professor Witherow, and we think he defends his positions with great success. The dogma of apostolical succession he very effectually demolishes; it is the merest dream that ever visited a silly brain, and yet it holds thousands of sensible men beneath its power. That the Anglican Church can claim any such succession is seen to be impossible in the following sentences:—

"The way in which most people of intelligence will regard the matter is this: The Roman Church is either a true Church or a false Church. If a true Church, it was schismatical to separate from her; if a false Church, it was not possible for her to transmit a divine Commission. If the popes were not usurpers, but honestly performing the duties to which God called them, then it was sin in Anglicanism to withdraw its allegiance from papal rule; if, on the other hand, the pope is the man of sin, sitting in the temple of God, he must be Antichrist; and a commission to preach Christ, which is derived from Antichrist, is not much to boast of. In either case, what the pope gave, the pope can take away; and in this case he has taken away."

The boastful claims of certain high churchmen, which they put forth when they denounce all dissent from their community, are sarcastically stated by Bishop Hoadley.

"As for us of the Church of England, we have bishops in a succession as certainly uninterrupted from the apostles as your Church could communicate to us; and on this bottom we have a right to separate from you; but no flesh living has any right to differ or separate *from us*."

Those who are studying church government cannot afford to overlook this thoroughly able work. If they master this volume, they will hardly require anything else.

The True Psalmody; or, The Bible Psalms the Church's only Manual of Praise. Edinburgh: J. Gemmell.

FROM a forensic point of view we may admire the argument of an able *defence*, when we are quite sure that the verdict will go in an opposite direction. Here we have an instance. Perhaps this is the best book that was ever compiled in favour of the exclusive use of the Scotch metrical version of the Psalms of David, as a complete manual of praise. No other, it is alleged, ought to be used in public or in private worship. Paraphrases are poisonous; hymns are heresy. The good Presbyterians of Philadelphia, U.S., published this treatise thirty years ago. It is re-published now for the special benefit, we presume, of their brethren in Belfast. If not a lively oracle, it is at least a learned oration. To repeat a scratch proverb: "*Credula res amor est*"; or to adopt the free translation of an old author, for the sake of its aptness: "The man who loves is easy of belief."

Conquests of the Cross. Part I. (including Presentation Plate). Price 7d. Cassell and Co.

THIS opens well, and promises to be a grand advocate for missions. We trust the work will be read by the millions. The engravings are of fine quality.

An Old Testament Commentary for English Readers. Edited by C. J. ELLICOTT, D.D. Cassell and Co.

ELLICOTT'S Commentary stands very high. Our own opinion of it has greatly risen since its first issue. The publication in parts is now far advanced, even to the Psalms; but it is not too late for our readers to obtain it in bound volumes, or in parts, if they prefer it in that form.

Anecdotes on Bible Texts: St. Mark. By J. L. NYE. Sunday School Union.

A GOOD shilling's-worth. Mr. Nye is now nearly through the New Testament. Teachers with these collections of anecdotes ought never to be dull in their talks with their classes.

The Path of Wealth; or, Light from My Forge. A Discussion of God's Money Laws. By a Blacksmith. With an Introduction by Rev. A. CARMAN, D.D. Brantford, Ontario: Bradley, Garrepon, and Co.

A CAPITAL book upon tithing and systematic giving. The subject is handled in a lively and earnest manner. We cannot say that the portrait looks much like a blacksmith, neither is the style of the book such as to sustain that character; and yet we do not doubt that the author is a very superior son of the forge. The work is got up in an original, not to say homely, style; but we should like to see it in thousands of Christian homes. Should the principle of regular systematic tenth-giving be taken up by all Christians, *as it ought to be,* we should hear no more of bazaars and entertainments, for the treasury of the Lord would be filled in a manner more pleasing to God, and more honourable to his church. Our friends in *the Dominion* should not let this book be overlooked: it will do them great service if they scatter it widely.

The Way Back. By JAMES L. STANLEY. Religious Tract Society.

VERY evangelical and spiritual. The rising steps which lead from conviction to consecration are well described, and an earnest effort is made to help the weak ones in the ascent. The work is issued in very neat form.

Words of Life: Sermons on Christian Doctrine, Experience, and Duty. By DAVID MERSON, M.A. Dickenson.

THESE seem to be good sermons, sound and practical. We rejoice that the English Presbyterian pulpit can show so good an average of excellence; for we suppose these discourses to be very near the general level of the body to which the preacher belongs; and this is saying no small thing.

David: the Man after God's own Heart. A Book for Young Men. By Rev. H. E. Stone. Nisbet and Co.

GOOD practical observations, intended to promote faith and holiness. A thoughtful comment upon a great and chequered life. Mr. Stone has read carefully, and has written admirably. Believers will read with profit what he has written with prayer.

David: his Life and Times. By Rev. W. J. DEANE, M.A. ["Men of the Bible" Series]. Nisbet and Co.

THIS is a more learned work than the former, and will meet the demands of quite another class of readers. But we draw no comparisons, each is good in its own line. One could hardly get better change for half-a-crown than this well-condensed, instructive, and suggestive epitome of the events of a right royal life.

Memorable Bible Nights: Sunday Afternoon Talks in the Chapel of the Children's Home. By NEHEMIAH CURNOCK, F.R.M.S. Methodist Sunday School Union.

YOU who want a series of holy talks to the young should get this, for it will put you on a tram-line, and you can engineer your own cars by the help of it. The work is specially well done, and is worthy of the audience to which it was addressed, namely, the officers and children of Mr. Stephenson's Home, and a number of well trained children who dropped in.

Real Life Stories. Illustrated. Alfred Holness.

CAPITAL! Just the thing to give to the careless, with earnest prayer for their conversion. The pictures will attract, and the stories impress, and the cost is only one-and-six. Some of the stories brought out for a penny are written by an excellent member of our own College Conference, with the view of taking men from evil novels.

Short Biographies for the People. By Various Writers. Religious Tract Society.

A SELECTION from the series of short biographies already issued. In this list we have lives of Reformers. First-rate. Cheap and good.

Barton Memorials: Works of Mr. Samuel Deacon. Published under the direction of Mr. THOMAS COOK. Elliot Stock.

THIS literature deserved reprinting, but it needed a helping hand to secure the publishers from loss; and this the venerable Thomas Cook has supplied, very much to his own honour. Mr. Deacon's writings do not rise into the highest class, but they were on a level with the understandings and tastes of those to whom he addressed himself, and were calculated to do them real good. We trust that, with a new lease of life, the usefulness of these books will be repeated.

In the Far East: Letters from Geraldine Guinness. Edited by her SISTER. Morgan and Scott.

WHAT pathos there is in this plea for China! A consecrated woman here tells her experience, and that of her comrade, and tells it in bravely modest language. She has upon her heart the pressure of the awful fact that a million of people die every month in China without the knowledge of salvation. She is on fire with this burning fact. She longs to bring to them the Word of life; and her friend, Miss Read, has the same soul-hunger. It seems a strangely cruel thing to these earnest young ladies that so many of us should stay at home, and work over and over again the fields which are of such slender acreage, while boundless leagues of our Lord's

estate have never felt the gospel plough, nor received a handful of seed. May these pleadings be prevalent in the church of Christ!

The book is handsomely brought out, and exceedingly well edited. If it charms others as much as it has edified *us*, it will have a great sale, and will be of the utmost service to Chinese missions.

The Children's Champion and the Victories he Won. Nelson and Sons.

VERY good indeed. "The righteous shall be in everlasting remembrance." Shaftesbury deserves to be the subject of many pens and pencils. This pretty volume is chaste in its illustrations, handsome in its binding, and elegant in every part of its get-up. A suitable wreath to be laid upon the tomb of the beloved earl.

Andrew Gillon; a Tale of the Scottish Covenanters. By JOHN STRATHESK. Edinburgh: Oliphant and Ferrier.

A TRUE tale of the Covenanters exceedingly well told by a writer who has a charming pen. Well worth the shilling asked for it. Be sure to buy it.

The Autobiography of a Soldier in India, with his Conversion or Call by Grace and Subsequent Experience and Call to the Ministry. By THOMAS WITTS, Minister of the Strict Baptist Church, Sydney, N.S.W. Part I. F. Kirby, 17, Bouverie Street.

THOSE who belong to "the Gospel Standard" company may enjoy this bit of biography, but we hardly think that any one else will do so. This first portion is the journal of a soldier who has had terrible conviction of sin, and many soul conflicts, but holds firmly to predestination, and that side of truth which goes therewith. All the other part of the Word of God is outside the boundary of his faith, and he severely censures those who receive it. He is very hard upon "the Brethren," "Temperance men," "Arminians," and others who are not up to his mark.

More Precious than Gold. By JEANNIE CHAPPELL. Partridge and Co.

A STORY which rises above the common level, and is sure to win attention.

Our Little Dots. Religious Tract Society.

A SPLENDID book for the times. The cover, with its silk and satin, beats all former attempts at pretty binding.

The Juvenile: a magazine for the young. London Missionary Society. Snow.

THIS little monthly strikes us as having much vivacity about it. The engravings are novel and striking. The volume for 1888 is one shilling.

The Homilist. Edited by Rev. DAVID THOMAS, D.D., and Rev. J. J. S. BIRD, B.A. Vol. LIX. Houlston.

THERE are difficulties connected with a double editorship, but in this case they are softened, for Dr. Thomas writes with righteous indignation against the degeneracy of the age, and Mr. Bird inculcates old-fashioned doctrine with all his might. We are glad to see this magazine upon the right side. It is sure to lose many of its former purchasers; but we trust new ones are forthcoming.

The Homiletic Magazine. Vol. XIX. Nisbet.

THIS is a rich volume, both for continuous expositions and for sermon outlines. One needs to discriminate, and leave out here and there that which is not up to the mark; but so far as we can see, this is a help which ministers may safely use, and gather from it most valuable hints in the composing of their sermons.

Old Jonathan. Collingridge.

A LIVELY magazine, with a clear gospel ring about it.

Our Own Magazine. Published by the Children's Special Service Mission, 13, Warwick Lane.

THIS magazine has an immense circulation, and it deserves it; for it goes straight at the mark, and aims at the spiritual good of its young readers.

The Child's Companion. Vol. for 1888. Religious Tract Society.

OUR old friend grows better and better, and its dress surpasses all we have ever seen. We also heartily recommend *The Cottager and Artisan.*

Horner's Stories for the People. Third Series. W. B. Horner and Sons.

HORNER AND SONS have tried, with popular stories of a high moral and religious tone, to cut out the vicious catchpennies which are depraving our boys and girls. They have gained an immense circulation for some of their stories, and so far they must have been successful, since a market for the good leaves so much less sale for the bad. In a bright cover, twelve of the stories are issued for one shilling. We do not care for such literature for our own perusal; but so far as it supplants the filthy fiction of the period we wish a large success to its spirited publishers.

Practical Essay-writing, for the use of Candidates for Competitive, Qualifying, and other Examinations. By A. W. HOLMES-FORBES, M.A. Sonnenschein.

THIS is a very sensible, useful, practical treatise. Young men who wish to write well should not fail to read this most wise and instructive handbook. It costs one shilling and sixpence; but to the young essayist it will be worth much more, if he carefully follows its directions.

Saved by Love. A Story of London Streets. By EMMA LESLIE. Nelson.

TELLS how the little orphan child of a very poor Christian woman was led to consort with one of the wildest and worst girls in the street — "Street Rubbish" she styled herself. How this semi-savage was Christianized by the patient love and simple Bible words of her little friend is well told.

Baptist Hymn Writers and their Hymns. By HENRY S. BURRAGE, D.D. Portland, Maine, U.S.A. London: Marlborough and Co.

A VERY interesting work. We marvel how Dr. Burrage could make so much out of Baptist hymn makers. Certainly, all that diligence and affection could accomplish has been wrought by his facile pen. Baptists should not neglect to purchase this portly volume. We hardly think that C. H. Spurgeon deserved a portrait and a memoir *as a hymn-writer:* he has not often figured in that capacity, and may be forgiven for the little he has in that way inflicted on the public.

Robert Aske: a Story of the Reformation. By ELIZA F. POLLARD. Partridge and Co.

THE story of Robert Aske, the leader of "The Pilgrimage of Grace," who was executed at York, in 1537, for the part he took in that insurrection, is thrillingly interesting, whether we accept the author's account of his secret marriage, by Cardinal Pole, to a daughter of the Earl of Essex, as historically correct, or not. The story embraces a miniature biography of Tyndale, and an account of "the ups and downs which attended his efforts for the publication of the Bible"; for as of "The Word made flesh," so of the inspired Word, it might have been said, "They seek the young child to destroy it." The book—a handsome volume for three-and-six—is full of stirring incident, and wise observations on the events of the period, and will greatly enhance the writer's reputation.

Higher Up. By NELLIE HELLIS. Religious Tract Society.

"A LITTLE child shall lead them," is the appropriate motto of this ingenious story. It is not altogether a child's book, though the central figure is a little gentleman who takes an omnibus ride in search of his mother, who had gone "higher up"—to heaven—a few days before. His strange talk to the old 'bus conductor sets that worthy thinking about his last journey, and how it will fare with him when death stops him.

The Christmas Child, and *Only a Dog.* By HESBA STRETTON. Religious Tract Society.

Two stories precisely what you would expect from the pen that wrote *Jessica's First Prayer.* They are very short, very sweet, and, at sixpence, very cheap.

Following Heavenward; or, the Story of Alfred Reid. By PANSY. Nelson and Sons.

"PANSY" books need no commendation in America: proprietors of religious periodicals are offering them as "premiums for subscribers." *Following Heavenward* is by far the best of those we have yet seen. It is the experience of a Christian lady with a class of roughs, or rowdies; and judging from the descriptions we have read of the New York article, our home-grown rough is "nowhere" in comparison. Mrs. Roberts needed divinely-inspired tact, inventiveness, love, and patience in dealing with these incorrigibles; and that these were liberally given in answer to prayer is evident in every one of the telling instances recorded. The book is full of stimulus and suggestiveness to Christian workers, and should be so to "out-of-workers."

The Little Woman in Grey. Scenes and Incidents in Home Mission Work. By CHARLES R. PARSONS. Stirling: Drummond's. London: Partridge.

As delightful a book of experience in the gospel harvest-field as the "Pansy" book just noticed, and much on the same lines. Coming from Drummond's, we need not say that there is the clear ring of sound gospel truth in it.

Among the Turks. By V. L. CAMERON, C.B., D.C.L., Commander, Royal Navy. Thomas Nelson and Sons.

WELL done, Commander Cameron! You convey to the boys a world of information in such a form that they must take it in. You are a master magician, and you use your art well. Don't draw the long-bow more than you can help. For illustrations this is a volume in Nelson's best style.

Oliver's Old Pictures; or, the Magic Circle. By EMMA MARSHALL. Nisbet and Co.

THE words "Second Edition," on the title-page, are good evidence that some connoisseurs have put an exceptional value on *Oliver's Pictures.* We are not much struck with the story; but then, we have had to devour such quantities of story-teller's sweets, that probably our palate is out of order.

The King's Daughters. By EMILY S. HOLT. John F. Shaw and Co.

MISS HOLT always writes what we can heartily recommend. We are told, by those who read carefully, that there is some careless writing in this story; and we do not wonder that it should be so, when one pen produces so very much. Miss Holt's writing is all well meant, and of good quality.

The People of the Pilgrimage. An Expository Study of the "Pilgrim's Progress" as a book of Character. Second Series: Helpers, False Pilgrims, &c. By Rev. J. A. KERR BAIN. Hodder and Stoughton.

ANOTHER good book. Mr. Kerr Bain appreciates the Dreamer's Allegory, and looks lovingly at its moving characters. Every true Bunyanite will rejoice that such a commentator upon our great author has arisen: a man who is himself almost an allegorist, and, therefore, drops into the Bunyan line of things. As he proceeds with his writing, Mr. Bain takes fire, and brightens in thought and style. His two volumes make up an exposition of "Pilgrim's Progress" second to none. They cost six shillings each, and are worth it. Quiet readers, who enjoy a suggestive book at the fireside, will take much pleasure in these two sets of lectures.

A Short Life of Christ for Old and Young. By CUNNINGHAM GEIKIE, D.D. Hatchards.

THIS is not an abridgment of Dr. Geikie's great work, but quite a new one. In our judgment, no one has ever written a satisfactory "Life of Christ," and nobody will ever do so. The evangelists will ever be the only worthy chroniclers of the Lord's career. Still, among those who have done well, we give the preference to Dr. Geikie; his book is much more reliable than that of Farrar, and far more full of teaching than any other we have ever perused. We do not profess to have read through this shorter "Life of Christ," but we have cut into the book in many places, and have always struck upon something excellent. It seems to us to be condensed, full, plain, devout, and in every way instructive. Those who cannot buy a larger work may be well content with this.

On the Book of the Prophet Daniel. Brief Comments. "Christian Commonwealth" Publishing Company.

PUTTING our paper-knife here and there into this book, we have come across many passages containing excellent teaching. The book is well condensed in its historic portions, and useful lessons are drawn from the prophet, which thoughtful men and devout students of the sacred Word will know how to estimate. We cannot here attempt to go into the merits of the author's impressions as to the relation of the wonderful prophecy of Daniel to present-day questions; nor are we prepared to fix the exact meaning and reference of all the passages quoted by the author; but we commend to our readers the prayerful study of Daniel's own book, together with all the other prophetical books, each of which exhibits some special side of the truth which the Holy Spirit has revealed for our benefit. *All* Scripture is given for our instruction, and therefore all should be studied. We should not neglect any part of the divine Word.

Every Morning: First Thoughts for First Hours. By JOSEPH PARKER, D.D. Charles Burnett and Co.

VERY Parkeresque. We do not think that this book will cut out Jay, or Hawker, or Mason; but there are many who will enjoy it, and be edified by it. It is exposition, meditation, prayer: in fact, many good and striking things combined. We like it better than the doctor's usual productions. It is original in method and in general style, as might have been expected from the author's individuality.

Elijah the Prophet and *Daniel the Beloved.* By W. M. TAYLOR, D.D. Charles Burnet and Co.

OUR esteemed friend, Dr. W. M. Taylor, has a genius for Bible Biography. He makes his characters fascinating, but not by what he heaps upon them. He goes deep, searches all the literature of his subjects, and brings out of the inspired narrative that which charms the reader. Here we have Elijah and Daniel, but aforetime we have had Joseph, David, Moses, Paul, and Peter. Any one of these can be had for 3s. 6d., and we very cordially recommend their purchase. Young men will meet with no modern nonsense here; but they will find a noble intellect, consecrating all its wealth of originality and acquirement to the cause of God and truth, and therein honouring itself and benefiting men.

Miller Manning; or, A Story of Cornish Life. By MATTHEW FORESTER. Bible Christian Book Room.

THIS shilling book must become popular, for it is the story of a real live man. Common sense and uncommon piety were the main characteristics of Walter Manning, the miller. He had his own way of doing things, and it was straightforward and full of force. Lovers of true stories, in contradistinction to fiction, will find a refreshing feast in these pages. We extract a bit of a sermon, and a specimen of his sensible advice:—

"It was quickly published throughout the town that 'Miller Manning,' of whom they had heard so much, was the preacher that day. In the evening the chapel was greatly thronged. His text was Isaiah xxv. 6: 'And in this mountain shall the Lord of hosts make unto all people a feast of fat things, a feast of wines on the lees, of fat things full of marrow, of wines on the lees well refined.' 'Religion is something to eat,' was his opening sentence. 'There is a reality about it. It is satisfying. Whoever goes to a feast and is not satisfied, is not a proper person to be there. Something is the matter. He is either unwell, and can't eat; or he is sulky, and won't eat. 'Religion,' he continued, 'is something not only for the mind to understand, but for the soul to live upon. A lot of people, nowadays, are very knowing, and talk fluently about doctrines and creeds; but the enjoyment of Christ is better than all the disputations in the world. Who would be guest at a feast merely to *talk about* the fat things and dainties? There be many deep mysteries about religion, and it is very profitable to meditate upon them, and to talk about them; but we must not allow the desire to fathom the deep things of God to deprive us of the marrow and fatness of his glorious gospel. GOD maketh the feast. You would do a foolish thing were you to refrain from eating because you did not know the art of the cook and confectioner. The guests are not required to know all that. Now here is pardon and peace—will you have them? As I was coming on last evening (I did part of the journey yesterday, 'cause the "merciful man is merciful to his beast"), I overtook a young man on his way home to his parents, after three months' absence. I found he had been in the company of unbelievers; for when I inquired if he was converted, he said, "Ah, the Bible! the Bible! There's a bone in the Bible I can't swallow." "Well," said I, "to be sure there is. And what of that? You are going home to spend Sunday, and you expect father will have dinner for his dear boy. But how father would be surprised to hear you say, 'Ah, father, none of that leg of mutton for me—there's a bone in it I cannot swallow!'"

"WALTER'S CURE FOR A GOSSIPING NEIGHBOUR.

"One of his class sought his advice in the trouble which is common enough in country villages, viz., newsing neighbours, who are not 'keepers at home,' but busy-bodies in other men's matters. The good woman—Jane Parsons—was anxious to be at peace with all; and particularly wished to be on good terms with those who lived near. But Agnes Saundry was such a great news-bag, that her calls on Jane were 'neither few, nor far between.' Nor did she appear to 'know the way out when once she got in.' Jane found Agnes's conversation both unprofitable and disagreeable; for she made so free with other people's names. This made Jane unhappy; so much so that she dreaded Agnes's coming. She resolved to lay the matter before her leader, who was not long in prescribing a remedy. 'Jane,' said he, 'keep your family Bible on the table, and, when she has been in the house long enough, ask her to read a chapter, or a psalm, and pray with you.' Jane followed this excellent advice. 'Agnes!' said Jane, 'you are a good scholar. I wish you would read a chapter, or psalm, and pray with me; it might do both of us good.' Agnes excused herself on the ground that she was *very busy*. She would gladly do so another time when she could stay. We need scarcely say that Jane had no further cause to complain of Agnes's gossiping in her house."

The Holland Road Pulpit, Brighton. Talks with Men, Women, and Children. By Rev. DAVID DAVIES. Stock.

MR. DAVIES, of Brighton, is publishing his sermons at a penny weekly. This is rather a bold venture for a provincial town; for even London penny pulpits do not live long, as a rule. Our friend is so bright and fresh that he may survive where others expire; at any rate, he has our best wishes, for we found him true to the gospel when others fought against it.

Flora's Feast: a Masque of Flowers. Penned and Pictured by WALTER CRANE. Cassell and Co.

WALTER CRANE is, in this instance, a poet with his pencil. This "Masque of the Flowers" is beyond description delicious. Our favourites of the garden here live before us in human, superhuman form, and charm us with their beauty. This is a crown's worth of delight.

Notes.

FRIENDS will have noticed the anxiety of the public press to put us into some ecclesiastical position which they can understand. To be the pastor of a church of Christ is enough for us; but it seems to them that we must join some one of the great religious communities: one day it is the Presbyterian, and the next the Episcopalian. Meanwhile, nothing has been said or done by us indicating any alteration in the position we have always held as to doctrine and church government. *When* we make a change, our friends will not need to learn it from the secular press: that *when* will not, probably, occur in this century, nor in the next. It does not yet dawn upon some minds that to quit a society like *the Baptist Union* involves no change in our position or sentiments. Baptist ministers are pastors of separate churches, which may associate with other churches, or cease to associate with them, as they judge best; but the minister and the church are not dependent upon the associations they may choose or decline. We are in fellowship with all the churches of our Lord Jesus which hold the truth, but have never entertained the thought of changing this way or that. Certainly we never dreamed of entering the Church of England.

The Baptist Union President, Dr. Clifford, took one of a series of Sunday afternoon addresses at South Place, Finsbury, a chapel which belongs to a people who are something more, or worse, than Unitarian. He figures with Messrs. Voysey and Picton, and others of the exceedingly broad school; and this not merely in his private capacity, but the bills are made clearly to state that he is President of the Baptist Union. This chapel is adorned with tablets, bearing the names of Moses, Voltaire, *Jesus*, Paine, Zoroaster, &c. The blasphemous association of our Lord with Thomas Paine and Voltaire creates an indescribable feeling in a Christian mind, and makes us wonder how a man, professing to be a servant of the Lord Jesus, could associate himself with such a place. Well might the Union resent our complaints against its more obscure wanderers, when its President, before he closed his year of office, would thus publicly associate himself with the deniers of our Lord's divinity. Has the body of Baptists over which this gentleman presides become so easy-going and docile that it will by its silence endorse the action of its President? Is it really so, that to preserve their confederacy any amount of looseness will be tolerated? We do not see that anything worse can be invented than that which the governing party either condones or admires. On the "Down-Grade" the train travels very fast: another station has been passed. What next? And what next?

We would like to agree with one who says that the bulk of our church-members love the old gospel; but we are not quite sure of it. If there were so general a soundness in the rank and file, would they quietly endure the abounding errors of the pulpits, and the babyish amusements with which congregations are being drenched? We fear the plague is among the people as well as among the priests. Yet, surely, there must be some who will fling aside the dastard love of peace, and speak out for our Lord, and for his truth. A craven spirit is upon many, and their tongues are paralyzed. Oh, for an outburst of true faith and holy zeal!

In *The Sunday School Chronicle*, of April 12, occurs an editorial note, which concludes as follows:—"Almost all writers now recognize the *human* element in the Bible, and see that this brings in human infirmity in matters of detail. We had a letter from a friend the other day, and there were several mistakes of spelling in it, but the letter quite fully conveyed to us our friend's thought. And if there are some inexactnesses, and even some mistakes, in the Bible, it carries to us, nevertheless, the mind and will of God. A lamp may give light to the feet on a dark night, even if the tin is a little bent in, and one of the panes is cracked."
Is the Sunday School Union going to teach our youth that the Bible is like an old

cracked lantern? To this we call the attention of those who are charged with the superintendence of the Union literature. Surely there are members of the Committee who cannot allow such teaching to pass unchallenged.

The Pastor has been sitting at the Tabernacle every Tuesday to see those who wished to confess the Lord Christ, and a large addition has been made to the church each month. The two months have yielded one hundred and forty two who have been actually enrolled, besides others who are waiting till they can come and receive the right hand of fellowship. This number is equal to many a church.

On *Monday evening, March* 25, the annual meeting of the TABERNACLE SUNDAY-SCHOOL was held in conjunction with the prayer-meeting. A number of the scholars sang some of their hymns very sweetly, and prayer was presented by the superintendent, Mr. Pearce, and several of the teachers. Mr. Wagstaff, the secretary, read the annual report, which stated that there are 102 teachers and officers, and 1,422 scholars, 141 of whom are church-members, 37 having been received during the past year. £150 has been raised for home and foreign missions during the year, in addition to £50 from Mr. Wigney's class for Mr. Easton, in China. The report gave interesting information about the various branches of the work, all of which appear to be in a healthy condition, except the library, and for that we have now provided, by the generous contributions of friends at the Tabernacle. Addresses upon Sunday-school work were delivered by Pastors C. H. Spurgeon, and David Davies, of Brighton. Our friends will like to know that this relates to the Home School only: the children in all our Sunday-schools, added together, nearly reach 8,000 in number. God be thanked for this blessed agency!

On *Monday evening, April* 1, a number of brethren, who were about to sail for China, in connection with the CHINA INLAND MISSION, came to the Tabernacle prayer-meeting, and so gave additional interest to the gathering. One of them was Mr. G. A. J. Huntley, a student in the Pastors' College, who spoke of the benefit he had received in that institution, and of his joy in going to the foreign mission-field. Other brethren told how the Lord had led them to give themselves to this work; and one friend, who is at home for rest after several years' service in China, gave a very graphic description of his experiences in that strange land. Several petitions on behalf of foreign missions were offered, and the Pastor prayed for each of the missionaries individually, and bade them farewell. At the close of the meeting, a number of believers put on Christ by being baptized on profession of their faith, as there were so many candidates

that it was necessary to administer the ordinance on one Monday and three Thursday evenings during the month.

The Pastor's heart, and the hearts of all his people, go lovingly forth to the China Inland Mission, which we regard as one of the Lord's most powerful instruments for gathering together his chosen from among that vast mass of human beings.

On *Monday evening, April* 15, the new members who had been received into the Tabernacle church during the past quarter were invited to meet the pastors and officers at tea. The time was inconvenient for several who wished to be present, but out of the one hundred and eighty-seven entitled to come, over a hundred were in attendance. After tea, short addresses upon the privileges and responsibilities of church-members were given by the pastors and Mr. William Olney, and by this means much useful information was conveyed, and the young members were made to feel at home in their new relationship. Our desire is that all who join the church may do so intelligently, with full resolve to be true working members of the community. Church-membership is far too lightly treated nowadays. Where it is so easy to come, it is equally easy to go; and people pop in and out of the churches, and do not give themselves heartily to them as once they did.

At the prayer-meeting, in the Tabernacle, there was a large attendance, and an earnest spirit of supplication prevailed. Mr. Harrison, one of our College evangelists, gave us interesting incidents which had occurred in his work in Australia and England. This very able brother is prepared to labour in congregations which need an extra worker for the ingathering of undecided ones. For this service he is peculiarly fitted.

Another box of books from C. B. has arrived. The contents will be given to a poor country minister, as requested by the donor.

OLD TUNES.—Will all lovers of the old tunes note that, on *Tuesday evening, June* 4, we shall have a special gathering at the Tabernacle, when Mr. Courtnay and his friends will help us to praise the Lord by singing a number of the fugal tunes mentioned in our review last month? Full particulars will be duly announced.

COLLEGE.—The following students have accepted pastorates:—Mr. G. Curtis, at Sheerness; Mr. G. A. Miller, at Rochester; and Mr. C. Stanley, at Bouverie Road, Stoke Newington. Mr. D. Tait, who has been for some time preaching at Millom, Cumberland, has settled there. Mr. C. Boyall is leaving the College, and holding services in connection with the Evangelization Society.

Mr. G. W. Ball has sailed for the United States. We commend him to brethren there.

Mr. J. O'Neill Campbell is removing from Sussex Street, Brighton, to Portslade-by-Sea; Mr. G. J. Knight, from Weymouth, to Newbury; and Mr. A. Mills, from Chester, to St. Mary's Gate, Derby. May the divine blessing rest upon them in their new spheres!

We earnestly entreat the very special prayers of all the Lord's people on behalf of the Conference, which is to commence on May 6; and we trust that, at the supper on May 8, we shall have fresh evidence of our friends' determination to help us in our important work of training preachers of the old gospel. Our sorrow, arising out of the breaches in our ranks, would crush us did we not know that the like has happened aforetime in other ages of the church; but the Lord has appeared and vindicated his own cause. He will again. However many may forsake the glorious gospel, the Lord will abide by those who are faithful to his unchanging truth!

EVANGELISTS.—During the first half of the past month, *Messrs. Fullerton and Smith* have been at the Conference Hall, Mildmay Park. Great crowds have attended the services; and the many earnest Christian workers, who have helped the evangelists, have met with large numbers who were either seeking the Saviour, or rejoicing in having found him. Next month we may be able to give fuller particulars of the mission, and also of the services at Devonshire Square and Salters' Hall Chapels. This month our brethren go to Dr. Barnardo's Mission Hall, "The Edinburgh Castle."

Mr. Burnham was at Hungerford Congregational Chapel during the first half of April. His health has been so unsatisfactory that he must take a season of rest before he undertakes further missions.

Mr. Harmer had successful services at Tewkesbury, where his help was heartily welcomed by Pastor A. Graham. He afterwards went, with *Mr. Chamberlain*, to Lydgate, Todmorden. Pastor W. L. Stevenson writes:—"We thank God for the rich blessing attending the services of Messrs. Harmer and Chamberlain, and rejoice that such men have been raised up and sent forth in connection with the work of the Metropolitan Tabernacle. It would be a grand thing if your evangelists could visit all the churches annually; it would result, I am sure, in an increase of spiritual life, of religious fervour, and of the membership of the churches, as well as an increase of brotherly love."

Pastor M. Cumming writes concerning *Mr. Harrison's* visit to Bury St. Edmund's:— "Many gathered to hear the gospel, which was most powerfully preached by our brother; and the abiding results are manifested not only in souls converted, but in deepened interest in Christ's work, and in enlarged congregations." Pastor J. T. Mateer sends a glowing account of the mission at Vernon Chapel, Pentonville. He says:—"I have much confidence in Mr. Harrison's work, for he does not deal in mere sentiment, or appeal only to the feelings of his audience; he convinces their judgment, and aims at their conscience, the Word of God being the quiver from which he draws the arrows of truth. It would have rejoiced your heart to have seen the joy of the new converts at the praise-meeting held specially for their benefit. Altogether, it was a glorious mission, and we are expecting to receive quite a number of members as the result of it."

In addition to his work at Farnworth, and Radcliffe, Lancashire, *Mr. Carter* has held a mission at St. Helens, concerning which Pastor J. Cottam sends us a very cheering report. Mr. Carter has just issued No. 2 of *The Quarterly Pioneer*, and he has also published *The Pioneer Hymn and Tune Books* for use in mission work. He judges that this small collection would suffice for churches at their first formation till they could afford something larger.

Mr. Parker has recently conducted missions at Aylsham, Norfolk; and Melbourne, Derbyshire; and in each place many were brought to decision for Christ. He has since been at Old Chesterton, Cambridgeshire.

We expect to have all our evangelists with us at the Conference, when their reports of what the Lord has done through them will give additional interest to the meetings, and brethren will be able to secure their services for any dates they have at liberty.

ORPHANAGE.—A good number of friends attended the *Collectors' Meeting, on Friday, April 5*, and enjoyed a very pleasant evening. Tea was provided at five o'clock, after which the guests roamed over the various departments, and were much pleased with the appearance of the children, and the arrangements made for their comfort. The President was present, and, as usual, was beset by the children, all of whom were eager to shake hands with him, and to hear his cheery voice. The programme for the meeting was full of interest. Several pieces were performed with the bells, the children sang splendidly, and the recitations were first-rate—for matter and delivery. One, written by the head-master, entitled, "Oh, what a mistake, to be sure!" caused a good deal of merriment. It is published in "The Stockwell Reciter." Addresses were given by Pastors F. H. Smith, of Peckham, and G. D. Hooper, of Hendon; and Benjamin Clarke, Esq., secretary to the Home for Little Boys, Farningham. The President was greatly cheered, and expressed the hope that the collectors would persevere in their good work. We should be glad to see the number of collectors largely increased, for it needs £10,000 a year in free-will offerings to provide for the Orphanage. Collecting-boxes and books may be had on application to the Secretary, Stockwell Orphanage, Clapham Road.

On *Friday evening, April* 12, the President again visited the Orphanage, in order to preside at the annual distribution of prizes in connection with the Orphanage Sunday-school. This was an exceedingly interesting meeting, both to the children and their teachers. On Sunday afternoons, for many years, Christian ladies and gentlemen have come to teach the orphans, so as to give the regular staff a rest, but principally with the object of leading the children to the Saviour. Marks are given for lessons and good conduct, and prizes are provided by the teachers for those whom they consider entitled to them. Those prizes were so very many that we had therein the best proof of the good behaviour of the children.

After brief addresses by the President; Mr. Evans, the superintendent of the school; Mr. J. Manton Smith; Mr. Harmer; and Mr. Lake, one of the Orphanage "old boys"; the prizes were handed by Mr. Spurgeon to those to whom they had been awarded.

Mr. Charlesworth and the choir propose to be absent on a visit to the Channel Islands from May 17th to 29th.

Will our friends kindly notice that the ANNUAL FESTIVAL will take place on the President's birthday, *Wednesday, June* 19?

PERSONAL NOTES.—Our friend, who daily distributes our "Illustrated Tracts," and extracts from our sermons, informs us that during the past four years he has given away 90,000 copies, and has thus been enabled to personally address thousands of persons upon the most important subjects. He drops his tracts into letter-boxes, leaves them from house to house, or gives them to individuals wherever he has the opportunity. Are there not other Christian men or women who can go and do likewise?

The sermon No. 2,078, "The Believing Thief," is specially adapted for large distribution. We gave eight hundred to the butchers, at their festival. We intend to issue it in book-form.

A bush-missionary, in Queensland, writes:—"In several places that I have visited, hundreds of miles from the coast, it is the regular practice for 'all hands' to be brought together for service on the Sabbath. The portions of Scripture you have read on the occasion of your preaching the sermon are read, a prayer—probably from a Church of England prayer-book, or some other—then the sermon, that you have preached in the ears of thousands in your Tabernacle, is carefully and solemnly read, although, perhaps, only in the hearing of half a dozen men. But who can estimate the good done?

"I know a man who rides twenty-five miles every Sabbath to attend one of these services at a neighbouring station, making, with the return journey, fifty miles, to hear one of your sermons read, and join with a few others in the service I have described.

"I will not weary you with other instances that have come under my personal observation, though I could mention several. My object in writing at all was to assure you that this branch of your work is bearing rich fruit, the quantity and quality of which will only be known when the precious sheaves shall be gathered home."

A Christian lady writes:—"I have long wished to let you know the blessing your sermons have been. Rather more than a year ago, I started a prayer-meeting in this village; and, as I am very busy, I had not time to prepare an address, nor do I think I have the ability. My husband bought me two or three volumes of your sermons, and since then I have used them. I do not read them to the people; I read them myself, and try to understand them as thoroughly as possible, and then *tell* their contents to my hearers. I know what they do for myself, and I do believe they have been the means of blessing souls here. Every week I just seem to find the very thing I want to say." Could not other friends follow this good example? Many a lonely hamlet might thus be blessed.

A clergyman writes to tell us of the wife of an ecclesiastical dignitary, who has read all our sermons that have been published since the year 1861. He says:—

"The origin of her reading them was this; her father was in the habit of giving the sailors in his employ something to read while at sea. As a rule, they would accept no religious literature, except your sermons, with any relish. His daughter was chosen to select from your sermons; so she read all, and does so to this very day."

Baptisms at Metropolitan Tabernacle:— March 21, twenty-one; March 28, eighteen; April 1, twelve; April 4, sixteen.

𝔓astors' College, 𝔐etropolitan 𝔗abernacle

Statement of Receipts from March 15th to April 15th, 1889.

	£ s. d.		£ s. d.
Collection at Campsbourne Road Baptist Chapel, Hornsey, per Mr. S. J. Jones	1 16 4	Collection at the Lord's-table, Baptist Chapel, Bridgwater, per Rev. C. H. M. Day	1 4 0
Collection at Union Church, Shefford, per Pastor A. Smith	0 17 6	Pastor A. H. Stote	1 0 0
		Mrs. Hulett	1 0 0

	£	s.	d.
Postal order from Thaxted	0	10	0
Mr. A. J. Score	0	2	6
H. D.	5	0	0
Miss Traill	5	0	0
G. L.	5	0	0
Mr. R. S. Gould, per Pastor R. M. Harrison	0	4	0
Mrs. Wilkinson	5	0	0
Thankoffering for Messrs. Page and Gordon's services at Collingwood Street Mission	2	2	0
Part collection at Wallington, per Pastor J. E. Jasper	2	2	0
Mr. George Green (for Students' Sermon Distribution Fund) ...	0	2	6
Mr. and Mrs. P. C. Rutherford. ...	5	0	0
Mr. W. Michael	2	0	0
Mr. Charles Barker...	1	0	0
Mrs. Cartwright	0	10	0
Collection at Manvers Street Chapel, Bath, per Pastor H. F. Gower... ...	6	6	
E. K. G.	40	0	
Edward Ridgway, Sheffield	10	0	
S. M.	5	0	0
Mr. Thomas Gregory	1	0	
Matthew xxv. 40 ...	1	0	
A sermon-reader	0	10	0
Collection from Hampton Court Baptist Chapel, per Pastor A. Hall	0	7	6
Rev. C. Hewitt	0	3	0
Mrs. Rainbow	1	0	0
Collection at Cottage Green Chapel, per Pastor J. A. Brown, M.R.C.S. ...	2	2	
Pastor R. J. Williamson	1	0	
Mr. C. L. Kaufmann	5	5	0
Mr. T. M. Whittaker	5	5	0
Mrs. Phillips, per Pastor C. L. Gordon	1	0	
Pastor E. Spanton... ...	0	5	0
Contribution from East Hill Baptist Chapel, Wandsworth, per Pastor J. W. Ewing	3	7	6
Contribution from Bromley Baptist Chapel, per Pastor A. Tessier ...	2	0	0
Mr. and Mrs. Grange, per J. T. D. ...	5	0	0
Rev. J. Burnham	2	2	0
Rev. A. H. King	0	3	0
Miss Rickwood, per J. T. D.	0	2	0
Miss Dawson	1	0	0
Mr. E. Cross	1	0	0
Mr. T. Harrison Evans	2	2	0
Pastor J. L. Bennett	1	0	0
Mrs. Jennings	5	0	0
Mrs. Dent, per Pastor T. W. Scamell...	2	0	0
Contribution from Esher Baptist Chapel, per Pastor J. E. Perrins ...	0	10	0

	£	s.	d.
Collection at Lower Edmonton Baptist Chapel, per Pastor D. Russell ...	1	14	3
Mr. J. Garner Marshall	5	0	0
Mr. C. Tyrrell Giles	2		
Mr. Edwin Jones	2		
Madame Blim, per J. T. D.	0	1	
Mrs. Charles Burt...	5		
Mr. I. Mannington	5		
Mr. E. Townshend	2	1	
Mr. Everett's Bible-class	3		
Mrs. Mizen	0	1	
Mrs. Willis	5		
Mr. and Mrs. Grey	1		
Mrs. Elgee	0	1	
M. L. C.	0	1	
Mr. E. Harris	5		
Mrs. Pepys	5		
Miss Hadfield	10		
Mrs. Pool	0	1	
Mrs. Lees	1		
Miss Descroix	0		
Mrs. Murray	2		
V. S.	5		
One blessed by the sermons	0		
Mr. E. W. Jacob	0		
Mrs. Brown	0		
Mr. R. Scott	5		
Miss Sillibourne	2		
Miss Cochrane	2	1	
Miss C. Coleman	1		
Highgate Road Chapel, per Rev. J. Stephens, M.A.	7	4	0
Mrs. Lewis	1	1	0
Miss L. Jones	0	5	0
Mr. J. Wilson	1	11	0
Mrs. Potter	2	0	0
Mr. J. Holt Skinner	5	0	0
Nameless	0	10	0
Mr. C. Hunt	3	0	0
The widow's mite	3	3	0
Mr. T. G. Owens	5	0	0
Quarterly Subscription:—			
Adelphi	1	10	0
Monthly Subscription:—			
Mr. R. J. Beecliff (two months)	0	5	0
Weekly Offerings at Met. Tab. :—			
March 17	28	0	9
„ 24	30	6	1
„ 31	6	13	5
April 7	29	4	8
„ 14	25	14	6
	119	19	5
	£364	**8**	**0**

£25 received from Mr. J. Dodson in October was thankfully placed to the funds of the College Missionary Association, the accounts of which will be published in the Annual Report of the College.

Stockwell Orphanage.

Statement of Receipts from March 15th to April 15th, 1889.

	£	s.	d.
Exors....	86	4	4
Jack, South Lambeth	0	5	6
Orphan girl's collecting-card 0 10 0			
Mrs. Eddy 0 10 0			
	1	0	0
Collected by Miss E. Lewis	0	5	0
Orphan girl's card, R. Pearce ...	0	12	0
Orphan girl's card, M. Corbett ...	0	5	0
Executors of the late Mrs. E. Douglas	300	0	0
Rev. W. Sexton	0	5	0
A widow, per Mrs. Wood, per J. T. D.	5	0	0
Mrs. Sparrow	0	10	0
Mr. F. H., Marychurch	1	0	0
Collected by Miss Bickmore ...	1	10	0
Sillyearn Sunday-school, per Mr. E. McDonald...	0	5	6

	£	s.	d.
Mr. T. A. Flitton	0	10	0
Mr. F. S. King, per Mrs. J. A. Spurgeon	1	1	0
Collected by Mrs. Jarman	0	5	0
Collected by Mr. J. Binstead ...	1	2	0
Per Mr. Gracey:—			
Agnesetta Gracey 0 9 4			
Lillie Gracey 0 10 8			
	1	0	0
Collected by Mr. S. C. White ...	1	10	0
Collected by Miss Stammers ...	0	3	3
Mr. G. H. Quincy	2	0	0
Collected by Mr. H. Payne	0	4	0
Mrs. Rettie	1	0	0
H. D.	10	0	0
Mrs. Parson...	1	0	0
A friend, Ross-shire	1	0	0

	£	s.	d.
Mr. C. Ibberson	0	2	6
Mrs. Wornell	1	1	0
Mr. W. Williams	0	10	0
J. B. C.	1	0	0
Miss F. M. E. Goodchild	0	10	0
Grateful	1	0	0
Mr. T. Wallis	4	0	0
Mrs. Cloat	1	0	0
Mr. H. Doorbar, jun.	0	5	0
Mrs. James Battershill	5	0	0
Mr. J. W. Davies	0	3	6
Miss Thornton	1	0	0
Mr. G. Eves	0	1	6
Mrs. Ord, per Mr. Thomas Newlands...	1	0	0
Miss Macfadyen	1	0	0
Miss E. E. Strowger	0	3	0
Miss H. Inglis	1	0	0
Mr. Thomas Jephcoat	1	0	0
Postal order from Waltham Abbey ...	0	10	0
Albert P.	0	5	0
Mr. H. W. Hour	0	10	0
Mrs. Beattie...	1	0	0
Postal order from Sittingbourne ...	0	7	6
Mrs. Garner	1	0	0
Mrs. Fairweather	0	4	6
In memoriam, Ethel Bertha ...	1	1	0
West Calder Free Church Sabbath-scholars	0	5	0
F. G. B., Chelmsford	0	2	6
Miss Farley	1	0	0
A friend in Norfolk	0	10	0
Mrs. Gray	0	5	0
Mr. G. H. Laurie	0	5	0
Mr. Samuel Bown	0	10	0
Mr. John Hill	2	0	0
Mr. John Hooper	2	0	0
J. S.	1	0	0
Mrs. Yates	0	10	6
Miss A. Rogers	0	2	6
Mrs. Barnes...	0	10	0
Mr. R. Pope Froste	5	0	0
A grateful grandmother	0	10	0

Per F. R. T.:—

	£	s.	d.
Mrs. Collingwood	0	5	0
Mr. T. R. Johnson... ...	0	5	0
	0	10	0

	£	s.	d.
Miss E. A. Fyah	0	1	0
Mr. L. Shepherd	0	10	0
Mr. C. L. Jones	0	10	0
E. K. G.	40	0	0
W A. M.	0	5	0
Miss Lizzie Thompson, per Rev. James Blythe	0	5	0
Miss Duncan	0	10	0
Miss M. Tillotson	0	5	0
Mr. and Mrs. Bibby	0	5	0
A widow's mite, J. R.	0	2	6
Matthew xxv. 40	2	0	0
Collected by Miss E. Hardwick... ...	1	5	0
Collected by the teachers and scholars at the Old Baptist Chapel Sunday-school, Guildford :			
Girls' box	2	9	3
Boys' box	2	1	10½
Infants' box	0	8	8½
Mr. P. Pickett's box ...	1	12	6
Mr. G. P. Pickett's box ...	0	10	8
Mr. G. Walker's box	0	5	6
	7	8	6
Mr. Robert Turnbull	1	0	0
A sermon-reader	0	2	6
Mrs. J. Wenham	0	13	0
Sandwich, per Bankers	2	2	0
Collected by Miss E. E. Jones	2	4	1
Young women's Bible-class at the Orphanage, per Mrs. James Stiff ...	0	16	4
Collected by Mr. E. R. Pullen	0	3	0
Mr. E. K. Stace	0	10	0
Miss M. E. Jenkins	0	3	6
A friend	0	1	0
	0	4	6

	£	s.	d.
Collected by Miss F. Dunster	0	6	0
Per Mr. J. Robinson :—			
Collection in Paglesham Chapel	0 11 0		
A lady friend	0 5 0		
	0	16	0
Collected by Mrs. F. Battam	1	2	6
G. C. G. Colliery Company, per Mr. Richards	1	1	0
Collected by Mrs. Laker	1	0	6
Collected by Miss W. Bagshaw ...	0	4	6
Mrs. Morris...	0	5	0
Collected by Pastor J. H. Barnard ...	0	3	0
Orphan girl's card, L. Richards ...	0	13	0
Collected by Miss G. S. Brown	0	1	0
Collected by Miss F. E. Barker ...	0	10	0
Collected by Miss Fitzgerald	1	2	6
Collected by Mrs. and Miss Houston ...	0	8	0
Collected by Miss L. Battam ...	1	1	9
Collected by Master Dowen ...	0	9	10
Collected by Miss A. Parker ...	0	2	5
Collected by Miss Nutt	0	1	0
Collected by Miss L. Matthews ...	0	10	3
Collected by Miss Greenop ...	2	0	0
Collected by Mrs. Roberts	0	12	0
Collected by Miss Florence Jeffery ...	0	10	6
Mrs. Burton's school-room box ...	1	8	0
Collected by Miss Helen Figg ...	0	8	6
Collected by Miss M. Saunders... ...	0	6	6
Collected by Mrs. W. E. Barnard ...	0	4	6
Collected by Mr. H. Teverson	0	17	0
Collected by Mr. W. Dixon ...	1	0	0
Collected by Mrs. Jackson ...	0	10	0
Collected by Miss S. Jones	0	13	0
Collected by Mrs. Robins ...	1	13	9
Collected by Mrs. E. Castell ...	0	6	0
Collected by Miss E. S. Girdlestone ...	1	0	0
Collected by Miss A. Burton	0	2	11
Miss Jones	0	2	6
Mr. T. M. Whittaker	3	3	0
Collected by Mrs. Welford ...	0	10	3
Miss Scates	50	0	0
Mrs. Raybould	1	0	0
Collected by Mr. Garrett... ...	0	8	6
Collected by Mrs. Ewen	2	15	0
Collected by Mrs. E. Luxford	0	10	6
Collected by Mr. W. Bragg ...	2	8	0
Collected by Miss Livett... ...	0	15	0
Collected by Mr. S. Snape ...	0	12	0
Collected by Miss Bennett ...	0	10	8
Mr. J. Williams	0	10	0
Orphan boy's card, F. Gant ...	0	1	0
Collected by Mr. L. A. Spiller ...	0	10	6
Mr. James G. Romang	0	10	0
Collected by Mr. James Hooker, jun...	0	10	6
Collected by Mr. A. G. Edgerton ...	0	12	0
Collected by Miss Rintoul ...	0	6	0
Collected by Miss Pavey ...	0	12	0
Collected by Mrs. Cowen ...	1	5	0
Miss Lennard, per J. T. D. ...	0	5	0
Collected by Mrs. Wilmot ...	0	15	0
Collected by Miss Dora ...	0	19	8
Collected by Miss Linderman ...	0	5	6
P. O., Govan Road, Glasgow (Jack and Maggie)	0	8	6
Mr. Huntington Stone	5	0	0
Collected by M. Chance	0	4	9
Collected by E. Chance	0	5	3
Collected by Sarah Jackman ...	0	5	9
Collected by Leonard V. Palmer ...	0	10	0
Collected by Miss L. Morgan ..	0	3	2
Collected by Miss E. K. Rawlins ...	0	12	
Collected by Mrs. Penning ...	0	7	0
Collected by Mrs. Perry ...	0	7	6
Madame Blim, per J. T. D. ...	0	10	0
Mrs. Moore	0	2	6
Box at Tabernacle gates	0	6	9
Mr. and Mrs. Kay	0	2	6
Mr. George Turner	0	10	0
Collected by Mrs. Jno. Lord ...	0	7	0
Collected by Miss E. M. Prior ...	0	12	1

	£	s.	d.
Miss E. Clover ...	0	6	0
Proceeds of halfpenny entertainment given by six little girls in the Chesterfield silk-mill ...	0	4	0
Mrs. Elgee	0	0	6
Mr. R. Snell	0	0	0
H. M., Camden Town	0	0	0
Collected by Miss Barker ...	1	18	6
Collected by Mr. James Simpson	1	0	0
H. H., Aberdeen	1	0	0
Collected by Mrs. G. Halsey ..	0	10	0
Collected by Mrs. S. T. Pocock...	0	17	0
Mr. T. G. Owens	5	0	0
Collected by Miss E. Tyler ...	1		10
P. and P.	0		0
Miss Hadfield	10	0	0
Collected by Mrs. W. Jones ...	1	8	7

Collected at Richmond Street Sunday-school:—

	£	s.	d.
Young Men and Women's Bible-classes	10	6	4
The school	11	18	8
	22	5	0

	£	s.	d.
Collected by Miss S. Gilpin ...	0	10	6
Mr. Sutherland	1	0	0

Bouverie Road Baptist Chapel Sunday-school

	£	s.	d.
school	1	0	0
H. E. S.	10	10	0
In memoriam	0	5	0
Pence from sermons	0	11	0
Miss Corkett	0	2	6
T. R.	0	5	0
W. and J. E. M.	1	0	0
Mr. Chatterton	0	10	0
Mr. S. H. Dauncey	0	2	6
Mr. G. Smith	0	10	0
Mrs. T. Thomas	1	1	3
Collected by Mrs. J. T. Crosher ...	13	4	10
Mrs. Spencer	0	5	0
Collected by Miss C. M. Bidewell ...	0	7	0
Mrs. Woolland	0	10	0
Miss Symington	1	0	0
V. S.	10	0	0
Mrs. Williams	0	2	6
Sabbath-school children at Bogmoor	0	8	0
Mrs. William Low...	0	10	0
Mrs. Watson	0	5	0
Mrs. Cooper	0	5	0
Mr. E. W. Jacob	0	10	0
P. A. L. M.	1	0	0
Mr. Charles Stewart	1	5	0
E. M. R.	2	10	0
E. I. M.	5	0	0
Collected by Pastor S. J. Baker	2	0	3

Teachers and children of Halbeath Sabbath-school

	£	s.	d.
Sabbath-school	0	2	3
A country minister	0	3	0
Mr. J. Meader	1	1	0
Mrs. Lewis	2	2	0
A thankoffering from three ...	0	5	0
Mrs. Bowie...	0	5	0
S. and N.	10	0	0
Mr. J. Wilson	0	10	0
Maggie	0	2	6
Miss I Anderson	0	3	0
A Dorset friend, Anon.	0	5	0
Miss E. Miller	0	10	0
JNO., Newcastle-on-Tyne ...	0	5	0
A member of the Church of England...	0	5	0
Mr. R. Middleton and friends ...	1	0	0
Mr. J. W. Kirwan...	1	0	0
The late Mrs. John Rinder, Leeds, per Mrs. Walker	1	0	0
Mr. William Morris	1	0	0

Meetings by Mr. Charlesworth and the Orphanage Choir:—

	£	s.	d.
Sale of programmes	7	19	7
New Malden	5	14	5
Westminster	2	8	9
Hull, part proceeds	18	15	6
Mr. Veitch's mission, Chelsea	10	0	0

	£	s.	d.
Crouch Hill (donation) Mr. W. Sissons	1	0	0
Metropolitan Tabernacle United Christian Brothers' Benefit Society ...	2	15	6
Grimsby and Cleethorpes ...	48	14	0

Received at Collectors' Meeting, April 5th.

Collecting Boxes:—

	£	s.	d.
Adlard, Miss A.	0	1	3
Abbey, Mrs.	0	2	2
Amies, Miss	0	2	2
Austin, Miss	0	7	9
Ayliffe, Miss	0	5	0
Belleini, Miss	0	3	0
Brown, Mr. J.	0	7	11
Barnden, Mrs.	1	1	8
Brice, F. and G. ...	0	3	4
Butler, Mrs.	0	10	8
Brewer, Misses A. and L.	0	13	0
Barber, Miss	0	6	7
Boot, Miss N.	0	18	5
Buckingham, Miss ...	0	6	0
Buswell, Miss	1	19	9
Bilby, Miss	0	5	11
Boswell, Mrs.	0	10	3
Bell, Mrs.	0	12	0
Beecliff, Mr. J.	0	18	5
Bruin, Miss E.	0	18	7
Brice, Miss C.	0	4	3
Beale, Miss J.	0	14	7
Brice, P. and A. ...	0	2	3
Burton, Mrs. W. ...	2	14	5
Belleini, Miss	0	2	8
Brooks, Miss	0	6	11
Burrage, Mrs.	0	3	9
Cooper, Mr.	4	4	11
Collins, Mrs.	0	9	4
Call, Mrs.	0	9	7
Combs, Mrs.	2	1	7
Cross, W.	0	2	5
Charlesworth, Miss F. ...	0	1	4
Conquest, Mrs.	0	13	8
Chard, Mr. T. P.	1	18	2
Caragerard, Miss ...	0	2	3
Curtas, P. W.	0	1	9
Cook, Miss	0	6	7
Cairns, Miss L.	0	18	4.
Cook, Miss A.	0	9	7
Davie, Mrs.	0	7	8
Dolman, J.	0	2	10
Deacon, L. and F. ...	0	12	0
Everitt, Miss	0	7	0
Ellerington, Mrs.	0	5	6
Esling, Miss E.	0	5	4
Field, Mrs.	0	2	2
Fuller, Miss E.	0	4	2
Furness, Mrs.	0	10	9
Frost, Miss	0	5	5
Fowler, Miss E.	0	9	3
Fathers, Mrs.	0	2	6
Foster, Miss E.	0	3	11
Goetz, Miss	1	1	0
Gage, S. V. L.	0	7	7
Guyer, Mrs.	0	3	4
Hartley, Miss E. ...	0	2	0
Hawgood, Miss	2	2	1
Henderson, Mrs.	0	6	1
Hill, Miss L.	0	1	0
Hoyles, A.	1	0	7
Hertzell, Mrs.	0	4	3
Hillen, Mrs.	0	10	5
Hall, Miss L.	0	1	1
Hillier, Mrs.	1	6	4
Hannam, E. H.	0	1	0
Hartley, F.	0	2	4
Hartley, E.	0	0	9
Kingholme, Miss ...	0	4	0
Larkman, Miss B. ...	0	6	1
Lockyer, Mrs.	0	12	3
Lansdale, Miss A. ...	0	0	10
Landford, Master J. ...	0	0	9
Lansdale, A.	0	0	7
Lowne, Mrs.	0	4	6

	£ s. d.
Limebeers, Miss ...	0 2 0
Landford, J. ...	0 0 2
Laundry box, S.O. ...	0 7 4
Matthews, F. and W. ...	0 4 3
Mallison, Mrs. ...	0 2 7
Mills, F. ...	0 6 0
Middleton, Mrs ...	0 2 0
Morgan, Mr. ...	0 13 6
Mackay, Mrs. ...	0 7 0
Monk, Mrs. ...	1 10 8
Moore, Miss E. ...	0 5 8
Missing, Mrs. ...	0 1 7
Miss Ivimey's mothers'- meeting ...	0 16 0
Oliver, Miss F. ...	0 3 7
Palmer, Mrs. ...	0 2 9
Price, Miss E. ...	0 5 8
Pitt, Mrs. ...	0 19 8
Philp, Miss ...	0 5 7
Pearmain, Miss ...	0 6 0
Pearce, Mrs. ...	0 16 2
Preedy, Mrs. ...	0 3 6
Parker, F. ...	0 1 6
Prior, Mrs. ...	0 6 1
Probyn, Miss G. ...	0 4 6
Phillips, Miss ...	0 3 10
Peters, Miss F. W. ...	0 13 2
Pike, Mr. G. H. ...	0 6 8
Price, Miss F. ...	0 2 6
Podmore, Mrs. ...	0 4 4
Paviour, H. ...	0 2 1
Quennell, Mrs. ...	0 6 0
Rowe, Mr. ...	0 2 9
Rayner, Mr. ...	0 5 1
Ridley, Mrs. ...	0 3 10
Round, Miss E. ...	0 11 1
Ransom, Miss E. ...	0 3 2
Rose, Miss B. ...	0 2 1
Russell, Mrs. ...	0 4 2
Rose, Miss H. ...	0 2 1
Roper, Mrs. ...	0 8 0
Staines, Miss C. ...	0 7 2
Stratford, Miss E. ...	0 5 7
Smith, Miss G. ...	0 1 9
Sheard, Miss F. ...	0 2 3
Smee, Miss C. ...	0 5 0
Smith, Mrs. C. J. ...	1 3 11
Selth, Miss ...	0 5 2
Spencer, Mrs. ...	0 8 10
Smith, E. H. ...	0 4 0
Stewart, Mrs. ...	0 15 2
Sidery, Mrs. ...	1 3 0
Smith, Mrs. G. ...	0 3 6
Soulsby, Miss ...	1 0 4
Terrell, Mr. E. ...	0 5 0
Turner, Mrs. ...	0 4 8
Tyson, Mrs. ...	0 10 4
Taylor, Mrs. ...	0 4 1
Turner, Miss M ...	0 4 11
Thomas, Miss A. ...	0 3 10
Thomas, Miss G. ...	0 1 5
Wells, Miss ...	0 3 0
Walter, Mrs. ...	1 5 0
Wickham, Miss L. ...	0 1 1
Wickham, Mrs. ...	0 1 0
Wild, Miss M. ...	0 5 0
Watts, Mrs. ...	0 7 4
Warren, Miss M. ...	0 11 8

	£ s. d	£ s. d.
Wingate, Miss N. ...	0 9 1	
Watling, Mrs. ...	1 9	
Weekes, Miss ...	0 5	
Young, Mr. ...	0 1	
Young, Mr. J. A. ...	0 6 0	
Odd farthings and halfpence	0 0 10	
		66 0 8
Collecting Books:—		
Andrews, Mrs. ...	0 8 5	
Alderton, Miss ...	0 5 6	
Bonser, Miss E. ...	0 6 0	
Broughton, Miss ...	0 8 6	
Barrett, Mr. H. ...	3 8 0	
Brown, Mr. J. H ...	1 9 0	
Charles, Miss F. B. ...	0 7 6	
Chew, Miss ...	0 5 0	
Colman, Mrs. ...	0 6 6	
Dee, Mrs. ...	0 10 0	
Frost, Miss ...	1 0 0	
Fowler, Miss N. ...	1 5 0	
Fryer, Miss S. ...	0 17 6	
Fairey, Miss...	1 11 6	
Good, Miss ...	0 6 0	
Hallett, Miss ...	0 10 6	
Hoare, Miss ...	0 12 0	
Jephs, Miss ...	2 10 0	
Lawson, Mrs. ...	1 7 0	
McDonald, Mrs. ...	0 10 0	
Miller, Mr. C. ...	1 0 0	
Scutt, Mrs. ...	0 6 10	
Saunders, Mr. E. W. ...	5 0 0	
Walters, Miss ...	0 8 0	
Willis, Mrs. ...	1 0 0	
		25 18 9
Donations:—		
Barrett, Mr. ...	0 10 0	
Jones, Mr. W. Corden ...	0 5 0	
Per Mrs. Charlesworth:—		
Aukland, Mr. J. L.	1 1 0	
Darling, Mr. Jas.	0 10 0	
Everidge, Mrs. ...	1 0 0	
Halsey, Mrs. ...	0 10 6	
A friend, per Mrs. Halsey ...	0 2	
Houghton, Mrs. E.	0 5	
Mills, Mrs. T. ...	0 10	
Mursell, Mr. G. A.	1 1	
Olney, Mr. Jno. ...	2 2 6	
Pocock Brothers, Messrs. ...	2 2 0	
Phillips, Mrs. ...	0 5 0	
Smith, Mr. G. R.	1 1 0	
Thompson, Mr. W. W. ...	1 1 0	
		11 11 0
Johnson, Mr. A. C., Sunday morning breakfast box	1 0 0	
Olney, Mr. T. H. ...	3 0 0	
Stevenson, Mrs. ...	0 10 0	
Teddington Baptist Sunday school, per Mr. F. Rose...	1 0 0	
Townsend Street Sunday- school	3 17 6	
Tea tickets sold ...	0 19 6	
		22 13 0
		£956 9 9

List of Presents, per Mr. Charlesworth, from March 15th to April 15th.—PROVISIONS :—1 dozen Hens, Mr. W. J. Graham ; 20 Pork Pies, 1 dozen Stilton Cheeses, and 1 dozen packets Hayes' Food, Mr. J. T. Crosher ; 28 lbs. Baking Powder, Messrs. Freeman and Hildyard ; 2 sacks Potatoes, Mr. H. Watts ; 1 New Zealand Sheep, Mr. A. S. Haslam ; half-chest Tea, Messrs. Pannett and Neden ; 1 sack Potatoes, Mr. W. Cutler ; 1 Cake and 1 pot Jam, Mrs. E. Lovell.

BOYS' CLOTHING.—20 Flannel Shirts, Mrs. Sifton ; 12 Shirts, Mrs. E. H. Williams ; a box of Ties, Mr. C. E. Garner.

GIRLS' CLOTHING.—5 pairs Stockings, Mrs. Johnston ; 57 Articles and 1 Dress, The Ladies' Working Meeting at the Metropolitan Tabernacle, per Miss Higgs ; 6 Articles, Miss F. M. E. Goodchild ; 19 Articles, Mr. E. McDonald ; 138 yards Dress Material, 2¾ yards Calico, 1 piece Red Braid, Mr. Hall ; 25 Articles, the Cheam Baptist Working Society, per Mrs. E. Cox ; 2 Articles, Mrs. E. Lovell ; 8 Pinafores, Mrs. Loosely ; 6 Articles, Miss A. Thatcher ; 66 Articles, Miss Salter's Bible-class ;

18 Articles, Mrs. Watling; 6 Articles, Miss McLaren; 3 Articles, E. Rickwood; 6 Articles, Mrs. J. Goodwin.

GENERAL.—3 dozen Tennis Balls and 2 Rackets, Mrs. A. Edmeades; 1 Article, Miss F. Sutton; 4 volumes "Girl's Own Annual," 2 volumes "Every Girl's Annual," Mrs. W. S. Caine; 25 volumes, Messrs. J. F. Shaw and Co.; 1 Bat and Ball, 1 Scrap Book, Mrs. Loosely; 200 copies of "Perfect Peace," Mr. H. Putman.

Colportage Association.

Statement of Receipts from March 15th to April 15th, 1889.

Subscriptions and Donations for Districts:—

	£ s. d.		£ s. d.
Okehampton district ...	10 0 0	Friends at Maldon...	15 0 0
Bower Chalk district :—		Essex Congregational Union, Pitsea ...	10 0 0
Miss Hardiman	0 10 0	Mr. W. H. Roberts, for Ilkeston ...	10 0 0
Mr. Martin	0 10 0	South Devon Congregational Union,	
	1 0 0	Newton Abbot	10 0 0
Rendham, per Rev. G. Hollier ...	5 0 0		
Worcester Association	30 0 0		£216 0 0
Great Totham district	10 0 0		
Bethnal Green :—		Subscriptions and Donations to the General Fund:—	
Mr. W. R. Fox 5 0 0			£ s. d.
Mr. C. E. Fox 5 0 0		Mr. John Lister	2 0 0
	10 0	E. K. G.	20 0 0
Norfolk Association, for Neatishead ...	10 0 0	Mr. A. Todd...	0 5 0
Estover district, per Mr. H. Serpell ...	40 0 0	Mr. T. G. Owens	5 0 0
Mrs. H. Keevil, for Melksham ...	10 0 0	H. E. S.	10 10 0
Greenwich, per Pastor C. Spurgeon ...	10 0 0	V. S.	2 0 0
Fairford district, per Captain Milbourne	15 0 0	Mr. E. W. Jacob	0 5 0
Yorkshire Association, Borobridge ...	10 0 0	Readers of "The Christian Herald" ...	29 7 6
Suffolk Congregational Union, Great			
Thurlow	10 0 0		£69 7 6

Society of Evangelists.

Statement of Receipts from March 15th to April 15th, 1889.

	£ s. d.		£ s. d.
Mrs. Walter	2 0 0	Mr. J. Sleigh	0 5 0
Thankoffering for Mr. Parker's services		Thankoffering for Messrs. Fullerton	
at Westbury	2 9 6	and Smith's services at Dalston	
Thankoffering for Mr. Parker's services		Junction Chapel...	18 0 0
at Deptford	3 6 0	Mr. T. G. Owens	5 0 0
Thankoffering for Messrs. Fullerton		V. S.	1 0 0
and Smith's services at Shoreditch		Mr. Jefferson	1 0 0
Tabernacle	16 16 0	Thankoffering for Mr. Parker's services	
Balance of collection after expenses of		at Melbourne	5 14 0
Mr. Burnham's visit to St. John's		Nameless	0 10 0
Congregational Chapel, Ipswich ...	0 2 6		
Thankoffering for Messrs. Harmer and			£65 4
Chamberlain's services at Lydgate,			
Todmorden, Yorks	9 1 0		

For General Use in the Lord's Work.

Statement of Receipts from March 15th to April 15th, 1889.

	£ s. d.
Sarah P.	0 10 0
I. C.	0 1 6
Mrs. Smith	5 0 0
Postal order from Fakenham ...	0 5 0
	£5 16 6

£1 received from a sermon-reader shall be used for the distribution of sermons, but we fear it will not be possible to get anyone to call at each station as desired.

Friends sending presents to the Orphanage are earnestly requested to let their names or initials accompany the same, or we cannot properly acknowledge them; and also to write to Mr. Spurgeon if no acknowledgment is sent within a week. All parcels should be addressed to Mr. Charlesworth, Stockwell Orphanage, Clapham Road, London.

Subscriptions will be thankfully received by C. H. Spurgeon, "Westwood," Beulah Hill, Upper Norwood. Should any sums sent before the 13th of last month be unacknowledged in this list, friends are requested to write at once to Mr. Spurgeon. Post Office and Postal Orders should be made payable at the Chief Office, London, to C. H. Spurgeon; and Cheques and Orders should all be crossed.

THE

SWORD AND THE TROWEL.

JUNE, 1889.

The Preacher's Power, and the Conditions of Obtaining it.*

AN ADDRESS BY C. H. SPURGEON, AT THE ANNUAL CONFERENCE OF THE PASTORS' COLLEGE, HELD ON TUESDAY, MAY 7TH, 1889.

RETHREN, we want to do our work rightly and effectively, and we cannot do it without *power*. Of course, no work of any kind is accomplished in this world without a certain expenditure of force, and the force employed differs according to the matter in hand. The sort of power of which we feel the need will be determined by our view of our work; and the amount of power that we shall long for will also very much depend upon our idea of how that work should be done. I speak as unto wise men, who know their object, and know also whence their strength must come. I speak also to men who mean to use their office as in the sight of God; but yet I think it desirable to stir up your pure minds, by way of remembrance, and put you and myself in mind of the grand design for which we need power.

We could be ministers, as some men are ministers, without any particular power, either natural, or acquired. Merely to perform services (to use an ugly word) " perfunctorily " does not require special endowments. Any speaking machine might do as well. There are ministers whose sermons, and whose whole services, are so much a matter of routine, and so utterly lifeless, that if power from on high were

---

* This address occupied one hour and thirty minutes in its delivery. The opening portion is all that we can give this month. It forms a subject by itself, and division further on was found to be too rough a breaking up of the discourse.—C. H. S.

to come upon them, it would altogether bewilder them. Nobody would know them to be the same persons; the change would seem too great. The same things are said, in the same tone and manner, year after year. I have heard of a preacher, whom one of his people likened to a steeple, which had but two bells in it, for, he said, "It is always ding dong, ding dong, ding dong, ding dong." "Oh!" said his friend, "you ought to be abundantly grateful that you have as much variety as *that*, for our man has only one bell, and his voice is for ever Ding, ding, ding, ding." When this is the case among Nonconformists it ruins the congregations, for it is death to every possibility of collecting people to hear ; and still more is it murder to all hope of their being improved if they do hear. I should think it is by no means difficult, with a liturgy, to be read without much alteration all the year round, to become a fine example of either the ding dong, or the ding, ding ; but with us, whose devotion is of a free sort, there is less excuse for monotony, and if we fall into the fault the result will be more disastrous. It is possible, even without a liturgy, to pray in a very set and formal style ; indeed, it is so possible as to be frequent, and then the long prayer becomes a severe infliction upon an audience, and the shorter prayers are not much better. When I have thought of the preaching of certain good men, I have wondered, not that the congregation was so small, but that it was so large. The people who listen to them ought to excel in the virtue of patience, for they have grand opportunities for exercising it. I have frequently said of myself that I would not go across the road to hear myself preach ; but I will venture to say of certain brethren that I would even go across the road in the other direction *not* to hear them preach. Some sermons and prayers lend a colour of support to the theory of Dr. William Hammond, that the brain is not absolutely essential to life. Brethren, I trust that not even one of you will be content with mechanical services devoid both of mental and spiritual force. You will, none of you, covet earnestly the least gifts, and the dullest mannerisms, for you can obtain them without the exertion of the will. You desire to do your Master's work as it ought to be done, and therefore you long for excellent gifts, and still more excellent graces. You wish that people may attend to your discourse, because there is something in it worthy of their attention. You labour to discharge your ministry, not with the lifeless method of an automaton, but with the freshness and power which will render your ministry largely effectual for its sacred purposes.

I am bound to say, also, that our object certainly is not to please our clients, nor to preach to the times, nor to be in touch with modern progress, nor to gratify the cultured few. Our life-work cannot be answered by the utmost acceptance on earth ; our record is on high, or it will be written in the sand. There is no need whatever that you and I should be chaplains of the modern spirit, for it is well supplied with busy advocates. Surely Ahab does not need Micaiah to prophesy smooth things to him, for there are already four hundred prophets of the grove who are flattering him with one consent. We are reminded of the protesting Scotch divine, in evil days, who was exhorted by the Synod to preach to the times. He asked, "Do you, brethren, preach to the times ?" They boasted that they did. "Well, then," said he, "if there are so many of you who preach for the times, you may well allow one poor brother to preach for eternity." We leave, without regret, the gospel of the hour to the men of the hour. With such eminently cultured persons for ever hurrying on with their new doctrines, the world may be content to let our little company keep to the old-fashioned faith, which we still believe to have been " once for all delivered to the saints." Those superior persons, who are so wonderfully advanced, may be annoyed that we cannot consort with them; but, nevertheless, so it is that it is not now, and never will be, any design of ours to be in harmony with the spirit of the age, or in the least desirous to conciliate the demon of doubt which rules the present moment. Brethren, we shall not adjust our Bible to the age; but before we have done with it, by God's grace, we shall adjust the age to the Bible. We shall not fall into the error of that absent-minded doctor who had to cook for himself an egg; and, therefore, depositing his watch in the saucepan, he stood steadfastly looking at the egg. The change to be wrought is not for the divine chronometer, but for the poor egg of human thought. We make no mistake here: we shall not watch our congregation to take our cue from it, but we shall keep our eye on the infallible Word, and preach according to its instructions. Our Master sits on high, and not in the chairs of the scribes and doctors, who regulate the theories of the century. We cannot take our keynote from the wealthier people, nor from the leading officers, nor even from the former minister. How often have we heard an excuse for heresy made out of the desire to impress " thoughtful young men "! Young men, whether thoughtful or otherwise, are best impressed by the gospel, and it is folly to dream that a preaching which leaves out the truth is suitable to men, either old or young. We shall not quit the Word to please the young men, nor even the young women. This truckling to young men is a mere pretence: young men are no more fond of false doctrine than the middle-aged; and if they are, there is so much the more necessity to teach them better. Young men are more impressed by the old gospel than by ephemeral speculations. If any of you wish to preach a gospel that will be pleasing to the times, preach it in the power of the devil, and I have no doubt that he will willingly do his best for you. It is not to such servants of men that I desire to speak just now. I trust that if ever any of you should err from the faith, and take up with the new theology, you will be too honest to pray for power from God with which to preach that mischievous delusion; and if you should do, you will be guilty of constructive blasphemy. No, brethren, it is not our object to please men, but our design is far nobler.

To begin with, *it is our great desire to bear witness to the truth.* I believe—and the conviction grows upon me—that even to know the truth is the gift of the grace of God; and that to love the truth, is the work of the Holy Spirit. I am speaking now, not about a natural knowledge, or a natural love to divine things, if such there be; but of an experimental knowledge of Christ, and a spiritual love to him : these are as much the gift of God in the preacher, as the work of conversion will be the work of God in his hearers. We desire so thoroughly to know, and so heartily to love the truth, as to declare the whole counsel of God, and speak it as we ought to speak. No small labour this. To proclaim the whole system of truth, and to deal out each part in due proportion, is by no means a simple matter. To bring out each doctrine according to the analogy of faith, and set each truth in its proper place, is no easy task. It is easy to make a caricature of the beautiful face of truth by omitting one doctrine and exaggerating another. We may dishonour the most lovely countenance by giving to its most striking feature an importance which puts it out of proportion with the rest ; for beauty greatly consists in balance and harmony. To know the truth as it should be known, to love it as it should be loved, and then to proclaim it in the right spirit and in its proper proportions, is no small work for such feeble creatures as we are. In this grand, yet delicate labour, we have to persevere year after year. What power can enable us to do this ? While so many complain of the monotony of the old gospel, and feel a perpetual itching for something new, this disease may even infect our own hearts. This is an evil to be fought against with our whole being. When we feel dull and stale, we must not imagine that the truth of God is so ; nay, rather by returning more closely to the Word of the Lord we must renew our freshness. To continue always steadfast in the faith so that our latest testimony shall be identical in substance with our first testimony, only deeper, mellower, more assured, and more intense—this is such a labour that for it we must needs have the power of God. Do you not feel this ? I pray you feel it more and more. O brethren, if you propose to be true witnesses for God, your proposal is a very glorious one, and it will tend to make you feel the truth of what I am about to say, namely, that a more than human power must guide you, and make you sufficient for the difficult enterprise.

Your object is, however, so to bear your personal witness *that others may be convinced thereby* of the truth of what is so sure to your own soul. In this there are difficulties not a few, for our hearers are not anxious to believe the revelation of God ; some of them are desirous not to do so. In the reign of Queen Elizabeth an order went forth that everybody should go to the parish church, at least, once on the Sunday. Of course, the bulk of the people were still Romish, and it went much against the grain for them to attend the Reformed service. I have read that when Romanists did go to the service prescribed by law, many of them put wool into their ears, that they might not hear. In a moral sense this practice is still in vogue. Certain parts of the truth men will hear, but other portions are disagreeable to them, and their ears are dull of hearing. You know—for you believe in the original sin of men (about the only thing original there is in many)—how Satan has most effectually blinded the minds of the ungodly, so that, speak we as wisely as we may, and as persuasively as we can, nothing but a miracle can convince men dead in sin of the truth of God. Nothing less than a miracle of grace can lead a man to receive what is so altogether opposite to his nature. I shall not attempt to teach a tiger the doctrine of vegetarianism ; but I shall as hopefully attempt that task as I would try to convince an unregenerate man of the truths revealed by God concerning sin, and righteousness, and judgment to come. These spiritual truths are repugnant to carnal men, and the carnal mind cannot receive the things of God. Gospel truth is diametrically opposed to fallen nature ; and if I have not a power much stronger than that which lies in moral suasion, or in my own explanations and arguments, I have undertaken a task in which I am sure of defeat. Well said the writer of one of our hymns, when he spake of the Holy Spirit,

> " 'Tis thine the passions to recall,
> And upward bid them rise;
> And make the scales of error fall
> From reason's darkened eyes."

Except the Lord endow us with power from on high our labour must be in vain, and our hopes must end in disappointment.

This is but the threshold of our labour: our inmost longing is *to call out a people who shall be the Lord's separated heritage.* A new theory has lately been started which sets forth as its ideal a certain imaginary kingdom of God, unspiritual, unscriptural, and unreal. The old-fashioned way of seeking the lost sheep, one by one, is too slow: it takes too much time, and thought, and prayer, and it does not leave space enough for politics, gymnastics, and sing-song. We are urged to rake in the nations wholesale into this imaginary kingdom by sanitary regulations, social arrangements, scientific accommodations, and legislative enactments. Please the people with the word "democratic," and then amuse them into morality. This is the last new "fad." According to this fancy, our Lord's kingdom is, after all, to be of this world; and, without conversion, or the new birth, the whole population is to melt into an earthly theocracy. Howbeit, it is not so. It seems to me that the Lord will follow up the lines of the Old Testament economy still, and separate to himself a people who shall be in the midst of the world as the Lord's kings and priests—a peculiar people, zealous for good works. I see, in the New Covenant, not less, but even more, of the election of grace, whereby a people is called out, and consecrated to the Lord. Through the chosen ones, myriads shall be born unto God; but beside these I know of no other kingdom. Brethren, the election of grace, which is so often denounced, is a fact which men need not speak against, since they do not themselves desire to be elected. I never can make out why a man should cavil at another's being chosen when he does not himself wish to be chosen. If he wishes that he were chosen to repentance, if he desires holiness, if he longs to be the Lord's, and if that desire be true, he is chosen already. But seeing that he does not desire anything of the kind, why does he cavil with others who have received this blessing? Ask an ungodly man whether he will take up the humble, often-abused, and persecuted position of a lowly follower of Christ, and he scorns the idea. If it were possible for him to get into that position for a time, how gladly would he shuffle out of it! He likes to be " in the swim," and to side with the majority; but to be a live fish, and to force his way up the stream, is not according to his desire. He prefers a worldly religion, with abundant provision for the flesh. Religious worldliness suits him very well; but to be out-and-out for Jesus, called out from the world, and consecrated to obedience, is not his ambition.

Do you not see in this your need of an extraordinary power? To call men out to a real separation from the world and a true union with Christ, apart from the power of God, is an utterly futile effort. Go, whistle eagles into an English sky, or beckon dolphins to the dry land, or lure leviathan till thou play with him as with a bird, and then attempt this greater task. They will not come, they have no wish to come; and even so our Lord and Master warned us when he said, "Ye will not come unto me that ye might have life." They will read the Bible, "Ye search the Scriptures, for in them ye think ye have eternal life"; but they will not come to the Lord himself; that is too spiritual for their tastes. No, the command, "Repent ye, and believe the gospel," is too hard, too sharp, too humbling for them. Is not this enough to appal you? Dare you go forward unless your Lord shall gird you with heavenly power?

Stop: we have only yet begun. They are called out; but there is something further to be done through the instrumentality of our ministry: *our hearers have to be born again, and made new creatures in Christ Jesus*, or else our preaching has done nothing for them. Ah, dear friends, we get into deep waters when we come to this great mystery! Does any unregenerate man know the meaning of being born again? Ask the learned doctors whether they know anything about it, and they will try to conceal their ignorance beneath a sneer. Ask them if they think there is anything in it, and they will perhaps reply, "Yes, there must be such a phenomenon, for many respectable and even scientific people have professed to be the subjects of it." Still they smile, and express their wonder that it is so. The confession of many a candid scientist is that it may be so, but he is not himself able to comprehend it. Why, then, do they not hold their tongues? If they have not experienced the new birth, that fact is no proof that others have not. Why do they sneer as if they were our superiors? The regenerate in this matter are necessarily their superiors. A person who has only one eye is a king among blind men; let not the blind affect to despise him. If any of us have personally experienced the new birth, even though we may be ignorant of many other things, we are in this point better instructed than those who have never felt the divine change. But, just in proportion as you know what it is to be born again, you will feel that herein is a task indeed. How sublime a position for you to become, under God, the spiritual parents of men! You could not create a fly, much less could you create a new heart and a right spirit. To fashion a world has less difficulty in it than to create a new life in an ungodly man; for in the creation of the world there was nothing in the way of God, but in the creation of the new heart there is the old nature opposing the Spirit. The negative has to be removed as well as the positive produced. Stand and look that matter over, and see if you are at all able in and of yourself to work the conversion or regeneration of a single child in your Sunday-school! My brethren, we are at the end of ourselves here. If we aim at the new birth of our hearers, we must fall prostrate before the Lord in conscious impotence, and we must not go again to our pulpits till we have heard our Lord say, "My grace is sufficient for thee: for my strength is made perfect in weakness."

Supposing that to be done, remember *those who are brought to God are to be kept and preserved to the end;* and your longing is that your ministry should be the means of keeping them from stumbling, and holding them fast in the way of righteousness even to the end. Do you propose to do that of yourself? How presumptuous! Why, look at the temptations which pollute this city; and I suppose that the seductions of evil are much the same in smaller towns, and in the villages, though differing in form. Their name is legion, for they are many. Look at the temptations which assail our youth in the literature of the hour! Have you even a slender acquaintance with popular literature? Do you wonder that weak minds are made to stumble? The wonder is that any are preserved. Yet this is only one of the many death-bearing agencies. How great is the leakage in our churches! The most faithful minister has to complain of the loss of many who appeared to run well, but have been hindered, so that they do not obey the truth. The great heap that we have gathered upon the threshing-floor is sadly diminished when he comes whose fan is in his hand. But we do propose, nevertheless, to be the means, in the hands of God, of leading the sheep of Christ to pasture, and continuing to lead them, until they feed on the hill-tops of heaven with the great Shepherd himself in their midst. But what a task we have undertaken! How shall we present them to Christ as pure virgins? How can we keep them from the pollution of the all-surrounding Sodom? How shall we, at the last, be able to say, "Here am I, and the children thou hast given me"? Brethren, we cannot do it at all; but the Lord can do it through us by the energy of his grace. If you have half-a-dozen converts, how greatly you will praise God, if you pass, with that half-a-dozen at your side, safely through the gate of pearl! Certain of us know many thousands whom we have instrumentally brought to the Saviour; but unless we have a power infinitely greater than our own, how shall we shepherd them to the end? We may announce them as our converts, we may associate with them as workers, and feel thankful for them as fellow-heirs, and yet bitter may be our disappointment, when all comes to all, and they turn aside unto perdition. How grievous to be, to all appearance, rich in usefulness, and on a sudden to find that our converts are like money put into a bag that is full of holes, and that our treasured converts fall out, because they were not truly gathered to the Lord Jesus after all! "Who is sufficient for these things." Weak we are, exceeding weak, every one of us. If there is any brother here who is weaker than usual, and knows that he is so, let him not be at all cast down about *that;* for you see, brethren, the best man here, if he knows what he is, knows that he is out of his depth in his sacred calling. Well, if you are out of your depth, it does not matter whether the sea is forty feet or a full mile deep. If the sea is only a fathom deep you will drown if you be not upborne; and if it be altogether unfathomable, you cannot be more than drowned. The weakest man here is not, in this business, really any weaker than the strongest man, since the whole affair is quite beyond us, and we must work miracles by divine power, or else be total failures. We have all set up in the divine profession of working by omnipotence, or rather of yielding ourselves up to omnipotence that it may work by us. If, therefore, omnipotence be not within hail, and if the miracle-working power is not within us, then the sooner we go home and plough the fields, or open shop, or cast up accounts, the better. Wherefore should we undertake what we have not the power to perform? Supernatural work needs supernatural power; and if you have it not, do not, I pray you, attempt to do the work alone, lest, like Samson, when his locks were shorn, you should become the jest of the Philistines.

This supernatural force is the power of the Holy Ghost, the power of Jehovah himself. It is a wonderful thing that God should condescend to work his marvels of grace through men. It is strange that instead of speaking, and saying with his own lips, "Let there be light," he speaks the illuminating word by our lips! Instead of fashioning a new heaven and a new earth, wherein dwelleth righteousness, by the mere fiat of his power, he couples himself with our weakness, and performs his purpose! Do you not marvel that he should treasure his gospel in these poor earthen vessels, and accomplish the miracles, which I have very briefly described, by messengers, who are themselves so utterly unable to help him in the essential parts of his heavenly work! Turn your wonder into adoration, and blend with your adoration a fervent cry for divine power. O Lord, work by us to the praise of thy glory!

(*To be continued.*)

The Up-Grade Journey.

"They go from strength to strength, every one of them in Zion appeareth before God."—Psalm lxxxiv. 7.

HEAVENWARD going, heaven still nearing,
    Journeying on the pilgrim's line,
Not by gradients steep and tortuous,
    But by beautiful incline.

Still progressing; golden sunshine
    Smiles upon me as I go,
Pleasant landscapes are around me,
    Bright in all their summer glow.

Blessed journey! upward, heavenward,
    To the palace of the King,
Marked by all that's fair and joyous,
    As upborne on eagle's wing.

Onward still, the goal approaching,
    There! it in the distance gleams!
More than filling up the picture
    Of the brightest, fondest dreams

Who would cling to earthly pleasures,
    Moving downward, downward still,
While the loftier joys are calling
    Every yielding heart to fill!

ALBERT MIDLANE.

Spiders.

BY THOMAS SPURGEON.

(*Continued from page* 164.)

REALLY, I thought I had said all that could be said on behalf of spiders in my previous paper. Hence I gave no intimation that they would be "continued" in our next. I fancied I had spun all my web. But it is with this as with our sermons, something has been omitted, and we wish we could have another say on the same subject. Moreover, I have been away from home! Home isn't the place to study the habits of spiders, at least, mine isn't, I'm glad to say. But my lot has been cast a while in a place where spiders most do congregate. There they flourished by the dozen and the score; on the verandah, all down the hall, and in every nook and corner.

> Spiders to right of us; spiders to left of us,
> I'm sure you'd have wondered
> Why the spiders weren't slain
> And their cobwebs weren't sundered.
> And you'd share my conclusion
> That some one had blundered
> In allowing such hangings
> To be there by the hundred.

It was the spiders' paradise surely. No unkind besom marred their peace, or interrupted their business. Men might come and men might go; but they held on for ever. Enemies from without there were, as we shall presently see, but fear of molestation from within the house there was none; for the owner thereof had a special dislike to flies, and spared the spiders on that account. I'm not positive that this was the sole reason, but charity suggests it. Ah, well! they were not there for nought. At all events, they served my purpose; I had not far to go, or long to look, for specimens and illustrations. There was one daring fellow, swinging like a pendulum at the end of his long line; there was another, scampering down to the citadel of his castle at express speed, so as to extend as early a welcome as possible to an afternoon visitor; while others watched like cats for mice, hungry hunters they were, and their more fortunate neighbours ruminated over their last fat fly, like Pharaoh's well-favoured kine "upon the brink of the river." Indeed, it seemed scarcely fair that there should be such manifest disparity in the fortunes of these creatures. There, standing out against the blue sky, was a tremendous fellow, a veritable Falstaff, as plump as a dumpling; while at scarce a hand-breadth from him was another, as thin as a whipping post. Is providence partial amid spiders as well as among men? Is that fellow Dives, and this Lazarus? And fat as he was, he got more spoil than the starveling. He worked no harder, indeed he seemed too corpulent to stir; while the other was always "on the go." Their "stand" must have been equally good, for the one was alongside the other. How was it, then, that one was rich, and the other poor? "Just luck," says one. Think you so, honestly and soberly? And are you a Christian? To believe in luck is tantamount to denying providence. Sir Thomas Brown has said, "Let not fortune, which hath no name in

Scripture, have any in thy divinity.   Let providence, not chance, have
thy acknowledgment."   We are not as shuttlecocks to the battledores
of frisky fairies and fickle chance ; and I, for one, find no difficulty in
believing that the God who rules on high looks after spiders as well as
sparrows.   Is it not written "The eyes of all wait upon thee . . . .
thou satisfiest the desire of *every living thing*" ?   Why, then, are not
all served alike ?   Wherefore this partiality ?   Why does one man have
to envy his fellow in such words as these :—

> "My house was still in the shadow,
>   His lay in the sun ;
> I long'd in vain ;—what he asked for
>   It straightway was done.
> Once I staked all my heart's treasure,
>   We play'd—and he won."

I know but one answer to the enquiry, and to the loyal heart it is
enough.   "*The Lord is King.*"   It is not for us to say, "What doest
thou ?" or, " Why hast thou made me thus ? "   " The Lord maketh poor,
and maketh rich : he bringeth low, and lifteth up."   Surely Joseph
might send Benjamin a mess five times greater than those of his
brethren, although he was the youngest, if he pleased !   The others did
not grumble.   Nor should we.   " Even so, Father : for so it seemed good
in thy sight."   Speaking of "luck" reminds me that spiders themselves
were once considered lucky.   Fancy a sensible man writing in his diary,
" I took, early in the morning, a good dose of Elixir, and hung three
spiders about my neck, and they drove my ague away ! "   What will not
some fond folk believe ?   Anything save the truth !
But I have wandered far from the spiders' paradise.   There they
were, as I have said, as plentiful as blackberries, and as "there is
nothing without voice," I listened for their lessons.   One of them said,
emphatically, " BE PATIENT."   There he stayed all the hours, day after
day.   Possibly he went for a stroll when my back was turned ; but if so,
he must have hurried home pretty smartly, for, on my return, he was
in statu quo.   I'm inclined to think that he never budged, until indeed
the long-looked-for game flew into his trap ; *then* he moved, I tell you.
His was a silent sermon, but it was very impressive.   The text was,
"Your strength is to sit still."   He showed me that all things come to
him that waits.   He bade me in quietness and confidence possess my
soul.   But I must own that what seemed as easy as kissing your hand,
to the spider, is no child's play for men and women.   To sit still !   Why,
as a boy, I was offered sixpence to sit still for five minutes ; and when,
by an almost superhuman effort, I once succeeded, dear father chalked
it up on the wall.   I remember it as if it were but yesterday.   Our
heavenly Father has very few children who are not fidgety.   Some of
them seem all on wires—regular spring-heel Jacks.   Not content with
doing their part, they must needs worry and fret about results and
issues.   Wiser would they be if, having spun the web, they watched
and waited.   " See," said the sensible spider, " I spread my toils, and
wait till God sends the fly."   " I will act similarly," thought I.

> " I'll do the little I can do,
>   And leave the rest to him."

I will take due precaution against accident, and then beg him to shield me from harm. I will exercise all possible effort in my life's work, be it temporal or spiritual, and leave results to heaven. Meanwhile, my soul shall wait only upon God. Dear reader, may you learn this lesson too! May you share in "the patience of the saints"! "The Lord direct your hearts into *the patience of Christ.*" (R.V.)

Then, all the spiders seemed to say to me, "BE VIGILANT." It was not possible to surprise them, or to catch them napping. They seemed all eye. And, as if that might fail, they had each a thread communicating with the centre of their webs. Not only were their ears and eyes open, but they had, so to speak, tied a string from the door to their toes, so that they might know if anyone came to the front door, even if they happened to be in the back kitchen. Friends or foes, by this means, received due attention without delay. The spider and Peter give the same advice, "Be vigilant." Don't miss any privilege or opportunity. Be prepared for every enemy. Keep your eyes open. Some there are who have eyes, but they see not. "The wise man's eyes are in his head." "The eyes of a fool are in the ends of the earth." Above all, see that that thread is not broken, or hangs too slackly. Conscience itself needs to be tightly strung.

> " Quick as the apple of the eye,
>   O God, my conscience make;
> Awake my soul when sin is nigh,
>   And keep it still awake."

Yet another of these unpopular insects said, as plainly as a spider can speak, "BE VALIANT"; and this is how he said it. A tremendous dragon-fly suddenly hove in sight. Thought I, "If that man-of-war should steer this way, good-bye to the web, and alas for the spider!" But I was wrong. Presently the bright wings dashed into the snare, and almost before one could say the proverbial "Jack Robinson," Mr. Spider had pounced upon his prey. I was disposed to urge him back to his den. Is not discretion the better part of valour? Surely such silvery wings, and such a length of tail could flash through the threads, and go on glistening in the sunshine; or, if the dragon waited, could he not demolish the spider? Had the little fellow counted the cost? Did this David know that that Goliath " had an helmet of brass upon his head, and was armed with a coat of mail, with greaves of brass upon his legs, and a target of brass between his shoulders"? Whether he knew it or not, out he rushed. With wonderful celerity he passed his ropes over and under the gauze-like wings, and soon the dragon was in the inner prison, as it were, with his tail made fast in the stocks. His travelling days were done. He might whirr and whizz as he pleased; his doom was sealed. "Well done, little spider! I admire your pluck; you evidently did not go by size, or weight, or looks. As for size, that dragon could have devoured you *holus bolus*; as to weight, it must be admitted he has shaken your castle from centre to circumference, while his appearance was that of a flash of lightning. True, your net helped you amazingly. You remind me of the old gladiators who fought with a trident and net; the net deftly flung entangled the swordsman, and then the big fork easily sucked his blood. So you first snare, and then slay your enemies. But you are brave for all that, else

you would not have tackled that glittering gladiator." I, too, would be
brave betimes. Everyone grows courageous when all is over. Anyone
can pursue the fleeing foe; but to seize the decisive moment, to act
and speak in the nick of time, to confront the foe without parleying;
this is the test of courage and capacity. We Christians ought to be
A 1 at this. Fear says, "All the Canaanites are sons of Anak"; but faith
cries, "We can lay them low." Fearfulness calls every gnat a dragon-
fly; while fearlessness says, "The bigger the better; there be more blood
in his veins. He'll last over to-morrow; whereas, a midge is. but a
mouthful." Oh, that believers were braver! Oh, that Christians were
courageous! We fly when we should fight, and run when we might
reign. Our valour has evaporated. We do not attempt such great
things for God as he deserves, and as his cause demands. Besides, he
is our helper, so we need not fear. As Jehoshaphat said to the priests
and Levites, so saith the Lord to every saint, "Deal courageously, and
the Lord shall be with the good."

My sympathy for spiders is getting (as the Yankees say) "pretty
considerable." I confess I had little enough to start with. I find that
they have enemies not a few—hence my sympathy. Amongst these is
a bee, who is both a mason and a murderer. A mason he certainly is,
for he builds his house himself of clay, and a murderer, too, for his
house is full of dead spiders. I saw at least a dozen fall out of a
waterproof which had been hanging in the hall, and in which these
building bees had made their home. There could be no mistake—the
spiders were "as dead as door-nails." Alas, poor spiders! there had
been foul play some dark night; and, like the Assyrians, "When they
arose early in the morning, behold, they were all dead corpses." But
who has not enemies? Only those who have not grit enough to say
"No," and to stem the current. "Life is strangely beset with enemies.
No man is too contemptible to have one. Even humble creatures like
the caterpillar have enemies." So says the Rev. J. G. Wood, of whose
decease we have heard with deep regret.

"The last enemy that shall be destroyed is death." Like these bees,
he slays and bears us off to our lodging in the clay; but that, thank
God, is not the end. "The skies, not the grave, are our goal," and
they who see our sepulchres need not say, "Alas! poor mortals"; for,
unlike the spiders, we shall not have ceased to be, though some would
relegate us to such a lot. Souls, with such materialistic minds, are as
these spiders were. We believe it not. When our bodies are as lifeless
as they, encased in clammy clay like them, our souls will be on high.
The spirit shall return unto God who gave it.

> "Thanks be to God, there is no death
> For all who trust his Word;
> Thanks be to God for victory,
> Through Jesus Christ our Lord."

Why always Whisper?

AN esteemed evangelist, a member of the Tabernacle church, sends the following interesting items :—

While reading the short article in this month's *Sword and Trowel*, entitled "Why always Whisper?" a similar incident occurred to my mind, and as you express a wish that other correspondents would favour you with such, I make bold to send you the following :—

Some five years ago, I was preaching in the South London Palace. One Sunday night, amongst the audience were some personal friends of mine, a mother and two daughters ; also a near relative of my own, a poor fellow who had been afflicted with paralysis. One result of his affliction was that he *could not whisper*, but always talked very loudly. Under the preaching of the Word, that night, one of the daughters above-mentioned, was deeply impressed. I had some conversation with her, but she did not seem to grasp the truth. They left, accompanied by my poor friend, who, being very anxious for the salvation of this dear girl, went all the way home with the sisters, telling them all the way about the Saviour he loved so well. When he arrived at their home, he continued to urge this young woman to decide for Christ, and eventually she did so. Now comes the most wonderful part of the story. While telling them of Jesus, and praying with them, which, owing to his affliction, he did very loudly, they were rather startled, by hearing someone sobbing in an adjoining room. Upon going to see what was the cause of this sobbing, and who it was, they found it was a young woman, a niece of the landlady of the house, who, having heard through the wall all this poor brother had said about Jesus and his love, was thereby brought to see herself a poor, lost sinner. She was pointed by him to the sinner's Saviour, and was led there and then to trust in Jesus for salvation. She, with the others, came on the next Sunday to the South London Palace. I saw her then, and several times afterwards, and she appeared to be a bright, happy Christian. How wonderfully God works, using the very affliction of our poor friend for his glory!

It is sometimes a good thing to *sing* aloud, as well as *pray* aloud, as the following, I think, will show. David says, "I will sing *aloud* of thy mercy " (Psalm lix. 16).

Some little time before the former fact occurred, I went to work in a new shop, where none of the nine or ten men were on the Lord's side. By his grace I did not hide my colours. As soon as I got on speaking terms with the men, which I soon did, one of them said to me, " We knew you were an old *ranter*, as soon as you came into the place." "Indeed," said I; "how ? " " Why," said he, " you commenced *singing* Sankey's hymns as soon as you commenced work." It was true, and by God's help I *kept on singing aloud* at my work, and sometimes talking with them a bit, and the Lord, in his own good time, brought every one in that shop to himself. (See Spurgeon's sermon, " Beginning at Jerusalem.")

I trust you will pardon me in thus writing, but I thought these true incidents might interest and encourage you.

Believe me to be your obedient servant,

C. LAZENBY.

"The Greatest of these is Love."

HOW free in gift is Love!
        Not like the host
        Who counts the cost,
And fears lest he should give too much;
Love comes behind, with timid touch,
And breaks the vase, in haste to pour
On the dear feet its fragrant store,
        Unmindful of the glance
        That clouds the countenance
Of him who scorns her in his arrogance:
        More than content that he,
        Who thought and heart can see,
Accepts the tribute of her loyalty.

        How brave of soul is Love!
        When, cowardly,
        The strong men flee,
Love, bold in weakness, ventures nigh
Where hangs her Lord in agony,
Braving the brutal ribaldry
Of rabble and of soldiery;
        And while the quaking earth
        Rebukes their heartless mirth,
Love gazes sadly on the gentle face
        Once so divinely fair,
        But now enlined with care
And suffering, borne to save a guilty race.

        How true of heart is Love!
        When faith has fled,
        And hope is dead,
Love lingers at the empty tomb,
Unmindful of the cheerless gloom,
Unwilling to forsake the place
Till she her missing Lord may trace.
        Her eyes o'erfilled with tears,
        And heart oppressed by fears,
She waits without a thought of self or home,
        Till by his voice most sweet
        She knows, and at his feet
Adores, him newly risen from the tomb.

April 18, 1889.   E. A. TYDEMAN, Bacup.

Unconscious Sanctification.

A PAPER READ AT THE SECOND CONFERENCE OF THE PASTORS'
COLLEGE EVANGELICAL ASSOCIATION,

BY PASTOR THOMAS GREENWOOD, CATFORD HILL.

NOTHING in the whole realm of Christian experience can compare in importance with sanctification. It is a great thing to be reconciled to God and accepted in the Beloved ; but forgiveness and reconciliation may be regarded more as a means than an end. We were predestinated to nothing less than to be conformed to the image of God's Son. Our sins are blotted out, and all hindrance to fellowship is removed, that the Holy Spirit may be given to us, and the Divine image renewed. If this be not done, forgiveness has not accomplished its purpose. Fully realizing the importance of holiness, we welcome every movement whose aim is to increase it in ourselves or in others.

But I fear that many of these efforts suffer by a forgetfulness of the fact that true holiness, like every true greatness, is unconscious of itself. The endeavour to increase sanctification is confused with the desire to increase the consciousness of sanctification, which is a very different thing. We want to feel more consecrated, to know that we are growing ; and if we have not this feeling, or are not passing through experiences such as some one whom we admire describes, we begin to question if our sanctification be real. It may be we look back on our own history, and call to mind how at one time we had to invoke God's special aid in doing certain actions ; while we did them, then, consciously for Christ, we fear lest now we are led by mere force of habit. But may we not have formed the habit of serving Christ ? If so, the ease and persistency of our actions indicate a real advance. Perhaps we had, for example, a covetous disposition, and found it very hard to give liberally to any cause ; we then had to look right back to the grace of our Lord Jesus Christ in order to gain the necessary impulse. The only question we *now* ask is as to the proportionate claims of, say, the Pastors' College, as compared with the Orphanage. You have probably read the American story of the man who had listened to a sermon containing a powerful appeal ; at its close he was heard to say, " I'll give five dollars." But while the plate was coming he changed it to three dollars. A moment after he said to himself, " I'll only give two dollars." Evidently, there was a struggle going on within him between the old nature and the new. The collecting-plate soon brought it to a crisis. He flung ten dollars into the plate, and said, "Now, squirm, old natur'!" My acquaintance with Yankee classics is not enough to enable me exactly to translate "squirm" into vulgar English ; but its meaning is sufficiently evident : having given twice as much as he at first intended, his old nature was made to squirm. Such a struggle might take place again, but not often. One or two more victories as complete as this would end the strife, and then, without an effort, he would give to every cause as far as he was able. But would he then be less holy ? Assuredly not. Still, if you had offered him your congratulations that Sunday on his generosity, he would have accepted them. God had enabled him to be liberal, and he rejoiced in it, giving God the praise. But if, years afterwards, when greater liberality was habitually exercised, you should speak in the same way, he would repudiate the idea of praise altogether, and only bemoan that he could do no more.

Any man who has become a disciple of Christ will, before long, be confronted by a difficulty with regard to his old companions. Two paths lie before him: in one is continued honour from his friends, in the other is Christ's reproach. He finds it hard to follow his Master. He cries for help and is strengthened, then bravely undergoes all ridicule. After a while another crisis arises, and yet another. In them fidelity to Christ may involve a greater loss, and yet the struggles may be less keen, because the world has come to be less valued and Christ more. He has now learned to make his boast in the Lord. Is he, however, less holy because the struggle is less? Unquestionably the reverse. But here again, if at first you said, "What a consecrated man you are!" he would accept your praise, and he might, perhaps, go to the next Holiness Convention, tell of his difficulties in putting his earthly prospects on the altar, and declare he was now fully consecrated. But afterwards, he would disclaim all title to commendation, and say, "To follow Christ was so evidently better that I did it naturally; but as for complete consecration," he might add, "if I were put into the position some have occupied, and had to 'turn or burn,' unless God gave me more grace, my faith would waver."

The recently-converted thief is always struggling against dishonesty, but it is not so with the thoroughly honest man. He acts honourably without consideration. If a temptation arises to which his honesty is barely equal, then comes conflict; but while he is superior, he knows nothing of either battle or victory.

At first success causes delight, but afterwards it is tinged with shame. Instead of rejoicing that God gave us the victory, we mourn that we had to struggle over so small a matter. "After all the grace God has shown me, to think that for a moment I withheld what He asked! If I had only loved the Lord more, I should have rendered it without an effort!"

Struggles will not cease while we aim at actual conformity to Christ. He who, in this life, has come to complete repose, is drifting down the stream. But while struggles remain, their causes will change. Paul had his agony, but the occasion of it in his case was not the same as with us. Many things which we can only accomplish by a supreme effort of faith had become habitual to him. It was the loftiness of his ideal which made him groan as he did. If we have not now the same signal victories that we once had, if we are unable to say, "I have realized what I was aspiring to," the reason may be that we are no longer occupied in meeting definite actual transgressions; our ideal is higher now, and we are endeavouring to bring every thought and emotion into captivity to the obedience of Christ.

It is very difficult to reckon our advances in spiritual things, or to compare our position with that of others. There are height and weight machines for the body; examinations serve the same purpose for the intellect; but there is nothing to test or compare the growth of the spirit. A man may be exulting in progress when there has really been decline; or he may be bemoaning his dissimilarity to Christ when he has been increasing in His likeness. The little shallow brook makes a great noise as it ripples over the stones and down its diminutive cataracts

—you can hear it at a distance, it attracts attention to itself. But wait until it becomes a huge river, on which navies can float, whose flow is irresistible, and it will be so quiet that you are unaware of its presence until you stand on its banks. When love works great effects, it is greater than when it is emotional and self-conscious. If it has become so powerful that dams are impossible, and little impediments cause scarcely a ripple, it is because its volume has increased.

Struggles, then, while they indicate growth, show also a lack of complete attainment. We might further say that when we rejoice in our attainments, it is questionable if we have really made them. If a man tells you joyfully his liver is working well, it is evidently not accustomed to do so ; and you would not be surprised if a change of wind made him less jubilant about his health. When a man declares he is fully consecrated, that his all is on the altar, and he is waiting for the fire, he may be perfectly sincere ; but I fear his consecration is a little precarious, he is not so thoroughly devoted as he thinks, or he would not remark it so much. When a child begins to walk, every step is a triumph ; he stands at one chair, another is two feet away, he hesitates, balances himself, takes three steps, and looks up delighted ; and rightly so, his father thinks, at any rate. But when he *knows* he can walk, he walks but little. When he is thoroughly able to do it, he does not congratulate himself upon taking three or three thousand steps without falling ; he never thinks of it, and is unconscious of danger or success. If he makes one fall, his mind dwells on that more than on the miles he has gone without stumbling. When a man says, "I have been three months without a conscious transgression," we are glad to hear it ; but it is evidently a new experience. We hope he will find that this should be the normal condition of Christian men, and not remark every day of success, but be very humiliated for every failure.

Paul described his position thus :—" One thing I do, forgetting the things which are behind, and stretching forward to the things which are before, I press on toward the goal unto the prize of the high calling of God in Christ Jesus." His past achievements he does not think of so much as the distance which still separates him from the goal, that to which he has been called, that for which he was apprehended of Christ. Generous men have sometimes, on the summits of mountains, provided a seat on which is written, " Rest and be thankful." When you have reached the highest peak you may do this appropriately, but in spiritual climbing you never arrive there. While in the valley below you see the mountain is high, but clouds limit your vision, and you cannot tell how high it really is. As you ascend, the air becomes clearer, and you realize more and more how far you are from your destination. Never mind what is behind ! If it be a great advance, thank God, and take courage, but do not sit down and contemplate it.

The man who knows he is humble has lost his humility. The man who thinks of himself as kind, loving, gentle, moral, honest, has these graces in the smallest degree. They are not fully attained until they have become natural and unobserved. When the Saviour commends those on His right hand for their generosity and love, they feel themselves altogether unworthy of His praise. True, they had helped the poor, they could do no less ; but they were not conscious of serving the Lord as He indicates. Their well-doing had become a holy and blessed

19

habit with them, they had no anticipation of reward. This I take to be the perfect condition—that holiness should be our very nature, and we should be so accustomed to serve Christ as not to notice it in every particular action.

Certainly, the converse of this is the deepest degradation. While a man feels the shame of drunkenness, there is hope of his reform. While a man blushes at his dishonesty, you may bring him back to upright-ness. But when the drunkard feels no shame, when the man looks on dishonesty as a necessary condition of his business, and glories in his sharp practice, then he is as low as he can be; there is no hope for him. God must convince him of sin before he will turn. And as unconsciousness of sin is the deepest degradation, so unconsciousness of purity is the highest holiness.

In proportion as we attain to likeness to Christ, we cease to observe that likeness; but our failures stand forth prominently in our daily thoughts. Men talk of "the second blessing"; but there is a third blessing, of which, I am told, our President spoke in one of his ser-mons. Job had his first blessing when he became a God-fearing man; he had his second blessing when the lamp of God shined on his head, and the secret of God was upon his tent, when everyone rose at his presence, and accorded him honour because of his many and signal virtues. But a third, and higher, blessing he received when he was made to say, "I have heard of thee by the hearing of the ear: but now mine eye seeth thee. Wherefore I abhor myself, and repent in dust and ashes." Brethren, it is this third blessing we prize. It is not our ambition to have attainments to dwell upon, or to "delight in a sense of inward purity," as one wrote; rather would we have a sense of inward *im*purity wherever it exists, and feel more keenly when we fail to resemble our Master. We would be holy—not as Mr. So-and-so is holy—but as HE is holy whose whole nature it is to be holy.

Beholding the Lord not only makes us abhor ourselves, but trans-forms us into His image from glory to glory; and this is real sanctification. In Israel's last era they lost that vivid conception of God which patriarchs and psalmists enjoyed. They would not use the august name of "Jehovah," lest it should be degraded, but substituted for it the name of "Lord." Refusing to look into the face of God, or to call Him by His true name, they lost sight of Him more and more. One consequence of this was that the very idea of holiness was changed, high moral principles ceased to be esteemed, and trifles were lifted into prominence. So will it be with us; if we lose sight of Him in His unspeakable holiness, we shall be pedantic, squeamish, and censorious in our own holiness, instead of being deeply, freely, and joyfully holy. A little self-introspection is good; better have much than be indifferent to one's condition; but divine contemplation is most to be desired. It was not while Elijah abode in the cave, but when he went forth and stood upon the mount before the Lord, that his petulance was dissolved, and he was qualified to fulfil fresh duties.

This is the will of God, even our sanctification. There is no sin which is unconquerable, no failure which is irremediable. If we attain to nothing higher it is because our willingness, or our faith, is at fault. Robert Murray McCheyne asked himself, "Is it the desire of my heart to be altogether holy? Is there any sin I wish to retain? Is sin a grief to me?" To this he answered, "Lord, thou knowest all things. Thou knowest that I hate all sin, and desire to be made altogether like Thee." Can we say the same? Am I really wishful, not for a sense of superiority over others, not for a comfortable feeling of having made progress, but for a complete likeness to Christ? Lord, reveal my shortcomings to me! Lord, remove them from me!

Sanctification is the essential thing, not consciousness of it. Let us be careful to discern what it is we are really desiring, lest, grasping at the shadow, we risk the loss of the substance.

John Newton's Preaching.

THE passage which we submit to our readers is from certain letters written by John Newton to Rev. W. Barlass, of New York. We transcribe it, not for the imitation of any, but as an instance of a method of preaching which most teachers would condemn, but which, in Mr. Newton's case, was satisfactory to his large audience. The good man was full, and could readily overflow; he was also a practised and experienced speaker, and did, in his ripe age, what no young man could attempt without extreme folly. We give the passage, not only as a curiosity, but as a counterblast against that absurd elaboration which is so much cried up. As we said the other day, "Our preachers are not satisfied unless they can plant boiled potatoes: but boiled potatoes never grow."

Let the venerable Newton tell his own tale.

"I compare the rules which have been, or may be offered, either to ministers or believers, to lasts for shoes; they must be accommodated to the foot, or else, though the shoe may *look* well, it will not *set* well. The rules of God's Word, indeed, discover their divine origin in this respect, that, being founded upon an exact knowledge of the heart of man, and the nature of his present state, they are applicable to all persons, times, and circumstances : no real inconvenience follows from observing them; but the neglect of them is always of ill consequence. But the rules of men are too personal, partial, and short-sighted to deserve our notice any farther than as hints, which we may follow, or not, just as we find them suit. I should be glad to entrust you with my judgment *pro re natâ*, in any point which might occasionally arise. But to offer you such copious advice as you desire, concerning the matter and manner of preaching, would not only be assuming too much, but would be acting contrary to my judgment and professed principles. I have formerly fettered myself by following other people's rules, and therefore ought not to shackle my friend by prescribing to him. You have the word of grace, the throne of grace, and the Spirit of grace with you. Under this divine direction, what passes within you and around you, will furnish you with better rules for your own management, than you could possibly receive from the wisest man upon earth, who was not exactly in your situation.

"The one question you have specified, rather surprised me as coming from Scotland, where I thought written sermons were only of a late

date, and even now only in use amongst those who, having departed
from the great truths of the gospel, are, of course, necessitated to live
upon their own funds. I will so far answer it, as to tell you simply how
I have been led. My first essay as a preacher was in 1758 (six years
before my admission into the Established Church), in a Dissenting
meeting-house at Leeds. I attempted it wholly extempore. But I
thought I had my general and particular heads very methodically ranged
in my mind. I set off tolerably well, though with no small fear and
trembling. I soon feared and trembled much more; for, after speaking
about ten minutes, my mouth was stopped. I stared at the people, and
they at me, but not a word more could I speak. I was forced to come
down and leave the people, some smiling and some weeping. My pride
and self-sufficiency were sorely mortified, and for two years afterward
I could not look at the place without feeling the heart-ache, and, as it
were, saying to myself, *Hic Troja stetit.* The disaster made me conclude
it would be absolutely impossible for me ever to preach without book.
Accordingly, I began to compose sermons at full length. The next
time I was asked to preach, I did not feel much trepidation. I had my
discourse in my pocket, and did not much doubt but I was able to read
it. And I read it sure enough. But being near-sighted, and rather
ashamed to hold up my notes in view, I held my head close down to the
cushion; and when I began, I durst not take my eye off for a moment,
being impressed with a fear that I should not readily fix it again upon
the right part of the page; so that I hardly saw anybody in the place
during the whole time; and I looked much more like a dull schoolboy,
poring over his lesson, than a preacher of the gospel. I was not much
less disconcerted this time than the former; and applied to my notes
the poet's words, *Nec tecum, nec sine te.* "Nor with thee, nor without
thee." At length the Lord put it into my heart to have a meeting for
a few select friends in my own house, on the Lord's-day evening, which
I continued for about the last three years I lived in Liverpool. And
in these exercises he was pleased in some measure to open my mouth.
When I came to Olney, and long afterward, I used to write about as
much as I have now written, upon the text before I preached; but for
some years past I have seldom written a page. Very often I cannot fix
upon my text before I am in the pulpit; and frequently I have begun
when I have known no more what I should say, or how I should handle
the subject, than any of the people before me; and this not of choice,
nor through indolence, but of necessity. At some such seasons, so far
as I can judge of myself, I have preached to as much advantage as if I
had studied my sermon for a month. Various have been the methods
my wise and gracious Lord has taken to break down my spirit of self-
dependence, and to hide pride from me. Of all the maxims I have met
with about preaching, I most admire that of Luther, *Bene precasse, est
bene studuisse.* "To have prayed well is to have studied well."

"If my mind was in a right frame towards the Lord, I think I should
not be greatly embarrassed if called to preach at five minutes' warning
to the most respectable congregation. But often it is otherwise with
me, and I am forced to venture with my heart sadly out of tune. How
often, and how justly, might he stop my mouth, and put me to shame
before the people! But he is merciful."

Ecclesiastical Amusements.

FROM a tract entitled "Ecclesiastical Amusements," by E. P. Marvin, Lockport, we cull the following. It is clear that America is in the same boat as England, and that in Mr. Marvin it finds the counterpart of our own beloved Archibald Brown. May some of these hot shots work havoc among the masqueraders of the sanctuary, who set up the image of Baal in the house of the Lord!

"What shall we say, what would the Master say, of a bevy of vain and bedizened young ladies, fascinating and cornering susceptible young men, to sell them commodities above value, and which they did not want? or a dance gotten up by the ' King's Daughters'? What of the many devices like grab-bag, fish-pond, bean-counting, ring-cake, and raffle, involving the gambling principle? What of the Church of God showing wax-works, and peddling small wares and fun to the world? or getting up a variety show of Mother Goose, a Fan Flirtation, a Donkey Social, a Punch and Judy Show, or a gathering of Merryandrews and Belly-worshippers (Phil. iii. 9), to replenish her treasury?

"At one of them a lady sang the song beginning with 'Lord, send me a husband!' An owl is supposed to respond, 'Who, who?' She answers: 'Almost any one, Lord, will do.'

"Comic songs, humorous recitations, dramatic exercises, and operatic selections are employed, often with the help of professionals, and sometimes advertised as ' Howling Entertainments.' A certain Y.M.C.A. held a Smoking Concert, and an entertainment by a popular actress and dancer; and another in Mexico, when all else seemed too tame, held a Bull Fight, and 'made a pot of money.'

"Said an infidel to me: 'I think your God must be in great need of money, by the tricks the churches practise to get it for him.' Many of the pious grieve over these things, and hang their heads for shame. Even those who aid and attend these performances cannot well approve them. Why have they not conscience and courage enough to witness against them? No intelligent Christian can ask God's blessing upon such practices, nor expect it to rest upon money so procured.

"Amateur dramatics to please the world and put money in the purse of the Church, *silence the testimony of the pulpit against the stage, and even promote its interests.* The theatre has always been a school of immorality, from the time when the Greeks sang and danced around their wine-god Bacchus until now, and these performances are training-schools for the play-house. A young man who had been employed in a Brooklyn theatre told me that he received his first training and taste for the stage in Sunday-school concerts. A Sunday-school in Hamilton, Canada, has lately furnished three actors for the stage.

"In fact, most of these leading ecclesiastical play people attend the theatre and the dance, and play cards, and not a few leading pulpits are weakened or silenced in their testimony against these things.

"And this babel cry for 'amusements,' with the frenzy of enterprise in the Church to meet it, has not yet culminated. God only knows where it will lead! It is world wide. I am told that a Coloured Church, South, lately dramatized and acted the Prodigal Son, actually killing and eating the Fatted Calf. It is said that their Church festivals are often characterized by the vilest orgies. Eph. v. 12."

275

"The C. H. Spurgeon."

AT the College meeting, at Dalston Junction, May 6th, Mr. Lauderdale, of Great Grimsby, greatly interested the people by the story of the fishing-smack *The C. H. Spurgeon.* That vessel has endured exceedingly rough weather, of which we gave some account in a former number : we now add a photograph. The damage is evident to every eye. *The C. H. S.* seemed done for, and indeed, had it not been exceedingly well-built, it must have gone to the bottom. In the picture, Mr. Empson, the owner, is standing in the companion, and boxes and tools are lying about, belonging to the carpenters, who lost no time in getting to work with repairs. It is wonderful how soon the boat was restored to its former glory. Long ago, what seemed a wreck has been so completely restored as to be as brisk as any other of all the fleet in fishing the deep sea. Long may the good ship be profitably occupied for its master in taking multitudes of fishes! We need not indicate the way in which Mr. Lauderdale turned the vessel *C. H. S.* into an emblem of the preacher C. H. S. Storms have happened, but the flag of C. H. S. is still flying, and his net returneth not empty. Praise the Lord!

Fighting the Dummy.

DURING our visit to Mentone we frequently saw the French soldiers at drill. The recruits were made to go through certain exercises, with sticks for swords. These men were raw recruits indeed—many of them fresh from the country, where they industriously till the soil, and lead frugal and quiet lives. The conscription compels them to quit their peaceful avocations, and come to learn the "art of war." Alas that it should be so! When will men learn war no more? As we stood, one day, looking at the young soldiers at drill, we observed them performing a certain exercise which greatly interested us for the moment. A dummy was made to represent a soldier, and was set upright with supports. The soldiers "formed into line," and at a distance of some two or three hundred yards the word of command was given, and on rushed the heroes with their weapons, to attack—what? The aforesaid dummy! As they neared the effigy a great shout was raised, one or two leading the attack; a fierce onslaught was made upon—what? The dummy! We suppose this exercise is useful in training the raw recruit, but we could not help reflecting thereon. How much this is like some of the preachers and teachers of the present day! Are they not fond of setting up all sorts of dummies to attack? spending time and energy in raising dummies of doubt and philosophy, in order to show their cleverness in destroying them. Theories of which nobody ever heard before are set up to be knocked down, and doubts are suggested, of which no one in the congregation ever dreamed, that they might be demolished. Oh, that these good people would not waste their energies upon such foolish work! Let them preach Christ and him crucified, and maintain his everlasting truth. So will his name be glorified, and the sons of men be blessed.   F. G. LADDS.

V. J. CHARLESWORTH.

V. J. Charlesworth:

MR. SPURGEON has been greatly favoured of the Lord by obtaining the help of co-workers singularly loyal and devoted, who, under his infectious zeal, work the innumerable societies clustering round the Tabernacle, each individual being strikingly suited to his position.

Conspicuously has this been the case in reference to the large orphan family of five hundred boys and girls at Stockwell. From its opening, in 1869, the Orphanage has enjoyed the wise guidance, the sympathetic control, and the enthusiastic service of the Rev. V. J. Charlesworth, as Head Master. He this year celebrates his personal jubilee, and twenty years of service at the Stockwell Orphanage.

Looking over the years that have passed since 1839, the thoughtful mind can trace the divine hand which trained Mr. Charlesworth for his special service, and the divine strength which has upheld him therein.

Like Mr. Spurgeon, Mr. Charlesworth is an Essex man. He was born April 28th, 1839. In 1858 he entered Homerton College as an educational student. His first experience of orphanage work was gained with Dr. Laseron, at his Training Home and Schools at Tottenham.

In 1864 Mr. Charlesworth became co-pastor with Mr. Newman Hall, at Surrey Chapel, and for five years found a congenial training-school, where all his sympathy for the poor and the sad might be exercised; so that, when, in 1869, Mrs. Hillyard's splendid gift of £20,000 compelled Mr. Spurgeon to begin his Orphanage, and it was necessary to find the man who could nurture it into vigorous life, the unerring hand of God led the Pastor to Mr. Charlesworth, and in him to the right man for the place. We have a quaint sense of ancient history as we read in *The Sword and the Trowel* for June, 1869: "Mr. Charlesworth, late assistant minister to Mr. Newman Hall, has now become the resident Master of the Stockwell Orphanage;" and, three months later, another "Note," also by the President, saying, "Mr. Charlesworth is a great acquisition as Master." In this, as well as in other matters, the convictions of former years are, with Mr. Spurgeon, only deepened by the lapse of time.

Here, then, began the life-work by which Mr. Charlesworth will be best remembered. Most readers of *The Sword and the Trowel* have seen the fruits of his labours, either at the Orphanage itself, or during the visits of the Choir of boys to the provinces.

Mr. Charlesworth is eminently a man of fatherly kindness and sympathy. If the face be "the index of the soul," then he is one with whom no lad would presume to take liberties, but from whom he would never shrink in cringing fear. Cross the quadrangle of the Orphanage when you will, you shall hear the merry laugh that tells of the happy and free domestic life of the Institution.

Here, at any rate, there is no "great gulf fixed" between the palace of the master and the prison of the children; the Orphanage is only an enlarged home. In latter years the return visits of "old boys" to the scene of their former days, have been very frequent, for "Stockwell is a fragrant memory."

The same kindly urbanity has secured for the inner working of the Institution that "absence of history" which constitutes the bliss of a community. Wise tact and sympathy have established mutual regard between the master and his fellow-workers. Revolt and revolution have never looked within its gates, and even serious friction has never been reported. Among the larger anxieties of such a work, the placing out of the lads and girls in suitable situations is a very real one; but herein Mr. Charlesworth has been signally successful. As a rule, far more applications for the youths and girls are received than can be met.

Growing out of the increased financial necessities of the Orphanage, as well as from the desire to let the people in the provinces have eye-witness of its work, have sprung up the visits of the Choir and Hand-bell-ringers all over the United Kingdom. This has created an interest in the Orphanage never known before, intensified it where already existing, and brought in *annually hundreds* of pounds to the exchequer. In all these things the special genius of Mr. Charlesworth has been manifest, and his zeal as a coadjutor of Mr. Spurgeon put beyond question. We gladly echo, as his fiftieth birthday goes by, the wish we once heard Mr. Spurgeon express concerning him, "O king, *live for ever!*"

The other works in which Mr. Charlesworth has engaged are neither few nor insignificant. *The Sword and the Trowel* has often carried his pen-productions, prose and poetic, to its readers. Many of the "Stock-well Orphanage Tracts" are the work of his busy brain; and often does he render a friendly turn to a tired minister by his acceptable pulpit services. His "Life of Rowland Hill," a permanent reminiscence of his Surrey Chapel associations, is the raciest book on that racy man that we know: it will pass through more editions yet. As a man, as an author, as a preacher, to know him is to esteem him; but his chief honour is that for twenty years already—and, we trust, for many, many more —he was, and will be, " the much-esteemed Head-master of the Stock well Orphanage."

The Butcher and his Coat.

BY PASTOR F. E. MARSH, SUNDERLAND.

" IF I were to take off my overcoat, you would be able to see of what trade I am." So said a good Christian brother—a butcher by trade—and, he continued, "If Christians would only take off the coat of selfishness, which many of them wear, the world would be able to see that they are the followers of Christ indeed."

Let us take off the coat of selfishness, and deny self once for all. Say of self as Peter said of his Master, " I know not the man." Sinners will not believe what we say, but they cannot deny what we do. The say of the lip must be proven by the sanctity of the life. John commended the elect lady for walking in the truth, not for talking about it (3 John 3, 4). We must keep upright in our walking, or our head will go before our heels, and we shall soon be grovelling.

Selfishness is the curse of the world, and the cause of all the division in the church. Let us be unselfish, and so be in unity with him who humbled himself to the death of the cross.

" Know thy Opportunity."*

BY MRS. REGINALD RADCLIFFE.

FOR many years Sailors' Homes and excellent Seamen's Missions, with painstaking and laborious missionaries, have been a blessing to our seaports; but in 1876 an additional institution, on quite a different plan of action, was opened in Liverpool, and called a " Strangers' Rest," followed, about a year after, by a similar one in London ; then by several other Strangers' Rests in Hull, Sweden, Denmark, Germany, Smyrna, Constantinople, the Cape, &c., &c.

The Rest in Liverpool is furnished very plainly, and does not supply food or beds, but offers a hearty welcome, a warm fire in winter, and a fountain of pure water. Upon its windows is painted, in several languages, the following invitation :—

" STRANGERS' REST.
" Seamen and Foreign Emigrants may read or write their letters, or rest.
" NOTHING TO PAY."

Inside they find a row of Bibles, in many languages, for their use in the house, and others are sold or given away with tracts.

Of the band of workers in Liverpool, numbering, perhaps, as many as seventy brethren and sisters, no one but the brother who keeps and cleans the house is paid. These workers come from the congregations of various denominations; and we would fain hope that the friendly churches who have thus contributed helpers have themselves been stimulated thereby.

The house is open every week-day from ten a.m., and on Sundays from two p.m. The harmonium, at the upper end of the general reading-room, is a great attraction. The hymns are mostly led by a lady ; and I have seen men of four or five different nations, each from a book in his own language, joining in the same tune at the same time.

Paper, envelopes, pens and ink are supplied gratis; and many a son is thus induced to write to his father or mother after years of silence.

As the general reading-room fills, the workers invite the men upstairs, each nationality going to a separate room. There the workers read the Bible, and speak and pray with the strangers in their own tongue. During the last twelve years many have so been led to Jesus, and thus the gospel, free of cost, is carried to the far-off parts of the world.

To the London Rest the Jews habitually resort, and several have been converted. At times of hardship or persecution in Russia, many Jews are welcomed at the Liverpool Strangers' Rest.

When Mrs. Osborne was working at the London Rest, Miss Lowe asked her if she had ever thought of the foreign field. This suggestion was prayed over, and Mrs. Osborne started, at her own charges, for the Cape of Good Hope, and opened a Soldiers' and Sailors' Rest at Table Bay. For years there has been much blessing there. She writes home of a young soldier, a private in the ordnance corps, converted on

---

* With the hearty desire that friends will be moved to aid this institution, and others like it, we gladly insert this article. The honoured name of the writer will command special attention.

Mr. Varley's subsequent visit to the Cape, who, from that moment, began to work earnestly amongst the poor natives in Cape Town. He did not live long afterwards; but both black and white people were weeping over his grave. Every corps in the garrison was represented at his funeral. During his three weeks' illness it was most touching to hear the constant enquiries from the poor natives at the Military Hospital. The work this soldier began has spread abundantly.

A Russian sailor, converted at the Rest in London, translated two English tracts given him there, and sent his translation to his parents in Russia, whereby they were both brought to the Lord. This sailor now writes from his Russian home :—"My heart is still overflowing with gratitude to my King of kings for his keeping power, and his loving-kindness and tender mercies to me. Hallelujah ! Glory be to God alone for evermore, for I am safely home now, and all is 'well with my parents, and they are living for Jesus ; but, oh, do pray for me, that our heavenly Father may grant it, and give this blessing for it, that I may be allowed to speak *here* for Jesus in public. Oh, my heart weeps over these erring ones here, but I can't do anything for them yet. O Lord, Lord, have mercy on them, with death's shadow covered over the people here. Yes, Lord, I keep believing that they will see that real light."

From my own experience of Russia, I can sympathize deeply with this heart-prayer; for when in Russia, not long ago, with my husband and daughter, the police kept a very sharp look-out on all attempts to preach the gospel publicly. One evening, when we had, with other friends, met more than, perhaps, one hundred people in a house, the police surprised us. The meeting had been a very blessed one. We were all so happy together, singing and praying, and seekers finding the Saviour, that we for a time had quite forgotten the police. Suddenly a loud knock reminded us where we were, and an officer, with his men, entered, crimson with passion. He stamped up and down, his sword clanking at his side. Words poured out like a torrent, but fortunately some of us did not understand Russian. The meeting was, of course, suppressed, names and addresses of the people present taken down; and shortly afterwards our host of that evening was compelled to depart from his beloved Russia.

Mr. Torre, who has been for six years a devoted and wise helper at the London Rest, believing that the Lord would have him go and tell of his mighty love where there are fewer Christians, began, two years ago, to look for an opening so to do, where he could support himself and his family. He is now sailing immediately with his wife and children for South America. He intends to be a self-sustaining missionary, and expects, also, to open a Strangers' Rest at Buenos Ayres.

At the Liverpool Strangers' Rest, one of the most blessed branches of the work has been to extend a hand of love and sympathy to the crowds of foreign-speaking emigrants on their way to America, who stay about two nights. Their hearts are often made tender by recent partings, and so they listen most gratefully to words of comfort from Christian friends, and many write back of blessing received. On arriving in Liverpool, they go to their boarding-house, and, after refreshment, have a long evening to pass. In nearly every group of emigrants some one who can interpret is often to be found, and is of use when our foreign-speaking workers are not present. These strangers need no formal service, but real, earnest helpers to draw them to Jesus. Just now is the emigrant season with us, and thousands of these foreign-speaking men, women, and children are passing through Liverpool to the far West.

The Rev. Josiah Strong, D.D., of New York, thus writes in *Our Country*, p. 39 :—"The United States has many attracting influences, while the influences of Europe are expellent, and the facilities of travel are increasing year by year. . . . These threefold influences, therefore, which regulate immigration, all co-operate to increase it, and insure that for years to come this great gulf-stream of humanity will flow on with a rising flood. . . . . In view of the fact that Europe is able to send us nearly nine times as many immigrants during the next thirty years as during the thirty years past, without any diminution of her population, and in view of all the powerful influences co-operating to stimulate the movement, is it not reasonable to conclude that we have seen only the advance guard of the mighty army which is moving upon us ? "

Now, it will be asked, What is the object of this appeal ?

1st. That similar Strangers' Rests should be commenced in all suitable seaports of Britain and the world.

2nd. That in those comparatively few ports of Britain and Europe through which emigrants stream to America and our colonies, special efforts should at once be made on behalf of the emigrants, and particularly on behalf of the foreign-speaking ones.

3rd. That whilst the above-named efforts are being made in Europe, our zealous Christian friends of America and our colonies should be entreated to make corresponding and greatly-increased efforts for the evangelization of the masses they may expect shortly to pour into their country from the kingdoms of Europe.*

Difficulties—How can they be overcome ?

As step number one, get alone into your closet and pray ; then try to get one or two out-and-out Christian brothers or sisters to join you, such as will feel it a privilege to work without any pay, in the same way that you will propose to do yourself. If they object, and say, " That is very novel ! " reply, " It was novel a hundred years ago, when Raikes, on initiating Sunday-schools, arranged that all his Sunday-school teachers were to be paid, and his scheme collapsed, being brought down by the cost of the teachers' salaries; and so his movement stopped till another head suggested that none of the teachers should be paid." Since then the Sunday-school movement has rolled on gloriously ; and what would the churches in Britain or America have been these hundred years but for Sunday-school teachers ? Now, all that you will be proposing is merely an extension of the Sunday-school principle, viz., enlarging it to week-days as well as Sundays. This we accomplish, not, of course, by each worker coming every evening of the week, but by relays. Such has, for years, been the practice in many of our Ragged-schools.

---

* When lately in America with the Rev. J. Hudson Taylor and my husband, I was greatly impressed on finding myself amongst a hundred thousand foreigners massed in one city, forming about a third of its population.

Next, inquire for the use of a room, or house, or school-room, in a convenient situation. The situation must be convenient for the *strangers*. Be very slow to build or buy. In Liverpool and London we have never bought, but secured suitable shops or houses. If it should be determined to hire a house, it should contain one large room and several smaller ones, in order to deal with different languages at the same time.

Foreign Missions are the question of the hour; but have we not here many of the nations of the world brought to our very doors in Britain and Europe, and afterwards massed in hundreds of thousands at the doors of our American friends, manifestly indicating that we should let them hear that Jesus Christ came into the world to save sinners? As the church of the living God, *we* have thus a great responsibility, whilst our beloved friends in America have a wondrous opportunity; and, taught of God, they will know how nobly to improve it, ever remembering that their country doubles its population in the extraordinarily short period of twenty-five years.

"The stranger that dwelleth with you shall be unto you as one born among you, and thou shalt love him as thyself."—Leviticus xix. 34.

A Student's Impressions of the 1889 Conference.*

THE long-expected day has dawned, and on Monday afternoon, May 6th, we came together for our second Conference on the new foundation, which is simply the old one emphasized. It certainly seems strange to older brethren, who have gathered at this season, year after year, that the Conference should have a new name, for that is the only thing new in it. The President is the same; how ridiculous to suppose it could be otherwise! In belief, and in object, it is the same; and, except that a few well-known brethren are not here, the faces are much the same. Yet there is great significance in our now being called members of the Pastors' College *Evangelical* Association, for it marks an era in the history of the brotherhood.

Last year we were in a ferment. The fierce waters of controversy made some of us, who had not found our "sea legs," wish for a quiet haven; but now we are in smoother waters, with the same captain and much the same crew. Certain foreigners, who were going the same way, have been invited on board by the captain; and right good brethren they seem to be. My endeavour shall be to give an outsider some idea of the reason why these four hundred brethren came together during the happy week which is now ended.

The Conference is generally invited for the first day to one of our larger London chapels. On Monday, May 6, we went to Dalston Junction Chapel, a very bright, roomy, and artistic building, which looks well when filled, as it was in the evening, and is on the Lord's-day. By-the-by, Pastor Burton's place of worship suffers, in common with many other chapels in the metropolis, from too close proximity to the railway. The frequent puffs, snorts, and screams of engines, as they passed almost under one end of the building, did not deepen devotion, although they ensured wakefulness. When any of us set about erecting a chapel, our experience at Dalston will serve as a caution, and prevent our selecting a site upon the banks of a railway. It must be hard to keep the pastures green and the waters still by the side of an iron way which is enlivened by such vigorous sounds.

---

* This paper is the unsolicited contribution of a student. Friends will, we think, be interested in it, and they will forgive our inserting certain enthusiastic expressions, so natural to a student, though so complimentary to ourselves.

·Our first meeting was for prayer; and here is the key to the whole position. We come together as men of God, and prayer is our first thought. The Conference, first and foremost, is intended to deepen piety and intensify zeal. We want the Conference to lead us to the heights of spiritual communion; and for this we cry to God. As one brother said, "We want to stand on the mountain where heavenly breezes blow"—so we began with an earnest climb up the hill-side of fellowship, along the path of prayer. A good beginning is not everything, but to us it means a great deal. This is our *touch* meeting: here we get in touch with one another, for our brother over there prays just our prayer, tells out precisely our difficulties, and breathes exactly our desires. Here we get in touch with the spirit and aim of the Conference, for deep conviction of the truth, earnest faith in God, a sense of great need, and wrestling importunity, speak in every prayer. Something definite is being prayed for, and that something definite is what *we* want. This gathering might very truly have been called a *waiting* meeting, for we waited on the Lord for his inspection, and correction, and then for the baptism of his Holy Spirit. Persuaded that the divine blessing was coming, we did not want to block the passage, and so we joined in the prayer, "O Lord, let us get ourselves out of thy way, so that we may not hinder thee from blessing us!" This meeting was full of power from beginning to end, and was to the rest of our meetings like the servant's lighting the morning fire for the family.

Dalston friends provided a bountiful tea, for which we thanked them. We met in the chapel for the public meeting at seven. It was a fine gathering of people, who evidently appreciated the work of the College, and loved its President. The burst of enthusiasm which greeted Mr. Spurgeon, as he rose to explain the nature and object of the meeting, did our hearts good. If a meeting starts in a cold and formal way, it takes twice the effort to make it blaze. After prayer and praise, Mr. Spurgeon said that exactly eight hundred men had been sent out by the Pastors' College, and that since 1865, when the first Conference met, 83,037 had been added to the churches by baptism, and there had been a clear increase of 68,784. During the President's soul-stirring address, on "Reality in Religion," the puff and snort of the passing locomotive were not unwelcome, for they touched that inexhaustible spring of wit and humour in our President, which is so ready to act, and is so frequently used for good purposes. The address was with power, and stirred the inmost souls of the hearers. The speeches to-night were all of a very high order, and we especially enjoyed the incisive remarks of Pastor W. Julyan (Trowbridge) on "Reality in Prayer." Among other good things, he said, "Some pray for the 'masses' to be brought in, and then speak slightingly of a congregation of poor people; others pray earnestly for the conversion of our elder scholars, and then speak disparagingly of those who gathered a crowd of boys and girls." "Reality" was the keynote of all the speeches on Monday night, and the desire to be more real Christians must have entered many a heart! Our conviction is that many of those who heard will be more real from that night. One of the best things said in the evening was a remark of our noble host, Mr. Burton. He said, "I have been called a follower of Mr. Spurgeon; but that is not true: *I have never followed him, for he has never moved.*" It was a sight indeed to see the dense crowd blocking the street to bid farewell to our President as he came out; they did so with loud and long-continued cheers.

Tuesday is our first day in the College Conference Hall. Many brethren were unable to be at the meeting of the previous night, but they were forthcoming on the Tuesday morning. To-day is the time for pleasant recognitions, and for renewal of old acquaintances; and you must know that a great deal of such "conference" goes on outside the College walls. We want to know how our country brethren are doing, and we would fain cheer them, and learn from them. At 10.30 we were trooping into our spacious

Conference Hall—hallowed by precious memories. We had a season of close fellowship with God in prayer and thanksgiving.

One of the pastors said, "You who are yet in College do not know how we who are out in the field long for this Conference. The reason is that the Conference is generally an extraordinary experience, and we long for it as a season of refreshing in the midst of exhausting toil." Ministers working on alone from the beginning to the end of the year are apt to run down; and that testimony must be true which says, "Churches never suffer by sending their ministers to the Conference, for there they get such a spiritual filling, that the influence is seen in their ministry for many a day after."

We were led in prayer by some brethren well known to us—all must have been well known to God, for they prayed as only those can do to whom prayer is a life habit. What power there was in those deep-sounding "Amens" which rolled over the assembly! The burden of the prayers was for our own spiritual state, and for more power in our ministry. The hall was quite full, and as we looked into the visitors' gallery, and saw that to be full also, we thought that it was a good thing that our congregations should be thus represented; for when they hear the prayers, they must say, "Why, these ministers' prayers are just like other men's prayers; these ministers have like passions as ourselves, their hearts throb as do ours." This season of devotion brought such blessing that it was profitably prolonged until noon.

Then followed the great event of the Conference—the President's address. Englishmen know how to pay honours where they are due. It was no pre-arranged matter, but a spontaneous outburst of loving sympathy that brought us all to our feet, as our President stood before us, to begin his address. Soon cheers gave place to song, as the hall rang with the strains of the doxology.

About the address itself, what can we say? Readers of *The Sword and the Trowel* will have it in full, so they can read it for themselves, though they cannot expect to feel it as did those who had the privilege of listening to it as it gushed from the living fount.

The address lasted more than an hour-and-a-half. Did someone whisper that both speaker and hearers must have been tired? You would not suggest that if you had listened to one of these Conference addresses, and especially to this one.

After a brief recess, the Conference business was transacted. We know societies that waste much valuable time over jots and tittles; but the business of our Conference was got through in a very short space, and yet was by no means hurried.

After dinner we made our way to the Orphanage at Stockwell. You know what a model institution that is. Like everything else connected with the Metropolitan Tabernacle, it bears the mark of a master-hand. There is nothing like an apology anywhere: things are done boldly, and done well.

After tea came another meeting, characteristic of the aim of the Conference—a gathering for prayer and mutual stirring-up.

The Orphanage choir was there to sing. We enjoyed the jumping, shouting, laughing, and cheering of the children as the President came in, for they thus showed their love without restraint.

Brethren who had specially interesting accounts of pastoral work, gave them to us. There was no programme, any brother could speak; but we admired the forethought which invited Dr. Sinclair Paterson and Rev. David Davies (Brighton) to be present.

Mr. Davies said he liked our College because we were "pulpit-makers," rather than "pulpit-seekers," referring of course to the many churches founded by our men. Dr. Paterson said many things which we cheered to the echo. We felt the force of his question when he asked, referring to

those who explain away the substitutionary work of our Saviour, "What
are they doing but repeating the cry of those mockers at the crucifixion
of our Lord—'Let Christ the King of Israel descend now from the cross,
that we may see and believe'"?   "No," said the doctor, "we believe Him
on the cross."

This happy gathering closed at 8 o'clock, so that from 8 to 9 we might
be in the girls' play-hall to see Mrs. Allison's exhibition of eastern manners
and customs. It was a very picturesque scene. We shall be pardoned for
saying that the charming voice and manner of Mrs. Allison, engaged almost
as much of our attention as the eastern curios. We heartily thanked her
for her kind thoughtfulness in arranging and explaining this exhibition.

On Wednesday, we came together by eleven o'clock, expecting great
things from this day's programme; but we received far more than our
highest anticipations. We always commence with a season of prayer; it
would be unnatural not to do so. The spirit of prayer soon flooded the
large assembly. After the consciousness of the divine presence in this first
half-hour, the deeply wise and gracious paper of Pastor T. Greenwood, on
"Unconscious Sanctification," was just the thing. This will be published,
and you will read it as eagerly as we listened to it.

The next event was thus described on the programme: "The morning is
to be dedicated to conference upon the work of the Holy Spirit in relation
to our service." It *was* a dedication. Our President's opening remarks
must have been the work of the Holy Spirit. How else could we have been
hushed into that divine calm? How we felt the need of reverence as we
approached the subject! Almost as soon as the conference commenced, we
had a great consciousness that the Lord was present, and with deep seriousness of heart, and solemnity of spirit, we desired to put our shoes from off
our feet, for this was holy ground. We remembered the vision of Isaiah,
chapter sixth, and thought we heard voices saying, "Holy, holy, holy, is
the Lord of hosts, the whole earth is full of his glory!" It seemed as if
the posts of the door were moving. The coming of the Majestic One over-
awed us. The introductory remarks of the President seemed to bring the
great Spirit of God to our spirits—we say *great*, for everything was great
during that memorable conference. It was a great sound, as of a mighty
rushing wind. It was a great filling of a place that seemed suddenly to
burst its limited dimensions, and become the greater temple of the infinite
Jehovah. We thought of Moses, and his vision of God from the cleft of the
rock, and with him we bowed our heads and worshipped; then we rose up
for deep, solemn, and subdued praise. Some of us felt, when the President
sat down, that we might have closed the meeting then, for the Spirit of God
had really been discerned by our spirits.

Still, we were glad that the Conference continued. Pastor A. G. Brown
was the first speaker after the President. We were very receptive at the
time; but had we not been, his remarks would have stirred us. He raised
a high platform for us when he said, "We have to perform our service in the
same spirit in which our Lord worked, and our measure of power will be
according to the measure of Christ's Spirit which we possess." Prayer followed, for the further we ventured into this sacred enclosure the more
sacredness must be about us. Pastor Frank H. White then spoke. We never
hear our brother speak without admiring his beautiful spirit. In gifts he is
a man above many, yet he has a way of making you feel that it is almost
better to be an ordinary than an extraordinary man. His treatment of the
subject was most encouraging. Again we engaged in prayer, and the power
of the Spirit awakened the brethren as to the future, for they prayed for
faithfulness to live and work out the convictions of the moment. Then followed an impressive paper by Pastor J. A. Brown upon the Holy Spirit's
help in our preaching. The Conference was fulfilling its mission: we were
getting nearer to the Lord, and knowing more of the ways of God.

20

This extraordinary meeting is over; but it will ever stand as a joyful memory if we are faithful to its impressions, or as a constant rebuke if we are not obedient to its quickening influences.

The meeting and supper for subscribers, which took place in the evening of this day, hardly come under this brief review : accounts of these must be given by those who were present at them. We can only say that the gifts to the College were princely, and worthy of the entertainment at the supper, which was a right royal one. Those who have never seen it can hardly imagine how splendid our Lecture Hall becomes on the festive night. We must not forget to say that on this evening Evangelistic meetings, with collections for the College, were held in several chapels in London and the suburbs, the services being conducted by our own brethren.

On Thursday we met at 11 o'clock. Going into the hall about a quarter to the hour, it was pleasant to see the visitors' gallery already occupied. As the hour struck the hall was full of men, who expected again to go into the presence-chamber of the King. It is difficult to make everybody punctual, but at our Conference the bulk of the men are true to the moment. The influence of yesterday was yet upon us, and the opening season of devotion was again very precious. A prayer for Ireland, by a brother from that country, drew forth many hearty "Amens." We longed for the light of God to break up on that gloom-girt isle.

After this half-hour's devotion, Pastor H. O. Mackay read a paper, written by the venerable G. Rogers, formerly Principal of the College, on "Encouragement for the Discouraged." The paper had a special charm for those who knew Mr. Rogers; and those of us who have never seen him understood at once why they thought so much of him. The fact that this paper was prepared for ministers will remind our churches that there are such persons in the world as discouraged ministers, who need the prayers and sympathy of their people. Though Mr. Rogers is closing his 90th year, it was remarked that few men with 50 years deducted could produce such a paper.

Mr. W. Y. Fullerton, whose wonderful success as an evangelist has made him known all over the land, next read a characteristic paper on "The Life which is Life Indeed." It was the work of sanctified sense and joyful experience. Next came a lesson from Pastor J. S. Morris on "The Vision of the King, the Preparation for Service." This paper was a careful exposition of that glorious sixth chapter of Isaiah, to which we have already referred. After the very wholesome feast of this morning, it was suggested that we should sit still to digest the truths; and we were silent until a brother was moved to pray. Several others followed; then, for the third or fourth time this morning, our President led us in prayer. We shall not soon forget it. The voices of men and children were heard in the street below, and these he regarded as appeals to us to present the cases of the young and the poor before the Lord. They seemed to say, "Ask a blessing for us!" "Ask a blessing for us!"

In the evening we gathered for the great public meeting in the Tabernacle. The best seats were occupied nearly an hour before the meeting commenced. Those who thus waited were kept from weariness by the songs of the Orphanage children. After singing and prayer, Pastor G. Samuel (Birmingham), who has just returned from a voyage to Australia and New Zealand, gave an account of noble work already done by Pastors' College men in the colonies. His remarks about Mr. Thomas Spurgeon were much appreciated. During the singing of our College anthem, "Hallelujah for the Cross," we heard a sound as of a trumpet. We looked, and we saw the glowing face of Mr. Smith, Mr. Fullerton's genial companion, and we understood why Mr. Spurgeon says it is as good as a half-holiday to look at him. Mr. Graham spoke to us of Congo work, and delighted the audience by singing, "Peace, be still!" in the Congo language. Speeches by Pastor C. B. Sawday (Leicester) and Mr. Julyan, were much appreciated by the enthusiastic audience. The last speaker was Pastor F. C. Spurr, whose account of the great Revival in Cardiff was listened to with eager interest by all. We thought of the great American Revival, and wished for a similar work in the metropolis.

On Friday, our last day, we assembled in the hall for " devotion, a sermon by the President, communion, and farewell." During the first half-hour, grateful thanksgivings were specially prominent. Why ? The fact was, the prayers of Thursday and of to-day, were warm with Wednesday's baptism of fire. We heard such phrases as, " the marvellous coming of God," " that most remarkably-blessed season" ; but no words can tell what it was. The prayers of to-day were expectant, as well as thankful, for the Conference order is " from strength to strength." This last day is no gathering round the dying embers of a fire, but it is the full blaze of a furnace, heated seven times hotter. In prayer, one asked for a " crowning blessing," another for " the vision of the King " ; another was sure " the best wine was kept until the last." At the closing service, the President called up Mr. Archibald G. Brown, to be his curate, and we were glad to see him in that capacity. One expression in his opening prayer was, " From thee, O Lord, we are always receiving, even from the first tear in the eye of penitence, to the crown upon the brow in glory ! "

Mr. Spurgeon preached from Jeremiah xxxii. 14. The heavy labours of the week must have taxed our President's strength, but we saw no signs of it, even at the close of an hour's discourse. Those who will read the sermon, will see in what a wonderful manner Christian experience is dealt with. How graphically was the dark night of conviction described ! How rapturously the fulness of day when, before the cross, guilt is removed ! How the strong grasp of spiritual things was shown to be the joy of life ! We enjoyed the remark, " The law that prayer is heard, is better established than the law of gravitation." But it was when the intense delights in Christ were spoken of, that we were made to recline on beds of spices within the heavenly banqueting-house.

After the sermon, we gathered round the Lord's table. It was a touching scene as, with hands linked all round, we rose to sing the Scotch version of Psalm cxxii., to the familiar tune " Martyrdom," with the well-known refrain, " I do believe, I will believe." At the last verse the grasp was tightened, and the electric current of Christian sympathy and love, which passed all along our ranks, made strong men bow their heads and weep. A few words of farewell were spoken, and one of the most delightful Conferences was over. Walking away, we thought:—Next Lord's-day, these ministers will see the congregations for whom they have earnestly prayed during the Conference ; will they see *all* their hearers around the throne of God ? God grant it, for his dear Son's sake ! Amen.

Notices of Books.

On the Way to the Throne. *Being Practical Expositions of Outstanding Events in the Life of our Lord on his Way through the World to his Throne.* By the Rev. R. BALLANTINE, M.A. Edinburgh : Oliphant & Anderson.

OUR excellent brother, Mr. Ballantine, has to confront, in Scotland, the same spirit of refined infidelity which rages in England ; and he does so bravely.

His addresses were suggested by the subjects of a painted window, which was given to his church. We do not care for painted windows ; but when they become suggestive of such discourses as these, we are not inclined to throw a stone at them. These pages are full of solid evangelical truth, very admirably put. They deserve a wide circulation.

The Personal and Pre-Millennial coming of our Lord. Edinburgh: Macniven and Wallace. London: Hodder and Stoughton.

Prophetic Notes: an Exposition of Sacred Prophecy. By Rev. HENRY STURT. Elliot Stock.

THE former of these little books (or rather large pamphlets) contains the record of a Conference held at Edinburgh, in the autumn of last year, not for controversy, but for fellowship. Assembled there, for five days, were venerable disciples of Christ, vigorous students of Holy Scripture, and valiant defenders of the faith—brethren whose praise is in all the churches. These made up a platform of representative men, each ardent in some special department of Christian service, but all animated by that one blessed hope, "the coming of the Son of man in his glory."

It seems almost invidious to mention names, but James Drummond, Andrew Bonar, G. H. Pember, and Grattan Guinness, are too conspicuous to pass unnoticed. The printed pages retain so much of the spiritual unction which flowed through their simple words, that we heartily commend them to the perusal of any of the Lord's disciples who languidly listen to the eager cry of the Spirit and the Bride, as they say, "Come," and have never themselves uttered, with tremulous voice and thrilling emotion, an eager, hearty "Amen" to the last prayer of the Apocalypse, "Even so, come, Lord Jesus."

The other book consists of "*Notes on Chief Parts of Sacred Prophecy*"; brief, but generally judicious. Mr. Sturt wisely asks his readers to have the Bible open in front of them. The commentators he refers to are well approved by pre-millenarians, especially those of the "Futurist" school. A long address he delivered, four or five years ago, from the chair of the Yorkshire Congregational Union, furnishes a supplement.

The Poets' Bible. Selected and Edited by W. GARRETT HORDER. Old Testament Section. W. Isbister, Limited.

ON the appearance of the New Testament portion of this work we began to use it, and we have often referred to it since with much content. We have often found an appropriate stanza or poem placed by the compiler in connection with a portion of Holy Scripture; and this is extremely helpful to a preacher who is not ashamed to use every stone that comes in his way.

It is a great mistake not to have arranged the poems in Scriptural order: for practical purposes this would have been by far the more useful method. The absence of a textual index leaves the work imperfect as a Preacher's Book, whatever it may be as a "Poet's Bible."

The Bible-Work: Old Testament: Exodus xii. — Deuteronomy. Prepared by J. GLENTWORTH BUTLER, D.D. Funk and Wagnalls.

WE have highly commended former volumes of this great work. It is a compendium of all the good and gracious things which have been written upon this portion of Scripture. Brethren whose libraries are rich in exposition may not need this collection of comments; but to men who are not thus favoured, it will be a great inheritance. Testing the matter at various points, we find that the extracts have been wisely chosen, and well placed; and we were not long before we found a discourse fashioning itself out of the suggestions which we had gained in reading. This is a large volume, and deals with the latter and larger part of the Pentateuch.

Scripture Scenes and their Lessons. By Rev. ANDREW CARTER, M.A. Drummond's Tract Depôt, Stirling.

To Him that Overcometh. Same Author and Publishers.

TWO tasteful books, at a shilling each. Just the thing for little presents. Full of gospel teaching. May be distributed with confidence.

The Dairyman's Daughter. By the Rev. LEGH RICHMOND. Cloth, sixpence. Houlston and Sons.

THIS favourite story will never die out. At sixpence, very nicely bound, it ought to have another triumphant progress through the land, and its number should be counted by hundreds of thousands.

The Imperfect Angel, and other Sermons.
By THOMAS G. SELBY. Hodder and
Stoughton.

*The Baptism of the Spirit, and other
Sermons.* By CHARLES NEW. James
Nisbet and Co.

Two substantial volumes, the former
containing twenty, the latter twenty-
five sermons, each modestly issued
without preface, or plumes of dedication, or other paraphernalia, but both
far above average mediocrity. Mr.
Selby excels in intellectual force. For
clear thinking, for choice metaphor
(when an apt illustration helps you
better than an argument), and for
accurate expression, at once simple
and scholarly, he commends himself
to our conscience. On some dark
texts he throws a flood of light. In
this he does good service. As he
shrewdly observes, in one of his discourses, "A passage of Holy Writ, to
which we attach no clear and definite
significance, is an empty house in
which the devil of fatal error is always
free to instal itself" (page 264). Mr.
Charles New's sermons are ripe and
rich in unction—full of sanctified experience. Our Wesleyan friend is a
valiant champion, whom preachers of
the Word may well be pleased to see
in the van. Our Independent brother
has a mission to the pews. Did our
space permit, we could cull from each
of these many a passage worthy of
quotation.

Landmarks of New Testament Morality.
By Rev. GEORGE MATHESON, M.A.,
D.D. Nisbet and Co.

THIS is a stimulating book. The
name of the author guarantees depth
of insight, delicacy of touch, and
felicity of expression; and we rise from
the perusal of these pages with a
keener sense of the practical power of
the religion of Jesus. The standpoint
of the author is solely ethical and
philosophic. "All doctrines of a
purely dogmatic theology we here pass
by on the other side, for the simple
reason that, in relation to our subject,
they are on the other side." Laying
a broad foundation, by showing that
Christianity absorbs the good points
of Stoicism, Epicureanism, and Pla-
tonism, "gathering together in one
all things in Christ," the author

proceeds to construct a solid pyramid,
having love as its apex. The definition
of sin as a dissonance between self-
love and universal love, is suggestive;
but we wonder how many of our
readers will be the wiser when they
find faith characterized as "the vision
of an ideal." Two of the positions of
the book seem to us mutually destructive. If a man invariably chooses
good when he sees it, and if "he does
not choose it one whit the less should
he continue to follow the lower path,"
and if he thus, though choosing good,
continues to do evil only because his
vision of vice is dim, then, surely, all
he needs to wean him from sin is a
clear sight of it. But the whole argument is, that Christ came to reveal, not
sin, but goodness; and that "he
desired to be loved, not because he
was a person, but because he was a
personification." How do these things
work in harmony?

We rejoice to see that the need of
the revival of primitive conscience is
recognized; but we must hark back to
our fathers' grasp of dogmatic truth
if we are to regain their massive morality. This volume is worthy of a
place in Nisbet's "Theological Library"; the price is six shillings.
There is a slight misprint on page 142.

Future Probation Examined. By
WILLIAM DE LOSS LOVE, Pastor at
South Hadley, Mass. London:
Funk and Wagnalls. Price 6s.

THE doctrine of everlasting punishment is distinctly proved to be the
doctrine of the earliest followers of
Christ. The oldest writings are abundantly quoted, together with the
sacred Scriptures, and the novel
theories of annihilation, future probation, and restoration are shown to
be interlopers in the domain of theological teaching. Such a work ought
to have weight with the "modern"
men, but it will not; for they are
carried away by Satanic delusion, bewitched by a spirit of falsehood which
will not let them bow before any
authority but their own vain
"thought." The giant evil which
now rules the age must run its
mischievous course. May that course
be short!

The Christian Conscience : a Contribution to Christian Ethics. By Rev. W. T. DAVISON, M.A. T. Woolmer. 3s.

THIS "Fernley Lecture for 1888" is an eloquent and exhaustive treatise—scriptural in design, scholarly in execution, shrewd in the detection of philosophical subtleties. The lecturer has spared no pains in consulting authors of repute, be they Coryphæans, chorus-leaders of the religious or of the rationalistic schools. Any effort to combine the pious and the philosophical points of view, the sacred and the secular, he rightly conjectures is prone to incur the censure alike of saints and scientists. To obviate this dilemma, he has fenced two out of the ten sections into which his book is divided, namely, iii. and ·iv., because, as he alleges, the Biblical lines are complete without them. Does this arrangement whet your curiosity? Well; the chapters relate to *the hypothesis of evolution*, as it passes over from the region of *physical* observations into that of *moral* apprehensions. He meets the moral claim of those whose speculative disposition is so determined that they would hazard their eternal destiny upon the truth or falsehood of the theory "which *evolves* human conscience out of animal instincts, and makes our judgment of right and wrong depend upon our feelings of pleasure and pain."

Barring needless controversy with apostates, the study of this *sense of the soul* as an element of technical education, might be profitable in the churches at large. If it be the author's purpose to edify the many, he is strangely handicapped in this course; for "The Fernley" is obviously an endowed "lecture" of the Wesleyan Methodist Society, and its arrangements confine its usefulness. When delivered, the lecture, we suppose, is held within moderate compass; when published, its dimensions and digressions are uncertain. It may appear as a sixpenny pamphlet, in paper covers, or as a seven shilling volume, in cloth binding. Ought not this to be rectified? Surely, a twopenny tract, reporting the discourse as delivered, would be the most useful. It would reach the homes of the people in towns and villages where Methodism flourishes, and prove an advertisement for the more elaborate essays which appeal to a smaller and more select circle interested in the contributions of the dons of the denomination to the wider domain of Christian literature.

The Sermon Bible. Psalm LXXVII. to Song of Solomon. Hodder and Stoughton.

IT must be of great service to a minister to know who has preached aforetime upon his text. He knows where to look if he possesses the volume mentioned, and he is helped still more when in this work he finds notes of a discourse by an abler divine than himself. We don't *endorse* all the sermons here given; but we heartily recommend those who have three half-crowns to spare to secure this book. The only peril is that they will then be led to wish for the first and second of the series. Ministers with books are like ladies with bonnets, very apt to wish for what they admire. We often pass a book-shop which the proprietor has labelled, TEMPTATION WAREHOUSE. "The Sermon Bible" is a necessity rather than a luxury.

The Child's Life of Christ. With Original Illustrations. Cassell and Co.

THIS is a grand volume artistically. With its splendid engravings, and large clear type, we were charmed, and as we read the first seventy pages we were pleased. All of a sudden, when we came to the circumcision of the infant Christ, we were assailed by god-fathers and god-mothers, and annoyed by a sprinkling ceremonial. What this had to do with the Lord Jesus, or his circumcision, we cannot tell; we see no sort of connection. We think it a great pity that such a noble volume should be rendered useless to a large number of good people by the introduction of this romancing. We like the style and tone of the work except that it is of the Anglican Church churchy. Church friends may like it, for the very reason which, in our case, grievously detracts from its value.

Bible Briefs; or, Outline Themes for Scripture Students. By G. C. and E. A. NEEDHAM. James E. Hawkins.

OUTLINES for addresses or sermons. Not a word redundant : these frameworks are terse—almost too much so. Here you buy meat without bones, and land without stones. Mr. and Mrs. Needham will have the gratitude of many a hard-pressed teacher when he is hard up for a talk to the school. They generously invite other people to use their handiwork, and promise that they will not consider it "borrowing." A certain minister says, somewhat spitefully, that Mr. Spurgeon's sermons are largely used in many pulpits, and we confess that we are not grieved by the information. If the Lord has ever given to his servant a thought or an expression which tended to edification, it is the common property of the church of God. We will raise no cry of plagiarism. We have never taken out letters patent. He who pays his penny, and buys our sermon, may preach it if so it pleases him.

A Concordance to the Holy Scriptures : with the various Readings both of Text and Margin. By SAMUEL NEWMAN. Reprinted from the Second Edition of 1762. Corrected and enlarged. John F. Shaw and Co.

CRUDEN mentions this Concordance in his preface, saying, "Mr. Cotton published a pretty large Concordance, which has been often printed ; afterwards Mr. Newman published one more complete."

Cruden is in no danger of being cut out by his predecessor ; but we are glad to possess Newman as a relic of the Puritanic age, and of the New England portion of Nonconformity. This is a fine edition, in beautiful type. We trust that the friend who issues it will sell a sufficient number to repay his costs.

The Expositor's Bible. The Book of Isaiah. By the Rev. GEORGE ADAM SMITH, M.A. Vol. I. Isaiah i—xxxix. Hodder and Stoughton.

WE felt pleased with this volume until we came upon a passage which seems to reduce the inspiration of Isaiah to a sort of foresight which he obtained through his moral and religious convictions. The prophets were the keenest and largest-hearted observers that ever appeared, and they inferred from certain general principles, grasped by their faith, that such and such events would occur. No doubt, some of the prophets had great natural foresight, but surely they had much more, or they could never have written the minute details which their prophecies indicated, and history recorded. How the prophet could have written the famous prophecy concerning our Lord in his fifty-third chapter, we are quite at a loss to conceive. From what conspicuous principles, clear to him as the laws of nature, he could have gathered that our Lord would "make his grave with the wicked, and with the rich in his death," it is hard to imagine. Mr. Adam Smith has, in somewhat veiled language, taken away from Holy Scripture the inspiration which is the foundation of our faith. We are too grieved to say more about his learned book : the better the book, the more harmful will be the evil.

A Manual of Introduction to the New Testament. By Dr. BERNHARD WEISS. Translated from the German by A. J. K. DAVIDSON. Vol. II., completing the work. 7s. 6d. Hodder and Stoughton.

DOUBTLESS there are people in the world to whom this work will be delightful reading : to us it is painful and unprofitable. We do not want to know all that can be said against the priceless Book which is the charter of our joy ; and, however ably the objections may be met, we had rather not have heard of them. It is like going through a puddle for the sake of being washed. The style of the criticism of Weiss is not to our mind. He may be very reverent, according to modern notions, but he is not reverent enough for us. He handles the inspired books as if they were essays from Tom, Jack, and Harry, instead of being the writing of the Holy Ghost. We do not say that Weiss is intentionally irreverent ; but we cannot get on with him, and we do not see any particular reason for translating his book.

Media, Babylon, and Persia. ["The Story of the Nations" Series]. By Z. A. RAGOZIN. T. Fisher Unwin.

WE like this the least of the series. For some reason, principally lack of information, the course of this history is not clear. The historian has little religious reverence, and his spirit is not that which we can fraternize with. He charges Ezekiel with error. The book, no doubt, contains the gist of what the sceptical and learned think they know about the Medes, but we are not satisfied with it. In this volume of "The Story of the Nations" the author says that Nebuchadnezzar never invaded Egypt; but in the volume upon EGYPT, by Canon Rawlinson, we read that he completed the ravages of that country which had been foretold by Ezekiel. To say the least, the author of "Media" might have spoken a little less positively; but it is of the nature of writers of this class to be most dogmatic where they are least to be relied on. We believe in Rawlinson rather than in Ragozin; and we believe in Ezekiel more than in all the historians put together. In almost every book we find the rank poison of modern doubt in some form or other, but as a rule so craftily insinuated that it is easy to pass it unobserved.

The Religious Census of London. Reprinted from "*The British Weekly.*" Hodder and Stoughton.

A VALUABLE collection of statistics, which workers in London should purchase, peruse, and preserve. It cannot possibly pay the publishers, and must be regarded as a gift to the students of the numerical condition of the churches. Price 3s. 6d.

The Nine Famous Crusades of the Middle Ages. By ANNIE E. KEELING. T. Woolmer.

THE Crusades are that portion of actual history which reads most like romance. How the narrative makes the blood to tingle in the veins! The fanatics of Christendom in those wars foreshadowed the mad heroism of Moslems in our own day. This was as much their strength as their internal dissension was their weakness. A crusade was the boiling over of the

world's caldron of bigotry; and, notwithstanding all the cruel mischief which it wrought, it probably caused less misery than the steady boiling of that same caldron in the perpetual persecution of all who differed from the dominant church.

Our authoress has studied her subject thoroughly, and has prepared this summary with commendable care. Our readers will find a world of interest in this book if they are historically inclined.

A Peep into Russia, with Journey there and back. By ALEXANDER G. BURNETT. Edinburgh: James Murray.

VERY quaint and chatty. The author writes with the personal detail of a Boswell, and manages to gain and hold one's attention to very small matters. He aims at exciting interest in the German Baptists; and this is an admirable design, in which we wish him God-speed.

The Young Man's Text Book and Birthday Calendar. Simpkin & Marshall.

THE beloved George Williams writes an introduction, and the profits go to the Swansea Y.M.C.A. The texts are well selected, and the book is neat and cheap. It is to be had, in various bindings, from 1s. to 2s.

Poems. By ARTHUR VINE HALL. Simpkin, Marshall, and Co.

FLASHES of true poetic fire from the pen of our friend Newman Hall's nephew.

The New Popular Educator: a Complete Encyclopædia of Elementary and Advanced Education. Vol. I. Cassell and Co.

"THE Popular Educator" has been the ladder by which thousands have climbed to knowledge. Where a tutor cannot be obtained, it largely fills the vacancy; and even where the living teacher is near it is a noble help. Messrs. Cassell and Co. are re-issuing this great work, and the first volume is now before us. They take care to keep it up to date. It has never yet been surpassed, and we do not think it will be. Young men who wish to intermeddle with all knowledge should invest in this great mine of instruction.

Tom's Nugget; a Story of the Australian Gold Fields. By Professor J. S. HODGETS.

The Old Lock Farm; a Story of Canal Life. By ANNIE GRAY.

Who was Guilty? The Story of a School Mystery. By WILLIAM J. LACEY.

Ethelwyn's Light; or, "Honesty's the Best Policy." By LUCRETIA MAYBURY.

Lindéman Brothers; or, Shoulder to Shoulder. By JESSIE SAXBY.

"Doctor Phill"; or, As in a Mirror. By Mrs. SKINNER. Sunday School Union.

THE first of our Sunday School Union packet that would tempt a boy to break the fourth commandment is "*Tom's Nugget.*" We hope and believe that the state of things now at the Australian Gold Fields is vastly better, from a moral point of view, than at the period of the gold fever of thirty or forty years ago, which Mr. Hodgets describes as one of "dreadful sights" and "grisly horrors." Master Tom's wonderful adventures, and how he helped in the capture and conviction of a notorious band of Bushrangers, will be read and re-read by boys, big and little. Professor Hodgets ought to be professor of archery, for he can draw a long bow that would tax the strength of a Strongbow. It would require the credulity of a regiment of Marines to believe some of his yarns. But, then, it's real story, don't you know?

"*The Old Lock Farm.*" Everybody ought to know and bless God for the work of George "*Coalville*" Smith among the "Brickies," and "Boaters," and Gipsies. Here is a heart-stirring story, founded upon incidents in the Canal Mission work. Among other good things, it contains a real ghost story, and real gospel.

"*Who was Guilty?*" Mr. Lacey has a turn for concocting mysterious stories and strange coincidences, to illustrate profitable lessons for youth, in a "taking"—or is it not now a fetching?—style. But what would story-tellers do if there were "no more sea"? Here we have another instance of the treacherous tide cutting off the retreat of a too-trusting traveller. Of course he was saved, so we save our tears.

"*Ethelwyn's Light.*" Another Sunday School Union seaside story, full of smugglers, and mysterious caves and vaults.

"*Lindéman Brothers.*" A pretty story of fidelity to conscience, and self-sacrificing brotherly love.

"*Doctor Phill.*" A short story, which may be briefly described as "A Prodigal Son and a Good Elder Brother."

The Earls of the Village. By AGNES GIBERNE. Shaw and Co.

THESE Earls were not members of the aristocracy, but tradesfolk. In each house of the Earl family there was sore trouble, chiefly owing to unequal yoking, or evil companionships. Miss Giberne's stories all contain wise counsels, faithful warnings, and clever writing.

In Spite of Himself. By AMELIA E. BARR. James Clarke and Co.

A VERY improbable story. Not to our taste.

The Foster-brothers of Doon. A Tale of the Irish Rebellion of 1798. By the Author of "Golden Hills." Religious Tract Society.

THE tragic events of "ninety-eight" might furnish superabundant material, not only for the novelist, but for the historian. Our author has undoubted qualifications for the production of a first-class historical story; for, while taking advantage of "the wonderful Irish genius for wit and humour to brighten up any sombreness in the narrative," he tells us that no pains have been spared to preserve minute accuracy in all that concerns the history of the Rebellion. This half-crown book is a marvel of cheapness.

The Latch-Key; or, Too many by Half. By the Rev. T. S. MILLINGTON. Religious Tract Society.

A STORY of what the writer calls "a large little family" of eleven children, or, "too many by half," as some folks would say: but how would you halve eleven? Mr. Millington does not profess to give us the "latch-key" to the problem; but he does give us a book half-full of fun and half-full of feeling —the work of a rare humorist and a real Christian.

The Life of Timothy Coop; or, The Story of a Consecrated Business Career, with which is Connected a Brief Account of a Religious Reformation. By W. T. MOORE, M.A., LL.D. Christian Commonwealth Publishing Company.

TIMOTHY COOP was a man who followed his convictions promptly, and with vigour. Strength of mind enabled him to be highly prosperous in business; but, under the sanctifying influence of divine grace, it did much more for him, for it made him faithful. He was led to adopt very much the same views as those held by Mr. Archibald Campbell; and he became a great helper of the body of people who call themselves "Christians," or "Disciples." But he was by no means narrow in his sympathies, for he was always a generous helper of his friend, Mr. Spurgeon. The late President Garfield was his great friend. He always struck us as a man both shrewd and spiritual, committing himself to no one party without reserve, yet loving heartily the friends with whom he had deliberately associated himself. We generally agreed with his sentiments when he explained them in his own way, although there were points upon which we differed regretfully.

His biographer must excuse our saying that the general interest of the book will be greatly diminished by the introduction of so large an amount of matter which bears peculiarly upon the section of the church to which Mr. Coop belonged. It makes the volume bulky, but does not increase its interest. We do not *blame* Mr. Moore for introducing it; for a man has a fair right to make use of such a biography to make known the views of the person thus portrayed; but still, the number who will understand the interior discussions of the American and English "Disciples" are not very numerous in this country. Our joy in Timothy Coop lies in the combination which we saw in him of faithfulness to convictions, and freedom from bitterness. He dwelt among his own people, but he urged them on to larger enterprise. He loved his own way of working, but he was liberal in his help to those who worked after

other methods. He deserved a memoir, and Mr. Moore has displayed considerable ability in its compilation.

The Life and Letters of Mrs. Sewell. By MRS. BAYLY. Nisbet. Price 6s.

A QUIET domestic life. If the autobiography with which it commences had only been continued, what a book it would have made! Mrs. Sewell belonged, originally, to the Society of Friends, but quitted them because she saw it her duty to be baptized. She joined none of the denominations, but was somewhat eclectic in her beliefs. She was influenced by our honoured brother B. W. Newton, but also by Robertson, Henry Dunn, Pulsford, and others: the mixture we by no means commend for general consumption, but her vigorous spiritual life survived it. She was ever the animals' friend, and the helper of the poor: a character in which she may be safely imitated. Here we have a life, uneventful because happy, and happy because useful. This will not attain to a front rank among memoirs—there is no reason why it should, but it will greatly interest the many who knew Mrs. Sewell and her gifted daughter.

The Jerusalem Sinner Saved, and, *The Heavenly Footman.* By JOHN BUNYAN.
Paradise Regained, Samson Agonistes, etc. By JOHN MILTON.
Practical Social Science. By HARRY JONES, M.A.
Natural History Notes and Anecdotes. First Series. Religious Tract Society.

THESE are numbers 12, 13, 14 and 15 of the R. T. S. Library; and wonders they are for sixpence. The Natural History Book is one of the most charming we have ever read. It is the sort of book that one might get up in the night to read. Young men, if you don't read nowadays it must be because of the donkey that is in you; for, surely, any rational animal would count his cash well invested in such volumes as these, and would never allow the investment to lie idle for want of diligent study.

"Emmanuel" Series of Intaglio Texts. Sixpence each. Partridge and Co.

VERY suitable for hanging up. Chaste and ornamental.

Pictures from Eastern Lands. A Book for Boys and Girls. By A. E. K. G. Morrish.

THIS work is written in plain and simple language containing no hard words, and so boys and girls will like to read it. When they do so, it will be understood by them, and will fill their minds with instruction of the best kind. Not only is the book well-intentioned, but it is really rich in eastern illustrations and in Scriptural truth. It ought to be purchased and given as a present by believing parents who desire their children to read the Bible intelligently, and with pleasure. This is a good book—a specially good book. We feel no hesitation in commending it to everybody. Alas! in these evil times we are apt to be taken in, if we cannot read a book quite through—and how are we to do this with the hundreds which are sent to us? We tremble lest there may be unknown to us a deadly pill inside the sugar-coating: but in this case we are at our ease. It is a child's book, but by no means childish: good, but not goody-goody.

The Contents and Teachings of the Catacombs at Rome: a Vindication of Pure and Primitive Christianity; and an Exposure of the Corruptions of Romanism. By BENJAMIN SCOTT, F.R.A.S., Chamberlain of the City of London. Morgan and Scott.

THERE is a great wealth of information in this well-condensed, well-written book. Think of 587 miles of passages in the catacombs! How much must lie there yet undiscovered! How much that is instructive both as to ancient heathenism and early Christianity! Although the most of the choicer inscriptions have been carried off to the Vatican, many miles of catacomb remain untouched, and full of antiquities. If anything could be found in these streets of subterranean tombs, which would support the errors of Popery, they would be opened up; but as the inscriptions are more after the manner of Baptists, and Baptists are poor, they will be left in darkness.

Mr. Scott here gives materials for capital lectures, which while they would please would also edify and impress an audience. His stories of the follies of Rome ought to be told by a thousand tongues; for they reveal not only the idolatry of the Papacy, but the stupid blundering of the makers of saints, and the certifiers of their relics. The catacombs have been a hiding-place for truths as well as for martyrs, and the sermons in stones, which have been there preserved, preach very forcibly against certain of the errors of the apostate church. Half-a-crown will bring a large return if spent upon this book, if the reader becomes a lecturer, borrowing the diagrams to illustrate his theme.

"Many Infallible Proofs": their Evidences of Christianity; or, The Written and Living Word of God. By ARTHUR T. PIERSON, D.D. Morgan and Scott.

AN invaluable work. The price is low at half-a-crown. It is the book which the present period needs. It is solid, plain, conclusive argument. Of course, the down-graders will dodge it, or admit it in phrases, and then proceed to deny it by their interpretations. Their haughty assumptions of culture and profound knowledge would be amusing, if they were not amazing. To those who retain candour, although somewhat shaken by the present earthquake of doubt, such infallible proofs as these will be greatly reassuring, and we believe they will return to the old faith with increased confidence. To spread such a treatise as this will be a very gracious work, and the results must be beneficial.

Select Sermons. By Rev. CHARLES B. W. GORDON, Pastor, First Baptist Church, Petersburg. Vol. I. Gordon and Co., Petersburg, Virginia.

THIS is said to be the first volume of sermons published by a coloured Baptist. It is a very good beginning. Many white preachers would preach better if they were as much up to the mark as our dusky brother. We do not think a discourse is any the better or the worse because of the colour of the preacher's nose. The sermons are very short, but they are evangelical and instructive. We do not think we could laud them to the skies, as some critics have done; but they are creditable to their author.

Decisive Events in History. By THOMAS ARCHER. Cassell and Co.

A BOOK which every youth and maiden should read. So tersely, and withal so vividly written, that once let the reader touch a page, and he will be entangled in the meshes of the story, and will not escape except by going through it all.

Old Wang, the First Chinese Evangelist in Manchuria. By Rev. JOHN ROSS. Religious Tract Society.

A PRECIOUS piece of missionary biography. More of such lives will enrich the Church in years to come; and the more the better, if this be a sample of what we may expect. Old Wang was a man of distinct personal character, endowed with force and pertinacity, and sanctified by grace. The remarks of Mr. Ross, which follow, are worthy of serious attention in this present evil hour :—

"Without ignoring the fact that there are nominal conversions from improper motives, experience testifies that the one outstanding influence, in changing the temple-frequenting Chinaman into a worshipper of the true God, is that which converted Old Wang—the revelation in Jesus of the mercy of the one living and true God. The love of the Father manifested in the loving Son is that which makes men here break their idols, and cast their chanted prayers into the flames. The first inciting motive is that which many brave Christians sneer at as a selfish, and, therefore, an unworthy one : that which urges them to seek salvation now in this way, now in that, and finally to believe in the Lord Jesus Christ, is the fear of future suffering on account of sin. Theoretically it is more noble to be indifferent to personal suffering, or the fear of it, and to seek rather 'to be virtuous for virtue's sake.' Yet, somehow, humanity presents but rare cases of such nobility. The first cry now in the hearts of millions of Chinese, and often on their lips, is that which rang in the ears of the apostles, 'What must we do to be saved ?' 'How shall I escape from the wrath to come ?' is but the articulate expression of the soul-fear of the conscience-stricken. And this, after all, is but natural. The man who, far out at sea, is overtaken by a tempest, every wave of which threatens to engulf his tiny boat, is not in the least anxious whether the brine is damaging his clothing ; and when he beholds a ship in the distance, he cries at the pitch of his voice, not to have his face washed, but his life saved. Once on board, the feeling of security admits of his paying attention to his garments and personal appearance."

Half-Hours with the Early Explorers. By THOMAS FROST. Cassell and Co.

ANOTHER book of a class which cannot be too largely multiplied. Readable, and even romantic, and yet historically true, such works do not confuse the mind and bewilder the memory. The constant reading of tales leaves the intellect almost unable to separate fiction from fact, and we are sure that the moral result cannot be good. The world of novels is not the world which God has made; but is the embodiment, if not of a lie, yet of a dream: it is a pity to conduct our youth into the region of the false and unreal. We fear that grave evil is being done by means which it would be hard to load with indiscriminate condemnation. The very heart of truth is being eaten out by the worm of fiction, and much of the utter indifference of the present age to everything solemn and true, is due to the surfeits of fancy with which men are indulged, bringing with them long fasts from the wholesome diet of the mind. This record of Marco Polo, Sir John Mandeville, and the long line of pioneer explorers, is well written and will win many readers.

Samuel Rutherford. By Dr. ANDREW THOMSON. Fourth Edition. Hodder and Stoughton.

OUR shelves are so crowded with books awaiting our notice, that we cannot, as a rule, write upon each edition of any publication ; but whether it be the fourth edition or the fortieth, we must say a good word for Rutherford, as he is set forth by Andrew Thomson. This is a notably excellent life of a great saint.

What is implied in "Preaching Christ"?
An Address to the members and friends of the Open-air Mission. By ADOLPH SAPHIR, D.D. Morgan and Scott. Price one penny.

A CLEAR and able testimony, to the eternal truth. Mr. Saphir has a happy way of communicating the deepest truths in the simplest words.

We hope the Open-air Mission will distribute this sermon by tens of thousands.

Christ the Light of the World, and *The Acts of the Apostles*. Dean and Son.

PRETTY books, with coloured pictures, and the stories nicely told; and all for sixpence.

Notes.

OWING to the extreme pressure upon us this month, the notes are necessarily brief.

In *The Freeman*, April 19, in an article referring to the appearance in South Place Chapel of the then President of the Baptist Union, it was said, "these lectures, it should be stated, are arranged by 'The Ethical Society,' of which the Archbishop of Canterbury is the president." Something else also should be stated. In answer to a letter, asking if the Archbishop was indeed in connection with the Ethical Society meeting in South Place, Finsbury, we received for answer: "His Grace is much obliged to you for giving him the opportunity of correcting the rumour as to his connection with the Ethical Society you mention. The report is, as you suppose, quite untrue—this being the first time the Archbishop has heard of the Society in question." It does not matter much, but we may as well know the truth.

We receive daily notes concerning the departure from the truth of preachers in England and Scotland; and though the subject is wearisome to our heart, we cannot forbear entreating the Lord's people to pray day and night for the afflicted church of God. He alone can stay the ever-growing evil, but he would have his people cry to him concerning it. The evil is by no means imaginary, but all too real. Our protest came not too soon, nor could it be too forcible. At this moment, those who have quitted the old faith may do what they please to silence papers and periodicals, but the evil reeks before high heaven. We trust it will not be long before the lovers of the gospel will awake to the danger, and speak out so as to be heard.

In the first week in June there are to be two special services at the Tabernacle. On *Tuesday evening*, 4th inst., Mr. John Courtnay and the Southwark Choral Society are to help us praise the Lord with some of the grand old fugal tunes that ought never to have gone out of use. We shall be glad to see a large muster of friends who love those ancient melodies.

On *Thursday evening*, June 6, C. H. S. has promised to preach another sermon for the British and Foreign Sailors' Society, when Mr. Matthews, the energetic secretary of the Society, has promised to bring as many sailors as he can muster. He is anxious to distribute the sermon, when it is published, among those that go down to the sea in ships; and he will be very grateful for all contributions that are given to him for that object.

The secretary of the Tram-car and 'Bus Scripture Text Mission, Mrs. Wood, 53, Paternoster Row, E.C., asks us to call our readers' attention to the fact that for 10s. a text can be placed in a tram or 'bus, and maintained in a good position for a year. She will be very glad to receive donations.

COLLEGE.—Mr. A. G. Haste has settled at Carrickfergus; and Mr. Joseph Young has sailed for Jamestown, St. Helena.

Mr. F. R. Bateman has removed from Twickenham to Henley-in-Arden. Mr. F. Dann, who returned from Minnesota some months since, for his health's sake, has now sailed again for the United States.

Will all the members of the Pastors' College Evangelical Association kindly note that *Monday, June* 24, has been fixed for the day of SPECIAL UNITED PRAYER? Will our brethren everywhere try to make this a day of real wrestling prayer? If all the churches take it up heartily, we may look for large blessing.

EVANGELISTS.—Mr. J. E. Mathieson closes a very appreciative report of *Messrs. Fullerton and Smith's* services at Mildmay Park Conference Hall, as follows:—" I had not previously met with your valued evangelists, but I soon learned to appreciate and to love them. . . . . I know of no two brethren more fitted for great and important work for the Master than these two. I wish friends in every large town in our land would seek to share in the benefit which a visit from them is likely to impart."

Since the Conference, our brethren have been at Dr. Barnardo's Mission-hall, The Edinburgh Castle, where great crowds attended the services, and many received the truth. They also conducted services on two afternoons and evenings at Beulah Chapel, Thornton Heath, where much blessing resulted.

Their future engagements are : June 1—9, Kilburn Hall; June 15—23, Bath Street Chapel, Poplar; June 30, Mildmay Park

Conference Hall; Saturdays and Sundays in July, the Polytechnic, Regent Street; August, for rest; September, Paris; October, Tunbridge Wells and Stowmarket; November, Oxford and Carlisle.

Mr. Burnham's services at Hungerford Congregational Chapel were greatly blessed. The minister (Rev. J. S. Haggett) writes:— "It was a grand time for benighted Hungerford. . . . . We had a very rich season of blessing." Mr. Burnham has now gone for a voyage, which we hope will restore him thoroughly to health.

Pastor A. Graham, Tewkesbury, writes:— "*Mr. Harmer's* visit has been productive, through God's mercy, of much good. The members of my church were greatly blessed, and a considerable number, who were brought to listen to Mr. Harmer's plain gospel addresses, profess to have been led to Christ. We have had a gracious revival, and shall know the beneficial results of the mission for some time to come."

Pastor W. Glanville reports as follows concerning Mr. Harmer's services at East Surrey Grove Chapel, Peckham :—" We thankfully acknowledge the services of Mr. Harmer, who conducted a fortnight's mission for us, commencing April 14th. Throughout, the meetings were well sustained, and a considerable number professed to find peace. There is no doubt that we have been greatly helped and blessed by the ministry of our able and earnest brother."

This month and next Mr. Harmer is to be at Commercial Street, Whitechapel; Dartford; and Crewkerne.

Mr. Harrison has held an eight days' mission at Kidderminster. Believers have been revived, and a good number of unconverted persons passed through the enquiry-room. The end of this month, and the beginning of next, Mr. Harrison is to hold tent-services at Clapton.

ORPHANAGE.—All our friends, both in town and country, will be sure to remember the *Annual Festival*, which will (D.V.) be held on the President's birthday, *Wednesday, June* 19. Full particulars will be duly announced. If the vast assemblies of past years should be exceeded this year, it will be great joy to the President's heart. Why not?

In another part of the magazine we have referred to Mr. Charlesworth's jubilee. Another friend, who this year completes his twentieth year of service to the Institution, is our honorary dentist, W. O. Hinchliff, Esq., to whom we are immeasurably indebted for his care of the children's teeth. It is interesting to note that the Stockwell Orphanage was the first public institution that had a dental surgeon on its staff; but many others have followed our example. Our friend, Mr. Hinchliff, of Kennington Park Road, has had no honorary post, except in the sense of being unpaid, for youngsters have many teeth to pull out, or put in, or stop, and he has done all for all without fee or reward. God bless him!

COLPORTAGE. — The Annual Conference was held on the 19th and 20th of May. On Sunday morning, at ten, a number of the colporteurs assembled with members of the committee for prayer, and again in the afternoon, when the presence of the Lord was very manifest in the earnest pleadings of the brethren, who were also greatly refreshed by the President's sermons in the Tabernacle.

On Monday afternoon the men again met, and related their experience, much to the enjoyment of Mr. Spurgeon, who delivered an address of much power upon the text, "Have faith in God." The evening meeting in the Tabernacle was largely attended, and was presided over by the President, who gave an address upon the evils of reading trashy fiction, and the blessings of the Colportage Association. The Secretary, W. Corden Jones, read a portion of the Annual Report, which we shall give entire next month.

Several of the colporteurs described their work, and gave illustrations of the way in which God was using their labours in combating the evils of unhealthy literature, and in the conversion of sinners. It was a very cheerful meeting, Mr. Stops, of Bethnal Green, especially causing much amusement by the graphic sketches which he gave of his methods of gaining the attention of the people.

PERSONAL NOTE. — A Scotch friend writes :—" Testimony meetings are very common here in various parts of our city. Last Saturday I went to the meeting at the Seamen's Chapel. A deputation of converted carters, slaughterhouse-men, and colliers, came to testify of Christ's power to save. They were all young men, except their leader, James W——, the carter, who had seen more than fifty years. He, an uncultured man, but transparent with a living Christianity, and a love for souls, told how he was arrested and converted, fourteen years ago, sitting reading, at his own fireside, Spurgeon's sermon on, 'My grace is sufficient for thee.'

"'Before that,' he said, 'I could not go home sober on a Saturday night; but grace has wrought a great change—all things are made new.'

"I asked, at the close of the meeting, if he had ever written to tell you? He said, 'No, I am not given to letter-writing ; I am no scholar.'

"I thought I would write to tell you of this one more trophy you had won for Christ before you go to the other side, where you will see what has been gathered into the kingdom of God by your instrumentality."

Baptisms at Metropolitan Tabernacle:— May 2, thirty.

Pastors' College, Metropolitan Tabernacle.

Statement of Receipts from April 16th to May 14th, 1889.

	£	s.	d.
Mr. J. B. Crisp	1	0	0
Miss Mackintosh	0	5	0
Miss S. Revell	0	1	11
Miss Maclean	0	10	0
Contributions from Longcross Baptist Chapel, Cardiff, per Rev. F. C. Spurr	15	0	0
G. C.	0	2	0
Mrs. F. Heritage	2	2	0
Dr. E. Cronin	1	1	0
Mr. James Collingwood	3	3	0
Pastor N. Papengouth	1	0	0
Pastor W. B. Nichol	0	10	0
Mr. Jno. A. Arnold	2	2	0
Mr. J. G. Hall	1	1	0
Mr. H. Keen	3	3	0
Mr. James W. Wolfe	1	1	0
Miss E. E. Jones	0	5	0
Mr. E. Gammon	1	1	0
Mr. J. Allder	1	1	0
Mrs. Griffiths	1	0	0
Contribution from Elgin Baptist Chapel, per Pastor R. E. Glendening	5	0	0
Mr. G. Harris	2	0	0
Mr. J. Whittle	5	0	0
Mr. and Mrs. Kelley	5	0	0
Mr. Jno. Moser	10	10	0
Messrs. A. Straker and Son	3	0	0
Mr. and Mrs. Horn	1	1	0
Mr. William Edwards	21	0	0
Mr. Pankhurst	1	1	0
Mr. and Mrs. C. H. Price	5	5	0
Mr. C. Buchell	2	0	0
Contribution from Fraserburgh Baptist Church, per Pastor W. Richards	0	16	0
Mr. J. T. Crosher	3	0	0
Mr. Jno. Nelson	0	2	0
Mr. and Mrs. A. Norman	2	2	0
Mr. and Mrs. E. S. Boot	3	3	0
Collection at Philip Street Baptist Chapel, Bristol, per Pastor H. Moore	1	1	0
From Eythorne Baptist Chapel, per Pastor G. Stanley		15	0
From Rayleigh, per Pastor I. Bridge	0	5	0
Collection at Dartmouth Baptist Chapel, per Pastor F. J. Greening	1	6	0
Collection at Westbourne Baptist Chapel, Bournemouth, per Pastor G. Wainwright	4	0	0
Collection at Southend Tabernacle, per Pastor H. W. Childs	2	0	0
Mrs. Ryder	1	1	0
Mr. Charles Jones	1	1	0
Mr. and Mrs. J. Brown	5	5	0
Mr. J. Tansley	0	5	0
Pastor W. Gillard	0	5	0
Mr. and Mrs. Annison	1	1	0
Mr. and Mrs. Perry	1	1	0
Miss A. Norris	0	10	0
Rev. Jno. Green	0	5	0
Pastor G. T. Ennals	0	10	6
Contribution from Salem Chapel, Dover, per Pastor E. J. Edwards	3	0	0
Collection from Ashdon Baptist Chapel, per Pastor R. Layzell	0	12	9
Contribution from Limpsfield Baptist Chapel, per Pastor F. M. Cockerton	0	10	0
Mr. Samuel Spurgeon	0	10	0
Collection at Grafton Street Baptist Chapel, Northampton, per Pastor S. Needham	1	0	0
A friend, per Pastor G. Wright	1	0	0
Collection at Orpington Baptist Chapel, per Pastor J. Scilley	2	2	0
Rev. E. A. Carter	1	1	0
Pastor J. B. Warren	0	10	0
Mr. and Mrs. Potier	10	0	0

	£	s.	d.
Contribution from Southwood Lane Baptist Chapel, Highgate, per Pastor J. H. Barnard	0	1	0
Children's Bible-class, East Dereham, per Pastor N. T. Jones-Miller		5	7
Contribution from East Dereham Baptist Chapel, Pastor N. T. Jones-Miller	0	15	6
Lord's Supper collection, Peckham Public Hall, per Pastor Frank Smith	1	1	0
Mr. and Mrs. Mallett	2	0	0
Mr. Vaughan	5	0	0
Mr. J. E. Potter	5	5	0
Mr. Jno. Carter, jun.	1	1	0
Mr. W. C. Greenop	3	3	0
Miss Greenop	1	1	0
Mr. Thomas Kennard	0	10	0
Mr. and Mrs. Chisholm	1	1	0
Mr. M. H. Hodder	2	2	0
Mr. T. W. Stoughton	2	2	0
Collection at Waterbeach Baptist Chapel, per Pastor F. Thompson	2	0	0
Contribution from King's Langley, per Pastor D. Macmillan	0	6	0
Subscriptions from Stockton-on-Tees, per Pastor T. L. Edwards	2	13	0
Pastor E. J. and Mrs. Edwards	2	2	0
Proceeds of lecture at Stow-on-the-Wold, per Pastor F. E. Blackaby	1	5	0
Collection at Baptist Chapel, Folkestone, per Pastor R. F. Jeffrey	5	10	0
Contribution from New Brompton Baptist Chapel, per Pastor W. W. Blocksidge	2	2	0
Pastor E. S. Neale	1	0	0
Old Baptist Chapel, Rushden, per Pastor W. J. Tomkins	3	7	6
Pastor J. Dupee	0	0	0
Pastor J. M. Cox	0	15	6
From Shipton-on-Stour, per Pastor R. T. Lewis		16	6
Collection at Salem Baptist Chapel, Boston, per Pastor W. Sexton	1	1	1
Mr. and Mrs. Marden	1	0	0
Mr. George Palmer	20	0	0
Collection at Faringdon Baptist Chapel, per Pastor H. Smith	1	0	0
Per Pastor W. Hackney, M.A.:—			
Mr. H. O. Adams	0 10 6		
Mr. Branscombe	0 10 6		
Mr. Devenport	0 10 6		
Two friends	0 10 6		
	2	2	0
Collection at Octavius Street Baptist Chapel, Deptford, per Pastor D. Honour	1	15	10
Collection at Devonshire Square Baptist Chapel, per Pastor E. H. Ellis	3	13	6
Pastor C. A. Ingram	0	5	0
Pastor James Smith (Tunbridge Wells)	1	1	0
Mr. T. Braithwaite	1	0	0
Contribution from Attercliffe Baptist Chapel, Sheffield, per Pastor J. G. Williams	0	5	0
Collection at Leafield, Oxon, per Pastor W. J. N. Vanstone	1	10	0
Mr. Thomas Lea, M.P.	2	2	0
Mr. James Smith, per Pastor W. Ruthven	1	1	0
Pastor G. Smith	0	10	0
Contribution from Hay Hill Baptist Chapel, Bath; per Pastor W. Pettman	1	0	0
Pastor J. B. Hockey's Bible-class, Brentford	1	0	0
Pastor R. S. Latimer	0	10	0
Mr. H. R. Colbeck	2	2	0

	£	s.	d.
Pastor F. C. Carter	1	1	0
Mr. and Mrs. Walter Mills	5	5	0
Contribution from Melksham Baptist Church, per Pastor G. A. Webb	2	4	6
Mrs. J. Manton Smith	1	1	0
Per Pastor A. W. Wood:—			
Mrs. Whicher and Miss Tomkins 1 0 0			
Messrs. Southwell, Lockerly 0 10 0			
A. W. W. 0 10 0			
	2	0	0
Pastor J. T. Swift	1	1	0
Contribution from Putney Baptist Church, per Pastor W. Thomas	1	1	0
Mr. T. A. Denny	50	0	0
Mr. G. Finch	1	1	0
Contribution from Talbot Tabernacle, per Pastor F. H. White	5	0	0
Contribution from Burton-on-Trent Baptist Chapel, per Pastor J. Askew	0	10	0
Collection at Ilfracombe Baptist Chapel, per Pastor J. W. Genders	2	1	9
Pastor A. Knell	0	9	0
Mr. T. H. Olney	25	0	0
Miss Spliedt	6	0	0
Mr. John Short	2	2	0
Mrs. W. B. Head	1	1	0
Mr. Buckley	1	1	0
Mr. and Mrs. Narraway	2	2	0
Mrs. Buckmaster	1	1	0
Miss Croose	1	1	0
Mrs. Jenkins	3	3	0
Mrs. Scard	1	1	0
Mrs. Norman	1	1	0
Miss Norman	1	1	0
Miss M. A. Norman	1	1	0
Rev. J. E. Perrin	0	10	6
Rev. E. J. Farley	5	5	0
Mr. and Mrs C. Goddard Clarke	2	2	0
Mr. and Mrs. J. G. Taylor	5	0	0
Mr. W. Busbridge	2	2	0
Mr. John Ridge	0	10	0
Mr. G. H. Judd	2	2	0
Mr. John Pearce	10	0	0
Mr. Edward Clark	5	0	0
Mr. W. T. R. Knapp	1	1	0
Mr. F. Rouse	3	3	0
Mrs. Rouse	1	1	0
Miss Rouse	1	1	0
Mr. T. Mullis	5	0	0
Mrs. Parker	5	5	0
Mr. F. Sexton	2	2	0
Mr. and Mrs. Green	2	2	0
Pastor and Mrs. Joseph Benson	2	2	0
Pastor James and Mrs. Douglas	2	2	0
Mr. and Mrs. Hellier	5	0	0
Mr. William Olney	5	5	0
Mr. William Olney, jun.	1	1	0
Miss E. A. Gilbert and friend	5	0	0
Mr. H. Foster	3	3	0
Mr. and Mrs. Meakins	1	1	0
Mr. T. D. Atherton	3	0	0
Mrs. Moore	1	0	0
Miss F. Burdett	2	0	0
E. R. L.	5	0	0
Mr. G. C. Heard	5	5	0
Miss Heritage	2	2	0
Mrs. Ellwood	5	5	0
Mrs. Rowton	0	10	6
Mr. T. Frisby	1	1	0
Mr. and Mrs. Frisby	10	0	0
Mr. Theodore Barnes	1	0	0
Mr. J. Howard Barnes	0	10	6
Mr. R. A. James	5	5	0
Mr. and Mrs. A. W. Lovell	1	1	0
Mr. and Mrs. W. A. Lovell	5	0	0
Mr. and Mrs. G. J. Russell	2	2	0
Rev. W. Tyler, D.D.	2	2	0
Mrs. Dumbleton	1	0	0
Mr. Godfrey	1	0	0
Mr. R. Abraham	5	0	0

	£	s.	d.
Mr. S. Field	2	2	0
Mr. and Mrs. W. Stubbs	10	0	0
Mr. and Mrs. Dipple	5	5	0
Mr. Wollacott	5	0	0
Miss Wollacott	1	0	0
Miss May Wollacott	1	0	0
Mr. and Mrs. Kerridge	5	0	0
Miss Kerridge	1	1	0
A friend	1	0	0
Rev. W. L. and Mrs. Lang	25	0	0
Mr. and Mrs. G. S. Everett	15	0	0
Mr. and Mrs. Hale	5	5	0
E. W.	0	10	0
Mr. and Mrs. James Withers	5	5	0
Miss Toward	2	2	0
Mr. and Mrs. G. S. Phillips	2	2	0
Mr. and Mrs. Clewley	2	2	0
Mr. and Mrs. Winckworth	5	5	0
Mr. E. Russell	0	10	0
Mrs. Macpherson	1	0	0
Mrs. Cuthbert	1	1	0
Mr. G. H. Atkinson	5	5	0
Mrs. S. E. Goslin	0	10	6
Mr. J. C. Goslin	1	1	0
Mrs. Scandritt	0	10	6
Mr. Frank Fisher	4	4	0
Mr. G. Newman	2	2	0
Mr. T. Kelk	1	1	0
Mr. S. Thompson	2	2	0
Mr. and Mrs. F. Thompson	3	0	0
Mr. G. Andrews	1	10	0
Mr. F. L. Edwards	25	0	0
Mr. John B. Meredith	5	0	0
Two friends	1	1	0
Mr. J. Leaver	2	10	9
Mrs. W. Evans	7	7	0
Mr. William Evans	15	15	0
Mr. Richard Evans	20	0	0
Mrs. E. Stevens	1	1	0
Mrs. H. H. Garrett	4	0	0
Mr. and Mrs. J. R. Thomas	2	2	0
Miss A. E. Thomas	0	10	6
Mr. Henry Thomas	1	1	0
Miss Pitt	0	10	6
Mr. and Mrs. John Dyer	5	5	0
Mr. and Mrs. Henderson	3	0	0
Miss Smallridge	2	2	0
Mr. and Mrs. W. Payne	5	5	0
Mrs. Butcher	1	1	0
Miss Butcher	1	1	0
A friend	1	0	0
W. S. L.	1	1	0
A friend	2	0	0
Mr. Alfred Wright	1	1	0
Miss Sheldrake	1	1	0
Miss Frisby	1	1	0
Miss Coker	1	1	0
Mr. Isaac Rogers	1	1	0
Rev. Joseph Lanman	1	0	0
Mr. and Mrs. R. Hayward	10	0	0
Mrs. Rust, sen.	5	0	0
Mr. and Mrs. Gray	2	2	0
Mr. G. Ingle	0	10	6
Mr. J. W. Everidge	3	3	0
Mr. and Mrs. Wayre	5	0	0
Mr. W. Johnson	10	0	0
Mrs. Charlesworth	1	1	0
Mr. W. J. Graham	25	0	0
Mrs. Higgs and family	50	0	0
Mr. and Mrs. W. Higgs	25	0	0
Mr. Thomas Greenwood	20	0	0
Mr. and Mrs. Joseph Hill	10	0	0
Mr. Edmond Hill	2	0	0
Miss Ethel Hill	1	0	0
A friend	10	0	0
Mr. G. W. Mitchell	5	0	0
Mr. Philip A. Houghton	10	0	0
Mr. S. Irwin	1	0	0
Teddington Baptist Church, per Mr. S. Irwin	1	10	0
Mr. and Mrs. Duncan Miller	2	0	0

Name	£	s.	d.
Rev. J. M. Hewson	1	1	0
Mrs. Keeley	1	1	0
Miss Thorpe	1	1	0
Mr. and Mrs. R. Hawkey	5	5	0
Messrs. Bourne, Johnson, and Latimer	5	5	0
Miss Morrison	1	0	0
Miss Parnell	1	1	0
E. Y. E.	10	0	0
Mr. R. Sortwell	2	2	0
Mrs. Sortwell	2	2	0
Miss Annie Sortwell	1	1	0
Miss Nellie Sortwell	1	1	0
Miss Elsie Sortwell	0	10	0
Philadelphia	1	0	0
Mr. and Mrs. Moss	3	3	0
Mr. and Mrs. Fowler	5	0	0
Pastor W. Williams	2	2	0
Mr. and Mrs. G. T. Congreve	10	10	0
Mr. Bigwood	5	0	0
Mr. Buswell	5	0	0
Mr. and Mrs. A. Clarke	5	0	0
Mr. and Mrs. Alderton	3	3	0
Mr. George Pedley	5	5	0
A friend	0	10	6
Mr. John Hall	5	0	0
Mr. David Hall	2	0	0
Mr. and Mrs. Summers	5	5	0
Mr. Thomas Sutcliff	2	0	0
Mr. George Hollands	2	2	0
Mr. James Clark	10	10	0
Mr. R. W. Harden	4	0	0
Miss Darkin	1	1	0
Mr. and Mrs. Downing	2	2	0
Mr. and Mrs. Essex	6	6	0
Mrs. Tinniswood	3	3	0
Mrs. G. H. Virtue	5	0	0
Rev. R. Collins	2	2	0
Mr. George Apthorpe	2	0	0
Mr. William Chivers	2	0	0
Mr. T. G. Ackland	2	0	0
Mr. W. Ackland	3	3	0
Mr. C. Nuille	5	0	0
Mr. and Mrs. James Hall	20	0	0
Dr. Dunbar	5	5	0
Miss E. McDowall	5	0	0
Cash	1	0	0
Miss K. E. Buswell	1	1	0
Miss A. Buswell	1	1	0
D. S.	3	3	0
Mrs. Alfred Boot	1	1	0
Miss L. E. Boot	0	10	6
Mr. and Mrs. C. F. Alldis	3	3	0
Mr. and Mrs. George Creasey	2	2	0
Mr. R. Collins	5	5	0
Mr. and Mrs. Gyles	5	5	0
Mrs. Collins	1	1	0
Mr. George Redman	5	0	0
Mrs. Bartram, per Mr. George Redman	2	0	0
Mr. W. Fox	1	1	0
Mr. Joiner	1	1	0
Mrs. Joiner	1	1	0
Mr. Williams	1	1	0
Mrs. Williams	1	1	0
Mr. R. G. Hobbes	1	0	0
Mrs. C. Fellows	1	1	0
Mr. William Vinson, sen.	5	0	0
Mr. and Mrs. Warren	5	0	0
Mrs. E. Raybould	5	5	0
Mr. and Mrs. C. Parker	5	0	0
Mr. and Mrs. C. Bond	5	0	0
Mr. H. L. Bartlett	1	1	0
Mr. R. Stocks	1	1	0
Mr. and Mrs. H. Smith	25	0	0
Mr. and Mrs. J. G.	2	0	0
K. G.	0	10	0
A. G.	0	10	0
Mr. M. Romang	2	2	0
Mr. M. Romang, jun.	1	1	0
Miss M. Romang	1	1	0
Mr. E. Romang	2	2	0
Mr. J. T. Dunn	1	1	0
Mr. A. Rust	5	0	0
Mr. W. H. Wisker	0	10	0
Mr. Jno. Bygrave	1	10	0
E. E. P.	1	1	0
Mr. Henry Hoare	0	10	0
Mr. J. Muir Leitch	2	0	0
Miss Clarkson	1	1	0
Mr. and Mrs. Barrett	2	2	0
Mr. J. Chamberlain	1	1	0
In memory of the late Mr. Chas. Davies	5	0	0
Mrs. Newstead	1	1	0
Miss Giles	1	1	0
Mr. Burnett	2	2	0
Mr. and Mrs. Gibbons	1	1	0
Mr. Opie Rodway	2	2	0
Mr. William Williamson	3	3	0
Mr. G. M. Rabbich	1	1	0
Mr. W. Davis	1	1	0
Mr. and Mrs. Grose	5	0	0
Mr. James Grose	3	3	0
Messrs. Morgan and Scott	10	10	0
Pastor J. A. Brown	6	6	0
Mr. E. Graves	1	10	0
Mr. and Mrs. George Higgs	5	0	0
H. O. M.	1	1	0
Rev. A. A. Harmer	2	2	0
A. P.	0	10	0
Mr. Jno. Roberts	1	0	0
Mr. Robert Adams	5	5	0
Miss Chenoweth	1	0	0
Mr. J. P. Coe	5	0	0
Collection at Parson's Hill Baptist Chapel, per Pastor Jno. Wilson	6	0	0
From Epping, for May 8th	5	0	0
Rev. W. C. Jones	0	10	0
Mr. and Mrs. Smithers	3	3	0
Mr. George Lester	1	1	0
Subscription from King Street Baptist Chapel, Oldham, per Pastor W. F. Egerton	1	1	0
Not Damaris	1	0	0
Mrs. Hudson	2	0	0
A. S.	0	2	6
A sincere friend, Abergavenny	1	0	0
Miss Love	1	0	0
Pastor N. Heath	0	10	6
Collected at Fleet, Hants, per Pastor N. Heath	4	6	9
Mrs. Sims	5	0	0
Miss Gould	2	0	0
Mrs. Wilson	2	0	0
Mr. W. Rainbow	0	7	6
Sunday-school teacher	0	5	0
Mr. and Mrs. B. W. Carr	1	0	0
Miss Carr	1	1	0
Mr. B. W. Carr, junr.	1	1	0
Miss Agnes Oakey	1	1	0
Mr. and Mrs. Rains	5	0	0
Miss Rains	1	1	0
Collection at Ridgmount Baptist Chapel, per Pastor W. J. Juniper	1	0	0
Pastor William Slater	0	5	0
Pastor J. T. Mateer	1	0	0
Pastor F. James	0	5	0
Mr. W. Johnson	10	0	0
Mr. George Williams	100	0	0
G. T.	10	0	0
B.	100	0	0
Pastor and Mrs. C. H. Spurgeon	10	0	0
The Right Hon. Lord Kinnaird	100	0	0
A friend	50	0	0
An old Independent	20	0	0
Mr. B. I. Greenwood	10	0	0
Mr. J. Alabaster	25	0	0
Mr. James Mote	2	2	0
Mr. W. Turnbull	50	0	0
Mr. Samuel Barrow	25	0	0
Mr. and Mrs. George Gould	2	2	0
Mrs. Fordham	4	0	0
Mr. T. Burrows	2	2	0
The Misses Dransfield	2	2	0

	£	s.	d.
Mr. Fred. Howard...	2	2	0
Mr. F. J. Wood	5	0	0
W. S. ...	5	0	0
Mrs. Reed	50	0	0
Mrs. Faulconer	50	0	0
Miss Steedman	50	0	0
Mr. Thomas R—	20	0	0
Mr. T. D. Galpin	10	0	0
Mr. G. F. White	5	5	0
Miss M. Heath	5	0	0
Mr. R. R. Nelson	2	0	0
Mrs. J. R. Prentice	3	0	0
Mr. Martin J. Sutton	5	0	0
Mr. John Marsh	1	0	0
Mrs. Calder ...	20	0	0
T. J. P.	5	0	0
Mr. Thomas Cook ...	5	0	0
Mr. G. W. Rabbeth	1	1	0
Miss Petter ...	3	0	0
Mr. G. Gibbs	1	1	0
Mr. H. Hudson	1	1	0
Pastor Hugh D. Brown, M.A. ...	1	0	0
Mr. and Mrs. W. R. Fox (for the support of one student for a year)	50	0	0
Mr F. W. N. Lloyd	10	10	0
Hall Lane Mission, Liverpool ...	5	0	0
Lady F.	5	0	0
Mrs. Altham	5	0	0
Dr. and the Misses Habershon ...	10	10	0
Mrs. Pepys ...	5	0	0
Mr. J. D. Link	2	2	0
J. M.	5	0	0
Mrs. Bennetts	5	0	0
Pastor J. Benson ...	5	0	0
Mr. E. Marsh	10	0	0
Mr. H. J. Atkinson, M.P.	5	0	0
Mr. C. E. Smith	20	0	0
Mr. and Mrs. J. Marnham	10	0	0
Mr. T. W. Doggett	5	0	0
C. A. M.	25	0	0
Mr. and Mrs. W. R. Huntley ...	21	0	0
Mr. G. Wheeler	2	0	0
Pastor J. W. Harrald	2	2	0
Mr. W. Clissold, per Pastor W. T. Soper	4	0	0
Dr. Swallow	3	0	0
Collection at Lake Road Chapel, Portsmouth	7	11	8
Mrs. C. Ball	3	0	0
Mr. Walter Hinson	5	5	0
Mr. Robert Ryman	5	0	0
Mr. Joshua Keevil...	10	0	0
Mr. John Neal	3	3	0
Messrs. Wills and Packham	10	0	0
Mr. and Mrs. G. H. Dean	12	12	0
Mr. Martin H. Sutton	1	1	0
Mr. W. H. Stevens	5	0	0
Mr. H. S. Pledge	3	3	0
Mr. A. Macnicoll ...	2	0	0
Mr. A. Blackwood...	5	0	0
Pastor J. J. Kendon	2	2	0

	£	s.	d.
Mr. W. Fox	10	10	0
Mrs. May	10	0	0
Mr. Joseph Corpe ...	2	2	0
Mr. J. C. Wadland	2	2	0
Pastor E. T. Davis	2	2	0
Mr. and Mrs. R. Johnson	2	2	0
N. Y.	1	1	0
Mr. J. A. Balfour ...	2	2	6
Mr. A. Woollard	5	5	0
Mr. C. W. Roberts	4	4	0
Mr. G. D. Pearman	5	0	0
Mr. E. Falkner	2	2	0
Mr. E. P. Fisher	15	0	0
Mr. F. G. S. Norris	1	1	0
Mr. H. M. Leslie ...	1	1	0
From Scotland	25	0	0
Mr. B. I. Greenwood	5	5	0
Mr. Robert Paton ...	5	0	0
Mrs. Aitken...	2	0	0
Mr. J. Stiff	25	0	0
Mr. T. Freeman, F.G.S., F.S.S., per Pastor J. Briggs .	1	1	
Mr. and Mrs. J. S. Price...	4	4	
Mr. Dougall	0	10	
Pastor J. Bennett Anderson	0	10	0
Pastor A. E. Johnson's Bible-class	1	3	
Miss Mann ...	0	10	
Part collection at South Stockton, per Pastor H. Winsor	0	10	
Pastor W. Jackson	2	2	
Mr. R. Booth	1	0	
Mr. E. Webber	0	5	
Mrs. Knott ...	0	5	
Mrs. Wells ...	1	0	
Mr. W. Cochrane, per Mrs. Wells	1	0	0
Pastor G. T. Bailey	0	5	
Mr. Walter Tucker	0	5	
Collection at Conference meeting at Dalston Junction Chapel, per Pastor W. H. Burton ...	23	18	8
Collection at the College Conference Public Meeting ..	37	1	
Mrs. MacGregor	1		0
Prayer-meeting collection at Mansion House Mission, per Pastor G. W Linnecar ...	0	12	
Mr. J. R. Bayley ...	1	0	
Rev. Louis Liesching	0	10	
Two brothers in Christ ..		15	
Mr. T. T. Price	0	12	
Adelphi	0	10	0
Weekly Offerings at Met. Tab. :—			
April 21 ... 23 0 9			
„ 28 ... 10 5 0			
May 5 ... 23 14 6			
„ 12 ... 21 16 0			
	85	16	3
	£2968	7	6

Stockwell Orphanage.

Statement of Receipts from April 16th to May 15th, 1889.

	£	s.	d
Mrs. Macpherson ...	0	2	6
Jack, South Lambeth	0	4	6
Collected by Miss E Dowding, per Pastor C. L. Gordon	0	10	0
Collected by Miss N. Martin	0	1	10
Mr. W. J. Lewis ...	2	2	0
Mrs. Filby ...	0	2	6
Mr. James Duke and Mrs. Duke	3	0	0
Collected by Mr. Farley ...	4	5	0
Mrs. S., "A tenth"	0	3	6
Collected by Miss Jessie Bennett	0	5	11
Mrs. E. Salt...	0	4	6
Bethesda Free Chapel, Sunderland, per Mr. H. W. Cothay, junr.	0	2	0

	£	s.	d.
The Misses N. White and Florence Day, proceeds of Dolls' Bazaar	0	12	0
Collected by Mr. W. Morris	0	4	6
"One of his stewards" ...	1	0	4
L. Cargill (orphan boy's collecting card)	1	1	0
Bonnington Sunday-school, per Mr. R. Sutherland	0	1	0
Mr. J. Goodchild	1	1	0
Mr. E. K. Stace	0	10	0
Collected by Mrs. Copping	0	10	0
Mr. S. Slodden	0	2	6
Collected by Miss Stientz...	1	3	1
Mr. T. S. Hardman ("An old boy")	1	1	0
Mr. E. C. Bowtell ("An old boy") ...	0	10	0

	£	s.	d.
Melbourne Hall, Leicester, per Mrs. Simpson	2	0	0
Young Women's Bible-class at the Orphanage, per Mrs. J. Stiff	0	13	6
Mrs. S. F. Davey (Bible-class)	0	13	9
Collected by Mr. W. J. Gardner	0	16	2
Sale of S. O. tracts...	0	1	6
Pastor R. S. Latimer	0	0	0
Miss Mary Ingle	0	0	6
A friend, per Pastor T. L. Edwards	1	0	0
Mr. J. S. Crisp	0	0	0
Mr. W. White	0	10	0
From Dorton	3	3	0
Mr. W. Kelley	0	10	0
Mr. and Mrs. George Gould	2	2	0
The Misses Dransfield	2	2	0
Lady West	2	2	0
Mr. C. Ibberson	0	2	6
Miss M. Butcher	0	5	0
Miss. E Williams	0	10	0
Rev. Charles Bullock, B.D.	1	1	0
Mr. T. Fawkes	4	0	0
R. H.	1	0	0
Miss Pinckstone	0	5	0
Mr. J. Meader	0	5	0
Hawick Working Boys' and Girls' Religious Society	3	2	0
Mr. J. Wickham	1	0	0
Pastor Hugh D. Brown, M.A.	1	0	0
Mr. H. C. Bridgman	0	2	0
Mrs. Green	1	0	0
Mable, Jan, and Duncan Matheson	1	0	0
Mr. Thomas R——	5	0	0
E. C.	0	10	0
A. R. C.	0	10	0
Mr. H. Ellis	0	4	0
A. S.	0	2	6
Mrs. Mold, per F. R. T.	0	5	0
Mrs. McKenzie	0	10	0
Mr. S. Gammon	1	5	0
Mr. T. Muir Dalziel	3	0	0
Every little helps	0	10	0
Miss Kelland	1	0	0
Mrs. Dewar	1	0	0
Mr. J. W. Jackson	1	0	0
Mr. J. Holt Skinner	3	0	0
Mr. Walter Heath	0	5	0
Miss Martha Greenaway	0	10	0
Mrs. Richards	1	0	0
Mrs. Sims	5	0	0
Mrs. Wilson	1	0	0
Mrs. Rogers	0	10	0
Mrs. Allen	0	2	6
Mrs. Biddall	0	10	0
Mr. W. A. Harding, per Mrs. E. Stevens	1	1	0
Miss C. Selby	0	7	6
Mr. W. Alexander	0	10	0
Mr. G. Alexander	0	1	6
A sermon-reader, Malham	1	0	0
Mrs. Nicholl	0	6	6
Mr. C. Brown	0	10	0
Mr. G. Smith	0	10	0
In memory of dear Caroline Achateny	1	0	0
Mrs. Winsor's collecting-box	0	13	6
Mr. J. Gwyer, sale of poems	1	10	0
Mrs. R. Booth	1	0	0
Mrs. Hague	1	0	0
Executors of the late Mr. J. H. Tarrant	10	0	0
H. T., Exeter	1	0	0
Reader of " Christian Herald "	0	0	0
Mr. D. Camps	3	0	0
Mr. C. Adlem	0	15	0

	£	s.	d.
Mr. J. M. Wilson	0	5	0
Mr. R. E. Walker	5	0	0
F. G. B., Chelmsford	0	2	6
" A friend of orphans "	1	0	0
Collected by Mrs. R. C. Allen	0	7	0
Mr. W. Underwood	1	0	0
A constant reader, per Mr. W. Underwood	1	0	0
Mrs. Gunn	5	0	0
Mr. R. G. Glendinning	20	0	0
Mr. J. G. Priestley	3	0	0
Miss I. Cooper and friend	0	1	6
Mr. A. G. Wing	0	0	0
Mrs. Knowles	0	10	0
Pastor C. B. Allen	0	8	0
Mr. S. H. Dauncey	0	2	6
Mrs. Pentelow	0	5	0
Mr. H. J. Atkinson, M.P.	15	0	0
Mr. T. W. Doggett	5	0	0
Miss Castle	1	0	0
Bert and Norman Wells	1	0	0
Mrs. Walker	2	2	0
Mr. J. O. Tonkin	1	0	0
Janet Wood	0	10	0
Mrs. Barkwell	0	5	0
South Street Baptist Sunday-school, Greenwich	2	2	0
Mr. J. Wheatcroft	100	0	0
Mr. T. Pattison	0	10	0
Mrs. Wood	0	10	0
Mrs. Pester	0	5	0
Postal order from Edinburgh	1	0	0
Mr. E. P. Fisher	6	0	0
Mr. T. Penny	2	2	0
Mrs. Pickering	0	5	0
Mr. T. Jephcoat	0	10	0
Mr. W. Benfield	1	0	0
A friend, Edinburgh	1	0	0
Mr. and Mrs. F. Sellar	2	2	0
Mrs. Rutherford	0	10	0
Mr. W. Brown	0	2	6
Mrs. Norris, per Mr. D. H. Gill	1	0	0
H. Jackson and friends	0	10	0
J. R. M.	1	0	0
Mrs. Randall	1	0	0
H. W.	0	1	0
E. and C. Hoddy's Sunday-dinner collection	1	0	0
Millom Baptist Sunday-school, per Pastor W. Tait	0	18	7
Box at Orphanage gates and office box	4	8	
Meetings by Mr. Charlesworth and the Orphanage Choir :—			
Crouch Hill Baptist Chapel, part proceeds	3	0	0
Sale of programmes, Drummond Road	0	7	9
Proceeds of meetings at Merthyr (less expenses)	22	1	4
Donations :—			
Mr. John Jenkins	5	5	0
Mr. P. Morgan, M.P.	5	0	0
Mr. C. H. James, M.P.	1	0	0
Mr. C. Henry James	0	10	6
Mr. Francis	0	10	0
Mr. Sarvis	0	10	0
Mr. George James	0	5	0
Mr. D. Evans	0	2	0
	35	3	10
Mr. G. Hatton's Mission	8	5	6
Brixton Auxiliary Sunday-school Union	2	2	0
	£315	3	7

List of Presents, per Mr. Charlesworth, from April 16th to May 14th.—PROVISIONS :—A small hamper of Buns, Mrs Brame; 224 lbs. Rice, Mr. J. L. Potier; 1000 Buns, Mr. W. Medcalf; 1 New Zealand Sheep, Mr. A. Seale Haslam; 1 hamper Bread, Mr. N. Read; 36 lbs. Butter, Mr. E. Sparrow; 1 sieve Cabbage and 1 sieve Rhubarb, Mr. W. Taylor.
BOYS' CLOTHING.—3 yards Cloth, Miss Dickerson, per Pastor F. Thompson; 6 Flannel Shirts, The Ladies' Working Meeting at Oaklands Baptist Chapel, Surbiton, per Mrs. Baster; 1 dozen Flannel Shirts, The Misses Dransfield.

GIRLS' CLOTHING.—A quantity of Hats and Gloves, Mrs. Higgs; 48 Articles, The Ladies' Working Meeting, Metropolitan Tabernacle, per Miss Higgs; 2 Articles, E. Rickwood; 34 Articles, The Ladies' Working Meeting at Oaklands Baptist Chapel, Surbiton, per Mrs. Baster.

GENERAL.—A box of Flowers, L. H.; 8 yards Tatting, J. D.; 3 boxes Flowers, The Sunday-school at Cowbeach, per Mr. James Newnham.

ERRATUM.—May "Sword and Trowel," page 248, Orphanage account, "A Widow, per Mrs. Wood, per J. T. D. £5. should be Mrs. Ward.

Colportage Association.

Statement of Receipts from April 16th to May 14th, 1889.

Subscriptions and Donations for Districts:—

	£	s.	d.
Mr. R. W. S. Griffith, for Fritham ...	10	0	0
Mrs. Allison's Bible-class, for Orpington	4	12	0
Southern Baptist Association	50	0	0
Mr. George Williams, for Peckham and East Dulwich	2	2	0
Ludlow District:—			
Mr. E. Fitzgerald ... 1 0 0			
Per Mr. James Evans 10 0 0			
	11	0	0
Kettering, per Mr. W. Meadows,	10	0	0
Somers Town, per Miss Griffith	10	0	0
Weston Turville ..	1	5	0
Mr. Thomas R——, for Bower Chalke	5	0	0
Rendham, per Rev. George Hollier ...	5	0	0
	£108	19	0

Subscriptions and Donations to the General Fund:—

	£	s.	d.
Stockwell Orphanage Young Christians' Band	0	4	6
Mrs. Raybould	1	0	0
Mr. C. W. Roberts...	2	0	0
The Misses Dransfield ...	1	1	0
Mr. Thomas R——	10	0	0
Mrs. Hassall... ...	1	0	0
"A hyssop growing out of the wall," and a friend	1	0	0
Mrs. Wilson	1	0	0
Mr. A. Todd	0	5	0
Mrs. Gunn	10	0	0
Mr. J. G. Priestley	2	0	0
A friend	2	0	0
North Britain	5	0	0
Annual Subscription:—			
Mr. John Powell ...	1	1	0
	£37	11	6

Society of Evangelists.

Statement of Receipts from April 16th to May 14th, 1889.

	£	s.	d.
Thankoffering for Mr. Parker's services at Old Chesterton	1	6	1
Mrs. Wilson ...	1	0	0
Thankoffering for Mr. Harmer's services at Tewkesbury	3	3	0
Thankoffering for Messrs. Fullerton and Smith's services at Mildmay Park Conference Hall...	40	0	0
The Misses Dransfield ...	1	1	0
Mrs. Spencer	0	2	6
Mr. Thomas R——	5	0	0
Mr. C. E. Smith	5	0	0

	£	s.	d.
Thankoffering for Mr. Burnham's services at Hungerford Congregational Chapel	1	1	0
Thankoffering for Messrs. Fullerton and Smith's services at Devonshire Square Chapel	15	15	0
Mr. W. Bradstock...	0	10	0
Mr. J. Atkinson	1	0	0
North Britain	10	0	0
	£84	18	7

For General Use in the Lord's Work.

Statement of Receipts from April 16th to May 14th, 1889.

	£	s.	d.
Postal order from Queen Victoria Street	0	5	0
Postal order from Aberdeen	0	2	6
Mrs. Pearce	0	5	0
Mr. T. G. Owens	5	0	0
An old friend, per Mr. W. Michael ...	1	0	0
S. A. H., Hornsey...	1	0	0
Miss E. Emsden	0	5	0
Miss Hall	0	12	0
Mrs. Brown...	0	5	0

	£	s.	d.
Mr. E. Kent	1	0	0
Mr. E. Trim	1	0	0
The Misses Symington	2	0	0
Mr. D. Anderson	0	10	0
Mr. D. A. McDonald	0	5	0
	£13	9	6

Friends sending presents to the Orphanage are earnestly requested to let their names or initials accompany the same, or we cannot properly acknowledge them; and also to write to Mr. Spurgeon if no acknowledgment is sent within a week. All parcels should be addressed to Mr. Charlesworth, Stockwell Orphanage, Clapham Road, London.

Subscriptions will be thankfully received by C. H. Spurgeon, "Westwood," Beulah Hill, Upper Norwood. Should any sums sent before the 13th of last month be unacknowledged in this list, friends are requested to write at once to Mr. Spurgeon. Post Office and Postal Orders should be made payable at the Chief Office, London, to C. H. Spurgeon; and Cheques and Orders should all be crossed.

ANNUAL PAPER

CONCERNING

THE LORD'S WORK

IN CONNECTION WITH

THE PASTORS' COLLEGE

NEWINGTON, LONDON.

1888-89.

THE PASTORS' COLLEGE.

Printed for the College by
ALABASTER, PASSMORE, AND SONS, FANN STREET, E.C.

1889.

COLLEGE BUSINESS OFFICERS.

President.
C. H. SPURGEON, "Westwood," Beulah Hill, Upper Norwood, S.E.

Vice-President.
J. A. SPURGEON, White Horse Road, Croydon.

Trustees in whom the Property is vested.
THE PASTORS AND DEACONS OF THE CHURCH AT THE
METROPOLITAN TABERNACLE.

Mr. WILLIAM P. OLNEY, 9, The Paragon, New Kent Road, S.E.
Mr. JOSEPH PASSMORE, 4, Paternoster Buildings, E.C.
Mr. T. H. OLNEY, 9, Falcon Street, Aldersgate Street, E.C.
Mr. W. PAYNE, 350, Kennington Road, S.E.
Mr. B. W. CARR, 60, Josephine Avenue, Brixton Hill, S.W.
Mr. C. F. ALLISON, 7, Eccleston Square, S.W.
Mr. H. SMITH, 159, Clapham Road, S.W.
Mr. J. STIFF, 197, Clapham Road, S.W.
Mr. J. BUSWELL, 20, Stockwell Park Road, S.W.
Mr. W. HIGGS, Sussex Lodge, Binfield Road, Clapham, S.W.
Mr. J. HALL, 2, Grantley Villas, Larkhall Rise, S.W.

Financial Committee.

C. H. SPURGEON.	J. PASSMORE.
J. A. SPURGEON.	J. BUSWELL.

Solicitor, and Secretary for Students' Applications.
Mr. T. C. PAGE, 92, Newington Butts, S.E.

Secretary.
Mr. H. HIBBERT, Metropolitan Tabernacle.

The work of the College has for many years been adopted by the Church at the Tabernacle as its own. The various accounts are examined with those of the Church by auditors chosen by the Church, and are read and passed at the Annual Church-meeting in the beginning of the year.

Report of Pastors' College, 1888-9.

BY

C. H. SPURGEON.

———◆———

FOR many years I have devoted the best of my thoughts to the work of furnishing young preachers with a better equipment for their life-work, so far as that can be done by human instruction. Perhaps one of my heaviest tasks has been to give in an annual account of my stewardship in the form of a Report. I would far sooner do the work than talk about it. Not that I have any dislike to rendering in my account of service done, but the difficulty lies in making an interesting business of common, every-day service. Who can say anything fresh about his constant occupation?

Everybody, nowadays, wants to see people clothed in costumes, or to hear the banging of drums : we have nothing sensational to exhibit, and no trumpet to sound, and, therefore, ours is a tame affair. If our readers are interested in the work of the Lord, they will wade through our prosaic account : but if not, they will perhaps go to sleep before they get half-way through our Report. One consideration is very cheering : we are writing for subscribers, people who have proved their interest in our labour of love by giving of their substance to it ; and they will read attentively, whether our style should prove sparkling or flat.

Long years ago I commenced to educate young brethren who showed preaching ability. I was young myself then ; and therefore, at the close of many days, those of my early pupils who survive are now my equals, and some of them even my superiors, in age. I had in those early days but one object, namely, to help them to preach in better style the gospel which I then loved as my own soul—which I now love even more ardently. I have not changed as to that object, nor as to that gospel ; but very great, and, to my mind, very sad, changes have occurred elsewhere. Against those changes I have made such protest as I could, and have confirmed what I said and wrote, by taking up my position "without the camp." It has been a painful business, but it has not arisen from any change in my faith, but from the "progress" which others have made—a progress which might be better described as sliding backward. I hoped that the brethren educated in the Pastors' College would stand firm, amid the general unsettlement ; and so they have done, in great numbers, to the glory of God. My longing is that in the future we may take in and send forth more of the sort of men who know the truth in the power of it in their own souls, and will therefore abide by the faith once for all delivered to the saints, and so provide a breakwater which, in a measure, may resist the onrush of error. For certain of my brethren the torrents have been too furious, and they have gone with the stream, to my immeasurable grief. Indeed, it seemed to me, in one dark hour, as if no man would stand with me ; but I encouraged myself in the Lord my God, and found that the defections were not to be so numerous as I feared. It was a sharp trial, but by no means an unexpected one : dark signs had been increasing. In any case, I should have gone on with my work ; for if some depart from the faith, it is still our duty to commit the divine oracles to others, hoping that they will prove faithful. No leader of any large number of men has been altogether without trials such as mine. No strange thing has happened unto me. Therefore, cheered by the large measure of success in the existence of so many steadfast witnesses, and hopeful of the return of certain of the wanderers, we hold up our banner still, and press forward without fear. The heart-break and disappointment cannot harm us if they do not dispirit us ; and they have not done *that*. We know now more clearly how much of our harvest is true wheat, and we also see and feel how little reliance is to be placed on men, and how only those will stand whom the Lord himself is pleased to keep by the Holy Ghost.

Our venerable friend, Mr. ROGERS, though he has passed his ninetieth year, is still clear in intellect, and strong in heart ; and with singular pleasure I here insert a letter which I received from him in reference to the College, which he has watched over from its infancy until now. His words are so appropriate to the occasion, and say so plainly what ought to be said, that I am glad to step aside, and let a grand old man speak in my stead.

Letter from Rev. George Rogers.

DEAR MR. SPURGEON,

A FEW observations, upon the occasion of another anniversary of the Pastors' College, may not be unacceptable from one who continues to be greatly interested in it. " Days," we are told, " should speak, and multitudes of years should teach wisdom." Recent days have loudly spoken of the wisdom of the institution of the Pastors' College, and it has been confirmed by the teaching of recent years : not the wisdom of this world, which comes to nought, but that which is of God only. This wisdom has been displayed in the origin of the College, in its constitution, in its extension, and especially in its influential position in the present day.

Its origin was unpretentious, the smallest seedling from which a college could have been expected to grow. It was not the result of human foresight, contrivance, or design. It was as if a man should cast seed into the ground, and should sleep and rise, night and day, and the seed should spring and grow up, he knoweth not how. There was first the blade, then the ear, and then the full corn in the ear. The providence and grace that led to its formation, have been its guidance and support hitherto. No one takes credit to himself for its origin or increase. Its most prominent agents, instead of influencing it, have been influenced by it ; and instead of honouring it, have been honoured by it.

Its constitution, like that of every plant, was the development of its seed after its own kind. That seed was the good seed of the kingdom, which alone, in a fallen world, has its fruit unto righteousness, and its end everlasting life. "Salvation by grace alone" is its distinguishing peculiarity. It was designed for the promotion of this, and to this it has faithfully adhered. It has given life to all its movements. It has been its bond of unity, unaffected by distance of time or place. It has been its preservative from the undue influence of reason, and human learning, and from the evils of a Christianity which wears the name without the power. The grace of God, which is the gospel's chief glory, has also been its chief offence in every age of Church history; and it is so still. "The preaching of the Cross is to them that perish, foolishness; but to them that are saved it is the wisdom of God and the power of God." There is a savour, too, in "salvation by grace alone," by which it becomes experimentally distinguished from its numerous imitations and perversions, and by which all who experience it are brought into close and inseparable union with each other. Difference in doctrine cannot fail to produce a corresponding difference in experience and practice; and it is absurd to endeavour to substitute freedom of enquiry, or the claims of humanity, or universal charity, in its place. Union without a creed is as when there was no king in Israel, and every man did that which was right in his own eyes. It is well that the Pastors' College has a creed, and the most well-defined and scriptural of all creeds, by which, in the uniformity of its constitution and influence, amidst all surrounding changes, it has remained unchanged, and, having obtained help from God, has continued to this day.

To its dependence upon the wisdom of God, rather than of man, the Pastors' College owes its prominent position amidst the theological conflict of the present times. Who knoweth whether it has not come to its maturity for such a time as this? If we would know what kind of influence it has had, and to what extent, upon the Christianity of the present age, we have only to suppose it to have never existed, and all its direct and indirect effects upon the Church and the world to be withdrawn. Let the seven or eight hundred ministers who have gone from it, some of whom have been favoured with special honour and usefulness, in chapels that have been built, in churches that have been formed and in the souls which have been saved by their instrumentality, be as though they were not, and we may easily imagine the state of Nonconformist Christianity. It is not improbable that a considerable proportion of those who were trained for their office in the Pastors' College might have obtained an introduction to the same office by other means; but their ministry could not be supposed to be precisely of the same kind. They might have obtained superior "culture"; but judging by the mixed character of similar institutions, they would not have been so decided in their views, so exclusive in their teaching, and so zealous in their defence of the glorious gospel of the blessed God.

This distinguishing peculiarity of the Pastors' College has been severely tested by the theological theories and speculations of modern times. It has been weighed in the balance, and has not been found wanting. It has been compelled to close its ranks, to become more united in itself, and to present a bolder front to its adversaries than before. Some few have gone from us, not we from them. They went out from us because they were not wholly of us. Of these, even, some are still with us in like precious faith, who, when let go by local and temporary associations, will return to their own company. If they are not of the same faith, there can be no desire for their return. It is a matter of unspeakable gratification, and beyond what we could have anticipated, that the representatives of the Pastors' College in this and other lands, uninfluenced by time or place, and the more subtle attractions of new theories and speculations, should, with so few exceptions, have continued to be of one mind and of one heart with their collegiate training, and with each other, and resolved to hold the beginning of their confidence steadfast unto the end.

It is no new contest in which the Pastors' College has been engaged, but such as it must have clearly foreseen, and such as the doctrines of grace have encountered in every age. Had it been for some minor and non-essential doctrine or duty, it would have said, "I am doing a great work, and I cannot come down"; but when its own work was interrupted and assailed, it boldly stood forth in its defence. The battle was the Lord's. It was the old and ever-returning conflict between reason and revelation; between the righteousness of the law and the righteousness of faith; between nature and grace. Its warfare is not for its own denomination, though chiefly within it, but for the common salvation, in which all men are equally concerned. It deserves, therefore, the sympathy and support of all to whom its principles are precious, and who are zealous for their preservation for the benefit of others.

Well would it have been for my own denomination (the Independent) if, while being still more carried away by errors of modern times, some one of its colleges had been equally true to the old gospel, and equally obstinate in its defence; it would then have left some witness within itself of the evangelical purity and independence from which it has receded, and have provided for itself, ere it had gone beyond recovery, a way of safe and honourable retreat. Should these remarks be attributed to the natural tendency of old age to say, "The former times were better than these," or to impaired faculties of body or mind, they must at the same time be admitted to have been the result of an unusual length and extent of observation, and of goodwill to all and ill-will to none. Grace be with all them that love our Lord Jesus Christ in sincerity: so says,

Yours, with unabated confidence and fidelity,

GEORGE ROGERS.

The design of the Pastors' College has, from the beginning, been to help *preachers*, and not to produce *scholars*. There are plenty of institutions for the promotion of learning for its own sake; ours is a part of the work of the church at the Tabernacle, and church-work is gospel-work, and nothing else. Let the world educate men for its own purposes, and let the church instruct men for its special service. We aim at helping men to set forth the truth of God, expound the Scriptures, win sinners, and edify saints. Hence it is as important that men should be prayerful as that they should be studious, and as needful that they should be gracious in soul as healthy in body. No matter how clever a man may be, if there be a general levity of behaviour, and conspicuously, if there be any token of uncleanness of life, he must be dismissed; for he cannot have been ordained to bear the vessels of the Lord. Even where there is nothing overtly evil, a low state of piety, a want of enthusiasm, a failure in private devotion, a lack of consecration, will be as great a defect as the absence of mental ability, or difficulty of utterance. This makes the tutors' work specially anxious. It is easy enough to teach the Greek grammar and the Bible Hand-book, compared with watching over the moral and spiritual state of the student. Very occasionally, it has been my painful duty to expel a man; but happily of late I could have heartily accepted each brother day by day, had there been seven examinations upon this score in each week. None are perfect; all of us are faulty; but, personally, I have enjoyed fellowship of the holiest kind with many of the men, and have been the better for it. This is a subject for great thanksgiving.

Very anxious are we that the inner life should be vigorous, and that the heart should be growing as well as the head. Our brethren, on leaving us, have frequently cheered me by the observation, " I feared that in coming to College I might lose my simplicity of faith and spirituality of mind; but there has been no danger in this place. It would have been my own fault if I had declined in grace; but as it is, I feel that I have been greatly helped in the heavenly life." This testimony has been quite spontaneous, and very hearty, and we have been more pleased with it than words can tell. Our subscribers will read the two following letters from my brother, the Vice-President, and from Principal Gracey, with this view of the case in their mind's eye, and they will see how satisfactory they are to my heart. Neither of them would wink at evil, or commend where they saw cause for censure, or even suspicion.

Vice-President's Report.

HAPPILY there is nothing new to report of the work done in the College during the past year. We have matured our plans in the past, and are now engaged in steadily working along the old lines. The health of the men has been affected by the long-continued and trying winter, and we have been obliged to ease the studies of some few of them, but trust that the return of warmer and more genial weather will see our invalids once again at the post of duty, which it has been a trial to them to leave unoccupied while seeking renewed strength at the seaside.   The spiritual tone of the College greatly delights us.   A prayerful and devout feeling pervades our young brethren ; and many of them are looking forward to the Mission field, with all its dangers and trials, as the future sphere for their self-denial and complete consecration to the Master's will.   Those who have left us this year for pastorates bear away our entire confidence and esteem, and are heartily commended to the brotherly love of those who are already in the field.   Our thanks are due to kind helpers, such as our brethren David Davies of Brighton, Dr. Sinclair Paterson, James Douglas, M.A., and others, who have aided us when our dear President's absence has made a gap which required some outside help to fill up.   The contact with fresh minds and varied modes of thought is not without great benefit to our young brethren. We welcome all new light upon the old truths, and, in the fervent wish to know all that is revealed, we continue to labour on, so that each of our students may be "a workman that needeth not to be ashamed, rightly dividing the word of truth."

JAMES A. SPURGEON.

The illness mentioned in the above letter has this winter been more common than usual, and we are now forced to have a medical certificate of sound health with each man when he enters, since the severity of our studies and the length of the time occupied in each year tries too heavily men who are not robust.   Our vacations are brief, the students do not shirk their abundant class-work, and many of them have congregations to look after at the same time, and all this takes it out of them.   This is a digression.   We now add the Principal's Report.

Mr. Gracey's Report.

THE College year began, continued, and now closes under many tokens of the favour of the Great Head of the Church.   Chief among these is the presence on our benches of men endued with such gifts and faith as, we fondly hope, may well fit them to be good pastors, missionaries, and evangelists.   All of them, it is true, are not possessed of "all the talents," any more than all the trusted servants of old were. But if the sermons preached during the year, and the class-work done, be taken in evidence, they show a good average capacity on the part of most, and a high order of ability on the part of not a few, to bear the severe strain of the ministry of to-day, and perform its hardest tasks. There is, of course, a great variety, and sometimes a notable peculiarity in gifts ; but it has very seldom happened, in the whole course of our history, that we have had a brother so very peculiar that the message has not at length arrived—" The Lord hath need of *him*."

During the year, as men have been ready to enter upon pastorates, invitations have come without any plan or network of influences being used to obtain them.   Had more men been fully ready, more settlements might have taken place.

I owe it to the students to say that earnest and diligent work is a tradition in the College.   On this score tutors have very seldom indeed to utter a complaint; for should the rare appearance of a drone be detected, the busy workers would speedily make him feel anything but comfortable.   To preserve an easy mind, every man must work, and work hard ; such are the conditions the very atmosphere of the place imposes on the students.   And it is not the least among the blessings we enjoy, that the spirit of true Christian brotherhood pervades the whole College, making the intercourse of students with each other the means of shaping and strengthening their Christian life and character.

Prayer has been maintained, and zealous efforts for the salvation of men.   Some decayed, and weak, and several young churches have received regular ministrations of brethren throughout the year ; and some of these have grown so strong as to be nearly able to support their own pastors.   Very rich has been the blessing outpoured upon the work done at some of these " advanced posts."   Equally cheering have been the results of Evangelistic services held in various parts of the country, as well as in London, and in other denominations besides our own, by some of the brethren specially gifted for this department of labour.   Right heartily did all the brethren enter into the mission services conducted by Messrs. Fullerton and Smith at the Tabernacle during the Autumn, dividing among them the whole of the surrounding districts, and visiting from house to house in order to invite all non-churchgoers to the meetings, and then speaking with the anxious enquirers afterwards.   It was a labour of love, and brought with it its own reward in an increased joy and stimulus in the service of our Divine Master.   This contact with the vigorous life and activity of the Tabernacle Church we count among the choicest of our blessings, especially as it enables the students more fully and constantly to come under the stimulating power of the ministry, example, and character of the beloved Pastor, our President.

The same or similar subjects of study have been adhered to as in former years.   On one of the mornings when I meet the whole College I have used Dr. Hodge's Handbook of Theology, and on the other I have delivered my own lectures on the Mediatorial work of Christ. I am now delivering a course of lectures on Baptism.   With the middle and advanced classes our subjects have been Homiletics, Church History, Synonyms of the Greek Testament, the exegetical study of the Greek text of the Gospels according to Matthew and John, the Acts, and the Epistle to the Hebrews.   In the classics we have had Virgil's Æneid, Cicero De Senectute, Xenophon's Cyropædia, and Plato's Phædo.   In Hebrew, besides spending considerable time over the grammar, we have read selections from Genesis, Joshua, the Psalms and Prophets.

D. GRACEY.

The preceding pages will, in some measure, have shown what the men are studying, and the letters from other tutors will serve to complete the information. My own work is that of addressing the men on Fridays, and giving them readings upon subjects connected with preaching. After I have had some two hours of lecturing, the men come to see me one by one upon their work; and after spending the first hours of the day in preparation, and then the rest of it in hard work, I feel that Friday is one of the heaviest, and yet one of the happiest days in my week. The private talks with so many, upon matters requiring a clear judgment, involve more wear and tear than anything else.

Our friend Mr. RICHARDSON pursues his work in voice-training, and many men have derived manifest benefit from his class-teaching and private instruction. It has been a main point with us to attend to elocution. It seems to us that in every college this should have a very prominent place. If our men cannot speak, what is the good of them? Happily, they are, as a rule, distinguished by their clearness of utterance; and this, we think, must be, in a measure, attributed to the trouble taken with them while with us. In some cases of brethren who can sing, we have not hesitated to employ the ablest professional teachers of music, and trainers of the voice, and we have seen the best results following from their able assistance.

Mr. CHESHIRE works on with his Science classes, and has this year taken *Light and Heat*, certain matters connected with *Human Physiology*, and *Scientific Aspects of the Temperance Question*. The last subject is specially useful to men who are all abstainers, and all anxious to affix to other coats the little bit of blue.

Mr. FERGUSSON, whose lively Report we put into this place, is spared to us, and after many years of diligent service, is full of devotion to the grand old cause. Indeed, all our tutors not only hold the faith, but love it in their very souls.

Mr. Fergusson's Report.

THE amount of work done in our department this year has risen above the average of other years, on account of a higher previous education in the case of the Students before entering on the studies of the College. The course of the brethren has been marked by uncommon thoroughness, unflinching and unbroken steadiness, stimulated by a strong desire to get as much as possible out of their studies. The spirit in which the work has been done has been strongly marked, on the part of our Students, by a sense of personal need of what they are called upon to study; and a feeling of responsibility as to the best use to be made of the present opportunities for self-culture, and mental discipline.

A particularly pleasing feature of this year's work has been a pronounced definiteness of purpose. Every piece of work done has tended in one direction—to help them to exalt the Lord Jesus Christ.

Not less definite in expression than their purpose are the methods by which they intend to achieve that purpose. They are few, they are simple, but they are strong. They are these. Witness-bearing for that Master to whom they owe everything, and for Him alone ; a determination by prayer, by example, and by genuine work, to deepen, widen, and accelerate the stream of spiritual life among the people of God in the churches to which they may be called; and watching, working, and striving above everything, for the conversion of sinful men unto God. Equally plain and outspoken are they, as to the weapons and instruments with which they hope to carry out their one purpose, and which, at all hazards, they resolve to use. They are few, but they believe they are mighty, through God, to the pulling down of strongholds. They are these. Faith in the Lord Jesus Christ, who by suffering became the substitute for sinners ; who also by service became the sinner's righteousness, and thereby gave him a legal right to an inheritance in heaven ; also dependence on the constant supply of the Spirit of God, who alone can make the man a new creature, and by dwelling in his renewed breast, turn him into a temple of the Holy Ghost. They believe in the complete adequacy of a Bible inspired by the Holy Ghost, and profitable for doctrine, for reproof, for correction, for instruction in righteousness ; and with this in their hand, they go forth to conquer.

Another feature in the work of the year which pleased us much was the absence of all dreamy expectation or morbid dread as to the future. They are fully aware of the signs of the times in which they live. They know that their ministry will begin in a wintry season, and be overhung by dark and cloudy skies; and they know, and are fully prepared to encounter, undisguised hatred to the doctrines of the cross of Christ, and bitter prejudice against the College which maintains those truths ; neither are they ignorant of the devices employed to keep them out of vacant churches, by leagued professionalism and secret societies of disappointed men. They know all this. They laugh at the threat of boycotting; for, on entering College, they are informed that it never has applied to vacant churches, and that it does not intend to do so; and yet the men go forth to pastorates. They believe that, if the Head of the Church sent them to College, to be prepared as preachers for Him, He will also provide spheres of usefulness for them; and out of these spheres no associations of mortal men, of whatever sort, shall be able to keep them, or to thwart the purpose of Christ concerning them.

On the whole, this year has been one of much promise, in our judgment, both as to work and students. The men, as far as we can see, are so devoted to their Master as to be prepared to go anywhere and do anything for Him. Once more we erect at our class-room door our " Ebenezer," and as He has hitherto helped us, so will He to the end.

Subjoined is a list of the books used in our department. Fleming's Analysis of the English Language, Bain's English Composition, Angus' Hand-book of the Bible, Taylor's Elements of Thought, Whately's Logic, Sir William Hamilton's Metaphysics, Butler's Analogy, Wayland's Ethics, and in English History—Green and Smith's.

ARCHIBALD FERGUSSON.

Mr. Marchant's Report.

BEING now well on in the tenth year of my tutorial work at the
College, I do not think I have ever made any report of a year's
labour with more pleasure and confidence than now. The feeling that
we are wanted in the world, and that no other institution is doing our
work, is our deep-seated conviction. That God can do without us is,
doubtless, true every day ; that he has graciously wrought very largely
by means of our brethren from the College, can hardly be other than
evident to all parts of the Church of Christ. There is an old and
familiar saying—" It takes all sorts of people to make a world " ; surely,
if this is true, it ought to follow that it needs all sorts of preachers to
minister to such a world. Our preachers are to be found labouring in the
lowest slums of London, in the poorest hamlets of the country, and also in
the foremost pulpits of our largest and most distinguished cities. The
fruits of the gospel are manifest and abundant alike among all classes of
the people. God has said to the slums, " Give up," and to the squares,
" Keep not back; bring my sons from the crowded cities, and my
daughters from the dispersed of the villages." We have sometimes been
supposed to send forth our labourers fettered with the bonds of ignorance.
Even if that were so, our bonds have become manifest, in Christ, in
palaces and in all other places. Geography gives its witness, no less
than social grades. Europe, Asia, Africa, America, Australia, and the
islands of the sea, thank God for the Sons of the College. Thus, while
rich and poor are glad of our message, we can bear, with no great effort,
the lofty carriage of our supposed superiors. The witness of God is
sufficiently helpful to us all.

But far better than any help which this divine testimony may be
affording us without, is the strength which it imparts within the College
itself. We cannot be daily hearing our Lord say, " Lo, I am with you
alway," and be as though we heard it not. It is really a delight to hear
the brethren pray over Greek and Latin difficulties as though these too,
like hard hearts, had to be won for Christ and brought in submission to
his feet. Our discipline, while full of liberty, under the skilful hand
of our deeply-esteemed Principal, has never, I think, been more encouraging than now. Love leads us, love binds us together, and the joy of
the divine presence finds us, day by day, with a common purpose. We
are such as love his salvation, and we agree to say, " Happy is that
people whose God is the Lord."

The text books for the year have been much the same as those named
in the last Report :—Xenophon's Anabasis, and Lucian's Dialogues, in
Greek ; Eutropius, Cæsar, and Virgil in Latin, and Arnold's Exercises
in both languages. Two or more books of Euclid have been worked
through by different classes, while the usual elementary work has
occupied the attention of Juniors. In my opinion the work has been
well done by nearly all the brethren, and good progress has been made.

F. G. MARCHANT.

The Evening Classes.

AT the commencement of the College, we instituted classes, which were held in the evening, that young men might gain an education *gratis*. There was greater need in those days than now for such an opportunity; and we found more young men ready to attend than at this present. Board Schools and Polytechnics now supply the lack which in former years was grievously apparent. Hundreds who have been useful deacons, teachers, preachers, and workers received their first training in these evening classes. All that we asked of them was that they were believers in the Lord Jesus, and were anxious to improve their gifts, that they might serve him better. Joyfully they were received, heartily they worked. Many passed from these classes into the College proper, and much drudgery was spared the tutors. Others felt that their *forte* would be to serve the Lord in a secular calling; and they have done so. We constantly meet with men in good positions who gratefully ascribe their rising in the world to the education obtained at this evening seminary. Their grateful guineas have not failed to find their way to the institution which helped them in their beginnings. At present the number of evening students is fewer than it was wont to be; but we hope to beat up recruits, and to start afresh with renewed vigour. Here is the Report of the Tutors :—

During the past year our young men have given diligent application to the work of all the departments of these classes, and noticeable progress has been made. Many have testified that the education received in these classes has been most useful to them in their work for the Lord, and especially in their evangelistic labours. We are glad to observe that again this year another student has been drafted into the Pastors' College.

In the Theological Class, lectures have been given on "The Attributes of God," "Christian Evidences," "The Trinity," and "Providence."

Our Discussion Class is greatly appreciated, and the papers read have shown much improvement in the style of their composition, and in the manner of their delivery.

Lectures have been given in Mental Science.

The Elementary Greek Class has studied the "Initia Græca" and John's Gospel; the Advanced Class is now reading Anabasis III. Some of the students have made really good progress in this subject.

Lectures have been given in Elizabethan History and Literature, with special reference to Spenser's works; in Grecian History to the Supremacy of Sparta; and in English Grammar.

S. JOHNSON
THOS. F. BOWERS.

22

Work by brethren after leaving College.

OF the service rendered by the brethren who have entered the ministry, we cannot pretend to present even a summary; it would occupy much more than a College Report. Churches have been revived which were almost extinct, and others have made a solid advance. Alas! there are failures, as we sadly know; but the progress has been none the less a subject for overflowing gratitude to the Lord of the harvest.

We can only mention new work. To raise a new church and house is no small labour; but this has been done, with the help of all sorts of agencies and friends, under the lead of our own brethren at Barnes, Battersea, Bermondsey (two places), Rotherhithe, Blackheath, Burdett Road, Brixton (four places), Bromley-by-Bow, Bromley (Kent), Camberwell, Catford, Chalk Farm, Cheam, North Cheam, Chelsea, Chiswick,. Dalston, Deptford, Ealing Dean, Enfield Highway (Totteridge Road), Edgware Road, Enfield, Erith, Finchley (two places), Greenwich, Hampton Court, Hounslow, Hornsey Rise, Norbiton, Mitcham, Merton, Norwood,. Notting Hill (Talbot Tabernacle), Old Ford, Paddington (St. Peter's Park), Peckham (two churches), Penge, Plaistow, Putney, Silvertown, Streatham, Surbiton, Teddington, Tooting, Thornton Heath, Vauxhall, Wallington, Walthamstow, Wandsworth (two chapels), West Ham Park, Westminster, Willesden, Wimbledon, Woolwich (Joseph Street). These are not all which we have founded in the Metropolitan district. Some of these are now in the hands of brethren not from our College; but they were nursed by us till they could run alone. Others we have not mentioned, because we are only, in a smaller degree, partners in the work, in some instances stepping in when they would otherwise have been abandoned. In other cases we have had long preaching, and souls have been saved; but churches have not been formed. Our policy has been to plant many slips, assured that some would take root, and that good would come of the preaching of the Word.

Outside of the home region, we cannot even mention all the churches which, in whole or in part, are due to the earnest efforts of our brethren; but the following are notable :—Maidenhead, Winslow, Willingham, Carlisle, Brentwood, Grays, Hornchurch, Southend (two places), Maldon (Essex), Nailsworth Tabernacle, Bracknell, Gosport, Sandown, Ventnor, Redbourne, St. Alban's Tabernacle, New Bushey, Dover Tabernacle, Faversham, Herne Bay, Sittingbourne, Loose, New Brompton, Orpington, Sheerness, Tunbridge Wells, Tunbridge, Whitstable, Rochester, Manchester (Coupland Street), Melton Mowbray, Burnley, Morecambe, Ulverston, Holbeach, Northampton (Mr. Bradford's), Henley, Oxford (Commercial Road), Shepton Mallet, Cheam, Dorking, Aldershot, Redhill, Crawley, Eastbourne, Portslade, Shoreham, Worthing, Hull (Frank Russell's), Middlesbrough, Nottingham Tabernacle, and others.

In Scotland, we have made several attempts, and not without success, while in the colonies we have a goodly list to present, but our space fails. We will give one or two instances in detail.

Hampton Court Baptist Chapel.

THE Lord's work here is an excellent sample of what he will do by the prayer, faith and diligence of his people. Four years ago we came to hold services in this locality; and, for that purpose, we rented a "Lyceum," whose uses were alternately evangelical and theatrical. The gospel was preached without any fuss or specious attraction, and, by its essential power, the work grew, and souls were won to Christ. The latter was to us the supreme seal of God's approval, and we began to think of establishing a home for the church which was evidently to be gathered. A freehold site was secured, though at heavy cost, and in twenty-one months from the commencement, our new chapel, seating three hundred, was opened. In March, 1887, a church of baptized believers was formed, numbering forty-three members. Hundreds of pounds were raised for the Building Fund; and the work was continued down to December, 1887: all having been done so far during our College course. The Student became the Pastor in January, 1888. Sixty-nine members have joined during two years, sixty-one being at present on the roll. All our expenses have been met, with the exception of £850, on Freehold Site and Building. There is a great field here for an earnest church; the district was formerly called "The Devil's Freehold," but now the Lord has a portion in it.

ALFRED HALL, Pastor.

Baptist Tabernacle, Aldershot.

IN the early part of 1883, a few Baptists began to meet together, and, feeling their need of a home of their own, applied to the College for a student to be sent down. Accordingly, in February, 1883, Mr. Cooper—now of Portland, Victoria—was sent, and he conducted services every Sabbath in the Foresters' Hall. Twelve months after, a church of about twenty baptized believers was organized. On the Monday following, at a public meeting held in the Wesleyan Soldiers' Home, a Baptist Tabernacle Building Fund was started. The chairman, W. Allden, Esq., kindly gave a corner plot of ground worth £300, and W. Hawley, Esq., £100, so that the fund was started in a very hopeful manner. From this time forward the friends endeavoured, by every lawful means, to augment the funds.

My connection with the church began in September, 1884, and on January 1st, 1885, I was elected to the pastorate. In May, 1886, we entered upon the work of erecting our present chapel.

The opening services took place in the September following. The chapel is capable of seating three hundred, and cost £800. This sum merely represents the bare cost of labour and material; for the builder who erected it was a very generous friend. Towards the payment of this we obtained £250 as a loan from the Metropolitan Tabernacle Loan Building Fund, ten per cent. on £500 from Mr. Spurgeon, £100 from Mr. Hawley, as already mentioned, and the remaining sums we have been trying to raise by our own individual efforts. Our liabilities now are about £280. We are all poor, and sorely in need of help, and sadly in need of school-rooms.

So far, as will be seen, we have only spoken of the material building; a word or two is now necessary as to the spiritual.

When it is known that we are in the largest garrison town in the kingdom, with its attendant evils, surrounded by drink-shops, music-halls, and, until very recently, houses of ill-fame, with an exceedingly migratory population, it will at once be understood that our work is very hard, and at times very disappointing; yet we must praise God, and will.

Since we have been here, 97 persons have professed their faith in Christ, 41 of whom have been baptized, and, with 23 others, received into fellowship.

But where are the ninety-seven? Forty-nine have left to join other churches, and forty-eight are with us to-day. These constitute the number of our present membership. But no figures can give any real idea of the work done. I believe many come in, as we say, just casually, and get the "harpoon" stuck into them; we see them no more, but by-and-by, we believe that they will come home to God.

Our work is emphatically a Home and Foreign Missionary work. We can never, therefore, get a settled congregation for any length of time, nor a permanent membership. But we are on the winning side, and believe and work for better things.

JESSE AUBREY.

Bunyan Baptist Chapel, Norbiton.

Pastor—JOSEPH CLARK.

THIS cause was started at the close of the year 1881, by a few friends who met in the Assize Courts, Kingston. The Church was formed of 30 members. The Pulpit, or rather the Judge's bench, was supplied by members of the Tabernacle Evangelists' Association, and of the Country Mission, and also by Students of the Pastors' College, one of whom, Mr. A. C. Chambers, now of Rhyl, served the people with much acceptance for twelve months. The Assize Courts, however, were unsuitable for public worship; but there are many who bless God, that while they entered those Courts "condemned already," they left them acquitted by "the Judge of all the earth."

After a time, a site was secured in a suitable locality, under circumstances which evidently indicated that the good hand of the Lord was in the matter. The late highly-esteemed W. Higgs, Esq., offered a piece of land in Norbiton at cost price, and forthwith arrangements were made with Messrs. Higgs and Hill to build a School-chapel. The foundation stone was laid by our generous friend J. T. Olney, Esq., and it was ready for occupation in January, 1885.

Mr. Joseph Clark accepted the pastorate, and entered upon his labours at the opening. Our heavenly Father's approval of the choice may be seen in the blessing which has rested thereon.

We entered the present chapel with 39 members; since then, 230 have joined the church: the majority having been drawn from the world. We have a large Sunday School, good Bible Classes, a Christian Band, a Band of Hope, and a local Preachers' class, whose members conduct services at a Mission Hall, and evangelize the neighbourhood.

We owed for the Chapel and land at the beginning of 1885, £1,800; we have since paid £1,500, and this chiefly by the self-denying efforts of our church and congregation; for helpers outside who have assisted us in sums above ten pounds could be counted on the fingers of one hand. We were favoured with a loan of £350 from the Metropolitan Tabernacle Loan Building Fund, for which we are deeply grateful, as we have no interest to pay on it, and we are regularly diminishing the debt. A balance of £300 remains to be paid before we may venture to contract another debt, in building the sorely needed larger chapel, which we think the previous statements would justify us in beginning straightway, but for our poverty. For months, we have been uncomfortably crowded. In summer time we utilized the adjoining ground, with heaven for a roof, wood and canvas for walls, and rough timber for seats, providing accommodation for 900 persons. Here it was our great joy to assemble each Sunday evening, so long as the weather permitted, after which we were painfully obliged to say good-bye to our new friends, because we had no place in which to receive them.

We are forbidden to steal, we are afraid to borrow, we therefore beg. We should be glad of speedy help from the Lord's stewards.

Union Church, Northampton.

THIS church had its rise under peculiar circumstances. Northampton, as is well known, has obtained notoriety through the majority of its electors choosing Mr. Bradlaugh, as their representative. Many who have no sympathy with his atheism, support him for political reasons, but others feel compelled to oppose him on account of his hostility to all that they hold sacred. Mr. Henry Bradford, while minister at Prince's Street Baptist Chapel, aroused the hostility of those members of the congregation who were supporters of Mr. Bradlaugh, by a sermon on "The duty of Christians to separate themselves from unbelievers." They secured an adverse vote, which led to Mr. Bradford's withdrawal. At the urgent request of many of his hearers, and other Christians, he consented to remain in the town, and form a new church on Union principles. This was in 1884, since which time a substantial chapel, holding a thousand worshippers, has been erected, at a cost, including land, of £4,000. It was opened, free of debt, in 1886. A minister's house has since been added. Much of this was due to the enthusiastic help of our late beloved friend Admiral King Hall. There is a membership of about 140. In the church covenant, to which adherence is required, there is not only a profession of evangelical faith, but a prohibition of those worldly entertainments and practices which injure the spiritual life of a church.

Wallington Baptist Church.

THIS church originated in some open-air services held in Carshalton about the year 1875 by a member of the Metropolitan Tabernacle Country Mission—formerly a very fruitful society. After a while, a room in a cottage was hired to hold the services in; but the room becoming too small for the congregation attending, the Carshalton public hall was engaged, in which the services continued to be held until March, 1888, when a handsome and spacious chapel was opened in Queen's Road, Wallington, which is an adjoining district, the population of which is rapidly increasing. The cost of the freehold site was nearly £600, and of the chapel, about £4,300, about half of which remains on mortgage.

Since the chapel was opened, the congregations have largely increased, the income has more than doubled, and 44 new members have been received into fellowship, making the present number of members 148. Bible Classes for Young Men and Women have been commenced, which, together, have a membership of nearly 80, and several from these classes have recently been baptized on a profession of faith. A Band of Hope, a Young Christians' Band, and a Young Men's Prayer Meeting, have also been started, and are each doing well. Our Foreign Mission Auxiliary has more than trebled its contributions during the year, and a Young People's Missionary Working Party has been commenced.

Despite the heavy debt on the chapel, we have decided to commence the building of School and Class Rooms *at once*, the need being very great; but we are pledged to open them *free of debt*, so as not to increase our present liabilities. Several generous friends are promising liberal help on this condition, but we need still larger aid. We have about £550 in hand, or promised, towards the £750 required, and we hope that many to whom God has entrusted wealth will come to our aid in this undertaking.

The present Pastor (J. E. Jasper) commenced his ministry here in July, 1880, while a student in the Pastors' College; and contributions will be gratefully received by him at "Fernilea," Clifton Road, Wallington, Surrey. No cause can better deserve aid.

Baptist Chapel, Carlisle.

SEVERAL unsuccessful attempts had been made to establish a Baptist cause in Carlisle, previously to Mr. A. A. Saville being sent by the President to endeavour to plant a church there: this was about nine years ago. Mr. Saville endured great straits, but by his perseverance proved himself to be the man for the place. He and the friends he has gathered round him have lately entered their handsome new stone chapel at the corner of Warwick Square. The present building is seated for 414 people, but will admit of galleries for 290 more; there is ground for schools, but until the heavy debt is greatly reduced, this necessary work must be deferred. The chapel and land cost nearly £3,000. We believe this to be a solid spiritual work, and the man by whom it has been wrought is worthy of the practical commendation, which shows itself in help.

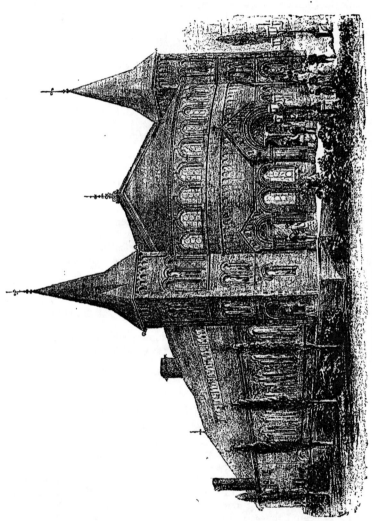

TALBOT TABERNACLE, BAYSWATER.

Talbot Tabernacle.

Pastor—FRANK H. WHITE.

THE old iron building, which had been in use for about 20 years, has now given place to a noble and substantial structure. The new Tabernacle is situated on the old site, Talbot Road, Bayswater. It is somewhat Byzantine in its architecture, with a semi-circular frontage of red brick and terra-cotta. Externally, it presents a most inviting appearance. The interior shows an open roof of pitch pine, with a clear span of 62 feet, capable of being thrown open to form part of the general auditorium. The seating capacity is for 1000 persons, but quite 200 more can be accommodated. Its entire cost, inclusive of furniture, heating apparatus, architect's fees, &c., is £6,500.

With its splendid proportions, the uniqueness and simplicity of its arrangements, the comfortable feeling created as you enter, the fact that not a single column or pillar is to be seen, to obstruct sight and deaden sound, so that from every part of the building one can both see the preacher and hear his message, makes the Talbot Tabernacle a model building. Our honoured American brethren, Drs. Gordon and Pierson, who preached at the opening, paid a graceful tribute to its rare excellence, the latter remarking that it was both stately and symmetrical, good enough for the wealthiest, and not too good for the poorest.

The building is practically free of debt,' there being but a small deficiency of about £500, which is met by a loan from the Tabernacle Building Fund. "Two things we determined on," says Mr. White, "from the beginning—(1) that we would not go into debt, and (2) that we would resort to no doubtful expedients for raising money. From both of these we trust we have been preserved. So freely have the Lord's people sent me of their substance, that I have not needed to call on a single donor in request of money. Indeed, my heavy responsibilities in the care of the Church and other labours in the gospel, rendered this an impossibility. It would fill a volume to tell how the Lord has appeared for us in every step of the way. Although the cost far exceeded the sum at first estimated, yet never once have we been without the means to pay the contractor as amounts became due. The money reached me in sums varying from a few pence sent all the way from China, by a Native Bible-woman, whose annual stipend does not exceed £4 a year, to £500 from 'a lover of the old gospel' at home. £80 were subscribed in pennies. The cost of the baptistery was sent me from the sick bed of one 'whom the Lord loveth.' Indeed, the whole is made up of free-will offerings, given for love of Christ and His Ancient Gospel. This makes every brick in the place most precious to me. Like the stones in Madame Guyon's prison, they shine in my eyes like rubies.

We have abundant tokens of the Lord's presence and blessing. The congregations are large, and nearly 80 believers have professed their faith in baptism. For all this I can only cry in the golden words which sweep the facia of our gallery, 'Not unto us, not unto us, O Lord, but unto Thy name be all the glory, for Thy mercy, and for Thy truth's sake.'"

Baptist Chapel, Cambridge Road, Worthing.

THE Worthing Baptist Church originated in the blessing of God which attended the labours of Mr. W. F. Stead, who left the Pastors' College some eleven years ago, and commenced his ministry in a little room in this town. The work grew sufficiently to warrant his hiring the Montague Hall, where services were held until a good central site was secured, and a school-room built. Here Mr. Stead continued his ministry till the Autumn of 1883, when he resigned, and was succeeded by Pastor C. Douglas Crouch, of Shoreham. Discovering that the cause was burdened with a debt of about £1,100, Mr. Crouch saw that the congregation he would be able to gather in the school-room would find the interest of the debt, together with the working expenses of the church, too much for them, and that his only hope of success lay in the immediate erection of a commodious chapel. He therefore set to work to collect funds on the distinct understanding, that the new chapel would not be opened before the whole of the contract price was provided by cash or promise. Through the divine favour so manifestly seen in the generous response which the Lord's people gave to the appeals for help, the new building (of which the above is a picture) was within a few months opened by the Rev. A. G. Brown, the whole of its cost (£2,200) being promised by the close of the opening day. The congregations have ever since been good, souls have been saved and added to the church, and the old debt, which has been somewhat increased by extras, such as furniture, boundary walls, &c., is now being gradually reduced; *help towards the complete discharge of this liability would be very gratefully received by Mr. Crouch.*

Kensington Chapel, Jubilee Drive, Liverpool.

PERHAPS one of the quietest, yet most effective efforts in connection with our College, is that of Brother Walter, of Liverpool. For seventeen years he has with untiring zeal continued a work which would have disheartened most men, and have made them seek a more inviting neighbourhood. During the early part of his ministry, the chapel in Soho Street filled with casual hearers, and many of these were converted to God. Very gradually a church of earnest people grew up, and institutions usual to a living church appeared, until it was regarded as a centre of Christian activity, and its pastor a power for good in the district. While most of the Nonconformist churches in Liverpool have had a hard struggle to maintain their former status, Soho Street is growing and enlarging its sphere, notwithstanding its dark, dingy chapel, and its depressing surroundings of narrow, densely populated streets, from which the people are continually migrating. Our friend told us, a few days ago, that his congregation had completely changed at least three times during his 17 years' ministry. Under these circumstances a site for new chapel and schools was sought, and Kensington being in every way a desirable district, and convenient of access for the Soho Street worshippers, a site was purchased, and chapel and schools are now nearing completion. The total cost is estimated at £4,000, towards which £2,000 has been received for the old chapel from our Wesleyan friends, who will use it for home mission purposes. The new chapel will seat eight hundred persons, and the schools will accommodate four hundred scholars. Mr. Walter is highly esteemed by his ministerial brethren, and has held the office of President of the Liverpool Baptist Union, of which he is now the Secretary. The writer (a neighbouring pastor), has no words sufficiently warm in which to commend the labours of this faithful preacher of the old-fashioned gospel, to those who desire to aid him in his present undertaking.

Abbey Street Chapel, Bermondsey,

IS at the far end of the famous tannery district, in which 89,000 souls live. The chapel was erected when fair gardens adorned the place where now stand a thousand houses. Congregationalists, Baptists, and Christians of all sorts worshipped together, until 1870 or 1871. Then the Baptists of *Deptford Lower Road* were induced to dispose of their building and unite with the church at *Abbey Street;* from that time Baptists have been in the large majority. Several ministers held the pastorate for short periods until 1885, when the prospect was very gloomy. An almost empty chapel, in bad repair, a considerable debt, and an undesirable reputation, crippled all efforts. At this time Mr. Spurgeon sent Mr. Carlile, then a student, to try to put new life into the cause. The results show the wisdom of this action. Mr. Carlile was familiar with the neighbourhood, for he was born in the street where the chapel stands.

The work has grown steadily and solidly; the debt has gone, the building has been renovated, and now its interior is as pleasant and pretty as almost any chapel of its size. Nearly 200 believers have been received into church fellowship, and not a dozen of them have come from other churches. It is often the joy of pastor and people to lead souls to the Saviour. The people have learned to contribute cheerfully to the support of the work. The Sunday-school is well attended, there being no lack of children in Bermondsey. The superintendent, an earnest worker, is an old student of the Tabernacle evening classes. There is a Young People's Society, numbering from 60 to 70, many of whom have found " The Friend " whose friendship is better than riches. The children have their Band of Hope, which attracts about 200 to its weekly meetings. The week-day services and prayer meetings are well sustained. Three years ago Mr. Carlile started a new work, which has grown to considerable proportions. During the winter months there is much poverty in the district, and many feel the pangs of hunger. The friends at Abbey Street provide *Free Dinners* for the genuine unemployed men and women who need help. After the dinner, a service is held for half an hour. The fruits of this effort give much encouragement to the workers. In one month nearly 2,000 adults attended the dinner services.

The *Fatherless Children's Society* has for its objects the clothing and aiding of fatherless children, who are not able to enter institutions like the Stockwell Orphanage. It holds its festivals at stated seasons, when from 50 to 100 poor little ones are fed and clothed. It is a right royal feast that the little ones have. The clothes are made by the members of the churches for Jesus' sake, and not a penny has been paid for labour, though over 600 little bodies have been clothed.

In Bermondsey, men of all creeds and no creed have held their meetings and preached their views. The Drill Hall, Town Hall, and Music Hall, have seen the advent of men with new gospels, aided by band and choir. They came, they preached, they retired, or, more correctly speaking, the people retired. We were told that the old gospel of free grace and dying love," was dead; but the people still come to the chapel, and bless God for leading them where He saved their souls.

Baptist Tabernacle, New Brompton.

IN 1878 two students—Messrs. Blackaby and Blocksidge—went to this town, and alternately conducted services in a small hall seating 100 persons. Through the blessing of God on the preaching of the gospel, a church was formed in 1879, consisting of 16 members.

In January, 1881, Mr. Blocksidge became the pastor of the church, then numbering 46 members.

In October, a school-chapel was built and opened, and a Sunday-school commenced. In time the congregations so increased that the sitting accommodation was inadequate, and the school outgrew the capacity of the room. A good friend then built a gallery, and that being at once filled, the Town Hall was hired for Sunday services.

The idea entertained at first, was to build a chapel adjoining the school-room, on the piece of land in front; but it was found that it would not be large enough for the congregation waiting to enter it.

After earnest prayer and deliberation the church resolved to pull down the school-room, and build a chapel as large as the site would permit, with school-rooms underneath.   This has been successfully accomplished: the Tabernacle was opened on January 30th, 1889, when Rev. C. Spurgeon preached in the afternoon, and Mr. C. F. Allison presided in the evening over crowded congregations.   The chapel will seat 638 persons; and the school-room, with six class-rooms, will accommodate 600 scholars.   The cost was about £3,600, toward which we have raised about £1,700, leaving a debt of nearly £2,000.

Ten years ago a few friends were struggling to commence this cause, to-day there is a church of 235 members, a school of 400 scholars, and kindred institutions.   To God be praise.

W. W. BLOCKSIDGE.

The Baptist Temple, Ayr.

ON June 21st, 1886, a few baptized believers met together, and re-solved to form a Baptist Church in Ayr.   Mr. Spurgeon was communicated with in July, as the result of a visit from Mr. Horne, the present pastor, then a student in Pastors' College.   The outcome of the correspondence was, that Mr. Spurgeon promised to aid, and Mr. Horne began work on September 26th of the same year, with 27 members.   The membership and gatherings commenced to grow right away, and ere long it became necessary to look out for a larger hall. This was secured; but it also became too small, and an exodus was made to a still larger place—"The Queen's Rooms."   This edifice was formerly used as a theatre, and at that time was being let for lectures, &c. The friends were not long in it before they found that it suited them admirably, and had every convenience for a church, and they entered into negotiations with the proprietor for the purchase of it.   The result was, that the building was bought for £1,350, including the site, which is the most choice in the town.   When it was resolved to purchase the building, plans were immediately set on foot to raise the sum necessary to get possession, viz., £500, which was done in about six months' time. Since then about £130 more has been raised, which has mostly been expended in alterations, so that the debt is still slightly over £800. Efforts to reduce the debt, however, have never ceased, and in course of time this sum will be lessened.   The building—since christened "The Ayr Baptist Temple"—is quite fresh and strong, has a good appearance from the outside, and holds 500, with room for extension. There is also a good hall which seats fully 200, three vestries, a kitchen with every appliance for tea-meetings, &c.   Although paying interest on borrowed money just now, the church has no more expense to face than formerly, when one hall was rented for Sabbath, and another for Wednesday evening.   The baptistery had to be erected in a private house, as liberty would not be granted to bring it into either of the halls.   There have been 152 additions to the membership, which, at the present time, is 147.   The increase goes on steadily.   It must be remembered that, although it was resolved to form the church on June 21st, 1886, work did not begin until September 26th, so that the above has been accomplished in a little over two years.   "Christ crucified" has been, and ever will be, at once the theme and inspiration of the Baptist Church in Ayr.

High Street Baptist Chapel, Tring.

THIS Hertfordshire town, of four thousand inhabitants, has been called "Baptist-Chapelled Tring"; for there are in it four Baptist churches, owning five chapels, with accommodation for over two thousand persons. One of these churches is of the General Baptist order, and until a few years back was the "little one," and a rather despised little one, among its wealthier neighbours. The chapel was small, ill-ventilated, and so close to the road that the noise outside often drowned the voices inside.

The history of the present pastor's connection with the church is somewhat singular: He was a Methodist, and had been a local preacher up to the time of his going to Tring, where he had purchased a drapery business. Methodism has never been able to get a foothold in this town, so Mr. Pearce wandered from chapel to chapel in search of a home. On one occasion he was selected by the pastor of the little General Baptist church to preach a missionary sermon. Not long after, the good old pastor, Mr. Sexton, was suddenly called home, and the deacons sought Mr. Pearce's services on the following Sabbath. For two years he supplied the pulpit, and was frequently urged to become pastor of the church. Here it must be noted that Mr. Pearce, who, before residing at Tring, had never thoroughly studied the Word of God on the subject of Baptism, there saw for the first time the ordinance administered in the primitive manner, and prayerfully reviewed his opinions. The result was, that he felt it to be his duty to be baptized.

In 1876 he became pastor of the church. From that time to the present the work has shown a steady growth, far exceeding the highest expectations of the friends. Mr. Pearce felt constrained to give up his business to devote himself wholly to the work of the Lord, beginning his ministry upon the proceeds of the weekly offering—£50 per annum.

Mr. Pearce sought admission to the Pastors' College, and for three years pursued his studies without neglecting his pastoral work. So greatly was the work prospered that a new chapel became a necessity. A site in a prominent position was secured, a school-room, for temporary use as a chapel, erected at the rear thereof, and now a handsome chapel is rapidly approaching completion. The total cost of the land and buildings is about £3,100, towards which sum about £2,000 have been obtained. The majority of the people are of the poorer sort, and have, says the pastor, "exercised heroic self-denial, depriving themselves not only of comforts, but necessaries," that they might help in this much-needed work. They have had generous help from friends connected with the other churches in the town, but will need the aid of the Lord's stewards in other places to enable them to open the chapel in September free of debt.

Baptist Church, Brentwood

THE work in this Essex town began on this wise. Certain Baptists sought opportunity to worship together. The Tabernacle Country Mission took the work in hand in 1884, but in a short time handed it over to the College. Several brethren took an evening service in the Town Hall. Mr. Broad (now Pastor at Poplar) was the preacher for some months, and gathered good helpers. In 1884, the present pastor, then in College, undertook the work. The Town Hall was hired for morning as well as evening service, and the Lord owning the Word, the work took a definite form. After consulting our President, and securing his sympathy, we set about building a chapel, in the most central part of the town. In October, 1885, we entered the new chapel—a neat iron building holding 300 persons. Here we have grown in number and influence, and are still growing.

The church, in July, 1886, consisted of 19 members. We now number between fifty and sixty. This does not give a fair gauge of the work done, for many have been converted, who have removed.

The chapel is a centre of Christian influence and work. There is a Sunday-school, a Band of Hope, Bible Classes, &c.

Last year the debt was cleared off; but the ground is mortgaged. The work is almost self-supporting, the only outside help coming from the Pastors' College and the Baptist Fund. We hope, in a short time, to run alone.

This work is the direct outcome of the Pastors' College; and it has been performed in a district saturated with Ritualistic teaching, and in a town which has never been affected to any great degree by Evangelical doctrine. Surely all who value the faith of our fathers must bless the earnest preachers of the Word, and cry, "Happy is the College that hath its quiver full of them."   J. W. WALKER.

Baptist Church, Rotherhithe New Road.

THIS cause was commenced in 1883. A number of friends, anxious to begin Christian work in the neighbourhood, assembled in hired rooms, in Bramcote Road. Mr. F. Tuck, now Pastor at Gravesend, was sent by Mr. Spurgeon to minister to this people. The first day's services were opened with a prayer meeting, a goodly number assembling to implore divine blessing upon this new enterprise. That was the origin of a work which has hitherto proved itself to be a blessing in a new and rapidly-increasing neighbourhood. Notwithstanding difficulties, which to many might have appeared insurmountable, this small cause has pushed forward by the help of God. The ministry has been blessed, and souls have been saved. Perhaps, by reason of incessant trial and poverty of financial position, the progress has been slow; yet we may, with confidence, say it has been sound. Soon, the rooms became too small, and a plot of land was secured from the South Eastern Railway, at a yearly rental, for the purpose of erecting a temporary Iron Chapel. With the help of Mr. Spurgeon and a few other influential gentlemen, combined with the earnest efforts of our own people, a building was erected at a cost of £380, the whole amount being raised within two years.

Many changes were witnessed, amongst others was the removal of Mr. Tuck to Gravesend. Mr. Dewdney succeeded him, and laboured hard for two years. His College course being completed, he sailed for Christchurch, New Zealand. The present Pastor then settled, and continues to labour among this people. Last September, we were formed into a Church by Mr. Dunn, of the Metropolitan Tabernacle. We then numbered 55 in all; the Lord has since added to our number 21 souls. Helped by the College, we are labouring to support our own pastor ourselves. We have a good Sunday-school and Tract Society; Open Air Services are also a regular institution among us just now. We are about to secure a site, on Ilderton Road, for the building of a permanent chapel. The site is well situated, almost in the centre of three large estates, upon which there is no other dissenting place of worship. Believing that God is with us, we press forward, hopefully trusting in divine power to make this work a great success.

W. WALKER.

Baptist Church, College Park,
WILLESDEN JUNCTION.

MR. J. W. THOMAS commenced a series of evangelistic services about four years ago, in a chapel previously used by "The Brethren." He has gathered round him a band of about forty baptized believers, who are earnestly working to extend the cause of Christ in the vicinity. There is a Sabbath-school of about one hundred children. The friends are working under difficulties, as their meeting-place is only hired: they need help to purchase the building. This is a very hopeful beginning.

The Tabernacle Church, Hull,

MEETING AT THE CENTRAL HALL, PRYNE STREET.

WE were earnestly urged, at the beginning of 1885, by a few
friends, supported in their application by the Revs. E.
Lauderdale, of Grimsby, and W. Y. Fullerton, to commence a Baptist
Church in this town. The President was consulted, and consented to
my giving up itinerant work for this important sphere, generously
promising liberal aid for the first few months. We commenced our work
hopefully in June, 1885, and a church was formed in July, when thirty-
four united in church fellowship. Some of these had recently come into
Hull to reside, and, being Baptists, requested to unite with us in the formation of the church. It was the day of small things with us, but we
walked by faith, and not by sight. Our faith was soon rewarded, and
believers were constantly added to the church. During the remainder
of 1885, we received thirteen more into fellowship, most of whom were
gathered from the world.

During the year 1886, we received forty-four new members, most of
whom we baptized, on the profession of their faith in Christ. From the
beginning to the end of the year, a stream of blessing refreshed the
church. This was the year when we were favoured with a visit from
Messrs. Fullerton and Smith, whom God has so greatly owned in His
service. About one hundred and fifty gave in their names as having
received good at the circus, and we sent letters to the different ministers
of the town, respecting about a hundred of these, commending those
who attended their respective churches to their special care. We ourselves
received about thirty-five from that mission.

In the autumn of 1887, we engaged the Alhambra Music Hall, for
Sunday afternoon and evening services. We were supported by large
congregations, and many souls were added to the Lord.

The year 1888 was most happy and successful in every way. We had
the Presence of God in a very marked manner, and many were constantly crying, "What must we do to be saved?" Our temporary home
had been long too small for us, but we knew not how to get a better.
We, however, made it a matter of prayer, and the Central Hall, Pryne
Street, was opened up, and we have engaged it for our services. Our
congregations doubled at once on Sunday nights, and many have been
born again there. It is not all that we desire, as we are often disturbed
on the week evenings with the noise in the large hall, which is then let for
dancing, etc., whilst we worship in the smaller room upstairs. We,
however, recognize the hand of God in leading us there, and we still
wait upon Him for help to erect, ere long, a suitable sanctuary. We
received 30 into fellowship last year, and 1889 bids fair to be more
prosperous still. We have received already, or are about to receive, 22
additional members, making the total membership 135. We eschew all
doubtful practices, and confine ourselves to prayer and to the preaching
of the Word. Oh, for a baptism of fire!

FRANK RUSSELL.

Mission Chapel, New Beckton.

A MOST interesting and successful mission has been carried on at New Beckton by the flourishing and earnest church at Parson's Hill, Woolwich, under the pastoral care of our friend Mr. Wilson. One of the members went to reside in the district in 1885, and was surprised to find no religious agency whatever at work there. The place seemed to have been entirely neglected—a dark spot left without any Christian influence. He resolved to commence a Sunday-school, and at first was obliged to hold it in a field until a Christian gentleman kindly came forward and offered the use of a carpenter's shed, which was gladly accepted. Meetings were then started in the evening for adults, a number of the members of Parson's Hill going over to conduct them, and the work has been so greatly blessed, that two hundred children have been gathered into the Sunday-school, and forty persons have been brought to the Saviour and have joined the church at Parson's Hill. The carpenter's shed was sold in 1887, and we were compelled to erect an iron chapel and schools at a cost, including site, of £570. Five hundred pounds were raised by the end of last year, leaving a debt of only £70. The population is a migratory one, and many who are brought to the Saviour move to other parts of London. It is sad that in a place where a large proportion of the gas is made wherewith to light London there should be spiritual darkness; but to a large extent we can say, "The darkness is past, and the true light now shineth."

Baptist Tabernacle, Burton-on-Trent.

THE church worshipping here was formed by the late Rev. T. Hanson, assisted by Mr. Testro, of the Pastors' College, on April 7th, 1872, the members numbering twenty-three. Mr. Hanson resigned through ill health, and was followed by the Rev. J. D. Rodway, after whose removal, in 1873, the church was pastorless for a period of nine months, and many members were of opinion that, as prospects looked so dark, it would be better to give up. Such was the state of things when the present pastor was sent from College in 1874. The church, numbering twenty-five members, was worshipping in an iron chapel burdened with a debt of more than £400. Since then, by God's blessing, the debt has been paid, and 379 have been received into fellowship.

In 1885 plans were prepared for the new Tabernacle and schools; and our beloved President kindly gave us £50 towards the estimated expenditure of £3,000. The memorial stones were laid in July, 1886, and the Tabernacle was opened for public worship on February 8th, 1887, by Pastor C. Spurgeon, of Greenwich, and on the following Sunday the Rev. E. Parker, D.D., of Manchester, preached. Since then we have continued to receive God's blessing. The church is now full of spiritual life, and numbers about 160 members.

JOHN ASKEW, *Pastor.*

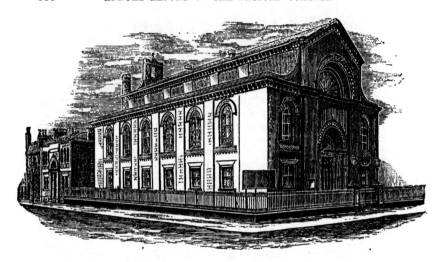

Coupland Street Baptist Church, Manchester.

AT the commencement of the year 1886, Pastor Geo. Wainwright felt himself compelled to resign his position as pastor of Grosvenor Street Baptist Chapel, the craving for amusement being the chief source of disquietude. Over 100 members resigned with him. At the unanimous invitation of this company he consented to stay with them, and to form a new church. Such was the origin of Coupland Street Baptist Church. The building in which the church meets was formerly occupied by the United Presbyterians, and is admirably suited for the purposes of the church. The block includes a chapel, capable of seating about 700; lecture-hall, with accommodation for 300; five well-furnished class-rooms and vestries, and chapel-keeper's house. It is situated in the centre of a large middle and working-class population, for whose spiritual necessities very little provision exists in the immediate vicinity. There is a ground rent of £50 per annum upon the building; and with this embargo the whole has been purchased for the sum of £1,750; and the only debt remaining on the building is due to the Baptist Building Fund, from which £500 was received, to be repaid without interest in five years. Through the breakdown of Pastor Geo. Wainwright's health in March, 1888, the work suffered a considerable shock; but under the spiritual charge of Pastor E. Morley, formerly of Halstead, Essex, there are signs of increasing blessing. The annual chief rent of over £50 on the land considerably increases the difficulty of this young church. The friends are deserving of hearty and practical sympathy. In their case a brave faith has been rewarded by the divine blessing.

Northcote Road, Wandsworth Common.

THIS building was erected by the church worshipping in Chatham Road. It will be remembered that Messrs. C. and T. Spurgeon, while yet lads, began their ministry in this place. They took up a little mission, which had been started by a devoted servant of God, and carried it on so successfully, that they raised the Chatham Road Chapel, and opened it free of debt. This chapel still remains in the hands of the energetic church, though they have shifted their quarters. When they left for wider spheres of usefulness, Mr. Harmer became pastor of the young church; and on his resignation, after successful labour, Mr. Mummery of Eynsford, succeeded him. On his death, in 1883, Mr. Stone became the third pastor, and a very efficient one he has proved. In the first year of his pastorate, an aggressive effort was made upon the neighbourhood, in the form of Tent Services, for a month. These were so successful that a large hall had to be hired for the evening services, and these were well attended. Souls were saved. Soon the membership equalled the number of sittings in the little chapel, and under these circumstances it was thought wise to rise and build. New estates have been opened up, and the builder is incessantly at his work. There was great need to supply the religious wants of the people. A Building Fund was started, with C. H. Spurgeon for treasurer, and afterwards O. V. Morgan, Esq., M.P. In 1886 a plot of freehold land was purchased for £850. In 1887, a contract for £5,200 was accepted, and the building was commenced; and in 1888, it was opened by C. H. Spurgeon. During this, the first year of its occupation, the work has progressed rapidly; 76 have joined the church. The various societies have been largely increased, and the church, amid its other labours, has been able to hire, furnish and open, a Young Men's House; and there is every prospect of a strong and useful church filling the new house.

The style of the building is Early English. Its interior is in the form of a half-circle, with gallery. It is seated throughout with chairs. Under the chapel is a schoolroom, holding 250, a large infants' room seating 100, and five class-rooms; while behind there are three vestries for the use of church officers. The whole cost, including builder's extras, architect's fees, and the ground, has been £7,416.

Mr. Stone, the pastor, is exercising a self-denial, which we think too severe. We know of no man who more fully lays his all upon the altar of the Lord. The debt is the trouble which burdens him, and he both stints himself and wears himself out in the effort to remove this load. He commends himself to us as one of a thousand, and we hope he will continue to receive the help of all our friends in his specially arduous enterprise.

Queen's Road, Wimbledon.

BELOVED PRESIDENT,

WITH alacrity I respond to your invitation to give an "outline" of the work here at Wimbledon.

Space forbids anything but an "outline"; but it will be one which might be filled up with delightful testimony to the consecration of many faithful hearts, and, above all, to the covenant mercy of God.

The varying fortunes of the church from 1871, when the work was started, to December 1880, when the present pastorate commenced, need not now be dwelt upon. Suffice it to say, that friends from the Tabernacle formed the nucleus of the church; funds from the Tabernacle aided the work; students from the Tabernacle filled the pulpit.

Since December, 1880, we will speak with greater fulness. The testimony will be as to things heard, seen, handled.

A church of between twenty and thirty members; a chapel of only two hundred sittings, and these needing to be let; an income of £50 per annum, and a debt of £400 was our beginning then. From that time up to the end of 1886, events may be catalogued as follows: pewing and alteration of chapel, costing about £200; extinction of debt £400; building up of church to about two hundred members; gathering Sunday-school of three hundred and fifty scholars and teachers; and establishing two missions, one at Morden, the other at Merton, where a site has been secured, sufficient for larger chapel and schools, but on which, at present, a good iron hall, seating one hundred and eighty people, is standing, and in full use.

At the end of 1886 a new start was made. For three years a suitable site had been sought, but to no purpose, nine plots of ground in succession had been either rejected by us, or we had been rejected by the owners. Then, however, the fog lifted. A fine site was secured; our old building sold, plans prepared, work begun. We had by this time learned the necessity of doing things thoroughly, so that there would be no need for starting afresh a few years hence. Consequently, we sought to lay our foundations broad and deep. The site is sufficient for schools to accommodate six hundred, and chapel to seat one thousand; the cost of the land was £1,000. The building at present erected has cost £3,200, and consists of eight class-rooms, one prayer-meeting room, and a main assembly hall, capable of seating four hundred people.

Unfortunately, we have a heavy debt. Just at the crisis when the building was being erected, my strength failed, and instead of being on the tramp seeking aid from outside friends, I was just bidden to "stand still." This continued seven months, *i.e.*, till the best opportunity for soliciting aid was gone. Out of a total expenditure of about £4,200, we owe now about £1,950, of which £500 is due to the builder, and is therefore urgently needed. May some of the Lord's stewards see our difficulty and come to our help, for we greatly need it.

We are still pushing on; in fact, endeavouring to follow *your own advice* to me at the outset,—" *Go and blaze away.*"

With earnest prayers, in which all the church unites,

I am, my dear President,

Yours to serve,

C. INGREM.

[Friends will note that only the left-hand portion of the design has as yet been carried out, and this has laid upon our friends so heavy a burden that they need assistance in removing it. The town of Wimbledon, being a central railway junction, is growing rapidly, and it needs the complete building; but this must be delayed till the first portion is paid for, or nearly so. May this be very soon. Mr. Ingrem's ministry is as attractive as it is solid, and a career of remarkable usefulness is before him. To raise money is a dreary task, sadly wearying to a young and zealous spirit. How much we wish that some wealthy child of God would undertake to find the needful funds for such a work as this! The spiritual forces are vouchsafed us. Must the holy work linger because of the silver and the gold?]

The Tabernacle, Southend-on-Sea.

UNTIL the year 1876 there was no Baptist church in this rapidly-growing town, when a few friends, assisted by Mr. Spurgeon and his friend, the late Mr. John Edwards, hired the Public Hall for services to be conducted by students of our College. After a time an iron chapel on freehold ground, vacated by the Episcopalians, was purchased, and a school-room added thereto, at a total cost of about £1,000. Mr. J. G. Wilson was then pastor of the church. In 1885 the dilapidated iron building gave place to a permanent structure, costing £1,000, with sittings for four hundred and eighty persons, with provision for galleries when needed. This work has been accomplished under the direction of the present pastor, Mr. H. W. Childs. Last year, land for much-needed school and class accommodation was purchased, and funds are now needed for clearing off the debt of £248, and providing means for building operations.

The population is continually shifting, so that the good done is not expressed in the number in membership, which is nearly one hundred. During the summer, thousands of visitors throng the place, and a rare opportunity is presented of preaching the truth as it is in Jesus. Testimony has been borne from all parts as to the good received.

Clarence Road, Southend.

THERE is also another healthy church in Southend, under the care of our esteemed brother Mr. Hogbin; and there seems to be no reason why they should not both prosper with the increase of God. This cause was started by Mr. Wilson when he left *The Tabernacle*, and we much regretted it; but we believe that division will be overruled for good. The present pastor is one whom the Lord will greatly bless

Gipsy Road Baptist Chapel, Norwood.

THE church worshipping here (under the pastorate of the Rev. Walter Hobbs) was formed in March, 1879, and was then holding services in the Paxton school-room, Hamilton Road, conducted by the Rev. E. H. Ellis (now of Devonshire Square, Stoke Newington), but at that time a student in the College. Only sixteen members joined the church at its formation, but there were many indications that God was blessing the work, and active steps were taken to raise funds for the erection of a permanent chapel. In June, 1880, Mr. Ellis resigned his ministry here, to accept the pastorate of his present church; and, in November of the same year, Mr. Hobbs, of Newtown, Upper Norwood (who also had been a student in the College), commenced a pastorate which has been greatly blessed to the salvation of many. The handsome chapel in Gipsy Road, with sitting accommodation for 750 persons, and a lecture-hall seating 550 persons, has been built during Mr. Hobbs's ministry, at a cost of over £5,000, and the whole of this sum has been raised. The friends have "had a mind to work," and have cleared off a portion of debt every year, considerable impetus being given to these efforts by the grants from the London Baptist Association Debt Relief

Fund. In less than six years from the time of opening, the entire cost of building and furnishing has been met, and the chapel enlarged.

About 520 persons have been received into church-fellowship during Mr. Hobbs's pastorate, and the membership now stands at about 326. In the Sunday-school there are 597 names on the books, the school-room and class-room being uncomfortably crowded every Sunday. It is hoped that during the present year increased accommodation will be provided by the erection of new class-rooms on the vacant ground at the back of the chapel. "Young People's Societies of Christian Endeavour" (of both sexes) have been recently established, and are doing excellent work in sustaining the younger members of the Church in the faith they have professed, and in leading others to a knowledge of the Saviour.

Beulah Baptist Chapel, Thornton Heath.

ONE of the latest churches formed in connection with the College is that at Thornton Heath, a region between Norwood and Croydon. From his garden at Beulah Hill, Mr. Spurgeon often looked down upon this region, and from various quarters he received reports of the spiritual destitution of the district. Towards the close of 1886, he purchased a large plot of freehold ground, in an admirable position, and erected upon it a substantial school-chapel, accommodating about 300 people. On May 3, 1887, the anniversary of the day when he was baptized, Mr. Spurgeon opened the chapel by presiding at a prayer-meeting at six o'clock in the morning, and by preaching in the afternoon. At the service, he announced that, with the help of friends, he had the pleasure of presenting the land and building, free of debt, for the use of the church afterwards to be formed. Mr. J. W. Harrald, Mr. Spurgeon's private secretary, took charge of the work. The chapel has been well filled; many who did not previously attend any place of worship have been induced to come, although none of the modern expedients for attracting a congregation have been tried. The Word preached has been blessed to the conversion of many souls; and much earnest Christian work has been brought to bear upon the neighbourhood. In February, 1888, Mr. Spurgeon paid another visit to the chapel, and presided at the formation of the church, when 79 members were enrolled, and Mr. Harrald was elected pastor. There are now 111 members. The Sunday-school contains 360 scholars, and 30 teachers. An infant school-room has been built, and opened free of debt, and the church is about to spend £250 more for new class-rooms, &c. Several prayer-meetings are held every week, and there are also a Gospel Temperance Society, a Band of Hope, a Dorcas meeting, and all the agencies of an aggressive Christian church. Mrs. Spurgeon renders great help to the work by supporting an efficient Bible-nurse, whose services are in great request, and much appreciated. As Mr. Harrald's duties continue to increase, arrangements have been made for Mr. Minifie, one of the missionary students of the College, to relieve him of the week evening services.

Work of our Brethren abroad.

IN former reports we have viewed the outcome of the College from a more distant point of view, and have seen with pleasure the labour of brethren in the foreign field. We will not attempt to go over this again, for we could not do justice to it in so short a space. Our missionary brethren fall not behind in holy effort and self-sacrifice. China, India, Japan, the Congo, and North Africa, can bear witness to their fitness for pioneer work, and to the blessing which the Lord is ready to bestow upon them. In this they are partakers with their brethren of other colleges.

In the United States many of our men are found plodding away. In some cases new churches have been formed by them, and the hard work of the laying of foundations has been sustained. In Nebraska, and California, congregations have been gathered out of the world, and churches built up.

In Tasmania, the princely generosity of Mr. Gibson and family has opened up many fields for our men. They can give a good account of themselves in New Zealand, where our dear son is not alone, in Australia, Canada, and the Cape Colonies. There is still a great lack in reference to the colonies for a society to assist struggling churches in the first years of their existence, when they greatly need external aid. Empires are born, and the babes lie neglected in the cradle. There is very much land to be possessed, and those who enter first upon the new countries will for ages hold the leading place in them; this we should covet for the pure and undefiled Evangelical faith.

Last year Mr. George Harris went out from us to the Falkland Islands, not so much with the hope of founding a self-supporting church, as in the hope of preaching the gospel among the scattered people, and reviving their interest in religion. One earnest brother, Mr. Natt, guaranteed him a home and board, and he has most liberally kept his word. Mr. Harris has improved in health, and has gathered an earnest company of people, who are anxious to retain him. He himself is diligent in going about as much as he can in those islands seeking souls for Jesus. What may ultimately come of the effort it would be hard to tell, for we have not the gift of prophecy. It is ours to sow beside all waters, but not ours to know whether shall prosper, this or that, or whether they both shall be alike good. No part of the earth, be the population great or small, should be left without the gospel. Happily, many agencies are at work to secure the spread of the truth in every quarter. There is room for us all, and for many more. The command of our Lord is still binding : "Pray ye, therefore, the Lord of the harvest, that he would send forth labourers into his harvest."

Pastors' College Society of Evangelists.

ALL our College Evangelists have been kept fully occupied during the past year, except when they have been taking necessary rest. The strain of the work has told rather severely upon one or two of the brethren; but they have all been greatly blessed in their services, and this has amply compensated them for anything they have had to suffer. There appears to be, practically, no limit to the extent to which the churches and pastors are willing to avail themselves of the help of well-qualified and trustworthy evangelists, for most of our brethren have had many more invitations than they could accept; and the fact that they are invited again and again to the same places, shows in what estimation their labours are held. Every month the "Notes" in *The Sword and the Trowel* bear witness that outsiders are induced to listen to the Word preached and sung, that many yield themselves to the Saviour, backsliders are reclaimed, pastors encouraged, and churches quickened and revived by the visits of the evangelists. Sometimes the funds of the Society run rather short, but we have hitherto managed to keep a balance in hand. If some of our friends could form an accurate idea of the great good accomplished by this useful agency, they would subscribe still more largely, and enable us to extend its beneficent operations. The visit of an evangelist is, under the divine blessing, the means of awakening the interest of the church members in the work of conversion. Under the same ministry, time out of mind, hearing is apt to become monotonous, and the vivacity of religious feeling is somewhat weakened. The new voice startles the sleepers, and refreshes even the most watchful. Extra efforts are put forth, ardour is increased, hope is kindled, and the church is put in working trim.

Outsiders are invited to attend at special meetings. Persons who did not imagine that anybody cared a pin about them, find themselves pressed to attend meetings conducted by persons of whom their friends speak with enthusiasm. They yield to the gentle persuasion, come where the gospel is simply and faithfully preached, and are impressed. From this class, who are not yet hardened by refusing the sacred message, large harvests are sure to be gathered. The very fact that the gospel is new to them, gives the preacher a better prospect of succeeding with them.

Nor is the evangelist less useful under God to the regular hearer whose hesitation has become chronic. The Lord employs the special address "to precipitate decision." We borrow the phrase from a leading minister, who described one of our evangelists as having peculiar gifts in the direction of precipitating decision. It is a tough phrase, but it means a good deal. The Holy Spirit uses this chosen messenger to put the last ounce into the scale, and the balance turns. The agency of the after-meeting, with its personal talk, accomplishes what the Sabbath preaching has been driving at. The minister sows; the evangelist reaps. The constant shining of a gospel ministry ripens the corn, but the special service thrusts in the sickle. Many are truly converted, but are too timid to come forward : these are encouraged. Many more are sinfully procrastinating ; and these are led to end their hesitancy, and at once decide for the Saviour.

Those pastors who have had visits from our evangelists are the best judges of their character. They, almost invariably, write in glowing, grateful terms of the help they have received, and frequently mention the satisfactory character of such an agency, which does not draw people away from the regular means of grace, but ·does its work strictly in connection with churches, and with an eye to their support and increase. Considerable friction has been produced by random efforts of a class of spiritual adventurers—good or questionable, as the case may be, but quite dissociated from the churches, and working rather to their detriment than to their benefit. There are brethren who wish only to be helpers of the regular workers, and will be so wherever they are allowed to occupy that place. They would preach the gospel even if the regular authorities opposed them ; but they would far rather labour in glad harmony with their brethren in Christ, the pastors of the flocks.

The places visited during the past year by MESSRS. FULLERTON AND SMITH are Huddersfield, Greenock, Oban, Taynuilt, Tobermory, Penge Tabernacle, Bromley (Kent), Talbot Tabernacle (Notting Hill), Trinity Presbyterian Church (Bayswater), Westbourne Grove Chapel, Upton Chapel (Lambeth), Christ Church (Westminster Bridge Road), the Metropolitan Tabernacle, Bloomsbury Chapel, Peckham Park Road Chapel, Westminster Chapel, Exeter Hall (Y.M.C.A.), Shoreditch Tabernacle, Dalston Junction Chapel, Devonshire Square Chapel (Stoke Newington), Salters' Hall Chapel (Islington), and Mildmay Park Conference Hall.

Mr. BURNHAM has been at Shefford, Gosport, Ruardean Hill (Gloucestershire), Goudhurst and neighbourhood (among the hop-pickers), Bradford, Cotton End (Bedford), Tottlebank and Ulverston, Ashdon and Radwinter, Puddletown and Bere Regis, Rotherhithe New Road, Harefield (Middlesex), Ipswich, Amersham, and Hungerford.

Mr. HARMER has held services at Bishop's Stortford, Drummond Road Chapel (Bermondsey), Acton, Dartmouth, Thornton Heath, Hull (with Mr. PARKER at Queensbury, Sandy Lane, Denholme, Allerton, and Clayton, near Bradford, also at Crewkerne ; and with Mr. CHAMBERLAIN at Redditch and Lydgate, Todmorden), Orpington, March, Cheddar, Tuddenham, Crown Street, Ipswich, Belstead, and Washbrook (Suffolk), Tewkesbury, and East Surrey Grove, Peckham.

Mr. CARTER has conducted missions at Yalding (Kent), Watlington (Oxfordshire), King's Langley, Hunton Bridge, and Leavesden (Hertfordshire), and St. Helens (Lancashire) ; and he has spent some months at Farnworth and Radcliffe (Lancashire), where his labours have been the means of greatly strengthening two weak churches.

In addition to the meetings he held in conjunction with Mr. Harmer, Mr. PARKER has been to Falmouth, Bourton-on-the-Water, Ringstead, Haddenham, Westbury, Aylsham, Melbourne (Derbyshire), Deptford, and Old Chesterton (Cambridgeshire).

Since his return from Australia, Mr. HARRISON has held services or missions at Mr. Charrington's Assembly Hall, Dalston Junction Chapel, Tottenham, Northampton, Staines, Bath, Keighley, Romford, Bristol, Redditch, Sittingbourne, Bury St. Edmund's, and Vernon Chapel, Pentonville.

Will our friends specially pray that this sacred and Scriptural agency may be still more greatly blest? When they have prayed, let them help us in the support of the work.

Pastors' College Missionary Association.

WHEN the Lord puts it into the heart of men in the College to go to some foreign land, and no Society is prepared to help, we have often longed for the means of aiding them to go forth and freely preach the Word where the Lord seems to direct them. We could not do this without means, and, after some little waiting, we are now able to commence the work. As the means come in, this form of service will be sure to extend in such ways as God, in his Providence, shall point out. We have now started, and we shall not let the grass grow up to our ankles.

Receipts from April 17th, 1888, to April 15th, 1889:—

G. T.	250	0	0
Mr. Arthur Hall	50	0	0
Mr. J. Dodson...	25	0	0
In memory of the late Mrs. C. F. Belsey,			
Rochester, per Miss Belsey	10	0	
Mr. C. Matthews	5	0	
Dr. Alfred Fennings	5	0	
Mrs. Shurmer	0	3	
Mr. W. Parlane	10	0	
Mr. D. J. Pillai	10	0	
Mr. E. Marsh	20	0	
Friends at Lincoln, per Mr. A. Jackson	0	12	
Mr. C. F. Allison	5	0	
Mrs. Milligan	1	0	
Mrs. Wight	1	0	
Beulah Chapel Auxiliary, Thornton Heath ..	6	6	8
	£399	1	6

Of this amount we have expended £50 in paying for Mr. Patrick's outfit and passage to North Africa, and £30 for instalments of his first year's salary. It was necessary to have some capital before undertaking liabilities, and we are now fairly at work.

Support.

THIS work has been conducted by me in faith in the living God. Having no foundation fund or endowment to fall back upon, I have to look up to the Lord from day to day. Hitherto, every necessity has been met before it has been felt. Trials of faith have been singularly few, for I am so weak. The College was erected, and paid for when opened. The building is used for a hundred and one purposes, beside college work proper, and there is a small income for keeping it in repair, but this is all our property. For many years the church at the Tabernacle subscribed some £1880 *per annum*. Because of the demands of other agencies, this sum was not realized last year, and thus one brook is diminished in its flow. God will either fill up this brook Cherith, or cause another to run with the needful supplies. Perhaps friends at Tabernacle will renew their zeal, and help their Pastor as they once did.

At the Annual Supper, a large sum is always given; last year more than ever. A few helpers have ceased to give because of the President's protest against Down-Grade tendencies. In this matter they have a right to do as they think proper, and I shall not complain; but what they may do or not do does not alter my duty. My protest would be repeated more vigorously than ever to-day, if the cost were sure to be ten times as great. Monetary considerations will not close my mouth, or make me bate a word of a witness which I feel forced to bear. The evil which I exposed grows worse and worse, and my one regret is that I did not drag it into the light long before. I hoped for better things, but they came not, and I was compelled to cry aloud and spare not. However, if some few returned me wrath for my indignation, I did not wonder, and certainly did not feel dismayed. Nor was there the slightest cause; for numerous friends came to the rescue, and of their own loving wills last year caused the amount to pass the usual limit. To God be praise.

At the present our balance is much less than appears in the accounts, for four months have passed since then: months of expenditure rather than of income. I am looking up for some large sums to be given. If they do not come at the supper, the Lord will send them in other ways: but send them He will, so long as He wishes the work to go on.

Many young men are applying. The churches will soon be needing preachers of the old faith. The Down-Grade craze will run itself out, and thoughtful people will become weary of it. There are signs of revolt from the rule of unbelief, and then will doors be open to firm believers. I trust friends will help me to keep guns on the battery, and supply me with ammunition. Whether or no, as I am the Lord's servant, I will abide by His truth, and labour for its advancement as God shall help me; and if I stand alone, I will abide on the rampart, come what may.

C. H. Spurgeon

Summary of Results

DURING the thirty-three years of our existence as a school of the prophets, seven hundred and ninety-nine men, exclusive of those at present studying with us, have been received into the College, " of whom the greater part remain unto this day; but some (sixty-three) have fallen asleep." Making all deductions, there are now in the work of the Lord, in some department or other of useful service, about six hundred and forty brethren. Of these, six hundred and one are in our own denomination as Pastors, Missionaries, and Evangelists. They may be thus summarized :—

Number of brethren who have been educated in the College... ...	799
„ now in our ranks as Pastors, Missionaries, and Evangelists	601
„ without Pastorates, but regularly engaged in the work of the Lord	21
„ not now engaged in the work, but useful in secular callings	23
„ Educated for other Denominations ... ... · ...	2
„ Dead—(Pastors, 56 ; Students, 7)	63
„ Permanently Invalided...	12
„ Names removed from the College List for various reasons ...	77

These last are not removed from our list in all cases from causes which imply any dishonour, for many of them are doing good service to the common Lord under some other banner. We are sorry for their leaving us, and surprised that they should change their views ; but this also is one of those mysteries of human life which are beyond our control.

FORM OF BEQUEST.

*I Give and Bequeath the sum of*_____

pounds sterling, to be paid out of that part of my personal estate which may by law be given with effect for charitable purposes, to be paid to the Treasurer for the time being of the Pastors' College, Metropolitan Tabernacle, Newington, Surrey, and his receipt shall be a sufficient discharge for the said legacy ; and this legacy, when received by such Treasurer to be applied for the general purposes of the College.

STATISTICS.

Return for the year.	Number of Pastors making returns.	INCREASE.					DECREASE.					CLEAR INCREASE.	Total Number of Members in Church Fellowship.
		By Baptism.	By Profession of Faith.	By Letters from other Churches.	By Restoration.	Total Increase.	By Death.	By Dismission to other Churches.	By Exclusion.	By Erasure for Non-Attendance.	Total Decrease.		
1865	71	1,224	224	367	47	1,862	100	195	89	67	451	1,411	7,359
1866	101	1,774	218	544	51	2,587	133	309	168	111	721	1,866	10,222
1867	121	2,098	208	593	67	2,966	138	347	93	150	728	2,238	12,502
1868	140	2,175	186	529	43	2,933	158	364	92	257	871	2,062	14,716
1869	150	1,958	244	670	92	2,964	202	433	79	404	1,118	1,846	15,784
1870	157	2,032	236	602	73	2,943	234	460	84	511	1,289	1,654	17,536
1871	169	1,768	299	648	72	2,787	295	495	94	417	1,301	1,486	18,640
1872	172	2,053	222	741	98	3,114	255	580	95	416	1,346	1,768	19,925
1873	197	2,633	334	899	150	4,016	337	731	88	455	1,611	2,405	24,435
1874	230	3,173	358	1,134	109	4,774	368	813	134	486	1,801	2,973	29,746
1875	237	4,284	317	1,242	208	6,051	426	886	119	534	1,965	4,086	32,263
1876	264	3,752	456	1,322	148	5,678	446	943	172	902	2,463	3,215	35,812
1877	283	3,555	479	1,456	193	5,783	447	1,121	146	921	2,635	3,148	39,121
1878	296	3,600	557	1,655	142	5,954	487	1,097	114	1,095	2,793	3,161	39,951
1879	305	3,479	701	1,631	121	5,932	487	1,279	159	1,402	3,327	2,605	42,324
1880	330	3,950	699	1,723	156	6,528	500	1,386	156	1,354	3,496	3,032	46,185
1881	363	4,042	838	2,196	232	7,908	636	1,608	225	1,270	3,739	4,169	53,660
1882	387	5,000	935	2,014	203	8,152	654	1,650	200	1,670	4,174	3,978	56,264
1883	387	5,008	1,065	2,046	191	8,310	699	1,871	153	1,769	4,492	3,818	59,524
1884	397	5,338	880	2,126	257	8,601	738	1,788	174	1,959	4,659	3,942	62,478
1885	398	5,522	1,020	2,338	305	9,185	748	2,113	402	2,046	5,309	3,876	67,334
1886	421	4,852	968	2,451	236	8,507	829	2,167	246	1,964	5,206	3,301	71,266
1887	381	5,014	1,022	2,258	299	8,693	708	1,747	308	1,890	4,653	4,040	63,419
1888	382	4,053	1,023	2,080	191	7,347	648	1,933	245	1,797	4,623	2,724	58,531
TOTAL		88,037	13,489	33,255	3,684	133,465	10,673	26,316	3,845	23,847	64,681	68,784	**58,531**

382 Churches furnish returns for 1888 : of these, 265 show an average increase of 13 members per church ; 81 an average decrease of 10 members per church ; 36 show the same numbers as in previous return ; thus giving an average INCREASE OF 7 MEMBERS PER CHURCH.

SWORD AND THE TROWEL.

JULY, 1889.

The Preacher's Power, and the Conditions of Obtaining it.

AN ADDRESS BY C. H. SPURGEON, AT THE CONFERENCE.

(Continued from page 260.)

E now purpose to consider the way in which we are to obtain the power we so much desire. WE NEED TO FEEL IT WITHIN OURSELVES WHEN WE ARE RECEIVING OUR MESSAGE. In order to have power in public, we must receive power in secret. I trust that no brother here would venture to address his people without getting a message fresh from his Lord. If you deliver a stale story of your own concocting, or if you speak without a fresh anointing from the Holy One, your ministry will come to nothing. Words spoken on your own account, without reference to your Lord, will fall to the ground. When the footman goes to the door to answer a caller, he asks his master what he has to say, and he repeats what his master tells him. You and I are waiting-servants in the house of God, and we are to report what our God would have us speak. The Lord gives the soul-saving message, and clothes it with power: he gives it to a certain order of people, and under certain conditions.

Among those conditions I notice, first, *a simplicity of heart.* The Lord pours most into those who are most empty of self. Those who have least of their own shall have the most of God's. The Lord cares little what the vessel is, whether golden or earthen, so long as it is clean, and disengaged from other uses. He sees whether there is anything in the cup; and if so, he throws it all out. Only then is the cup prepared to receive the living water. If there is something in it before, it will adulterate the pure word; or if what was there before was very

24

pure, it would, at least, occupy some of the room which the Lord seeks for his own grace. The Lord therefore empties us, that we may be clear from prejudice, self-sufficiency, and foregone conclusions as to what his truth ought to be. He would have us like children, who believe what their father tells them. We must lay aside all pretence of wisdom. Some men are too self-sufficient for God to use. If God were to bless them largely, they would talk in Wolsey's style of *"Ego et meus rex"* (I and my king); but the Lord will have none of it. That straight-backed upstart letter I must bow itself down into its lower-case shape, and just look like a little pot-hook (*i*) of a thing, and be nothing more. Oh, to be rid of self! Oh, to quit every pretence of wisdom! Many are very superior persons, and so when they get God's message they correct it, and interpolate their own ideas; they dream that the old gospel cannot be quite suitable to these enlightened days, when "everything is done by steam, and men are killed by powder." They not only interpolate, but they omit; because they judge that certain truths have become obsolete by the lapse of time. In this way, what with additions and subtractions, little is left of the pure words of God. The apostles are generally the first to be sent adrift. Poor Paul! Poor Paul! He has come in for very hard lines just lately, as if the Spirit of God did not speak through Paul with as much authority as when he spake through the Lord Jesus. Note well how our Lord deigns to put himself on a level with his apostles when he says, "The word which ye hear is not mine, but the Father's which sent me"; and in his final prayer he prayed for those who would believe on him through the apostles' word, as much as to say, that if they would not believe on him through the word of the apostles, they would not believe at all. John, speaking of himself and his fellow-apostles, has said by the Holy Ghost, "He that knoweth God heareth us; he that is not of God heareth not us. Hereby know we the spirit of truth, and the spirit of error." This is *the* test of believers at the present time: the rejection of the apostles condemns the modern school.

Brethren, may the Lord give us *great humility of mind.* It ought not to be an extraordinary thing for us to accept what God says. It ought not to take much humility for such poor creatures as we are to sit at Jesus' feet. We ought to look upon it as an elevation of mind for our spirit to lie prostrate before infinite wisdom. Assuredly this is needful to the reception of power from God.

I have noticed, too, that if God's power comes to a man with a message, he not only has childlikeness of mind, but he has also *singleness of eye.* Such a man, trying to hear what God the Lord shall speak, is all ear. He honestly and eagerly desires to know what God's mind is, and he applies all his faculties to the reception of the divine communication. As he drinks in the sacred message, with a complete surrender of soul, he is resolved to give it out with the entire concentration of his mental and spiritual powers, and with a single eye to the glory of God. Unless you have but one eye, and that one eye sees Christ and his glory in the salvation of men, God will not use you. The man whose eyes cannot look straight on, must not be admitted a priest unto the living God. There are certain defects which cut a man off from the divine employ, and anything like a sinister motive is one of them. If you aim at making money, winning ease, securing approbation, or obtaining position, or even if you aim at the exhibition of rhetorical talent, you will not be fit for the Master's use. God would not have us entangled with subordinate designs. You do not keep a servant to go to the door that people may say, "What a fine girl she is, and how charmingly she dresses!" You may smile if it is so, and put up with it; but your sole wish is to have your message promptly and faithfully delivered. How contemptible it is when a minister so acts as to give the idea of childish display! He stands up to deliver his Lord's message, but his hope is that people will say, "What a nice young man! How properly he speaks, and how prettily he quotes Browning!" Self-display is death to power. God cannot largely bless men with such small ideas. It were beneath the dignity of the Godhead for the Lord largely to use an instrument so altogether unadapted for his sublime purposes.

Beloved, I notice that God imparts his messages to those who have *a complete subordination to him.* I will tell you what has often crossed my mind when I have talked with certain brethren, or have read their lucubrations : I have wondered which was the Master and which was the servant, the man or God. I have been sorry for the errors of these brethren; but I have been far more distressed by the spirit shown in those errors. It is evident that they have renounced that holy reverence for Scripture which is indicated by such an expression as this, "*That trembleth at my word.*" They rather trifle than tremble. The Word is not their teacher, but they are its critics. The Word of the Lord is no longer enthroned in the place of honour with many ; but it is treated as a football, to be kicked about as they please; and the apostles, especially, are treated as if Paul, and James, and John were Jack, Tom, and Harry, with whom modern wise men are on terms of something more than equality. They pass the books of Scripture under their rod, and judge the Spirit of God himself. The Lord cannot work by a creature that is in revolt against him. We must manifest the spirit of reverence, or we shall not be as little children, nor enter the kingdom of heaven. When some men come to die, the religion which they have themselves thought out and invented will yield them no more confidence than the religion of the Roman Catholic sculptor who, on his death-bed, was visited by his priest. The priest said, "You are now departing out of this life"; and, holding up a beautiful crucifix, he cried, "Behold your God, who died for you." "Alas!" said the sculptor, "*I made it.*" There was no comfort for him in the work of his own hands; and there will be no comfort in a religion of one's own devising. That which was created in the brain cannot yield comfort to the heart. The man will sorrowfully say, "Yes, that is my own idea; but what does God say?" Brethren, I believe in that which I could not have invented. I believe that which I cannot understand. I believe that which compels me to adore, and I thank God for a rock that is higher than I am. If it were not higher than I, it were not a shelter for me.

"But still," says one, "we must be earnest students of the literature of the period, and of the science of the age." Yes: I did not say you were not to be so; but keep them in subordination to the Word of God. When the Israelites took captives in battle, it sometimes happened that among the prisoners there was a woman whom the captor might desire to marry, and the Lord did not forbid the alliance; but have you ever noticed the command to shave her head, and pare her nails? This must be done most carefully with all the literature of this period, whether it be secular or religious, whether it deal with fact or fiction. The shaving will need to be very close, and the paring to be very careful. Even when these operations are performed, a wise man will still see reason to question whether the subject of them had not, after all, be better let alone. There is an instructive precept of the ceremonial law which shuts out some things from ever being used in the service of the Lord. I quote it with trembling: "Thou shalt not bring the hire of a harlot, or the price of a dog, into the house of God." I question whether, in quoting certain poets and authors, we may not be contravening this statute. When men's lives have been foul, and their principles atheistic, there should be great hesitation as to quoting their language. The blasphemer of the living God is hardly to be mentioned in the Lord's house, however fine may have been the product of his rebellious heart. At any rate, all that is of man, even the best of men, must be altogether subordinate to the Word of the Lord.

I have mentioned simplicity of character, singleness of eye, and subordination of mind; and next to these, I notice, also, that, if God will speak to us, there must be a *deep seriousness of heart.* Let me remind you again of that text: "That trembleth at my word." When George Fox was called a Quaker, because he trembled at the name of God, the title was an honour to him. The man was so God-possessed that he quaked, as well he might. Habakkuk describes the same feeling as having been his own; no unusual experience with the true child of God. In fact, God never comes to us without our trembling. The old Romish legend is that the tree that bore the Saviour was the aspen, whose leaves continually quiver. He that bears Christ within him, and feels the weight of the divine glory, must be filled with awe. Our brother Williams just now said that he feared and trembled for all the goodness that God had made to pass before him: this is my feeling and yours. We are so weak, and these divine inspirations are so weighty, that we are subdued into awe, and there is no room for levity. Brethren, avoid anything like trifling over sermon-making. Someone says, "Well, I take very little time over my sermon." Make no boast of that; it may be your sin. Listen! If a man had been put apprentice to cabinet-making, and had worked at it for a lifetime, it may be he would have a great deal of skill and a store of prepared material, so that he could turn out a chair in a short time; but you must not, therefore, think that you could do the same, and that cabinet work is mere child's play. A certain minister may compose a sermon in a short time, but you must remember that this is the result of the labour of many years. Even he who, according to common parlance, speaks quite extemporaneously, does not really do so: he delivers what he has in previous years stored up. The mill is full of corn, and, therefore, when you put a sack in the proper place, it is filled with flour in a short time. Do not regard preparation for the pulpit as a trifling thing; and do not rush upon your holy duties without devout fitness for the hallowed service. Make your waiting upon God a necessity of your calling, and at the same time the highest privilege of it. Count it your joy and honour to have an interview with your Master. Get your message fresh from God. Even manna stinks if you keep it beyond its time; therefore, get it fresh from heaven, and then it will have a celestial relish.

One thing more upon this head. This power, which we so greatly need in getting our message, will only come where there is a *sympathy with God*. Brethren, do you know what it is to be in tender sympathy with God? Perhaps no man among us knows what *perfect* sympathy with God means; yet we must, at least, be in such accord with God as to feel that *he* could not do or say anything which we would question. We could not doubt any truth which he could reveal; neither in our heart of hearts would we quarrel with anything which his will could appoint. If anything in us is not in perfect agreement with the Lord, we regard it as evil, and groan to be set free from it. If anything in us contends against God, we contend against it, for we are one with God in intent and desire. We hear much nowadays of sympathy with man; and in a measure we agree with it. Sympathy with the fallen, the suffering, the lost, is good. But my sympathies are also with the Lord my God. His name is dishonoured; his glory is trailed in the mire. It is his dear bleeding Son that is worst used of all. Oh, to think that he should love so well and be refused! That such beauty as his should be unacknowledged, such redemption rejected, such mercy scorned! What are men, after all, compared with God? If they are like myself, it were a pity that they were ever made! As for God, does he not fill all things with goodness as well as with being! To me Calvinism means the placing of the eternal God at the head of all things. I look at everything through its relation to God's glory. I see God first, and man far down in the list. We think too much of God to please this age; but we are not ashamed. Man has a will, and oh, how they cry it up! One said the other day—and there is some truth in it, too—"I attribute a kind of omnipotence to the will of man." But, sirs, has not God a will, too? What do you attribute to that will? Have you nothing to say about its omnipotence? Is God to have no choice, no purpose, no sovereignty over his own gifts? Brethren, if we live in sympathy with God, we delight to hear him say, "I am God, and beside me there is none else."

I can hardly tell you how high a value I set upon this enthusiasm for God. We must be in harmony with all his designs of love towards men, whilst in secret we receive his message. To become apparently warm in the pulpit is not of much account unless we are much more intense when alone with God. Heart-fire is true fire: a housewife who perseveres in the old method of making her own bread, does not want a great blaze at the mouth of the oven. "Oh, no," she says, "I want to get my fagots far back, and get all the heat into the oven itself, and then it becomes of use to me." Sermons are never baked by the fire and flash at the mouth; they must be prepared through the heating of the inmost soul. That precious Word, that divine shewbread, must be baked in the centre of our nature by the heat that is put there by the indwelling Spirit.

The Lord loves to use a man who is in perfect sympathy with him. I would not say anything unbecoming, but I believe that the Lord finds pleasure in the sympathy of his children. When you have been very heavy of heart, even to weeping, if your little child has said, "Dear

father, don't cry," or has asked, "What are you crying for, father?"
and then has broken out into sobbing himself, have you not been comforted by him? Poor dear, he does not understand what it is all about;
but you say, "Bless you, my dear child"; and you kiss him, and feel
comfort in him. So doth the Lord take up his poor weeping minister
into his bosom, and hear him cry, "Lord, they will not come to thee;
Lord, they will not believe thee. They are running after evil, instead
of thee. Lord, if I gave them a play, or a peepshow, they would come
in crowds; but if I preach thy dear Son, they will not hear me."
The great God enters into your sorrows, and finds a content in your
heart's love. God is not a man; but as man was made in the image of
God, we learn something of him from ourselves. He loves to clasp a
sympathizing one to his bosom, and then to say, "Go, my child, and
work in my name; for I can trust my gospel in thy hands." Be with
God, and God will be with you. Espouse his cause, and he will espouse
yours. There can be no question about this.

Follow me, my brethren, while I speak upon THE POWER THAT IS
NEEDED WHEN WE ARE DELIVERING THE MESSAGE ITSELF. Brethren,
if there is to be a divine result from God's Word, the Holy Ghost must
go forth with it. As surely as God went before Israel when he divided
the Red Sea, as surely as he led them through the wilderness by the
pillar of cloud and fire; so surely must the Lord's powerful presence
go with his Word if there is to be any blessing from it. How, then,
are we to get that priceless benediction? Great natural forces are in the
world, and when engineers wish to employ those forces, they go to work
in a certain manner suitable thereto. They cannot create power by
mechanism, but they can utilize it, and economize it. For instance, the
wheel and pulley do not produce power; but by diminishing friction,
they prevent the waste of power, and this is a great matter. We, also,
can be great gainers by using methods to minimize friction with this
present evil world, with which we unavoidably come into contact. Your
own experience will teach you the wisdom of this. Look earnestly to
that holy separateness of spirit which shall preserve you from the dis-
tracting and down-dragging tendencies of things seen. Happily there
is another kind of friction which has great power in developing latent
force. Just as a certain form of electricity is produced by friction, so
can we obtain power by coming in contact with God, and by means of
the spiritual effect of truth as it operates upon a willing and obedient
heart. To be touched by the finger of God, yea, to come into contact
with even the hem of our Master's garment, is to obtain heavenly
energy; and if we have much of it, we shall be charged with sacred
strength in a mysterious but very palpable way. Be much with God
in holy dialogue, letting him speak to you by his Word while you speak
back to him by your prayers and praises. So far you will obtain force.

The greatest generator of force which is available to man is heat. I
suppose that nothing produces so much power for human purposes as
fire; and even so, the burning and consuming element in the spiritual
world is a great factor in the development of spiritual strength. We
must be in downright earnest, and *must* feel the burnings of a zeal which
consumes us, or we shall have little force. We *must* decrease: we must
be burning if we would be shining lights. We cannot save our lives

and save others : there must be a destruction of self for the salvation of men.

Many other things suggest themselves to me on this point; but I waive them all, to come distinctly to the one most real and most sufficient power, namely, the Holy Ghost, to whom be glory evermore !

In order to have the Holy Spirit with us, there must be *a very close adhesion to the truth of God,* with clearness, boldness, and fidelity in the utterance of it. Do not dream that to have a formal creed, or a something which is said not to be a creed, but " a declaration," or some other style of confession—I know not how to mention the nondescript invention—is enough. Without intensely hearty belief of truth these precious documents are wretched affairs. Declarations of the kind I refer to may be compared to flags, which may be useful if carried by brave standard-bearers, or they may be tawdry ornaments, used for meaner ends. A teacher was once instructing a class in patriotism and nationality. He happened to see the national flag hanging up upon the wall, and he asked a child, " Now, my boy, what is that flag ? " " It is the English flag, sir." " And what is the use of it ? " The truthful boy replied, " It is used to cover the dirty place in the wall behind it." I need not interpret the parable. Let modern ecclesiastical history point the moral.

Do not let it be true of any of you, that a loudly professed orthodoxy is a mere coverlet for error, which is secretly held. No, dear brethren, stick to the truth, because the truth sticks to you. Wherever it leads you, follow it ; down into the valley, or aloft upon the hills. Follow close at its heels, and only fear to be left behind in its course. When the road is miry, never fear that you will ever be hurt by the splashes of truth.

The truth of God is the best of all guests : entertain it, as Abraham did the angels. Spare not the best you have for its maintenance ; for it leaves a rich blessing with those who deny themselves for it. But do not entertain any of the inventions of man ; for these will betray you, as Judas betrayed Christ with a kiss. Do not be dismayed by the caricatures of truth which are manufactured by malicious minds. Nowadays it is the policy of men to misrepresent gospel doctrines. They remind me of Voltaire, of whom it is said that he could take any book that he read and make whatever he liked out of it, and then hold it up to ridicule. Remember the Roman practice in persecuting times : they wrapped the Christians in skins of bears, and then set dogs to tear them to pieces. They treat us the same, morally, if we hold by unpopular truth. I have seen myself in several skins lately : I can only say they were no skins of mine. I return them to those who arrayed me in them.

If our declarations of truth are fairly and honestly stated, and then argued against—well and good ; but when they are misrepresented, and tortured to mean what we never meant them to mean, then we are not careful to reply. When this happens to you, count it no strange thing. Reckon that because they cannot overcome the truth itself, they fashion an image of it stuffed with straw, and then burn it with childish exultation. Let them enjoy their game as they may. Brethren, I do not believe that God will set his seal to a ministry which does not aim at being strictly in accordance with the mind of the Spirit. In proportion as a ministry is truthful, other things being equal, God can bless it. Would you have the Holy Ghost set his seal to a lie? Would you have him bless what he has not revealed, and confirm with signs following that which is not truth? I am more and more persuaded that if we mean to have God with us we must keep to the truth. It is an almost invariable rule, that when men go aside from the old faith they are seldom successful in soul-winning. I could appeal to all observers whether it is not so, and whether men, powerful in other ways, do not become barren and unfruitful as to the salvation of others when they become doubters rather than believers. If you enquire into the worm which has devoured the root of their usefulness, you will find that it is a want of faith upon some great, cardinal principle—a want of faith which may not be displayed in their public ministry, but lurks within, poisoning their thoughts. You must be with the Holy Ghost if you are to have the Holy Ghost with you.

Beloved, *have a genuine faith in the Word of God, and in its power to save.* Do not go up into the pulpit preaching the truth, and saying, "I hope some good will come of it"; but confidently believe that it will not return void, but must work the eternal purpose of God. Do not speak as if the gospel might have some power, or might have none. God sends you to be a miracle-worker; therefore say to the spiritually lame, "In the name of Jesus Christ of Nazareth, rise up and walk," and men will rise up and walk; but if you say, "I hope, dear man, that Jesus Christ may be able to make you rise up and walk," your Lord will frown upon your dishonouring words. You have lowered him—you have brought him down to the level of your unbelief, and he cannot do many mighty works by you. Speak boldly; for if you speak by the Holy Spirit you cannot speak in vain.

Oh, that we could make our people feel that we believe what we are saying! I have heard of a little girl, who said to her father, who was a minister, and who had been telling her a story, "Pa, is that real, or is it preaching?" I cannot object to your smiling at my anecdote; but it is a thing to weep over, that preaching should be suspected of unreality. People hear our testimony, and ask, "Is it a matter of fact, or is it the proper thing to be said?" If they saw a statement in a newspaper, they would believe it; but when they see it in a sermon, they say, "It is a pious opinion."

This suspicion is born of want of fidelity in ministers. I saw, just now, outside the shop of a marine-store dealer, a placard which runs thus: "Fifty tons of bones wanted." "Yes," I said to myself, "mostly back-bones." Fifty tons of them! I could indicate a place where they could take fifty tons, and not be overstocked. As for us, let us be able to say, "I believed, therefore have I spoken." Let us have a genuine faith in everything that God has revealed. Have faith, not only in its truth, but in its power; faith in the absolute certainty that, if it be preached, it will produce its results.

Closely adhering to the truth by a dogged faith, we are in the condition in which God is likely to bless us. But then, there must be in the preaching *a concentration of heart upon the business in which we are engaged.* We shall never do well in our sacred calling if half our energy goes to something else. The man who is doing half-a-dozen things generally fails in them all. Of course he does. We have not enough water in our streamlet to drive more than one mill : if we let it run over one wheel, that one wheel will turn to purpose ; but if we divide the water, it will do nothing. God's message deserves every fragment of my ability ; and when I deliver it, I ought to be "all there," every bit of me ; none of me should go astray or lie asleep. Some men, when they get into the pulpit, are not there. One said to me, in conversation, "I do not know how it is, but I feel so different when I shut that pulpit-door." I answered, "Have the door taken off." That might not, however, produce the effect ; it would have been better if it could be said of him as of Noah, "The Lord shut him in."

Do not some show by their preaching, that their heart is not in it? They have come to preach, and they will get through what they have to say: but their deepest thoughts and liveliest emotions would come out better at a political meeting. They have not all their wits about them when preaching. They remind me of the legend of the two learned doctors down in the fen country, who thought that they would have a day's shooting of wild ducks. They were extremely learned, but they were not at home in common pursuits. They came to a piece of water, into which it was necessary for them to wade to get at the ducks, and one said to the other, "I have not put on my water-boots." The other replied, "I have forgotten my boots, too ; but never mind." They both waded in, for they were keen sportsmen. They reached a sufficient nearness for shooting the ducks. Then one whispered, "Now, brother, fire at them." The brother replied, "I've forgotten my gun. Haven't you brought yours?" "No," said the other, I did not think of it." There were sportsmen for you ! Their deep thoughts had made them unpractical : their Hebrew roots had displaced their common sense. Have you never seen such preachers ? They are "not there" : their minds are in the profound abysses of critical unbelief. The Holy Ghost will not bless men of this sort. He spake by an ass once, but that ass showed its sense by never speaking any more. I know creatures of like kind not half so wise.

Now, dear friends, see what I am driving at. I hope that I shall not miss it. It is plain to every thoughtful mind, that if we are not altogether in our work, we cannot expect a blessing. God the Holy Ghost does not work by a torso, or a bust ; he uses our whole manhood. See a tradesman in our poorer quarters, on a Saturday night, outside his shop. He walks up and down, and cries, "Buy, buy," with vehemence ; he salutes every passer-by ; he presses his commodities ; he is everywhere at once ; he compels men to come in ; he urges each one to be a purchaser. So, also, must we serve the Lord with all diligence, if we hope for success in our sacred calling.

(To be continued.)

My Friend Jack.*

I USED to call him Jack. But that was just like me, for I was always rude and uncouth as a lad, and, I fear, much of my boyish abruptness has followed me into my manhood; for I still have a very awkward way of doing most things. It must have been born in me; and, perhaps, much of my awkwardness may be more my misfortune than my fault.

The real Christian and surname of my friend is John Early, and his location, Leicester. Though Mr. Early was somewhat late in coming to Christ, I am glad to say he has come at last. His conversion has greatly cheered me, and I feel sure that to relate the record of his coming to Christ will interest, and, I trust, profit you also. Anyhow, I am writing it with that object in view. John and I were constantly together, from the age of five to fifteen; after that time, for the next five years, we only met occasionally. Of course, there was a reason why we did not meet quite so often. I will tell you why, or you may, perhaps, think we had quarrelled; but not so, such a thing we never did in all our lives, and I am sure we shall not do so now we both love Jesus. Oh, dear no. The cause of our separation was quite different. The fact was, John found a little sweetheart; and they have a saying down where I was born, that "two's company and three's none." I believed this myself, so I deemed it wise not to call upon him so often, and I saw no relief but to look for a suitable one for myself; and this I did, with a grand result—quite a success, I can assure you; so from the early age of fifteen to manhood, I courted hard, and then made my sweetheart my wife, and I would do the very same thing over again, if I had to live my time over again, whatever people might say about it; for I am one of those who believe that, with love in the home, and Christ in the heart, early marriage would be a real boon to any man. When people wait so long for positions, and conditions, they often get to think more about the cage than the bird, and many of the blessings attached to an honourable marriage are lost for life. The foolish customs of this country keep our young men waiting and watching till they gain a position which will enable them to furnish a big house, with Brussels carpets, and piano and servants complete, till many a young man loses heart, and the home-bird loses all her song before they really start life.

It was not so with either John or myself: we both started early at the Cape of Good Hope, and entered into the United States as soon as we became men, each making up his mind to work hard; and God has blessed our efforts, and that right gloriously. But, there, that is just like me, I have run right away from my subject, you see. I do not know how it is, but my life seems full of interpolations. However, I will return at once to my narrative.

Having explained how it was I lost John's company, you will see it was quite natural for each of us to turn his attention to his newly-formed companion; so, like the animals in the ark, we decided to walk together two and two, in a most orderly manner, each in his own

---

* Mr. Manton Smith is now issuing a second volume of his personal memoranda. It is entitled, "More Stray Leaves from my Life Story."

direction. For the next twenty years, so far as I can remember, John and I never saw each other, till we met face to face in a large meeting— the one as a preacher of Jesus Christ, and the other as a seeker of that same Jesus. It is to this most interesting meeting I should like to invite your attention. Mr. Early was one of the three boys I refer to in "My Life Story" (page 17), who smoked a cigar with me in the cemetery the Sunday prior to my father's funeral. I mention this fact because of the strange way in which we met again after twenty years' separation from each other. It happened on this wise. Some four years ago, my esteemed friend, the Rev. F. B. Meyer, invited my colleague and myself to conduct a special gospel mission at Leicester. It was also arranged by him that, on Sunday morning, he and Mr. Fullerton should conduct the usual service at Melbourne Hall, and that my dear friend Chamberlain and I should conduct a mass meeting for non-church goers, half an hour later than the usual service time, in the large skating rink.

It was a great success, thank God, though a strange sight; for we had no seats, worth naming, and quite two thousand persons had to stand the whole of the time. During my address on this occasion, a flash of thought struck me, and caused me to relate my truant Sunday's experience while a school-boy. Just then, looking down that sea of faces, I saw one face that looked to me like my companion John. I became more and more impressed that it was he, till at length I paused, and said, "I believe I see in this audience one of the very boys I have been speaking about, if so, he can verify my statement; and if it should be my friend, I trust that at the close of this service, he will come and grip my hand once again. And now," said I, "let me tell you, my dear friend, before this vast crowd, I can, by God's grace, stand here this morning, and, without boasting, declare that through the precious blood of Jesus Christ I am a saved man. Can you say that much, friend? It is the very same Jesus that you and I heard our teacher speak about in the Sunday-school, years ago. If you have given your heart to Christ, come and tell me; if not, let me, I beseech you, have the joy of telling you, in private, of his goodness to me, and his willingness to save you."

I was not mistaken in my hearer's identity; and at the close of the service, up came John, weeping and trembling, to the platform, and took my hand. He burst into tears, and said, "O dear friend, I am so pleased to see and hear you once again; but I am not a Christian myself. Tell me, now, what must I do to be saved?"

I commenced, and thought I could tell him so much, but not a word could I say. My heart was too full, and my feelings got the better of me, till all I could do was to weep with him. Happily, my friend Chamberlain, the sweet tenor singer from the Tabernacle, was by my side, and he has always a most clear and loving way of putting the truth to anxious souls. It was he who, after an address by myself to several thousands of children, at the Metropolitan Tabernacle, turned to my dear son George and led him to Christ. In like manner Mr. Chamberlain took my friend at Leicester by the hand, saying, "Well, friend, are you willing here, and now, to take Jesus Christ to be henceforth your Saviour and Lord?" "I will, I will!" was the sobbing, but solemn reply. Then, taking us both by the hand, John said, amid many tears, "I call these friends on this platform to witness that I will, God helping me, I will, O Lord, be thine." And from that time I believe he and all his household have become regular attendants at the Melbourne Hall church. How often are we reminded by many incidents in our daily life, that God still moves in a mysterious way his wonders to perform!

This emphatic "I will" was a grand sound to all who witnessed the scene on the platform of the Skating Rink. It reminded me of a boat I once saw launched. When the dockmaster said the word "Go," away she went, leaving the old stocks behind, and floated gracefully into deep waters. It is just like that when a sinner comes with his penitent prayer to Christ, and then resolves, in the Lord's name, to give up all for Jesus; when the "I will" comes straight out from the heart, and the mind acquiesces in the solemn decision, then all that is required to complete salvation is the tongue to confess that trust unto others. Sinner, will you not say now, "I will, I will, God helping me, I will, O Lord, be thine"? If you do so with all your heart, then shall the truth of that text be fulfilled in your experience: "If thou shalt confess with thy mouth the Lord Jesus, and shalt believe in thine heart that God hath raised him from the dead, thou shalt be saved: for with the heart man believeth unto righteousness; and with the mouth confession is made unto salvation" (Rom. x. 9, 10). J. MANTON SMITH.

Trialogue on a Wet Sabbath Morning.

SCENE, the minister's vestry; *time,* half-an-hour before beginning of the service. *Present*—Pastor, Deacon, Elder.

Pastor. I am always sorry when we have such a wet and dreary Sunday. It will keep many away most properly, and more will make an excuse out of it for stopping at home.

Deacon. Don't take a gloomy view of it. I think we must call it fine growing weather, though it is certainly rather soft.

Pastor. Yes, I hope it may prove growing weather. Oh, for spiritual growth in us all!

Elder. Which way would it be best for us to grow? Larger, or smaller?

Pastor. If I had my choice, I should say—let us grow smaller. For this is a necessary growth; as John the Baptist said, "He must increase, but I *must decrease.*" I think we should choose that growth which is absolutely necessary; and we may do so the more cheerfully, since, in growing less, we really grow greater in the only way which is desirable. If it is a growing day, we must not let it be a groaning day, unless it be with growing pains. Oh, for a blessing!

Deacon. You are sure to have it; for I often notice that when you are most depressed, and come to us crying to the Lord in weakness, we always get a better sermon than ever.

Pastor. So may it be again! Call in the brethren, and let us pray.

C. H. S.

Open-Air Preaching in and about London.

THE annual meeting of the Open-Air Mission reminds us that this primitive mode of preaching the gospel is in much greater favour than of old. The association has now an effective membership of one thousand and sixty-four ; and during the year, congregations amounting in the aggregate to three millions, have been addressed, and upwards of a million small publications have been circulated. The secretary, Mr. Gawin Kirkham, has, on the average, travelled more than a thousand miles a month, and has given three hundred and twenty-four addresses in the course of the year. Long life to him !

As every one knows, in the old times, before the Reformation, open-air preaching flourished in London as it has never done since, the two great stations being Paul's Cross and the Spital, the farmed land around the latter naturally taking the name of Spitalfields. At both places much besides theology was dealt in ; for, in at least one instance, we find a preacher at the Spital making reference to the repairing of the conduit in Fleet Street. Many comical or semi-tragic scenes took place ; and the manner in which an unpopular preacher would be dealt with was seen in the case of Bourne, soon after the death of Edward VI. As Foxe says, " The stir was such that the preacher plucked in his head, and durst no more appear in that place." It bordered on the comical when Queen Elizabeth called on Dean Norvell to keep to his text when he was discoursing on Ash Wednesday, 1565. More than twenty years later, when the Queen was also among the throng that assembled to celebrate the defeat of the Spanish Armada, it was one of the most noteworthy congregations that have assembled in the open-air.

Although the battle of the Reformation was ardently fought at the Spital and Paul's Cross, the practice of open-air preaching in London proper was not long kept up with energy. In the seventeenth century, the Quakers and others did something in this direction ; but we have to come down to the days of George II. to find ourselves in the golden age of preaching in the open air.

Leaving the wonderful field-preachers of Wales out of the account, the greatest open-air evangelist of whom our Christian annals tell is Whitefield ; and if that laborious veteran did not actually make his start in London, his chief triumphs over sin and the devil were made in Moorfields. In the time of George II. Moorfields was the principal playground of the citizens, and at Easter-tide, more especially, the fair that was held on the open space attracted a vast concourse for three days. In 1742 the preacher himself described Moorfields as " a large, spacious place, given . . . by one Madam Moore, for all sorts of people to divert themselves on." The array of booths was very great, and from twenty to thirty thousand persons would be attracted to the ground. It is a striking testimony to the power of Whitefield's eloquence when we find that he successfully rivalled in attraction showmen and merry-andrews. From all directions people would be seen running from the theatres and wild-beasts' shows, not to miss the opportunity of hearing the preacher. No wonder that such an evangelist retired from the field with pockets filled with notes from enquirers !

In our own day, the city is by no means neglected by the preachers, who use portable pulpits, and give their messages in the open-air. Nor are congregations wanting in the forenoon of Sunday, either in the city itself, or close to its boundaries.   What a congregation there is, for example, at Petticoat Lane, or at Whitecross Street, or at the so-called bird-fair, which is now a veritable Sunday-morning market, hard by the ancient Spital! At all of these places services are held. On warm Sunday evenings, when weather permits, a preacher may be heard on the steps of the Royal Exchange: that great centre of life being on the Sabbath a quiet sanctuary for an open-air congregation.

The preachers who carry on their work in and about London are encouraged to persevere in their service by the conversions which frequently reward them, many of which are of a striking kind. One of these, which lately happened in the so-called Green Lanes, was a true "prodigal's return." The preacher had taken his stand near one of the entrances to Finsbury Park; and the prodigal came out of the Manor House Tavern, which he had entered to "have a drink." Attracted by the crowd and the singing, the man, who was about thirty years of age, heard a discourse on the Prodigal Son; and he did not leave the spot until he had accepted Christ as his Saviour. Six months later, that convert wrote to the preacher who had been instrumental in his conversion :—

"You know what a wretch I had been for fifteen years—a drunkard, a gambler, a Free-thinker, a would-be atheist, living only for drink, dancing, cards, and every form of vice. You know also how the devil, that father of lies, had brought me down to despair and misery. You know all this, and you know what a picture of a poor outcast prodigal I presented on that blessed Sunday morning, the 10th of June last, at the Manor House. . . . It was there that that story broke my heart, destroyed my evil will, and caused me to cry out with great agony of soul, 'My God, if there is a prodigal in London, it is I ! ' "

That man is now a volunteer worker among the poor and degraded in common lodging-houses; and his mother is rejoicing in his reclamation.

On Sunday, the 17th of last June, a meeting was being held at Stoke Newington, when one who joined the congregation was a man who came out of a public-house, smoking a pipe. A Christian postman, who was present, asked this stranger what hindered him from accepting Christ ? Further conversation revealed the fact that here was another wasteful prodigal; a backslider, who was not only spending a large proportion of his earnings in drink, but who had also deserted wife and children in the country.   In his more calm and sober moments, the man had felt remorse for his conduct, and had then been in a mood for committing suicide. Now, however, the postman spoke to him about the Prodigal Son, and that touched his heart; and at length he gave up drink, and became a changed character. The postman talked much with his new friend, prayed with him, and introduced him to the Sunday-morning Bible-class, at Mildmay Conference Hall. On the August Bank-holiday, the man brought his wife and family up from the country, found a new home for them, and they are now living happily together. That family, at all events, will be able to testify to the good and lasting effects of open-air preaching.

Being instant in season and out of season, certain of the members go out in exceptionally severe weather ; and find that fruit comes of their labours. A Battersea member reports a case of this kind which happened at a service held during a severe frost. Notwithstanding the cold, people opened their windows to hear what was said, and one man, who benefited by the address, for ever after reckoned that day as a memorable period in his experience.

Another case of listening at an open window, was that of a man who did not like to join his wife in the more public assembly of the street. At length, however, courage came, and he went boldly down, and not only heard, but accepted the word, and was renewed in heart and life. That man is now a church-member and a ready helper at open-air services.

The conversion of a gambler from the error of his ways, was the occasion of a striking scene at Holloway, only a few months ago. Among the crowd there stood a man who struck observers as being unusually hard and sullen in appearance. He looked like a man who might interrupt, but happily was now not in such a mood. He had had a Christian mother, and the time for the devoted woman's prayers to be heard had come. After listening a while, his features seemed to soften, then tears gathered in his eyes ; and at length, in the light of day, and before all the people, he confessed what a life he had lived. In addition to other things, he had been a gambler; "But no more of that for me," he cried ; and, suiting the action to the word, he took from his pocket a betting-book, tore out the leaves and scattered them in the breeze over the heads of the congregation. This was an unmistakable case of repentance.

In a memorable instance, at the East End, a poor woman, who was bent on committing suicide, was arrested in her downward course, saved, and turned into a helper of those who rescued her.

At Clerkenwell, a man was attracted to an out-door service, who, having "been on the drink" for ten months, resolved to kill himself out of his misery ; but before carrying out that resolve, he determined to throw a brick at the preacher, because he felt confident that there had been unfair advantage taken of him. The preacher, for example, had evidently heard all about what had been going on, and he had published the news to the world without asking permission. The scene of this service was in Coldbath Square, and the preacher at the time in question was a Scripture Reader. Something in the prayer so touched the man's heart, that he did not throw the brick ; but when the service was ended he made a full confession of his guilt and wretchedness. The preacher became so interested in the man's case, that he raised over £20, to send the convert and his family to Canada. Since then the emigrant has remitted £4 to the same Scripture Reader, to help any others in a similar way. "God bless the open-air service," the man remarked, when writing from his new home, "for that night it saved my life; and, what's more, my soul was owned by the Lord Jesus Christ. No more drink for me. We have had a prayer-meeting in our log-cabin. Tell the people," he adds, "that open-air services are good, and thank the Open-Air Mission for sending out preachers to preach such good news."

From the above, we may infer that open-air preaching is a very needful institution for these times. The veteran traveller and charming writer, John Macgregor, M.A., or Rob Roy, is generally regarded as the founder of the Mission, and no one can expect ever to see a more devoted and capable secretary than our friend Gawin Kirkham. May the work and the workers prosper more and more !

G. H. P.

"Polish and Power."

THE other Saturday evening, feeling tired and overworked, I went to the Turkish Baths, to get freshened up for the Sunday services. I sat in the beautifully-furnished heating room, quietly waiting my turn to go through the mysterious process of cleansing, when my attention was called to two gentlemen, whose conversation I was obliged to hear. "Well," said the shorter of the two, "I don't get much out of his preaching now."

"How is that ? " asked the other ; "does he neglect the sermon preparation ? "

"No. I think he prepares too much ; he says he wants more time for study, and he can't visit the old folks like he did when he came fresh from college."

"Perhaps he feels running dry," significantly remarked the little man, as he wiped the perspiration from his face.

"I tell you what it is, Mr. S——," said the first speaker, with emphasis, "our minister thinks a lot too much about polish ; he makes splendid sentences, but there's no power in them. He used to quote the Scriptures at first, now he puts in bits of poetry: all are very nice and pretty, but no power. What is the good of preaching when there's no power about it ? I like polish, but I like it on something."

I went to take my turn in the bath, but not to forget the old man's words about polish and power.

J. C. C.

Make Points.

WITHOUT points a sermon is fatally defective. A few weeks ago a candidate stood in a Brooklyn pulpit. He was young, he was pious, and said many good things, but failed utterly. One of his hearers remarked of him, " He talked, and talked, and talked, but said nothing." That is, he made no points. The query of any common mind, " What is he driving at ? " could not be answered.

Lecturing before a class of coloured students of theology, the late Dr. Colver remarked, in that vivid, quaint style for which he was distinguished, "Always have at least two mule's ears to every sermon." The white visitors saw no sense in the simile, but the students seemed to enjoy it greatly ; for they were wont to ride mules with neither saddle nor bridle, and were compelled to lay fair hold of the two ears in order to keep their seat.—E. P. T., in " *Homiletic Monthly.*"

More Fishers than Fishes.

THERE is a legend that in some remote age a fish found its way into our harbour at Mentone, and this suffices to attract quite a company of anglers to the breakwater. Our friend photographed this College of Fishermen just at the right moment; and here we see the devoted men just as they appeared, fully absorbed in their uneventful sport. Hour after hour they sit, and bait after bait they place on their hooks; but their baskets go home empty again and again. Many a time have we seen more than a score rods in a few yards all aimed at some little unknown fish, who nevertheless had escaped the peril of these terrible engines of destruction. The bait alone must have been worth ten times the value of the fish, to say nothing of those magnificent cans and baskets so thoughtfully provided for bearing home the spoils.

Thus have we seen the waters of trade, honour, and pleasure surrounded by great companies of enthusiastic competitors even when the best gain that could be hoped for was utterly insignificant. Hundreds of candidates for one paltry situation; dozens of shops competing for a slender trade hardly sufficient for one; troops of simpletons, old and young, crowding a place of amusement where the mirth was of the dreariest order! Wherefore do they spend their time and care to catch the half of nothing? There are noble pursuits which abound with true profits, and real pleasures; but these are passed by because they are too spiritual, while the foolish multitude tread one upon another in their eagerness to find a prize where nothing is to be gained. They seek the living among the dead. Oh, that men would look to infinite and eternal things! Then would they win a reward for their watching and waiting such as they will never find in the waters of this poor passing world.　　　　　　C. H. S.

A Sunset in the Southern Sea.

ALL the passengers aboard are gazing at the orb of day setting in gorgeous splendour. The western skies are ablaze with rosy light, which is mirrored in the ocean around us, and we look upon "a sea of glass mingled with fire." Attendant clouds wait upon the departing luminary and are transfigured by its glory. A painter would go into ecstatic raptures over such masses of brilliant colouring, and long to reproduce them upon canvas. "Mr. Turner," said a would-be lady critic to the great artist, "I never see in nature the peculiar lights and shades you put into your pictures." The reply was crushing—some might think cruel—"Madam, don't you wish you could?" The trained eye of the artist might see *more* of the beauty of the scene before us; but so divine a spectacle would surely arouse the most careless and superficial observer from apathy to enthusiasm.

It has been a beautiful day, and never were sunbeams shining on a rippling sea more welcome. For two days previous to this, we have been running before a gale and have had a taste of the "roaring forties." Many of the sails were furled, and the others were reefed, the hatches were battened down, and our good ship, under storm-canvas, scudded along, now on the top of some mountain wave, and anon with heavy seas breaking over her. But, to-day, we have been favoured with a splendid illustration of the fact that, whatever pessimists may say, life is not all storm; but that the sunshine, which always bathes the upper surface of the darkest clouds, breaks through them ever and again to gladden us with its glory. Sometimes, "men see not the bright light which is in the clouds"; *but it is there.* "Let patience have her perfect work": seasons of trial herald "times of refreshing from the presence of the Lord."

We also feel that the sunset before us is a fitting climax to the beauty of the day. A sunset may be visible after a day of gloomy and repellent fog. At the eventide of a sinful life it may be light through the abounding mercy of God. To the dying thief the crucified Saviour said: "Verily I say unto thee, To day shalt thou be with me in paradise." But it should never be forgotten that "one such case is recorded to teach men not to despair, and *only one* to warn them not to presume." And it should likewise be remembered that though in the sovereignty of God, men repenting at the close of life may be saved, yet such sunsets are clouded and darkened with bitter remorse and painful regrets. On the other hand, those "that love God are as the sun when he goeth forth in his might." And a life of unalloyed sincerity, of unstained purity, and of unselfish labour, a life resting on the infinite merits of the Saviour and inspired with his Spirit, will most probably be crowned with a glorious departure into the unseen. Men vainly pray like Balaam, "Let me die the death of the righteous, and let my last end be like his!" unless they live the life of the righteous. Let a man's career be consecrated to the service of God, and it will be no idle boast for him to say, as sick Addison did to the gay young peer he had summoned to his presence, "See in what peace a Christian can die."

As the great disc of fire descends partly below the horizon, the semi-circle we see looks like a vast gateway of gold. A passenger remarks,

"We are sailing on the voyage of life, and yonder is the gate of the Celestial City." "Yes," we reply; "but unfortunately we are sailing from, and *not* towards, that beautiful haven of rest." Alas! how many people there are, who like to gaze upon pictures of heaven, love to hear sermons about the glories of heaven, talk glibly about meeting their friends in heaven! but a moment's serious reflection should convince them, that they are travelling in another direction altogether, rushing, or it may be drifting towards the blackness of eternal night. *Siste, viator, i.e.,* "Stop, traveller," began most of the old Roman epitaphs; and we too would urge, "Stop, traveller," pause and consider. "Heavenwards must our journey tend." "Turn ye, turn ye, why will ye die?" Not only "ask the way to Zion," not only "let your faces be thitherward"; but recollect that to reach that home you must daily travel towards it.

The after-glow is most beautiful. Gorgeous cloud-curtains hang over the radiant light that lingers lovingly where the sun dipped. Some of these clouds present surfaces of sapphire colour; others are of a slaty hue, edged, as it were, with pink coral. Feathery bands of dark crimson float here and there athwart the scene. The sun is hidden from our gaze, but he is evidently still glorifying the sky around us. The fact is, the sun has only apparently set; he never really sets, it is always high noon with him. In like manner, though the Christian sinks behind the horizon of this world, and at death vanishes from mortal ken, he really lives on, but with added glories; for "the path of the just is as the shining light, that shineth more and more unto the perfect day." And when heaven is reached, the words of the seer will be amply verified: "Thy sun shall no more go down" (not even apparently), "and the days of thy mourning shall be ended."

The sun has departed now. A single line of light alone remains to show where he set. Darkness covers the face of the deep; but it is a darkness illuminated by the lights that rule the night. As the passengers walk the deck, their eyes are fixed, not upon the Southern Cross and other constellations new to several of us, but upon a clearly-defined halo round the moon, so immense that all declare they have never seen the like before. The captain's explanation is, that this halo, combined with the beautiful sunset we have witnessed, portend more rough weather. Let it be so. In this chequered life, sunshine follows storm, and storm succeeds sunshine. Still, "this is not our rest," but "there remaineth therefore a rest to the people of God."

> "Then let the wildest storms arise,
> Let tempests mingle sea and skies;"

"The Lord reigneth." "The sea is his, and he made it." Winds and waves are under his control. The ship may go down in the boiling surge, but we shall only sink into the "hollow of his hand." And calmed with this thought, we seek our cabin to sleep, "rocked in the cradle of the deep," many thousands of miles from our English home.

ROBERT E. CHETTLEBOROUGH.

The Life which is Life Indeed.

A PAPER READ AT THE SECOND CONFERENCE OF THE PASTORS'
COLLEGE EVANGELICAL ASSOCIATION, BY W. Y. FULLERTON.

IT is a common-place amongst us that there is a life which is death. She that liveth in pleasure is dead while she liveth ; and he who lives the prodigal life of the far country, is likewise dead. The "son which was dead, is alive again" only when he comes home to his Father ; and if he does not return at all, he enters on a second life, which is the second death. For there is a life which is death.

And there is a life which is life. Before the Spirit of God takes hold of a man, and he is born again, the man exists ; then he lives. His dormant spirit is quickened, and he knows the power of the world to-come. His life is hid with Christ in God. For there is a life which is life.

And there is a life which is life indeed. As a man with a meagre physical life, often depressed with langour, or racked with pain, sometimes, it may be, on a Highland moor, or on a Swiss mountain, feels the luxury of living, and almost imagines he has wings; so there are moments in some Christian lives, and months and years in others, when "heaven comes down our souls to greet," and a rapturous royal life surges in our spirits, raising us far above the mean world around us.

> "I cannot tell the art
> By which such bliss is given,
> I only know Thou hast my heart,
> And I have heaven."

This is the life which is life indeed, not in word only, but in deed and in truth. And when we make a stand for truth, it is more than ever necessary that we back it with life, so that our formation may not be like the order of a hospital, but like the precision of a regiment as, obedient to the least word of the Captain, it marches to victory.

Alas ! in the case of many a man, and in the case of many a preacher, too, when the experience of this heavenly life is spoken of, the tense of the verb has to be altered, and it becomes, "The life which WAS life indeed." Doubt has found an entrance, or sin, and the bloom and fragrance of the better being is gone. The mischief was not wrought, perhaps, at the moment it first became apparent, but further back, at some time of carelessness, or neglect, or trifling. Just as a railway carriage, slipped from a train, does not stop at the moment of its detachment, but runs almost as quickly for a while, and then imperceptibly becomes slower, until it finally stands still, so some know what it is to have all their present impetus—not from present experience, but from the past; and gradually the impulse becomes less, because more distant, until it ceases to be a power in the life at all; and the man, looking round for the cause of the weakness, fails to find it. He begins to doubt whether he ever had the experience, or whether he only dreamt it ; whereas, the failure is the result of the slip which took place long ago. Oh, what a number of worn-out spiritualities there are in the church, both in pew and pulpit, and because no "old clo'" man comes round to buy them, the saints are arrayed in threadbare garments !

Like the little girl, who, when asked if her father was living, said, " He is not very living"; so some are alive, and perhaps live long, but do not live much. Concerning the life more abundant, they only say, the life which *was* life indeed.

Or in the midst of present despondency, the whole thought is of the life which WILL BE ; and while none are without the need which the thought of the future glory supplies, it is sad when the present glory loses its power over our hearts. To become languid and unjoyous, is the worst thing that can happen to us, for it makes anything heroic impossible. The vanquished army is easily beaten by the victorious one, just because of the lack of that moral power which the anticipation of victory would supply. The pulseless life leads its victims to hurry and impatience, and they do their present work badly, because they are always thinking, not of it, but of the next thing. If a preacher, the man becomes prosy; for while it is true that out of the abundance of the heart the mouth speaketh, it is also possible to speak out of the emptiness of the heart very wearily and very often. It is even possible to become a sermon-machine, and be so taken up with heads and tales, as to have life only in outline, without any fulness or beauty.

In these cases the life is the life they hope *will be*, not the life that *is*. In St. Giles's, Cripplegate, there is the tomb of a man, whose name there is no need to remember, though it is on the marble tablet which records the date of his birth and death. Beyond that there was, I suppose, nothing in his life to remember; so the curt inscription finishes with the three words, "That is all." To be born and to die ! That is *not* all, when a man knows the life which is life indeed, and which, though a man die, is still the life which IS. Seth lived and died ; Cainan lived and died ; Mahalaleel lived and died ; Jared lived and died ; Methuselah lived and died ; but Enoch walked with God—he lived the life which was life indeed—and was not; for God took him.

> " One crowded hour of glorious life
> Is worth an age without a name.",

It is scarcely necessary to remark that the title of this paper is taken from the Revised reading of the closing clauses of Paul's first letter to Timothy. "Lay hold on eternal life," is the unrevised version; but the new, combined with the old, is, perhaps, an advantage, as it directs our attention, not only to the duration of the life, but to the essence of it. During each separate moment it is life indeed, and in length it is to be life eternal.

In either case, it has to be laid hold of; and it is in the hope of stirring my own soul, and yours, to take a firmer grip of this superlative life that these lines are written. God has a high purpose for us, when he takes hold of us. Happy is the man who apprehends that for which he is apprehended; who, when the strong hand above grasps him to raise him higher, enters into the divine purpose, and wills to do his will, knowing that he is predestinated to be conformed to his image, and at length to stand on the same height. Thus we lay hold on the life which is life indeed.

The exhortations which surround the text may help towards its fulfilment. We are not to set our hope on riches, but on God. And yet

we need not despise the good things of this life, for he gives us all things
richly to enjoy.   To do good, like our Master, who went about doing it ;
to be ready to distribute, for the life hoarded becomes stagnant ; willing
to sympathize with others, because we are in sympathy with Christ ; not
setting ourselves up as better than our fellows ; sociable.

Gliding from the mention of life indeed, Paul urges Timothy—if he
were here, he would, doubtless, urge you and me—to keep that which was
committed unto him—he was put in trust with the gospel—avoiding
profane and vain babblings, and oppositions of science falsely so called,
which, even then it was true, some professing have erred concerning
the faith.

The fact that some have erred is a loud call to us that we should not
rest content till we have a more healthy, whole-hearted life. They have
turned back ; let us not sit down in sluggish contentment.   We are
familiar enough with the fact that error in faith often leads to a frustrate
life; but it becomes quite a question whether the process is not oftener
reversed, and the lack of life preceding leads to the lax doctrine. When
a man's heart-fervour wanes, and the truth ceases to influence his own
soul, he is apt, first to doubt it, then to despise it, and presently to dis-
card it altogether ; and then there appear "all the blind creeping things
which spring up when life goes and corruption comes."

They tell us that doubt is in the air. And so it always is. The
prince of doubt reigns there supreme. Yet a vigorous life, though surrounded by fever germs, is unharmed ; it is only when the life is low that
disease gains the ascendency. If the living corpuscles of the blood are
strong and healthy, they devour the noxious matter, and positively grow
stronger because of it; if weak, they are overcome, and the man is instantly ill.   The process with the doubt-germs is exactly analogous ; if
a man has the life which is life indeed, he strangles the suggested evil,
and becomes stronger to oppose other sophistries; but if his life be puny,
the doubt conquers him, and he becomes more sickly still.   *The life
which is life indeed is the antidote for doubt,* and except ye eat the flesh
and drink the blood of the Son of man ye have not that life in you.

It is this life, too, which lends value to doctrine. Our belief is what
we live by (by-lief) ; but a rule of life presupposes the life to be ruled.
Doctrine is not much by itself ; but devotion without doctrine is generally, in the long run, rather unsatisfactory. In fact, life without doctrine needs a good deal of doctoring. A good rule is a good tool ; and
though they say it is the deed, and not the creed, which meets the world's
need, yet surely the deed is all the better in being the outcome of life
according to law ! Our creed thus becomes our guide, and not our
chain.

Still, we need to beware of making sound doctrine, in any sense, a
substitute for the life which is life indeed. It is easy enough to imagine
that because we have the head right the heart is right also. And the
dead hearts in the churches work more havoc than all the dead hands.
Yet, it must be confessed, that some men's doctrine is like an ice-crust
over a brook, which has since shrunk away from it, leaving the hollow-
sounding surface frozen. Oh, for an influx of the life which is life
indeed, to bear upon its bosom the doctrine which, in its turn, will bear
all those who venture to trust it !

' Again, *this life is the first essential to usefulness.* When Napoleon was asked' what was the best style of gun, he said, "it greatly depended on the man behind it"; and after our most elaborate arrangements for the furtherance of God's work, success greatly depends on the men behind them. An all-alive man infuses his spirit into every enterprise. We have been told that, in the world, "the true veins of wealth are purple; and not in rock, but in flesh. There is no wealth but life." Which, if we believed, we might be more careful of human life than we are; while, if we realized that, in the spiritual world, our true wealth is the royal purple of an indwelling Christ, we should, doubtless, be more sensitive about our spirituality.

Further, *life is the true bond of union.* As we have no infallible measure for a man's spiritual life, we band together according to our doctrine, which is the nearest and truest guage possible in present circumstances. But life is the true affinity, and in these days it is splendid to see the live men in all the churches drawing nearer to each other, that together they may oppose the world's death. Had we but more of the life which is life indeed, perhaps our hearts would fuse even more rapidly.

And *this life indeed, is the foretaste of heaven.* There is no "Hitherto shalt thou come, but no further" concerning it. An illimitable vista of glory opens up before our wondering gaze, and what we now enjoy is like Rembrandt's pictures, which, it has been well said, never seem to be imprisoned in their frames, but convey an idea of wider space beyond them. And, most of all, like his picture, "The School of Anatomy," representing a group of doctors around a dead body, and in its wonderful art annihilating the power of death by strongly rivetting the attention to the living. So the blessed life which may be ours in Christ, anticipates heaven in neutralizing the power of sin, though it cannot here eradicate it.

Now, survey this fair field, and having seen its many glories, notice its cardinal points. There are four.

The life which is life indeed is *a life of ever-deepening knowledge of God.* It is eternal life to know him at all; to know more of him is to have the perfect life grow fuller and richer every day. In this sense we believe in progress. This is the true science, and the man who has this knowledge the true scient. God becomes to us less distant every day, and in him we live, and move, and have our higher being. This knowledge is deep; but the Spirit searcheth even the deep things, and knowing these, we are not so much taken up with the advancing times as with the unchanging God. Novalis calls Cromwell "a God-intoxicated man"; and we, having this life indeed, though not filled with wine, wherein is excess, yet can be so filled with the Spirit that, in our rapture, it were little wonder if some around us should say, "These men are full of new wine." But, living that life, we cease to care what they say. That life is God-centred, and encircled by God.

> " It fortifies my soul to know
> That, though I perish, Truth is so:
> That, howsoe'er I stray and range,
> Whate'er I do, Thou dost not change.
> I steadier step when I recall
> That, if I slip, Thou dost not fall."

This life indeed, moreover, is *a life of ever-increasing faith upon the Son of God.* No man knoweth the Father save he to whom the Son will reveal him. And the Son only reveals him to those who accept the invitation he gave in the next breath, "Come unto me, and I will give you rest." So we come to him ; and accepting the Revealer, have the revelation ; trusting the Saviour, receive the salvation; and, resting on the Redeemer, rejoice in the redemption. "Being crucified with him, I live; yet not I, but Christ liveth in me : and the life which I now live in the flesh I live by the faith of the Son of God, who loved me, and gave himself for me." We glory in the cross ; and where knowledge ceases we believe.

Not only do we believe in the sacrifice, but we learn to sacrifice because of our belief. We go with Christ that we may die with him. For he died that they which live should not henceforth live unto themselves, but unto him who died for them and rose again. Hence, the life which is life indeed becomes *a life of continuous sacrifice of self.* We lose our life that we may save it. We give light by being ourselves consumed.

> " The vine from every living limb bleeds wine.
> Is it the poorer for that spirit shed ?
> The drunkard and the wanton drink thereof—
> Are they the richer for that gift's excess ?
> Measure thy life by loss instead of gain.
> Not by the wine drunk, but the wine poured out :
> For love's strength standeth in love's sacrifice ;
> And whoso suffers most hath most to give."

Father Gossner used, in bidding farewell to his missionaries, to charge them—BELIEVE, HOPE, LOVE, PRAY, BURN. That is the life indeed, which, between a plough and an altar, is ready for either.

Thus, either in sacrifice or service, this life becomes *a life of constant and instant obedience to the least commandment.* Our Lord himself said, " I know that his commandment is life everlasting"; and, as he spake not his own words, nor did his own works, but the Father's; so we, following him, must wait attentively until we hear his word, that we may do only and always his bidding. Oh, this dear Word, every word of which is precious, and from none of which can we ever part ! You say the letter killeth ! Then that is just why we keep it, for we want our old self to be killed, that the Spirit may make us alive with life indeed.

To those who are willing to take God's least word, much blessing comes from things which might else seem trivial. For instance, our Lord said, " Enter into thy closet, and when thou hast shut thy door, pray to thy Father which is in secret." Take the general sense of that, and it only means we are to have private prayer, and that is life. But if, in child-like simplicity, we lovingly obey the very words of it, surely it becomes life indeed. Oh, what a sense of God's presence rushes down upon the worshipper as, inside the room, he turns the handle of the door ! There is a blessing promised, and a time named—"When thou hast shut thy door." Shut it thyself ; and then, kneeling, realize that thy Father is in secret. He was there before thee, and there as he was not outside ; there to enrich thee unto all bountifulness, and give new supplies of grace and power. Open thou thine heart wide to receive them. *The life which is life indeed is the life with a shut door and an open heart.*

Into the open heart Jesus comes himself. He is the eternal life which was with the Father, and which was manifested to us. So our constant prayer is :—

> "Be thou beside us, and in all our need
> Suffer us not to fall away from thee.
> And if at any hour, at any pass
> Of our extremity, our hearts should fail,
> And the betrayal tremble on our lips,
> Turn on us thy reproachful eyes again—
> Whose least sad look can strike the falsehood back,
> Sharper than many swords ; whose least low word
> Sets the face steadfast through the thundering storm ;
> Whose least light touch can smooth the bars of fire
> Into a bed of roses—look on us !
> O Lord, stay with us, and we ask no more ! ''

Church of the Holy Refrigerator.

IT is not easy to hatch chickens in an ice-house, or nurture lambs in a snow-drift ; and it is equally difficult to train young converts in churches which have the atmosphere of cellars. Many a strong Christian looks back with thankfulness to the warmth of a living church which cast its protection around him when he was but a babe in Christ ; while others, who were born strong and vigorous, are almost frozen to death in some "church of the holy refrigerator."

The *Golden Rule* quotes a remark made at a recent convention, that much of the discredit thrown upon evangelistic labours results from the cold state of the churches into which the new convert is ushered. Everything is warm in the revival meeting ; after the revival, everything is coldly formal in the regular meetings of the church. The utmost that can be said of some churches is that they are eminently respectable. Into this atmosphere comes the young convert ; and no wonder that his spiritual life-blood is congealed, and that people say in future years, " I don't believe in revivals. We had a great awakening, but where are the converts now ? The fault lies quite as much with the church as with the superficial nature of the revival. The speaker put the matter in a nutshell when he remarked, "The wise raiser of poultry does not take his chickens out of the incubator and put them into a refrigerator." —*The Armory*.

Counterfeit Gospels.

THE very commendations which some people give of the so-called gospel they preach arouse our suspicion. When we hear of its recent and human origin, we at once begin to doubt its validity. We are reminded of the boy who went into a shop to change a sovereign. "Are you sure it is a good one ? " asked the man behind the counter. "*Oh, yes, quite sure, sir ; for I seed father make it this morning.*" We do not believe in a gospel which was coined but this morning. We preach a gospel which was minted in heaven, which bears the image and superscription of Christ, which has the ring of true metal, and which will pass current in all the dominions of the King.   C. W. TOWNSEND.

Borrowing a Knife.

A SATIRE.

I HAPPENED to be in a garden some time ago, and a friend of mine was also there, busying himself with the shrubs. Presently he came to me with an extraordinary look on his countenance; and with a singular movement of his body, he addressed me thus:—

"O thou, who art standing on this gravel path, bearing thereon with light tread, and who art carefully surveying the surrounding landscape with eager and all-seeing eye—thou who didst this morning partake of thy breakfast, and who will shortly partake of thy middle meal, give heed to me, I beseech thee, who am only a man with a thirty-five shilling suit of Scotch tweed on my body.

"Thou art well acquainted with shrubbery, and knowest full well that certain specimens of the same cannot be removed except by the sharp, incisive application of a certain instrument. That instrument thou possessest. It is thine. Thou didst purchase it—the receipt for the same thou holdest in thy possession. Thou art under no obligation to transfer the same to thy unworthy suppliant for his temporary use. And yet with boldness I approach thee. Ah! grand instrument, both blunt and sharp, whichever way it is handled. Instrument of fame, instrument of honour, yet instrument of shame; for have not some men violated its functions even to their own destruction? And yet I approach thee. Let not my request be ignored by thee; but let it be gloriously answered. Yea, even now. Be pleased to turn unto me a favourable ear, and grant the request I now humbly present unto thee. Amen."

The above is *part* of this man's speech—only part; it would distress me to give it all. I was amazed, saddened. What did the man mean? At first I thought he must have suddenly become affected in his head. It was such an extraordinary rigmarole, reeled off at a good speed, and in a monotone. When I had recovered sufficiently, I asked, in subdued tone, "What on earth do you mean?" He smiled, and then innocently said,

"I WANT TO BORROW YOUR KNIFE."

*　　*　　*　　*　　*　　*

The above story is made up—purposely so. It happened *mentally;* and that is all the claim it can make to be a FACT. Nobody supposes that any man wanting to borrow a knife would be such a fool as to ask for it in the manner indicated above. When men have occasion to ask for anything of the sort, they are usually more explicit and brief.

This story has been invented as a *satire* upon a good deal that passes as PRAYER! With this key let the reader re-read the knife story, and think if there be not some connection between the absurdity of that preposterous concoction and the "prayers" of some men he may know. Take any ordinary, old-fashioned prayer-meeting, and condense the petitions into the actual necessities of the people. How few sentences would be left! We want *directness* in prayer; but how few possess it! The "bore" is an institute in many prayer-meetings. Whatever anyone else may do, *he* is sure to come in; and you know exactly how he will begin, what he will say, and how he will finish.

It is dreadful to think how men sport before the throne of grace ; they offer to God what no fellow-man would stay a minute to listen to ; and, besides that, they kill a good prayer-meeting.

I knew a man whom, for distinction, we will call the "WATER-POT." He was rightly named. Sure as any fire came to any meeting, *he* would come out and operate, and soon the thing would be spoiled. In vain the boys put glue on his seat—he *would* rise, and risk the consequences. He was a nuisance, and he is not the only one of the sort.

Many prayer-meetings are languishing for want of spirituality and common sense. The offender may be a useful deacon, one with whom you could not afford to part : he would be mortally offended if you stopped him in his twenty minutes of "prayer." There is yet room for genius to invent a machine that will *silently*, yet effectually, stop these bores. Such an inventor could rely upon each minister in this country, at least, procuring one.

The writer knows churches where the young people never came to a prayer-meeting ; it was a physical impossibility for them to sit out the monotony induced by the old cronies who reeled off the same stereotyped phrases week after week. These old parties frowned upon the younger members who ventured to pray, and they seemed to think that young Christians had no moral right to approach God in the public meeting. And yet, some of the most touching petitions are often presented by young, tender, guileless Christians in secret, which, if presented to God in the presence of a number of Christians assembled for prayer, would have a remarkable effect upon the company.

Unfortunately, this word-spinning is found in the pulpit—a place it ought never to enter. The writer once heard a "prayer" offered by a "D.D." (he played the violin, and therefore may be rightly named a "*fiddle* D.D.") which had not one word of supplication or praise in it from beginning to end. It was a literary effort, designed to inform the Almighty on a few obscure points in astronomy and theology As a prayer, it was a failure. The American boy was right. One morning, after leaving church, he turned to his father, and said—

"Father, does God know everything ?"

"Certainly, my boy," replied *pater;* "why do you ask ?"

"Oh, nothing," said the boy, "only our minister told him such a lot of things this morning, that I thought may be *he wasn't posted.*"

It was a noticeable feature about Mr. Moody's prayers, that they were *direct*, and very comprehensive. Moody asked for what he wanted, and, generally, he got it. Is it not often so, that we are disappointed about the answers because God is disappointed about the prayers ?

Oh, for directness, brevity, earnestness, spirituality and faith, in our prayers ! Then we might expect good times. But no good can come of this intolerable mumble, mumble, and roundaboutness. When you want a knife, ask for it straight.

F. C. SPURR.

An Old-Time Negro Sermon.

ON a Sabbath afternoon, in a town at the extreme south of the States, Dr. J. M. Ludlow wandered into a Methodist meeting-house, and heard a sermon, of which the following is an outline. As "Brother Yerkes," the preacher, "took his stand beside the desk," he "began a teetering motion, swayed, perhaps, by his feelings, as a balanced rock might have been by an earthquake." After a while, he broke into rapid and rhapsodic speech, the words pouring forth as through a mill-race. "The run of the sermon," says the doctor, " may be gathered from the following scraps, which have lingered in my memory" :—

"Behold, *I stand at the door and knock*." " O chillern, *whar* am de door ? Speks yer t'ink it am de door of bebbin. Oh, dem gates ob pearl into de golden city ! Oh, de door inter de Fader's house ! Oh, let de angels swing 'em wide open on ter de hinges ob redeemin' lub ! But, chillern, dat's not de door dat yer and I is a watchin' yet.

"Speks yer t'ink it am de door ob de church. Wide door shua nuff! big as de door ob de Ark ob de Cubbinant; an' inter it go all de walkin' an' de creepin' tings, great an' small, rich an' poor, flyin' saint an' a-crawlin' sinner. But dat's not de door we's a watchin' dis arternoon.

"No, chillern ; de door is de door inter de heart.

"But *who* am a stan'in' at de door ? 'Tain't no tramp come ter de shanty, like de debbil, a-standin' 'roun' to eat up suthin' what he may devour. 'Tain't no thief a-hangin' 'bout waitin' ter snatch some soul wid de claws of de great temptation. 'Tain't no' cendiary ter set yer on fire wid de 'ternal burnin'. But, it's jus' de bestest frien' yer ebber could hab ; wiser dan de white folks, kinder dan de fader what toted yer when yer was a baby, an' more lubbin' dan de mudder what nussed yer. It's de Lor' Jesus a stan'in' at de door; his head white as de light ob de noonshine, an' a-glisterin' wid de dew, an' all ober as lubly as de rose ob Sharon. An' he done brung de bread fur de soul, an' de wine fur de sperrit, an' de pearls ob great price fur de eberlastin' rejoicin'.

"An' *what am he doin'* at de door ? Only jus' a knockin' an' a sayin', ' O poor sinner, let me in ! I'se come ter supper wid yer ! ' Did yer nebber hear him a-knockin' ? He knocks wid de conscience when de sin am a-troublin'. He knocks wid de fear when de doctor am a-feelin' ob de pulse, an' he say, ' I am de great physicianer.' He knocks wid de hungerin' an' de thirsterin' arter righteousness, when de husks ob de worl' turn de stomach. He knocks soft an' gentle when dar's a coffin in de cabin. He knocks like de thunder when yer won't hear him in no tudder ways.

"Better let him in ! Let him in, Susan ! Let him in, Daniel ! He's a callin' yer by yer name, fur he aint no stranger ; knows everybody a heap sight better than the critter knows hisself. O chillern, let in de Lor' Jesus; an' when de front door ob de heart swings wide open, de hull sky full of glory will come a rushin' in too, fur de Lor' Jesus am clothed wid de rainbow, an' walks in de shoes ob sapphire.

" Now, *why don't* yer let him in ? Oh ! it's 'cause yer got de bar up— bar ob yer selfishness, bar ob yer drinkin', bar ob yer dancin', an' de bar ob yer foolin'. Oh, take de bar down, chillern! Did yer yar de screechin' dis mornin', when de fire done burnt up de cabin an' de little baby in it ? O Lor', help Aunt Rachel, an' don't keep her refusin' to be comforted 'cause her baby ain't no more. Mudder lef' de chile in de cabin an' locked de door. When the fire was a-shootin' from de winder, big men said, ' Open dis door, an' we'll save yer.' But de baby couldn't open de door. Oh, how de tears run down yer cheeks, all fur dat baby ! But better cry some fur yerself, now, 'cause de flames ob de eberlastin' burnin' has a-cotched on ter de cabin ob yer own life ; an' de Lor' Jesus he's a-stan'in' at de door. But some of yer can't let him in, any more dan dat baby. Yer's frowed away yer strength ; yer's lost yer resolution ; or yer's all upsot wid de suddingness ob de hell a-bustin' out in yer. O chillern, open de door this yer bressed minit, before it am eberlastin'ly too late," etc.

The swaying motion was kept up for a few moments after the preacher ceased speaking, when he suddenly dropped into the chair from utter exhaustion.

"An' now," said the pastor, "when de choir hab stopped cryin', dey will sing a hymn, an' we'll put all de pennies we's got inter de box, and de white folks will put in de silber, for de relief of Aunt Rachel."

Our Countrymen in India.*

BY H. RYLANDS BROWN, OF DARJEELING.

THE following brief account of a recent four months' tour, in connection with the Anglo-Indian Evangelization Society, has been written with a view to calling forth a deeper and more prayerful interest in our own countrymen in India.

When visiting a young man about twenty years of age, living all alone, far away from any railway-station, on the borders of Bhootan, the words, "Look unto me, and be ye saved, *all the ends of the earth*," came home with a new appropriateness. How wonderfully the Word of God fits in with all the scenes and circumstances of life !

Not a few of those visited last winter are the sons of godly parents— a grandson of a missionary who translated the Scriptures into Mongolian, and a son of a Disruption minister, of 1843, being of the number. When visiting such, it is encouraging to know that one's efforts are backed by the prayers of the loved ones at home ; but it is distressing to know that the character of many is far other than those would wish, or than they probably think it is. One young fellow told me that he did not tell his friends of his illnesses because he did not want to trouble them, and I felt sure he would not hint at his moral delinquencies. Here and there a godly man is to be found, who is as a lump of salt, but they are few and far between; and, alas ! even such too often very sadly deteriorate. The late Mr. Alexander Balfour, of Liverpool, wrote : "Englishmen rapidly deteriorate abroad, and they must return home, else they degenerate." This is, doubtless, true ; but in the many cases

* Mr. H. R. Brown will be remembered by many of our readers as one of our College men. We rejoice that such a worker went out from our midst. The Lord be with him !

where "returning home" is not practicable, God's grace will be found sufficient, if only he be waited upon and trusted. His promises are as valid in India as elsewhere; still the hot-house Christians at home little know what the extremes of trial and temptation in an idolatrous country are. A good man said to me that, without acting on the aggressive, he hoped to stand as a witness for God. I fear for him. One and another before him have thought to shirk the reproach of the cross, and yet live usefully; but the ill-marked line of distinction between them and their neighbours, has gradually been obliterated, and they have been carried away with the stream. Now and then, but very occasionally, a man is met with who is willing to admit that he is dissatisfied with the life he is living. One such told me that he was ashamed of his manner of life; and he mentioned that a few weeks before, when on a sporting expedition, he had shared the tent of a certain major who, morning and evening, read a portion of Scripture, and knelt in prayer. The young fellow said, "I felt miserable when I saw the man do that." My heart went out in love for him, and I pleaded with him to decide for Christ, and we prayed together: but he procrastinated, and said, "I am afraid of what my companions will say." I entreated him not to risk his soul's salvation for fear of man; but in vain. Next morning, after again pleading with him, and getting from him an "I can't," I left him still in bondage.

The vast mass of Europeans in India, whether soldiers, tea-planters, officials, or commercial men, are living un-Christian lives. Should any resent this charge, I would appeal to their neglected Bibles and prayerless lives in support of it. When in Sikkim lately, visiting the men of the Mule Battery, recently engaged against the Thibetans, I went into a tent and got into conversation with the men. One said, "There's not a Christian in our Battery." I said, "That's a serious thing to say"; but he replied, "My father and mother in Yorkshire are real Christians, and I know what I am talking about. I know what a Christian is. I'm not one myself, and there's not one here; there's one teetotaler, but not a Christian." I said, "It's time there were some: who will lead the way?" I found out the teetotaler, and spoke to him of Christ; but he seemed quite satisfied with himself, and with a form of religion. The afternoon I rode into the camp I came upon twenty or thirty men sitting in rows on the grass, with two or three standing in front, as if teaching them; but on making enquiries, I found they were engaged in a gambling game, which they daily play at. The officer in command kindly dispensed with a parade, that I might hold a service, which was well attended. Here, and in other places, I gave away a number of Mr. Spurgeon's sermons, and other good literature, largely through the generosity of Mr. E. G. Glazier, a civilian, who delights to help forward every good work.

It will interest some to know that in two instances I found that hymns had been a source of comfort. A lady, so dangerously ill, that on my first visit I was not allowed to see her, though my voice must have reached her as I prayed with her husband in the verandah, told me, on a second visit, that she had got much comfort in the night from, "Just as I am, without one plea." Poor soul, she needed comfort! There she was, lying in a solitary house in the jungle, seemingly at the point

of death, her husband out of a situation, and her four children far
away in England. The other case was that of a homely Scotch wife,
broken-hearted at her husband's having broken out in drink after two
years of sobriety. On my quoting to her the hymn beginning, "What
a friend we have in Jesus!", she was much touched, and told me that she
had first heard that precious hymn from her boy, who learned it at the
Sabbath-school in Lucknow.

On one occasion I spent a couple of hours with the son of a praying
mother, who was rapidly imbibing infidel principles. After talking and
praying with him, he promised, ere I left, to return to his former practice of regularly reading the Bible. Was this in answer to his mother's
prayers?

At times it seemed manifest that God was directing my steps. At
one time I unexpectedly came across a mother sorrowing over the death
of her son, a young man whom I had met in another part of the country,
and who, I fear, is filling a drunkard's grave. What could I do but
join her in asking his aid who binds up the broken in heart. On another
occasion I visited a planter who had recently lost his wife, living in a
very out-of-the-way place, at a long distance from any centre. His
three affectionate children gathered about my knee, and I sang to them,
and told them of Jesus and his love. When we knelt in prayer the
father joined us. He was completely broken down, and yet, I trust,
helped on his way.

In every place where I stayed the night I was able to read and comment on the Scriptures, and pray.

It is not always an easy matter to arrange for services, but in answer
to prayer doors are opened. In the middle of a week I was at a house
where I wanted to hold a service. I asked the hostess, recently from
Scotland, if she had heard Mr. McNeill preaching. "No," said she,
"he's a Baptist, isn't he?" "No," I said, "a Free-Churchman."
"Oh, I never hear any but Established Church ministers and Episcopalians." This did not seem hopeful for an opening; however, I did
not despair. Next day I met several planters at breakfast, and spoke to
one about a service on the following Sunday. He said, "You can have
my bungalow, but Mrs.—— will not be able to come, as her trap is
away." "Well, could we not have it at her house? Will you ask her?"
"All right, and I'll let you know to-morrow." The answer came that
the lady and her husband were willing, and I at once set about making
it known. We had most of those in the neighbourhood who could
attend, and after the service I received a hearty invitation to return.

On another occasion, when a service I had hoped to hold fell through, I,
being eager not to miss a Sunday, went to a man who I am pretty sure
wished me further, and asked the use of his bungalow. "Well, yes,"
he said, "you can have it, but I won't be present, I am going to So-
and-so; but my assistant will be at home." "Thank you, very much,"
said I, and then proceeded to visit in the neighbourhood, with the result
that we had a very good service, the gentleman himself being present.

The men often look very awkward at these services, and I am not surprised. Think of a number of men who know one another's lives well
enough, brought face to face at one of their own bungalows for a religious service! Of course, they are uneasy.

Here's an odd incident. I remember once announcing a meeting by post-cards, which were not delivered until after it was over. On enquiring of the Post Office babu the reason of the delay, he said, "I thought they were complimentary notices, and that it did not matter, so I sent them next day!" Fortunately, I was not altogether depending upon these notices, for I had been visiting in the neighbourhood, and a good service was held.

In some places, where there were only one or two Europeans, I had meetings for babus. At R. the courts were closed an hour before the usual time, that pleaders and others might attend, and we had a crowded school-room. At another small place, where a meeting for babus had never been held, it was difficult to find chairs for the audience. After one of these meetings, a Hindoo followed me and said, "You have urged us to do what is right, but my difficulty is to *know* what is right." "I think not, my friend," said I. "Though you do not admit it, I fancy your difficulty is to be willing to *do* what is right. If a man really wants to do right, he will not be left in ignorance of what is right." I went on to say, "We have in Jesus Christ a perfect standard." "Yes," said he, "I admit that Christ was a perfect man; but we, too, have our good and great characters." "Such as"—"Well, Ram is one," said he. "Are you prepared to defend all you know of Ram?" "No." "I am prepared to defend all that is recorded of Jesus Christ," said I; "and you admit that you have no fault to find with him. Am I not right, then, in saying that it is not that you cannot find out what *is* right that is your trouble, but that you lack the will to *do* it?" I then sought to set before him what a perfect Saviour Jesus is.

Though glad of interesting opportunities for work amongst native gentlemen, my time was mostly spent with our own countrymen. For months I lived with them, and received not a little hospitality at their hands. Some of my travelling was by rail, but most on horseback, often twenty, thirty, and, on one occasion, forty miles a day, over hill and dale, through jungle, and, in the end of January, for two days, in pouring rain, so that I was drenched through three times. Notwithstanding that I was for nearly two months in the unhealthiest district of India, the Lord spared me in health and from accident.

It would be pleasing to flesh and blood to say smooth and comfortable things of our fellow-countrymen out here, and far be it from me to be other than grateful for all the kindness I have received at their hands. But let any man spend several months yearly in travelling about India, intent on the best interests of his fellows, and eagerly on the look-out for signs of interest in spiritual things, and his heart will be made sorely to ache. The strain on one's spirit is great, and often have I been ready to faint and give up under the trial. But God has marvellously helped me by granting seasons of happy fellowship with himself, when on these long, solitary journeys. After having a wide experience among all classes—planters, railway employés, commercial men, and soldiers— I grieve to say that their moral condition is deplorable, and their spiritual state appalling.

"Oh, that my head were waters, and mine eyes a fountain of tears, that I might weep day and night for the slain of the daughter of my people!"

Group of Orphan Girls at Stockwell Orphanage.

WHEN this magazine reaches our readers, our Orphanage Fête Day will be over and gone. What a day it is when it is fine! Think of some twelve thousand friends coming together, all full of enthusiasm, to help Mr. Spurgeon in his good work! It is a high day also for the children, who greatly enjoy the march past, and the kindly notice of the visitors. No one can estimate the heart-cheer this great and glorious gathering brings to us amid the care of such a service. Ten thousand thanks are hereby presented to all our hearty helpers. The Lord's name be praised, not only for the moneys brought in, but for the love with which every gift is perfumed. Many who are not with us in person remember us with fervent Christian love, and we feel enriched by the blessings which their prayers bring down upon us. Thanks to them all.

To keep our 250 girls and 250 boys in full going order costs a large sum; for we do not starve or stint them. We have no notion of making our Orphanage into a Workhouse with a fine name. We therefore need many liberal gifts. Friends who were not with us on the 19th, please send us your purses if you could not bring us your persons—at least we don't want the purses, but as much out of them as you can afford, for *the Lord's boys and girls!* Is he not the Father of the fatherless?

Throughout the year every want has been supplied right royally, and a large sum has been added to the Foundation Fund. . Our source of income is the source of all things; and with Him there can be no failure, nor even delay. With joy do we put on record our happy experience of "streams of mercy never ceasing," which "call for songs of loudest praise." Our soul doth magnify the Lord, and our spirit hath rejoiced in God our Saviour.

Notices of Books.

The Salt-Cellars. Being a Collection of Proverbs, with Homely Notes thereon. By C. H. SPURGEON. Passmore and Alabaster.

WE have just published our new book, "The Salt-Cellars." It is the first of two volumes, and the second is almost ready. The many years of "John Ploughman's Almanack" are here preserved and arranged so as to make a dictionary of ·proverbs. This work has answered its purpose in relieving the mind of its author during a time of severe pressure. We might call it, "The Recreations of a City Parson." Many an hour, when the heart has been heavy, and the brain weary, we have wandered among the heather and the gorse of these quaint proverbs, and have forgotten our cares awhile. In the judgment of many friends, this new book is sure to command a large sale; and if we prognosticate by the large number subscribed for in the trade, there cannot be much doubt about it. The public will, we trust, serve themselves with our "salt, without prescribing how much." We have all through the book aimed at moral and spiritual results in a cheerful way. We are not here handling the Psalms, nor lecturing after the manner of Ecclesiastes, but we have set in order many Proverbs, and have added interpretations of them. We shall amuse; but we hope, also, to instruct, and to impress. Here we bring our light-armed troops to the front, and our trust is that some may be wounded by an arrow of reed who have escaped the sword of steel. The book is most handsomely got up: the binding is the best that Passmore and Alabaster have yet done. The price is three-and-six.

Plenary Verbal Inspiration of the Scriptures: its Nature, Evidences, Difficulties, and Objections. By J. ANDERSON, M.D. Brighton: D. B. Friend.

To this admirable treatise we wish a very wide circulation, for it ably defends the Plenary Verbal Inspiration of Holy Scripture. We are much pleased with the soundness of the writer upon this foundation doctrine,

and with the clear and decided way in which he defends it. Dr. Anderson asks a correction of our review of his works in our May number. His idea of a future probation for those who quit this life unsaved has *exclusive* reference to the thousands of millions who have never heard the gospel, and not in any way to those who have heard, and have deliberately rejected it. We cannot refuse to insert the correction; but we see no trace of any such teaching in the inspired volume to which Dr. Anderson most properly ascribes such high authority. There is a mystery before us, no doubt, but our God knows how to deal with it. Our notice now refers to the Inspiration book, which is all we could wish it to be.

Blots and Blemishes. The Leadenhall Press, and Simpkin, Marshall, & Co.

WE do not like the peculiar form in which this book is cast, which has a look of irreverence about it; and there are one or two expressions to which we take exception, for they are themselves "blots and blemishes"; but the observations are on the right side of most questions, and are pithy, full of common sense, and piquant. The publishers get up their work well; they are in the front row for good and tasteful printing. We have had a good shilling's-worth of pleasure out of these pages, and we commend them to readers who want something original and racy.

Notes on Superstition and Folk Lore. By JEANIE M. LAING. Introduction by D. H. EDWARDS, F.R.H.S., F.A.S. Edinburgh: John Menzies.

A CURIOUS record of superstitions, which, we trust, are extinct, but which are always ready to revive as gospel light grows dim. This little book has more in it of odd and out-of-the-way lore than we have found in many a costly pretentious volume. It gives no countenance to the silly fears about Friday, spilling salt, sitting down with thirteen, &c., all of which are simply degrading to human beings and wicked in Christians.

The Women Friends of Jesus; or, the Lives and Characters of the Holy Women of Gospel History. By HENRY C. MCCOOK. Hodder and Stoughton.

DR. MCCOOK *can* preach and write. He is observant and poetical, and, with so rich a theme before him, he is at home, and does his best. Every page is alive. Like beds of flowers, his chapters are vivid in colour, and glowing with beauty. This ought to be one of the most popular books in the catalogue of Messrs. Hodder and Stoughton. During the period of religious revival, the women-friends of Jesus have their true successors in the women-workers of the Church, whom may God multiply a thousand-fold! We have lent this book to two or three friends to hear the opinions of sensible, Christian readers, whose judgments have never been perverted by the habitude of professional criticism, and they have all been greatly pleased and edified. Here is a fair specimen of the style of the book:—

"A painting exposed in a shop window attracted my attention. The artist had evidently sought a theme which would enable him to lay a wealth of colour on his canvas. He had chosen a garden scene; and flowers, plants, climbing-vines, the house and window-drapery, even the coat of an old gardener trundling his barrow along a walk, fairly blossomed over with bright tints. A peacock perched upon the garden wall, whose plumage drooped almost to the ground. Near by, the central figure of the sketch, walked a woman gorgeously apparelled from hat to slipper. She held over her head a glaring parasol, and her face was ruddy with health and beauty.

"Has the artist any lesson for me underneath this mass of colour? I pondered. As I looked at flower-beds, growing plants, and climbing-vines, even at the bird's plumage, the effect of the brilliant hues was only pleasant. No sense of repulsion was stirred at the sight of these dumb things, wearing a livery upon which nature had lavished her utmost wealth of colour, and rejoicing seemingly in the same. But as I looked again upon the woman, I was conscious of a feeling of disapprobation and sorrow. Here was a creature with an immortal soul; endowed with power of heart and mind which might have lifted her into a realm of lofty thoughts and spiritual communions, whose holy of holies no beast of the field, nor fowl of the air, nor flower of the garden or woodland, can approach unto! Yet, there she walks, mincing through life, like the woman of Isaiah's picture (ch. iii. 16), a thing of colour alone, and no stability; all glitter, and no gold! Oh! it is pitiful to see an immortal flitting across life with no higher aim and issue than a blossom or a bird!"

The Preacher's Commentary on the Gospel of St. John. One hundred and thirty homiletic sketches. By the REV. GORDON CALTHROP, M.A. Hodder and Stoughton.

SCARCELY a commentary. Some one hundred and thirty interesting topics are selected and treated as themes for discourse. Good—very good. For their purpose, namely, to help preachers to discourses, these condensed summaries of thought are very excellent. We have seen better; but when a work is so full of grace and truth we are not in the humour to set up comparisons. *The Clergyman's Magazine,* in which these sketches first appeared, must have carried manna to many a study and pulpit.

The Temple of Solomon. By THOMAS NEWBERRY. James Nisbet and Co. *Herod's Temple.* By Rev. J. G. KITCHIN. M.A. Church of England Sunday-school Institute.

JUNIOR teachers and senior scholars in any of our evangelical Sunday-schools will find here admirable keys to a technical acquaintance with the Temple buildings severally referred to in Old and New Testament Scriptures. However clear and concise the descriptions, they will not enable anyone to dispense with the wholesome labour of diligent study. We are glad it is so. Grudge not your pains in mastering a subject, for you make more progress and realize more satisfaction when you train yourselves to teach by setting yourselves to learn.

The Threshold of Manhood. A Young Man's Words to Young Men. By W. J. DAWSON. Hodder and Stoughton.

MUCH that is good and telling will be found in these discourses, but there is an undertone which we greatly deprecate. We must reckon the author among those who are against the old faith, though he is not so far gone as many. In some passages we demur to his statements as much as to his opinions. For instance, is this true? We protest that we have neither felt nor seen anything of this Jewish gloom:—"The God Cromwell worshipped was the God of the Hebrews, who was clothed with thunder; the God Milton believed in was the great Taskmaster, in whose eye he sought to live. The age demanded a stern ideal of God to inspire the valour of the battle-field, and the strenuous agonies of renunciation unto death, and it found it in the ancient Scriptures of the Hebrews. And that is the idea of God which still prevails in every land where the Reformation was triumphant—God is still worshipped with fear and trembling. It is from the Hebrew Scriptures preachers take their texts, and it is the Hebrew idea of God which is set before the people. And what is the result? At its highest, life is elevated by a stern ideal of duty; at its lowest, life is crushed into a slavish and joyless round of formality. But the ideal Christ has given us in the parable of the Prodigal Son, or that of Paul, when he says, 'We have not received the spirit of fear, but the spirit of adoption, whereby we cry, Abba, Father'—this is forgotten; and so the joy is taken out of piety, and the sunshine out of life; and instead of being Christians, we are really Jews, permeated with Jewish ideas of God, and forgetting, if not repudiating, the very different idea of God which is set before us by him we call Master."

This statement we utterly deny. If any have a deeper and more overflowing joy than believers in the grand old faith, we have not yet come across them. The more closely we keep to the old orthodoxy, the more wells of comfort and joy do we see springing up around us.

Blackie's Modern Cyclopædia of Universal Information. Edited by CHARLES ANNANDALE, M.A., LL.D. Blackie and Son. Vols. I. and II.

THIS cyclopædia, in eight compact volumes, consists of concise and tersely written articles. It must be of great use to a man who cannot buy the larger cyclopædia, and even to one who can. It is a library in itself, and contains something upon everything: history, geography, biography, literature, science, politics, commerce, all have their place. At six shillings a volume it is cheap. We are reminded by this work of those country shops where they sell everything, from cheese to corsets, from a box-iron to a wedding-cake. A wag once asked for a pennyworth of tinder at one of these emporiums, and to his discomfiture it was presented to him, the ingenious shopman having manufactured it in no time. You have only to "enquire within," and this work will tell you about as much on any subject as an ordinary reader will need to know. We have only two volumes out of eight; but the publishers are sure to complete the work in a style equal to its first portion.

Fifteen Hundred Facts and Similes for Sermons and Addresses. By J. F. B. TINLING, B.A. Hodder & Stoughton.

A COLLECTION of illustrations which will be useful to those who know how to weave them into their instructions. Some fools are too dignified to condescend to tell a story; but wise men tell a great many, and are therefore glad to meet with new ones worth the telling. We do not believe the assertion of De Quincey, that "all anecdotes are false"; though we fear that many are home-made, and others are considerably tinkered. Surely there are plenty of instructive incidents which are genuine: the most of those which are here collected are of that sort. Mr. Tinling has made a fine selection. Many of the similes will be quite new to the general reader: and they are so well arranged and indexed, that their value for practical purposes will be greatly enhanced. This is a good minister's book. Make your pastor a present of it.

To the Lions. A Tale of the Early Christians. By the Rev. ALFRED J. CHURCH, M.A. Seeley and Co.

THIS story might be described as "No fiction"; for the like of it has been transacted a thousand times over. It is a fine classical narrative of the persecutions in the days of Trajan and Pliny; it has enough of plot in it to win the attention, and no more. We can introduce it to our readers without fear of creating an appetite for novels. May the spirit of those who faced the lions for the Lord 'Jesus return into our churches!

An Account of Missionary Success in the Island of Formosa : published in London in 1680, and now reprinted with copious Appendices. By Rev. W. CAMPBELL, F.R.G.S. Trübner.

Two beautifully printed volumes. When the Dutch possessed Formosa, some two hundred and fifty years ago, there were flourishing Christian churches in the island: of this religious movement we have here a quaint, methodical, and somewhat dreary record, adorned with the regulation classical effigies of the Puritan period. Our Dutch friends of the olden time evidently aimed at the spread of the 'Reformed faith in connection with their trade-settlement in Formosa; and they would seem to have gone about it in a very orderly ecclesiastical manner—a manner which had more of the form of godliness in it than of the power, though it was not utterly devoid of that latter necessary. Unfortunately the Dutch were expelled by the Chinese, and their work in the island was stamped out by persecution. It is a curious record. We always feel our interest aroused when we come across anything Dutch: it has an air of the old world, and a touch of quaint, dignified homeliness which gives pleasure. Something of this clings even to the story of the Dutch preachers in Formosa.

We trust that the present endeavours of our Presbyterian friends will be more permanent than those of former centuries; indeed, rich promise is with both the Canadian and English efforts. Formosa will, by this work of Mr. Campbell, be made better known to the circle of believers to whom all missionary work is dear. The observation which we quote from these volumes is very much to our mind :—"There is need for giving much greater prominence to the written Word—less answering of heathen objections, of moral discourse, and even of mere expounding; and more, much more, prayerful selection of, and clear distinct reading of God's own message to sinful men."

Garenganze ; or, Seven Years' Pioneer Mission Work in Central Africa. By FRED. S. ARNOT. Hawkins.

WHAT a world this Africa is! Here is a missionary pioneering for seven years in a region which seems far removed from the Congo, and all other missionized regions. We read this volume with the conviction that the church must wake up, and send out a hundred men where she has hitherto sent only one. This is a valuable addition to the missionary literature of the Dark Continent, and another blow at the Arab rule, which seems to be Satan incarnate. We are half inclined to apologize to the foul fiend for making the comparison; for in reading such a fact as that which follows our blood boils :—"Large numbers of slaves are brought into the capital every year by returning war parties, and are sold chiefly to Arab traders from Zanzibar, and to Ovimbunden traders from Bihé. Strong young men have been sold for ten or twelve yards of cotton cloth. Children able to walk are perhaps worth a little, but infants are considered a drug in the market, and it is generally to the advantage of the slave-dealers to make away with them. They will not often allow a mother to carry her own child, thinking to employ her more profitably by making her carry ivory, or food; and so these little ones are generally cast out to the hyenas, or thrown into the rivers."

Harold's Bride. A Tale, by A. L. O. E. Nelson and Sons.

WOMAN'S work in an Indian village: an account of the trials of missionary life, written by a devoted labourer. Capital reading for Zenana working parties.

The Cry of Christendom for a Divine Eirenikon. A Plea, with all the Churches, for the Rights of the People, Christianity and Peace. R. D. Dickinson.

OUR author's protest against Popery and Sacramentarianism leads him so far, that he discards both Baptism and the Lord's Supper. Here we cannot follow him, neither do we see any force in the arguments with which he supports his views; yet it is not to be marvelled at, that the revolting notions which turn the two ordinances into a sort of religious witchcraft should drive men to doubt the perpetuity of the ordinances themselves. To us it seems impossible to erase these two instructive rites from the teaching and example of our Lord and his apostles. Our hatred of ceremonialism would lead us to overlook them if we could, but we dare not be wiser than what is written.

Scotland's Part and Place in the Revolution of 1688. By CHARLES G. M'CRIE. Edinburgh : Elliot.

A VERY instructive piece of history, throwing light upon many things in connection with the Scotch churches. We confess to much enlightenment by this record.

The Scripture Mother's Help. By Mrs. NEW. Houlston and Sons.

CARDS in a box. Questions on Evangelical truth, and their answers. Intended to be used on Sundays. They do not look to us very fascinating, but the proof of every pudding is in the eating : they may be so handled as to interest children, for we know a case in which it has been done. Price two shillings.

Our Celestial Home. An Astronomer's View of Heaven. By JERMAIN G. PORTER, A.M., Director of the Cincinnati Observatory. Nisbet & Co.

A BOOK in blue, with many stars glittering upon it. It deals with the question of *Where is heaven?* and handles it very reasonably. After reading the book, we do not see that we know any more about the matter in hand than when we first opened it. Perhaps this is our stupidity ; perhaps not. At any rate, Mr. Porter does not

bamboozle us with vain speculations ; but he writes soberly, with wide astronomical knowledge, and with reverent mind towards the Word of the Lord. The author does not know *where* heaven is, nor do we. So far as it is a place, we must wait till we get there before we shall learn its longitude and latitude ; but we know *with whom* it is, and we therefore rejoice in it, because we shall be "for ever with the Lord."

Scripture Animals, and the Lessons Taught by Them. By the late Rev. RICHARD NEWTON, D.D. Nisbet.

Bible Animals (same book). Oliphant, Anderson, and Ferrier.

Two editions of this last of Dr. Richard Newton's works for children. Like a certain pure tea, they are "always good alike." Dr. Newton was made on purpose to preach to children, and he answered to his Maker's design admirably. Everything of Richard Newton's should be in the hand of every child unless it is a downright idiot. Nisbet's edition, at 2s. 6d., has fine clear type, good for the eyes ; Oliphant's, at 1s. 6d., is in small print ; but then it has pictures. Either of them is cheap. As a spectacle-wearing man, the editor of *The Sword and the Trowel* gives his verdict for Nisbet ; but if he were younger, he would save his shilling, and deal with Oliphant. "How happy could I be with either ! "

An Old Pastor's Testimony ; or, Witnessing for God and Truth, upon his Seventy-eighth Birthday. By DAVID A. DOUDNEY, D.D. Book Society.

IT is strengthening to read the witness of an old man concerning the faithfulness of the Lord his God. For many a year Dr. Doudney has been among our beloved friends. He is a man of a choice spirit ; there are few like him. He has now been editor of the "Gospel Magazine" for fifty years ; and has reached the ripe age of seventy-eight. His words will be very sweet to those who look not for the delicacies of poetry and philosophy, but for the solid fare of living testimony to the living God. Many plain believers will feast on this testimony. The Lord bless the writer of it !

Among the Palms; or, Stories of Sierra Leone and its Missions. By ROBERT BREWIN. Andrew Crombie.

ONLY one shilling. Strikingly full of detail. Genuine missionary stories. *Buy it at once.*

Stories for Bible Readers. By J. L. NYE. Sunday School Union.

WHEN so many are trampling on the Old Book, or picking it to pieces with their critical beaks, we are glad to meet with an author who does it honour, by narrating facts concerning its value and influence. True, the stories are rather worn; but they will be new to new readers, and they are sure to do them real good. A verse on the opening page is worth copying—

"Study it carefully;
Think of it prayerfully;
Deep in thy heart let its precepts dwell;
Slight not its history;
Ponder its mystery;
None can e'er prize it too fondly or well."

Some Exhibition of God's Power to Save, and of his Enemies' Hatred: being the Report of the Work of the Salvation Army, in France and Switzerland, in 1888. By Maréchale BOOTH-CLIBBORN and Colonel BOOTH-CLIBBORN.

Experiences of a Slum Pioneer. International Headquarters, 101, Queen Victoria Street.

THE literary work of the Salvation Army is exceedingly well done: the engravings are remarkably telling, and the writing is always lively. These two books plead well for their work, and as they are only twopence each, and yet profusely illustrated, they will have a wide sale.

Young Plants and Polished Corners; or, Nature in the Light of the Bible. By CHARLES HEWITSON NASH, M.A. A Book for Sons and Daughters. Nisbet and Co.

MR. NASH has a dash of poetry in his style, and this makes his pages pleasant. We notice a naturalness and simplicity in his language which will commend him to our sons and daughters; and better still, he has a fulness of gospel truth which commends him to our conscience. We know our

neighbour as a man after our own heart, and we wish him good success in his endeavours to bless our youth.

The Homes, Haunts, and Battle-fields of the Covenanters. By A. B. TODD. Edinburgh: James Gemmell.

WE thought we had reviewed and highly commended, both the first and second volumes of this most pleasing work. We feel as fascinated with these pages as in former days we were with Sir Walter Scott; but the charm is not that of a minstrel's words, but of holy fact and gracious truth. Oh, for another twenty years of the Covenanters! This generation builds their sepulchres, but acts towards their testimony as their persecutors acted towards the men themselves. Mr. Todd is a literary "Old Mortality," and diligently keeps alive the memories of the brave men of God. Purchase and read his books, and their influence will be salutary and strengthening. There is a denomination in America called Hard-shelled Baptists; but in this country few have any shell at all. The Covenanters were Hard-shelled Presbyterians. Oh, for a second edition of the breed! There will have to be a Disruption *from* the Free Church before long if any men remain of the old stock.

The Saving Spirit. What the Spirit of God does for the Sinner, and what the Sinner must do for himself in the whole matter of Salvation. By Rev. JOHN HARRIES. Elliot Stock.

WITH very much that Mr. Harries has to say upon the blessed Spirit we heartily agree, but we cannot think that he succeeds in trying to define the exact relation of the Spirit to the will of man. Perhaps he gets on as well as anybody else, for no one knows much about it. If we were to attempt to define the mysteries of birth, we should flounder into the deeps of controversy; and it is much the same when we offer to define the divine and the human in conversion. To us it is enough to know that he worketh in us to will, and to do, and therefore we both will and do. Our Methodist friends will enjoy the book, and take no exception to it. In many respects it is good and profitable.

God in Business. By H. J. LATHAM.
Nisbet and Co.

THIS is a very telling book upon a
practical subject; but the fact that it
contains a story about C. H. Spurgeon,
which is quite new to the said C. H. S.,
and for which, so far as he knows,
there is not one iota of foundation,
leads us to fear that more of the
"facts" stated are of an apocryphal
character. This is a great pity; pity
it is that it is not true.

The Triumph of Grace over Sin. By
the Rev. ALEXANDER FORBES, M.A.
Hamilton, Adams, and Co.

A TREATISE which is likely to be of
much service to seekers, and to be a
sweet morsel to all who love the doctrines of grace. It has already had a
large sale, and deserves a larger one.

Living Springs. By the Rev. HENRY
BONE. T. Woolmer.

MR. BONE's little book is full of marrow. He has a rich, racy way with
him: he deserves to be read, for he
well repays his reader. Here are some
tit-bits from a short paper on "The
Family Altar": such jewels abound
through all his pages :—
"It was once surmised, in the years
long past, that beneath the hearthstone
of many a dwelling some sacred
treasure lay. It is so yet, if the altar
be built upon the hearthstone. Divine
favour, immutable promise, sacred
purpose, sufficient grace, lie hidden
there."
"It is said that one of our missionaries, conducting Sir A. Gordon on
to a lofty hill in Fiji, said to the illustrious Governor, pointing to the town
beneath, 'There is not a family in that
town that will not close this day with
the Bible and prayer.' Do we wonder
at the success of that beautiful little
colony? Could that be said of any
village, even much less town, in the
kingdom? Better a home without a
roof, without bread, without fire, without light, than a home without God.
Family devotion becomes a chain that
links the home to heaven."
"In some of the old country mansions visitors are shown the room
where once slept the good Queen Bess,
Cromwell, or George. But the home

consecrated entirely to the King of
kings is better far."
"My 'acquaintances' should be
those who would join with me and mine
in the morning and evening sacrifice.
Prayer must not be set aside because
there is 'a party' to-night. It is the
better opportunity for conducting it.
The altar and the Bible would be out of
place, I think, in the midst of a ball.
Which shall it be, then, *no ball*, or *no
Bible?* 'Zacchæus, . . . to-day I must
abide at thy house.' No, Lord, not to-
day; we have a party; there will be
dancing—quite a social evening."
"In some of the old castles there
was a subterranean passage, by which
the family went from the house to the
chapel. So a hidden way is found
from the home of prayer to the church,
and to the life of earnest service."

*Do Something for Jesus: a Book for
Sunday - school Teachers, Church
Members, and the Young in general.*
By Rev. E. BALLEY. Tunbridge
Wells: A. K. Baldwin.

VERY good indeed. An edition at a
penny should be brought out by the
Sunday-school Union and scattered by
thousands. It should not be confined
to the local circulation which renders
it needful to charge fourpence for it;
for it is too good to be read by the few
only.

A Physician's Sermon to Young Men.
By WILLIAM PRATT. Ballière, Tin-
dall and Cox.
Forbidden Fruit for Young Men. By
MAJOR SETON CHURCHILL. James
Nisbet and Co.

AN earnest tract and a more elaborate
essay, in both of which delicate subjects
are decorously handled. The bud and
bloom of manhood are rife with temptation; it is well, therefore, for our
youngsters, while breathing the atmosphere of social purity, to master
the codes of health and the counsels
for longevity. Moses, the servant of
the Lord, spoke sharply in a postscript to his swan-song (Deut. xxxii.);
"*It is not a vain thing for you; because
it is your life: and through this thing
ye shall prolong your days in the land.*"
No expression of ours can be more
emphatic.

Gideon Strong, Plebeian. By SILAS HOCKING. Andrew Crombie.

A SENSIBLE story of a young fellow who was so wicked as to be "a plebeian by birth," and to entertain opinions, on matters social and political, very divergent from those of the squire and the parson. Worse still, he dared to open his mouth for the right and the true. How he had to learn the meaning of "justices' justice," and to quit the village, is very well told. We suspect it is the experience of many a village Hampden.

"By a Way she Knew not." By the AUTHOR of "The Bairns." Hodder and Stoughton.

"THE way" here described is certainly a strange one. The tempests and tossings are many, but the vessel at last enters the desired haven.

Little Miss Wardlaw. By LOUISA M. GRAY. Nelson and Sons.

A HIGH-SPIRITED girl, by self-will, gets into trouble, and through trouble is led to Christ. A well-told story: good for headstrong young ladies.

Notes.

MY name appears upon the Father Damien Committee; but incorrectly. The objects aimed at in connection with the memory of that philanthropic hero are most excellent; but they can be effectively carried out by the many other gentlemen selected by the Prince of Wales. I can honestly say that I am not able to do more than I have to do already. I have a strong objection to bearing a nominal office, and taking credit and responsibility for doing what I am unable to do; and therefore I declined the position so kindly allotted to me.

We may all thank God that Father Damien, who deserves high honour, is not the only one who has heroically devoted himself to live and die among the lepers. Our Moravian brethren did this long ago, and others are still doing it. If ten thousand persons acted thus heroically, it would not diminish the honour due to each self-sacrificing lover of his race; and it would only increase the necessity to deal with the disease itself, which is still so fearfully prevalent in various parts of the world, and is not altogether absent even from this favoured island. Leprosy has been regarded as hopeless until now, but by God's grace the minds of physicians may be guided to a cure. Much has been done in late years to relieve pain, and some of the deadliest of pests have been subdued; and we therefore trust that our gracious God may remove this plague also. The design of bringing medical thought and experience to bear upon it is a Christlike one; and therefore this *Lepers' Friend Society* deserves the best aid of Christian people everywhere.—C.H.S.

When friends read such a heading as "Mr. Spurgeon in the Law Courts," they may suppose that we are going to law with somebody. Nothing can be more contrary to our mind. The fact is that, when moneys are left to the Orphanage, the wills are sometimes so complicated that executors dare not act except as a Court of Law directs, and in such cases the Trustees of the Orphanage may be compelled to be parties to the suit; not with the view of getting anything by litigation, but simply to obtain an authoritative interpretation of doubtful codicils. Friends had better give their money while they live. No one can tell the worry that one contested will brought upon the President of the Orphanage for years. It is all over now; but it tried him very sorely to know what to do.

The meetings of the Surrey and Middlesex Baptist Association, held on *May* 21, came just too late for our June magazine. They took place at *Brentford*, and were of a very hearty and spiritual character. The members of the Association are of one heart and of one soul in the things of God; some of them have suffered much to maintain the truth, and keep themselves clear of the deadly errors of the period. It is true that many of the churches are poor, and little esteemed among men; but they are faithful, and for this reason our heart is knit to them. Their confession of faith is not hidden in a corner, nor looked upon as a chain; but the gospel of the grace of God is that which they unite in holding and proclaiming. *Mr. Hockey*, the Moderator, conducted the business with a happy geniality, when, in the morning, the brethren looked about them to see what they could do for the spread of the Redeemer's kingdom. In the afternoon the sermon was listened to by a crowded audience. We feel happy to be numbered with a set of brethren among whom the evil spirit of unbelief is not courted and honoured. All the proceedings of the day had in them the heartiness which belonged to Baptists of the old school, who were evangelical not in name only, but in deed and of a truth. Here is provided for the faithful a city of refuge, where they can enjoy Christian association without sacrificing their consciences by fellowship with that which they do not believe. The day will come when those who think they can repair a house which has no foundations will see the wisdom of quitting it altogether. All along we have seen that to come out from association with questionable doctrines is the only possible solution of a difficulty which, however it may be denied, is not to be trifled with by those who are conscious of its terrible reality.

On *Tuesday evening*, May 28, between 500 and 600 of the pastors and officers of metropolitan churches connected with the Pastors' College Evangelical Association met at the Tabernacle for prayer and conference. There was no pre-arrangement as to speakers, but every brother who rose, or was asked to speak, seemed to have just the right word given to him. All were moved to consider the relationship of the Holy Spirit to ourselves and our work. The brief addresses by Pastors J. A. Spurgeon, J. Douglas, M.A., W. Williams, and F. H. White, were interwoven with prayer and praise, and the meeting was closed with a short sermon by C. H. S. on the passage, "Be not drunk with wine, wherein is excess; but be filled with the Spirit." Altogether, the meeting was one that will long be remembered. From many quarters the most enthusiastic thanks for the meeting have been sent in, and it strikes us that a repetition would be most useful. Some other church will perhaps invite the brethren.

On *Tuesday, June 4*, Mr. Spurgeon preached in the afternoon, at 3 o'clock, at Collingwood Street, New Cut. Mr. T. A. Denny, and Mr. R. K. Causton, M.P., assisted. It was a real working-class congregation. The Brothers Young are doing a remarkable work in that dark neighbourhood: workingmen preaching to working-men in their own style. This is as it should be. They have the fervour of the Salvation Army, combined with solid doctrine: sinners are saved, and a body of earnest believers trained to service.

Mr. S. presided at a tea, with some sixty of the door-keepers and pew-openers of the Tabernacle, at six. These kind friends were thanked for their hearty, self-denying services, and asked to suggest improvements. Some very sensible suggestions were offered. Mr. Higgs and Mr. Hall, the deacons who superintend worship arrangements, were introduced to the workers, and received with hearty goodwill. The brethren were urged to use their office well, and so to treat all comers that they would be in a fit condition to hear the Word preached without distraction. The position is a very arduous and unthankful one, but the Lord can be greatly honoured in it. It was a pleasure to meet this set of earnest men, and to mark the enthusiasm with which they devote themselves to helping the Pastor, by watching over the crowds who throng our house of prayer. Our friends and hearers should help to make this work as light as possible.

At half-past 7, the Pastor presided at a meeting for hearing a selection of the old fugal tunes. Mr. Courtnay brought with

him a very capital choir, to whom we are very grateful. The announcement of the meeting gathered together a very large number of friends. As the meeting went on, great enthusiasm was apparent, and the old tunes were taken up with hearty spirit. Mr. Spurgeon spoke between the various tunes, which were Cranbrook, America, Derby, Calcutta, Nativity, Hampshire, Lonsdale, Praise, and Refuge. No one wishes these tunes to be the staple of our psalmody; but we ask to be allowed to enjoy them occasionally, and to let them have a fair field. The gist of what was said by Mr. Spurgeon will be found in the notes which we subjoin. The old men who remembered these tunes in their younger days were present in great force, and were moved to tears; while those whose tastes will not allow them to praise were forced to confess the power which this despised music has over the souls of men.

Fugal tunes have been sneered at because of the ridiculous effects which might be produced by the repetitions of certain parts of a line. Absurd incidents may have happened; but we do not believe a tithe of the silly stories which are hawked about. They were made up by foolish persons, who had nothing better to do. When an accident does occur, it is the fault of the person who was so unwise as to put the wrong music to the hymn. Ludicrous results may follow from the misuse of a tune which has no repeats, as, for instance, in the admirable tune Darwells. Should it be sung to the hymn which has the line, "The year of Jubilee is come," the break in the tune would make the congregation seem to say, "Billy is come." In any form of singing, common-sense must be used, or it will certainly turn out that fools will sing foolishly. The present tunes are, many of them, excellent, but they are often rattled through at a pace which looks as if the leader said, "We have in hand the task of praising God; let us knock it off as sharp as we can." There is no time to drink in the spirit of the song: everything is done at a gallop. The fugal tune enables you to taste the words, and emphasize them. There are, at least, some hymns in which a repetition would naturally suggest itself to any devout mind, and the more natural we can be the better.

Fugal tunes require to be well learned and practised; and so much the better. A congregation always confined to baby tunes is apt to follow mechanically, especially if an organ not only leads them, but does most of the business for them. Singing which will exercise the people in tone and time is all the more likely to arouse attention and care. Of course, the tune must not be too difficult; and that these are not of that kind is evident from the fact that they were once so popular, and so earnestly taken up. Modern music has nothing whereof to glory while it gives us the same tune for a funeral and a wedding: "The voice that breathed 'o'er Eden" is sung to have the same strain as "Brief life is here our portion." One has only to criticize the new as the old has been criticized, and plenty of laughable anecdotes will be forthcoming.

Mr. John Curwen said: "If I may again plead for variety, while keeping within the range of what is practical, I should ask for the occasional use of the fugal form—that is, of the entering of voices one after the other. Few musical forms better express the rising emotion of a multitude than this. The first psalmodists of the Reformation wrote many tunes in this shape."

Rev. E. D. Ford, of Manchester, wrote: "I especially like what you say as to the total banishment of repeats and fugal passages. In that direction modern usage has taken all the life out of our psalmody. The fact is that, under the new mode of administration, our singing is becoming a bore instead of a blessing. Grand old tunes of the funereal cast are hurried through like jigs; and new ones of the humdrum type are introduced, utterly destitute of melody, with nothing but their harmonies to recommend them, and those harmonies rarely filled in anywhere save in the note-book."

Our departed friend, Rev. D. Katterns, in addressing the congregation at the laying of the foundation-stone of the Baptist Chapel at Stepney Green, said: "He congratulated the pastor and people upon the hearty manner in which they joined in the singing. He thought that such tunes as Nativity had been forgotten, but from the hearty way in which all joined in, he was mistaken. It was such singing as must have greeted the ears of Wesley and Whitefield at their great open-air gatherings, and was obtained only by consulting the tastes of the people."

Much more was said by the Chairman, but we have no room for it. There is no use in disputing concerning tastes in music, or in anything else; and as this is a matter of taste, all we ask for is a little candour, and as much freedom for the old fashion as for the new. At any rate, the Chairman takes that liberty. He announced his hope and expectation that before long another evening could be given to the same kind of sacred song. May we all be there to hear!

On *Thursday evening, June 6*, Mr. Spurgeon preached a sermon for sailors in connection with the British and Foreign Sailors' Society. A contingent of mariners from the East was present, with a regiment of Scandinavians. The sermon will be printed as soon as time can be found for passing it through the press. Our excellent and enthusiastic friend, Mr. Matthews, the Secretary of the Society, wants to give it away by tens of thousands. Any sums sent to us for that purpose shall be remitted to him. We have been much cheered of late by meeting with one and another who were blessed by our North Sea Fishery Work years ago, when we gave the vessels a

Communion Service. Mr. Mather's much greater work has risen out of it, and has gone far, far beyond it. The Lord bless the men, whether of Grimsby or London, or any other port; and may his blessing rest on all attempts to do them good!

COLLEGE.—Mr. L. S. Steedman has been accepted by the Baptist Home Missionary Society of Scotland, and placed in charge of the islands of Eday and Sanday, Orkney. He has been in Orkney already some six months, filling a vacancy. Mr. R. B. Morrison has gone to Bournemouth, to superintend the work in the hall erected by our Brother Wainwright's friends.

Mr. R. Yeatman, who sailed for Canada a little while ago, has settled at Minnedosa, Manitoba. Mr. C. Joseph is leaving Birmingham, having accepted the unanimous invitation of the church at Lake Road, Portsmouth. Mr. C. Chambers, late of Perth, has become one of the Travelling Secretaries of the Baptist Total Abstinence Association.

On *Friday, June 14*, the summer session of the College was formally closed by the students spending the day at "Westwood." So many brethren have lately completed their course, that our numbers have been greatly reduced. We have therefore accepted a considerable number of men, who will come to us in August, when our students return from their holidays. It will be useless for candidates to apply for some time to come, as we are not likely to be able to receive any more before August next year.

Brethren who think of competing for the prizes for the *essays upon the Sabbath* may be glad to know that no limit is assigned to the length of their papers.

Thinking that our readers would like to see the poetical message that our venerable friend, Professor Rogers, sent to the Conference, we insert it here. We are happy to say that the Grand Old Tutor remains in fine condition, though he has entered upon his 91st year.

Dear Brethren, though unseen by sense
I'm with you at your Conference:
And surely more may claim to be
Present with you, than you with me.

I'm with you, when with soul intent,
You listen to the President!
And marvel at the wondrous store
Beyond what you had heard before.

I'm with you in some humble place,
When prostrate at the throne of grace;
And aid your anthems as they rise
To join the songs above the skies.

I'm with you when in converse sweet,
Your holy aspirations meet,
And "suddenly, with one accord,"
Are in the presence of your Lord.

I'm with you, when the joyful sound
Of gospel grace moves all around;
And when with genuine grief of mind
You mourn for those you leave behind.

:I'm with you, as an unseen guest,
"When present at the sacred feast :
And none who doubt my right t'appear
·Can hinder me from being there !

:I'm with you, when with hand in hand,
You form one consecrated band,
And one electric glow of soul
'Unites and animates the whole.

And when you to your homes repair,
I still am present with you there :
For why should not such joy be given,
·When old on earth, or young in heaven?

GEO. ROGERS.

EVANGELISTS.—In sending a thankoffering of £60 for *Messrs. Fullerton and Smith's*
services, Dr. Barnardo writes :—

"My dear Friend,—I have tried, during
the last few days, to get a moment in which
:to write to you to acknowledge the very deep
debt under which you have placed us all at
the Edinburgh Castle, through the visit of
the beloved brethren, Messrs. Fullerton and
Smith. If I say that we have *all* been refreshed and stirred up to greater earnestness, that numbers of backsliders have been
drawn to the feet of Christ, and that a great
many of the unconverted have become new
creatures in Christ Jesus, you will understand that the surest proofs of a divine work
have been graciously given of God, as the
result of our brethren's sanctified labours.
I cannot say all I would of them, but in a
word I must say this—they have endeared
themselves greatly to us all. They are
lovable, simple-minded, godly men, consecrated to the holy task of winning souls.
They seem to think nothing of themselves.
'The only pain we had during their visit was
at *parting*. I would fain have kept them
altogether with us, and so have robbed
you, if I could ! But you know better than
I do how vain any such attempt would be.
Coming to Stepney at a time when I was
greatly harassed and pressed with outside
public affairs, their visit was a very special
relief and comfort to my mind, and I personally received not a little good from
fellowship with them."

During the past month, our brethren have
been at Kilburn Hall and Bath Street
Chapel, Poplar. On Saturdays and Sundays
:in July, they are to be at the Polytechnic,
Regent Street, and they will take week-
evening services at Falcon Square Chapel
and Thornton Heath.

Mr. Burnham has been for a voyage up
the Baltic, which has been very beneficial to
his health.

Mr. Harmer was at Commercial Street,
Whitechapel, for the first half of June. A
good number gathered at the open-air
services, and listened to the Word preached
and sung. It is a hard soil both for the
pastor and the evangelist ; but the Lord can
give a harvest even there. Mr. Harmer has
since been to Dartford ; and this month he
goes again, with *Mr. Chamberlain,* to
Crewkerne.

Mr. Harrison paid another visit to Mr.
Charrington's Hall from June 9 to 13. He
is to hold tent-services at Clapton from June
30 to July 10.

Mr. Parker has held missions at Gordon
Road, Peckham, and Waltham Abbey,
during the past month.

Mr. Spurgeon hopes to visit the island of
Guernsey, July 9 to 11, to serve the newly-
formed church under Mr. Snell.

ORPHANAGE.—The Orphan Choir visited
the Channel Islands at the end of May.
Successful services and meetings were
conducted in Jersey and Guernsey. Our
brethren in both places were cheered and
helped by the visit. Applications from
friends who can arrange meetings for the
Orphanage, to be held in the coming season,
should be sent to Mr. Charlesworth as early
as possible.

The Annual Festival, on *June* 19, was a
great success, for which, may the Lord be
praised ! The weather was all that could
be desired ; the crowd was larger than ever,
between ten and eleven thousand persons
having been admitted during the day ; and
the total receipts amounted to about £1,200.
Everybody seemed to be there with loving
hearts and generous hands. James Stiff,
Esq., presided at the afternoon public
meeting, when the President, and the Revs.
John McNeill, J. B. Meharry, and G. D.
Hooper spoke ; and Pastor W. Williams, in
the name of the ministers educated in the
College, and a few private friends, presented to Mr. Charlesworth £50, and an
illuminated address congratulating him
upon his Jubilee, and the completion of
20 years' service as Head Master of the
Orphanage. The President's verdict was—
"It serves him right."

While this meeting was going on in the
open-air, three other gatherings were
crowding our three large halls. There were
Mr. Walter Mayers with a Service of Song
by Dr. Barnardo's boys, and our own bell-
ringers and choir delighting their enthusiastic audiences. Even then, there were
bands of visitors who could not find standing room at any of the meetings, but were
content to survey the houses, and peram-
bulate the grounds.

At the evening meeting, the Vice-President, J. A. Spurgeon, occupied the chair,
and addresses were delivered by the Revs.
John Bond, E. H. Ellis, E. Roberts, W.
Cuff, and W. Stott ; and the President, on
behalf of the Trustees, presented Mr.
Charlesworth with his portrait, suitably
framed and inscribed. To Mr. Hinchliff,
the honorary dentist, the Trustees presented *The Treasury of David.* Mr. Spurgeon thanked this generous gentleman in
warm terms. For those who could not
get near enough to hear the speeches, there
was plenty to interest them in the children's

processions, singing, reciting, handbell-ringing, musical drill, &c. The band of Highland pipers from Dr. Barnardo's Homes, the brass band lent by the same kind friend, the music by the Southwark Choral Society, under the leadership of Mr. John Courtnay, and the illumination of the grounds when the shades of evening fell, all added to the enjoyment of the visitors. To all who helped in any way to secure the success of the day's proceedings we desire to express our heartiest thanks.

The President seemed to shake hands *ad infinitum*, and the next day he felt as if he had been chopped up into small pieces, and could not put himself together again. A paper describes him as having lost all his friends by his action concerning the "Down-Grade," but assuredly, when he was struggling as for life itself among the thousands who pressed to grasp his hand, things wore a very different complexion. It will be time to pity him when God forsakes him. Till then, let no man's heart fail him, for the battle is the Lord's.

The Report of the Orphanage will be inserted in the August number of *The Sword and the Trowel*.

The Orphanage excursion to Herne Bay will take place on *Tuesday, July 9*. Friends wishing to accompany the party can obtain particulars on application to the Orphanage.

The holidays commence on *July* 16, and we shall be glad to hear from friends who can receive either boys or girls who have no relatives to take them. We pay the railway fare, if necessary. Kindly address your letter, Head Master, Stockwell Orphanage, London.

COLPORTAGE.—The secretary desires us to call our readers' special attention to the Annual Report, which is given in full with the present number of the magazine.

PERSONAL NOTE.—A country minister writes:—" A few weeks ago, as I was going from door to door exchanging your sermons, which I lend about, I called upon a woman who showed me a letter from her son in London, by which I judged that he had begun to realize his state as ' without God.' I said, ' This young man needs a little help. If you will allow me, I will send him Spurgeon's *All of Grace:*' and I did, his mother paying for it. It went from the publishers, and took him greatly by surprise. He read it, and it was used of God to lead him to Jesus by faith. He is now happy in the Lord, and has since confessed Christ in baptism."

Baptisms at Metropolitan Tabernacle :— May 30, twenty-six.

𝕻astors' 𝕮ollege, 𝕸etropolitan 𝕿abernacle.

Statement of Receipts from May 15th to June 14th, 1889.

	£	s.	d.
Subscription from Faversham Baptist Chapel, per Pastor C. A. Slack	0	10	0
Part collection at Broad Street Chapel, Ross, per Pastor W. A. Wicks	1	1	0
Mr. Robert Miller	10	10	0
Collection at St. Ann's Road Baptist Chapel, Brixton, per Pastor W. Sullivan	1	1	6
Pastor J. J. Irving, Illinois	0	10	0
Mr. and Mrs. W. H. Haydon	5	5	0
Collection at Romney Street Chapel, Westminster, per Pastor G. Davies	1	5	0
Mr. A. Rhodes	0	5	0
Rev. W. Y. Fullerton	5	5	0
Balance of Residuary Estate of the late C. W. Dalton	4	7	11
Readers of " The Christian," per Messrs. Morgan and Scott	0	15	0
Rev. Jno. Jackson	2	2	0
Mr. W. S. Cowell	2	0	0
Mr. J. E. Colvin	5	0	0
Mrs. Salt	0	5	0
Sir Donald Currie, M.P.	5	0	0
Mrs. Hislop	1	0	0
Tenth	2	10	0
Rev. R. Taylor, Norwood	3	3	0
Miss Lillie Petter	5	0	0
Mrs. Mills	5	0	0
Mr. W. G. Nash	5	0	0
Mr. Henry Hayward	5	5	0
Mr. G. E. Elvin	2	2	0
Mr. James Toller	2	2	0
Mr. W. H. Seagrave	5	0	0
Mr. G. Kingerlee	1	0	0
Collected by teachers and children at the Almshouses Sunday-school	4	10	0

	£	s.	d.
M. W. R.	1	1	0
A brother who desires to do all things Scripturally	1	0	0
Mr. Frank Dodwell	0	10	0
Mrs. Johnson	1	0	0
Miss Rickwood	0	2	0
A Halesworth friend	0	5	0
Mrs. Matthews	0	10	0
Mr. William Buchan	0	10	0
Mrs. S. Dunn	0	10	0
A friend, Motherwell	1	0	0
Mr. H. Coghill	30	0	0
Mr. R. Dawson	0	4	0
Mrs. Ambler, per Rev H. L. Wayland, D.D., Philadelphia	11	0	0
Rev. W. Stott	2	2	0
Mr. John Chapman	5	5	0
Mr. John Anderson, Glasgow	5	0	0
Mr. H. J. Mansell	5	0	0
Pastor and Mrs. J. A. Spurgeon	5	5	0
J. A. Spurgeon, jun.	1	1	0
Daisy Spurgeon	1	1	0
In memoriam	1	1	0
Dr. R. F. Weymouth	1	1	0
Mr. R. J. Beecliff	0	5	0
Weekly Offerings at Met. Tab. :—			
May 19	40	0	0
,, 26	30	17	10
June 2	21	1	0
,, 9	32	0	0
	129	18	10
	£291	6	3

Stockwell Orphanage.

Statement of Receipts from May 15th to June 14th, 1889.

	£	s.	d.
Balance of residuary Estate of the late late C. W. Dalton	2	12	9
Christian Police Association, per Mrs. Dorin	0	10	0
Jack, South Lambeth	0	4	0
Lewisham High Road Congregational Sunday-school, per Mr. R. J. Thompson	2	16	3
Mr. G. F. Dean (an old boy) ...	1	1	0
Bessell's Green Baptist Sunday-school, per Mr. E. Greenway	1	1	6
Collected by Mrs. C. Wood	0	15	0
Mrs. Oxer	1	0	0
Collected by Mrs. Rhodes	1	3	8
P. O., Exmouth	0	10	0
Rev. H. H. Veder	0	4	0
Mr. E. K. Stace	0	10	0
Miss E. M. McDowall	3	0	0
Collected by Miss M. Warren	0	9	0
S. W. London Band of Hope Union, per Miss Carr...	2	2	0
Mr. D. D. Sinclair	0	5	0
"Gershom"...	0	1	0
Young Women's Bible-class at Orphanage, per Mrs. J. Stiff	0	11	3
Sandwich, per bankers, April ...	2	2	0
Sandwich, per bankers, May ...	2	2	0
Collected by Mr. H. W. Spice ...	0	7	2
Miss Walker, per J. T. D.	1	10	0
Miss Dunn	0	10	0
Collected by Mr. T. E. Inwood ...	1	1	0
In memoriam, 17th July, 1885 ...	1	5	0
Mr. M. Brown	0	2	6
Mr. M. D. King	1	1	0
One of his stewards	1	13	6
Mr. Wm. Norton	0	10	0
Miss M. E. Jenkins	0	3	0
Mr. E. Puttock	0	2	6
Townley Street Mission Hall, per Mr. R. H. Tomkins	0	16	0
Friends at Risby	1	0	0
Collected by Mrs. Maxted	0	14	7
Mrs. Potter (children's box) ...	0	10	0
Miss Scarfe	0	1	0
Mrs. and Miss Stewart	0	10	0
Donation from a friend	20	0	0
Collected by Mrs. Laker	0	10	0
Mrs. Lloyd...	0	5	0
Mrs. Morden	0	3	0
Collected by W. J. T., Charles H., and Emily Jackson	0	13	0
Per Mrs. J. A. Spurgeon, West Croydon :—			
Mrs. Colman 5 5 0			
Miss Toward 2 2 0			
Mrs. Ferne 1 0 0			
Mr. Pelton, J.P. 2 12 6			
	10	19	6
Orphanage box at Tabernacle gates ...	1	15	3
Mr. J. Denham	1	0	0
Mr. W. D. Crowhurst	0	10	0
Mr. R. Parsons	0	5	0
Sale of S. O. tracts	0	1	6
Mr. D. Thomas	1	0	0
Mr. J. Buik	0	3	6
Mr. T. P. Potts	1	0	0
Readers of "The Christian," per Messrs. Morgan and Scott	17	13	0
Mr. George Reid	10	0	0
Mrs. Breakwell	0	5	0
Mr. John Ramsay	0	7	6
Mr. C. Ibberson	0	2	6
A thankoffering, Plymouth	1	0	0
Executor of the late Miss Catherine Rogers	90	0	0
Mr. P. Wallis	0	10	0

	£	s.	d.
Mrs. Mitchell	0	10	0
Mrs. Holcombe	0	5	0
Collected by Mr. I. Horn	0	7	6
Mr. W. S. Cowell	5	0	0
Collected by Master Herries ...	1	4	8
Mr. Thomas Chamberlain ...	0	7	0
Mr. R. Greenwood...	0	2	6
Mrs. Ferguson	0	3	0
Mrs. Webb	2	0	0
Miss Wilford	1	0	0
Mrs. Mundy...	1	1	0
M. N. W., Berbice	2	10	0
Mansfield Street Sunday-school children	2	0	0
Nemo	0	10	0
Mrs. Thorne	0	10	0
Helen Taylor Memorial Trust	2	0	0
A constant reader of sermons and "Sword and Trowel"	0	10	0
Mr. James Frame	1	0	0
Miss Bonfield	0	10	0
Mr. E. Reynolds	0	2	6
Miss M. E. White	1	10	0
From the poor to the poor	0	6	0
Mr. L. Shepherd	0	10	0
Mr. R. Lievesley	1	0	0
Mrs. Smith	1	0	0
Mrs. Dobbs	2	0	0
Mrs. Cracknell	1	1	0
Mr. A. Glastonbury, per Mrs. Angus...	1	0	0
Shoreditch Tabernacle Young Women's Bible-class, per Mr. J. Frost ...	1	13	6
Mrs. Barry	1	1	0
Miss Key	3	0	0
Proceeds of juvenile sale of work at Wellington Street Baptist School-room, Stockton-on-Tees	23	16	3
Tortoise, Hawick	1	0	0
A thankoffering from a servant ...	0	2	0
M. W. R.			0
J. S.	0	2	6
From Charmwood	0	2	0
Postal order from Irvine... ...	0	5	0
F. G. B., Chelmsford	0	2	6
Collected by Mr. Clark, per Mrs. Charles Spurgeon	0	17	0
Mrs. Higham	3	0	6
Collections at Surrey Square Mission	2	8	6
Mr. H. C. Jenkins	0	5	0
Collected by Miss E. Botting ...	1	6	0
Mr. E. J. Reed, per Pastor J. A. Spurgeon	1	1	0
Sarah Evans	0	10	0
Mrs. Shaw	0	15	0
Mrs. Johnson	2	0	0
Mrs. Bell	1	0	0
Mr. William Newton	0	5	0
Gildencroft Baptist Sunday-school, Norwich	0	10	0
Collected by Miss M. J. Ashton ...	3	0	6
Mr. E. Brown, per Rev. George Kerry	3	0	0
The birds from Paradise	2	0	0
Mr. George Smith and a friend... ...	0	11	0
Collected by Mrs. R. Long	5	2	5
Mrs. Matthews	0	10	0
B. G., Norwich	1	0	0
Mr. P. L. Hankin	1	1	0
Mr. E. Adam	1	0	0
Mr. A. W. Arden	0	5	0
Readers of "The Christian Herald" ...	8	9	9
A reader of "The Sword and the Trowel," King's Lynn... ...	0	2	6
A friend, Edinburgh	1	0	0
Mr. Dixon	1	1	0
Colonel Sir H. Yule, C.B., R.E. ...	1	10	0
Collected by Miss Jordan	0	12	0
A poor woman at Mildmay	0	1	0

	£	s.	d.		£	s.	d.
Miss R. Gould	3	0	0	Mrs. G. Colyer	0	10	0
Miss L. Belough	0	1	0	Mrs. Hewkley	1	1	0
Collected by Mrs. Fred. Norris ...	1	0	0	A well-wisher, per Mrs. Hewkley ...	2	0	0
Mr. H. Coghill	30	0	0	Mrs. Knott	1	0	0
Mr. and Mrs. Baker	1	0	0	Mr. A. E. Walker, balance of money			
Mr. D. W. James	2	2	0	left by a friend ...	25	1	1
Miss E. Ellis	0	10	0	E. R., Sheffield	10	0	0
Mr. R. Dawson	0	4	0	Mrs. Hoyle	1	0	0
Rev. A. Macdonald	1	0	0	Collected by Mrs. Lang :—			
Mr. G——, Wells, Norfolk	0	1	0	Miss Falkner 0 10 0			
Eythorne, Ashley, and Wollage Green				Mrs. A. Beckingsale ... 0 5 0			
Sunday-schools	4	10	0	Miss Wyatt 0 2 6			
Collected by Mrs. James Withers :—					0	17	6
Mr. M. J. Sutton 3 3 0				In memory of little Seymour	0	10	0
Mr. W. I. Palmer 1 1 0				Miss R. Daniell	0	5	0
Mr. M. H. Sutton 1 1 0				Mr. A. Lawther	5	0	0
Mr. Alfred Sutton 1 0 0				Mrs. Fryer	0	10	0
Mrs. James Withers ... 1 1 0				Mrs. Garner...	1	0	0
Mr. E. Harvey 0 0 6				Mr. S. Jones	1	0	0
Mrs. Walter Palmer ... 0 0 0				Mr. G. Kingerlee	10	0	0
Mr. Alfred Palmer... ... 0 0 0				Mrs. Gooser	0	10	0
Mr. Herbert Sutton ... 0 0 0				M. and W. S., Glasgow	0	10	0
Mrs. C. Simonds 0 10 0				An aged sister	0	2	0
Mrs. Lowsley 0 5 0				Mrs. Bridgman	0	2	0
Mr. Beecroft 0 5 0				Mrs. Robertshaw	0	2	6
Mr. W. Cowslade 0 5 0				Collected by Miss May Williams ...	0	15	
Mrs. Collier 0 5 0				Sabbath-school girls, The Priory,			
Mr. Leslie 0 3 0				Abergavenny	1		6
Mrs. Parfitt 0 2 6				*Meetings by Mr. Charlesworth and the*			
Mr. W. Ravenscroft ... 0 2 6				*Orphanage Choir :—*			
Mrs. W. Shepherd... ... 0 2 6				Bexley Heath (for expenses) ...	2	10	0
Mrs. J. Davis 0 2 6				Donation, Mr. H. J. Bristow ...	1	1	0
Mr. Brigham 0 2 6				Channel Islands :—			
Mr. Turner 0 1 0				Jersey (less local expenses)	12	0	8
	11	13	0	Guernsey	16	10	0
Mr. and Mrs. T. W. Beveridge... ...	2	2	0	A friend, per V. J. C.	1	0	0
Mr. and Mrs. Stephenson	0	2	0	Peckham Public Hall, per Pastor F. M.			
Mrs. Garroway	5	0	0	Smith (for expenses)	2	0	0
Mr. W. T. Phillips...	0	10	0	Sale of programmes	0	2	6
Mr. G. Wright	1	0	0	Mildmay Park Conference Hall ...	10	10	0
Miss Barker...	1	0	0				
Miss H. Fells	0	10	0		£472	16	1
Miss E. A. Fysh	0	1	0				

List of Presents, per Mr. Charlesworth, from May 15th to June 14th.—PROVISIONS :—1 box of Fish, Mr. T. R. Watkinson ; 1 churn Milk, North Hants Dairy Co. ; 2 sacks Potatoes, Mr. J. Walker ; 1 New Zealand Sheep, Mr. A. S. Haslam ; 8 cwt. Potatoes, Anon. ; 2 sacks Flour, Messrs. Clover and Son ; 6 Stilton Cheeses, Mr. J. T. Crosher ; 12 quarterns Bread, Miss A. J. Fuchs ; 6 tins Castle Cakes, Messrs. Peek, Frean & Co. ; 3 sacks Potatoes, Mr. J. Hall ; 24 lbs. Butter, Mr. F. Barnes ; 8 jars Jam, Messrs F. W. Beach and Sons ; 1 churn Milk, Mrs. C. Harris.

BOYS' CLOTHING :—13 Shirts, Mrs. Holcombe ; 36 Bows, Mrs. S. E. Knight ; 1 overcoat, Mrs. Paul.

GIRLS' CLOTHING :—A few articles, Miss J. Dickson ; 76 articles, The Ladies' Working Meeting at the Tabernacle, per Miss Higgs ; 92 articles, the Juvenile Working Society, per Miss Woods ; 50 articles, Miss A. E. Jones and class ; 6 articles and 12 Handkerchiefs, Mrs. A. R. Smith and friend ; 4 articles, Mrs. Oakley ; 18 articles, Mrs. Rees ; 19 articles, Mrs. Watling ; 1 dozen Aprons, Mrs. E. Baxter ; 101 Garments, the Reading Young Ladies' Working party, per Mrs. James Withers.

GENERAL :—A hamper of Flowers, The little Common Wesleyan Sunday-school children per Mrs. Barton ; a box of Flowers, Mrs. E. Parsons ; a box of Flowers, Mr. E. Greenway ; 16 Toys, Miss A. E. Jones and class ; 5 Dolls and 2 Aprons, Mrs. S. E. Knight.

FOR SALE ROOM :—1 Scrap Book, Mr. J. Trickett ; 5 articles, Miss J. Workman ; 5 articles, Mrs. Shipway ; 21 articles, Miss Mares ; 12 washing Gloves, J. P. Oxford ; 14 articles, The Misses Milner ; 2 articles, M. B. C. ; 11 articles, Miss Marsh ; 7 articles, Mrs. Howard, Mrs. Stone, and Miss Davy ; a box of Hats and fancy articles, Mrs. Feltham.

Colportage Association.

Statement of Receipts from May 15th to June 14th, 1889.

Subscriptions and Donations for Districts :

	£	s.	d.		£	s.	d.
Sandown and Ventnor, per Colonel				Sellindge, per Mr. Thomas R—— ...	10	0	0
Birney	9	10	0	Wolverhampton District	10	0	0
Oxfordshire Association, Stow and				Fairford, per Captain Milbourn ...	10	0	0
Aston District	10	0	0	Wilts. and East Somerset Association	25	0	0
Bromley, Kent, Congregational Church	10	0	0	Newbury District	10	0	0
Great Yarmouth Town Mission ...	7	10	0	Portsmouth District :—			
South Devon Congregational Union,				Miss Robinson 5 0 0			
Newton Abbot 10 0 0				Mrs. T. Tufnell 1 10 0			
					6	10	0

	£	s.	d.
Cambridgeshire Association	10	0	0
Ironbridge and Coalbrookdale	15	0	0
Repton and Burton-on-Trent, per E. S.	20	0	0
Worcestershire Association	30	0	0
Mr. R. Cory, for Cardiff and Pen-rhicweiber	10	0	0
Mr. John Cory, for Castleton, Cardiff, and Penrhicweiber	20	0	0
Metropolitan Tabernacle Sunday-school, for Tring	10	0	0
Yorkshire Association, Boroughbridge	10	0	0
Miss Lassell, for Maidenhead	10	0	0
Borstall District	20	0	0

Bethnal Green District:—

Mr. C. E. Fox	5	0	0			
Mr. W. R. Fox	5	0	0			
				10	0	0

	£	s.	d.
Mr. R. Scott, for Langham and Dedham	10	0	0
Home of Industry, Bethnal Green	10	0	0
Orpington, M. A. H., quarterly	5	0	0
	£308	**10**	**0**

Subscriptions and Donations to the General Fund :—

	£	s.	d.
Mr. J. Hindsput	0	1	0
Friend, Brabourne	0	5	0
Mr. F. Cockrell	0	5	0
Collection at Annual Meeting	21	14	0

	£	s.	d.
M. V., West Norwood	0	5	0
Balance of the residuary Estate of the late C. W. Dalton	1	15	2
Readers of " The Christian," per Messrs. Morgan and Scott	3	10	0
T. G. T., Birkenhead	5	0	0
Mrs. Webb	0	10	0
Miss Banfield	0	10	0
M. W. R.	1	1	0
Mr. A. Todd	0	5	0
Mr. H. Coghill	10	0	0
Mr. G. Kingerlee	1	0	0
Annual Subscriptions :—			
Miss E. M. Macdowall	2	0	0
Miss Norris	0	10	6
Mr. W. H. Ell	1	1	0
Mr. W. G. Macgregor, 1888	1	1	0
Mr. W. G. Macgregor, 1889	1	1	0
Mr. W. Izard	2	2	0
Mr. G. F. Satchell	2	0	0
Mrs. John Olney	2	2	0
Messrs. W. Kent and Co.	1	1	0
Mr. Thomas H. Olney	10	0	0
Miss Newman	5	0	0
The Misses A. and E. Newman	2	0	0
Mr. W. Payne	1	1	0
Mr. B. P. Bilborough, 1888	1	1	0
	£78	**1**	**8**

Society of Evangelists.

Statement of Receipts from May 15th to June 14th, 1889.

	£	s.	d.
" H."	1	0	0
Thankoffering for Messrs. Fullerton and Smith's services at Beulah Baptist Chapel, Thornton Heath	1	11	6
The readers of " The Christian," per Messrs. Morgan and Scott	0	10	0
T. G. T., Birkenhead	5	0	0
Messrs. Alexander and Wood	4	0	0
Mr. and Mrs. Green	0	2	6
Mr. C. Hunt	5	0	0
Mrs. Dobbs	0	10	0
J. B. G.	5	0	0
Dr. Kenderdine, per Pastor T. Spurgeon	10	0	0
Mr. G. Shaw	5	5	0

	£	s.	d.
Thankoffering for Messrs. Fullerton and Smith's services at the Edinburgh Castle	60	0	0
Mr. W. Tennant	0	5	0
John Malyon	1	0	0
Mr. H. Coghill	30	0	0
Thankoffering for Mr. Parker's services at Gordon Road, Peckham	1	0	0
Thankoffering for Mr. Harmer's services at Ipswich	1	6	8
Mr. and Mrs. Haynes	0	10	0
	£132	**0**	**8**

For General Use in the Lord's Work.

Statement of Receipts from May 15th to June 14th, 1889.

	£	s.	d.
Mr. S. R. Turner	2	0	0
Miss S. Green	0	1	0
Mr. James Wilson	0	15	0
A friend, per Miss Harrison	0	10	0
Postal order from Hawick	0	2	6
Scotch notes from Collace	2	0	0
Mr. J. A. Menzies	0	5	0

	£	s.	d.
John F. H.	1	0	0
Postal order from Newport (I.W.)	0	1	6
Mr. J. McElkinney	0	10	0
	£7	**5**	**0**

Friends sending presents to the Orphanage are earnestly requested to let their names or initials accompany the same, or we cannot properly acknowledge them ; and also to write to Mr. Spurgeon if no acknowledgment is sent within a week. All parcels should be addressed to Mr. Charlesworth, Stockwell Orphanage, Clapham Road, London.

Subscriptions will be thankfully received by C. H. Spurgeon, " Westwood," Beulah Hill, Upper Norwood. Should any sums sent before the 13th of last month be unacknowledged in this list, friends are requested to write at once to Mr. Spurgeon. Post Office and Postal Orders should be made payable at the Chief Office, London, to C. H. Spurgeon ; and Cheques and Orders should all be crossed.

THE

TWENTY-SECOND ANNUAL REPORT

OF THE

Metropolitan Tabernacle

COLPORTAGE ASSOCIATION,

1888.

President.

REV. C. H. SPURGEON.

Vice-President.

REV. J. A. SPURGEON.

Hon. Treasurer.

MR. C. F. ALLISON.

Committee.

MR. J. BUSWELL.	MR. S. JOHNSON.
„ C. CARPENTER.	M. LLEWELLYN.
J. J. COOK.	WALTER MILLS.
J. T. CORSAN.	J. PASSMORE, Junr.
G. EVERETT.	S. R. PEARCE.
G. GOLDSTON.	F. THOMPSON.
J. HALL.	C. WATERS.

MR. WOOLLARD.

General Sec.

REV. W. CORDEN JONES.

OFFICE AND DEPÔT:—

TEMPLE STREET, ST. GEORGE'S ROAD,

SOUTHWARK, S.E.

THE OBJECT OF THIS ASSOCIATION

Is the increased circulation of *religious and healthy literature* among all classes, in order to counteract the evil of the vicious publications which abound, and lead to much immorality, crime, and neglect of religion.

This object is carried out in a twofold manner :—

1st.—By means of Christian Colporteurs, who are paid a fixed salary, and devote all their time to the work, visiting every accessible house with Bibles and good books and periodicals for sale, and performing other missionary services, such as visitation of the sick and dying, and conducting meetings and open-air services as opportunities occur. This is the most important method, enabling the Colporteur to visit every part of the district regularly.

The average total cost of a Colporteur is from £75 to £80 ; but the Committee will appoint a man to any district for which £40 a year is guaranteed, if the funds of the Association will permit.

2nd.—By means of Book Agents who canvass for orders for periodicals, and supply them month by month ; these receive a liberal percentage on the sales, to remunerate them for their trouble.

This second method is admirably adapted to the requirements of districts where the guaranteed subscription for a Colporteur cannot be obtained. Shopkeepers or other persons willing to become Book Agents may communicate with the Secretary.

The Association is unsectarian in its operations, " doing work for the friends of a full and free gospel anywhere and everywhere."

RATE OF PROGRESS.

This may be seen from the following Table :—

Date.	Colpor-teurs.	Sales.			Visits to Families.	Date.	Colpor-teurs.	Sales.			Visits to Families.	Services and Addresses
		£	s.	d.				£	s.	d.		
1866	2					1878	94	8,276	0	4	926,290	
1867	6	927	18	1	114,913	1879	84	7,661	16	0	797,353	8,244
1868	6	1,139	16	3	91,428	1880	79	7,577	7	10	630,993	6,745
1869	11	1,211	10	6	127,130	1881	78	7,673	3	6	624,482	7,544
1870	9	1,056	11	4	92,868	1882	79	8,038	2	2	620,850	7,149
1871	10	1,110	3	4	85,397	1883	76	7,921	9	3	592,745	7,514
1872	12	1,228	10	11	121,110	1884	78	8,760	15	9	626,348	7,627
1873	18	1,796	2	2	217,165	1885	76	9,525	16	2	552,677	8,458
1874	29	2,937	1	7	217,929	1886	87	9,601	13	7	560,750	11,952
1875	36	4,415	8	7½	360,000	1887	80	9,166	8	3	831,130	9,742
1876	49	5,908	1	9	400,000	1888	80	8,916	11	1	624,989	9,352
1877	62	6,950	18	1½	500,000							

Cheques may be crossed London and County Bank ; and Post Office Orders made payable to W. C. JONES, *at the Chief Office, St. Martin's-le-Grand. All communications should be addressed to* REV. W. CORDEN JONES, *Colportage Association, Temple Street, St. George's Road, Southwark, London, S.E.*

Metropolitan Tabernacle
COLPORTAGE ASSOCIATION.
TWENTY-SECOND ANNUAL REPORT, 1888.

HE twenty-second year's work of the Association haviug been brought to a successful close, the committee are glad to report to their friends and subscribers some of its salient and most interesting features.

They desire to do this with sincere gratitude to God for His rich blessing, which has manifestly rested upon the labours of the colporteurs, both in stimulating the taste for reading of a sound beneficial character, and in the direct conversion of souls to Jesus Christ.

The number of colporteurs employed in various districts during the year was 80, being the same as the previous year. Considering the difficulty experienced in some localities to raise the necessary contributions, it is so far encouraging, that the numbers have not decreased; but if the nature and claims of colportage were better understood, the committee believe that the comparatively small sum of £40 per annum, needed towards the support of a colporteur, would be easily raised, and that a larger number of agents would be applied for, particularly as the work of the Association is not confined to any one denomination.

A special feature, during the year, has been a very extensive sale of penny books, happily published in profusion by several leading firms of publishers. These books have been found by the colporteurs adapted to the people whom they visit, especially among the poor, and in the rural districts, and have, doubtless, done much to supplant "penny dreadfuls" in many instances. Of course a large quantity has had to be sold to produce similar monetary results. The total value of sales for the year was £8,916 11s. 1d., and the approximate quantities of books and periodicals are as follows:—Bibles, 7,948; Testaments, 9,460; books over 6d., 58,121; books under 6d., 105,055; magazines, 328,065. These have found their way to hundreds of towns and villages, many of them into remote and neglected districts, and constitute so much good seed scattered broadcast through the land, the harvest of which is not doubtful.

Illustrations of the evils which colportage aims to combat have been very numerous of late. The vendors of pernicious literature have been particularly bold and aggressive. The translation and sale of vicious foreign novels in this country became so great a disgrace to social morality that a public prosecution was instituted, which, happily, resulted in the confiscation and suppression of some of the worst kinds. The American plague of the Sunday newspaper, with its attendant evils, also threatens to increase; while there does not appear to be any diminution in the issue of unhealthy sensational periodicals, which have an immense influence for evil, especially amongst the young of both sexes. The daily papers have recorded repeated instances of crime, both in town and country, directly attributed to the reading of such publications.

Bearing these facts in mind, and knowing, from long experience, that colportage affords an effectual means of neutralizing and supplanting baneful literature, besides being a distinctly evangelistic agency for winning souls to the Saviour, the committee are increasingly desirous to extend the operations of the Association as far as possible.

They therefore trust that friends in all the districts now occupied, will give their utmost support to the Society, and so enable it to encourage new and additional efforts to extend the benefits of colportage to fresh localities.

Attention is particularly called to the fact that, in the cash account, the general subscriptions and donations are considerably less than during the previous year. This produced a deficiency of £872 6s. 4d., which would have seriously hindered the progress of the work but for the exceptional legacies received. The committee hope, therefore, that, this year, increased support will be given, to enable them to maintain their present undertakings, and to utilize the resources placed at their disposal for the extension of the work.

The committee tender their hearty thanks to all their numerous helpers in the enterprise—to the committee of the Religious Tract Society, who have kindly continued their supply of books, &c., on favourable terms, besides making a free grant of tracts for distribution ; to the committee of the British and Foreign Bible Society, who have given special and increased facilities for the sale of their publications ; also to those kind friends who have acted as local superintendents and collectors ; and to the large number of generous contributors to the finances of the Association.

In conclusion, the committee appeal to all who value the promotion of purity in reading and morals, and the evangelization of their country, to support the Association by their prayers and practical efforts for its extension.

Below will be found illustrations selected from colporteurs' reports for the year, which, it is hoped, will be read with interest.

EXTRACTS FROM COLPORTEURS' LETTERS AND REPORTS, &c.

WORK IN THE EAST END OF LONDON.

Experience has proved that the colporteur is an invaluable worker among the crowded streets and alleys of London, as well as in the scattered rural districts. Three agents of the Association are now engaged regularly in the neighbourhood of Bethnal Green.

Mr. STOPS, who works under Miss Macpherson, of "The Home of Industry," writes, concerning a visit to a shop and

THE CONVERSION OF A YOUNG MAN :

" Spiritually I have not seen such results as one would wish, although I have had some encouragement in that respect, for one young man has professed conversion. In one of the shops I went into I noticed a card with this text, ' In God we trust.' I asked the lady if that was her motto. She said, ' Yes.' Whilst talking to her, a young man came into the shop. I asked her if it was her son. She said, ' No.' I said, ' Is he a son of God?' She said, ' No.' I spoke to him, and found he was anxious about his soul. I asked him if he had got a Bible. He said, ' No.' I asked his mistress to buy him one, and by persuasion she did. I asked him to read it, which he promised he would. By persuasion I sold the lady four text cards to put up in the shop. I have seen the young man since, and he said he had found peace. Some of the people do not seem to know what I have got in my pack. One lady said, ' Don't want you to play to-day. What music have you got there ? ' I said, ' Some books. If you buy one, and read it, and believe it, you will have music in your heart.' Sold her a Testament. One woman looked out of window, and said, ' It is that tally man ; tell him, Not at home.' I heard what she said, and said, ' I am not the tally man, but have got some pictures for you to look at.' Whilst looking at them, the tally man came. I sold her some cards. Young woman asked me : 'Have you got a dream-book—Mother Shipton's ? ' I said, ' No, not Mother Shipton's, one by father somebody else '—' Waking Dreams,' which I sold her.''

Mr. HEATH labours in connection with James Street, St. Luke's, where he frequently assists the Pastor, E. J. Farley, but is chiefly engaged in visiting the neighbourhood to sell good literature. He says there are always

LARGE NUMBERS OF SICK AND DYING,

the most urgent cases of which he tries to visit. He writes :—"On February the 8th I visited Mr. B——, Cowper Street, Finsbury, whom I found very ill, suffering from an attack of bronchitis. I have reason to believe that my former visits to this man have been used of God in awakening him to a true sense of his need of the Saviour, as he now takes a great delight in reading the Word of God, and has marked many passages in the Bible which are full and clear as to the ground of a sinner's acceptance with God. I read to him part of the 53rd of Isaiah, and spoke a little as I read, especially fixing his attention to the sixth verse ; and I may say I never saw a more attentive listener, and never saw more rich meaning in these words than while I was speaking to him. It seemed as though new light came to my own soul as I read the words, ' The Lord hath laid on Him the iniquity of us all.' The Spirit gave me utterance, and the Word, I am sure, was applied to his heart, for as I rose from my knees he exclaimed, ' Glory be to God for His mercy.' ''

Another colporteur labours under the superintendence of Rev. W. Cuff, of the Shoreditch Tabernacle, and does good service. A feature of his work has been a stall in Brick Lane on Saturday evenings, which must do much good among the crowds who frequent that thoroughfare. Mr. Thorn writes concerning his visitation :—"Visited two sick men, both of whom are Christians. One of them is very bad, his life having been despaired of. Conversed, read, and prayed with them, which was a joy and an encouragement to them both. One has since died. Visited a man in Whitechapel Infirmary. He has been lying there for ten months, suffering from consumption, and is now sinking rapidly. I read, prayed, and conversed with him, and during my conversation with him the tears came to his eyes ; may they be the first emotions of his conviction of his sinfulness, and may he find peace in believing in the Lord Jesus Christ ! Called upon a person whom I found to be paralyzed, and in a very sad condition. I spoke to her ; but she is so very bad that she could not converse with me, although she gave evidence of being pleased with my visit. Before leaving I committed her, in prayer, to our heavenly Father's care. Have visited, on several occasions, the widow of the man I visited and waited upon some time ago, and have spoken and prayed with her. I regret to say she cannot read, hence this is a great barrier to her, and one which she readily makes use of to excuse herself looking at the Word or other good books.''

Mr. HOLLOWAY, of Peckham and East Dulwich, has had much encouragement in his work, under the superintendence of Rev. F. M. Smith. Local funds are much needed to continue his services. He reports :—"I am thankful to report that God has been pleased to use me in winning two precious souls to Jesus, one a soldier and the other a dear mother, at the London City Mission, Nunhead Green, where I have several times taken the meeting for the Missionary, who has been ill. I have, also, several times spoken at mission meetings, Sunday-schools, cottage meetings, and temperance meetings, and have induced many to sign the pledge. I have been much encouraged in my work, in speaking to people about their souls at their doors. Several, I am thankful to say, who did not read the Word of God, have been much impressed, and have purchased Bibles from me, and I trust they will soon be led to the feet of Jesus. I have also visited many sick, and read the Word of God with them, and prayed with them. I am sorry to say that there are, in the neighbourhood,

A GREAT MANY SHOPS SELLING BAD LITERATURE,

which is doing a very great deal of harm. I have been often told, when offering the Word of God for sale, that they do not want that rubbish; if they want to read, they will get a penny novel. There is also a great deal of poverty, and much of it is caused through drink. A servant girl, in East Dulwich Grove, told me, that her mother had lost all love for her father, and brother and sisters, through drink, and pawns every-thing that she can get hold of for it ; and when she went home to see her a few days ago, she threw a large jug at her head because she would not give her money to get drink with. I could speak of many others, who have lost all love for their children through the accursed drink ; and I do trust that God will use me in winning some of those precious souls to Jesus, and unto his name shall be all the praise."

STREET STALLS.

Passers-by are often attracted by a display of books, &c., on a stall among the costermongers.

Mr. EDGSON, of Somers Town, working under the superintendence of Miss Griffith, sends the following account of

A DAY'S WORK AT THE STALL.

" I thank God my stall is proving a blessing to the many who are attracted by it. I will just give you a brief account of a day at the corner of Euston Road, where I stand on Saturdays, that you may know the kind of work that is being done. In the first place, it is near to the three Great Northern Railways, so I meet with all kinds of people. In taking up my stand on Saturday, as soon as I arrived and exhibited the placard advertising New Testaments, a cabman pulled up his horse, and jumped down. He said, ' Give me one of your New Testaments ! ' which I did ; and when he got it, he was surprised at the size, and went away quite pleased. I had not been there very long when a man came to me and asked me for a New Testament in the German language, as he was going by train, and wanted to take one with him. After selling several books and Scripture texts, there came a man, who seemed very interested, looking over my stock. I spoke to him, and showed him several special things ; but he made no answer, and I soon found he was deaf and dumb. He selected a book, and a New Testament, of which I had to write down the price on a piece of paper. He had not gone away many minutes before another young man came up who was afflicted in the same way. He, too, selected a book, and went away quite pleased. Later on, a servant girl (who, a fortnight ago, bought from me a book called ' The Prince of the House of David ') came to me, and told me she had not known, until she had read that book, how much the Saviour had suffered, and that she realized it was for her, and she wanted to be a Christian. Then she told me the difficulties in the way, which were soon cleared away. I could tell, by her manner, that she was in real earnest about her soul ; and she thanked me very much for the help I had rendered her, and promised to see me again. To finish the day, a socialist came and stood by the side of my stall, offering to the people their organ called ' Justice,' and calling out, ' Salvation for the body. Never mind about the soul ; we know nothing about that.' So, to counteract that, I took up some penny Testaments, and offered them for sale, as salvation of body and soul, for one penny; and I sold all I had with me. Thus ending my day, I packed up and came home."

ASSOCIATIONS OF CHURCHES.

The following Associations employ colporteurs from this Association, and others would do well to try the work as an Evangelizing Agency:—Yorkshire, Norfolk, Suffolk, Worcestershire, Oxfordshire, Cambridgeshire, Essex Congregational, Kent and Sussex, Wilts and East Somerset, The Southern Baptist and Devon Congregational. As the reports would fill a goodly volume, only brief extracts can be given from a few.

BOROUGHBRIDGE, Yorkshire.—MR. POWELL, while working regularly as a col-porteur, has given special assistance with the services at Dishforth Chapel, recently re-opened. He says:—" We have had some very good services in this place, and are looking for a blessing. We keep sowing the seed, and labour and pray for a reaping time. I visit once a month (some twice a month) about 27 villages and hamlets. I am thankful to report signs of blessing, as the result of my visits and the books sold. An old lady told me that a ' Friendly Visitor' she had bought from me had done her good ; and she had lent it to a neighbour, where she hoped it may do good also. I called upon a woman who is a Roman Catholic. She, after a little persuasion, purchased two little books. We had some conversation together, and she wished me to call again."

" I have been very much interested in this man. He keeps the general stores, and has bought many of my books. I have often had serious conversations with him about his soul, and I have very good hope that he is resting on Jesus, and that the light is breaking in upon his soul. I am always glad to visit him, as it often gives me a good chance to speak to others also, who congregate together in his work-shop."

NEATISHEAD, Norfolk.—MR. SLAYMAKER is doing good service here, helping at the chapel on Sundays and visiting during the week. The local report states that " MR. SLAYMAKER, the colporteur, is still working very successfully at Neatishead, and is doing great good by his visits, and the books he is persuading the villagers to buy from him."

GREAT THURLOW, Suffolk.—MR. BARKER'S labours under the direction of the Congregational friends, are highly appreciated. He reports an encouraging case of conversion through visitation. " When visiting this place I met with a very encouraging result, I had visited an old lady for months ; and I made it my business to speak to her about her soul, and I was pleased to learn from her that the few words I had spoken had been made a blessing to her soul, and that she had found peace through believing in Jesus. By her bedside, the little book called "Christianity, the poor Man's Friend,'' has been attended with great blessing ; the poor people prize it highly ; many have found great comfort through reading it. I am pleased to inform you that God is blessing the work in Thurlow."

DROITWICH, Worcestershire.—MR. WHARMBY'S report is a sample of several others. He writes :—" The time having again come round when you expect to hear something of the details of our work, it affords me much pleasure to be able to say that the district in which I labour is in a better condition now than at any period since I have known it. This is especially so, with respect to the sale of books, there having been a steady and substantial increase in the sales during the last six months. This is a gratifying result, when we take into consideration the poverty and depression against which we have had to fight. Amongst the labouring class, perhaps, I sell fewer books than I once did ; for they are feeling the pinch of poverty very acutely, and are therefore, prevented buying as they otherwise would. But my circle of acquaintance amongst the middle or higher classes of my district has widened considerably, and amongst these I have disposed of a good few books ; many of which, I believe, have been afterwards given to the poorer people. I am also much encouraged, as I look back over the pages of my journal, and read the expressions of joy uttered by sick people whom I have visited. One man, who has recently gone to heaven, said, a short time ago, my monthly visit was, to him and his wife, a season of delight, and was looked forward to with feelings of joy. Many others express themselves in a similar way. An old man of 89 years takes hold of my hand when about to leave him, and makes me promise, before he looses his grasp, that I will, if possible, visit him next month ; and I know he has been looking for me, because, if I happen to be a day later than usual, he says, ' I was afraid you wasn't going to call.' I believe, in this department of our work, much real good has, and is being done. I am engaged, most Sundays, preaching the gospel somewhere, chiefly in some obscure village. I visit all my places regularly every month."

PEWSEY VALE, Wilts and East Somerset Association.—Mr. MOODY, one of the colporteurs, reports as follows :—" I am pleased to tell you that the little book, ' Come Home, Father,' has been the means of creating deep impressions, which I trust may result in lasting good. A Mrs. C—— H—— bought the book, and read it to her husband and children, and it brought the tears from all eyes ; or, as Mrs. C—— says, ' We was all crying together on account of that beautiful little book.'

TEXT CARDS USEFUL.

" Two text cards that I sold to a Mrs. B——, of H——, namely, ' My grace is sufficient,' &c., and ' My strength is made perfect,' have been the means of much blessing to her during her severe illness.

BRANCHES RUNNING OVER THE WALL.

" The little book, ' Saved through a Dream,' has been much blessed. Mrs. S—— H—— bought a copy. Being deeply impressed with it herself, sent it to her sister, who has received still greater blessing through reading it ; and having lent it to all her neighbours, sent it by post to her relative."

THE COLPORTEUR AS A SICK VISITOR.

"A Mrs. H—— has been very much blessed through my visiting her during illness. Hearing that she was ill I went and saw her. On the following Sunday she sent for me again. On the following Monday her husband came to see me, saying that neither his wife nor himself ever heard the way of salvation set forth so plainly and clearly. He said his wife had been like a different woman since my visit on Sunday night, and was most anxious to see me again. I went same evening, and found her much changed, and I believe a saved woman. Shortly afterwards she died, and her husband feels satisfied she is gone to rest."

BOURTON - ON - THE - WATER, Oxfordshire, Association.— Mr. C. BARTLETT writes :—" In visiting the village of C——, I called at the house of two old people who had been ill. The woman met me at the door, and, taking me by the hand, said .' O sir, I am so glad to see you ! I wanted to thank you. Your words last Sunday night, when preaching, did me so much good. Come in and see my husband ; he is downstairs. I went in, and asked him how he was getting on. He said, ' I'm better in health, thank you.' I said, ' How about the soul now? Is that all right?' He said, ' I'm afraid not, sir. I can never forget what you said to me when I was ill in bed; but somehow I can't feel right.' ' But are you trusting in Jesus?' He said, ' I try, and sometimes I think I can ; but then I can't feel as I want to.' After conversation and reading a few passages of Scripture, I said, ' Let us tell the Lord about it.' We all knelt down and prayed ; and, rising from our knees, the old man, with tears, said,·' God bless you, sir ! I feel much happier. I wish you lived nearer, and could come oftener. Be sure and call again.' Another old man said : ' My wife did talk about you, sir, even with her last breath, and said she should like to have seen you once more, and have you read and pray with her ; but she is gone.' I entreated him to seek the kingdom of God at once, that he may be ready when called."

SWAFFHAM PRIOR, Cambridgeshire, Association.—Mr. COLLIER perseveres in a difficult work with many tokens of blessing. He reports :—" We find it hard work to sell, on account of labour and money being scarce in the neighbourhood. We have many things to cheer us in our work. We endeavour to recommend the best books we know of to the people, from whom we continually hear of good received through reading them. ' Little Dot,' ' Loved unto Death,' ' Satisfied,' ' Brighter than the Sun,' ' Charlie Coulson,' which is a great favourite everywhere it goes. A little while ago I sold two of Mr. Spurgeon's Sermons, ' No. 2,000,' and ' The Way of Salvation,' to an aged man, who was so taken up with them that he ordered three monthly parts at sixpence each, saying he and his wife could read them on Sundays, and get more good from them than they could by going to church, being both of them deaf, and unable to hear what the minister says. During the past two months we have had a larger number of sick people to visit, who have been greatly helped and cheered in their sorrows by our visits to them, especially among the aged sick."

DOWNTON Southern Association, one of five districts worked by the colporteurs.— Mr. MIZEN writes cheerfully as follows :—"The Lord is still blessing me in my work. I was never more heartily received than at present, both in the villages and homes of the people." After describing some services, the colporteur writes :— "I gave away two dozen of ' Charlie Coulson ' and ' Promoted,' Horner's Penny Stories. The next morning I heard of one young person who had found the Saviour through hearing her aunt read ' Promoted.' She had been seeking the Lord for sometime. At both services that day God's spirit was striving with her. Horner's stories are well spoken of, and sell well. At Redlynch things are going on well. We want more room. Fourteen years to-day I came here. I thank God for ever sending me, I have been very much blessed in my work, and others have been blessed through my labours. To God be all the glory and praise."

POOLE DISTRICT.—MR. LLOYD sends a very encouraging report. He writes :— "My report for last year (1888) will, I believe, be found very encouraging in many ways. The year has been—though not the most productive by sales—the best in reaping and ingathering of precious souls for the Master. I will take first the work at Corfe Mullen Chapel :—Little more than a year ago the work there was at very low ebb ; not more than seven or eight attended the Sunday morning services, seldom twenty on Sunday evenings, and there were no week-night services. I began by walking the roads of the village with my little boy and girl on Wednesday evenings, repeating portions of Scripture as loud as I could, interspersed with singing and earnest appeals to the soul. After doing so a few times, several persons accompanied us, and in a few weeks we had quite a large party in the chapel on Wednesday evenings, and the attendance increased on Sundays. Then I got a grant of 500 of Mr. Spurgeon's sermons, got a local cover for them, and started a Loan Tract Society with them. Then I commenced giving away fifty copies a month of *The Baptist Visitor*. I afterwards got a grant of tracts (15s. worth) from the Baptist Tract Society, and lent them with the sermons—divided the village into parts, and obtained the help of several female members of the congregation, who have since become members of the church. By this time the year 1888 had begun; the preaching was kept up, and the public were becoming interested, and not a few concerned about their souls. Then we had special services every night for four weeks, and well attended to the last, during which, several persons professed to be converted. By the month of March, at our week-night prayer-meetings, several new converts—men and women—would pray. The good work still keeps up; the Sabbath-school has doubled during the year, and is still increasing. I have a Bible Class of eighteen, nearly all adults, five of whom are married men." The above is in addition to what may be called my own regular work, the report of which now follows :—"As I walked down Market Street, Poole, on the 3rd June, a man asked me if I remembered, six years ago, being overtaken by a ginger-beer van and asking the driver for a lift ? I could not, till he said that I got down at Bushels Hill Farm, and asked his acceptance of a little New Testament, which he took. He said :—'I am the man. I laughed at you as a soft one then. I was a wretched drunkard and swearer. I have drunk two businesses, and had scarcely any home, my wife was in rags— I spending what I earned at the publics I called at with my goods. I put that Testament in my pocket ; that night in the stable I thought of it, and read a bit—had not read one for many years before. I began to be miserable ; I read bits many times a day. I kept thinking I had it in my pocket, then I resolved to throw it away ; but before doing so, I would read a bit, then I could not destroy it. After several weeks I became so miserable that I cried to God for mercy. He heard me, and had mercy on me, showed me my condition, made me hate it, repent, and believe the gospel. I have been a member of a Christian society more than five years, and have been the means of the conversion of several of my neighbours. My wife is happy, my home comfortable, and myself in a good position again ; and that Testament did it all.' Many more or less interesting incidents from my visiting might be related, showing God's blessing upon the work, which increases in magnitude, causing me to be always busy—wearing to the flesh, but cheering to the spirit—making me very tired and very happy." The following is an account of my visits, services, &c., during the year :—Visits as missionary and salesman of Bibles and other books, 4,494 ; total amount realized by sales during the year 1888, £124 7s. 1d.

NEWTON ABBOT, South Devon Congregational Union.—MR. TURNER, who has laboured there long and earnestly, writes :—"I have frequently visited a poor old man, residing at T———. He held some peculiar ideas about Christ and salvation. I did my best to explain the way of salvation, according to the teaching of the New Testament ; after many visits, and in answer to many prayers, he was able to believe and be saved, which for some time seemed very difficult. He has passed away, leaving behind him a glorious testimony that ' all is well.' Another very wicked old man I visited during an affliction ; I found his mind was very dark, and knowing his previous mode of life, I knew how much he needed a Saviour. After a long conversation, I commended him to God in prayer. When I called again, he thanked me for my visit, and said I was the means of doing him much good. A young man came to me in the market, the other week, and asked me if I remembered what I said to him ten years ago, when his work-mate wanted him to have a quart of cider for dinner. I simply said, ' Don't you have it, Jim.' God blessed those few words. He was a wild, reckless fellow, often the worse for drink. He said, 'Whenever I was tempted to drink after that, I fancied I could hear, "Don't you touch it, Jim." ' This proved the turning point in his life. He gave himself to the Lord, and is an earnest worker in one of our Sunday-schools. In connection with Sunday work, God has blessed me very much. Two young women have been converted and are giving evidence of it by Christian living."

It is hoped that these reports from agents connected with associations, will lead other County Associations to employ colporteurs. Space forbids the multiplication of reports from the many remaining districts, in all of which, similar results have been realized.

TABLE OF COLPORTEURS' SALES.

A complete list is impracticable, on account of the number and variety of Books sold, but the following table indicates the number of Books and Periodicals sold in considerable quantities during the year 1888 :—

BOOKS.

Bibles...	7,948	Books under 6d.	...105,055
Testaments (various) ...	9,460	Books over 6d.	... 58,121
Mr. Spurgeon's Book Almanack	1,629	,, in Packets ...	... 40,070
,, John Ploughman's do.	9,787	Scripture Texts... ...	... 83,387
,, Books (various)	3,824	Cards in Packets ...	...105,340
Almanacks (various)	14,765		

TOTAL BOOKS AND PACKETS   439,386

MAGAZINES.

A 1, The	4,369	Mothers' Companion	10,453
Adviser	3,575	Mothers' Treasury ...	4,944
Appeal	2,952	Notes on Scripture Lessons ...	4,460
Band of Hope	12,011	Old Jonathan	2,493
Child's Own Magazine	10,718	Prize	11,763
Herald of Mercy ...	3,480	Sunshine	12,792
Baptist Messenger ...	4,812	Chatterbox	5,328
British Workman	10,835	Our Darlings ...	3,129
British Workwoman	11,388	Sword and Trowel	5,469
Child's Companion	9,195	Friendly Greetings	3,048
Children's Friend ...	11,199	Young England	3,824
Cottager	6,780	Boy's Own Paper ...	4,496
Family Friend	12,612	Girl's Own Paper ...	10,485
Friendly Visitor	6,904	Quiver	13,483
Home Words	4,367	Spurgeon's Sermons...	11,002
Infants' Magazine ...	3,816	Sunday at Home ...	9,900
Mothers' Friend ...	5,469	Miscellaneous Magazines...	79,806
Our Own Gazette	6,708		

TOTAL MAGAZINES...   328,065

These figures give some idea of the sales made by 80 Colporteurs. In addition to this, they distributed gratuitously upwards of 215,000 Tracts, and made about 624,989 visits.

Value of Sales from the commencement of the Association :—

£121,801 6s. 7d.

LIST OF COLPORTEURS, WITH DISTRICTS,

OCCUPIED DURING 1888.

DISTRICT.	COUNTY.	COLPORTEUR.	OPENED.	LOCAL SUPERINTENDENT OR GUARANTOR.
Warminster	Wiltshire	S. Kg	1867	Mr. W. C. ...
Swindon	Do.	B. Slatter	1869	W. B. Wearing, Esq.
Ros	Herefordshire	W. J. Singleton	1872	Thmas ..., Esq.
Riddings and keston II		Bort Hall	1872	W. H. ..., Esq.
Cheddar	Somersetshire	E. Garrett	1873	Rev. J. B. Field.
Dorking	Surrey	H. Witton	B73	Mr. C. Peirson.
Maldon	Essex	J. Kd	873	Friends at Maldon.
Cardiff	Glamorganshire	S. Shaw	1873	R. Cory, Esq., J.P.
Ryde	Isle of Wight	W Ford	1873	Mr. Jacobs.
Minchinhampton	...	H. May	1874	Rev. W. G. Smith.
...	...re	G. Athay	1874	
Alcester	Warwickshire	C. Skinner	1874	Local ...
Evesham	Worcestershire	T. Boulton	1874	
Droitwich	D.	J. Wharmby	B74	
...	Wiltshire	C. Mn	1874	Southern Baptist A ... an.
Brentford	Middlesex	H. Mears	1874	T. ...d, Esq.
Wellow	Hare	W. Hge	B74	Southern ... st Association.
Witney	...hire	L. W. Smith	B74	Oxfordshire Association.
Stow and Aston	...re	C. Bartlett	1875	Mr. J. B. Ransford.
Castleton	...re	T. Sabin	1876	John Cory, Esq.
... and Evill	Kent	J. Hines	1876	Rev. E. J. Edwards.
Wolverhampton	Staffordshire	A. Frost	1876	M ... Thas Bantock.
Ironbridge	Shropshire	L Gilpin	B76	A. ..., Esq.
Pewsey Me	Wiltshire	R. Mly	1876	Mr. Sharman and L ad ... &c.
Mn	Somersetshire	{ H, C. Waller and A. J. Mpton }	1876	Mr. W. Hannam.
Hmim	—	R. Bellamy	1876	R. W. Griffith, Esq.
Lymington	Do.	G. right	1876	Rev. J. Collins.
Ludlow	Shropshire	S. ncck	B76	James Evans Esq.

DISTRICT.	COUNTY.	COLPORTEUR.	OPENED.	LOCAL SUPERINTENDENT OR GUARANTOR.
Hadleigh	Suffolk	E. ...	1876	R. H. ... Esq.
Halesowen	Warwickshire	A. ...	1877	Local ...
Poole	Dorset	W. Lloyd	1877	Southern Association.
Salisbury	Wiltshire	T. Richards	1877	
High ...	Bucks	D. ...	1877	R. ..., Esq.
Bower Chalk	Dev n	H. ...	1877	Josh. Bolton, Esq.
...	Salisbury	E. G. Lawson	1877	Mr. ...
Newbury	Norfolk	W. ...	1877	... Mission, S. W. Pag ...Esq.
...	Berkshire	H. Grimwood	1878	A. Jackson, Esq.
...	Ess ...	M. Frost	1879	Ess ... Congregational Union.
Bethnal ...	Middlesex	R. Thorn	1879	Messrs. Fox. S par. Rev. W. Giff.
Kettering	...ton	A. Portingall	1879	Rev. I. M. ...
...	Derbyshire	R. Beard	1880	Anonymous.
Orpington	Kent	T. Bign ...	1880	C. F. ..., Esq.
Swaffham	Cambridgeshire	F. Collier	1880	Cambridge Association.
Repton	Staffordshire	J. P. Allen	1880	E. S., Anonymous.
Sandown	Isle of Wight	W. Coleman	1881	... Birney
...	Do.	W. ...	1881	Mr. G. Sparks.
Sellindge	Kent	J. W. Andrew	1882	Mr. Sharwood.
Tewkesbury	...	Thos. Nelmes	1882	Rev. A. Graham.
Thornbury	Do.	C. G. H...	1882	E. Cullimore, ...
Tring	Herts	C. ...	1882	Metropolitan Tabernac e Sunday S hooe
Calne	Wilts	W. Slaymaker	1883	J. Chappell, Esq.
Great Totham	Norfolk	T. Bendall	1883	Norfolk ...
Penrikyber	Ess ...	J. W. Knee	1883	Rev. H. J. Harvey.
Aberdare		J. ...th	1883	... J. and R. Cory.
... and ...	...		1883	J. E. Taylor, ...
Meyseyhampton	Gloucestershire	C. Ma ...	1884	Captain Milbourn.
Borstal	Kent	E. R. ...	1884	Lieut.-Col. Plummer.
Melksham	Wilts	A. ...	1884	Rev. G. ...
Stratford-on-Avon	Warwickshire	S. Bartlett	1884	Mr. W. E. ...
Lond ...	St. Luke's	E. J. Heath	1885	Rev. E. J. Farley.
Bromley	Kent	W. Hardiman	1885	Rev. R. H. Lovell.

District	County	Agent	Year	Agent
Okehampton Sol-	Devon...	G. J. Witing	1886	Mr. R. V. B ay.
Portsmouth Sol- diers' Home	Hants..	B. Neal	1886	Miss Robinson.
Thurlow	Suffolk	J. H. Barker	1886	Mr. F. Pratt.
Uxbridge	Lancashire	F. W. Singleton	1886	J. Dodson, Esq.
	Mex	S. Rss	1886	D. M, Esq.
	eRks	G. Duckett	1886	Miss Lassells.
*Weston - super - Mare	Somerset	E. Owers	1886	Rev. Spencer Mch
*Thornton Heath	Surrey.	G. Barnes	1886	Rev. C. Spurgeon.
Greenwich	Kent .	W. Beer	1886	H. Serpell, Esq.
Estover	D vons	H. Cope	1887	Rev. F. M. Smith.
Peckham	Surrey.	J. Holloway	1887	R. Scott, Esq.
Langham	Essex Mex	F. Hyatt	1887	Ms El.
Somers Town		R. Edgson	1888	Yorkshire Association.
Boroughbridge	Yorkshire	J. Powell	1888	J. J. um, Esq.
Burstow	Surrey...	W. H. Chillman	1887	Miss Macpherson, "Home of Industry."
Bethnal Green	Middlesex	J. Stops	1888	Rev. G. Hollier.
Rendham	Suffolk	W. Bird	1888	Rev. E. J. Edwards } Kent and Sussex Association.
St. Ngis	Kent	L. W. Reed	1889	
Cowfold	Sussex...	W. Brooker	1889	Rev. J. S. Geale

No. of Districts occupied during 1888 : 89.

* The Districts mark d with an asterisk have been suspended or d from lack of Local Subscriptions.

BOOK AGENTS :—

	COUNTY	AGENT	DISTRICT	COUNTY	AGENT
Braintree	Ess x e..	F. W. Fenton	Reigate	Surrey...	G. Bass
Newington	Kent ...	L. Bw	Mes	Lancashire	W. Johnson
Histon	Cambridgeshire	G. Mansfield	Snailbeach	Shropshire	W. Jenkins
Presteign	Radnorshire	S. Watkins			

SUBSCRIPTIONS AND DONATIONS

Received from 1st January to 31st December, 1888.

FOR DISTRICTS.

	£	s.	d.
Burstow and Horley, per Mr. J. J. Tustin	40	0	0
Borstal	20	0	0
Bromley (Kent) Congregational Church	30	0	0
Bethnal Green:			
W. R. Fox	20	0	0
C. E. Fox	20	0	0
Brentford, per Mr. Thos. Greenwood	40	0	0
Bethnal Green Home of Industry	10	0	0
Bower Chalke:			
Mr. Butler	1	0	0
Mr. Thos. R—for 1889	6	0	0
Baptist Church	5	0	0
	12	0	0
Calne:			
Per Mr. J. Chappell	7	10	0
Per Mr. H. Wilkins	22	10	0
	30	0	0
Castleton, Cardiff, and Penrhiwceiber, per Messrs. J. and R. Cory	110	0	0
Cambridge Association, Swaffham Prior	50	0	0
Cheddar:			
Per Mrs. Clark	2	2	0
Rev. J. Renney	0	5	0
Mrs. Webb	0	5	0
Rev. D. F. Field	0	2	6
Mrs. Davies	0	2	6
Mr. Jeffries	0	2	6
	2	19	6
Dorking	15	0	0
Epping, per Mr. H. B. Brown	20	0	0
Estover, per Mr. H. Serpell	20	0	0
Fritham, Mr. R. W. S. Griffith	30	0	0
Fairford and Meyseyhampton, per Cap. Millbourn	35	0	0
Greenwich, per Pastor C. Spurgeon	40	0	0
Great Yarmouth Town Mission	37	10	0
Great Totham District Subs.	21 12 0		
Per Rev. H. J. Harvey	18 0 0		
	39	12	0
Hadleigh, per Mr. R. H. Cook	40	0	0
High Wycombe, per Mr. R. Collins, jun.	40	0	0
Halesowen, per Mr. J. Hawkes	27	7	0
Ilkeston and Riddings, per Mr. W. H. Roberts	40	0	0
Ironbridge and Coalbrookdale, per Mr. A. Maw	30	0	0
Kettering	40	0	0
Ludlow District:			
Collected by Mrs. Fitzgerald	1 8 0		
Mr. W. Mainwaring	0 10 0		
Subscriptions for 1887	25 0 0		
Subscriptions for 1888	10 0 0		
	36	18	0
Littledale, per Mr. J. Dodson	60	0	0
Langham, per Mr. R. Scott	10	0	0
Melksham, per Mrs. H. Keevil	40	0	0
Maidenhead, per Miss Lassells	40	0	0
Maldon, Friends at	30	0	0
Minchinhampton	40	0	0
Newbury	40	0	0
Norfolk Association, Neatishead	40	0	0
Nottingham Tabernacle	10	9	0
Orpington:			
Mrs. Allison's Bible Class	21 1 3		
M. A. H.	20 0 0		
	41	1	3
Oxfordshire Association:			
Witney	30 0 0		
Stow and Aston	30 0 0		
	60	0	0

	£	s.	d.
Okehampton	40	0	0
Pitsea, per Essex Congregational Union	40	0	0
Portsmouth:			
Per Miss Robinson	15 0 0		
„ Mr. T. Hogben	12 0 0		
„ E. M.	5 0 0		
„ Mr. W. Harmsworth	0 2 6		
„ Mr. G. Beavis	1 1 0		
„ Mr. W. Tuffnell	0 10 0		
	33	13	6
Ross:			
Per Miss J. Ball	0 2 6		
„ Mr. Thos. Blake	20 0 0		
	20	2	6
Repton and Burton-on-Trent, per E. S.	80	0	0
Rendham, per Rev. J. Hollier	10	0	0
Somers Town, per Miss Griffiths	40	0	0
Stratford-on-Avon	25	0	0
Southern Baptist Association	200	0	0
St. Luke's, Pastor E. J. Farley	50	0	0
Sellindge, per Mr. Thos. R—	40	0	0
South Devon Congregational Unio	40	0	0
Suffolk Congregational Union	40	0	0
Sandown and Ventnor, per Col. Birney	27	15	0
Thornton Heath, per A Sympathizer with Mr. Spurgeon	50	0	0
Tewkesbury:			
Per Mr. T. White	40 0 0		
„ Pastor A. Graham	2 10 0		
	42	10	0
Thornbury	7	10	0
Tring District:			
Mr. W. Humphrey	0 10 0		
„ F. Buther	2 0 0		
„ T. J. Elliman	1 0 0		
„ Thos. Glover, 2 years	1 0 0		
Metropolitan Tabernacle Sunday School	40 0 0		
	44	10	0
Uxbridge, Mr. D. White	10	0	0
Wolverhampton, per Mrs. T. Bantock	40	0	0
Wendover and Neighbourhood	40	0	0
Wilts and East Somerset Association	110	0	0
Worcester Association	120	0	0
Weston Turville, Friends at	3	15	0
Yorkshire Baptist Asstn., Borobridge	40	0	0
Total	£2,482	12	9
Differences between the amount of Arrears and Advances at the beginning and end of the year	56	11	4
See General Account	£2,539	4	1

GENERAL SUBSCRIPTIONS AND DONATIONS.

	£	s.	d.
Blyth, Miss	5	0	0
Bank of England Notes S.W. Post Mark	10	0	0
Billing, Mr. Josh.	1	0	0
Baker, Mrs.	2	10	0
Cockrell, Mr. F. H.	2	0	0
Collection, at Annual Meeting	13	15	3
The "Christian Herald," Readers of	14	9	3
Cairngorm	0	10	0
C. A. M.	25	0	0
C. W., Collecting Box	0	8	3
Devonshire	1	0	0
D. E. G., Wilts	0	10	0
Dore, Mr. Jas.	1	0	0
E. S.	2	0	0
E. K. G.	20	0	0
Evans, Mrs.	0	5	0
Ealing Collection	0	17	0

	£	s.	d.
Francis Miss	0	5	0
Fox, Mr. C. E.	5	0	0
Fox, Mr. W.	5	0	0
Fox, Mr. W. R.	5	0	0
Fennings, Dr. Alfred	5	0	0
Gunn, Mrs.	10	0	0
Gibson, Mr. John	10	0	0
Gardiner, Mrs.	2	2	0
Heelas, Mr. D.	1	0	0
H. M., S.E. Post Mark	5	0	0
H. E. S.	10	10	0
H. I., Malta	0	10	0
Hill, Mr.	0	5	0
Hadfield, Miss	5	0	0
Hector, Mr. J.	2	0	0
H. B.	50	0	0
Jessie	1	0	0
Jenkins, Pastor W.	0	5	0
Jones, Mr. and Mrs. W.	5	0	0
J. S.	5	0	0
L. K. D.	1	0	0
Long, Mr. A.	1	1	0
Menzies, Mrs.	2	2	0
Marshall, Mr.	1	1	0
Matthew, 25 and 40	0	10	0
Miller, Mr. and Mrs. G.	0	15	0
Mounsey, Mr. E.	2	10	0
Memory (in loving)	50	0	0
M. C. S. F.	0	10	0
Neal, Mr. Jno.	1	1	0
Newell, Mr. E.	2	10	0
Norman, Mr. F. A.	0	10	0
O. B., per Pastor J. A. Spurgeon	10	10	0
O. B., per Pastor J. A. Spurgeon	10	0	0
Ormond, Mr. H.	2	0	0
P. W. A.	5	5	0
Pole, Mrs. L. W.	0	5	0
Priestley, Mr. J. E.	2	0	0
Parken, the late Miss, instalment of legacy	1	16	
Peek, Rev. R.	0	5	
Roberts, Mr. C. W.	5	0	
Raybould, Mrs.	4	0	8
Readers of the "Christian," per Messrs. Morgan & Scott	1	10	
Rayson, Mrs.	0	10	
Raven, Mrs. M.	0	10	
R. P.	10	0	
Scotland	5	0	
S. H.	5	0	
Stephens, Mrs. E.	0	5	
S. W., per Mr. S. R. Pearce	1	0	
T. A., a friend	0	5	
Townsend, Mrs.	1	1	
Thos, R., Mr.	5	0	
Todd, Mr. A.	0	5	
Wyman, Mrs.	1	0	
W. M.	5	0	
Watcham, Mr. H.	1	10	
W. J.	0	10	
Webb, Mrs.	0	10	
Websdale, Mrs.	1	0	
Willcocks, Mr. W. H.	1	0	
Wood, Mr. and Mrs. Henry	1	1	
Williamson, Mrs.	0	15	
York, Miss R.	0	10	8

	£	s.	d.
York, Miss E.	0	10	0
Sums under 5/-	1	6	10

ANNUAL SUBSCRIPTIONS.

	£	s.	d.
Allison, Mr. C. F.	5	0	0
Barrett, Mr.	0	10	0
Brown, Mr. and Mrs. G.	1	1	0
Brayne, Mr. E.	0	10	6
Casson, Mr. W.	0	10	0
Chamberlain, Mr. A., for 1887	1	1	0
Chamberlain, Mr. A.	1	1	0
Calder, Mrs. G. A.	5	0	0
Cook, Mr. J. J.	1	1	0
Cassell & Co., Messrs., Limited	2	2	0
Davies, Mr. T. E.	2	2	0
Frearson, Mr. H. B.	15	0	0
Fishwick, Mr. F.	2	2	0
Harling, Miss	0	10	0
Harrison, Mr. W.	1	1	0
Hall, Mr. J.	1	1	0
Hellier, Mr. R.	0	10	6
Hellier, Mrs. R.	0	10	6
Izard, Mr. W.	2	2	0
Jenkins, Mrs.	1	1	0
Kent, W. & Co., Messrs.	1	1	0
Liberty, Mr. Charles	0	10	0
Lang, Rev. W. L. and Mrs.	2	0	0
Lloyd, Mr. E. W. N.	10	0	0
Mead, Mr. John	1	1	0
Mead, Mrs. John	1	1	0
Murrell, Mr. W. C.	1	1	0
Norris, Miss	0	10	6
Newman, Miss	5	0	0
Newman, the Misses A. and E.	2	0	0
Olney, Mr. Thos. H.	10	0	0
Olney, Mrs. Jno.	2	2	0
Palmer, Mr. Geo.	20	0	0
Perren, Mr. A.	10	0	0
Parry, Mr. and Mrs. J. C.	0	10	0
Powell, Mr. J.	1	1	0
Penston, Miss	0	10	6
Payne, Mr. W.	1	1	0
Partridge, S. W. & Co., Messrs	2	2	0
Pearce, Mr. S. R.	1	1	0
Passmore, Mr. J. Junr.	1	1	0
Rodgers, Mr. J. J., for 1887	1	1	0
Rodgers, Mr. J. J.	1	1	0
Satchell, Mr. G. F.	2	0	0
Smallridge, Miss	0	10	0
Tucker, Mrs.	0	5	0
Thompson, Mr. F.	1	1	0
Woollard, Mr., for 1887	1	1	0
Woollard, Mr.	1	1	0
Waters, Mr. C., for 1887	0	5	0
Watts, Mr. H. M.	0	5	0
Wayre, Mr. W.	1	1	0

Total   £505 8 1

Legacy and Interest per Executors of the late E. Boustead, Esq. ... 3,039 15 9

METROPOL TAN TABERNACLE COLPORTAGE ASSOCIATI O.

General Account, December 31st, 1888.

Dr.

	£ s. d.	£ s. d.
To Colporteurs—		
Wages ...	946 12 8	
Expenses ...	283 9 0	
New Packs and Repairs ...	55 1 9	5 385 3 5
To Depôt and General Expenses—		
Salaries, Secretary and Assistants ...	524 0 0	
Printing, Stationery, and Annual Reports ...	30 18 7	
Postages and Telegrams ...	22 4 0	
Cleaning, and Al ... ns ...	23 15 0	
Advertising and ...	7 4 6	
... ing and ... ference ...	28 5 1	636 7 2
		£6,021 10 7

Cr.

	£ s. d.	£ s. d. £ s. d.
By Gross Profit on Sales ...		2,051 11 2
By Subscriptions and Donations—		
For Districts ...	2,539 4 1	
For General Purposes ...	505 8 1	3,044 2 2
By ... st on Deposit with Bankers ...	11 15 5	
Interes on Stock Victoria 4% ...	41 5 6	53 0 11
By ... n e Deficiency ...		872 6 4
		£6,021 10 7

Balance Sheet, December 31st, 1888.

Dr.

	£ s. d.	£ s. d.
To ...		
Dist ... ions (in advance) ...	145 19 4	
Publishers, Printers, &c., ...	1,250 9 3	1,396 8 7
To Capital Account—		
Bal ... ce, December 3 st, 87 ...	3,162 15 7	
Balance Deficiency, December 31st, 1888 ...	872 6 4	
	2,290 9 3	
	3,039 15 9	5,330 5 0
* To Legacy, 1888 ...		
This Legacy is ... ted to Curren Expenses.		£6,726 13 7

Cr.

	£ s. d.	£ s. d.
By Stock—		
At Depôt ...	597 13 9	
Wi ... Ag	1,152 18 11	1,750 12 8
By Debtors—		
Colporteurs' Balances (in transit) ...	555 0 9	
Book Agents' ", ...	25 6 2	
District Subscriptions (due) ...	261 4 0	841 10 11
By Investment—		
Victoria 4% Stock ...		1,200 0 0
By Cash—		
At Bankers and on Deposit ...	2,904 10 0	
Wi ... al Secretary ...	30 0 0	2,934 10 0
		£6,726 13 7

Examined with vouchers a d fnd correct,

JAMES A. SPURGEON,
BENJN, WILDON CARR,

W. CORDEN JONES General Secretary.
April 1888.

THE

SWORD AND THE TROWEL.

AUGUST, 1889.

The Preacher's Power, and the Conditions of Obtaining it.

AN ADDRESS BY C. H. SPURGEON, AT THE CONFERENCE.

F we would have the Lord with us in the delivery of our message, *we must be in dead earnest, and full of living zeal.* Do you not think that many sermons are " prepared " until the juice is crushed out of them, and zeal could not remain in such dry husks? Sermons which are studied for days, written down, read, re-read, corrected, and further corrected and emended, are in great danger of being too much cut and dried. You will never get a crop if you plant *boiled* potatoes. You can boil a sermon to a turn, so that no life remaineth in it. I like, in a discourse, to hear the wild-bird notes of true nature and pure grace: these have a charm unknown to the artificial and elaborate address. The music which we hear of a morning, in the spring, has a freshness in it which your tame birds cannot reach; it is full of rapture, and alive with variety and feeling.

It is a treat to hear a really good local preacher tell out his experience of how he came to Christ; and relate it in his own hearty, unaffected way. Nature beats art all to nothing. A simple, hearty testimony is like grapes cut fresh from the vine : who would lay a bunch of raisins by the side of them? God give us sermons, and save us from essays! Do you not all know the superfine brother? You ought to listen to him, for he is clever ; you ought to be attentive to his words, for every sentence of that paper cost him hours of toilsome composition ; but somehow it falls flat, and there is an offensive smell of stale oil. I speak advisedly when I say that some speakers want locking out of their studies, and turning out to visit their people. A very good preacher once said to me, " I feel discouraged ; for the other Sunday I did not feel at all well, and I preached a sermon without much study ; in fact, it was such a talk as I should give if I sat up in bed in the middle of the night, and in my shirt-sleeves told out the way of salvation. Why, sir, my people came to me and said, ' What a delightful sermon ! We have so enjoyed it ! ' I felt disgusted with them. When I have given them a sermon that took a full week, and perhaps more, to prepare, they have not thought anything of it ; but this unstudied address quite won their hearts." I replied to him, " If I were you I would accept their judgment, and give them another sermon of the same sort." So long as the life of the sermon is strengthened by it, you may prepare to the utmost; but if the soul evaporates in the process, what is the good of such injurious toil? It is a kind of murder which you have wrought upon the sermon which you have dried to death. I do not believe that God the Holy Ghost cares one single atom about your classical composition. I do not think that the Lord takes any delight in your rhetoric, or in your poetry, or even in that marvellous peroration which concludes the discourse, after the manner of the final display at old Vauxhall Gardens, when a profusion of all manner of fireworks closed the scene. Not even by that magnificent finale does the Lord work the salvation of sinners. If there is fire, life, and truth in the sermon, then the quickening Spirit will work by it, but not else. Be earnest, and you need not be elegant.

The Holy Spirit will help us in our message, *if there is an entire dependence upon him.* Of course, you all receive this at once ; but do you entirely depend upon the Holy Spirit ? Can you? dare you, do that ? I would not urge any man to go into the pulpit and talk what first came into his head, under the pretence of depending upon the Holy Spirit ; but still, there are methods of preparation which denote the utter absence of any trust in the Holy Spirit's help in the pulpit. There is no practical difficulty in reconciling our own earnest endeavours with humble dependence upon God ; but it is very hard to make this appear logical, when we are merely discussing a theory. It is the old difficulty of reconciling faith and works. I heard of a good man who had family prayer, and commended his house and household to the care of God during the night-watches. When burglaries became numerous in the neighbourhood, he said to a friend, " After you have asked the Lord to protect your house, what do you do ? " His friend answered that he did nothing more than usual. " Well," said the first, " we have put bolts, top and bottom, upon all the doors, and we have a lock and also a chain. Besides that, we have the best patent fastenings on all the windows." " All that is well enough," said his friend ; " is not that enough ? " " No," said he ; " when we go to bed my wife and I have two bolts on the door of the bedroom, and a lock and chain on the door. I have also got a spear-head fixed on a pole, and my wife has an electric apparatus which will ring a bell, and give an alarm outside." His friend smiled, and said, " And all that is faith in God, is it ? " The good man replied, " Faith without works is dead." " Yes," said

AND THE CONDITIONS OF OBTAINING IT.

the other, "but I should think that faith with so many works would be likely to be smothered."

There is a medium in all things. I should not pray God to take care of me, and then leave my front door unfastened and my window open. So I should not pray for the Holy Spirit, and then go into the pulpit without having carefully thought upon my text. Still, if I had prepared thoughts and expressions so minutely that I never varied from my set form, I should think that my faith was, to say the least, encumbered with more works than would allow her much liberty of action. I do not see where the opportunity is given to the Spirit of God to help us in preaching, if every jot and tittle is settled beforehand. Do let your trust in God be free to move hand and foot. While you are preaching, believe that God the Holy Spirit can give you, in the self-same hour, what you shall speak; and can make you say what you had not previously thought of; yes, and make this newly-given utterance to be the very arrow-head of the discourse, which shall strike deeper into the heart than anything you had prepared. Do not reduce your dependence upon the Holy Ghost to a mere phrase; make it more and more a fact.

Above all, dear friends, if you want the blessing of God, *keep up constant communion with God.* We get into fellowship with God at this Conference; do not let us get out of communion with God when we go home. When may a Christian safely be out of communion with God? *Never.* If we always walk with God, and act towards him as children towards a loving father, so that the spirit of adoption is always in us, and the spirit of love always flows forth from us, we shall preach with power, and God will bless our ministry; for then we shall know and utter the mind of God.

I must add here, that if we are to enjoy the power of God, *we must manifest great holiness of life.* I would not ask any brother to profess that he has a higher life than other believers; for, if he did so, we might suspect that he had no very eminent degree of humility. I would not invite any brother to talk about having more holiness than his brother-ministers; for, if he did so, we might fear that he hung out the outward sign because the inward grace was absent. But we must have holiness to a high degree. Unholy living! How can God bless it? I heard of one who, on the Sabbath morning said to his people, "I was at the play last night, and I saw So-and-so"; and he used what he saw as an illustration of his subject. It saddened me to hear the story: may the like never be done again. Alas! acts of worldly conformity are not only tolerated nowadays, but they are, in some quarters, commended as signs of a large mind. If a man can enjoy the theatre, it is his own concern; but when he invites me to hear him preach, I decline to accept his invitation. Even worldlings look with scorn upon loose habits in a preacher. I know a certain clergyman who is fond of cards. Speaking to a man-servant, a friend said, "Where do you go on Sunday; I suppose you attend the church?" —the place being very near. "No," said the man, "I never go and hear that gentleman." "Why not?" "Well," he said, "you know he is very much taken up with card-playing." "Yes," said my friend, "but you play cards yourself." This was the answer: "Yes, I play cards; but I would not trust my soul with a man who does it. I want a better man than myself to be my spiritual guide." The remark is open to many criticisms, but there is about it a ring of common sense. That is how the world regards matters. Now, if even men of the world judge trifling preachers to be unfit for their work, depend upon it the Holy Ghost has not a better opinion of them, and he must be sorely vexed with unspiritual, unholy intruders into the sacred office. If we can lie; if we can be unkind to our families; if we do not pay our debts; if we are notorious for levity, and little given to devotion; how can we expect a blessing? "Be ye clean, that bear the vessels of the Lord." As I have said before, he does not mind what the vessel is, even though it be but of earth or of wood; but it must be clean. It is not fit for the Master's use if it is not clean. Oh, that God would keep us pure, and then take us in his own hand for his own purposes!

Once more: if we are to be robed in the power of the Lord, *we must feel an intense longing for the glory of God and the salvation of the sons of men.* Even when we are most successful, we must long for more success. If God had given us many souls, we must pine for a thousand times as many. Satisfaction with results will be the knell of progress. No man is good who thinks that he cannot be better. He has no holiness who thinks that he is holy enough; and he is not useful who thinks that he is useful enough. Desire to honour God grows as we grow. Can you not sympathize with Mr. Welch, a Suffolk minister, who was noticed to sit and weep; and one said to him, "My dear Mr. Welch, why are you weeping?" "Well," he replied, "I cannot tell you"; but when they pressed him very hard, he answered, "I am weeping because I cannot love Christ more." That was worth weeping for, was it not? That man was noted everywhere for his intense love to his Master, and, therefore, he wept because he could not love him more. The holiest minister is the man who cries, "O wretched man that I am! who shall deliver me from the body of this death?" No common Christian sighs in that fashion. Sin becomes exquisitely painful only to the exquisitely pure. That wound of sin which would not be a pin's prick to coarser minds, seems a dagger's wound to him. If we have great love to Jesus, and great compassion for perishing men, we shall not be puffed up with large success; but we shall sigh and cry over the thousands who are not converted.

Love for souls will operate in many ways upon our ministry. Among other things, it will make us very plain in our speech. We shall say to ourselves, "No, I must not use that hard word, for that poor woman in the aisle would not understand me. I must not point out that recondite difficulty, for yonder trembling soul might be staggered by it, and might not be relieved by my explanation." I heard a sentence the other day which stuck to me because of its finery rather than its weight of meaning. An admirable divine remarked, "When duty is embodied in a concrete personality, it is eminently simplified." You all understand the expression; but I do not think that the congregation to which it was addressed had more than a hazy idea of what it meant. It is our old friend, "Example is better than precept." It is a fine thing to construct sounding sentences, but it is only an amusement; it ministers nothing to our great end. Some would impress us by their depth of

thought, when it is merely a love of big words.   To hide plain things in
dark sentences is sport rather than service for God. If you love men better,
you will love phrases less.   How used your mother to talk to you when
you were a child ?   There ! do not tell me.   Don't print it.   It would
never do for the public ear.   The things that she used to say to you
were childish, and earlier still, babyish.   Why did she thus speak ? for
she was a very sensible woman.   Because she loved you.   There is a
sort of *tutoyage,* as the French call it, in which love delights.   Love's
manner of addressing men disregards all the dignities and the fineries
of language, and only cares to impart its meaning, and infuse the blessing. To spread our heart right over another heart is better than adorning it with the paint and varnish of brilliant speech.   If you greatly
love, you are the kind of man that knows how to feel for men, and with
them.   Some men do not know how to handle a heart at all.   They are
like a stranger at the fish-market, who will so touch certain fish, that
they at once erect their spines, and pierce the hand that touches them.
A fishwife is never hurt in that way, for she knows where to take them.
There is a way of handling men and women, and the art is acquired
through intense love.   How do the mothers of England learn to bring
up their children ?   Is there an academy for maternal tuition ?   Have
we founded a guild of motherhood?   No; love is the great teacher, and
it makes the young mother quick of understanding for her babe's good.
Get much love to Christ, and much love to immortal souls, and it is
wonderful how wisely you will adapt your teaching to the need of those
around you.
    I will mention a few things more which are necessary to the full
display of the power which regenerates sinners, and builds up saints.
Much care should be bestowed upon our surroundings.   Brethren, do
not think that if you go, next Lord's-day, to a place you have never
visited before, you will find it as easy to preach there as it is at home
among a loving, praying people.   Are you not conscious, when going into
some assemblies, that they are cold as ice-wells ?   You say to yourself,
" How can I preach here ? "   You do not quite know why, but you are
not happy.   There is no quickening atmosphere, no refreshing dew, no
heavenly wind.   Like your Lord, you cannot do anything because of
the unbelief around you.   When you begin to preach, it is like speaking
inside a steam-boiler.   No living hearts respond to your heart.   They
are a sleepy company, or a critical society ; you can see it, and feel it.
How they fix their eyes on you, and concentrate their spectacles !   You
perceive that they are in what a countryman called " a judgmatical
frame of mind."   No good will come of your warm-hearted address.   I
have had great success in soul-winning, when preaching in different
parts of the country ; but I have never taken any credit for it; for I
feel that I preach under great advantages : the people come with an
intense desire to hear, and with an expectation of getting a blessing ;
and hence every word has its due weight.   When a congregation expects
nothing, it generally finds nothing even in the best of preachers ; but
when they are prepared to make much of what they hear, they usually
get what they come for.   If a man goes fishing for frogs, he catches
them ; if he fishes for fish, he will catch them, if he goes to the right
stream.   Our work is, no doubt, greatly affected, for good or evil, by the

condition of the congregation, the condition of the church, and the condition of the deacons.

Some churches are in such a state that they are enough to baffle any ministry. A brother minister told me of a Congregational chapel in which there has not been a prayer-meeting for the last fifteen years; and I did not wonder when he added that the congregation had nearly died out, and the minister was removing. It was time he should. What a blessing he will *not* be somewhere else! "But," said he, "I cannot say much about this state of things; for in my own church I cannot get the people to pray. The bulk of them have not been in the habit of taking public part in the prayers, and it seems impossible to get them to do so. What shall I do?" "Well," I replied, "it may help you if you call in your church officers on Sunday mornings, before the service, and ask them to pray for you, as my deacons and elders do for me. My officers know what a trembling creature I am; and when I ask them to seek strength for me, they do so with loving hearts." Don't you think that such exercises tend to train men in the art of public prayer? Besides, men are likely to hear better when they have prayed for the preacher. Oh, to get around us a band of men whose hearts the Lord has touched! If we have a holy people about us, we shall be the better able to preach. Tell me not of a marble pulpit; this is a golden pulpit. A holy people who are living what you preach make the best platform for a pleader for Christ. Christ went up into the mountain and taught the crowd; and when you have a company of godly people around you, you do, as it were, go up into the mountain and speak with the people from a favoured elevation. We need a holy people; but, alas! there is too often an Achan in the camp. Achan is more generally harboured than he used to be, because goodly Babylonish garments and wedges of silver are much in request, and weak faith feels that it cannot do without these spoils. Carnal policy whispers, "What shall we do with the chapel debt if the wealthy deacon leaves, and his silver goes with him? We should miss the respectability which his wife's goodly Babylonish garment bestows upon the place. We have very few wealthy people, and we must strain a point to keep them." Yes, that is the way in which the accursed thing is allowed to debase our churches and defeat our ministries. When this pest is in the air, you may preach your tongue out, but you will not win souls. One man may have more power for mischief than fifty preachers have power for good. May the Lord give you a holy, pleading people, whom he can bless!

For large blessing we must have union among our people. God the Holy Spirit does not bless a collection of quarrelling professors. Those who are always contending, not for the truth, but for petty differences, and family jealousies, are not likely to bring to the church the dove-like Spirit. Want of unity always involves want of power. I know that some churches are greatly at fault in this direction; but certain ministers never have a harmonious people, although they change frequently: and I am afraid it is because they are not very loving themselves. Unless we are ourselves in good temper we cannot expect to keep the people in good temper. As pastors, we must bear a great deal; and when we have borne as much as possible, and cannot bear any more, we must go over it again, and bear the same things again. Strong in the love which "endureth all things, hopeth all things," we must quietly resolve not to take offence, and before long harmony will be created where discord reigned, and then we may expect a blessing.

We must plead with God that our people may be all earnest for the spread of the truth and the conversion of sinners. How blessed is that minister who has earnest men around him! You know what one cold-hearted man can do, if he gets at you on Sunday morning with a lump of ice, and freezes you with the information that Mrs. Smith is offended, and all her family, and their pew is vacant. You did not want to know of that lady's protest just before entering the pulpit, and it does not help you. Another dear brother tells you with great grief (he is so overcome that it is a pity his voice does not fail him altogether) that one of the best helpers is very much hurt at your not calling to see him last Friday, when you were a hundred miles away preaching for a struggling church. You ought to have called upon him at any inconvenience, so the brother will tell you, and he does his duty with a heart "as cool as a cucumber." It may even happen that when you come down from the mount where you have been with God, and preached with your soul on fire, that you come right down into a cold bath of commonplace remark, which lets you see that some of your hearers are out of sympathy both with your subject and yourself. Such a thing is a great hindrance, not only to your spirit, but to the Spirit of God; for the Holy One notices all this unkind and unspiritual behaviour. Brethren, what a work we have to do! What a work we have to do! Unless the Spirit of God comes to sanctify these surroundings, how can it ever be done? I am sure you feel the necessity of having a truly praying people. Be much in prayer yourself, and this will be more effectual than scolding your people for not praying. Set the example. Draw streams of prayer out of the really gracious people by getting them to pray whenever they come to see you, and by praying with them yourself whenever you call upon them. Not only when they are ill, but when they are well, ask them to join in prayer with you. When a man is upstairs in bed, and cannot do any hurt, you pray for him. When he is downstairs, and can do no end of mischief, you do not pray for him. Is this wise and prudent? Oh, for a pleading people! The praying legion is the victorious legion. One of our most urgent necessities is fervent, importunate prayer.

Brethren, in addition to co-operation in service, we need that our friends should be *looking out for souls.* Whenever a stranger comes into the chapel, somebody should speak to him. Whenever a person is a little impressed, an earnest brother should follow up the stroke. Whenever a heart is troubled, some genial voice should whisper to him words of comfort. If these things were so, our ministry would be quadrupled in effort, and the result would be fourfold. May all our chapels be co-operative stores for zeal and earnestness, wherein not one man but every man is at work for Christ!

I have done when I say just this. *Let each man bethink him of the responsibility that rests upon him.* I should not like to handle the doctrine of responsibility with the view of proving that it squares with the doctrine of predestination. It does do so, assuredly. I believe in predestination without cutting and trimming it; and I believe in responsibility without adulterating and weakening it. Before you the man of God places a quiver full of arrows, and he bids you shoot the arrow of the Lord's deliverance. Bestir yourself, and draw the bow! I beseech you, remember that every time you shoot there shall be victory for Israel. Will you stop at the third shooting? The man of God will feel angry and grieved if you are thus straitened, and he will say, "Thou shouldest have smitten five or six times, and then Syria would have been utterly destroyed." Do we not fail in our preachings, in our very ideal of what we are going to do, and in the design we set before us for accomplishment? Having laboured a little, are we not very satisfied? Shake off such base content! Let us shoot many times. Brethren, be filled with a great ambition; not for yourselves, but for your Lord. Elevate your ideal! Have no more firing at the bush. You may, in this case, shoot at the sun himself; for you will be sure to shoot higher if you do so, than if some grovelling object were your aim. Believe for great things of a great God. Remember, whether you do so or not, great are your responsibilities. There never was a more restless time than now. What is being done to-day will affect the next centuries, unless the Lord should very speedily come. I believe that if we walk uprightly and decidedly before God at this time, we shall make the future of England bright with the gospel; but trimming now, and debasing doctrine now, will affect children yet unborn, generation after generation. Posterity must be considered. I do not look so much at what is to happen to-day, for these things relate to eternity. For my part, I am quite willing to be eaten of dogs for the next fifty years; but the more distant future shall vindicate me. I have dealt honestly before the living God. My brother, do the same. Who knows but what thou art come to the kingdom for such a time as this? If thou hast grit in thee, quit thyself like a man. If thou hast God in thee, then thou mayest yet do marvels. But if not, bent, doubled up, proven to be useless, thou shalt lie on that foul dunghill which is made up of cowards' failures and misspent lives. God save both thee and me from that!

I would enhance our sense of responsibility by the remembrance of the death-beds of our people. Unless we are faithful to them, it will be a painful sight to be present when they come to die. Suppose that any one of our hearers should stretch out his bony hand, and say, "I am lost, and you never warned me; you always gave me some idea that it might be a little way round-about, but I should get right all the same; and I chose the round-about way of the 'larger hope,' instead of the divine hope that is set before us in the gospel." I would rather never have been born than have anybody speak thus to me when he shall come to die. My brother said to me the other day what Charles Wesley said to John Wesley: "Brother, our people die well!" I answered, "Assuredly they do!" I have never been to the sick bed of any one of our people without feeling strengthened in faith. In the sight of their glorious confidence, I could sooner battle with the whole earth, and kick it before me like a football, than have a doubt in my mind about the gospel of our Lord. They die gloriously. I saw, last week, a dear sister, with cancer just under her eye. How did I find her? Was she lamenting her hard fate? By no means; she was happy, calm, joyful, in bright expectation of seeing the face of the King in his glory. I talked with a tradesman, not long ago, who fell asleep, and I said, "You seem to have no fears." "No," he said, "how can I have any? You have not taught us what will make us fear. How can I be afraid to die, since I have fed these thirty years on the strong meat of the Kingdom of God? I know whom I have believed." I had a heavenly time with him. I cannot use a lower word. He exhibited a holy mirth in the expectation of a speedy removal to the better world.

Now, dear brethren, suffer one last word. You and I will soon die ourselves, unless our Master comes; and blessed will it be for us, if, when we lie in the silent room, and the nights grow weary, and our strength ebbs out, we can stay ourselves upon the pillows and say, "O Lord, I have known thee from my youth, and hitherto have I declared thy wondrous works; and now that I am about to depart, forsake me not." Thrice happy shall we be, if we can say, in the last article, "I have not shunned to declare the whole counsel of God."

Brethren, I resolve, God helping me, to be among those that shall walk with our Lord in white, for they are worthy. "These are they," it is said, "who have not defiled themselves," entered into no contracts and confederacies that would have stained their consciences, and polluted their hearts. These are they who have walked apart for his dear sake, obeying this word, "Come out from among them: be ye separate, touch not the unclean thing; and I will be a Father unto you, and ye shall be my sons and daughters, saith the Lord Almighty." A special enjoyment of adoption is given to the conscience that is true to the separated path, and is never degraded by compromise. God help you in this! I believe that in fidelity will be your power. "You may well make a little slit in your conscience," said one to a Puritan, "for other people make great rents in theirs." "Yes," said he, "you call me precise; but I serve a precise God." Hear you that solemn word, "I the Lord thy God am a jealous God." This jealousy burns like coals of fire, and it is cruel as the grave; for God is so sternly jealous of those he loves much, that he will not bear in them that which he will endure in others. The greater his love, the more fierce his jealousy if in any way his chosen depart from him.

I shall be gone from you ere long. You will meet and say to one another, "The President has departed. What are we going to do?" I charge you, be faithful to the gospel of our Lord Jesus Christ, and the doctrine of his grace. Be ye faithful unto death, and your crowns will not be wanting. But oh! let none of us die out like dim candles, ending a powerless ministry in everlasting blackness. The Lord himself bless you! Amen.

Mosquitoes.

BY THOMAS SPURGEON.

YES, I hear him! There is no mistaking his war-song. He is, as yet, a good way off; but that distance lessens every moment, and the dismal noise increases. He will be digging into my epidermis, in an instant, with his long proboscis! No; he is away again. Hurrah! But not for long. Nearer, and yet nearer, he approaches, until he blows his unwelcome trumpet in my very ear, and I can bear it no longer. I madly dash my hands about my head, in the hope of annihilating my invisible foe. But I succeed only in hitting the place where he *was*. I fight as one that beateth the air. However, he retires for a while, and gives me space wherein to re-compose myself for sleep.

But all too soon he, or some of his companions (for, like the locusts, "they go forth all of them by bands"), renew the attack. The sound of the trumpet waxes exceeding loud and long, and the unhappy victim is beset on every side by *musketeers* who never miss their aim, and whose bullets are poisoned, every one.

It is all very well for you, dear reader, whose happy lot is cast in so cool a climate, to say, "What a fuss to make over a trifle! Much ado about nothing! How foolish to be fearful of such insignificant things!" and the like. Let me tell you that to be pestered with these little vampires is no joke. There is something horrific in their hum. "Perhaps their bark is worse than their bite," you suggest. To which I reply: they are both bad, and the worst of it is that, like Mary and her little lamb, the one nearly always accompanies the other.

But you say, "After all, it's only a mosquito bite." Yes, but that reflection affords small comfort when that same bite has raised a lump as big as a florin, which stings and smarts with utmost irritation. And when some extra sweet individual, of whom the mosquitoes are evidently specially fond, has to wear dark spectacles to hide the excrescences all around her eyes, and cannot go to meeting because she is "such a sight," surely the bite is bad enough, say what you will of the bark.

For my own part, it is the "bark," the war-whoop, which troubles me. For more than one reason, *my* beauty has never suffered because of the bites, and the poison doesn't "take" with me as with most. But oh! that terrible tattoo, that indescribable slogan, rising and falling, waxing and waning. Farewell sweet sleep, while such music (?) is about. True, the thing that creates all this trouble is tiny and fragile. A touch will silence him. He knows that too. Hence he takes good care that you don't touch him.

By the way, it is a great mistake to measure influence, either for good or ill, by size. Just as these little things prove great nuisances, so some of our lesser troubles are really the most annoying. Hearing of them, one might say, "Oh, those are the merest trifles!" But experiencing them, we discover that small vexations and little worries are tantalizing in the extreme. If little foxes spoil the vines, little trials spoil our rest and mar our peace. Getting rid of these pests is no easy matter. Do not I know from experience that mosquito nets will sometimes shut them *in*, instead of out? Am I not aware that

eau-de-Cologne and oil of lavender soon lose their virtue ? Need I still
to be convinced that you may fumigate your dormitory by burning
Persian insect powder till suffocation threatens, and that in spite of it,
by early morning the 'squitoes will be as lively and hungry as ever?

The plan of the American patentee for killing cockroaches is about
the best for these things too. He provided each eager applicant with a
couple of pieces of wood, with directions to get the insect on to one,
and to pound it with the other. One thing I know is, that it is perfectly useless to send your arms flying round like the sails of a wind-
mill. Your enemy will be back directly. But then, it is not easy to
lie still, and be bitten. The most successful hunters I know are they
who have sufficient presence of mind, coupled with nimbleness, to allow
their tormentor to settle on cheek, or brow, or *nose,* and then, by a well-
directed smack, to take him in the very act, with the blood upon his
blade. None but the strong-minded and agile need attempt this. It
is as well if they are thick-skinned also. But herein is a moral. We
miss much by being in too much of a hurry and flurry. Oh, if we could
only wait our opportunity !

One of the worst features in the character of these bloodsuckers is,
that they do not attack till the shades of night are falling, and the stars
begin to blink. They love darkness rather than light. But *they* are
not the only creatures who, stabbing in the dark, are the more dangerous
and detestable. These I can pardon (especially if I catch them) on the
score that

" 'Tis their nature too."

But as for the others—well, the difficulty is to catch them; and you
must catch your hare before you cook him.

There is a theory—I do not know how true it is—that if you let these
fellows have their fill their fate is sealed. I could hope that this is so.
I have killed a lot at that rate, by allowing Providence to avenge me.
Is not this the best way to treat other foes ? I know some who have
only injured themselves by a vindictive spirit, while others have had
the work done for them far more effectually. "Vengeance is mine; I
will repay, saith the Lord." The vampire will get a drop too much
presently. The oppressor will overreach himself.

The irritation caused by mosquito bites is, to some, unendurable.
They must tear, and rub, and scratch the place. No sooner is the itching
felt, than on come the finger-nails, themselves poisonous, to the relief(?)
of the wound. My advice is that which *Punch* once gave on quite
another subject—"DON'T !" Does not your vade mecum, treating of
irritation, say, with underlined words, " *scratching must be avoided* " ?
If you can only bear without rubbing (ay, there's the rub), the inflam-
mation will subside the sooner. This advice holds good in other cases
also. Once stung by treachery, or unkindness, or misrepresentation, it
is generally better not to meddle with the wound. The relief resulting
from thinking over and talking about the injury is only temporary.
In reality it only stokes the fire, and spreads the poison. Bear the
wound bravely, good friend. Apply a little lotion in the shape of faith
and prayer, and the burning will soon depart, and your flesh shall be
again as the flesh of a little child.

To my intense astonishment, I find it recorded in natural histories that only the female mosquito stings—that she alone is the bloodsucker. If this be so, there is a large preponderance of the weaker—I had almost said gentler—sex. I look in vain for a complete parallel to this fact (if fact it be) amongst human beings. *Men* can be sharp, and say cutting things, without doubt. Still—shall I say it?—the palm must be yielded to woman. Did I not speak her praise when I wrote of glow-worms? Yes, and truly. But this is true as well. Let it be admitted that a woman who, for the time being, has laid aside the ornament of a meek and quiet spirit, cannot be equalled for caustic retort and stinging insinuation if she has a quarrel, especially with another of her sex. It is said that the mouth of a mosquito, under the microscope, is a perfect case of surgical instruments. Saws and knives, and lancets, and scalpels—they are all there; and to these must be added a phial or two of poison.

Alas! it is true of men as well as of women, "their teeth are as swords, and their jaw teeth as knives; while the poison of asps is under their lips." Ah, these tongues of ours! Would that their edge were dulled, and their venom extracted! Let him that stung sting no more.

What is the possible use of mosquitoes? God created not the earth in vain, and we may be sure that if the house is not purposeless, its furniture and occupants have each their place and office. Suppose we say we know not the reason. We thereby only confess our ignorance. But we can guess, at all events.

Be it remembered that the larvæ of mosquitoes and gnats have their home in stagnant pools and miry swamps. These they help to purify, and to some extent hinder the fearful forces of infection. From their arks among the bulrushes they issue in countless myriads when their wings are grown, each one blowing his own trumpet, and proclaiming clearly enough that there are marshes near that ought to be drained, and pestilential waters that should be cleansed. They have themselves done their little best to clarify and purify, so they can now the more freely urge the authorities to use their stronger power for the good of the people. Bravo, little buglers! Let us hope you will trumpet to some purpose. But city councils, and road boards, and vestries, are hard to influence. Thank you for your warning voices! While that deceiver, "Jack-o'-Lantern," beckons travellers into the bog, you warn the unwary not merely of the mire and slush, but of the malaria which lurks therein! So, if "the cholera is God's protest against dirt," it may be that mosquitoes remonstrate, at his command, against stagnation and miasma, and the neglect that too often causes them.

I have heard it hinted, too, that but for bees and butterflies we should be sickened with the overpowering sweets exhaling from the flowers, and that we have to thank gnats and mosquitoes (bloodsuckers though they be) for helping in this task.

Who knows but that the sweets of life would sicken us but for the many things that help to remove the dangerous honey? Some of these may bite and sting us, but such treatment we can bear if they also prevent us from sipping too much nectar, and inhaling the overpowering redolence of earthly flowers. Anything that relieves us of a super-abundance of merely worldly joy is a real blessing. Oh, that we may ever hail it as such, and thank our Father for it!

"A Short Life and a Merry One."*

"A SHORT LIFE AND A MERRY ONE." Such was the frequent ejaculation used by my school-fellow Tom after he had once got into the full power of the whirlpool of pleasure and sin which surrounded him in this big city of London. The beginning of his life was bright with promise. He was welcomed into the world by parents who were blessed with many social comforts; so that from early childhood Tom might truly have said with the Psalmist, "The lines have fallen unto me in pleasant places."

In our school days we had many things in common. Amongst other things, a goodly share of the schoolmaster's long cane fell to our lot; and sometimes he distributed to us our portion in a most unmerciful manner. Those were the days of instruction through the flesh. In the Sunday-school we were taught, as boys, many gracious lessons; and had we heeded them, we should have been saved many a pang in after-life.

On reaching our teens a great trial fell to the lot of each of us. I lost my father by death before I was fifteen, and about the same time Tom was called upon to commit all that was mortal of his dear mother to the cold grave. This was indeed a loss for him. None are in greater danger than boys who have lost their mothers. We need earnestly pray, "O God, help the dear boys, who are early bereft of the care and love of a mother." A boy may manage to struggle on fairly well without the guardian care of a father ; but what can make up for the loss of a mother's tender care and loving influence ? Nothing but God himself.

After the home had been broken up by death, Tom set off for London. Just about this time I left my country homestead for this great centre, which seems now to have no circumference. By God's grace, and to him be the praise, I was carried, after a time, by a gracious guidance, within the reach of Christian influence ; and in answer to my godly mother's daily prayer, was sought and found by the great Seeker of souls.

Unhappily for poor Tom, his lot was like that of the man who went down from Jerusalem to Jericho : "He fell among thieves." The good seed sown in early life was soon plucked up by the fowls of the air, in the form of evil companions, who led him to become familiar with the pipe, the pot, the play, the song, the dance, and other things. Low pursuits engrossed the whole of his time and attention, till he became a complete tool in the hands of his evil companions, whirled rapidly round like a child's toy in the wind. Tom was like a boy's whipping-top, constantly being whipped into wicked activity by the lash of the tempter.

After a few years of gay life, the marks of the task-master were visible in his person to all who saw him ; and the truth of that text, "The way of transgressors is hard," had come home to him with a bitter experience. Still he would not acknowledge it. He tried hard to brave it out by a toss of the head, and a jest. With a don't-care kind of manner he would continually repeat his flippant prayer, "A short life and a merry one is the sort of life for me." The last time I was in his company was before my conversion to God. The chorus of the song he sang I cannot forget. It has often struck me and stung me since. It ran as follows :—

---

* See Review of "More Stray Leaves," and purchase the volume.

> "So let the world jog along at its will,
> I'll be free and easy still;
> Free and easy, free and easy,
> I'll be free and easy still."

Poor fellow! He knew little of true ease, for he had no peace of mind. He was then like many to-day who think they are free, while they are the bondslaves of the devil. The servants of sin are neither free nor easy; for all the time they think they are pleasing themselves, they are pleasing and serving Satan.

"Oh!" says the poor slave to sin, "I can do what I like; and that is liberty." Nay, friend, it is the very reverse of liberty. Doing what is *right* and doing what you *like* are two very different things. Doing what you like is liberty run wild. When liberty leaps into licentiousness at a bound, it ceases to be liberty. Licentiousness forges fetters from which no human power can free a man. Easy you never can be whilst living in sin, for the conscience you now manage to drug will awake one day, and the ease you thought to have gained will prove to be only the forerunner of sorrow.

Soon after my companion had reached his majority, a lawyer called upon him and told him that he had in his possession upwards of £1,000, which was his share of his grandmother's property. This unexpected news Tom called a slice of good luck; and on hearing it he exclaimed, "Bravo! Here goes, then, for a short life and a merry one!" Of the latter part of this sentence I will say nothing; but the first part was true enough, too true for poor Tom, for before two months had passed away, his decision, so flippantly uttered, was unexpectedly fulfilled.

The details of his life during that short time are better not told. During the six weeks after receiving his property he was never once sober. For three weeks his clothes were never taken off his body; his end came suddenly while surrounded by sin in a low public-house. The details of his death are too revolting to repeat, and no purpose would be served by the narration. But for the sake of any young man who may have started on the inclined plane, which proved the ruin of my school-fellow, I must give another word by way of solemn warning. I trust I have already said enough to warn any who may be under a similar temptation. May the red light of danger be seen by those who are choosing the downward road which leads to destruction!

Reader, do you know anything of God's saving and keeping grace? If so, thank God daily for this blessed privilege. If not, "Seek the Lord while he may be found, call upon him while he is near." But for God's grace my fate and portion might have been the same as that of my early companion Tom. I would adore that grace, and live to its praise. Tom was always good-natured, and in this lay much of his peril. The lines of our life led to different destinations: they were once parallel, but he yielded little by little till he was carried by the current of sin from bad to worse.

Reader, do you ever pray? If not; let me suggest a prayer for you to pray at once, *just now*. It is not original, it was once prayed by Peter, and answered immediately. It is a prayer of three syllables. "*Lord, save me.*" I have known many pray this prayer, and receive the answer right away. If you have already prayed it, and have received

the answer in your soul, let me ask you to add to that prayer this one—
"Lord, keep me and use me daily for thy glory." Expect an answer to
the prayer which you present, for according to your faith it shall be unto
you.   J. MANTON SMITH.

That Cheering Look.

I REMEMBER to have preached, years ago, at a watering-place in the
Virginia Mountains, at the dedication of a new church. The people
were all strangers to each other; and, as we went away, my friend said
(who had a right to speak so familiarly), "I wonder, my dear fellow,
that you could be animated at all to-day; for we are all strangers, and
things were pretty cold, I thought." "Ah!" but the preacher replied,
"you did not see old brother Gwathmey, of Hanover, who sat there by
the post. The first sentence of the sermon caught hold of him, and it
kept shining out of his eyes and his face, and he and the preacher had
a good time together, and we didn't care at all about the rest of you."
Sometimes one good listener can make a good sermon; but ah! sometimes
one listener, who does not care much about the sermon, can put the
sermon all out of harmony! The soul of a man who can speak effectively is a very sensitive soul, easily repelled and chilled by what is unfavourable, and easily helped by the manifestation of simple and unpretentious sympathy.—*Dr. J. A. Broadus.*

Aërated Rationalism.

DR. JOHN KER, in his admirable "History of Preaching," gives a
description of Karl Schwarz, which might, perhaps, be applicable
to some preachers even in this country. "Schwarz is the exponent of
The Newest Theology, a kind of manifesto of his party, and his sermons
have already passed through several editions. He is a man of sharp
intellect, ready and eloquent of utterance, while a breeze of imagination
fills the sails of his speech, and makes up for the want of real warmth
and light. His principle is, that a preacher must translate the spirit of
Christ into the wants and feelings of his time, by which he means the
adaptation, not of language, but of the substance of Christian doctrines.
He would take the ideas of sin and atonement, the death, resurrection,
and ascension of Christ, and, having stripped them of what he calls their
mythical dress, he would apply them to the human nature of our day.
Thus, for the Holy Spirit, he substitutes 'the higher reason of Christianity'; for the sinful heart 'the laxity of modern life'; for regeneration,
'the beginning of nobler impulses'; instead of Christ's ascension, we have
'the elevation of humanity'; instead of personal immortality, we have
'corporate immortality.' The old words are very often so skilfully used
that the superficial hearer thinks he is getting the Bible, and it is only the
hungry heart which feels the want of living bread. There is, at the
same time, a constant repetition of scorn for traditionalism and Phari-
saism, with a claim to superior enlightenment and culture. But it is
simply the old rationalism aërated—Hegel in the pulpit instead of Wolf;
and when it stands awhile, or comes from an unskilful imitator, it is as
dead as such teaching was in the middle of the last century."

GROUP OF LEPERS IN INDIA.

The Leprosy.

THE painful subject of leprosy has, of late, been forced upon public attention. The united recognition of the heroism of Father Damien will have the best permanent result if it moves the heart of Christendom to compassionate the leper. Although unable to serve on the committee, we can heartily co-operate in their main object; and we can do so all the more freely when the subject takes a wider scope, and does not gather around a single individual. There were heroes before Damien, and many of them; but as they did not happen to belong to the Romish church, they were left to work and suffer without recognition. We do not envy the Catholic, but we feel aggrieved for the Moravian; and we hope that henceforth philanthropy may receive due honour, whatever the religious opinions of the man who, for its sake, makes a sacrifice of himself.

The picture on the opposite page is a very terrible one, but it is the copy of a photograph sent home by Mr. Potter, who went to Agra from our College, having earned the love and esteem of us all. In the view as we received it, there were three Baptist missionaries (including Mr. Potter) on the right of the lepers, but these made the picture too long, and therefore we have left them out. At the risk of causing painful feelings, we insert the photograph that it may call forth the fervent prayers of our readers for all who enter upon the trying work of dealing with the lepers of heathendom. If our Lord were here, he would not pass them by, but visit them, and heal them; and therefore we are sure that he would have his servants preach his gospel to them, and also aid every effort by which it is hoped that the disease may be alleviated, if not stamped out.

The following letter from Mr. Potter is deeply interesting.

"MY DEAR MR. SPURGEON,—I have been much interested in reading the two articles in The Sword and the Trowel, with reference to the lepers of India. As an old student of the College, and one who has had a share of work among the lepers, perhaps I may be allowed to add a few words to what has been already written. Since my arrival in India, seven years ago, I have become sadly familiar with the sight of leprosy. Of lepers, there are many, and of asylums for them, few. Hence they may be seen in almost all Indian cities and towns, and often in villages also. They live mostly by begging; hence they try to occupy the most prominent places in busy thoroughfares. To move the pity of passers-by, they expose their fingerless hands and decaying feet; hence the sight is a very painful one. Loathed and hated by their own countrymen, and often driven away from the places they would fain occupy, their case is sad indeed. Moreover, being left to themselves, they often marry, and are given in marriage. One sees, therefore, little children nursed and associated with their leprous parents. Yet such is their love of freedom, that they mostly prefer this wandering life to the confinement and discipline of the asylum, where shelter, food, and clothing are all provided freely. When too weak to beg, or too ill to move about, as a last resort, oftentimes, they make their way to the leper-house.

"The Agra leper-house stands in an out-of-the-way place, away from
29

the city and the public road ; hence I had been in India five years before I heard of its existence. It contains about thirty-five lepers, of whom five are women. These people are placed under the medical care of a native Mohammedan doctor. They are provided freely with a small room, and sufficient food and clothing. About two years ago we commenced work among them. Before we began to visit them, they might well have cried, 'No man careth for our souls.' In the bazaar, near by, where we often preach, we are frequently regarded as enemies, and hated as those who are trying to turn away the people from the religion of their fathers. But in the leper-house, which no kind friend ever visits, we are at once received as friends, and thanked for the trouble we take in visiting it. With so little in this world to live for, it was comparatively easy to turn the attention of the poor lepers to the world to come.

"The depravity of human nature, and the defilement of sin, they could realize more easily than others, for they had such a vivid picture of it in their own bodies. They felt their need of healing, both for body and soul, so listened attentively whilst we told them of Jesus, the Healer. After having heard many times of the way of salvation, some of them seem to have gained a very intelligent grasp of the main facts of the gospel. They tell us that they have no faith in idols now, and some tell us that they do believe in Jesus, and pray for pardon in his name. We expect to meet many of these poor lepers in heaven. One gentleman, who had visited many asylums, and knew a good deal about leper work, said he had not met with a more interesting group anywhere. He urged that they should be baptized. It will be our delight to baptize some of them when they request it. It is not difficult to prove to these poor people how much they owe to Jesus Christ. Had they lived about fifty years ago, they might have shared the fate of so many other lepers in India in being buried alive. An old preacher of our mission, who was formerly a Brahmin priest, spoke to them of this, one day, and then, with deep emotion, added, 'With my own hands I have assisted in the burial of a living leper.' Such a thing is now forbidden by law; yet there are not wanting many to this day who would practise it if they dared. Only a few weeks ago a Hindoo asked me why it should be forbidden. 'The lepers,' he said, ' are cursed of God, and ought to be buried away out of sight.' These words sounded to me strange from the lips of one who would, probably, call the killing of an ant sinful, and the killing of a cow the greatest of crimes. Yet so it is, that Hinduism ' strains out the gnat and swallows the camel.' Moral leprosy of the worst type abounds to-day, both among our own so-called Christian fellow-countrymen, and also amongst the Hindoos and Mohammedans. Yet, whited sepulchres as they are, the people think themselves to be very righteous and holy, when inwardly they are full of rottenness and corruption. In the religion of this country morality is of little concern. Hence it is that the heart-religion of Jesus Christ is hated and despised, and his precious blood is trampled under foot. Would that the leprosy of sin were realized by the people as the leprosy of body is by those of whom I have been writing ! It is our privilege to tell of a fountain opened for sin and for uncleanness; yet we have often to cry, with bitterness of soul, 'Who hath believed our report, and to whom is the arm of the Lord revealed?' I am sending a photograph of the Agra lepers, so that they themselves may plead for your prayers and sympathy. "JAMES G. POTTER."

We are glad to receive the Fourteenth Annual Report of work done among the suffering lepers of India. The committee seem to reside in Dublin,. but the secretary is Wellesley C. Bailey, Esq., 17, Glengyle Terrace, Edinburgh. There are said to be five hundred thousand lepers in India, men and women. This society seeks to carry the gospel to them, to relieve their sufferings, and to supply their simple wants. It seems that £6 will support a leper for one year, and £20 will supply a Christian teacher to an asylum for the same period. This is practical information, and we doubt not that many will act upon it. Will they be so good as to write to the above-named secretary, and not to us? The mission appears to work in connection with the great missionary societies, and we doubt not it does great good.

A valuable work has been sent to us for review, entitled, "Leprosy." By W. Munro, M.D., Manchester. It is published by John Heywood, Manchester, and is a very helpful contribution to the science of this horrible disease. Of course, much which is advanced by Dr. Munro is tentative, and will require further testing; but his great theory is certainly a striking one—*the primary probable cause of the disease is a want of salt, combined with a deficient vegetable diet.* This can in due time be tested, and if it should prove to be true, we may yet see leprosy as rare in India as in England, only the Government must remove the Salt Tax, which has always seemed to us to be a mean and cruel impost, getting comparatively little benefit out of a great denial of an article so needful to human health and comfort.

We may return to this subject on another occasion. Meanwhile, we ask the prayers of our subscribers for Mr. Potter, and all who go in and out among the poor victims of this loathsome malady.

C. H. S.

Our Treasure-trove.

"O LORD, THOU ART OUR TREASURE-TROVE," said a devout man in prayer. The expression was somewhat new; but, better still, it struck a chord in our heart. It was a memorable day when first we found our Lord Jesus, and saw in him our all in all. By that discovery we rose from poverty to wealth. Many a time had we ploughed that field and never dreamed of treasure; but our plough struck on a stone and at the moment we were vexed, for we thought it would break the share. We passed by the obstacle; but when we returned in the next furrow we struck on it again with a jerk which threw the whole plough out of gear. A stone of stumbling was in our way : we must needs see into the matter. Ah! then it was that we perceived the great prize, " the treasure hid in a field." What a mine of wealth he has been to us no pen can write, nor tongue can tell! "Unto you which believe he is precious ;" but how precious no arithmetician can compute.—C. H. S.

Cases of Providential Provision.

THE following instances are recorded of provision made for those servants of God, the ejected ministers, in circumstances of want and difficulty. They might be multiplied a thousand-fold. Great as were the sufferings of these holy Nonconformists, their Lord did appear for them in many marvellous ways; and in no case did the Lord leave them to lament their bold adhesion to the way of truth.

1. After Mr. Edmund Matthews was ejected from Wollaston, in Northamptonshire, he was reduced to great straits. By the practice of physic he barely earned a livelihood. But he ever expressed a strong confidence in God; and at the lowest ebb of his affairs manifested no desponding fears respecting the subsistence of himself and his family, which consisted of his wife and seven children. He cheerfully committed them to divine Providence, and God cared for them; for when Mr. Matthews was on his death-bed, a message came from two of his relations, one of whom sent him word that he would clothe his wife and children, and the other, that he would provide them with food. They in fact never afterwards wanted, and some of them rose to exalted stations in life. In this instance, the Lord displayed, not only his faithfulness to such as trust in him, but his mindfulness of their labours of love; for when this good man was in affluence he was noted for his great charity to the poor.

2. Mr. Whiting, of Aldwinkle, in the same county, had great offers from the Earl of Peterborough, if he would conform; but the voice of conscience was too powerful for the suggestions of interest; and he was ejected. Though his wife's friends were rich, they gave him no fortune with her, of which she frequently complained to him: but he used to reply, "We have no need of it now; it will come, perhaps, when we need it more": and it pleased God that, just when he was ejected from his living, her parents died and left them all their property. Mr. Whiting seems to have been one of those true Christians, who, in every situation, say of their heavenly Father, "He hath done all things well"; for the minister, who preached his funeral sermon, said that "He had often heard him mourn, but never heard him murmur; and that he was much taken up in admiring the goodness of God."

3. Mr. Mortimer, ejected from Sowton, in Devonshire, found much difficulty in providing for his large family, and was at last reduced so low, that he was under the necessity of leaving the place of his residence to avoid an arrest. As he walked along the road, he met a man driving some sheep. Mr. Mortimer was desirous of avoiding him; but the man came up to him, and put a paper into his hand, which he found to contain a sum of money. He immediately returned home to his dejected wife and family, praising God for this seasonable relief. On the paper there was nothing written but these words, "To preach Providence."

4. Many instances are recorded of the interference of divine Providence for Mr. Maurice, of Stretton, in rescuing him out of the hands of persecutors. This good man was wonderfully supplied in time. On one occasion, when he was in prayer with his family, and representing their necessities to his heavenly Father, a carrier knocked at the door, and

delivered to him a handful of money, which he said was a present from some friends, but would not tell who they were. The same person was, at another time, the instrument of relief in a similar manner.

5. After the ejection of Mr. Thomas Perkins, from Burley, in Rutlandshire, he was often in great straits; but his faith was unshaken and constant, and he manifested much cheerfulness and pleasantness in all conditions. His niece being once on a visit to him, he, in the course of their friendly conversation, said to her, "Child, how much do you think I have to keep my family? But poor threepence!" Observing her to appear affected at this, he very cheerfully exclaimed, "Fear not, God will provide": and, in a little time, a gentleman's servant knocked at the door, and brought him a side of venison, with wheat and malt. The good man then took his niece by the hand, and said, "Do you see? Here is venison, which is the noblest flesh, the finest of wheat for bread, and good malt for drink. Did I not tell you God would provide?"

"Ye Must be Born Again."

ABOUT eighteen years ago, when in the north of England, at one of our minister's fraternal gatherings, I heard the following, which, as near as I can remember, I relate for the benefit of those who delight in variety at the expense of truth, and to encourage those who keep pegging away with one aim only, namely, the gathering out of God's elect from the ruins of "The Fall."

In a rather fashionable and wealthy circuit among the Methodists, a good brother had recently been invited or appointed; his fame as a preacher had preceded him; in his last circuit it was said he drew persons from all denominations to hear him, and his chapel, when he preached, was always full. Many gathered to hear him on his first Sunday. In the morning he preached from the words, "*Ye must be born again*," dwelling upon the last two words, showing the analogy between the natural and spiritual birth. Some praised it, saying they had heard nothing like it for long enough; others said it smacked rather too much of Calvinism. The unusual manner of dealing with the subject, and the deep thoughtfulness shown in its preparation, caused many to talk of it and him; and as a consequence, a larger congregation came to hear him in the evening. Then he took the same text, this time dwelling upon the results in the individual life of those who were "*born again*," urging his hearers to personal examination, repeating his text often during the sermon. Many of those who praised in the morning held their peace at night. What was "Calvinistic" then, was "too personal" now.

Notwithstanding adverse criticism, a still larger congregation gathered the next time he preached, when he for another sermon chose the same words for his text, this time enforcing the *necessity* for the new birth by emphasizing the "*must*." Many and various were the comments at the close of the service. To many lovers of the truth it was as "marrow and fatness." These also talked about the "three wonderful sermons" they had heard from the same text. But that evening the preacher announced for his text, John iii. 7, "Marvel not," &c.

This time he emphasized the "I," opening up the character of the wonderful person speaking. "Marvel not that *I* said," &c., following up the argument to its logical issue—that for *him* to say so, IT MUST BE SO. "He who formed the body and filled it with the soul, who came from heaven's glory for the express purpose of redeeming both to God the Father, ought to know what he was talking about when HE said, '*Ye must be born again.*' "

Some of the leaders and stewards of the chapel thought they had heard enough of this text; all agreed that the subject was "well handled," "nicely put," "cleverly thought out," but "rather dogmatic"; and some suggested they might have "too much of a good thing," and hoped they had heard the last of that text. Judge of their surprise the next Sunday morning, when, for the fifth time, their new minister took "the same old text." Everybody agreed that it was a wonderful sermon—logical, incisive, and experimental; and not by any means a repetition of any former sermon.

In the evening of the same day he made a most earnest and eloquent appeal to the unconverted from the *same* words, "Ye must be born again," defining the condition of various classes to whom the words applied. At its close he asked any who "WISHED *they were born again,*" to come to the front; while those who *knew* they were, were requested to remain to pray for the power of the Spirit. Large numbers of both kinds remained, while the majority of the congregation left the building. Many entered into peace that night, and a grand awakening had begun.

At a stewards' meeting during the following week, this matter of three Sundays with their new minister and only one text, was a subject of discussion; and after the proper business of the meeting had been transacted, one of them ventured to ask him, in the presence of the others, if he could find but one text in his Bible? "Well," said the minister, "I might find another, and possibly shall do so; but answer me this—are all our people born again yet? Why did they all troop out of chapel, last Sunday, immediately after the sermon?" Several replied, they did not suppose the majority were regenerated. "Then," said he, "I must tell them their need, and *preach the new birth* TILL THEY ARE."

The next Sunday, just before the sermon, this new minister leaned over the desk, and confidentially asked them all to give him their attention. Of course, they gave it; when he spoke words to this effect, "I have been asked during the week if I cannot find another text in my Bible besides John iii. 7. I NEVER FIND TEXTS. I study my *people* and my *Bible*. I pray to be guided to the right subject for them. When a text lays hold on me, I preach the truth it contains. *When it drops me, I drop it.* Your position as a church and congregation is an honourable one. Good Sunday-school; good staff of teachers; large income from seat-rents; good collections for home and foreign missions, and for all charities. You have a good organ and a good choir; a good house for your minister. In every way you are a pattern for other congregations, except for one thing, and that is the prayer-meeting. I could count easily all who were present at the one *preceding* my first sermon here. *I found this;* and my text fell upon me. I was compelled to preach the most important and fundamental doctrine in the

Bible. If we are not born again, we have no true religion; our profession is simply dressing up an enemy in the regimentals of the Queen's troops; we have not the Spirit of Christ, therefore we are none of his. Now, no one can be born again long without knowing it; therefore, I ask a favour of you this morning, and that is, that all of you dear people who *have been born again* will raise your hands; and, let me say, you will not be ashamed to let others know it, if you are. May God help you to testify of his grace in you!"

Amidst profound silence, nearly one-third put up the hand.

"I see," said the minister, "that more than one-half of you are not born again yet; will you that *are*, unite in prayer for those who *are not*, while I preach to them, for they are yet dead in trespasses and sins." After a short and earnest prayer, he again announced as his text, "Marvel not that I said unto thee, Ye must be born again."

In the evening, to a crowded congregation, he preached from the words, "He that hath the Son hath the life; he that hath not the Son hath not the life" (1 John v. 12. R.V.). In consequence of this man of God's earnest, though eccentric manner, his preaching was the means of a very gracious awakening and revival in that neighbourhood; and nearly every Sunday, for a considerable time, there were persons remaining after the services asking, "What must I do to be saved?" We are led to cry often, "Oh, for more of the old-fashioned *discriminating* kind of preaching!" We have plenty of generalities; there appears to be a widespread fear of offending "the pew" by supposing that any members of our congregations are not Christians; even the prayers offered from most of our pulpits suppose that all present are children of God, while some go even further than that, and teach the pernicious doctrine of the universal fatherhood of God. Not long ago I myself heard a leading minister in Bristol declare to his people—a large and mixed congregation—as follows :—"God is your Father; if he is not, who is? Certainly not the devil; he could not beget such a wonderful, comprehensive combination of body, soul, and spirit. Should anyone come to you and say that God is not your Father, tell him it is a lie. Never give up this heritage, your birthright."

Such men ignore the plain teaching of the Word of God; they cannot read such portions as John viii., 1 John iii., or Paul's arguments to the Romans and Galatians. Thank God, there are those who are not afraid to make a distinction between Christ and Beelzebub; between saint and sinner; between "those called out" (Ecclesia), and those left; between *pardoned* sinners and rebels; not following the majority, who only distinguish between the copper and silver; the silver and gold; the silk dress and the merino; the gold-headed cane and the hazel staff; the working-man and the gentleman; the servant and the lady, in the church and assembly of believers. Oh, for more of the Spirit of the Master in all our membership, that we all may be one, making a distinction where our Lord made one, but not dividing what he hath joined together!

WILLIAM M——.

In the Forest.

DWELLERS in grimy cities sigh for the fields and floods. Tens of thousands must thus sigh in vain. Pity them, ye whose ways are free, and who feel the grass and moss beneath your up-springing feet, instead of the hard granite, or the Dead Sea asphalte of our endless streets. Oh, for a ramble through the woods, and a glimpse at the deer as they fly from the sound of the branch you have broken beneath your tread! It is refreshing to think that the piler of bricks has not yet engrossed the whole of God's fair earth, and that here and there spots remain to remind us of the world of angels and their songs, which long preceded the reign of steam-engines and their yells. At the very thought of the great beech-trees, and the bracken, and the fallow deer, our heart bows down and worships God.

Those who are so happy as to have a holiday, should more and more see to it that they sanctify it by peaceful devotion. The beneficial effect of a quiet day of prayer and praise is far greater, even in a physical direction, than that of a month amid the crowd and noise of a seaside resort, where, instead of real rest, one hunts for fresh excitements. Only the truly devout Christian can know the marvellous restorative power of nature, when she is enjoyed in all her delicious quiet in communion with nature's God.

Lines for the Times.

SUCCESS is sad defeat when truth is maimed,
And offerings dissolute bedeck the fane,
Where disbelief, too oft, alas! has claimed,
And, shameless, vaunted a debasing gain.

'Tis not in numbers to outweigh the right,
Weighed in the balance, numbers are but nought;
'Tis not in darkness to accord with light,
Nor conscience can, at any price, be bought.

Deep cunning, artifice, duplicity,
A guise of false adornment may display;
But not for ever; the glad time shall be,
When all earth's sin-blights shall have passed away.

When the Judean Monarch gave the head
Of the stern Baptist at a wanton's quest,
It was the witness, not the truth, lay dead;
Truth cannot perish, though by might oppressed.

What though the crooked ways of guile succeed,
And truth and justice fail of victory—
Better be faithful, ruled in heart and deed
By law divine, not crafty policy.

Better be met with sneers and proud disdain,
Of those in thin conceit so very wise,
Than bear upon the soul the guilty stain
Of bartering right for wrong, and truth for lies.

—*Selected.*

Elihu; an Example to Young Men.

(Job xxxii.—xxxvii.)

BY JAMES L. STANLEY.

THERE is perhaps nothing which so quickly and so completely reveals a man as his *words*. "Thy speech bewrayeth thee," said the maid to Peter ; and in so saying she illustrated a common principle of judgment. What is *in* generally comes out ; if not at once, yet in the course of time ; and we know the good or evil which lies in the heart. "A good man, out of the good treasure of the heart, bringeth forth good things ; and an evil man, out of the evil treasure of the heart, bringeth forth evil things." And what is *not* in, cannot come out ; and so we know the wisdom or ignorance, the depth or shallowness, of the man. "Out of the *abundance* of the heart, the mouth speaketh."

It is by his speech that we must know Elihu ; for we have no other means of knowing him. His discourse, and a few attendant circumstances, make up the whole material available for forming an estimate of his character. The address is left to speak for itself ; and this it does emphatically.

The conduct of Elihu, indicated in his opening remarks, recalls the words of Psalm xxxix. : "I said, I will take heed to my ways, that I sin not with my tongue : I will keep my mouth with a bridle . . . I was dumb with silence, I held my peace, even from good. . . . My heart was hot within me, while I was musing the fire burned : then spake I with my tongue."

The introductory sentences of Elihu's speech are in full accord with the Psalmist's language, and reveal the first striking characteristic of his utterances, viz., *Modesty*. Can anything exceed the charming simplicity of these words—"Then Elihu answered, and said, I am young, and ye are very old ; wherefore I was afraid, and durst not show you mine opinion." I said, "Days should speak, and multitude of years should teach wisdom." Here are a becoming reserve, a wholesome diffidence, a suitable deference to the opinions of others ; characteristics which would adorn persons of any age, but which are eminently appropriate in youth. Elihu acted in the spirit of Solomon's words, "A wise man will *hear*, and will increase learning." With him, there was not only a "time to speak," but a "time to keep silence." All through the long speeches of Job's other friends, Elihu remained a patient listener, and if he did not learn by their wisdom, he learned by their folly. It is of immense importance to ourselves, and to others, to know when to keep silence. Bishop Butler says : "The wise man observes that there is a time to speak, and a time to keep silence. One meets with people in the world who seem never to have made the last of these observations ; and yet these great talkers do not at all speak from their having anything to say, as every sentence shows, but only from their inclination to be talking ; their conversation is merely an exercise of the tongue, no other human faculty has any share in it. . . . . Is it possible that it should never come into people's thoughts to suspect whether or no it is to their advantage to show so very much of themselves ? Oh, that ye would altogether hold your peace, and it should be your wisdom ! . . . . But one would think that it would be obvious to every one that, when they are in company with their superiors of any kind, whether in years, knowledge, or experience; when proper and useful subjects are discoursed in which they cannot bear a profitable part—that these are times for silence, when they should learn to hear, and be attentive, at least in their turn." That quaint and holy poet, George Herbert, says:—

> " If thou be master-gunner, spend not all
> That thou canst speak, at once, but husband it,
> And give men turns of speech : do not forestall
> By lavishness thine own, and others' wit
> As if thou mad'st thy will. A civil guest
> Will no more talk all, than eat all the feast."

Silence at times is *courteous;* for it has respect to the claims of others. It is *modest;* for it indicates a moderate estimate of one's own powers. It is *wise;* for it increases our means of gaining knowledge by attending to the wisdom of others.

Elihu's conduct also exhibits *Veneration for Age.* " I am young, and ye are very old," says Elihu. Therefore he paused, as he says it is said of him, "because they were elder than he." This regard for age is not a mere sentiment ; but a healthy moral instinct, based upon the relations of inferior and superior. Elihu himself explains, " I said, Days should speak, and multitude of years should teach wisdom." But it may be argued, Elihu's experience did not confirm his expectation. He had to say, " Great men are not always wise: neither do the aged understand judgment." Then, we say, all the more honour to Elihu that he gave them credit for wisdom, and did not judge them unfavourably until he had proved them at fault. To honour old age is not only to obey a natural instinct, but to submit to the Word of God. " Thou shalt rise up before the hoary head, and honour the face of the old man." (Lev. xix. 32.) Multitude of days gives a natural advantage to their possessor. The mental powers, by exercise and cultivation, become matured ; and a long experience furnishes ample material to guide the judgment. True it is that old age does not always realize this ideal; and hoar hairs are not always combined with those high moral qualities which command respect; nevertheless, the general obligation is not thereby cancelled. We must be guided by the rule, and not by the exception. To say the least, it is probable that, in the majority of cases, the old man will prove the abler counsellor, and the young man will lose nothing by recognizing and acting upon that probability. There was a king once, as Old Testament history shows, who "forsook the counsel of the old men," and soon after he had done so his subjects forsook him. Yet we would by no means imply that wisdom only resides beneath the snows of age; for the histories of Daniel and Joseph show that it dwells in those who still possess the dew of youth.

Elihu's conduct also exhibits a beautiful and exemplary *Self-restraint.* His self-restraint would have been most commendable had Job's friends been other than they were, and he had listened quietly to the teachings of wisdom. But there was an element in their utterances which, to a mind like his, must have proved a sore test of patience. They were all wrong in their conclusions, and Elihu saw it; he could see their mistakes as they went on, and yet he held his peace.   His self-restraint was wise in *two* ways.   *He heard all they had to say, before he came to a final conclusion.*   Then he appears to have indulged the hope that they would say something to the point : "Behold, I waited for your words; I gave ear to your reasons, whilst ye searched out what to say." It was *just* to hear all ; it was *kind* to hope for something good.   It is well to feel the stirrings of indignation, enthusiasm, sympathy, affection, and the like ; but it is also well to have these emotions under the control of reason, and the fear of God.   Self-control in any direction is no easy matter, and there is plenty in Scripture and experience to show that one of its most difficult tasks is with the tongue.   But Elihu succeeded well under the circumstances of strong temptation in which he was placed; so may we.   Let us try.

But, let it be observed, there was a limit to this restraint.   He spoke at last, and here we see his *Courage*.   There was nothing sullen or morose about the silence of Elihu.   He did not belong to that

> " sort of men, whose visages
> Do cream and mantle like a standing pond;
> And do a wilful stillness entertain.
> *   *   *   *
> That therefore only are reputed wise
> For saying nothing."

Nor was there aught of servility, or meanness, or idolatry of men about him.   It is true Elihu says, " I was afraid; " but that did not mean that he was afraid of *men*.   When the proper time came, he was prepared to utter his opinion, although that opinion was totally opposed to the elders to whom he had listened.   Elihu had clear convictions, and he had the courage to avow them ; he had formed a judgment, and he feared not to express it.   In his conduct we see a . just balance of behaviour.   There is not, on the one hand, the insolence of conceit and forwardness; nor on the other hand is there the obsequiousness of a slavish spirit.   He knows how to treat men with respect ; and he knows how to maintain a due respect for himself.   There was true courage in Elihu's conduct.   Some can only express dissent under the influence of strong passionate feeling ; but this is much the same as for a man to nerve himself for some disagreeable work by the use of stimulants.   In both cases there would be excited feeling impelling the will, and in all probability the will would be in a mischievous condition.   He is truly courageous who, taking a calm view of all circumstances, and fairly estimating consequences, deliberately resolves to speak the truth.   Elihu was no trimmer.   Not only did he refuse to suppress his convictions ; but he did not shape them in order to please anybody. "The fear of man bringeth a snare " ; and one snare consists in the temptation to cut, and pare, and tone down truth to curry favour with others.   It becomes us always to be temperate in language, and no right-minded person would be reckless of the feelings of others ; yet, at the same time, we should never shrink from avowing what we believe to be right.

So far, we trust, we have shown that Elihu is a pattern to young men.   Imitate him.

The Bible in France

RIGHTLY to understand the vast religious needs of France, when the agents of our great Bible Society commenced their work of systematic distribution, we have to look back for a century or two in the general history of the country. The great false step was taken when the Papacy found more favour than the Reformation; and when the massacre of St. Bartholomew became the fruitful cause of bitterness and calamity. Just before our own civil troubles commenced, in the seventeenth century, the so-called Grand Monarch, Louis XIV., was born, and that heartless, short-sighted king prepared the way for the disastrous times which followed. Utterly without feeling, he was content to pursue a course of luxurious ostentation. Even when the peasants were on the brink of famine, he never thought it worth while to curtail, in the least, the expenditure of his profligate court. He may be said to have been the pupil of Mazarin, the minister of his minority, a man who amassed an enormous fortune, literally wrung out of the miseries of France. When Louis XIV. lost his great minister by death he was hardly more than twenty years of age; and the disastrous policy he at once adopted in regard to religion entailed evils on the country which are still visible. The Protestants of France were then called after Calvin; and it was of these that Louis said: "My grandfather loved the Huguenots without fearing them; my father feared without loving them; I neither fear nor love them." The persecution which followed drove away from France the flower of her subjects. Had the humane and statesmanlike policy of Richelieu and Mazarin been continued, the religious history of France would have run on different lines, and probably the horrible Reign of Terror might have been averted.

Louis XIV., and his equally infamous successor, were the chief authors of the Revolution. France underwent centuries of preparation for the Revolution—and for centuries more she will feel the effects of that mighty upheaval. That catastrophe was promoted by the selfishness of the court, the nobility, and the upper clergy; but, although in the first instance the movement was a reaction against priestcraft and political wrong, the springs by which it was nourished were anti-Christian. In the earlier part of the century, such writers as Voltaire, Diderot, and many more, found congenial occupation in acclimatizing in France the destructive theological criticism of the English deists. While all things were going from bad to worse in the country, the seeds thus sown were sure to ripen into revolution. Voltaire was not an atheist; but he harboured detestation for the upper clergy, who lived scandalous lives of luxury. No wonder that the church sunk still lower in the estimation of the people, when her only defenders were Jesuits; and no wonder that the atheism which those disseminated who came after Voltaire found ready acceptance. Instead of finding a cure, patriots aggravated the disease. A civilized community without the gospel is a suppressed volcano which may at any time break forth with destructive energy.

About two hundred and fifty years ago the Huguenots had more than seven hundred churches in France; and true religion appears to have flourished in their midst in proportion as avenues to emolument and distinction were closed to them. Evil days were coming upon them, however, and one by one their liberties were curtailed, until at length the temper of the court found expression in actual persecution. The fanatical king endeavoured to "convert" his Calvinistic subjects by the aid of "missionaries," whose efforts were seconded by dragoons; little thinking that by driving a million of his best subjects out of the country he was impoverishing France by paralyzing her industries, and enriching his enemies, with whom the exiles took refuge.

The rights of the Huguenots were fully restored at the Revolution of

1789. There are now about a million of so-called Calvinistic Protestants in France; but a century of freedom from persecution has made them less zealous in the cause of truth than their fathers were. Some of the churches have degenerated into Rationalism, not a whit more desirable than the Romanism it has superseded. The Protestants are now divided into two sections, Evangelical and Rationalistic. The Calvinists have about six hundred pastors, and the Lutherans about a tenth part as many. Both of these sections are assisted by the State.

One of the first to become interested in the work of Bible distribution in France was Pástor Oberlin, of the Ban de la Roche, whose work among the inhabitants of that wild but picturesque district constitutes one of the most striking romances of modern church history.

In 1820, the British and Foreign Bible Society opened its own depôt at Paris, under the superintendence of Professor Kieffer. According to the early accounts, the French people received the copies of what was virtually, to many of them, a new revelation, with great gladness; and certain individuals, including the brothers Courtois, the famous bankers of Toulouse, by their freely-rendered services greatly promoted the circulation. With hearts fired with old Huguenot enthusiasm, the Christian bankers seem, as it were, to have exhausted the old methods, and then to have invented new ones in their ardent desire to have the Scriptures scattered among the people.

As the capital of Upper Garonne, the seat of a university, and a centre of trade, Toulouse was favourably situated for Bible distribution. The bankers employed colporteurs to sell copies in the great square of the city; while others, also in their employ, penetrated into every street and lane in order to dispose of copies of the New Testament to the lowest classes of the people. The Revolution of 1830 rendered such operations somewhat easier of accomplishment, and the brethren were able to send word to England, "The Word of God has now penetrated into places where it had never been heard of before." Nor was there even a tinge of exaggeration in such a boast; for their colporteurs were found in the Pyrenees; they appeared in remote and retired villages, and they set up Bible-stalls in fairs and markets, where such wares had never been offered before. Soldiers passing through the town also received attention; copies passed the frontier of Spain; the general result being that large numbers were spiritually enlightened.

In 1832, after having been instrumental in circulating nearly 350,000 copies of the Scriptures, Professor Kieffer died. This celebrated Oriental scholar was succeeded by M. Pressensé, a man of good family, a convert from Romanism, and a former pupil of the Jesuits. Soon afterwards, or in 1833, the French and Foreign Bible Society was founded; and colportage became more fully organized, and was carried on with more ardour. The first colporteur engaged was a convert from Romanism. In those early days, the friends of the Bible were less astonished and gratified at the achievements in the way of sales of their itinerant booksellers, who disposed of hundreds of thousands of copies.

Nor were the colporteurs Bible-sellers merely; they were converted men who were not backward in testifying what God had done for their souls. One of the most remarkable among the pioneer band of colporteurs was one who had fought under Napoleon, a man named Ladam, who quitted the army in 1815. Five years later he was converted; before he died, in 1846, he had himself circulated 12,000 copies of the sacred Book. In all directions whither this man went persons were awakened, and evangelical congregations were gathered as the fruits of his labours.

Many incidents of those days illustrated the truth of the old adage, that "truth is stranger than fiction." A veteran soldier who had learned to value the Scriptures as his chief treasure, would be found buying copies for those who had been less favoured. A young man of fair worldly prospects would be found carrying the colporteur's pack out of sheer gratitude for the good he had derived from reading the inspired Word. In numbers of instances the reading of the Scriptures created a desire for evangelical preachers; and in one memorable instance the members of a commune 600 strong, after being visited by a colporteur, assembled and declared themselves favourable to the Protestant religion.

At the present time, there is nominally more liberty in France than ever before in the history of the nation; but, as no one can say how long the present state of things may last with a people so erratic, the friends of the Bible have for long past been doubly anxious to turn golden opportunities to the best possible account. Indeed, the excess of liberty on the one hand, and the fanaticism which threatens to harden into bondage on the other, show that certain characteristics which gave a colour to the first Revolution are still to be found in France. While permission to hold religious service in an apartment at Versailles will readily be granted, and while evangelistic meetings can be held in any part of Paris without opposition from the authorities or the people, there is nevertheless a growing hostility to revealed religion, which will yet bear disastrous fruit. We find a number of the Paris Municipal Council speaking of the desirability of suppressing the "beliefs and the superstitions of the supernatural." Another public authority who, of course, like Voltaire, confounds Christianity with popery, and the gospel with priestcraft, says that "a religious man is the enemy of all progress." The result is, that sales of the Scriptures are effected with greater difficulty than before; and contempt for sacred things is more openly expressed by the workpeople than formerly. The gospel meetings of Mr. McAll and other evangelists are largely attended, and their remarkable development since the siege of the capital has been quite remarkable; but no less noteworthy, on the other hand, has been the growing hostility to religion. Take, by way of one illustration, what we see in the schools. Since the war, elementary education has made such rapid strides that the expenditure of Paris under this head is probably larger than London in proportion to the population; but, instead of New Testaments being circulated among the children, as was the case fifty years ago, the Scriptures are rigidly proscribed in all the National Schools.

Restrictions on book selling have been removed; the colporteur may freely offer his wares in the streets without the police interfering, as was formerly the case; or he may move about rural districts without fear of either magistrate or *curé*; but the Republic would have consulted its own interest had the advice of Victor Hugo been acted upon: "Give the working man, to whom this world is hard, the notion of a better world prepared for him, and he will be quiet and patient. Patience springs from hope. Therefore spread the gospel in villages. Put a Bible in every house, and every field will show the moral result." The Republic has not sown according to this counsel; and, therefore, the harvest is not such as he predicted. The main body of the people have lost all faith in the priests and the system they represent; and unless we can show them that the gospel is essentially different from Romanism, they will have no ear to listen to our message. Their present religious condition may be inferred from the fact that, instead of there being "a Bible in every house," there are, Mr. McAll assures us, hundreds of thousands in Paris who have never had a Bible in their hands.

In taking account of the irreligion of France, we should note that it is more demonstrative in the case of such an impulsive race than with ourselves; and in the capital more especially, unbelief is more fully organized. If the paradox may be allowed, the average workman makes a religion of unbelief; and while anticipating his materialistic millennium, copies many things from the church itself. Speaking of the Parisian Freethinkers, not very long ago, a writer in an influential London newspaper remarked: "They have divided the capital into parishes, and there is at least one association in every arrondissement. Before a man can enter the association he must make a profession of the materialistic faith. The members hold periodical meetings, which are conducted by regular preachers or lecturers, and money is raised by collections, just as in churches. They even celebrate baptisms and marriages, and conduct funeral services." There would be something excessively ludicrous in all this if the consequences were not so terrible; but we shall be prepared to learn that persons who can go to these lengths in folly, also attain to a fervour of bigotry which has never been surpassed. It is said that the bare mention of the name of the Supreme Being will cause some of these people to change colour with anger.

One of the chief curses of France at the present time is its corrupt Press. In one of his letters from Paris, M. de Pressensé refers to "the turbid stream of infamous productions which appeal directly to the vilest passions, and stir up the foulest dregs of poor human nature"; and the historian adds, that a daily paper in the French capital is entirely devoted to a kind of literature "which is purely and simply an incentive to debauchery." Zola and his followers of the so-called Realistic-school, have degraded the high office of the *littérateur* by corrupting the public mind, until even the courts of justice bear testimony to the havoc that is being made. The Realistic-school is said to be declining; but whether this is so or not, the mischief they have done in promoting immorality and crime, and also in searing the national conscience, will remain for many a long day. In addition to the novels of sensualism, come the halfpenny political newspapers, which flood the country, and effectively draw away the artisans from better reading.

Thus we see that, in any case, a dearth of the Scriptures means that something else will take their place: if what is good is absent, the area will be occupied by what is bad. The Press, whether for good or for evil, will never be inactive; and the Bible-seller needs to be maintained in order to counteract, in some degree, the colporteurs of evil, who are always busy. It is, no doubt, much easier to sell the bad than the good; but none the less on that account, and in spite of the fact that the sales of Scriptures are decreasing, should the staff of colporteurs be maintained.

The fruits of the corrupt Press are continually appearing, and are becoming more universal. Thus, when M. Watrin, the colliery engineer, at Decazeville, was murdered some years ago, one member in the French Chamber spoke of the crime of the savage Socialist workpeople as though it had been a legal "execution." More reasonable were the representations of others, that the real inciters of such crimes were writers like M. Zola and his imitators. Some of the most enlightened citizens of the country see in what direction things are tending; and they utter the necessary warnings. Not very long ago a deputation waited upon the Prime Minister, at the French Foreign Office, for the purpose of drawing attention to the inflammatory language used in newspapers, and at public meetings. As the language used frequently degenerated into "incitements to sedition, murder, and pillage," the public peace was thought to be endangered. Contrast all this with what has taken place in the once cannibal communities in the South Seas, and we shall be able to trace things to their cause. Islands which were once centres of terror and bloodshed, have been raised by Christianity into thriving trading stations, where education and commerce are daily extending. France will be troubled until she recognizes the fact that the same gospel which has subdued savages is also the panacea for her own sufferings and perils. The outlook might become one of despair, if it were not still true that "the word of God is not bound."

From what has been said, it will be inferred that colportage is the main channel through which the Scriptures can be circulated in France. Some good people who visit the Continent, expect to see Bible-depôts in commanding situations, and also to find copies in the windows of ordinary booksellers. Under existing circumstances, this cannot be the case; and

M. Monod, the representative of the Bible Society in France, has to depend upon his colporteurs.

The adventures of the colporteurs, as narrated by themselves, make very entertaining reading ; and, did space permit, many good stories might be quoted from their diaries. The itinerants hold meetings, as well as sell books ; and in an outbuilding, borrowed from a friendly innkeeper for the purpose, or beneath the village trees, with lanterns hanging from their boughs, many memorable scenes may be witnessed. Striking testimonies are frequently given to the light-giving power of the Word. One Bible-seller expended 1,200 francs in the purchase of a donkey and covered cart, in which he travels and lives. " I am the happiest of men," he says, " being no longer under the obligation of lodging in all kinds of dirty inns, where drunkards and scoffers abound ; but I have always at my disposal a peaceful home, where I can read, and write, and pray."

We hear of one veteran who has a genius for finding out places where a colporteur has never penetrated before, and in one such secluded hamlet a copy was sold to every one of the inhabitants. A man who travels among the Vosges left a certain village in despair, because he was unable to sell a single copy. He was soon befogged in the hills, and wandering until he came to a house, which he entered, he found he had come to the spot whence he started. In the meantime, the minds of the people had undergone a change in regard to purchasing ; they took all the man's copies, and sent the agent on his way rejoicing, with an empty bag.

In estimating the value of such an agency as this, we must ever bear in mind the altered character of the times, and also what has been already intimated respecting the booksellers being divided into two bands—good and evil. " Formerly, when travelling was tedious, and postage dear, the country farmers and peasants used to hear but little of what was published at the great centres. But now, the moment a scandalous book is published in Paris, it is sure to be circulated in a cheap and attractive form through all the villages of France. What, then, are we to do ? " asks M. Monod. " Sermons and discussions are very good, but clearly they can benefit only the people who are already disposed to attend them. If we want to put the good side by side with the evil, we must go where the evil goes, and circulate the Scriptures in the remotest hamlets, where, I venture to say, no other Christian agency but Bible Colportage can find access, or do an efficient work."

We wish to all such work the blessing of God.

"Seeking to Save."

A REMINDER: BY J. BURNHAM.

SEPTEMBER is close upon us again, and we are still bent upon the sacred errand suggested by the above title.

FIFTY THOUSAND HOP-PICKERS

will be imported to Mid-Kent, for the month, from our large crowded centres of population ; and, by the help of God, we do not intend they shall be able to say (as they might have done a few years ago), " No man careth for my soul."

Of all the solutions of the great problem of to-day, " How to reach the masses," with the exception of the London City Mission, we venture to believe none better than

"THE HOP-PICKERS' MISSION."

Indeed, we have opportunities for pressing the Word of God upon the people which even the City Missionary has not ; for the people, far removed from the vice and drunkenness of large towns, breathing the wholesome and invigorating air of the "Garden of England," and surrounded by the works of God in their loveliest form, and at the most attractive season of the year, are far more susceptible to kindly influences, and more ready to listen to those who seek their good, than they can possibly be in their homes amid sinful associations and surroundings. Moreover, we possess an advantage in this work through our

VISITS TO THE GARDENS,

which is lacking at other seasons and under other circumstances, viz., that while we stand and talk to the "pickers," we are helping to swell the heap in the "bin"; and, on this account, if for no other reason, they are willing to listen, and *may* listen to profit, as "faith cometh by hearing."

CAMP-VISITING

on Sundays is an interesting feature of the work. Accompanied by a little band of singers, and a portable organ, two companies usually start at the same time, in opposite directions, each company visiting from six to eight camps during the morning's march. Soon a savoury smell greets us across the field, and behind yonder high hedge we come upon a camp of some ten or a dozen families, variously engaged. So thoroughly un-English is the scene about us, that it requires but little stretch of imagination to believe ourselves suddenly transported to a Hottentot settlement. Here are a number of boys and girls, stripped to the waist, making the best use of a tub of dirty water in the absence of soap; while three or four men, similarly semi-attired, are bending over the brook close by for their weekly ablutions; here are half-a-dozen men grouped upon logs, or faggot bundles, smoking and listening to a "chum," as he reads *Lloyd's, Reynolds'*, or the *Police News;* and here are the wives around the camp-fire, preparing the savoury meal, the scent of which greeted us on our way to the camp; while Susan Jane, but partially dressed, is "tittivating" before a twopenny mirror hanging on the door-post, for is she not expecting her "Joe" down from St. Giles' by the Sunday-morning "Hoppers' Train"? Then, in dangerous proximity to a group of women at the huge wash-tub, are three or four "neither men nor boys, but hobbledehoys," playing at "tip-cat," and courting anything but kindly compliments as now and again they tumble over the nether limbs of a sleeper, stretched at full length on the grassy carpet.

A hearty "Good morning, sir; how are yer? Glad to see yer agin!" and like expressions, tell the tale that we are not strangers, and are welcome as ever in their midst. Our errand is well known, and by the time our organ is open, the sundry duties and pleasures are waived for a time, and, eagerly accepting the hymn-sheets, they are ready to help in the singing of some familiar strain. A portion of Scripture, special hymn for the "bairns," brief prayer, and ten minutes' homely talk (not "preachment"), and we leave with kindly proof of appreciation ringing in our ears, "Come agin, sir, next Sunday!"

OPEN-AIR SERVICES

in the surrounding villages are also an important part of this mission. Each afternoon (weather permitting), with a light van (which furnishes a platform for speakers, and the band of singers who will walk out in the evening), we visit the village, where we hope to "hold forth." We go from door to door with hand-bills and personal invitation (or "cry" the announcement through the streets, if driven for time); then, after a quiet cup of tea, we "open fire," at seven o'clock, on the village green. By the time we have sung two or three good opening hymns, we have a large congregation ready for the message. On the whole, we have orderly services, and little interruption. Occasionally the drink-devil enters our extemporized sanctum, and tries to divert attention. In the midst of a service at Marden, a half-intoxicated woman broke into the throng, and sorely nonplussed one of our brethren, who was a novice at the work, and hardly yet equal to the occasion. He was earnestly pleading with the unsaved, upon the ground that God had "made provision for us in his Son," when a shrill voice exclaimed, "And what of that? *I* have made provision, too" (holding up a big lapful of vegetables); "I have provided taters and cabbage for dinner to-morrow." Our good brother tried to proceed, but only to be again startled by the laughter of the crowd, as she called out, "Have some taters, guv'nor?" She persisted in the interruption, and we deemed it wise to "sing a hymn" —our usual resort whilst measuring our way through a difficulty. Meantime, one of our workers sidled up to the woman, and suggested that if she wished to speak it would better become her to face the audience, only she must use choicer language than she had thus far lavished upon us. Boldly she stepped to the front, planted herself back to the van, and faced the crowd. With the full light of our lamp upon her face, and the people gazing at her, she was cowed; sneaking into the shade behind, she muttered, half aloud, she "wasn't going to stand there, and make a fool of herself"; whereupon the young speaker, who had "recovered himself" during the singing, retorted that "it was too late for her to make that discovery."

At another village, a man with a cornet was engaged to play on the steps of a public-house opposite our stand, to prevent the people hearing us; but cornet-blowing taxes the wind more than speaking or singing, and he got tired first; and, 'tis worthy of note, the publican, who hired him on that occasion, is now very friendly toward us, and both receives tracts himself, and allows us to leave them on his table, and talk to the people at his bar.

On another occasion, one of our workers had been distributing tracts in a public-house, when some men barred his way at the door, declaring he should not pass out till he "paid for a drink" for them. "Very well," he replied; "I will stay here, and you will have to hear what I say"; and, while speaking kindly, he yet aimed his words so well that soon the men were glad to clear the way, and wish him "Good-night."

Think not, courteous reader, that ours is simply a gospel of *words* and *tracts*—

BOOTS, CLOTHING, AND MEDICINE

also form part of our gospel errand to these poor "strangers." Of course, we use these things discriminately, but still find sad cases of need for each and all of these "occasions" in turn; and by them we are better able to win the confidence of the people, without which we certainly could do them no good with our message. James ii. 15, 17.

Yet one other scene let us introduce to the reader ere we close this page. 'Tis Sunday afternoon, 3.30, and crowds of "hoppers," washed, and many decently "got up for the occasion," are pressing through the gateway into a large meadow, in the centre of which is a hurdled enclosure, with a policeman at its entrance. Within the enclosure are rows of seats, widely set, to allow of rows of children on the grass between the seats; at the end is our van, with portable organ, open and ready for use. At four o'clock our esteemed friend, Mr. Kendon (President of the Mission), with a large band of his scholars, and Miss Kendon, with many of her young ladies, step into the scene, and straightway we begin with a few inspiriting songs; while the space outside the enclosure is soon crowded with "home-dwellers" and village stragglers, who have come miles this bright Sunday afternoon to witness this scene and hear the singing and speaking. By five o'clock we have about five hundred men, women, and children, seated and orderly, and after grace is sung,

"THE HOP-PICKERS' FREE TEA"

is served, which to these immigrants is "the great event of the season." Does the reader ask *Cui bono?* Very much, dear reader. Of necessity, much of the seed is sown, of which *here* we may not meet with the harvest; and yet, never a season passes without our meeting with cases of blessing from the work of former years.

That all this varied work entails heavy expense, must be at once evident; especially as we now have *three centres* of operation in all, covering a very wide area.

WHO WILL HELP US?

Parcels of clothing, boots, or tracts and Testaments, may be sent, *carriage paid*, to the Rev. J. J. Kendon, Marden Station, S. E. R. Contributions (naming this mission) to C. H. Spurgeon, Westwood, Upper Norwood; Rev. J. J. Kendon, Goudhurst, Kent; or to the Secretary of the Mission, J. Burnham, "Fernbank," Brentford.

Notices of Books.

The Pearl of Days; or, 575 Illustrations of the Sabbath. Vols. I. to VIII. Compiled by CHARLES HILL. Partridge and Co.

THIS very excellent periodical makes a handsome, well-illustrated, and instructive volume. As a defence of the Sabbath, it will be extremely valuable. We wish we could see more care among Christians to give their servants the rest of the Lord's-day. Less cooking would be a great reform. Everything possible should be done to release every one from needless labour on the Lord's-day. Horses which, of necessity, must be used to take persons to the place of worship who cannot walk by reason of distance or infirmity, should rest on Saturday, so as to maintain to the full the spirit of the command, where the letter cannot be unreservedly carried out. A certain amount of work must be done on the Sabbath; acts of necessity, mercy, and piety must ever be lawful: but even in reference to these, it will be well to get, at some other time, the rest which is destroyed by their service. The seventh part of time is due to divine worship and hallowed repose. Let it be carefully reserved.

Buddhism in its connection with Brahmanism and Hinduism, and in its Contrast with Christianity. By Sir MONIER MONIER-WILLIAMS, K.C.I.E. John Murray.

A GREAT book: worthy to be called the standard work upon its own subject. We judge that no one can write with fuller information, or with greater impartiality, than Sir Monier Monier-Williams. His witness for ever extinguishes the foolish notion that Buddhism is worthy to rank with Christianity. A lot of nonsense has been talked of late, and ignorance might have been pleaded as the excuse for it; but now that the facts are clearly set forth, ignorance will not be the cause of this glorification of a lie, but sheer malice against the one true faith. The volume teems with valuable information, and it should be placed in every scholar's library. Here is a statement which will correct the notions of most of us in a very agreeable manner. "The best authorities are of opinion that there are not more than a hundred millions of real Buddhists in the world; and that Christianity, with its four hundred and thirty to four hundred and fifty millions of adherents, has now the numerical preponderance over all other religions. I am entirely of the same opinion. I hold that the Buddhism, described in the following pages, contained within itself, from the earliest times, the germs of disease, decay, and death; and that its present condition is one of rapidly increasing disintegration."

Bible Talks. By GEORGE CLARKE. Marshall Brothers.

VERY good spiritual conversations, with some striking stories, very well told. Rich in edifying experience.

Westwood Leaflets. By Mrs. C. H. SPURGEON. Twelve varieties. 2d. per dozen; 50 for 6d. Passmore and Alabaster.

IN several instances we have heard of the divine blessing resting upon these leaflets, which are attractive, and a little out of the ordinary line of tracts. Being tasteful in appearance, and exceedingly well written, they will be sure to be accepted and read. The writer of these parables would be greatly cheered if her friends would widely circulate them, so that she might be encouraged to send forth more of a like character. Her own husband hereby expresses his editorial judgment, which is, of course, impartial, that these tracts are as good as the best he has ever met with, and deserve to be scattered everywhere. A packet of fifty can be had of the publishers for sixpence. Any bookseller will get them for you.

More Stray Leaves. By J. MANTON SMITH. Passmore and Alabaster.

MANTON SMITH'S powers of story-telling are as indisputable as his skill upon the cornet. His unaffected, natural style carries the reader away with the writer, and makes him laugh or cry, whether he will or not. The twenty thousand people who are familiar with his first stories, will welcome a second batch. We generally gather stray leaves into heaps for burning; but these, it seems, from the design on the cover, are to be threaded into wreaths. Very well, they deserve it: they will keep fresh and flourishing for years. Our readers have seen some of these stray leaves among the ever-green leaves of this magazine; and we have given one more this month, just as a specimen. The men in the streets with their walnuts, allow you to crack and eat one as a temptation to buy a score, and this is why we put one of the chapters of Mr. Smith's new book into this month's number.

The Story of Jesus. By RICHARD B. COOK, D.D. Baltimore, U.S.A.: R. H. Woodward and Co.

As a short life of Christ this is worthy of commendation, if only for its admirable pictorial instruction. The cuts are numerous and good. The reading matter is largely a compilation, very well put together.

John the Baptist; a Contribution to Christian Evidences. The Congregational Union Lecture for 1874. By HENRY ROBERT REYNOLDS, D.D. London: Memorial Hall.

WE remember reading this noble life of John the Baptist some fourteen years ago. Not always agreeing with every utterance of Dr. Reynolds, we were greatly edified by his instructive teachings, and clear insight into the character of the Lord's forerunner. The large edition cost 12s.; the present one is sufficiently clear in type, but from its somewhat smaller form they can offer it at half the former price. The new Preface is very courteous to the modern school; but they will not at all enjoy it. We cannot say that we are very charmed with it; but portions of it are most trenchant. We like the doctor's remarks on the foolish dream of the hour, from which many scientific men have already awakened to despise the image which appeared in its vision. Here are Dr. Reynolds' remarks:—"Evolution comes to a most difficult pass, when challenged to account for the variation of the highest species of brute into the humblest species of man. It is more at fault still, when striving to link together, by natural selection, the functions of the most vegetal sort of animal with those of the most animal phase of vegetation; still profounder is the gap between the living and non-living kingdoms, while that between 'nothing' and 'something' yawns wider than ever. But even if all these perplexities were solved, and science could show us, in its laboratory or records, the missing links of which we are in search, there are no two successive or co-existent phenomena, vital or physical, physiologic or psychical, which satisfy any mind which hungers for a solution of the underlying mystery of all things, which refuses to be comforted with the mere story of Evolution, or with a record of the complexity of natural movements, clash of atoms, and the unspeakably wonderful harmony of organ, function, and environment."

A New Commentary on Genesis. By FRANZ DELITZSCH, D.D. Translated by SOPHIA TAYLOR. 2 Vols. Edinburgh : T. and T. Clark.

DELITZSCH is a master in Scriptural exposition, and far too sound to please the men of the hour. All his commentaries are weighty and powerful; and the present work is not the least of them. Of course, they are not meant for the masses, and could not be understood by them; but to scholars they are exceedingly valuable and helpful.

To us it is hard work to read Delitzsch consecutively ; but it is a privilege to consult him, to see how he explains difficult passages. The tone of the author of the commentary now before us is that of one who desires to follow truth wherever it leads him, but also of one who is not sure that, as yet, he has assuredly found it in reference to the matter in hand. Concerning the resurrection of our Lord, and the divine gospel of which that fact is the keystone, he is quite certain, on evidence which no criticism can disturb ; and hence he has no sympathy with those who treat holy Scripture irreverently, and dissect it with their critical knives as they might cut up the writings of uninspired men. But his position is not so far apart from theirs as to leave him unaffected by the spirit of the age. He defines his position in the following sentences :—

"We do not belong to those moderns who, as the children of their age, are so charmed by the most recent stage of Old Testament science as to see therein the solution of all enigmas, and to disregard, with an easy mind, all the new enigmas. But as little, too, are we of those ancients who, as the children of an age that has been overtaken, see in the new stage a product of pure wantonness, and are too weak-brained, or too mentally-idle to take up an independent position with respect to the new problems by surrendering their musty papers."

We are obliged to our learned brother for his courteous epithet of "ancients," but not quite so much so for the words " weak-brained," and " mentally-idle." He will, probably, upon reflection, correct this estimate ; for,

among the "ancients" are some of whom he has, in former days, formed no such a judgment. In his candid pursuit of truth he must not forget to be just to those among his brethren who are as sincere, and even as thoughtful, as himself. He will hasten to withdraw the expression, for he has no wish to assume the airs of those great infallibles who denounce as ignorant all who will not accept their idle speculations. The Delitzsch of our heart's memory is nearer akin to these "ancients" than he dreams ; although he is, by no means, amenable to the charge which he, in an impatient moment, has fixed upon them.

The Bibles of England : a Plain Account for Plain People of the Principal Versions of the Bible in English. By ANDREW EDGAR, D.D. Alexander Gardner.

GOOD reading for those who like to know the story of all English Bibles from the beginning ; and surely none is more full of interest. The subject has been written upon by many ; but this is a clear and condensed statement, and will be helpful to students and lecturers. Plain people, whose brains have not been exhausted by growing heavy crops of Hebrew and Greek, will get on with this volume ; but they will enjoy it all the better if they know a little Latin.

The Law of Liberty, and other Sermons. By JAMES MORRIS WHITON, Ph.D. James Clarke and Co.

THESE pulpit exercises are remarkable. Ten out of the twelve discourses were delivered at Anerley Congregational Chapel, last August : those who know the place and its minister will infer the style. Dr. Whiton hails from New York. Very properly he is a doctor of philosophy, and not a doctor of divinity. He excels within his own lines, but those are not the lines of the gospel. Where Christian ethics are concerned he is eloquent ; where Christian doctrines are involved he is evasive. He belongs to the school which teaches "the New Theology." This name is doubly incorrect ; for in these modern notions there is no theology, and nothing new.

Dogmatic Theology. By WILLIAM G. T. SHEDD. Edinburgh: T. and T. Clark.

Two huge volumes of Biblical theology —is there really any other theology than that which is Biblical? Is not all else a dream? Dr. Shedd sets forth the Augustine-Calvin view of the teachings of Holy Scripture in the most clear and forcible manner. Time was when these volumes would have been prized at their weight in gold; but now, we fear, the publishers will find the publication a costly venture. The books have a hearty welcome to our library; for, in almost all respects, they are after our own heart. We commend them to all students and preachers whose purses are long enough to allow of their purchase: twenty-five shillings is the price. They are a mountain of sacred truth, and we value the whole mass, with the exception of some very poor stuff upon Baptism. How can anything be said worth saying with Infant Baptism as its teaching? That portion of this great work we dismiss, and then our rejoicing in the remainder is exceeding great. On those grave questions of future retribution which have become the centre of controversy in this "progressive" age, our author is very positive and sound; and this is exceedingly to his honour. He is not ashamed of those ancient truths which are now derided and even abhorred by the free-thinking spirits who have usurped our pulpits. Here is a passage which ought to be carefully noted, although we do not suppose it will be:—

"That endless punishment is rational, is proved by the history of morals. In the records of human civilization and morality, it is found that that age which is most reckless of law, and most vicious in practice, is the age that has the loosest conception of penalty, and is the most inimical to the doctrine of endless retribution. A virtuous and religious generation adopts sound ethics, and reverently believes that 'the Judge of all the earth will do right' (Gen. xviii. 25); that God will not 'call evil good, and good evil, nor put darkness for light, and light for darkness" (Isaiah v. 20);

and that it is a deadly error to assert, with the sated and worn-out sensualist, 'All things come alike to all: there is one event to the righteous, and to the wicked' (Eccl. ix. 2).

"The French people, at the close of the last century, were a very demoralized and wicked generation; and there was a very general disbelief and denial of the doctrines of the divine existence, the immortality of the soul, the freedom of the will, and future retribution. And upon a smaller scale the same fact is continually repeating itself. Any little circle of business men who are known to deny future rewards and punishments are shunned by those who desire safe investments. The recent uncommon energy of opposition to endless punishment, which started about ten years ago in this country, synchronized with great defalcations and breaches of trust, uncommon corruption in mercantile and political life, and great distrust between man and man. Luxury deadens the moral sense, and luxurious populations do not have the fear of God before their eyes. Hence luxurious ages and luxurious men recalcitrate at hell, and 'kick against the goads.' No theological tenet is more important than eternal retribution to those modern nations which, like England, Germany, and the United States, are growing rapidly in riches, luxury, and earthly power. Without it they will infallibly go down in that vortex of sensuality and wickedness that swallowed up Babylon and Rome. The bestial and shameless vice of the dissolute rich, which has recently been uncovered in the commercial metropolis of the world, is a powerful argument for the necessity and reality of 'the lake which burneth with fire and brimstone.' "

Devoted; or, Working for God. Some Reminiscences of Mrs. Thomas Boyd (*née* Chassie McNaughton). By her HUSBAND. Nisbet and Co.

SKETCH of the life of a beautiful Christian woman. It will have a charm for her friends in London, Oldham, and elsewhere. The lesson of the brief narrative is the power of a consecrated life.

The Peshito-Syriac New Covenant Scriptures. BY W. NORTON. W. K. Bloom, London.

THE chief design of this short treatise is, in the author's own words, "to aid in defending the true text of God's Word by means of the Peshito-Syriac." Mr. Norton deems that too much authority is allowed to the Greek MSS. in determining the text of the New Testament, and he adduces the evidence of this most ancient version by way of counterpoise. It is beside our veteran author's aim to state fully the case of the Greek MSS.; but, consciously or unconsciously, he makes up for this by conducting his readers into a region of investigation little visited. As he cites authorities on the origin and history of the venerable Syriac version, he gives glimpses of apostolic and other early missionary labours in Central Asia and on the coast of India of the deepest interest, especially now that, after the lapse of many centuries, the tide of missionary effort is again flowing towards these same lands.

The English Revisers' Greek Text. By G. W. SAMSON. Moses King, Cambridge, Mass.

ANOTHER contribution to the already voluminous literature designed to prove that the revisers have not yet reached finality in fixing the Greek text of the New Testament, any more than they have attained perfection in the English of their version. Professor Samson is interesting even when he is not convincing.

Modern Church Amusements: are they Scriptural or Devilish? Frank Ballard's Protest against A. G. Brown, and "The New Theology," Answered. By a Preacher of the Gospel. Manchester: Brook and Chrystal. London: F. Pitman.

MR. ARCHIBALD BROWN has done great service to the church of God, but it was hardly possible that he should escape opposition. We are sorry that such a protest should come from a Wesleyan minister. We did not think that one of that honourable confraternity would thus have written. In itself considered, Mr. Ballard's pamphlet did not deserve the honour of a reply; but as one was judged needful, this is assuredly faithful enough. It would be a good work to scatter the Answer in the region where the Protest is likely to do mischief. Mr. Archibald Brown has struck home: the irritation of the new-theology men in many quarters is sufficient evidence of his success.

A Short Analysis of the Old Testament. By PRINCIPAL DOUGLAS, D.D. J. and R. Parlane, Paisley.

VERY lucid and helpful. This admirable analysis takes chiefly the form of headings to the chapters of the Old Testament. In its present form it is manifestly at a great disadvantage: yet even so, many Bible readers will esteem it a boon. But if Dr. Douglas could succeed in placing the headings at the beginnings of the chapters, where headings ought to be, his work would, we venture to think, receive an almost universal welcome, despite the alarm felt in the breast of his co-Revisers concerning such annotations.

Sunbeams from Heaven for Darkened Chambers. By HESTER DOUGLAS. With a Preface by the BISHOP OF SODOR AND MAN. Swan, Sonnenschein and Co.

WRITTEN by an invalid, out of the depths of her heart, and therefore full of tender sympathy. It is of that gentle, simple character which is likely to suit sufferers. They cannot bear deep divings, or high soarings, but want the plain truths of the gospel, put in an experimental form. There are certain rough women abroad who will write to sick ladies and tell them that it is their own fault that they are ill. If these well-meaning but coarse enthusiasts had a touch of real pain themselves, they would know better than to vex those whom the Lord tenderly loves. From the fancies of hysteria to the brutalities of egotism, there is but a step, and a fanatical confidence enables idle women to take it, and then to cry themselves up as wonders of faith. There is nothing of this in these sweet Christian pages. Some, for their own reading, would prefer something deeper; but many an invalid lady will find here just the very word she needs.

Phœnicia (The Story of the Nations series). By GEORGE RAWLINSON, M.A. T. Fisher Unwin.

THE history of Phœnicia is so linked with the story of God's chosen people, that it becomes peculiarly attractive to the student of Holy Scripture. Tyre and Sidon were in league with Solomon, and, no doubt, felt something of the influence of the true religion; but later on, in the days of the proud Sidonian queen of Ahab, Baal and Ashtoreth ruled in the court of Israel, and all Elijah's indignant zeal could not drive out the foul invaders. Later on, Judah turned aside to the worship of the accursed Moloch, another "king," or deity of Phœnicia. The story of Nebuchadnezzar's unprofitable victories over Tyre is here given, and the expedition of the Tyrians, when they circumnavigated Africa, with a courage perfectly marvellous for the period of its accomplishment. Professor Rawlinson narrates Alexander's conquest of the island city, and then traces the history down to the present condition of the ruined spot. Our reading has been most delightful. We could wish it were in our power to convey some portion of it to our subscribers; but as we cannot, we would urge upon them the expenditure of a crown upon the purchase of the volume, and a steady perusal of the book. It is a feast for intelligent students, who wish to know the history of their fellow-men. With great pleasure we learn that the "Story of the Nations" will be continued, without any fear of cessation for lack of materials. Before all the stories are told which are now extant, more will have been fashioned by the energy of men under the hand of Providence.

History of the Presbyterians in England: their Rise, Decline, and Revival. By the Rev. A. H. DRYSDALE, M.A. Publication Committee of the Presbyterian Church of England, 14, Paternoster Square, E.C.

A VALUABLE addition to our church histories. We have been much struck with that part of the narrative in which the old Presbyterian churches in England became Unitarian; for there is a clear parallel between the commencement of that period and the present time. The ministers gloried in freedom from religious enquiry and profession. They did not at first quit the orthodox faith, but they denied the binding nature of it, became intoxicated with the new principle of untrammelled ministry, and worshipped the idol of "free and candid religious enquiry." The race to Socinianism was as rapid as it was ruinous. Once abandon the authority of Scripture, and the need of fundamental doctrine, and the drift towards fatal error is strong and sure.

The Presbyterian Church of England has issued this historical document, which is by no means a dry digest, but has about it a sufficient quantity of lively detail to make it good reading. We accept with thankfulness this history of a church to which we desire abounding increase and prosperity, so long as it abides by the old faith; and we trust this will be evermore. Alas! Scotland has furnished sorrowful proof that no form of church government can secure spiritual love to the truth; and nothing but the life of God by the Holy Ghost's abiding in the church can do it. Yet we cannot persuade ourselves that the Free Church can have really come down from its original platform. There must be some mistake: the sons of Knox are not going to leave the solid doctrine of their fathers for the dreams of the moderns. God forbid it should be so!

First Steps to God. A Guide for Beginners in the Spiritual Life. Second and abridged Edition of "Home to God." By SAMUEL PEARSON, M.A.
The Way Back. By JAMES L. STANLEY. Religious Tract Society.

Two books of the best order. We cannot speak too highly of them for sound doctrine and holy tendency.

Indian Missions, and their Latest Critics. By G. MACKENZIE COBBAN. Elliot Stock.

A PAMPHLET on the question of the day. It is well to hear both sides.

454 NOTICES OF BOOKS.

Through Cloud and Sunshine. By E. G. SARGENT. Elliot Stock.

HE who publishes poems in these days had need be a brave man, a soldier, or even a *sergeant.* These hymns and poems are good, and deserve to live; but they are not sufficiently striking to attain to any high degree of fame. They will minister to the spiritual growth of those who will read them with care.

The Boatswain's Mate; a Dialogue between two British Seamen. By G. C. SMITH, R.N. W. Wileman, 34, Bouverie Street.

IT carries us back many a year to meet with a book by old Boatswain Smith. We can remember him with the half-dozen sailor boys that he took about with him; and, better still, we recall the old man at the laying of the first stone of the Metropolitan Tabernacle, when nearly 80, trying to preach an open-air sermon, and subsiding into a prayer by himself, which we doubt not was heard in heaven, but was quite lost to the hearing of anybody upon earth by reason of the great crowd, and the old gentleman's feebleness. He did a good work in his day. Good people in our young days were wont to speak of him with great respect. A sixteenth edition of his shilling book proves that there is something vital in it.

Chronicles of a Quiet Family. A Temperance Story. By SALOME HOCKING. Andrew Crombie.

NOTHING striking or sensational; probably all the more true to life: a temperate Christian temperance story.

Rhys Lewis, Minister of Bethel. An Autobiography. By DANIEL OWEN. Translated from the Welsh by JAMES HARRIS. Simpkin, Marshall, and Co.

WE do not know what to say of this story, which has been so greatly extolled by Welsh critics. We yield to the superior judgment of those who praise it; but we confess that it would never have occurred to us to rate it so highly; in fact, we do not know how to rate it at all. It is a regular rigmarole of common-place talk, and yet it is profoundly interesting; it is eminently life-like in its descriptive parts, and yet we do not think that, as a whole, it is true to probability; it is religious, and yet it does not leave a holy impression upon our mind. These contradictory judgments make our estimate of the book quiver in the balance. Many who read the story will wonder at our hesitancy; but all the same, we must give our own opinion candidly. The excellence of the writing lies in its fine colouring of home-life in Wales; we hope, however, that it does not truthfully describe the religion of the Nonconformists of the Principality. We have spent a considerable time over this book, by earnest request, but we have not obtained an adequate return. This may be our own fault, and it may be Daniel Owen's.

Frolic; or, the Adventures of a Water Spaniel. By ADA HITYER.
Our Garden and its Feathered Families, and other Stories. By the author of "Moravian Life in the Black Forest." Dean and Son.

TWO beautiful books for boys and girls. To teach children to love animals and treat them kindly, is one of the first duties of parents, and they will be much assisted by such pleasant reading as this. The stories are delightful. If these books only cost sixpence, as we suppose, they are beyond all praise for cheapness and every other virtue.

Little Folks. A Magazine for the Young. Cassell and Co.

GOOD as ever; ever so good.

Town and Sea-Side. Dean and Son.

ONE of the most resplendent playbooks ever issued. The coloured pictures are enough to make a child's eyes water with sheer delight. And all for a shilling!

Longley's Holiday Guides. F. E. Longley, 39, Warwick Lane.

WHAT can you expect for a penny? Well, here is a brief but instructive guide to almost any place that you can select for your holiday. A guide for a penny? A blind man could hardly borrow a dog for less.

George Washington: His Boyhood and Manhood. By W. M. THAYER. Hodder and Stoughton.

The Pioneer Boy, and How he became President. The Story of the Life of Abraham Lincoln. Same author and publishers.

TWO popular books at an extremely low price, namely, eighteen-pence each. Here are two great lives from the land of Go-a-head, which are calculated to stir up our youngsters in a healthy manner. Either of them will make a present which will be jumped at.

Impressions of Australia. By R. W. DALE, LL.D., Birmingham. Hodder and Stoughton.

THE impressions made upon such a mind as that of R. W. Dale, while personally traversing Australia, cannot fail to interest readers who care about that southern world; and who among us does not? This volume contains much valuable information, but we found ourselves getting sleepy while trying to read it. Dr. Dale is just a little dull upon this topic; and yet we like him better here than when he preached to the Baptist Missionary Society. When he would not have us speak of " a lost world," we began to ask whether he had not lost his way.

War: its Causes, Consequences, Lawfulness, &c. An Essay. By JONATHAN DYMOND. With Introductory Words by the Right Hon. JOHN BRIGHT. John Heywood.

THE Peace Society should take means to scatter this book like snow-flakes over the land, and every lover of peace should aid its endeavours. The introductory words of John Bright contain a passage which is characteristic of him, and gives sound advice in a forcible form:—" I have been asked on several occasions, 'What do you think about the doctrine of the Peace Society, or of your own religious body, in their opposition to all war, however necessary, or however just it may seem to be, or however much you are provoked or injured?' I think every man must make up his own mind on that abstract principle; and I would recommend

him, if he wants to know a book that says a good deal upon it, to study the New Testament, and make up his mind from that source."

Helpful Truth for Removing Doubts and Fears Concerning Personal Salvation. By THOMAS MOOR. Nisbet.

JUSTIFIES its title. A bit of genuine old-fashioned theology and experience. We trust it may comfort many troubled hearts.

Will-Making made Safe and Easy. With a Great Variety of Forms. By ALMARIC RUMSEY, Barrister-at-Law. John Hogg.

RATHER out of our line; but as friends have to make their wills, a shilling's-worth of instruction may save a good many shillings. We should like the book better if it gave actual forms of wills as well as directions. One thing we may say seriously, Let no Christian man neglect to make his will, lest he should die suddenly and cause a world of sorrow through his neglect. Our sad witness is that this has been the case through the delays of very good men, and their dearest ones have had to suffer severely, when all might have been happily arranged.

The Missionary Year-Book for 1889. Religious Tract Society.

THE missionary societies should be heartily grateful to the Religious Tract Society for bringing out this Year-Book; and all who wish to have at hand full information as to all missionary work should purchase a copy. Here will the faithful see how the armies of the Lord go forth to battle. What hosts they are, and yet how few amid so many adversaries!

Christian Progress in China: Gleanings from the Writings and Speeches of Many Workers. By ARNOLD FOSTER, B.A. Religious Tract Society.

LOVERS of China, here is another store of provision for your thoughtful compassion. Here you will see what the Lord has done, and is still doing, for the crowded population of the Flowery Land, where the dragon devours the souls of men. Here are many special items of information upon Jews in China, and other interesting matters. '

Lionel Harcourt the Etonian; or, "Like other Fellows." By G. E. WYATT. Nelsons.

THE weakness and wickedness of the youth who impoverishes his parents, or defrauds his creditors, that he may be and do "like other fellows" with larger means, is very well illustrated in this tale of public-school life.

Houses on Wheels. By EMMA MARSHALL. Nisbet and Co.

AN attractive tale for children. It will enlist their sympathy in behalf of the little ones in travelling vans, who are in the very van of the army of ignorance. Our legislature should civilize the bairns who go a-gipsying, or they will grow up like the wild creatures of the woods. Mrs. Marshall's hand has not lost its cunning.

St. Yeda's; or, the Pearl of Orr's Haven. By ANNIE S. SWAN. Edinburgh: Oliphant and Anderson.

MENTAL sweetstuff of good quality. "Scotch mixture, warranted pure."

Molly's Heroine. By FLEUR-DE-LYS. Nelson and Sons.

A NOVEL, slightly spiced with religion, containing some rather good sketches of Cornish character, but without plot or purpose. The binding is fine.

Notes.

MEETING the other day with this portrait in an American paper, we thought we would preserve it as a memorial of ten years ago. The frost lies on the head and beard now, and the eyes call for the aid of the optic-glass; but there is work in the man yet, if it please God to grant it to him. It may be, life will be spared till better days have dawned for the faith and the faithful, or till HE comes who has so long been coming quickly to his waiting Church—coming more really than she has been watching.

June 27 was a grand time at MILDMAY PARK CONFERENCE. The friends who meet there are among the choicest of Christians: elect out of all the evangelical denominations, and wedded to the old faith. The meetings were good throughout. Our part in them was most pleasant to our own heart; and in looking back upon it, our record is—*the*

Lord hath helped us. What an audience! If counted,—some three thousand. If weighed,—equal to any audience on earth. The friends need no effort to win their attention: they are the most appreciative of hearers, and receive with eagerness all that is sound and Scriptural. It is both an honour and a pleasure to talk with a company of godly people so united in the faith, and so alive to holy service. An immense amount of charitable work and missionary enterprise finds its centre in this home of evangelical doctrine and effort. Blessed was the day in which Mildmay was founded by Mr. Pennefather! He is now with God; but his much-beloved widow remains to rejoice over the growing cause.

A full account of all the addresses is published, and can be purchased of Shaw & Co., and all booksellers.

On *July* 1, with great pleasure we preached for our beloved brother, NEWMAN HALL, after our own prayer-meeting. We cannot tell how much we honour this veteran servant of God, who is one of the few who remain upon the old lines, testifying to the faith which was dear to Rowland Hill and James Sherman. It were ill indeed if the son of the Author of "The Sinner's Friend" had forgotten to proclaim the great atoning sacrifice. The church over which Mr. Hall presides is feeling the terrible pressure occasioned by all the wealthier folks going into the suburbs; and it would be wise if some of the Lord's stewards considered the fact that our churches in the poorer regions, while most needed, will not be able to hold their ground among the poor unless sustained from without. All places of worship situated like our own Tabernacle, and Christ Church, and Mr. Brown's Tabernacle at Bow, would find it difficult, if not impossible, to keep up their institutions, if they solely depended upon their immediate neighbourhoods, since they are becoming poorer and poorer. In our own case, we cannot but see that the tendency to live in the suburbs must in the future operate to make it hard work to keep all things going. Still, when a man is far into the 36th year of his pastorate, and finds all things prosper, he may hopefully expect that the stress and burden of this continuous exodus will not fall so heavily upon himself as upon his successors.

On *July* 2, the good people of SOUTH STREET CHAPEL, GREENWICH, welcomed their pastor's father, who found it a joyful task to preach to them, and to mark their loving attachment to their absent pastor. They are unanimous in their anxiety to see him return in health; and we believe they will have that pleasure about the time that this magazine is published. Our son has had to bear the ills of exaggeration and falsehood, through the eagerness of reporters to create a sensational paragraph; but no one who knew him has ever suspected him of an indiscretion in the manner mentioned, much less of a wrong. His receptions throughout his American journey have been of the heartiest kind, and we hope he will return in fine spirits and sound health. Yet are we not without a grave trial in the ill-health of our second son, whose bright papers are always welcome to *The Sword and the Trowel*. He has been so depressed that he felt that he must seek a change. We do not know from his personal inform-ation that he has resigned; but as we see it announced in the papers, we suppose they have received the news by telegram. He has done good service during the years of his sojourn at Auckland; may the Lord direct his way, restore his strength, and make him a still greater blessing somewhere else!

July 9, 10, 11.—This week was, as to its work-days, all given to GUERNSEY. Mr. Snell was sent by us to commence a church in this delicious island, and he has started two centres of assembly. In St. Peter's an Episcopal church has been bought, and a congregation gathered which will support the minister. Some £300 is needed to com-plete the purchase, and it would be a great relief if some friends would help us to remove that load. In raising £350 we have gone as far as we can for the present; but we cannot be happy till the rest is given. The other work at St. Sampson's will also grow.

What a week we had in Guernsey! Crowds to welcome us, and crowds to say "Fare-well"! Friendship in Christ is sweet. Wesleyan friends lent their finest chapel, and were with us at the services; in fact, believers of all sorts were fervent in fellow-ship in the gospel. It was a week of strong excitement, and it called forth all our strength, and brought down fresh power from on high. Our dear French Baptist friends have won our heart. Two of their

chapels we were able to visit, and it was a joy to preach to such a sincere and open-hearted people. Travelling to Guernsey by night is the *crux* of the affair when we cannot sleep; but when the Lord's presence is with us, fatigue and weakness are for-gotten. We look to have two good English Baptist churches in the island; our French brethren have already five places of worship. Oh, for the blessing of God upon the whole island!

On *July* 16, it fell to our lot to stand in the pulpit where, 36 years ago, we preached the Word of the Lord in WATER-BEACH. What a rush of grateful memories! Here were the children's children of our former friends and converts. Many have gone, but some few of the very oldest are yet lingering. There seemed to be a loving unanimity among the people. Our beloved brother, Ellis, of Stoke Newington, took the evening service to allow us to get home. Even then it took us from 9.30 a.m. to 10 p.m. to go to and fro, and preach one sermon. To rise early, and sit up late, is involved in this; for how else is the excessive ordinary work to be got through? *Having had a feast of work through July, we must now keep at home; and therefore we hope our friend will not post that letter which he has prepared, inviting C. H. S. to take anniversary services at his place.*

Large numbers of the foreign delegates to the World's Sunday School Convention came to the Tabernacle services, both on *Lord's-day June* 30, *and July* 7. On the latter occasion some hundreds filed through the vestry, and gave their loving salutations to the pastor: there is no "Down-grade" among *them*. On *Monday evening, July* 8, two of them, Drs. Peloubet and Dixon (Baltimore), spoke at the prayer-meeting. Dr. Dixon especially interested the people with his account of how *their* pastor had been for years *his* pastor. He remembered the time when his father's library consisted of his Bible, hymn-book, and "Spurgeon's Sermons", each volume of which was bought as it appeared. Before he began to read the newspaper he read the sermons; they led him to Christ; his first desire to be a preacher of the gospel came through reading them; and as a minister he had often been helped by them in his work for the Lord.

On the following Monday evening Dr. Dixon was again present, when he gave an admirable exposition of Acts ii. 25-28, and afterwards took part in the open-air service on the Tabernacle steps. He is a brother as great in heart as he is tall in body, and he is considerably over six feet high. On two Sabbath mornings he offered the longer prayer, and so helped the minister. What prayers they were! His heart bubbled up with a good matter, and overflowed in fervent petitions of affection. Two doctors of divinity said to Mr. Spurgeon, "Your sermons brought us to Christ, led us into the ministry, and have helped us to carry it out." What words of cheer!

On *Monday evening*, *July* 15, the annual meeting of the POOR MINISTERS' CLOTHING SOCIETY was held in the Tabernacle lecture-hall. There was a large attendance, and additional interest was given to the proceedings by the bringing in of the garments promised at the last annual meeting. A large number of friends agreed to give one article each, and in this way 137 garments were added to the Society's stores, to which there will, doubtless, be a much larger addition by the time this magazine is published, as the Pastor reminded the friends at the prayer-meeting that they also had promised to help, and asked them to bring their contributions to the prayer-meeting on July 29. If each reader sent, for the first Monday in August, one garment for man, woman, or child, the store would be well filled.

Addresses were delivered by the Pastor, and Mr. Harrald, who also read the report. From this it appears that, for twenty years, the Society has been engaged in the good work of helping to clothe poor ministers and their families, and that, during the past year, fifty-three parcels, of the value of £279 12s. 8d., have been sent out. The total expenditure of the year was about £105, and the small balance due to the treasurer was contributed at the meeting. New and partly-worn clothing of all kinds, and materials that can be made up, are always welcome. Parcels should be addressed to Mrs. Evans, Metropolitan Tabernacle, Newington, London. While agriculture pays so badly, farmers have little to give, and country pastors pine. Now is the time to help village Nonconformity, and this good work is one which meets a great and very urgent need in a kind and thoughtful way. The work deserves help, does it not?

COLLEGE.—Mr. E. R. Pullen has settled at Shirley, Southampton; and Mr. F. T. B. Westlake at Radcliffe, Lancashire. Mr. G. H. Carr, late of Bow, has gone to Barking Road Tabernacle; Mr. E. Spanton has removed from Dawley, to Hatherleigh, North Devon; and Mr. H. C. Field has taken charge of the work at Harefield, Middlesex. Mr. G. W. Ball, who sailed recently for the United States, has accepted the pastorate at Pike, Wyoming County, New York State; Mr. F. Dann, at Cherry Creek, Chautauqua County, in the same State; and Mr. R. Yeatman, at Minnedosa, Manitoba, Canada. We are always glad to hear from churches needing pastors; and from populous places where there is need of a Baptist church, which would not interfere with other gospel preaching. There are still large towns which should have in them a gospel church of the New Testament sort.

Many brethren have written about the great blessings experienced by their churches on the day of united prayer, *Monday*,

June 24. In several places meetings were held at unusual hours—early in the morning, at dinner-time, or in the afternoon—while the regular evening meetings were characterized by more than usual fervour. At the Tabernacle, we had not many students with us, as they had gone to the country for their holidays; but earnest prayer was presented on their behalf, and also for the brethren who are labouring as pastors, evangelists, and missionaries. Oh, for a blessing from on high, a genuine revival of religion!

EVANGELISTS.—Mr. C. Russell Hurditch writes concerning *Messrs. Fullerton and Smith's* services at Kilburn Hall:—

"It is the first time I have ever arranged for a special mission in any of our halls in London so late as June, as midsummer is scarcely the time to gather London congregations, night after night, in *any* building. Notwithstanding this, however, there were large attendances on the week-nights; while on Sundays, the new building was packed, and overflow-meetings were held.

"It is with joy I add that the labours of these beloved brethren were crowned with success in the winning of souls. We have many cases before us where the changed life seems indicative of solid conversion to God, as the result of the gospel which they so ably preached, for which we do heartily praise God, and also thank you and our brethren for the visit that proved so acceptable."

Mr. Hurditch came to the Tabernacle on *July* 14, and took part in the service. We wish him God-speed in his far-reaching evangelistic work.

The minister of Bath Street Chapel, Poplar (Mr. Myers, United Methodist Free Church), sends us a long report of the eight days' mission held by our brethren. We have not the space for the full account; but we may mention that Mr. Myers calls special attention to the children's service conducted by Mr. Smith, when some 2,000 were present; the men's meeting on Sunday afternoon, when 800 gathered to listen to Mr. Fullerton's wise and weighty words; and the closing service, when the spacious building was not large enough for those who desired to be present. Many were brought to decision at the services.

On the day that Mr. Spurgeon spoke at the Conference Hall, Mildmay Park, Mr. Fullerton conducted an overflow-meeting "under the mulberry tree"; and on the following Lord's-day he and Mr. Smith held services in the hall, which was crowded both morning and evening. Collections for the Orphanage realized £30 13s. 1d. Friends at Mildmay thus a second time had fellowship with us in our work, and we thank them heartily.

During July, on Saturdays and Sundays, our brethren have been at the Polytechnic, Regent Street, where large numbers have gathered to hear the Word. In the intervals between these services they held meetings in Falcon Square Chapel, in connection with Mrs. Fisher's work among young women ; and from July 15 to 17 paid a second visit to Beulah Chapel, Thornton Heath. Special efforts had been made to bring in those who attend no place of worship, and many of these were induced to be present. Many were brought to immediate decision for Christ, and others were seriously impressed at the services. We were pleased to see both these workers at "Westwood" looking in better case than ever we remember to have seen them before at the close of a campaign.

This month the evangelists hope to enjoy their much-needed and well-earned rest. In September they will probably go to Paris. October is to be devoted to Tunbridge Wells, Tonbridge, Stowmarket, and Hadleigh; November to Oxford and Carlisle; and December to Ashford (Kent), and Gravesend.

Mr. Burnham desires us to call special attention to his article on the Hop-pickers' Mission, in which he expects to be engaged next month.

Mr. Harmer and *Mr. Chamberlain* during the early part of July, were at Crewkerne, where the attendance was good for summertime, and the results encouraging.

Mr. Carter is continuing his "Pioneer" work with much success. Through the blessing of the Lord upon his efforts, the churches at Harefield, Middlesex, and Radcliffe, Lancashire, have been so strengthened that they now have pastors of their own ; and it is hoped that Farnworth, Lancashire, will soon be in the same condition. Meanwhile, Mr. Carter is at work in other places where Baptist churches are needed.

Pastor W. Jackson sends us the following cheering account of the mission conducted by *Mr. Parker* at Waltham Abbey:—
" He sang and preached the gospel on each occasion with much acceptance and power, and he dealt with enquirers in an effective manner. Some were convicted of sin, others were converted to God, and obtained peace ; and several who had been in a hopeful state were brought to decision. It was with great joy that we witnessed the ingathering of precious souls. Elder scholars, former scholars, the second daughter of the pastor, the second daughter of one deacon, the third daughter of one elder, and the eldest daughter of another elder, were drawn by the uplifted Saviour. Strangers also were brought nigh, and some who had previously manifested a spirit of indifference, if not open hostility to the Redeemer, were made willing in the day of his power."
Mr. Parker has since visited Sandhurst, Berkshire, where successful services were held both indoors and in the open-air. Mr. Parker will be glad to hear from brethren desiring his services in the autumn and winter. His address is 13, Doddington Grove, Kennington, London, S.E.

ORPHANAGE.—On *June* 23, Mr. Charlesworth conducted the anniversary services at Llanwenarth, Monmouthshire, of which church the Rev. T. H. Williams, formerly a boy in the Orphanage, is the pastor.

On *July* 2, the children enjoyed their annual strawberry feast. The fruit was supplied by Mr. A. Ross, who hopes to be able to keep up the custom, in memory of his father, who has gone home, after having, in many ways, proved himself to be the friend of the orphans.

The children's holidays commenced on July 16, and will terminate on August 15. A few boys and girls have no relatives to take them : will not friends come forward to give these poor unfortunates a short holiday? An application addressed to the Head Master, the Orphanage, Clapham Road, S.W., will receive prompt attention. In all cases, where necessary, we will pay the railway fares.

COLPORTAGE.—*Special offer to extend Colportage work in new districts.*—The Committee desire to call the attention of all who are interested in trying to mitigate the frightful evils arising from the widespread circulation of trashy and immoral literature, to the necessity for pushing the sale of sound and healthy books and periodicals by means of Christian Colportage.

This is the mission of the Association, which employs seventy-eight men in various districts, whose business it is to try and create a taste for reading of a better class. They are Christian men, of various denominations, who visit from house to house for the sale of the Scriptures and healthy literature, caring specially for the afflicted and aged, besides conducting occasional services, as required, for gospel preaching in the open-air and cottages.

Since the commencement of the Association, 318,768 Bibles and Testaments have been sold, besides 1,961,873 books, and 4,099,195 periodicals, to the value of £121,801 6s. 7d.

The funds of the Association will not enable it to support a colporteur permanently unless £40 per annum can be guaranteed for a district.

The Committee have, however, much pleasure in stating that, owing to an exceptional legacy, they are prepared, for a limited period, to entertain offers for about twenty additional districts, to send a colporteur for the first year at a greatly-reduced rate, if there is a reasonable prospect of the full £40 per annum being raised during the second or third years.

The whole amount guaranteed need not be remitted at once, but can be paid quarterly in advance.

Applications should be addressed to the Secretary, W. Corden Jones, Pastors' College, Temple Street, Southwark, S.E.

PERSONAL NOTES.—An American Chief Justice, who is also a Presbyterian Elder, writes as follows to one of our friends:—"To meet an unexpected emergency, I had to fill the pulpit by reading a sermon. I had some volumes of Spurgeon's sermons, and I went into them vigorously. I had to study them to see what could be left out without injury to the force of the discourse; and I was greatly gratified to find that my mind and my heart soon became much interested and profited by the exercise; and much more impressed than I had before been with Spurgeon's power as a preacher. 'To make a long story short,' I filled the pulpit in the morning of seven Sabbaths, and gave our people such preaching as they had never heard there before. The result to myself was every way beneficial spiritually, and I thanked God that he gave me the opportunity of giving and receiving good. If the way should be providentially opened, I would be not only willing, but glad to perform just such a service every Sabbath in the year."

A City Missionary sends us the following cheering instance of the usefulness of our magazine:—"I take the *Sword and Trowel* regularly, and am in the habit of giving it to a poor blind man (rich in grace) after I have read it myself. He has many visitors to read to him, among them a Scripture Reader. This servant of God, calling one day, was requested by my blind friend to read a discourse from the magazine I had left. He did so; and strange to say, an address he had prepared to deliver in his Mission Hall at night was completely driven from his mind, your sermon he had read taking its place. There was no help for it, he could only preach your discourse, or remain dumb. He chose to do the former, and at the close two souls professed to find the Saviour. "Thus the *Sword and Trowel* is becoming the mouth-piece of the Lord in more ways than one. May God bless it, and its Editor!"

A friend gives us the following particulars of the conversion of a persecutor:—"A few years since, there dwelt in London a Christian woman whose husband was opposed to religion, and at times would taunt his wife about it. If he could hear any statement disparaging to Mr. Spurgeon, he would say, on his return home, "There's your Spurgeon again"; and thus would wound the feelings of his pious wife. A brother of the woman, residing in Suffolk, paid them a visit; and the husband was induced by him to go to a service at the Metropolitan Tabernacle. Mr. Spurgeon had been preaching only about a quarter of an hour when the husband was observed to be in tears; the Word had taken effect. It was the starting-point of a new life, and the man lived and died, to all appearance, a sincere Christian."

A sister in Christ sends us the following account of her conversion, and apologizes for not having written before to tell us the cheering news:—"For many years I longed for something that I did not possess, feeling something was wanting. I felt a burden heavy on my heart; but one blessed Sabbath morning, 30 years ago, going up to my bed-room, I picked up one of your sermons, and sat down and read it. It was entitled 'The Separation of the Chaff from the Wheat.' I was delighted to feel love, joy, faith, and peace, rush into my soul on reading the words, 'Believe on the Lord Jesus Christ, and thou shalt be saved.' "Bless the dear Lord Jesus, my burden rolled away! I felt the happiest person in the world for two hours. I could not stop in the house: I walked up and down the garden rejoicing; I was overcome with my new-found happiness. I have passed through great trials since—loss of property, loved ones gone home with Jesus—but that blessed faith and love have been renewed day by day."

Baptisms at Metropolitan Tabernacle:—June 27, seventeen; June 28, one; July 4, five.

Pastors' College, Metropolitan Tabernacle.

Statement of Receipts from June 15th to July 15th, 1889.

	£	s.	d.		£	s.	d.
Per Pastor A. W. Wood, of Broughton	0	4	0	Mrs. Drayson	0	10	0
Mr. H. R. Cooper ..	1	1	0	Friends in Senekal, Orange Free State,			
Mrs. Websdale, per J. T. D.	2	0	0	South Africa, per Mr. H. Gudath ...	10	0	0
Part of Lord's Supper collection, Peck-				Pastor C. J. Fowler	0	10	0
ham Public Hall, per Pastor Frank				Nameless	0	10	0
Smith (previously omitted) ...	0	10	0	A friend, Highbridge	0	2	6
A sermon-reader ...	0	3	0	Mr. Thomas Gurney	0	10	0
Mr. and Mrs. Miller ...	1	0	0	Mr. F. S. Shields, R.W.S.	1	0	0
Mr. W. N. Finlayson	0	5	0	Mr. J. T. Cook	2	2	0
Mr. G. Harris	1	0	0	Mr. John Twaites...	1	0	0
Mrs. Shearman	3	0	0	Mr. James Alabaster ...	10	0	0
Mrs. Tunbridge	0	10	0	In memoriam	5	0	0
Mr. John M. Cook...	5	0	0	Mr. and Mrs. J. H. Alabaster ...	5	0	0
Mr. E. Mounsey	2	0	0	Mr. Passmore	10	0	0
Mrs. Allard	1	0	0	Mrs. Passmore	5	0	0
Mrs. Watcham	1	0	0	Mr. and Mrs. J. Passmore ...	5	0	0

	£	s.	d.
Mr. and Mrs. James Passmore ...	5	0	0
Adelphi	1	10	0
The executors of the late Mrs. Sheridan			
Knowles	896	17	0
Miss B. Heering	0	10	0
It.	1	0	0
Miss Wyburn	1	1	0
Miss E. Cross	0	5	0
Mr. and Mrs. Clarke ...	1	0	0
Mrs. Elgee	0	10	0
Mrs. Durrant	10	6	9
Mrs. Lloyd	0	5	0
Mrs. Leask	1	0	0
Mr. E. Newell	2	10	0
Mr. Robert Fergus...	5	0	0
Mrs. Bell	0	10	0
Mr. John Hosie	1	0	0
Mrs. C. Norton	0	2	6

	£	s.	d.
God's tenth ...	0	4	0
Mrs. Bainbridge ...	2	2	0
A reader of "The Sword and the			
Trowel" (with box of jewellery for			
sale)	0	5	0
Mr. George Norton ...	2	10	0
The executors of the late Mr. W. H.			
Roberts	500	0	0
Weekly Offerings at Met. Tab. :—			
June 16 ...	39	3	11
„ 23 ...	16	14	8
„ 30	38	13	4
July 7	28	0	9
„ 14	30	6	1
	152	18	9
	£1,661	4	6

Stockwell Orphanage.

Statement of Receipts from June 15th to July 15th, 1889.

	£	s.	d.
In memoriam, E. ...	0	10	0
Jack, South Lambeth	0	2	0
Collected by Miss Sharp	0	11	6
Collected by Mrs. Cable	0	5	3
Collected by Miss E. Sherrard ...	0	12	6
Gershom	0	1	0
Mr. James Bristow	2	2	0
Collected by Miss Moore (No. 8 Boys')	0	17	2
Mr. Cooper	1	1	0
Collected by Mr. Cooper ...	0	13	6
Staines Baptist Sunday-school, per Mr.			
J. McKee....	1	13	0
Mr. Smithers, per Mr. Cockrell ...	1	1	0
Mrs. Robson...	0	2	0
Mr. S. Short...	0	10	6
Collected by Miss Fitzgerald ...	0	2	0
Young Women's Bible-class, per Mr.			
John Brash	0	5	0
Collected by Miss E. Hinton ...	0	15	0
Mr. W. E. R. Hoskin	1	0	0
Collected by Mrs. Oxenbridge	0	3	0
Dr. G. Saunders, C.B.	1	0	0
Mr. James W. Marshall	1	0	0
Collected by Miss W. Bagshaw ...	0	2	7
Collected by Charlie and Elsie Garrett	0	10	6
Collected by Mr. Morris	0	11	0
Collected by Miss S. H. Pickering ...	0	9	0
Collected by Miss Keay ...	0	5	0
Mr. J. Lothian	0	7	0
Collected by Mrs. Coles ...	0	10	6
Mr. C. Ibberson...	0	2	6
Collected by Mr. W. Smith ...	0	15	0
Mr. T. Weir...	0	10	0
Collected by Mrs. Walker	0	11	6
Collected by Master Crisp ...	0	4	3
Mr. E. Longmore	1	0	0
Collected by Miss Greenop ...	1	0	0
Collected by Mrs. Roberts ...	0	4	6
Collected by Mrs. Penning ...	0	5	0
Per Pastor J. Rankine :—			
Collected by Mrs. Rankine	0 16 2		
Collected by Mrs. McDonald	0 8 0		
	1	4	2
Collected by Mrs. J. L. Blake :—			
Peterborough box	2 17 5		
Claxton box	0 2 7		0
	3	0	
Masters Harry, Charlie, and Bertie			
Curtis	1	0	0
Mrs. H. Warriner	0	2	0
Mr. T. Greening	1	6	0
Mr. T. Pask	0	5	0
Wishaw Baptist Church, per Pastor G.			
Whittet	1	3	6

	£	s.	d.
Collected by Miss Ellwood ...	0	5	0
Collected by Mr. J. Harman ...	0	5	0
Mrs. Parkes...	1	0	0
Miss Parkes	0	10	0
Miss B. Parkes	1	0	0
Collected by Mr. A. Jungling ...	1	0	0
Mrs. M. Munro	0	10	0
Collected by Miss Bennett ...	0	5	6
Collected by Miss C. M. Stevenson ...	0	16	8
The infant class, Baptist Sunday-school,			
Chipping Norton, per Mr. E. Burbidge	0	13	6
Collected by Mrs. Welford	0	12	0
Miss Day	0	2	0
Collected by Miss D. Martin ...	0	6	6
Mr. C. B. Casey (children's box) ...	1	5	0
Collected by Mrs. Burton ...	0	13	3
Collected by Mrs. Bullock ...	0	4	3
Collected by Miss E. Clarke	0	12	0
Mrs. Angell...	0	3	0
Collected by Mrs. Jarman ...	0	3	0
Mr. G. G. C. McKenzie ...	0	2	6
Collected by Miss M. Waterman ...	1	5	0
Rev. Marcus Rainsford	1	1	0
Mr. H. R. Cooper	1	1	0
Collected by Miss Wain	7	0	0
Collected by Mr. P. Wooltorton ...	3	10	0
Mrs. Baker	0	5	0
Collected by Mr. S. T. Hudson ...	0	8	0
Collected by Mrs. S. E. Smith .	0	10	0
West Croydon Baptist Sunday-school,			
per Mr. W. S. Durrant...	5	5	0
Collected by Mrs. Gallyon ...	2	10	3
Collected by Miss Luxford ...	0	6	0
Mr. Michael Cook	1	0	0
Mrs. Clements	1	1	0
Collected by Mrs. Robins ...	0	10	0
Collected by Mrs. E. Offer ...	0	5	0
Miss Josie Arnold's box	1	0	10
Collected by Miss E. A. Earl ...	0	13	0
Collected by Miss E. M. Elford...	1	5	0
Mr. C. Hill	0	0	6
Miss N. Matthews	0	10	0
Collected by Miss M. A. Weatherhead	0	11	0
Collected by Miss E. Epps ...	0	5	6
Collected by Miss J. Pearce ...	0	12	7
Mr. M. Stroud	2	2	0
Mr. J. G. Romang (first day's takings)	1	0	0
Collected by Miss E. Salmon	0	6	2
Collected by Miss C. M. Bidewell ...	0	5	6
Collected by Miss K. Smith ...	0	2	0
Collected by Miss L. Staveley ...	3	10	0
Mr. F. Paterson	0	10	0
Sale of S. O. Tracts ...	0	3	0
Mr. S. Priddy	0	10	0

	£	s.	d.
From a friend to the little orphans ...	0	5	0
"We are seven" ...	5	0	0
Young Women's Bible-class, Lewin Road, Streatham, per Mrs. Davis	0	13	2
Collected by Miss Hunt (No. 5 Girls')...	0	6	0
Collected by Miss Maxwell ...	0	3	3
Miss A. A. Roberts, per Miss Maxwell	2	2	0
Collected by Miss Jeffery	0	7	0
Collected by Mrs. A. Walker ...	0	5	7
Collected by Mrs. Cooper (No. 6 Girls')	0	9	3
Collected by Miss M. Passmore...	0	4	11
Collected by Master J. Walker...	0	1	6
Mrs. N. Sparrow ...	0	10	0
Collected by Miss L. Johnson ...	2	7	0
Collected by Miss A. A. Hall ...	0	8	6
"One of his stewards" ...	3	12	0
Miss Brady ...	1	0	0
Collected by Masters M. and E. Chance	0	7	6
"Better late than never" ...	0	10	0
Mr. J. Clunie ...	0	5	0
Collected by Miss Davis ...	0	15	8
Miss Stirling ...	0	3	0
Sale of S. O. Tracts ...	0	6	6
Collected by Mrs. Medland ...	0	11	0
Jack, South Lambeth ...	0	2	0
Collected by Mrs. Clarke (No. 2 Girls')	0	5	1
Mr. E. K. Stace ...	0	10	0
Gershom ...	0	1	0
Rev. S. R. Young ...	0	10	0
Mr. Isaac Watts ...	2	2	0
Young Women's Bible-class at the Orphanage, per Mrs. J. Stiff...	0	14	0
Miss Martineau ...	2	2	0
Collected by Mr. H. Andrew ...	1	2	0
A friend, Ebury Bridge ...	0	10	0
A friend at the Sunday-school Union bazaar, per Mr. C. J. Smith ...	0	10	0
Mrs. Eaton ...	0	5	0
Collected by Mrs. Tiddy...	2	8	6
Mr. J. Gray ...	0	6	0
Adelphos ...	5	0	0
Mrs. Campbell ...	0	2	6
Capt. C. M. Möller (for boy E. Cliffe)	10	0	0
Mr. J. Cameron ...	0	5	0
Mr. W. D. Crowhurst ...	1	0	0
Collected by Mrs. H. Critch ...	2	1	3
Mrs. R. Smith ...	1	0	0
Collected by Mrs. Evans...	0 0 0		
Mrs. J. A. Pash	0 0 0		
Mr. G. Hadnutt ...	0 0 0		
Mrs. Salter ...	0 0 0		
A servant ...	0 10 0		
	2	10	0
Mr. Ranford ...	1	0	0
Mr. J. C. Wadland ...	1	0	0
Mrs. Websdale, per J. T. D. ...	1	0	0
Mrs. Raybould ...	1	1	0
The Unity Bible-class ...	1	1	0
Mr. Wollacott, per J. T. D. ...	5	0	0
G. T. ...	0	10	0
Orphanage boxes at Tabernacle gates	0	17	6
Collected by Miss Lennard ...	0	11	0
Ashwell ...	1	0	0
Collected by Mr. F. Brown ...	0	16	0
Master Gordon Roberts ...	0	7	7
Miss Clara Donaldson ...	1	0	0
A thankoffering ...	0	4	0
Mr. C. R. White (for 1888-9) ...	2	2	0
Collected by Master C. Twort ...	0	1	4
Collected by Mrs. Wilmot ...	0	5	6
"This is David's spoil," Cambridge-shire...	0	5	0
L. K. D. ...	0	5	0
Miss S. Porter ...	0	0	0
Mr. S. D. Lamb ...	0	10	0
Miss E. Cross ...	0	5	0
Mrs. Elgee ...	0	10	0
Messrs. Morgan and Scott ...	5	5	0
Collections at Mildmay Park Conference Hall, after services conducted by Messrs. Fullerton and Smith...	30	13	1

	£	s.	d.
Mr. George Palmer, J.P....	50	0	0
A commercial traveller ...	25	0	0
In memoriam ...	1	1	0
Mrs. Baines ...	2	0	0
Mrs. Bayley ...	1	0	0
Miss Bayley ...	2	0	0
Mr. Hartswell ...	0	2	0
Mrs. J. G. Blake ...	0	5	0
Lottie ...	0	2	6
Rev. W. Harris ...	1	0	0
Mr. James Johnman ...	0	2	6
A lover of Jesus ...	0	10	0
A friend of the orphans ...	0	10	0
P. and P. ...	0	5	0
Mr. G. D. Forbes ...	0	2	6
Miss E. Hudson ...	0	7	0
Mr. W. Brown ...	0	2	6
Mr. Crouch ...	20	0	0
Mr. G. Smith ...	0	10	0
Mrs. Moubray ...	1	0	0
Mr. E. Newell ...	2	10	0
Mr. T. Jephcoat ...	0	10	0
St. John's Green Baptist Sunday-school, Colchester ...	0	10	0
Mr. R. Fergus ...	10	0	0
Collected by Pastor W. Gillard...	2	4	6
Mr. John Weir ...	1	0	0
Mr. William Church, jun. ...	0	2	6
Mr. B. Carey ...	1	0	0
Mr. C. F. Pfeil ...	1	1	0
Mr. John Hosie ...	0	10	6
Mrs. Spencer ...	0	2	6
Mr. H. Jackson ...	1	0	0
One from the shores of Bude ...	0	10	0
Mrs. Hall, per C. H. S. ...	1	0	0
Collected by Mr. John Beecroft ...	0	5	0
Pastor E. T. Davis ...	1	1	0
Mrs. Fraser...	0	7	0
H. Humber and friends ...	0	5	0
Mrs. C. Norton ...	0	5	0
Mr. and Mrs. Collin ...	1	0	0
Miss Maxwell ...	1	1	0
Mrs. Cooper ...	0	5	0
J. W., Barrow-in-Furness ...	1	0	0
Mr. George Norton ...	2	10	0
Miss M. Hyatt ...	1	0	0
Mrs. Cowell ...	1	0	0
A poor member of the Tabernacle church ...	0	2	0
Jewellery sold :—			
Miss Amey ... 10 0 0			
Mrs. Lewis ... 0 14 0			
	10	14	0
A friend ...	2	0	0
Mrs. Hatchard ...	1	0	0
Mr. George Baker ...	1	0	0
Mr. S. H. Dauncey ...	0	5	0
Mr. I. Cox ...	1	0	0
A country minister ...	0	3	0
Mr. W. Simmons ...	2	0	0
Executors of the late Mr. W. H. Roberts	100	0	0
Executors of the late Mrs. Sheridan Knowles ...	896	17	0
Miss Dixon, per J. T. D. ...	0	10	0
Mr. A. B. Todd ...	0	7	6
Miss Buckle ...	5	0	0
Mrs. Clews ...	1	0	0
Mrs. White ...	0	2	6
Mr. and Mrs. Scruby ...	0	10	0
Pastor W. Parry ...	0	5	0
Mr. George Tingey ...	20	0	0
Mr. and Mrs. W. R. Fox, for the support of one child for a year ...	20	0	0
Mr. William Graham ...	1	0	0
Mr. and Mrs. Miller ...	1	0	0
Mr. William Crawford ...	0	10	0
Mrs. Cracknell ...	1	1	0
Mr. W. N. Finlayson ...	0	5	0
Mrs. Keylock ..	0	2	0
S., from America ...	0	2	0

	£	s.	d.
Pastor F. M. Smith	0	10	0
Currant trees	0	10	0
Pastor A. Tessier	0	10	0
Miss S. M. Stedman	0	5	0
Mrs. J. Roberts	0	2	0
Nurse Rickwood	0	2	0
Mrs. Watson and Mr. James Watson	0	7	6
Mr. P. Cockerill	0	10	6
Mr. R. P. Hicks	1	1	0
Mrs. Fairey	1	0	0
Mr. A. Davis and friend	3	3	0
Mr. C. W. Roberts	5	0	0
Mr. and Mrs. M. G. Hewat	2	0	0
Mr. F. Freeman	10	0	0
Mr. G. Harris	1	0	0
Mrs. Shearman	2	0	0
Mr. J. Holt Skinner	25	0	0
Miss Turner and friends	0	13	0
Mr. Egerton Burnett	3	3	0
S. D. C.	0	10	0
Miss J. Allan	0	2	6
Miss H. Hopperton	0	10	0
Mrs. Dodwell	1	0	0
Mrs. Milligan	2	0	0
H. M. F.	0	3	0
Collected by Miss Ann Mackay	0	12	0
Friends at Great Barton, per Mr. R. M. Scott	1	5	4
Mr. A. Pearson, sen.	1	1	0
Mrs. Thorndike	0	5	0
Mr. S. Tutcher	2	0	0
An invalid	0	10	6
Mr. and Mrs. D. Baker	0	10	0
Mr. G. Bantick	1	0	0
Mrs. Clarke and Mrs. Bubb	0	10	0
Mr. and Mrs. Cracknell	1 1 0		
Sunday offerings	0 13 6		
	1	14	6
Collected by Master O. J. Rossiter	8	5	0
Mr. and Mrs. Proctor	1	0	0
Miss Royle	0	5	0
Miss Spliedt	1	0	0
Miss H. Husk	0	7	6
Adelphi	2	2	0
Mrs. R. Taylor	0	5	0
Mrs. McKenzie	0	10	0
Rev. J. and Mrs. Adams	0	5	0
Miss Adams' Bible-class	0	3	0
In loving memory of Frankie Joscelyne	1	0	0
Miss Mary Hay	0	5	0
Mrs. Boyle	0	5	0
Mrs. Tunbridge	0	10	0
Miss Jones' evening class	1	3	0
M. F.	0	5	0
Miss Morrison	1	1	0
Miss E. Clover	0	7	6
Miss M. E. White	1	10	0
Mrs. Walters	0	10	0
J. D., Cranbrook	0	1	0
A servant	1	0	0
Mrs. C. Ware	0	2	6
Mr. C. Cutchlan	0	5	0
Mr. John M. Cook	5	0	0
Edith, per Mrs. Walker	0	5	6
Mrs. Walker's collecting-box	4	12	9
Rev. C. B. and Mrs. Lewis	2	2	0
Mr. E. Mounsey	2	0	0
Miss Lizzie Samuel's collecting-box	1	10	0
Mrs. Watts	1	1	0
Mrs. Calder	21	0	0
Pastor G. Cobb	0	10	0
Miss M. A. Hardy	0	2	0
Mr. A. Todd	0	10	0
Mrs. Williams	0	5	0
Miss Anne Baker (presentation almanacks)	0	6	6
Mrs. M. Smith	0	1	6
Mrs. Knott	1	1	0
Miss Sarah Gray Hill	2	2	0
Mr. John Best, J.P.	1	0	0
Mr. C. W. Smith	2	2	0

	£	s.	d.
Miss A. M. Morris	0	3	6
Mr. and Mrs. T. A. Kelly	1	1	0
Miss J. Harding	0	10	0
Mrs. Chapman	0	2	6
Mrs. C. Dales	1	0	0
Pastor and Mrs. A. Hall	0	5	0
Mrs. Couttie	1	0	0
Collected by Miss May Turner	1	0	0
Miss Eveline Davies	1	0	0
Miss Janet Chalmers	0	3	3
Mr. and Mrs. Jeffery	1	1	0
Mr. G. Cooper	2	0	0
Miss M. F. Lindsay	0	10	0
Miss M. J. Maynard	0	5	0
Mrs. England	1	0	0
Mr. C. J. Curtis	1	0	0
Rev. John Spurgeon	1	0	0
Mr. C. F. Alldis	1	1	0
Given to Mr. C. F. Alldis, at the Tabernacle, June 16	0	10	0
Mrs. Irwin	0	3	0
Miss K. B. Webb	2	0	0
Collected by Master M. Herries	0	8	2
Mr. Henry Doorbar, jun.	0	5	0
Mrs. E. Underwood	0	5	0
Mr. J. W. Mottershead	0	10	0
Mr. Edwin Davis	1	10	0
Mr. and Mrs. J. Dickey	1	1	0
Rev. Duncan and Mrs. Sharpe	0	10	0
Mrs. Lane	0	5	0
Colonel A. R. Clarke, R.E.	3	0	0
J. F.	0	10	0
Mr. James Smart	0	10	6
Mrs. Fry	0	5	0
Miss Effie Preston	0	2	6
Mr. F. Mullis	1	1	0
Mrs. Spindler	5	0	0
For Jesu's lambs	0	5	0
Mr. J. G. Wilkins	1	0	0
Mrs. Lutley, Sunday table offerings	1	1	0
Mrs. Allard	0	5	0
Mrs. Watcham	2	0	0
Mrs. Drayson	0	10	0
Postal order from Penpont	0	5	0
Mr. W. Jones	15	0	0
Mrs. Pearce	0	7	6
Mr. George Ranson, Kansas	2	1	1
Mrs. Tompkins	1	0	0
Mr. D. A. McDonald	0	5	0
Rev. J. M. Hewson	0	10	0
Mr. W. Williamson	3	0	0
Entertainment given by the masters and pupils in Bethany House School, Goudhurst, Kent, per Pastor J. J. Kendon	5	0	0
Mr. F. W. N. Lloyd	10	10	0
Mr. J. W. Green	1	0	0
Mr. J. Wood	0	10	0
Pastor C. J. Fowler	0	10	0
Poly	0	7	6
Mrs. Bell	2	10	0
A thankoffering from three	0	5	0
Mr. and Mrs. D. Bloomfield	0	2	6
Mrs. Heffer	2	0	0
Collected by Mrs. Bonsema	2	13	0
Mr. John Reid	0	2	0
Mrs. White	1	0	0
Mrs. Lane	1	0	0
Ruthie and Jackie	2	2	0
Mr. James Morrison, Panama	1	0	4
Mr. W. Howard	1	1	0
Mr. James Scott	10	0	0
Collections at Beulah Baptist Chapel, Thornton Heath, per Pastor J. W. Harrald	3	13	6
Collected by Miss Newbold	0	15	1
Collected by Miss J. Gardiner	1	2	6
Mrs. Foster	1	0	0
Nameless	0	10	0
Stamps from Newport, I.W.	0	1	0
Mr. Waters	1	1	0

	£	s.	d.
Mr. F. A. Fawkes ...	1	1	0
Mrs. Mills ..	2	2	0
Mrs. Williamson ...	0	15	0
Miss Sarah Brown ...	0	10	0
A friend ...	2	0	0
Widow Smith ...	0	2	6
Collected by Miss Zurhorst ...	10	11	6
Mrs. Yates ..	0	10	6
Miss A. Lloyd ...	0	10	0
Mrs. Williams ...	0	5	0
Mrs. Barnes ...	0	10	0
F. G. B., Chelmsford ...	0	2	6
Mrs. Mitchell ...	0	10	0
Mrs. Ferguson ...	0	5	0
Mrs. J. Whittuck Rabbits ...	10	10	0
Sandwich, per Bankers ...	2	2	0

Meeting by Mr. Charlesworth and the Orphanage Choir:—

	£	s.	d.
Moiety of proceeds, Southampton ...	1	12	10

Amounts received at the Annual Festival, June 19th:—
Donations:—

	£	s.	d.
A friend, Southampton ...	0	1	0
A friend ...	0	0	0
Anon., collected ...	0	1	0
A. T. ...	0	2	0
Anderson, Mr., per Mr. Cornell ...	1	0	0
Briers, The late Mr. Jno., Shenley, per Mrs. Jones	1	1	0
Bailey, Mrs. ...	0	4	9
Barnard, Pastor J. H. and Mrs. ...	0	1	0
Descroix, Miss ...	0	1	0
Davies, Mrs., per Mrs. Mott	1	0	0
Devenish, Mrs. ...	0	5	0
Deacon, Misses Lilian and Florence ...	0	5	0
E. A. S., per Mr. S. Johnson	1	1	0
Evans, Mr. Richard ...	20	0	0
E. and M. A. S. ...	1	1	0
E. C. ...	0	2	6
F. H. ...	0	10	0
Friends, per Mr. Cook ...	1	2	6
G. M. ...	0	10	0
G. B., 146, Trinity Road, Upper Tooting ...	0	1	0
Healey, Mrs. ...	2	0	0
Hoare, Mr. ...	0	10	6
Hillen, Mrs. ...	1	1	0
Hill, Mr. W. ...	0	5	0
Hammerton, Mrs. ...	0	10	0
Jones, Mrs. ...	0	5	0
J. W., family box ..	0	13	6
Jenkins, Mrs. ...	2	2	0
M. M., per Mr. S. Johnson	1	1	0
Moulton, Miss ...	0	3	0
Miller, Mr., per Mrs. Mott	0	10	0
Newman, Mrs. ...	0	10	0
No name ...	2	2	0
N. M., Clapham ...	0	10	0
Norris, Miss ...	0	5	0
Olney, Mr. T. H. ...	10	0	0
Providence Baptist Sunday school, Hounslow, per Mr Yeates ...	0	10	6
Perrett, Miss ...	1	3	0
Romang, Mr. ...	0	10	0

Per Rev. J. A. Spurgeon.

	£	s.	d.
Miss Croose ...	1	1	0
Mrs. Scard ...	1	1	0
Mrs. Buckmaster ...	1	1	0
	3	3	0
Spurgeon, Mr. Joseph, per Mrs. Goslin	2	0	0
Smith, Mrs. ...	0	5	0
Stiff, Miss E. ...	0	2	0
S. B. and C. B. ...	0	10	0
The widow's gift from one of your children...	1	12	10
Turley, Mr. ...	1	0	0

	£	s.	d.
Teddington Baptist Sunday-school, per Mr. F. W. Rose	0	7	0
Tinniswood, Mrs. ..	1	1	0
Thick, Miss ...	0	5	0
Perry, Mr. ...	0	5	0
Willis, Miss Ada .	0	5	0
Wayre, Mr. and Mrs. ...	2	2	0
Wayre, Miss and Master...	1	1	0
Williams, Mrs. H. ...	0	10	0
Wood, Mr. W. ...	0	10	0
Weller, Mr. ...	0	2	6
Wall boxes ...	0	3	6
Webber, A. and C. (boy's card) ...	0	7	0
	71	8	7
Mr. Passmore—book-stall ...	14	14	0
Mr. Pascall—confectionery	6	1	0
Mr. Hines—scent-stall ...	1	15	0

Collecting Books

	£	s.	d.
Allum, Mrs. ...	3	17	0
Bonser, Miss ...	0	9	6
Balls, Mr. T. T. ...	1	12	2
Broughton, Mrs. ...	0	0	0
Brown, Miss J. H ...	0	5	6
Barrett, Mr. H. ...	1	4	0
Cockshaw, Miss J. ...	1	7	0
Cockshaw, Miss ...	0	0	0
Corsam, Miss B. ...	0	7	0
Cann, Miss ...	0	17	10
Clayton, Miss H. W. ...	4	4	0
Charles, Miss F. B. ...	0	7	0
Cunningham, Mrs ...	1	15	0
Cox, Miss ...	0	3	2
Dee, Mrs. ...	0	8	0
Duncombe, Mrs. ...	1	1	0
Edwards, Miss ...	1	3	0
Evans, Mr. S. T. ...	2	13	0
Evans, Mr. W. J. ...	2	12	8
Fowler, Miss N. ...	0	8	0
Figg, Miss H. ...	0	8	0
Freeman, Mr. G. (book-binder) ...	4	12	6
Goslin, Mrs. ...	0	7	0
Godbold, Mrs. ...	0	13	6
Good, Miss ...	0	4	0
Honour, Miss ...	1	1	0
Horn, Mr. J. ...	0	12	6
Hawthorne, Mrs. ...	0	18	0
Hobbs, Miss...	1	3	0
Jephs, Miss ...	1	0	0
Knight, Mrs. J. E. ...	0	5	0
Lawson, Mrs. ...	0	17	6
McDonald, Mrs ...	0	15	0
Mann, Miss ...	6	2	0
Mott, Mrs. ...	1	2	0
Miller, Mr. C. ...	0	15	0
Miller, Miss H. ...	0	11	4
Noble, Mr. A. ...	0	3	9
Richmond, Mrs. ...	0	14	0
Spurdens, Miss ...	0	4	0
Scutt, Mrs. ...	0	2	0
Saunders, Mr. E. W. ...	2	10	0
Taylor, Miss...	0	7	0
Wheeler, Miss ...	1	10	0
Willis, Mrs. ...	1	0	0
Wilson, Miss ...	1	15	0
Walters, Miss ...	0	12	8
	56	17	1

Collecting Boxes:—

	£	s.	d.
Ayliffe, Miss ...	0	7	7
Apted, Mr. ...	0	13	2
Armstrong, Mr. ...	0	10	9
Allen, Miss ...	2	11	11
Ansell, Mr. ...	0	5	1
Atkins, Master E. ...	0	1	8
Bates, Miss ...	0	5	1
Black, Miss ...	0	5	11
Barnden, Mrs. ...	0	10	1
Brake, Miss G. ...	0	5	3
Branscombe, Master R. ...	0	3	11
Bygrave, Master C. ...	0	1	9

		£	s.	d.
Butcher, Master W.	...	0	4	6
Buxton, Mr. S. A.	...	0	10	2
Brice, Miss C.	...	0	5	5
Bruin, Miss E.	...	0	11	3
Baldock, Mr. H. A.	...	0	13	2
Boswell, Mrs.	...	0	3	5
Boot, Miss N.	...	0	8	1
Beale, Miss	...	0	15	3
Betts, Mrs. ...	...	0	2	8
Beaumont, Mr. E.	...	0	2	11
Brown, Miss R.	...	0	7	6
Betts, Mr. W.	...	0	1	9
Box, Miss J.	...	0	4	0
Benham, Miss	...	0	3	0
Barr, Master	...	0	3	0
Bartlett, Master E.	...	0	3	2
Bevan, Mrs. A.	...	0	3	2
Bailey, Mr. G.	...	0	6	6
Brooks, Miss	...	0	4	9
Brice, G. and W	...	0	2	0
Burrage, Mrs.	...	0	4	4
Butcher, Master H.	...	0	1	1
Bond, Master F.	...	0	0	11
Briggs, Miss	...	0	11	10
Bucknole, Miss	...	0	9	11
Buckingham, Miss	...	0	7	9
Butler, Mrs.	...	0	8	4
Bygrave, Miss F.	...	0	2	7
Baxter, Miss E.	...	0	8	8
Brown, Mr. I.	...	0	4	11
Box, Mr. J. ...	...	0	2	2
Bellefontaine, Master	...	0	0	11
Brice, Master A. and P.	...	0	2	9
Bennett, Mrs. R.	..	0	1	10
Baskett, Mrs.	..	0	6	7
Barnard, Miss N.	..	0	6	9
Bygrave, Miss B.	...	0	5	0
Bygrave, Master H.		0	3	9
Baldock, Master A. W.	...	0	8	10
Ballands, Miss A. ...	...	0	4	8
Bowles, Mrs.	...	0	4	4
Blandford, Mrs.	...	0	7	10
Barnes, Mr.	...	1	0	0
Cairns, Miss M.	...	0	8	
Carpenter, Miss	...	0	6	0
Cairns, Miss C.	...	0	9	0
Causton, Miss E.	...	1	10	
Cowell, Mr. ...	...	0	6	11
Chisholm, Master W.	...	0	10	9
Collier, Mr. ...	...	0	14	0
Cockshaw's, Miss J., pupils		0	15	0
Clark, Miss ...	...	0	4	5
Cook, Miss ...	...	0	4	4
Clay, Mrs. ...	...	0	4	3
Chandler, Miss M.	...	0	6	7
Conquest, Mrs.	...	0	6	1
Castell, Mrs. E.	...	0	5	7
Craggs, Master C.	...	0	2	1
Cairns, Misses J. and L.	...	1	6	0
Crane, Mrs. ...	...	0	4	8
Chapman, Miss H.	...	0	13	6
Charles, Miss L.	...	0	2	6
Charles, Master J. G.	...	0	1	7
Coker, Miss ...	...	2	4	0
Crane, Master W. ...	...	0	10	0
Caragerard, Miss ...	...	0	4	2
Coe, Miss ...	...	0	0	5
Crow, Mrs. ...	...	0	1	8
Cranch, Master R.	...	0	2	4
Cross, Master	...	0	2	8
Craggs, Master H.	...	0	1	5
Chapman, Mrs.	...	0	10	10
Craggs, Master C. ...	...	0	7	0
Charlesworth, Miss F.	...	0	3	5
Craggs, Master	...	0	4	9
Cornwall, Mrs.	...	0	6	0
Colman, Miss E. ...	...	0	2	5
Chamberlain, Miss	...	1	2	1
Cullingham, Mr. J.	...	0	7	6
Cranch, Master B. ...	...	0	0	11
Collins, Miss	...	0	3	10

		£	s.	d.
Dalton, Mr. R.		0	4	11
Dice, Masters S. and E.				
and Miss...		2	15	5
Durwin, Mrs.		0	10	11
Davies, Master T. ...	...	0	6	1
Debenham, Mr. A. W.		0	8	4
Druce, Miss ...		0	6	1
Dolling, A. W.		0	17	3
Deakin, Miss	...	0	10	7
Dury, Mrs.	...	0	6	4
Essex, Mrs. ...	...	0	10	10
Ellerington, Mrs. ...	...	0	3	7
Eyles, Misses A. and A.	...	0	1	3
Edmonds, Miss A.	...	0	5	3
Esling, Miss	...	0	4	6
Edginton, Miss L	...	0	9	5
Evans, Master S. H.	...	0	2	6
Everitt, Mr.	...	1	0	5
Everitt, Miss	...	0	14	7
Forsdike, Miss S. ...	...	0	1	11
Fraser, Miss	...	0	11	7
Field, Miss K.	...	0	17	1
Fairbairn, Miss	...	0	1	1
Field, Miss ...	...	0	19	8
Fremlin, Miss	...	1	11	2
Fuller, Mr. A.	...	0	9	1
Fox, Miss A.	...	0	0	6
Finnis, Miss D.	...	0	2	8
Fowler, Miss	...	0	2	11
Froggatts, Master T.	...	0	4	0
Farmer, Miss	...	1	1	11
Fairy, Master H.	...	0	6	8
Foster, Miss E.	...	0	10	4
Fuller, Miss E.	...	0	4	0
Forsdike, Miss	...	0	8	0
Fellowes, Mrs.	...	0	19	0
Fitness, Master A		0	1	4
Fern, Mr. C.	...	0	8	2
Gosling, Miss	...	0	7	9
Gowers, Mrs.	...	0	6	7
Grimes, Miss	...	0	7	11
Goodwin, Miss	...	0	0	2
Gosling, Miss H. E.		0	17	0
Goetz, Miss		0	9	6
Green, Miss		0	6	9
Graves, Master P. ...		0	2	3
Grant, Miss ...		0	12	3
Gouldy, Miss	...	0	6	1
Gant, Mrs. ...	...	0	2	5
Grose, Miss G. M. ...		1	2	9
Gray, Mr. A.		0	0	
Giles, Master H.	...	0	0	
Harrald, Master C.		1	0	0
Harrald, Master E.	...	0	1	3
Harrald, Misses L. and M.		2	15	0
Huitt, Miss E.	...	0	3	10
Higgs, Miss C.	...	9	1	5
Hartley, Master E.	...	0	0	11
Hayler, Mrs.	...	0	7	1
Hale, Miss	...	0	11	6
Hardy, Master B. ...	...	0	11	0
Hodly, Mr. J.	...	0	2	2
Harris, Miss	...	0	6	5
Hill, Miss L.	...	0	1	9
Hunt, Miss	...	0	12	3
Hart, Mrs.	...	0	4	9
Hollobone, Mr.	...	0	19	3
Hillier (No. 3 Girls'), Miss		0	14	6
Herman, Mrs,	...	0	9	1
Howard, Master W.	...	0	1	5
Hall, Miss ...	...	0	1	6
Hicks, Miss E.	...	0	3	7
Hoyles, Master	...	0	8	0
Hewson, Master A. W.	...	0	3	3
Hogbin, Mr.	...	0	5	1
Hare, Miss	...	0	14	8
Hewett, Miss L. ...	...	0	5	1
Hartley, Master F.	...	0	1	4
Howlett, Miss	...	0	6	5
Hartley, Miss E.	...	0	0	8
Hudson, Miss	...	1	17	8

Name	£	s.	d.
Holland, Master P.	0	3	9
Higgs, Master W.	1	6	0
Harmer, Miss A.	0	7	4
Jervis, Miss	0	3	6
Jones, Miss	0	4	11
Johnson, Miss S. A.	0	3	10
Jordan, Miss V.	0	6	5
Joupees, Master F.	0	1	9
Jago, Mrs.	1	14	3
Jones, Miss L.	0	3	1
Joyce, Mrs.	0	6	0
Johnson, Mr. and Mrs.	0	16	0
Kerridge, Mrs.	0	9	3
Keys, Mrs.	0	5	6
Knowles, Master C.	0	2	10
Knight, Miss M	0	2	5
Kaines, Miss	0	5	8
Keys, Master C.	0	11	6
Keevil, Miss E.	0	6	2
Kerridge, Mr.	0	15	0
Luscombe, Miss	0	3	0
Little, Miss	0	8	3
Larkman, Miss B.	0	8	2
Lambert, Mrs.	1	12	7
Laurance, Mr.	0	8	5
Long, Mrs.	0	1	8
Lance, Mr. H. W.	0	6	1
Lucas, Miss A.	0	0	10
Lucas, Miss	0	1	1
Lansdale, Miss	0	6	1
Lansdale, Master	0	4	11
Mills, Mr. F. C.	0	3	3
Morgan, Miss	0	4	8
Middleditch, Masters C. & W.	0	2	2
Mycroft, Miss	0	4	11
Morgan, Miss L.	0	2	5
Mellor, Mrs.	0	8	8
Morgan, Miss	1	9	2
Moppett, Mrs.	0	3	1
Mills, Mr. W. R.	0	6	1
Matthews, F. and W.	0	5	3
McCombie, Mrs.	0	11	3
Mills, Mr.	1	1	6
Messant, Miss A.	0	6	6
Munro, M. and E	0	7	0
Mills, Master F.	0	4	3
Medland, Miss	0	10	6
Marsland, Mr.	0	6	3
Merritt, Miss	1	2	7
Milner, Miss G.	0	5	0
Moser, Master G.	0	1	3
Maynard, Mrs.	0	16	0
Mann, Miss	1	3	10
Neville, Miss E.	0	3	2
Northcroft, Mrs.	0	8	8
Nell, Miss	0	7	4
Nicholas, Miss A.	0	4	8
Orford, Master E. II.	1	1	0
Oliver, Miss F.	0	9	2
Oliver, Miss Florence	0	8	2
Oxenford, Mrs.	0	16	1
Probyn, Miss	0	6	10
Pratt, Mr.	2	1	4
Poole, Master W.	0	5	7
Pavey, Miss S.	0	6	0
Pitt, Miss M.	0	8	8
Powell, Miss E.	0	15	1
Pearce, Misses J. and L.	0	11	6
Parling, Miss	0	3	6
Pain, Miss C.	0	7	5
Powell, Miss L.	0	14	4
Perry, Master J.	0	2	4
Pearce, Mrs.	0	3	5
Pritchard, Master J.	0	1	8
Parker, Miss E. F.	0	12	1
Pearce, Misses C. and P.	0	9	7
Platt, Miss	0	5	8
Piggott, Miss A.	0	4	2
Parker, Mr. F.	0	0	11
Prestland, Master	0	5	0
Price, Miss E.	0	10	5
Pepler, Miss	3	3	2
Prebble, Mrs.	1	2	2
Payn, Miss A.	0	1	11
Partridge, Masters E. and W.	0	3	1
Pawsey, Misses A. and E.	0	11	5
Payne, Mr. H.	0	6	0
Peters, Miss F. W	0	4	10
Pearmain, Miss	0	3	6
Parsons, Miss	0	12	11
Parsons, Miss	0	0	5
Quennell, Mrs.	0	7	3
Reverley, Mrs.	1	4	11
Raiman, Mrs.	0	14	7
Round, Miss	0	4	5
Roberts, Mrs.	1	7	0
Reading, Mr. W. H.	0	3	4
Russell, Mrs.	0	2	6
Riddell, Master P.	0	0	9
Rawle, Mrs.	0	4	5
Rose, Miss B.	0	1	5
Roberts, Mrs.	0	3	11
Roper, Mrs.	0	2	1
Rogers, Mrs. G.	1	2	4
Ransom, Miss E.	0	1	5
Ransom, Master	0	6	6
Robson, Master H.	0	4	0
Rickett, Master W	0	10	4
Roberts, Mrs.	0	7	3
Speller, Mr. R.	0	12	6
Spender, Mrs.	0	7	0
Shepherd, Miss F.	0	8	3
Smith, Mrs.	0	0	11
Staines, Mrs.	0	5	6
Sillito, Miss	0	3	3
Spiller, Mr. L. A.	0	7	1
Smith, Miss R.	1	1	8
Stone, Mr. C.	0	5	4
Stocks, Miss	2	0	2
Shepherd, Master H.	0	5	5
Stanard, Master F.	0	5	0
Smale, Miss M.	0	19	10
Swain, Miss	0	5	0
Sage, Miss	0	2	10
Shenton, Miss	0	1	7
Shenton, Mrs.	0	3	3
Smee, Miss E.	0		4
Sutherland, Miss D.	0		10
Stewart, Mrs.	0	10	10
Smith, Miss R.	0	3	1
Smee, Miss C.	0	4	1
Smith, Mrs. C. J.	1	1	0
Slade, Miss	0	11	10
Summers, Miss L.	0	2	7
Saunders, Mrs.	1	4	2
Smith, Mrs.	0	5	6
Sidery, Mrs.	0	16	1
Smith, Master E. L.	0	3	1
Silverlock, Master J.	0	6	9
Speh, Miss	2	10	10
Sculfor, Miss	0	3	4
Sarel, Mrs.	0	5	9
Salkeld, Miss	0	1	1
Sayers, Master P.	0	1	2
Stevens, Mrs. J. E.	0	8	3
Seacombe, Mr. A. W.	0	13	6
Smith, Mrs.	1	2	6
Sullivan, Master H.	0	0	4
Sullivan, Miss L.	0	0	6
Swain, Mrs.	0	9	2
Sayers, Miss A. J.	0	1	7
Sorrell, Mr. F. S.	0	1	5
Soar, Master W.	2	0	7
Sortwell, Miss A.	1	1	0
Tucker, Mr.	0	2	6
Thomason, Miss	0	7	10
Thwaites, Miss E.	0	3	5
Turner, Miss M.	0	6	11
Taylor, Mr. F. W.	0	1	3
Toms, Miss L.	1	0	9
Taylor, Miss H.	0	4	8
Thomas, Miss E.	0	5	10

			£	s.	d.
Taylor, Master A. ...	...		0	8	3
Thomas, Mrs.	...	...	0	3	7
Unwin, Mrs.	...	...	0	1	8
Vero, Miss ...	...	...	0	6	7
Vears, Mrs. ...	...	...	0	11	2
Vander, Master A....	...		0	4	7
Walker, Miss D. ...			0	15	0
White, Mrs. ..	...	...	1	3	4
White, Miss M. A....	...		0	2	10
Wilkinson, Mrs.	...		0	7	0
Wyld, Miss M.	...	...	0	5	3
Weekes, Miss J.	...		0	4	9
White, Miss E.	...		0	0	9
Watson, Master W. J.	...		0	4	7
Watson, Master R.	...		0	9	2
Weekes, Miss F	...		0	4	9
Weare, Mrs....			0	6	3
Watts, Mrs....		...	0	4	9
Waddell, Mrs.		...	0	17	11
Woodcock, Mr. J. W.		...	1	9	6
Watling, Mr.		...	0	14	3
Wilkin, Miss A. ...		...	0	2	8
Walker, Master J...		...	0	4	1
Willis, Mrs. ...		...	0	14	0
Wheeler, Mr.	...		0	2	10
Wright, Mrs.			0	6	3
Wall, Master H		...	0	0	4
Wells, Miss	...	...	0	2	11
Williams, Miss J. ...		...	0	2	11
Wingate, Miss N. ...		...	0	3	10
Weekes, Miss		...	0	6	1
Waite, Miss ...	...		0	3	3
Ward, Miss ...	...		0	9	8
Wilkins, Mrs.	...	...	0	19	2
Warrington, Miss A.	...		0	1	10
Woods, Miss			0	15	1
Wessell, Miss	...		0	5	6
Whiffin, Mr....	...	...	0	14	0
Webster, Mr.	...	...	0	16	8
Warner, Master C.	...		0	2	4
Walter, Miss Z.	...	,	0	11	0
Webber, Miss	..		0	10	0
Young Women's Bible-class at Leyton Baptist Chapel			0	6	6
Young Women at Messrs. Freeman and Hillyard's, per Miss Marshall			1	18	8
Young, Mr. ...		...	0	3	1
Collections at musical drill			7	11	10
Cash received in excess of above	...	...	2	19	2
			188	19	9

Given to Mr. Spurgeon at the Orphanage, June 19:—

		£	s.	d.
Mr. James Stiff	...	20	0	0
Mr. Moore ...		1	0	0
An old friend	... ...	2	0	0
A country visitor	...	0	14	0
E. S. and E. Rutty...	...	1	12	5
Miss Tilley ...	...	5	0	0
Mrs. Ellwood	...	4	0	0
Mr. Gihon ...	...	3	0	0
Mrs. Harris, a thankoffering		5	0	0
Mr. William Aiken	...	1	0	0
Captain Clarke	...	0	10	0
Rev. R. Shindler	...	0	5	0
A friend ...		5	0	0
Mr. William Ings (New Zealand) ...		5	0	0
Mr. T. Alp ...		1	0	0
Mrs. Samuel Dunn	...	0	6	6
Mrs. Heritage		2	15	0
Mr. G. F. Pringle		1	0	0

			£	s.	d.
A friend	...	...	1	0	0
Lydia ...	...	...	0	10	0
A friend	...	...	0	3	0
A friend	...	...	1	0	0
Mrs. Gibbon...		...	1	0	0
Young friends at Hampstead			0	17	0
Robert and Ann Gallant ...			0	18	0
A Suffolk friend			2	0	0
Miss Walsh ...	...	...	0	10	0
A friend		...	0	2	6
Mrs. Reynolds	.	...	0	2	0
Two friends ...		...	0	2	0
John Frew ...	.	...	0	3	0
Miss Hill		...	0	10	0
Some friends in fellowship at Clapton Hall, per an old student	...		29	0	0
A friend from the country			0	10	0
Miss Shaw ...	...	...	0	10	0
Mr. Simpson		...	0	10	0
The Misses A. and E. Newman ...	...		3	0	0
Miss Newman		...	5	0	0
Daisy and Willie	...		0	8	0
Miss Geikie ...	...		2	0	0
Mr. Noah Keevil ...			2	2	0
Rev. John McNeill ..		...	1	1	0
A friend	...		1	0	0
Archie	...	...	1	0	0
Mr. Longbothum ...			5	0	0
Mrs. Halcrow		...	0	10	0
Miss Gurney	...	...	0	5	0
Mr. James Jackson		...	1	1	0
H. E. S. ...		...	10	10	0
Ps. xxxiv. 11		...	0	2	0
Edith ...	...	...	0	2	6
A constant reader ...		...	1	0	0
B. ...	...	...	0	10	0
C. ...	...	...	0	10	0
D. ...	...	...	0	2	0
A. Y. ...	...	...	0	3	0
R. W. ...	...	...	0	2	0
N. ...	...	...	0	2	0
G. ...	...	...	0	5	6
L. ...	...	...	1	0	0
Nellie Hill ...		...	0	2	0
Martha	...	...	0	2	0
Two sisters ...	.	...	0	2	0
R. S. ...	...	...	0	10	0
H. ...	...	...	0	2	0
S. T. ...	...	...	0	2	6
Mrs. Budd ...	...	...	0	2	6
No name	...	...	0	5	0
E. P. ...	...	...	0	2	0
N. C....	...	...	0	2	0
A servant's mite ...		...	1	0	0
L. ...	...	...	0	10	0
Mr. F. R. Ginn ...		...	0	5	0
Mr. Letham ...		...	1	0	0
An old friend		...	0	2	0
L ...	...	...	0	2	6
W. M. ...	...	...	0	4	0
Mr. and Mrs. Essex		...	1	1	0
Collected by the Misses Crumpton...		...	3	5	0
Collected by Miss Kate E. Buswell	...	...	3	3	0
Sums under 2s.	...	...	0	12	7
			148	3	6
			£2,165	15	10

List of Presents, per Mr. Charlesworth, from June 15th to July 15th, 1889.—PROVISIONS :—6 large Pork Pies, Mr. J. T. Crosher; 1 New Zealand Sheep, Mr. A. S. Haslam; 28 lbs. Baking Powder, Messrs. Freeman and Hillyard; 9 quarterns Bread, Miss A. J. Fuchs; 162 punnets Strawberries, Mr. A. C. Wilkin; 1 lb. Tea, Mrs. Allen; 86 pecks Strawberries, Mr. A. Ross and friends; 1 box of Eggs, Mr. W. Paxman; 1 hamper Strawberries, for No. 3 Girls, Miss Woods; 1 hamper Aërated Bread, Mr. N. Read; 2 boxes Gooseberries, Mr. D. Camps.

BOYS' CLOTHING :—6 Shirts, S. H. L. ; 11 Articles and 1 Suit, Mrs. Looseley ; 2 Suits, 3 pairs

Trousers and 1 Vest, The Ladies' Working Party, Winscombe Chapel, per Mrs. P. J. Wilkins; 6 Shirts, E. C.

GIRLS' CLOTHING :—6 Articles, Mrs. Beall ; 3 dozen Pinafores, for Nos. 1 and 6 Girls, Mrs. Moss ; 101 Garments, The Reading Young Ladies' Working Party, per Mrs. J. Withers; 10 Articles, Mrs. Robertson; 5 Articles, Mrs. Wicks ; 9 Articles, M. O. S. ; 28 Articles, The Ladies' Working Meeting at the Tabernacle, per Miss Higgs; 15 Pinafores, Mrs. Looseley; 7 Articles, The Ladies' Working Party, Winscombe Chapel, per Mrs. P. J. Wilkins; 100 Garments, Miss Salter's Bible-class; 13 Articles, Mr. J. Hall (for the late Mrs. J. Hall) ; 36 Articles, The Cheam Baptist Working Society, per Mrs. E. Cox; 8 Articles, Miss Bennett; 30 Aprons, The Juvenile Working Society at the Tabernacle, per Miss Woods ; 12 Articles, Mrs. Kidner.

GENERAL :—6 Fancy Articles, Mr. C. A. Pavey; 1 hamper Flowers, Friends at Baptist Chapel, Tewkesbury ; 9 Fancy Articles, Mrs. Hitchman ; 6 Articles, Mrs. Crickmer and friend ; 5 baskets Flowers, Mr. J. B. Le Maître; 1 Rug. Mr. Cadman; 1 box Flowers and 2 Dolls, Pastor C. J. Bougourd; 10 Ladies' Caps, Mrs. Castle; 1 Woollen Wrap, Mrs. W. Coward; 100 sheets Scraps, Mr. J. Cooper.

Colportage Association.

Statement of Receipts from June 15th to July 15th, 1889.

Subscriptions and Donations for Districts :—

	£	s.	d.
Mr. J. J. Tustin, for Burstow	10	0	0
Wilts and East Somerset Association...	5	0	0
Tewkesbury District, per Mr. Thomas White	7	10	0
Greenwich, per Pastor C. Spurgeon ...	10	0	0
Kent and Sussex Association, for St. Margaret's and Cowfold	26	1	0
Mr. Thomas Greenwood, for Brentford	10	0	0
Norfolk Association, for Neatishead ...	10	0	0
Mrs. H. Keevil, for Melksham	10	0	0
Minchinhampton District	20	0	0
Suffolk Congregational Union, for Great Thurlow	10	0	0
Dorking, per Mr. W. Drane ...	15	0	0
Great Yarmouth Town Mission ...	7	10	0
Essex Congregational Union, for Pitsea	10	0	0
Okehampton District	10	0	0
Pastor E. J. Farley, for James Street, St. Luke's	20	0	0
Worcestershire Association	30	0	0
Great Totham District ...	10	0	0
Ross, per Mr. Thomas Blake	10	0	0
Mr. R. W. S. Griffith, for Fritham ...	10	0	0
	£241	1	0

Subscriptions and Donations to the General Fund:—

	£	s.	d.
Mrs. Websdale, per J. T. D. ...	1	0	0
A friend, per Mr. J. Wharmby	0	10	0
Mr. Richard Evans	0	7	6
Mr. and Mrs. Miller	1	0	0
Mr. H. I. Parker	0	2	6
Mr. John M. Cook... ...	5	0	0
Mr. E. Mounsey	2	0	0
Mrs. Watcham	1	0	0
C. A. M.	25	0	0
Mrs. Drayson	0	10	0
Mr. W. Jones	5	0	0
Mrs. Williamson	0	15	0
L. K. D.	0	10	0
Mr. George Palmer, J.P ...	20	0	0
Mr. E. Newell	2	10	0
The Executors of the late Mr. W. H. Roberts	100	0	0
Annual Subscriptions:—			
Miss Penston	0	10	6
Mr. F. W. N. Lloyd	10	0	0
	£175	15	6

Society of Evangelists.

Statement of Receipts from June 15th to July 15th, 1889.

	£	s.	d.
Thankoffering for Mr. Parker's services at Aylsham	1	0	0
Mrs. Johnston	5		
Mrs. Shearman	3		
Miss Spliedt	1		
Mr. John M. Cook	5		
Mr. E. Mounsey	2	0	
Mr. J. Everett	2	0	0
H. E. S.	5	5	
Mrs. Websdale, per J. T. D.	1		
Thankoffering for Messrs. Fullerton and Smith's services at Bath Street Chapel, Poplar	6	0	
Mrs. Binck	1	0	0
Miss E. Cross	0	5	0

	£	s.	d.
Thankoffering for Mr. Parker's services at Waltham Abbey ...	2	10	0
Thankoffering for Mr. Harmer's services at Commercial Street Chapel, Whitechapel	1	2	6
Mr. Charles Barker	1	0	0
Thankoffering for Messrs. Fullerton and Smith's services at Kilburn Hall	10	0	0
Thankoffering for Mr. Parker's services at Sandhurst, Berks.	3	10	0
Mr. T. Fenwick	1	0	0
	£51	12	6

Friends sending presents to the Orphanage are earnestly requested to let their names or initials accompany the same, or we cannot properly acknowledge them ; and also to write to Mr. Spurgeon if no acknowledgment is sent within a week. All parcels should be addressed to Mr. Charlesworth, Stockwell Orphanage, Clapham Road, London.

Subscriptions will be thankfully received by C. H. Spurgeon, "Westwood," Beulah Hill, Upper Norwood. Should any sums sent before the 13th of last month be unacknowledged in this list, friends are requested to write at once to Mr. Spurgeon. Post Office and Postal Orders should be made payable at the Chief Office, London, to C. H. Spurgeon ; and Cheques and Orders should all be crossed.

ANNUAL REPORT

OF THE

STOCKWELL ORPHANAGE,

1888-9.

London:

PRINTED BY ALABASTER, PASSMORE, & SONS, FANN STREET, E.C.

The Stockwell Orphanage,

FOR 500 FATHERLESS CHILDREN

CLAPHAM ROAD, LONDON, S.W.

———◆———

Applications for the admission of destitute Fatherless Children (boys between the ages of six and ten, girls from seven to ten), should be addressed in writing to the Secretary, and full particulars must be given. As the number of candidates is far in excess of the accommodation, the Trustees may decline to issue a form of application. If a form should be granted, it must not be regarded as a guarantee that the application will succeed.

The questions must be fully and frankly answered by the applicant, and the form of application should be returned as soon as possible. The slightest untruthfulness will necessitate the rejection of the case. Unhealthy, deformed, and imbecile children are not eligible. Only children born in wedlock can be received. Children whose fathers are living cannot, under any circumstances, be admitted. Whatever the plea may be, no exceptions can be made to this rule, as the trust is definite and unalterable.

If the case is entered on the list of approved candidates, the Trustees appoint a visitor to make personal enquiries. Should these be satisfactory, the child will appear before the Committee in due course; and if it is then among the most needy and deserving, it may be accepted for admission to the Institution, as soon as there is room.

Friends who are only acquainted with the case in which they are specially interested must not be surprised at its rejection by the Trustees at any stage if it proves to be less necessitous than others; nor must they wonder if the child is declined because of unsuitability; for the Institution is neither Hospital, Reformatory, nor Idiot Asylum. The Trustees maintain the strictest impartiality while considering the claims of the various applicants, and the greatest need always has the loudest voice with them; hence many needy ones must be refused because there are others in still more deplorable circumstances.

Applicants are requested *not* to call upon the Trustees privately, as they are bound *not* to attend to them otherwise than officially. Cases will be considered on their own merits, and applicants will derive no advantage from personal solicitation. Mr. Spurgeon cannot personally see any applicants, and should not be written to. All letters on this business must be addressed to the Secretary at the Orphanage.

Subscriptions will be gratefully received by C. H. SPURGEON, Westwood, Beulah Hill, Upper Norwood, S.E. Gifts of Food, Stores, Clothes, Books, Toys, and useful articles, are always welcome, and should be sent to the Head Master.

———————

NOTE.—Letters requiring an answer should contain a stamped directed envelope.

ANNUAL REPORT.

1888-9.

"HE Lord hath been mindful of us." When the history of a year can be compressed into such a sentence, our friends may know that all is well, even though we do not put on record all the instances which have, day by day, revealed the ever-watchful care and gracious provision of our God. When love cherishes such a precious memory, and faith grasps the promises, then hope may sing, "He will bless us." Our retrospect embraces the long period of twenty-two years, and our testimony as to the last year equally applies to the whole of the series. Faith honoured, prayer answered, and promises fulfilled—these are the summary of the history of our work for God in caring for the fatherless. Blessed be the Lord that such a burden was laid upon us! As the Lord Jesus showed the speciality of his love, in confiding to that disciple whom he loved the care of his widowed mother, so humbly, but gratefully, we venture to feel that we are partakers in a similar peculiar favour, by being permitted to take in charge the children of the great Father of orphans. Surely he has said to each trustee of the Orphanage, and every worker in it, "Take these children, and train them for me, and I will give thee thy wages."

In issuing the present Report, the President would lovingly invite the many friends who have had fellowship with him in the work, to unite in an ascription of praise. "O magnify the Lord with me, and let us exalt his name together!" Look at the dear boys and girls now in this happy home, and sing concerning each one of them, and the many who have preceded them—*These are poor and needy; yet the Lord thinketh upon them.*

At one period the Church of Christ is called to suffer martyrdom with patience, and then grace is given her to supply heroic spirits. These are milder times, when the great demand is for the generous graces, that the awful mass of poverty and ignorance around us may have its misery assuaged. Now is an hour peculiarly fitted for that pure religion and undefiled before God and the Father, which displays itself in visiting the fatherless and the widow, and keeping one's self unspotted from the world. We are not called upon to shed our blood; but we should freely scatter our money. Ours is a joyful sacrifice, shall we fail in it? Our fathers laid down their necks on the block, or gave their bodies to be burned: shall we not with delighted alacrity yield of our substance a double tithe for the Lord and the poor?

Many have felt the power of divine love, and have cared for the fatherless, as a charming way of giving vent to their gratitude. Hence the noble orphanages which are the glory of our land. They are everywhere; and, alas, everywhere needed! The Christian Church has entered upon a career of generosity which is her glory. The Stockwell Orphanage, suggested by the consecration of one saintly woman, has been carried on by the absolutely spontaneous gifts of the godly even unto this day. Its real founder was the Lord of love, and HE has found all its supplies.

During the past year we admitted 52 boys and 33 girls, thus bringing up the grand total to 962 boys and 367 girls, or 1329 Orphan Children in all. What an amount of misery averted, and good bestowed !

To have been the means of providing a Christian home and training for so large a number, must ever make music in the heart by night for all who have taken a share in such holy, happy service.

The joy to the many widowed mothers, who were thus relieved of a portion of their burden, found expression in the grateful " Thank you, and God bless you ! " as they brought their children to our gates. To make " the widow's heart sing for joy " is a joy in which perfect saints and holy angels cannot share. Let us drink deep draughts of it while we may. It is a Godlike ministry, a true fruit of the faith of God's elect ; let all of us to whom Jesus has said, " I will not leave you orphans," enter into the benign service.

From a long list of children received during the year we give particulars of a few cases, taken without any special selection, just to show of what sort they are who are partakers of the benefit : they will arouse tender thoughts for that mass of needy Orphanhood brought to light by the operations of the Institution.

E. V. M., Wood Green.   Second of five children under 11 years of age.   No provision whatever.

A. E. C., Sittingbourne.   Third of six children under nine years of age.   Mother earns five shillings per week.

W. G. S., Grimsby.   Third of six children under 12 years of age.   Father drowned at sea.

W. H. J. L., Brixton.   Second of six children.   Father died of consumption, mother goes out washing.

F. E. F., Highbury Hill.   Eldest of four children.   Mother insane.

R. W. G. C., Hatcham.   Fourth of six children under 13 years of age.   Father a Railway Guard, one child is deaf.

E. W. M., Southampton.   Fifth of seven children.   Father a custom-house officer. Delirium tremens cause of death.

S. P., Matlock Bath.   Fifth of eight children under 16 years of age ; youngest one year.   Father died of sunstroke.

P. E. A., Wandsworth.   Fifth of eight children.   All depending on the mother.

E. E. M., East Ham.   Fourth of seven children under 14 years of age.   The mother has been in good circumstances, but now takes in washing.

K. H., Camberwell.   Fourth of seven children, unprovided for.

B. M. J., Lambeth.   Fifth of eight children.   Visitor writes—"They have no income of any kind now, and six of the children are too young to be of any help."

These are specimens of those admitted, but we sorrowfully add that they are also specimens of many hundreds who have been declined, since we had not room for them. There are thousands upon thousands of fatherless children who have to pine in poverty, and to drag down their poor widowed mothers ; and these grow up, with the training of the streets, to become a danger to the community.   There is room for much more of the kind of work which many are now doing, and all such efforts deserve help.   In our case the fact that there is no collecting of votes draws to us a mass of applicants, numbering nearly a hundred times as many as those whom we can receive.   The mothers apply first to us, and then to other Institutions.   While this involves great labour for the Secretary, it is a compliment to the Institution, and shows that we are in good repute in the world of widowhood.   We do not propose to enlarge, for we have many other things to do, and we are convinced that we shall effect a better result by managing 500 children well than by having two or three times that number and getting into confusion.

If we could have our way we would conduct a model orphanage, whose plans and arrangements would be helpful to others.   It is a high ambition, but it would be a serviceable one if we could attain to its fulfilment.   It never was our idea that we should show how closely expenses could be cut down, and how little of comfort could be afforded. Let children be referred to the Poor Law Guardians, if that is the object aimed at.   We will not preside over a herd of starvelings: we want a company of happy children, in whom can be nurtured hopeful prospects in life, and for whom there shall be a future with which they are prepared to grapple by good health, cheerfulness, education, and true religion.

We have no list of subscribing voters to fall back upon, and are driven and drawn to look to the Lord alone as the great fountain of supply ; but we are not without many human conduit-pipes through which the " streams of mercy never ceasing " flow to us.   We mention some of these with deep gratitude for assistance past, and with a lively expectation of further help to come.

Friends living have given differing amounts.   Some have cheerfully brought hundreds of pounds, and others have sent shillings, with warm wishes that they could contribute thousands.   We thank them all. Friends who have gone to heaven have remembered us, even in their last moments, and we are, this year, remarkably helped by specially large legacies ; at the same time, it is better to give in life than to run the risk of a contested will.

Our collectors, with boxes and books, have, during the year, brought in the sum of £780 12s. 6d.   Meetings are arranged for the collectors from time to time, when the President rejoices to see his cheery circle of helpers, and personally to thank them for their efforts in a cause which is so dear to his own heart.   Many more of our young people might help us by joining this Regiment of Regulars.   Friends residing at a distance, who are not able to attend the meetings, write to the President personally, and have special collecting books from him.   He has quite a large connection of loving friends whom he would never have known had it not been for their coming to the help of the Lord in this matter. This is very pleasant, and brings the Pastor and his people, the Preacher and his readers, into a holy fellowship which will last throughout eternity.

The children in the Orphanage were supplied with cards, and their friends collected £247 5s. 9d. This is a very choice offering, for it was for the most part collected in pennies, and was in almost every case a hearty expression of true gratitude. The mothers of our children are a grateful band. We frequently have very cheering letters from them. God bless them, every one!

Altogether, the amount received during the year from collecting-cards, books, and boxes, reached the noble sum of £1,027 18s. 3d. This is substantial help : but could it not be very easily doubled ? We wish our friends would try. Will you take a card or a box, dear reader ?

The Young Ladies' Working Associations at the Metropolitan Taber-nacle, Brixton, Reading, and other places, continue to render consider-able help by their loving labours, and their services are greatly valued by us. But "yet there is room." Friends who have not much society can work single-handed, and do a good deal for us if they make up articles of clothing suitable for boys and girls between the ages of 6 and 15. Please put good work into the articles, and do not make them fine, but useful. This is not looking a gift-horse in the mouth, but merely saying what sort of harness we should like it to wear.

During the year, Mr. Charlesworth has journeyed to many places with a Choir of Boys, and he has met with enthusiastic receptions. The addition of £513 2s. 2d. to our funds from this source, after deducting all expenses, and the cost of the musical training of the boys, moves us to say, very earnestly—"Thank you heartily, beloved friends, for thus helping us!" Could not friends in other towns arrange for the boys to visit them ? Can they not be asked again where they have gone before ? Yes, the Lord will arrange all this for us.

It is no slight thing to have 500 children, and a large staff to be provided for year after year; but it is refreshing to remember that the Lord has carried us on without a hitch. The cash has run low, but the cruse of golden oil has never been absolutely dry. Our heavenly Father has always found a messenger who has hurried up with the supplies when there seemed likelihood that the barrel of meal would run out. We have made no frantic appeals, for we have had no need to do so. Blessed be the Lord ! We have never had to beseech our friends *to get us out* of debt ; they find a joy in *keeping us out* of it, and this is exactly to our mind, for we believe in the precept, "Owe no man anything." Howbeit, we owe a wealth of love to those who care for our orphans' charge with all this care. God bless them !

The work within the Orphanage has its own anxieties, and there is little need to go into particulars for the information of those who know by experience the care which even a small family involves. Children are not angels ; and when boys and girls do not come to us "out of the every-where," as little babes, but come out of the streets, and even from the slums, they do not bring with them the fragrant influences of a garden walled around; but at times we meet with a child who reminds us of one that has been plunged in the Dead Sea, and has the slime of the Lake of Death upon him. To cleanse away the evil which has been gathered by the little ones so early is a task impossible to flesh and blood; and even the grace of God in such a work abounds in all wisdom and prudence before the work is done. The members of our staff devote themselves to the moral and spiritual training of the children with commendable zeal and patience, watching for souls as those who must give an account. It is a good cause for thanksgiving that our failures are so few, and our successes are so many that we pray and labour on. We look with fatherly pleasure on our old boys, and rejoice to see their success in life, and in many instances their devotion to Christian work. Some of those now living praiseworthy lives once caused us anxious solicitude. After leaving us they wandered far, but the Good Shepherd found them out, using as his means the teaching of their early days. Bread cast upon the waters has been seen after many days. Again has the divine assurance been verified—" My Word shall not return unto me void."

Many of the letters received from the old boys from time to time breathe a grateful spirit, and afford encouragement to the workers. The following will be read with special interest.

DEAR MR. SPURGEON—

A few weeks ago, I paid a visit to the Stockwell Orphanage, at which place some seven years of my life were spent. In talking with my former matron, I told her that I had been led to become a Christian, and was anxious to do all I could in the service of Jesus Christ. She at once expressed a wish that I would write and tell you this, assuring me that it always did your heart good to hear of the conversion of those who had been brought up in the Orphanage. I believed this readily enough, and could only reproach myself for not having personally thought of what she suggested.

At the same time, it occurred to me that a few notes upon the Stockwell Orphanage, written by an old boy, would not be altogether devoid of interest to yourself, and to the many friends of the Institution.

I should be very glad if you could use the enclosed article in any way to make known the Orphanage.

Yours thankfully,

H. G.

We feel quite pleased to put in H. G.'s article, since it will give our friends some idea of how our boys regard the Orphanage.

RECOLLECTIONS OF THE STOCKWELL ORPHANAGE.

BY AN OLD BOY.

When, for the first time, I found myself away from home, and alone amongst strangers, it was as much as I could do, in spite of the kindness with which I was treated, to refrain from crying. I can readily recall the feeling of bewilderment and utter loneliness that came upon me when I stood within the great play-hall, and looked up at the lofty rafters, and saw, with wondering eyes, the enormous fire, piled high with wooden logs, that blazed at one end of the room. How strange, too, and unlike all that I had ever known before, the dining-hall seemed, with its long tables, spread with row after row of mugs and slices of bread-and-butter; and the dormitories, neat, clean, and comfortable, but so different to the little bedroom I had been accustomed to at home! On Sunday mornings it was usual to select about thirty of the bigger boys to go to the Tabernacle. My pride was great when, for the first time, I found myself one of the lucky thirty. I had heard much of the extraordinary size of the place, and had been told how fine a thing it was to sit facing thousands of people, and to see their eyes fixed with one accord on the preacher in the pulpit; but when I found myself actually within the walls, the reality surpassed all my imaginings. There is an inspiration in numbers. "Where two or three are met together in my name, there am I in the midst of them," is a comforting assurance; but who does not feel that in God's house the more there are the merrier? It was simply grand to hear, as I heard then, thousands of men and women singing unitedly, to the praise of God, such a hymn as "All hail the power of Jesus' name"—the "Crown Him, Crown Him" resounding from one part of the building to the other.

Those who are sufficiently interested in the Stockwell Orphanage to read the reports that are published from time to time, cannot have failed to notice the extraordinary immunity from sickness and death that the Institution enjoys. But death pays occasional visits; and at such times the place wears an air of impressive solemnity, all play is suspended, and the boys stand in little knots, discussing in subdued tones the characteristics of the departed one, and the circumstances attending his end. It is a sad thing when a boy whom one has known and played with, is suddenly laid aside, his seat at table unoccupied, and his bed vacant for perhaps several weeks, until the intelligence leaks out that "So-and-so is *dead*." I remember well, on such an occasion, standing, hat in hand, with a group of other boys, gazing upon the cold and rigid features of one who had lived in the same house as myself, and to whom I had been indebted for many small favours and acts of protection, such as only a little fellow, fresh from the indulgence of home, and left to fight his own battle in a strange place, can appreciate. My friend, happily, had died "looking unto Jesus," and praying earnestly that those he was leaving might, without exception, rejoin him in the mansions eternal in the heavens.

Calendars were always in great demand at Stockwell, and some of the boys gained no small amount of popularity by the facility with which, owing to constant practice, they could arrive at the number of days from a given date to the time fixed for the holidays. "How long is it to the holidays?" you would ask. "Three weeks and four days, the day after to-morrow," would perhaps be the reply. All calculations were based on to-morrows. On Monday, the following Saturday was said to be the day after to-morrow, the day after to-morrow, to-morrow. As the holidays drew near, the excitement grew daily more intense. Brown paper was hoarded carefully, string could only be obtained at six times its weight in sweetmeats, while the fortunate owners of carpet bags and tin boxes became enviable mortals indeed. Packing up! The very thought sent a thrill through one's veins. But one dread ordeal had always to be undergone before the final preparations for departure could be made. Examination by the doctor! We were all drawn up in line, and as the doctor passed through the ranks, each boy extended his hand, and protruded his tongue for inspection. Unhappy he whose tongue or pulse betrayed some lurking indisposition, and many the assertions of such a one that his health was all that could be desired, and that no reason whatever existed for his detention. Our doctor, I fancy, was fond of a joke. Some boys who had been laying the dinner on one of these examination days, had helped themselves rather freely to the pickles, and, as a matter of course, their tongues betrayed the fact. Out he stood them, and proceeded to ask all manner of questions as to the ailments which the appearance of their tongues justified him in supposing them to have.

"Do you suffer from head-ache?"

"No, sir."

"Nor stomach-ache?"

"No, sir."

"Why, then, has your tongue such an unnatural colour?"

"Please, sir, I've been eating pickles."

A secret society. Boys have always a fondness for mystery and romance. No page in history possesses such charms for them as that which tells of the deeds of the knights-errant in the brave days of old. Some youthful genius once conceived the idea of establishing a secret society amongst the boys at Stockwell; the members of the said society being bound to succour and sustain one another in times of difficulty, to protect the weak and helpless, and—unromantic provision—to pay one half-penny per week for the privilege of membership. The society was duly started, a knight-grand-commander appointed, with sundry less grand knights-commanders to assist him, and all necessary rules and regulations laid down. But a difficulty presented itself at the outset. It was, of course, essential that the members should wear some distinctive badge by which they might be known to their fellow members. But how could such a badge be worn without attracting the attention of outsiders? After much careful consideration, the device was hit upon of tying a piece of string in the lowest button-hole of the waistcoat. This answered well enough, until our knight-grand-commander, growing ambitious, insisted on wearing his string a button-hole higher than his fellow members. Then schism began its deadly work. After much wrangling and discussion, a compromise was arranged. Our president was not to wear his string in a higher position than his humbler brethren, but *he could wear a thicker piece.* Determined to avail himself to the utmost of this privilege, he foolishly appeared next morning with a small rope tied in his waistcoat. This the master at once detected, the secret of the string leaked out, and the society's career was summarily closed.

Christmas at Stockwell was the best of days. Friends, masters, matrons, vied with each other in doing us honour. Everything that kindness could suggest, or ingenuity devise, was provided for our pleasure. The dinner was a memorable affair, looked forward to for weeks. Roast beef and pudding were supplied with reckless profusion.

Every boy was presented with a new shilling, a box of figs, and sundry oranges, bon-bons, Christmas cards, and other good things too numerous to mention.

An important part of the day's proceedings was the ceremony of cheering the friends who had contributed so liberally to our happiness. The President came first. The Head-master, with smiling face, would take his stand upon the platform, and, as soon as silence was obtained, would begin :—"Boys and girls, although we cannot have Mr. Spurgeon with us at this time, I know you will be glad to hear that he has sent this letter which I hold in my hand all the way from the south of France that it might be read to you to-day."

And then he would read aloud the few loving and manly words that our President almost always addressed to us on such occasions.

"Now boys, three cheers for Mr. Spurgeon. Hip, hip, hur—!" and the hurrahs were instantly caught up and repeated, and renewed again and again with undiminished vigour, until the majority of our visitors, and even some of the boys, were compelled to stop their ears.

"That will do very nicely, boys ; and I think our friends here will agree with me that if Mr. Spurgeon didn't hear your cheers in Mentone, it was not *your* fault. Now let us give three cheers for these friends themselves."

Then followed cheers for the givers of the pudding, the beef, and all the other good things; and then, as in reverent tones the grace was repeated, our heartfelt thanks were offered to the giver of all good, the Father of all mercies, who had thus put it into the hearts of kind men and women to forego much of their own pleasure, that they might contribute to that of the poor and fatherless. "Inasmuch as ye have done it unto one of these, ye have done it unto Me."

H. G.

EDUCATIONAL CONDITION.

The education of the children is always a matter of some difficulty, from the facts that so many of them are of delicate constitution, and that their schooling was neglected during their mother's widowhood. Still, we have great cause for thankfulness in the results we are able to record, and in the fact that there is no difficulty in procuring situations for our boys when their time has come to leave the institution.

Our subscribers will be interested in the following tables :—

SCRIPTURE EXAMINATION, MARCH, 1889.

In connection with

Brixton Auxiliary Sunday School Union.

Number of Prizes.	First-class Certificates.	Second-class Certificates.	Totals.
Girls: 3	22	33	55
Boys: 5	26	67	93
8	48	100	148

SCIENCE AND ART EXAMINATIONS, MAY, 1888.

SCIENCE TEACHERS: Mr. J. J. Thompson, and Mr. A. Simmonds.

Subjects: Sound, Light and Heat; Magnetism and Electricity.

First-class Certificates	0
Second-class ,,	55
Total	60

Classes were held during last winter, and the Examinations took place in May, 1889. The results will not be known till July next. Subjects —Physiography, Geology, Magnetism, and Electricity.

BAND OF HOPE EXAMINATION, NOVEMBER, 1888.
Subject—" Food and Drink."

Number of Prizes.	First-class Certificates.	Second-class Certificates.	Hon. Mention.	Totals.
Girls: 1	5	9	1	16
Boys: 3	10	13	2	28
4	15	22	3	44

The health of the children is wonderful. Thanks be to our heavenly Father for results as to physical condition, which surprise the most sanguine hopes. Many weakly children have grown to be robust, and many have attained maturity who must have fallen in their earlier years but for the advantages of the Orphanage as to food, air, clothing, and general cheerfulness. Our indefatigable doctor writes as follows:—

307, CLAPHAM ROAD, 5th June, 1889.

Gentlemen,—I have the honour of submitting to you my Annual Report, ending March, 1889. As in the past, so have we in the present a cause of thankfulness for our great immunity from sickness. One little boy (Ireson) passed on his way, and to the end expressed his gratitude to all about him. We have had no case of epidemic disease, and the general condition of the children is most satisfactory. My continual thanks are due to the officers and trustees for their kind aid. To the Honorary Medical and Surgical Staff I feel an ever present indebtedness.

I have the honour to be, Gentlemen,

Your obedient Servant,

WILLIAM SOPER.

The President and Committee cannot be too thankful for the kindness and skill of the Medical Staff. The members of our Consulting Honorary Staff rank high in the profession, and we are most grateful for their generous services. For his skilful treatment of the children's teeth the Honorary Dentist has placed the Institution under an obligation which the Managers desire to acknowledge. The health of the children is a matter of primary importance, and the officers are unremitting in their efforts to promote it. We warmly thank all.

PART II.—STATISTICAL.

It is a common saying that Statistics may be made to prove anything, but this is only a figure of speech. The following Tables are compiled with care, and are left to speak for themselves : a careful perusal will satisfy our constituents as to the maintained activity and usefulness of the Institution during another year. Our record has always been as simple as possible, and we have erred perhaps, in the judgment of some, in making our reports too prosaic : but this is an error in the right direction, for the friends who are won to a charity by sensational statements and appeals, are not likely to preserve their interest, or continue their help when the excitement has died away. A sober statement of facts is all that is demanded by common-sense and justice; and those whose judgments are convinced as to the merits and claims of the work itself, are likely to render permanent and not merely spasmodic assistance. The careful perusal of the following Tables of Statistics is requested by the President and Board of Management.

BOYS RECEIVED DURING THE LAST 7 YEARS :—

No. of Report.	Date.	Annual Admissions.	Total Admissions.	Annual Removals.	Total Removals.	In Residence.
14	April, 1882, to March, 1883	38	702	48	468	234
15	April, 1883, to March, 1884	47	749	44	512	237
16	April, 1884, to March, 1885	43	792	37	549	243
17	April, 1885, to March, 1886	40	832	44	593	239
18	April, 1886, to March, 1887	37	869	34	627	242
19	April, 1887, to March, 1888	41	910	44	671	239
20	April, 1888, to March, 1889	52	962	47	718	244

GIRLS RECEIVED DURING THE LAST 7 YEARS :—

No. of Report.	Date.	Annual Admissions.	Total Admissions.	Annual Removals.	Total Removals.	In Residence.
14	April, 1882, to March, 1883	41	135	2	4	131
15	April, 1883, to March, 1884	40	175	5	9	166
16	April, 1884, to March, 1885	45	220	4	13	207
17	April, 1885, to March, 1886	47	267	17	30	237
18	April, 1886, to March, 1887	15	282	29	59	223
19	April, 1887, to March, 1888	52	334	41	100	234
20	April, 1888, to March, 1889	33	367	36	136	231

Boys, 962.   Girls, 367.   Total, 1329.

PARENTAGE OF THE CHILDREN :—

Mechanics...	307	Accountants	...	15
Manufacturers and Tradesmen ...	203	Commission Agents	...	12
Shopkeepers and Salesmen	190	Postmen and Sorters	...	8
Labourers, Porters, and Carmen	187	Soldiers	...	8
Warehousemen and Clerks ...	142	Solicitors ...	...	7
Mariners and Watermen ...	46	Surgeons and Dentists		6
Ministers and Missionaries ...	34	Journalists	...	6
Commercial Travellers ...	29	Architects and Surveyors	...	3
Railway Employés ...	29	Fireman ...	...	1
Farmers and Florists ...	28	Cook		1
Cab Proprietors and Coachmen...	26	Photographer	...	1
Schoolmasters and Teachers ...	18	Gentleman	...	1
Policemen & Custom House Officers	20	Butler	...	1

TOTAL... 1,329

RELIGIOUS PROFESSION OF PARENTS :—

Church of England	514	Presbyterian	25	Bible Christian ...	2
Baptist ...	330	Brethren ...	7	Society of Friends	1
Congregational ...	145	Roman Catholic ...	3	Salvation Army ...	1
Wesleyan...	126	Moravian ...	2	Not specified ...	173

TOTAL... 1,329

THE INSTITUTION IS FOR THE UNITED KINGDOM.

PLACES FROM WHICH CHILDREN HAVE BEEN RECEIVED :—

Balham	8	Highbury	2	Pimlico	6
Barnsbury	2	Holborn	9	Plaistow	1
Battersea	21	Holloway	17	Poplar	6
Bayswater	7	Homerton	3	Rotherhithe	11
Bermondsey	82	Hornsey	4	Shadwell	1
Bethnal Green	6	Horselydown	6	Shoreditch	4
Bloomsbury	2	Hoxton	11	Soho ...	2
Borough	10	Islington	31	Southwark	32
Bow ...	15	Kennington	12	Spitalfields	1
Brixton	33	Kensington ...	7	Stepney	6
Bromley	1	Kentish Town	9	Strand	2
Camberwell	42	Kilburn	9	Streatham	3
Camden Town	7	Kingsland	3	Stockwell	5
Chelsea	7	Lambeth	62	Stoke Newington ...	8
Clapham	13	Lewisham	5	St. John's Wood	1
Clapton	6	Limehouse	6	St. Luke's ...	2
Clerkenwell	12	Marylebone	20	St. Pancras ...	5
Dalston	3	Mile End	8	Sydenham ...	2
Deptford	8	Newington	15	Vauxhall	5
Dulwich	6	New Cross	12	Walworth ...	48
Finsbury	4	Norwood	11	Wandsworth ...	17
Hackney	19	Notting Hill ...	10	Westminster ...	10
Haggerston ...	1	Nunhead	2	Whitechapel ...	3
Hammersmith	5	Old Ford	1		
Hampstead	4	Paddington	6	LONDON... TOTAL 835	
Hatcham	1	Peckham	42		
Haverstock Hill	3	Pentonville ...	3		

Bedfordshire, Bedford	5	*Berkshire*, Uffington	1	*Buckinghamshire*,	
„ Luton	1	„ Wantage	1	„ Princes Risboro'	1
Berkshire, Maidenhead	2	„ Wokingham ...	1	„ Winslow ...	2
„ Newbury	2	„ Wargrave	1	*Cambridgeshire*,	
„ Reading	23	*Buckinghamshire*,		„ Cambridge ...	4
„ Slough	1	„ High Wycombe	1	„ Cottenham ...	1

COUNTRY—*continued.*

Cambridgeshire, Histon	1	
„ Soham	1	
„ Wisbech ...	1	
Cheshire, Birkenhead	1	
„ Chester ...	1	
Cornwall, Falmouth	3	
„ Penzance ...	3	
„ Porthleven ...	1	
„ Truro ...	2	
Derbyshire, Belper ...	1	
„ Derby ...	5	
„ Matlock Bath	1	
Devonshire, Appledore	1	
„ Bideford ...	1	
„ Brixham ...	2	
„ Devonport	3	
„ Exeter ...	1	
„ Plymouth	1	
„ Stoke...	1	
Devonshire, Torquay	4	
Dorsetshire, Poole	2	
„ Portland	2	
„ Swanage	1	
„ Weymouth	2	
Durham, Durham	1	
„ Stockton	4	
Essex, Barking	1	
„ Boxted	1	
„ Braintree	1	
„ Brentwood ...	1	
„ Chelmsford ...	1	
„ Chingford	1	
„ Coggeshall ...	1	
„ Colchester	3	
„ Dunmow ...	1	
„ East Ham	1	
„ Halstead ...	1	
„ Hatfield Heath	1	
„ Ilford... ...	1	
„ Leyton ...	3	
„ Leytonstone ...	5	
„ Loughton	1	
„ Maldon ...	8	
„ North Woolwich	2	
„ Paglesham ...	1	
„ Plaistow ...	1	
„ Rayleigh ...	1	
„ Romford ...	3	
„ Southend ...	1	
„ Stratford ...	3	
„ Upminster	1	
„ Walthamstow	6	
„ West Ham ...	1	
„ Witham	2	
„ Woodford ...	1	
Gloucestershire, Bristol	4	
„ Cirencester ...	2	
„ Gloucester ...	2	
„ Nailsworth ...	1	
„ Painswick	1	

Gloucestershire, Stroud	2	
„ Weirstone ...	1	
„ Wotton ...	1	
Hampshire,		
„ Bournemouth...	2	
„ Christchurch...	1	
„ Farnboro' ...	1	
„ Hayling Island	1	
„ Landport ...	1	
„ Lymington ...	1	
„ Newport, I.W.	1	
„ Pokesdown	1	
„ Portsmouth ...	3	
„ Portsea ...	1	
„ Ryde, I.W.	1	
„ Romsey	1	
„ Sandown	2	
„ Southampton	6	
„ Southsea ...	2	
„ Totton ...	1	
„ West Cowes, I.W.	1	
„ Winchester ...	1	
Herefordshire,		
„ Ledbury ...	1	
„ Berkhampstead	1	
„ Dunstable	1	
„ Hoddesdon ...	1	
„ Redbourne ...	1	
„ St. Albans ...	1	
„ Ware	1	
Huntingdonshire,		
„ Fenstanton ...	1	
Kent, Ashford ...	3	
„ Bexley Heath	2	
, Boughton	1	
„ Bromley	3	
„ Canterbury	1	
„ Charlton ...	3	
„ Chatham ...	5	
„ Cranbrook	1	
„ Crayford	1	
„ Deal	2	
„: Dover ..	2	
„ Eltham	1	
, Eynsford	2	
„ Eythorne	1	
„ Folkestone ...	2	
„ Goudhurst ...	1	
„ Gravesend ..	3	
„ Greenwich ...	12	
„ Maidstone ...	3	
„ Margate ...	7	
„ New Brompton	5	
„ Northfleet ...	2	
„ Orpington ...	1	
„ Plumstead ...	4	
„ Ramsgate ...	2	
„ Rochester ...	1	
„ Sittingbourne	3	
„ Swanscombe...	1	

Kent, Tonbridge ...	1	
„ Tunbridge Wells	1	
„ West Wickham	1	
„ Woolwich ...	5	
„ Wrotham ...	1	
Lancashire, Ashton-under-Lyne	2	
„ Blackpool ...	1	
„ Bolton...	1	
„ Liverpool ...	5	
„ Manchester	4	
„ Morecambe	1	
Leicestershire,		
„ Leicester ...	1	
„ Lutterworth ...	1	
Lincolnshire, Boston...	2	
„ Grimsby ...	2	
„ Lincoln ...	1	
Middlesex, Acton ...	1	
„ Barnet ...	1	
„ Chiswick ...	1	
„ Ealing ...	1	
„ Edmonton ...	2	
„ Finchley ...	1	
„ Fulham ...	1	
„ Harlington ...	1	
„ Hampton-Wick	1	
„ Harrow ...	2	
„ Hendon ...	1	
„ Hounslow ...	2	
„ Isleworth ...	3	
„ Tottenham ...	6	
„ Walham Green	1	
„ Whetstone ...	1	
„ Wood Green...	1	
Norfolk, Dereham ...	1	
„ Holt ...	1	
„ Lynn... ...	1	
„ Norwich ...	1	
„ Yarmouth ...	1	
Northamptonshire,		
„ Brackley	1	
„ Kettering ...	1	
„ Northampton	1	
„ Oundle ...	3	
„ Peterborough	1	
„ Thrapstone	1	
„ Walgrave	1	
Northumberland,		
„ Newcastle ...	1	
Monmouthshire,		
„ Blaenavon ...	1	
„ Newport ...	1	
Nottingham,		
„ Nottingham ...	1	
„ Retford ...	1	
„ Sutton ...	1	
„ Worksop ...	1	
Oxfordshire, Banbury	1	
„ Chipping Norton	3	

COUNTRY—*continued.*

Oxfordshire, Kidlington	1	*Surrey,* East Moulsey	1	*Warwickshire,*	
„ New Headington	1	„ Godalming ...	1	„ Birmingham	4
, Oxford ...	1	„ Godstone ...	1	Coventry	1
„ Thame ...	1	„ Guildford ...	1	„ Leamington	1
„ Witney ...	1	„ Horley ...	1	„ Oxhill ...	1
Rutlandshire,		„ Kingston ...	3	„ Quinton ...	1
„ Uppingham ...	1	„ Leatherhead	1	„ Wolverhampton	1
Salop, Aston-on-Blim	1	„ Norbiton ...	1	*Wiltshire,* Calne ...	1
„ West Felton ...	1	„ Penge ...	1	„ Chippenham	1
Somersetshire, Bath ...	2	„ Red Hill	1	„ Pinton Stoke	1
„ Taunton ...	3	„ Reigate ...	1	„ Salisbury ...	2
„ Yeovil ...	1	„ Richmond ...	1	„ Summerford	
Staffordshire, Bilston	1	„ Surbiton ...	1	Magna	1
Suffolk, Aldborough...	2	„ Sutton ...	3	„ Swindon ...	1
„ Bury St. Edmunds	1	„ Tooting ...	3	„ Warminster	1
„ Fressingfield	1	„ Wimbledon ...	1	„ Westbury	
„ Halesworth ...	1	„ Woking ...	1	„ Leigh ...	1
„ Ipswich ...	6	*Sussex,* Brighton	8	„ Wroughton...	1
„ Southwold ...	1	„ Chichester ...	4	*Worcestershire,*	
„ Stanstead ...	1	„ Hailsham	1	„ Cradley	1
„ Stowmarket ...	4	„ Hastings	3	*Yorkshire,* Bedale	1
Surrey, Addlestone ...	1	„ Lewes	1	„ Burley ...	1
„ Barnes ...	2	„ Newhaven ...	1	„ Leeds ...	1
„ Bletchingley	1	„ St. Leonard's	1		
„ Catford ...	1	„ Seaford ...	1	COUNTRY... TOTAL 473	
„ Croydon ...	13	„ Worthing ...	1		

Wales, Aberystwith	1	*Wales,* Haverfordwest	2	*Wales,* Llanelly ...	1
„ Bridgend ...	1	„ Hay	1	„ Rhyl ...	1
„ Builth ...	1	„ Llanbister ...	1	„ Swansea ...	3
„ Cardiff ...	5	„ Llandudno ...	1		
		Scotland, Dunfermline ...	1	*Ireland*	2

SUMMARY OF ADMISSIONS.

London	...	835	Wales	...	...	18	Ireland ...	2
Country	... ...	473	Scotland	...	...	1	
		TOTAL	...	...	...	...	1,329.

PART III.—DESCRIPTIVE.

Our experience continues its confirmation of the practical superiority of THE SEPARATE HOME SYSTEM over every other. We have not wildernesses of wards, nor leagues of barracks, but homes and families, after the fashion of society as God would have it. The loss of parental influence is a calamity to a child, and the wisest course is to make that loss as little as possible by keeping up the family form and spirit. Covering an area of nearly four acres, in one of the healthiest suburbs of London, the Orphanage is admirably adapted for its purpose. Each home is complete in itself, and each family has its own "mother." The boys dine in one common hall according to families; the girls' meals are all prepared in their respective houses; and it is a rule that both boys and girls assist in all the domestic duties of the establishment. Family worship is conducted in each department morning and evening, and the children learn the text for the day from Mr. Spurgeon's Almanack.

Though we cannot change human nature, nor make even good children perfect, we can do better for them in family groups than if we had them in great masses, and packed them away in grosses, like steel pens. Individual character comes out better in small groups than in large regiments. The teachers of our Sabbath School can bear witness that our children are the best of pupils, and that a spirit is felt within our little kingdom, which it is hard to find anywhere else. The present results are most pleasing.

The Institution is UNSECTARIAN. No child is injured as a candidate by the creed of his parents. Why should he be? In a matter of pure charity, sectarian preferences have no weight. Although the characters of the parents and their usefulness in the church of God constitute in some cases a plea for a more speedy reception of their little ones, yet if Christian principles were lacking in the father the child should not be punished on that account; on the contrary, there may be all the greater need that the little one should come under religious training.

The supreme desire of the Committee of Management is that the children shall not only be thoroughly fitted for the struggle of life, but that they shall be instructed in the truths of our common Christianity, renewed in spirit by the Holy Ghost, and brought up in the nurture and admonition of the Lord. We are more concerned that the children should become disciples of Christ than members of our church; and for this we both pray and labour.

Ours is a work for Jesus, carried on in the spirit of faith and love, and in it we have the hearty confidence and co-operation of Christians of all denominations. Upon the ground of our common faith in the cross, and our possession of the one life whose very breath is love, we unite in helping the widow and the orphan for Christ's own sake. His approval is our chief reward, but it is an additional joy to know that the Orphanage is an eloquent answer to the sneers of infidels and scoffers of the modern school who would fain make it out that our charity lies in bigoted zeal for doctrines, but does not produce practical results. Are any of the new theologians doing more than those of the old Orthodox faith? Is not theirs the religion of "talkee, talkee"? What does their Socialism amount to beyond words and theory? At any rate, we care both for the bodies and souls of the poor, and try to show our love of truth by truthful love.

The Institution is OPEN TO ALL CLASSES OF THE COMMUNITY. It will be seen in the table that, while almost every grade of society has been represented, by far the greater proportion of children belong to the most necessitous classes. When a family has been dependent upon the weekly wage of the father, which leaves but a slender margin for saving, the whole of the support ceases at his death, and the savings scarcely suffice to pay for the funeral. When the income has been larger, a long illness, which often attends consumption, has eaten up all the savings, and left nothing in store. But for the orphanage, a widow with many helpless little ones would despair. What can she do? With the children clinging around her how can she even go out to work? She is, herself, weakly, it may be, how is she to earn bread for so many? Oh that our riends could see the widows, they would be ready to give all that they have to help them! We should have to hold them back from bestowing all their goods upon the needy ones. Frequently have we seen the hand of the Lord helping choice saints by means of our Institution, and then we have been exceeding glad. These sisters of ours, it is a joy to make their burden lighter. Are there not thousands who will share our burden and our blessing? Will not our readers begin to do so, if they have not done so already? Our faithful subscribers may rejoice with us that the Institution has sheltered no less than 1,329 fatherless children up to April, 1889.

To secure the admission of a destitute fatherless child, No PATRONAGE IS REQUIRED, AND NO PURCHASE OF VOTES. The most helpless and deserving are *selected* by a Committee, who give the first place to the greatest need. This is our rule, and we desire ever to abide by it. In this way help is given to those least able to help themselves. Applicants are put to no expense, beyond providing necessary certificates. It is better that the admission of a child should be an answer to the bitter cry of need rather than a reward for diligence or a repayment for postage spent in worrying subscribers for votes. The amount expended, directly and indirectly, in gaining admission to some institutions, is in some cases almost equal to the value of the benefit secured. As it is impossible for us to receive all who apply, there is this satisfaction—the candidates are only declined for want of room, and not because they have failed to buy sufficient votes. The Trustees devote much time and anxious thought to this department of their work, and they endeavour to choose the most worthy cases. The President wishes here to say that, to the Trustees belongs the credit of managing all the interior arrangement of the Orphanage, while he is, himself, only the General Manager, and the Receiver of the gifts by which the institution is carried on. The Trustees manage the steamship and the President is the stoker of the fires. Friends must be patient with us, and believe that we do our best.

The Children are NOT DRESSED IN A PECULIAR UNIFORM, to mark them as charity children. We have no admiration for this bit of absurdity. Orphanhood is a child's misfortune, and he should not be treated as though it were his fault. In a garb which marks him out as poor, it is not easy for a child to acquire self-respect. We wish some of the older institutions could break through the traditions which turn the objects of their charity into grotesque figures, or mark them out as charity boys. We mean to steer clear of that sort of display.

In the arrangements of the Schools our object is to impart *a plain but thorough* ENGLISH *education*, in order to fit the boys for commercial pursuits. In addition to the ordinary subjects, they are taught elementary science, drawing, shorthand, and vocal music. As the boys attain the age for leaving, little or no difficulty is experienced in finding employers who are willing to receive them. Many of the old boys are now occupying good positions in large houses of business, and it is a joy to know that many are engaged in works of usefulness; a large number are members of the Christian Church, and three are Pastors of Churches.

For the girls, a plain solid education is attempted in the Schools, and thorough domestic training in the Homes. The Trustees will be glad to give special training where there are special capacities, and as

33

openings occur for female talent they will be glad to have girls able to enter them. The special vocation of the girls must be left to their friends to determine on leaving : our usual plan is to ensure that, as far as possible, they shall be thoroughly fitted for domestic service in good families; but we are anxious to be guided by the providence of God, and the opportunities which offer themselves. No doubt, the better the education, if it be of a really practical kind, the better is the child's chance in life.

The moral and religious training of the children is a matter of primary concern ; and the earnest efforts of the matrons and teachers are supplemented by the labours of a staff of gracious Sunday-school teachers. Detachments of the children attend the Tabernacle and the neighbouring chapels on Lord's-day mornings, and Special Services are conducted at home, morning and evening. A children's week-night service is held every Wednesday. Several earnest friends give much attention and prayer to this department of the work. Once a quarter the entire household is assembled to hear a special address. Leading ministers of all denominations and distinguished laymen have rendered important help in this matter.

A Young Christians' Band holds a monthly meeting, and there are frequent meetings for the Members of the Band of Hope.

As the Orphanage is maintained by free-will offerings, we may indicate several methods by which our friends help us:—

(1.) By **Donations and Subscriptions.** All sections of the Church and of the community are laid under obligation, and we gladly add that members of every communion contribute to the funds of the Institution.

(2.) By **becoming Collectors.** Mr. SPURGEON will be glad to send special Collecting-books. Collecting-boxes and cards may also be obtained on application to the Secretary.

(3.) By **arranging for Public Meetings,** to be conducted by the Head Master with a choir of Orphan boys. The entertainment given by the boys is of a first-rate order, and is calculated to do moral and spiritual good. Our bell-ringers add to the attraction of the singing, and help to charm the ears of the audience. Mr. V. J. CHARLESWORTH will be happy to supply all particulars.

(4.) By **Gifts of Useful Articles.** Sometimes a friend can spare material who could not give actual cash. Food, clothing, toys, fuel, furniture, books, and all other useful articles can be used on the premises, and fancy goods can be sold at the annual sale. All is grist that comes to this mill.

(5.) By **Birthday and New Year's Offerings.** A festive season suggests a fitting opportunity for sending help to those whose orphanhood calls for special sympathy and succour. Our mercies are doubly sweet when they are shared with those who would otherwise feel the bitterness of want. We minister not to ourselves, but to the poor and needy. The Lord accept our work of faith and labour of love !

A WORD TO OUR DONORS.

(1.) The name should be legibly written, and a sufficient designation uniformly given.

It is unfortunate when *Smith* is mistaken for *South,* or *vice versâ.* Where an *initial* only is given, we may not know whether to address the reply to Mr. or Mrs, or by any other designation.

(2.) As two persons may bear exactly the same name it is important the address should be given. Where a donor has a *business* and a *private* address, it is desirable one or other should be uniformly used.

(3.) Change of address, or the death of a donor, should be promptly reported for the correction of our books.

(4.) We would respectfully urge our donors to advise us of the despatch of gifts in kind by letter or post card.

TO INTENDING BENEFACTORS.

As it is most important to comply with legal conditions, in order to secure the validity of a legacy, we append the necessary form. Persons deviating from such form are likely to frustrate their own intentions; and no sane person would wish to do that. It cannot be too clearly understood that bequests of land or houses for charitable purposes are null and void. By forgetting this fact, friends have put the President to serious trouble, involving him in actions at law, and all sorts of unpleasantness. He has too much to do already, and does not want to have his back broken with the proverbial last straw. Those are wisest who are their own executors, and distribute their money in their own lifetime; but if this cannot be accomplished, friends should at least make their wills, and see that they are plainly drawn up and properly executed.

FORM OF BEQUEST.

I Give and Bequeath the sum of⸺⸺⸺⸺⸺⸺⸺⸺⸺⸺ pounds sterling, to be paid out of that part of my personal estate which may by law be given with effect for charitable purposes, to be paid to the Treasurer for the time being of the Stockwell Orphanage, Clapham Road, Surrey, and his receipt shall be a sufficient discharge for the said legacy; and this legacy, when received by such Treasurer, to be applied for the general purposes of the Orphanage.

Stockwell Orphanage.

GENERAL ACCOUNT FOR THE YEAR ENDED MARCH 31st, 1889.

	£	s.	d.		£	s.	d.
To Maintenance and Education:—				**By Subscriptions and Donations:—**			
Salaries and Wages	2,009	15	0	General	5,145	7	8
Provisions	4,224	19	6	Boxes and Books	1,027	18	3
Clothing	1,760	2	10	Services of Song (less expenses)	513	2	2
Laundry	446	10	1		6,686	7	8
Fuel, Gas, and Water	882	0	1				
Books and School Requisites	160	19	11				
Medical Expenses	140	17	8	„ Legacies	9,363	17	3
Excursions and Travelling	62	19	8	„ Balance of Dividends and Rents (less Repairs and Insurance)	1,921	1	6
Situations, Outfits, Gratuities, &c.	62	7	9				
Gardening and Sundries	49	1	0				
	9,789	13	6				
„ Printing, Stationery, Publications, Office Expenses, Collecting Boxes, &c.	563	1	1				
„ Repairs, Alterations, Furniture, &c.	1,190	14	5				
„ Poor and General Rates	173	2	6		17,971	6	5
	11,716	11	6				
„ Transfer to Foundation Fund	6,000	0	0	„ Balance at Credit March 31st, 1888	2,339	1	5
„ Balance at Credit, March 31st, 1889	2,593	16	7				
	£20,310	8	1		£20,310	8	1

Audited and found correct, this 7th day of June, 1889.

WM. IZARD, 147, Cannon Street, E.C. } Auditors.
WM. WILCOCKS, 47, Cornhill, E.C.

JOSEPH PASSMORE,
WILLIAM HIGGS, } Trustees.
HENRY SMITH,
JAMES A. SPURGEON, Acting Treasurer.

FREDERICK G. LADDS, Secretary.

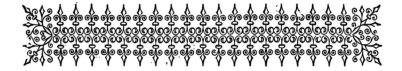

THE

SWORD AND THE TROWEL.

SEPTEMBER, 1889.

Peculiar Power in Prayer.

A THURSDAY EVENING SERMON BY C. H. SPURGEON.

"And it shall come to pass, that before they call, I will answer; and while they are yet speaking, I will hear."—Isaiah lxv. 24.

HE prophet is foretelling happy days for Israel, when the elect out of her should be visited in great mercy, and should enjoy the presence and blessing of God. He gives a very wonderful list of favours which would be enjoyed by these chosen people. There shall be for Israel as great a change as if there were new heavens and a new earth. The Lord's people shall spring into new life, created anew by him who saith, "Behold, I make all things new."

Coupled with this new creation, there would exist peculiar happiness; for the Lord says, "I create Jerusalem a rejoicing, and her people a joy. And I will rejoice in Jerusalem, and joy in my people: and the voice of weeping shall be no more heard in her, nor the voice of crying." When sin departs, sorrow goes also. Happy age, when tears shall cease because all cause of weeping will be removed!

With this happiness there will be, in the millennial period, a lengthening of human life. "The child shall die a hundred years old," and "there shall be no more an old man that hath not filled his days." When the grace of God has renewed both the heart and the world, the longer men live on earth the better. In many cases, a shortening of human life has been a blessing, since it has stopped the more terrible development of evil. Men grow bad enough in sin in seventy years; what would they become if they could spend seven hundred years in educating themselves in wickedness? But when they shall be all gracious, then shall the hoary head be indeed a crown of glory.

34

With this length of age shall come continued prosperity. "They shall not build, and another inhabit; they shall not plant, and another eat; they shall not labour in vain, nor bring forth for trouble." God will be able to bestow temporal blessings without the check which evil now lays upon his bounty. Then will come the age of gold, which is not fabled, but is prophesied in the Scriptures of truth. Then shall there be universal peace : "The wolf and the lamb shall feed together, and the lion shall eat straw like the bullock." Dawn on us, blessed age! Why dost thou delay?

It is singular that, in the midst of these special benedictions, there should occur this high privilege of remarkable power with God in prayer: "Before they call, I will answer; and while they are yet speaking, I will hear." It is evidently no every-day boon. It is the peculiar gift of a time of special grace.

Upon this blessing we will meditate at this time ; not dissevering it from its connection, but taking it as the Lord gives it. Our first remark shall be that, when and where this is the case, *great grace must have been given to the pleaders;* and, secondly, when and where this is the case, *great grace is seen on God's part.* In the third place, the verse itself shows us *the great value which God attaches to prayer,* since he will, in some cases, stand ready to reply to it with unexampled speed.

I. First, then, the giving of this promise implies GREAT GRACE WROUGHT IN THE PLEADERS. It is not fair to view these words as a promise to everybody. God does not say of all men, "Before they call, I will answer ; and while they are yet speaking, I will hear." God's servants are called upon to practise importunity, and this would not be needful, or even proper, if God had promised to answer every prayer at once. We are to be intense in prayer, to wrestle with the angel, and to bring forth our strong reasons while we plead. God is not slow to answer ; but for wise purposes he withholds the blessing till we are better prepared to receive it. Many of God's children are in such a state of mind that it would not be safe to make this promise to them. They will be heard when they pray, but they may not be answered for many a day, or even for many a year. Whenever God can say of any people, "Before they call, I will answer," it shows that they are well-grown in grace, and far in advance of the most of believers. We may not pluck up texts by their roots, and make them mean what they do not mean. We must understand them as God meant them to be understood. All that the words here mean is this—that to persons to whom the Lord has given a great measure of grace, he will give such wonderful power in prayer, that before they call, he will answer them.

This can be the case, first, because *these people will seek right objects.* If we go to God asking for what it would not be seemly in him to give, nor wholesome for us to receive, we shall be sent from the mercy-seat to mend our prayers. The people of whom the text is spoken were evidently so well instructed that they would only ask for such blessings as the Lord would instantly bestow. Their minds had become perfect reflectors of the eternal purposes of God. A correct prayer is the herald of divine action. Coming events cast their shadows before them, and God's benediction when it is coming shadows itself in prayer. A believing man in prayer is a prophet to himself. His prayer is the foretelling of what God is about to do. That is great grace which makes our desires coincide with the designs of the eternal God. Is not this the fulfilment of the promise, "Delight thyself also in the Lord; and he shall give thee the desires of thine heart"? When a man has lain so long in God's bosom that the secret of the Lord has penetrated his soul, then he asks for right objects, and for these only; and then the Lord says, "Before they call, I will answer; and while they are yet speaking, I will hear."

Next, it is clear that when the Lord can thus unconditionally promise a prompt answer to men's prayers, *they will pray in right order.* It is not every prayer that can enter heaven. There are prayers which ought not to be heard. "Ye have not, because ye ask amiss." Prayers which are not fervent ask to be denied: if you have not heard yourself, you cannot expect that God should hear you. Prayers that are not humble cannot be allowed an audience with the High and Lofty One. If we are impertinent and arrogant in prayer, how can the Lord hear us? Those prayers must be of a right order, to which the Lord can promise an immediate reply.

What is the right order of praying? It is to pray in the name of Jesus, not pleading our merit, but urging the person, righteousness, and sacrifice of Jesus as the argument for a gracious reply. We must also address our prayer to the Father, bowing low before him, seeing he is in heaven and we are upon the earth. A true prayer must begin with "Our Father," and keep its face towards heaven. So, also, must prevailing prayer be dictated by the Holy Spirit. When the Holy Spirit helps our infirmities, and teaches us what we should pray for as we ought, then our prayer expresses the desire of the Holy Spirit himself, and he "maketh intercession for the saints according to the will of God." Then may we be sure that before we call, the Lord answers; and that while we are yet speaking, he hears.

Dear friends, I fear that many of our prayers have not sped, because they were not sprinkled with the precious blood; they were not set on fire by the Holy Ghost; they were not directed to the Father. How often have our prayers been put back that the suppliant might amend his plea, as they say in courts of law; prayers which might have been heard at once had they been presented in due order.

When God hears all the prayers of men immediately, it shows that *they are in a right condition.* As I have already said, such a prevailing man must be in earnest, and thus one reason for delay is gone. One design of prayer towards ourselves is to make us see our need of the blessing, and feel the value of it, so that we may ask with intensity of mind. Prayer is for our sakes, and not because God needeth it; and when a man is evidently conscious of his need, and able to appreciate the blessing, then there is no reason for protracting his prayer; and the answer is given at once. Humility is needful; but when a man is already humble, and lies low before God; when, like Abraham, he speaks of himself as "dust and ashes," then God may give him his desire without fear that he will be puffed up. He must be lowly, reverent, and full of holy tenderness, to whom the Lord can promise instantaneous answers to prayers.

Want of faith is the ruin of many a prayer; the Lord delays his answer till we plead in faith. "According to your faith be it unto you," is the rule of the kingdom ; and if, at any time, God answers a man while he is yet speaking, it is because the man is full of faith. Prayer is intended to exercise faith, and so to strengthen it ; but when faith is already strong, and in active exercise, then it becomes a fitting thing for the Lord, if so he pleases, to answer the prayer directly, by saying, " Be it unto thee even as thou wilt." Little faith cannot find the key-hole ; but great faith puts the key into the lock and opens the door at once. To the knock of little faith the door of grace will open; but great faith carries a latch-key, and enters at once. It is plain that the man to whom our text is a personal promise, is possessed of mighty faith.

Beloved, prayer is often hindered by sin. God's own people have to come again and again to him, because he says to them, "I cannot give you that blessing until you put away that sin." Whenever God says, " Before they call, I will answer; and while they are yet speaking, I will hear," it is evident that sin has been put away from the suppliant's heart. He has been sanctified and cleansed by the Spirit of the blessed God, and therefore he may have his way in prayer. If you think that you can have power in prayer without holiness, you are very much mistaken. If you imagine that God will bind himself to grant your requests, while you are setting up idols in your heart, you are much mistaken. Beloved, this is a great subject : I cannot enter fully into it; but I beg you to think it over. What must be the holy and happy state of that man to whom the Lord can say, " Before he calls, I will answer him; and while he is yet speaking, I will hear"! Seek to be in that state yourself.

We may say of such favoured persons, that *they are living very near to God*. He must be walking in the closest fellowship with God, to whom God can give so full, so speedy a reply. He must be where the heart of God influences his desires and longings; he must, in fact, be like the apostle John, when his head was pillowed on the bosom of his Lord. Some of God's own beloved are not always on good terms with the Lord Jesus. Sad for me to say it. I do not mean that they are lost ; or that they ever will be ; but I mean that sometimes they go day after day without speaking to the Well-beloved. What would a wife think if we could say to her, " You live in the same house with your husband, but you do not treat him lovingly " ? She would feel deeply ashamed. What an unhappy household her's would be ! But what shall I say of some who profess love to Jesus, but who have no real fellowship with him ? They do not give up prayer, or the reading of the Word of God; but there is little communion with God in their devotions. It must not be so. O friend, say it shall not be so ! If we are the Lord's, and have been bought with his blood, we must draw near to him, we must joy in his joy, and live in his love. When it is not so, things are not going well with us, and the Lord cannot say of us, " Before they call, I will answer; and while they are yet speaking, I will hear."

Use the text aright, and it is seen to be the property of the man who is made fit to be trusted with such a heritage ; and if you feel that you have no such character, seek after it by the Spirit of God.

II. Secondly, so large a promise shows GREAT GRACE ON GOD'S PART.

How gracious that the Lord should say of any, " Before they call, I will answer"! *Great is God's grace to hear prayer at all!* If he said to me, " Go and cry to me, and I will hear you after a month of pleading," I would bless his name. Ay, and if he said, " Cry to me day and night, and I will hear you at the end of the year," I would accept his offer, for it is infinitely more than I deserve. If lost souls could have the word, " Cry to me for a thousand years, and after that I will grant your petitions," the abode of wrath would not be so encircled with despair. But our Lord does not thus postpone his gifts. If there is a postpone- ment, there is always a reason for it, and that reason usually lies in ourselves. We are not straitened in him. What a wonder that the Lord should hear a sinner's prayer ! Whoever you are, if you cry, he will hear you. It is written, " He that asketh receiveth ; he that seeketh findeth ; and to him that knocketh it shall be opened." No man on earth, no man in hell, will dare to say that he sought the Lord with all his heart, and that the Lord would not be found of him. You may have to come again and again ; but the Lord will hear you. What matchless mercy is this ! Child of God, he will hear you. He that made the ear, shall he not hear ? He that caused you to plead has not led you to plead in vain. He that gave you a thirst for his grace, intends to satisfy that thirst.

It is great grace that God should dwell so near men to be more than prepared to hear their prayer. He must love greatly, or he would not perceive their prayer afar off, before it was actually made manifest by a call upon him, or a speech to him. " Before they call, I will answer ; and while they are yet speaking, I will hear." He so earnestly waits to be gracious, that he is beforehand with them ; before their prayer has gone up to heaven, the answer has come down from heaven. It takes longer for a prayer to come from our heart to our mouth, than it does to go from our heart to God's ear. So quick is God in observing all the movements of the mind of his children, so intimately near is he to them in love, that before they can get the words from their tongues his blessings are in their laps.

How great is the grace of God in watching for the coming needs of his people ! Before they become painful wants, they are met and supplied. Some of us know what it is never to feel the rough side of need ; indeed, we never feel anything more of it than that which we infer from the divine supply. We guess how naked, and poor, and miserable we should be without Christ, when we look on the dress in which he has arrayed us, the wealth with which he has endowed us, and the joy with which he has filled our hearts. Before we reach the halting-place, at the end of the day's march, we can see that entertainment is prepared. Do not I see " The House Beautiful" at the end of the road ? The bread is made, the evening meal is prepared, the damsels stand ready to wait upon us in the banqueting-hall of the Lord of the way. Our table is prepared, our cup overflows. Blessed be the Lord !

In many matters *God is prepared for prayer before the prayer is pre- pared for him.* For instance, if you seek pardon, the means for your being forgiven were provided more than eighteen hundred years ago on the cross: there sin was put away, and a cleansing fount was opened by your Lord. Long before you call for pardon, absolution is waiting.

When you seek peace with God, you may remember that Jesus is our peace, and was so from of old.

Suppose your prayer is of another kind, " Lord, give me wisdom, light, and grace. Work in me all thy will, and help me to work out that will in my life." Before that prayer is uttered, all grace is given you in the bestowal of the Holy Ghost. The Holy Ghost has never left us since he came down at Pentecost: he abides still with his people, and will abide with them for ever in all fulness of gift and grace. You have in the Spirit all the grace and all the help that you will ever want between this place and glory. By his indwelling the prayer is born and fulfilled: " Before they call, I will answer."

I think I hear you say, " Well, these are all high spiritual blessings." I have often found it so with regard to temporal blessings. Providential aid is sent to us in the very nick of time; yea, while we are seeking it. I prayed, on one occasion, when in great need, for the Orphanage, and I had my answer that very day. But, look you; that money was set apart, and was on its way days before, so that before I called the Lord had answered me. I knew a minister of Christ to whom his cow was the great support of his family. It fell dead on a sudden. That day he received a letter containing more than enough to buy another cow, which sum had been sent him unsolicited from a Pastors' Aid Society in London. That money was on the road before the cow died and the cry of need had been uttered. That minister was my grandfather.

You should hear my father's story of returning from his preaching one cold night in November, and when he had some twelve miles to go his pony was taken very ill, and he feared it could go no farther. Out in a country road, in the pitiless wind, with the fear that he would lose his pony, and be unable to go on with his good work, the tears stood in the good man's eyes. Deliverance came; but the point I want to note is this, that, on the previous night, a wealthy and generous man had been kept awake by thinking of poor Mr. Spurgeon, who would the next day be out in the snow with his pony. His impression was that he ought to send him money to buy a horse which could do the journey quicker. So that, while the servant of God was fearing, his Master had already made provision for him. God knows how to bring his children out of their troubles; and if we would trust him more, we should see greater things than these. The Lord foresees the prayer, and has the answer ready before the prayer is actually uttered. Glory be to his great grace!

We close our happy talk by noting THE GREAT VALUE THAT GOD SETS ON PRAYER. This in the text ? Let us see.

It is clear that prayer is most needful. Those to whom the promise is made were *the best of saints;* they had been so sanctified and taught of God that it was safe for God to say, " Before they call, I will answer," *and yet they must pray.* I heard of one who was so sanctified that she had hardly any need to pray. Her corruption was all gone, so that she had not to watch and pray; and her will was so in harmony with the will of God, that she hardly believed it right to ask anything of God, but preferred to leave him to do as he pleased. What proud folly ! That sanctification which makes you leave off praying, comes from the devil. The sooner you are rid of such sanctification the better. It is not divine sanctification, or it would lead you to pray with greater frequency and fervency than ever you did before. Beware of that kind of holiness which makes you think you are above prayer. When you are truly holy, you will pray to real purpose.

Notice that those were *the best of times*—millennial times—the time when the wolf had come to lie down with the lamb, and the lion was eating straw like the bullock. Will men pray then? Assuredly. Intercession is the holy service of saints, so long as there remains a soul unsaved, or a promise unfulfilled. We shall not, in this life, reach a period in which prayer will be out of date.

Is it not a wonder that prayer should be so acceptable? Observe that God has answered a man, and yet he lets him pray afterwards. This is clear from the expression, "Before they call, I will answer." The man does not need to call, does he? Oh, yes, just as much as before. If your prayer is heard before you pray, still pray, but pray in the key of praise. Though God may answer before we call, he means us to call all the more for that. He loves our prayers so much, that though he may have already answered them, he does not tell us so, but lets us pray on. He loves to hear us cry, "My Father, give me this blessing," although he has already given it. The voices of his children's hearts are full of music to his ears. How sweet to pray to one who so greatly loves to hear!

Mark in the text another fact, which shows the glory of prayer, for it *sets the time of the blessing*—" *While* they are yet speaking, I will hear." The time for God to give is while we are yet speaking. Prayer is the stroke of the clock of mercy. When the church of God is aroused to pray, a revival is near. When a man arrives at the condition of a peculiarly earnest prayerfulness, it is a token for good to him. When a sinner begins to cry for mercy, it is the token that mercy is at work with him. David gives us an instance when he only said that he intended to pray for forgiveness, and it came while he was speaking. "I said, I will confess my transgressions unto the Lord; and thou forgavest the iniquity of my sin." He did but resolve to confess, and he received absolution. The blessing is coming if we are praying; nay, it is come. Prayer itself is the receiver of the blessing. While they are praying their mouths are open, and God fills them.

Here is the wonder of it all, and with this I have done—*that prayer should bring God into the field, personally and actively.* Let me read the text again: "It shall come to pass that before they call, *I* will answer; and while they are yet speaking, *I* will hear." He does not say, "While they are praying, an angel shall come," but "*I* will answer." He does not say, "While they are yet speaking, they shall be heard by a seraph," but, "*I* will hear." Surely the Lord might have delegated this to one of the angels standing at the top of the ladder which Jacob saw. He might have said, "Gabriel, when a prayer ascends the ladder, hasten down with a blessing." No: he himself will be engaged—"*I* will answer." Prayer has an effect upon God himself; it comes into his ear, it moves his heart, it stretches out his hands. Let us not doubt this. The life of prayer is gone if we cease to believe that God is, and that he is a rewarder of them that diligently seek him. Our prayers are much more to God than we dare hope. He evidently values them for the sake of his Only-begotten Son, in whose name they are presented.

Now, beloved, do you believe all this? If so, then go and pray mightily. Do you say that you cannot? Well, then, ask for more sanctification, more growth in grace. All spiritual blessings are grouped together. You can no more have power in prayer without the other forms of spiritual power, than a man can be strong to reap a harvest without being strong to dig or plough. May God make us strong in faith and mighty in prayer, and then it may be said that, like Luther, we can have of God whatever we desire. We shall go into our secret chamber, and come back from the mercy-seat, crying, like Luther, "*Vici! Vici!* I have conquered." When the battle is won on our knees, it will not be lost in any form. Oh, for the prayer whose answer comes with it, or even before it!

"The Renewal of the Heart."

Psalm li. 10.

MY heart is hard, a very flint,
   Soften my heart, Lord Jesus;
Then, with a hand of love, imprint
   Thine image there, Lord Jesus.

My heart is foul, defiled by sin,
   Oh, cleanse my heart, Lord Jesus;
Then come thyself, and enter in,
   And dwell with me, Lord Jesus.

My heart is weak, to evil prone,
   Strengthen my heart, Lord Jesus;
Centre my love in thee alone,
   Nor let me fall, Lord Jesus.

My heart is mute, I cannot sing,
   Retune my heart, Lord Jesus;
Then touch the chords, till every string
   Thrills with thy praise, Lord Jesus.

My heart is cold as northern ice,
   Inflame my heart, Lord Jesus;
Then, as a freewill sacrifice,
   Accept my heart, Lord Jesus.

Though hard, and foul, and weak, and cold,
   My heart is thine, Lord Jesus;
And thou art mine, to have and hold
   For evermore, Lord Jesus.

E. A. TYDEMAN.

"We have lost our Boats!"

BY THOMAS SPURGEON.

THERE she lay like a log on the billows. The noble craft that, erstwhile, "walked the waters like a thing of life," was now as helpless as a bird with broken wings. Her towering masts and graceful spars had gone by the board in a fierce tempest, which had scarcely yet subsided. Her rigging still strewed the decks, though the weary crew were doing their best to clear away the wreckage. Worst of all, the water was gaining on the pumps, and the ship was slowly, but surely, settling down. What hope had the hapless mariners of saving themselves or their ship?

But while there is life there is hope! Presently, through the rack, there loomed up the stately form of another vessel. She saw her sister in distress, and, sister-like, hove to, and stood by as close as safety would permit. Soon she ran up a signal to the effect that she would take the shipwrecked crew if they would come on board. Then it was that the bitter·wail came flying on the squall's white wings: "*We have lost our boats!*" and louder yet: "WE HAVE LOST OUR BOATS!"

How utterly helpless was their state! A saviour had at length appeared, yet salvation seemed no nearer, for a great gulf of hissing waters lay betwixt them and the boats by which they might have bridged that gulf were wanting. The shattered bones of one still hung about the starboard davits, but of the others there was left not a wrack behind. Some frightful seas, more mighty than the rest, had torn them from the chocks, and flung them on the main. Alas, poor shipmen! bereft of all means of communicating with those who fain would pluck them from between the teeth of death. They were unable to do so much as a hand's turn towards their own deliverance—dependent entirely on the sympathy and skill of others. What if the master of yonder vessel could not have manned his boats, or would not have run the risk? What if, in the brave attempt, the would-be rescuers had perished? It was not so, thank God. Almost as soon as their helplessness was known, the risks were willingly encountered; and though the seas ran mountains high, all the wet and weary men were transferred to the place of safety.

Such is the story: we must not miss its moral. Think again of the pitiable plight of the boatless mariners. Not less desperate is the sinner's state. Sin has wrecked him totally. Dismasted and dismantled, as it were, he is tossed to and fro, the sport of evil passion, the toy of the tempest of unrighteousness. And he has lost his boats! The disaster is so complete that what else had helped him to salvation is now rendered useless—stove in by the storm. Mind, memory, will, conscience —all are rendered unseaworthy. What though the Saviour stands beside him, as indeed he does, and bids him come? He cannot come. He has lost his boats. Unless that same Saviour send further succour, the sinner must perish quite as surely as if deliverance had never sailed in sight. What, then, is the sinner's part? Why, to put the speaking trumpet of full confession to his lips, and shout aloud, "I have lost my boats!" "God be merciful to me a sinner!"

"At last I own it cannot be
That I should fit myself for thee ·
Here, then, to thee I all resign;
Thine is the work, and only thine."

What else can he do? He must depend upon the free favour and gracious help of him who comes to save. And what if he is unable or unwilling so to do? Ah, no! there is no such *if* to dread. The sailors in my story soon heard the welcome sounds of the tackle running through the blocks, the splash of the boat dropping on the wave, the measured beat of the oars, and the shout of the rescuers: "We've come to save you; do not fear." Is Christ less willing? Is Jesus less able? Behold, O helpless, guilty one, the endeavours for your complete salvation! The Spirit strives with you, the Saviour pleads for you, the cross attracts you, the gospel lifeboat nears you; and see! the motto on its bows reads thus: "The Son of man is come to seek and to save that which was lost."

One only thing was necessary with the sailors in our narrative. They had to step into the boats. And the poor sinner must act similarly. He must believe to the saving of his soul. Oh that the reader would do so now! Meritless and helpless, jump in! jump in! Free grace and dying love—the lifeboat and the longboat—await that trustful leap.

One cannot help thinking that it was just as well that those on the foundering ship had no boats to trust to. They would hardly have been equal to the task of launching them, and more than likely the frail craft would have proved unseaworthy.

Certainly, it is well for us to discover that we are without resource. Our boats, at best, are leaky and dangerous. Happy they who see a Saviour near, and come to the refuge he provides, not with effort and merit of their own, but by the faith and love which he imparts. As Joseph sent waggons to bring his starving friends to the land of plenty, so Jesus enables those to come who know and feel their need. "Children, get on board!" "Children, get on board!"

Fetch them in.

A FEW years after the American war, at the White Sulphur Springs, in Virginia, was a venerable man, the celebrated General Robert Lee. He was a devout Episcopalian. One day a Presbyterian minister came to preach in the ball-room. He noticed that General Lee, who was a particular man about all the proprieties of life, came in late, and he thought it was rather strange. The general had waited till all the people who were likely to attend the service had entered the room, and then he walked in the corridors, and out under the trees, and wherever he saw a man or two standing he would go up and say gently, "We are going to have divine service this morning in the ball-room; won't you come?" And they all went. To me it was very touching that that grand old man should quietly go around—and for a minister of another denomination, also—and persuade the loiterers to go in. Should we not take means to help our pastor to draw a congregation? Are there not some whom we could bring with us?—*Dr. J. A. Broadus.*

A Noble Woman, and One of Her Hymns.

THE volume on "English Hymns: their Authors and History,"* by the late Rev. S. W. Duffield, who died at Bloomfield, New Jersey, soon after he had written the preface to the second edition, is a work full of interest for all students of hymnology, and for many besides. It contains reliable information concerning a very large number of English hymns, which the author has been at great pains to verify.

It is to be regretted that several apocryphal stories have found currency in relation to some of our well-known hymns, both those from German sources, and those which have been English-born. Those who touch this subject should, at least, aim to be accurate as to incidents and dates. Carelessness in such matters is hardly pardonable. But it is a still greater transgression when writers suffer their imaginations to run away with them, and when an incident, interesting as a simple fact, is woven into a story in which fact and fiction are so blended that the latter gains the ascendency, like the Irishman's apple-pie, which was mostly quinces. From these defects this work is happily free.

Many well-known stories connected with English hymns—that is, hymns by English authors—are here repeated, in connection with others which have American surroundings; but one important feature of the work is, that it gives us English hymns from more than two hundred American pens. Some of these productions will never take rank with those of Watts, Toplady, Wesley, Cowper, Newton, Lyte, Miss Havergal, and other hymnists of high repute, but others of them have already become classic; and, better than that, have been enshrined in the hearts of hundreds of thousands everywhere, as having been the means of leading them to Christ, and into the fellowship of his redeemed. It is enough to mention, "My faith looks up to thee," as an illustration of the statement.

Some of the poetic productions treated in this volume are not in reality hymns at all, and yet their associations are such that no work on Hymnology should exclude them from notice. We shall mention one of this character which has a touching history connected with it. It is the hymn commencing :—

"I love to steal a while away."

This is the first line as it stands in American hymn-books, but the original begins—

> "Yes, when the toilsome day is gone,
> And night, with banners grey,
> Steals silently the glade along,
> In twilight's soft array,
> I love to steal a while away," &c.

The piece was written by Phœbe Hinslade Brown, born in Canaan, New York, 1st May, 1783. The *time* of her birth—May-day, the first day of the month of flowers—and the *place*, Canaan, were not

---

* "English Hymns: their Authors and History." By Samuel Willoughby Duffield. Third edition. Revised and corrected. Funk and Wagnalls, New York, and 44, Fleet Street, E.C.

foreshadowings of a life of brightness, and beauty, and rest; not, at least, in relation to earthly things. She was left an orphan when only two years old. Education she had very little of, some three months at school only; and reading was acquired only when she was eighteen. Writing to a friend in after life, she said, "As to my history, it is soon told. A sinner saved by grace, and sanctified by trials."

Her father, George Hinslade, had the gift of song, and composed a tune which bears his name. When Phœbe Hinslade became the wife of T. H. Brown, a house-painter, she did not much improve her condition. Poverty and care were her daily lot for many years. She began her married life at Ellington, Tolland Co., Connecticut, and here she began to use her pen. Near the house where she lived was a grove, and to this place she resorted oftentimes at dusk, for meditation and prayer. Her purpose was misconstrued by some of the gossips of the village, who attributed to her evil designs. We can well understand that a Christian woman, with her fine mind, and often disagreeable surroundings, would take delight in any convenient place where she could have communion with God in his works and Word, and pour her cries and sorrows into his ear. What devout soul, with a mind capable of the highest culture, would not "love to steal awhile away"?

The unsympathetic conduct of one of her neighbours led to the composition of the verses which we give below. She says in her account of the hymn :—

"I had, while living in East Windsor, kept a kind of diary, and continued it in Ellington. I wrote several scraps of poetry in Ellington, which were published by my brother, Nathan Whiting, in the *Religious Intelligencer*, at New Haven. It was in Ellington that I wrote the 'Twilight Hymn.' My baby-daughter was in my arms when I wrote it. I had been out on a visit at Dr. Hyde's, and several were present. After tea, one of my neighbours, who I ever felt was my superior in every way, came and sat down near me, chatting with another lady, without noticing me. Just as I was rising to go home, she turned suddenly upon me, and said, 'Mrs. Brown, why do you come up at evening so near our house, and then go back without coming in? If you want anything, why don't you come in and ask for it? I could not think who it was, and I sent my girl down the garden to see; and she said it was you. That you came to the fence, but, seeing her, turned quickly away, muttering something to yourself.' There was something in her manner, more than in her words, that grieved me. I went home, and that evening was left alone. After my children were all in bed, except my baby, I sat down in the kitchen, with my child in my arms, when the grief of my heart burst forth in a flood of tears. I took pen and paper, and gave vent to my oppressed heart in what I called 'My Apology for my Twilight Rambles, addressed to a lady'":—

"Yes, when the toilsome day is gone,
    And night, with banners grey,
Steals silently the glade along,
    In twilight's soft array,

"I love to steal a while away
    From little ones and care,
And spend the hours of setting day
    In gratitude and prayer.

"I love to feast on Nature's scenes,
    When falls the evening dew,
And dwell upon her silent themes
    For ever rich and new.

"I love in solitude to shed
    The penitential tear,
And all God's promises to plead,
    When none can see or hear.

"I love to think on mercies past,
    And future ones implore,
And all my cares and sorrows cast
    On him whom I adore.

"I love to meditate on death!
    When shall his message come
With friendly smiles to steal my breath,
    And take an exile home?

"I love by faith to take a view
    Of blissful scenes in heaven;
The sight doth all my strength renew
    While here by storms I'm driven.

"I love this silent twilight hour
    Far better than the rest;
It is, of all the twenty-four,
    The happiest and the best.

"Thus, when life's toilsome day is o'er,
    May its departing ray
Be calm as this impressive hour,
    And lead to endless day."

For some years this piece remained in manuscript; but when the evangelist Nettleton was compiling his "Village Hymns," he was advised by Mrs. Brown's brother-in-law, Dr. Ely, who was pastor of a church at Monson, where she afterwards lived for thirty years, to apply to her for some hymns. She gave him the above, and three others. She lived to see her son, Samuel R. Brown, D.D., sent out as the first American missionary to Japan. It is a singular fact that the above incident, and, indeed, nearly all the particulars of her life, were first published in the Sandwich Islands. Dr. Damon, of those Islands, sent to Dr. Brown, of Yokohama, Japan, requesting particulars of his mother's life. Dr. Brown wrote from her autobiography, which she penned in Chicago, in 1849, at her children's earnest request. The account was printed in *The Friend*, Honolulu, April, 1879.

The version of the hymn in Nettleton's "Village Hymns" is compressed, and a few expressions altered. Mrs. Brown tells us that, at the time the hymn was written, she had four children, and lived in a small, unfinished house; her sick sister occupying the only finished room. She says:—

"There was not a place, above or below, where I could retire for devotion without a liability to be interrupted. There was no retired room, rock, or grove, where I could go, as in former days; but there was no dwelling between our house and the one where the lady lived. Her garden extended down a good way below her house, which stood on a beautiful eminence. The garden was highly cultivated with fruit and flowers. I loved to smell the fragrance of both, though I could not see them, when I could do so without neglecting duty; and I used to steal away from all within doors, and, going out of our gate, stroll along under the olives that were planted for shade on each side of the road. And, as there was seldom anyone passing that way after dark, I felt quite retired and alone with God. I often walked quite up (to) that beautiful garden, and sniffed the fragrance of the peach, the grape, and the ripening apple, if not the flowers. I never saw anyone in the garden, and felt that I could have the privilege of that walk, and those few moments of uninterrupted communion with God without encroaching upon anyone; but after once knowing that my steps were watched, and made the subject of remark and censure, I never could enjoy it as I had done. I have often thought that Satan had tried his best to prevent me from prayer, by depriving me of a place to pray."

Mrs. Brown was a member of the Congregational body, and a very godly, humble, holy, and devoted woman. Though always poor, she was never idle. At Monson she was the teacher of an infant-class for many years. She ended her days at Henry, Illinois, 10th October, 1861. Her son has recently passed away. In writing to Dr. Damon, the latter gives an incident which shows what was the deep, holy, abiding influences of his mother's teaching, character, and example. He says:—

"A month ago, I received a sprig and clover blossom from her grave, sent me by a gentleman in Walton, New York, who always visits the spot when he goes to Monson, his birth-place, because he cannot forget his teacher, having been a member of the infant-class she taught. It was a large class, and she proposed lessons for them that were published by the Massachusetts Sunday-school Society." The son adds:—

"Her record is on high, and she is with the Lord, whom she loved and served as faithfully as any person I ever knew; nay, more than any other. To her I owe all I am; and if I have done any good in the world, to her, under God, it is due. She seems even now to have me in her hands, holding me up to work for Christ and his cause with a grasp that I can feel. I ought to have been, and to be, a far better man than I am, having had such a mother." Mothers, imitate her! Children, pray that your mothers may be such as Phœbe Hinslade Brown was!

R. SHINDLER.

A Missionary's Appeal.

IT is sad beyond all telling to be a missionary in India at the present moment, and know Hindu life below the surface, and see confusion and bewilderment on all sides, and hear old men talk sadly of the evil times, and the sure signs that the end of the age and Hinduism has come, and feel how little is being done after all by England and America to save this land, full of sadness, and without hope. For the sake of India, for the sake of God, let not any criticism of us and our methods stop your gifts or slacken your prayers for its salvation. For us, we will continue to do our duty as God shall reveal it unto us, praying that all India may *soon* see the salvation of God.—*G. M. Cobban, in the closing sentences of "Indian Missions and their Critics."*

Bernard Gilpin.

MOST people know the story of Bernard Gilpin, who was laid hold of by the arch-persecutor, Bonner, in gentle Queen Mary's time, with the vow that he would "have him at a stake in a fortnight." His life was saved by the breaking of his leg; for his journey to London, for the purpose of being burned, was thus painfully delayed; and, meanwhile, Queen Mary died, and the persecution ceased. This man "worth remembering" was born in 1517, early in the reign of Henry VIII., at the family estate of Kentmire Hall, in Westmoreland, which had been given to an ancestor by a baron of Kendal, in King John's time, for his prowess in killing a wild boar that infested those parts. Bernard was a contemplative, reserved, and serious boy. A characteristic story of his infancy shows that his eyes were open early, and his moral sense awake. A begging friar came, one Saturday evening, to his father's house, and was received in a very hospitable manner. The plenty set before him was a temptation too strong for his virtue, of which it seems he had not sufficient even to save appearances. The next morning, however, he ordered the bell to toll, and from the pulpit inveighed against the debauchery of the time, and particularly against drunkenness. Little Bernard was seated on his mother's knee, listening intently to the sermon, and presently cried out, he " wondered how that man could preach against drunkenness, when he himself had been drunk only the night before."

His college life at Oxford began at sixteen. He had been brought up in the Romish church. The reformed doctrines had made little progress in England; but Erasmus was at the time attracting the eyes of the learned world. Many hated the satirical Dutchman; many admired his bold and witty exposure of the lazy and illiterate churchmen, and the outrageous superstitions of the day. Gilpin found in Erasmus a treasure of real learning, and under his guidance entered upon a path of free enquiry. The times were favourable for intellectual awakening. The air was astir. Stagnation was gone. Peter Martyr came to Oxford, and began a series of divinity lectures in a strain quite novel to the university, attacking the doctrine of the corporeal presence. The indolent heads of the Popish party were roused to a strenuous opposition. Chedsey, Morgan, and Tresham, men whose bigotry kept pace with their learning, entered the lists against the Reformer; and, after long persuasion, gained the reluctant help of Gilpin, whose credit stood high in the university. His zeal, however, was much cooler than theirs. He had discovered that some Romish doctrines were not so well supported by Scripture as was commonly imagined. Entering thus into a controversy against his inclination, he determined to make it as useful to himself as he could, and to bring his old opinions to the test, that he might discover whether antiquity or intrinsic worth gave them their supposed value. His adversaries' arguments, weighted with the authority of the Word of God, proved too strong for him, and the disputation was soon over. Gilpin gave up his cause with the grace that attends sincerity. He owned publicly that he could not maintain it; and then, retiring to his study, entered upon a thorough re-examination of the Romish doctrines. He soon discovered that seven sacraments had never been heard of

before the time of Peter Lombard, eleven centuries after Christ; that
of the denial of the cup to the laity, a doctrine intended to give a
mysterious superiority to the clergy, no trace existed till a thousand
years after the sacrament was instituted; that transubstantiation and
the propitiatory sacrifice of the Lord's Supper were dogmas no older
than the eighth century. He grew disgusted at indulgences, prayers
before images, and the disallowance of the public use of Scripture.
Many of the rites and ceremonies of the Romish Church, as he examined
them, appeared trifling, ridiculous, or impious; and, as he plainly
perceived, led the people from the practice of virtue to put their trust in
outward performances.

While he was thus engaged, the Council of Trent passed the bold
decree that the traditions of the Church should be esteemed of equal
authority with the Scriptures themselves. Gilpin and many more were
scandalized by this proceeding. When he found Rome carrying her
authority to such a height of arrogance as to set up her own unwritten
word against the Scriptures, a word which he said "was in no degree
comparable to the word of an honest man," he thought it high time
for good Christians to take alarm.

This was his mental condition when, at the age of thirty-five, he was
presented to the vicarage of Norton, in the diocese of Durham, of which
Cuthbert Tunstall, his uncle, was bishop. It was the rule that none be
presented to a living in the gift of the Crown without first preaching
before the King. Gilpin's sermon before the Court of Edward VI. was
a bold invective against the avarice of the times, as seen in the clergy,
the Court, and the magistrates and gentry.

Tunstall, the bishop of Durham, was a man of marked individuality.
Humane and broad-minded as it was possible for a Romanist to be, he
was yet a shrewd and politic man of the age. He had been in high
credit at Court during Henry VIII.'s time, and at his death had been
left one of the regents of the kingdom. But in Edward's reign he was
dissatisfied with the changes daily made in religion, and, though willing
enough to give up the grosser tenets of Popery, was no Protestant. The
Romish party, who greatly valued him, made him privy to some of
their treasonable designs, which he, in his cautious way, neither
approved nor betrayed. The plot miscarried, and the bishop, being
implicated, was committed to the Tower, where he lay when Gilpin was
appointed to Norton.

Going down to his parish, Gilpin entered upon its duties fervently,
but with an incompleteness of spiritual preparation which he deeply
felt. He made it his principal care to inculcate moral virtue, seldom
handling controversial points, lest he should mislead his people. For
though resolved against Popery, he saw not as yet the Protestant cause in
its strength, and was not settled in some of his religious opinions. Growing more and more unhappy on this matter, he at length sought counsel
of his uncle the bishop, who, as we have seen, was no bigot; and by
his advice determined to travel in Germany, France, and Holland, and
converse with some of the most noted leaders on both sides of the
question. Unable to bring himself to make use of any part of the
income of his living while he was absent from its duties, he resigned
it, to the disgust of the bishop, who was horrified at his reckless

disinterestedness. "You will bring yourself to a morsel of bread," said he. Gilpin pleaded a scrupulous conscience, which really would not permit him to act otherwise. "Conscience!" replied the bishop; "why you might have had a dispensation." Three years were spent on the Continent, and Gilpin returned still more a Protestant than before. King Edward had meanwhile been succeeded by Mary, and Tunstall, released from the Tower, had been sent back to Durham, with strict injunctions to purge it of heretics. Loudly proclaiming that the heretics should find a warm reception there, he came down to his diocese; but nothing was further from his intention than persecution. Fuller says of him, that he wished to *bark* the more, that he might be at liberty to *bite* the less; and so the reports from his diocese were filled with encomiums of its orthodoxy, interspersed here and there with the trial of a heretic; but either the depositions against him were not sufficiently proved, or there were great hopes of his recantation, no mention was made of any burnings.

The bishop bestowed upon Gilpin the archdeaconry of Durham and the rectory of Easington. The archdeaconry brought upon him a responsibility which he scorned to shirk. The manners of the clergy were scandalous, the pastoral care was totally neglected, and it was hard to say whether vice or ignorance was more remarkable in them. Gilpin could not sleep for concern at this state of things. He endeavoured to call the clergy to a sense of their remissness, and rebuked the laziness of the wealthier part of them. "While three parts out of four of the clergy," he said, "were picking what they could off a common, the rest were growing wanton with stall-feeding." The prudent bishop, observing his zeal, failed not to furnish him with cautions in abundance; but Gilpin could not temporize, and soon found himself in a ring of enemies, who hated his preaching of repentance and salvation by Christ, and loudly proclaimed that all who preached against pluralities and non-residence became heretics soon after. They lost no time in accusing him of heresy before Tunstall. The good-hearted and wily bishop received them blandly, and said that, if found guilty, Gilpin should find a very severe judge in the Bishop of Durham. He then took care to examine his accused friend in points only on which he knew him able to bear examination, brought him off innocent, and dismissed the cause, telling the accusers, "He was afraid they had been too forward in their zeal for religion, and that heresy was such a crime as no man ought to be charged with but upon the strongest proof."

The rectory of Houghton falling vacant, the bishop transferred him to that extensive parish, which embraced fourteen villages. He repaired and enlarged the parsonage-house, and entered upon a course of earnest labour and hospitality to the poor, which increased the ire of his foes, whose laziness and avarice were condemned by his example. They accused him again before the bishop, but again he was acquitted. His enemies now saw that they could not get him burnt in Durham; the bishop was evidently too cool in his zeal; and they determined to accuse him before a very different man—Bonner, Bishop of London. Here they went the right way to work. Bonner was an inquisitor by nature. The fierce zealot at once promised that the heretic should be at a stake in a fortnight. Gilpin's friends apprised him of his danger,

35

and begged him to fly. "That," he replied, "would be denying the faith." He called his steward, William Airay, and, laying his hand on his shoulder, said, "At length they have prevailed against me. I am accused to the Bishop of London, from whom there will be no escaping. God forgive their malice, and grant me strength to undergo the trial." He then ordered his steward to provide a long garment for him, in which he might go decently to the stake. This he wore every day till he was apprehended. On the way to London, his leg was broken, as we know, and his enemies took occasion to retort on him a favourite observation of his, that nothing happens but for our good, asking him whether he thought his broken leg was so intended? He answered, he made no question but it was. And so it proved; for before he was able to travel, Queen Mary died, and he was set at liberty. He returned to Houghton amidst crowds of people blessing God for his deliverance.

Under Queen Elizabeth, Gilpin was offered the bishopric of Carlisle, and soon afterwards, the provostship of Queen's College, Oxford, but declined both preferments, and sat down content with his one living, fulfilling its duties with an industry and generosity unsurpassed by any clergyman in England. The value of the living was £400 a year, and with this he accomplished an extraordinary amount of good. He built and endowed a grammar-school, and so great was the resort of young people, that the town was not able to accommodate them; and he maintained twenty or thirty children in his own house—some, whose parents could afford it, at easy rates, but the greater part at his own expense. The more promising scholars he sent to the university, and maintained them there, nine being on his list at his death. Broth was provided for the poor daily; every Thursday a large quantity of meat was cooked for them; a dinner was given them once a quarter, with a gift of corn and money; and at Christmas time, an ox was divided amongst them. In his walks he would often give his cloak to a destitute person, or bring home poor folk to be fed and clothed. His hospitality was boundless. Strangers and travellers were welcome, and even their beasts had such care taken of them, that it was said, "a horse turned loose in any part of the country would immediately make its way to the Rector of Houghton's." Every Sunday, from Michaelmas to Easter, he expected to see his parishioners, for whom three tables were spread, one for gentlemen, one for farmers, and one for labourers. But the best investment was, in his opinion, the money that encouraged industry. He loved to make up the losses of his laborious neighbours. If one had lost a beast, he gave him another. He bestowed his horse one day on a poor man, one of whose team had fallen dead. His own parish did not exhaust his labours. The neglected state of the country round appealed to his warm heart, and he used to visit, every year, the most neglected parishes in Northumberland, Yorkshire, Cheshire, Westmoreland, and Cumberland, leaving his curate in charge at home. In each place he stayed two or three days, and preached in the churches or barns, visited the gaols, and composed quarrels. On his way to church, in one place, he observed a glove hung up, as a challenge. He took it down himself, and, holding it up in the pulpit, rebuked the inhuman custom, and exhorted to mutual love. His name was greatly revered. On one occasion, his horses were stolen. The news quickly got wind, and every one was indignant. The thief, learning from the report of the country, whose horses he had taken, came trembling back and returned them, declaring that he believed the devil would have seized him had he carried them off knowing them to be Mr. Gilpin's. He was known and loved as the "NORTHERN APOSTLE."

The Treasurer, Lord Burleigh, travelling from Scotland on one occasion, visited Gilpin, whom he held in high esteem; and after spending a few days in the generous rector's parsonage, and observing the order, simplicity, and benevolence of all the arrangements, and the crowds of persons of all kinds who came there for advice and help, took his leave; and, turning his horse on the hill-top, which commands the view of Houghton, exclaimed, "There is the enjoyment of life indeed! Who can blame that man for not accepting a bishopric! What doth he want to make him greater, or happier, or more useful to mankind?"

C. A. D.

What Church? A Word to Converts.

SAYS one: "I think I'll join the —— church, for that is the most popular church in town. They have the finest building and the largest congregation." Says another: "I shall join the —— church, for their minister is an interesting preacher, and I like his social qualities." Still another: "I shall join the —— church, for I was converted there, hence feel most at home." And another: "I shall join the —— church, for my deceased parents belonged to that church. What was good enough for my father is good enough for me." And yet another: "I shall join the —— church, for they are not so strait-laced as the others. One can go to a social dance, if he wishes, and no fault is found. The preacher plays a game of cards occasionally, just for fun. I like to see churches tolerant." Another: "I shall join the —— church, for all my preferences lead me in that direction."

But another thoughtfully says: "This matter certainly demands consideration. I shall take time to examine the New Testament carefully and prayerfully, and then offer myself to that church which, in my view, comes nearest to the gospel in its doctrines and practices." The last speaker alone takes a consistent position. No one can deny this. He seeks the Lord's will rather than his own. If all Christians would pursue the same course, "denominations" would soon begin to fall out of sight, and there would come a true union among God's people, even a union *in the truth*. Such a union, however, will never be accomplished while professed Christians make popularity, likes and dislikes, personal preferences, the practices of honoured parents, and a desire for comfort, the rule of their action, rather than the Word of God. These things serve to keep up divisions among God's people. If all converts would go to the New Testament, and study it prayerfully, and then follow its teachings, this would do more to bring about a true "Christian union" than a thousand debates upon church union. What is the Bible given us for, if not to be studied and followed as the Lord may help us to understand it? W. C. PRATT.

𝕿𝖍𝖊 𝕱𝖑𝖔𝖜𝖊𝖗-𝖌𝖎𝖗𝖑𝖘 𝖔𝖋 𝕮𝖑𝖊𝖗𝖐𝖊𝖓𝖜𝖊𝖑𝖑.*

ON a Saturday morning of last July we were betimes at Covent Garden; and, having been acquainted with the market as it was some years ago, we were much struck with the changes which have taken place in the last few years. London has grown so fast during the last generation, that we cannot wonder that this great market has also extended beyond its ancient bounds, and appears to be still too straitened for the enormous business transacted therein. Many houses have been taken down, but still the area is too small for public requirements. The chief thing, however, which will strike a visitor who only knew the market years ago, will be the remarkable extension of the trade in flowers. Then this business was so small,' that it was easily carried on in front of the old church; but now there is a spacious covered building devoted to this department, and on a favourable morning the interior is a refreshing sight, while the air is filled with Nature's sweetest scents.

The money daily expended on flowers in London would represent quite a respectable fortune. The market scene is a lively one; well-to-do purveyors for fashionable patrons are there seeking supplies, on the one hand, while, on the other are the more numerous flower-girls of our great leading thoroughfares, who part with their scanty capital with anxious faces, because every penny must be laid out to the best advantage. A few years ago there was hardly a flower-seller to be seen in the streets of London, and now there are thousands of them.

They are a class by themselves; and their great need has given rise to "The Watercress and Flower-girl Mission," of which Mr. John A. Groom is the honorary superintendent. The headquarters of the Mission are just off Clerkenwell Green, close to the parish church of St. James, which has long been a centre of evangelical teaching: as the parishioners themselves choose their own rector, they take care to have one who is on the side of the gospel. Here, those who have an eye for the interesting in the byways of London, may see the Flower-girl Brigade at work, making artificial flowers for milliners and others who represent the home market for such productions. These young creatures are reclaimed from the streets, with their many temptations and dangers, and hundreds of them have passed on to fill useful situations in life.

Though Mr. Groom's work begins with flower-girls, it does not end with them; his mission is as comprehensive as any in London. There are over a thousand scholars in the Sunday-school; a great deal is done through the winter in the way of giving early breakfasts to board-school children, who would otherwise have to go to their lessons without breaking their fast; and the missionary and the Bible-woman spend a great part of their time in house-to-house visitation. Apart from this and other branches of service, Mr. Groom might fairly claim to rank among the popular preachers of London; for on successive Sunday nights throughout the year he preaches to a thousand persons at Foresters'

---

* Nothing pleases us better than to bring works of charity and piety before our readers. They will never cease to be interested in the labours of consecrated men among the children of poverty.—C. H. S.

Hall, in Clerkenwell Road. He faithfully preaches tho old truths of the gospel which, in his case, prove themselves to be as fresh and as attractive as ever to the common people. The crowd not only comes to hear, but many are gathered into the church, and the Lord is glorified. The mission chiefly seeks to benefit the most needy class of female street-traders ; but in reality many classes are reached, and the work will extend. When it was commenced, nearly a quarter of a century ago, attention was confined to one market and one district ; but to-day an influence is exerted throughout the whole of London.

In what degree flower-girls, as a class, have created a demand for flowers in the streets it would be impossible to say, though it is plain that they represent a new industry. In our opinion, the streets are all the prettier for their presence ; and it is a healthy sign that a regular demand for flowers should have arisen. These lovely products of nature now meet us at every turn. Flowers have come to be the pleasures of the poor as well as the luxuries of the rich. You may have flowers brought to your door ; and if you go abroad, flower-girls will wait upon you. Where the tide of life runs fullest, the flower-girl endeavours to ply her trade. In every main thoroughfare, at crossings, hard by an obelisk or a statue, at railway stations and omnibus stands, the industrious sisterhood are found, early and late. The principal stand of all is in front of the Royal Exchange ; and we believe that no one with an artistic eye would deny that the crescent of flower-girls, with their baskets on the ground before them, sets off that stately edifice to advantage on a summer morning.

The number of the flower-girls has increased at a greater rate than the resources of the Mission which exists for their benefit. Who is there, that knows anything about the temptations of the streets, that will not pity them ? They deserve the help which the right-minded Christian gives to the poor ; the more so because so many of them exhibit those virtues which are supposed to command success in life. They are not only patterns of industry, in an ordinary sense, but they are abroad during excessively long hours. They are at market in the early hours of each morning to buy their stock ; and until late at night they linger where people congregate, still trying to sell the stock which will spoil if kept through the night. The flower-girl's posies add charms to many a suburban mansion, but her own poor room is hardly worthy of the name of home. Both at home and abroad most things seem to be against her : there are the squalid surroundings of her abode, the want of helpful friends, and, perhaps, the still heavier drawback of a drunken father or a degraded mother. It is but natural that the temptations of the town should come to such with tenfold more force than they would to others. If some are led astray, or make foolish alliances with lazy fellows who have a fancy for them, it is only what might be expected from young girls who have to get their livelihood on the streets until late at night. Hundreds have been saved for something better than they could have ever known if left to themselves, and in this way God has been glorified and the community benefited. What has been done in the past may be repeated in the future, if Mr. Groom and his committee have their hands sufficiently strengthened to enable them to persevere, and extend their enterprise.

The girls are not all of one class or quality. What may be called the *bond fide* flower-girl follows her business through all the four seasons ; but there are many others who, as interlopers, are selling flowers during the best months, and in the winter seeking indoor work. Some of these are of a lower class than the flower-girls proper; and instances occur in which they bring discredit on the sisterhood to which they do not properly belong. There are even strong and lazy young men who take to flower selling; but they do not deserve encouragement. Flower-girls must not be judged by the evil ones among them: there are bad and good of all classes.

It is singular that a large proportion of the girls are Irish and Catholics. Why Irish girls should be attracted by flower selling more than others is not easily to be explained, unless it be owing to the wit and poetry which are characteristic of the Irish nation. In any case, we have to deal with things as we find them; and there is nothing discouraging in the fact of these young creatures being mainly Irish. It rather tells the other way when so many of them have already yielded to Christian influences. If they ask for our sympathy, and sometimes for a little help, both together are little enough for us to give, although, what is given will go a long way among such recipients. If it be asked, What can be done for them? the readiest answer is found in what Mr. Groom and his helpers are doing, from early morning till late at night, throughout the year. The missionary and the Bible-woman are continually ministering to these poor women and girls in a way that is always valued. They receive many a word of good cheer or Christian counsel while at their business in the streets ; and they are visited in their own homes. It may happen that a girl will be found at her work faint from want of food; or her eyes may tell of despair, because night is coming on, and her perishable stock remains unsold.

In the one case the girl will be supplied with a plain meal at a coffee-house ; in the other case, if her flowers are actually spoiled, the loss, almost overwhelming in her case, will be made up. Such practical Christianity the girls can understand, and it finds a ready response in their hearts, especially when, in case of exceptional distress or sickness, they are efficiently helped. So far as our observation goes, no class of the poor more deserves what is done for them than these girls; and to this Mr. Groom would himself bear witness. It is a hopeful circumstance that the police so readily extend their protection to the girls, and, as a rule, give them a good character. It is, of course, inevitable that improprieties will occur ; but where this is the case, the offenders are commonly found to be interlopers, and not members of the regular flower-selling sisterhood.

The saddest side of the general life of flower-girls is seen in the unhappy lot of little children who thus trade in the streets. The Bill for the Prevention of Cruelty to Children will somewhat affect these little ones; but it will not remove them from the streets, and their evil influences. The " cruelty " from which they suffer not only consists in their being driven abroad at untimely hours in the great public thoroughfares, but in the way in which their earnings are used by their elders who send them out. Their parents are, in many instances, degraded people, who are willing to sacrifice their children to their own self-indulgence ; and being lost to all feelings of shame or self-respect, they do not care whether the little adventurers earn money or steal it. To reach, and in some degree to cure, this great wrong, Mr. Groom and his committee propose to establish a Home for little girls of the flower-girl class, children whose surroundings in the world are far more disastrous than those of orphans. Their ages are from twelve to sixteen, and their present hardships are not the worst part of their lot : they are in imminent danger of swelling the ranks of the fallen unless they are rescued as children once and for all. If taken in hand in time, they are excellent material for the Christian philanthropist to work upon. It is calculated that the proposed Home could be started with £1,000, and efforts are being made to raise a special fund.

These children have a claim on Christian people ; for they are really an ill-used class, who cannot help themselves. The Society for the Prevention of Cruelty to Children could tell some harrowing stories about individual cases, brought before police magistrates. So important is this scheme of a Home for Little Girls, that Mr. Groom and his committee regard it as the missing link in their chain of service ; and they consider that no branch of work will yield a greater return. At all events, it is felt that there is no alternative ; these poor children must either be left to go their own way towards perdition, both in this world and the next, or they must be altogether removed from the evil associations of the streets, which are at once their curse and snare.

When we take an all-round view of Mr. Groom's manifold operations in connection with "The Watercress and Flower-girl Mission," the closely-packed precincts of Clerkenwell Green become invested with new interest. A generation ago, before any clearances of its rookeries were made, the entire area north of the Holborn Viaduct, was the retreat of squalor, vice, and crime, and the outlook was enough to fill the worker with despair. The "Green" had long since ceased to be carpeted with grass ; the population had gone on growing around the church and Sessions House ; but at the same time, there were dotted about, here and there, old houses, curious in their construction, or interesting as landmarks in our social history. The transformation which has taken place in regard to buildings is so wonderful, that the district would hardly be recognized by persons who remember it thirty years ago. The Thieves' Houses, over the Fleet river, are no longer to be seen ; and the dangerous streets are now as safe as any leading thoroughfare. But while in outward appearance the place has so strikingly changed, and in some respects changed for the better, we must not be deceived by mere appearances. The people are still there in overwhelming numbers, the children especially mustering in such force, that nearly a dozen large buildings of the School Board are to be seen within half-a-mile of Mr. Groom's head-quarters. Despite "improvements," there is as great a work as ever to be done ; and those who are willing to do it should be encouraged. G. H. P.

Again in the Woods.

AUTUMN begins to lay its hand upon all things. The beech trees, which tower aloft like clustered columns in the heart of the wood, bear up bravely against the cold night winds. The bracken, and the ferns, and the soft green moss will not yet believe that summer has left them. But for all that, the vigour of the year is past, and the sabbath season of the woods has come—a sabbath upon which man makes sad inroads with his murderous gun. Now is a fine season for the solitary glades. Every falling leaf is a sermon. "Far from the city's dust and din" we wander till our feet are arrested by the tiny tarn which gives drink to bird and beast; and by its brink we sit us down and muse upon a fading world, and the generations of its life which rise like the waves of the sea only to die upon the shore. Yet life abides, and death cannot drive it from the throne. The leaves fall, but the forest lives on : men perish, but the race survives. Better still, the Lord of all things lives ; and as his watchful eye watches over the floweret which blooms in the innermost wood, so does he care for me. Lost as I might well be amid these pathless forests, yet he broods around me, and I am at home in him. When, like a faded leaf, I hang a while upon the tree awaiting my end, I will not fear ; for when the time shall come for me to flutter to the ground, he will be with me, and direct my way, as surely as if I were the only creature he had ever made. Here then, at the foot of your polished pillars, O beeches of the forest, I am at home with the living God, and yet learn the lesson of the fading leaves.   C. H. S.

Never Bring your Cares Indoors.

AN aged believer whom I have just seen on what is probably his dying bed, remarked to me that he had no cares, "and," added he, "I never have fretted, for I made it a rule never to bring my cares indoors." His house stands within his timber yard, and I smiled to think of his home as being a sacred enclosure around which care might wander, but into which it could not enter. It might deal with the deals, and concern itself with the planks, but could not come upon the carpet. How fine it would be if when we scraped our boots we cast care under the scraper ; and by a believing prayer left it with the dust which is the serpent's meat, and not ours ! What is the use of fretting ! It never coined a penny for our poverty, nor prepared a slice of meat for our hunger. It is a killing thing, and is to be avoided by all who love life. We do not waste strength by labour, for there is a recuperative power within which restores us after activity ; but we lose life by anxiety, and lose it fast. Worry is a form of suicide. Don't repine, for it takes so much out of you. A calm, contented life is worth far more to the insurance office, as the tables of probabilities go, than the life of one who drains his soul away by anxiety. Besides, a believer glorifies God by being always restful in faith. His peaceful life is a sermon with a quiet but irresistible eloquence in it which wins men to a desire after his holy secret.   C. H. S.

WILTON HOUSE OF REST, ST. LEONARDS.

A House of Rest.

OUR beloved friend, ARCHIBALD BROWN, has conferred inestimable blessings upon the poor by his Convalescent Home at Herne Bay. Many a sick minister has also found repose beneath that hospitable roof. We have now the pleasure of telling weary workers of a further door of hope for them. There can hardly be too many places for godly men who have spent their strength in the Master's service, and need refreshment.

On the first of August there was opened, at West Marina, St. Leonards, a newly-built and conveniently-planned house, delightfully situated facing the sea, which is henceforth to serve as a place of entertainment and rest for Christian workers who may need such reviving as change of scene on the sea-shore commonly ensures. The founder of this pleasant holiday-house is our well-known friend, Mr. C. Russell-Hurditch, who, four years ago, opened, by way of beginning, a smaller house in Devonshire Road, Hastings. In the course of two years some four hundred Christian workers availed themselves of its advantages. The house was well furnished, and the table was liberally supplied, while the charges, which varied according to the rooms occupied, ranged from about ten to twenty-one shillings per week, an additional advantage being obtained by the railway company granting tickets from London at five shillings each. Miss Helen Hurditch, the founder's sister, superintends the arrangements.

The House of Rest was so greatly valued, that it was felt desirable to increase the accommodation, and Mr. Hurditch was encouraged to proceed with this enterprise by having £1,000 left for the purpose. The premises form the two end houses of a terrace in course of erection, forming the western boundary of the green and garden now being laid out close to the sea. Accommodation will be provided for thirty visitors, in addition to the usual staff, the rooms commanding bright and extensive views, while every possible convenience will be found for their comfort.

The total cost of this freehold property, including £750 for furniture, will be £4,500, and as only £1,300 of this sum is at present in hand, Mr. Hurditch adds that he is "now praying the Lord to move his people to contribute the remaining sum required, to enable us to enter upon this work free of debt."

Friends wishing to contribute, or desiring further information, should send to Mr. C. Russell-Hurditch, 164, Alexandra-road, St. John's Wood, London, N.W.

Parrot-like Reading.

OF all books that are publicly read for the edification of the people, none, ordinarily, is so badly read as the Bible. It is not merely that public readers fail to give to words the fulness of power and beauty that is in them. It is not merely that the reading lacks rhetorical elegance and finish, and that Holy Writ, as uttered by such persons, ceases to charm and captivate. The Scriptures are often read as one would read a formula in an unknown tongue, whose alphabet and pronunciation he had mastered, but without having the slightest idea what the words meant, or whether they had any meaning.—*Dr. J. S. Hart.*

𝔓astor 𝔍. 𝔍. 𝔎endon,

PRESIDENT OF THE HOP-PICKERS' MISSION.

BY the Editor's kind indulgence, we have been permitted to plead the cause of "The Hop-pickers' Mission" repeatedly in the pages of this magazine during the past eleven years; and thus, of necessity, there has constantly been before our readers the name of

PASTOR J. J. KENDON;

and now we are glad to be able to present a fairly good portrait of him,

as a further "reminder" to those good friends who have this year forgotten to forward their contributions for our work in Kent.

"Them that honour me, I will honour," is a text which finds practical illustration in the life and work of our dear friend. Like many a worker for God, he was led to Christ in early life; and, from his conversion, manifested an intense desire for soul-winning. In the East of London, he began his life-work as a missionary; here he was greatly used by the Master, and his name became a household word in many a home.

Twenty-eight years ago severe family affliction and bereavement rendered a change necessary, and through his visit to a dying man (to whom he had been made a blessing), he made the acquaintance of a gentleman of wealth and influence who gave Mr. K. a letter to the Secretary of the "Town and Country Mission," who (as our friend called) had just received a sum of money from a Christian lady, a native of Goudhurst, to send a Christian worker for three months into that neighbourhood. Accepting this as the direct intervention of God on his behalf, he gladly went. He found the people very dark and destitute in spiritual things, and not a door in the place open to him. He rented a labourer's cottage for himself and his young family, at two shillings per week; and then commenced preaching in the streets. By degrees he won the hearts of the people, and in growing numbers they gathered about him. By the time the dark, cold days of winter rendered open-air work impracticable, God had touched the heart of the squire's wife, who pleaded with her husband for the loan of an empty oast-house to shelter this poor pastor and his little flock.

Up a rickety ladder, into this poorly-lighted and draughty place, the people gathered for upwards of three years. The interest of this godly lady next built him a little room, to serve as a day-school through the week, and for services on Sunday; and here, in 1864, the little band of believers was formed into a church.

Those were days of sore struggling for our friend, and often he found it extremely difficult to "make ends meet"; yet his trust in God remained unshaken, and his daily motto was, "Jehovah-Jireh." Referring to those days, he says, "How often, when we have been brought to our last penny, and have not known how to provide for our little ones, have we been enabled to go to our heavenly Father, and tell him all our wants in simplicity and in confidence; and, in his own time and way, he has graciously sent the needed help!"

With the hope of augmenting his meagre income, he "took a bin," for himself and family, in the hop-garden; and each September, for years, found him and his, toiling hard, in sunshine or shower, from morn till eve. His advent provoked the exclamation from a burly fellow, "Hello! Hi, Bill! here's *a parson* come to pick hops!"

In *that* day the annual influx of 50,000 from our London slums brought an alarming amount of sin and suffering into the county; and, as "the parson" stood at the bin, his ears often tingled with the profane jest, oath, and bawdy song, greeting him on all sides. At length, unable to bear it longer, and regardless of loss; he left his family at the bin, and commenced trudging the gardens hour after hour, pausing at each bin to "speak a word for Jesus," and to leave tracts. Opposition and insult soon yielded to the forcible argument of a godly life, and his very presence became a check upon their sin. From this small beginning sprang

"THE HOP-PICKERS' MISSION,"

now so widely known, and an example of service that is now followed in various hop-growing centres by earnest brethren each returning season.

The Lord has smiled on our friend, rewarded a thousandfold the sacrifices he so willingly made, and his position and circumstances are greatly improved. His school has grown, as well as the mission, and some five hundred scholars have passed through his hands, and are honourably filling posts of usefulness in life, and most of them in Christian service; notably so his own sons, the elder of whom, after three years' successful course in the "Pastors' College," is now pastor of a group of churches in Jamaica, numbering one thousand two hundred in their membership.

Those of us who have known this work from its beginning, often stand amazed, as we look on the fine block of buildings, now accommodating sixty boarders; and, near by, a neat, commodious chapel (with Sunday-school room adjoining), in which gathers a warm-hearted band of worshippers weekly, from many miles around.   Whereas he found, at starting, not a door open to him, now there is not a door closed against him in the whole neighbour-hood; and we are led to exclaim, "What hath God wrought?"

We cannot do better than close this brief sketch with a quotation from the pen of our worthy editor:—"The story of Mr. Kendon's labours at Goud-hurst is exceedingly full of interest, and is an instance of how a determined, zealous man may, under the divine blessing, surmount difficulties, and make the influence of the gospel to be felt in an agricultural district with few to help."

We may add, for the information of any who may wish to send help for the mission, Pastor J. J. Kendon's address is Goudhurst, Kent.

Brentford.   J. BURNHAM.

Experience of James Fraser, of Brea.

Declaring such things as, through the Lord's blessing, have done me good.

I CANNOT deny but the Lord hath shown me kindness and done me good, and that a little one hath become a great nation, and that, however "I am poor and needy," yet "the Lord remembers me."   And notwithstanding "I came over this Jordan with my staff," yet now am I, by the Lord's bless-ing, "become two bands."   But whatever good it be that the Lord hath shown me for the benefit of others, and confirmation of myself, I have thought fit to show and set down these things, which, in my experience, through the Lord's blessing, I have found to be most helpful unto me in furthering me in the ways of holiness, peace and fellowship with God.   And I have found these twenty-seven things especially concur, and blest for doing me good :

1. The society of saints : When they have been full in communicating their cases, they have encouraged me, my griefs have been eased by them; I have by their godly conversation, been provoked to good works; I have been kept in life by them, recovered out of decays by them, enlightened and edified by them. Eccl. iv. 4, 9, 10, 11 ; 1 Cor. xii. 7; Heb. x. 24, 25; Prov. xxvii. 17. "Iron sharpeneth iron."

2. I have found much profit by observing the Lord's providences, by search-ing into God's ends in dispensations, whether good or evil; this hath made me see much love in things, freed my judgment from confusions, and made me know my duty. Micah vi. 9 ; Hosea xiv. 9 ; Psalm cvii. 43 ; Jer. viii. 7; Gen. xxv. 22 ; Exod. iii. 3, 4.

3. I have found meditation on the attributes of God to do me much good, especially his love, power, sovereignty, and holiness, Job xxii. 21 ; John xvii. 3, for thereby have I been made conformable to his image, and my love, fear, and faith, have been begotten and increased. Eph. iii. 18, 19.

4. I have found much good by a long and serious study and pondering of the covenant of grace ; the freedom, fulness, and unchangeableness thereof; the condition (faith), and nature thereof.   By meditation on the gospel, gospel-promises, offers, and invitations; this hath strengthened and sanctified me, given me more knowledge of Christ and of his ways than anything that ever I was exercised in.   I have found it indeed the "ministrations of life." Gal. iii. 2 ; Heb. xi. throughout ; Rom. i. 16, 17.

5. I have found the Lord confining me at home, in not calling me abroad ; ordinarily this hath been a gathering time, and never ordinarily better than when alone.   Abstraction and solitude hath done me good.   Prov. xviii. 1 ; Numb. vi. 2, 3 ; Hos. ii. 14.   God hath oftentimes visited me in a solitary wilderness.

6. I have found outward afflictions and hard measure from the world doing

me good, humbling my soul, mortifying me to the world, making Christ and his consolations sweet, whom before I cared not much for; I found it good to bear the yoke in my youth; I have thereby learned dependence on God, and have had much experience of his love in supporting me under afflictions, sanctifying them to me, and delivering me out of them. Lam. iii. 27; Psal. xciv. 12; Heb. xii. 11; Psal. cxix. 67, 71; Prov. xxix. 15; Hos. v. 15.

7. I have found quietness in spirit, moderation and calmness in speaking, and advisedness doing me good; and, while thus in silence I have waited on God, his Spirit hath breathed. Isa. vii. 4, and ix. 15; Exod. xiv. 13; 2 Chron. xx. 17; Phil. iv. 7; Lam. iii. 26; 1 Pet. v. 7.

8. I have found much good by the diligent practice of private duties, such as prayer, meditation, reading, self-examination, and such like. I have thereby been strengthened, quickened, and drawn near to God; they have been as meat and drink. Mat. vi. 6; Luke xxii. 46; Psalm i. 2, 3; Job viii. 5; Prov. xviii. 1.

9. I have found extraordinary duties of fasting, and improving other occasions over and above the morning and evening sacrifice, do me much good; much of the Lord's mind by these hath been revealed, Dan. x. 12, and strong lusts have by these extraordinary occasions received a dead stroke. I have been sensibly comforted at these occasions; these, after long sickness, have given me health. Psalm cxxvi. 6; Jer. 1, 5, 6; Isa. lviii. 7, 8; Mark ix. 29.

10. I have found the Lord kind to me since I left off hearing of the conformists; since that day the scales have been falling from my eyes: whilst I heard, I was still kept in bondage. 2 Cor. vi. 17, 18; 1 Cor. v. 7.

11. I have found much good from and by the prayers of others; for since I did employ some for that effect, I have found much good. And I have observed, that those of us who do seek the benefit of other's prayers were the most thriving Christians: and those who neglect this do decay and wither. Job xlii. 8; James v. 16; Eph. vi. 19; Rom. xv. 30; 2 Thess. iii. 1, 2.

12. I have found very much good by doing good to others, by instructing, exhorting, and teaching of them, and praying for them, especially the poor ignorant people. Yea, in the very time while I have been speaking to them, a glorious light hath shined upon my soul, and made me apprehend those things I have been declaring to them more clearly; yea, when full of confusions and sorrows going about this duty, my heart hath thereby been lightened, my talents improved. Isa. xxxii. 20; Eccl. xi. 1; Prov. xi. 25.

13. I have found the serious consideration of true Christian liberty, and of the easiness of Christ's yoke, and Christ's love in commands, in opposition to a slavish spirit and scrupulous fearful conscience, do me very much good, and make my heart engage in the service of God. 1 Kings xii. 4; Luke i. 74; Rom. vii. 1, 4, 6 and vi. 14; Neh. ix. 35; Deut. xxviii. 48; as likewise using considerations against discouragements, 1 Sam. xii. 19, 20.

14. I have found much profit and strength by considering of baptism, and what it sealeth; cases and scruples thereby cleared and removed, and faith of interest strengthened, and I thereby emboldened to draw near to God. Rom vi., first twelve verses.

15. The Lord hath blest the reading of practical writings to me, and thereby my heart hath been put into a frame, and much strength and light gotten; such as Isaac Ambrose, Goodwin, Mr. Gray, and very much by Rutherford's above others, but most of all by Thomas Shepherd of New England his works; he hath by the Lord been made the "interpreter, one of a thousand;" so that, under Christ, I have been obliged to his writings as much and more than to any means whatsoever for wakening, strengthening, and enlightening of my soul; the Lord made him a well of water to me in all my wilderness straits.

16. I have found it good to put a good construction on the Lord's ways, when they have been outwardly very sad. Exod. xx. 19.

17. I have found much good by speaking to the praise and commendation of God. When many times not so affectionately, yet sincerely out of the sense of duty, I have begun to praise him to others, I have found my tongue to have affected my heart. James iii. 2; Psalm cv. 3, and cxlv. 5, 6, 11. The Lord hath sensibly rewarded me for this.

18. I have found much good by sore and long inward temptations, being "poured from vessel to vessel," changing and being changed, lifted up, and casten down; the greatest settlement is by these. Isa. xxxviii. 16, "By these" (saith Hezekiah) "shall men live." These humbled me, and kept me waking, and ever crying to the Lord; and have given me much experience of the Lord's kindness, and acquainted me with the exercise of saints in the Scripture. James i. 2.

19. Resisting of strong temptations, and engaging with difficult duties, and struggling against all indispositions within, loss and contempt from the world without, and so taking up the cross; the Lord hath signally owned me in these, and the fruits of them have been very great; such as, praying under indispositions, reproving of acquaintances, forsaking of ways and thoughts very pleasing to the flesh. Jer. ii. 1, 2; Heb. xi. 6; Rom. ii. 7; Mat. v. 10, and xvi. 24.

20. I have found much good by studying and exercising the duty of humility and submission. James iv. 7. Duties are easy to a humble spirit; it eases the soul of disquietments, and makes burdens easy. Hell is not hell to a humble soul, saith Shepherd. I have ever found help when humbled.

21. The calling to mind and seriously meditating on the Lord's dealings with me as to soul and body, his manifold mercies, has done me very much good, cleared my case, confirmed my soul of God's love, and my interest in him, and made me love him. Oh, what good hath the writing of this book done me! and what wells of water have mine eyes been opened to see which before were hid! Psalm cvii. 4, and xviii. 1, 2. Scarce anything hath done me more good.

22. Making and renewing of vows and covenants with God, though gone about in much weakness, and but weakly performed, yet hath it begotten life, and kindly thoughts of God, and hath been a means to recover me out of decay, and to keep from further backsliding. Deut. xxix. 12, 13.

23. Meditation on the most common and general truths hath done me good, such as death, heaven, judgment, sin, God's being and providence, man's fall, and Christ's death, &c.

24. Speedy going about duties, without trifling or delaying. A duty done in time is worth twice so much delayed.

25. By writing on points of divinity; as on the Scriptures, on God's attributes, on Christian duties, sermons, cases, and the like; these, like fresh water, have refreshed my heart.

26. Serious and deliberate self-examination, and, while thus exercised, trying myself, looking to the qualifications of saints and hypocrites in Scripture, their sins and failings; studying the nature of true saving grace, the difference, according to the Scriptures, betwixt false and true grace; this hath contributed much to my settlement.

27. I have found much good by being abstracted from meddling in temporal or civil business. That I had not great meddling in affairs in the beginning of my Christian course, partly that others did not employ me, but took all to their own hand; partly that I was indifferent, and had no heart while I had so great things to do in reference to my soul. And although my private affairs called for diligence, yet do I not now repent it; for I thereby got my heart wholly taken up with my soul's condition, and was not diverted therefrom. Prov. xviii. 1.

Notices of Books.

Memoirs of the Rev. James Fraser, of Brea (A.D. 1639—1698). Written by himself. With Introductory Note by Rev. ALEXANDER WHYTE, D.D. Edinburgh: Religious Tract and Book Society. London: Marlborough and Co.

VERY great has been the reviewer's refreshment while examining this choice book. As a record of human thought and emotion it is of great interest to the mental philosopher; but as a description of the experience of a deeply tried believer, it is exceedingly precious to the Christian. No wonder that Dr. Alexander Whyte calls it one of his prime favourites: it is a kindred volume to Bunyan's "Grace Abounding." We do not grow these deep, soul-conversing men nowadays: the moderns would not know them, but would ridicule them as morbid, visionary, unpractical, and the like. The true-born heir of heaven, in whom there is spiritual life, is aware of secret sorrows and inward pinings which the bastard professor never feels; and, on the other hand, he is cognizant of secret joys and raptures which the mere pretender cannot even imagine. We do not wish any reader to imitate James Fraser any more than we would desire to see him confined on the Bass Rock; but we greatly pity any professed Christian who will not be the better for marking the way of inward tribulation in which the Lord led his faithful servant. We have given, in earlier pages, a chapter from this instructive memorial.

Our Senior Scholars: How to Retain them in Connection with our Sunday Schools. (First and Second Prize Essays, 1888.) By FRANK S. GARNICK and J. W. THOMAS, F.C.V., F.I.C. Sunday School Union.

THE two prize essays contained in this book strike us as being both bold and judicious. The writers urge certain admirable methods very earnestly, hint at others with diffidence, and dismiss doubtful expedients with short shrift. The subject treated on is one of vital importance. A link must be found between the growing scholar and the public means of grace, or else Sunday-school work will be pouring water into a leaky bucket. The ministry must become more plain in its language, and more earnest in its spirit, so that our hopeful youth may be interested and impressed. The writers of these essays do not lay blame on ministers, but they keep to their own department, and handle the matter with deep earnestness and practical wisdom. A shilling will be well spent by any teacher of a senior class upon the purchase of this timely work.

The Story of Jesus in the Words of Scripture, illustrated, for Lord's-day Use in Home and School. By ALEXANDER MACKEITH. Black-board Drawings by DAVID PRATT. Glasgow: Maclure, Macdonald, and Co.

WE do not marvel that this work is marked "15th thousand," for it should go to the 150th at least. Never have we seen so much for one shilling of really usable and striking instruction. If the drawings can be bought as large diagrams, and exhibited to the children, we have here a systematic method of setting forth the Life of our Lord of the first order of usefulness. Apart from its Sunday-school use, this volume is of great illustrative value; and to ask a shilling for it is next door to giving it away. A great deal of real art is displayed in the multitudinous engravings.

The Gospel in Song: a Hymn Book for Mission and Revival Services. Sunday School Union.

IT is no easy matter to compile a good hymn-book which in small space shall cover the varied needs of a congregation, and fitly express their praise and prayer in song. This becomes even more difficult when the larger share must be of a distinctly evangelistic type, as suitable for "Mission and Revival Services." But the compiler of the present book of praise has distinctly succeeded in giving this special character to his collection of hymns, whilst retaining many of the more solid and endeared ones. It is an unusually good compilation, is splendidly printed, and absurdly cheap at a penny a copy. May the Sunday School Union have a large sale to cover its necessary cost of production!

36

The Written Word. By SAMUEL G. GREEN, D.D. Sunday School Union.

THIS is such a treatise, brief, yet full, as only an intellectual mastery of the subject-matter, and a well-practised pen, could produce. Every thoughtful reader of the seventeen chapters into which the book is divided may make himself thereby intelligently, if not exhaustively, acquainted with those great topics of Biblical criticism usually spread over volumes of Introduction to the Old and New Testaments. In the midst, however, of so much that is excellent and helpful, for which we feel the sincerest thankfulness, we grieve to see a man of Dr. Green's standing so far yielding to the miserable cant of the day as to parade, with a solemn air, the mistakes in matters of science made by Christian expositors of former ages; as if such mistakes were peculiar to Christian teachers, and were not committed as the result of giving way to the then fashionable science. Surely, enough has been done by Christian apologists of these days in immolating their predecessors at the shrine of scepticism. Sceptics are not propitiated, and believers are not purified, by such sacrifices. On the other hand, we notice Dr. Green puts on, here and there, an authoritative air towards *believing* critics, whose view-point does not happen to be his own. This may be effective in some connections, but in dealing with Sunday-school teachers it scarcely tends to edification.

What are we to think of Dr. Green's doctrine of inspiration? What is it? Properly enough, we are urged to apply the inductive method, and only to attempt a definition after the investigation of the phenomena of Scripture. The meaning of this, simply put, is, that inspiration is a doctrine of Scripture; and all that Scripture says on the subject should go to form our conception of the doctrine. Or, is something more intended? If so, what is it? In indicating the "phenomena," Dr. Green exhibits a strangely narrow range of vision, to use no harsher word. Evidently, to Dr. Green's mind, when the Scriptures affirm that "God spake by Moses," that "holy men of old spake by the Holy Ghost"; and

when the prophets introduce their communications with a "Thus saith the Lord," and the apostle declares that "All Scripture is given by inspiration of God," &c., these affirmations of Scripture are to be distinguished from the "phenomena," and the "phenomena" sought elsewhere. Whatever may be found elsewhere, the induction cannot be sound, since it is not complete, for it does not recognize these authoritative statements as among the most vivid and expressive "phenomena" of the Scriptures. To the last citation given above (2 Tim. iii. 16), Dr. Green emphatically calls our attention in a note, that he adopts the Revised Version of the passage "without hesitation." We do not object to Dr. Green as a teacher being "without hesitation"; but we may ask, Was it hesitation as to the *extent* of inspiration in the Scripture that fortified him, in the presence of the context of the verse, its own remarkable structure, and all the controversies concerning it, to depart from the Authorized Version, and unhesitatingly to adopt the new version of it? We ask this the more seriously because Dr. Green immediately affirms that, in a passage like this, the *extent* of inspiration is not plainly stated. Comparing this important *inference* with one of his concluding sentences on this subject, we should like to be assured of Dr. Green's real, or "unhesitating" sentiments on this vital point. We do not wish to press his words beyond their fair and obvious meaning, but what are we to conclude when he says: "He (*i.e.*, God) employs human instruments, and it is not for us to say how far he will permit the human element—the element of imperfection—to characterize the vehicle of his communications"? If Dr. Green means to tell us that human nature, even when employed as a vehicle of the Divine mind, is, after all, *limited*, then no one denies so obvious a truth. But how did so skilful a writer descend to such a platitude at the very moment when he was giving us a hint that he was saying something unspeakably mysterious and profound? But if Dr. Green intends by these words to convey something else, namely, that human nature *contaminates* with its imperfection the divine message it is employed to convey, then the purity of Scripture is, at one stroke, surrendered. It is all one as if truth were poisoned at its very spring. And the superhuman task is thrust upon us, in these latter days, of determining between divine truth and human error under the most disadvantageous circumstances; that is to say, when the very men who made the mixture, the prophets and apostles, "who spake as they were moved by the Holy Ghost," did not, because they could not, avoid the adulteration. Are we wiser than they? The purity of Scripture was the great weapon used by our Protestant fathers against the pretended infallibity of Rome. Have we abandoned this also? If so, what now is our supreme and unerring guide in religion and morals? Our own individual reason? This is the only resort left, since there is no such thing as a consensus as to the teachings of reason in general. We do not wish to disguise our alarm at the issue of such teaching as this by a corporation like the Sunday School Union, and by a teacher like Dr. Green. If the chapter on which we have animadverted is only ambiguous, then the book ought. to ,be recalled, and this chapter re-written with a phraseology that shall not only have reference to the criticisms of the day, but shall also distinctly and expressly set forth the things most assuredly believed amongst us.

Tea Meeting Talks with my Bible Class. By ALFRED DICE. With Preface by Pastor J. W. DAVIES. Simpkin, Marshall, and Co.

MR. ALFRED DICE must surely be one of the best of teachers, and by no means afraid to teach his young people all the truths of Scripture, even to the deep things of God. "Tea-meeting talks" are generally weaker than the tea; and if they have any flavour, it is that of milk-and-water, drops of milk and pails of water, with three spoonfuls of sugar; but these "talks" are so solid, that we are inclined to think that at Bromley Road they have meat-teas for a shilling, which is the price of the book. We fear the *public* taste is not at this time up to the mark for food of this sort; but among his own friends, we hope Mr. Dice will command a sale, especially as the profits will go to build the chapel which the Bromley Road friends so greatly need. The author himself will send the book, post free, for fourteen stamps, and his address is, Mr. Alfred Dice, Bromley Road, Lee, S.E.

Pulpit Notes. By Rev. B. D. JOHNS. Alexander and Shepheard.

THESE outlines, we doubt not, were the frame-works of excellent discourses. They are such as many of our useful brethren would make for themselves; but we do not know how far others would get on with them if they tried to use them. Everything depends upon the filling up. Mr. Johns would be sure to set them blazing with truth earnestly uttered, but that cannot be seen in these notes. The bare outline must remain like a brazier when the burning coals are out of it, till some fervent spirit fills it up and sets fire thereto. Here are notes of a hundred and one discourses by a young minister whose opening ministry is full of promise.

The Questions of the Bible arranged in the Order of the Books of Scripture. Compiled by W. CARNELLEY, with Preface by S. G. GREEN, D.D. T. Fisher Unwin.

IT is handy to have the questions of the Bible made into a separate volume, but we greatly question whether any considerable number of persons will spend 7s. 6d. in the purchase of a book which simply contains the questions and their connection.

The Authorship of the Fourth Gospel, and other Critical Essays. Selected from the Published Papers of the late EZRA ABBOT. Boston, U.S.A.: G. H. Ellis, 161, Franklin Street.

THESE essays display the ripest scholarship united with sound divinity. We do not wonder at their separate publication; though we fear that in England they are not likely to meet with a remunerative sale. The brief paper on Dr. Tregelles is specially interesting.

The City of Faith; or, Notes and Gleanings in Religious Inquiry. By S. B. BLEAU, M.A. Elliot Stock.

A THOROUGHLY educated spiritual man, of a highly thoughtful order, will relish this book. It is rather too deep for the plain believer; but he will rejoice to see that the author argues for faith, and almost everybody who does this is pretty sure to argue for *the* faith. Error cries up doubt: it is truth which demands and honours faith. This is one of Elliot Stock's neat little volumes, of which he has issued quite a series. The paper and type are of a very superior order, as they should be to be in harmony with the excellent matter with which Mr. Bleau has stored his pages. We could not keep our hands off the few paragraphs which follow—they are so exactly to our mind :—

"What, then, is the so much vaunted process of Evolution but a phantasmal process? What does it present us with but a groaning and travailing universe? Within its own dreary limits it contains a measure of *truth,* but in relation to the true being it is but the phantasy of a disordered universe, of that creation which was, through sin, ' made subject to vanity.' It is destitute of hope; its final word is a ceaseless ' struggle for existence'; its pictures are of creatures that through primeval ages ' tear each other in their slime'; of men who .

' Perished in winter winds, till one smote fire
From flint-stones, coldly hiding wh at they hold.'

However fair nature's aspect, it ever veils

' One vast, savage, grim conspiracy,
Of mutual murder from the worm to man.'

And it is a science with these consolations with which many within the Christian church are so fascinated! And a ' liberal theology' would seem to rely more upon the processes of nature and the discoveries of science, upon the offered panaceas of a time, doubtless, described by the prophet in the words, ' Many shall run to and fro, and knowledge shall be increased '—a

time of feverish haste—than upon the great apocalypse, the miraculous manifestation of ' the powers of the world to come,' that is finally ' to end the strife.' Verily, under the spell of the Gorgon-eyes of present-day science, the sense of the mystery and misery of evil—supernatural evil, and the infinite pathos of that supernatural suffering which met and vanquished it, are in danger of fading from the mind even of ' liberal Christianity.'

" But the cry of progress is miserably insufficient wherewith to confront the sufferings of nature, and the misery and sin of man.

" The grandeur which Darwin saw in the Evolutionary ' view of life ' is a horrible grandeur. Were scientific Evolution the original and divinely-chosen order of things, then Pessimism would be the most reasonable frame of mind. ' The sense that there is something wrong that needs to be put right—something in men and in the world which makes the thought of life very sad, and crowds it with terrible liabilities to failure and agony—this has weighed often very heavily upon the human mind; it has driven some men into hopelessness . . . . others into blank atheism; it is a view of things . . . which has had no small share in producing that pessimist view of all life and nature . . . .which finds vent in the philosophical dogma that proclaims this to be the worst of all possible worlds.'

" Only a supernatural gospel is the answer to this dread conclusion."

The Story of Jesus for Little Children. By Mrs. G. E. MORTON. Partridge.

THE story of stories is told in simple words, and it makes a very handsome book. It may be to some mothers a great help if they read it to the tinies ; but it would be better still if, after reading it, they told the story in even simpler language of their own. Each set of children has a *patois* of its own, with which the mother alone is fully acquainted. How wonderful that the biography of the Son of the Highest is better adapted than any other to be told to little children ! Angels study it ; divines dive into it ; babes love it. Blessed is the story of Jesus !

John Bright, the Man of the People. By JESSE PAGE. Partridge and Co.

VERY good for a popular sketch ; but it is like putting a sea into a saucer, to give us John Bright in such small space. He was a politician who scorned policy and did the right ; a statesman who abhorred state-craft, and had no craft but simple honesty. Where shall we find the like of him ? Mr. Page writes very well, but he is hardly in sympathy with this good great man in all his conscientious acts. We go with him all through ; but we leave party politics to partizans. Very happy is our recollection of an hour spent with John Bright in the Hotel Italy at Menton. At that time he, himself, was somewhat depressed, and we were not much better, so that our spirits were in unison. Again we have lost a friend.

Bertram de Drumont : a Mediæval Tale. By the late ELLA BAKER. Kegan Paul, Trench, and Co.

Kingscote Stories. (Same author and publishers.)

FROM the memorial preface to these two volumes, we learn that Miss Ella Baker " died from the sting of a bee," at the early age of twenty-nine, and that " these posthumous productions are published by a proud but sorrowing father." We jot down a few items concerning this " quiet, unselfish life," very largely occupied with domestic and filial duties, just to show *lawn-tennisiennes* what may be done : *pour encourager les autres*, in fact. Ella mastered (self-taught) French, Italian, and German. One " instance of memory is given "—*we* add, " and of industry " : at the age of thirteen she repeated the whole of " The Lady of the Lake " ; and where she substituted any words for those of the original, the rhythm and meaning were correct. She assisted her sister in preparing her " History of the English People " for young persons, besides writing, as a recreation, the books at the head of this notice. Of these stories and biographical sketches we have but this to remark, that they are in no sense *religious ;* indeed, the absence of any teaching which could be so described, has, to our mind, great

significance. On the other hand, it is but scant praise to say that her writings fully justify her father's words : " She was highly intellectual, with a fine taste, and poetic imagination."

Kensington Picturesque and Historical. By W. J. LOFTIE, B.A., F.S.A. With upwards of Three Hundred Illustrations by WILLIAM LUKER, Junr. Field and Tuer.

THIS is a noble volume, worthy of its dedication, by command, to Her Gracious Majesty. The illustrations, some of them in colours, make the book a delight for the artist as well as for the student. Kensington is unusually rich hunting-ground for the writer of a topographical book. Its past was not without points of interest, but its present bristles with them, since so many of our great painters have their studios in that region, and art itself has set up its throne in that western suburb. Mr. Loftie has laboured assiduously to gather materials, and to make them correct. He gives us little or no guess-work, but confines himself to facts. He has practised a self-denying condensation ; for he appears to have collected matter enough for four such books as the present. Our impression is, that the amount of compression is, nine times out of ten, a fair gauge of the value of writing: the test is accurate in the present instance. This volume is not quite in the usual line of those which we review : it is not an article of necessity, but of pure luxury. It was published by subscription, but can be purchased for £2 5s.

As it Should Be : Aunt Rachel's Advice to Her Niece. T. Woolmer.

WE have never seen a better book for servants. It is saturated with the essential oil of wisdom and perfumed with kindness.

Who is the White Pasha ? a Story of Coming Victory. Nisbet and Co.

WE cannot say that we have been edified by this conjectural treatise. We do not think that Gordon is the White Pasha. We hardly see the propriety of interweaving Scripture with a pleasing fancy with regard to that brave soldier. There is really nothing in it, as far as we can see.

Toilers in London; or, Inquiries concerning Female Labour in the Metropolis. By the "BRITISH WEEKLY" COMMISSIONERS. Hodder and Stoughton.

THE more of such information the better. Our well-to-do folks ought to know how the toilers fag and fast. Much good may come of increased acquaintance with the poverty of workers; for the miserly may be shamed, and the generous may be aroused. A little ingenuity in the mode of helping the poor is often of more value than a large amount of money; and such books as this give suggestions to kind hearts, which active hands soon carry out.

Our Wee Boy. Earnest Thoughts for Young Mothers, gleaned from a Brief Motherhood. With Introduction by JOHN LOWE, F.R.C.S. Edinburgh: James Thin.

A MOTHER's story of her boy's brief life; told with holy simplicity. It must have cheered the sorrower to write the little narrative, and it will comfort many more to read it.

Hoyle's Hymns and Songs for Temperance Societies and Bands of Hope. Partridge and Co.

THE name of William Hoyle is well known as a composer and compiler of music for temperance meetings, and this revised and enlarged edition of his hymns and songs will keep up his deservedly high reputation. There are now two hundred and seventy-five pieces in the collection, but the price is still the same—1s. 8d. in paper covers, and 2s. 6d. in cloth. We heartily commend this book to any temperance friends who are asking, "What shall we sing at our meetings?" There is sufficient variety in it to make it suitable for adults or children, and it is equally adapted for public gatherings or the home circle.

Rockville. A Temperance Story. By an A. C. P. Manchester: Brook and Chrystal.

WE must sorrowfully confess that we do not know what an "A. C. P." is; but whatever it is, he, she, or it is a first-rate story-teller. The title of this shilling book does not convey a full idea of its contents; for while it is a Temperance story, it is much more. The heroine of the tale is a governess to the children of a drunken major, and she, or an "A. C. P.," manages to weave four other capital stories into the principal narrative. We recommend an "A. C. P." to write some more Temperance books in this fashion, and to get Messrs. Brook and Chrystal to publish them. Brook and crystal stream are always in the Temperance line.

Captain Lobe; a Story of the Salvation Army. By JOHN LAW. Hodder and Stoughton.

SALVATION ARMY means to most people a great braying of trumpets and thumping of the big drum; we may add, too, the harassment of sick and dying persons, notwithstanding the earnest protests of their friends. But, happily, there's quite another side of the business, and we have it here in this blood-red book. By its help, you may mentally make a personally-conducted tour in "Slumdom," with an active and intelligent officer, whose heart bleeds for the sin and misery ever before his eyes. It seems that there are those in the Army who hate its noise and parade, and rather *suffer*, than favour, many of its methods, which most Christian people object to. We commend the book to our readers for its own interest, and that they may see somewhat of this wonderful organization with its friends' eyes. We are sure it will cause them to admire and sympathize with the heroic women, ay, mere girls, who spend their lives among the degraded and dangerous classes of our great city. The writer assures us, that though there is a spice of romance in the story, the bulk of the book is verily and indeed fact.

Jacky: a Story of Everyday Life. By SALOME HOCKING. Andrew Crombie.

THIS is not exactly a Temperance tale, although the principal character, little humpbacked Jacky, and his violin, are both won over to the side of total abstinence. There is nothing very notable about the book; but it conveys some useful lessons in a pleasing manner.

"In all our Doings;" the *Golden Links of the Collects.* A *Story for Boys.* By G. STEBBING. Shaw and Co.

THE author devotes much labour and pious skill to the task of commending the collects of the prayer-book, to boys especially. Probably she had been pained by learning that one of the most distasteful tasks of "church boys" at school is that of committing to memory the collect for the Sunday; and further, that to the great majority of attendants at church these ancient prayers are incomprehensible. All through the book the clergyman is represented as taking "the little black prayer-book" from his pocket, or from the table, and reading a collect, which the trembling parishioner says fits his case wonderfully *when very much explained.* There is no word about *praying* for saint or for sinner; it is the beautiful collect, ever and always. It is not, "Lord, teach us to pray," but, "Show us the fitting collect;" not, "Behold, he prayeth," but, "Hark! he's saying the collect for Quinquagesima." We wish that our friends who believe in the power of prayer would let their hearts flow out freely, trusting the Spirit of God to help their infirmities of thought and speech.

Bishop's Cranworth; or, Rosamond's Lamp. By EMMA MARSHALL. Shaw.

MRS. MARSHALL has the happy art of writing seriously without being dull. This tale deals with the troubles of the noble family at "the Castle," and those of the vicar under the shadow of the castle walls. The plot of the story lies in the return of the *prodigal father* to the all-forgiving son, with the refusal of the elder *sister* to join in the family joy. Our readers will not look for religious teaching in perfect accord with our own; for Mrs. Marshall is a consistent Episcopalian, and sees some things in the "dim religious light" of the church rather than in the cloudless light of the Word.

The Shadow of Nobility. By Mrs. EMMA E. HORNIBROOK. T. Woolmer.

THE story of a daughter forced into a *mariage de convenance* with one of the "nobility," only to find that rank is but a "shadow," and that "society never deals with hearts," much less

with the soul and God. Mrs. Hornibrook's creations are of a very high order, and religious truth pervades all her writings.

Raromi; or, the Maori Chief's Heir. By A. A. FRASER. Tract Society.

INTIMATE knowledge of Maori life and character is evident in every chapter, and the blood-curdling stories of the old chief, Dog's-Ear, and his black and white friends and foes, will be read and re-read by boys, till the book is all dog's-ears. There should have been a glossary of Maori words, and a somewhat smaller demand upon our idea of the possible.

Geoffrey Heywood; or, "The Right Way." By Mrs. COOPER. Religious Tract Society.

THIS is a Scotch story, dealing with a hardly supposable case of conscience, that of a young man confronted with the temptation to retain possession of a large fortune, although he, and *he alone,* had reason to doubt that he was the rightful heir. How he was enabled to overcome the temptation is well told, and the religious teaching is clear and Scriptural; but the story overtaxes our credulity.

All for Number One; or, Charlie Russell's Ups and Downs. A Story for Boys and Girls. By HENRY JOHNSON. Religious Tract Society.

AN amusing, though overdrawn story, of the vain attempt of a low, selfish, petty tradesman, who has "come in" to a hundred thousand pounds, to be a gentleman of great importance, and to train his grandchild Charlie to be what he called "upper-tenish." The real gentility, of kindness of heart and consideration for others, is exemplified in the cook to his swellship, and in a poor little street-singer, "Skylark," whose sayings and doings will please the boys and girls.

Hugh Axe of Hephzibah. By Rev. JOHN BAMFORD. T. Woolmer

THE author of "Father Fervent" and "Elias Power" exhibits both power and fervour in this little book about "Christian citizenship"; which, though it reads just like a story, the writer styles an allegory.

That Boy Jack! A story for Young Folk. By HELEN H. ROGERS. Hogg.

THERE is not much in this story, but it would do a boy good. We like the honest manliness which it sketches.

Dulcibel's Day-Dreams; or, the Grand, Sweet Song. By EMMA MARSHALL. Nisbet and Co.

A PRETTY story of a young girl—of clerical family, of course—who wished to live to purpose, but could find no opportunities in her sleepy little village for the great deeds she was always dreaming of. How she was taught "that all lives can be made rich in service, noble in effort, and rich in the highest gifts," is the lesson of the book.

Humpty-Dumpty's Silver Bells. A Story illustrating the Lord's Prayer. By MARGARET HAYCRAFT. Religious Tract Society.

A LITTLE gem of a story. Poor little "Humpty-Dumpty," if he ever lived, must have been an angel in very strange disguise. It may be that the reading of this pathetic narrative will make at least some human beings more angelic.

The Fairy of Rose Alley. By J. F. HIGGS. Sunday School Union.

FANCY a fairy whose name is Mary! It was only in fancy that Mary was a fairy, for she was a little crippled girl, just the counterpart of "Humpty-Dumpty," only, of course, more angelic, because she was a girl and he was a boy!

Nellie O'Neil. By AGNES C. MAITLAND. Nelson and Sons.

ANY girl who deserves a book will be delighted with this charming story; and if she is not the better for reading it, she does not deserve to have another.

Vera's Trust. By EVELYN EVERETT GREEN. Nelson and Sons.

EXTERNALLY, this book is in keeping with Messrs. Nelsons' high repute; and internally, it is worthy of the gifted authoress. Vera, true to her name, is true to her trust; and in due season restores to its rightful owner the money of which his father had been defrauded, and he rewards her faithfulness by marrying her; and no doubt "they lived happy ever afterwards," though the story does not say so.

The Story of a Cuckoo Clock. By ROBINA F. HARDY. Edinburgh: Oliphant, Anderson, and Ferrier.

THE cuckoo in the clock was always up to time, and so taught a needful lesson to Master Lazybones, who was always late. This little book might be useful to any of that young gentleman's relatives, who may be known to any of our readers.

The Jessamines. By GRACE STEBBING. Sunday School Union.

JESSAMINE BURDON was not at all worthy of such a sweet name as Jessamine, and she was very much of a burden to her friends, until her cross and disagreeable ways gave place to a happier and kinder mood.

Vashti Savage. By SARAH TYTLER. Partridge and Co.

THIS is not the story of the savage Vashti, who refused to obey the commandment of King Ahasuerus; but it is the tale of a gipsy girl, who fled from her brutal father, and was cared for by a kind gentleman who found her. The only name she owned was that of Vashti; so, as a surname, she was called Savage, because of her character. By gentle and loving training she became greatly altered. The story is well told, and the book is nicely got up and capitally illustrated.

Dolly. By M. F. W. Religious Tract Society.

THE writer of "Dolly" entitles it "a quiet story for quiet people." One might do worse than use it for whiling away a quiet half-hour.

Aunt Diana. By ROSA NOUCHETTE CAREY. Religious Tract Society.

A SENSIBLY-WRITTEN story, showing that the rough way may be the right way, and that they who bravely choose the path of duty will find refreshment at the well of blessing.

The Lads of Kingston. A Tale of a Seaport Town. By JAMES CAPES STORY. Partridge and Co.

A LIVELY, likely Yorkshire temperance story, full of sound common sense; especially suitable for young lads.

The Life of Submission, Dependence, and Rest: a Clergyman's Personal Testimony. Marshall Brothers.

WE cannot say that we care much for the pietism of these pages. They are a record of the experience of a good brother who has obtained "a clean heart," in some sense or other, above what he received at his conversion. His life will be the best proof of the truth of his estimate of his own excellent condition. He complains that older brethren do not give him more sympathy: but what if the older brethren think him rather weak, and apt to be carried away with new theories? At any rate, the older believers are not necessarily the least wise, or the most dull. Let the brother receive his sanctification from the Lord by the Spirit, and if he says as little about his own holiness as ever he can, we think it will be a sign that he is doing so. The brother means well, and is, perhaps, quite as good a man as he thinks he is; but, not knowing him, we cannot say. The holiness which we should all aspire after is not quite the same as that which we hear so much about.

The Trinity of Evil: Infidelity, Impurity, Intemperance. By the Rev. Canon WILBERFORCE, M.A. Hodder and Stoughton.

CANON WILBERFORCE hits hard. In each of the three directions in which he turns his gun, he discharges such heavy bolts that he makes all men know that he *will by force* drive out the deadly foe of man. We do not wonder that these lectures are in a third edition; but, as a result, the preface has become a little stale.

The Story of Christian: Life Pictures from "The Pilgrim's Progress." By SAMUEL GREGORY. 2, Castle Street.

BUNYAN is not only instructive himself, but the suggester of instructive teaching to others. Not Bunyan and water, but brief discourses in which the illustrations from the Pilgrim are made use of as aids to thought. Very good reading for Ladies' Working Meetings.

Notes.

OUR publishers, on seeing the likeness of ten years ago which occupied this place at the head of last month's notes, suggested that another should follow representing the man as he is. Here he is, then, thanks to the goodness of the Lord, preserved unto this day, "witnessing both to small and great; saying none other things than those which the prophets and Moses did say should come." It is no small mercy to have enjoyed thirty-five years and a half of successful service over one church, and to have seen the sermons printed week by week during all that period except the first year.

As a general rule rumours and reports are not true, and may be at once dismissed. More and more the daily press craves sensational stories, and hence a supply is forthcoming from the factory of imagination. In general, it is better to let all stories live or die by their own innate truth or falsehood; but, occasionally, it may be as well to speak.

Some reports may need correcting lest any should be misled upon an important point. A congregational minister lately immersed two young believers who saw it to be their duty to be baptized. At their baptism he is reported to have said, "Dr. Davidson sends any one at his church that wants to be baptized to Mr. Spurgeon's Tabernacle, and *I believe* if any of Mr. Spurgeon's people have an infant they would like to have baptized, he sends them to Dr. Davidson." Our good brother may *believe* what he pleases; but he has no facts upon which to base his faith, and it is the reverse of truth. We have never yet met with a baptized believer among our friends who also believed in infant baptism: the two beliefs are at opposite poles. If any one of our members, who are all baptized, could be in so curious a state of mind as to wish to have his infant sprinkled, he would be sure not to tell his Pastor of it; and if he did venture upon such a thing, he would certainly find that no Anabaptism would have him for its accomplice. We do not believe in two baptisms. A man can only be either baptized or buried once. If either of the two baptisms now before us is Scriptural, the other is unscriptural. We would not have any man, for the sake of a supposed charity, act so inconsistently as to promote two baptisms : let him cleave to the one which he believes to be of the Lord's ordaining, but let him not flirt with the other. Trifling with conscience and with the laws of God's house has become far too common in these days. Let each man learn for himself the will of the Lord, and then let him abide by it, and by no means become a partaker in the acts of others when he considers them to be mistaken.

The tithe-collecting difficulty perplexes Parliament, and no one can tell how to dispose of it. Suppose there were no tithes to collect, would not religion be relieved of a scandal, national peace be promoted, and Churchmen be benefited by having the privilege of supporting their own ministers? No evil-disposed person could invent another cause of dissension and strife so productive of ill-will among Christian people as is the compulsory support of a church by people who differ from it. All lovers of true religion should unite in seeking a speedy end of the present grievous state of things. The land will not pay the tithe now that its produce fetches so little money; and, therefore, apart from the question of right or wrong, something will have to be done.

Monday evening, July 29.—Very singular was the scene at the Tabernacle prayer-meeting this evening. The Pastor had requested each friend to bring some article of clothing for the Poor Ministers' Society, and the friends did so with happy alacrity. The great table was piled so high that the Pastor said he could not see over it, and felt like being buried alive; so other tables were filled, and the stair-cases on each side of the pulpit were covered deep from top to bottom. There were coats and capes, trousers and hats, pinafores and petticoats, and all sorts of garments for men, women, and children, to the number of more than six hundred in all. It was a very gracious blend of raiment and reverence, that meeting for prayer.

The meeting was memorable for a speech by Mr. Coles, a negro missionary on his way back to Africa. He showed us the difficulty the missionary has in preaching, since he has to explain to the people the meaning of the words God, sin, soul, &c. And as these ideas are foreign to them, and their language cannot readily express them, it is a labour indeed to make the truth to be understood by them. For instance, to set forth the notion of a soul, Mr. Coles told them that there is a little man inside every man, which looks out of his eyes, and hears through his ears, &c. At death this little man goes to God; and if good, it stops with him; but if bad, the devil drags it down into the fire. The illustration was so given as to make us see the teacher's difficulty far better than if we had read of it in books. Between the prayers, Mr. Chamberlain and Mr. Parker sang like angels. Mr. Scilley, of Orpington, gave instances of the power of the cross to save both rich and poor, careless and despondent. Dr. Peloubet, from America, interested us all by describing this mortal life as a school. Our heavenly Father places us in peculiar conditions, which are advantageous for certain points of knowledge, not to be acquired in any other position. What with the Pastor's talks, the many prayers, and, above all, the sweet presence of the Lord, we said, "Master, it is good to be here."

On *Tuesday, July* 30, Mr. Spurgeon saw friends who wished to join the church. There were several who were brought into our neighbourhood by providential removal from other churches, and there were others who were hardly ready to make an open confession; but there remained enough to rejoice the church with its increase. Some were very special : a lady, educated for the stage, led to seek more enduring pleasures; one who had lived all his life without religion, brought to delight in divine things; two wives, newly led to Jesus, anxious about their husbands; a young gentleman made to weep for sin by the sermon on "Jesus wept," &c.

Friends coming on these days are first seen by one of the staff of elders in attendance, and then pass in to the Pastor. This is essential, for otherwise persons come to sell tea, to ask alms, to get subscriptions for a book in parts, or some other of the endless ways of soliciting help. But as many come as can be seen in the time, and the cry is, "Still they come." The Word seems to be used for conversion with a regularity of abundance, which calls for the adoring gratitude of all who delight to see Jesus glorified by the salvation of his redeemed.

On *Monday evening, August* 5, although it was the Bank Holiday, and many Tabernacle friends were out of town, there was a large attendance at the prayer-meeting. Pastor Bœckmann, of Sweden, gave an account of the work he is trying to do in that country, and spoke of the great usefulness of the Pastor's sermons. Mr. Dunster, who is leaving the College, and settling at Soham, expressed his gratitude for the help he had received from the College, and asked the prayers of the people for his future work. Earnest supplication on his behalf was presented by Brother Clarence Chambers. Our Brother Carter gave some details of the "Pioneer" work which he has been doing in several large towns where no Baptist church existed, or where it had greatly declined. This part of our College and Evangelists' labours has not long been commenced; but it already gives promise of great blessing. Much prayer must be offered that the right men may be selected for the work, and we shall also need the generous help of the Lord's servants in raising the necessary funds for the hire of halls, and the various expenses that must be incurred in connection with such efforts.

Several prayers and hymns were interspersed between these accounts of Christian service, together with appropriate remarks by the Pastor, and gospel solos by Mr. Chamberlain, with choruses in which the congregation joined. Our attention was then turned from home affairs to the foreign field. Pastor Brooks, of Grand Rapids, Michigan, who had assisted the Pastor on the previous day, said that for twenty-three years he had been looking to Mr. Spurgeon and the Tabernacle church, and now that he could actually look upon them, he felt quite overwhelmed. Ever since his conversion, he had been reading the Pastor's sermons, and he could not tell of all the help he had derived from them. He had been on the Continent, and seen many of the marvels of Paris, Rome, &c., but the greatest sight he had witnessed since he left home was the work that was being done by Mr. Spurgeon and the Tabernacle church. This very loving speech did not exalt us above measure, for we made liberal allowance for the warm brotherly love which viewed matters in the light of generous partiality.

China next occupied our thoughts and prayers. In introducing the subject, the Pastor reminded us of Brother Stubbs, of Patna, who asked that, whenever we had rice on the table, we would pray for him; and said that it would be a good thing if we prayed for China every time we drank a cup of tea. He then referred to a letter received that morning from Brother Macoun, who left some months ago for China, and who begged earnestly for many more labourers for that great harvest-field. Mr. George Clarke, who has been labouring there for fourteen years, and who is shortly going back to his loved work, gave us some striking statistics to illustrate the fewness of the missionaries and the vastness of the population amongst which they labour. Speaking of the trials of the work, he said that he had often comforted himself with the words of a Christian soldier, at Woolwich, to an evangelist, whose congregation had been drawn away by a military band, "Go, on, brother, the Father loves to hear about the Son." If the Chinese would not hear about Christ, the Father would be pleased to hear the preacher's testimony to his dear Son. There was much more said at the meeting, for which we have not space; and, truly, it was good to be there. Before closing, the Pastor shook hands with Mr. and Mrs.

Clarke, and their little boy, and Miss Dunn, the daughter of Elder J. T. Dunn, who is going out to labour in connection with the China Inland Mission, and to be married to our Brother Huntley; and after bidding them farewell, in the name of the whole assembly, commended them to the Lord in prayer.

On *Monday, Aug.* 12, Mr. William Olney, at 5.30, invited to tea a number of well-known Christian brethren from all the churches to meet Mr. Spencer Walton, who, with six other friends, is going to South Africa, to form "The Cape General Mission," under the presidency of the beloved Andrew Murray, author of *Abide in Christ,* and other gracious books. At the prayer-meeting which followed, much business was transacted at the throne of grace. First came Mr. Soper, from *Rio,* with pleadings for *Brazil.* He has been for seven years preaching Christ in that great empire. He needs a tent—not a very large one—who will give us one for him? Then came a group of *five friends who had travelled from the South of Russia* to see the Christians of England. They were made the subject of special prayer. They had come all that distance to see Mr. Spurgeon, and the Quakers, and the Salvation Army. Three of them were *Molokani,* or Russian Quakers, and two were baptized believers. Although we could not communicate in their language, we felt union of heart with them in the Lord, and one of the sisters acted as an interpreter. We must pray for Russia. Next came *The North Africa Mission,* for which Dr. Eccles prayed: this mission deserves the generous aid of Christian friends, since it intrudes on no man's foundation, but succours a needy region. Last came *The Cape General Mission,* which promises well. Mr. Spencer Walton is a tried evangelist, sound in the faith, and zealous. His helpers are of the right sort, and they go with large purposes, and complete freedom of action. They will look up our own countrymen, and go to the heathen just as the Lord shall open the way. Dr. Dixon and Dr. Nelson, from the United States, both gave warm-hearted speeches, and kept the meeting alive. Much prayer was offered, and we felt that never was time better spent, or more filled with holy enjoyment.

COLLEGE.—The following students have accepted pastorates:—Mr. F. W. Dunster, at Soham, Cambs.; Mr. A. W. L. Barker, at Emsworth, Hants; and Mr. I. S. Watson, at Syston, Leicestershire. Mr. C. A. Dann sailed on the 16th of August for the Bahamas, to take the place of Mr. Wilshere (of the Baptist Mission), who is obliged for a time to relinquish his work through ill-health.

Mr. T. W. Scamell has removed from Barton Cliff to Ashley, Lymington. Mr. H. W. Childs, of Southend, has sailed for the United States. Mr. Perrins, who lately went to the States, has settled at New London, Huron Co., Ohio.

On *Tuesday, August* 6, the students returned to College after their vacation, and on the following day they assembled at "Westwood." It was a fine day, and the men much enjoyed themselves. Three meetings were held outside the President's study, and addresses were delivered by the President, the tutors, and others, all calculated to excite in the men an enthusiasm for the ministry, and a firm attachment to the old and tried gospel. Our readers are earnestly requested to pray for the College, to which the Editor of *The Sword and the Trowel* devotes so much care, and thought, and time. Oh, that the Lord may raise up many witnesses for his truth in these evil days! Great attempts are made to keep our brethren out of pulpits, but opponents might as well endeavour to keep the sun from shining on the fields.

College Missionary Association. — Mr. Patrick, who went out in January to Tangier, has been greatly blessed in his work there. We think our readers will be interested in the following extracts from a letter recently received from him:—

. "Honoured and dear President, — By yesterday's post I received a letter from the Council of the *North Africa Mission*, asking me to devote myself entirely to work among the Spanish-speaking people of Tangier. I had, for some time, quite expected to be asked to do this, and the Lord's leading has seemed to be so plain that I feel I dare not refuse to do so.

"I came out here fully intending to devote myself entirely to work among the Moors; and, desiring this, I refused many times to take any part in the Spanish meetings that some of the missionaries were holding. In the absence of Dr. Churcher and Mr. Hamilton, I at last consented to conduct a meeting. God blessed the word spoken. Other meetings followed, and men almost daily professed conversion. We felt constrained to start meetings each night, and each night our mission-hall was filled. Then came the persecution from Jews and Jesuits, but our converts have all stood firm. The meetings are again large, and souls are being converted. In this way the Lord has forced me into the work; and now, for a month, I have been preaching seven times a week. God seems to have given me a special power in these meetings, and though all through I have spoken through interpreters, yet I have had great liberty of speech, and great blessing to my own soul. To-day I believe we have from thirty to forty true Christians attending our meetings.

"I believe there are about 15,000 Spanish-speaking people in Tangier, *i.e.*, 5,000 Spaniards, 8,000 Jews, and 2,000 Moors, while in all the coast towns Spanish is being spoken more largely each day.

"So, dear Sir, I write to ask for your consent to give myself entirely up to this work. It isn't what I thought I was coming out for, but I am persuaded it is what the Lord has brought me out for. The work must necessarily be a hard one, but I am persuaded there is great blessing awaiting us."

Mr. Patrick then gives us full particulars of the *café* which he has felt it needful to secure for the proper working of the mission, and closes his letter as follows:—

"I trust that you will be able to say that you feel I am doing the right thing in devoting myself to the Spanish work, and is it too much to hope that another brother may come out this autumn to take up the Arabic work in my place?"

We have consented to Mr. Patrick's wish, and have promised to help in paying the rent of the new premises; and as funds come in, and suitable brethren offer themselves, we shall be glad to extend our operations. We hope soon to be able to give further details of this interesting mission. We have lost none of our interest in the work of the Baptist Missionary Society; but this is a little work which has arisen among ourselves, and we believe that, without intruding upon any other, it will grow. It will certainly do so, if friends think fit to find the means.

Letter from China.—Our late student, Mr. Thomas Macoun, writes most interestingly. He is under the care of the China Inland Mission.

"Shanghai, 17th June, 1889.

"Dear Mr. Spurgeon,—Since my arrival in China, some five months since, I have been at the 'Training Home,' Gan K'ing, in the province of Gan Hull (four hundred miles from the coast), and expect to remain here till the summer is through. The language is my present Hill Difficulty, but so far I do not object to it; in fact, I rather like it. I fancy it is quite as good a mental discipline as are the dead languages we studied in College!

"Gan K'ing is a delightful place from the point of view of its being really a 'home,' where we are gradually introduced to heathenism. As yet, I am afraid, we know nothing of 'missionary hardships'; but, as the Chinese say, 'Man-man-tih' (wait a while). From the point of view of the cross, the city of Gan K'ing is an exceedingly sad place. The natives are kind, enquiring, and not by any means unlovable— *i.e.*, more so than sinners at home. As far as I can find out, they are much the same. They do not *flock* to hear the gospel: the 'natural mind' in China is quite as opposed to the things of God as the 'natural mind' elsewhere. Praise God, however, the gospel is quite as well adapted for the Chinese as for ourselves at home. As I daily meet these Chinamen, I cannot help feeling that we, in England, have been, and are, intensely selfish and disobedient in leaving this tremendously populous nation all these years in such horrible darkness. Oh, it is sad to see them worshipping the spirits of their ancestors, not because there is no God to be worshipped, but they know nothing of him! I think it argues very poorly for the worshippers of Jesus at home that such a thing should be possible in this advanced stage of the world's history; and it certainly makes one think they do not believe very much in Jesus, or they would do more to spread the knowledge of him in this and other heathen lands. It *would* rejoice my heart if I knew half the men at College now were coming into the mission field. At Gan K'ing a large native house is being built for the accommodation of something like fifty men, who can all be here studying at the same time, so there will be plenty of room in case twenty or thirty men should come from the College in the coming autumn. At present there are seventeen men in ' the home,' besides Mr. and Mrs. Wood, who are at the head of it. Amongst the number there are two grocers; two clerks (one of them studied in T. C. Dublin for the C. I. ministry, but got put right on the question of baptism before his ordination took place); one commercial traveller, and one wholesale warehouseman; one apothecary; one barrister (an Oxford M.A.); one architect (who is building house already alluded to); one solicitor (formerly in practice near London); one Y. M. C. A. secretary; one doctor (L. R. C. P. and S., &c.); one *lay assistant* (Ch. of E.); another barrister (at least, before he was ' called ' he heard God's call to China, so was not ' called' by man); and, with two men from the Pastors' College the list is complete. You will see by this what kind of men are *at present* learning the language in ' the home.'

" Brother Huntley is doing good work with his medicine. One patient he has at present had his leg fearfully scalded '(almost the entire leg), but is coming round nicely, through the little skill H. was able to pick up, in a few weeks, at the London Hospital. The patient's father had covered the boy's leg entirely with mud, and for more than a month the poor boy suffered intensely—they are very ignorant of the simplest rudiments of medicine and surgery.

" China is a fearful place; and if Jesus Christ is not everything to a man, he had better stay at home.

" I hope, by the next time I write, to be able to tell you something about my location. So far, my experience of the C. I. M. has been everything in its favour; and I think if the men at College understood its principles and practices better, they would, many of them, come to China through it!

" With warm Christian love, hoping, dear Sir, you are very well,

" I remain, dear Mr. Spurgeon,
" Yours very faithfully,
" Thos. Macoun."

Evangelists.—Mr. J. E. K. Studd sends us the following cheering account of *Messrs.*

Fullerton and Smith's services at the Polytechnic, Regent Street:—

" My dear Sir,—It is with much pleasure that I enclose you a cheque for £30, as a thank-offering for the services lately held here by your evangelists, Messrs. Fullerton and Smith. They have spent the last four Saturdays and Sundays with us; and the services throughout have not only been most enjoyable and well-attended, but we have had the added pleasure of seeing many young men and young women deciding for Christ, and confessing him before their friends. Last night, being the closing one of the mission, our hall was not nearly large enough to contain those who wished to attend; and at the close of this service, when those who had decided for Christ during the past month were asked to signify it by standing up, quite a number did so, and many more joined them when an invitation was given to those who wished to decide the question to do so.

" You will, I know, be glad to hear that we are also holding meetings for the converts every Wednesday evening, and these have been steadily increasing in numbers, until last Wednesday, the converts, together with one or two Christian workers, must have numbered over a hundred."

Pastor T. A. Carver writes concerning *Mr. Harmer's* mission at Dartford:—" We were delighted with our dear brother's visit. He preached the gospel with very great clearness and power, and is, I am sure, the very man for the work in which he is engaged. The time of year was very much against us; but, on the whole, the services were well attended, and there was a holy, solemn feeling pervading the whole of the meetings."

Messrs. Fullerton and Smith, and most of our other evangelists, have been resting during the past month. They are now all resuming work for the autumn and winter. Any brethren who desire their services should apply at once, as there are not many vacant dates.

During September, Messrs. Fullerton and Smith will probably conduct services in Paris, Mr. Burnham will be in the hopgardens in Kent, Mr. Harmer will be at Stonebroom and Burton-on-Trent, and Mr. Harrison at Mr. Charrington's Hall, Mile End Road.

Many of our readers will be interested in the resolution passed by the church at Auckland, at a meeting specially convened for the purpose of taking into consideration the letter from Pastor T. Spurgeon. Our son feels that he must rest a while. He was never strong, and he feels weary and depressed. May the Lord direct his way! The resolution is as follows:—

Resolution passed at Church Meeting.

" In accepting from the Pastor the notice of his resignation, the church desires to express:—

"1. Its heartfelt sorrow and regret at the continuance of physical weakness and ill-health which the Pastor conscientiously believes precludes him continuing the various obligations of the Pastorate. The church tenders him its affectionate sympathy in this, and his other troubles, and in the bereavement he has lately suffered, and prays that divine comfort may be sent, and the great Physician vouchsafe unto him increased strength and good health; so that he may be spared to labour yet many years in the Lord's vineyard.

"2. The church most gratefully records its thanks to its great Head for the abundant success that has attended the preaching of the gospel by the Pastor during his eight years' ministry in this city. God's people have been built up, and strengthened, and edified, and large numbers have been won for Christ and the church. We earnestly thank the Pastor for his untiring devotion to the limit of his strength in all he has done in the various departments of our church work, and for the good that has been accomplished under his care and oversight.

"3. We desire to recognize the most earnest desire of the Pastor at all times to spread out before the people the truths of the Word of God pure and unadulterated, and to preach the gospel of the grace of God in all its fulness and freeness, so as to win souls for Christ the Lord.

"4. There are still some six months during which we shall be privileged with the continuance of our Pastor's presence and labours. The church expresses its determination to uphold his hands, and to accord him a continuance of its affectionate sympathy and love."

COLPORTAGE ASSOCIATION.—During the past month three new districts have been opened, and enquiries have also been made in reference to several others, which it is hoped may be started shortly.

The Surrey and Middlesex Baptist Association has guaranteed £40 a year for a colporteur, and the President, C. H. Spurgeon, £40 for a second, who are stationed respectively at Egham and Sunbury, where good results are expected.

The Western Association has also guaranteed £40 a year, and a colporteur has been sent to Chard, to work under the direction of the local Association.

The attention of the readers of *The Sword and the Trowel* is again requested to the special offer made in the August number to encourage a still further extension of the work.

In the meantime, our friends will not forget that the General Fund will need sustaining. The Secretary, W. Corden Jones, will gladly correspond with any friends wishing further information. Address, Colportage Association, Temple Street, Southwark, London, S.E.

PERSONAL NOTE.—One of our College brethren writes:—

"My dear Mr. Spurgeon,—You will see, by the enclosed card, that my dear uncle has gone home. Your sermons, and *Morning by Morning*, and *Evening by Evening*, were greatly used of God in his conversion; and I promised to let you know that he was happily delivered from the doubts and fears that had so long troubled him, and brought into assured belief in the Lord Jesus as his Saviour, by your delightful sermon on, 'With His Stripes we are Healed' (No. 2,000). After hearing it read to him, he said, 'I can never despair again.' We are all very grateful to you for the blessing your works have been to him."

Baptisms at Metropolitan Tabernacle.—August 1, six.

Pastors' College, Metropolitan Tabernacle.

Statement of Receipts from July 16th to August 14th, 1889.

	£	s.	d.		£	s.	d.
Contribution from Baptist Church, Bacup, per Pastor E. A. Tydeman	1	1	0	Mrs. Rathbone Taylor	2	10	0
Contribution from Higham Hill Baptist Chapel, per Mr. T. Cox	0	10	0	An afflicted missionary in India	1	0	0
Miss Jephs	1	1	0	Mansion House Mission, Camberwell	0	12	0
Mr. John Masters	3	0	0	Mr. Levi Haigh	0	5	0
Dora, Isabel, and Grace Walker	0	5	0	From Scotland	25	0	0
Mr. R. Greenwood	0	5	0	Miss Katie Lockett	0	10	0
Mr. John Smith	1	0	0	Mr. W. Fowler	50	0	0
Mrs. H. Keevil	5	0	0	Mr. D. A. McDonald	0	5	0
R. P.	10	0	0	D. L. A., Aberdeen	0	10	0
Mr. Edward Ford Duncanson	50	0	0	Mr. and Mrs. Watts	0	10	0
"Ebenezer," an old friend	0	10	0	Mr. C. F. Allison	20	0	0
"The Freeman" Newspaper Company dividend	0	8	0	Weekly Offerings at Met. Tab.:—			
J. S.	5	0	0	July 21	28	14	4
Mr. R. J. Beecliff	0	5	0	,, 28	32	0	0
A tenth, from Ipswich, less 2d. paid for postage	0	9	10	Aug. 4	28	14	6
Mrs. Watcham	0	10	0	,, 11	10	5	0
Mr. J. Wilson	1	9	6		99	13	10
					£281	10	2

Stockwell Orphanage.

Statement of Receipts from July 16th to August 14th, 1889.

	£	s.	d.
Gershom	0	1	0
Collected by Mrs. Webb	3	0	0
Collected by Miss J. Cowie ...	1	3	0
Jack, South Lambeth	0	2	0
W. W., Kettering	0	2	6
From Mr. Charlesworth's letter-box ...	0	2	0
Mr. C. Ibberson	0	2	6
Mr. W. J. Stockwell	0	2	0
Miss B. Lewis	1	0	0
Mr. B. A. J. Paxton	0	10	0
Miss E. Moses	0	2	6
Mr. H. A. Gribbon	1	0	0
The Netherlands	0	16	0
Stamps, Anon.	0	1	0
Orphanage boxes at Tabernacle gates	0	15	0
Collected by Mr. George Yates... ...	0	4	0
Collected by Mrs. Ansell...	0	7	3
Collected by Mrs. S. T. Barrah	0	8	0
Sale of S. O. tracts	0	1	0
Mr. John Noble, for Stockwell Orphan-			
age day in the country...	1	0	0
Parsons Heath School, per Mr. H.			
Letch	0	11	0
Mr. J. Parkinson	1	0	0
Mr. E. K. Stace	0	10	0
Collected by Mrs. Perry	0	10	0
Mrs. Larlham	2	2	0
Miss Scoles	2	10	0
Mr. John Masters	3	0	0
Mr. George Armstrong, per Mr. Joseph			
Corrie	2	0	0
Mr. Edward Webber	0	10	0
Mrs. Scott	0	7	0
Mrs. Latta, per Mr. A. Allan	0	10	0
Scotch note from Aberdeen ,... ...	1	0	0
In loving memory of Pattie	0	13	6
Executor of the late Miss A. G. Birt ...	5	0	0
Mr. Charles Mackson ... ,... ...	0	5	0
In memoriam	1	1	0
Herne Hill communion collection, per			
Pastor F. Carter	2	2	6
Collected by Mrs. R. C. Allen	0	12	0
Mr. R. Greenwood...	0	2	0
Mrs. Browne	10	0	0
Miss Smither	1	0	0
Executor of the late Miss A. Forret ...	2)	0	0
A widow's mite, Dundee...	θ	5	0
Mr. E. Sparrow	0	0	0
In memory of a friend	1	3	0
Sabbath morning children's service,			
Moray House, Edinburgh	2	5	0
Miss Shaw	⅟	0	0
Mr. W. Woolidge	0	10	0
Mr. Lawrence Shepherd	0	10	0
Mr. F. Ansell	0	3	8
Lilla, Bertie, Jessie, Arthur, and			
Winnie Nash	1	18	6
A sermon-reader	0	5	0
Mr. J. Crocker	3	0	0
Mr. N. J. Baxter	1	0	0
Mr. R. Beattie	0	10	0
Mr. F. Hallett	0	5	0
Mr. S. Cornborough	5	0	0
Mr. and Mrs. F. Sellar	2	2	0
R. P.	10	0	0

	£	s.	d.
Collected by Miss A. H. Rust ...	0	6	0
Collected by Master Herries	0	4	4
Rookery children's box	0	18	0
Mrs. Sole, per Miss M. Porter	0	5	0
Mr. T. F. Bromham	0	2	6
The late Miss Porter	1	0	0
Mr. H. J. Atkinson, M.P., per Pastor			
J. A. Spurgeon	10	0	0
R. H. W.		10	6
Mr. J. P. Duggart...		2	6
Mrs. Hopkins	0	10	0
For conscience sake	0	2	0
Executor of the late Miss Catherine			
Rogers	80	0	2
C. B. M.	5	0	0
Mr. G. Smith	0	0	0
"Ebenezer," an old friend	0	1	0
Contributions, after services held by			
Messrs. McPherson and Smale, at			
Brora, N.B.	1	16	6
Mrs. Cripps	0	5	0
Mrs. Tyson	1	0	0
G. N., Edinburgh	1	0	0
Mr. Robert Morgan	0	12	9
Executor of the late Mr. Thomas			
Jenkins	22	10	0
J. S. ... ...)	5	0	0
Sandwich, per Bankers	2	2	0
G. H.	0	2	6
F. G. B., Chelmsford	0	2	6
Mr. A. More	0	10	0
Mr. J. Wilson	0	10	0
Mr. T. B. Trotter	0	18	9
Mrs. Rathbone Taylor	2	10	0
Welsh minister's wife	0	2	6
Mrs. M. D. Macleay	2	0	0
Mr. Robert Jones	1	1	0
Mrs. Renshaw	1	0	0
Mr. Edward Chew	0	10	0
T. P., Warrington...	0	7	0
Mr. Bartlett...	1	1	0
The Misses Horton	2	0	0
Mr. William Burnett	1	16	0
A servant near Forres, Scotland ...	0	2	0
A thankoffering	0	10	0
Miss T. A. Urquhart	1	0	0
Miss Pentelow	0	5	0
Mr. S. H. Dauncey	0	2	6
Miss Drake	0	5	6
Mr. H. C. Bridgman	0	2	0
Mr. M. Jones	0	2	6
Rev. Charles Miller	0	10	0
Mr. J. Wickham	1	0	0
Misses E. and J. Foster's box ...	0	15	0
Mrs. M. Horn	0	2	6
Mr. J. Robson	0	5	0
Miss M. Williams	0	2	6
J. B. C.	1	0	0
Mr. and Mrs. Watts	0	10	0
Mr. F. Duffell	0	5	0
Executor of the late Miss Mary Dunning	18	0	0
	£270	10	11

List of Presents, per Mr. Charlesworth, from July 16th, to August 14th, 1889.—PROVISIONS:—6 lbs. Tea, Mr. J. Cooper; 1 Cake, Miss Dawson; 1 New Zealand Sheep, Mr. A. S. Haslam; a quantity of Fruit, Mr. W. E. Vinson; 2 sacks Cabbages, Mr. H. Watts; 1 churn Milk, Mr. C. Harris; 90 gallons Milk, Mr. R. Higgs.

BOYS' CLOTHING:—2 Flannel Shirts, Mrs. Coath; 1 Vest, Mrs. Wilkin.

GIRLS' CLOTHING:—70 Articles and 1 Dress, The Ladies' Working Meeting at the Tabernacle, per Miss Higgs; 43 Garments, The Fleet Baptist Chapel Working Society, per Mrs. Aylett; 54 Bathing Dresses, Miss Hadland; 1 dozen Aprons, Miss Descroix.

GENERAL:—1 box of Shells, Mr. T. McMahon; 2 loads of Firewood, Mr. J. Cooper; 14 Dolls,

Miss L. Adams; 14 Fancy Articles, Miss Dawson; 1 Scrap Book, A friend; 2 dozen Comb Bags and 2 dozen Iron Holders, Miss Descroix.

ERRATUM:—August "Sword and Trowel," page 465, Mr. Everett £1 0s. 5d. *should be* "Robert Street Sunday and Ragged School," per Mr. Everett.

Colportage Association.

Statement of Receipts from July 16th to August 14th, 1889.

Subscriptions and Donations for Districts.

	£	s.	d.
Wendover and neighbourhood, per Mr. J. E. Taylor	10	0	0
Orpington District, per Mrs. Allison's Bible-class	2	17	6
Kettering, per Mr. W. Meadows, sen.	10	0	0
Stratford-on-Avon District	7	10	0
Mr. John Cory, for Castleton, Cardiff, and Penrhicweiber	20	0	0
Mr. Richard Cory, for Cardiff and Penrhicweiber	10	0	0
Newbury District	10	0	0
Mr. D. White, for Uxbridge	20	0	0
South Devon Congregational Union	10	0	0
Somers Town, per Miss Gritfith	10	0	0
Borstall District	20	0	0
Surrey and Middlesex Baptist Association	15	8	4
Southern Association	50	0	0

	£	s.	d.
Cambridge Association	10	0	0
Weston Turville Baptist Church	1	5	0
	£207	0	10

Subscriptions and Donations to the General Fund:—

	£	s.	d.
Mr. John Masters	3	0	0
Executor of the late Miss A. G. Birt	5	0	0
R. P.	10	0	0
Mr. A. Todd	0	5	0
Mrs. Watcham	0	10	0
Mr. Henry Wakeling	3	11	6
Mr. and Mrs. Watts	0	5	0
Annual Subscriptions:—			
Mr. and Mrs. J. Brown	1	1	0
Pastor J. A. Spurgeon	0	10	6
	£24	3	0

Society of Evangelists.

Statement of Receipts from July 16th to August 14th, 1839.

	£	s.	d.
Thankoffering for Messrs. Fullerton and Smith's services at Beulah Baptist Chapel, Thornton Heath	3	3	0
Mr. William Donaldson	5	0	0
Mrs. Robert Wilson	2	0	0
Mr. Charles Carter	5	0	0
R. P.	10	0	0
Thankoffering for Messrs. Fullerton and Smith's services at the Polytechnic, Regent Street	30	0	0

	£	s.	d.
Mrs. Wightman	1	0	0
J. S.	5	0	0
Mr. John Currie, per Mr. J. Louson	1	0	4
Mr. Norton	5	0	0
Miss T. A. Urquhart	1	0	0
Thankoffering from a mother	5	0	0
	£73	3	4

For General Use in the Lord's Work.

Statement of Receipts from July 16th to August 14th, 1889.

	£	s.	d.
"Beauty for ashes"	6	0	0
Mrs. Hayes	5	0	0
Mrs. H. Keevil	5	0	0
A sermon-reader	0	4	6
	£16	4	6

HOP-PICKERS' MISSION.—Mr. Bettison, £3; J. S., Edinburgh, £2; Mrs. Watts, £1; Mr. Hopperton, 5s.—£6 5s.

Friends sending presents to the Orphanage are earnestly requested to let their names or initials accompany the same, or we cannot properly acknowledge them; and also to write to Mr. Charlesworth, Stockwell Orphanage, Clapham Road, London.

Subscriptions will be thankfully received by C. H. Spurgeon, "Westwood," Beulah Hill, Upper Norwood. Should any sums sent before the 13th of last month be unacknowledged in this list, friends are requested to write at once to Mr. Spurgeon. Post Office and Postal Orders should be made payable at the Chief Office, London, to C. H. Spurgeon; and Cheques and Orders should all be crossed.

THE

SWORD AND THE TROWEL.

OCTOBER, 1889.

The Coming Day.

A SERMON, DELIVERED APRIL 18TH, 1855, BY C. H. SPURGEON,
PASTOR OF NEW PARK STREET CHAPEL, SOUTHWARK,
AT THE INDEPENDENT CHAPEL, WIVENHOE, NEAR COLCHESTER.*

"The night is far spent, the day is at hand."—Romans xiii. 12.

HESE are short words, but full of meaning. He who lieth tossing on his weary couch at midnight is glad when he seeth the coming morn. The warder on the castle top, who all night long keeps sentinel with the stars, rejoiceth when he finds that "the night is far spent, and the day is at hand." "The morning cometh" is a gospel to a fainting spirit.

I shall speak, first, of *the night of the heart;* secondly, of *the night of the world;* and thirdly, of *the night of our existence as to time.*

First, THE NIGHT OF THE HEART. The heart is a little world in itself; it has its days and nights, its summers and winters. I shall speak of that dark night through which the Christian has to pass when conviction throws its dark shadow over his heart. When the Lord begins to deal with a sinner, he takes away all his boasted self-righteousness, and often brings him into such a low and desponding state that he loathes his very existence. I do not believe in a man's being born again without pain. Many of us passed through great distress and affliction before we knew that our sins were pardoned. For months I wished I had been born a dog instead of a man, whilst my sins made midnight in my soul. It is not every convert who has to go through the same burning fiery furnace, but every person has, in a

---

* We met with the following report of a sermon preached by us more than thirty-four years ago. It was taken down by a local reporter, and has remained buried among our old papers. It may be viewed as a curiosity of youthful preaching, and therefore we print it.

measure, to pass through the dark night of conviction. We must all feel that godly sorrow which needeth not to be repented of; otherwise we shall know nothing of the saving power of Christ. There may be persons here present who are passing through the state I have just mentioned. You are beginning to feel a night in your heart. It was all light a little while ago, when you felt you were as good as other people; and if I had called you a sinner, you would have said, " and so is everybody else"; but you did not consider yourself much to blame. Now you feel that all the Bible says of you is true, and that you are worse than you could have imagined. You fear that you will be lost for ever: you feel yourself to be so vile. Yet your self-despair and bitter grief are not evidences of eternal darkness, but the rather they are tokens that " the night is far spent, the day is at hand." I would say to every poor creature groaning under corruption, and bowed down with heaviness by reason of sin, " The night is far spent, the day is at hand."

You say, " How am I to know this?" I will give you three or four signs by which you may tell when your night is nearly over, and your day is coming. When your night is far spent, *it is the darkest with you.* They tell us that the darkest part of the night is that which precedes the dawning of the day. I know it is so in the heart. Are you getting worse than you were? Do you feel yourselves more deeply lost than ever? Man's extremity is God's opportunity. Therefore, despair not, thou trembling one. Say not that God will not have mercy upon you. When you are cast down, God will help you up. If you are brought down to self-despair, now is the day of deliverance. When the iron enters into thy soul, then shalt thou come forth from the prison-house. Some have gone so far in despair, that they have been ready to destroy themselves; and yet they have been saved. I beseech you, never listen to the suggestion of the foul spirit, who is both a liar and a murderer: keep your hands off your own life, and believe that the despair which now makes existence itself a burden is meant to drive you to the Saviour.

Another sign that " the night is far spent, the day is at hand," is when' *your candle is burning out.* I was hesitating one night about a text, and I sat up late, when I noticed that my candle was dying down, and flickering in the socket; then these words forcibly struck me as most appropriate, " The night is far spent, the day is at hand"! If I were to question the people of Wivenhoe as to their spiritual state and condition, they would probably say, " We are as good as other people. We pay twenty shillings in the pound, and hope to go to heaven." What is this but trusting to your own righteousness? Have you not discovered that, though you may be as good as other people, you will not be measured by them, but by the standard of the Bible. If you have found out your true condition, your candle is not quite so bright as you thought it was; in fact, it is burning low. Once your character shone like the stars ; but now its glory has departed, and your own esteem is lost in darkness. Is the candle of your righteousness burned out ? If so, " the night is far spent, the day is at hand "; and it will not be long before you will rejoice with God's people.

Another sign by which you may tell when the morning is coming, is *you will see the morning star.* The morning star! What is that? Jesus Christ is the Morning Star! Poor sinner! hast thou had a glimpse of Jesus? Hast thou had a sight of the bleeding Saviour? If you have seen the Morning Star, the day has come. That man who puts his trust in Jesus is saved. The gospel is simply, "Look unto me, and be ye saved, all the ends of the earth." There is nothing to do but look; look, and be saved. I lately saw a fine picture representing Moses lifting up the serpent in the wilderness. He held up the brazen serpent with one hand, and pointed to it with the other, and cried to the wounded Israelites, "Look! look! and live." A poor man lay before him with his arms encircled with serpents; but as he was looking at the brazen serpent, the venomous reptiles were falling off him. Another man was trying, with all his might, to untwist the serpents which had fastened around his body; but they were twisting themselves around him all the tighter for his efforts. A poor mother was holding an infant in her arms over the tops of people's heads, to let it see the brazen serpent, whilst she was gazing at it most earnestly herself. O mother, hold up your child to let it look to the cross, for there is life for your child as well as for you! It is "look," my brethren. Have you seen enough of Christ to rely upon his virtue and merits? Can you put your trust in his power? Can you venture to repose wholly upon him? If you can, "the night is far spent, the day is at hand."

In the country, we can tell when the morning cometh *by the twittering of the birds around our window.* When little-faith cries, "cheer up, cheer up," and faith sings its carol, and love gives forth its note, the morning has come. The devil has been a liar from the beginning, and is so to-night, for he tells you that you are hopelessly lost in darkness. Tell him, no; you have a little hope yet, and will have more by-and-by, for "the night is far spent, the day is at hand." I fear there are some here who no more understand what I am saying than if I spoke to them in an unknown tongue. With all solemnity, let me tell you that, if you have never been convinced of sin, of righteousness, and of judgment to come—if you have never been ploughed in conscience by the Spirit, never wounded by the sword of the Lord, you have neither part nor lot in this matter, and are in the gall of bitterness and the bonds of iniquity. May God, in his mercy, send you a night of darkness, that you may long for a morning with Jesus! "The evening and the morning were the first day"; and if you have no evening, no morning will come to you. With this part of the subject I have done.

Secondly, THE NIGHT OF THE WORLD. O poor world! thou hast had a long, long night since the time when mother Eve stretched out her hand, and plucked the fruit of the tree.

> Oh, what a fall was there, my brethren!
> Then you, and I, and all of us, fell down,
> While sin and Satan triumphed over us!

From that moment the sun of earth's true light was quenched, and its heaven was veiled in darkness. Since that time darkness has covered the earth, and thick darkness the people. We see in various directions Romanism, Mahommedanism, and Paganism in their thousand forms,

making night hideous. It is enough to make a Christian weep tears of
blood to think how long this world's night has lasted. He who feels
aright will feel the deepest woe at heart when he thinks of the sad consequences to his fellow-creatures of these ages of midnight. Since the
days of Noah, how many millions of men have been swept into eternity
without hope! O night of sin, dark thou art! But my text says, "The
night is far spent, the day is at hand." Let us hope that the night of
the world is nearly spent, and that a glorious day is dawning. The
Psalmist tells us of the beasts of the forest, that "The sun ariseth,
they gather themselves together, and lay them down in their dens.
Man goeth forth unto his work and to his labour until the evening."
    These are two signs which show us that the day is coming. *The beasts
are lying down.* The Church of Rome has, in many places, lost its
former power : it has no such sway as it had before the Reformation.
It may roar as it pleases, but its power is broken wherever the gospel
is faithfully preached. It can make no progress where there is light ;
and to me it seems to be making for its den. Soon, by God's command,
the angel will cast the millstone into the flood, and Babylon the great
shall be fallen.*
    Once Mahommedanism could have caused ten thousand scimitars to
flash from their scabbards, and strike deep for the false prophet ; but now
Islam is as a wolf which would raven if it could ; but its teeth are drawn.
Where are the gods of the heathen ? Are they not falling ? True,
Juggernaut may still stand up, but not in its former honour. The
beasts are hastening to their lairs. Take courage, Christians, for "the
night is far spent, the day is at hand," and the latter-day glory will
speedily come !
    The church is assuredly going forth to her labour. There never was
a time when God's church was doing more than now, although it is still
doing little enough. Christians have too often been a lazy set, and the
conduct of some of them is enough to make observers infidels. I
recollect hearing of a colloquy between an infidel and a Christian minister,
who were in the constant habit of passing each other. "Do you preach
the gospel ? " asked the infidel, one day, of the Christian. "I do," replied the latter. "And do you believe there is a hell ? " "Most certainly I do," rejoined the Christian. "Then how is it," said the infidel,
" that you have been in the habit of seeing me every day for many years,
and have never once warned me of it ? " What a question to answer !
Might it not be put to some of you ? We have a great deal of profession, but where is the power of religion ? Think of the days of
Whitefield and Wesley ; there were giants in those days ; twenty
modern Christians tied up in a bundle would not make one of them.
Dealing with Christian professors in masses, have we not reason to be
disgusted with them, and, most of all, with ourselves ? Yet the church
was never more active than now ; and, save in apostolic times, never
was more accomplished. Fifty years ago, where were our Missionary
Societies, our Sunday-schools, Ragged-schools, Tract Societies, and Bible
Societies ? There were but faint foreshadowings of them. It was a happy

---

* We should hardly speak in this fashion now. Romanism is crippled, but the
essential doctrines of Popery are spreading in the Church of England, and elsewhere.

day when the sun began to shine, and saints began to quit their couches, and go forth to serve their Lord. Blessed is the prophecy which lies within foreign missions. Our Sabbath-schools are also most hopeful signs. I am no fortune-teller, neither do I profess, like some popular preachers, to predict the end of the world, or to know the date of the second coming of our Lord. There are so many opinions about it that I dare not venture a new one ; but I do venture to hope that the general activity of the church of God is a sign that the day of the Lord is drawing nigh. There are many other hopeful signs. Christian people are working together, and more unity is seen. The church is awaking, and we hope it cannot be long ere travailing Zion shall bring forth her children. Oh, that the nations of the earth may bow before Jesus, and rejoice in his marvellous light ! " The night is far spent, the day is at hand."

In a happy, hopeful frame of mind, we may feel like the Greek soldiers returning from the Persian wars, when at last they beheld the sea which washed the shores of their beloved country. They clapped their hands, and, with loud voices, cried, " The sea ! the sea ! " I see the waters of that great sea of glory which will spread from pole to pole. I hope to live to see Christ in his glory yet upon the earth, and to hear the song, " The kingdoms of this world have become the kingdoms of our God, and of his Christ." May revolving years' prove that we are right in the hope that " the night is far spent, the day is at hand " !

If I had time to-night, I would give you three or four proofs of the fulfilment of the prophecies, and show you that the glories of the latter day are hastening on. The prophecies of God are the figures upon the clock of time. In the times of our Lord a star pointed out the place of his nativity ; and now a star of promise may be seen moving towards the hour of his glory. If you are a reader of the prophecies, and a watcher of events, you will be apprehensive that the Lord is coming quickly. "The night is far spent, the day is at hand." Cast your eyes over the world, and in every country you will see stars of hope. When we look at China, we cannot help saying, " Verily, the night is far spent, the day is at hand." Keep on with your gifts, and labours, and prayers, and hopes. Although the vision tarry, it must come at last.*

Thirdly, THE NIGHT OF OUR EXISTENCE IN THIS DYING WORLD IS FAR SPENT, and the day is at hand. In a certain sense, while we live upon this earth, we are all in the night. This time-state is, comparatively, darkness. Here we have nights of sickness, care, trial, and weariness. This life is, indeed, to many, a dreary night. Still, it is not altogether night, for—

> " The men of grace have found
> Glory begun below."

This world is a howling wilderness to those who go howling through it ; but the wilderness and the solitary place rejoice and blossom as

---

* To the ungodly the day of the Lord will be darkness, and not light. The signs of the Lord's coming which we would now mention lie rather in the deepening darkness than in any growing light. This is a deep subject, for it is not for us to know the times and the seasons ; but yet there are reasons for cheering expectation.

the rose when faith is in full exercise. The believer is happy; but still, as compared with the glory to be revealed hereafter, his present life is a night. The night with many is far spent, and the day is at hand. May I not say to many a grey-headed sire, "Brother, thy night is far spent, and thy day is at hand"? I am afraid that, to some, the grey head, instead of being a crown of glory, is only a fool's cap. I once heard Mr. Jay say that, if a man had lived sixty or seventy years, and not loved Jesus, nor made his heaven secure, to call him a fool was to call him by his right name. I recollect reading of a certain fool who was kept in a nobleman's palace, and because he was so clever, his lordship gave him a walking-stick, and told him that whenever he found a bigger fool than himself, he was to give him that stick. Some time after, his lordship was taken dangerously ill, and calling the fool to his bed-side, he said, "I am going to die." "And what provision have you made for your long journey?" said the fool. "None at all," said his master. "Have you a home in the other country?" asked the fool. "No," replied his lordship. "Then take this stick: whenever I go a journey, I make provision for it." I tell you, friends, if your silver locks are not a crown of glory, they accuse you of gross folly. If you are saved in the Lord, I would willingly change places with you, because you are nearer to the eternal day; but if you are not in Christ, I feel a trembling compassion for you. To die in the Lord is sweet; but to die without hope, how terrible! May you all be ready for the eternal morning!

To certain others "the night is far spent, the day is at hand," not because of age, but because of illness. She whose cheek is blanched with fell disease, upon whose face there comes the hectic flush, the faint memory of health; she has the token of the rising sun, if she be the Lord's daughter. Glory shines in those eyes. She is melting away into the eternal. To her "the night is far spent, the day is at hand." He who has long nursed a cancer near his heart, or whose languid frame shows that death has marked him for its own, if he be a believer, may congratulate himself upon the speedy coming of the glorious morrow. But let us all look to ourselves, my friends, and recollect that, if we are Christians, we are nearer to the land of the unfading day than we may think. O man, dost thou think that thy bones are iron, and thy ribs steel? No, thou art dust, and unto dust thou shalt return. Perhaps before another week has tried us, we may have entered upon the endless Sabbath! Young as we are, we may have passed beyond the region of clouds and gloom before another year begins. How bright will be the day! Oh, if we could see a day in heaven! It is a day at which the sun might turn pale with envy. A day with Jesus—what felicity! "There shall be no night there"—no night of fear, no night of sorrow, no night of death. There they neither see mattock, nor shroud, nor coffin, nor hearse. Let us rejoice that every hour shortens the night, and hastens on the day. Let us triumph in the prospect of life's new morning. "The night is far spent, the day is at hand."

With some of you, your present night is far spent, and no morning is coming! Would to God that this were not so! Must I, my Lord, at last speak like Boanerges, when I would sooner be a Barnabas? Must I close with anathemas? Must I speak to those who love not the Lord

Jesus? Help me, O Lord, to speak with power! Some of you may expect no day when you die, but a dark and endless night. You may die in a moment! O sinners, you are standing over the mouth of hell upon a single plank, and that plank is rotten! You are hanging over a yawning gulf, by a single rope, and the strands of that rope are snapping! You are in awful danger—in danger of eternal destruction—and yet you make mirth! You will go away to-night, and the wind will blow away from you what I have said; and every warning will be forgotten. But, mark my words, the hour will come when you and I shall meet again. You say, "When shall we meet again?" Beware of the judgment!

At the bar of God I shall confront you; before the judgment-seat of Christ I shall meet you. The thought staggers me! I shall have to stand in the witness-box against your souls, and say, "I warned them, but they would not hear. I bade them fly to Jesus, but they refused." If I am unfaithful you will lay your blood at my door, and I shall sink with you to well-deserved perdition. I cannot bear it! If you are lost, it shall not be for want of calling upon you to repent of your sins, and to believe in Jesus for salvation. It shall not be for want of telling you that the wages of sin is death, but the gift of God is eternal life through Jesus Christ our Lord. Drunkard, is thy cup so sweet that thou wilt drain it to the dregs? O thou filthy man, is there anything so sweet in thy lasciviousness as to make thee barter away thy soul and heaven for ever? O thou miser, idolizing thy gold, is it more precious than the bliss of heaven? And thou, young man, without a thought of God, will you venture thus to die? Will you dare to die without a refuge to flee to in the great and terrible day of the Lord? "Turn ye, turn ye, for why will ye die, O house of Israel?" God's power alone will turn you from your evil ways. If you heave a sigh to the Lord Jesus, he will come and save you. He who lifts up his soul to God, and cries, "Lord, save me, or I perish," shall be heard and answered. It matters not that words fail you; only tell the Lord that you are a wretch undone, and that if you perish, you are resolved to perish at the foot of the cross of Christ, and you shall never be cast out.

I have heard that when Mrs. Ryland was dying she was in great darkness of soul. Her quaint husband, John Ryland, went to her bedside, and said to her, "You are going to heaven, my dear" "No," cried she, "I am going down to hell." "And what will you do when you get there? Do you think you will pray there?" She replied, "I am sure I shall pray as long as I exist" "Why, then," said her husband, "if you pray in hell, they will say, 'Here is praying Betty Ryland come here; we cannot have praying people here; turn her out.'" It is impossible for a praying soul to be lost; for a praying soul has a measure of faith, and faith saves. A praying heart is a token that for you there is day coming, and not night.

Behold, at this very hour, Jesus cries again to sinners upon earth, "Come unto me, all ye that labour and are heavy laden, and I will give you rest." May God, in his infinite mercy, lead you to the only true rest—rest in Jesus! May the good Spirit apply these rambling remarks to all your souls, and may the seafaring men of Wivenhoe find a port in Jesus, when all the night is over, and the day of glory dawns upon us in Immanuel's land! Amen.

544

"Lovest thou Me?"

"Lovest thou me?"—John xxi. 15.

MY heart shall answer, but with silence only,
        For speech could ne'er impart
How drear my future life would be, and lonely
        From thee apart.

Thine eye alone can read the inmost feeling,
        For thou Creator art;
Answer with searching glance my mute appealing,
        Behold my heart!

My guilt I own, and, bitterly repenting,
        I turn to thee for grace;
Have mercy, Lord; to prove thy true relenting,
        Show me thy face!

I did not realize the utter madness
        Of that deep sin of mine,
Till on thy face I saw the look of sadness
        And grief divine.

Yet hadst thou not then turned, and looked upon me,
        I too had gone away,
And, Judas-like, the enemy had won me,
        A castaway.

Love thee? The barest doubt of it is madness,
        For thou art all to me;
Nor earth, nor heaven could bring me aught of gladness,
        Apart from thee.

I will not grieve thee by again comparing
        Mine with another's love;
But humbly wait till I, thy passion sharing,
        Its truth shall prove.

Bacup.   E. A. TYDEMAN.

Mark this!

HEAVEN is a prepared place for a prepared people, but the grace of God is prepared for unprepared sinners. You need a Mediator between your souls and God, but you need no mediator between your souls and Christ. Fitness for the presence of the Father you do require; but you may come to Jesus just as you are. The way to heaven may be long, but the way to Christ is but one step of faith. Saints will be and must be fruitful through the Spirit of God, but sinners are wrought upon by the Holy Ghost when they are as yet barren and unfruitful. In a word, there is a reward which is of grace; but before it is gained, grace comes to us freely, not of reward at all, but as the free gift of God to the undeserving.   C. H. S.

Butterflies.

BY THOMAS SPURGEON.*

BUTTERFLIES are, to my mind, among the most beautiful things that God has made. If I were asked to name two objects in the natural world that charm me most, I think I would say, " Flowers and Birds ; " but if my questioner asked for only one, I would certainly answer—"Butterflies." For do they not combine the charms of the other two ? Are they not flowers on wings?

"It flies, and seems a flower that floats on air."

True, they are scentless, and herein are below the flowers. True, they are songless, and, so far, fall short of the birds. But flowers must tarry at their posts or die ; and birds, for the most part,, have not the glorious hues and sylph-like loveliness of butterflies.

Certainly, of all insects, the butterfly would win the first prize in a beauty show. How resplendent some even of the commonest are! and all fast colours, too ! There, for instance, is our little yellow friend, the brimstone butterfly, the harbinger of spring, as yellow as if he sipped only at the buttercups. He might, indeed, be a buttercup transformed by some strange spell into a flying thing—a butterfly. How often have I chased him in the meadows, the little sunbeam ! Then, there were those little blue fellows, like blue-bells winged. And into what ecstasies we used to go when a Tortoise-shell, or an Admiral, with his scarlet stripes, or a Peacock, with his varied shades of blue and red, happened to come along!

But, oh ! if these common types are lovely, what shall be said of those that flutter and zig-zag in foreign lands, filled, as many of them seem to be, with the flaming colours of the tropic sunsets, the bright blue of the cloudless skies, and the tender tints of the virgin forests ?

Some there are which, in certain lights, seem gilded o'er, while the wings of others are, for all the world, as if from some decorator's hand there had fallen on to them some little bits of highly burnished silver leaf. David's description of the dove would not be inappropriate to this frail sister—" Her wings covered with silver."

Then there are some clad in imperial purple, of so rich a hue that man can by no means imitate it. The dyes of Tyre, wonderful as they were, could not match it. Lydia's wares would look dull and dim beside the regal splendour of these fragile wings.

I have heard tell of butterflies (would that I might see them!) whose wings are opaline, burning with many colours, like that wondrous gem, and iridescent as a pigeon's neck. Try to imagine an insect of which the admiring naturalist writes : " The upper wings are of the richest azure, glittering like burnished metal, and iridescent as the opal, but with far greater intensity of hue."

But who could tell the varied charms of butterflies ? Surely every colour, in all possible tints and tones, are on them, in every conceivable pattern and device. Some are clad in velvet, some in silk.

---

* The initial letter is contributed by the writer.

Here is a list of favourite hues :—Sooty black and snowy white ;
flaming crimson and tender pink ; martial scarlet and navy blue ;
homely brown and jealous yellow; orange, deep enough for the most
zealous Protestant ; and green, verdant enough for the most patriotic
Irishman. Moreover, all these colours are cunningly arranged in spots
and stripes, and bars and bands, and edgings and marblings, and half-
moons and festoons, and streaks and patches, with every tint harmonizing
and blending most perfectly. Who, but the Great Artist, could paint
like this ? With such lovely wings in view, their " gorgeousness of
colouring almost inconceivable," we do not wonder that Linnæus
dubbed them Knights, and gave them Homeric names.   Hector and
Thais, Dido and Thetis, Pollux and Archippus, together with many
other classic notables, live again in the fair forms of butterflies, which,
trembling in the summer sunlight, prove themselves by no means
unworthy of their illustrious namesakes.

What puzzles me beyond measure, is the fact, that some dull hearts
refuse to stir at sight of them—ay, that some dull eyes scarce note
them when the meadow glistens with their quivering glory. I can
comprehend the prophet's servant failing to observe the cavalry of God
on the ranges, until his eyes were opened ; but how some folk can walk
through fields bedight with beauties fluttering at their feet, and never
see them, I cannot understand. They have no eye for the beautiful !
And oh, how much they miss ! I feel inclined to say, as Elisha did
for the young man, " Lord, I pray thee, open their eyes, that they
may see ! "

> " Who loves not the gay butterfly that swims
>   Before him in the ardent noon, arrayed
>   In crimson, azure, emerald, and gold ;
>   With more magnificence upon his wing—
>   His little wing—than ever graced the robe
>   Gorgeous of royalty ; is like the kine
>   That wander 'mid the flowers which gem the meads,
>   Unconscious of their beauty."

Still more surprising is it, that others see only to hunt and hurt.
Let us hope, in thoughtlessness rather than with wantonness, they chase
the flying flowers, and crush them in their cruel hands. I know something of the fascination of such pursuit, and must plead guilty to having
imprisoned many a frail fairy, though all the harm it did me was to
herald, by its own bright presence, the opening spring-time. It was
boy-like, I suppose ; yet I had been taught, as many are not, that we
ought never to sport with pain and distress in any of our amusements,
or treat even the meanest insect with wanton cruelty ! To destroy
insects that are destructive is pardonable ; but even they should not be
tortured. To collect specimens is, of course, allowable ; but to chase
and capture, and imprison butterflies, for mere sport, is surely inex
cusable. A Society for the Prevention of Cruelty to *Insects* is not
uncalled for, each member to pledge himself in Cowper's words :—

> " I would not enter on my list of friends
>   (Though graced with polished manners and fine sense,
>   Yet wanting sensibility) the man ·
>   Who needlessly sets foot upon a worm."

"It is a very serious thing," says Madame Michelet, "to imprison a bird born free ;" and what she says of birds, holds good of every butterfly. Born free, gloriously free, he is. Liberty is his happy birthright.

> "Frail beauty of the spring and summer's sun,
> Oh, that I could the youthful hands exhort
> To leave thee to thy pleasure sweet, which none
> Can give thee back when 'tis for ever gone ! "

It can hardly be doubted that the main reason for which butterflies exist is that their beauty may gladden us. It would be difficult, indeed, to discover any other purpose in their creation. True, some of the caterpillars, from which they spring, devour odious plants. (The grub of the Peacock Butterfly, for instance, lives on stinging-nettles.) But the majority of them destroy leaves which are lovely to behold, or fit for food. True, the butterflies help to hold in check the surfeit of sweets, which else might sicken us ; but this service, surely, is not indispensable. It remains, therefore, that their beauty is their excuse for living. And is it not a sufficient one ?

We have abundant evidence that our glorious Lord would have his people's eyes delighted with the beautiful, else had he dressed this world in garb as simple as the Quaker's grey, and made all forms " as ugly as a satyr." "He hath made everything beautiful in his time." Some there are who seem to regard it in the nature of a crime to be lovely. It need hardly be added that they are not Apollos or Venuses themselves. If Ovid recognized loveliness as " a favour bestowed by the gods," surely we Christians ought not to refuse to see in it one of our living God's best gifts, and to prize it accordingly. Let us admire it in flowers, and skies, and seas ; in beasts, and birds, and insects; and, not least, in human kind, the noblest of God's works. If the devil has too often used personal charms as a soul-destroying bait, it follows not that beauty is of the devil. Rachel, and Abigail, and Esther, received their loveliness from above. It was God our Father who made Moses " a proper child," and Joseph " a goodly person," and David of " a beautiful countenance."

> " The lesson which the many-coloured skies,
> The flowers, and leaves, and painted butterflies,
> For evermore, repeat,
> In varied tones, and sweet,
> That beauty, in and of itself, is good."

But be it remembered that though *the butterfly* may have no other office than to be beautiful, this should not be the only aim of any human being. This is where the error lies. Men and women, who have no aspiration higher than show and vanity, are mere butterflies; but *they* have not the butterfly's excuse.

Moreover, it is essential that the beauty be perfectly natural. We speak of " the painted butterfly," but God's pencil is alone responsible for its lovely hues. Natural comeliness is of God, paints and pigments are of the devil. I read, with some amusement, that an old colonial statute has been discovered in New Jersey, which provides " that all women, of whatsoever age, profession, or rank, whether maids or widows, who shall, after this Act, impose upon, seduce, or betray into matrimony any of his Majesty's subjects, by virtue of scents, cosmetics, washes, paints, artificial teeth, false hair, or high-heeled shoes, shall incur the penalty now in force against witchcraft, and like misdemeanours." This law is, apparently, still unrepealed, but, doubtless, remains a dead letter. It is as well it should. If reason will not teach, force will entirely fail. Oh, when will mortals come to see that "beauty unadorned is adorned the most"; and that any made-up loveliness is positively detestable ?

The beauty of the butterfly is not, however, so useless as it seems. The wings are covered with brilliant scales, overlapping each other like the slates on a roof, or as the plates of a coat of mail. Beautiful as they are, their use is evident. They serve as protection as well as adornment. They are the dazzling armour of these glorious knights. Beauty is doubly beautiful when.it is useful too. That it may be turned to good account we know. "Beauty, if given to God, is, indeed, a talent not to be despised; it adds a grace to our actions, a lustre to our virtues, an eloquence to our words." "But it," says one, "brings so many risks and trials." Yes, verily, the butterfly finds that out, too. His beauty endangers him. The capturing net, the suffocating spirits, and the show case—these are penalties consequent upon wearing such bewitching wings. Flattery and envy, selfishness and pride, are among the perils to be feared for those who are beautiful; and against them divine grace is the only sufficient guard. "Beauty, if it be not dedicated to the service of God, becomes a deadly poison, both to ourselves and others."

Again, virtue must be with loveliness, or what avails the prettiness ? The butterfly could only have our hearty dislike if, in spite of its graceful form and brilliancy, it had habits and tastes repulsive. "Beauty is vain : but a woman that feareth the Lord, she shall be praised." The best style of beauty is the beauty of holiness. "How goodness heightens beauty ! "

These remarks on butterflies would hardly be complete without, at least, a reference to the well-worn but striking emblem they afford us of the resurrection. The creeping worm, whose only business is to eat, by-and-by prepares itself for burial. It is its own undertaker. It makes its own shroud and coffin, digs its own grave, and conducts its own funeral. In due time its long sleep terminates ; it tears its grave-clothes off, and comes forth with fourfold wings, to flutter in the sunshine, and to sip ambrosia from the cups of Flora; a fair, if faint, image of "the glorified spirits in heaven."

> "Child of the sun, pursue thy rapturous flight,
> Mingling with her thou lov'st in fields of light,
> And when the flowers of Paradise unfold,
> Quaff fragrant nectar from their cups of gold :
> There shall thy wings, rich as an evening sky,
> Expand and shut with silent ecstasy.
> Yet wert thou once a worm—a thing that crept
> On the bare earth; then wrought a tomb, and slept !
> And such is man ! Soon from his cell of clay
> To burst a seraph in the blaze of day."

A Chat in Havre-des-Pas.

"CAN you speak French?" said a tall man, whom I chanced to meet in Havre-des-Pas, Jersey.

"No, sir, I cannot," I replied; "but I can say, 'I am saved,' in English, and that is something to be thankful for."

"Indeed!" said he; "I should think that assertion comes either from ignorance or presumption."

"Not so, sir, but the very opposite," I replied. "As far as my French is concerned, my ignorance is just about complete; for all I can say is 'Oui' (yes). But as regards my soul's salvation, I am happy to say my education has not been neglected; for I have been taught by God's good Spirit to know that those who believe God's Word, and trust it, can not only say they are saved, but may know with assurance it is so, and have God's Spirit bearing witness with their spirit that they have become children of God. And I can assure you, sir, I have now no anxiety about my own salvation; all my anxiety and concern now is about the salvation of others; and that is what has brought Mr. Fullerton and myself over to this island."

Whilst I was thus speaking, up came a lady by my side, and said, "That's right, sir; I am glad you are having a word with my brother, for he needs it. He is always ready to give coals to the poor, bread to the hungry, and money to the church; but he will not give himself to Christ."

"There you go, again," said this tall Jerseyite; "you first take this gentleman round to your brother Fred, and you will do some good if you can get him converted; for he has a bad wife, and that drives the poor fellow to the drink; and, goodness knows, he has a poor home, and a miserable life of it, altogether."

"Yes, indeed, John," said the lady, "that is quite true; but I believe Fred, with all his faults, will be saved, and enter the kingdom of heaven before you. He, poor fellow, does know he is a sinner, and you are so self-satisfied; and, what's more, Fred has been to one or two of their meetings, and has promised to go again; and you will not even promise to go and hear the gospel."

During this conversation, up came a second lady, and commenced to speak to the first lady in a most excitable manner in French. Not a word did I understand, but I saw the man was much interested by what she was saying. At length she said to me, "What do you think this lady says?"

"I don't know; but it is evidently something that seems to interest you both."

"Yes, indeed," she says; "my brother Fred went to your meeting last night, and found the Saviour, and he is at home singing and praising God, and wants to see me; so I must go and see him at once. And now, John, we will pray till we get you to Christ."

And away the two women went, talking together in French.

"Ah, yes! there you go; there's quite a swarm of you now," said her brother, as she passed on.

"Yes," I replied, "and your last remark reminds me of an incident that occurred in Scotland. I will tell it you before I go, if you will let me."

"Yes, say on," said he.

"I know a well-to-do gentleman in England; and one day he thought he would like to take two of the Lord's evangelists for a trip down the Clyde."

"A very wise and good thing to do," said the Jersey gentleman.

"Yes, and so say I. Well, you must know, upon stepping on board, at Greenock, one of the evangelists took a seat on one side of the deck to view the landscape of that lovely country, whilst the other evangelist took his seat on the opposite side of the ship to view the rugged rocks and mountains beyond. The gentleman meanwhile was very busy running up and down the deck in a rather excited manner, giving away tracts, and speaking a word for Christ to the pleasure-seekers on board. After a time, a man who had been closely watching the movement of this gentleman, took a seat beside one of the two evangelists. Soon the evangelist put his hand on his knee, and said to him, ' Do you see that gentleman running about the deck ? Is not that man a fool ? '

" ' You're right. I have been watching him some time, and I think he's the biggest fool I have ever met with.'

"After a brief pause, the evangelist said, ' Friend, whom do you think that man is a fool for ? '

" ' I don't know,' said the stranger.

" ' Then, I will tell you,' said the evangelist ; ' he is a fool for the Lord Jesus Christ's sake.'

" With this remark, the man sprang to his feet ; and, without another word, dashed off to the other side of the deck, and took a seat beside the other evangelist.

"He had not sat there long before the second evangelist, who had noticed what had been going on, turned towards him, and placing his hand on his shoulder, said, ' Brother, is your soul saved ? '

"Like a savage tiger he sprang to his feet, and exclaimed, ' Goodness gracious ! Why, there's a gang of them ! ' "

So, turning to my Jersey friend, I said, "And I do assure you there is quite a gang of us over here just now, seeking souls for our Master."

"Well," said he, "I have heard that young Mr. Fellowes, and a fine fellow he is, indeed. I like his preaching, though I am not of the same persuasion as he is."

"Well," said I, "I am sure he won't mind that, if you only give yourself to Christ ; for that is the main thing after all. But I fear, my friend, you are something like the boy with the sweet plums."

"What is that ? " said he. "Tell me about the plums."

And I did, for it was just what I wanted to do. You can often put in a point, and make it stick in a story, where you would fail by argument :—

"There was a lad, whose mother was very fond of him, and one day, seeing he was not very well, she was most anxious to give him a pill, but she did not know how to get her pet lad to take it. But you know, sir, love is very ingenious, and she thought of a very happy plan. She took a large plum, made a slit in the side, put in the pill after taking out the stone, and then placed it on a plate beside his bed, and said, 'Willie, dear, when you go to bed to-night, you will find a nice plum on the plate beside your bed ; you may have it, dear.' 'Oh, thank you, mamma,' said Willie, 'that is so nice ; I am very fond of plums.' And in the morning the anxious mother said, 'Willie, dear, did you eat the plum last night ?' 'Yes, mamma dear, all but the pip, and I spat that out.' The poor mother was much disappointed, and I fear many a faithful minister often shares a similar disappointment."

Reader, do not miss the point ! We are most anxious for you to have as many sweet plums as will do you good; but only Christ can save the soul.

J. MANTON SMITH.

The Human Side of Inspiration.

ONE might suppose that believers in Plenary Inspiration were all idiots; for their opponents are most benevolently anxious to remind them of facts which none but half-witted persons could ever forget. Over and over they cry, " But there is a human side to inspiration." Of course there is ; there must be the man to be inspired as well as the God to inspire him. Whoever doubted this ? The inference which is supposed to be inevitable is—that imperfection is, therefore, to be found in the Bible, since man is imperfect. But the inference is not true. God can come into the nearest union with manhood, and he can use men for his purposes, and yet their acts may not in the least degree stain his purposes with moral obliquity. Even so he can utter his thoughts by men, and those thoughts may not be in the least affected by the natural fallibility of man. When the illustration of the Incarnation is quoted, we remark upon it that the Godhead was not deprived of any of its moral attributes by its union with manhood; and even so, in the union of the divine and human in the inspired Word, the thoughts of God are in no degree perverted by being uttered in the words of men. The testimony of God, on the human as well as the divine side, is perfect and infallible; and however others may think of it, we shall not cease to believe in it with all our heart and soul. The Holy Spirit has made no mistake, either in history, physics, theology, or anything else. God is a greater Scientist than any of those who assume that title. If the human side had tainted the lesser statements we could not be sure of the greater. A man who cannot be trusted as to pence is hardly to be relied on in matters which involve thousands of pounds. But the human side has communicated no taint whatever to Holy Scripture. Every Word of God is pure and sure, whether viewed as the utterance of man or as the thought of God. Whatever of man there is in the enunciation of the message, there is nothing which can prevent its being implicitly received by us, since the man saith nothing on his own account, but covers his own personality with the sacred authority of, " Thus saith the Lord."

C. H. S.

"See what there is to be Seen."

"GOD couldn't arrange it more beautiful," said a poor old blind man, as he sat in the chimney-corner of his cottage. "Arrange what?" said the visitor. "Why, *I'm as blind as a mole,* but *I can hear well;* and my old woman there," pointing to his wife in the other corner, "is *as deaf as a post,* but *she can see well.* Could God Almighty a' done it better?" This blind, bright saint could certainly see beauty in God's arrangements where it never would have been suspected by on-lookers. It need hardly be said that sightless J. revels in the light where mere sight-seers would grumble at the darkness. His natural blindness seems to have given a quick, keen perception to his spiritual sight. "No walls around me now," he says; "I'm never hemmed in. It's all brightness. Bless'e, I'd ten times sooner be as I be, than have my sight, and not see my Saviour!" He is—speaking after the manner of men—at poverty's door, yet he has luxurious faith; and, in truth, his bare home is hard by the jewelled-walls of the pearly-gated city. Listen to his thankful, contented talk : "They allows the old woman and me two shillings and ninepence, and two loaves, and we can manage on that ; and what more do we want?

> ' I must have all things and abound,
> While God is God to me.'"

Christian friend, did you ever take your stand beside your God, and see what there is to be seen? Do so ; and it may be that, in your deprivations and disappointments, you will behold a wonderful and beautiful arrangement by which you can glorify God far better than by the gratification of your own selfish and earth-bound desires. Never were the Israelites better off than when they had just enough manna for the day, and not a morsel over; and it may be you are richer and happier in your present condition than you could have been in any other. See if it be not so!

"I thank God!" said one, "that I lost my all; for it has led me up into many blessed experiences with my God which I never knew while I was held down by the golden chain of worldly possessions. Then my affections were set on things on the earth, but now they rise to heaven."

If you see things from God's standpoint, your black trouble will appear fringed with brightness, relieving the monotonous darkness upon which you have fixed your steady gaze far too long already. Look at your prolonged affliction from this point of view, and you will discern secret fingers carving the delicate "lily work" which shall adorn you in the upper sanctuary, when you become a pillar in the temple of your God. It may be, by the very method so distasteful to you, the cherubim of adoring reverence are being woven into the texture of your being. Yes, *do* see what there is to be seen, for in every dispensation there is the hand of a divine purpose, full of love, and wisdom, and grace.

> "O little heart of mine! Shall pain
> Or sorrow make thee moan,
> When the great God is all for thee,
> A Father all thine own?"

F. E. B.

Cheering Words from our Missionary in North Africa.*

AT present our encouragements in the work of God in Tangier far exceed our discouragements. Generally speaking the Spaniards are glad to hear the gospel, and our hearts have been rejoiced by many believing.

One Sunday evening, I preached from John iii. 36, and among those who professed to accept Christ was a bricklayer. He went home, and immediately told his wife of his conversion. They came together to our Monday meeting, and the wife professed to give her heart to Christ. The next day, while working at the top of a house, the poor fellow lost his balance, and fell heavily to the ground. Bruised, bleeding, and unconscious, he was carried home. I visited him the next day, and found him in great pain, with his wounds still undressed. When I spoke to him about his soul, he drew his Testament from under his pillow, and opened it at John iii. 36. His eyes sparkled with joy as he put his finger first under the word "HATH," and then on his heart. A few weeks since, a Moor said to us, "It is easy to die if the heart is right." One of our lady missionaries visited him later, and, thanks to her nursing, he gradually recovered, giving glory to God. But while it is grand to see men prepared to die trusting in Christ, it is equally grand to see them living with Christ.

N. H. PATRICK.

* Mr. Patrick is a man of our own College, and is our own missionary, working in connection with the North Africa Mission. We hope that this work will grow till we have many such men in the field. This must, of course, depend upon the amount of money which we receive for this object. We would not deprive any one of the societies of a single shilling ; but, at the same time, we desire to have independent missionaries of our own wherever a door is opened. This work, in the nearest of unchristian lands, has taken a deep hold on our heart. ALGIERS AND MOROCCO FOR CHRIST is our cry Mr. Patrick began to work among the Mahometans, but it is thought better that he should now give his attention to the Spaniards. He begins with happy tokens, and a lady has just gone out to be his wife and fellow-labourer. We hope to give particulars from time to time. Please, dear friends, note this work, and pray for its prosperity.

F. P. F——— was my servant for some months. He was only twenty, but gave evidence of true conversion. He slept at home, but was so persecuted there that he could find no opportunity for quiet prayer; but every morning he knelt down in the kitchen, where the day's work was to be done, seeking strength for that work. He earnestly desired his mother's conversion, and prayed for it without ceasing. She, however, was extremely bitter with her son, and endeavoured to get him sent into the Spanish army, but failed. The home became almost unbearable to him. About three weeks ago he received orders to join the Spanish navy. He came to say good-bye. Rising from our knees, I begged him to be faithful to Christ. Tears were in his eyes, but he replied firmly, "God helping me, I will, sir. I will tell everybody the truth about Jesus." May God keep him faithful!

The simple faith of some of these men is grand. A. C——— was working for me, and one evening, with a bright look, he said, "God does answer prayer, sir." "Yes, he does," I replied. And then he told me how, that morning, when drawing water from the well, he had dropped the bucket. It was full of water, and sank. He knew it would soon be in the sea, and so ran hastily for the hook. It was a very bad one, and he felt certain he would lose the pail; but then he prayed about it, and to his delight, the first time he let the hook down, he pulled the bucket up. "God does answer prayer, sir," he said. The week before this happened, I had dropped a bucket down the same well, had used the same hook, and, after trying for nearly an hour, had given it up; but I hadn't prayed. I learned a lesson that day.

Our converts have been much persecuted. For following Christ, men have been turned out of their homes. Others have been reviled, beaten, or excommunicated; while others, again, have been deserted by their friends, and dismissed by their employers. But perhaps the most severely tried have been an old shoemaker and his daughter. The poor girl fell sick, and they were too poverty-stricken to provide her with proper nourishment. Some of our enemies had threatened and warned them to leave our meetings; but finding this of no avail, attacked them from the other side. The father was given plenty of work, and paid very handsomely for all he did. His heart was gladdened, for he was able to give his sick child all she required; but, after a fortnight, his employers informed him that, if he wished to have any more work, he must leave those Protestants, once and for all. It was a hard struggle, and, at one time, it seemed as if the devil was to be victorious. He remembered how poverty had pinched, and how they had starved; but grace was given according to his need. He lost his work, but kept his Saviour.

We look forward with confidence for great blessing here. We have large premises, good health, and over and above all else, the everlasting gospel. This is what Tangier needs, and the people are beginning to feel this to be the case. Pray for us!

N. H. PATRICK.

Here and There.*

BY H. RYLANDS BROWN, DARJEELING.

IT is not always an easy thing to get a man to open his bungalow for a service; and when that difficulty has been got over, it is not easy to get together an audience. Thinking it would be well to have a service in a bungalow where I had not had one before, I went to the occupant, from whom I could not be sure of a welcome, and asked him if he would let me use his bungalow for a service the following Sunday. He looked as if he would have liked to say, "No," but said "Yes, if you like, but I expect I shall be away." I thanked him heartily. The next thing was to call upon the planters of the district, and invite them to attend. In addition, notices on post-cards were sent all round. I took care to send them in good time, for, on a previous occasion, a Babu postmaster had put my notices on one side, and when I asked him the reason of the delay in their being sent out, he said, "Oh, I thought they were merely complimentary notices!" This was fine fun for the planters when given as the explanation of their getting the notices after the service had been held.

Well, on the Sunday, eight planters assembled, including the gentleman in whose house we were. He sat in front of me, looking very uninterested, and I wondered how I could awaken his interest. Towards the close of my address I said, "Whatever any of you may think of this service, it is a fact in your history; and though other matters, such as getting in coolies, pruning, building factories, putting up machinery, the breaking down of machinery"—that last phrase did what I wanted, for the man's machinery had broken down last year, and he had been put to great inconvenience. His face lit up, and I held his attention to the close. I went on, "The fact of this service may be buried under these other facts, and hidden from you, but it cannot be obliterated. Now, you think it small in comparison with these other more important matters, but in the great judgment day, when they shall have sunk into their real insignificance, this service will stand out, and it will be a terrible thing if it should be found then that you disregarded God's warnings, and wilfully pursued a course of forgetfulness of him." The good friend who had lent his bungalow was very cordial after the service.

Occasionally I have pleasant rides through very lovely scenery, but it is not always so. Once, during last cold weather, having to meet an appointment, I was riding the greater part of two days in pouring rain. Three times I was wet to the skin, and had to beg changes of clothing at as many different houses. At the first I had to get into the clothes of a man who stands six feet three! At the second, my kind benefactor was about twice my breadth, so when I got into his things, I remarked, "Not lost, but gone inside!" At the third, next morning, by way of keeping up an average, I had to make an effort, and get into the garments of a man even smaller than myself. Late on the second day,

* Our readers will remember that Mr. Harry Brown went out from our College, and has laboured on in India for many years as pastor at Darjeeling in the summer, and evangelist for the Anglo-Indian Society in the winter. The Lord blesses his work.

after being ignominiously thrown from my pony, I reached my destination, after some as uncomfortable and difficult riding as I have ever had.

One learns to be thankful for very small mercies when on tour. A young fellow's giving up an evening at cards to spend it with me was as cold water to a thirsty soul. The other men who had their nice little arrangement broken up did not, I fear, pour blessings on my head. It once fell to me to be left alone in a bungalow for the night, because every one in the neighbourhood had gone to a dance. The fact of there being lady visitors was an opportunity not to be missed. They did not risk an invitation to me, for had I accepted it, I should have been sadly in the way. The Lord's saying, " Blessed are ye when men shall separate you from their company," appeared very full of meaning to me that night.

The tour referred to was taken in connection with the Anglo-Indian Evangelization Society.

Richard Baker: Nobility in Humble Life.

BY R. SHINDLER.

THE old church at Eythorne, near Dover, has been a mother of churches. During the thirty-four years' ministry of Rev. John Giles it flourished greatly. Three hundred and forty members were added to the church, an average of ten per year ; and churches were founded at Dover, Deal, and Canterbury, which have flourished and borne fruit.

Mr. Giles was set apart to the ministry by the church at Carter Lane, afterwards meeting at New Park Street, and now at the Metropolitan Tabernacle. Dr. Rippon, Mr. Giles's pastor, was much attached to him ; and well he might be, for he was a faithful and earnest preacher of the blessed gospel, and was honoured in the conversion of many. The church then held, and it holds still, and all its ministers have held and taught, the great truths of the everlasting gospel of God's free grace in Christ Jesus.

The village of Eythorne is seven miles from Dover, Deal, and Sandwich, and from these towns it has always had hearers in attendance, the bulk of the congregation being made up from the scattered villages of the rather thinly-peopled country around. It has been the centre of blessed influences throughout the whole district, and of hundreds it may be said, " This man was born in her."

Among the members of this church, God has raised up some whose names have been, and one or two are still, well known in Baptist circles. Rev. Daniel Clarabut, who laboured with such zeal and divine success as pastor of the church at New Mill, Tring, Herts, was a member at Eythorne, and was set apart by the church to the ministry. He married Miss Giles, who was residing at Canterbury in 1873. The old church at Tring—herself the mother of many churches in Herts and Bucks—never flourished more than it did under Mr. Clarabut's earnest and faithful ministry.   His name is still fragrant there, though more than half a century has passed since his rather early death.

Rev. George Pearce, for so many years a missionary in India, was a member at Eythorne, before he, with some others, was dismissed, to found the church at Pentside, Dover.   He was baptized, with five others, on 23rd September, 1819, when Queen Victoria was a baby in arms.   Two of the five others were George Baker and Richard Baker. George Baker became a village preacher.   After a few years he undertook the charge of the church at Romney Marsh, as mission pastor, and subsequently he presided over the church at Sutton-at-Hone, and still later he commenced a Baptist interest at Dartford.   For many years he was engaged as an evangelist, and was made useful to many.

It must have been in 1840, or 1841, that the writer, having been raised from the brink of the grave, and delivered from the "horrible pit" of overwhelming soul distress, gained some help from George Baker's humble and faithful efforts, when he was preaching on Sunday afternoons, in what was then a gravel pit, nearly opposite the spot now occupied by Trinity Baptist Chapel, Bexley Heath.   Though a mere youth, his long severe conflict of soul, and subsequent enlargement and deliverance, made the truths of the gospel very precious to him, and he hungered for solid food, though he got but little.   George Baker's plain preaching of the gospel was, therefore, the more acceptable.   Mr. Baker died some years ago.

Richard Baker, the subject of this sketch, was in many respects a remarkable man ; and, though he occupied only a very humble station in society, it may be truly said that " he was a faithful man, and feared God above many."   For more than sixty-nine years he maintained an honourable character and position as a member of the same church, and lived to see all his children, and some of his grandchildren, united with their parents in the same fellowship.   For many years he was a Sunday-school teacher, and for forty years a village preacher ; and was known and respected by all, and beloved by many, as a humble, faithful, earnest Christian man ; a good neighbour ; an affectionate husband and father ; a careful, industrious, painstaking workman, who never needed his master's eye for the due performance of his allotted task.   All his life he was a labourer in some capacity or other, on various farms within a radius of five miles from Eythorne.   If the writer had been asked to select a man as a type of a good, industrious, faithful farm-labourer, from the great number he has known in various parts of the country, he would at once, and unhesitatingly, have named Richard Baker.   He esteemed him very highly, respected him very greatly, and loved him as a friend and brother in Christ.   His work on a farm was invaluable, as there was nothing that came amiss to him, from ploughing and sowing to reaping, stack-building and thatching, mending fences, gates, and stiles, gardening, pig-killing, measuring land, setting out piece-work for other men, and calculating work and wages.   A young nobleman came to reside on an estate which fell to him by inheritance ; he was a careless spendthrift, and after a season of enforced economy, as the result of his lavish expenditure, he died from a fall in the hunting field.   The writer has often contrasted the fast-living, improvident, pleasure-loving peer of the realm with the humble and far more happy farm-labourer, who toiled all the week for his family, and was always willing, indeed pleased, to take a village service on the evening of a Lord's-day, though it entailed, as it sometimes did, a walk of six, eight, ten, or even twelve miles, out and home. Without wishing to cast any reflection on the aristocracy as a class, for the gifts and grace of some have shone conspicuously, and with no wish to decry any one, or give to any more than is meet, he has sometimes asked the question, of himself and others, "Which of the two men was the true nobleman?"

But let us give a brief sketch of the life of this unpretentious, good man. He was born at Upper Deal, in 1799, one of three children, his mother dying when he was a child of four or five years. The only thing he could remember about her was that she taught him to repeat the Lord's Prayer. His father was a farm-labourer, and the home was far from a happy one, for his step-mother took to drink, and the children were neglected. A short time at a dame's school, and a few months at a common elementary school, was all the training he had, for he had to turn out as a farm-servant at a very early age. His first place was at Walmer, his second at Northbourne, covering five years, when he went to Woolwich Green, Womenswould, where he lived many years, and where most of his children were born.

The life of a farm-servant is not an easy one, and where the master and mistress, and fellow-servants, are not actuated by the fear of God, it is commonly far from conducive to good impressions and anything like true godliness. At the time of Richard Baker's boyhood, it certainly was not, as a rule, a school for piety, though fine specimens of Christian men and women might be found in connection with it. The writer has known many such in the county of Kent and elsewhere, during a ministry of more than forty years.

The parish of Womenswould, in which Woolwich Green is situate, and the adjoining parish of Nonington, were then, as now, in the hands of a lay-proprietor, who spent about a fifth of the income, or less, on clergymen who did the spiritual work of the parishes. Some very good men have laboured there, especially at Nonington, in which parish Bishop Ryle married his late excellent wife, a Miss Plumptree. At the time of Richard Baker's youth, Womenswould had to do with one service in three weeks. As a consequence, the farm-servants met together on Sunday afternoon for play, or to hunt squirrels, or such-like amusement, and there was no fear of God before their eyes. Richard joined them two or three times, but his conscience told him he was wrong. After a time, the Wesleyans, of Dover, took pity on the place, and commenced a service in a house. After some persuasion, Richard went to hear the preaching. No particular impression was made until, one day, the preacher gave out the text: "And as he reasoned of righteousness, temperance, and judgment to come, Felix trembled, and answered, Go thy way for this time; when I have a convenient season, I will call for thee" (Acts xxiv. 25). This text, and the home appeals of the preacher—a layman, as unordained preachers are sometimes called—were God's message to the soul of Richard Baker. He says, in some notes of his life, written in his eighty-sixth year, "I felt this was my case, and I made up my mind, there and then, that I would do no more squirrel-hunting on Sundays." He found it hard to persevere; but he did, though the farm-servants of the village persecuted him after their rude manner. His master and the housekeeper both encouraged him to persevere. He now began in good earnest to seek the Lord, and cry for mercy. His elder brother George was also awakened, and they met together to pray, sometimes behind hedges, and sometimes in outhouses.

About this time God sent three excellent clergymen into the neighbourhood ; one to Kingston, one to Upper Hardes, and one to Womenswould. God blessed the labours of these good men ; their churches were well-attended, and much good was done.

The time for changing servants came round, and a better set of young fellows came to Woolwich Green, who did not oppose religion. The masters, too, gave them a room where they could spend their spare time, and provided them with a fire and candles, a very unusual thing in those days.

Strange as it may seem, to people of the present generation, especially, up to this time Richard did not possess a Bible. Copies of the Holy Scriptures were costly, and therefore somewhat rare. He soon, however, became the owner of one, and applied himself with great diligence to learn to read it. The little learning he had when a boy he had almost forgotten, and it was a toil, on winter evenings, to master the art of reading and spelling, to which he afterwards added ciphering.

Like the celebrated Welsh girl, Mary Jones, the obtaining of a Bible marked a period in his history. He had already begun to attend the Baptist Chapel, Eythorne, and his desire to obtain a Bible led to his introduction to "that dear good man, Rev. John Giles, the pastor." A member of the church told Mr. Giles of Richard's great want, and he sent for him, that he might receive it from his own hand. The good pastor talked to him tenderly and lovingly, and won his heart at once. He got his Bible, made a new friend in the pastor, and went home singing—

"Holy Bible, book divine,
    Precious treasure, thou art mine ! "

Ah, how he read that Bible ! And how he prayed, "Open thou mine eyes, that I may behold wondrous things out of thy law " ! Witnessing a baptism, he was impressed with a desire to walk in the same blessed path of obedience. After some further instruction in divine things, he was baptized, as mentioned before ; and now he, the last of the six, has gone to unite with those who preceded him in reaching home.

It would appear that when the earnest, godly minister came to take charge of Womenswould church, the Wesleyans ceased their preaching services there, and it does not appear that they were ever renewed, though for many years afterwards the pastor at Eythorne visited the hamlet of Woolwich Green, and sent his lay-helpers ; at least, it was so during the writer's labours there. But now a little chapel has been erected, and a Sunday-school is conducted by one of the farmers, and other friends.

Soon after joining the church, Richard took to himself a wife, who was a member of the church at Deal. They lived together more than sixty-five years, walking together in the fear of God, and in the peace and hope of the gospel. The rest of his life he lived and worked either at Woolwich or Eythorne.

His first regular Christian work was Sunday-school teaching. He felt his unfitness, and so began with the lowest class, and then rose until he had the highest class under his care. Referring to the " Fourth Report of the South Kent Sunday-school Union (1823)," embracing schools within a line drawn from Folkestone to Sandwich, and round to Deal and Dover, it is evident that the work was earnestly, zealously, and efficiently conducted.

Our friend Richard, when he went to reside at Woolwich the second time, commenced a Sunday-school of an evening, in his own cottage. The good minister at the parish church commended his humble brother and fellow-worker ; and afterwards, by a very pleasant arrangement, the school was removed into the centre of the parish, under the care of some ladies, who had more time at their command. Richard, however, would not be idle, and as the services at Eythorne were over by three o'clock, he thought the long evenings gave him an opportunity to benefit his neighbours, so he opened his house for prayer, and the reading of such sermons as those by George Burder, whose plain evangelical discourses have been made abundantly useful.

There have always been a number of preaching-places in connection with the Eythorne church, especially when the pastor has given himself, as Mr. Giles did, and as some others have done, to this blessed evangelizing work. During the writer's pastorate this kind of work was revived and extended, and it has been carried on since, though less as the work of the pastor, and more as the work of the church, which is as it should be. During the writer's pastorate a chapel was built at Ashley; another, which had been closed thirty years, at Eastry, was first leased, and has since been bought and enlarged; a third was restored to the control of the Eythorne church; and in all these, and in two other places, where chapels have since been erected, Sunday-schools are flourishing.

Our friend Richard was regularly called by the church, and set apart as a village-preacher, and he continued it for forty years ; and even when he was considerably over seventy years of age, he has often walked ten or a dozen miles to and from a Sunday-evening service, and then been up at four o'clock the next morning in preparation for his work on the farm.

Our friend was never censorious, nor eager to find fault, nor in any sense narrow-minded ; but he knew that those who follow Christ must renounce the vanities and foolish usages, as well as sinful customs, of worldly people, and he framed his life accordingly. One of his employers said of him, " He is a wonderful man ; he can do anything on a farm ; he knows the Bible from beginning to end ; he can preach and pray : but there are two things he cannot do—he cannot swear nor get drunk, as many men do."

Harvest-suppers have often put a man's religion to the test. On one occasion, at a harvest-supper, Richard Baker was asked by his master, who was at the head of the table, to sing a song. Several foolish songs had been sung, and Richard at once responded in his own way, prefacing his song by saying, " Dear friends, when I was a wanderer from God, I used to sing foolish songs, such as we have heard, because I did not know any better; but since then God has brought me out of the horrible pit, set my feet upon a rock, and put a *new song* into my mouth, and I think I will sing you a song of two verses." He immediately struck up—

> " 'Tis religion that can give
> Sweetest pleasures while we live ;
> 'Tis religion must supply
> Solid comfort when we die.
>
> After death its joys will be
> Lasting as eternity:
> Be the living God my Friend,
> Then my bliss shall never end."

This put a stop to all other songs that night.

It is remarkable that the little hymn just quoted was composed, excepting the last two lines, which have been added by another hand, by Mary Masters, an uneducated servant.

Richard Baker had eight children, two of whom died young ; one of the others is in America, one has been a Scripture-reader and home-missionary. and another is one of the village-preachers in the Eythorne district. Three daughters are also walking faithfully in God's ways, and six of his grandchildren are church-members. When, at eighty-four, he was no longer able to work, the church made him a liberal allowance, and his single daughters and other children made his home happy, and his last days pleasant. After a long illness his wife died 14th November, 1888, and on the 17th of the following month he was called home, having entered his ninetieth year.

The scene at his funeral was remarkable, and such as is seldom witnessed at the interment of a farm-labourer. His fellow-workmen bore the body to the tomb, the deacons, elders, and many members and others in the congregation, including his late master and mistress, followed, and almost the entire village were spectators. Rev. George Stanley, his pastor, improved his death by an appropriate sermon from Acts xxi. 16, when some of his favourite hymns were sung, among which was the old pilgrim song—

> " Jerusalem, my happy home !
> Name ever dear to me."

Dear old Richard Baker was a liberal-minded man, but he was sound in the truths of the gospel, and his heart responded to the sweet notes of sovereign grace and redeeming love. Of all the eight pastors during his time, Mr. Giles stood first, but we forbear to say who stood next ; and of all living preachers, Mr. Spurgeon stood, in his opinion, more than head and shoulders above the rest. He read his sermons with delight when he could no longer distinguish the sounds of the living voice. Mr. Spurgeon had his hearty sympathy, too, in the noble testimony he has recently borne in defence of the everlasting gospel.

The example of this good man as a humble, fervent-spirited, and consistent disciple of Christ, may well be followed. Whoever was absent from the Sunday-morning prayer-meeting, Richard Baker was there ; and when he could no longer hear others, he loved to pour out his own heart in supplication. Strange to say, too, when his mind had become weakened, and often wandered as to all other things, the prayer-meeting and the blessed truths and promises of the gospel always held their place in his thoughts. There were two great truths in which he ever rejoiced, and delighted to hear and speak of—"No condemnation *in* Christ; no separation *from* Christ." Well, therefore, his last words might be—"Praise! Praise! Glory!"

"At home with Jesus! He who went before
  For his own people mansions to prepare;
The soul's deep longings filled, its conflicts o'er,
  All rest and blessedness with Jesus there;
What home like this can the wide earth afford?
  'So shall we be for ever with the Lord.'

"With him all gathered! to that blessed home,
  Through all its windings still the pathway tends;
While ever and anon bright glimpses come
  Of that fair city where the journey ends;
Where all of bliss is centred in one word—
  'So shall we be for ever with the Lord.'"

Meta Heusser, in "Hymns from the Land o Luther."

A Church that will Hold.

THE need is not a minister that will draw the people, but a church that will hold them for God. The following hits the matter:—
"A man came up to my study the other day, from one of the churches near Murray Hill that is vacant, and he said: 'I wish you could recommend us a minister for our church.' I said: 'I can recommend a dozen.' He seemed rather bluffed at that; thought that was a large number, and said: 'Won't you suggest a name?' And I went on suggesting one name after another. I suggested one man, and he said: 'I understand that man has not a very strong voice.' I suggested another. 'Well, I understand that man wears a black cravat in the pulpit.' Another man. 'Well, I understand that man is not a very good reader.' And another man. 'Well, I understand that man has a very stiff and formal delivery.' Finally he said: 'Well, what we want in our church is a minister that will draw.' 'Oh, no, my Christian friend; what you want is a church that will hold. You haven't it. Twenty congregations have passed through your church in the last twenty years, and they have passed through because you have not had a church that will hold. You want a church that will hold the people when they get into it. The minister cannot hold. Success depends not half so much upon the minister as upon you, the church.'"

We take this from *The St. Louis Advocate*, and call attention to it because we believe it indicates one of the main causes of the want of growth in churches. The churches must make their membership into a pastorate by universal mutual care and communion. The minister may catch fish, but the church must be the basket to carry them home. Let every believer take his place in the body, for its supply and edification, and then "the one-man ministry" will simply be the leadership in an every-man ministry.

Interesting Notes on Foreign Missions.[*]

THE remarkable letter of Colonel Charles Denby, to his friend General Shackleford, appears in the February number of the *Missionary Review*. The following are extracts from it :—

"Believe nobody when he sneers at the missionaries. The man is simply not posted on the work. I saw a quiet cheerful woman teaching forty or more Chinese girls; she teaches in Chinese the ordinary branches of common school education. Beneath the shadow of the 'forbidden city' I heard these girls sing the Psalms of David and 'Home, Sweet Home.' I saw a male teacher teaching forty or more boys. The men or the women who put in from 8 o'clock to 4 in teaching Chinese children, on a salary that barely enables one to live, are heroes, or heroines, as truly as Grant or Sheridan, Nelson or Farragut; and all this in a country where a handful of Americans is surrounded by three hundred million Asiatics, liable at any moment to break out into mobs and outrages, particularly in view of the tremendous crimes committed against their race at home.

"I visited the dispensaries, complete and perfect as any apothecary's shop at home ; then the consultation-rooms, their ward for patients, coming without money or price, to be treated by the finest medical and surgical talent in the world. There are twenty-three of these hospitals in China. Think of it ! Is there a more perfect charity in the world ? The details of all the system were explained to me. There are two medical missionaries here who receive no pay whatever. Who can rival the devotedness of these men to humanity ? I have seen missionaries go hence a hundred miles, into districts where there is not a white person of any nationality, and they do it as coolly as you went into battle at Shiloh. And these men have remarkable learning, intelligence, and courage. It is perhaps a fault that they court nobody, make no effort to attract attention, fight no selfish battle. It is idle for any man to decry the missionaries or their work. I can tell the real from the false. These men and women are honest, pious, sincere, industrious, and trained for their work by the most arduous study. I do not address myself to the churches ; but, as a man of the world, talking to sinners like himself, I say that it is difficult to say too much good of missionary work in China."

UNSALARIED MISSIONARIES IN INDIA.

The Rev. M. M. Carleton writes as follows to the editor of the *Missionary Review* concerning the unsalaried missionaries in India : "We find in the foreign field men and women from England who have gone out among the heathen with independent fortunes of their own. They give their wealth *plus themselves* to missionary work. During the thirty-two years I have been in India, I have known several of this class of English missionaries. They are among the best workers in the mission-field. They come from old English families distinguished for generations both in Church and State. Some of them enter the mission-

---

[*] From "The Great Value and Success of Foreign Missions, proved by Distinguished Witnesses." By Rev. John Liggins. (See Review.)

field with private fortunes of half a million of dollars, and with this wealth they give their own lives freely to the cause of missions."

THE CHANGE IN TORRES STRAITS.

As a boy, one of my earliest remembrances is that of being told the tragic history of the *Charles Eaton.* A large merchantman of that name, bound for China, was wrecked among the dangerous reefs of Torres Straits. A raft was hastily made, on which the crew and passengers all escaped to a small island, where they were treacherously welcomed by the natives. On the first night after their arrival, the savages, having seen that all their visitors were asleep, set upon them with clubs. With the exception of one little boy, every one of the white men was killed, and the bodies were eaten. The child was carried off with the skulls of the murdered people to Murray Island. A schooner sent out by the British Government rescued the boy ; and finding the skulls piled as a trophy, brought them to the Cape of Good Hope, where they were buried.

The facts are impressed on my mind because an uncle of my own was one of the victims, and his death must have occurred about the same time I was born. Now, through the heroism of missionaries who, fearless of its evil reputation, and of the blood of some of their own number, persisted in occupying that ill-omened region for Christ, Murray Island is civilized ; it has become an educational centre ; industrial and other schools are planted there, regular reports are issued of the work carried on by native teachers, and it is a well-known place of call for traders. It is quite as safe to-day for a stranger to be wrecked in Torres Straits as in Boston Harbour ; and a merchant is in more danger of being clubbed on Broadway than on those once murderous shores.—*Dr. T. Harwood Pattison, quoted in the Sunday at Home, March,* 1887.

CIVILIZATION WITHOUT THE GOSPEL DOES NOT CIVILIZE.

At the last annual meeting of the London Missionary Society, the Rev. James Chalmers, the "Apostle of New Guinea," said : "Two years ago, from this country they sent out the British flag to that country, and they told the natives of New Guinea that the British Queen Victoria —God bless her !—was going to protect them. Have you considered it ? I have had twenty-one years' experience amongst natives. I have seen the semi-civilized and the uncivilized ; I have lived with the Christian native, and I have lived, dined, and slept with the cannibal. I have visited the islands of the New Hebrides, which I sincerely trust will not be handed over to the tender mercies of France ; I have visited the Loyalty Group, I have seen the work of missions in the Samoan Group, I know all the islands of the Society Group, I have lived for ten years in the Hervey Group, I know a few of the groups close on the line, and for at least nine years of my life I have lived with the savages of New Guinea ; but I have never yet met with a single man or woman, or with a single people, that your civilization without Christianity has civilized. For God's sake let it be done at once !—Gospel and commerce, but remember this, it must be the Gospel first. Wherever there has been the slightest spark of civilization in the Southern Seas, it has been where the Gospel has been preached ; and wherever you find in the island of New Guinea a friendly people or a people that will welcome you there, it is where the missionaries of the Cross have been preaching Christ. Civilization! The rampart can only be stormed by those who carry the Cross."

THE WONDERFUL RESULT OF A LOVING ACT.

Mrs. Jennie F. Willing, in a late missionary address in New York city, related a story of a missionary and his wife in one of the South Sea Islands, where Dr. Crocker, of Michigan University, narrowly escaped being eaten by cannibals. Dr. Crocker and a friend lived to tell the story of their adventures in England. Moved by love, and under the guidance of the Holy Spirit, a clergyman and his wife decided to go out as missionaries to that very island. Embarking on a merchant vessel, they succeeded in inducing the captain to put them ashore where none of the inhabitants were visible.

Seating themselves on a box that contained all their earthly possessions, they watched the ship spread its white sails and disappear below the horizon. When the savages, accompanied by their chief and his daughter, came on the scene, they felt the limbs of the missionary, and evidently thought that in him was material for a good dinner. The daughter ran her fingers through the long, silky hair of the lady, who, impelled by Christian love, drew the girl to her, and imprinted a kiss upon her lips. That natural act won the heart of the daughter. For three days the debate on eating the unexpected guests went on, and at last was decided in the negative by the pleading eloquence of the chief's favourite child. The missionaries lived long enough to see the people of that island converted to Christ, and sending out missionaries to other islands still in heathen darkness. Thus that little act of love was the means, through God, of saving many precious souls.

MR. M. D. CONWAY'S EXPERIENCES IN HONOLULU.

One cannot help being amused at reading a letter of Mr. Moncure D. Conway's, the "Liberal" preacher of London, describing his experiences at Honolulu, at which port the steamer, which was carrying him from San Francisco to Australia, touched. The vessel stopped there only over a Sabbath, and the disgust of this traveller at the strictness with which the people kept the day is very great. He expected on landing to witness "merry scenes, islanders swimming around the ship in Arcadian innocence, the joyous dance and song of guileless children of the sun"; but his anticipations were rudely destroyed by finding a "silent city," "paralyzed by piety." "Never in Scotland or Connecticut have I seen such a paralysis as fell upon Honolulu the first day of the week." This traveller found the stores shut, and in a druggist's shop they would not even sell him a glass of soda. No one being willing to show him the sights of the place, he was compelled to go to church in order to look upon the people. He was impressed by what he saw there, especially at the Chinese church under the care of Mr. Damon, whose work in elevating the people he cannot help praising. But, after all, he can enjoy little where the Sabbath is kept so strictly, and complains bitterly of the "pietistic plague" which prevails on the island. This testimony to the success of Christian efforts in the Hawaiian Islands is undesigned, but not the less valuable.—*Missionary Herald, February,* 1884.

The Pardon of Sin under Law.

BY PASTOR R. GOVETT, NORWICH.

THE law of Moses contained the shadows of the gospel. The primary covenant of Israel at Horeb was, indeed, a solemn promise not to sin. "All that the Lord hath said we will do, and be obedient." If law is broken, penalty must follow. Forgiveness does not appear as part of it. So, in the original draught of the covenant, God says, "Behold, I send an Angel before thee. . . . . Beware of him, and obey his voice, provoke him not; FOR HE WILL NOT PARDON YOUR TRANSGRESSIONS: *for my name is in him*" (Ex. xxiii. 20, 21). Hence, the worship of the golden calf was not pardoned, though Moses himself pleaded for its forgiveness. The penalty has yet to be exacted.

After the breach of the first covenant, a new one was made with Moses, as the representative of Israel (Ex. xxxiv.). Under that, Israel was directed to construct an abode for her God, in the midst of the tribes; and the promise of forgiveness first appears.

But not every sin was pardonable: sins of wilfulness admitted of no forgiveness (Num. xv.). Sins of ignorance alone might be forgiven. *In what way?*

I. Was the sinner to appear before God at his altar, and on bended knees, with fasting, tears, and groans, solemnly to vow that he would never sin again?

By no means! His solemn promise made at Sinai was already broken. Where would be the use of solemnly promising again? God could find no satisfaction in such vows. The secret of failure lies very deep. "Because the mind of the flesh is enmity against God: for it is not subject to the law of God, neither indeed can be" (Rom. viii. 7).

In what way, then, were sins of ignorance pardonable? We find the mode set forth in the fourth of Leviticus. Four different views of the pardon are given, varying with the importance of the case. It is enough for our present purpose to take the last of these, a sin committed by one of the common people.

27. "*If any one of the common people sin through ignorance, while he doeth somewhat against any of the commandments of the Lord (Jehovah) concerning things which ought not to be done, and be guilty.*"

An act against human law is a crime avenged by human magistrates. But an act against the laws of the divine Lawgiver, is a *sin* entailing penalties beyond those of man. He is "*guilty.*"

The act makes him a debtor to law; he is bound to suffer the penalty of death, by way of satisfaction to the good law which he has broken. On the observance of God's laws the welfare of the universe turns. And within the offender arise fears, wherever sin has not hardened the heart.

28. "*Or if his sin, which he hath sinned, come to his knowledge.*"

Men's thoughts of sin differ greatly from those of God. Many philosophers will teach you that sin is committed only where there are full knowledge and deliberation. *Now, for such sin there was no forgiveness, under Moses* (Num. xv. 30). "The soul that doeth ought presumptuously, whether he be born in the land, or a stranger, the same reproacheth the Lord; and *that soul shall be cut off from among his people.*"

Many sins take place unknown to us; many are forgotten. But vainly do men forget, if God remembers, and has all sins in his books. "*Though he knew it not, he is guilty, and shall bear his iniquity*" (Lev. v. 17—19). Such were the circumstances of the sin: how was it to be pardoned?

"*He shall bring his offering, a kid of the goats, a female* without blemish, *for his sin which he hath sinned.*"

· 1. Not every animal was admissible for a sacrifice; some kinds, as the swine, the dog, the camel, were unclean. It must be one, then, of a kind specified by the Lord. The offender was to lead it with him to the place of meeting appointed by God. Only there might the business be transacted.

2. Might the creature that he brought be "*accepted for him,*" that is, as his substitute? *That* was the question which at once engaged the attention of the priest, the executioner of the law of Jehovah. When the sacrifice of Isaac was stopped by the angel, Abraham offered up a ram, caught in the thicket by his horns, "*for a burnt offering, in the stead of his son*" (Gen. xxii.).

The question to be decided by the priest was, "Is the creature perfect?" If it had anything superfluous or lacking in its parts, it was not to be accepted (Lev. xxii. 21—25). "WITHOUT BLEMISH" is the condition, and it is some forty times demanded in the law. Jehovah will accept only what is perfect. He complains of Israel presenting to him creatures for sacrifice which their governors would reject (Mal. i.). It is not—"God will accept us if we do our best." You have committed sin, and sin is *not* "*doing your best.*"

So, before our Lord Jesus Christ was offered as a sacrifice, he was presented before both Caiaphas and Pilate; and each found no fault in him.

The offender here presents himself before Jehovah as a sinner confessed, desirous of obtaining pardon for this one offence. He proffers a perfect animal to be his sacrifice. The priest pronounces it without fault, and it is accepted as his substitute.

What is the next step?

29. "*He shall lay his hand upon the head of the sin offering.*"

The act is a carrying out of his desire for forgiveness. "Let this creature bear my sin, which I thus, by thy permission, lay upon it. My sin is now *on my own head,* and I bear sin, and I lie under the sentence of death." "The soul that sins shall die," is the ordinary current of law. But does law admit of substitution? May the Lawgiver show mercy to the sinner? And the answer of Scripture is, that God does delight to do so; and that another's bearing the sins of the offender, and suffering for them, is his way of salvation.

The meaning of the act, then, is clear: "O God, let my sin be imputed to this perfect creature!"

1. This view is established by the sin offering of the second goat, on the day of atonement. "And Aaron shall lay both his hands upon the head of the live goat, *and confess over him all the iniquities of the children of Israel, and all their transgressions in all their sins, putting them upon the head of the goat.* . . . . *And the goat shall bear upon him all their iniquities*" (Lev. xvi. 21, 22).

2. In the trespass offering, where hands are not imposed, we have instead *confession of sin,* before atonement is made by the priest, and the sacrifice is presented (Lev. v. 15, 16).

3. In the case of an uncertain murder, where the elders declare their *innocence* of the crime, there is no laying on of hands, but a washing of them, in the presence of the priests, the executioners of God's law (Deut. xxi.). They deprecate in prayer the wrath of God, "and the blood shall be forgiven them."

The testimony of Jewish teachers is, that such is the meaning of the laying on of hands. It appears, also, that confession in words was made to God, desiring that the victims might be the substitute of the offender.

But some have objected—"Scripture makes the *blood* and the fat, and the flesh of the sin offering, to be *holy.* How can that be?" Because the sin is *borne on* the *head* of the goat. It is not said that it *penetrates into its heart,* and defiles its blood. The perfect goat still remains perfect within.

Look at the matter from another point of view.

Why is the sacrifice slain, and that *before the Lord ?* The goat is *perfect.*
Perfection does not deserve death at the hand of the Lord, but life. Why
does not the Judge of all interfere, then, to save its life ? "Ye shall therefore keep my statutes, and my judgments : which if a man do, he shall *live*
in them" (Lev. xviii. 5). "What good thing shall I do, that I may have
eternal *life ?* " "If thou wilt *enter into life,* keep the commandments"
(Matt. xix. 17). "In the way of righteousness is *life ;* and in the pathway
thereof is *no death* " (Prov. xii. 28). Why ? Because something evil has been
laid upon it ; for at once great changes ensue. *That* is slain that deserves
not to die : the *offender,* who deserves to die, is *forgiven,* and *lives.* Sin, then,
has been passed over to it, and that by the offerer. Yes ! He brings the
animal "*for his sin which he has sinned."*

As soon as hands have, by God's direction, and in his presence, been laid
on the creature, it "*bears sin."* We know how oft this phrase occurs in
Scripture. The Lord hath "*laid upon him the iniquity of us all."* "By his
knowledge shall my *Righteous Servant* justify many ; for he shall *bear their
iniquities*" (Isa. liii. 6—11). "He made him to be *sin for us,* who knew *no
sin,* that we might be made the righteousness of God in him."

Herein shines out the love of God.

But some object—"*That is unjust !* " We ask, *To whom is it unjust ?*
1. To *Christ ?* Nay, he voluntarily, deliberately took the sinner's place and
doom ! 2. To the *Father ?* Nay ; for he and the Son are agreed. The plan
of grace is his. And the principle of law is, "*Volenti non fit injuria."* " No
injustice is done to a man who desires you so to act as you have done." The
Father and the Son are in this salvation abundantly glorified. And the
Saviour's reward of suffering has yet to be bestowed. "*He shall see of
the travail of his soul, and shall be satisfied."*

"*And slay the sin offering in the place* [*where they slay*] *the burnt
offering."*

The meaning of the next step is apparent enough. The animal now,
despite its perfection, "*bears sin."* And to bearing sin *belongs death.*
"Neither must the children of Israel henceforth come near the tabernacle
of the congregation [the tent of meeting,] lest *they bear sin, and die* "
(Num. xviii. 22). Priests might not eat any defiled meat, "*lest they bear sin
for it, and die therefore*" (Lev. xxii. 9). The "blasphemer should *bear his
sin, and be put to death*" (Lev. xxiv. 15). For, as the New Testament
declares, "*The wages of sin is death."*

And the death is inflicted by the sinner's own hand. Death is what he
deserves. In the fulfilment, in our Lord's sacrifice, Peter can say—"Jesus
the Nazarite, a man approved by God . . . . . ye have taken, and *by*
wicked hands have crucified and slain" (Acts ii. 22, 23).

By this one observation alone we may see the error of a learned German,
who teaches, that the animal slain represents *the wicked wilfulness of the
sinner,* which he puts an end to by slaying it ! Nay ; what is *slain* is *perfection,* in order that the *sinner* may *live !* Nor does any sinner slay the evil
in himself ; he slays his substitute, after it has been accepted in his stead.
God's scheme stands on two pillars, seemingly opposite to one another :—
(1) PERFECTION before God, and (2) DEATH inflicted in his presence, and
by his order. Why ?
Of grace : "The priest shall make atonement for him, and *it shall be
forgiven him."* When Isaac escaped death as the sacrifice, Abraham offers up
the "*ram in the stead of his son*" (Gen. xxii. 13).

30. *And the priest shall take of the blood thereof with his finger, and put
it upon the horns of the altar of burnt offering.*

Here "the priest"—God's officer, set apart to execute his orders, and
especially his wrath—steps on the scene. The priest is of a special race,

selected and peculiarly cleansed by Jehovah, in order to draw near himself, and attend at his altar. None else might presume to approach, under penalty of death. And the priest must be perfect of flesh; several defects would shut him out from the priesthood (Lev. xxi.). How great an offence Jehovah judged it to be to invade the priest's office, we see by the cutting off by fire of Korah, and his two hundred and fifty princes; and by the smiting of Israel with leprosy to the day of his death. Out of the censers of Korah and his company were broad plates made as a covering of the altar, "to be a memorial, that no stranger, which is not of the seed of Aaron, *come near* to offer incense before the Lord; that he be not as Korah, and as his company " (Num. xvi. 40).

In the New Testament fulfilment, the priest is the sinless Son of God, who atoned by his blood, and is now seated at the right hand of the Most High.

The priest alone might present the blood of the perfect one to God. The *priest* cannot make atonement *without blood.* "Without shedding of blood is no forgiveness." And *none but the priest* might offer the *blood* of the perfect one, shed in death.

The death is a judicial one, a violent outpouring of the soul. In most deaths by disease, no blood is shed.

At this point many mistake and stumble. They say, "'The blood'—as Scripture teaches—' is *the life.*' It is, then, *the life of Christ,* and *not his death,* that brings pardon, when presented to God."

Not so! Scripture never speaks of the Saviour's *life* as procuring the sinner's forgiveness. It is always "his *blood,*" "his *death.*" "This is my *blood* of the New Testament, which is being *shed* for many, *unto remission of sins*" (Matt. xxvii. 28). "We have *redemption through his blood, the forgiveness of sins*" (Eph. i. 7). "Ye who once were far off are made nigh *by the blood of Christ.*" How presented? When shed in death. "That he might reconcile both [Jew and Gentile] unto God in one body *by the cross,* having *slain the enmity thereby*" (Eph. ii. 13—16). "Having made peace *through the blood of his cross,* by him to reconcile all things to himself" (Col. i. 20, 22).

Would any cite the words, "We shall be saved by *his life*"? One look at the context turns over this citation to establish the other side. "While we were yet sinners, *Christ died for us.* Much more then, being *now justified by his blood,* we shall be saved from wrath through him. For if, when we were enemies, *we were reconciled to God by the death of his Son,* much more, *being reconciled,* we shall be saved by his life" (Rom. v. 8—10).

Blood, while it is flowing in the veins of the living creature, is the support of its life. *But while so coursing in its veins, it effects no pardon.* Not till it is poured out in death does it bring forgiveness. "*Without shedding of blood is no forgiveness*" (Heb. ix. 22).

The priest is to put the blood on "*the altar.*"

The altar was the appointed place of presenting the blood, the fat, the flesh of the sacrifice. There abode the fire that consumed the sacrifice. The fire came forth from God, and it was always to be tended by the priests, and never allowed to go out (Lev. vi.).

Now, fire is terrible both to man and animals. It represents the wrath of God. Death by fire from the Lord bespoke his wrath against the sinner. So were Nadab and Abihu cut off; so Korah and his company. "Lest my *fury* come forth *like fire,* and burn that none can quench it, because of the evil of your doings" (Jer. iv. 4; xxi. 12; Sam. ii. 4). "For, behold, the Lord will *come with fire,* and with his chariots like a whirlwind, to render *his anger* with fury, and *his rebuke with flames of fire*" (Isa. lxvi. 15). "Their worm shall not die, neither shall *their fire be quenched*" (Isa. lxvi. 24). "I will blow against thee *in the fire of my wrath*" (Ezek. xxi. 31; xxii. 21).

More definitely, the blood of the sacrifice was to be put on the four horns

39

of the altar. The altar had a projection at each of its corners. In those horns seemed to be centred the power of the altar to produce death. The horns just above the fire were the places on which the blood was to be set: the blood, proof of the death of the sacrifice, in pursuance of the demand of the Judge.

In its New Testament fulfilment, the altar is the cross; instrument of death and the curse. The cross had four ends; and on each of these blood was put. On the highest point there was blood of the Saviour, drawn by the crown of thorns; on the ends of the transverse beam, there was blood from the nails. At the foot of the cross, there was again blood drawn by the nails.

" *And he shall pour out all the blood thereof at the bottom of the altar.*"

The whole of the ransom must be paid. The blood is the ransom-price. " For the *soul* of the flesh is in the *blood;* and *I have given it to you upon the altar to make an atonement for your souls;* for it is the *blood* that maketh atonement *by the soul.* Therefore I said unto the children of Israel, No *soul* of you shall eat blood, neither shall any stranger that sojourneth among you eat blood " (Lev. xvii. 11, 12). " He shall even pour out the *blood*, and cover it with dust. For it is the *soul* of all flesh; *the blood of it is for the soul thereof.*" " For *the soul of all flesh is the blood thereof*" (Lev. xvii. 13, 14).

In this passage the argument is obscured unless we render the Hebrew, *nephesh* (soul), by one word throughout. Man is described here as a " *soul.*" The blood, which is the creature's visible " *soul,*" was reserved by God to himself, on purpose that it might atone for guilty *souls.*

The New Testament fulfilment of these two commands shows how clearly Christ our Lord is pointed out as the GREAT SIN-OFFERING. One of the soldiers sent to break the legs of the culprits, when he found that Jesus was dead already, " with a spear pierced his side, and forthwith came there out *blood* and *water*" (John xix. 34). The rest of the blood fell, then, at the foot of the cross—" the bottom of the altar."

31. " *And he shall take away all the fat thereof, as the fat is taken away from off the sacrifice of peace offerings; and the priest shall burn it upon the altar for a sweet savour unto the Lord.*"

After the blood of the sacrifice had been taken, its skin was rent off, and the animal was cut up. There is thenceforth no care for the creature's welfare; its soul and body are both forfeit.

There is external perfection visible, before the creature's slaughter. But after its slaying, there is manifested *inward* perfection beside. For death is not the sum total of the dues of justice against the transgressor. " It is appointed unto men once to die; *and after death, judgment.*" The priests, the ministers of judgment, must give the fat to the *fire of the altar.* A new phase of judgment begins after death—the victim's fat is laid on the fire. " The priest shall burn it upon the altar, according to *the offerings made by fire unto the Lord* (verse 35)." Thus the sin offering takes its designation from its burning by the priest—it is " *an offering made by fire.*"

There is One only who, tried under the wrath of God, could show perfection. Job, when tested, and not under the wrath of God, was advised to " curse God and die ": and, while he did not do that, yet he cursed the day of his birth. But Christ was perfect. Seven words of his while on the cross are given us. And they were a " savour of rest " to God, and to man. The first four respect man; the last three, God.

1. Jesus prays for his crucifiers! 2, 3. He provides a protector and an abode for his mother. 4. He promises Paradise to the penitent robber.

Then we have his words:—

5. " I thirst"—as fulfilling the Scripture; the only point as yet unfulfilled in his life (John xix. 28).

6. " My God, my God, why hast thou forsaken me ? "

7. "Father, into thy hands I commend my spirit." In all this God could find full complacency. Here he could rest.

"*And the priest shall make atonement for him, and it shall be forgiven him.*"

It is not, "*the sinner shall make atonement for himself.*" He is doubly disqualified; by his *act* of disobedience, and by his *state* of enmity. "If ye then, being *evil.*" "The mind of the flesh is enmity against God." (Rom. viii. 7.) He is both guilty and polluted; unfit to draw near to God, and unacceptable to him.

What is the sense of "atonement"?

The Hebrew word signifies to *cover.* The perfect soul of the creature is given by God on the altar to cover the guilty soul. Its blood is given to *blot out the offender's sin.* "I have *blotted out*, as a thick cloud, thy transgressions, and, as a cloud, thy sins" (Isa. xliv. 22).

"Repent ye therefore, and be converted, that your sins may be *blotted out*, that the times of refreshing may come from the presence of the Lord" (Acts iii. 19).

Attempts in that day to atone in any but God's way would have been unbelief. Much more is any attempt now to put away sin, save by the blood of Christ.

Thus there are *two coverings* here presented.

1. The passive one—the *blood* of the victim (Lev. xvi. 11, 27).

2. The active one—the *priest.* He was set between God and man, to regard the interests of both: to uphold the demands of law, and yet to bring in grace in God's way. And God's way of covering sin was by presenting the blood and the fat on the altar

"*It shall be forgiven him!*"

Joyful words! 1. The penalty has been borne by another. 2. The merits of another have prevailed to restore the lost favour of God.

All others "die in their sins." And then we see, in the treatment of the sacrifice, the deserts of the unforgiven sinner.

Forgiveness of transgression is not the usual course of law. Pardon is grace undeserved. This passage tells of the forgiveness of but *one* act of sin, while the sins of men are more in number than the hairs of the head.

Thus the whole ends in God's testimony to the sinner of pardon. What a boon to the offender! And if that were granted under law, how much more under the gospel! The Perfect Priest and the Perfect Sacrifice are come, and have brought forgiveness! The High Priest is even at God's right hand! He has given "*knowledge of salvation unto his people by the remission of their sins*" (Luke i. 77). "*Having forgiven you all trespasses*" (Col. ii. 3). "*Go in peace; thy sins are forgiven.*"

"Shall I, then, go *to the priests of Rome to get forgiveness ?*" Yes; if Christ has not perfectly satisfied God for sin! Yes; if the Perfect Priest has not perfectly atoned! Yes; if Jesus our Lord is not now ever living, seated in heaven at the right hand of God! Yes; if God owns any sinful, dying men, down on the earth, as his atoning priests! "By one offering he [Christ] hath for a continuance perfected them that are sanctified" (Heb. x. 14).

Notices of Books.

Echoes from Japan. By M. McLean. Passmore & Alabaster. Cloth, 3s. 6d., paper boards, 2s. 6d.

The object of this lively and instructive book is to arouse missionary zeal for Japan. Our earnest hope is that the excellent authoress will not have written in vain; certainly she has found one interested reader in the writer of the present notice. What with gracious reflections, noteworthy observations, memorable histories, and a personal narrative running right through, the book has many charms. The cover is Japanese of the Japanese, and represents a fish going up a waterfall. Some of the illustrations are quite as special: we append a specimen.

JAPANESE NURSE AND BABY.

Present Day Tracts on Subjects of Christian Evidence, Doctrine, and Morals. Vol. X. Religious Tract Society.

THE high value of these tracts is not allowed to decline. They are among the best of the good things which the R. T. S. has issued. The tract on *Socialism* is very timely, and that on *the Age and Trustworthiness of the Old Testament Scriptures* is equally so. Six first-rate essays, neatly bound, for 2s. 6d.: nothing can be more worthy of the notice of the thoughtful believer. We have now before us the tenth volume of the series, and it is an exceedingly good one. If our friends possess these ten volumes, they will not need the other form of them, for these are the same tracts arranged according to subjects. Happy is he who has the tracts in either form.

The Obedience of a Christian Man. Set forth by William Tyndale. ["Christian Classics" Series, V.] 2s. 6d. Religious Tract Society.

THE Tract Society will do great service to the higher class of students if they continue to reproduce choice pieces of the classical divinity of past ages. Of course, there will be found in such works things with which none of us will altogether agree; but we want to know what holy men of old thought; and when their writings are difficult to obtain, we are grateful for a re-issue which puts them within our reach. Students are generally as poor in coin as they are hungry for learning. You can cultivate literature "upon a little oatmeal"; but some books require for their purchase more than a little gold. He is a public benefactor who reprints a noble book at a small price. All the renowned works of antiquity are not of equal value to all, but a judicious choice will produce an invaluable series. So far that choice has been good.

Tyndale's "Obedience of a Christian Man" is one of the few books which deserve to be immortal. It has the life of the Holy Spirit in it, and hence it has quickened martyrs and confessors, and will, we trust, continue to inspire witnesses for the truth of God. Its English is pure, strong, racy, vigorous: if a man should read it for style alone, he would grieve the shade of the writer, who cared nothing for literary honour; but he would greatly profit himself by seeing what can be done with our dear mother tongue—that strong Saxon speech, which may not suit courtiers, but is a fitting language for brave men.

Tyndale hits hard, and may be judged to be coarse by our modern gentility; but when a man has to deal with the errors of Rome, he may safely leave soft gloves to be worn by his adversaries. He loved his Bible; its plain sense was his sheet-anchor. He cared nothing for the schoolmen, with their allegorical, tropological, and anagogical interpretations, which he sarcastically calls *chop*ological; but he bows with lowly reverence before the manifest meaning of the Holy Ghost in the words which he gave to the inspired writers. Burning with hatred towards sin and error, he is willing to sacrifice himself to redeem his fellow-men from the bondage of priestcraft, and he sets forth the gospel in the clearest terms. Tyndale is as transparent as glass, and we read him with extreme delight.

A man who would meet the errors of the ritualists would find many weapons in this work; and he would be refreshed by some fine bits of gospel truth, which would make him indignant with those who ruin souls by perverting the sacred Word.

The present edition will be prized by bookish folk who like margins and rough edges, and the old style of printing. We ought to add that this is a clear and beautiful style.

Our Present Hope and Our Future Home. A series of fifty-two papers. By REV. JAMES STURROCK, M.A., Paisley. Alexander Gardner, Paternoster Row.

A PASTOR of considerable ability finds his people desirous of seeing certain of his addresses and short sermons in print; he therefore collects them into one volume, and issues them under a title which he thinks appropriate. This is, we suppose, the origin of the book before us, which contains many good things, but has not much relation to its title, so far as we can see. Our author is outspoken as to the divine authority of sacred Scripture, and by no means conceals his hearty agreement with the old faith; moreover, he gives forth no uncertain sound as to the vital experience necessary to salvation, and he puts his thoughts in pleasing language; and therefore we believe that he has succeeded in his one design, for he says, "All I aim at is to provide profitable reading for the Christian fireside." It is well to have many such books as food for every day, for every-day people. If they are not among those writings which influence an age, and settle great principles for generations to come, they do at least supply the daily need of the spiritual life among a number of the godly who are the mainstay of the churches.

Epistolary Studies; or, an Alphabet of Ethics for Young Thinkers. By JAMES SMITH, Newmarket. Jarrold and Sons. Price 2s.

These brief essays are by no means dull. They teach high morality and practical godliness; and from their abundant incident and their judicious brevity they secure attention. In the essay on gambling we note the following curious fact:—"On the laying of the foundation stone of the Congregational Chapel, on the site of King Charles's palace at Newmarket, two betting men, standing near the writer, actually laid a wager as to the probable length of the dedicatory prayer, as soon as the Rev. J. Raven, of Ipswich, was well into it." Think of two fellows betting on the length of a prayer!' This 'beats racing with snails, or laying odds upon which drop on the window would first run down to the bottom of the pane. If Mr. Smith had not himself overheard this betting about a prayer, we should have hoped, for the sake of human nature, that the story could not be true.

Pen Pictures from the Life of Christ. By the Rev. JOHN CULLEN, M.A. R. D. Dickinson.

PICTURES by no means badly drawn. Comparable to those sketches with which our daughters adorn the walls of a loving father's house: they hardly vie with those exhibited in the Royal Academy, but by loving friends they are justly valued. To the general reader these will be profitable pages; but the minister or student will not need them. Hearers of such discourses are highly favoured; there is in them good current money of the merchant, though not many nuggets of gold.

Farmer George, of Devonshire. By HENRY DENING. J. Kensit.

MR. DENING does not perfectly carry out his character as a rustic, for he lets expressions slip in which are too refined for the country; but still, he has done amazingly well. John Ploughman accepts imitation as the sincerest form of flattery, and he is delighted when he sees the thing done as well as in this case. The stories which are worked in are capital, and the holy lessons, which are deftly inserted, are better still. "The worst of it is," said the boy when he was finding fault with his pudding, "there's such a precious little of it" —sure sign that he liked what there was. It is a book which farming folk will read, and it will do them good. Here are two of the stories:

"It was a rare meeting, sir, I can tell you," says Jack, "and the people were packed together like sheep in a pen; because last week an infidel got up at the end of the meeting, and said he did not believe that a word of the Bible was true; and so the preacher said that if the infidel chap would come again last night, he would prove that the Bible was true with a pair of pincers. So he said 'all right,' he would be there. And so he was, and stuck hisself in front of the platform, as impudent as you please. When the preacher comed in, there was a bit of a titter; but he soon got to work, and tackled his man in workmanlike style. He went at him like this: he says, 'You don't believe a word of the Bible to be true'? 'No, I don't.' 'And I said I would prove the Bible true with a pair of pincers'? 'Yes.' 'Now,' says the preacher, 'I am going to read a verse out of the Bible from the book of Proverbs; and out of the three thousand proverbs that Solomon wrote, this one suits me best to-night; it is found in the thirtieth chapter and the thirty-third verse: "The wringing of the nose bringeth forth blood." Now,' says the preacher, catching up the blacksmith's pincers, and going towards the infidel, 'let me have a go at your nose, and the audience will see in two seconds whether the Bible is true or not.' Oh! sir, you should have seen his face,

looking as long as a fiddle, and his nose cocked up in the air, afeard that the preacher would lay hold on it. He pretty quick took a back seat for the rest of the meeting, for he saw that the preacher could practise as well as preach."

"I know of a clergyman, who was strong in health, who said he required a small amount of stimulants before starting on his rounds, as it was as good as a pony to him. One day he was shocked at finding one of his leading parishioners in the ditch the worse for liquor. The parson asked him how such a sad event happened? The farmer replied, 'I was riding your pony, sir, and he threw me off.' The parson resolved that, if that was the effect on his parishioner, he would give up his pony altogether. And so he did, and found that he could do his work much better in consequence, and with no ill effects on others."

The England of Shakespeare. By EDWIN GOODBY. Cassell and Co.

CHATTY and lively; with more about plays and players than we care for; but this could not well be otherwise when we have "The England of Shakespeare" for a theme. Our author makes us see those memorable days with our own eyes. Stirring times, sir, with a lioness on the throne, and brave sea-dogs around it. The Spanish king's beard was singed by Drake, and at last all the hair of his head was burnt off as the Armada was destroyed. One does not feel fascinated with the age when one looks under the surface, and sees the cruelty, drunkenness, and servility which were common everywhere, especially when "the lioness" was gone, and the man with the big tongue poured forth his inflated pedantry, and wanted all England to adore his wisdom. Lovers of real history, who are aweary of the made-up stories which swarm around us like the frogs of Egypt, will spend pleasant hours with this book before them.

Hold the Fort. Practical Suggestions for Abstainers. By MARY PRYOR HACK. Hodder and Stoughton.

A VERY practical shilling's-worth. Deals not only with the morals but with the medicine of total abstinence.

The Beginnings of Religion. An Essay. By THOMAS SCOTT BACON. Rivingtons.

SUCH is the modest title of a really magnificent volume. In so saying we refer less to the bulk of its contents than to the breadth of its conception. Are you surprised that a work of five hundred pages, admirably constructed and copiously indexed, is termed "an essay"? It is because of the simple aim to give the *results* rather than the *processes* of investigation and reflection, and so to keep within a compass which ordinary readers will appreciate. The author, an American clergyman, surveys a field of literature familiarly known to us as "*Comparative Theology.*" It is needless for us to say that this subject has been peculiarly attractive to scholars of the present century; and yet our author claims—fairly, we think—that he is breaking up fresh ground, or at least, taking a new departure. Specialists have pursued their studies in various departments, and enthusiasts have attempted to subvert our old traditions by their modern thoughts. The writer starts with an assumption—call it an axiom, if you like: "*There must be specialists in study.*" Of course there must. This is as obvious in mental pursuits as it is in mechanics. You do not suppose that your pocket-knife was manufactured by one artisan, but many specialists united in its production. The question arises—"How much deference do the specialists demand of us?" Here our author steps in to give us the net result in one case, as manufacturers would supply us with the finished article in the other. The bulk of our best educated men are not content with the fractional studies of any specialist, but take the wider view. They do not despise poetry, because they have a passion for philosophy; they do not eschew Scripture, because they esteem science; they do not impugn the Pentateuch, because they are Egyptologists. Are we all to renounce the right of private judgment because Darwin is eminent as a Naturalist, Huxley as a scientist, or Max Müller and Whincy as philologists? This is the point discussed in these chapters. The summing-up of our modern Bacon, after a survey of wide regions of phantom and fiction, of whim-whams and mysterious myths, traces back true religion to its indubitable source, not to the discovery or invention of mortal men, but to the revelation and inspiration of God the only wise. Lovers of pure literature, who give attention to reading, will do well to make note of the publishers, and procure the essay.

A Protestant Dissenter's Catechism. By JAMES ROSE, Baptist Minister, Sandhurst, Wokingham, Berks. Price one penny, from the author, or W. Webb, Yorktown, Surrey.

THIS is a tract concerning Mr. Gace's Catechism. In the year 1870 we exhibited this dead rat on the end of our barn. See *The Sword and the Trowel.* Evil things have the knack of keeping long above ground, and so this precious catechism is in its twelfth edition. Godly churchmen are ashamed of the thing, and would gladly suppress it. Mr. James Rose has taken the trouble to answer it in this penny catechism: it is giving the concern more honour than it deserves; and yet it may be a necessary condescension. Although a creature may not be worth hunting, the hunting may be beneficial to the huntsman in other ways. We doubt not that the superstitions of Baptismal Regeneration and Apostolical Succession will be damaged by the doughty blows of our worthy brother, and this will be no small benefit to the cause of the gospel. Wherever bigotry has been displayed by the priestly party, Mr. Rose's neat little catechism should be widely diffused as an antidote to the poison.

Modern Miracles: being Manifestations of God's Love and Power. By LEILA THOMSON. Nisbet and Co.

SKETCHES from the actual experience of a believing worker. Not dreams of a Mrs. Bat's-eyes, but marvellous works of Almighty grace, such as they see whose lives are consecrated to the Lord. "Impossible! Only I saw it!" Romantic to the theorist; matter-of-fact to the believer in the divine Saviour.

The Preaching Tours and Missionary Labours of George Müller, of Bristol. By Mrs. MÜLLER. Nisbet and Co.

THESE descriptions of fifteen great evangelistic tours must, of necessity, be mere sketches. Our venerable brother, whose very presence is a testimony for God, has persevered, in his old age, in travelling throughout all lands, bearing witness to the faithfulness of the Lord God, in whom he has trusted so long, and so fully. Seeing he must be in his eighty-fourth year, we can hardly expect that he should do much more; but it is delightful to observe how strength has been given him unto this present. His esteemed wife, by answering his letters, and other helpful service, makes his work more easy, and thus keeps his mind more free for labour. He has thus time for prayer and preaching, and bearing witness to the many who gather about him. It was a great means of grace to hear and see our friend, some ten years ago, at Mentone. It was not only his word, but the man himself that spake to our heart; for he has tried and proved the promises of God.

This second edition of George Müller's Travels will, we have no doubt, command a large circulation in the vast circle of Christian people who love the man, and value his work. His *Reports* are not ordinary books, but powerful pleas for faith in the living God, and this record of "Preaching Tours" is a reflection of the Acts of the Apostles.

Notes on the Shorter Catechism. By Dr. MACKAY. Hodder and Stoughton.

The author of "Grace and Truth" has done good service by these brief explanations of the catechism. We regard The Shorter Catechism as one of the strongest bulwarks of the faith. South of the Tweed it is little known; but it has been the backbone of Scottish Calvinism. Alas! without spiritual life even a backbone is only so much dead matter. Leave out infant baptism, which is here in its very mildest form, and we commend these Notes to all who would teach their children the faith of their fathers.

Handbooks for Bible-classes. Exodus. By Rev. JAMES MACGREGOR, D.D. Edinburgh: T. and T. Clark.

BIBLE-CLASS teachers need just such notes as these — short, pithy, and reliable. We have been pleased to watch the issue of these Handbooks; and on the whole we have been satisfied with them. Of course, we believe that a man would get more out of Matthew Henry of deep, spiritual, practical instruction; but supposing him to be destitute of that great mine of Scriptural exposition, and to be only able to lay out a few shillings, we do not know that he could do better than buy these notes by Professor Macgregor. Though the space occupied is small, the labour has been great, and the products of that labour are given in terse sentences, by no means easy to write. To expound Scripture is no holiday task; for, as Lightfoot says, "Inspired writings are an inestimable treasure to mankind; for so many sentences, so many truths. But, then, the true sense of them must be known, or, otherwise, so many sentences, so many authorized falsehoods."

The Great Value and Success of Foreign Missions. By Rev. JOHN LIGGINS, New York. The Baker and Taylor Co.

THIS is a splendid defence of missions. It places the fact of their success so clearly before us that it needs no further demonstration. We are glad to hear that the book is to be had in London, of *Mr. Nisbet*. It is a wonderful gathering up of the most telling incidents in missionary work. It is well-nigh powerful enough to induce Mr. Caine to go for a missionary himself. He has had the moral courage to stir the committees up with a pole, and they have not been peculiarly grateful. We don't think he meant to oppose missions; but if he did, this book would be a very hard nut for him to crack. If the missionary societies are up to the mark as commonsense people, they will spread this vindication by hundreds of thousands. We have culled a few of the stories, and made an article of them for this month's magazine. See page 563.

WE have received from *Drummond's Tract Depôt, Stirling*, several *assortments of tracts*, all of which we can heartily commend. The packets of booklets, 50 for sixpence, by H. K. Wood, and those of four pages by Wm. Luff, are specially excellent.

The Floral Wall Cards in shilling packets containing six, are excellent and cheap. Much spiritual education may be unconsciously received by looking upon texts and hymns attractively set forth upon the wall. The more of such silent sermons the better. We wish the Stirling enterprise ever growing success.

Messrs. Hodder and Stoughton have issued their *Annual Monotint Books ;* and beautiful productions they are. The two at sixpence each are little beauties, and the other two which are priced at a shilling each are exceedingly good for the money. This method of sending books forth in paper covers enables the publishers to keep the price down, and the public seem to like the plan ; but to us it seems like driving out pretty children into the cold without proper garments : the sweet creatures soon perish in the rough world upon which they are cast. Still, as it brings poetry and art in their undress where else they might not come at all, it is not for us to object, but rather to speed the thinly clothed sprites upon their way :—Go, things of beauties, and be joys while ye may !

Horner's Penny Stories for the People have now reached No. 43, and have enjoyed a sale of 5,000,000. We do not recommend anyone to read stories at all ; but as the public will have such things, these are the sort which we recommend. Here the reader has plenty for his money ; and nothing of taint in it, but much that will improve him both morally and spiritually. As boys will be story-readers, give them these.

The British Weekly Pulpit. Vol. I. 27, Paternoster Row.

A VAST mass of preaching, prayer, and exposition for six shillings. We do not endorse it all ; but it is all valuable as a record of the ministry of the times, and much of it as gospel teaching for all time.

Herald of Mercy. One shilling. Morgan and Scott.

THIS makes a capital book. It is beautifully illustrated, strikingly written, and full of the gospel.

The Prophet Jonah : his Character and Mission to Nineveh. By HUGH MARTIN, D.D. Edinburgh : James Gemmell.

THE second edition of this useful exposition appeared in 1877, and it is well that there is a sufficient demand for it to encourage the publishers to reissue it. We have in former issues of this periodical warmly praised Dr. Martin's work ; and we again commend it to those who are not yet acquainted with it. The style is not brilliant, but the matter is excellent.

Daily Thoughts for Morning and Evening. By TWO MEMBERS OF THE YOUNG WOMEN'S CHRISTIAN ASSOCIATION. Marshall Brothers.

DAILY portions for a month for young women in business. Very good, but not very striking.

The World's Sunday School Convention, July, 1889. *Complete record of its proceedings.* Sunday School Union.

THE World's Sunday School Convention was a happy idea carried out with great success. The record of its proceedings will be of permanent interest. The papers and speeches as a whole are most instructive reading. We have before us the two-shilling edition in paper, and we like it so well that we recommend everybody else to find up another shilling, and buy it as a bound volume. Here is much seed corn, which will produce, both in our own time and in years to come, most blessed fruit in the form of new enterprises which are herein suggested, but are not yet carried out. Much to our regret we did not feel strong enough to attend the Convention, though pressed to do so most vigorously by our well-beloved friend, Mr. Belsey, the President. To read the report is some consolation for being deprived of the great pleasure of hearing the words of wisdom. Sound doctrine was evidently in the ascendant, and nothing gained such hearty applause as a clear statement of the old gospel.

North Country Poets. Edited by W. AN-
DREWS, F.R.H.S. London: Simpkin,
Marshall, and Co. Hull: A. Brown.
A FRESH and striking collection of
verses and poems.   Lovers of the
curious in literature should secure a
copy at once.   Hull possesses a band
of antiquaries and literary men which

may well suffice to make it notable
among English towns.   Mr. Andrews
is not the least among a distinguished
coterie.   His setting forth of some
of the humbler poets will, we trust, be
successful. These northern stars, if not
of the first brilliancy, nevertheless
make up a very striking constellation.

Notes.

HAVING given two likenesses of the editor,
we now give one of his beloved wife—such
as it is.   Friends may like to know that her
good works of "The Book Fund for poor
ministers" and "The Pastors' Aid Fund"
are still in full operation, and the need for
such labours of love rather increases than
diminishes.   To God be praise that more
than thirteen thousand parcels of solid
divinity have been sent to poor preachers of
the Word of God belonging to different
denominations.

From August, 1875, to September, 1889,
Mrs. Spurgeon has made 13,017 grants of
books, &c. to clergymen, ministers, and missionaries of all denominations, the total number of volumes given having been 113,023
beside 162,008 single sermons, and an
almost innumerable quantity of tracts,
pamphlets, &c.

In May, 1888, Mr. S. S. Bagster commenced "The Auxiliary Book Fund" for
the distribution of books to local preachers
and other Christian workers who are not
pastors.   Up to December 31st., he had
made 126 grants, comprising 1,142 volumes.
This work of helping unpaid workers
deserves to attain far larger proportions.

Some years ago my death was reported,
and a kind friend improved the occasion
with a funeral address, which turned out
to be rather premature.   Now the papers

announce that I am about to retire from
my post, and one of them even proceeds to
arrange for my early death and distribution of my worldly goods, with which it
liberally endows me, although, I am sorry
to say, only in imagination.   Now, all this
is utterly untrue.   I hope to work on for
many years, if my life be spared, and if the
present age be continued.   It came to pass
that, on a certain Sabbath morning, feeling
very unwell, I had forewarnings of a coming
attack of my constitutional ailment, and felt
that I should, probably, be soon laid aside
for a season by sickness.   I therefore begged
the friends to hear me while they could.
They very well understood what I meant;
but a strange newspaper-man did not; but
understood me to invite friends to hear my
sermons while they could, for I should soon
retire from the ministry.   To this first error
natural additions of talk have contributed
more and more of the false or exaggerated.

I have had nearly eight months' continuous preaching, and it is long since I
have been favoured with so great a privilege.   The fall of the year has come, and
with it symptoms that the old enemy is
lurking about—symptoms especially in the
hand which is needed every hour of the day
for writing.   But this is nothing unusual.
It is not even so bad as is generally the case;
and I am writing these lines with that suffering member, in the joyful belief that I shall
keep on with my preaching and other work
till the time arrives for me to take the holiday which falls to me about the middle of
November.   No idea of giving up my beloved
work has crossed my mind of late.   To
whom should I give it up?   Who will carry
on the Orphanage, College, Colportage,
Evangelists, &c., &c.?   Who will minister
to that tremendous throng which crowds the
great house as constantly as the doors are
opened?   When the Lord sends the manifest successor, the original worker will
cheerfully give way; but why should he do
so while, as yet, his years are only fifty-five,
and he is no worse in health than he has
been wont to be, but, on the contrary, has
had a better year than usual?   It will be
wise to believe nothing which is seen in the
newspapers until you have found out the
truth of it for yourself.

We have a programme of "The Christly
Ethical Church of England," to which

certain "Down-graders" are attaching themselves. It seems that the word "Christly" is preferred to *Christian*, "because the latter word, in its conventional sense, alas! has passed into reproach." This is, by no means, a piece of news. It was always so. This precious "Ethical Church" has, it seems, "*an ethically ideal Christ*," and thus it has the mind of Christ, though it announces that, "*This ideal Christ does not render it necessary that we should discuss the particulars of his written history, when, where, and how he came into the world, whether he wrought miracles, or not, was God or man, or both in one personality; we have the* IDEA, *it lives and works and grows in us.*" "The whole of religion may be reduced to two words, 'BE JUST.'" This is fine teaching, certainly!

That members of the Baptist Union Council should join this new "Church" does not in the least surprise us. We hear of one and another of our ministers quitting the Union as these things come under their notice; but nothing is said of it, and the most of the brotherhood sleep on while error is spreading within their ranks, and their churches are feeling the dry-rot of its influence. Some men teach the principle of separation from error, and yet remain its hearty allies. Surely, there will yet be an awaking!

Scotland has faithful men, and these not few in number; but what are they at? Save in the Highlands, they seem to be consenting to the general defection. Those who were accused of crying "Wolf!" need not answer the accusation, for the facts are very much worse than they represented them to be. The wolf turns out to be a pack of wolves. Those who were supposed to be sheep have allowed the skin to shift a little, and the wolf is now apparent enough. Have the modern gentlemen a legal right to the emoluments of the Free Church? It was not started to propagate their notions; indeed, it has boldly protested against the like of them. Nothing will probably touch some consciences but an appeal to the question of right in reference to the design of the Institution which they are beginning to pervert. Scotland will yet yield men of firm spirit, who will not see the heritage of believers rent from them, and divided among those who undermine the foundations of her ancient faith.

The prayer-meeting at the Tabernacle, on *Monday evening, August* 26, was specially devoted to supplication for children. A large detachment of boys and girls from the Orphanage attended, and added to the interest of the proceedings by singing several hymns very sweetly; and their presence reminded the brethren of the need of prayer for them, and for all children. Mr. Charlesworth spoke of the work at the Orphanage, and mentioned that one of the "old boys," Pastor T. H. Williams, had been preaching

at Upton Chapel for his namesake, W. Williams, on the previous day. Mr. Chamberlain appropriately followed by singing, "Suffer the children to come unto me"; and other petitions were presented. Among them was one asking that all Christians might realize the responsibility of speaking to sinners, upon which the Pastor briefly but forcibly spoke. He said that, when Messrs. Fullerton and Smith come to the Tabernacle, in November, there would be a fine opportunity of personally speaking to the unconverted; and meanwhile, every effort possible must be put forth with the view of bringing such people under the sound of the Word of the Lord.

Mr. Cooper, an American minister, gave a very enthusiastic account of his visit to the Orphanage. He said that, since he had been in Scotland and England, he had been saddened by what he had seen of the child-life in the great cities; but he considered that the Stockwell Orphanage was one of the brightest and most beautiful gardens in the whole of the metropolis. Mr. Cooper also bore testimony to the joy he had experienced on the previous day at the Tabernacle—a joy which had not been shared by some of his ministerial companions, who, as he expressed it, "kicked mighty badly" at the evening sermon, showing that "the offence of the cross" has not yet ceased. After the Pastor had again given a short address, Mr. Harrald presented several special requests for prayer which had been sent in, including one from China, and another from Scotland; the orphans sang the charming hymn about "Immanuel's land," and a most delightful evening was closed with the benediction. Friends may always send in special requests for prayer, and if they are proper ones, they will not be passed over.

The first part of the evening on *Monday, September* 2, was devoted to very earnest prayer for a blessing upon the sermon delivered on the previous Lord's-day morning. ("Pricked in their Heart," No. 2,102. Friends who have read the discourse have, no doubt, noted how calculated it was to lead to immediate decision for Christ.) The rest of the meeting was mainly occupied by students from the College. The Pastor thought it would be profitable for three of them, without any notice or preparation, to tell how they were brought to the Saviour. These testimonies were so singularly interesting that, after an interval of prayer, three more were asked to state how they were brought to the Saviour. This they did most touchingly. After more prayer, Mr. Parker sang, "How shall we escape if we neglect so great salvation?" The Pastor gave an address upon the way in which some parents hindered their children from coming to the Lord, instead of helping them, as the mothers of the brethren who had spoken had done; and also spoke of the ruin wrought by false professors of religion.

Mr. Harrald again summarized the written requests for prayer, and led the assembly in presenting them at the throne of grace. Thus closed another notable meeting. A great storm had been raging all the evening, the lightning flashes being visible in the Tabernacle, but there was quite as large a congregation as usual, and all appeared to enjoy the way in which the hour and a half had been spent.

On *Monday evening, September* 9, after quite a number of brief, earnest petitions for the salvation of sinners, the Pastor expounded Matthew iv. 24, which he called "a black bill with a blessed receipt at the bottom." He especially dwelt upon the words "*and he healed them,*" and applied them to sin-sick souls in London, and in other parts of the world's great spiritual hospital. He then said that, if any more of the students would like to tell how they found the Lord, they were at liberty to do so. Two of them accepted the invitation: and one of the two having mentioned that he was converted through a sermon preached by Pastor M. Cumming, at Bury St. Edmund's, Mr. Harrald, "another Bury man," was called upon to give his testimony. Then came one of the brothers Young, of the Collingwood Street Mission, who gave us a practical illustration of the way in which he pleads with the rough sinners of "the New Cut" to yield themselves to the Saviour; and he was followed by Mr. Charles Cook, of Hyde Park Hall, who gave an account of his work in Hyde Park, Edinburgh, and various foreign prisons where he has gone to carry the Word of God to the poor creatures who are immured under circumstances of peculiar horror and suffering. The Pastor then closed the meeting with a solemn appeal to those who are trusting in Christ, but have never confessed their faith, to come out and declare themselves on the Lord's side; and an earnest entreaty to any servant of Satan who might be present to "strike" at once, and quit the service of the old tyrant, whose wages are death.

Special Notice.—Several important meetings will shortly be held at the Tabernacle, and to these we call the attention of any of our readers who live in London, or who may be visiting the metropolis.

On *Tuesday evening, October* 1, the annual meeting of the Pastors' College will be held, when the President hopes to preside. Several of the students will speak, and Pastor Charles Spurgeon will give an account of his recent tour to New Zealand, America, &c., illustrated by specially-prepared dissolving-views. It would be a great cheer to the heart of the President to see the Tabernacle well filled. Adversaries have their little ways of being bitter; let hearty friends sustain by their presence and sympathy. Help is always welcome.

From *Tuesday, October* 8, *to Wednesday, October* 16, a Gospel Temperance Mission

will be conducted at the Tabernacle by Mr. G. F. Cook, a Blue Ribbon Missioner. The Pastor will give an address at the opening meeting. All temperance friends are summoned to the battle. Every one must help to gather in the people. They cannot get good from the missioner if they do not hear him. "Compel them to come in."

On *Tuesday, October* 15, there is to be an all-day Missionary Convention at the College and the Tabernacle, full particulars of which can be obtained of Mr. W. C. Minifie, the late Secretary of the College Missionary Association, who has been | for some time making the arrangements most energetically. Dr. Maclaren is to speak in the afternoon. At night, it is hoped that the Tabernacle will be crowded with young men for the public meeting, over which George Williams, Esq., has kindly promised to preside, and C. H. Spurgeon, John McNeill, Reginald Radcliffe, and other advocates of foreign missions are expected to speak. The object of the Convention is to arouse the young men of London to a sense of their responsibility with regard to the millions of heathen who have not yet heard the gospel. Representatives of all the great Missionary Societies will take part in the proceedings of the day. Will not our friends make this meeting a special subject of intercession, for great results may come of it, if the Lord will?

On *Wednesday, November* 6, Mr. Charles Cook, of Hyde Park Hall, will come to the Tabernacle to give an account of his visits to foreign prisons. Our friend has already told our readers something of this work through the pages of *The Sword and the Trowel*, and we shall be glad if the meeting in the Tabernacle will bring in funds to help Mr. Cook in the further prosecution of his mission to the criminals who are confined in dungeons abroad under circumstances of terrible suffering. Admission to Mr. Cook's lecture will be free, and a collection will be made.

Last, but certainly not least, from *Monday, November* 18, to *Sunday, November* 24, Messrs. Fullerton and Smith will conduct an Evangelistic Mission at the Tabernacle. We shall want the earnest help of all our friends in gathering in the non-church and chapel-goers, and in pointing seeking souls to the Saviour. Mr. Smith will conduct a special service for children on *Sunday afternoon, November* 17, at three o'clock. All Sunday-school teachers and children in the neighbourhood are earnestly invited to be present.

COLLEGE.—Mr. F. G. West has settled at Farnworth, Lancashire, one of the places which has derived great blessing through Mr. Carter's "Pioneer" work.

In response to a request from South Africa, we are, this month, sending out two of our students, Messrs. D. H. Hay and T. Adamson, one of whom will probably be located at King Williamstown, and the other at Port Elizabeth.

The following brethren have removed, or are about to do so:—Mr. H. J. Martin, from Arthur Street, King's Cross, to Conduit Road, Plumstead; Mr. J. S. Poulton, from Winslow, to Coate, Oxfordshire; Mr. T. E. Rawlings, from South Shields, to Idle, near Bradford; Mr. W. Thomas, from Putney, to Penzance; and Mr. J. C. Travers, from Holbeach, to Sherbrooke Road, Carrington, Nottingham. Mr. T. A. Judd, who has been supplying at Branderburgh, N.B., for the past six months, has now settled there.

Mr. H. Dunn, of Coseley, has sailed for the United States. Mr. G. Boulsher, who has been for 17 years in the States, has returned to this country for a season of rest, and further preparation for future service. He brings with him a very hearty letter of commendation from the Association in Columbia, Missouri, whose missionary he has been since November, 1886. Mr. Robert Spurgeon returns this month to India, after a brief visit to England, where he has to leave his wife and children.

On two Friday afternoons during the past month, the students were greatly interested in the accounts given by Mr. Albert Norton, an American brother, of his missionary labours among the hill-people of Central India. Without depending upon any Society, but in simple trust in the living God, Mr. Norton has laboured for many years among the poor people of the hills, whom he considers more ready to receive the gospel than the Hindoos or Mahometans.

EVANGELISTS. — *Messrs. Fullerton and Smith* have resumed work, after their summer holiday, by paying a short visit to Paris during the past month. They have since been at Cavendish, Suffolk, and Tonbridge: and this month they are going to Tunbridge Wells, Stowmarket, and Hadleigh. The early part of November they are to be at Oxford, and from November 18 to 24, they have promised to conduct another mission at the Tabernacle.

Mr. Burnham has been among the hop-pickers in Kent, and he notes with special gratitude that the weather has been unusually favourable for the many out-door meetings that have been held. He wishes us to intimate to brethren desiring his services, that he is now in good health, and will be glad to arrange for any vacant dates this winter.

Mr. Harmer conducted a few tent-services, at the end of August, at Peckham, in connection with Pastor F. M. Smith, and from August 29 to September 11, accompanied by *Mr. Chamberlain*, he was at Stonebroom, Derbyshire, among the miners and railwaymen, many of whom were brought to decision. Mr. Harmer has since been at Burton-on-Trent; he is to be at Wisbech, with Mr. Chamberlain, from September 28 to October 8; and from October 17 to 27 at Bath. He asks us to say that, in future, he will use, in his missions, a new edition of *Flowers and Fruits*, which Mr. Charlesworth has revised for him.

Mr. Harrison has been at Mr. Charrington's hall during the whole of September.

Mr. Parker will be in Edinburgh in October. He is now fully engaged up to the end of the year.

ORPHANAGE.—*Notice to Collectors and other Friends of the Orphans.*—On *Friday, October* 25, the QUARTERLY COLLECTORS' MEETING will be held at the Orphanage, when the President hopes to preside, and there will be an interesting programme. It has been suggested that, in connection with this meeting, friends might like to send in harvest thanksgiving offerings towards the maintenance of our large orphan family. The produce of the field, the garden, and the orchard will be welcome. All articles should be sent to Mr. Charlesworth, Stockwell Orphanage, Clapham Road, London, carriage paid, so as to arrive not later than noon on October 25. The President of the Orphanage appeals to his many friends in the country to make this a special occasion for helping the orphans. This is not to be a *religious parade of fruit and flowers*, in a place of worship, but a simple offering to the poor and needy who are gathered in the Orphanage.

Mr. Charlesworth and the Orphanage choir are engaged as follows during this month:—October 1, Bath; 2, Weston-super-Mare; 3, Wellington; 4, Taunton; 5—7, Truro; 8, Helston; 9, Hayle; 10, St. Ives; 11, Penzance; 12—14, Falmouth; 15, Redruth; 16, St. Austell; 17, Newquay; 18, Liskeard; 23, Tottenham; 24, Dalston Junction; 25, Orphanage; 28, Brixton; 30, Windsor. A choir of 200 children will take part in the Blue Ribbon Mission, at the Tabernacle, October 8 to 16; also in the Missionary Convention, October 15.

SPECIAL NOTE. — Our much-esteemed friend, Mr. William Birch, jun., has sailed for Auckland, to take the place of Mr. Thomas Spurgeon. Mr. Birch has occupied the Free Trade Hall, Manchester, for many years, and held a vast crowd together on the Sabbath. His sermons have been printed, week by week, for nearly 900 weeks. Souls have been saved under his earnest ministry in great numbers; and were it not for pressing considerations of health, we doubt not he would continue in the same laborious and useful sphere for many years to come. As it is, he goes forth with the love and prayers of thousands, and with the bright hope and loving confidence of the man whose son he is to succeed. Mr. Birch was baptized by Mr. Spurgeon many years ago; and though he has continued in business, he has done as much in the ministry and in orphanage work as the foremost man in England, and all upon the most self-denying terms.

Baptisms at Metropolitan Tabernacle.— August 22, twenty; August 29, eighteen.

Pastors' College, Metropolitan Tabernacle.

Statement of Receipts from August 15th to September 16th, 1889.

	£	s.	d.
From Crathie	0	2	0
Mr. J. G. Casswell...	2	10	0
Mr. John Gibson	10	0	0
New Zealand	3	0	0
Mr. A. Barr...	0	10	0
Postal order from Thaxted	0	10	0
Rev. G. H. Rouse, M.A.	1	0	0
Mr. J. R. Bayley	1	0	0
Tabernacle Church, Hull, per Pastor Frank Russell	1	5	6
Mr. E. Stanion	0	10	0
Mr. Councillor J. Crighton	5	0	0
Jno. F. H.	1	0	0
Mr. J. Billing	2	0	0

	£	s.	d.
Mr. John Cameron	3	0	0
Mrs. Fielder...	10	0	0
Mrs. Raybould	1	0	0
A. M. M.	0	2	6
Weekly Offerings at Met. Tab. :—			
Aug. 18 ... ... 48 15 7			
,, 25 ... ... 34 13 9			
Sept. 1 ... ... 27 1 0			
,, 8 ... ... 37 7 10			
,, 15 ... ... 6 13 5			
	154	11	7
	£197	1	7

Pastors' College Missionary Association.

Statement of Receipts since list published in College Report.

	£	s.	d.
Rev. W. L. and Mrs Lang	5	0	0
Mr. John M. Cook...	5	0	0
J. S.	5	0	0
Jane Anderson (for Spanish Testaments for North Africa)	0	5	0

	£	s.	d.
Miss Webster	1	0	0
"Come over, and help us" ...	2	0	0
	£18	5	0

Stockwell Orphanage.

Statement of Receipts from August 15th to September 16th, 1889.

	£	s.	d.
Miss Redman	0	10	0
Collected by Mrs. Rouse	0	10	0
Box at Orphanage gate, and office box	1	11	3
Miss E. Vivian	0	5	6
Mrs. Reed	3	0	0
Jack, South Lambeth .	0	4	0
Miss Amery, per Miss Ivimey	10	0	0
Collected by Mr. G. H. Knight ..	0	10	0
Mr. F. J. Mouat, M.D. (for excursion)	5	0	0
Mrs. Berry	1	0	0
Collected by Miss Bickmore	1	10	1
Miss C. Farley	1	0	0
Collected by Miss Bilby	0	1	1
Mr. and Mrs. J. Thomas... ...	2	0	0
C. A. M.	10	0	0
Mrs. Whatley	0	7	6
Miss Hall	0	12	6
Mr. J. Dickinson	0	10	0
Crew of the s.s. Brunswick, per Capt. J. Protheroe	3	0	0
Mr. Squibb	0	6	0
"The orphans' friend"	1	1	0
Miss Ellis	0	5	0
Friends at Free Church, Golspie, per Rev. J. Mackenzie ...	2	1	0
Mr. C. Ibberson	0	2	6
Mr. J. G. Casswell... ...	5	0	0
Miss Mead's collecting-book ...	9	12	0
Orphans at Tring, per Mr. Albert Mead	9	18	7
Mr. Albert Mead	40	0	0
A poor old woman...	0	2	6
A sermon-reader	0	10	0
Miss Mary Berry	1	0	0
New Zealand	2	0	0
Miss M. Smith	1	0	0
Dr. Bennet	1	1	0
Miss Agnes Mackenzie	1	0	0
Mr. J. Farley	2	2	0
Mrs. Gowing	0	10	0
"Woodside"	5	0	0
Mr. Samson Lucas...	0	10	0
Miss E. Pearce	1	0	0
Mrs. Parsons and friend	1	1	0
Mrs. Brown	0	5	0

	£	s.	d.
Miss Tolson, per Mrs. Greenwood ...	0	5	0
Mr. T. Porter	10	0	0
Collected by Mr. E. R. Pullen ...	0	4	0
Collected by Mrs. Rugg	1	2	8
Collected by Miss Martin ...	0	7	0
College Street Chapel Sunday-school, per Mr. C. Thomas	0	13	3
Mr. Mathias	1	1	0
Mr. Thompson (for excursion)... ...	10	0	0
Battersea Park Tabernacle Sunday-school, per Mr. Barfoot	2	0	0
Highbury Hill Sunday-scholars and friends, per Mr. T. Smith, jun. ...	0	12	0
Mr. E. K. Stace	0	10	0
Young Women's Bible-class at the Orphanage, per Mrs. J. Stiff ...	0	19	9
Sandwich, per Bankers	2	2	8
Executors of the late Mr. Joseph Parish	52	3	
Orphan boys' collecting cards, per list	66	12	
Orphan girls' collecting cards, per list	51	4	
Collected by Mr. R. Walter ...	0	1	
George Armistead (first earnings) ...	0	1	
Mrs. T. Thomas	1	0	
Collected by Miss Harbert ...	0	18	4
Collected by Mr. Ackland ...	0	0	
Collected by Mrs. Phillips ...	0	1	
Collected by Miss Sharp ...	2	1	
Miss R. A. Thomas	0	1	
An Ipswich friend... ...	0	1	
Mr. and Mrs. Harding ...	2		
Mrs. Chidlaw	0	1	
E. J.	0		
Rev. G. H. Rouse, M.A. ...	1		
Mrs. Hallett's children	0	1	
Mr. W. Woolidge	0	1	
Miss E. A. Fysh	0		
Mr. G. Smith	0	1	
Mrs. Duly	0	1	
Miss Morrison	0		
F. G. B., Chelmsford	0		
Mr. S. H. Dauncey	0		
Mr. G. R. Smith	3		
Mr. A. G. Jeynes	10		
Mr. George Reid	20		

	£	s.	d.
Mr. and Mrs. F. Nunn	1	1	0
Mrs. Ewart ...	1	1	0
Mr. W. Mingins, per Mrs. Ewart	1	0	0
Mr. J. Cutler	1	0	0
Mr. F. J. Rumsey ...	0	10	0
Mrs. M. A. Bucknell, per C. H. S.	2	0	0
Mr. Councillor J. Crighton	20	0	0
Miss Sarah Hughes (two canaries sold)	0	10	0
W. S.	5	0	0
Mrs. Edwards	2	0	0
Mr. J. Billing	5	0	0
Miss Lucy Avenell ..	0	1	0
Mr. E. J. S. Chappell	3	3	0
Mr. J. Mottershead	0	5	0
E. E. ...	5	0	0
Mr. J. C. Lance ...	0	6	0
Mrs. Bridgman	0	2	0
Collection on Yarmouth Beach, per Mr.			
Randolph ...	0	11	6
Loose Baptist Sunday-school ...	0	10	0
Miss Davis ...	0	10	0

	£	s.	d.
Mr. William Phillips	1	1	0
Mr. John Cameron	1	1	0
Miss Heap	2	0	0
Miss H. Heap	2	0	0
Miss A. Heap	1	0	0
West Brompton Railway Mission Sun-			
day-school	1	1	0
Mr. James Tutt	1	0	0
Mrs. Grimshaw	0	5	0
Houston Free Church Sabbath-school...	0	10	
Mr. W. Wooldge	1	0	
Per Pastor W. Jackson :—			
W. Jackson and family ...	0 16 0		
Mrs. H. Hall .	0 4 0		
	1	0	
Mr. E. J. Reed, a thankoffering, per			
Mrs. J. A. Spurgeon, W. Croydon ...	2	2	0
	£436	13	6

Orphan Boys' Collecting Cards.—Allison, S., 7s 10d; Abbott, H., 12s; Barter, A. S., 6s 3d; Beer, A. J., £1 1s; Bowles, E., 4s 7d; Bristow, J., 13s 6d; Brend, A., 7s 1d; Bowen, W. G., 7s 6d; Baker, J., 5s 6d; Buddle, W., 8s 3d; Barnard, D., 8s; Bromwich, A., 2s; Burnham, F., 5s 6d; Burgoyne, W., 10s; Barson, E. J., 14s 3d; Barrett, F. B., 9s; Burrows, L., 1s 1d; Cleaverley, J., 5s; Coman, E., 6s 4d; Cooper, C. W., 2s; Cook, C., 8s 7d; Carman, A. E., £1 1s; Constable, F., 12s; Clayden, W., 10s; Cordery, H. M., 11s; Challis, H., 10s 10d; Cambridge, H., 16s 3d; Clark, H., 6s; Carter, P. F., 5s 6d; Darling, E., 9s 3d; Deverall, G. F., 5s 1d; Davis, J., 3s; Edwards, G., 12s 6d; East, G., £1; Elder, J. H., 4s; Earthrowl,—, 3s 6d; Fyfield, F., 13s 5d; Fitch, E., 7s; Fullerton, H., 1s 3d; Green, A., 10s; Gammon, A., 3s 5d; Greenhough, G., £1 1s; Gant, F. C., 6s 3d; Golding, D., 3s 6d; Goatley, L., 2s; Gearing, F., 1s 7d; Green, W. S., 15s; Goddard, C., 4s; Henderson, G., £1 1s; Hadlow, E. J., 2s; Hills, E., 2s; Hill, G., 10s; Hart, A., 6s 3d; Harris, C., 3s 5d; Hilder, J. C., £1 7s; Hawken, L., £1 1s; Hodgson, W., £1 1s; Heath, W., £1 1s; Jansen, W., 4s 6d; Johnson, P., 7s 10d; Jenkin, F., 2s; Jarvis, H., 1s; King, A. T., 3s 9d; Knappett, E. C., 4s 4d; Kent, J. W., £1 2s; Lenderyou, A., 7s; Love, A., 10s; Langridge, J., 5s; Lenson, P., 12s 10d; Lawrence, H., 1s 8d; Legge, W., 3s 9d; Mansell, E., 11s; Moore, F., £1 1s; Metcalfe, T., £1 1s; Mitchell, B., 17s; Manktelow, P., 10s; Mac lean, C., 2s; McDonald, R., 1s 4d; Morton, P., 2s 3d; Moore, A., 2s; Mann, H. G., 5s; Moore, W., 3s; Martyn, W., £1 10s; Marks, A., 3s 4d; Manser, S., 8s; McArthur, K., 5s; Mitchell, G., 3s 1d; Nicholls, J., £1 1s; Newman, A., 14s; Ounsted, A. W., 3s 2d; Peveral, W., 19s 7d; Peachey, A., 6s 9d; Platt, A., £2 2s; Park, F., 3s 8d; Pinder, S., 4s; Ponton, M., 5s 7d; Parker, T., 10s; Pitney, F. G., 9s 10d; Pritchard, G., 4s 7d; Pegg, G. M., 7s 2d; Rye, Charles, 3s; Roberts, H., 14s 1d; Rosser, C., 8s; Rodwell, B., 6s 4d; Roe, F., 13s 4d; Runnacus, H., £1 1s; Rogers, W., £1 1s; Sharp, W., 2s; Surtees, J., 7s; Schumacher, J., 14s 1d; Sheen, H. E., 1s 2d; Suttle, R. J., 13s 5d; Start, P., 4s 1d; Smith, R., 13s; Schofield, J., 12s 10d; Stoner, W., 7s; Strike, A., 6s; Sparke, H., 13s; Stone, F., 6s 7d; Spurgeon, W., £3 0s 6d; Taylor, G., £1 1s; Taylor, F., 2s 6d; Virtue. E. F., 7s 7d; Walker, C, 4s 1d; Worker, S., 2s; Wincott, J. S., 1s 2d; Williams, A., 3s 10d; Wallis, H., £1 1s; Walter, P., 2s 3d; Winnen, J., 5s 10d; White, P., 1s; Williams, J., 4s; Woods, C., 1s; Webber, A., 3s 5d; Webber, C., 3s 5d; Wells, S. A., 4s 3d; Webb, E., 10s 9d; Wallis, F. G., 6s.—Total, £66 12s 3d.

Orphan Girls' Collecting Cards.—Arnold, S., 1s 6d; Attfield, B., 12s 9d; Allsop, M., 6d; Aldrich, M., 3s 3d; Attiken, E., 4s 3d; Arthur, H., 5s; Ayling, E., 5s 6d; Blake, L., 12s 2d; Boyles, L., 2s 2d; Bullock, L., £1 4s; Barlow, M., 6s; Beck, M., 1s 6d; Buddle, F., 9s; Butcher, L., 11s 10d; Bridgman, A., 6s 10d; Bond, N., 6s 7d; Bigglestone, M., 16s 6d; Bull, L., 5s 6d; Beetham, L., 3s 1d; Bishopp, L 5s; Burrows, F., 3s; Brown, R., 7s; Boorman, V., 2s 6d; Bertwistle, E., 13s 3d; Blatchford, H., £1 16s 9d; Cheshire, B., 3s 6d; Caister, E., 7s 3d; Coombes, E., 2s 6d; Cox, E., 5s; Clymer, A., 5s; Cousins, L., 5s 8d; Cooper, K., 2s 7d; Cable, F., 3s 6d; Crawford, S., 1s; Collis, H., 11s; Cordwell, H., 4s 6d; Donoghue, E., 3s 5d; Dickerson, E., 15s 3d; Doncaster, A., 3s 3d; Everard, E., 11s; Ellis, A., 6s 2d; Epps, F., 10s; Evans, A., 6s 1d; Filby, E., 6s; Freathy, E., 3s 9d; Fenn, A., 3s 6d; Fairhead, L., 2s 5d; Gregory, M., 17s 7d; Grimes, E., 11s; Haydon, L., 1s 5d; Holman, E., 10s 1d; Hoidge, A., 15s 8d; Houching, M., 10s; Hall, B., 6s 7d; Hofmann, D., 1s; Hunter, F., 4s; Hewitt, H., 18s; Hinchley, L., 4s; Hockley, L., 1s 6d; Haydon, E., 10s; Heath, K., 1s 6d; Ingle, F. 5s 6d; Jones, B., 7s; Johnson, A., 4s; Johnson, K., 2s 3d; Jackman, L., 5s 2d; Johnson, L., 10s; Jackson, L., 1s 6d; Jackson, A., 10s; Jessop, K., 5s 9d; Jacques, K., 4s 1d; Kenward, B., 3s 9d; Knowles, L., 4s 3d; Lyons, E., 3s; Logan, K., £1 1s; Larcombe, A., 3s 6d; Long, M., 4s; Lawler, R. 10s; Leitch, G., 11s 6d; Maynard, M., 3s 9d; Mockford, L., 4s; Mitchell, N., 3d; Miles, M., 7s, Maycock, W., 3s; Morton, E., £3 12s; Martin, A., 7s 1d; Newton, K., 1s 3d; Nobbs, T., 2s 2d; Neve, L., 10s; Nutt, C., 2s; Owen, D., 2s 2d; Parker, A., 1s; Pickering, E., 7s 2d; Payne, M., 5s; Pope, A., 7d; Price, S., 14s 6d; Player, E., 3s 1d; Parmenter, M., 4s 6d; Perry, R., 2s; Parker, A., 5s 9d; Parsons, B., 1s 1d; Pennington, F., 6s 3d; Rowbottom, G., £1 1s; Richards, K., 4s 2d; Rampling, S., 1s 8d; Seymour, I., 8s; Soper, A., 7s 3d; Steer, M., 2s; Spaughton, M., 1s; Smith, J., 1s; Sayers, A., 15s 6d; Shorter, S., 4s 8d; Sharland, H., 4s 2d; Searing, S., 2s 8d; Smith, M. A., 16s 6d; Smith, C., 10s 6d; Smith, A., £1 1s 3d; Scott, L., 12s 4d; Smithers, L., £1 1s; Trepte, E., 13s 6d; Thorp, E., £1 1s; Tiley, R., 6d; Thiel, D., 2s 6d; Unwin, M., 7s; Valler, C., 8s 10d; Woolfit, M., 2s 6d; Wright, K., 3s 6d; Woodcock, I., £1 1s; Witham, P., 10s 7d; Wilkins, E., 7d; Wilmore, E., 5s; Walker, K, 12s; Wren, M., 2s; Ward, M., 2s; Warwick, L., £1 1s; Williams, L., 11s 2d; Westwood, F., 13s; Wright, E., 4s; Williams, N., 2s 1d; Youens, L., 3s 1d.—Total, £51 14s 3d.

List of Presents, per Mr. Charlesworth, from August 15th, to September 16th, 1889.—PROVISIONS:— Three and a half churns Milk, Mr. G. Harris; 5 churns Milk, Mr. R. Higgs; 1 New Zealand Sheep, Mr. A. Seale Haslam; 224 lbs. Rice, Mr. J. L. Potier; 4 bushels Beans and 41 Marrows, Messrs. C. and A. Parker; a quantity Cabbages, Mr. J. Watts.

BOYS' CLOTHING.—40 pairs Socks, Mrs. Vinson; 12 Flannel Shirts, Miss Dransfield; 54 Ties, 18 Caps, Mr. E. Nye.

GIRLS' CLOTHING.—8 Articles, Miss Frances Hall; 10 Articles, Miss Hall; 83 Gifts, The Young Women's Bible Class at the Orphanage, per Mrs. J. Stiff; 6 Articles, Miss J. Z. Walton; 37 Articles, The Juvenile Working Society at the Tabernacle, per Miss Woods; 28 Ulsters, Mr. T. Yorath; 6 Articles, (for No. 1 girls') Miss Salter; 36 Articles, The Ladies' Working Meeting at the Tabernacle, per Miss Higgs; 72 yards Ribbon, 48 Silk Ties, Miss Higgs.

GENERAL.—A box of Toys, &c., Miss Rabbeth; a parcel Sundries, Mr. J. Batts; 1 load Firewood, Mr. S. Thompson; a quantity of Toys, Mrs. Sutherland; a box of Flannel Scraps, Anon.; a quantity Magazines, Miss Newton.

Colportage Association.

Statement of Receipts from August 15th to September 16th, 1889.

Subscriptions and Donations for Districts:	£	s.	d.	Subscriptions and Donations to the General Fund:—	£	s.	d.
E. S., for Repton and Burton-on-Trent	20	0	0	A thankoffering	0	10	0
Oxfordshire Association, Stow and Aston District	10	0	0	Postal order, New Bond Street... ...	0	10	0
Mr. R. W. S. Griffith, for Fritham ...	10	0	0	Mr. John Gibson	10	0	0
Wolverhampton and Shipley District ..	10	0	0	Mr. William Mainwaring	0	10	6
Mr. J. J. Tustin, for Burstow and Horley	10	0	0	New Zealand	3	0	0
Miss Lassell, for Maidenhead	10	0	0	Miss E. K. Morden	0	1	0
Portsmouth District	12	10	0	Miss Ward, collecting-box	0	3	0
For Tewkesbury District, per Mr. Thos. White	7	10	0	Mr. Councillor J. Crighton ...	5	0	0
Friends for colporteur at Rendham, per Rev. G. Hollier	5	0	0	Mr. J. Billing	1	0	0
Metropolitan Tabernacle Sunday-school, for Tring	10	0	0	Mr. A. Todd	0	5	0
Quarterly Subscription:—				Annual Subscription:—			
M. A. H., for Orpington	5	0	0	Rev. G. H. Rouse, M A. ...	1	0	0
				Half-Yearly Subscription:—			
				Mr. H. B. Frearson	.	7	10	0
	£110	0			£29	9	6

Society of Evangelists.

Statement of Receipts from August 15th to September 16th, 1889.

	£	s.	d.		£	s.	d.
Mr. J. G. Casswell...	2	10	0	Mr. Councillor J. Crighton	10	0	0
Mr. John Gibson	20	0	0	Pastor W. Jackson	1	1	0
Rev. R. Tutin Thomas	0	3	0	Miss Husk	0	5	0
Miss E. K. Morden	0	1	0	Mrs. Raybould	1	0	0
Mr. Robert Ryman	5	0	0				
Rev. G. H. Rouse, M.A.	2	0	0		£43	0	0
Mr. and Mrs. Horner	1	0	0				

For General Use in the Lord's Work.

Statement of Receipts from August 15th to September 16th, 1889.

	£	s.	d.
Miss E. Smith, per J. T. D.	1	0	0
Mrs. Hallows	0	5	0
	£1	5	0

HOP-PICKERS' MISSION.—Miss Yockney, 3s. 6d.; Miss V. G. Bridgland, 10s.; Mrs. Tebbutt, 5s.; Mrs. Kingham, £2 2s.; Mrs. Halcrow, 1s. Mr. Burnham also asks us to acknowledge the following anonymous contributions:—Bank-note from London, £5; stamps from Rugby, 5s.

£5 received from H. M. has been allotted to the London City Mission. 5s. from Jane Anderson will be sent to Mr. Patrick for Spanish Testaments for North Africa.

Friends sending presents to the Orphanage are earnestly requested to let their names or initials accompany the same, or we cannot properly acknowledge them; and also to write to Mr. Spurgeon if no acknowledgment is sent within a week. All parcels should be addressed to Mr. Charlesworth, Stockwell Orphanage, Clapham Road, London.

Subscriptions will be thankfully received by C. H. Spurgeon, "Westwood," Beulah Hill, Upper Norwood. Should any sums sent before the 13th of last month be unacknowledged in this list, friends are requested to write at once to Mr. Spurgeon. Post Office and Postal Orders should be made payable at the Chief Office, London, to C. H. Spurgeon; and Cheques and Orders should all be crossed.

THE

SWORD AND THE TROWEL.

NOVEMBER, 1889

Fighting and Praying.

A BUGLE BLAST BY C. H. SPURGEON.

"Then came Amalek, and fought with Israel in Rephidim. And Moses said unto Joshua, Choose us out men, and go out, fight with Amalek: to morrow I will stand on the top of the hill with the rod of God in mine hand."—Exodus xvii. 8, 9.

"THEN came Amalek"; that is, after the manna had fallen, after the rock had been smitten. First food, then conflict. God spared his people all battles in their early days. For a while their adversaries were as still as a stone. But when everything was arranged, and the commissariat of the camp was provided for, "then came Amalek." Brethren, in our march to heaven, it may happen that one part of the way is free from conflict; but let no man wonder if things change. One of these days we shall read this despatch from the seat of war, "Then came Amalek, and fought with Israel." Do not court attack, nor even desire it. When you hear the older folk talk about their inward conflicts, do not lament if your chronicle of wars is a short one. There is a time when kings go forth to battle, and that time will come to you soon enough. It has often been the Lord's way to give his people space for refreshment before trying them.

The same truth holds good as to service for the Lord. In the case before us, warfare was service. Some new-born converts rush to the service of God before their knowledge or their strength has fitted them for it. I want to speak very guardedly, for I have great sympathy with their zeal; but I wish to show unto them a more excellent way. Few begin work for God too soon. Ah me! Some professors have not begun

40

yet, after years of profession. What shall we do with old sluggards, who have been lying in bed for thirty years? Are they worth the trouble of waking? I fear not. May the Lord be gracious to them, and save them! We cannot work for God too soon; yet it is possible to go to work before you have sharpened your tools. There is a time for every purpose; and each thing is good in its season. Learn, and then teach. I would have you serve the Lord successfully: wherefore, as God gave to Israel manna and water before he sent them to fight with Amalek, so should every believer feed on the truth himself, and then go forth to teach others also. Feed, that you may work, and work because you have been fed.

After the manna and after the smitten rock, came the fight: "Then came Amalek." He was a descendant of Esau, full of his father's hate. This tribe fell upon Israel without proclamation of war, in a cowardly manner, and slew the hindmost of them, when they were not expecting an attack. They were the first of the nations that dared enter the lists against Jehovah. The others had been cowed by the wonders of the Red Sea; but Amalek was daring and presumptuous. According to the Hebrew, Amalek laid his hand upon the throne of God, and dared to molest his people.

Note well, that in this battle of the Lord, there were two kinds of fighting. The first was the Joshua-service; and that was done in the plain by the fighting men. The second was the Moses-service; and this was done upon the side of the hill, by the men of God, who communed with heaven. We need both modes of warfare.

I. To begin with, we want much of THE JOSHUA-SERVICE.

This is the service of many. Moses said to Joshua, "Choose us out men, and go out, fight with Amalek." We have a battle against sin, error, pride, self, and everything that is contrary to God and to his Christ; and in the Joshua-service many can be employed. As the Holy Spirit has given diversities of gifts, so are there varieties of agencies for battling for the truth. Every believer should be a soldier in Christ's own army of salvation. We must not join a church with the main design of our own edification: our chief point in life is far higher than the most spiritual form of self-interest. We must live to battle for Christ Jesus our Lord in all manner of ways. To feed on the manna of heaven, and then to wrestle with the evils of earth, is a healthy combination. We need, all of us, to stand up for Jesus in these evil days: the enemies are many and powerful, and no man redeemed by Christ must keep back from the conflict. Friend, what part will you take?

In this Joshua-service *all the combatants were under due command.* "Joshua did as Moses had said to him," and the people did as Joshua commanded them. In all holy service, willingness to be led is a great point. Certain workers may be very good personally; but they will never combine with others to make a conquering band. They work very well alone, or as fore-horses in the team; but they cannot trot in double harness. We most of all need men and women who can keep rank, who can do their work quietly and perseveringly, and are ready to follow the direction of those whom God may call to be leaders. A general can do nothing without such soldiers; and they feel that they can do little without him. Soldiers without discipline become a mob, and not an army. May the Lord send us troops of disciplined warriors prepared to chase the Amalekites! All at it, and always at it, and all for the love of Jesus: this makes a fine motto. Friend, will you be one of the steady workers?

In Joshua-work courage was required. "Go out, fight with Amalek." The Amalekites were fierce, cruel, strong. They are said to have been the chief among the nations; by which I understand first among the plunderers of the desert. The soldiers under Joshua had courage, and faced their wolfish foes. Saints need courage for Jesus in these days. May God, in his mercy, make his people bold against scepticism, superstition, and open wickedness! In these days boldness is a jewel, for men are not sure about anything, or they speak as if they were not; and when men are not sure themselves, they can never convince others. A modern-thought gentleman said in a paper, the other day, "We are not all so cocksure as Mr. Spurgeon." No; and the more's the pity. If ministers are not absolutely certain of what they preach, they are not likely to convince others. If you doubt a thing, let it alone till your doubt is solved one way or the other. He that doubts creates doubters. Only he that believes will make believers. In this age of unbelief, if you are to win victories, you must have convictions, and you must have the courage of those convictions, and refuse to bow down before the infidelity of the age. We are called, not to flirt with error and evil, but to fight with it; therefore, let us be brave, and push on the conflict.

Those fighting under Joshua did not grow weary. Moses had the more spiritual work, and his hands grew heavy: we sooner tire in private devotion than in public service. Joshua and his men were not weary: never let us be weary in well doing. Do you ever grow weary in one peculiar way of serving God? It may be useful to try something else. "You mean, drop what I am doing?" No; I do not. I mean, do something extra. It often happens that a man cannot do one thing, but he can do two things. Do you think the observation strange? It is true. Variety of labour serves for recreation. In the service of God it is a relief to turn from one consecrated effort to another; and so rest one set of faculties by exercising others. Throw your whole soul into the heavenly crusade, and weary not through your fight with Amalek from dawn to set of sun. Friend, will you be unwearied in the heavenly war?

In the Joshua-service *they were successful*, for "they discomfited Amalek and his people with the edge of the sword." Beloved workers for the Lord: may he grant you like success against evil! The devil goes to be beaten, and he shall be beaten. If we have but courage and faith in God, and can use the edge of the sword, we shall yet defeat the powers of darkness. Many evils are deeply entrenched in modern society: the drunkenness, the scepticism, the superstition, the vice around us are a tremendous force; but the gospel of our Lord Jesus Christ is equal to the emergency. If all professedly Christian men were actuated by the spirit of the gospel, many evils would be greatly diminished. If we also believed in the power of the gospel, so as to tell it out to our fellows with joyful confidence, in the power of the Spirit of God, we should soon see the wickedness and worldliness of the age put to the rout. Alas, brethren! the fault of many workers is that they do not use the *edge* of the sword. One does not like to think of the edge of a sword; but nothing else will serve in battle. One gentleman has preached a magnificent sermon, everybody admired it. Yes, that was the richly-adorned hilt of the sword; but nobody was wounded. Another man, in rough tones, boldly stated a naked truth, and pressed it home on the conscience, and that truth has pricked his hearer in the heart.

The edge of the sword means business, and people know it. They are not amused; but are made to mourn and repent. What cares the evil heart of man for the scabbard of our sword? it needs the edge, and must have it. In talking to people, are we not often afraid of using the edge of the sword? "Well," says one, "I try to bring in the gospel gradually." Quite right: but the best way to bring in the edge of the sword gradually is to cut with it at once. We are such a long while parading and parleying, that we do not come to the point, and tell men that they are lost in sin, and must immediately fly to Christ for refuge, or they will perish. We must bring forth the truth clearly. and boldly, if any good is to be done.. "Joshua discomfited Amalek with the edge of the sword." We must use the Word of God, which is the sword of the Spirit, and force it home upon the attention and the conscience of all we can reach. Give the people plenty of instruction as to the central truth of salvation through the blood of Jesus. We may do as we like about flags and drums—I mean, preach ing about this or that minor point—but we must come to the edge of the sword, the wrath to come for the ungodly, and salvation in Christ for believers. Give men plenty of that sacred command, " Believe on the Lord Jesus Christ, and thou shalt be saved." Strike home in the name of the Lord, and command all men everywhere to repent. Quote Scripture; quote it continually. Bring out the doctrines of grace, which are the burden of the inspired Book. It is the Word of God that saves souls, not our comment upon it. Smite them with the edge of the sword.

Thus I have spoken about the Joshua-work, wishing with my whole soul that every member of the visible church would enter the ranks, and use the sword with his whole heart. Oh, that those who are marching to the promised rest may serve the Lord valiantly while they are on the road thither! If you are saved yourselves, may the Lord employ you in his army, and glorify himself in you !

II. The second part of the subject is full of interest. It is THE MOSES-SERVICE—the service of Moses and his comrades. These did not go down to the battle-field themselves, but they climbed the mountain-side, where they could see the warriors in the conflict; and there Moses lifted up the rod of God.

Note, that *the Moses-service was essential to the battle;* for when Moses held up his hand, Israel prevailed; and when he let down his hand, Amalek prevailed. The scales of the conflict were in the hand of Moses, and they turned as his prayer and testimony failed or con- tinned. It was quite as necessary that Moses should be on the hill as that Joshua should be in the plain. This part of church-work is often overlooked; but it is quite as necessary as the activity of the many.

We need the secret prevalence of chosen servants of the Lord, whose business is not so much with men for God as with God for men.

This holy work was of *a very special character.* Only three were able to enter into it. I believe that, in every church, the deeply spiritual, who prevalently commune with God, and bring down the blessing upon the work of the rest, are comparatively few; I might almost say, are absolutely few. God lays his own hand upon one here, and another there, and causes them to approach unto him. Would God all the Lord's servants were prophets! But it is not so. The Lord uses many in his working-service, who, nevertheless, are not among his intimates. They do not hold high rank among the intercessors who have power with God. This service is peculiar; but the more widely it is exercised, the better for the cause of God. We want many who can draw down power from God, as well as many who can use that power against the enemy.

This Moses-service lay in *very close communion with God.* Moses, and Aaron, and Hur were called to rise above the people, and to get alone, apart from the company. They climbed the hill as a symbol, and in retirement they silently communed with God. That rod of God in Moses' hand meant this—God is here with these pleading ones on the mount; and by his powerful presence he is smiting the enemy. How blessed it is for a people to be led by those whom the Lord has honoured in former times, and with whom he still holds fellowship!

In this sacred engagement *there was a terrible strain upon the one man who led the others in it.* In the process of bringing down the divine power upon the people, the vehicle of communication was sorely tried. "Moses' hands were heavy." Beloved, if God gives you spiritual power to lead in Christian work, you will soon find out that the condition of such leadership is a costly one. Your case requires a deeper humility, a steadier watchfulness, a higher consecration, and a closer communion with God than that of others; and these things will try you, and, in many ways, put a heavy strain upon you. You will be like Elias, who, at one time, could run like a giant, and at another could faint and fly. The burden of the Lord is no feather-weight.

In this hallowed service *help is very precious.* When Moses' hands began to drop down, and he himself was faint, Aaron and Hur gave him substantial aid. They fetched a stone. and they put it under him, and they made him sit thereon, with his hands still lifted high, and his eyes towards heaven. When he stood in a sweat, because of his anxious prayer, and the muscles of his arms grew weary, his brethren stood by him, each one holding up an arm lest the rod should drop; for if it did, the cause of Israel dropped also. Are you a worker? Have you a leader fit to. lead you? Bring a stone and put under him: cheer his heart with some gracious promise from the Lord's Word, or with some happy sign from the work itself. Cheer the good man as much as possible. Do not throw a stone at him, as I have known some workers do; but put a stone under him, that he may sit down, and not be overcome. Copy Aaron and Hur, by staying up his hands, the one on the one side, and the other on the other side, so that his hands may be steady until the going down of the sun. Happy men, thus to sustain their leader! The sacred power with God which brings down victory for others is given to some, and they use it; but flesh is weak, and they faint. Let others of like grace gather to their help, and hold up their hands, one in one way, and one in another way, as Aaron and Hur held up the hands of Moses. Let spiritual men earnestly help those whom God calls into special spiritual communion with himself, that so the name of the Lord may be glorified, and victory may wait upon the banners of his people.

This is the pith of my address. The prayer-meeting is, after all, that spiritual power on the mountain-side which makes the workers strong. Do not let the praying work flag; and even if it seems to do so, let Aaron and Hur come to the rescue. Come, and help, with all your might, to keep the rod of the Lord still steady, that the battle of the Lord may be fought out victoriously. Go on, Joshua, and use the edge of the sword: the Amalekites need it. But take heed, you that are on the mountain-side, that *your* service does not cease. Humble men and women, unknown to fame, you may be called by God, like Moses, to hold up his rod, and bring down the blessing. If any of you grow faint, I pray that others may come forward, and keep the rod of God in its place. The prayer-meeting must be maintained at all cost. The communion of the church with God must never be broken. If you visit a factory, you may see thousands of wheels revolving, and a host of hands employed. It is a wonderful sight. Where is the power which keeps all this running? Look at that slated shed! Come into this grimy place, smelling of oil. What is it? It is the engine-house. You do not think much of it. This is the centre of power. If you stop that engine every wheel will stand still. Some good people say, "I am not going out to-night. It is only a prayer-meeting." Just so. It is only the engine. It is everything. Go on board a great ocean steamer, bound for New York. You say, "I have been in the saloon. I have seen the wonderful luxuries provided for the passengers. It is a marvellous vessel." Did you look at her engines? "What! go down that ladder? I saw some black fellows below, stoking great fires; but I did not care for that." Talk not so. If it were not for those sooty stokers the grand saloon and the fine decks would be of no use. Prayer is the engine. It supplies the force. I like to see the engines going— praying, praying, praying, praying! Then the hidden screw, down under water, drives the huge ship, and causes it to speed towards the appointed haven. Keep the Moses part of the work going; and let not the Joshua-work be slack.

Beloved in the Lord, let us hearten one another in our warfare. Let us each stand in his office, and do the part to which the Lord has called us. Let us take courage. We are sure of victory. In the margin of our Bibles we read, "Because Amalek had laid his hand upon the throne of Jehovah, the Lord will have war with Amalek from generation to generation." Sin lays its traitorous hand upon the very throne of God. Will he allow it? The unbelief of the age has laid its hand upon the holy sacrifice of Christ. Will the Lord be quiet concerning this? Scepticism has dared to assail the inspired Word. Will the Lord endure it? Is not the time of his coming hastening on when men grow bolder in sin? May we not, from the very infamy of the age, gather that it is coming to its climax? The iniquity of the Amalekites is filling up. The Lord will surely smite the evil of the age with the edge of the sword. Let us not be afraid.

My firm conviction is, that the gospel is as powerful as ever. If we could but get it out of the sheath of so-called culture, and education, and progress, and questioning, and could use the bare, two-edged sword of the old-fashioned gospel upon the hearts of men, we should again hear shouts of victory. We have heard with our ears, O God, and our fathers have told us, what work thou didst in their days, and in the old time before them; and if we can get back the courage of the old times, and the gospel of the old times, and the Spirit of the old times, we shall see a renewal of those wondrous deeds. We must exert ourselves; for Joshua did so. We must lean upon the strength of God; for Moses did so. The two together—active warfare and prayerful dependence—will bring the blessing. We are more than ever forced into this fight to-day. Thirty years ago things were very different from what they are now. It was easy to gather a congregation then, compared with what it is now: the spirit of hearing is departing from our cities. Cavillers and questioners are to-day far more numerous than they were thirty years ago. One finds among Christian professors shoals of infidels. Ministers are, in large numbers, sowers of doubt. One who is reputed to preach evangelically told his young men the other day that a page of Huxley was worth all that Moses had written in Genesis. I know a convert from Mahometanism who has been greatly staggered while in England by what he has heard from Christian teachers. Many ministers are more at home in undermining the gospel, than in the conversion of souls. Let us, therefore, look well to our weapons, and be in earnest to defend the truth of God. I charge you, each one, to do his part, and play the man in this evil day.

Though myself only fit to be numbered with the least of my Master's servants, yet I am called to lead a great work, and therefore I beg my comrades to help me. Hold up my hands! My brethren, hold up my hands! Send up your continual prayer on my behalf. If the standard-bearer falls, what will the weaklings do? I am feeble in body, and sore pressed with anxious care; spare me what care you can by your brotherly aid, and specially by your loving words of comfort, and your pleadings in prayer. To the best of my ability I have held the fort, and kept the faith. Though, as yet, my protest seems unavailing, and Amalek prevails by reason of scientific unbelief, yet the Lord on high is greater than the noise of many waters. Truth must yet prevail, and error must be routed. In the name of the Lord let us set up our banners once again. Renewing the pledges of our brotherly covenant, let nothing but death divide us. Let us be one in this great conflict for the Lord and for his throne. Amen.

Drones.

A N average hive of bees numbers about seventeen thousand, seven hundred of which are drones. The bee-hive is a type of the Christian Church; only here the drones out-number the workers. Any church of five hundred members, will find that one hundred do all the work, and nearly all the giving, whilst the others, for a three shilling seat-rent, take out a license for universal grumbling. Gideon's three hundred fought the battle, whilst upwards of thirty-one thousand looked on and criticized. God's victories are always won by the few. Daniel's little band is to the front, whilst the hosts of the Merozites come not to the help of the Lord against the mighty.

Drones are more pretentious than working bees. They are bigger, stronger, and more showy.

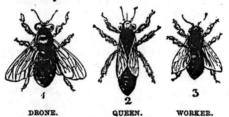

DRONE.   QUEEN.   WORKER.

It is the old story of ability to work and a will to be idle. In our churches we often find a strong hand joined to a weak heart, and a golden purse owned by a copper spirit. A mansion is required to accommodate the body whilst a pill-box would suffice as a temple for the soul.

But that is not all. Whilst their brilliant powers and rich resources are withheld from the church, they are often wasted upon inferior objects. Literally, the children's bread is taken and given to dogs. Christ's poor are starved, whilst puppies and pigeons, peacocks and pheasants are feasted. Athletics and operas, fine arts and concerts, are to-day absorbing talents which, if consecrated to gospel missions, would bring streams into the desert, and make the wilderness blossom like the rose. To see talents so rich in promise expended upon such trivial objects, reminds us of the Alpine shepherd, who spent fifteen years in trying to balance a pole on his chin, or the illustrious monarch who hunted through the whole of his kingdom to find a white mouse with green eyes.

But more than that. Not only does the church suffer the loss of this labour, but in this idleness there lurks the church's greatest danger. They that do nothing are sure to do worse than nothing; for an idle brain is the devil's workshop. Drones are destitute of stings; but in church life those who do the least, sting the most. When the ass refuses to draw, he often turns to kicking. Employment brings peace to the commonwealth, whilst its absence breeds riots and civil wars. A nation composed of retired tradesmen would be a sorry kingdom for any prince to rule, and a church composed of all drones would baffle the powers of a Paul and break the heart of a Peter.

Moreover, drones misrepresent religion. He that would eat the kernel must crack the nut; and that frightens them. They are like Solomon's slothful man, who roasteth not what he took in hunting. They go in for things raw, to save the trouble of cooking, and therefore always suffer from spiritual dyspepsia. No doubt they are apples of God's orchard; but they remain always in that transition stage when the apple is as sour as the crab; and this makes a great many say of the church militant, what the little boy said of the church triumphant—he "didn't want to go to heaven because grandfather was there."

A wise man once said that in a town of lazy people he should expect to find "crazy houses; ragged, dirty, and saucy children; the school-house empty, and the jail full; the church silent, the grog-shop noisy, and the carpenters, saddlers, and blacksmiths doing their principal work at the taverns." So much for a lazy town; and let all idlers beware. But what of a lazy church? It would be the sepulchre of death, and the sport of the world. Its excellency would consist in some of the following ornaments—A hideous debt astride a Gothic building; pitch-pine seats and a marble pulpit with a sleepy pastor feeding a drowsy people with an empty spoon; a quinquennial instead of a quarterly balance-sheet; an organ to do the praising, a book to do the praying, and five rich deacons to do the giving; all church missions and extra services amalgamated in one week-night lecture; but the Dorcas society continued as the best means of advertising the news of the neighbour-hood; strong bodies and weak souls; a laughing devil, and a weeping Saviour; astonished angels, and self-satisfied worshippers.

The man that lives only for himself is one of "the wastes and burdens of society." The paradise of the past would have excluded him; for there man had "to dress the garden and to keep it"; he is useless for the paradise of the future; for there God's servants are to serve him; he is out of harmony with God himself; for Jesus says, "My Father worketh hitherto, and I work." He is out of sympathy with mankind; for "no golden act binds him to the world's sad heart." The ant and the stork, the cat and the dog, the horse and the ox, the birds of the air and the fish of the sea, all unite in condemning him, and with ten thousand other forms of life would cry—

> "Go and toil in any vineyard,
>   Do not fear to do or dare
> If you want a field of labour,
>   You can find one anywhere."

LEVI PALMER, *Taunton.*

Saved from the Sinking Ship

"I'LL never do it again!" "I'll never do it again!" was my exclamation, as I walked along the esplanade, wet to my skin, after tugging away with all my might, without any breakfast, to assist in launching a Lifeboat during a severe gale. The storm was terrific. The picturesque bay where I was staying looked lovely to the artist eye; for ships were lying at anchor in such numbers, that it looked more like a naval review, than distressed mariners seeking shelter in a time of storm. Those who knew the coast well, said, "this is a bad sign." I had noticed the cone had been hoisted for several days, warning vessels of the approaching storm. Many seemed to have heeded the warning, and entered and anchored within the harbour. At length the testing time came ; for even in the harbour the tempest tossed the boats about with such violence, that the signal was given by the big bell for all the lifeboat men to be in readiness. Several ships drifted some distance from their anchorage, and large cables snapped through the violence of the waves, which caused the greatest fears for the lives of the sailors. Hundreds of spectators thronged the beach, and soon the air was full of the cries of the people. "Launch the Lifeboat ! Launch the Lifeboat ! Launch the Lifeboat ! A ship has gone for the rocks ! " I had just taken my seat at the table, feeling quite ready for my morning meal; but the shrill cry, on all sides, "Launch the Lifeboat ! " took away all my desire for my fresh herring and tea. I ran helter-skelter to the boat-house, and pulled and pushed with might and main to help to launch the lifeboat. I assisted the crew in donning their cork jackets, and fastening on their life-belts. With all possible speed, at the command of the captain, these brave fellows dashed into the foaming spray like true heroes, amid the cheers of the spectators. I stood knee deep in the water, and shouted at the top of my voice, " God speed you, my lads "; but the human voice could scarcely be heard amid the dashing and roaring of that angry sea.

Wind and wet had no effect in quelling our excitement while lives were to be rescued. Standing on the beach, we saw the big vessel drift across the bay, towards the rocks like an express train. It was quite evident that no power on earth could save her from destruction. Fortunately for the seamen, there was, just in front of the rugged rocks, a sandbank, on to which this vessel struck. We saw her bump, bump, bump, like a child's toy boat, so fierce was the gale. As she stranded on the sands the sailors hoisted the signal of distress. Meanwhile, the brave fellows in the lifeboat, which had been unobserved by the crew, were pulling towards them with all their might, every now and then lost to view in the trough of a mighty wave, but again rising on the angry crest of the next mountainous billow, and looking like a cork or a bird in the distant storm. Many eager eyes looked on the scene, watching their movements from the shore, while fervent prayers went up to God for their safety and successful return. Through a powerful glass, my colleague and I watched most anxiously to see the poor shipwrecked crew taken into the lifeboat. We saw the boat get within speaking distance of the wreck, then there seemed to be some great delay, as if some unseen barrier prevented their rendering assistance. After a time the lifeboat put back to sea, tossing and lurching in a marvellous manner, trying to hold her position about a quarter of a mile from the sinking ship. The spectators became furiously excited, crying out, "Why ever don't they save them?" Some said, "It is too rough to get alongside." Others said, "They will yet fire rockets and use the cage." Some thought they must have secured a life-line from the ship, and the men would yet swim to the boat. But with all our speculations and waiting, and watching, nothing further seemed to be done towards saving the crews. At last the harbour captain saw through his glass the danger of the lifeboat and the exhaustion of the men. He signalled them back to the harbour to learn the cause of their delay. They saw his signal and obeyed his instructions. As they pulled towards the shore, we saw the crew of the sinking ship climb the rigging and watch their deliverers returning without them. No wonder that our excitement increased and our anxiety ran high. I was among the first to greet the lifeboat crew, and enquire the cause of their failure from the coxswain. My curiosity and sympathy at once turned into vexation when he assured me that these seafaring men on a sinking ship would not accept their offer of salvation.

"Not accept salvation?" I indignantly enquired, "after all your brave efforts to save them."

"No, sir," said the coxswain, "they positively refuse my conditions."

"You astonish me," I said, "whatever are your conditions of salvation which could cause these men to refuse them?"

"Simply, sir, that they get into the boat."

"And do you really mean to tell me, that these men, on a sinking ship, positively refuse your offer?"

"Yes, sir," replied the coxswain, "that is so; unless I promised to bring with them their big boxes and personal belongings. I told them I could not do it; I dare not do it; I must not do it. My orders, sir, are to save life, not boxes and property. They must leave them behind; but every man I would willingly take on board. I told them I would try and lay by for a time, as I knew without my boat they must perish; and if they were willing to accept my terms, and leave their boxes and save themselves, they had only to hoist their flag of distress while we were near them, and we would make for their help at once. And this is why we have been lying out in the gale so long."

"Tell me," said the harbour-master, "is there any chance for them?"

"None, sir," said the coxswain, "apart from us. The ship has broken her back, with her bumping on the bottom; she is full of water, right to the deck. It is impossible for them to get into the cabin for food. They must receive help from without, or perish with their boat."

"Coxswain," said the harbour-master, "are you and your men willing to go out once more, and give them one more chance to be saved?"

"What say you, lads?" said the coxswain."

"Ay, ay, sir," from the brave fellows, was the unanimous cry.

Their numbed hands were rubbed, and warm refreshments were supplied, while the life-boat was bailed out. The withdrawal of the life-boat was the best possible sermon to these men in distress. When help was withdrawn, their position seemed to be realized; for before the lifeboat had time to get round the promenade of the pier, the flag of distress was hoisted from the wreck.

"Pull, my lads!" said the coxswain: "they are now calling for aid."

Thud, thud, thud, went the oars, with as much precision as that of soldiers' footsteps. With renewed interest we watched her as she feathered the waves towards the sinking ship. No sooner had she come alongside, than we saw distinctly through the glass one after another being lowered into the boat. Then came a pause; and then a shout: "They've got them! They're saved!" was the cry from many voices, as the boat came heading towards the harbour. Cheer after cheer, accompanied with waving pocket-handkerchiefs, encouraged the brave-hearted-crew that manned the lifeboat.

Awaiting on the shore were many warm-hearted people to welcome them. In the seamen's Bethel, hot coffee and refreshments had been prepared for them prior to their arrival. The number rescued that day from a watery grave was thirteen. Though fourteen lives were that day saved from that ship, the fourteenth life would be considered by some people hardly worth the saving; but to the sailors it was much. Although the coxswain refused to take on board their boxes, he welcomed into the lifeboat, with their long bags of clothing, the ship's favourite cat, which poised himself on his master's knee, and sat gracefully watching the storm.

We were privileged to greet these sailors on landing, and were invited into the Seamen's Home, to give them a word of welcome. They seemed sad at the loss of their vessel and much of their personal effects, which were left to the mercy of the waves. But when once safely housed on shore, they seemed full of gratitude to the lifeboat-crew for their own salvation, and that of their favourite cat.

As I witnessed the effort put forth, and the hundreds of eager eyes that watched for the salvation of these men, and then learned with bitter disappointment that they first refused the salvation offered them, unless their property also was saved, I thought within myself, "How must God feel, after giving his Only Son a ransom for sinners, to hear the paltry excuses men will make for not accepting his salvation!" But our God is full of mercy, and slow to anger.

You, dear reader, have, doubtless, proved this again and again, in your own experience. Like the men with the offered lifeboat, you have not only had a second opportunity to receive salvation, but, it may be, you have refused, or neglected, hundreds of such invitations. Thank God, to-day you have still another opportunity; for God still stands beseeching you to be saved. He challenges your very objections; for he says, in Isaiah v. 4, "What could have been done more to my vineyard, that I have not done in it?" Here is the challenge of Omnipotence; is there any answer to such an enquiry? No, verily; for God has done all that his mercy and his justice could do to save sinners. He has provided a way of escape from the storm of sin. He has brought a very sea of salvation to our lips; and yet how madly men refuse or neglect his great salvation! Oh, that to-day some may see their real condition by nature—ruined, lost, and undone—and accept God's mercy, which, by grace, he still offers to them. This acceptance would cause the very bells of heaven to ring, and the angels to sing, "Saved, saved, completely saved, through Christ's redeeming love!"

J. MANTON SMITH.

A Child Born a Hundred Years Old.

SOME Christian teachers, and other persons, have repeatedly avowed the difficulty, if not the impossibility, of conversion at an advanced age. We have no wish to give the least encouragement to delay in the things of God, because we have no claim to any time but the present and passing moment. God's time for every duty, and especially the great concern of the soul's salvation, is "now," and "to-day." "Come, now, let us reason together," &c.; "Choose you, *this day*, whom ye will serve"; and, "*To-day*, if ye will hear his voice, harden not your heart." That is, clearly enough, the rule he has given us, and we have no right to presume on any good coming to us while in the path of disobedience.

But when we come to talk of the operations of divine grace, and God's exercise of his sovereign prerogatives, there are no difficulties, no limitations, no impossibilities. His own law to himself is, "I will work, and who shall let it?" And so, when we set any limits, of age or otherwise, beyond which God does not, or will not, go, we are approaching ground which we have no business to tread; and we had better take off our shoes and be silent.

God does convert and save some at a very advanced age, for he knows no limit but his own sovereign will.

When the excellent Countess of Huntingdon resided at Oathall, she had a place of worship built on her own estate, and the pulpit was supplied by her chaplains and others. Numbers were made partakers of the grace of God. Among these was a very old man, whose name was Abraham. He was born in Sussex, and grew up an idle youth, and entered the army, in which he served fifty years. After his discharge he married, and settled in a village near Oathall. Here he was awakened to a serious state of mind. He attended his parish church, but found neither guidance nor comfort. He then went round to the other churches in the neighbourhood, but with no better success. He could not find peace for his soul. Law and grace, morality and sacraments, were strangely mixed up, and his mind was confused.

Abraham had heard of the Methodists, but he did not like them; however, when Lady Huntingdon's chapel was opened by Mr. Venn, vicar of Huddersfield, he thought he would go for just once. He was then just a hundred years old, and in possession of all his faculties. Mr. Venn's discourse was as cold waters to a thirsty soul. The truth was brought home to him with power, and he drank it in with delight. He could hardly contain himself. When the service was over, he laid his hand on the shoulder of one who sat next him: "Ah, neighbour!" said he, "this is the very truth of God's Word, which I have been seeking, and never heard it so plain before. Here will I abide."

And so he did, attending regularly for more than five years, making happy advances in knowledge and experience. His great age, and his white hair, made him conspicuous in the congregation, and he was equally remarkable for his humility and simple faith. He spoke of the day when he found Christ as the day of his birth, and used to say that he was a child born at a hundred years old.

One day, the Countess was talking with him, and he was giving her an account of some of his domestic trials. "Ah, my lady!" said he, "it is my grief that my old partner is a little too apt to run ahead sometimes, and go against me. But I will tell you what happened the other day, when that remarkable darkness and tempest came over us here. She was terribly frightened, and thought it was the day of judgment. In she ran, with another woman of like mind, and down they fell upon their knees on the floor. 'Abraham,' said she, 'come and pray for me.' 'What is the matter, dame?' said I.

"'Oh, it is the day of judgment! it is the day of judgment! Ar'n't you afraid?' 'Afraid!' said I, 'no; what should I be afraid of? If it is the day of judgment, then I shall see Christ Jesus my Lord, and that will be a joyful sight.' So, my lady, I began to sing a hymn. By-and-by the storm was over, and then they both forgot the fright it had put them into." Abraham persevered in his Christian walk, adorning the doctrine of his Saviour, and, at last, was gathered into his bosom in peace; like a shock of corn, coming in his season, he passed away peacefully when in his 106th year.

Truly, we may say, "What hath God wrought!" And, again, "Is there anything too hard for the Lord?"

Cases such as the above may be few and far between; but it suffices to show that there is neither limit nor end to the power and grace of "the Holy One of Israel."

To people of all ages we have this message: "It is time to seek the Lord."

The Father's Love.

"I have declared unto them thy name, and will declare it: that the love wherewith thou hast loved me may be in them, and I in them."—John xvii. 26.

FREELY loved; no claim whatever
   Have I on God's precious grace;
All I have, or am, or shall be—
   All to his free love I trace.

DEARLY loved; my soul, adoring,
   Owns his love, so tender, true;
Love, wherewith his Son he loveth;
   Love wherewith he loves me, too.

SWEETLY loved; a joy responsive
   Fills his heart, and filleth mine;
Clouds may pass, but faith, triumphant,
   Bids me on his love recline.

EVER loved; a love eternal
   Stamps its impress on my soul;
Earth may pass, his love shall ever
   Like a ceaseless river roll.

Freely, dearly loved, and ever!
   Loved for all eternity!
FATHER, let my heart be daily
   Serving, praising, loving thee.

ALBERT MIDLANE.

1689 and 1889 : Then and Now.

BY R. SHINDLER.

THE accession of William III. and Mary to the throne of England marks an era in the history of Great Britain ; and not less is it a landmark in the history of British Nonconformity. The reigns of the four Stuart kings had been alike dishonourable to royalty, damaging to all the interests of the nation, deeply injurious to true religion, and perversive of the rights of conscience and the claims of liberty. Nonconformists had suffered greatly ; and among them, the Baptists and the Quakers had to endure the most rigorous hardships, and the bitterest persecutions. Imprisonment had been the lot of thousands, many more suffered fines and other restrictions, while not a few—and some of the best of men and women—endured death in various forms. This—and the tale of horrors and misery is all too painful to repeat— this was all done in the name and interests of the Church of England as by law established.

And yet, notwithstanding all the rigorous enactments, and often their high-handed administration, nonconformity flourished, taking root downward, and bearing fruit upward. The Baptists were conspicuous, alike in their endurance and their increase, and not less in their loyalty to the sovereign, and their zeal for God and the spread of the gospel.

The Toleration Act of 1689 removed many disabilities and restrictions from Nonconformists, and was the occasion of almost unbounded rejoicings, though it left them, in many respects, still burdened and fettered. However, it afforded them an opportunity to come to the front, to show themselves in their real character, as loyal, law-abiding, earnest-spirited Puritan Christians ; to hang out their flag, and in the name of their God, to set up their banners. They did so ; and, in reading the history of their movements, we see distinctly their fidelity to conscience and to God, taking, as they did, such Scriptures as these for their mottoes : "We ought to obey God rather than man"; and, "Whatsoever he saith unto you, do it."

Hence it was that, with an eager readiness which admitted of no delay, they published a "Confession of their faith"; not so much in any case for themselves, or to bind their adherents, as to avow their real sentiments, for the information of others, that any unwarrantable stigma as to doctrine and practice might be removed.

The General Baptists, those professing to hold Arminian sentiments, were a somewhat numerous and not uninfluential body, and had already, during the easier times of Charles II., published what they called their "Orthodox Creed" (1678), which would be considered as verging towards Calvinism in these days. The Particular Baptists, who held, in the main, to the Calvinistic faith, were more scattered about the country ; but were not wanting either in men of learning and talent, or in some amount of social influence. They at once drew up and published their Confession. It is prefaced thus :—"We, the ministers and messengers of, and concerned for, upwards of one hundred baptized churches in England and Wales (denying Arminianism), being met together in London, from the third of the seventh month to the eleventh of the same, 1689, to consider of some things that might be for the glory of God, and the good of these congregations, have thought meet (for the satisfaction of all other Christians that differ from us in the point of baptism) to recommend to their perusal the confession of our faith, which confession we own, as containing the doctrine of our faith and practice, and to desire that the members of our churches respectively do furnish themselves therewith."

Then follow the names of twelve London, and twenty-five country or provincial ministers.

The Confession contains thirty-two articles, harmonizing in most particulars—baptism, of course, excepted—with the Westminster Confession. In 1855, Mr. Spurgeon republished this Confession in a cheap form, with a letter of introduction, to his own church, and to the " Household of Faith " generally.*

It would be a good thing if this " Confession" were read, and better still, if read and received by every Baptist. It is worthy of the men, and the times, when it was produced, and worthy of all Baptists everywhere and always. Had it been held and practised, as it ought to have been, we should have heard nothing about " Down-Grade," and no one would have whispered a word about the amalgamation of so-called Particulars with the Generals. Those who wish for the amalgamation will, no doubt, find their home on the Low Level line.

Before we place the dates 1689 and 1889 in contrast, it may be well to glance at the progress, or otherwise, immediately following the earlier date. One observation must be made, too, in reference to the order and government of the General Baptists and the Particulars.

The former retained a considerable portion of the element of Presbyterianism in their assembly. The whole assembly was, as it were, one church, and though individual churches or congregations exercised some amount of independency, they were under the control of the assembly. Some held, and, to a certain extent, it was admitted, that an elder or minister of any one congregation, was an elder of all churches. Such, at least, was the notion of Smyth. The spirit of centralization prevailed in that body, as it did not among the Particular Baptists, and by degrees the entire assembly, with few exceptions, proceeded from Arminianism to Arianism, and thence to Socinianism, until the few remaining orthodox formed the new association in 1770.

The same deadening influences which produced such evil results among the General Baptists, wrought sad havoc among the Particulars. They did not give up Calvinism, or, in other words, renounce the Confession of 1689, but they overlaid it with an incrustation of something which approached Antinomianism, and ate out the life of the churches, and of the gospel as preached by many of the ministers. Divine sovereignty was maintained and caught, not only in exaggerated proportions, but to the practical exclusion of moral responsibility ; the obligation of sinners to " repent, and believe the gospel," was ignored, and even denied, and all gospel invitations and pleadings were restricted to those who were supposed to give evidence of a gracious state. The

---

* "The Baptist Confession of Faith." Spurgeon's Edition. 4d. Passmore and Alabaster.

writings of Dr. Crisp, too, reproduced by his son, and lacking the revision which the father would most likely have given them, aided the mischief in some directions, men taking crude expressions out of their surroundings, and torturing them into what seemed to favour Antinomian doctrines.

Amidst it all, however, there were churches and ministers who maintained the proportion of faith as set forth in the 1689 Confession ; and this more healthy state of things was aided, no doubt, by the preaching of Whitefield and the ministers both in and out of the Establishment, who were sound in the faith, and co-operated with the excellent Countess of Huntingdon in her evangelical efforts.

At the present date, 1889, a very large number of so-called Particular Baptist churches and ministers have very little practical acquaintance with the 1689 Confession ; they know very little about it ; and, if we are to judge them by their words, have very little, if any, sympathy with the Confession as a whole, and deny *in toto* some of its articles, such as relate to Election, Particular Redemption, Final Perseverance, and the Punishment of the finally impenitent. It is only in keeping, therefore, with their avowed sentiments that they should seek amalgamation with the Generals ; for in openly disavowing all faith in the Calvinistic sentiments of the Confession, they would be acting more honestly than they now do ; and in uniting with the Generals they would simply go to their own place. It has always been open for ministers and church-members to go from one body to the other, and there is no legal hindrance to their doing so; but the present action, in the direction of wholesale amalgamation, has no basis of legal authority or right, and proceeds upon the assumption that the Baptist Union is the Baptist denomination, which is very far from being the case. The whole of the churches never have been united in one body, and there is less likelihood of their being so united now than ever. A strong centralizing force has grown up within the Baptist Union ; but apart from the funds entrusted to its administration, it has no legal authority to say yes or no in reference to amalgamation. It cannot exclude a member for decadence of sentiment, and probably would not if it could. As a matter of fact, it would be convenient, and so far well, for all who disown the Confession of 1689 to class themselves with the Generals ; and all who own that Confession to bear the appellation of Particulars; and, probably, if the current still sets in the direction of Arminianism, or something worse, and there be a nominal amalgamation of the so-called Particulars and Generals, there will be a plainer course indicated for all who hold to the old Confession, to march under that standard in their various enterprizes for the subjection of the nations to the faith of Christ.

It would be a sad sight, however, one that might make angels weep, if such a thing were to be—and it seems as though it will be—that the nominal sons and successors of the venerable fathers who laid the foundation of the Particular Baptist denomination, and built the solid castle, and fortress, and massive walls of the old city, should just simply and complacently vacate the entire premises, and, so far as they are concerned, leave them to decay and ruin.

But if they will do so, they must ; and what then ? What will follow ? They will learn, and we shall see. But, anyhow, " the foundation of

41

God standeth sure, having this seal, The Lord knoweth them that are his." The truth will not, cannot falter nor fail. "All flesh is as grass, and all the glory of man as the flower of grass. The grass withereth, the flower thereof falleth away: but the word of the Lord endureth for ever. And this is the word which by the gospel is preached unto you." Of course, it is readily admitted that men may reject, as tens of thousands have rejected, the distinctive doctrines of the Particular Baptist Confession, and yet be true Christians, and accomplish much good in the cause of God ; still, however, holding fast the proper Deity and Atoning Sacrifice of our Lord Jesus Christ. But it is quite another thing to enter a denomination holding such a Confession as that of 1689, and then to complacently surrender the name and the doctrines it represents. It reminds one of the story of the widow who had had made a large wooden image of her deceased husband, whom she familiarly called "Simon." After some years, she was reduced in circumstances, and was short of many things. One morning her maid shouted upstairs that there was no wood to light the fire. "Oh, dear!" said the old woman, "I suppose you must take a chip or two off Simon." And so, by degrees, Simon fell into such reduced circumstances that he eventually disappeared altogether.

We have no fear, however, for the truth: that will stand; it cannot be overthrown. The mischief accrues to those who renounce it, and to those from whom it is withholden, as well as to those who turn away their ears from it, and give heed to fables. But, however dense the clouds behind which the sun has set, it always rises again, with glory undiminished ; and however long and dreary the winter, spring returns in due season. So will it be with the truth of God. And so will it be with all who believe, and hold, and confess the truth. May God grant it specially to all Baptists !

The Interpreters of the Scriptures.

RICA, having been to visit the library of a French convent, wrote thus to his friend in Persia concerning what had passed:— "Father," said I to the librarian, "what are these huge volumes, which fill the whole side of the library?" "These," said he, "are the interpreters of the Scriptures." "There is a prodigious number of them," replied I; "the Scriptures must have been very dark formerly, and very clear at present. Do there remain still any doubts? Are there now any points contested?" "Are there?" remarked he, with surprise. "Are there? There are almost as many as there are lines." "You astonish me," said I. "What, then, have all these authors been doing?" "These authors," returned he, "never searched the Scriptures for what ought to be believed, *but for what they did believe themselves*. They did not consider them as a book wherein were contained the doctrines which they ought to receive, but as a work which might be made to authorize their own ideas."—*From J. L. Nye's "Stories for Bible Readers."*

England in the Fifteenth Century.*

MANY years ago the late John Cassell, the illustrious pioneer of cheap literature, projected an illustrated History of England, which should successfully appeal to the popular taste. By this he hoped to supersede the pernicious reading of the Jack Sheppard and Newgate Calendar order, which was then widely circulated in town and country, though not in such large quantities as is the case at the present hour. Being well written, attractively illustrated, and issued at the popular price of a penny a week, the enterprise at once succeeded, and the sale of the History exceeded the great publisher's expectations. Readers found out that there was quite as much fascination in the history of their own country as in sensational stories—and a little more. The History was originally designed to be of modest dimensions; but since its first appearance, its story has been continued down to the present day, and it now extends through ten ample volumes. While the book is full enough for all English purposes, it is really one of those "big" things which might excite the admiration of Americans. The present re-issue, which has extended as far as the second volume, has been carefully revised throughout, as regards both the text and the engravings. The improvements are so great, that the History comes to us with the face of a new book; and, quite apart from the text, the gallery of pictures is a history in itself.

To look back upon that older world of four hundred years ago, in which so many noteworthy persons lived and worked, is to find ourselves, as it were, in times of promise which we can now understand far better than those who lived in them. As is shown by our engraving, the shops and thoroughfares of London were much as they had been for centuries; the houses in which the great traffic of the city was carried on being of that rough, shed-like pattern which was shown in the Old London street at the late Inventions Exhibition. The roughly-paved streets were without pathways; and though the overhanging houses were much more picturesque than our present buildings, their dreadfully unsanitary condition made them oftentimes the harbourers of plague, and other infectious diseases. If we could have walked the streets, we should have been struck by the large proportion of ecclesiastical personages among the foot-passengers. There was advantage, either real or imaginary, in belonging to the clerical order, because they were answerable only to the canon law, which was somewhat less harsh than that to which ordinary people were subject.

The century is chiefly interesting to us, however, as the age of the invention of printing, before the advance of which the darkness and superstition of the mediæval ages gave way, like unwholesome night-mists before the morning sun. While the printing-press, "God's modern miracle" and "the church's lever," as it has been called, certainly made the rapid multiplication of books easier, we have to remember that literary treasures were not at all times so scarce as is usually supposed. The historian says of four and five hundred years ago, respecting the

* "Cassell's History of England." The Jubilee Edition. Vol. II. From the Wars of the Roses to the Great Rebellion. Cassell and Company. Price 9s.

A LONDON STREET IN THE FIFTEENTH CENTURY.

(From "Cassell's History of England.")

friends of learning—who, in that age, were commonly also the friends of religion :—

"Not the least meritorious benefactors of their country, next to the writers and printers of books, were those who collected them into libraries, and the most munificent patron and encourager of learning in this manner was the unfortunate Duke Humphrey of Gloucester. He gave to the university of Oxford a library of six hundred volumes in 1440, valued at £1,000. Some of these very volumes yet remain in different collections.. Duke Humphrey not only bought books, but he employed men of science and learning to translate and transcribe. He kept celebrated writers from France and Italy, as well as Englishmen, to translate from the Greek, and other languages; and is said to have written himself on astronomy, a scheme of astronomical calculations under his name still remaining in the library of Gresham College. The great Duke of Bedford, likewise, when master of Paris, purchased and sent to this country the royal library, containing eight hundred and fifty-three volumes, valued at 2,223 livres."

The setting-up of the printing-press in Europe may be looked upon as the end of the dark ages, and the dawn of better days. Wickliffe had been dead over half a century, a like period was to pass before Luther would stand forth as the champion of truth, so that the newly-constructed printing-press, which, under God, was to prove so powerful an instrument in the hands of Luther to defeat the legions of Rome arrayed against him, was a sort of intermediate landmark between the preacher of Lutterworth and the monk of Wittenberg.

It is said that the Chinese had used wooden types from which to print for centuries; and the wonder is that such an idea did not sooner occur to a western mind. When it did really occur, metal was used instead of wood, and so carefully was the art perfected, that the Mazarin Bible, which may be regarded as the first production of Gutenberg's press, has never been excelled as an example of sumptuous printing. In connection with the fact that the new invention was the greatest event of the century, is there not something truly significant in the Scriptures having been the first book sent forth into the benighted world? This fact makes the heart sing as we spy it out on the page of history; and it is one of the things belonging to the days of old which should prevent our despairing for the present or the future. In what to us may appear to be the darkest times, the Lord is at work to further his gracious purposes, and his truth will stand fast for ever.

"Cassell's History of England" is the more acceptable, because separate chapters are devoted to such things as these, or to the progress of the people; things which are far more interesting than the pageantry of princes, or the ravages of armies. As a popular history it deserves all the praise which we can give it, and we commend it to our readers who have not already seen it.

The Colporteur in London.

MR. STOPS AT BETHNAL GREEN.

VERY few of the many who come to London for business or pleasure, care to acquaint themselves with the characteristics of a place like Bethnal Green, which, from a pleasant semi-rural suburb of the old city, has come to be one of the most densely-populated areas in England.

The rapid growth of the population deserves notice. At the commencement of the present reign, the population was 74,000, probably not more than half of the present total. House-room, of course, is proportionately more expensive, and the labour-market is more overcrowded.

By an entry in his diary (June 26th, 1663), Samuel Pepys enables us to realize, in some degree, what the place was like before its fields and gardens were covered with houses. " Sir W. Batten, Sir J. Minnes, my Lady Batten, and I by coach to Bethnal Green, to Sir W. Rider's to dinner, where a fine place, good lady mother, and her daughter, Mrs. Middleton, a fine woman. A noble dinner, and a fine merry walk with the ladies alone after dinner in the garden ; the greatest quantity of strawberries I ever saw; and good. This very house was built by the blind beggar of Bethnal Green, so much talked of and sung in ballads ; but they say it was only some of the outhouses of it."

Those were the days when farmers might still be found in the parish of Shoreditch. The palace of Bishop Bonner is said to have given a name to Bonner's Fields which surrounded it ; and there, at one time, could have been pointed out the house of Sir Thomas Gresham, and the school of Ainsworth, the lexicographer. The parish generally has gone from bad to worse. In the earlier years of this century, when little or nothing was done for the common people, either by schoolmaster or philanthropist, Bethnal Green fell into very evil repute; and its general condition, at that time, showed to what dangers a great city becomes exposed when children are allowed to grow up without Christian teaching. In 1826, there was organized, on this very ground, a gang of thieves some six hundred strong, who were a terror to the metropolis. They plundered shops, robbed and half-murdered passengers in the streets, and even stole cattle on market-days from droves which might be passing along. Such outbreaks were the symptoms of a disease that ragged-schools and similar institutions have, for half a century, been seeking to cure. Unless the only cure had been applied, there can be little doubt that, by this time, London would have become one of the most criminal and dangerous cities on the face of the earth.

In a general way, colportage would seem to be better suited for country districts than for the poorest quarters of great and overcrowded towns ; but after the work had been successfully revived in England, it did not seem to be quite right that London, and the populous suburbs, called Greater London, should be altogether neglected. The inhabitants of crowded streets, courts and alleys, are very different from country people, although they suffer from the same shortcomings, and have the same needs. On the whole, there will be more to discourage and to depress the worker's spirits. On country roads, and in villages, his call is looked upon as a relief to the monotony of life ; but amid scenes of squalor, where hundreds of families have each only a single room, the possibility of selling books is diminished. Having to go up and down dingy stairs to knock at doors, is very different from calling at wayside cottages, at whose porches, in summer weather, one may sit and read a book from the colporteur's pack. Hence, a man like our friend, Mr. Stops, in Bethnal Green, merits a full share of sympathy ; for he has difficulties to cope with such as might damp anyone's enthusiasm.

We first met with Mr. Stops at the annual meeting of the colporteurs last May. He is a man below the middle height, but he is a person of strong individuality. He has an eye for the humorous, as well as a mind for the serious side of his work. Being thoroughly in earnest, he is able to tell a story to which a large and mixed audience will always be willing to listen. Mr. Stops has the advantage of thoroughly understanding the ways of the London poor ; for he is one of the people, a native of Hoxton, and has lived in and about London all his life. He is also an encouraging example of how the teaching of a Christian mother will bear fruit after she has gone to her rest. If the good seed is sown, the harvest is surely reaped, sooner or later.

When the godly mother passed away, she asked her children to meet her in a better world, and they made a promise to do so, without, probably, fully comprehending what the promise involved. The son was a child of twelve, and, being of that age, he was told by his father that he must henceforth " do " for himself—a very common-place intimation of a certain class of widowers to their children when there is no mother to look after them. In the case of our young hero, there was nothing like dismay at his prospects ; on the contrary, he bravely entered upon an adventurous course. Religious impressions came and went, and he was exposed to various temptations, the reading of bad books being a chief danger. While he was in one situation, his master's wife died without hope ; in another, the master himself died, after he had served the Lord for forty years. This scene left an impression on the assistant's mind ; but the change needed did not yet occur. He went from one situation to another; and it so happened, on one occasion, that he met with a colporteur, whom he tried to tease, but of whom he bought a Testament. This man stated that the Bible should be treated like any other book, by being read through. The reasonableness of such advice was perceived and acted upon; preachers were listened to; and the Metropolitan Tabernacle was visited. When he was once convicted of sin, the distress of mind which the young convert passed through seems to have been very great. On a certain day, while on London Bridge, he put down a load he was carrying, with the intention of jumping into the water; but just at that moment the words came into his mind, " And after death the judgment," and he was saved from the crime of suicide. Soon after that he found the peace of God which passeth all understanding. This he has never lost. Since he became a Christian himself, our friend has been instrumental in the conversion of father, stepmother, brother, and three sisters.

Such is another addition to those " short and simple annals of the poor," which, to a Christian mind, are ever of interest. Immediately after his conversion, Mr. Stops engaged in Christian work; he distributed tracts, and undertook preaching in the streets, first at Walthamstow, and then in London. He then became acquainted with Miss Macpherson, who employed him during two months in lodging-house work, in connection with her own institution. It was through the recommendation of Miss Macpherson that arrangements were made for Mr. Stops to enter the Colportage Association. When he first saw Mr. W. Corden Jones, the secretary, and went before the committee, the candidate's being below the middle height was thought to be a serious drawback, as a heavy pack would have to be carried; but as a set-off against such a drawback, it was soon seen that Mr. Stops could hold his own by speaking for himself, while he evidently desired, above all things, to be engaged in the Lord's service.

When he entered upon the Bethnal Green district, in November, 1888, Mr. Stops was trying an experiment, so far as he was himself personally concerned; but now that he has extended his acquaintance with the people, and knows more about the difficulties which have to be overcome by a colporteur in such a situation, our friend sees no reason to regret the choice he made. While he never disguised the fact that he would have preferred a country district, he nevertheless resolved that, in God's strength, he would succeed in London. From the outset to the present time, he has been working as a pioneer, and gaining experience, without which a man cannot hope permanently to succeed. When he has perfected his plans, and tested methods of working, he will make his mark, even in Bethnal Green. As we have already pointed out to Mr. Stops, in private conference, the missing link in regard to sales will be found in the setting up of a Saturday-night stall in the thronged thoroughfare of the Bethnal Green Road.

Some of the general characteristics of the people, and of the densely-packed streets they live in, may be noticed; for only in proportion as these are understood shall we also comprehend what the colporteur has to contend with while carrying on the work committed to him. London, it should also be remembered, is a congregation of towns; and just as one town may differ from another, so do the quarters of this great metropolis. In regard to their slums, East and West may be equally squalid, but in certain tastes and fashions they may be quite opposite. The denizens of St. Giles's are not in love with Whitechapel.

In and about Bethnal Green, Monday is the best day for going from door to door; for the people have then a proportion of their money left which will, in some instances, go in drink, if not invested in wholesome reading, such as these people may be induced to purchase. Of course, there are streets in the poorest quarters in which it is hopeless to think of selling even penny books at any time; and in these the colporteur is simply a visiting missionary, who may leave a tract at one place, and speak a good word at another. This is trying work; but then it is some compensation, that the poor receive the bookman better than the middle-class. When all allowances are made, however, who would not feel discouraged when a penny represents the entire takings of eight hours? By way of relief, the man will retreat with his pack to what is conventionally called "a better neighbourhood"; but even in such pleasant thoroughfares as the Victoria Park Road and its side streets, he can never be sure of sales.

The general hindrances to the work are very apparent in such a parish as Bethnal Green. Chief among the obstacles in the way of the colporteur's happy progress, are Sunday newspapers and sensational novels. Large numbers read these who can hardly be persuaded to read anything else. Not being able to allow quite so large a discount on books as the shops, and as the Sunday-schools allow to their scholars, is another disadvantage. The public would not have lost much if the threepence in the shilling discount on books had never been introduced; but as it is so generally given, the Bethnal Green people not only think much of it, but they are even disposed to buy such works as give most paper for their money. Cheap lots, which have been reduced in price, sell more readily than anything else.

As would be naturally expected, a great many different kinds of characters are met with : some being friendly, others hostile. Perhaps the most difficult to deal with, because they are the most intolerant and unreasonable, are Romanists and Socialists. While the latter would like to pull down all our institutions, the Romanist will sometimes express the warm-hearted wish that he could burn the colporteur and his pack.

At the same time, many Romanists are far from bigoted. Towards the end of last November, a young lady was met with at Hackney who had recently been converted to what is wrongly called "the old faith."

"We do not want any of your books; we are Catholics," she said.

"I am sorry for you," bluntly replied the colporteur; "you are in the wrong."

"I used to belong to your faith," continued the girl, "but I have been staying with some friends here who have lent me their books, and I have come to the conclusion that they are right."

"They are wrong."

"You believe that to be once saved is to be always saved?" asked the young woman.

Yes; if you have been *once* saved, that is the question. Perhaps you never were saved?"

"You sin after you're saved?" she asked.

"Yes; but we don't go to the Virgin Mary : we go to Jesus."

"You are too sinful to go straight to him; you must go to the Virgin Mary first," said the young woman; "she has got power to help us."

"It does not look like it in the second chapter of John," replied the colporteur. "She could not turn water into wine, but said to the people, 'Whatsoever he saith unto you, do it.' If she could not do that which was least, she cannot grant the pardon of sin."

This interview ended by the young Romanist buying a shilling Bible and some text-cards. Like many others who are spoken to, this young woman has not been seen again; but the colporteur's services are not likely to be without results.

On another occasion, a lady of quite a different sort appeared at a house in the outskirts. "What sort of books have you got?" she asked. "We are Jews, and do not buy Gentile books. You are not a Jew?" she added, looking at the intruder with some incredulity. Then she quite lost her temper when the colporteur intimated that, in the Christian sense, he was a Jew.

"You are a liar!" she bawled out.

"Thank you," was the quiet reply; "thieves and liars always think other people are the same."

"Are you a Jew, then?" was asked, in softer tones.

"Yes," said the other; "'For he is not a Jew which is one outwardly . . . but he is a Jew which is one inwardly.'"

While talking with this woman, the fact came out that she had a brother in Australia. There happened to be a book in the pack on that country : it was purchased; and thus even the Jewess was pleased.

While going on his way, the man with the pack will at one house encounter a woman who is violently opposed to Mr. Spurgeon, but who, in time, has her prejudice softened down, until she becomes a customer. Some amount of business is done in the shops. A shopman is interested in the pack because it is such an odd-looking thing; and when his curiosity is satisfied by having it opened, he becomes a buyer.

Of the excessive folly of some who read merely for "pleasure," in their sense of the word, many examples might be given; and, although we are supposed to be living in the era of education, enquiries after silly songs, and even after "dream-books," are by no means obsolete. There is a sense in which mere sensual reading becomes little, if anything, better in its effects than excessive drinking. In one instance a youth of eighteen was discovered, who confessed to being "a great novel reader;" and in this indulgence he had squandered as much as five shillings a week. Of course, he did not like religion, being under the impression that it drove people mad, never for a moment suspecting that he was himself losing his senses through fiction. Let us hope that a turn for the better was made when this youth made a friend of the colporteur, and purchased a Bible and other books.

But the colporteur is an open-air preacher as well as a bookseller and house-to-house visitor; and, while out in such service in Bethnal Green, he is not likely to lack aught in the way of adventure. Whether they are well disposed towards religion or not, people are sure to be attracted by an open-air service; and hence it is important that colporteurs should be able to hold their own as street-preachers.

On one occasion, our colporteur was standing by while a student from a London college was getting through his sermon, perhaps almost too creditably. A working man, whose head was affected with what he had taken, perceived what was going on; and made straight for the service, with the intention of silencing the preacher, and giving some of his own notions to the congregation. After he had held forth for a time in his own style, denouncing the Bible as false, and so on, the college preacher, who, till this time, had been making such satisfactory progress, was so upset that it was necessary for Mr. Stops to stand forward.

"Did you ever know of a thief who liked a policeman?" he asked the man who was interrupting the service.

"No, yer fool, no more did you!" was the reply.

"We are a pair properly matched, then: we shall get on well now," said our colporteur. "But why don't a thief like a policeman?" he went on. "It is because he has broken the law. Now, that is just like you," he added, looking well at his man. "*You* don't like the Bible because you have broken God's law." He then went on to quote how men loved darkness rather than light, because their deeds were evil; the result being that the disturber was silenced, and on parting accepted a tract, and shook hands.

The colporteur, in a crowded London district like Bethnal Green, thus engages in a many-sided service, which is altogether of a very arduous kind. As regards Mr. Stops, we believe him to be a man of enterprise, who will gradually conquer difficulties, and make his own way. What our friend needs to make his success more complete is a Saturday-night book-stall in the thronged main thoroughfare of his district, and we would respectfully beg the parish authorities to find room for such a stall. On Saturday night working people are more in a humour to buy than at any other time. Mr. Stops well understands how to make both himself and such a stall attractive, so that if this suggested innovation is ever carried out, we believe that he will give a better account of himself and his sales than he has found it possible to do up to this present.   G. H. P.

Search-lights.

WITH the sparkling, foam-flecked sea for a setting, and the sylvan shores and verdant heights of the Isle of Wight for a background, the recent naval display at Spithead, presented an imposing spectacle to the sight-seer. Feelings other than those of personal pleasure or patriotic pride were stirred in the hearts of those who deemed the name of "Devastation," borne on the prow of one of the vessels, a fitting designation for the whole fleet, and mourned the evil which called for such a display.

Amongst the most interesting features of the spectacle were the search-lights, which were generally in full play in the Solent at night-time. They consist of electric lamps, fitted with powerful reflectors, so that their rays can be thrown to great distances; and having a double movement, they can be turned to all points of the compass, or flashed at any angle like a huge policeman's "bull's-eye." The effects produced, and the reflection cast in the sky, are remarkable. A stranger to their presence and purpose, walking in the neighbourhood at night, might be startled at seeing a cloud above him grow mysteriously luminous, as if some wonderful phenomenon had appeared in the heavens; then, in an opposite direction, a still brighter body of light might be suddenly seen, as if a door had been opened in heaven, and some of the "inner radiance" were flowing forth earthwards. Yet again, a single yet highly brilliant beam appears, strongly suggestive of the flaming sword wielded by the angel at the gate of Eden, or of a comet reposing beneath the horizon, and shooting its vast tail upwards towards the dome of night. This, also, may be succeeded by a combined display of all the lights in full play together, presenting a pyrotechnic spectacle of signal splendour. The utility of these wonderful accessories, in scanning the ocean or coast-line in the darkness, and thus detecting the presence of any lurking foe is obvious, and not without spiritual parallel.

What a marvellous "search-light" is the all-seeing eye of God! This was realized by the Psalmist, when he wrote—"O Lord, *thou hast searched me, and known me.* Thou knowest my down-sitting and mine uprising, thou understandest my thought afar off . . . . If I say, Surely the darkness shall cover me; even the night shall be light about me. Yea, the darkness hideth not from thee; but the night shineth as the day" (Psalm cxxxix. 1, 2, 11, 12). And again (Psalm xc. 8.) "Thou hast set our iniquities before thee, our secret sins in the light of thy countenance." Would that men generally were made conscious of this searching gaze! Surely they could do no other than surrender, even though in fear and trembling; and this should soon give place to fullest confidence and peace, as the look they had thought to be only wrathful, toned into tenderest compassion and love.

The Divine Word is also a most powerful and effective "search-light." It is, in fact, a wondrous combination, supplying all the needed adjuncts of our warfare. In Hebrews iv. 12, where the apostle enumerates, in symbols of the strife, the mighty qualities of the truth of God, he seems to anticipate this modern equipment of a campaign. At any rate, the concluding words of the verse are strikingly apposite to the parallel we are suggesting :—"The word of God is quick, and powerful, and sharper than any two-edged sword, piercing even to the dividing asunder of soul and spirit, and of the joints and marrow, *and is a discerner of the thoughts and intents of the heart.*"

Oh for holy skill in flashing this all-revealing light into the dark hearts of men! Most marvellously does it make manifest their hidden thoughts and secret sins; but it can flood them, too, with the joy-light of forgiveness and reconciliation.   A. G. BARLEY.

Monday Meditations.

"WELL! I don't know, it seems to me I am not what I seem;
My preaching yesterday *to-day* seems like a passing dream:
The morning's text was sweet, I know, and people seemed to hear;
But there was little unction in the opening, I fear.

"Where are my notes? (just one or two, for *order's* sake, I make;
A little wax in case the thread of memory should break).
How poor they look! I really think the veriest child could say
As much as *that*; and this is *all*, perhaps, that lives to-day.

"What if my preaching should be proved *mechanical*, and I
A creature of ambition, *not* "the legate of the sky"?
What if these midnight watchings, and this unappeased desire
For truth and godly language, prove to be but fleshly fire?

"God's truth is all too precious for my few poor struggling words;
Nature *will* move her iron hand, and touch discordant chords.
I am so great a sinner, Lord, and tremble as I see
The vast *responsibility* that preaching lays on me.

"What has it brought me? shattered nerves, seared hopes, and weary wife,
Creating an unfitness for the *common* things of life.
Were it not well that I should seek in commerce, or in trade,
A livelihood for those I love, and for myself—*the shade?*"

So broods the weary pastor; so, the Monday hours roll by,
But th' old men's prayers at eventide chase out the misery;
And he goes home oblivious quite of commerce or of trade,
Wondering what sermon next shall spring from out the midnight shade.

Be comforted, O man of God! and is it nothing worth
Safely to pilot God's redeemed among the wrecks of earth?
In spite of Monday's moanings, friend, a *blessed* lot is yours,
And recompense of grace shall crown the labourer that *endures*.

Our hearts are worn with earthly care, and steeped in worldly things,
And it is almost heaven at times to fold our weary wings, .
While Gilead's balm and Hermon's dew from yon cool heights are driven
Across our sultry atmosphere till every cloud is riven.

Oh, never heed the weariness; *be* weak, the weak to gain.
The glorious work of God the Son is surely worth the pain.
While every mercy you unfold, and every hope you show,
Falls to *yourself*, be comforted, and bid the tempter *go*.

God renovate the shattered nerves, and rest the weary brain,
And soothe with his approving smile the *unsuccessful* pain;
And make himself so precious, by a whisper or a smile,
That you shall wish a *thousand* lives, to *preach* HIM *all the while*.

Galleywood, Chelmsford.   M. A. CHAPLIN.

𝔄 𝔚ord for my 𝔄lma 𝔐ater.

BY AN OLD STOCKWELLITE.

IT is customary, in speaking of the good that is done by means of Orphanages
and kindred institutions, to dwell almost exclusively upon one part of
their work; the relief given to poor widows and other relatives by the
removal of children, and the happy translation of the children themselves
from homes of want and privation to places of comparative comfort and
plenty. Were this all that had to be seen to, the conductors of orphanages
would lead far easier lives than they do. The children have not only to be
rescued *from* poverty, but taught to ward poverty off: in other words, they
must be educated, and fitted to fight their own battles. If they are not
trained with this object distinctly in view, much of the labour on their behalf
must necessarily be lost. Unfortunately, it is but too apparent that in the
matter of education many institutions make a fatal mistake, and unwittingly
injure those they intend to benefit.

An orphanage differs materially from an ordinary public school. A great
number of the children have lost both parents, all have lost one. It can
hardly be expected, therefore, that they should possess that refinement of
character which is generally to be found in those who are subject to the soft-
ening influences of home. Many of them, too, are taken from a lower class
of society. A discipline more than usually stern is therefore considered
necessary.

The institutions, moreover are generally large; and as without method
and regularity the staff would be powerless, it is thought wise to lay down
numerous rules and regulations, extending to the minutest details of daily
life. The children are taught to do this thing in one way, and that thing in
another way: they are drilled, and drilled, and drilled, until all individuality
is lost, and they become mere automatons, acting only as another directs.

The system, doubtless, answers admirably for securing order, but it is attended by serious consequences. A boy leaving school obtains, it may be, a
subordinate position in some mercantile office. He is asked to do certain work
to which he is unaccustomed; not having been shown how to do it, and his
tutors having deliberately smothered what little power he had of thinking
for himself, he of course makes a muddle of his task, and not only loses
favour with his employer, but becomes the butt of his companions. This, of
course, to a certain extent, is true of all boys entering an office fresh from
school; but the ordinary school-boy adapts himself in a few days, or, at
most weeks, to the new order of things, while the other lad takes months.

As if this were not enough, the early business life of many boys is blighted
and embittered by another cause, for which there is really no excuse: I
allude to the manner of clothing orphan children. It is little short of cruelty
to send boys and girls to work amongst others of their own age, dressed in
the absurd uniforms that many institutions have adopted. The "charity
badge" carries with it almost ceaseless ridicule and discomfort. The case
occurs to me of a boy who, on leaving a well-known institution in the north
of London, was provided with an outfit consisting of two new suits of clothes,
with the monogram of the school embossed on the buttons, an Inverness-
cape of the unmistakable "charity cut," and several hats, collars, and other
articles of clothing that must have brought up the total cost to something
over £5. This outlay was practically money thrown away, for the poor boy
found his position so intolerable that he plainly told his friends he must
either have some suitable clothing or give up his situation. Think of the lad
whose friends cannot go to this expense, and who is compelled to bear the
jeers of his companions, until he has saved sufficient money to clothe himself! How can he be expected to make headway in the world, when his
best friends place such obstacles in his path?

These remarks have been made, not in a spirit of antagonism to existing institutions, but rather to show how even the very best-intentioned people may, by attaching too much importance to discipline, and yielding a too ready obedience to precedent in the matter of clothing, seriously mar their own work, and stand in the way of those whose progress they desire.

That these are not necessary evils the Stockwell Orphanage amply proves. I was myself brought up there, and can gratefully render my tribute of praise to the excellent system of training there in force. Let me touch briefly upon its principal points.

The Institution is conducted on what is known as the cottage system. The children are not placed in one large building, like soldiers in a barrack, but are allotted to different houses, each of which is presided over by a Christian matron. Thus no one is lost sight of in the multitude, and a certain amount of home feeling is introduced, which goes far to remove the necessity for that strict discipline which has been objected to.

A spirit of self-reliance and independence is encouraged. The children are not subject to endless drills and parades. So many hours a day are given to school, so many to work, and the remainder can be spent just as the children please. They are not watched at every turn by a master, but are allowed as much freedom as possible. Healthful sports are encouraged, but not insisted on. There are a swimming-bath, a gymnasium, and a cricket club. There is a playground for the boys, and another for the girls, and spacious playhalls for use in wet weather. The children make their own beds, sweep and scrub the floors, clean windows, light fires, and lay their own meals. Anyone visiting the Orphanage can see for himself that the work is efficiently done.

A plain and practical education is given. Latin and Greek do not form part of the school curriculum; for, however desirable the acquirement of these and other languages may be, it must be admitted that such subjects as handwriting, arithmetic, and shorthand are of more use in after-life, and therefore entitled to greater prominence.

No uniform is worn. It would be untrue to say that there is not often a *similarity* of dress. This is almost unavoidable. But the clothes provided are such as almost any English boy or girl might wear. They are not always cut after the latest fashions, neither are they made of the finest possible material. Why should they be? The clothing is simply serviceable and unconspicuous. No red waistcoats are worn, nor yellow stockings, corduroy trousers, or sackcloth dresses.

The Stockwell Orphanage, according to its published prospectus, receives boys between the ages of six and ten, and girls over the age of seven. As a result of the system of training its managers have adopted, it sends out into the world, at the ages of fourteen or sixteen—what? Machines? Soldiers in embryo? Guys? No; *boys and girls.* This may seem to some a very commonplace achievement; but there are few institutions of which the same could be justly said.   HARRY GOLDING.

Notices of Books.

Spurgeon's Illustrated Almanack for 1890. Passmore and Alabaster. Price one penny.

OUR friends will like this pennyworth. To give away this almanack will be one of the very best ways of doing good; for the teaching is simple and attractive, and the fact of its being an almanack will secure its preservation and its perusal. The texts for every day have been carefully selected by Mrs. Spurgeon.

John Ploughman's Sheet Almanack. Passmore and Alabaster. Price one penny.

THIS is a grand pennyworth. Better than ever. There ought to be at least a million copies sold. No kitchen, workshop, or stable should be without it. Kind souls should see it put up, in cab-shelters, lodging-houses, and wherever working people congregate.

Second volume of Salt-Cellars is ready.

The Salt-Cellars. Being a collection of Proverbs, together with Homely Notes thereon. By C. H. SPURGEON. Vol. II.—M to Z. Passmore and Alabaster. Price 3s. 6d.

Early copy just to hand. The second volume will be on sale on the first of November.

Religious Teaching and Modern Thought. Two Lectures. By J. R. LEEBODY, M.A., Professor of Mathematics and Physics, Magee College. Henry Frowde.

REVEALS a great deal of careful thought, and a measure of faith; but there is nothing in it which a thorough believer would think worth the reading. We care not for adaptations of the gospel, or attempts to commend it to unrenewed human nature: it is ours to preach it, and God's to bless it to his own, as he will most surely do. This little book may serve the purpose of letting the secure among our churches see for themselves what unchristian teaching is rife in our midst —so rife that even those who may be counted Broad are obliged to bear their protests against the deadly thing.

The Faith Mission. Report of Conventions at Rothesay and Kinross. Marshall Brothers. Fourpence.

VERY nicely got up. We don't know what Pilgrim This and Pilgrim That means. There are traces in the speeches of things which we should probably question; but the report shows that earnest living believers said many good and helpful things to each other, and doubtless "the Lord hearkened and heard."

Trophimus; or, a Discussion of the Faith-cure Theory. By WILLIAM GRIBBON. 1263 Lexington Avenue, New York. Price five cents.

MR. GRIBBON has little patience with the mad sort of Faith-cure brethren whom he meets with in America. If all may be cured by faith, why did Paul leave Trophimus at Miletum sick? If medicine is wrong, why anoint with oil? Why "take a little wine for thy stomach's sake"? Why command Hezekiah to take a lump of figs, and lay it upon the sore? Mr. Gribbon lays a very heavy indictment against the Faith-cure people in encouraging false faith, and so bringing discredit upon true faith. He mentions some grievous cases of failure; and who cannot? If we go beyond the plain promise of the Word of God, we may be as enthusiastic as we please, but God will not act according to our notions. While one of the most devoted and useful women in this world lies dying of a cancer, it is idle to tell us that in every case the prayer of faith can be offered for the sick. When persons are assuredly in the power of an incurable disease, there is no more space for the prayer of faith than in the case of the dead. When the prayer of faith is offered, the sick are raised; but this lies in no man's power, but is a special gift from God. We may desire it, but command it we cannot. We cannot endorse all that Mr. Gribbon says; but his tract may prove a suitable antidote for a wild fanaticism. It is curious that, while so many are refusing to believe anything, we witness at the same time an outburst of amiable credulity which is eager to accept signs and wonders. They are wise who, in such seasons, possess their souls in patience.

"Out of the Depths." A Message to a Backslider. [Anon.] R. J. Masters, 32, Wilton Road, Victoria Station.

LARGE type. Plenty of the Word of God. Faithful and tender admonitions for those who have wandered. A very useful shilling's-worth.

A Handbook of Christian Baptism. By the Rev. W. EDWARDS, B.A., President of the Baptist College, Pontypool. Alexander and Shepheard.

JUST the kind of work that was needed to be circulated in our churches. We fear that the young people are not generally instructed upon the point of baptism, or they would not so readily forsake the New Testament rule. Mr. Edwards has made a full and clear summary of the subject, and nothing remains but to have it read and studied by our rising youth. It can be had in paper for sixpence, and in boards for a shilling.

The Coming Prince, the Last Great Monarch of Christendom. By ROBERT ANDERSON, LL.D. Third edition. Revised. Hodder and Stoughton.

THIS is a valuable work, by an author highly esteemed in our churches. More than seventeen years ago (in our June number for 1872, page 309) we reviewed a new and revised edition, of which the present appears to us to be almost a fac-simile. On the cover and title-page of both there is a medallion of Antiochus Epiphanes, "the Antichrist of the Old Testament." The engraving is taken from a coin in the British Museum. In the forefront of many a modern volume we meet with a table of errata, and we make a rule of rectifying such mistakes as we cut the leaves, that our attention may not be distracted in the subsequent perusal. But when by inadvertence "the title of a book" is embarrassing, some curious device must be adopted.

The last four verses of the ninth chapter of Daniel supply the text of Dr. Anderson's disquisition. In the twenty-fifth verse we read of "Messiah the Prince": in the twenty-sixth verse of "THE PRINCE THAT SHALL COME." Had the Doctor so entitled his work, a multitude of his friends would have known what Prince he intended to designate. We may as well mention that the word "Prince," in the original, is the same; and the translation, "Prince that shall come," is to be found alike in the Authorized Version and the Revised Version. By "the last great Monarch of Christendom" our readers will, therefore, please to understand "the wilful king" of prophecy, who is depicted to us as blasphemer and persecutor, warrior and diplomatist. In nothing is the sacred narrative more precise than in its dates; but yet chronology has been a weak point with the majority of Christian writers. These four verses of Daniel are remarkable, alike for the extraordinary historic interest and the excessive hostile criticism they have excited. The enemies of the cross of Christ know the vantage ground they gain if they can assail the prediction of "Seventy weeks." In the judgment of Dr. Anderson, this prophecy has suffered nothing from the attacks of its assailants, but much at the hands of its friends. The difficulties raised by Christian expositors have been stumbling-blocks in the pathway of clear exposition. "*Mine*," says he, "*has been the humble aim of 'sorting,' as Bacon phrases it, one great prophecy, 'with the events fulfilling the same, for the better illumination of the church touching those parts of the prophecy which are yet unfulfilled.*'" Our readers can refer back to our former record. We have no space for more criticism. In vain does any one ask us to tell him, in a few words, what this or that sentence of prophecy means. Why, Albert Barnes, in his notes on Daniel, devotes thirty-seven pages to these two verses, the twenty-fifth and twenty-sixth of Daniel, ninth chapter. But this need not discourage the study; for the key and the clue to Modern Infidelity and Indifference can only be found in the verbally inspired pages of Prophecy.

Not Cunningly-devised Gospels. Being a Concise Epitome of Early Historical Evidence attesting the Genuineness and Antiquity of the Four Gospels. By C. UNDERWOOD. John Kensit, 18, Paternoster Row.

WE do not know how it has come to pass that this very useful little work has escaped our notice. It is specially prepared for young men in our churches, or in the Y.M.C.A., and it cannot fail to aid them in resisting the perpetual assaults of modern unbelief. Historical testimony to the existence of the books of Scripture in the first Christian centuries is valuable, and proof that such writings were accepted as authentic and inspired is also much to be prized. Mr. C. Underwood has used both head and heart in the compilation and the argument, and we trust he will see the fruit of his labour in many being grounded in the faith. When will there be no need of these arguments? Oh that the Lord would convert the crowd of ministers who are deluded by Satan into becoming doubt-sowers! All things are possible to faith; but the proud unbelief of modern culture limits the Holy One of Israel. Let lovers of the Lord scatter the remedies, for the disease is everywhere. Paper, 9d.; and cloth, 1s. 3d.

Memorials of the Baptist Church worshipping in Eld Lane Chapel, Colchester. T. Wright, 18, Head Street, Colchester.

THE more of such memorials the better. The church-history of earnest believers ought not to lie in oblivion. Colchester Baptist Church has had an honourable history, and has taken the lead among the Essex portion of the denomination. Having fulfilled two hundred years of witnessing, it was time that a chronicle was written. Many were the good old men whom we knew, who were connected with this church, but these have fallen asleep. May those who now fill their places be as faithful as their fathers! In this record, as in all others of Baptists of former ages, we find articles of faith, confessions, and creeds. The silly boast of "We have no creed" is in itself absurd enough; but to fix this upon Baptists, as one of their fundamental principles, is to give the lie to history. The modern creedless Baptist is a production of the age of shams. He has no predecessor. May he have no successor!

Lovers of Baptist history should purchase and preserve this history of the Colchester church.

The Church History Series. V. Athanasius, his Life and Life-work. By HENRY ROBERT REYNOLDS, D.D. Religious Tract Society.

A BRIEF but exceedingly well-written life of Athanasius, the hammer of the Arians, and the father of orthodoxy. It might be of service to our "Downgraders," if they would read such a life; but as they have no sympathy with any man who has a fixed belief, they are not likely to try the virtues of such a biography. Athanasius is the sort of man that the age requires; but we question if it has a corner left in its all-pervading doubt to allow breathing-space for such a hero.

Summer Musings and Memories Dear. By W. T. M'AUSLANE, LL.D. Glasgow: Maclure, Macdonald, and Co.

THE author is the brother of the late Dr. M'Auslane, formerly of Finsbury chapel. This volume is a memorial for certain of the writer's departed friends, and it will, therefore, have the most interest for members of his own circle. His prose is always on the right side; he departs not from the good old way. His verse is flowing and poetical, and will be best appreciated by those familiar with the glorious scenery of Scotland, of which he sings. We note that Mr. Sankey has set some of the hymns to music, for use in his services.

Anecdotes of the Wesleys. By the Rev. J. B. WAKELEY. Eleventh Edition. *Anecdotes of Whitefield* (same author). Hodder and Stoughton.

THE price of these volumes has something to do with their large sale; but yet they are in themselves exceedingly attractive. At one-and-six they are really sold at half-price.

Glimpses of Fifty Years. The Autobiography of an American Woman. By FRANCES E. WILLARD. Published by the Woman's Temperance Publication Association, H. J. Smith and Co. (Agents), Chicago, Philadelphia, &c., &c.

THE life of a splendid woman, brought out at her jubilee, in a style worthy of a lady. Miss Willard could only have been produced in America, but she would have honoured any nation in which she might have been born. She was born to lead. Gloriously did she head the Women's Christian Temperance Union in its very wonderful crusade; and she remains ready still to lead, as we hope she will do for many a year to come.

This is a grand book: in size, in artistic enrichment, and in matter, it is a book of the first magnitude. We do not know whether it is to be bought in England; but it comes to us with a priceless missive from the queenly woman whom it commemorates. May her second fifty years be richer than the first—if they can be!

Fallen on the Field. Being Memorials of the Rev. Alfred Henry Clegg, Missionary to the Gambia. By JOHN S. PAWLYN. T. Woolmer.

ANNALS of a brief life, which had opened with much sweetness of consecration. From the banks of the Gambia he has gone home early in the morning of life. We cannot explain these removals of the useful: there is no reason why we should.

Alone with the Word: Devotional Notes on the New Testament. By G. STRINGER ROWE. Hodder and Stoughton.

THIS strikes us as being an exceedingly valuable book. It is just an outline of the New Testament, a summary and explanation of its books and chapters. Something of the kind was needed to assist readers who desire to become intelligent students of the sacred Word; and it is here supplied in admirable form. So far as we can judge, Mr. Stringer Rowe has impartially given the sense of the sacred writings. We turned to the ninth of Romans, to see how he would describe that chapter. Had he been a Calvinist, he could not have been more faithful to the spirit of the passage! This is as it should be. "Alone with the Word"—in the presence of infallible Scripture—we are neither of this party nor of that, but we sit at Jesus' feet and receive his Word. This is a solid and useful work.

The Shepherd Psalm. By F. B. MEYER, B.A. Morgan and Scott.

THIS needs no letter of commendation. Mr. Meyer is at home with this sweet Psalm, and pours forth holy thought in streams. A pretty little book for 1s. 6d.

A Homiletical Commentary on the Book of Judges. With Critical and Explanatory Notes, Several Hundred Outlines, &c. By the Rev. J. P. MILLAR, M.A. R. D. Dickinson.

WE have not seen a fresh volume of "*The Preacher's Homiletical Commentary*" for quite a long time. We are glad to see the enterprise resumed. We hope that its success may encourage Mr. Dickinson to proceed with the series, and to employ authors of a high class upon it. We cannot think that anyone would read this comment without seeing sermons flitting all around him, or, at least, those midges of thought from which sermons are developed. JUDGES is a grand book for illustrating the characters of men, and the eras of human history. Mr. Millar has not produced anything dazzling or original; indeed, we hardly think that he has reached the standard required in an expositor; but yet his devout observations, and the notes which he has collected, make up a mass of material, which a true preacher will turn to good account. If a preacher does not use what is here given, he will, at least, be assisted in his own personal researches; and this is a good thing.

The Epistles of St. John. Twenty-one discourses. By WM. ALEXANDER, D.D., Lord Bishop of Derry and Raphoe. (The Expositor's Bible.) Hodder and Stoughton.

THERE is a great deal of learning and eloquence in this book, but as a commentary it seems to us to be fragmentary. It contains a fine set of spasmodic expositions; the intervals being filled up with original thoughts upon all sorts of things. We are sorry to see Baptismal Regeneration in a somewhat mitigated form; but yet in quite unmistakable distinctness. We do not specially care to have it explained to us why "the Christian church" has neither a fast nor a feast for the first and last days of the year: especially when we perceive that the usage of the Episcopalian body is thus referred to. Other churches have their Watch-nights, and these churches are even more numerous than the Anglican community, and might as correctly have been called "the Christian church." There are rushes of poetry and bursts of devotion in this volume which redeem it from all its faults; but we must confess that we do not understand some of its explanations— as, for instance, of "the sin which is unto death." We hope we may pray for the slothful with whom the Bishop deals with such proper severity. All that is said upon the subject is good, but we question its relation to the matter on hand. The entire work is eccentric: good, but jerky; instructive, but not always to the point. We can hardly regard it as a part of "The *Expositor's* Bible." Though it is a very remarkable addition to our store of comments upon the Epistles of John, and contains much expository matter, it is not an Exposition of those Epistles as a whole. Dr. Candlish's volumes are worth a Bodleian of such writings.

Popular Sociology. By ARTHUR FISHER, M.D., L.R.C.S. Hamilton, Adams.

THE suggested method of preventing theft is to abolish all private property: "A consummation devoutly to be wished" by all the loafers in the universe. We shall see such sociology when men are no longer men; but not till then.

The Hansa Towns. ["Story of the Nations" Series.] By HELEN ZIMMERN. T. Fisher Unwin.

FEW of our readers will be acquainted with the history of the Hanse Towns. The story is as instructive as it is interesting. It is told in a very fascinating manner, and is never allowed to sink into dulness. The material of the history is ample, and therefore the more telling passages could be selected. Lubeck and the other cities combined for mutual protection, and to preserve their commerce: then they were the pioneers of liberty. The League became powerful, aspired to make and unmake kings, and refused to adjust itself to the alterations of society; and then it became a tyrannical power. In the end its use ceased, and by degrees it decayed into a mere name. The story of the Hanse towns is not unlike that of Venice. Warrior-merchants defied emperors and armies. The clustering bees held their hives against the wasps, and made honey for themselves. Our subscribers should buy this volume. If they desire instructive reading, this is one of the best of a series which is first among popular historical publications.

The Cup and the Kiss, and other Sketches. By REV. P. B. POWER, M.A. Religious Tract Society.

A GRACIOUS shilling book, containing ten chatty "sketches" on matters of practical and experimental godliness; very homely, and yet striking, as are all Mr. Power's writings.

Is Bad Sight on the Increase? The *Philosophy of Sight.* By A. FOURNET. Swan Sonnenschein and Co.

THIS seems to us to be an argument for the use of spectacles before the absolute need of them becomes painfully apparent. They are to be used because the eyes are good enough to be benefited by them. This is what we make out of the tractate; but we do not feel sure that we have hit the mark, for an optician of whom we asked a judgment, as from a specialist, "failed to understand it." The work is hardly in the line of books which we propose to review, and we must be excused offering an opinion. Where doctors differ, the man unskilled in optics is barely modest if he forms a judgment.

Henry M. Stanley, the African Explorer. By ARTHUR MONTEFIORE, F.R.G.S. Partridge and Co.

A LIFE of Stanley, nicely illustrated, for eighteenpence, cannot but find thousands of purchasers. He has accomplished great things for civilization; but we question whether his high-handed and warlike show will not hinder rather than promote the advance of the missionary. The servant of Christ will be supposed to be in alliance with the user of the rifle, especially when steamers which were sent out to bear only the heralds of peace are seized by sheer force, and degraded into bearers of fighting men. In Stanley's rougher acts we do not doubt that he has had high philanthropic motives, and that he has done that which commended itself to him according to his light; and, therefore, we honour him as a man of the world, daring, energetic, and self-sacrificing. May the Lord use him as a pioneer, despite the errors at which we have hinted!

The United Presbyterian Church: a Handbook of its History and Principles. By Rev. WILLIAM BLAIR, D.D. Edinburgh: Andrew Elliot.

ENGLISHMEN are greatly puzzled to distinguish between the Frees, the U. P.'s, and the Established; here is a singularly complete manual, which will enable an unenlightened southron henceforth to know the history and nature of the United Presbyterian Church.

"Every Day." By M. F. W. Religious Tract Society.

THIS book kept a restless little niece as "still as a mouse" for three quarters of an hour! Could anything written for children have a better recommendation?

The Birds in my Garden. By W. T.
GREENE, M.A., M.D. Religious
Tract Society.

THINK of Peckham Rye having its
own Gilbert White, after the manner
of Selborne! And why not? In that
garden, which is one of many strips
of ground, Dr. Greene has noticed
far more birds than we should have
thought possible. What with his
aviary, and the outsiders who come
and go, he has made up a very respectable list of British birds, and he
has both watched them with care, and
written upon them in a pleasing manner. We like him well, except when
he attempts to correct the Scriptures.
David speaks of "the sparrow alone
upon the housetop" as a melancholy
watchman, and our author talks at
once of the sparrow as being a cheerful
bird, and having his mate near. What
if the Psalmist thought of a bird which
had lost its mate, and therefore sat
pining alone? Anybody who tries to
rectify the Scriptures will be found
either to misunderstand them, or to be
in error himself. Taking out this fly,
this is a good pot of ointment. We
have read the book with all the more
interest because the locality is so near
London, and because it needs a very
intent observer to make a readable
record of a district so ravaged by
blacks, boys, and cats.

The Onward Reciter. A Choice Collection of Recitations, Readings, and
Dialogues, for Band of Hope Meetings, &c. Edited by T. E. HALLS-
WORTH. Vol. XVIII. Partridge.

WE always like this Reciter, which is
still well up to the mark. It must
surely come to an end through sheer
exhaustion of materials. Vol. 18 is
not so good as earlier numbers, but
it is far better than we could have
expected it to have been.

*The Wonderful Box and its Marvellous
Lids.* By the Author of "Loving
and Fighting." John Haddon and
Co., 3 and 4, Bouverie Street.

TALKS to children of first-rate kind.
If anything, these pages are overdone
with anecdotes. Anyone looking for
incidents and illustrations will here
find enough to last him a month, with
liberal allowance.

Romance of Psalter and Hymnal. By
Rev. R. E. WELSH, M.A., and F. G.
EDWARDS. Hodder and Stoughton.

THE subject of "Hymn-writers and
their hymns" has been thoroughly
worked out. The present authors
have, however, by the freshness of
their style, and by adding Hymn *Tune*
Composers, acquired a place for themselves. The work is lively, and exhibits a competent knowledge of the
matters in hand. We cannot forgive
the unworthy remarks upon Dr. Watts,
and the quiet snubbing of Miss Havergal, in the chapter entitled "General
Survey." It is true, better things are
said of these pre-eminent singers
further on; but this does not erase
the former undeserved censures. The
writer, with all his professions of
catholicity, is evidently of the bitter
Broad school. He is liberal to every
one who has been, in any way, off the
old lines; but he will strike, if he can,
at the orthodox. We suppose his book
will thus command the attention of the
"men of culture." For our own part,
we regret that these wanton offences
against the harmony which the subject suggests should mar an otherwise
interesting volume. The part of the
work which deals with composers is
specially instructive, and in it we meet
with many opinions which give us pleasure. Persons who are old-fashioned
in their ideas of congregational singing,
will be surprised to see how far their
untutored judgments have been sanc-
tioned by the great masters of music.
Perfection of taste full often agrees
with the natural instincts of simple
folks.

*The Quiver: an Illustrated Magazine
for Sunday and General Reading.*
Cassell and Co.

A YEAR'S issue of "The Quiver"! A
delightful book! Just the thing to
give to brother Charles on his birthday! He likes engravings and tales;
and I think these will lead him to read
those earnest words upon the gospel
with which the magazine abounds.
Just the thing I should like to give
the dear boy: but can I afford it?
What! Only seven-and-six! I'll take
the book away with me at once, if
you please, for fear it should be sold
out.

Original Fables. By Mrs. PROSSER. Religious Tract Society.

WE need no second invitation to read a book by Mrs. Prosser. Outwardly this is a beauty, and within it is a joy. The pictures are first-rate, and the fables are better still. Here is a short one :—

HOW TO WORK.

" ' Sukey, you've got an easy life of it,' grumbled the pot to the kettle, 'sitting there like a lady all day long, with nothing to do but to boil a little water and sing a pretty song.'

" ' I do what is given me to do, and do it cheerfully,' said Sukey. ' One can but be employed ; and you, when you are sputtering over your pudding or potatoes, and the frying-pan, when he is spitting with his cakes, are on no harder service, really, than I am ; but everything depends on the way you take work. *I sing over mine !* ' "

Bird-Preachers. Friendly talks with Little Folks about Bible-Birds. By Rev. A. N. MACKRAY, M.A. Religious Tract Society.

ONE of the best of the Tract Society's shilling volumes. A great deal of Biblical information is given in connection with earnest instruction. Engravings good, and a neat shilling's-worth in all respects. The young people will read it.

Our Dumb Companions ; or, Conversations about Dogs, Horses, Donkeys, and Cats. By T. JACKSON, M.A. New edition. Partridge and Co.

WE must have seen and commended this long ago. We delight in all these books, which bring the animal world within the circle of our loving consideration, and teach young folks to regard them as friends.

Readings with our Mothers on Women of the Bible. By Mrs. S. O. HABER-SHON. Partridge and Co.

VERY choice. A wise, motherly mind dictated these chapters, which are full of Scriptural exposition, and yet come home to the wants of working mothers with wonderful power of adaptation. We judge that this little book would be just what many a lady wants who feels it is difficult to interest her Mothers' Meeting.

Blackie's Modern Cyclopedia of Universal Information. Edited by CHARLES ANNANDALE, M.A., LL.D. Vol. III. Blackie and Son.

THE more we look into this Cyclopedia, the better we like it. The little wood-cuts are very good, and the whole affair is as condensed and complete as can be. The third volume reaches FIR. We wish the enterprise large success. Six shillings is little enough for each volume, and in eight the purchaser will have the whole of it.

Martyrs to Freedom : or, Struggles for National Liberty. By Rev. PHILIP BARNES. John Hogg.

A SERIES of thrilling stories, reaching from the brave deeds of Sir William Wallace, down to John Brown of Harper's Ferry. The young will read to be amused, and the older folk to be instructed. The shrine of Freedom is sacred, and her hero-martyrs deserve to be had in remembrance. Mr. Barnes has raised a fit memorial to the soldiers of Liberty. His book has a manly ring about it, and will help to train men.

Romance of the Forests. By ASCOTT R. HOPE. John Hogg.

MR. HOPE has looked up a capital subject. Is not the forest the chosen home of romance? Is it not the palace of the imagination, the hunting-ground of fancy? We hardly think our author has done the best that might be done with such a theme ; but he has accomplished what he aimed at ; he has made a book which young and old will read with minds upon the stretch for wonderful adventures and incidents. This is the kind of book to turn over on a holiday, when one wants even his reading to be a part of his rest.

Under False Colours. By SARAH DOUDNEY. Blackie and Son.

WE like everything about this book. Its cover and contents, together with the printing and pictures, are all good. There is a healthy sentiment in it which makes it eminently suitable for the reading of elder girls, and at the same time the style is calculated both to impress the fancy and touch the heart.

The Century Dictionary: an Encyclopedic Lexicon of the English Language. Prepared under the superintendence of WILLIAM DWIGHT WHITNEY, Ph.D., LL.D. T. Fisher Unwin.

THIS a great work in every respect. Here is a mass of instruction for half-a guinea, and there are to be twenty-four of such parts, or six quarto volumes. We know of nothing which can lie side by side with this Dictionary in all respects. It is to contain some 200,000 quotations; and it aims at a complete list of technical terms up to the date of publication. How it may succeed in theological terminology we can hardly judge from looking through a single part; but the principle upon which the work is to be carried out is fair and right. Altogether we have great expectations as to this elaborate publication. We trust that "The Century Dictionary" will be the dictionary of the century. The illustrations are to number about six thousand, and are well fitted to throw life into the letterpress. The work is almost an encyclopædia, and in some respects it is better, for the information is found distributed under the leading words, and you need not wade through a long article to get at what you want. This is one of those publications which will become a literary necessity to all writers for the press.

OUR friends at *The Deaconess House, Mildmay Park*, produce cards with a tender beauty about them which compels our admiration. The six bevelled cards, *Feathered Messengers*, with birds upon them, are delightful, and are very cheap in a packet at 2s. *The Calendar* at 1s. is beautiful. The two packets entitled *Under his Wings* are 3s. each, and each contains three tasteful cards, large and striking. We like the *Quietness and Confidence* packet, with sheep, at 1s. There is nothing strikingly fresh in the Mildmay issues of the year; but our friends can judge for themselves, if they write to Miss E. St. B. Holland for the new list.

Into all the World. Griffith and Farran.

AN account of St. Andrew's Waterside Church Mission, and of all that has come of it. The illustrations are good and abundant; indeed, we think them better than the book itself, which is thoroughly earnest, but does not exhibit the skill of a practised writer. The work described is upon thoroughly "*Church lines*," and it is evident that the writer is not over-fond of undenominational societies, though he speaks courteously enough of them. For our own part, we rejoice in every effort to make known the gospel of our Lord Jesus Christ; but we feel gladdest when we see the churches themselves taking up the work which the Lord has committed to them. All the works of gospel teaching which societies have undertaken, should have been done by the churches, as such; and so far we agree with the writer, though we greatly differ from him as to what "the Church" really is.

This Mission is itself very like a society. We do not know how *low* or *high* it may be; but as the book is sent for review, we cannot say less than that it has greatly interested us as a record of the struggles and successes of earnest Churchmen in a zealous attempt to benefit our sailors.

Treasure Book of Consolation for all in Sorrow or Suffering. Compiled and Edited by BENJAMIN ORME, M.A. T. Fisher Unwin.

A RICH store-room, wherein are laid up cordials, balsams, and ointments for the wounds of suffering humanity. Similar collections have been made by other hands; but this is not excelled by any that have gone before it. The extracts are from all quarters, and are wisely made.

Lady Missionaries in Foreign Lands. By Mrs. E. R. PITMAN. Partridge.

WOMEN are not a whit behind men in the display of heroism on the mission-field. This book ought to bring out many a brave woman from the hearths and homes of our churches.

The Child's Own Magazine. Sunday School Union.

THE youngsters will enjoy this shilling annual. Lots of cuts and stories.

The Sunday-School Union Motto Cards for 1890 are exceedingly attractive. Schools can have them adapted to their use.

God's Jewels: their Dignity and Destiny. By W. Y. FULLERTON. Passmore and Alabaster.

THERE are several books upon the subject of precious stones, in which these choice things are made to flash with the light of holy instruction; but this little work is equal to any one of them. It is replete with interest. Everything about jewels which can be used for sacred service is turned to account. Mr. Fullerton has not hammered out gold leaf, but he has given solid gold—nuggets of it. He has so many illustrations that he does not linger long on any one, but passes on to the next, and the next. Having studied this subject carefully, and having lectured upon it at considerable length, we are in the position of a qualified judge, and we award a first prize to this very beautiful book. Price 1s. 6d.

The Rosebud Annual, 1890. James Clarke and Co.

LAST year we incurred wrath by wishing that some little instruction had mingled with the mirth of this most amusing book. The irate gentleman imputed to us the desire to have the whole system of Calvinistic theology put before the little ones. He knew that we never intended anything of the kind; but being out of temper, he must needs say something sour. We still think, as we did last year, that ROSEBUD is a wonderful magazine for the little mites, that it is marvellously full of merry things, and, finally, that it would be a little better if it had even a taste of something above the downright babyish. Does the good man look angry again? Yes; but it is not at us, but at the artist who made the children on the cover of his Annual to be all left-handed.

Notes.

THERE is no truth in the statement that Mr. Thomas Spurgeon is on his way to England. He will rest in the colonies, and in due time, when his strength is fully recruited, the Lord will direct him to a sphere of service. Prayer is requested that it may be so.

Friends may as well believe nothing which they see in the papers in reference to the Editor and members of his family. In reading the news, it is a startling sensation to come across personal acts of which you are not aware, incidents which never occurred to you, letters which you never wrote, follies of which you are not guilty, and virtues which you dare not claim. Spurgeon is a good subject for stories. Possibly there is not enough of real interest about the man, and therefore a lavish invention supplies the deficiency. Long before a purpose has been conceived in his mind, it is shaped into a plan for him, and fathered upon the innocent individual, who has then to answer letters of rebuke or advice upon a matter with which he has no connection whatever. When so many sheets have to be filled, and truth is so scarce, the romancing faculty is very apt to be called into play. The other day our niece was rescued from drowning at Boulogne; but we had no niece in the place. One Sunday evening a lady was advertised to preach in the Tabernacle; but we did not know the lady, and had no thought of abdicating in her favour. What next?

Mr. John Urquhart, of Weston-super-Mare, has bravely borne his witness as to doctrinal declensions in the Baptist Union, and therefore deserves the thanks of all who hold by the truth of God; but nothing will come of it. The most honoured brethren are treated as nobodies the moment they differ from the dominant party. Deep sleep has fallen upon many who are themselves sound in the faith, so that they dream that all is well when the enemy has already wrought grievous mischief in the churches. It can scarcely be possible that they still doubt the fact of a sad apostasy; but they try to persuade themselves that it is not very widely spread, nor very serious. The day will come when they will awake to the sad truth; and then they will have themselves to blame for crying, "Peace, peace," where peace could not be.

Several denominations have held their autumnal gatherings, and seem greatly pleased with themselves. We do not wish to be censorious; but if we were in that humour, we should find justification on every hand. That an assembly of Church of England divines should at one time be listening to an actor as he pleaded for the stage, and at another time should be present at High Mass, is cause for great searching of heart among godly evangelicals. That which would, a few years ago, have provoked loud protest, is now quietly passed over, and, for the sake of gathering large congresses, all sorts of vagaries are allowed. Worldliness is to the front, and truth is fallen in our streets. The deterioration is not in Nonconformity only, nor in the Establishment alone: the fashion of the hour is so generally followed as to seem well-nigh universal when denominations hold their field-days. Nevertheless, a goodly number are of another mind. Truth has yet its advocates; worldly amusements are not admired by all: and the day may come, sooner than anxiety imagines, when the Lord will turn his hand upon his people, purge them of their idols, and restore his truth to its throne.

As we hope soon to be resting in the South of France, we commit the College, Orphanage, Colportage, Evangelists, &c., to the care of our heavenly Father; but it would be a peculiar boon to see the treasury replenished during the first fortnight of November, that we might take our time of retirement without even the temptation to a single care in reference to pecuniary supplies. God has been specially gracious, and therefore we look for a continuance of his bounty.

Special Notice.—We again call our readers' earnest attention to the following announcements:—

On *Wednesday evening, November* 6, Mr. CHARLES COOK, of Hyde Park Hall, will lecture at the Tabernacle upon his visits to foreign prisons. The Pastor hopes to preside. There will be no charge for admission, but a collection will be made in aid of the fund for the visitation and relief of prisoners abroad, and for the distribution of the Scriptures amongst them. Mr. Cook will be greatly cheered if large numbers gather to hear the remarkable story of his prison experience. He has been almost everywhere. "In prisons oft," he has been as a visitor and messenger of mercy. There is room for another Howard in reference to the prisons of certain nations, which linger in the march of civilization, and yet would be highly indignant to be thus described. Mr. Cook ordinarily carries on preaching in Hyde Park, and in his hall in that region. To those services persons of all nations resort, and are blessed. A young woman who had sought recreation in the Park, on the Sabbath, was impressed at one of the open-air services, and is now a member of the church at the Tabernacle.

MESSRS. FULLERTON AND SMITH will be at the Pastor's farewell services on *November* 17; and in the afternoon of that day, at three o'clock, Mr. Smith will commence the mission by conducting a special service in the Tabernacle for children and young people. Every night, from November 18 to 24, the evangelists will be at the Tabernacle, and there will also be special afternoon meetings, of which full particulars will be duly announced. Will all the Lord's people pray for a great blessing upon this visit of our beloved brethren; and will all who can, help to gather in the unconcerned and unconverted, that they may hear words whereby they may be saved?

The preachers at the Tabernacle during the senior Pastor's absence will (D.V.) be as follows:—November 18 to November 24, Messrs. Fullerton and Smith; November 28, Mr. W. C. Minifie (Secretary of the Missionary Convention); December 1, morning, Dr. Pierson (of Philadelphia); evening, Pastor J. A. Spurgeon; December 5, Pastor E. H. Ellis (of Stoke Newington); December 8, Pastor Hugh D. Brown, M.A. (of Dublin); December 12, Pastor W. Williams (of Upton Chapel); December 15, Rev. John Bond (Wesleyan Minister); December 19, Pastor W. Pettman (of New Park Road, Brixton); December 22, morning, Dr. Sinclair Paterson; evening, Rev. John McNeill; December 26, Mr. W. C. Minifie; December 29, morning, Rev. J. B. Meharry (of Crouch Hill); evening, Rev. Mark Guy Pearse; December 31, Watch-night service, Messrs. Fullerton and Smith; January 2, 1890, Pastor J. Clark (of Norbiton); January 5, morning, Pastor C. Spurgeon (of Greenwich); evening, Pastor J. A. Spurgeon; January 9, Pastor E. Roberts (of South London Tabernacle).

The past month has been such a busy time at the Tabernacle, that we can only give brief notes of the many important meetings that have been held, although there is ample material to fill far larger space than can be spared for this purpose. We put the MONDAY EVENING PRAYER-MEETINGS together, for they are all worthy of note.

On *Sept.* 16, the senior Pastor did not feel well enough to be out, and therefore his brother, J. A. S., presided. After several hymns and prayers, Mr. Burnham gave an interesting account of his recent experiences among the hop-pickers in Kent. Mr. Harrald presented the special requests for prayer, in which Ned Wright also joined. Messrs. Chamberlain and Parker sang together the sweet hymn commencing "I am thine, O Lord," and the congregation joined in the refrain, "Draw me nearer, blessed Lord." More supplications followed, and then Pastor J. A. Spurgeon delivered an address, founded upon Psalm cii. 16, and closed the meeting with prayer, in which the absent Pastor was specially remembered, as he had been all the evening.

On the following *Thursday, September* 19, C. H. S. was able to preach. He has seldom escaped a severe attack when once the evil has lodged in hand or foot; but on this occasion, it is the hope of all friends that he may hold on till his winter rest comes on. Will those who love him ask this boon for him at this hour? Prayer calls in the great Healer, and he, in his own way, and by the use of his own means, can prevent as well as cure.

On *Monday, Sept.* 23, the Pastor was delighted to be again in his accustomed place. In commencing the meeting, Mr. Spurgeon stated that, since his arrival that afternoon, he had seen fourteen candidates for church-fellowship. There is a continued forthcoming of men and women bearing testimony to what the Lord has done for their souls. Several prayers were presented, and hymns sung—

all short and stirring; after which the Pastor spoke of the great power of the hosts of men who recently marched through the streets, all bent on one object, and said that the Church of Christ ought to be even more united and earnest in pursuit of its great aim. He looked for times when great armies of men would seek the Lord through the impulse of the Holy Spirit. More petitions followed, and then the Pastor gave an address upon the mischief that may be done by little neglect, and unseen falsehood, illustrating his subject by an incident that had happened at "Westwood" a few days before. Walking in the garden with his father, he was just passing the corner of a building when a large vase fell down from the top quite close to them, and with sufficient force to have killed anyone whom it might have struck. On examination it was found that where there ought to have been an iron rod there was only a piece of wood, which had rotted away, till the touch of a workman's hand was all that was needed to overturn the vase. Mr. Spurgeon warned his hearers against doing Christian work scampingly. Let all be done at the very best; for sooner or later some one would have to suffer if bad work was put into our life-building. Mr. William Olney gave an interesting account of the children's services on the sands at Llandudno, and the meeting closed with many supplications and thanksgivings.

On *September* 30, the special subject for supplication was the NORTH AFRICA MISSION. Mr. E. H. Glenny, Dr. Eccles, our own brother Hamilton, and several ladies who are about to go to North Africa, were at the Tabernacle. Mr. Hamilton gave a brief account of the work in Morocco, and pleaded very earnestly for more labourers to reinforce the little band of workers there; and the Pastor bade good-bye to each of the missionaries, and commended them individually to the Lord in prayer, the congregation joining in a hearty "Amen" at the close of each petition.

On *October* 13, various missions connected with the Tabernacle were described, and prayer for increased blessing on their work was presented. Mr. Allison pleaded for Ebury Mission, Pimlico; Mr. William Olney gave an account of the progress at Haddon Hall, Bermondsey; Mr. Moore spoke of his work in Union Street; Mr. Passmore appealed for more labourers for Lansdowne Place Schools; and Mr. Trevett gave a report of the City Mission work at Red Cross Street. All these efforts were remembered in prayer by various brethren; several written requests were presented by Mr. Harrald; and the Pastor delivered two brief addresses, one upon creating an appetite for Christ in man, and the other with special reference to the claims of Gospel Temperance upon Christians. Mr. Chamberlain delighted us by singing a quaint Methodist melody, with a rousing chorus, which had been much blessed in the mission at Wisbech.

On *Tuesday evening, September* 24, the annual meeting of the METROPOLITAN TABERNACLE EVANGELISTS' ASSOCIATION was held in the lecture-hall, which was crowded with an enthusiastic audience. Pastor C. H. Spurgeon presided, and expressed his gratitude to Mr. Elvin for the admirable manner in which the work had been carried on, and also to all the brethren and sisters who had, in various ways, assisted the Association. The annual report, presented by Mr. Elvin, showed that there are now 111 workers, and that during the year they had held 2,070 Sunday services, and 1,428 on weeknights, an increase of 137 on the previous year. The cost of the work, for rent, gas, travelling expenses, printing, postage, &c., has been about £170, and the Secretary was able to report a small balance in hand. In addition to this general account, the sum of £223 1s. has been collected and expended by the workers at the various mission-halls. Representatives of the different missions were present, and sang at intervals during the meeting, and addresses were delivered by Messrs. Figg, Gregory, Court, Hammond, Pummell, and Johnston. This is a thoroughly "live" work, and the meeting was quite in harmony with it. We have need of more speakers and singers, more places for them to speak and sing in, and more helpers to rally round them, and form new mission-stations in this ever-widening city.

On *Tuesday evening, October* 8, the Pastor delivered the inaugural address of the nine days' GOSPEL TEMPERANCE MISSION, conducted at the Tabernacle by Mr. G. F. Cook. Each evening a stirring speech was given by Mr. Cook, and he also conducted a service on the Sunday afternoon. Altogether, 579 persons signed the pledge, and many were conversed with about their souls. It is believed that the Mission will give an impetus to the work of the Tabernacle Gospel Temperance Society during the coming winter, and that the influence of it will be long felt. Since the Society was organized, between seven and eight years ago, six Missions have been held, at which nearly 22,000 pledges have been taken. Still, there are numbers of honoured Christian folk who are not with us. They bid us reclaim the drunkard; but they do not help. Betty may go on beating the bear; but her good man is still up the ladder giving her the benefit of his encouraging words. We pause, lest we grow intemperate.

On *Monday evening, October* 14, the annual meeting of the LADIES' MATERNAL SOCIETY was held in the lecture-hall, under the presidency of the Pastor. The report stated that about two hundred poor women had been helped during the year. The Bible-woman's account of the visits paid by her to those who were relieved by the Society was very interesting. The Pastor gave an address upon the raising to life of Dorcas, and the importance of carrying on the work begun by that holy woman.

Pastor J. C. Carlile, of Abbey Street Chapel, Bermondsey, related some of the sad instances of distress that had come under his notice during the recent strike; and Mr. William Olney impressed upon the ladies the importance of visiting personally those whom they helped through the Society, and incidentally remarked that the Maternal Society was the oldest of the institutions connected with the Tabernacle church. In the poor neighbourhood in which our great house is placed, the boxes of clothes are always being wanted. We wish more could have this alleviation of their need in the hour of nature's travail. Constantly are we compelled to feel that the region is becoming poorer and poorer, and destitution is surging around our gates. Where once were respectable citizens, there is now a far poorer and less provident class of people.

Undoubtedly, the MISSIONARY CONVENTION FOR YOUNG MEN, held at the Tabernacle, on *Tuesday*, *October* 15, has been *the* event of the month. Mr. W. C. Minifie undertook the whole of the arrangements, and he carried them out to a most successful issue. Was ever such a missionary meeting held in London before? We question it. The list of speakers indicates the character of the gatherings, and the audience was certainly a very special one. Young men were there in large numbers, and leaders in religion and philanthropy. Clergymen and ministers of all denominations were well represented. We need not give here details of the meetings, for the press, both secular and religious, has notified the names of those who took part, and a verbatim report of the proceedings will be published as soon as possible. Dr. Maclaren's address will long be remembered by all who had the privilege of hearing it; in fact, the same remark might be made of almost all the speeches. The meeting at night, when the Tabernacle was crowded with a most enthusiastic company, marks the high tide of missionary enthusiasm; and it is not surprising that the earnest appeals of Mr. Spurgeon and Mr. McNeill have already called out a number of willing workers, each of whom, in response to the divine call, "Who will go for us?" answers, "Here am I: send me." Our prayer is that every Missionary Society may gain workers by this Convention; that believers, who have means, will go forth at their own charges, while others, trusting in the Lord, will hasten to the foreign field, and labour, on their own account, making known the gospel. The church of God must get at the nations. Whether organized or disorganized, Christian effort must be put forth at a far greater rate till the gospel is preached to every creature.

COLLEGE.—Several students have accepted pastorates, or completed their College course during the past month. Mr. A. Priter has settled at Bethel Chapel, Shipley, Yorkshire; Mr. W. L. Mackenzie, at St. Peter's, Isle of Thanet; Mr. G. Freeman, at Halstead, Essex; and Mr. W. Maynard has become co-pastor of the group of Baptist Churches in Westmoreland.

Mr. W. T. Wotton has sailed for the United States; and Mr. A. Day sails this month for India, to take charge of Havelock Baptist Church, Agra.

Mr. D. Mace, late of Stotfold, has removed to West Malling, Kent; Mr. E. Dyer, of Atherton, is going to the Tabernacle, Southend; and Mr. W. Pettman is leaving Bath for New Park Road, Brixton.

On *Tuesday, October* 1, the annual meeting of the College was held. A large number of friends met for tea, which was generously provided by ladies of the congregation; and the assembly gradually increased until the greater part of the Tabernacle was filled. The Vice-President, J. A. S., opened the meeting with prayer; and the President, C. H. S., read the list of students who had settled since the last annual meeting, and gave an address upon the work of the College, specially thanking all who had, by the weekly offerings, or otherwise, helped to maintain the institution. Five of the students had been selected to speak, and every man acquitted himself nobly. Mr. Jones took for his topic, "The aim of the College"; Mr. Godfrey, "The work of the College inside"; Mr. Page, "The work of the College outside"; Mr. Donald, "The influence of the College"; and Mr. Minifie gave some information concerning the Missionary Convention, and sought to stir up the audience to greater zeal in the cause of foreign missions. Pastor Charles Spurgeon, of Greenwich, then delivered an interesting and instructive lecture on his recent tour to New Zealand, the United States, &c., which was illustrated by magnificent dissolving-views, produced from photographs that he had brought home. At the close, he was very heartily thanked by his father in the name of the whole audience, whose appreciation had been already manifested by frequent applause. We are sorry to add that Mr. Charles is not so well as we could wish. His journey round the world has not fully restored his strength.

EVANGELISTS.—During October, *Messrs. Fullerton and Smith* have conducted missions at Tunbridge Wells, Stowmarket, and Hadleigh. This month they go to Oxford, and then come to the Tabernacle for the special services mentioned in a previous column.

Mr. Burnham has been at Leicester and Sutton St. James, during the past month. He is at Dunstable from November 13 to 24.

In sending a thankoffering for *Mr. Harmer's* services at Burton-on-Trent, Pastor S. S. Allsop writes:—"May I say how pleased I was with his admirable adaptation to his work? He has left memories that will not easily die, and not a few souls who have been blessed by his visit."

Mr. Harmer, in conjunction with *Mr. Chamberlain*, has also conducted a most successful mission at Wisbech; and he has since been holding services at Manvers Street Chapel, Bath.

Mr. Harrison's five weeks' mission in Mr. Charrington's Great Assembly Hall, Mile End Road, has been attended by large numbers. On Sundays, hundreds have been turned away, unable to obtain admission. The result of the services has been very encouraging, many having professed to find the Saviour. During the past month, Mr. Harrison has been at Cross Street Chapel, Islington; the Polytechnic; Exeter Hall; and Talbot Tabernacle. This month he is to be at Bath.

Mr. Parker has been holding special services at Duncan Street Baptist Chapel, Edinburgh; and on Saturday evenings he has been at the Carrubbers' Close Mission meetings, speaking and singing the gospel to large numbers.

Mr. Carter reports continued progress with his pioneer work at New Brighton, Waterloo, Birkdale, and Horwich. His desire is to see Baptist churches in all these populous places; and we hope this may be realized without entrenching upon the domains of any other workers.

ORPHANAGE.—On *Wednesday evening, September 25*, the President preached to a crowded congregation in the West Croydon Baptist Chapel (Pastor J. A. Spurgeon's), and at the close of the service the sum of £42 16s. 4d. was collected for the Orphanage. We are very grateful to our dear brother, and his wife, and all Croydon friends, for this generous help for our work for the fatherless. It was delightful, also, to see all sorts of Christians in Croydon come up to the service with loving enthusiasm.

On *Wednesday evening, October 2*, Dr. H. Soltau, of Mildmay Park, gave his interesting lecture, "Burma and the Burmese," to the orphan children. They were greatly entertained and instructed, and we thank Dr. Soltau heartily for his kindness.

Our list of contributions this month includes quite a number of harvest thank-offerings for the orphans; and we expect that, after the collectors' meeting, on October 25, there will be still more of these acceptable gifts. May the Lord of the harvest abundantly repay those who have cared for the fatherless. We cannot mention each place, but Semley took the lead with hard upon a ton weight of produce. Hearty thanks to Semley!

Mr. Charlesworth and the orphan boys have had a grand tour in the West of England. The accounts are not complete at the time these Notes have to be made up; but we have received sufficient already to make us praise the Lord and thank the hosts of generous donors who have expressed such hearty sympathy with us in this part of our work. This is one of the most effectual cheer-ups we could possibly receive.

The following are among the recent entries in the Orphanage visitors' book:—

August 19—"I have always considered this to be one of the best of its kind which I have ever visited—officially or privately. It is some time since I have seen it, and it continues to maintain its high character.
"F. J. MOUAT, M.D.,
"Late of the Local Government Board."

September 7—The following entries are by members of the council of the Teachers' Orphanage, London, who paid a visit of inspection on this date:—
"The visit was thoroughly enjoyed. It is a home for the children in every respect.
"S. HALE."
"Have been deeply impressed with the ability and skill which direct, and the loyalty which characterizes the carrying out, of details of this excellently-organized, though home-like, institution.
"W. G. WELLS."
"With the hope that in the near future we may be able to copy this happy home. May prosperity and peace continue here!
"(Mrs.) E. M. BURGWIN."
"I go away simply delighted with all I have seen. "(Miss) E. CARTER."
"I am greatly pleased with the thorough home-like appearance of this delightful place. "(Miss) E. ANSELL."

COLPORTAGE.—The following letter may suggest to other friends, far away, a method of helping the Lord's work in the homeland they have left:—
"New Zealand, Aug. 19, 1889.
"Dear Mr. Spurgeon,—I have great pleasure in enclosing draft, value £40, for the Colportage Association, with which, if the funds will allow, I should like a new district opened, that I may have the privilege of maintaining a man to preach the old gospel in my native land, and do something to stem the tide of Popery and Infidelity, and keep old England true to the faith for which the martyrs died. . . . I propose, the Lord helping me, to do the same yearly."
It so happened that the friend who had paid £40 a year for one of our districts had died, so the New Zealand amount came just in time to enable the work to be started anew in a place which has been tried.

POOR MINISTERS' CLOTHING SOCIETY.—The parcel from W. L. H. has been safely and gratefully received.

PERSONAL NOTES.—Mr. Robert Spurgeon writes:—"Only eternity can reveal the gracious work being accomplished in *India* through your sermons. I often hear of things that would cheer your heart. Just before leaving India, a young Eurasian woman wrote and entreated me to send her your sermon entitled, 'A child of light walking in darkness' (No. 1985). I got it from the publishers, and sent it as soon as I landed. I baptized her and her father ten years ago, and have not seen her since. Two years ago she was in great mental trouble. Special prayer was offered for her, and she attributes her recovery to the reading of the sermon above-mentioned."

M. Gustav Haupt, a missionary on the Congo, writes us from *Stanley Pool,* that, in passing through the town of Kintamo, he saw at a hut one of Spurgeon's printed sermons. It was stuck there in order to protect the hut against evil charms, or thieves, as the owner had left it. The sermon is No. 2,025, from Jeremiah xlvii. 5. "How long wilt thou cut thyself?" The missionary who sends the information remarks, "What an appropriate question for those who, in an awful way, destroy their own souls!" This remarkable circumstance is a proof of the way in which the printed sermons circulate everywhere, and, like those seeds which are carried on wings of down, fly far beyond all expectation. Oh, that the sermon *fetish* might in very deed become a terror to the evil spirit, and a blessing to many souls!

This postcard was shortly after followed by a letter from a young Dutchman in the *Orange Free State, South Africa,* who says: —"When you preach there, in far-off London, your words are here within a few months, giving weary and sad souls food and medicine. I have a dozen or more of your sermons in English preached this year, and my father has three volumes of your sermons in Dutch."

A Wesleyan minister in *New South Wales* sends us the following cheering letter:— "Dear Mr. Spurgeon,—At an evangelistic service, held last evening, a well-known saw-mill proprietor, who is an esteemed local preacher in this circuit, made a brief reference to his own history to this effect:— ' For twenty-five years of my life I lived in the darkness of sin. I had never been inside a Protestant place of worship. *I had never, in all that time, met a Christian man.* I knew nothing of the distinction between Methodist, Presbyterian, Baptist, &c.: they were all alike despised in my eyes as being all in gross error. About that time, five of my companions were drowned together at Port Stevens. The occurrence made a deep impression upon my heart. The thought would force itself upon me, "What if you had been among the number? Would you not now have been weeping and wailing among the lost souls in hell?" I was greatly troubled, and did what alone I could do— prayed to God; but not knowing anything of the way of salvation through faith in Christ, and having no one to guide me, I lived for two years in the most awful agony. I would rather die than live those two years over again. I knew nothing of the great preachers of the day, until I happened to near of Spurgeon, and a friend being about

to visit Sydney, I asked him to get me a volume of Spurgeon's sermons. I read those eagerly, and received much light and comfort from them. At length I read one bearing the title, "Seeking for Jesus" (No. 947), and as I read, God spoke peace to my troubled heart. I felt that my sin was pardoned, and I could sing aloud for joy. It was about noon on a glorious Sabbath-day when the great change took place, and I well remember the spot on which it occurred. Since then, ten years ago now, I have been telling the story of the cross wherever I can.'

" I was much impressed by the incident, and resolved to let you know about it, as I thought it would both afford matter for praise to God, and prove an encouragement to trust in, and labour for, him, ' knowing that your labour is not in vain in the Lord.'

"P. S. *July* 25th. At our meeting last night, an old gentleman stated, that, 21 years ago, in this district, he was led to decision through reading a sermon of yours, entitled ' Now' (No. 681). He is to-day a consistent Christian. To God be the praise and glory!"

The secretary of a Young Men's Christian Association, in the country, writes:—" Dear Sir,—I met with a young man, a few days ago, whose case will interest you, as you have much to do with his present position. W. T—— was converted seven years ago. He was manager of a large brewery. As he was not happy, he commenced to read your sermons week by week. These made him more unhappy, because they showed him that he had not made a full surrender to the Lord, and he felt that he could not continue in his business and serve the Lord fully. The time came when he saw that one or the other must go, and he told his uncle, who is the principal partner in the firm, that he must leave, giving his reasons for so doing. Father and uncle persuaded him not to be so foolish as to throw away his only chance in life; but the answer was, ' I must throw away this or Christ: the one I cannot, the business I must.' His uncle then offered him as many shares in the firm as he liked to name, free; but still his answer was, ' No, I must wash my hands of the trade'; and he left, not knowing where he would go, or what he would do; but confident that the Lord, who had given him grace to take this stand, would help him through his one desire to please his Lord and Master. The way was opened for him to enter the City Mission, where he has been working for the last eighteen months with much success. I asked if he had told you the benefit your sermons had been to him, and finding that he had not done so, suggested that he should write, knowing that you are encouraged by every fresh case of blessing."

Baptisms at Metropolitan Tabernacle. September 26, seventeen; September 30, seven; October 3, seventeen.

Pastors' College, Metropolitan Tabernacle.

Statement of Receipts from September 17th to October 14th, 1889.

	£	s.	d.		£	s.	d.
Mrs. Baker	0	10	0	Pastor R. Turner Sole	1	0	0
Miss Hadfield ...	10	0	0	Mr. James Fish	0	10	0
Mrs. McSkinning ...	0	10	0	Miss Rayner...	5	0	0
Part collection at New North Road				Mrs. Elgee	0	10	6
Chapel, Huddersfield, per Pastor F. J.				A church-member, per C. H. S. ...	0	5	0
Benskin	4	6	6	Collection at Toowoomba, Queensland,			
" Adelphi "	2	2	0	per Pastor W. Higlett	1	12	6
Miss H. Thomas	2	0	0	Anti-Down-Grade, Edinburgh ...	0	10	0
Mr. R. Greenwood	0	5	0	" Adelphi "	1	10	0
Half collection at St. Andrew's Street				Weekly Offerings at Met. Tab. :—			
Chapel, Cambridge, per Pastor T. G.				Sept. 22 ... 41 16 7			
Tarn	5	13	0	„ 29 ... 32 0 0			
Mr. James Nutter	1	1	0	Oct. 6 ... 27 1 0			
Mr. C. Hunt..	1	0	0	„ 13 ... 23 10 0			
Mrs. Wilkinson	1	0	0		124	7	.
Mr. J. Wilson	2	1	1				
Mrs. Townsend	2	2	0				
Mr. Walter Mills	5	0	0		£173	6	8
Mrs Yates	0	10	6				

Pastors' College Missionary Association.

Statement of Receipts from September 17th to October 14th, 1889.

	£	s.	d.		£	s.	d.
Mr. E. Preston	0	6	0	Readers of " The Christian," per Messrs.			
Mrs. Townsend	1	1	0	Morgan and Scott	0	5	0
Aunt Fanny...	0	10	0				
Mrs. Rogers...	0	10	0		£2	12	0

Stockwell Orphanage.

Statement of Receipts from September 16th to October 14th, 1889.

	£	s.	d.			£	s.	d.
Miss S. A. Hunt, per J. T. D.	0	5	0	Per Mrs. J. A. Spurgeon				
Jack, South Lambeth ...	0	6	0	Collection at West Croydon				
Collected by Messrs. Clement and New-				Baptist Chapel, after				
lings' ticket writers, per Mr. Hawkins	3	10	9	sermon by C. H. Spurgeon	42 16 4			
Collected by Miss S. J. Jones ...	0	12	6	Less expenses	3 10 0			
Mrs. M. Cowan	0	5	0			39	6	4
Miss G. Lawson	2	0	0	Collected by Mrs. Penning		0	6	0
Collected by Mrs. Stopford	8	0	0	J. H. R.		1	0	0
Young Women's Bible-class, Lancaster,				Mr. C. Ibberson		0	6	0
per Mr. J. Brash... ...	0	1	4	Ethel Butler's savings		0	6	0
Orphanage boxes at the Tabernacle gates	0	1	4	A mother and daughter, Hawera ...		2	0	0
Collected by Mrs. Whittaker	0	14	0	Miss Hadfield		10	0	0
Young Women's Bible-class at the				Mrs. Allan		10	0	0
Orphanage, per Mrs. Stiff	0	17	9	Mr. Thomas D. Adams		1	0	0
Mr. H. J. Atkinson, M.P., per J. A. S.	1	0	0	Miss Lizzie Caffyn		1	0	0
Ebenezer	1	0	0	Mr. J. Gilmour		1	0	0
Mr. E. R. Porter	1	1	0	Mr. H. Jackson		0	1	0
Friends at Station Hill Baptist Sunday-				Mr. M. Jones		0	6	0
school, Chippenham, per Mr. A. B.				Mrs. Adlem (produce of pear-tree) ...		0	6	0
Turpin	8	6	Postal order from Edinburgh ...		0	1	0
Mr. E. K. Stace	10	0	First-fruits, Thornton Heath ...		0	6	0
Mrs. Sparrow	10	0	Mr. and Mrs. Henry Wood		1	0	0
Collected by Mrs. Pegg	0	7	6	Miss M. A. Nunn		1	0	0
Mr. W. F. Turner	6	0	0	W.		2	0	0
Collected by the Misses Bessie and May	0			Mr. R. Greenwood...		0	6	0
Harrison	6	0	D., Kendal		5	0	0
Collected by Mrs. Ansell...	4	5	Mr. T. Jephcoat		0	1	0
Mr. W. Park...	1	1	0	Mr. and Mrs. Haynes		0	1	0
Coastguards and Coastguards' Sunday-				Pastor J. A. Brown, M.R.C.S. ...		2	0	0
school, Shellness, per Mr. T. McMahon	0	5	0	Mr. E. M. Absolom		0	1	0
Messrs. A. and L. de Rothschild ...	2	2	0	S. and N.		10	0	0
S. O. laundry-box	0	2	0	Miss Jane Elliott		1	0	0
Mrs. Dewey	0	2	6	Mr. Philip Hooper...		0	1	0
Box at Orphanage gates	0	15	3	Mr. Lawrence Shepherd... ...		0	1	0
Miss Hine	1	0	0	Mrs. H. Watt		0		6
Collected by Mr. E. Seal... ...	0	4	0	In Beulah Baptist Chapel offering-				
Mr. James Larard...	0	10	0	box, Sept. 29th		0	2	0

	£	s.	d.		£	s.	d.
Miss Watts...	1	1	0	Collected by Master Herries	0	7	0½
Collected by Sunday scholars, Charles Street Baptist Chapel, Camberwell ...	1	6	0	Mrs. Timms	0	5	0
Mr. Walter Martin	0	8	1	Miss B. Hoering ...	0	10	0
Mrs. Birrell ...	1	0	2	Readers of "The Christian," per Messrs. Morgan and Scott ...	2	4	6
Collection at harvest thanksgiving service at Denmead, per Rev. J. P. Williams ...	1	4		Collected by Mrs. Roby (spots on the table-cloths)	1	0	0
Mr. J. Wilson	0	10		Mrs. Terrell (threepenny-pieces) ...	0	5	0
Mr. George Smith ...	0	5		Sandwich, per Bankers	2	2	0
Mr. Thomas Davies	5	0		*Meetings by Mr. Charlesworth and the Orphanage Choir:—*			
Mr. George Fryer ...	0	12		Bath ...	20	11	0
Mrs. Townsend ...	1	1		Mr. W. Taylor ...	52	2	0
Mr. Charles Mackson	0	5		Mr. W. Lewis ...	0	10	6
Mr. William Tennant	0	5		Mr. Moody ...	0	4	6
F. G. B., Chelmsford	0	2		Anon. ...	0	2	6
Postal order from Hawick	0	2				73	10 6
Collected by Miss E. M. Dalton	0	5		Weston-super-Mare	31	0	0
Orphan boys' collecting cards (2nd list)	3	13		Mr. James Pemell...	2	2	0
Orphan girls' collecting cards (2nd list)	0	18		"From Weston " ...	0	5	0
A friend from Shepperton	1	0				33	7
Mr. W. Hillier ...	1	0		Wellington ...	23	17	4½
Mrs. Yates ...	0	10		Mr. Egerton Burnett	2	2	0
Odd Fellows' Building Society, St. Julian's Hall, Guernsey	0	10	0			25	19 4½
Mr. S. H. Dauncey	0	2		Taunton ...	17	16	0
A brother in Jesus	0	5		Truro—collections :			
Mr. J. Alabaster ...	10	0		New Connexion Chapel ...	3	5	3
Mrs. Faulconer ...	100	0	6	Wesleyan Chapel ...	11	12	7
Miss E. Dumaresq	0	10	0	Baptist Chapel ...	4	19	5
Pastor W. Thomas's Bible-class, Putney Baptist Chapel	1			Meeting ...	27	15	1
The Lord's portion	0	1		Donations ...	5	16	6
A friend ...	0				53	8	10
Mr. and Mrs. H. Nichols	1			Less expenses	5	18	10
Mr. and Mrs. Underwood	0				47	10	0
A country minister	0			Helston ...	22	1	3
Miss Cox ...	10			Collected by Mr. Best :—			
Mrs. Chenery ...	0	1		Mr. Cotton ...	5	0	
Mr. James Campbell	2			Mrs. Cotton...	5	0	
Mr. D. Stewart, per Mr. Jas. Campbell	0	10	0	Mr. R. S. Martyn, J.P. ...	5	0	
Mr. I. Kipling ...	0	10	0	Mr. John Best, J.P. ...	5	0	
Collected by Mrs. James Withers :				Miss Best ...	1	1	
Mr. J. H. Fuller ...	2	2		Mr. E. P. Kendall	1	10	
Mr. J. R. Grubb ...	1	1		Mr. Heynes ...	1	10	
Mrs. Collier ...	0	5		Mr. J. L. Sleeman ...	1	1	
Mrs. Deane ...	0	2		Mr. H. Rogers ...	1	0	
Mrs. Cox ...	0	2		Rev. J. E. Hargreaves ...	0	0	
Mrs. J. Davis	0	2		Miss Richards ...	0	0	
	3	15	6	Miss Michell ...	0	0	
Rev. E. J. Farley ...	10	0	0	Mr. T. Davey ...	0	10	0
Mr. J. H. Church ...	1	0	0	Rev. H. V. Hobbs...	0	5	0
Mrs. Elgee ...	0	10	6		50	8	3
Sale of work at Londonderry, per Miss Sandes and Miss Mizen ...	4	0	0		£562	2	1

Orphan Boys' Collecting Cards (2nd list).—Inward, W., 4s ; Long, H., 12s 6d ; Mannell, W., £1 1s 2d ; Ponsford, H., 16s 9d ; Sambell, F. J., 10s ; Uren, G., 6s ; Westhrop, S., 3s.—Total, £3 13s 5d.
Orphan Girls' Collecting Cards (2nd list).—Carr, A., 6s ; Pearce, R., 2s ; Thirkell, R., 10s.—Total, 18s.

List of Presents, per Mr. Charlesworth, from September 16th to October 14th, 1889.—Provisions :— A quantity of Fruit, Vegetables, &c., proceeds of Harvest Thanksgiving, Friends at Lilliput Mission Hall, Parkstone ; 2 bags Apples (for No. 2 Girls'), Mr. George Keep ; 2 sacks Onions, Mr. D. Parkius ; 28lbs. Baking Powder, Messrs. Freeman and Hillyard ; a quantity of Fruit, Vegetables, Bread, Cake, Jam, Sweets, &c., proceeds of Harvest Thanksgiving, Baptist Church, Semley, Wilts, per Pastor J. Stanley ; 1 New Zealand Sheep, Mr. A. Seale Haslam ; 2½ bushels Apples and a quantity of Pears, Mrs. Ellwood ; a quantity Fruit and cut Flowers, proceeds of Harvest Thanksgiving, Friends at Baptist Sunday-school, Hetherland, per Pastor R. B. Morrison ; a quantity of Fruit, Vegetables, Bread, &c., proceeds of Harvest Thanksgiving, Corton Baptist Chapel, per Mr. J. Barnes ; 3 hampers of Apples, Friends at Station Hill Baptist Sunday-school, Chippenham, per Mr. A. B. Turpin ; a quantity of Vegetables, &c., proceeds of Harvest Thanksgiving, Baptist Chapel, Chitterne, per Mr. F. Maidment ; 40 Pork Pies, Mr. J. T. Crosher ; a quantity of Cabbages, Mr. J. Watts.
Boys' Clothing.—200 yards Narrow Cloth, Messrs. H. Fisher and Co. ; 13 Shirts, Mrs. Holcombe.
Girls' Clothing.—6 Articles, Mrs. Lamb ; 44 Articles, The Ladies' Working Meeting at the Tabernacle, per Miss Higgs ; 16 Articles, The Girls' Sewing Class, at Penge Tabernacle, per Rev. J. Wesley Boud ; 8 Articles, Mrs. Ford ; 33 Articles, The Cheam Baptist Working Society, per Mrs. E. Cox ; 25 Articles, The Wynne Road Ladies' Working Society, per Mrs. R. S. Pearce.
General.—1 cask of Blacking, Messrs. Carr and Sons ; 1 load of Firewood, Mr. J. Cooper.

Colportage Association.

Statement of Receipts from September 17th to October 14th, 1889.

Subscriptions and Donations for Districts:

	£	s.	d.
Cheddar District, per Rev. T. B. Field:			
Mrs. R. Clark	2	0	0
Mrs. Day	0	10	0
Mr. E Spencer	0	5	0
Mrs. Webb	0	5	0
Mrs. Tapscott	0	5	0
Mrs. J. Tilly	0	5	0
Rev. S. P. Jose	0	5	0
Rev. E. Edginton	0	5	0
Rev. T. B. Field	0	5	0
Mrs. Davies	0	2	6
Mr. C. B. Churchill	0	2	6
Mr. T. Boley	0	2	6
Rev. C. Merrick	0	2	6
Mr. R. Sherrey	0	3	0
Mrs. Jeffries	0	2	6
	5	0	6
Less expenses of collecting	0	2	6
	4	18	0
Tewkesbury, per Rev. A. Graham	3	0	0
Boroughbridge, Yorkshire Association	10	0	0
Bushton, per Mr. Thomas Harris	10	0	0
Oxfordshire Association, Witney District	20	0	0
Bethnal Green District:—			
Mr. C. E. Fox	5 0 0		
Mr. W. R. Fox	5 0 0		
	10	0	0
Great Totham, per Rev. H. J. Harvey	10	0	0
Home of Industry, Bethnal Green, per Miss A. Macpherson	10	0	0
Mr. R. Scott, for Langham and Dedham	10	0	0
Kent and Sussex Association, for St. Margaret's and Cowfold	12	10	0
Wolverhampton and Shipley	10	0	0
Wilts and East Somerset Association	25	0	0
Mrs. H. Keevil, for Melksham	10	0	0

	£	s.	d.
Mr. Thomas Greenwood, for Brentford	10	0	0
Norfolk Association, for Neatishead	10	0	0
Ironbridge and Coalbrookdale	7	10	0
Suffolk Congregational Union, for Thurlow	10	0	0
Mr. T. Hogben, for Portsmouth	3	0	0
Wendover and neighbourhood	10	0	0
Orpington, per Mrs. Allison's Bible-class	3	0	0
Okehampton District	10	0	0
The Western Baptist Association, for Chard	10	0	0
Friends at Maldon, Essex	15	0	0
Greenwich, per Rev. C. Spurgeon	10	0	0
Thornbury District, per Mrs. S. Taylor	5	0	0
A friend, New Zealand, for Riddings and Ilkeston	40	0	0
	£283	18	0

Subscriptions and Donations to the General Fund:—

	£	s.	d.
Readers of "The Christian," per Messrs. Morgan and Scott	1	0	0
Miss Hadfield	5	0	0
Mr. and Mrs. Henry Wood	1	1	0
H. B.	50	0	0
Mrs. Townsend	1	1	0
Mrs. Knott	0	10	0
Mr. Walter Mills	3	0	0
In loving memory	50	0	0
Annual Subscriptions:—			
Mrs. Jenkins	1	1	0
Mr. W. Harrison	1	1	0
Mrs. E. H. Tucker	0	5	0
Mrs. B. P. Bilborough	1	1	0
Messrs. S. W. Partridge and Co.	2	2	0
	£117	1	0

Society of Evangelists.

Statement of Receipts from September 17th to October 14th, 1889.

	£	s.	d.
Thankoffering for Messrs. Fullerton and Smith's services at the United Churches at Bayswater and Notting Hill	45	0	0
Mr. A. G. Jeynes	10	0	0
Miss Shaw	1	0	0
Mrs. Allan	50	0	0
Mr. and Mrs. Henry Wood	1	1	0
Mr. T. Chesters	5	0	0
Mrs. Cleminson	1	0	0

	£	s.	d.
Stamps from H. G.	1	0	0
Mrs. Townsend	1	1	0
Mr. Walter Mills	2	0	0
Mr. George Smith	0	10	0
Mr. James R. Bayley	1	0	0
Mrs. Pepys	10	0	0
	£128	12	0

For General Use in the Lord's Work.

Statement of Receipts from September 17th to October 14th, 1889.

	£	s.	d.
Mrs. Spencer	0	2	6
Sarah P., Warrington	0	12	0
	£0	14	6

Friends sending presents to the Orphanage are earnestly requested to let their names or initials accompany the same, or we cannot properly acknowledge them; and also to write to Mr. Spurgeon if no acknowledgment is sent within a week. All parcels should be addressed to Mr. Charlesworth, Stockwell Orphanage, Clapham Road, London.

Subscriptions will be thankfully received by C. H. Spurgeon, "Westwood," Beulah Hill, Upper Norwood. Should any sums sent before the 13th of last month be unacknowledged in this list, friends are requested to write at once to Mr. Spurgeon. Post Office and Postal Orders should be made payable at the Chief Office, London, to C. H. Spurgeon; and Cheques and Orders should all be crossed.

THE

SWORD AND THE TROWEL.

DECEMBER, 1889.

𝔗𝔥𝔦𝔰 𝔪𝔲𝔰𝔱 𝔟𝔢 𝔞 𝔖𝔬𝔩𝔡𝔦𝔢𝔯𝔰' 𝔅𝔞𝔱𝔱𝔩𝔢.

BY C. H. SPURGEON.

NE who is very valiant for the truth said to us, "*This must be a soldiers' battle.*" In that utterance we heartily concur. The gospel of the Lord Jesus is now assailed all along the line. Scarcely a denomination is free from the enemies of the truth : they are within our ranks. In the Church of England the superstitious errorists are more to the front than the sceptical ; and it is not an easy warfare which falls to the lot of Evangelicals within the Establishment. How is it they are there ? Those who are seeking a decision upon the matters raised by the action of the Bishop of Lincoln, are going straight to the point, and raising the question of Mass or no Mass in the most plain and practical manner. But if the result of the episcopal trial should be unfavourable, every Protestant man and woman should look upon the case as one for the personal conscience, and should, by individual action, drive the Evangelicals to a plain and unmistakable course of action.

Among Baptists, the great need is the personal investigation of the matters in debate by the members of our churches. It is clear that the members of the Council have nothing to say except by way of rebuke of any who protest against the growing error. The ministers also cry, "Peace, peace, where there is no peace." If sturdy individuality took up the matter, and godly men were determined not to remain in league with those who depart from the truth, the issues would be speedy.

A Congregational minister asks for an opportunity for the rank and file of the ministry to speak ; and his impression is, that ninety-five per cent. would be found to be on the old lines. We sincerely wish that we could believe it; but we think he puts his percentage far too high. Still, if in our free churches there were fair opportunities for utterance, either by the voice or through the press, we feel confident that the Broad School gentlemen would find themselves very much in the minority. But the hour of free speech will not come till the old Nonconforming spirit asserts itself in the pastors, deacons, and church-members, and the gag is taken off from the religious press. We are glad to hope that by other organs the truth will yet gain liberty to speak through the press. It is possible that a clique is now predominant, and that the mass of the people are misrepresented by them : if it be so, let them declare themselves.

The Free Church of Scotland must, unhappily, be for the moment regarded as rushing to the front with its new theology, which is no theology, but an opposition to the Word of the Lord. That church in which we all gloried, as sound in the faith, and full of the martyrs' spirit, has entrusted the training of its future ministers to two professors who hold other doctrines than those of its Confession. This is the most suicidal act that a church can commit. It is strange that two gentlemen, who are seeking for something newer and better than the old faith, should condescend to accept a position which implies their agreement with the ancient doctrines of the church; but delicacy of feeling is not a common article nowadays, and the action of creeds is not automatic, as it would be if consciences were tender. In the Free Church there is a Confession, and there are means for carrying out discipline; but these will be worth nothing without the personal action of all the faithful in that community. Every man who keeps aloof from the struggle for the sake of peace, will have the blood of souls upon his head. The question in debate at the Disruption was secondary compared with that which is now at issue. It is *Bible or no Bible, Atonement or no Atonement*, which we have now to settle. Stripped of beclouding terms and phrases, this lies at the bottom of the discussion ; and every lover of the Lord Jesus should feel himself called upon to take his part in an earnest contention for the faith once for all delivered to the saints. From the exceeding boldness of Messrs. Bruce and Dods, we gather that they feel perfectly safe in ventilating their opinions. They evidently reckon upon a majority which will secure them immunity ; and our fear is that they will actually gain that which they expect. We are not sanguine enough to believe that they are mistaken. Unless the whole church shall awake to its duty, the Evangelicals in the Free Church are doomed to see another reign of Moderatism. Have they suffered so many things in vain ? Will they not now make a stand?

Finding ourselves in a community which had no articles of faith, and seeing deadly error rising up, we had no course but to withdraw. Whether others think fit to do so or not is no part of our responsibility ; but nothing can free any true believer from the duty of maintaining pure and undefiled religion in its doctrine, as well as in its practice, by every means in his power. The most quiet country minister, the most retiring deacon or elder, the most obscure Christian man or woman—each one must come up to the help of the Lord against the mighty. The crisis becomes every day more acute : delays are dangerous ; hesitation is ruinous. Whosoever is on the Lord's side must show it at once, and without fail. Let those who so sadly pine for "another reformation," and a remodelled creed, stand out and say so, and no longer conceal their sentiments, or eat the bread of men at whose most cherished convictions they are stabbing with might and main. Let these be honest, and let the Evangelicals be true. The church expects every man to do his duty.

Three Fingers for Christ, and One for a Friend.

IT is written concerning Jesus, "He needed not that any should testify of man: for he knew what was in man." Testimony such as this can be asserted of no one else. Curiosity, however, has very frequently attempted to mount the same altitude with our Lord, and has endeavoured to obtain a view of all the operations going on in the town of Mansoul. It is asserted by one that he can give the most important features of a person's character, by simply glancing over one of his letters, and observing the formation of each word. A man who looks us "straight in the face" is sufficient evidence to some of genuine sincerity. A third class is quite satisfied of the existence of certain heart qualities by the manner in which a person shakes hands. A good hearty grip is enough to convince many of candour and undoubted esteem, and the careless limp-handed shake is ample evidence of indifference, and lack of social feeling. It is possible, however, that facts may be the opposite of appearances, and the unnoticed of more intrinsic worth than that which is at once perceptible. Take an example:—We shook hands with a very sincere friend, one Sunday evening, after the service. We knew his heart was right, and true as steel; yet, when we offered our hand, he gave his finger, accompanied with a smile. His usual course was to greet us full-handed, and make no mistake about the pressure or vibration. Why this exceptional mode of showing brotherly love? Was it absent-mindedness, or was it an acquired novelty in etiquette? We could not help noticing the change, and even speaking about it. The problem was solved in this way: our friend had three fingers enclosing the contribution which he was about .to drop in the weekly-offering box for the Lord's work; and consequently had only one finger at liberty to shake hands with. What an unspeakable and glorious change we should witness in the church of Christ if the same ratio were always observed in our relationship to Jesus, and in that which is subordinate to him! If in all thoughts, desires, words, acts, love, with even those who profess to follow the Master, it were "three fingers for Christ, and one for a friend," the Saviour would be more known and honoured, and the church would never lack diligent and earnest labourers, nor would it fail for silver and gold to carry on the Lord's work at home and abroad. One finger for Christ and three for self, is, alas! a great deal more common than "three for Christ, and one for a friend."   R. T. LEWIS, Shipston-on-Stour.

The Martyr's Seed a Martyr;

OR, JOHN WILLIAMS A RESULT OF PURITANISM.

IN the days of King James the First two yeomen were expelled from the diocese of Bangor for their Nonconformity. The brothers, for such they were, were Anabaptists, and therefore especially obnoxious to the bishop. The Establishment in Wales was served at that period by ignorant and ungodly men ; some of them were even drunkards. From the journal of the bishop himself, we learn that in some parishes the graveyard was reserved for stacking hay ; and the church was even the storehouse for the vicar's saddles and beehives. There were no Bibles among the people, and in some villages there had been no pretence of preaching for five or six years. The clergyman could seldom speak the tongue of the people. He was therefore disliked by them as of the " seed of the coiling serpent," and was himself a stranger to the grace of God. Earnest men like the two yeomen met together for mutual prayer and fellowship, and for this offence they were expelled from their native place. They thus suffered the loss of all things, and wandered penniless and friendless through various parts of England. They united themselves to a Baptist Church at Langworth, Berks, but they were not allowed to remain long in that locality. Driven forth from Langworth after similar experiences, they found themselves one evening in the neighbourhood of Witney, Oxon. They knelt down by the road-side, and prayed for divine guidance and help, and rising from their knees they asked for a sign from God. They threw a straw into the air, and walked at once towards the direction in which it fell. After sunset they reached the village of Coate, Oxon, and there they found shelter in a farmer's barn. As God would have it, the farmer was interested in them, and inquired into their history. He offered them work, which they accepted, and they settled in Coate. One of the brothers, James Williams by name, married the farmer's daughter, and appears to have prospered in the world ; for there is a record of his having purchased land. Thus even in temporal things God rewarded their sacrifices for the truth. But the brothers did not forget their principles when they prospered in the world : the use to which they devoted their wealth was the erection of a Baptist Chapel, which is still employed for the worship of God. A grandson of this James Williams was one of Cromwell's Ironsides ; Block Williams, as he was called, retired to Coate after the Restoration. Richard Williams, a descendant of James and of Block Williams, was the father of John Williams, the missionary. John Williams was born in a little house near Tottenham Green on the 27th of June, 1796. With his mother, John Williams attended the Independent Chapel at Edmonton, which was some two miles from his house.

On the 27th of March, 1810, he was apprenticed to a furnishing iron-monger named Tonkin, in the City Road, London. His parents then moved to Goswell Road, presumably in order to be near him. John Williams said of this period of his life, " My course, though not outwardly immoral, was very wicked. . . . I often scoffed at the news of Christ and his religion, and totally neglected those things which alone can afford solid satisfaction." On Sunday evening, January 3rd, 1814, he was waiting for some companions, with whom he intended to spend the Sabbath evening in the Highbury Tea Gardens, which were attached to some public-house. His friends were late, and as he chafed at their delay, his employer's wife spied him. She recognized the lad, and after much persuasion, induced him to accompany her to the Tabernacle, City Road. There God met with him, and saved his soul. In speaking of the good woman's deed, "It shows," said Mr. Williams, "what may be done for God by persons who are of no note in the Christian Church."

On the 17th of November, 1816, he sailed for the South Seas, accompanied by his young wife, whose family history also contains a remarkable leading of God's Spirit. On the 16th of November, 1819, he reached his destination, and commenced the enterprises which have never been surpassed in the records of missionary service. He built five vessels for missionary purposes; in fact, the record of his various labours is almost incredible.

On the 20th of November, 1839, he was killed, while endeavouring to carry the glad tidings of the gospel to the natives of Erromango.

John Williams is a conspicuous proof of the grace of God. Without a doubt he was what he was as a reward for the self-sacrifice of his ancestors; and he is an illustrious instance of a holy mother's influence. A careful study of his private journals has made the writer feel that while he was industrious, lovable, a mechanical genius, and a successful preacher of the gospel, he was above all, a man of God. He expressed his own personal conviction when he said, just before leaving England for the voyage which ended for him in martyrdom : " In comparison with the great truth of salvation by the death of Jesus Christ, the universe itself appears a bauble. I LOVE THE DOCTRINE : and I determine never to preach a sermon in any language, where the great doctrine of salvation through the blood of Christ is not the sum and substance of that sermon. WE THINK THAT THIS IS A TRUTH. WORTH CARRYING ROUND THE WORLD ; it is the soul of religious effort."

JAMES J. ELLIS.

"Godliness with Contentment is Great Gain."

VISITED a poor woman, who had received a shilling in the hour of her great need. She had fasted for twenty-four hours, and had neither coal nor candle in the house. When she received the shilling she procured the following articles :—Half-a-loaf of bread, half-a-pound of sugar, half-an-ounce of tea, half-a-cwt. of coal, and a candle. What a blessing a shilling is to a destitute *sober* person! but if given to an intemperate person, it just affords the means of self-murder. This poor woman can and does make an ounce of tea serve *twenty-four times*. She divides it into eight equal parts, one of which she infuses. The next time she boils the same leaves for some time; the third time she boils them again, but for a longer time. She says that even after this third boiling, "it's still proon" (brown). A knowledge of the above convicted me of the sin of ingratitude for my far greater mercies.—*From the Diary of a City Missionary.*

A Bundle of Papers.*

A STRANGE bundle of papers has come to my hand, nothing less than letters, and other matters, picked up in the town of Vanity Fair—not the modern creation of fancy, but the real town of Vanity Fair, set up by Beelzebub, Apollyon, and Legion, on the road by which all pilgrims must pass to the Celestial City.

The town seems strangely like that of the time of Christian and Faithful, though such things as the burning of the latter have not only passed into the region of the impossible, but would, I think, have been entirely forgotten, had not a memorial been recently erected on the supposed site to the memory of the martyrs. The Fair, however, from which the town takes its name, is still carried on, and is kept up, as it was then, all the year round. But it is doubtful if the pilgrims of those days would recognize it. The principal streets then were Britain Row, the French Row, the Italian Row, the Spanish Row, the German Row. The first still holds its supremacy, though it is now vastly more important than it was; but the new thoroughfares of America, Russia, &c., have also come into fashion. Many of the things Christian and Faithful mention would, as I judge from the advertisements in the newspapers which I have before me, no longer be known by their own and true names, though it is possible they are still for sale; for instance, such as preferments, titles, bawds, wives, and so forth. Many of the things, too, that they name, seem to have gone out of fashion, such as juggling, cheats, games, plays, fools, apes, knaves, and rogues. Jesters and fools have, at any rate, changed their character, as also, for the matter of that, have cheats, games, and rogues.

But from what I can glean, perhaps the greatest change is towards the pilgrims themselves. In the olden time, we read—and, after all, it is not so long ago:—

" The pilgrims were clothed with such kind of raiment as was diverse from that of any that traded at the Fair. The people, therefore, made a great gazing at them. Some said they were fools; some said they were bedlamites; and some, they were outlandish men."

Now, not only can there be no question that pilgrims are dressed exactly similar to the citizens of the Fair, but I should question whether more than about one-hundredth part of the inhabitants of the town would be offended if they were taken for the said pilgrims. That small and insignificant minority might refuse allegiance to the King of the Celestial City, but all the rest of the people would be vastly indignant if they were called by any other name than that of Pilgrim; at any rate, in that part of the Fair that we read of in the " Pilgrim's Progress." The naked fact is, that times have changed, and the name that was so abhorred in the earlier ages, has, by a turn of the wheel of time, become at last quite a fashionable one. So much so, indeed, that now, to all intents and purposes of ordinary life, the bystander is unable to recognize who are pilgrims, and who are traders in the Fair. Their

---

* We received this paper by the hand of one Trusty; but how he came by it we know not, neither can we understand all that is written therein.—C. H. S.

dress is the same, their language in ordinary conversation seldom differs, while to the superficial observer even their aims and objects seem too often alike. For be it observed, that what used to characterize the pilgrim, has now disappeared :—

"These pilgrims, which did not a little amuse the merchandisers, set very light by all their wares ; they cared not so much as to look upon them ; and if they were called upon to buy, they would put their fingers in their ears."

Alas ! I am half tempted to say, that if it were not for the pilgrims' many of the streets, and certainly many of the stalls, would be deserted. As for returning answer, "We buy the truth," there would be nothing strange in that'; all in the Fair profess to do the same. I should rather guess that this conformity to the world is carried to such an extent that even in the pilgrims' resting-places, their conversation and language are such that you would see little to confirm you in their profession of pilgrim. Not that the language of Canaan is extinct; far from it, you would hear much of it in their places of worship on the Sabbath, and it is even now constantly used by many of the Fair's citizens at such times ; but for colloquial conversation it is practically dead.

Again, there is evidently a striking change as regards the sovereignty of the town. Beëlzebub having at present, for reasons of his own, allowed his royal claims to lapse for a little, his very name is now scarcely heard.

Of the three famous witnesses at the trial, Superstition is dead, and his heirs banished to the outskirts of the Fair. Pickthank's descendants have taken the name of Forgetfulness. Envy has still numerous representatives.

The names of the jury are still common names. Live-loose, High-mind, and Implacable are to be seen on every side. While Love-lust is so often met with, that even his name has almost ceased to answer its purpose of distinguishing its owner.

Amongst the letters, is one from a gentleman living in the neighbouring town of Fair-speech, which is evidently now a populous district, forming, in fact, a suburb to the town of Vanity Fair, and maintaining the reputation Christian gave it of being a wealthy place. Possibly it is the original dialect of Fair-speech that has come at last to be the language of the Fair. Much that was mentioned of the former is certainly now true of the latter ; as, for instance, people there being most zealous when religion goes in silver slippers. In fact, the doctrines of By-ends have largely prevailed there. He finally became Mayor of Fair-speech, and was sent as the town's representative to the Chamber at Vanity Fair. Here he made his mark, and much of the change of opinion in the Fair must be put down to him and his followers. Their old chief's saying, that "he is for religion only as far as the times and safety will bear," is yet quoted, and one of the principal squares still goes by his name.

Money-love and Save-all are now the names of the principal private banks, and Lucre Hill, with its silver mine, has again come round to be the latest place of resort. The name, however, of Demas is quite forgotten. Not a street or public-house appears called by his name, let alone a church ; but yet in its modern form of "popular" the name is the almost universal motto of the town.

Giants are esteemed as merely allegorical fancies; but from the papers we gather that now, instead of a Giant Despair, there is a whole nation of people called by that name, dwelling, too, in the land of Doubt, through which the river of Diffidence runs.

I am puzzled by Atheist : I can still trace the name, but in most cases it has lapsed into other forms, such as Agnostic. On the whole, I should doubt whether the clan has much increased. Not so with Ignorance, or its more modern name of " Secular Education." A very large district seems peopled by his descendants. I believe the answer given to Hopeful—" I will never believe my heart is bad "—might be engraved on their door-posts, so generally is it accepted.

I have been most puzzled by a scrap of paper purporting to be part of a bill which I presume must have been carried away unsettled by a pilgrim from the City of Destruction. It is so disfigured and torn that I may have interpreted it wrongly ; for it is not written in the language of Canaan. As far as it goes, I here append it :

Dr. to Stephen Evangelist, 1st month.

	£	s.	d.
To preaching at corner of Broad Road, from 3.30 to 4.30, and vigorously urging people to leave the city	0	10	6
For being pelted while there, and otherwise vilified	0	5	6
For being detained in the common jail for 48 hours on a charge of obstruction, and for loss of time while there, and being prevented going to Carnal Policy, say	2	2	0
For loss of reputation through not being properly advertised at Royal Assembly Rooms, Town of Morality	5	0	0

The remainder of the account is torn off.   Granting that the labourer is worthy of his hire, there is yet something here that is strangely different to the days of Evangelist and Greatheart. Perhaps the individual has been somewhat scurvily treated ; yet it reads strangely. I can see from the papers, that some evangelists now live on what they term "faith "; but, after all, most people do that, who preach at all. The knowledge of salvation, and retailing it at so much an hour, is, to me, like selling the water of life. Whether it would be wise or possible for the pilgrims to take again to simpler ways and habits, I must leave to others to decide. At present, rightly or wrongly, money seems a measure for much that should be kept clear of it.

Another thing that may surprise some, is, that the pilgrims freely use the courts of law at the Fair for the adjustment of their own claims, instead of telling these things to the church. A lawyer is called in, and the contention becomes public property. The present Lord Chief Justice, or whatever title the chief legal officer holds, is a very different man to my Lord Hate-good ; and matters are, no doubt, settled fairly enough, though, in some cases, especially relating to pilgrimage, he seems at sea.

On the whole, the aim of too many of the pilgrims seems to be to possess a double citizenship—to be Citizens of the World, and Citizens of Zion, to be conformed to this world instead of being transformed. Thus, as the wish of most of the dwellers at the Fair is to make the best of both worlds, as By-ends of old taught, it is not surprising that, in one sense, the old quarrel between the rival races has almost died away, and, but for an occasional sneer or taunt, you would never have occasion to remember its existence ; yet that word must be as true as ever, which was spoken by the Prince of princes : " If ye were of the world, the world would love its own ; but because ye are not of the world, therefore the world hateth you."

Again, his saying, "No man can serve two masters," if not openly disputed, is often tacitly set on one side. Many study hard to do so.

Another curious phase of life that has been developed, is going at certain periods of the year to the Delectable Mountains. That the pilgrims go to have their souls strengthened, and to get a far-off glimpse of the Celestial City, cannot be doubted ; but I much fear that the gardens, orchards, and vineyards, which still exist there, are an attraction to many.

Some, certainly, live a very different kind of life there to what they are wont when at home ; and, to hear them talk, one would imagine the language of Canaan was their only tongue ; but, alas! too often, on their return to the Fair, they drop back into their old places, as if they had never been away. Yet, on the other hand, it is doubtless owing to these periodical excursions that, quite of recent years, many have started to go upon the King's errands to Dark-land, which, if you remember, lieth on the opposite side of the coast to the land which containeth the City of Destruction. So marked is this going forth of pilgrims charged with the royal mission, that Tell-tale declareth that it is beginning to exert an influence on the Fair itself, and to stir up a feeling of enquiry on the subject. It is even thought by some, that as the burning question of the hour seems to be how these pilgrims should be sent forth and equipped, it may, in time, stir up the nearer question, as to how pilgrims should live in the Fair itself ; *and soberly, it is high time that this should be considered.*

The Brass Kettle.

VISITED an old woman who had a complaint to make concerning a woman whom I have frequently met with, and who visits and prays with sick people, and others. She had been visiting this old woman, and had, the latter said, "made a very long prayer"; and before coming away had laid hold on a brass kettle, and asked the old woman if she would give it her. The impression left was mischievous.

"It was sic (such) a thing," said the old woman, "to be prayin' sae lang to get my bit kettle."

Indeed, I fear she will never hear another prayer without thinking of her kettle ; all that I could say to lead her mind away from the subject seemed of little avail ; again and again she recurred to her kettle.— *From the Diary of a City Missionary.*

"White already to Harvest."

(John iv. 35.)

BY W. Y. FULLERTON.

WE live in an age of crises; and it is the solemn and mature conviction of many of God's servants that we are on the eve of a
great movement of God's Spirit, and on the edge of a wonderful manifestation of grace. Divine providence, Scripture prophecy, and Christian
faith, all converge on this point, and cause us to expect, in the near
future, an overwhelming harvest of souls, which shall be as a kind of
firstfruits of the ingathering of the world.

And of all this harvest, Christ himself was at first the seed, the corn
of wheat in the ground, dying, and bringing forth much fruit. And of all
this harvest, Christ himself shall be at last the reaper, when, sitting on
the cloud, he shall thrust in his sickle and reap. In that glad day the
wheat shall be gathered into the garner; but meanwhile, the harvests of
the Spirit are gathered, not to be garnered, but to be sown. Elect
from amongst men, they are planted in the earth, that they may increase
and multiply. "The good seed are the children of the kingdom." The
harvest of to-day is the seed of to-morrow, which, in its turn, will yield
another harvest, and again be sown; and so on until the consummation
of all things, which may be nearer at hand than some of us imagine.

In a former paper, "Lift up your Eyes, and look on the Fields," we
found ourselves forced to the conclusion that only one-fiftieth of the
world could be counted as really Christian. If these thirty millions
of believers, out of the world's fourteen hundred millions, are looked
upon as *a harvest*, and as the sole result of all the centuries of toil, it is
enough to drive us to despair; but looked upon as *seed*, which may be
planted all over the earth, and which must be so planted, if our Lord's
command, "Go ye into all the world," is to be obeyed, there is
abundant reason for sanguine hopefulness and buoyant courage, if only
the church is alive to her opportunity.

And it is because the church is awakening to its privilege in this
matter; because she is arising and putting on her beautiful garments;
because there are signs of a new departure in carrying the gospel to
every creature, that we seem to have come to the fulness of time. "We
are living at the terminal point of the old and at the germinal point of
the new; and happy shall we be, indeed, if we know the time of our
visitation," and take the tide at its flood. "He that sleepeth in harvest
is a son that causeth shame."

So, while a review of the progress of the gospel leaves room for sorrow,
and room for rebuke, and room for humiliation, it leaves no room for
despondency or inaction. As a final result, we have achieved but little;
as a preparation for an expected end, much. "Let us take to ourselves
the great consolation, that to-day, as never before, the work is advancing.
The long and laborious process of undermining the chief strongholds of
heathenism will one day be followed by a great crash."

We must not deceive ourselves, as though the children of the wicked
one and the children of the kingdom were not both to grow together
until the harvest. In this age we can have no hope of getting rid of

evil men. What we may confidently expect is, to see the number of the saints mightily increase, in some places thirtyfold, in some sixty-fold, and in some a hundredfold; for "He reserveth unto us the appointed weeks of harvest."

Doubtless there are difficulties; but as "he that regardeth the clouds shall not reap," let us rather look for the glints of sunshine. Over the whole earth the fields are "white already to harvest." Oh, that the church would immediately put in the sickle, because the harvest is come!

"White already to harvest"! For although the souls already in-gathered are so few, among so many, let us remember that the work abroad has been accomplished principally within the last century—we might more truly say within the last thirty years—while at home it began only with the Reformation. And though there may be long delay during winter, when the harvest once begins the waiting time is over, and the song of "harvest home" is soon upon our lips.

"White already to harvest"! For although there are more people born into the world each year than are born into the church, we must not forget that it never was otherwise. Even in the most fruitful apostolic days, there is no reason to believe it was different. At the end of the first century, there were not more than half a million Christians in the world; and "during the first centuries Christianity increased, but Paganism increased far more rapidly." As the apostles were not discouraged, neither need we be, since our circumstances are, in this respect, alike.

"White already to harvest"! For although the population of heathen countries increases, the population of countries nominally Christian increases much more rapidly. There are yet, perhaps, three born in Pagan countries to every two born in Christendom; but the rate of increase in the latter is so much greater, that, at the end of the century, it is probable the actual increase will be as great, and, thereafter, it will gain ground more and more rapidly.

"White already to harvest"! For although there are actually fewer conversions than births in the world, yet the Christians increase in rapid and accelerating ratio to the heathen and unconverted. At home we have a slight balance of percentage in our favour, though it is difficult to say exactly how much: in India the general population increases at the rate of eight per cent., and the Christian population at the rate of thirty per cent.; while in China, the Christian community doubles itself in about eight years. And though the Roman Catholic and Greek churches are increasing, the Protestants are gaining upon them rapidly. There are of the latter four times as many, whereas of the former, only two-and-a-half times as many, as there were a century ago. Here, too, the ratio is increasing; for while, fifty years ago, Protestant population was to Papal as three to thirteen, it is now as one to three.

"White already to harvest"! For although in civilized countries many more profess Christianity than are truly born of God, in heathen countries it is precisely the reverse. There the consequences of an open declaration on Christ's side are so painful, that some observers even say there are ten times as many convinced in their heart as confess with their mouth. At any rate, there must be twice the number;

and some day, when the disabilities attending a profession of Christianity have disappeared, or when the Spirit of God shall baptize the
secret disciples into boldness, we shall have a large accession to the
visible church.

"White already to harvest"! For although the adherents of the
religions of the heathen outnumber those who follow Christ, yet all
over the world men are losing faith in their false systems; and, as
Gideon was encouraged by hearing the Midianite tell his dream of defeat
to his fellow, so may we be of good courage when heathens themselves
prophesy the final victory of our faith. "Let us alone," they say ;
"we are too old, but our sons and our grandsons are sure to be Chris
tians." A few extracts from competent standard authorities will best
establish the point. "The most acute observers have boldly declared
that Brahminism in India is dead or dying." "Both Buddhism and
Shintoism are crumbling into ruins." "The throne of Confucius, we
might almost say, begins to totter." "The outer shell of Hinduism may
remain, but the informing spirit has fled." The King of Siam, when
he lost his wife, sent to the missionaries for a New Testament, and his
brother gave as a reason that the king had lost faith in his own religion;
while a high-class Bombay paper says : "No one, we make bold to say,
believes in the Vedas as inspired." All this is just as true with reference to many Roman Catholic countries, especially in the white fields of
France ; and while the Mohammedans are, perhaps, less convinced,
they are much more accessible than formerly to evangelistic effort. In
a word, the nations are asking about Jesus as the Samaritan woman did,
" Can this be the Christ ? " (R. V.)

"White already to harvest"! For even when men do not change
their religion, the influence of Christianity changes it for them, robbing
it of its cruel and debased features, and giving a new direction to
thought, and conscience, and life. And if when the men of Sychar
were only *coming* to Jesus (John iv. 30, R. V.), the Master said the
fields were white to harvest, surely we may be sanguine that many of
those who are influenced by the contact of Christianity, though they
have not yet come to Christ, are coming.

"White already to harvest"! For in nearly every nation there is a
vague longing and expectation. The philosophers dream of a golden
age of universal culture, the Socialists of an age of common brotherhood. Mussulmans look for their coming Mahdi, while in Mexico the
natives vaguely expect the return of Montezuma to re-establish his
golden reign. In India, many still expect the incarnation of sinlessness,
and speak of the Ganges drying up. In Africa they look for the "White
Spirit " : a missionary there, exploring an unknown region, found a
chief who had never seen a white man, and yet had a house already
built for him when he should come. As in the village of Samaria, they
said, " We know that Messias cometh, who will tell us all things," men
yearn for the Coming One, over the whole earth to-day. Is not the
longing heaven-born, and shall not he who created it satisfy it, though
they worship they know not what ? Yea, verily ! Overturn, overturn,
overturn, until he come whose right it is to reign.

"White already to harvest"! For, in addition to home effort, which
cannot be tabulated, there are at this moment one hundred and fifty

missionary societies working for the evangelization of the world, besides many individual labourers. Surely, this fact is full of promise, especially when we remember that, with scarcely an exception, they have each greater resources than even their most sanguine friends ventured to hope for at their formation. Probably, in ten years, they will have greater influence than we even dare to expect now. With fifty-four societies in India, thirty-three in China, and thirty-five in Africa, what may we not hope for in days to come! See what has happened in days gone by. There are five times as many translations of the Bible, twenty times as many missionaries, forty times as much contributed, fifty times as many converts, and two hundred times as many schools as there were less than a century ago.

"White already to harvest"! For there is an increasing earnestness and enthusiasm for missions at home. This will prove an immense blessing to the churches here; for, as Dr. Duff says, "The church which ceases to be evangelistic, will soon cease to be evangelical." The man who has no sympathy with missions becomes the object of missions, rather than the subject of them. Self-propagation is the law of continued existence. "Now he that ministereth seed to the sower both minister bread for your food, and multiply your seed sown, and increase the fruits of your righteousness." It would be little wonder if the recent evangelical protest should result in a new evangelistic ardour; indeed, there are signs of such a movement already. But the direct influence of this increased sympathy with missions will tell most abroad. When we find a hundred new missionaries going to China in one year, in connection with the Inland Mission, and hear of two or three thousand young men volunteering in America for mission work, and of one firm of shipping agents alone engaging, for the accommodation of missionaries, seventy-seven berths in outward-bound vessels in two months, we cannot but think that the Lord, who thus arouses and equips his servants, has already some wide fields waiting for the sower, and some white harvest fields ready for the sickle.

"White already unto harvest"! For may we not expect apostolic success when we have restored to the church the gifts of healing and of tongues? Not in the old supernatural way, but in a most enduring, if more indirect, method. Medicine is enlisting on the side of Christ; already there are one hundred and seventy medical missionaries in the field abroad, and many more at home. And the Scripture is translated into two hundred and eighty different languages, so that most of the natives may now hear, in their own tongue, the wonderful works of God. As that was one of the marvels of Pentecost, the feast of first-fruits, may we not now hope, having the same sign, to reap the waving harvest? It is, indeed, probable, that every Lord's-day sees more souls ingathered than did that memorable Pentecost in Jerusalem, though not all being converted in one city, the mighty work attracts less attention.

"White already to harvest"! For the martyr spirit again rests upon the church. Witness the constancy of the native Christians during the Indian mutiny, when not more than two were known to apostatize, though in the face of terrible temptation. Witness the faith sealed with blood in Madagascar, and the more recent heroic confessions in Africa, at Uganda, where many accepted death joyfully—thirty-two being burnt at one time, and thirty at another, in two large funeral piles, under the most cruel and ingenious forms of torture—rather than renounce the Christ, their Saviour. And if Bor-Sing, heir to the Rajah of Cherra, in India, had only been one of our own countrymen, how it would have thrilled us to see him rejecting a crown for Christ rather than comply with the repeated entreaties to lay aside his religion, and become the lawful king of a willing people! But the Lord Jesus is made glad by such fealty as this, though we are so shamefully lethargic about it.

"White already to harvest!" For in nearly every nation Christ has his witnesses. And if one saved woman, witnessing in the village at the foot of Ebal, caused the Lord to say *those* fields were "white to harvest," surely wherever one true testimony is given, the fields there, too, begin to whiten in the warmth of the heavenly Sun. In our own favoured Protestant lands how many witnesses there are—alas, how many rejected! In France "there is Protestantism in the air"; and the McAll Mission, in that country, surpasses anything of the kind ever known in the annals of the church. Rome itself is invaded by a score of churches; and an ardent spirit prophesies that the Evangelical Alliance will yet meet in St. Peter's. Constantinople is encircled by the heralds of the Cross, before which the Crescent fades. The darkest places are in Central Asia and in the Soudan; but who can say how soon the fields there may be open to the gospel, which is able to civilize as well as save!

"White already to harvest"! For the newly-reaped churches in foreign countries are themselves becoming the seed of further harvests. Japan is taking the gospel to Corea. The Polynesian churches are carrying the glad tidings to the Caroline and Marshall Islands and to New Guinea, while they also contribute largely to the funds of the society at home. We hear of a man and his wife, at another place, converted from heathenism, living for three days on fivepence, and selling their bed and sleeping on a mud floor, that they might help to spread the news of salvation.

"White already to harvest"! For prudent men already speak of dividing the world amongst existing agencies, and evangelizing it before this century shall have run its course; and the recent Missionary Conference in London is a sign of the times full of hope.

"White already to harvest"! For already we have had glorious examples of what the gospel is able to accomplish on an extended scale. Who can, without devout gratitude, think of Polynesia, where, in a short forty-four years, the idolatrous cannibals have been turned into civilized Christians; the islands of Samoa, for example, where, out of thirty-five thousand inhabitants, twenty-seven thousand adhere to the London Missionary Society, and six thousand are truly converted! Or who can, without a glad exultation, remember Fiji, with its one thousand two hundred and sixty Christian church buildings, where before were heathen temples, or ovens to cook human victims! Or who can, without renewed confidence in the Word of God, meditate on Madagascar, where, even in times of persecution, and without a foreign missionary, the number of believers grew from one thousand to seven thousand, and where now those who were once counted as cattle take an honourable place amongst the Christian nations? Or who can, without admiring wonder, hear of Sierra Leone, where, in a brief seven years, brutal thieves and murderers were changed into earnest and devoted disciples of the Meek and Lowly One, until the woods resounded with their prayers and songs, and a church capable of holding two thousand persons was erected to accommodate the eager congregation? Or who can, without a fervent thanksgiving, look at Japan, from which, two hundred years ago, all Christians were banished, and where, it was said, that even the Christians' God, should he come, would lose his head : where the good seed was only admitted thirty-five years ago ; where, during the last sixteen years, eleven converts have increased to twenty thousand, and which now is, perhaps, on the eve of being to Asia what our own land has been to Europe and the world? Or who can, without holy inspiration, learn that in Formosa twelve hundred disciples were baptized in ten days? Or who can, without a thrill of delight, contemplate the work amongst the Karens of Burmah, where twenty thousand worshippers of demons have turned to the true God, and are now spreading their faith on every hand? Or who can, without sacred emotion, recall the news which from the Congo came but yesterday to gladden the heart of a sorely tried church—the news that at Banza Manteka there are over one thousand disciples, and many enquirers all along the river? But, perhaps, chiefest of all towers the mission to the Telegus, in India, where, in one day, two thousand two hundred and twenty-two persons were baptized by immersion (two men doing the whole work), and where, in forty-five days, nearly nine thousand were added to the Lord, and last year a thousand more? Who can face a fact like that without rapturous enthusiasm? Surely the fields are " white already to harvest " !

How important it is for us to seize the passing opportunity ! to lose no time ; to take part in the harvest, and hasten the ingathering. Even if only a fiftieth of the world is truly Christ's, yet if each one of those would reach but three with the gospel each year, the whole world would know of Jesus before the final hour of this century.

To accomplish this work we shall need to sacrifice ourselves, even as Rizpah did, when, in the beginning of the barley harvest, she took her place before her dead sons, and, until the water dropped from heaven, suffered not the birds by day, nor the beasts by night, to rest upon them. If she, all the harvest time, thus devoted herself for her dead sons, what shall not we do for our living Saviour, and for the souls of men which never die? Thus only can we know the joy according to the joy of harvest : " joy born of pain ; fruit found from buried seed : the corn of wheat falling into the ground, and *dying*, yields so rich a harvest."

In some parts of Scotland the school vacation begins only when the harvest is ripe ; and it is no uncommon thing for the master to find, towards harvest time, a few golden ears of corn laid on his desk—a gentle reminder from the longing, tired boys, that the days of toil should soon be over, and the holidays begin. Thus the weary church lays before the Lord the souls already ingathered, an ear or two from this country, and an ear or two from that; offering them, not as the fruit of harvest, but as a token that the harvest is ripe, and as a prayer that he would speedily end our labours, and usher in the harvest home.

The men of Beth-Shemesh, reaping their harvest in the valley, lifted up their eyes, and saw the long exiled ark returning, and rejoiced to see it. So may we labour on, gathering in the souls of men to the kingdom of God, until we too, and perhaps soon, shall lift up our eyes, and behold with joy our absent Lord return in glory! Then our harvest-time shall be over. May we not be ashamed at the end of the day's work!

"THE HARVEST TRULY IS PLENTEOUS, BUT THE LABOURERS ARE FEW; PRAY YE THEREFORE THE LORD OF THE HARVEST, THAT HE WOULD SEND FORTH LABOURERS INTO HIS HARVEST."

𝕹𝖊𝖙𝖙𝖑𝖊𝖙𝖔𝖓 𝕬𝖓𝖊𝖈𝖉𝖔𝖙𝖊𝖘.

FIRST SELECTION.

"IF HE HAD BEEN WICKED ENOUGH."

DR. NETTLETON was quite at home in every kind of theological discussion. With his little pocket Bible, or his Greek Testament, always in hand, he was at all times ready to stop the mouths of gainsayers, or to speak a word in season to such as might need instruction and advice.

He was once accosted by a *Universalist*, who wished to engage him in discussion on the doctrine of future punishment. Dr. N. replied, " I will not enter into any dispute with you at present, but I shall be pleased to have you state your views, that I may have them to think of." The man then proceeded to inform him that he did not believe in future punishment at all ; mankind, he believed, received all their punishment in this life, and all would be happy after death.

Dr. Nettleton then asked him to explain certain passages of Scripture, such as the account of a future judgment in Matthew xxv., and some other places ; merely suggesting difficulties for him to solve, without calling in question any of his positions. After taxing his ingenuity for some time in this way, and thus giving him opportunity to perceive the difficulty of reconciling his doctrine with the language of Scripture, he said to him :—" You believe, I presume, the account given by Moses of the deluge, and of the destruction of Sodom and Gomorrah ? "

" Certainly," he replied.

" It seems, then," said Dr. Nettleton, " that the world became exceedingly corrupt, and God determined to destroy it by a deluge of water. He revealed his purpose to Noah, and directed him to prepare an ark, in which he and his family might be saved. Noah believed God, and prepared the ark. Meanwhile he was a preacher of righteousness. He warned the wicked around him of their danger, and exhorted them to prepare to meet their God. But his warnings were disregarded. They, doubtless, flattered themselves that God was too good a being thus to destroy his creatures. But, notwithstanding their unbelief, the flood came, and if your doctrine be true, swept them all up to heaven ? And what became of Noah, that faithful servant of God ? He was tossed to and fro on the waters, and was doomed to trials and sufferings for three hundred and fifty years longer in this evil world; whereas, if he had been wicked enough, he might have gone to heaven with the rest.

"And there were the cities of Sodom and Gomorrah, which had become so corrupt that God determined to destroy them by a tempest of fire. He revealed his purpose to Lot, and directed him and his family to make their escape. 'And Lot went out, and spake unto his sons in law, saying, Up, get you out of this place; for the Lord will destroy this city. But he seemed as one that mocked unto his sons in law.' They did not believe that any such doom was impending. They, doubtless, flattered themselves that God was too good a being to burn up his creatures. But no sooner had Lot made his escape than it rained fire and brimstone from the Lord out of heaven, and they all, it seems, ascended to heaven in a chariot of fire; while pious Lot was left to wander in the mountains and to suffer many grievous afflictions in this vale of tears; whereas, if he had been wicked enough, he might have gone to heaven with the rest."

After making this statement, he requested the man to reflect on these things, and bade him a kind and affectionate adieu.

SOULS IN PRISON.

A *Restorationist* once attacked Dr. Nettleton, and quoted these words of the apostle Peter, in support of his doctrine: "By which, also, he went and preached to the spirits in prison." Dr. Nettleton observed to him, that the time was specified in the next verse when Christ preached to the spirits in prison. It was, "*When once the longsuffering of God waited in the days of Noah.*" It was by his Spirit, which dwelt in Noah, that he preached to those who are now spirits in prison. "No," said the man, "that cannot be the meaning of the passage. The meaning is, that Christ, after his crucifixion, went down to hell, and preached to the spirits in prison."

"Be it so," said Dr. N., "what did he preach?"

"I do not know," said the man, "but I suppose he preached the gospel."

"Do you think," said Dr. N., "that he preached to them anything different from what he preached on earth?"

"Certainly not," said he.

"Well, then," said Dr. N., "when Christ was on earth, he told sinners that if they should be cast into prison they should not come out till they had paid the uttermost farthing. If he went down to hell to preach to the lost spirits there, he doubtless told them, 'You will remain here till you have suffered all that your sins deserve.' What influence, then, would his preaching have towards releasing them from the place of torment?"

A WORSE CASE.

A stupid worldly man once said to him, "You know, Mr. Nettleton, that when we would do good, evil is present with us."

"Yes," replied Dr. N., "and that is a bad case; but it is worse when we would *not* do good, and evil is present with us."

[We hope to tell our friends about Dr. Nettleton next month, and to continue these excellent anecdotes concerning him.—C. H. S.]

The Flock in Winter.

WHEN snows descend and tempests blow, shepherds must look to their sheep with double care. When the grass cannot be reached, they must have other food; and when the blast is pitiless, they must have shelter. With the Lord's flock it must be so just now, for we have fallen upon cloudy and tempestuous days, when unbelief darkens the air, and chills the heart. We have a sharp spiritual winter upon us now, and the shepherds will have need of all their watchfulness and care, and of help from on high lest the flock should perish. Much prayer and personal piety should be set in action, and a sense of special dependence upon God should be aroused. Some of us who have been the first to discern the storm, have been made to feel an awful solitude from men, but a blessed communion with God, which cannot be better described than by the Ettrick poet's account of Highland shepherds in days gone by :—

"I know of no scene so impressive as that of a shepherd's family, sequestered in a lone glen, during the time of a winter storm. There they are left to the protection of Heaven alone; and they know and feel it. Before retiring to rest, the shepherd uniformly goes out to examine the state of the weather, and make his report to the little dependent group within. Nothing is to be seen but the conflict with the elements, nor heard but the raving of the storm. Then they all kneel around him while he recommends them to the protection of Heaven; and though their little hymn of praise can scarcely he heard even by themselves, and mixes with the roar of the tempest, they never fail to rise from their devotions with their spirits cheered, and their confidence renewed. Often have I been a sharer in such scenes, and never in my youngest years without having my heart deeply impressed. We lived, as it were, inmates of the cloud and the storm; but we stood in relationship to him who directed and governed them."

In this, as in a parable, let every faithful pastor and every believer in the faith of God, see his own condition in these perilous times. Spring may yet come, and summer also; but meanwhile let us "Feed the flock of God" in fellowship with God himself.   C. H. S.

The Work at Costers' Hall.

OUR friend Mr. W. J. Orsman, whose work among the street-trading classes and the poor generally at the north-east end of London has often been referred to in these pages, has now retired from the General Post Office after thirty-three years of active service; and as he has only just finished his fifty-first year, he will now be able to devote more time and energy to that work, among the poorest of the poor, on which his heart has been set ever since the time of his conversion under our preaching more than thirty years ago. Since his retirement, Mr. Orsman has been elected to serve on the London County Council, and he will evidently find a sphere of usefulness in connection with that body. Ever since his removal to North London, Mr. Orsman has counted it a privilege to remain associated with the Church at the

Tabernacle, so that Costers' Hall, with all its comprehensive work and agencies, is a station in which we are naturally greatly interested.

When Mr. Orsman commenced work in 1861, he had been five years in the Queen's service, "and four years in the service of the King of kings." In the account of his last year's work, just issued, he thus contrasts past times with the present:—"Twenty-eight years ago the term Mission was sparingly used ; in fact, excepting the Home and Foreign Missionary Societies, there were few ' Missions ' in existence. Undoubtedly in the Ragged Schools of that period, considerable evangelistic effort was carried on in the slums, but it was desultory in its character, and did not reach the concrete form of a large evangelistic centre, with its voluntary evangelist and pastor, and the converts bound together in a Mission Church by the holy ties of fellowship and discipline."

Experience has proved that the poor and over-crowded area of Hoxton is nothing like so popular with the charitable public as Whitechapel and the East-end ; but though there have been no tragedies at Hoxton, the needs of that quarter are exceeding great.

It will, of course, be clearly understood that the head-quarters of Mr. Orsman's service is not a mere mission hall, but the home of a working mission church. In the course of a generation the pastor of this church, who is assisted in preaching by Mr. Charles Hart, the theatre preacher, has had raised up around him a staff of one hundred and twenty-six helpers, many of whom are converts who have been brought in at the meetings. The voluntary services of the pastor and this large company of co-workers reduce the working expenses of what is really a large mission to the lowest point ; and "these voluntary workers are all hard-working men and women in the lower ranks of life." They not only work in this way, but they and the congregation generally regularly contribute on behalf of the general work, and also to the sick fund, their contributions last year reaching close upon £200. The Mission Church numbers three hundred and sixty-four *bonâ fide* members.

In addition to the meetings on Sundays, there are several gatherings for prayer and for Bible study during the week. The Christian Workers' Association has over ninety members. Some of these are tract distributors and visitors of the sick and needy ; others are open-air preachers who use the late Earl of Shaftesbury's barrow for a pulpit. The Sunday-school has about eight hundred scholars, or all that the building will accommodate, while the Bible-classes are so crowded that larger rooms will soon have to be found. The Free Library, the Young People's Christian Band, and Daniel Band, are all prosperous ; and care is taken that the singing at all of the services is bright and cheerful. As a pastor Mr. Orsman greatly values the services of those who take turn as door and landing keepers. "By this arrangement peace and quietness always reign at Costers' Hall, and strangers are sure to get a Christian greeting as they enter the building. These good brethren, for Christ's sake, freely relinquish their comfortable seats for at least two hours at a time, and march up and down the draughty corridors and landings. They are worthy descendants of the 'children of Shallum, who were porters in the king's gate, and keepers of the entry of the house of the Lord.' "

While heartily approving of Mr. Brown's tract on "The Devil's Mission of Amusement," Mr. Orsman goes on to say ·—"The Social aspect of the Mission we regard as that portion of the work which has either Thrift or Recreation for its basis, and which has grown out of the Spiritual work. The two are not naturally antagonistic to each other, although in some places we have seen the Social supplant the Spiritual. A wise and holy jealousy should always be exercised to keep the Lord's work in the foreground and distinct from mere creature enjoyments and benefits. This being granted, a skilful leader of Mission Work will find every operation within his premises helpful to Spiritual influence."

Hence, the Christian Helpers' Union holds meetings for study ; boys and girls in work have Evening Classes for their own benefit ;· and then come the Temperance Societies which meet at the Hall, the Costers' Benefit Societies, and the annual Donkey and Pony Show, which has exercised an immense influence throughout London in improving the condition of the animals of the street-traders.

The greatest boon is conferred on the people when children and adults are sent away from their over-crowded dwellings into the country for a short time. Thus, the Cottage for Convalescent Women at Shacklewell is much appreciated ; the children who go for a fortnight into the country return looking fresher and stronger; and the proposed Seaside Home for which donations are being received will no doubt soon be established.

The winter work in such a district includes timely help to the poorest of the people, especially when the weather is severe. Morning by morning one hundred and sixty Board School children have a Free Cocoa Breakfast given to them, the tickets being distributed by the masters of several neighbouring schools, who are hardly less gratified than the children themselves. The Irish stew sold at a low price is also exceedingly popular ; and our friend remarks, "Imagine the delight of a family in obtaining half a gallon of really good, thick, leg of beef and vegetable soup, flavoured with celery and mint, and half a pound of bread for 2d.!" The chief thing to be regretted is, that all who come cannot be served.

It will thus be seen that the work is about as comprehensive as it can well be ; and while the blessings of one year, through the Lord's favour, seem to be exceeded by those of the one following, all will pray that Mr. Orsman may long be spared to carry on the work to which he has put his hand. Hoxton is a poor place ; but how much poorer it would be without Costers' Hall, the people themselves would testify, if any were to question them. Mr. Orsman is a brother beloved, from whom we have received nothing but loving comfort. The very thought of him refreshes us, and to see him is a day's holiday. Whoever sends help either to W. J. Orsman, or Archibald Brown, may be sure that he is most effectively aiding the work of the Lord. The same may be said of Mr. W. Olney, jun., of Haddon Hall, Bermondsey, and others who work in connection with our Tabernacle. We glorify God in them.

Crouch Hill Baptist Chapel.

MANY Baptists in Yorkshire, and elsewhere, will long retain the memory of Henry Dowson, of Bradford, a fine, solid, genial soul, with deeply imbedded Strict Communion views. Coming to London in his latter days, he commenced a church in 1878. The meetings of this community were held in an iron building for some ten years. Iron buildings are too hot in summer and too cold in winter; and the very best thing that happens to them is to be pulled down, and done with. This auspicious end was reached in January of this year, 1889; and, like a phœnix rising from its ashes, the handsome red brick building succeeded the uncomfortable ironclad.

In this new building, Mr. Harry Pullen, once a student of the Pastors' College, is labouring with all his might among a people who hold fast the faith. We devote a little space in this magazine to this witnessing church, with the view of winning sympathy and help for them. They have expended nearly £5000 upon the chapel, schools, and so forth; but they have a debt of £1850, which they are anxious to discharge. "A debt is a sin where it can be paid, and an affliction where it must be borne": in the present case it is one of those afflictions which are a great trial of patience. If our wealthier members were truly consecrated, and gave at least a tenth to the Lord, debts would soon disappear; but in the case of the largely rich a tenth would never content their love and zeal; and if they quite fulfilled their indebtedness as stewards, the treasury would overflow. Our duty is. to recommend channels for liberality, and to stimulate its flow, as we do heartily in this case, knowing somewhat of both pastor and officers, and that somewhat being much to our heart's joy. Mr. Pullen, the pastor, lives at 91, Ferme Park Road, Hornsey, N.

The Gospel among the Letts.

THE following brief history of the people of Livonia, known as the Letts, was written in German by Pastor Rumberg, of Riga, and then translated into English; because he wishes to interest the readers of *The Sword and the Trowel* in these poor people, who seem to have been quite overlooked by Christian charity; for as far as he knows, no one has ever lent them a helping hand; and yet we are bidden to " do good unto all men, especially to them who are of the household of faith." Pastor Rumberg's story is a sad and yet an encouraging one: sad, because it tells of the sufferings and cruelties inflicted for centuries upon a poor helpless people; and encouraging, because it shows what the grace of God can do for the forlorn and down-trodden, and how, in spite of the modern criticism which makes the Scriptures out to be a mere work of man, the Word of God is still a power, not only to save, but to change a race of weak, enervated slaves, into men and women who do not flinch from truth, though persecution, stripes, and imprisonment be their lot.

The Letts dwell in the Baltic provinces of Russia, near the Prussian frontier. They are believed to have come originally from India, their language still showing some affinity to Sanscrit. Nine hundred years after Christ, they were a nation of considerable power; their ruler or " Crive," who was also their chief priest, resided in Romöe, which now belongs to East Prussia. Here was also the seat of their three chief gods, before whom a fire was continually burning, kept up by a priest, who, if he neglected it, and allowed it to go out, was himself burned before the gods. The people, strong by reason of their unity, and their absolute obedience to their Crive, carried on a successful war against the celebrated Danish king, Canute the Great, in the tenth century. Some time after, however, their power was broken by the king of Polen, who burned their gods in Romöe; from that time their unity was broken, and all attempts to restore it again were fruitless.

Towards the end of the eleventh century, Germans came over to Lirland, (or Livonia), and Courland, settling there and bringing their culture and their Christianity, such as it was, with them. The " Lires," another tribe of the original inhabitants, fought at first against the Germans; the Letts, however, never joined in these fights, but submitted without resistance to baptism; and were from that time slaves to the Germans, who did not care, neither priests nor nobles, to render Christian charity to the people they had compelled to become Christians. The great landlords, whose serfs they became, treated them no better than cattle, and would sometimes exchange them for dogs. If the grey rocks had tongues, they could tell many a sad story of the wrongs of the poor Letts, who frequently were driven away from their homes, whilst the cruel nobles and the godless priests took possession of their goods. Often, however, the robbers themselves quarrelled about the spoil; and at the time of the Reformation, things had come to such a pass between the priests and the nobles, that the latter requested Luther to send them some of his preachers. This was done, and now the people had to be turned into Lutherans; but the nobles did not find this an easy work, and therefore they built a public-house near every church, the people were made drunken, which was called a " church festival," and in this drunken state, they went to church and were " converted to the Lutheran faith " : the nobles were now the sole rulers over the people. A German author wrote in 1598: " A sadder and more unhappy people than these peasants (serfs), in Lirland, cannot be imagined on the face of God's earth."

In 1804, the emperor Alexander the First demanded the liberation of the serfs in the Baltic provinces, and in 1807 the law of liberation was signed; but it remained a dead letter, because the nobility were the lawgivers for the peasants, and did nothing to protect their rights. The peasants were not allowed to leave the province, nor to live in the towns, or to learn any other work than farming. They could not marry without permission of the lord of the manor, and no peasant could bring an action against his lord without having permission so to do. If the court decided against the lord, he was fined two or three roubles; but if the verdict was against the peasant, he was sentenced to sixty stripes. Until 1833, there were in Courland, a province of 460,000 inhabitants, only five public schools; afterwards, more schools were established, not by the Lutheran church, but by some benevolent noblemen. Virtually, the peasants were serfs until after the Crimean war, when Alexander II. made their emancipation a reality, and gave them the liberty for which they had been sighing so long. While cruelly oppressed, however, many were awakened to seek the salvation of their souls. In 1841, many emigrated to the interior of Russia, and others joined the Greek church, in order to get free from their German tyrants. But in 1847, a movement of another kind began, and rapidly spread. A schoolmaster, who was a believer in Christ, came to a place called Sirjen, in Courland. He led several of his pupils to the Lord, and these tried, in their turn, to bring others to him; and in a short time they commenced meetings for prayer and Scripture reading. The Lutheran clergyman, a good-natured man, considered these converts good church people; but after his death another clergyman came, who began to persecute them. He brought one of his own servants before the court, and had him punished with twenty-five stripes, for refusing to work in the fields on Sundays. Many believers were so shocked by this conduct of their pastor, that they kept away from church; the clergyman went from house to house, threatening them with severe punishment if they did not come, and if they would hold meetings anywhere else. But his threats were fruitless: in spite of them the people continued their meetings. Thereupon he ordered his clerk to take away all religious books from those who attended a meeting. However, even this measure had not the desired effect; the people bought new books, although with heavy hearts, for money was scarce at that time; and then they again attended the meetings. At last, on a very cold day, the pastor sent his clerk to take away from those who were present at the meeting, all their warm clothes—furs, mantles and woollen shawls, and they were obliged to go home in cold and frost, and neither clothes nor books were ever returned to them. Afterwards the clergyman made a complaint before the lord of the manor, that these people did not come to communion. His lordship ordered them thereupon to bring, within a fortnight, a certificate that they had partaken of the Lord's Supper, else they would be driven away from their homes. The pastor himself acting the part of persecutor, the brethren could not receive the communion from his hands, and four peasants were expelled from their homes, the lord of the manor taking possession of their goods, and all who attended the meetings received twenty-five stripes, or were sent to prison. At one time there were forty-two persons in prison, at another seventy; but when the brethren were nearly all expelled, or imprisoned, the sisters conducted the prayer-meetings, in winter-time generally on the frozen rivers.

Notwithstanding all this, the gospel spread from this place to the villages and towns of the neighbourhood; souls were converted everywhere; but persecution, stripes, and imprisonment were everywhere the portion of the converts. About fifteen years later, the brethren became acquainted with German Baptists in East Prussia, and were baptized, and thereby the hatred of the Lutheran clergy was still more increased. Meetings were strictly forbidden everywhere, the children were taken from the parents by force, and christened, and on their being brought back, the parents were told what names the clergyman had given to them. It was generally understood that a Baptist was to be considered like a dog, and might be ill-treated by every one, as he had no human rights. Baptists were not hired as labourers; they were expelled from their homes, their goods were taken, they were hunted up even in the woods where they met for prayer; their marriages were declared invalid, their children illegal, they could not be invested with any office; nothing was granted to them. One instance may suffice to show how exasperated the clergy were. In Sheden, a blacksmith was converted, and had a conversation about the sacraments with the Lutheran pastor, who, in the course of it, became so enraged, that he had the smith beaten until he was unable to rise; and, meanwhile, the pastor trampled with his feet on his head, exclaiming, "It is written, it is written." One brother was thrown into prison nearly every week, and usually left without food for two or three days; but he remained faithful to the truth once received.

However, all the persecutions, and the preaching of the clergy against the Baptists, only helped to make the truth spread further and further. In Riga, the residence of the Governor-General, there was no persecution of Baptists, as the petty tyrants could not have their way under the eyes of the governor; and here the Baptists had a good time from 1871 till 1883. In 1876, the first church was formed in Riga; in 1884, a second one; and in 1886, a third one, numbering together more than eight hundred members.

Since 1879, the Baptists have had religious liberty in Russia, yet they have still to endure oppression, chiefly by the Lutheran clergy. These have rarely a synod without speeches being made about the means of fighting against Baptists. In 1884 one clergyman blamed Lutheran masters for employing Baptist labourers, and proposed that no Lutheran should employ a Baptist. They have written many pamphlets against us which contain untruths, and frequently sent petitions to the Government in St. Petersburg asking that Baptists should not be allowed to receive Lutherans into their churches. Their children are called in the schools "unbaptized heathens"; sometimes they are excluded from school, whilst Baptists are still compelled to pay taxes for Lutheran churches and schools.

In Riga and the neighbourhood is a wide field for labour, but it cannot be worked as it ought, because most of the ministers have to earn their living by working. The first church in Riga built a chapel which is still burdened with a debt of £950, and is, therefore, unable to help others. The second church, of which the writer is the minister, has one hundred and forty members, of whom only fifty are able to contribute anything towards its maintenance. Until 1887, it was a genuine pilgrim church, and had to wander from one place to another. Now a chapel is built which is to be paid for by degrees; but there is no Sunday-school, and no house for the minister. The little church has given eight hundred roubles, but her resources are exhausted, and five thousand five hundred roubles (£550) are still required to complete and furnish it, and make it free of debt. This money it is not possible to get here in Russia, as all our churches are very poor; business is slack, employment hard to be got, all taxes are increased, and the people, having been serfs so long, have no means for building chapels. Many poor Lettish churches are at present in such a condition that they do not know how to get along. Still, they do all they can, and spread the gospel according to their ability.

Having laid the matter before the Lord in prayer, I apply, trusting in him, dear English brethren and Christian friends, to you to help my little church. The mission amongst the Letts is a blessed one; but, as far as I know, it is not supported by anyone. All they have they have gained themselves, struggling against many difficulties; therefore, I ask you again, dear brethren, to come to our help, for help is much needed here, and this poor little nation will never forget your Christian love. We have no money for the purchase of tracts for distribution. Another great and special need is the means for training young men for the work of the ministry. In a word, here is much to be done; and those who have brotherly hearts will find here a work for the Lord which will bear good fruit.

Commending myself and my work to your prayers and brotherly love,
27, Grosse Lagerstrasse, Hagenberg, Riga.   I. RUMBERG.

We will gladly forward any help which may come in for this worthy brother.—C. H. S.

Notices of Books.

Elijah and Ahab. By the late Rev. ALEXANDER EWING. With memoir by Mrs. EWING. Hodder and Stoughton.

IF this were only a wife's loving memorial of her husband, we would receive it with respect; but it is in itself well worth preserving. Mr. Ewing was not a brilliant genius, but he had the art of putting the gospel plainly and in a portable form, and hence he was useful to those who heard him. These sermons upon Elijah and Ahab are very good: condensed, instructive, and practical. Mrs. Ewing has prefaced the discourses with a vivacious and gracious memoir. The friends who bought the former memorial volume will be sure to purchase this also. The price is marked 2s. 6d., but surely this is an error: it is more like a four-shilling volume.

The Pulpit Commentary. Luke (2 vols). Kegan Paul, Trench, and Co.

THE huge enterprise of "The Pulpit Commentary" deserves success, if it were only for the perseverance brought out by it; but this is very far from being all that we can truthfully say of it. Many of the volumes are worthy of the utmost praise; and though others are seriously damaged by the dry rot of modernism, yet, as a whole, the series will prove to be most helpful to those for whom it was prepared. In these two volumes upon Luke, the same plan has been followed as in former portions of the "Commentary," but with rather less of confusion, as the contributors are fewer in number. The doctrine seems to be mildly orthodox, so far as we have been able to test it. Much of highly suggestive thought will be found by the preacher, and he will probably judge Luke to be as well worked out as any of the other books of the New Testament.

Gifford Lectures and Max Müller: their Religion Considered in the Light of Philology and History. By G. GREENLEES, Member of University Council, Glasgow. Simpkin. One shilling and sixpence.

THIS is a very laboured argument on the right side: so elaborate, that we are unable to follow it. Our author will not have it that true religion could be a product of the human mind; but he asserts that it must have come from God himself: this we fully believe. The reasoning of our author is too deep for us; but so is the abominable theory which he denounces. The error plunges into the obscurely profound, and we suppose that the hunter who would slay it must follow it to its lair. Mr. Greenlees' attachment to the Word of God has grown with his increasing years, and he feels it incumbent upon him, as a scholar, to strike at the specious errors which are undermining philosophy, as well as religion. His faith is fixed upon the substitutionary sacrifice, and therefore he speaks out at this crisis, and says, "It may be, my feeble cry will not be in the wilderness without an echo, but may tend to provoke those who ought to speak out—who can do it effectually—so that the crisis upon which we have entered may be passed in safety. May it be so!"

We fear that no protests will be regarded, come from what quarter they may. Judicial blindness has come to the teachers of the age: they have loved falsehood, and after it they will go. It is, however, the duty of every man, whatever the fashion of his mind, to speak out for the truth, whether men will hear or forbear.

Short Biographies for the People. Vol. VI. Religious Tract Society.

LIVES of good men all exhibit grace which made their lives sublime. Walking with God, they leave behind them other footmarks than men make on the sands of time. It is wise to set their shining way before their fellows, that they may learn to follow in their track of light. This is the sixth yearly dozen of brief but valuable biographies, and it is both good and cheap. Get it.

The Great Question Answered; or, God's Way of Salvation. By the Rev. A. METCALFE. Elliot Stock.

AN earnest, simple, little book, treating of the way of salvation. We rejoice to see so clear a testimony borne by a brother in the Church of England. Oh, that every vicar gave forth a certain sound!

Iris: Studies in Colour, and Talks about Flowers. By FRANZ DELITZSCH, D.D. Edinburgh: T. & T. Clark.

THE most profound students must have their recreations. Here we have Delitzsch, who is to our fancy a great deep of Hebrew scholarship—what shall we say?—tossing aloft a little of his spray in the form of right pleasant notes on colour, flowers, and beauty! It is well done. This learned man is as learned in his pleasantries as in his solemn commentaries. He explains to us in the first chapters why the distinctions of colours are so dim in all ancient literature. We see why the evangelists speak of the robe put upon our Lord as purple, and yet as scarlet. The want of colour-judgment, and of words to express shades of colour, is very remarkable: evidently the senses develop as they are exercised. Fancy the grass in Mark being described as of the same colour as the pale horse in the Revelation; yet green was to the ancients a pale colour, as compared with red or blue.

We judge that persons of taste will think this six shillings' worth of pleasant learning a special luxury. We have read it to review it; but our intent is to dive deeper into it when enjoying the light of the sun in our winter retreat. Who knows anything of Iris till he has basked in Italian sunshine?

Manliness, and other Sermons. By HUGH STOWELL BROWN. With Preface by ALEXANDER MACLAREN. D.D. Oliphant and Anderson,

A FAR better memorial of Hugh Stowell Brown than the unhappy life of him which was issued some time ago. In that biography the writer preserved that which should have been thrown away, and threw away that which should have been preserved. No report can preserve a sermon by our departed friend; for his personality, tone, gesture, and eye, all went to make it up; but these written notes are as good a revival of the preacher as we can expect. Mr. Brown was a man by himself, after no school or order. Sometimes you think he is going into the depths of spirituality, and he disappoints you by turning to

some practical matter: at another time he seems to threaten you with a bit of "Down-grade"; yet he gives you nothing of the sort, but the old gospel set forth in words of his own. *He was a man*, and his manliness was, perhaps, so conspicuous that some were frightened about his godliness: but this was strong enough to take care of itself after it had broken through all sorts of mannerisms which were thought to be essential to its life. The greatness of this brother's character refreshes us in the memory of it. There was nothing little about him. Like a colossal figure meant to stand upon a lofty column, there was a lack of finish, neatness, and propriety about him; but the great soul was there, and all Liverpool knew it. We do not feel that his sermons could be models to anybody else; but they did good service as clear testimonies for true religion. The ministry out of which they came was robust, forceful, free from cant, thoroughly English, independent, honest; hence its power.

Four Last Words from the Book of God. By SARAH GERALDINA STOCK. R. J. Masters, 32, Wilton Road, Victoria Station, S.W.

GRACIOUS reflections upon four important matters which come up in the closing verses of the Book of Revelation—such as *the Lamb* and *the Blood.*

The Mystic Voices of Heaven; or, the Supernatural Revealed in the Natural Science of the Heavens. By AN OXFORD GRADUATE. Elliot Stock.

SOMEWHAT mystical, but ever fragrant with reverence to the truth, and love to the Lord Jesus. The astronomical facts which make the warp and woof of this fabric are charming, and the use made of them is ever on the behoof of faith and worship. We have been made to think of Drummond's work while reading this; but we have felt none of the misgivings which haunt us when perusing that book of duplicate interpretations. It is a thick volume, full of quaint poetry, and special starry observations: it is not easy to describe it, but some minds will revel in it, and others will dismiss it as transcendental.

The Scripture Doctrine of the Two Sacraments. A Plea for Unity. By HENRY HARRIS B.D. H. Frowde.

MR. HARRIS wishes us to recognize that those who differ from us in reference to baptism are actuated by the same spirit of faith as ourselves. We do heartily recognize the fact; and we feel happy in living in daily and hearty fellowship with believers of every sect and name. We are one with him in the desire that the greater truths in which we are one should never be overshadowed by the minor opinions upon which we differ.

But these peace-seeking pages of Mr. Harris will not make peace. He fairly yields to us Baptists the points for which we contend, and then goes on with his argument as if his concessions were nothing. He coolly assumes what no mortal can ever prove, and as coolly ignores what none can honestly doubt. His head is as wrong as his heart is right. That he does not agree with us is nothing; but the dear, good rector does not agree with himself. He gives us a brotherly salutation, and we accept it heartily; but when he begins arguing, we do not laugh, for that would be discourteous, but we smile very heartily. Our differences are serious, and we must agree to differ; but we cannot agree to spirit our differences away. Dear Mr. Harris, we will go to the mercy-seat with you, but we shall never aid you in sprinkling an infant; and on that point we honestly feel that you make out a very weak case.

The Kingdom of God; or, Christ's Teaching according to the Synoptical Gospels. By ALEXANDER BALMAIN BRUCE, D.D. Edinburgh: Clark.

WE do not care for this book. It is another of the straws that show which way the wind is blowing. We may, after his "Life of William Denny," and the confessions of this volume, consider Dr. Bruce to be far gone on the same side as Marcus Dods. This would be a grievous fact if it stood alone; but what are we to say of the professor's position? He is not satisfied with the creed of his church, and yet he remains in it. He says, "What to do with our creeds has become, for all the churches, a burning question. That these creeds, centuries old, no longer express perfectly, or even approximately, the living faith of the church, is being frankly acknowledged on every side." Who makes the frank confession we do not know, but we hope they are outside the churches. Why do not those who make the acknowledgment cease from professing to hold such a creed, and so get rid of "the ecclesiastical scandal of making solemn pretence of receiving *ex animo*, what is only submitted to reluctantly as a condition of office"? This passage is Dr. Bruce's own. If that is his position, we feel too strongly to write more. By this professor, and another of the like order, the Free Church is training her future ministers! Those who think her creed antiquated, are to train the men who are to preach it! What the result must be it needs no prophet to foretell.

Raphael Tuck and Sons have aimed, in the first, second, and third place, at novelty, and their catalogue of cards, books, &c., of all sorts and sizes, is a proof of how hard they and their artists have laboured. We are glad to see a selection of religious cards under the head of MIZPAH, and the specimen sent, *Our Defender,* is very good. The two fine *panel cards* of the Madonna are quite out of our line; but the book in which the whole process of raising corn, from sowing to reaping, is set forth, is delightful: its title is, "*The Sower of the Seed.*" This firm issues a great variety of the card-covered books: well illustrated. *The Jackdaw of Rheims* is a work of great genius and humour; every page contains a masterly sketch.

But what can we say of the medley of cards sent us, which show that, while Messrs. Tuck go in for high art, and have cards at a guinea each, they also propitiate the masses with inventions at a penny, or less? *We* do not admire some of these things; but we have often remarked that there are people who think the odd, the comic, the grotesque, and the rough, to be the most striking. Well, everybody can get served here, even if he be refined as Raphael, or rough as a rustic.

The Unchanging Christ, and other Sermons. By Dr. ALEXANDER MACLAREN. Alexander and Shepheard.

WE do not review such sermons as these, but enjoy them. Dr. Maclaren we put in a niche by himself, among those whom we admire and reverence. The only fault we ever find with any sermon of his, is the fact that it comes to an end: we could wish the silver bell to ring on and on, for it never wearies the gracious ear. Friends are sure of the quality, and have only to remember the publishers' names.

Agnostic Fallacies. [Lectures delivered on Sunday evenings]. By Rev. J. REID HOWATT. Nisbet and Co.

WE will waive the question as to the suitableness of these addresses for Sabbath evenings; although we fear that those who could only get to the service once in the day would feel themselves badly fed, by hearing an argument against Agnosticism in lieu of a discourse upon our Lord. These lectures are first-rate; and the preacher was well advised when he agreed to print them. We have seldom seen a matter more wisely handled: the popularity of the lecture is not secured by flimsiness, neither is the clearness of the reasoning destroyed by depth. Reading as a cool critic, and becoming both interested and gratified, we were suddenly pulled up by the following welcome paragraph:—

"Going up the Clapham Road the other day with a friend, we turned aside to see Spurgeon's Orphanage. My friend looked silently for a time on that most touching spectacle of Christian compassion, translated into beautiful and solid deeds, and then he asked, 'Has Agnosticism done anything like this?' And I raked all the embers of history in my mind for a reply—but I have not yet found an Agnostic Orphanage. Have you? Yet Agnosticism is very loud-voiced in her cry that the chief end of man is to serve man. All honour to her cry, all honour to her cry!—but, if you please, we want something more than shouting here, we want *facts*; and this I say—it is the humble Christian worker, and the faithful Christian believer, who is to-day doing more for the benefit of humanity than the loudest-voiced Agnostic of them all. Deeds, if you please, brethren, not words; we are seeking just now for the fruits, and we are not going to be hoodwinked by the leaves."

This is not a big and expensive work; but is in every way adapted for giving freely to enquiring young men. Scepticism is everywhere, it pollutes the very air: so useful a remedy cannot be too widely diffused.

The Children's Angel: a Year's Sermons and Parables for the Young. By Rev. J. REID HOWATT. Nisbet.

MR. HOWATT is a genius in the direction of sermons for children. We do not wonder that he gives the little ones a sermonette at his Sabbath service, for he does the work surpassingly well. Here are fifty-two most useful addresses. Teachers, without actually appropriating Mr. Howatt's language and matter, might read his addresses, and find their own thoughts aroused, and so be directed to useful subjects for their next talks with the children. If anyone imagines that it is more easy to address children than adults, he is very much of a child himself. Our youngsters deserve our best: and, what is more, they will have it, or they will have none. We dare not envy Mr. Howatt, but we hold in high esteem the man who has so evidently received from the Master the commission, "Feed my lambs."

"The Christian" Portrait Gallery. Containing over 100 Life-like Illustrations, with Biographic Sketches. Morgan and Scott.

FOR half-a-guinea, a collection of one-hundred portraits of all the distinguished Christian workers of the period: a noble army indeed. We think the portraits are all good, except those of Mr. and Mrs. Spurgeon, and those are simply horrible. The pictures are well worked off. The difference between rough impressions, hurried off for *The Christian*, and copies carefully taken from the same blocks for this volume, is very great. This Portrait Gallery can claim a high artistic value, and yet the smallness of its price brings it within the means of many. What a capital Christmas-box it would make!

Messrs. Hildesheimer and Faulkner, 41, *Jewin Street, London,* have given a common-place reviewer an impossible task.⁴ Our proper sphere is theological, but this is a far more flowery region, where art, and poetry, and wit, all show their brightest tints, and set before us a Field-of-the-cloth-of-gold, suitable for the season of Christmas and New Year. Hildesheimer and Faulkner send us cards of surpassing taste—some silvered, with raised bronzed birds, are our favourites, and also those which glisten like jewels. The variety before us is well-nigh bewildering, for they run from the most amusing to the most æsthetic. We do not know what to write, but can only marvel that so much talent can find remunerative employment on cards. As for books and booklets, we cannot tell where to begin. Here is *Our Village, by Tom Hood, Illustrated by Sullivan*: a day's holiday. *In the Harbour : a Poem, by George R. Sims, Illustrated by W. Langley,* is as delightful in art as it is painful in subject. Some of the *Ballads* are beyond our range, but *The Shepherd's Daffodil* is marvellously fine. *Songs of the Birds* is a gem most lovely. So is *Happy Childhood,* all aglow with colours. There are four dainty religious booklets for children ; we wish there were more Scriptural cards. We cannot afford more space ; but we would say to those who need such things— write for a catalogue, or ask your bookseller to show you specimens.

"*A* 1." Vol. II.
The Family Friend. Vol. XX. New Series.
The Mothers' Companion. Vol. III.
The Friendly Visitor. New Series. Vol. XXIII.
The Children's Friend. Vol. XXIX.
The Infants' Magazine. Vol. XXIV.
The British Workman. Vol. XXXV.
The Band of Hope Review. Vol. XXXIX. S. W. Partridge and Co.

THESE magazines, as they lie before us in the form of gorgeous annual volumes, are beyond all praise. We do not single out one from the rest, because they are all equally good ; or, rather, each one is a little better than the other. Our marvel is that such a set of periodicals should have sprung up in one place. They are like a constellation of stars — bright, clear, sparkling. It requires no little talent to make one monthly succeed ; what must it be to carry on so many ? In the course of years serials wear thin ; the vein of originality is exhausted, and the life sobers down. But these periodicals renew their youth, and are as fresh as when they began their race. Many other publications have arisen, but none have excelled these messengers of grace, and temperance, and peace, and love. Spread them everywhere.

Boys and Girls who have Risen. A Prize Book for Mission Schools. Edited by G. H. PIKE. Passmore and Alabaster. Price 1s. 6d.

MR. PIKE has had a good sale for this little book which he has edited ; and we do not wonder, for it is full of stories of a sort which are not commonly met with. He has nearly sold all his edition of two thousand.

Cottage Lectures ; or, Short Readings for Mothers' Meetings. Ten Lectures on Health and how to keep it. By AGNES C. MAITLAND. Nisbet.

GOOD practical talk of the kind that most poor mothers need, about food, and air, and cleanliness, and housekeeping. Wise. Sensible.

After Shipwreck. By J. A. OWEN. Authors' Co-operative Publishing Company.

MRS. OWEN has gone through a great deal. We like her adventures better than the tales of fiction. She writes very well. The story of Mary Wallis, of Ewell, and her building the little chapel, and getting Rowland Hill to open it, is a really beautiful bit. She was a servant with only £8 a year, and yet built a little chapel, and kept the gospel lamp burning in Ewell. We have read "After Shipwreck" with considerable refreshment. Each article of the nine is first-rate.

Songs and Poems for Children. Edited by CARRIE DAVENPORT. John Hogg.

ALL the children's favourites of the olden time and now, with sixty pictures which will win their eyes as the verses woo their ears. Only three silver sixpences.

Upon the Religious Tract Society's four larger annuals we would briefly say that they are all noble volumes. We have always liked *The Leisure Hour*, it is so instructive and fresh: its range of subjects is wide, and its tone is high. *The Sunday at Home* appears to us excellent; but we had several complaints against it last year, and several friends say they do not like it so well as they used to do. From a literary and artistic point of view it can hardly be surpassed; but these are not the all-in-all for Sundays at home. *The Boys' Own Paper* and *The Girls' Own Annual* are all that boys and girls want for amusement and instruction. Wonderful are the pictures, and the tales, and the details of sports and handicrafts. Neither of the volumes can be charged with dragging in religion unseasonably; we half wish they could be, it would be like the Catholic's venial sin—a fault which deserves to be forgiven.

Sunlit Days. Selections of Poems from various authors.
Alpine Summits. Verses by Rev. CHARLES FOX, M.A. Sketches by E. St. B. H.
You may Pick the Daisies. By E. S. ELLIOTT.
Around the Throne.
Rest in the Lord. A Daily Text Book, with Verses by Mrs. PENNEFATHER and others. Illustrations by E. L., and E. St. B. H.
Silver Linings. Echoes of the Bells. Sowing. Reaping. Stepping Stones. James E. Hawkins.

SOME of these productions are real works of art; as, for instance, *Echoes of the Bells, Sowing, Reaping, Silver Linings*. But they are all excellent of their kind. The spiritual is blended with the beautiful. If our readers are giving presents, and like the order of publications which consist of verses, and pictures in Indian ink and colours, all done up in white paper covers, they should write to Mr. Hawkins for a price list.

The Century Illustrated Monthly Magazine. Vol. XXXVIII. T. Fisher Unwin.

THIS magazine is unique. In many features it excels all others. It has no claim on our pages from a religious point of view; but as a literary periodical, it is fresh and piquant.

"Our Darlings." Annual Volume. Shaw and Co.

OUR good friend, Dr. Barnardo, does everything in a marvellous style; he is not only a great worker, but a real genius. What a book for the young is this sparkling volume! Even in the paper binding which comes to us, it is sure to fascinate the youngsters. In pictures, coloured and otherwise, it abounds. How does the doctor manage it all?

Somebody's Darling. By C. SHAW. Shaw and Co.

THIS is so much in the same style, without and within, that we put it with the other darling of a book. It is an extraordinary production for two shillings. What a Christmas box! Somebody's darling shall have it. Bless her! That she shall.

Bemrose and Son again issue *three Calendars*, which we have long used with much pleasure. The bold figure for the date is visible from every part of our study, and catches the eye when a letter has to be dated. *The Scripture Calendar* has texts; *the Proverbial* has proverbs, and the *Daily* is simply the large figure for the day of the month.

The Sunday School Union also issues a similar *Calendar*, which bears, in addition, the afternoon subjects for the International lesson.

Sunshine for 1889. *Little Star for* 1889. Edited by W. M. WHITTEMORE, D.D. G. Stoneman.

Sunshine is cheap enough at 1s. 6d.—it is the next thing to giving it away. *Little Star*, at the same price, is all pictures and very large type, for the very little ones. Dr. Whittemore is never content unless he is editing periodicals: he is a born editor.

Early Days for 1889. 2 Castle Street, City Road.

THIS is not the very best or largest of juvenile magazines; but it has a freshness and an individuality about it which we like. It deserves a large constituency.

Follow the Right. A Tale for Boys. By G. E. WYATT. Nelson and Sons.

THE story of an almost impossibly gallant youth from Eton, who does everything that is true, noble, and self-forgetting, and, by this means, reconciles his father to the great lord who would not own the family because the mother's marriage did not please him. Boys who are at public schools will best appreciate the story. The printers and binders have done their work admirably.

The Sleepers Awakened; or, the Artist's Little Model. By ALFRED E. KNIGHT. Houlston and Sons.

A LITTLE story in which a holy child teaches an infidel father the way of peace. Touching and teaching, though the narrative is improbable. One of the best-intentioned tales we have ever read, and saturated with a faith which will make it live. A specially good shilling's-worth, because of the truths taught, and the necessity for laying emphasis upon them just now.

Timothy Tatters. A Story for the young. By T. M. CALLWELL. Nelson and Sons.

A CAPITAL Anglo-Irish story : comical, but good. If all Land-leagues would end as this does, England and Ireland would both be happy.

Master Travers. By FLORENCE M. STORY. Nelson and Sons.

ABSURD actions of a young gentleman, aged seven and a half, who comes in for a mansion, and a large estate. We cannot see any use either in writing or reading such nonsense.

Diarmid; or, Friends in Kettletown. By ROBINA F. HARDY. Oliphant, Anderson, and Ferrier. [Popular Shilling Series].
Kilcarvie. Same author and publishers.

MISS HARDY has a marvellous faculty for story-telling, and her facile pen runs on "from grave to gay, from lively to severe": here is Scotch humour at its drollest; and anon, touches of tearful pathos, and even tragedy. Throughout all we have seen of her lively character-sketches there runs a thread of pure religious teaching. We had just finished *Diarmid* when *Kilcarvie* found its way to the operating table; but *Diarmid* has disarmed us, and forced us to lay aside the scalpel, and commend this new subject to those who can spare five shillings.

Amaranth's Garden. By MARGARET SCOTT HAYCROFT. Partridge & Co.

THE teaching of this tender story is very salutary. It conducts a soul through doubt and hardness of heart back to faith and love. It is hardly probable that such a history could ever actually occur; but the fiction is extremely fascinating, and is exceedingly well told.

John Winter, a Story of Harvests. By EDWARD GARRETT. Partridge & Co.

A PRODIGAL returns converted, with the earnest desire to undo the mischief he has wrought; but things have gone beyond undoing, and, after attempting his utmost, he has to leave the scene of his former errors defeated, and sad at heart. This is a clever story, and an earnest spirit breathes through it; but, after admitting its singular talent and its good intent, we are forced to say that it is too much of a novel for our taste, and that we end it wearied of its strained positions and actions. The clothes of the characters are too tight, and they move with mannerisms too consistent, and too closely fitting, for real life. No; we do not think we should urge anyone to read it; and yet, if they are resolved to read a novel, they might go far before they found a better one.

The Yarl's Yacht. By JESSIE M. E. SAXBY, author of "The Lads of Lunda," &c. Nisbet.

A SINGULAR story, which some will greatly enjoy: we cannot say that we have done so. The style is laboured and wearisome, but the tone and spirit are healthy.

Aunt Kelly's Christmas-Box. By JENNIE CHAPPELL.
Ronald's Reason. By Mrs. S. C. HALL.
The Church Mouse. By Mrs. BURGE SMITH. Partridge and Co.

THREE sweet little sixpenny books. Very pretty without and within.

Around the Wicket Gate ; or, a Friendly Talk with Seekers concerning Faith in the Lord Jesus Christ. By C. H. SPURGEON. Passmore & Alabaster.

IT came into the author's heart to write a shilling book to help souls over the threshold, that they might really enter by the gate at the head of the way. To win eyes that look for pictures, a number of woodcuts have been interwoven with the simple, homely, earnest talk. In this way, the author, while away from his pulpit, hopes to keep on preaching. He begs his friends to scatter this little book in all directions.

The Salt-Cellars. Being a Collection of Proverbs, together with Homely Notes thereon. By C. H. SPURGEON. Vol. II.—M to Z. Passmore & Alabaster.

AN eminent and venerable writer, to whom we sent SALT-CELLARS, writes us in return, "*Salt-Cellars!* Why it is a mine of salt; and I shall descend into it for wisdom, for months to come, without reaching the bottom of it." He has prepared many a work himself, and knows what salt is.

The King's Own. A Monthly Magazine for the Study and the Home. Edited by Rev. JOHN URQUHART. No. 1, price sixpence. J. F. Shaw.

OUR excellent brother, John Urquhart, has now commenced a magazine of his own, where he may speak his mind and bear his witness without let or hindrance. This first number is a happy prophecy of what we are to expect. In *The King's Own, The Sword and the Trowel* welcomes an ally. Mr. Urquhart may be trusted to defend revealed truth against the flippant criticism of the period. He has courage, capacity, and dogged perseverance. We wish him the largest success in his venture, for the truth's sake, and for the church's sake. Every one who is attached to the orthodox faith should rejoice to see another publication pledged to its advancement, and he should, as far as possible, support it. *The King's Own* opens as a high-class magazine, worthy of the study and the parlour; and those who read its first number will confess that nothing better in religious literature has appeared for many a day.

The Nonconformist Historic Service of Song. By LIBERTAS. Price fourpence. F. S. Sheldrick, Cambridge.

WE had imagined that the "Service of Song" business, had been worked so threadbare that freshness could not possibly be introduced into it. But this present issue is, so far as we can see, an entirely new and singularly fruitful line of things. It is to give a brief but inspiring history of the brave endurance of our ancestors in securing for us our religious liberties, and to interweave with the story, specimens of the sacred songs in which their souls delighted. The literary portion is written in a fine, manly, breezy style, packed closely with solid information, whilst the music—mainly the good, old-fashioned hymns and tunes so sneered at by many to-day—has been chosen with excellent taste. Such a service of song could not fail greatly to edify all who hear it, and endear to them the principles of our holy faith. It ought to sell by thousands, and bring a good financial return, all of which, we understand, is to be used to cheer and help our village pastors. "Now, Mr. Superintendent and Mr. Choir-leader, give your orders, and get the thing done quickly."

My Strongholds of Love. Words of Good Cheer to the Suffering and Sorrowful. By the Rev. GEORGE EVERARD, M.A. Tract Society.

GRACIOUS and experimental. Will comfort mourners.

Beyond the Stars: or, Heaven, its Inhabitants, Occupations, and Life. By THOMAS HAMILTON. D.D. Edinburgh: T. and T. Clark.

WE remember enjoying this book at its first appearance. We are glad that there are enough thoughtful people left to warrant a second edition. It is a bright and hopeful book, but free from romance and idle dreaming.

The Sunday-school Teacher's Pocket-Book for 1890. Sunday School Union.

A SUNDAY-SCHOOL teacher who pockets this pocket-book, will be greatly helped in keeping his appointments; at any rate, he will keep them in memory, a great point in appointments.

45

What is a Christian? A Sermon preached in St. Giles' Cathedral, in connection with the Edinburgh University Gathering, September 29, 1889. By MARCUS DODS, D.D. Edinburgh : Macniven and Wallace.

As every man will endeavour to create Christians of the kind which he believes in, this Free Church professor will, no doubt, produce Christians and ministers who treat the Bible as they please, and doubt the Godhead of the Lord Jesus. Every seed produces after its kind, and the Free Church will soon be full of "true Christians who find much in the Bible which they cannot accept." Well may the Socinians sound their trumpets of victory. They could not find in all their ranks a scholar who could serve their cause so efficiently as Dr. Dods will do through this sermon.

One thing, however, is matter for congratulation : the sermon is issued by its author. He does not cavil about the inaccuracy of notes, and so forth, as a coward would do. Like a man, he throws down the gauntlet, and is ready to abide the consequences. This is as it should be. We shall now see where the Free Church of Scotland really is. Between the precious and the vile this sermon will develop a clear dintinction ; and we trust it will be thoroughly done. To stop the sifting would be the height of unwisdom. Anything is better than unholy compromise. The question at issue is well raised by this discourse, and it should be fought out with all calmness and good temper, but with the solemn resolve that truth shall be maintained, and all lowering of the standard shall be opposed, tooth and nail. The ages to come look down upon the conflict of the present : to-day is fashioning morrows of darkness or of joy. Let every man take his place, and do his work.

Word Studies in the New Testament. By MARVIN R. VINCENT, D.D. Vol. II. The Writings of John. The Gospel. The Epistles. The Apocalypse. New York: Charles Scribner's Sons.

A BOOK ! A book ! Dr. Vincent does not expound every verse at length, but he gives most thought-breeding notes on special verses as they occur. We hope this portly work will be published in England. It is the kind of book which we value beyond all others, a book which deals with the original, and fetches from its words the teaching which they were meant to convey— teaching which, in some cases, a translation does not present to us. Only the devout and thoughtful will care about such instruction, but *they* will prize it highly. The work is, in measure, a compilation from the best writers, but yet it has an originality about it which the reader will soon perceive.

Three Years in Central London. A Record of Principles, Methods, and Successes. By EDWARD SMITH, Wesleyan Minister. T. Woolmer.

A NARRATIVE full of interesting facts, handled by shrewd common sense. Mr. Smith writes from experience about matters which he has tested. God has blessed him, and he has succeeded in raising a church in Clerkenwell ; and in this record he narrates the results of experiments, as well as the outcome of that which is no experiment, namely, preaching the gospel, and visiting from door to door. He has tried the Social plans, and found them all failures. His testimony is invaluable as a support to those who keep on the old lines. Our heart has rejoiced as we have read views in which we perfectly agree, and stories which support them beyond dispute. Fiddling, and bagatelle, and comic singing, and all manner of dodges have been tried, but nothing succeeds like the gospel of our Lord Jesus Christ. We must make an article out of this book. Meanwhile, *buy it.* It is only 1s.

Hymns of our Pilgrimage. By Rev. JOHN BROWNLIE. Nisbet and Co. .

Too good to find fault with, but hardly good enough for unreserved praise. Like the most of modern verse, pleasing, but not of the first order of poetic thought.

The Yearly Bible Text-book for Children. G. Stoneman.

NOT worth publishing. As an exercise in finding texts, anybody could have prepared it.

Notes.

THRICE happy are we in having for a co-pastor one who is not only *our* brother, but is recognized by all the church-officers as *their* brother. We do not leave the flock without a pastor tried and proved, who will, for Christ's sake, look after every department of service with watchful care. We can never express our obligation to God for such a helper. The College has his constant attention in a thousand ways, which must remain unknown until the day declares it; and the same may be said of the Orphanage, wherein he is indefatigable in his watchfulness. We ask prayer for him that he may be sustained in health and vigour, both for the Tabernacle and for Croydon. Our hope is that, during our absence, nothing may flag, and specially that a great many may come forward to join the church.

We are not going to our quiet retreat because of ill-health, but in the hope of refreshment for that weariness of mind which is inevitable with such a charge as we have to bear. Many men have been taken away by death, or have been laid aside by failure of brain, through not taking rest. It is an economy of time to take off the collar for a little. Our vacation is mainly spent in gathering new subjects for another spell of sermonizing; and when we have been well enough to use it in that way, it has enabled us to keep on preaching and printing through the rest of the year. During our absence *the sermon comes out week by week* as usual, and some of those Thursday discourses which have been asked for are sure to appear.

"Christmas comes but once a year;
When it comes, it brings good cheer."

So have the children at Stockwell Orphanage found it hitherto. It has been a grand event in their lives, never to be forgotten. Kind friends, far and near, have generously made it a day of overflowing bounty, and hilarious delight. The new shillings and the boxes of figs have never failed; and there has been enough for poor mothers and aunts on the day after the feast. Our readers will not forget our family of five hundred. An old lady of ninety-nine said that, if she lived another year, she should be a *centurion*. Good for a blunder; but we are a five-fold centurion, for we lead a band of five hundred, besides women and men, who teach, manage, and nurse them. It needs a good deal of meat, pudding, cake, tea, and sweets to make up a merry Christmas : but it needs no wine or strong drink; the boys supply the spirits, nobody whines, but there are plenty of rum little fellows and funny folks, both on the girls' and boys' side. I am deputed to say to all and sundry, we, the children of Stockwell, wish you a happy Christmas, and we hope you will remember again those whom you have so kindly remembered in happy days gone by.

Volume the first of THE SALT-CELLARS met with so hearty a reception that the first edition of five thousand has almost all gone. This is encouraging. In our judgment the second is better. By long acquaintance with the proverbial lore of all nations and periods of time, we have been able to make these two volumes a storehouse of old saws, quaint sayings, folk-lore, and homely sentences.

We should be under great indebtedness to loving friends if they would use special exertions to get us new subscribers. All old magazines feel that the new ones make a draw upon them. We have no cause for complaint, but as the circulation of the magazine is, under God, the means of sustaining our various works, by interesting friends in them, we hope we shall not go backward, but forward, next year. Our endeavour is to keep our pages fresh and lively, and we judge that we succeed, because we constantly see our matter in newspapers, and other periodicals; and requests to reprint this, that, and the other, come so thick and fast that we cannot comply with them. What others borrow cannot be without value. Please get us new subscribers, and we will do better, if there be any better in us. To buy the volume for the year would also be most helpful to us; and we think the purchaser would have an interesting volume for his five shillings. The volume will be ready directly. Our appeal in this case is not to everybody; but to those choice friends who love us, and generously feel that our work is their work. In January we hope to sketch our journey to Mentone, with personal notes, that we may seem to visit our friends at the New Year. If critics grumble that we say much about Number One, we set over against it the fact that our readers ask for more of the same, and wish us to keep up the personal, almost family, character of our magazine. It is, and is meant to be, an autobiographical journal; and those who do not care for this feature can always escape the trial by letting it alone. To please everybody is a task we leave to our more severe critics, wishing them every success.

We are requested by our publishers to call special attention to the large number of literary advertisers who use this month's magazine. Christmas requirements are well provided for. We take pleasure in many of these works, because we have reviewed and commended them. Apologies are due to some publishers whom we are compelled to keep waiting. We have many notices in type for January. Our space is not adequate to the demand upon it made by books; but we will do our best to notice all that are fit for our pages.

Years ago, *the Surrey Gardens' Music Hall* was the scene of a great work of grace under our ministry. That building has utterly disappeared; but not so the result of the services held therein. Thousands remain to praise God for their conversion in the Surrey Gardens. For these twenty years we have had a school near the spot, in the Carter Street Lecture Hall; and the school would be there still, had not the clergyman of the district secured that building for church purposes. For this we do not blame him; but it has put our school to sad trouble. The workers have kept together in a Board School-room, and have been maturing their plans. Our deacon, Mr. Higgs, has secured ground for them; and now they propose to build a Mission Hall and Schools as *the Surrey Gardens' Memorial.* Some £2,000 will be required, and more than £600 is already promised to start with. Of that sum we have promised £100, and so we can fairly ask our friends at the Tabernacle to take the matter up, and carry it through, while we are absent. It may be we ask too much; but it would be a great pleasure if, in memory of the Lord's goodness to us in the Surrey Gardens, this affair were taken up, and carried through with a holy enthusiasm. Moneys should be sent to the superintendent of our Sabbath-school, Mr. S. R. Pearce, 426, Brixton Road, S.W., or to C. H. Spurgeon.

Week by week persons come forward to join the church at the Tabernacle. On the last Monday but one before leaving, Pastor C. H. S. saw a large number, and was able to accept twenty to be proposed for fellowship. Better than all other prosperity is this of soul-winning. A measure of blessing rests permanently on all the works. We have enjoyed one steady, unbroken Revival for some six-and-thirty years. Let the name of the Lord be magnified!

On *Monday evening, October* 21, the new members who have joined the Tabernacle church during the past few months, were invited to meet for tea and Christian counsel. Nearly two hundred were present, and a very profitable season was spent. Brief addresses upon the privileges and responsibilities of church-members were delivered by Pastors C. H. and J. A. Spurgeon, and Messrs. W. Stubbs and W. Olney. In so large a church as ours, it is necessary to make special efforts to enable the members to become acquainted with the officers, and with one another; and also to explain more fully than can be done in public all that is meant by joining the church.

The *prayer-meeting in the Tabernacle* was specially on behalf of Sunday-school and Ragged-school work. The Pastor presided, and he was supported by a goodly array of brethren connected with the home and branch schools. Several of them offered prayer. The Pastor spoke to teachers and parents upon the importance of putting the truth very clearly before the children entrusted to their care, and also upon the need of personal dealing with each one, with a view to their conversion while they are yet young. It was a good meeting, and much power was poured out upon those who led us in supplication. Some of us are burdened with the problem—How is it that the children of London pass through Sunday-schools, and yet so large a percentage of them never attend public worship after they have grown up?

On *Tuesday, October* 22, the annual meeting of Mr. DUNN'S BIBLE-CLASS was held in the Tabernacle lecture-hall, which was crowded. After prayer by Mr. Bullivant, Mr. Hudson, the secretary, presented the report, which was a very encouraging one. There are nearly one hundred and fifty members in the class, most of whom are engaged in Christian work. During the past year, the class has raised £65 for the College and Spanish Mission funds. In thanking the members for their generous gift, the Pastor spoke of the labours of our brethren, Wigstone and Blamire, in Spain, and then impressed upon his hearers the importance of thoroughly studying their Bibles, first for their own growth in grace, and afterwards that they might teach others also. After congratulating the class upon having such an excellent leader as Mr. Dunn, the Pastor, in the name of the members, presented a number of valuable books to Mr. Lee, who leads the singing. Addresses were given by Messrs. Allison, E. H. Bartlett, Dunn, Gray, Stocks, and Alderton; and Mr. Chamberlain, Miss Limbert, and other sweet singers lent their voices. Mr. Bartlett's account of a young man led into gambling by games which he learned at *an Institute,* was a truthful and seasonable warning against the methods so current at this hour. We will give the speech very soon.

On *Wednesday evening, October* 23, the annual meeting of MRS. STIFF'S BIBLE-CLASS, which meets in one of the rooms at the Orphanage, was held at 197, Clapham Road, under the presidency of Mr. Stiff. After singing and prayer, and an address by the chairman, the annual report was presented. This stated that there are now 45 members in the class, 38 of whom are in union with various churches. 234 articles have been made or given for the Orphanage, beside £10 5s. 2d. for the same object, £4 13s. 1d. for Zenana Mission, and £2 18s. 6d. for Lansdowne Place Ragged-school. During the ten years of its existence, 214 members have joined the class, 21 have become Sunday-school teachers, 30 have married, and 3 have gone to join the class above; while the sum of £130 14s. 10d. has been raised for various objects, and 2,243 garments have been presented to the Orphanage. Christian young women, residing in the neighbourhood of Stockwell, will be heartily welcomed any Sunday afternoon.

On *Monday evening, October* 28, at the Tabernacle prayer-meeting, after a few hymns and prayers, and a brief address by the Pastor upon the need of greater faith in God concerning our work, Mr. Millican, the secretary of the TABERNACLE LOAN TRACT SOCIETY, read the annual report of that useful portion of our service for the Lord. As the result of the tract-distributors' visits, many have been induced to attend the Tabernacle, or to send their children to the Sunday-school, while several have found the Saviour through reading the Pastor's sermons, which are left at 8,000 houses weekly. Mr. Harrald reported an expenditure of £26 6s. 6d., and £3 6s. 9d. balance in hand; and also gave particulars of the Mothers' Meeting, Maternal Society, and Sick Fund connected with this Tract Society, all of which had a balance on the right side. It is curious how each Society gets its surroundings after the manner of a church. God bless them all!

Mr. Cornell read the report and accounts of the SPURGEON'S SERMONS' TRACT SOCIETY. This Society supplies distributors at a distance with the Pastor's sermons in covers, so that they can be used as loan-tracts. During the past year 17,990 have been sent to various parts of the country; and in many instances they have been blessed to the conversion or comfort of their readers. All the funds needed for this work have been forthcoming, and the year closed with a small balance in hand. With more means, more sermons could be furnished to friends all over England, who lend them out.

Our thoughts were then directed to the foreign mission-field by the presence of Mr. Wilkinson, who was about to go to the Congo, and Mr. Robert Spurgeon, kinsman of the Pastor, who was returning, as a missionary of the Baptist Mission, to India.

On *Tuesday, October* 29, the autumnal meeting of the SURREY AND MIDDLESEX BAPTIST ASSOCIATION was held at Wimbledon. It was a joy to be present at the morning gathering for prayer and praise. There was a full muster of pastors and delegates, and from the opening hymn and supplication to the close of the hour of prayer, all were of one heart and one mind. The business of the Association was speedily despatched, and then Mr. Harrald read the Circular Letter on "The Atoning Efficacy and Vicarious Nature of the Death of Christ." This paper is admirably suited for distribution at the present time. It can be obtained of Pastor G. Wright, Kingston-on-Thames, for 1d., or in quantities at 5s. per hundred. In the afternoon, Mr. Spurgeon preached to a crowded congregation in the Congregational Chapel, and at night there was an enthusiastic public meeting in the Baptist Chapel. Mr. Ingram and his friends entertained the Association right royally, and we trust that the Wimbledon churches will be largely benefited through the day's proceedings. We wonder that more of our brethren do not join this Association: it seems ordained of God to be a refuge, and to become a power for good.

On *Monday evening, November* 4, after praise and prayer by various brethren, Mr. William Olney commended to the Lord Mr. A. Day, a student of the College, who was about to go to Agra. The Pastor delivered an address upon mission work, condemning erroneous notions with regard to missions to the heathen. He spoke of the plan of sending out men "without purse or scrip." He had no objection to those going out in that fashion who felt called to do so; but he would not like to have any part in inducing them so to go. When our Lord Jesus, on one occasion, gave the special command to certain evangelists (Matt. x.), the people generally were very favourably disposed towards him; but afterwards, when the chief priests had stirred them up to hatred of the Nazarene, the Saviour changed his message, and said, "But now, he that hath a purse, let him take it, and likewise his scrip." There are regions in which a man might safely trust to the kindness of the people to feed and lodge him; but in other parts, anyone following out a rule never intended to be general, would simply starve. Missionary heroism is to be commended wherever it is found, but no man should act contrary to the dictates of common sense. Prayer was offered for a young brother about to sail for the Cape Colony, and another for Mr. Read, one of the students, who was leaving for the United States. In a brief closing address, the Pastor referred to the resignation and faith of certain members of the church in times of trial. One brother had suffered severely through being run over by a reckless driver; but he had seen the hand of the Lord in it, since he was thus driven out of a business which was not helpful to piety.

On *Wednesday evening, November 6*, MR. CHARLES COOK, of Hyde Park Hall, delivered his lecture on " The Prisons of the World " to an audience which almost filled the Tabernacle. The Pastor presided. For nearly two hours, Mr. Cook kept us interested by his narration of experiences in visiting various prisons at home and abroad. In foreign countries, his object has been the distribution of bread, and the Scriptures, among the poor wretches who are languishing in horrible dens. To make public the condition of prisoners is a work which must have the best results. Mr. Cook's closing appeal must have left a deep impression on many of his hearers. A large company of Mr. Cook's co-workers at the Hyde Park Hall sang, and added greatly to the interest of the proceedings. A collection was made for the Prison Bible-distribution Fund ; and we hope that the story of the Prison-mission will move others to invite Mr. Cook to their chapels, or in some other way supply him with means for this Christ-like service.

On *November* 11, the Pastor presided at the last Monday evening prayer-meeting before his departure for a season of rest ; and this fact naturally gave the tone to the supplications. Mr. Allison, as one who had often been with him in his retirement, pleaded that this time his visit to the sunny South might be specially helpful ; and Mr. Young, of the Collingwood Street Mission, followed with a fervent prayer. Mr. William Olney, jun., gave an interesting account of Haddon Hall, and prayed for increased blessing upon the Pastor and the whole church. Mr. Burnham thanked the brethren and sisters for their constant remembrance of the Evangelists, and sang the hymn "In the hollow of his hand." Mr. Matthews spoke of his labours among the aborigines of Australia; Mr. Chamberlain sang in his own touching manner; Mr. Samuel Thompson and Mr. Charles Cook prayed ; Mr. William Olney impressed upon the members the importance of keeping everything up to the mark during the Pastor's absence; and the meeting was closed with the recital by the Pastor of some of his Mentone experiences, and a plea for undertaking the erection of "Surrey Gardens' Memorial Schools" while he would be away. It was a notable night, and fitly concluded a long series of prayer-meetings, which are probably without parallel in the history of the church of Christ.

COLLEGE.—During the past month Mr. A. J. Reid has accepted the pastorate at Shoreham, Sussex, and Mr. J. S. Adams, at Whitchurch, Shropshire. Mr. Albert Read has completed his College course, and sailed for the United States. We commend him to American friends.

Mr. A. G. Short, who has long been in feeble health, is now sufficiently restored to resume pastoral work, and he takes charge at Sandown. Mr. J. S. Morris has resigned his position at Leyton, to devote himself to the students at Harley House, Bow, where he will be theological lecturer, and superintendent of evangelistic work. He will also be pastor at Empson Street, Bow. We wish him the largest possible success in every part of his service for the Lord.

Two of our young brethren have been called home within the past few weeks. Mr. J. C. Travers was the earnest pastor at Holbeach for about three years; he had recently accepted an invitation to Carrington, Nottingham, but passed away in his sleep on October 24th, after suffering greatly through heart-disease. Mr. J. L. Keys, junr., only left the College in the beginning of this year, and settled at Tenbury, Worcestershire ; and on October 29th, after a brief but trying illness, he went to his rest and reward. We deeply sympathize with the bereaved relatives of both our brethren.

Mr. Patrick, our missionary in Tangier, writes:—" Many hindrances have come to us concerning the work in the last few weeks. A poor Spanish woman had medicine and lotion from our dispensary. In mistake, she drank the lotion, came to our hospital, and died in half-an-hour. No blame could rightly be attached to us, but many have kept away in consequence. Our caretaker has had a heavy fall. To-day our interpreter has gone down with fever. George Barlow, formerly belonging to Brother Carlile's church, but during the last year servant to Dr. Churcher, has been called home. Typhoid fever was the cause of death. The waters have been rolling over us, but we cling to the cross. Our meetings for a few weeks were much thinner, but last Sunday over one hundred and fifty gathered together. Two professed conversion. We have started an adult school."

We hope that we shall soon be able to send out to North Africa a second brother in connection with our College Missionary Association. An esteemed brother minister writes:—" I am deeply interested in the accounts I have seen of your missionary movement in Africa; and write to ask, if we could raise the salary, could you send out another man? I am more and more convinced that the right way to create a missionary spirit is to have a missionary sent out and supported by the church."

Mr. G. H. Harris, who went out to the Falkland Islands, has succeeded so well in forming a Baptist Church at Port Stanley, that he and his friends have resolved to build a chapel. Mr. Natt, the good brother who induced us to send out Mr. Harris, is now in England, and he has brought with him the money (partly borrowed) for the purchase and shipment of an iron building, which is now on its way to the Falklands. We have been able to contribute towards the cost; and our good deacon, Mr. Higgs, and his helper Mr. Cox, have assisted with their business knowledge. We trust this work will have a rich blessing resting upon it. If some wealthy brother would send £100 towards it, we should praise the Lord greatly.

On *Friday evening, November* 8, the London members and associates of the Pastors' College Evangelical Association met for tea, prayer, and conference at the College. A large number attended, and a most profitable season was spent. The President reminded the brethren that the Prize Essays on the Sabbath were to be sent in by January 1st, 1890, and announced that Professors Gracey, Fergusson, and Marchant, with himself if necessary, would be the adjudicators. Next Conference (D.V.) to be held on April 21—25, 1890. The President then suggested as a subject for meditation—*Serving Christ in Christ's company.* Brethren Douglas, Shindler, Williams, F. H. White, J. A. Brown, Lardner, and Keys took up the theme, and the President closed with a brief address. The Lord was with us, and we found it good to be there.

EVANGELISTS.—We have received cheering reports of *Messrs. Fullerton and Smith's* services at Tonbridge, Stowmarket, Hadleigh, and Oxford. In each place they have left behind them impressions that will not be erased, and some who will throughout eternity bless the Lord that they heard them preach and sing the gospel.

The great event of the past month has been the visit of our brethren to the Tabernacle. We have to finish the magazine so early that we must leave particulars till next month; but every effort has been put forth to ensure the success of the services; and we expect to hear of much blessing as the result of their coming. This month they are to be at Carlisle, and Gravesend; finishing the year, as usual, with the watch-night service at the Tabernacle.

Pastor W. E. Lewis writes, concerning *Mr. Burnham's* services at the Gospel Mission, Leicester:—" The Lord used him more particularly to the deepening of spiritual life in Christians; several backsliders were restored, and many unconverted ones deeply impressed." From Leicester our brother went to Sutton St. James, Lincolnshire, where Pastor D. C. Chapman reports that great blessing rested upon the Word preached and sung. Mr. Burnham has since been at Dunstable; and this month he will be engaged at Canonbury Hall, Lewisham; Stedham, Sussex; and Blindley Heath.

Pastor J. W. Campbell writes concerning *Messrs. Harmer and Chamberlain's* services at Wisbech:—" Their mission has been richly blessed to saint and sinner. Throughout the meetings we have had the grand old gospel forcibly and faithfully put before us in speech and song; saints have been refreshed and revived, and sinners have been convicted and converted." Mr. Campbell's deacon, Mr. R. B. Dawbarn, also writes, confirming his pastor's testimony to the usefulness of the mission.

Mr. Harmer's next engagement was at Manvers Street Chapel, Bath. Concerning the services there, Pastor H. F. Gower reports :—" We had enquirers after every meeting, and many professed decision. Our church, too, has been blessed with a quickening of earnestness and consecration." Mr. Harmer has since conducted a series of services at Kingston and Norbiton.

Rev. W. Tulloch, of Edinburgh, writes respecting *Mr. Parker :*—" He preached the gospel faithfully, and sang the gospel to the delectation of all. Several professed to have been awakened to spiritual concern, and some seemed to have closed with Christ."

ORPHANAGE.—The Collectors' meeting was held on *Friday evening, October* 25, and was thoroughly successful. Harvest-thanksgiving contributions have been received, and these made a glorious show. C. H. S. presided, and after prayer, thanked the collectors for their continued interest in the institution, and then commented upon a country bank-note which he had just received, accompanied by these words, "A picture for your little flock of kids." He would be happy to receive many more pictures of the same sort, and the "little flock of kids" would rejoice on every side Pastor F. M. Smith (Peckham) spoke on our Lord's command to Peter, "Feed my lambs." The children sang, recited, and played the hand-bells, and altogether it was a very lively evening. Total receipts about £120, an increase on last year.

Mr. Charlesworth and his choir are engaged this month as follows :—November 30, to December 2, Waterlooville; 3, Fareham; 4, Southsea, afternoon, Portsmouth, evening; 5, West Cowes; 6, 7, Bournemouth; 7-9, Southampton; 11, Downton; 12, Salisbury; 17, Battersea Park; 18, Erith; 19, 20, Dr. Laseron's Hospital, Tottenham.

The President very gratefully thanks all friends who helped at Windsor, Maidenhead, Thame, Newbury, Peckham, Acton, and Brixton.

Baptisms at Metropolitan Tabernacle:—Oct. 17, six; Oct. 31, twenty-seven; Nov. 7, eleven; Nov. 14, fifteen.

Pastors' College, Metropolitan Tabernacle.

Statement of Receipts from October 15th to November 14th, 1889.

	£	s.	d.		£	s.	d.
Miss Dixon, per J. T. D.	0	10	0	Miss H. W. C.	1	0	0
Mr. R. J. Beecliff ...	0	7	6	Mr. M. A. Jeph	1	0	0
Balsall Heath Road Baptist Church,				"Nameless"	1	0	0
per Pastor E. H. Hobby	0	8	10	From Scotland	25	0	0
Mrs. Ellwood	5	0	0	Mrs. Jackson	3	0	0
Mr. C. Barker	1	0	0	M. R.	1	0	0
From Wilts	1	0	0	Mr. W. N. Willcox	2	2	0
Mr. M. Hall	1	1	0	"Our dear Kate's own"	0	10	0
A. A. D.	0	5	0	Mrs. Grange	0	10	0
Mr. Dunn's Bible-class	26	10	0	Mrs. Johnston	5	0	0
A friend, Berwick	0	10	0	Mrs. Everest	0	10	0
From Ashford	1	0	0	Mrs. Annan	1	0	0
Mrs. Pool	1	1	0	Collected at Dalston Junction Chapel,			
Mrs. Wilkinson	1	0	0	per Pastor W. H. Burton	7	0	0
Mrs. Gardiner	2	2	0	From Catford Hill Baptist Chapel, per			
Mr. Thomas Gregory	1	0	0	Pastor T. Greenwood	2	5	0
Mr. Robert Miller	10	0	0	Dr. Pain	1	1	0
Mr. John Hector	2	0	0	Weekly Offerings at Met. Tab. :—			
Mr. E. Sparrow	0	5	0	Oct. 20	32	10	0
Mr. C. W. Roberts	10	0	0	„ 27	27	14	6
Prayer-meeting offerings at Mansion				Nov. 3	20	0	3
House Mission, per Pastor G. W.				„ 10	6	13	6
Linnecar	0	12	0				
Mrs. Smith	1	0	0		86	18	3
O. B., per Pastor J. A. Spurgeon	25	0	0				
M. C. S. F.	0	10	0		£240	18	7

Pastors' College Missionary Association.

Statement of Receipts from October 15th to November 14th, 1889.

	£	s.	d.		£	s.	d.
Mr. and Mrs. W. Pearce and Mr. J.				Miss Hall	0	5	0
Pearce	0	10	0	Beulah Baptist Chapel Auxiliary, per			
A reader of "The Sword and the				Pastor J. W. Harrald	4	4	0
Trowel"	1	0	0	In envelope at Tabernacle	0	0	6
Mr. Atherton	0	5	0				
C. A. M.	25	0	0		£33	14	6
Mr. John Hector	2	0	0				
M. R.	0	10	0				

Stockwell Orphanage.

Statement of Receipts from October 15th to November 14th, 1889.

	£	s.	d.		£	s.	d.
Mr. T. P. Alder	1	1	0	Collected by Mrs. Jarman			0
"Old boys"	1	2	0	Collected by Pastor J. H. Barnard			0
Sale of Fruit and Vegetables at Harvest				Collected by Mr. J. Garratt			0
Thanksgiving, Bugbrooke, per Rev.				Collected by Mrs. Laker		1	0
A. Millard	0	8	0	Collected by Miss L. Arnold		1	6
Collected by Mrs. Weeks	0	5	0	Mr. E. Bishop		1	0
Collected by Miss E. G. Comber	0	12	0	Mrs. P. Wooltorton		1	0
Mrs. Lee's box	0	1	0	Collected by Mrs. Bentall		1	0
Collected by Mr. J. Hooker	0	12	6	Collected by Miss L. A. Mansfield			1
Jack, South Lambeth	0	4	0	Collected by Mrs. E. S. Roberts			0
Anon., Metropolitan Tabernacle	0	5	0	Collected by Miss E. J. Farmer	1	3	
Collected by Mrs. T. Stringer	2	10	0	Collected by Mrs. Fakeley			0
Collected by Mr. N. G. Bridgman	0	4	0	Miss Smith			0
Collected by Miss E. Riddle	0	3	0	Collected by Mrs. Booker	1	0	
Collected by Miss S. A. Ackland	0	8	0	Collected by Mrs. F. Battam			0
Collected by Miss F. E. Barker	0	7	0	Collected by Miss W. Bughaw			0
Collected by Mr. A. Comber	0	6	6	Collected by Miss M. Bennett	1	0	
Collected by Miss Wolfenden	0	7	0	Collected by Mr. J. Harman			0
Collected by Mrs. Ashton	0	5	0	Collected by Miss E. Girdlestone	1	6	
Mrs. Best, per Mr. G. O. Heard	0	10	0	Collected by Mr. W. Armes			6
Mr. W. Dimock	0	2	6	Collected by Miss E. Wheeler			6
Collected by Miss F. Jeffery	0	10	0	Collected by Miss E. J. Brown	1	0	
Collected by Miss Pepler	1	9	6	Collected by Miss N. Burcher			4
Collected by Mrs. Jackson	0	7	6	Collected by Mr. G. Spooner			6
Collected by Mr. J. Simpson	0	15	0	Collected by Mrs. Welford	1	0	
A friend in the 'bus	0	5	0	Collected by Mrs. Robotham			8

	£	s.	d.
Collected by Mrs. Gallyon ...	1	1	4
Schoolroom collections at Ashdrane College, Croydon, per Mrs. Burton ...	0	14	6
Collected by Mrs. E. Luxford ...	0	7	6
Collected by Miss C. M. Bidewell ...	0	5	0
Collected by Mr. T. E. Inwood...	0	10	6
Collected by Miss E. Slade	0	16	0
Collected by Mr. W. A. Bragg ..	1	0	0
Collected by Miss S. Jackman ...	0	2	6
Collected by Miss Payn...	0	3	0
Collected by Miss E. Stokes ...	0	4	3
Collected by Mrs. D. Martin	0	0	0
Collected by Mrs. Down ..	0	2	6
Collected by Miss E. Jenkins ...	1	1	8
Collected by Miss Frost	0	4	0
Collected by the Misses Bailey ...	0	10	0
Mr. Robert Stewart's Bible-class, Regent Street Baptist Chapel, Belfast :—			
Miss E. Bradford 0 16 0			
Miss L. Gay ... 0 3 6			
Miss R. Melvin 0 6 8			
Miss A. Mulholland ... 0 3 6			
Miss M. Shaw... .. 0 2 4			
	1	12	0
Collected by Miss G. Puttock	1	18	6
Collected by Mr. I. J. Brown	0	5	4
Collected by Miss N. Matthews ...	0	10	0
Collected by Miss Warren	0	9	3
Young Women's Bible-class at the Orphanage, per Mrs. J. Stiff... ...	1	0	0
Collected by Master A. Partridge ...	0	2	2
Miss Ivimey's Mothers' Meeting, Metropolitan Tabernacle	1	10	1
Metropolitan Tabernacle office box ...	0	10	8
Collected by Masters M. and E. Chance	0	10	
A few friends' Harvest Home, per Mr. G. Gibb	0	10	0
Collected by Mr. W. Sherlock	1	16	1
Collected by Master A. Hoyles (penny collections at Sunday dinner-table)...	0	12	0
Collected by H. and F. Hoyles ...	0	3	2
Collected by Miss D. Sutherland ...	0	16	9
Sandwich, per bankers	2	2	0
Executor of the late Miss M. A. Aylward	17	19	
Executor of the late Miss Emily A. Whiteley	100	0	0
Collected by Mrs. Shipway ...	1	0	0
Collected by Mr. Funnell ...	0	6	0
Mr. E. K. Stace	0	10	0
Box at Orphanage gates	0		6
Collected by Miss E. K. Rawlins ...	0	7	8
Miss Dixon, per J. T. D.... ...	0	10	0
Mr. J. C. Wadland	1	0	0
Orphanage box at Tabernacle gates ...	2	2	6
Mr. W. Anderson, per Mr. Cornell ...	0	10	0
Collected by Mrs. Wilmot ...	0	11	0
A friend from Paris	0	3	0
P. and P.	0	5	0
R. W.... ...	2	0	0
Mrs. Cocker...	0	5	0
Mr. W. Lawrie	0	10	0
Mrs. Martin...	0	5	0
Mr. John Lamont, per Mr. William Olney	2	0	0
Miss M. A. Butterworth... ...	5	0	0
Mr. F. H. Butler	1	0	0
Mr. John Green	1	1	0
Mr. J. G. Van Rijn	4	0	0
Mr. C. Ibberson		2	6
Mr. J. Mee		2	6
A thankoffering from three ...	0	5	0
Miss Harrison		10	0
Miss H. Smith		5	0
Collected by Mrs. Norris	2	1	0
Collected by Mrs. Lang :—			
Mr. Whittend 0 5 0			
Mr. F. Beckinsale 0 5 0			
	0	10	0

	£	s	d.
Collected by Miss A. H. Rust	0		6
Mr. A. Beavam	1	1	0
Mr. M. E. Jenkins	0	6	6
Mr. and Mrs. W. Pearce, and Mr. J. Pearce	0	10	0
Mrs. Shearer, sale of jewellery... ...	1	4	9
"Thankoffering after harvest," per Pastor M. Matthews	1	0	0
J. B. C.	1	0	0
Miss Hawkes	0	5	0
Mrs. Scates	0	5	0
Mr. M. Hall...	1	1	0
Mr. W. Kay...	0	2	6
Mrs. Whittett	1	1	7
A friend, Berwick...	0	10	0
A. R., per Miss Allan	0	3	0
Mr. Edward Webber	0	10	0
Mr. H. Proctor	1	0	0
P. A. L. M.	1	0	0
"From one who heard your boys at Weston-super-Mare"	0	5	0
Collected by Miss M. Fitzgerald ...	0	12	0
Mr. N. Heath	1	1	0
Mr. H. Jackson	1	0	0
Mrs. J. Lord	0	10	0
T. A. H. P. W.	5	0	0
Mrs. Gardiner	2	2	0
Mr. A. Benton	1	0	0
Mrs. Pool	1	1	0
Mr. and Mrs. Bridgman	0	5	0
Mr. Hartswell	0	2	0
Collected by Mrs. R. C. Allen ...	0	7	0
Collected by Mrs. J. Withers :			
Mr. W. I. Palmer 3 0			
Mrs. Wilson 0 0			
Mr. Holmes 0 2 0			
	0	0	0
Mr. M. Jones	0	2	6
Mrs. Gulliver	8	0	0
A thankoffering from Mr. and Mrs. and the Misses S.	5	10	
Thankoffering for prayer answered ...	0	5	
Mr. D. Goodwin	1	0	0
Mrs. Bartlett	0	5	0
"A picture for your little flock of kids"	5	0	0
Mr. J. Hall	5	0	
Woodford Sunday-school, per Mr. W. French	0	12	6
Collected by Miss Good	0	4	7
O. R.	1	0	0
Collected by Master T. Watts, per Rev. T. H. Williams	0	6	2
E. B.	0	2	6
Collected by Mrs. Harris	0	1	4
Carl S. B.	1	2	0
Mrs. Mannington	1	1	0
Collected by Mr. R. Tomkins (Mission Hall)	0	18	0
Mrs. M. Macgregor	1	0	0
J. J., Harrogate	2	0	0
Mrs. Sharman's family box	1	10	7
Mrs. Bennett	0	5	0
Miss E. A. Fysh	0	1	0
Farley Green Mission	0	10	0
Rookery children's box	0	9	0
Mrs. Jackman	1	0	0
Mrs. Davies	2	0	0
Miss M. A. Lines	1	0	0
Miss E. Bickerton Evans... ...	8	0	0
Mrs. Mackenzie	2	0	0
Mr. Robt. Miller	10	0	0
"For the bairns"	0	10	0
Mr. C. Mackson	0	5	0
Mr. G. Bickerson	1	0	0
Mr. J. T. Waugh	1	0	0
Miss Hall	0	12	6
Mr. John Hector	1	0	0
Postal-orders from Liverpool	2	0	0
"Thankoffering for 71 years' mercies"	0	5	0
Mr. F. Howard	2	2	0
Mr. Henry Tribe	10	10	0

46

	£	s.	d.
Mr. D. Foord	5	0	0
Miss A. Hughes	0	10	0
Mrs. Spencer	1	0	0
Mrs. S. Dunn	0	10	6
O. B., per Pastor J. A. Spurgeon	50	0	0
F. G. B., Chelmsford	0	2	6
Miss Smither	1	0	0
M. C. S. F.	1	0	0
Mr. S. H. Dauncey	0	2	6
Mr. Cumpstey	0	10	6
Mr. G. Smith	0	10	0
X. S.	10	0	0
Miss E. Sizmur	0	5	0
B. G., Norwich	1	0	0
Miss E. C. Clatterbuck	0	5	0
Mr. D. C. Apperly	2	2	0
Mrs. Jackson	2	0	0
M. R.	1	0	0
Mr. W. N. Willcox	1	1	0
A Wellow friend, per Pastor J. Smith	0	5	0
Mrs. Hicks	0	10	0
Mrs. Veale	2	2	0
Miss E. Moses	0	2	6
"An aged Christian," Ludlow	0	5	0
Mr. T. Thomson	3	0	0
Postal-orders from Ipswich	0	13	0
Mrs. East	1	0	0

Collected by Miss K. Buswell:—

	£	s.	d.				
Mr. T. Woodley	2	0	0				
J. J. S.	0	10	0				
Mr. Meredith	0	10	0				
Mr. A. Lyon	0	10	0				
Mr. J. Buswell	0	10	0				
Smaller sums	0	6	0				
				4		0	

Per F. R. T. :—

	£	s.	d.				
Miss Winckworth	0	5	0				
Mr. and Mrs. Tidmarsh	0	10	0				
Mr. T. R. Johnson	0	5	0				
Mr. and Mrs. Jonas Smith	0	10	0				
				1	10	0	
Mrs. Mitchell				0	10	0	
Mrs. Fryer				0	10	0	
Mrs. Gregory				0	10	0	
Mrs. Annan				1	0	0	
Mr. E. Davis				1	0	0	
Collections at Dalston Junction Chapel, per Pastor W. H. Burton				10	0	0	
Orphan boys' collecting cards (3rd list)				2	11	0	
Orphan girls' collecting cards (3rd list)				2	14	5	
Mr. J. Coutts				1	1	0	
Miss A. Wilmot				1	0	0	
Mr. T. Vickery				1	1	0	
Mr. W. Kelley				0	10	0	
Executors of the late Mr. George Stevenson				50	0	0	

Christmas Festival Fund :—

	£	s.	d.				
Eskdale shepherd	0	10	0				
Mrs. Shearman	2	0	0				
Mr. E. Davis	0	10	0				
				3	0	0	

Meetings by Mr. Charlesworth and the Orphanage Choir :—

	£	s.	d.				
Hayle	22	5	0				
Falmouth	50	0	0				
Newquay	30	0	0				
St. Austell	42	6	4				
Per Mr. T. Stocker	0	10	0				
				42	16	4	
Liskeard				10	6	8	
St. Ives				13	13	6	
Penzance				19	5	0	
Bath (second amount)				4	1	4	
Maidenhead				20	7	0	
Windsor				14	2	3	
Thame				12	16	6	
Hanover Park Hall, Peckham				4	11	1	
Tottenham Baptist Chapel				8	14	11	
Sale of programmes :—							
Railton Road				0	11	4	

			£	s.	d.
Collyer Hall, Peckham			0	12	7

Received at Collectors' Meeting, Oct. 25th :—

Collecting Boxes—

	£	s.	d.
Abbey, Miss	0	3	1
Amies, Mrs.	0	0	8
Allen, Mrs.	1	5	1
Anthony, Mrs.	0	9	7
Belleni, Miss P.	0	2	6
Beard, Miss E.	0	2	6
Barker, Master H.	0	3	7
Brice, Miss C.	0	4	4
Buckingham, Miss	0	9	0
Blayney, Mrs.	0	3	0
Belleni, Miss	0	2	9
Brooks, Miss	0	6	8
Brice, G. and B.	0	3	2
Bruin, Miss E.	0	14	1
Beavis, Miss N.	0	8	9
Brice, Master A.	0	3	3
Brewer, Misses A. and L.	0	10	4
Barber, Miss	0	4	0
Brice, Master P.	0	6	10
Brice, Master G.	0	4	8
Brice, Master B.	0	2	1
Benson, Master S.	0	4	1
Bartlett, Master E.	0	6	6
Buchanan, Miss	0	1	9
Butler, Mrs.	0	13	3
Burrage, Mrs.	0	4	5
Barnden, Mrs.	0	15	1
Burton, Mrs. W.	1	19	0
Bates, Miss	0	2	5
Buswell, Miss	2	2	10
Bell, Mrs.	0	6	0
Clark, Master A.	0	3	10
Charlesworth, Miss F.	0	1	6
Cox, Miss A.	0	6	3
Cocking, Master E.	0	10	8
Cook, Misses A. and M.	0	5	0
Chapman, Mrs.	0	6	0
Cropley, Mrs.	0	2	2
Cowles, Miss A.	0	12	0
Combs, Miss	2	1	3
Chipperfield, Master J.	0	6	9
Crag~s, Master	0	2	7
Clarke, Miss M.	0	2	8
Crisp, Master E.	0	5	11
Cairns, Miss C.	0	13	9
Cretchley, Miss L.	0	2	1
Cretchley, Master H.	0	13	0
Cretchley, Master E.	0	2	10
Castell, Mrs.	0	4	10
Chapman, Miss H.	0	6	3
Conquest, Mrs.	0	10	6
Cruwys, Master	0	7	7
Cairns, Miss M.	0	11	5
Davis, Master T.	0	5	9
Dolman, Master J.	0	2	2
Davie, Mr.	0	7	9
Davey, Miss L.	0	6	6
Edmonds, Miss	0	2	8
Ellerington, Mrs.	0	3	8
Eyles, Miss A.	0	1	9
Eyres, Master C.	0	6	0
Elliott, Mrs.	0	2	8
Emerson, Miss L. F.	0	2	8
Emerson, Master S.	0	2	6
Eyres, Master N.	0	18	1
Farmer, Mrs.	0	3	8
Field, Mrs.	0	1	3
Fathers, Mrs.	0	1	8
Fuller, Miss E.	0	2	5
Frisby, The Misses	0	14	1
Grant, Mrs.	0	12	1
Goetz, Miss	0	10	1
Harris, Miss	0	7	3
Heron, Miss S.	0	2	4
Holland, Master P.	0	2	5
Hartley, Miss E.	0	2	1
Holland, Master J.	0	4	9
Hellier, Mrs.	0	16	0